CENTURIES OF

TRANSITION

The literature of the Middle Ages and of the Renaissance

ROBERT WARNOCK *The University of Connecticut*

GEORGE K. ANDERSON *Brown University*

BOOK TWO *of* THE WORLD IN LITERATURE

SCOTT, FORESMAN AND COMPANY

Chicago   Atlanta   Dallas   Palo Alto   Fair Lawn, N.J.

CENTURIES OF TRANSITION, *the second of a four-book series which includes* THE ANCIENT FOUNDATIONS, TRADITION AND REVOLT, *and* OUR HUNDRED YEARS, *presents against a background of cultural history the literary masters of the Middle Ages and of the Renaissance.*

The authors wish to acknowledge the courtesy of the publishers who have granted permission to reprint selections in copyright. Specific acknowledgment of these publishers is given on the pages where the selections appear.

CONTENTS

The selections listed in the table are complete except where superior letters appear: ᴬ indicates very long works of necessity abridged (with a preservation of the scope and continuity of the whole); ˢ indicates representative selection. A few negligible deletions are indicated in the text.

CHAPTER ONE CHRISTENDOM, ISLAM, AND THE MIDDLE AGES
200 TO 1350

INTRODUCTION 2

I   The Mohammedan World

The Koran ˢ 25

The Arabian Nights ˢ 28

Omar Khayyam 37
    The Rubaiyat ˢ 38

Hafiz 44
    The Divan (Odes) ˢ 44

II   The Christian Ideal

The New Testament 47
    The Gospel according to Saint Matthew ˢ 48
    First Epistle of Paul to the Corinthians ˢ 63

The Nicaean Creed 65

Thomas à Kempis 66
    The Imitation of Christ ˢ 66

Saint Francis of Assisi 74
    The Little Flowers of Saint Francis ˢ 75

III   The Knightly Ideal: The Fighter and the Lover

Sir Gawain and the Green Knight ᴬ 88

The Song of Roland ᴬ 110

The Nibelungenlied ᴬ 125

Aucassin and Nicolete 137

The Minnesingers 151
The Minnesingers: "O lady, long have I been fain" · "To
my lady's bower I crept" · "What sweetness into that
old word woman grew" · "Will you take this wilding
wreath?" · "Whatever be my faults" · "Who slays the
lion, who slays the dragon?" · "Went a maid fair to
behold" · The Ballad of Sir Tannhäuser · Life and
Death of the Noble Brennenberger 151–157

IV *Two Medieval Masters*

Dante Alighieri 157
The Divine Comedy ᴬ 160

Geoffrey Chaucer 201
The Canterbury Tales: Prologue, The Reeve's Tale, The
Franklin's Tale, The Nun's Priest's Tale, The
Pardoner's Tale 203

V *Popular Balladry*

British and Danish Popular Ballads 246
Riddles Wisely Expounded · Edward · Aage and Else ·
Thomas Rymer · Sir Patrick Spens · Niels Ebbeson ·
The Wife of Usher's Well · Bonny Barbara Allan ·
The Bride of Ribe · Robin Hood's Death and Burial ·
Bonnie George Campbell · Young Engel · Sir Luno
and the Mermaid · Kemp Owyne · Johnie Armstrong 248–263

CHAPTER TWO **REBIRTH AND DISCOVERY**
1350 TO 1650

INTRODUCTION 265

I *The Humanistic Spirit—Man's Search for Himself*

The Wandering Scholars 289
A Song of the Open Road · The Confessions of Golias ·
The Invitation to Youth · There's No Lust Like to
Poetry · Gaudeamus Igitur 289–291

Pico della Mirandola 291
Of the Dignity of Man ᴬ 292

Desiderius Erasmus 293
The Praise of Folly 294

Giovanni Boccaccio 300
   Decameron: The Three Rings, Don Federigo's Falcon,
   Friar Onion and the Relics of the Angel Gabriel,
   The Cradle 301

François Rabelais 309
   Gargantua and Pantagruel[s] 310

Michel de Montaigne 324
   The Author to the Reader 325
   Of Democritus and Heraclitus 326
   Of the Education of Children 327
   Of Age 340
   That We Taste Nothing Pure 341
   Of Three Commerces 342

II *From Knight to Courtier*

Miguel de Cervantes 346
   Don Quixote de la Mancha[A] 347

Baldassare Castiglione 388
   The Book of the Courtier[A] 389

Edmund Spenser 395
   The Faerie Queene: Cantos 1, 2, and 10 of Book One 396

III *Nationalism and Internationalism*

Niccolò Machiavelli 414
   The Prince[s] 415

Hugo Grotius 421
   Rights of War and Peace[s] 421

IV *Rise of National Drama*

Lope de Vega 425
   The Sheep Well 426

William Shakespeare 447
   Hamlet, Prince of Denmark 449

V *Emergence of the Scientific Spirit*

Nicolaus Copernicus 499
   The Revolutions of the Heavenly Bodies[s] 499

Giordano Bruno 503
   Of the Infinite Universe and Innumerable Worlds[s] 503

Sir Francis Bacon 505
   Novum Organum[s] 506

VI *The Religious Reformation and Puritanism*

Martin Luther 509
    Table Talk ^s 510

John Milton 514
    Paradise Lost: Books 1, 2, and 12 514

Jonathan Edwards 543
    Sinners in the Hands of an Angry God ^s 543

VII *The Renaissance Lyric*

Francesco Petrarca 548
    *Vision · Love's Inconsistency · Signs of Love · The
    Beauty and Virtue of Laura · Wherein His Heart, by
    Laura Rejected · Wherein He Pursues Solitude ·
    Wherein He Tells the Course · Wherein He Envies ·
    If It Be Destined · The Death-Bed of Laura · On
    the Announcement of the Death of Laura · He Thanks
    Her That from Time to Time · Wherein Laura Is
    Forever a Present Apparition · Wherein Soaring in an
    Ecstasy · The Spring Returns But Not to Him Re-
    turns · Wherein He Makes Confession* 548–551

François Villon 552
    *No, I Am Not As Others Are · His Mother's Service to
    Our Lady · The Ballad of Dead Ladies · Ballad of
    the Women of Paris · The Tree of Love · Ballad
    Written for a Bridegroom · Rondel · To Death, of
    His Lady · Villon's Straight Tip to All Cross Coves ·
    The Dispute of the Heart and Body of François
    Villon · Epistle in Form of a Ballad to His Friends ·
    Ballad of the Gibbet* 552–557

Pierre de Ronsard 557
    *Summer's Revel · Fragment of a Sonnet · Love's
    Charming · To His Young Mistress · Even unto
    Death · Love's Flower · Roses · The Rose · The
    Poet's Gift · Of His Lady's Old Age · To His Valet ·
    The Revenge · Deadly Kisses · His Lady's Death,
    His Lady's Tomb · Transit Mundus* 557–561

English Lyricists 561

William Shakespeare
    *Songs from The Merchant of Venice, Much Ado about
    Nothing, As You Like It, Twelfth Night, Measure for
    Measure, Cymbeline, The Winter's Tale, The Tempest* 562–564
    *Sonnets 18, 29, 30, 33, 54, 55, 60, 64, 66, 73, 95,
    102, 104, 106, 109, 116, 121* 564–567

Ben Jonson
  *To the Memory of My Beloved, Master William Shake-
  speare · Song: to Celia · Song to Celia · Simplex
  Munditiis · Epitaph on Elizabeth L. H. · It Is Not
  Growing Like a Tree · A Song* 567–569

John Donne
  *Song · The Ecstasy · Love's Infiniteness · The
  Funeral · Death* 569–571

Robert Herrick
  *The Argument of His Book · An Ode for Ben Jonson ·
  The Night Piece, to Julia · Delight in Disorder ·
  Upon Julia's Clothes · Cherry-Ripe · Upon Mistress
  Susanna Southwell Her Feet · To Daffodils · To the
  Virgins to Make Much of Time · To Dianeme · To
  Anthea, Who May Command Him Anything · To
  Electra · To Primroses Filled with Morning-dew ·
  To Daisies, Not to Shut So Soon · The Fairies · The
  Hag · His Prayer for Absolution · Litany to the Holy
  Spirit* 571–575

List of Illustrations

Five doorways of the Cathedral of Bourges. Photo cour-
  tesy of Compagnie des Arts Photomécaniques
  ....Front endpaper
The month of October, miniature by Pol de Limbourg
  and brothers, from *Les Très Riches Heures du Duc de
  Berry.* Photo Giraudon 3
The Last Judgment, relief over the central doorway, Ca-
  thedral of Bourges. Photo by François Haab from *La
  Cathédrale de Bourges* Éditions "Tel" 4–5
Double lancet window, La Tricherie, Vienne. Courtesy of
  the Metropolitan Museum of Art, New York 7
Monk, *pleurant* from the tomb of Philip the Bold of Bur-
  gundy. Statue by Claus Sluter. Photo courtesy of Max
  Epstein Archive, University of Chicago 9
Swiss wool tapestry, 1490, "The Lovers." Courtesy of the
  Art Institute of Chicago 11
Madonna and child, stone statue from Troyes, France,
  c. 1475. Courtesy of the William Rockhill Nelson Gal-
  lery of Art, Kansas City, Missouri 12
"The Morris Dance," engraving by Israhel van Mec-
  kenem. Courtesy of the Art Institute of Chicago, Clar-
  ence Buckingham Collection 14
Carcassonne, fortifications from the fifth, twelfth, and
  thirteenth centuries. Photo courtesy of the Max Epstein
  Archive, University of Chicago 15
Chartres Cathedral from the Northwest. Photo courtesy
  of Compagnie des Arts Photomécaniques 16–17
Chaucer. Courtesy of the National Portrait Gallery, London 18

A hunt at the court of Philip the Good, painting of the Bourgogne school, fifteenth century. Photo Giraudon 22

Mohammed besieging a fortress, miniature from an Arabic universal history of the fourteenth century. Reproduced from *Album Historique*, I, by Ernest Lavisse and A. Parmentier, by permission of Librairie Armand Colin 27

Interior of a harem in a palace at Damas. Reproduced from *Album Historique*, I, by Ernest Lavisse and A. Parmentier, by permission of Librairie Armand Colin 30

Portrait of a physician, school of Aqā Rizā. Persian manuscript 1925–4–20–01, British Museum 39

Pastoral scene from a Persian manuscript illumination, c. 1540. Oriental Manuscript 2265, Folio 157B (detail from top left corner), British Museum 42

St. Matthew writing his gospel, manuscript illumination, 12th century. Courtesy of Walters Art Gallery, Baltimore, Maryland 48

St. Peter, Italian Mosaic c. 600. Reproduced from *Album Historique*, I, by Ernest Lavisse and A. Parmentier, by permission of Librairie Armand Colin 63

A bishop, pen and brush drawing, English school, fifteenth century. From Canterbury Cathedral library, reproduced in *Vasari Society*, VII, No. 16 65

St. Francis of Assisi and a companion, from a painting by Giotto. Reproduced from *Album Historique*, II, by Ernest Lavisse and A. Parmentier, by permission of Librairie Armand Colin 75

Two knights fighting. Sketchbook. North French. c. 1390–1410. Courtesy of the Pierpont Morgan Library ...94

Carolingian warrior (Musée d'Artillerie) 113

Coin of Charlemagne (768–814), in the Archives Nationales 120

French tournament costume of the fifteenth century (Bibliothèque Nationale) 125

A tournament in the fifteenth century, German manuscript in the Germanic Museum, Nuremberg 127

German prince in tourney costume of the early fifteenth century (Musée d'Artillerie) 137

Siege of a city, from a manuscript of the *Chronicles* of Froissart (Bibliothèque Nationale 2645) 140

French *donjon* at Château-Gaillard, twelfth century ..149

Costumes of noble women, fifteenth century (Bibliothèque Nationale 156

The above eight pictures are reproduced from *Album Historique*, by Ernest Lavisse and A. Parmentier, by permission of Librairie Armand Colin.

Dante's Hell and Purgatory. Drawn by Seymour Fleischman 175

Dante's Heaven. Drawn by Seymour Fleischman ..195

Frontispiece of manuscript of the *Canterbury Tales*, about 1400. Courtesy of Harper Library, University of Chicago 223

Lorenzo de' Medici, by Verrocchio. Courtesy of the National Gallery of Art, Washington, D. C. (Kress Collection) 265

"The Banker and his Wife," painting by Quentin Matsys, Louvre. Photo by National Committee for Art Appreciation 267

Map, "Renaissance Europe, 1559." Drawn by Seymour Fleischman 270

Pope Julius II, painting by Raphael. Uffizi Gallery, Florence 275

Drawing of muscles of torso and legs, by Leonardo da Vinci. Now in Turin Royal Library 277

Interior of Ducal Palace, Gubbio. Courtesy of New York Metropolitan Museum of Art 281

Francis I on horseback, painting by François Clouet. Photo by Alinari 284

"Crucifixion with View of Toledo," painting by El Greco. Courtesy of Cincinnati Art Museum, J. J. Emery Collection 287

Erasmus, engraving by Albrecht Dürer, 1526 295

A page of the *Decameron*, 1729 facsimile edition of the 1527 edition. Courtesy of the Rare Book Room, Harper Library, University of Chicago 302

"Man with a Falcon," painting by Titian, c. 1525. Courtesy of the Joslyn Memorial Art Museum, Omaha, Nebraska 304

Friar John, caricature from the 1565 edition of *Droll Dreams of Pantagruel*. From *All the Extant Works of François Rabelais*, translation and notes by Samuel Putnam. Copyright 1929 by Covici-Friede, Inc. Reprinted by permission of Crown Publishers 320

A monk, caricature from the 1565 edition of *Droll Dreams of Pantagruel*. From *All the Extant Works of François Rabelais*, translated and notes by Samuel Putnam. Copyright 1929 by Covici-Friede, Inc. Reprinted by permission of Crown Publishers 321

Montaigne, portrait in the Musée Condé, Chantilly, school of Corneille de Lyon. Photo by Giraudon .335

Don Quixote and Sancho Panza. From the title page of *Don Quixote*, Lisbon, 1605 348

Don Quixote and the windmill, by Gustave Doré. From Cervantes, *History of Don Quixote*, published by Cassell and Co., London, 1864 355

Don Quixote and the prisoners, by Gustave Doré. From Cervantes, *History of Don Quixote*, published by Cassell and Co., London, 1864 364

St. George and the dragon, by Albrecht Dürer 404

"Four Soldiers," engraving by the Master MZ, German, about 1500. Courtesy of the Art Institute of Chicago, from the Mr. and Mrs. Potter Palmer Collection ..498

Copernicus, from *Tychonis Brahei, equitis dani, astronomorum coryphaei, vita . . . Accessit Nicolai Copernici . . . vita* by Pierre Gassendi, published at the Hague, 1655 (2nd edition) 502

Temptation of Adam and Eve, engraving by Albrecht Dürer, 1504 533

Three ladies, French fifteenth-century drawing 567

Interior, Hall of Mirrors, Versailles, decorated by Charles Le Brun, 1679–1684. Courtesy of Compagnie des Arts Photomécaniques ....Second endpaper

CENTURIES OF TRANSITION

CHRISTENDOM, ISLAM, AND THE MIDDLE AGES

300 TO 1350

THE Middle Ages in Europe constituted that long era of transition between the civilization of imperial Rome and the complicated modern world which has been developing for the past five hundred years. The Middle Ages was indeed a long era, covering as it did a full thousand years and a trifle more, from about 300 to about 1350. Essentially what characterizes this enormous span of years is the fact that men's efforts throughout these eleven centuries were directed toward the establishment of a new system of life after the older system had col-

lapsed amid the ruins of the classical world of Greece and Rome. The breaking up of the mighty Roman empire opened a chasm across the road which the Western world was traveling. And although this Western world had no clearer idea of the future at that time than is ever vouchsafed blundering mankind, still it had instinctively to move on, because the one great eternal verity is change. In order for Occidental man to continue along his appointed road, the chasm had somehow to be bridged. What we choose to call medieval civilization was the bridge which was eventually built.

A notable integration of life and thought remains the prime characteristic of this age. This unity is best illustrated by the power over the individual man wielded by the two great institutions of the Middle Ages—the Holy Catholic Church in the realm of the spiritual and religious life, and the feudal system in the secular sphere. Of these two institutions it is obvious that the Church was for the time the greater; it was able to partake of feudalism and yet rise above feudalism. It could bring kings and emperors to heel. When cracks began to appear in the central structures of these two institutions, the Middle Ages was nearing its end, and the modern era was about to begin. Although it is not possible to examine here the bricks and blocks which went to make up these two magnificent edifices, the Church and the feudal system, it is important to realize that both assumed the supremacy of a central authority —that of the Pope in the Church and that of the royal sovereign in the feudal system—and, further, that the authoritarian tendency is the leading motif in medieval culture and medieval learning.

RELIGIOUS HIERARCHY AND FEUDAL STRUCTURE

THE Church had emerged from the collapse of the Roman empire as the one universally accepted center of authority. Christianity, made the sole and official religion of the state by the emperor Theodosius in 395, had gradually developed an organized hierarchy. A basic doctrine, that the bishop at Rome was the heir to the power of Peter, the disciple whom Christ had appointed His successor, resulted in the acceptance of the Pope as head of the Church, at least in. the West. Conversion by the Church of the various "barbarian" tribes accompanied the development of its dogma, so that in the Middle Ages the people of Europe and their various rulers were Christian. What did such a status entail?

The Church took the position from the very beginning that it was the sole means which Christianity had at hand for the furtherance of God's plan on earth. No other plan, it maintained, was possible.

Salvation for the individual could be obtained only through the offices of the Church and by active participation in its ceremonies. The clergy administered the sacraments, by means of which Christians achieved grace necessary for happiness in the next world. The threat (implicit in interdict and excommunication) of being barred from the sacraments and from grace was equivalent to the threat of being barred from Heaven. The Devil, or Antichrist, was the perennial adversary; the world was a perpetual battleground in the momentous conflict between the Kingdom of God and the Kingdom of the Devil. The Holy Father in Rome was the spiritual and moral sovereign of Christendom, the exponent of divine affirmation. He was also the champion of mortal man against the onslaughts of the world, the flesh, and the devil—the very essence of the Antichrist. The vast and imposing hierarchy of the Church must administer the affairs of the Kingdom of God in this world; but to God Himself was due all the homage, the glory, and the wonder for the greatness of His manifold works.

The hierarchy of the medieval Church was an organization at once complex and compact. First there was God Himself in the Trinity. Then came the various orders of angels and then man, "a little lower than the angels"; and the relation of man to his superiors formed the pattern on which was planned the whole institution of the Church. Each official of the Church bore a direct responsibility to the official above him in the hierarchy—priest to bishop, bishop to archbishop, archbishop to cardinal, cardinal to pontiff. Eventually, of course, all responsibility was laid upon the shoulders of the Pope, who was the representative of God on earth, the spiritual ruler of Christendom—and, it should be added, in view of the tremendous material wealth of the medieval Church, a temporal ruler also who wielded immense power.

Such was the essential sameness of the design in the organization of medieval life, moreover, that the pattern from which the religious phases of this life were shaped served also as the design which determined the secular life of the time. In a more earthy way—as Caesar is earthier than God—the feudal system was the secular counterpart of the medieval Church. To be sure, the king of a country was not the vicar of Christ; he had no right to the keys of Heaven. Nevertheless, according to the social and political philosophies of the era, the sovereign was considered the material owner of every square inch of land within his domain, except for the estates of the Church. This ownership was his by divine consent and privilege granted; therefore, in spite of its material nature, it assumed also a spiritual significance. In the mind of a patriotic liegeman, at least, it might be called a spiritual entity. For the sovereign theoretically embodied his country.

To speak in more material terms, we may simplify the matter, admittedly to the danger point, by observing that the land was leased by its medieval sovereign to his hierarchy of nobility or vassals, who in turn subleased it; the nobility owed the sovereign, in return for the privilege of occupying and exploiting this land, homage and the tangible obligations of certain money payments and the defense of his realm, usually in the form of military service. Moreover, always keeping in mind the hierarchical aspect of the whole arrangement, we see that each lesser nobleman was responsible, in paying for his privileges, to the nobleman next above him in social rank. Thus a baron would owe an earl or a count; an earl would owe a duke; a duke would owe the king or emperor. It is impossible to consider here all the details of feudal returns or all the niceties of feudal

French peasants plowing and sowing on a strip of land with the lord's castle in the background. From the Très Riches Heures du Duc de Berry, *illuminated before 1416.*

organization, a complex study in itself; but the presence of the system in the social life of the Middle Ages must always be kept in mind, along with the submissive habits of thought and conduct which such a system must engender.

Obviously the feudal system worked to the benefit of the relatively infinitesimal number of the privileged aristocracy. The people as a whole, the masses of the population, had but little power until the Middle Ages had outlived its potency. Underneath the superstructure of feudalism labored the villein, or serf, as part of an economic unit called the manor. The serf was bound to the land allotted him by the local noble. He worked his own half-acre when he could and tilled the land of the noble, so that the lord of the manor could subsist on his expected higher level and pay his due to his superior. For the feudal system was based primarily on agricul-

This relief over the central doorway of the Cathedral of Bourges, shown on the endsheet, depicts the Last Judgment as the medieval mind pictured it. St. Michael weighs and separates the souls. The good souls are being received

ture, not on industry or commerce. The general effect was that the Middle Ages in its most characteristic aspects recognized but two classes of society—the nobility (among whom we must include members of the Church organization) and the people as a whole. Only among the freemen, who had been released from serfdom for special services signally rendered, was there a substantial foundation for a future middle class, and such freemen were extremely rare before the year 1000. When a middle class became truly discernible, the Middle Ages had entered its terminal stage.

MEDIEVAL THOUGHT, SPIRITUAL AND SECULAR

I N theory there was the understanding that one should render unto Caesar the things that were Caesar's and unto God the things that were God's. Yet, where the religious and secular powers were not distinct, since the Church's higher clergy were feudal lords as well, there were inevitable frictions, jealousies, and contentions. The eventual outcome of such jostlings and collisions, however, would in this era be usually a foregone conclusion. The Church, as the divine instrument of God, created to advance His purposes on earth, could brook no assumption of unauthorized power by a mere monarch, who, in the final analysis, was only a sinful mortal. No sovereign during the true ascendancy of the Middle Ages was ever able to combat successfully the power of the Holy Father. The Pope being the true overlord of all Christendom, the might of the Church would always, in the final test,

be victorious over the forces of the State. The Holy Roman Emperor himself, Henry IV, was obliged in 1077 to humble himself before Pope Gregory VII at Canossa after having been defeated in a controversy over the investiture of ecclesiastics with office by lay rulers. Archbishop Thomas à Becket, although martyred, won his battle with King Henry II of England; and Archbishop Stephen Langton humiliated King John.

Now what of the position taken by the medieval Church in reference to man's relation to man and his relation to God? While no complete exegesis can be compressed into a few sentences, still it is necessary for anyone interested in the Middle Ages to keep in mind some fundamental points about this attitude, since an understanding of the literature of the age is otherwise difficult if not impossible. The Church took the world in which we live for what it *by Abraham at the left as they enter heaven. The damned, being carried off by devils for suitable punishment, are shown at the right.*

was, dominated by the struggle between the Kingdom of God and the Kingdom of the Devil, and demonstrated how, by adhering to a particular belief and to a particular code of conduct, the world could be accepted and understood, against a final terrible Judgment Day. This coming of the Lord, this day of final ordeal, was inevitable; it awaited only God's pleasure. Certain interpreters of Holy Writ thought it likely that He would come at a particular time—in the year 1000, for example. The majority, however, preferred to think of the date of this divine event as indeterminate and indeterminable. At any rate, the belief in the body of doctrine established by century-old tradition and the code of conduct which served as the outward sign of this doctrine were both enforced under the strictest penalties for lack of faith or disobedience or too free subjective interpretation—heresy in the eyes of the Church.

And what of the world, which was man's immediate environment? There was some curiosity of varying degrees about the physical world. Most of the information about it was derived ultimately from sources which were either pre-Christian or non-Christian, such as the ancient Greek mathematicians, astronomers, and geographers, or the Arab scientists of contemporaneous fame. All this information, together with its dissemination, was monopolized by the Church. In the Middle Ages there was, to the

twentieth-century mind, an appalling unwillingness even to test or question this information or to speculate about the physically unknown except to relate it to the firmly established doctrine of the Church. It was deemed altogether sufficient to demonstrate that human reason would lead one inevitably to God, and this reconciliation of faith and reason is perhaps the greatest intellectual contribution of the Middle Ages.

As for the rest, the implication expressed in medieval teaching—and it is often far more than a mere implication—is that this world is at best temporary. Humanity, to take the long view necessary in all abiding faiths, philosophies, and religions, is therefore on its way to Heaven or to Hell, as the case may be. The world is a road of pilgrimage to the appointed lodging place. Certainly the world to come, for better or for worse, is a far more important consideration than this transitory life on earth. If the medieval teacher seems to think of man as more likely than not to end in Hell, that is because of his fundamental belief in man's sinfulness, an evil state that is attributable to the seduction by the Devil of man's first parents. Heaven is for the tried, the true, the privileged in God's sight; and before man can attain to Heaven, he must be put through the refining process of Purgatory—which is in itself no trifling ordeal—unless a man be so saintly that he can be borne away from this world direct to Heaven, as happened to a few saints and prophets. As a consequence of this attitude in so much of the moral and spiritual literature of the Middle Ages, it is the Other World, in contradistinction to the world in which man must live out his earthly span, that is the true end of existence.

At this point, however, a word of warning is due. To say that the world to come was more important in the eyes of the Middle Ages than the world of the present can be maintained, but only with some qualifications. Such was indeed the message of its moralists and teachers. But it cannot be believed, for instance, that men during this thousand-year period passed through life with hearts and minds fixed only on the Celestial City or on the lurid infernos conjured up by their poets and prophets. The mere experience of living is altogether too important to the average man and woman for such a way of life to be possible. The relation of man to man could never be made tolerable on such a basis. It is therefore proper to assume that the daily problems of life faced by the man and woman of the Middle Ages were then, as always, the usual familiar ones that were nevertheless immediate and urgent, and that human nature was basically the same then as it is now. There is ample evidence in the surviving works of Chaucer, Dante, the romance writers, and the tale tellers that such was the case, because, contrary to superficial impressions, the literature of the Middle Ages was not all didactic. It is true that the men of the Middle Ages did not invent the steam engine or the airplane; but they ate and drank and propagated themselves, transacted business, made homes and broke them up, practiced obstetrics, and buried their dead, as now.

Each significant age in the history of humanity has appreciated the world in which it lived; and the Middle Ages was no exception to this general rule. And so the sovereign, with all his advisers, agents, and sycophants, conducted the administration of his kingdom. The villein laboriously cultivated his master baron's strips of land, with a care for the soil which could teach some farmers of today a great deal; the tradesman, when he finally appeared, went about his needful occupations in the congested, dark, unsanitary towns, whose streets were crowded with domestic animals by day and infested by bandits at night; the housewife occupied herself with the usual meals and household tasks that have been the lot of women since time immemorial; the nobleman exercised his privilege of hunting, rode with his hawks and hounds or chatted with his ladies. There were always feast days, religious as well as secular, town fairs and market days, as well as days when nothing much occurred. There were violence, poverty, and filth beyond what a modern can easily imagine. There were also superstition, cruelty, treachery, selfishness, greed, and a numbing passivity which defies belief. There were hate and love and friendship as well. It is impossible that people in such an environment and with such matters to keep them busy should go about continually preoccupied with their immortal souls.

Still, most of the literature produced throughout the Middle Ages—a literature which was always the responsibility of the churchman or the teacher, since they controlled learning and literacy—is a stern reminder of the power of the pen. It is truly unfortunate that the commoners did not possess more vocal spokesmen. We might have now a much more accurate picture of the Middle Ages if they had been rather more articulate and more willing to speak out without fear or favor. The fact remains, nevertheless, that medieval teaching laid emphasis upon the life to come far more than did the teachers of the ancient world on the one hand or of the modern world on the other; and this emphasis assuredly colored medieval literature to a great extent.

PHASES OF THE MEDIEVAL LITERARY TRADITION

So much for suggestions concerning the social and intellectual fiber of the Middle Ages; what of the literature produced? The bastions of this literature are the Church and the feudal system, as they grew through the centuries of strife that went into their building. From the time of the permanent division of the Roman empire into two parts (395) until the coronation of Charlemagne by the pope as "Emperor of the Romans" (800), the Church had managed to hold together the remnants of the older civilization, in both the secular and the spiritual sense, spreading the word of God through missionaries and evangelists, defending itself against heresies which might split its unity, and preserving whatever learning it could salvage. In those earlier centuries of the Middle Ages, feudalism was only beginning; those were the days of absolute rule only, when a kingdom was scarcely more complex in its structure or its geographical extent than a mere barbaric tribe. In one sense, then, the ecclesiastical structure, as it developed through the first four centuries of the medieval era, was the predecessor of the feudal system.

As it happens, however, the years from 400 to 800 are not important to us as years of literary production in Western Europe. Epics and sagas un-

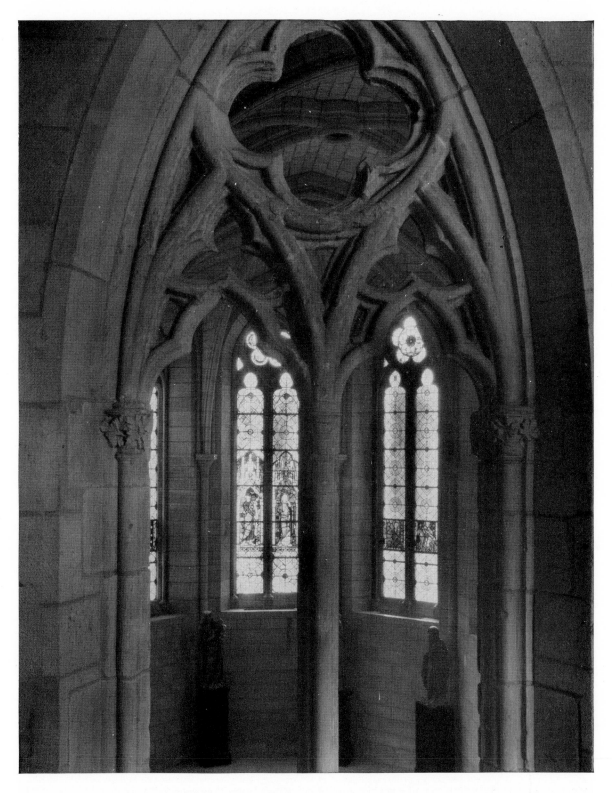

The beauty and religious conviction of medieval Gothic architecture is embodied in this thirteenth-century double lancet window from La Tricherie church, Vienne, France, now in the Cloisters, New York.

doubtedly flourished in oral tradition, very likely in much greater profusion than we realize today. In this type of literature the English took the lead, for the Anglo-Saxon epic poems, represented by *Beowulf* and the Caedmonian and Cynewulfian epic cycles,* all of which were originally composed by the end of the eighth century or shortly thereafter, are head and shoulders above contemporaneous continental literature. The superiority of these poems lies in the fact that their authors were men of talent belonging to a literary tradition both of artistic possibilities and of rigid standards; the Anglo-Saxon bard, or *scop,* had developed the potentialities of the Old Germanic alliterative verse to the point where it was expressive, elastic, and often extremely impressive. In addition to the writers of these epic poems, Anglo-Saxon England produced at least one unusual scholarly talent in the Venerable Bede, who died in 735. Bede's *Ecclesiastical History of the English People* was a model of historiography for centuries to come. On the continent before 800, on the other hand, the writing was almost exclusively of an ecclesiastical or academic nature—works on ecclesiastical policy; on doctrine; on the combatting of heresy; on the chronicling of historical events and the observation of basic natural phenomena, including geography, natural history, medicine, botany, and astronomy. Except for theological works, however, the total literary output of the continent until the year 800 is both highly derivative and essentially pallid. The single important exception is the work of Boethius, a Roman philosopher (d. 524), who wrote on music and rhetoric but is most valuable as a gifted transmitter of Platonic philosophy in his *De Consolatione Philosophiae,* which, translated into all the languages of Western Europe, exerted an influence of a diffused and secular kind as long as the Middle Ages lasted.

The unusual unifying power which was Charlemagne's introduces a second phase of development in the medieval tradition. From a political viewpoint, Charlemagne created a Frankish empire which was recognized by the Church as the heritage of the Roman empire,† and as duly sanctioned by God. With the strife which followed the death of Charlemagne, feudalism received its most powerful single impulse. But even more important to the history of Occidental civilization was Charlemagne's sincere desire to encourage learning in all of its

accepted forms. The founding of his Palace School was the first great milestone along the road which was to lead to the establishment of the University of Paris and thence to the spread of the Renaissance into Western Europe. It was an Englishman, Alcuin of York, who was his most useful and effective teacher. Unfortunately for the political harmony of the age, Charlemagne's empire after his death, becoming a bone of contention among his sons, was broken up. The struggles for leadership among its parts tormented the continent for centuries.

The years from 800 to about 1200 represent a second phase of the medieval tradition. To this period belongs the evolution of monasticism and Scholasticism.** Regardless of other developments, it was these particular manifestations of the medieval intellect which dominated the scene during these four centuries. During this time there came a revivifying of and stricter obedience to the monastic rules, as typified in particular by the reform of the Benedictine Rule in various parts of Europe during the ninth, tenth, and eleventh centuries. The monk in his cloister examined God's inventory and recorded the course of human events in chronicles, interpreted the Word of God as manifested in the Scriptures, pointed out the obvious superiority of the world to come over the world that was, preached how both reason and natural affection would draw men to God. This was the age of teaching by catechistic devices, dialogues, and debates; by the rigid application of logic, dialectics, and practical persuasion. In this age the orders of friars went forth to help found seats of learning in such widely separated places as Bologna, Paris, Oxford, Cambridge, and elsewhere; in this age were sown the seeds which bore fruit later in the lonely eminence of such theologians as Thomas Aquinas or Duns Scotus; such a talented investigating scholar, born before his time, as Roger Bacon; such possessors of "all knowledge" as Albertus Magnus or Vincent of Beauvais. This was the age of the churchman near the threshold of the Supreme, which he would approach but never quite cross.

Then came the thirteenth century, which many have regarded as the peak of medieval culture. Never again would there reign a Pope so absolute in his authority; never again would the Holy Roman Emperor be so potent in secular matters. Actually, in many quarters, the feudal edifice was being subjected to intense strain. The barons were becoming restive; the full prerogatives of the sovereign were in question. In England, early in this century, King John

---

* Caedmon was the earliest English Christian poet and his poems on Biblical themes date from about 1000. Cynewulf is the only Old English vernacular poet of whom we have undisputed extant works, written in the ninth century. The poetry of both is referred to as Old English Christian Epics.

† More than a century after the collapse of this "Roman Empire" of Charlemagne a new empire, ruled over by a German king, replaced it, 962. This came to be called the Holy Roman Empire, and lasted until 1806.

** Scholasticism was the study of philosophy aimed basically at reconciling Church dogma with Aristotelian logic, or faith with reason. It reached its zenith in the thirteenth century and then began to degenerate into formalistic arguing over minute points of dogma; as such it was ridiculed by many Humanist writers of the Renaissance.

was obliged to sign Magna Charta (1215), which was the opening wedge to weaken and destroy royal privilege. On the continent, the struggle continued between Pope and Emperor, as illustrated in Italy by the fierce local internecine warfare between Guelphs and Ghibellines;* and although the Pope, then at the height of his secular powers, was still supreme, the taint of worldliness was upon him, and the succeeding centuries were to prove that even his high office could become of the earth earthy. Yet it is entirely appropriate that Innocent III, the superb, should be the author of *De Contemptu Mundi,* a thoroughly characteristic document which states the medieval definition of this world as well as any.

This was the century of the great Scholastics, who continued to argue with infinite zeal and patience that the Kingdom of God was ascertainable through human reason, that it was essentially the reflection of God's relationship to man—the relationship of eternal love and well-being—and that man was truly blessed only when he withdrew himself from the temptations of the world, the flesh, and the devil, and regarded the present world as evil in contrast to the New Jerusalem flowing with milk and honey. And, in a narrower and more human way, it was dimly recognized that man, submitting to the decrees of omnipotent God, was blessed also when in the simplest terms he took comfort in the lesser things of nature, as was preached by Saint Francis of Assisi.

Still, side by side with the monasticism of the twelfth and thirteenth centuries, there was a secular compensation with more than one outlet. There was the chivalric movement, which gave prominence in fiction, as well as in courtly manners, to the aristocratic lady, giving her reverence and homage and joining the secular ideas of love to the divine concept of heavenly bliss. And while the thirteenth century produced Magna Charta and the revolt of the barons, thereby widening the base of the ruling power, it produced something else, the guildsman. Here was the first recognition of the social importance of the man of industry, the ancestor of the modern middle class, or *bourgeoisie;* and as this man's political and social position was enhanced—a process unquestionably helped along by the social, recreational, and religious organization of laborers called the guild— so much were medieval traditions weakened.

The advance of the guildsman to a position of importance in the medieval municipality coincided in the fourteenth century with early signs of weakness in the medieval Church—a confusion of authority, a

schism, which prevailed through a large part of the century (the Babylonian Captivity, 1305–1376). One faction professed spiritual obedience to a Pope in Rome; another to a Pope in Avignon while the courts of both Popes were remarkable chiefly for a cynical worldliness and luxurious display. Even when the Papacy returned to Rome, it was clear that the damage had been done. Almost immediately there-

A monk, one of the figures by Claus Sluter from the tomb of Philip the Bold of Burgundy, who died in 1404.

---

* These were two factions in the Italian city-states, the Ghibellines supporting the Holy Roman Emperors and the Guelphs backing the claims of the Popes.

after John Wycliffe in England began to preach what were termed heresies by the medieval Church and John Huss of Bohemia paid with his life (1415) for his revolt against the dicta of Rome. The Reformation was not officially recognized until a century later, but the essence of its thought can be found at this period.

If the twelfth and thirteenth centuries came to mean the greatest achievements of medieval theology and philosophy, then in comparison the fourteenth century, which happened to produce the greatest writers, if not the greatest thinkers, of the Middle Ages, was an era of transition to the Renaissance. Dante, who died in 1321, was the last and in every way the most typical great exponent of medievalism, with his rigid cosmography; his harsh, almost pedantic preoccupation with the sinful and the virtuous; his inspiration derived from the worlds still to come. Yet Dante had a noble admiration for poetry as poetry; and the later fourteenth-century authors like Boccaccio, Petrarch, and Chaucer have little to anchor them to the Middle Ages except their dates and the fact that they observed certain medieval conventions—an occasional concession to abstract teaching, allegory, and esoteric symbolism; a routine deference to the tenets if not the institution of the medieval Church. Yet these conventions, as these writers honor them, are not likely to strike one as anything more than external. By 1400 the Renaissance was already in the ascendant almost everywhere save in England, which suffered a temporary intellectual and literary stagnation during most of the fifteenth century.

We may safely conclude that the Middle Ages was primarily a period of constant struggle, both covert and overt, between the Church and outer paganism, or between the Church and the State. If Europe, from the eleventh to the thirteenth century, was split down the middle in the conflict between Pope and Emperor, Guelph and Ghibelline, what were the consequences of the conflict? For one thing, the growing city-states of medieval Italy, Venice, Florence, Genoa, for all their internal strife, cast off the restraints of the Middle Ages and became the birthplace of the individualism of the Renaissance; and here is an illustration of the truism that each age contains within itself the seeds of that which will later bring about its passing.

FROM EARLY EPIC TO CHAUCER

IT is a simple matter to ignore the literature produced in Europe before the year 800, for that is the interest of the confirmed specialist only. Its nature has already been briefly described; its expression was neither original enough nor powerful enough to stand the test of time. However, the epic tradition from non-Christian times and places, which is more vital than any other literary tradition in existence between the fall of Rome and the days of Charlemagne, showed itself in writing first in Anglo-Saxon England, as we have seen, and gradually emerged— as evidenced in their extant literature—among the continental nations and outlying Celtic lands, always, to be sure, under the auspices of an indulgent Christendom. This early epic tradition was first expressed compellingly in the true heroic style of *Beowulf*, from the eighth or ninth century; of the *Hildebrandslied*, in a mixture of Low and High German from about the same time; and of the Irish Finn and Cuchulain sagas, which were composed probably about a century later. The French *chansons de geste*, short epic poems, culminated in *The Song of Roland* in the eleventh century. In all these works, the hero is primarily a masculine hero; he typifies the ideals of his tribe or nation; he performs marvelous feats; he dies in the odor of sanctity. The English and Germans, in particular, carried over their epic traditions into heroic poems about Biblical characters; these survive as the poems of the Caedmonian and Cynewulfian cycles in Anglo-Saxon England and the Low German *Heliand*, from the late eighth and early ninth centuries.

During the eleventh and twelfth centuries— partly as a result of the revival of interest in the fiction of ancient Greece and Rome (typified, let us say, by the works of Ovid); partly as a result of the cult of the Virgin Mary which emerged during the later tenth century; partly as a result of the adventurous spirit which prompted the First Crusade; and partly because the feudal system had developed strength all over Europe—there evolved a type of epic poem in which the hero became a lover as well as a warrior and assumed the duties of a feudal servant to his lady love. From this type, which originated generally in Provence and southern France and spread thence throughout western Europe, grew the so-called medieval romance in all its varieties. Underlying most of these from the first was the concept of chivalry, in which the knight on horseback did valiant deeds for his sovereign lady. Although woman had appeared at times in the older heroic epic, she was now placed on a far higher pedestal than she had hitherto occupied and was looked up to as an ideal inspiration for a knight's greatest feats. Blending themselves with Celtic and general Germanic legendary narrative material, these new

Chivalric love as depicted on a Swiss wool tapestry. The words, translated freely, read: "In our sport will I be true; that indeed ye'll never rue." The tapestry is now in the Art Institute of Chicago.

epic poems, henceforth to be called romances, generated a powerful and pervasive influence over the whole of European literature. Therefore Lancelot loved and served Guinevere, and Tristan must follow Isoude, and Aucassin could think of no other woman but Nicolete. Older epic sagas, such as the famous *Volsungasaga* of Scandinavian origin, were integrated with a chivalric background into the famous *Nibelungenlied* of the thirteenth or fourteenth century. On the other hand, most of the Norse sagas themselves, relatively free from chivalric atmosphere because of their geographical remoteness, were written down about this same time and stand forth as epics in isolated grandeur.

The medieval romances represent the antithesis of the otherworldly literature which emanated from religious sources, because they glorified, in terms which none could fail to understand, the world in which we live, with its hopes and aspirations, its

dreams, its appetites, its disappointments, and its successes. These were love stories which signified an escape from reality, portraying the feudal world (in which most marriages were actually political) as a glamorous place where loving, handsome knights and loving, beautiful ladies lived together in amorous happiness amid infinite riches. To the medieval lady, who now had become an important segment of the audience and reading public, these romances no doubt satisfied a longing for an emotional outlet in real life, regardless of technical marriage ties. The illicit relationships so prominent in these chivalric narratives are doubtless explicable because even state marriages cannot quench love. These courtly, aristocratic romances and the ancillary lyrics following in their wake—the creations of the gifted Chrestien de Troyes or Gottfried von Strasbourg in the narrative poem and of Walther von der Vogelweide in the love lyric—were designed for women

A late medieval statue of the Virgin from Troyes, France.

as much as for men, and they called to the flesh as freshly and sincerely as does *The Song of Songs*.

The Church, however, did not approve of these romantic and erotic glorifications of human passion, for when all is said and done, it could legitimately insist that Lancelot and Guinevere or Tristan and Isoude were adulterers. Yet the Church was shrewd enough to know that prohibition is a poor way to stop the gratification of a human appetite. Instead, the clergy were encouraged to write their own romances, or to inspire the composition of romances by others, which would convey a moral message while at the same time they conformed to the aristocratic forms and frameworks of the true chivalric romance. And so we come to another type of medieval romance, with moral preachment sometimes couched in highly allegorical or esoteric terms, which produced such masterpieces as the cycle of the Holy Grail (later attached to the Arthurian saga) and the celebrated thirteenth-century French allegorical poem, the *Roman de la Rose,* which taught not only sacred love but a love of nature as well. In fact, the finest single example of a romance in medieval England, *Sir Gawain and the Green Knight,* of about 1370, is distinctly a "moral" rather than a "chivalric" romance. Ultimately, however, these two types of romance, originally quite different in purpose, were blended into a prose type of dissimilar elements—the original romances had been written in verse—and in this prose composition was achieved a compromise between the worldly and the didactic, with the moralistic element tending to predominate. By the fifteenth century, the prose romance was more and more the common form; and the type tended to go to seed in a prolix as well as pedestrian style.

All such fiction, whether secular or religious, whether for a moral purpose only or for the sake of entertainment and solace alone, was of a type originating among and belonging to the traditions of the feudal aristocracy and the clergy. What of the commoners? Unhappily, as we have seen, they were at this time relatively inarticulate. Enough has come down to us, however, to demonstrate that the ordinary individual in the Middle Ages could be entertained by tales, in verse or in prose, sometimes cruder interpretations of aristocratic romance, sometimes animal stories or beast fables of shrewd satirical import, sometimes flat narratives of the barrack room or the tavern. Among all these secular tales, the short, anecdotal type which was based upon either the sex intrigue or the practical joke, or on both—the so-called *fabliau*—was undoubtedly extremely popular. But so also were the innumerable little stories intended to illustrate some moral teaching—the *exempla*—which embellished virtually every kind of didactic writing and were especially common as teaching devices in the medieval sermons. The general basis for all of these tales of popular origin was their essential realism, often presented with savage satirical intent.

Beginning undoubtedly in the later Middle Ages among the Celtic and Germanic peoples, and to a limited extent also on French soil, were the so-called popular ballads, the true origins of which have never been fully explained. Their development at this time is obscure; nearly all surviving versions date from 1400 or later. It is clear that they come from the common people, but older theories about their actual genesis have now been largely cast aside. It is now generally agreed that they are the creations of village Miltons and rustic Homers; that they are of single authorship; that some employ a technique which suggests that they were originally intended for performance in a folk group, but that others are obviously of a more "literary" flavor. Yet all are primarily narrative, rather than lyric, and all were doubtless intended to be sung. In some there are clear indications not only of choral but also of choreographic elements of some sort. It seems reasonably evident that more than one type of narrative song has been included in this category, yet all are referred to as "ballads." At any rate, whatever their origin, they represent the fictional and epic instincts of the people as a whole rather than of the aristocracy or of the clergy, even though some are religious in subject matter; they are fascinating to the folklorist, but, although some possess an eloquence and a dramatic effectiveness altogether beyond the ordinary, they are to be referred to the backwaters rather than to the main stream of literature.

Also developing in western Europe during the Middle Ages was a native drama. There was a slight carry-over of classical drama through clerical channels during the early centuries of the era, but these surviving imitations of Roman comedy, for example, are isolated and altogether atypical. The most celebrated imitation of the classical is evident in the works of the German nun, Hrostvitha, of the tenth century. We may, however, dismiss the influence of Greece and Rome in this period and concentrate instead on the development of the new drama. Like Greek drama, medieval plays originated in religious observances, but there is no direct continuity from classical days. The theater made a fresh start. Certain dramatic and mimetic interpolations were made in the readings of the scriptures on special Church festivals, such as Christmas and Easter. This first ritualistic stage of medieval drama is usually assigned to the tenth century. It is a hazardous business to state categorically that the miracle or mystery plays grew directly out of the liturgical drama, yet such is most likely the case.

Unfortunately there is a gap of two or three centuries, from the tenth to the thirteenth, which cannot be filled in satisfactorily. It seems probable that the Christmas and Easter representations were followed by representations of other sacred material from the scriptures and that the dramatic business involved became more and more extensive and popular, until the representations themselves overflowed the church, pushed out into the church enclosure, and finally debouched into the market place. At this point in the thirteenth or fourteenth century, the guilds assumed the production of plays devoted to incidents from the Bible—usually to miracles or to the lives of saints. It was found both convenient and desirable to give these plays on feast days when there was good weather; and the presentation of these plays by the guildsmen therefore tended to group them together into cycles. An entire cycle of these miracle plays would then be performed by various guilds in a town on a given holy day; in the fourteenth and fifteenth centuries, the period of our surviving miracle plays, Corpus Christi Day, celebrated in June, became a favorite. The plays, well salted with lusty yeoman's humor, were then staged on floats or pageants, which moved about through the town. The actors were amateurs at first, but we hear of wages eventually paid them. Sooner or later the performances were held at a fixed place, such as the center of the town, perhaps the steps of the local church or cathedral or the courtyard of the local inn; but this is hardly likely to have happened before the fifteenth century.

During the later decades of this fifteenth century there emerged another type of play, in which the characters were abstract personages and in which the central theme was likely to be the struggle between God and the Devil for the possession of a human soul. The origin of these so-called morality plays, however, is most obscure. It seems probable that they arose independently of the miracle plays and that their authors were primarily clerics and teachers rather than laymen. Their messages are often ponderous and platitudinous and only occasionally endowed with the lusty humor of the miracle plays. By 1500, which is approximately the time of the most famous of morality plays, the Dutch *Elckerlijk* (translated into English as *Everyman*), it is evident that the miracle play as a type had died out except in isolated places. The Renaissance was to borrow elements from the moralities, from the slapstick of the older miracle plays, from the still more venerable folk drama (about which we know virtually nothing before 1500 at the earliest), and was to fuse these different elements with humanistic borrowings from classical drama, to achieve from this complex blend a modern European drama which was far advanced beyond anything produced in the dramatic field during the Middle Ages.

Even if the ballads, the tales, and the medieval plays owe their chief vitality to the common people, it still remains basically true that the stewardship over all writing in the Middle Ages, whatever the type might be, lay in the hands of the

"The Morris Dance," an engraving by Israhel van Meckenem, shows that medieval life was not entirely serious.

Church. These hands wrought sermons, homilies, commentaries on the scriptures, interpretations of monastic rule, and religious lyrics—some of which, such as the medieval Latin hymns like the *Te Deum*, the *Dies Irae*, the *Stabat Mater*, and the *Hora Novissima*, are of permanent value.

The scribe was, generally speaking, a cleric, either in a monastery or among the Church's secular clergy; and churchly tradition determined in the main what was to be written and what was to be cast into outer darkness. Furthermore, the survival to the present day of any piece of

medieval writing is a matter of the workings of Fortune. On a liberal estimate, it is probable that we have in our possession today only about one half of what was actually produced during the Middle Ages. From the earlier centuries of this era we doubtless know about much less than half. Was the lost half more worldly than otherwise? Possibly so, for the Church would naturally prefer to save only that which suited its purposes. As it is, the medieval Church has bequeathed to us a truly staggering amount of Christian commentary, monitory literature, precept, proverb, and the like. Some of all this

—that which represents common sense and the wisdom of the ages—may have come also from the people as a whole. But much of it originated in the monastery or the consistory. Little of it has any further appeal today than to the specialist who makes the Middle Ages his particular field of endeavor or to the enthusiast who sees the monastic and scholastic tradition as inherently superior to the modern.

This is all doubtless to be expected. It means in general, however, that the kind of medieval literature most deserving to live in the ages to come, on which we, for better or worse, are most apt to base our estimate of the net achievement of medieval civilization and traditions, is that literature which was produced during the later thirteenth century and the fourteenth century as a whole. Yet, as we have seen, it is the fourteenth century which foreshadows the collapse of the Middle Ages. Here at the beginning of the 1300's stands the great figure of Dante; at the end of the century stands another

figure, Chaucer, who is fully as great in a different way. Between these two giants come Boccaccio, Petrarch, Gower, the Piers Plowman Poet, and the Pearl Poet. Shortly thereafter appear the distinguished poet and chronicler Froissart, the romantic vagabond Villon, and the most readable today of the many writers in the tradition of medieval theology, scholasticism, and moral preachment—Thomas à Kempis.

To be sure, if we are to give the medieval Church its proportion just and due, we must still read Anselm and Thomas Aquinas and Bonaventura and Albertus Magnus and Duns Scotus and even Vincent of Beauvais and John of Salisbury. But they are a forbidding and—again except to the enthusiast—a strangely inhuman group of writers. On the other hand, the unknown authors of the Book of Lancelot and the *Conte del Graal;* the romantic and somewhat tedious Guillaume de Lorris and the sardonic Jean de Meun (sometimes known as the medieval

Grimly fortified strongholds testify to the constant feudal wars which endangered medieval life. This is Carcassonne.

II:16 CHRISTENDOM, ISLAM, AND THE MIDDLE AGES

CHRISTENDOM, ISLAM, AND THE MIDDLE AGES II:17

A portrait of Chaucer now in the National Portrait Gallery, London. It is probably an early copy from a miniature.

Voltaire), who between them were responsible for the *Roman de la Rose*; and such worldlings as Walter Map and the mysterious "Sir John Mandeville," to say nothing of the remarkable list of first-rate writers mentioned in the preceding paragraph —these are the men to whom we refer all the vital, abiding medieval literature of which we have knowledge. Which of these two groups represents the characteristically medieval?

The answer is, of course, that both groups are representative. Whatever the integration of thought in the Middle Ages—an integration adored in certain quarters today—the fact remains that no truly great period of human history is simple or uncomplicated, and the Middle Ages is no exception. It is equally true that while the theological and the scholastic held sway during the heart of the Middle Ages, still they are the most definitely limited by place and time. The more secular is the more nearly universal.

As an example, when the true medieval teacher, and he who is under his immediate influence, wishes to convey a piece of doctrine, what is the form he prefers? The dialogue, fresh from the center of the scholastic symposium. Perhaps he can secularize the matter into a debate between the body and the soul or between an owl and a nightingale, yet a dialogue it remains—the discussion between master and pupil or the controversy between master and master. Even in the courtly French love poetry the dialogue represents an influence from the teacher in love. But when Petrarch dedicates a new poetic form, the son-net, to his Laura's beauty; when Boccaccio turns over his narrative to the churls Calandrino and Bufal-macco; when Chaucer creates what is fundamentally a modern English novel, *Troilus and Criseyde*, and the first dramatic monologue of extensive self-anal-ysis, the *Prologue to The Wife of Bath's Tale*—then we have reached a stage of sophisticated literature which shows that the Middle Ages, in its last his-torical phases, cannot well be dissociated from the Renaissance.

THE IMPACT OF ISLAM

WE must remember that the terms "Middle Ages" and "medieval" can apply only to the world of western Europe. China, India, Per-sia, and the Moslem world in general would not be concerned with them. China and India were at that time proceeding unperturbed along their highly conservative courses. Persia was undergoing a true renaissance of arts and letters during these same centuries. The contributions of the Mohammedan civilizations to the sciences alone put them far ahead of European medieval culture in an intellectual sense. Indeed, the Near East in this period was an-ticipating the European Renaissance in most of the activities of the human mind. The obvious but sel-dom recognized fact remains that, except in the fields of theology and religious philosophy, medie-val Europe was relatively backward until near the close of the thousand-year era under consideration; and it may well be added that Dante and particu-larly Chaucer—by all odds the greatest writers of the Middle Ages—were as much a part of the Ren-aissance as of the European Middle Ages.

Before our final evaluation of the actual litera-ture of this age, therefore, we must turn our atten-tion eastward. The Byzantine Empire, during the approximately thousand years of its existence, be-came a symbol both of Eastern Christianity ° and of high artistic achievements. These achievements were confined to the fine arts, however, for Byzantine literature, as such, was of little worth except in so far as it served as a repository for the great contri-butions of ancient Greece and Rome. The greatest individual among the Eastern emperors, Justinian, left as early as 500 the reputation of a jurist, not of a man of letters.

The great factor in a versatile culture in Eastern lands throughout this era was the Mohammedan religion, whose influence from the seventh to the

° The long-standing split between the Eastern and Western Churches became official in 1054. Constantinople (Byzantium) was the religious capital of the Eastern Orthodox Church as Rome was of the Western Catholic.

fifteenth century was enormous. The teachings of Mohammed were in themselves fundamentally sim-ple. They were first preached among nomadic tribes-men in a bare and austere environment, but they spread like a forest fire over a huge territory, into all walks of life, and eventually came to be centered in a luxurious, opulent capital which gave the great-est possible encouragement to what we choose to call civilized thought. Mohammed (570–632) was him-self a builder of immense energy in the history of religions, and the *Koran* is important solely as a religious document, not as a work of literary art. As time went on, the rigor of Mohammed's teachings was blended with the worldly philosophies of other schools of Oriental thought, and the net resultant of these various forces was a civilization for which teeming, vivid Bagdad became the symbol. It was a world of practical living and idealistic thought, of commerce and trade, of materialism as well as mys-ticism. Haroun al-Raschid, Caliph of Bagdad, and Charlemagne communicated with each other, it is true, but there was little else in common between Moslems and Christians in the year 800. For in knowledge of the world and in knowledge of mankind, to say nothing of intellectual range and elasticity, the Moslem world was far ahead of the Christian world until the dawn of the thirteenth century.

It was not only the kind of work accomplished by Averroës or Avicenna, who in the eleventh and twelfth centuries pushed Arabic science and mathe-matics to the highest peak of development, that ac-counted for the difference between the Moslem and the Christian worlds. The Middle East had never dropped so far below the artistic and intellec-tual standards of Greece and Rome as had the west-ern world of Europe. On the contrary, it was in most respects, though perhaps not consciously, continuing the true classical traditions. Its literary achievement in particular culminated in the work of that re-markable quartet of Persian poets—Firdousi, Omar Khayyam, Sadi, and Hafiz—a group of writers of high order, who coincide approximately in time with the peak of Moslem scientific contributions. All of these men had passed away before the death of Chaucer in 1400, and in most ways the finest accomplishments of this neo-Persian literature had been completed by the middle of the fourteenth century.

From the time of Mohammed to the time of Haroun al-Raschid is nearly two centuries; and no religious faith, however simple, can remain either simple or unsophisticated for so long a time, especially when it has in the meantime become a world issue. The Bagdad of the days of Haroun al-Raschid was the locale of most of those remarkable narratives, partly satirical, partly erotic, partly adventurous and fantastic, which were ultimately collected and translated into European literature as *The Arabian Nights' Entertainment* or *The Thousand and One Nights*. It is manifestly unjust to think of these superb stories as mere juvenile fare—a fate which has overtaken both them and *Gulliver's Travels*, for example—because in their original and native state they combine the worldliness of Persius and Juvenal with the urbanity of Horace, the clarity of Ovid, and an exotic imagination which is in no way Roman or even Occidental.

After the close of the first Christian millennium the scene shifts from Bagdad to Shiraz. Now the romanticism of *The Arabian Nights* is mingled with the skepticism, the melancholy and world-weariness, and the paradoxical mysticism inspired by the Persian garden, the desert, the sun, moon, and cosmic universe—still romantic in essentials, but touched now with the restless, inquiring spirit of doubt questing after the unknown mystery of life and impregnated with fatalism. Here Omar Khayyam pondered his vision of the lion and the lizard in the ruined courts of Jamshyd, reflected upon the ineluctable moving finger of Time, begged God to forgive him for his carnality and then magnanimously returned that forgiveness, urged a stoical preparation for death, and mused in unforgettable words on how youth must pass forever. In this same kind of setting arose the vast epic by Firdousi, the *Shah Nameh*, the mighty songs of arms and the man—not Achilles, not Aeneas, but Rustum. Here the satirist Sadi, in his *Gulistan*, took his Moslem world for his province, seeing life steadily and as completely as one man can see it. And here Hafiz, the last of the great Shirazists and perhaps the most versatile poet of later Oriental literature, wrote odes to his mistress' eyebrows in precisely the same vein as that made famous centuries later by the courtly French poets of the Renaissance and the gifted singers of Elizabethan England.

Philosophically, the contrast between the Oriental and the Christian points of view at this stage of world history is not necessarily achieved by balancing the work of Omar Khayyam or Sadi against that of Thomas Aquinas, startling as the comparative study of such men will be. In any event, this contrast would have to be supplemented by a juxtaposition of the *Koran* with the New Testament—the naïve, austere, fanatical, yet at the same time sensual teachings of the *Koran* beside the poetic, subtle, withdrawing, yet practical Sermon on the Mount or Pauline Epistles. Compare and contrast, for example, the description of Paradise in the *Koran* with the New Jerusalem in the book of *Revelation*. The essential fact, in any thorough comparative study, will be that in the writings of Omar Khayyam and Hafiz we find a polish, a sense of life in this world, with all its strengths and weaknesses, and a *laissez-faire* attitude toward living which is altogether "modern" and not to be found in European literature until the fourteenth century. The reason for this is not that medieval Europe was essentially more inexperienced or more idealistic than contemporary Islam; it is only that Europe, due to historical circumstances, had developed a different approach, to cope with problems peculiarly its own.

At the same time, the Oriental mind from Haroun al-Raschid to Hafiz was by no means merely materialistic. The Persian writers in particular were powerfully influenced by a special brand of mysticism known as Sufism—a mysticism which, unlike the medieval vision of the New Jerusalem, affords the modern reader a remarkably liberal kind of spiritual experience. Sufism depends upon the character of the believer's mind and is equally at home in all doctrines and dogmas. It assumes that God, the nameless, undefinable core of being, is to be revered above all things, because He alone is worthy of adoration; and everything here below is to be subordinated, even sacrificed if necessary, to attain a recognition of God.

So far this is but little different from the medieval Christian point of view, except that the Christian insisted upon a personal kind of divinity, obviously anthropomorphic. Both points of view are clearly related to the Platonic theory of God as Love. The Persian Sufists, however, could at the same time express themselves in worldly and skeptical thoughts, which was not possible for a medieval Christian; religiously speaking, therefore, they were far more liberal than otherwise. The most that even so emancipated an individual as Chaucer could do, on the other hand, was to commit himself to a mild agnosticism about philosophical or religious matters— "I know not; such I leave to the divines." And this agnosticism would never be applied among medieval Christians to fundamental matters of Christian doctrine, except in the case of radicals like Wycliffe and Huss, who were obviously ahead of their times. The conclusion to be drawn from these comparisons is that the Persian of the year 1000 was able to make his transition to the modern era far more comfortably than his contemporary Christian enemy, who at that time was even fearful of the end of the world. It might well be argued that the Oriental had no transition to make. But, on the other hand, the European Christian was able to advance on seven-league boots after the fourteenth century, whereas Persian literature after the death of Hafiz in 1388 has remained fundamentally unchanged.

Crescent or Cross—until the eighth century it was a burning question which would dominate Europe, for Mohammedanism had penetrated from North Africa far into Spain. Charles Martel, ancestor of Charlemagne, settled this matter, as we can see now, on the fields about Tours in France in the year 732; and so the question as to what would have happened if the Universities of Paris, Bologna, and Oxford had been founded by Moslems remains a purely speculative matter. One must not, therefore, yield to Oriental literature at this stage of history any more than its just deserts, for the Western world has since passed it by.

To be sure, the inevitable impress of the Oriental upon European literature could never be lost, particularly in certain areas. The Crusades began in western Europe about 1100; they started as holy wars to wrest from the Moslems the Holy Sepulchre in Jerusalem, and they achieved a temporary success in the attaining of that immediate objective; but they ended as opportunistic junkets designed to increase the worldly power of Christian princes and the Christian Church. They often produced disillusioning spectacles like the Fourth Crusade of 1204 or the ghastly inhumanity of the fanatical Children's Crusade of 1212. But they brought western Europe into closer contact with the East than ever before; from the hated Saracen the European grudgingly and reluctantly learned much, for the Crusaders brought back with them to Europe fascinating Oriental stories and legends, and some few Europeans, at least, came to realize the importance of Arabic science.

In the meantime, the Orient was preparing a counterattack. The Ottoman Turks debouched upon the eastern extremities of Europe; they captured Constantinople (Byzantium) in 1453; they penetrated to the gates of Vienna as late as the seventeenth century. The Moors remained in Spain until nearly 1500. Interrelations between Crescent and Cross were therefore inevitable, in spite of the bigotry of the Christian and the fanatical intolerance of the Moslem. The plain fact remains, however, that from the later thirteenth century on it is medieval European literature which counts chiefly in the main sum. And after the Middle Ages had passed away, it was still European literature which was fulfilling a dynamic, penetrating role in the history of civilization.

THE MEANING OF THE MIDDLE AGES

In summary, we see now that the Middle Ages before 800 were, intellectually, comparatively barren everywhere in the European world. It is now out of fashion to refer to these centuries as "The Dark Ages"; and yet if there is any period of recorded history which deserves this epithet, it is still the period between 400 and 800. In the last analysis, we know of little that was contributed to the future during those uncertain years. Of course, if there is any special preëminence to be granted any segment of this early medieval literature, it should go to the Anglo-Saxons in England. During this monastic age, the most typical and withal the best examples of medieval literature are in Latin and therefore international in scope. The Scandinavian Eddic Poems came into being at the very end of this period, as did the continental and English romances, to say nothing of the Welsh and Irish legends; but these are grand examples of fundamentally isolated literature, with some of the virtues that derive from originality and yet with the parochialism that comes from their very isolation.

The significant literature of the later Middle Ages, at least after the year 800, is still in western Europe the work of the great Scholastics and the clerical writings on real and legendary history, as well as on the struggle between the Kingdom of God and the Kingdom of Satan. Near the year 1200 the romances of chivalric nature were flourishing, followed closely in time by the moral antiromances of clerical origins. At the same time there were outpourings of popular tales, generally in oral tradition, the beginnings of drama, the germs of balladry. In all these fields of literature, except for the ballad, France unquestionably assumed leadership; indeed, French influence is clearly the greatest in medieval literature. At this same time, too, came the full tide of Moslem science and belles-lettres.

During the thirteenth century, the massive contributions of Scholastic philosophy and theology, on the side of the otherworldly, were balanced by the continuous and increasing flow of romance material and popular fiction. Significant events, the rise of an industrial middle class, the growth of cities, and the ascendancy of a bourgeoisie, during this century and later, portended the end of the medieval era.

A hunt at the court of Philip the Good, a French painting of the Bourgogne school, fifteenth century.

In the fourteenth century, which witnessed clearly both a decay of the medieval and a promise of the Renaissance, the honors in literature were divided fairly between the Italians and the English; and, indeed, the honors in Renaissance art and literature were to be divided in similar fashion. If Italy produced her Dante and her Petrarch and her Boccaccio, England produced her Chaucer and her Piers Plowman Poet and her Pearl Poet. Chaucer looms more and more, as time goes by, a greater figure than Petrarch or Boccaccio and a formidable rival of Dante and the medieval mystics. Which of the two titans, Chaucer or Dante, by our twentieth-century standards is the more characteristically medieval? Probably Dante. Which is the greater poet as poet? Again, probably Dante. Which is the more comprehensive interpreter of humanity and critic of life? Unquestionably Chaucer. At this point we may leave the medievalists to wrangle among themselves.

As for the fifteenth century, which is already the time of the Renaissance in Italy, there can be little dispute. England went into a temporary eclipse; France, Spain, and Germany were not yet ready for this profound experience in the history of human civilization. But it was the century when Villon, Erasmus, Machiavelli, Ariosto, Rabelais, Cellini, Michelangelo, Raphael, and Leonardo da Vinci— to say nothing of Columbus and Copernicus—were born and bred, and the European mind at this time was entering one of the most brilliant periods in its development.

There is a certain tendency for some thinkers in our twentieth century to turn to the Middle Ages with something approaching veneration, as if this thousand-year period would be a desirable era to imitate. To some extent this feeling is the instinct of the latter-day orthodox Christian, standing embattled against new, urgent forces in the twentieth century which threaten the integrity of the Christian pattern. To others not thus religiously inclined, there remains still the fascination exerted by a unified program of living which the Middle Ages may seem to hold out. To such as these it will appear that no effective kind of civilization can exist without a culture, that this culture must depend upon a pattern, that a pattern necessarily assumes a hierarchy, and that the Middle Ages furnished a hierarchy in both Church and State. The fallacy in such reasoning lies in the assumption that a workable pattern must necessarily include a hierarchy. But more misguided than such an assumption is the hope that a return to the medieval way of life is either possible or profitable. The hands of the clock can never be turned back, and no self-respecting modernist could possibly be content in the Middle Ages, which was, after all, merely a transitional stage in the history of the world. The Middle Ages, to be candid, was an era of much ignorance, intolerance, and unquestioning acceptance of authority; no looking through rose-colored glasses, no plea for unity, no mystic communion with the saints and a personal divinity can alter those inescapable facts. If some deplore the coming of the Reformation and the releasing of powerful intellectual forces difficult to control, then they are a thousand years behind the times, or else they are gazing in wistful nostalgia at a bygone age which it would be impracticable and obstructive to renew; the Middle Ages died once and for all when Martin Luther nailed on the door of the church his theses and when it was finally realized that the world is too much with us, no matter how much we may prefer simple thinking and simple doing. A vast distance separates the Middle Ages from the Atomic Age.

The Koran

The *Koran* is the sacred book of Islam. It is a prose work in Arabic—the first important body of Arabic prose—consisting of one hundred and fourteen chapters, or *suras*, of varying length. Mohammedans everywhere accept it as the word of Allah, who established it in Heaven, where it is preserved in perfect, immortal form, and revealed it to his only prophet, Mohammed. Objective criticism insists that it was composed largely by Mohammed, who, though probably unable to read or write, had the undoubted talents of a brilliant prophet, as well as an oral knowledge of the Pentateuch and the Psalms from the Hebrew Old Testament, the New Testament, and other Oriental religious works, particularly those of the Persian Magians. It is therefore to be presumed that the *Koran* came into being during the active years of Mohammed as prophet, or between 610 and 632.

The *suras* of the *Koran* were very likely first written down in isolated pieces by Mohammed's scribe or scribes. Shortly after the death of the prophet in 632, a collection was undertaken by Zaid ibn Tabit, secretary to Mohammed—or so it is believed—under the guidance of Abu Bekr, Mohammed's father-in-law. To remove all possible dispute about sources and originals, the Caliph Othman in 650 sanctioned an authorized version. All previous copies of the *Koran* were then destroyed, and so the book as we have it in Othman's version is a remarkable example of a great religious source of authority which has remained intact to the present day.

Although it is a work in formal prose, the *Koran* in many of its *suras* has an unusually strong emotional and lyrical spirit, which is further enhanced by the frequent use of rhyme effects and refrains. The chronological order of the one hundred and fourteen *suras,* however, has never been satisfactorily determined. The speaker in virtually all of them is God. The tone of all is strikingly dogmatic and absolute. But in the varying degrees of this dogmatic quality some have seen a clue to the date of the composition of a given *sura*—the more assured and intolerant the tone, the greater the likelihood that the *sura* was written at Medina rather than at Mecca (that is, after 622, when Mohammed was established as the leader of a powerful political party). The whole matter is, of course, still open to liberal conjecture.

The *Koran* is, in any event, the great book of authority for the morals, laws, theological doctrines, and social ethics of the Moslem world. It is given more than is usual in such works to a consideration of the life to come. It is austere, unyielding, passionate as well as noble, fierce and cruel as well as sympathetic. From first to last it preaches the Unity and Soleness of the Most High, the Most Merciful and Most Compassionate God, Allah; to serve him and to die for him are the greatest of privileges, to neglect him and to disregard his commandments

are the unforgivable sins. The imagery of the *Koran* is the imagery of the desert, of the lonely places of body and soul, of the unsophisticated pastoral and rural scene rather than of the crowded bazaar and teeming Oriental city streets. It entertains the promise of an idyllic sensual existence for the Faithful after the great Day of Judgment. By its words billions have lived and died.

The Koran

CHAPTER 47. *In the Name of the Most Merciful God*

GOD will render of none effect the works of those who believe not, and who turn away men from the way of God: but as to those who believe, and work righteousness, and believe the revelation which hath been sent down unto Mohammed (for it is the truth from their Lord), he will expiate their evil deeds from them, and will dispose their heart aright. This will he do, because those who believe not follow vanity, and because those who believe follow the truth from their Lord. Thus God 10 propoundeth unto men their examples. When ye encounter the unbelievers, strike off their heads, until ye have made a great slaughter among them; and bind them in bonds; and either give them a free dismission afterwards, or exact a ransom; until the war shall have laid down its arms. This shall ye do. Verily if God pleased he could take vengeance on them, without your assistance; but he commandeth you to fight his battles, that he may prove the one of you by the other. And as to those who fight in 20 defence of God's true religion, God will not suffer their works to perish; he will guide them, and will dispose their heart aright; and he will lead them into paradise, of which he hath told them.

O true believers, if ye assist God, by fighting for his religion, he will assist you against your enemies; and will set your feet fast: but as for the infidels, let them perish; and their works shall God render vain. This shall befall them, because they have rejected with abhorrence that which God hath revealed, 30 wherefore their works shall become of no avail. Do they not travel through the earth, and see what hath been the end of those who were before them? God utterly destroyed them, and the like awaiteth the unbelievers. This shall come to pass, for that God is the patron of the true believers, and for that the infidels have no protector. Verily God will introduce those who believe, and do good works, into gardens beneath which rivers flow; but the unbelievers indulge themselves in pleasures, and eat as the beasts

*The Koran.*⁸ Translated by George Sale.
39–40. **indulge . . . eat.** Unbelievers, intoxicated with purely animal pleasures, will live in a merely animal state; the believers, whatever their physical pleasures, will have a spiritual euphoria as well.

eat, and their abode shall be hell fire. How many cities were more mighty in strength than thy city which hath expelled thee; yet have we destroyed them, and there was none to help them? Shall he therefore, who followeth the plain declaration of his Lord, be as he whose evil works have been dressed up for him by the devil, and who follow their own lusts? The description of paradise, which is promised unto the pious: therein are rivers of in-corruptible water, and rivers of milk, the taste whereof changeth not, and rivers of wine, pleasant unto those who drink, and rivers of clarified honey, and therein shall they have plenty of all kinds of fruits, and pardon from their Lord. Shall the man for whom these things are prepared be as he who must dwell forever in hell fire; and will have the boiling water given him to drink, which shall burst his bowels? Of the unbelievers there are some who give ear unto thee, until, when they go out from thee, they say, by way of derision unto those to whom knowledge hath been given, "What hath he said now?" These are they whose hearts God hath sealed up, and who follow their own lusts; but as to those who are directed, God will grant them a more ample direction, and he will instruct them what to avoid. Do the infidels wait for any other than the last hour, that it may come upon them suddenly? Some signs thereof are already come: and when it shall actually overtake them, how can they then receive admonition? Know therefore, that there is no god but God: and ask pardon for thy sin, and for the true believers, both men and women. God knoweth your busy employment in the world, and the place of your abode hereafter. . . .

CHAPTER 55. *In the Name of the Most Merciful God*

The Merciful hath taught his servant the Koran. He created man; he hath taught him distinct speech. The sun and the moon run their courses according to a certain rule, and the vegetables which creep on the ground, and the trees submit to his disposition. He also raised the heaven, and he appointed the balance, that ye should not transgress in respect to the balance: wherefore observe a just weight, and diminish not the balance. And the earth hath he prepared for living creatures: therein are various fruits, and palm-trees bearing sheaths of flowers, and grain having chaff, and leaves. Which, therefore,

of your Lord's benefits will you ungratefully deny? He created man of dried clay like an earthen vessel, but he created the genii of fire clear from smoke. Which, therefore, of your Lord's benefits will you ungratefully deny? He is Lord of the east and the Lord of the west. Which, therefore of your Lord's benefits will you ungratefully deny? He hath let loose the two seas, that they meet each another; between them is placed a bar which they cannot pass. Which, therefore, of your Lord's benefits will you ungratefully deny? From them are taken forth unions and lesser pearls. Which, therefore, of your Lord's benefits will you ungratefully deny? His also are the ships, carrying their sails aloft in the sea like mountains. Which, therefore, of your Lord's benefits will you ungratefully deny?

Every creature which liveth on the earth is subject to decay; but the glorious and honorable countenance of thy Lord shall remain forever. Which, therefore, of your Lord's benefits will you ungratefully deny? Unto him do all creatures which are in heaven and earth make petition; every day is he employed in some new work. Which, therefore, of your Lord's benefits will you ungratefully deny? We will surely attend to judge you, O men and genii, at the last day. Which, therefore, of your Lord's benefits will you ungratefully deny? O ye collective body of genii and men, if ye be able to pass out of the confines of heaven and earth, pass forth; you shall not pass forth but by absolute power. Which, therefore, of your Lord's benefits will you ungratefully deny? A flame of fire without smoke, and a smoke without flame shall be sent down upon you, and you shall not be able to defend yourselves therefrom. Which, therefore, of your Lord's benefits will you ungratefully deny? And when the heaven shall be rent in sunder, and shall become red as a rose, and shall melt like ointment, which, therefore, of your Lord's benefits will you ungratefully deny? On that day neither man nor genii shall be asked concerning his sin. Which, therefore, of your Lord's benefits will you ungratefully deny? The wicked shall be known by their marks, and they shall be taken by the forelocks and the feet and shall be cast into hell. Which, therefore, of your Lord's benefits will you ungratefully deny? This is hell, which the wicked deny as a falsehood; they shall pass to and fro between the same and hot boiling water. Which, therefore, of your Lord's benefits will you ungratefully deny? But for him who

28. **Some signs . . . come.** These include particularly the splitting in two of the moon, a grievous pestilence, and a peculiar smoke which will cover both the heavens and the earth. 31. **pardon . . . sin.** "Though Mohammed here and elsewhere acknowledges himself to be a sinner, yet several Mohammedan doctors pretend he was wholly free from sin, and suppose he is here commanded to ask forgiveness, not that he wanted it, but that he might set an example to his followers . . ." (Translator's note). 41. **balance,** justice and equity in dealings among human beings.

46–47. **Which . . . deny?** This refrain is addressed to men and *genii;* that is, to human and supernatural beings. 54. **two seas,** the Persian Gulf and the Mediterranean. 68–69. **every . . . work.** "In executing those things which he hath decreed from eternity, by giving life and death, raising one and abasing another, hearing prayers and granting petitions, etc." (Translator's note). 78–79. **smoke without flame;** possibly this signifies molten brass, which will be poured over the heads of the sinful. 85–86. **On that day . . . sin.** They will not be asked because their sins will be known by different marks stamped upon their bodies.

dreadeth the tribunal of his Lord are prepared two gardens (which, therefore, of your Lord's benefits will you ungratefully deny?) planted with shady trees. Which, therefore, of your Lord's benefits will you ungratefully deny? In each of them shall be two fountains flowing. Which, therefore, of your Lord's benefits will you ungratefully deny? In each of them shall there be of every fruit two kinds. Which, therefore, of your Lord's benefits will you ungratefully deny? They shall repose on couches, the linings whereof shall be of thick silk interwoven with gold; and the fruit of the two gardens shall be near at hand to gather. Which, therefore, of your Lord's benefits will you ungratefully deny? Therein shall receive them beauteous damsels, refraining their eyes from beholding any besides their spouses, whom no man shall have deflowered before them, neither any genii (which, therefore, of your Lord's benefits will you ungratefully deny?) having complexions like rubies and pearls. Which, therefore, of your Lord's benefits will you ungratefully deny? Shall the reward of good works be any other good? Which, therefore, of your Lord's benefits will you ungratefully deny? And besides these there shall be two other gardens (which, therefore, of your Lord's benefits will you ungratefully deny?) of a dark green. Which, therefore, of your Lord's benefits will you ungratefully deny? In each of them shall be two fountains pouring forth plenty of water. Which, therefore, of your Lord's benefits will you ungratefully deny? In each of them shall be fruits, and palm-trees, and pomegranates. Which, therefore, of your Lord's benefits will you ungratefully deny? Therein shall be agreeable and beauteous damsels (which, therefore, of your Lord's benefits will you ungratefully deny?), having fine black eyes and kept in pavilions from public view (which, therefore, of your Lord's benefits will you ungratefully deny?) whom no man shall have deflowered before their destined spouses, nor any genii. Which, therefore, of your Lord's benefits will you ungratefully deny? Therein shall they delight themselves, lying on green cushions and beautiful carpets. Which, therefore, of your Lord's benefits will you ungratefully deny? Blessed be the name of thy Lord, possessed of glory and honor!

CHAPTER 56. *In the Name of the Most Merciful God*

When the inevitable day of judgment shall suddenly come, no soul shall charge the prediction of

1–2. **two gardens.** The duality here and below is explained by the fact that one set of benefits will be decreed for men and another for *genii*. 47. **inevitable.** "The original word, the force whereof cannot well be expressed by a single one in English, signifies a calamitous accident, which falls surely, and with sudden violence; and is therefore made use of here to designate the Day of Judgment" (Translator's note).

An Arabic miniature showing Mohammed besieging a fortress, from a fourteenth-century universal history now in London.

its coming with falsehood; it will abase some, and exalt others. When the earth shall be shaken with a violent shock, and the mountains shall be dashed in pieces, and shall become as dust scattered abroad, then shall ye be separated into three classes: the companions of the right hand (how happy shall the companions of the right hand be!), and the companions of the left hand (how miserable shall the companions of the left hand be!), and those who have preceded others in the faith shall precede them to paradise. These are they who shall approach near unto God; they shall dwell in gardens of delight, reposing on couches adorned with gold and precious stones, sitting opposite to one another thereon. Youths who shall continue in their bloom forever shall go round about to attend them, with goblets and beakers and a cup of flowing wine; their heads shall not ache by drinking the same, neither shall their reason be disturbed; and with fruits of the sorts which they shall choose, and the flesh of birds of the kind which they shall desire. And there shall accompany them fair damsels having large black eyes, resembling pearls hidden in their shells, as a reward for that which they shall have wrought. They shall not hear therein any vain discourse, or any charge of sin, but only the salutation, "Peace! Peace!" And the companions of the right hand (how happy shall the companions of the right hand be!) shall have their abode among lotus-trees free from thorns, and trees of mauz loaded regularly with their fruits from top to bottom, under an extended shade, near a flowing water, and amidst fruits in abundance, which shall not fail, nor shall be forbidden to be gathered; and they shall repose themselves and enjoy damsels upon lofty couches. Verily we have created the damsels of paradise by a special creation, and we have

55–56. **right hand . . . left hand.** Compare Matthew, 25:33 ff. The *Koran* often acknowledges Moses and David as the authors of the Pentateuch and the Psalms, but makes no such acknowledgment of material to be found in the New Testament. Yet there is ample reason to believe that Mohammed was acquainted with the teachings of Jesus. 57–59. **those who . . . paradise,** possibly the first converts to Mohammedanism, or the prophets, or persons who were spiritual leaders through piety. 78. **trees of mauz,** acacia-trees. 84. **special creation,** created of finer materials than the females of the earth, and subject to none of those inconveniences natural to the sex.

made them virgins, beloved by their husbands, of equal age with them, for the delight of the companions of the right hand. And the companions of the left hand (how miserable shall the companions of the left hand be!) shall dwell amidst burning winds and scalding water, under the shade of a black smoke, neither cool nor agreeable. For they enjoyed the pleasures of life before this, while on earth, and obstinately persisted in a heinous wickedness; and they said, "After we shall have died, and become dust and bones, shall we surely be raised to life? Shall our forefathers also be raised with us?" Say, "Verily both the first and the last shall surely be gathered together to judgment, at the predestined time of a known day. Then ye, O men, who have erred and denied the resurrection as a falsehood, shall surely eat of the fruit of the tree of al Zakkum, and shall fill your bellies therewith; and ye shall drink thereon boiling water, and ye shall drink as a thirsty camel drinketh. This shall be their entertainment on the Day of Judgment.

We have created you; will you not therefore believe that we can raise you from the dead? What think you? The seed which you emit, do you create the same, or are we the creators thereof? We have decreed death unto you all, and we shall not be prevented. We are able to substitute others like unto you in your stead and to produce you again in the condition and form which you know not. You know the original birth by creation; will you not therefore consider that we are able to produce you by resuscitation? What think you? The grain which you sow, do you cause the same to spring forth, or do we cause it to spring forth? If we pleased, verily we could render the same dry and fruitless, so that you would not cease to wonder, saying, "Verily we have contracted debts for seed and labor, but we are not permitted to reap the fruit thereof." What think you? The water which you drink, do you send down the same from the clouds, or are we the senders thereof? If we pleased, we could render the same brackish; will you not therefore give thanks? What think you? The fire which you strike, do you produce the tree whence you obtain the same, or are we the producers thereof? We have ordained the same for an admonition, and an advantage to those who travel through the deserts.

Wherefore praise the name of thy Lord, the great God. Moreover I swear by the setting of the stars (and it is surely a great oath, if you knew it) that this is the excellent Koran, the original whereof is written in the preserved book; none shall touch the same, except those who are clean. It is a revelation from the Lord of all creatures. Will you, therefore,

despise this new revelation? And do you make this return for your food which you receive from God, that you deny yourselves to be obliged to him for the same? When the soul of a dying person cometh up to his throat, and you at the same time are looking on (and we are nigher unto him than you, but you see not his true condition), would you not, if you are to be rewarded for your actions hereafter, cause the same to return into the body, if you speak the truth? And whether he be of those who shall approach near unto God, his reward shall be rest and mercy and a garden of delights; or whether he be of the companions of the right hand, he shall be saluted with the salutation, "Peace be unto thee!" by the companions of the right hand, his brethren; or whether he be of those who have rejected the true faith, and gone astray, his entertainment shall consist of boiling water, and the burning of hell fire. Verily this is a certain truth. Wherefore praise the name of thy Lord, the great God.

The Arabian Nights

The huge collection of Oriental tales known in English as *The Arabian Nights' Entertainment,* or *The Thousand and One Nights,* has probably been in existence since at least the tenth century, but its actual origins are obscure. There is good reason to believe that it came into being among the Persians rather than among the Arabs, but, for that matter, much of its material can be referred to the folklore of ancient India. It is clear, however, that in its present form it belongs to the Moslem world, even if the Mohammedans themselves have never regarded the collection as constituting, on the whole, polite literature.

The Arabian Nights was first introduced to Europe through the French translation (1704–1717) by Antoine Galland and was an enormous success from the beginning. This version was translated into other European languages, including the English; but the best-known modern English versions are derived from a compilation found in Egypt in the later eighteenth century. It should be insisted that there is no authoritative text of this collection, only a kind of well-established tradition. Obviously nothing can be discovered about the authors of the many tales, who must have been legion. Several tales of precisely the same nature as those found in the traditional collection, such as the famous stories of "Aladdin and His Lamp" or of "Ali Baba and the Forty Thieves,"

---

1. **virgins,** perpetual virgins, no matter how much they may have to do with men. 17. **tree . . . Zakkum,** possibly the sycamore. 45–46. **admonition,** to put men in mind of the resurrection.

61–64. **would you not . . . truth?** This passage is obscure; one reasonable explanation would be that it means, "If you are not obliged to give an account of your actions on the Day of Judgment, as you seem to believe by denying the resurrection—you could as easily put the soul back into a dying man as avoid judgment." 64–65. **of those . . . God,** a leader or one of the first to profess the faith.

do not appear in either Galland's collection or the Egyptian version from which the modern English translations have been made. Such omissions, however, merely confirm the theory that *The Arabian Nights* is but a portion of the virtually limitless field of Oriental fiction.

This great collection comprises direct, fast-moving narratives of the greatest variety, clearly drawn from many different levels of society. Some are adventurous and fabulous (such as the most famous of them all, the tales of Sindbad the Sailor), some are supernatural, some are bawdy, some are romantic in a chivalric and aristocratic vein, some are trenchantly satirical. Quite apart from their intrinsic value as narratives, however, these tales serve as remarkable mirrors of the life of Islam during the past thousand years. The earthiness, the sensuality, and the sights and smells of the Orient must always be assumed here, no matter how much they may have been filtered out in polite modern English translations. All in all, they constitute the most celebrated single collection of popular fiction in the history of literature.

As is the case with many other similar collections, *The Arabian Nights* is integrated by means of the so-called "framework" device—that is, there exists a central story which is the frame on which the many canvases are stretched. Here the framework narrative has to do with a certain Sultan Shahriar, who caught his wife in adultery and killed her. In further revenge on womankind, he adopted the rather wasteful procedure of marrying a woman each night and then executing her the following morning. His realm was rapidly being depleted of marriageable females until the Princess Sheherezade, daughter of the Sultan's Grand Vizier, became his wife and entertained him on their wedding night with a marvelous narrative. So artfully did she contrive to have dawn interrupt her story at its most interesting stage that Shahriar postponed her execution for the moment to discover the end of the tale. Having finished one in daylight, she proceeded without a break to another and after a thousand and one nights, the Sultan abandoned his sanguinary program altogether, and he and Sheherezade remained married happily until the intervention of "the Separator of Friends and the Terminator of Delights."

The Arabian Nights

SINDBAD THE SEAMAN
AND SINDBAD THE LANDSMAN

THERE lived in the city of Baghdad, during the reign of the Commander of the Faithful Haroun Al-Rashid, a man named Sindbad the Hammal, one in poor case who bore burdens on his head for hire. It happened to him one day of great heat that whilst he was carrying a heavy load, he became ex-

The Arabian Nights. ⁸ Translated by William Lane.
2–3. Haroun Al-Rashid, Caliph of Bagdad from 786 to 809.
3. Hammal, a porter.

ceeding weary and sweated profusely, the heat and the weight alike oppressing him. Presently, as he was passing the gate of a merchant's house, before which the ground was swept and watered and there the air was temperate, he sighted a broad bench beside the door; so he set his load thereon, to take rest and smell the air,—And Sheherezade was surprised by the dawn of day and ceased saying her permitted say.

NOW WHEN IT WAS THE FIVE HUNDRED AND
THIRTY-SEVENTH NIGHT,

She said, It hath reached me, O auspicious King, that when the Hammal set his load upon the bench to take rest and smell the air, there came out upon him from the court-door a pleasant breeze and a delicious fragrance. He sat down on the edge of the bench, and at once heard from within the melodious sound of lutes and other stringed instruments, and mirth-exciting voices singing and reciting, together with the song of birds warbling and glorifying Almighty Allah in various tunes and tongues; turtles, mockingbirds, merles, nightingales, cushats, and stone-curlews, whereat he marvelled in himself and was moved to mighty joy and solace. Then he went up to the gate and saw therein a great flower-garden wherein were pages and black slaves and such a train of servants and attendants and so forth as is found only with Kings and Sultans; and his nostrils were greeted with the savory odors of all manner meats rich and delicate, and delicious and generous wines. So he raised his eyes heavenwards and said, "Glory to Thee, O Lord, O Creator and Provider, who providest whomever Thou wilt without count or stint! O mine Holy One, I cry Thee pardon for all sins and turn to Thee repenting of all offences! O Lord, there is no gainsaying Thee in Thine ordinance and Thy dominion, neither wilt Thou be questioned of that Thou dost, for Thou indeed over all things art Almighty! Extolled be Thy perfection; whom Thou willest Thou makest poor and whom Thou willest Thou makest rich! Whom Thou willest Thou exaltest and whom Thou willest Thou abasest and there is no god but Thee! How mighty is Thy majesty and how enduring Thy dominion and how excellent Thy government! Verily, Thou favorest whom Thou willest of Thy servants, whereby the owner of this place abideth in all joyance of life and delighteth himself with pleasant scents and delicious meats and exquisite wines of all kinds. For indeed Thou appointest unto Thy creatures that which Thou willest and that which Thou hast foreordained unto them; wherefore are some weary and others are at rest and some enjoy fair fortune and affluence, whilst others suffer the extreme of travail and misery, even as I do." And he fell to reciting:

The luxurious interior of an Arabic palace; the harem.

How many by my labors, that evermore endure—
    All goods of life enjoy and in cooly shade recline?
Each morn that dawns I wake in travail and in woe
    —And strange is my condition and my burden
      gars me pine;
Many others are in luck and from miseries are free—
    And Fortune never loads them with loads the
      like o' mine;
They live their happy days in all solace and delight
10   —Eat, drink and dwell in honor 'mid the noble
      and the digne;
All living things were made of a little pinch of dust
    —Thine origin is mine and my provenance is
      Thine;
Yet the difference and the distance 'twixt the twain
    of us are far—As the difference of savor 'twixt
      vinegar and wine;
But at Thee, O God All-wise! I venture not to rail—
    Whose ordinance is just and whose justice cannot
20   fail.

When Sindbad the Porter had made an end of reciting his verses, he took up his burden and was
about to trudge onwards, when there came forth to
him from the gate a little foot-page, fair of face and
shapely of shape and dainty of dress who caught
him by the hand, saying, "Come in and speak with
my lord, for he calleth for thee." The Porter would
have excused himself to the page but the lad would
take no refusal; so he left his load with the door-
keeper in the vestibule, and followed the boy into 30
the house, which he found to be a goodly mansion,
radiant and full of majesty, till he brought him to a
grand sitting-room wherein he saw a company of
nobles and great lords, seated at tables garnished
with all manner of flowers and sweet-scented herbs,
besides great plenty of dainty viands and fruits dried
and fresh and confections and wines of the choicest
vintages. There were also instruments of music and
mirth and lovely slave-girls playing and singing.
All the company was ranged according to rank; and 40
in the highest place sat a man of worshipful and
noble aspect whose beard-sides hoariness had
stricken; and he was stately of stature and fair of
favor, agreeable of aspect and full of gravity and
dignity and majesty. So Sindbad the Porter was
confounded at that which he beheld and said in
himself, "By Allah, this must be either a piece of
Paradise or some King's palace!" Then he saluted
the company with much respect, praying for their
prosperity; and, kissing the ground before them, 50
stood with his head bowed down in humble attitude.
—And Sheherezade perceived the dawn of day and
ceased to say her permitted say.

    Now when it was the five hundred and
      thirty-eighth night,

She said, It hath reached me, O auspicious King,
that Sindbad the Porter, after kissing ground between their hands, stood with his head bowed down
in humble attitude. The master of the house bade
him draw near and be seated and bespoke him 60
kindly, bidding him welcome. Then he set before
him various kinds of viands, rich and delicate and
delicious, and the Porter, after saying his Bismillah,
fell to and ate his fill, after which he exclaimed,
"Praised be Allah whatever be our case!" and, washing his hands, returned thanks to the company for
his entertainment. Quoth the host, "Thou art welcome and thy day is a blessed. But what is thy name
and calling?" Quoth the other, "O my lord, my name
is Sindbad the Hammal, and I carry folk's goods on 70
my head for hire." The house-master smiled and
rejoined, "Know, O Porter, that thy name is even
as mine, for I am Sindbad the Seaman; and now, O
Porter, I would have thee let me hear the couplets
thou recitedest at the gate anon." The Porter was
abashed and replied, "Allah upon thee! Excuse me,

65. **"Praised . . . case!"** This formula was supposed to avert the
evil eye.

for toil and travail and lack of luck when the hand is empty teach a man ill manners and boorish ways." Said the host, "Be not ashamed; thou art become my brother; but repeat to me the verses, for they pleased me whenas I heard thee recite them at the gate." Hereupon the Porter repeated the couplets and they delighted the merchant, who said to him: "Know, O Hammal, that my story is a wonderful one, and thou shalt hear all that befell me and all I underwent ere

10 I rose to this state of prosperity and became the lord of this place wherein thou seest me; for I came not to this high estate save after travails sore and perils galore, and how much toil and trouble have I not suffered in days of yore! I have made seven voyages, by each of which hangeth a marvellous tale, such as confoundeth the reason, and all this came to pass by doom of fortune and fate; for from what destiny doth write there is neither refuge nor flight. "Know, then, good my lords," continued he,

20 "that I am about to relate

THE FIRST VOYAGE
OF SINDBAD HIGHT THE SEAMAN

My father was a merchant, one of the notables of my native place, a monied man and ample of means, who died whilst I was yet a child, leaving me much wealth in money and lands and farmhouses. When I grew up, I laid hands on the whole and ate of the best and drank freely and wore rich clothes and lived lavishly, companioning and consorting with youths of my own age, and considering that this

30 course of life would continue forever and know no change. Thus did I for a long time, but at last I awoke from my heedlessness and, returning to my senses, I found my wealth had become unwealth and my condition ill-conditioned and all I once held had left my hand. And recovering my reason I was stricken with dismay and confusion and bethought me of a saying of our lord Solomon, son of David (on whom be peace!), which I had heard aforetime from my father, "Three things are better than other

40 three: the day of death is better than the day of birth, a live dog is better than a dead lion, and the grave is better than want." Then I got together my remains of estates and property and sold all, even my clothes, for three thousand dirhams, with which I resolved to travel to foreign parts, remembering the saying of the poet:

By means of toil man shall scale the height—Who to fame aspires must not sleep of nights;
Who seeketh pearls in the deep must dive—Winning

50 weal and wealth by his main and might;
And who seeketh Fame without toil and strife—Th' impossible seeketh and wasteth life.

39-42. "Three . . . want." Compare wording of Ecclesiastes, 7:1 and 9:4.

So taking heart I bought me goods, merchandise and all needed for a voyage and, impatient to be at sea, I embarked, with a company of merchants, on board a ship bound for Bassorah. There we again embarked and sailed many days and nights, and we passed from isle to isle and sea to sea and shore to shore, buying and selling and bartering everywhere the ship touched, and continued our course till we

60 came to an island as it were a garth of the gardens of Paradise. Here the captain cast anchor and making fast to the shore put out the landing planks. So all on board landed and made furnaces, and lighting fires therein, busied themselves in various ways, some cooking and some washing, whilst some others walked about the island for solace, and the crew fell to eating and drinking and playing and sporting. I was one of the walkers but, as we were thus engaged, behold the master who was standing on the

70 gunwale cried out to us at the top of his voice, saying, "Ho there! passengers, run for your lives and hasten back to the ship and leave your gear and save yourselves from destruction, Allah preserve you! For this island whereon you stand is no true island, but a great fish stationary a-middlemost of the sea, whereon the sand hath settled and trees have sprung up of old time, so that it is become like unto an island; but, when ye lighted fires on it, it felt the heat and moved; and in a moment it will sink with you

80 into the sea and ye will all be drowned. So leave your gear and seek your safety ere ye die!"—And Sheherezade was surprised by the dawn of day and ceased saying her permitted say.

Now WHEN IT WAS THE FIVE HUNDRED AND THIRTY-NINTH NIGHT,

She said, It hath reached me, O auspicious King, that when the ship-master cried to the passengers, "Leave your gear and seek safety, ere you die," all who heard him left gear and goods, clothes washed and un-

90 washed, fire pots and brass cooking-pots, and fled back to the ship for their lives, and some reached it while others (amongst whom was I) did not, for suddenly the island shook and sank into the abysses of the deep, with all that were thereon, and the dashing sea surged over it with climbing waves. I sank with the others down, down into the deep, but Almighty Allah preserved me from drowning and threw in my way a great wooden tub of those that had served the ship's company for tubbing. I gripped

100 it for the sweetness of life and bestriding it like one riding, paddled with my feet like oars, whilst the waves tossed me as in sport right and left. Mean-

64. furnaces, more properly braziers, pots full of charcoal sunk in the ground, or a little hearth of clay shaped like a horseshoe and opening down wind (Editor's note). 75-76. For this island . . . fish stationary. Popular lore is full of examples of great fishes or whales mistaken for islands, on which the luckless seafarers may land to their own destruction.

while the captain made sail and departed with those who had reached the ship, regardless of the drowning and the drowned; and I ceased not following the vessel with my eyes, till she was hid from sight and I made sure of death. Darkness closed in upon me while in this plight and the winds and waves bore me on all that night and the next day, till the tub brought to with me under the lee of a lofty island, with trees overhanging the tide. I caught hold of a
10 branch and by its aid clambered up on to the land, after coming nigh upon death; but when I reached the shore, I found my legs cramped and numbed and my feet bore traces of the nibbling of fish upon their soles; though I had felt nothing for excess of anguish and fatigue. I threw myself down on the island-ground, like a dead man, and drowned in desolation swooned away, nor did I return to my senses till next morning, when the sun rose and revived me. But I found my feet swollen, so made shift
20 to move by shuffling and crawling on my hands and knees, for in that island were found store of fruits and springs of sweet water. I ate of the fruits which strengthened me; and thus I abode days and nights, till my life seemed to return and my spirits began to revive and I was better able to move about. So, after due consideration, I fell to exploring the island and diverting myself with gazing upon all things that Allah Almighty had created there; and rested under the trees from which I cut me a staff to lean upon.
30 One day as I walked along the shore, I caught sight of some object in the distance and thought it a wild beast or one of the monster-creatures of the sea; but, as I drew near it, looking hard the while, I saw that it was a noble mare, tethered on the beach. Presently I went up to her, but she cried out against me with a great cry, so that I trembled for fear and turned to go away, when there came forth a man from under the earth and followed me, crying out and saying, "Who and whence art thou, and what
40 caused thee to come hither?" "O my lord," answered I, "I am in very sooth, a waif, a stranger, and was left to drown with sundry others by the ship we voyaged in; but Allah graciously sent me a wooden tub; so I saved myself thereon and it floated with me, till the waves cast me up on this island." When he heard this, he took my hand and saying, "Come with me," carried me into a great Sardab, or underground chamber, which was spacious as a saloon. He made me sit down at its upper end; then he
50 brought me somewhat of food and, being hungered, I ate till I was satisfied and refreshed; and when he had put me at mine ease he questioned me of myself, and I told him all that had befallen me from first to last; and, as he wondered at my adventure, I

42–43. **ship we voyaged in.** Note that Sindbad does not say that he was shipwrecked; in accordance with the tales of fabulous travelers, he often tells the truth when an untruth would not serve him.

said, "By Allah, O my lord, excuse me; I have told me the truth of my case and the accident which betided me; and now I desire that thou tellest me who thou art and why thou abidest here under the earth and why thou hast tethered yonder mare on the brink of the sea." Answered he, "Know that I am 60 one of the several who are stationed in different parts of this island, and we are of the grooms of King Mihrjan and under our hand are all his horses. Every month, about new-moon tide we bring hither our best mares for the purpose of having a breed between them and the sea-horses. The sea-horses try to drag them away with them, but cannot, by reason of the leg-ropes; so they cry out at them and butt at them and kick them, which we hearing, know that we must run out and shout at them, whereupon 70 they are startled and return in fear to the sea. Their colts and fillies are worth a mint of money, nor is their like to be found on the earth's face. This is the time of the coming forth of the sea-horses; and Inshallah! I will bear thee to King Mihrjan," —And Sheherezade perceived the dawn of day and ceased to say her permitted say.

NOW WHEN IT WAS THE FIVE HUNDRED AND FOR-
TIETH NIGHT,

She continued, It hath reached me, O auspicious 80 King, that the Syce said to Sindbad the Seaman, "I will bear thee to King Mihrjan and show thee our country. And know that hadst thou not happened on us thou hadst perished miserably and none had known of thee; but I will be the means of the saving of thy life and of thy return to thine own land." I called down blessings on him and thanked him for his kindness and courtesy; and, while we were yet talking, behold, the horse came up out of the sea; and would have carried the mare away with him, 90 but could not by reason of the tether. Thereupon the groom took a sword and target and ran out of the underground saloon, smiting the buckler with the blade and calling to his company, who came up shouting and brandishing spears; and the sea-horse took fright at them and plunging into the sea, like a buffalo, disappeared under the waves. After this we sat awhile, till the rest of the grooms came up, each leading a mare, and seeing me with their fellow-Syce, questioned me of my case and I re- 100 peated my story to them. Thereupon they drew near me and spreading the table ate and invited me to eat; so I ate with them, after which they took horse and mounting me on one of the mares, set out with me and fared on without ceasing till we came to the capital city of King Mihrjan, and going in to him acquainted him with my story. Then he sent for me, and when they set me before him and salams had

63. **Mihrjan,** probably a corruption of *Maharajah,* the Hindu word for "Great King." 81. **Syce,** a groom. 92. **target,** shield.

been exchanged, he gave me a cordial welcome and wishing me long life bade me tell him my tale. So I related to him all that I had seen and all that had befallen me from first to last, whereat he marvelled and said to me, "By Allah, O my son, thou hast indeed been miraculously preserved! Were not the term of thy life a long one, thou hadst not escaped from these straits; but praised be Allah for safety!" Then he spoke cheerily to me and entreated me with kindness and consideration; moreover, he made me his agent for the port and registrar of all ships that entered the harbor. I attended him regularly, to receive his commandments, and he favored me and did me all manner of kindness and invested me with costly and splendid robes. Indeed, I was high in credit with him, as an intercessor for the folk and an intermessary between them and him, when they wanted aught of him. I abode thus a great while and, as often as I passed through the city to the port, I questioned the merchants and travelers and sailors of the city of Baghdad; so haply I might hear of an occasion to return to my native land, but could find none who knew it or knew any who resorted thither. At this I was chagrined, for I was weary of long strangerhood; and my disappointment endured for a time till one day, going in to King Mihrjan, I found him with a company of Indians. I saluted them and they returned my salam; and politely welcomed me and asked me of my country.—And Sheherezade was surprised by the dawn of day and ceased saying her permitted say.

NOW WHEN IT WAS THE FIVE HUNDRED AND FORTY-
FIRST NIGHT,

She continued, It hath reached me, O auspicious King, that Sindbad the Seaman said: "When they asked me of my country, I questioned them of theirs and they told me that they were of various castes, some being called Shakiriyah, who are the noblest of their castes, and neither oppress nor offer violence to any, and others Brahmans, a folk who abstain from wine, but live in delight and solace and merriment and own camels and horses and cattle. Moreover, they told me that the people of India are divided into two-and-seventy castes, and I marvelled at this with exceeding marvel. Amongst other things that I saw in King Mihrjan's dominions was an island called Kasil, wherein all night is heard the beating of drums and tabrets; but we were told by the neighboring islanders and by travelers that the inhabitants are people of diligence and judgment. In this sea I saw also a fish two hundred cubits long and the fishermen fear it; so they strike together pieces of wood and put it to flight. I saw also another fish, with a head like that of an owl, besides many other wonders and rarities, which it would be

38. **Shakiriyah,** the second, or warrior, caste of Moslem society.

tedious to recount. I occupied myself thus in visiting the island till, one day, as I stood in the port, with a staff in my hand, according to my custom, behold, a great ship, wherein were many merchants, came sailing for the harbor. When it reached the small inner port where ships anchor under the city, the master furled his sails and making fast to the shore, put out the landing-planks, whereupon the crew fell to breaking bulk and landing cargo whilst I stood by, taking written note of them. They were long in bringing the goods ashore, so I asked the master, "Is there aught left in thy ship?" and he answered, "O my lord, there are divers bales of merchandise in the hold, whose owner was drowned from amongst us at one of the islands on our course; so his goods remained in our charge by way of trust and we purpose to sell them and note their price, that we may convey it to his people in the city of Baghdad, the Palace of Peace." "What was the merchant's name?" quoth I, and quoth he, "Sindbad the Seaman;" whereupon I straightly considered him and knowing him, cried out to him with a great cry, saying, "O captain, I am that Sindbad the Seaman who traveled with other merchants; and when the fish heaved and thou calledst to us, some saved themselves and others sank, I being one of them. But Allah Almighty threw in my way a great tub of wood, of those the crew had used to wash withal, and the winds and waves carried me to this island, where by Allah's grace, I fell in with King Mihrjan's grooms and they brought me hither to the King their master. When I told him my story, he entreated me with favor and made me his harbor-master, and I have prospered in his service and found acceptance with him. These bales, therefore, are mine, the goods which God hath given me."— And Sheherezade perceived the dawn of day and ceased to say her permitted say.

NOW WHEN IT WAS THE FIVE HUNDRED AND FORTY-
SECOND NIGHT,

She continued, It hath reached me, O auspicious King, that when Sindbad the Seaman said to the captain, These bales are mine, the goods which Allah hath given me, the other exclaimed, "There is no majesty and there is no might save in Allah, the Glorious, the Great! Verily, there is neither conscience nor good faith left among men!" Said I, "O Rais, what mean these words, seeing that I have told thee my case?" And he answered, "Because thou heardest me say that I had with me goods whose owner was drowned, thou thinkest to take them without right; but this is forbidden by law to thee, for we saw him drown before our eyes, together with many other passengers, nor was one of them saved. So how canst thou pretend that thou

103. **Rais,** the captain of the vessel.

art the owner of the goods?" "O captain," said I, "listen to my story and give heed to my words, and my truth will be manifest to thee; for lying and leasing are the letter-marks of the hypocrites." Then I recounted to him all that had befallen me since I sailed from Baghdad with him to the time when we came to the fish-island where we were nearly drowned; and I reminded him of certain matters which had passed between us; whereupon both he and the merchants were certified of the truth of my story and recognized me and gave me joy of my deliverance, saying, "By Allah, we thought not that thou hadst escaped drowning! But the Lord hath granted thee new life." Then they delivered my bales to me, and I found my name written thereon, nor was aught thereof lacking. So I opened them and making up a present for King Mihrjan of the finest and costliest of the contents, caused the sailors to carry it up to the palace, where I went in to the King and laid my present at his feet, acquainting him with what had happened, especially concerning the ship and my goods; whereat he wondered with exceeding wonder and the truth of all that I had told him was made manifest to him. His affection for me redoubled after that and he showed me exceeding honor and bestowed on me a great present in return for mine. Then I sold my bales and what other matters I owned, making a great profit on them, and bought me other goods and gear of the growth and fashion of the island-city. When the merchants were about to start on their homeward voyage, I embarked on board the ship all that I possessed, and going in to the King thanked him for all his favors and friendship and craved his leave to return to my own land and friends. He farewelled me and bestowed on me great store of the country-stuffs and produce; and I took leave of him and embarked. Then we set sail and fared on nights and days, by the permission of Allah Almighty; and Fortune served us and Fate favored us, so that we arrived in safety at Bassorah City, where I landed rejoicing at my safe return to my natal soil. After a short stay, I set out for Baghdad, the Palace of Peace, with store of goods and commodities of great price. Reaching the city in due time, I went straight to my own quarter and entered my house, where all my friends and kinsfolk came to greet me. Then I bought me eunuchs and concubines, servants and negro-slaves till I had a large establishment, and I bought me horses, and lands and gardens, till I was richer and in better case than before, and returned to enjoy the society of my friends and familiars more assiduously than ever, forgetting all I had suffered of fatigue and hardship and strangerhood and every peril of travel; and I applied myself to all manner joys and solaces and delights, eating the daintiest

viands and drinking the most delicious wines; and my wealth allowed this state of things to endure. This, then, is the story of my first Voyage, and tomorrow, Inshallah! I will tell you the tale of my second voyage. (Saith he who telleth the tale).

Then Sindbad the Seaman made Sindbad the Landsman sup with him and bade give him an hundred gold pieces, saying, "Thou hast cheered us with thy company this day." The Porter thanked him and, taking the gift, went his way, pondering that which he had heard and marvelling mightily at what things betide mankind. He passed the night in his own place and with early morning repaired to the abode of Sindbad the Seaman, who received him with honor and seated him by his side. As soon as the rest of the company was assembled, he set meat and drink before them and, when they had well eaten and drunken and were merry and in cheerful case, he took up his discourse and recounted to them in these words the narrative of

THE SECOND VOYAGE
OF SINDBAD THE SEAMAN

Know, O my brother, that I was living a most comfortable and enjoyable life, in all solace and delight, as I told you yesterday.—And Sheherezade was surprised by the dawn of day and ceased saying her permitted say.

Now when it was the five hundred and forty-third night,

She continued, It hath reached me, O auspicious King, that when Sindbad the Seaman's guests were all gathered together, he thus bespake them:—I was living a most enjoyable life until one day my mind became possessed with the thought of travelling about the world of men and seeing their cities and islands; and a longing seized me to traffic and to make money by trade. Upon this resolve I took a great store of cash and, buying goods and gear fit for travel, bound them up in bales. Then I went down to the river-bank, where I found a noble ship and brand-new about to sail, equipped with sails of fine cloth and well-manned and provided; so I took passage on her, with a number of other merchants, and after embarking our goods we weighed anchor the same day. Right fair was our voyage and we sailed from place to place and from isle to isle; and whenever we anchored we met a crowd of merchants and notables and customers, and we took to buying and selling and bartering. At last Destiny brought us to an island, fair and verdant, in trees abundant, with yellow-ripe fruits luxuriant, and flowers fragrant and birds warbling soft descant; and streams crystalline and radiant; but no sign of man showed to the descrier, no, not a blower of the fire.

109. blower . . . fire, a popular Arabic phrase to express desolation.

The captain made fast with us to this island, and the merchants and sailors landed and walked about, enjoying the shade of the trees and the songs of the birds, that chanted the praises of the One, the Victorious, and marvelling at the works of the Omnipotent King. I landed with the rest; and, sitting down by a spring of sweet water that welled up among the trees, took out some food I had with me and ate of that which Allah Almighty had allotted unto me. And so sweet was the zephyr and so fragrant were the flowers, that presently I waxed drowsy and lying down in that place was soon drowned in sleep. When I awoke, I found myself alone, for the ship had sailed and left me behind, nor had one of the merchants or sailors bethought himself of me. I searched the island right and left, but found neither man nor Jinn, whereat I was beyond measure troubled, and my heart was like to break for stress of chagrin and anguish and concern, because I was left quite alone, without aught of worldly gear or meat or drink, weary and heart-broken. So I gave myself up for lost and said, "Not always doth the crock escape the shock. I was saved the first time by finding one who brought me from the desert island to an inhabited place, but now there is no hope for me." Then I fell to weeping and wailing and gave myself up to an excess of rage, blaming myself for having again ventured upon the perils and hardships of voyage, whenas I was at my ease in mine own house in mine own land, taking my pleasure, with good meat and good drink and good clothes and lacking nothing, neither money nor goods. And I repented me of having left Baghdad, and this the more after all the travails and dangers I had undergone in my first voyage, wherein I had so narrowly escaped destruction, and exclaimed, "Verily we are Allah's and unto Him we are returning!" I was indeed even as one mad and Jinn-struck, and presently I rose and walked about the island, right and left and every whither, unable for trouble to sit or tarry in any one place. Then I climbed a tall tree and looked in all directions, but saw nothing save sky and sea and trees and birds and isles and sands. However, after a while my eager glances fell upon some great white thing, afar off in the interior of the island; so I came down from the tree and made for that which I had seen; and behold, it was a huge white dome rising high in air and of vast compass. I walked all around it, but found no door thereto, nor could I muster strength or nimbleness by reason of its exceeding smoothness and slipperiness. So I marked the spot where I stood and went round about the dome to measure its circumference, which I found fifty good paces. And as I stood, casting about how to gain an entrance, behold, the sun was suddenly hidden from me and the air be-

came dull and dark. Methought a cloud had come over the sun, but it was the season of summer; so I marvelled at this and lifting my head looked steadfastly at the sky, when I saw that the cloud was none other than an enormous bird, of gigantic girth and inordinately wide of wing, which, as it flew through the air, veiled the sun and hid it from the island. At this sight my wonder redoubled and I remembered a story—And Sheherezade perceived the dawn of day and ceased to say her permitted say.

Now when it was the five hundred and forty-fourth night,

She said, It hath reached me, O auspicious King, that Sindbad the Seaman continued in these words: —My wonder redoubled and I remembered a story I had heard aforetime of pilgrims and travellers, how in a certain island dwelleth a huge bird, called the Roc, which feedeth its young on elephants; and I was certified that the dome which caught my sight was none other than a Roc's egg. As I looked and wondered at the marvellous works of the Almighty, the bird alighted on the dome and brooded over it with its wings covering it and its legs stretched out behind it on the ground, and in this posture it fell asleep, glory be to Him who sleepeth not! When I saw this, I arose and, unwinding my turban from my head, doubled it and twisted it into a rope, with which I girt my middle and bound my waist fast to the legs of the Roc, saying to myself, "Peradventure, this bird may carry me to a land of cities and inhabitants, and that will be better than abiding in this desert island." I passed the night watching and fearing to sleep, lest the bird should fly away with me unawares; and, as soon as the dawn broke and the morn shone, the Roc rose off its egg and spreading its wings with a great cry flew up into the air dragging me with it; nor ceased it to soar and to tower till I thought it had reached the limit of the firmament; after which it descended, earthwards, little by little, till it lighted on the top of a high hill. As soon as I found myself on the hard ground, I made haste to unbind myself, quaking with fear of the bird, though it took no heed of me nor even felt me; and, loosing my turban from its feet, I made off with my best speed. Presently I saw it catch up in its huge claws something from the earth and rise with it high in air, and observing it narrowly I saw it to be a serpent big of bulk and gigantic of girth, wherewith it flew away clean out of sight. I marvelled at this and faring forwards found myself on a peak overlooking a valley, exceeding great and wide and deep, and bounded by vast mountains that spired high in air; none could descry their summits for the excess of their height, nor was any able to climb up thereto. When I saw this, I blamed myself for that which I had done and said, "Would Heaven I had tarried in the island! It was better than this wild desert, for there I had at least fruits to eat and water to drink, and here are neither trees nor fruits nor streams. But there is no Majesty and there is no Might save in Allah, the Glorious, the Great! Verily, as often as I am quit of one peril, I fall into a worse danger and a more grievous."

However, I took courage and walking along the wady found that its soil was of diamond, the stone wherewith they pierce minerals and precious stones and porcelain and the onyx, for that it is a dense stone and a stubborn, whereon neither iron nor hardhead hath effect, neither can we cut off aught therefrom nor break it, save by means of lead-stone. Moreover, the valley swarmed with snakes and vipers, each big as a palm-tree, that would have made but one gulp of an elephant; and they came out by night, hiding during the day, lest the rocs and eagles pounce on them and tear them to pieces, as was their wont—why I wot not. And I repented of what I had done and said, "By Allah, I have made haste to bring destruction upon myself!" The day began to wane as I went along and I looked about for a place where I might pass the night, being in fear of the serpents; and I took no thought of meat and drink in my concern for my life. Presently I caught sight of a cave near at hand, with a narrow doorway; so I entered and seeing a great stone close to the mouth, I rolled it up and stopped at the entrance, saying to myself, "I am safe here for the night; and as soon as it is day, I will go forth and see what destiny will do." Then I looked within the cave and saw at the upper end a great serpent brooding on her eggs, at which my flesh quaked and my hair stood on end; but I raised my eyes to Heaven and, committing my case to fate and lot, abode all that night without sleep till daybreak, when I rolled back the stone from the mouth of the cave and went forth, staggering like a drunken man and giddy with watching and fear and hunger. As in this sore case I walked along the valley, behold, there fell down before me a slaughtered beast; but I saw no one, whereat I marvelled with great marvel and presently remembered a story I had heard aforetime of traders and pilgrims and travellers: how the mountains where are the diamonds are full of perils and terrors, nor can any fare through them; but the merchants who traffic in diamonds have a device by which they obtain them, that is to say, they take a sheep and slaughter and skin it and cut it in pieces and cast them down from the mountain-tops into the valley-floor, where the meat being fresh and sticky with blood, some of the gems cleave to it. There they leave it till midday, when the eagles and

vultures swoop down upon it and carry it in their claws to the mountain summits, whereupon the merchants come and shout at them and scare them away from the meat. Then they come and, taking the diamonds which they find sticking to it, go their ways with them and leave the meat to the birds and beasts; nor can any come at the diamonds but by this device.—And Sheherezade was surprised by the dawn of day and ceased saying her permitted say.

NOW WHEN IT WAS THE FIVE HUNDRED AND FORTY-FIFTH NIGHT,

She said, It hath reached me, O auspicious King, that Sindbad the Seaman continued his relation of what befell him in the Mountain of Diamonds, and informed them that the merchants cannot come at the diamonds save by the device aforesaid. So, when I saw the slaughtered beast fall (he pursued) and bethought me of the story, I went up to it and filled my pockets and shawl-girdle and turban and the folds of my clothes with the choicest diamonds; and, as I was thus engaged, down fell before me another great piece of meat. Then with my unrolled turban and lying on my back, I set the bit on my breast so that I was hidden by the meat, which was thus raised above the ground. Hardly had I gripped it, when an eagle swooped down upon the flesh and, seizing it with his talons, flew up with it high in air and me clinging thereto, and ceased not its flight till it alighted on the head of one of the mountains where, dropping the carcass, he fell to rending it; but, behold, there arose behind him a great noise of shouting and clattering of wood, whereat the bird took fright and flew away. Then I loosed off myself the meat, with clothes dabbled with blood therefrom and stood up by its side; whereupon up came the merchant, who had cried out at the eagle, and seeing me standing there, bespoke me not, but was affrighted at me and shook with fear. However, he went up to the carcass and turning it over, found no diamonds sticking to it, whereat he gave a great cry and exclaimed, "Alack, my disappointment! There is no Majesty and there is no Might save in Allah with whom we seek refuge from Satan the stoned!" And he bemoaned himself and beat hand upon hand, saying, "Alas, the pity of it! How cometh this?"

Then I went up to him and he said to me, "Who art thou and what causeth thee to come hither?" And I, "Fear not, I am a man and a good man and a merchant. My story is a wondrous and my adventures are marvellous and the manner of my coming hither is prodigious. So be of good cheer, thou shalt receive of me what shall rejoice thee, for I have with me great plenty of diamonds and I will give thee thereof what shall suffice thee; for each is better than aught thou couldst get otherwise. So fear nothing." The man rejoiced thereat and thanked and blessed me; then we talked together till the other merchants, hearing me in discourse with their fellow, came up and saluted me, for each of them had thrown down his piece of meat. And as I went off with them I told them my whole story, how I had suffered hardships at sea and the fashion of my reaching the valley. But I gave the owner of the meat a number of the stones I had by me, so they all wished me joy of my escape, saying, "By Allah, a new life hath been decreed to thee, for none ever reached yonder valley and came off thence alive before thee; but praised be Allah for thy safety!" We passed the night together in a safe and pleasant place, beyond measure rejoiced at my deliverance from the Valley of Serpents and my arrival in an inhabited land; and on the morrow we set out and journeyed over the mighty range of mountains, seeing many serpents in the valley, till we came to a fair great island, wherein was a garden of huge camphor trees under each of which an hundred men might take shelter. When the folk have a mind to get camphor, they bore into the upper part of the bole with a long iron, whereupon the liquid camphor, which is the sap of the tree, floweth out and they catch it in vessels, where it concreteth like gum; but, after this, the tree dieth and becometh firewood. Moreover, there is in this island a kind of wild beast, called Rhinoceros, that pastureth as do steers and buffaloes with us; but it is a huge brute, bigger of body than the camel and like it feedeth upon the leaves and twigs of trees. It is a remarkable animal with a great and thick horn, ten cubits long, amiddleward its head; wherein, when cleft in twain, appeareth the likeness of a man. Voyagers and pilgrims and travelers declare that this beast, called Karkadan, will carry off a great elephant on its horn and graze about the island and the sea-coast therewith and take no heed of it, till the elephant dieth and its fat, melting in the sun, runneth down into the rhinoceros's eyes and blindeth him, so that he lieth down upon the shore. Then cometh the bird Roc and carrieth off both the rhinoceros and that which is on its horn to feed its young withal.

Moreover, I saw in this island many kinds of oxen and buffaloes, whose like are not found in our country. Here I sold some of the diamonds which I had by me for gold dinars and silver dirhams and bartered others for the produce of the country; and, loading them upon beasts of burden, fared on with the merchants from valley to valley and town to town, buying and selling and viewing foreign countries and the works and creatures of Allah, till we came to Bassorah-City, where we abode a few days, after which I continued my journey to Baghdad,—

And Sheherezade perceived the dawn of day and ceased to say her permitted say.

NOW WHEN IT WAS THE FIVE HUNDRED AND FORTY-SIXTH NIGHT,

She said, It hath reached me, O auspicious King, that when Sindbad the Seaman returned from his travel to Baghdad, the House of Peace, he arrived at home with great store of diamonds and money and goods. (Continued he) I foregathered with my friends and relations and gave alms and largesse and bestowed curious gifts and made presents to all my friends and companions. Then I betook myself to eating well and drinking well and wearing fine clothes and making merry with my fellows, and forgot all my sufferings in the pleasures of return to the solace and delight of life, with light heart and broadened breast. And everyone who heard of my return came and questioned me of my adventures and of foreign countries, and I related to them all that had befallen me, and the much I had suffered, whereat they wondered and gave me joy of my safe return. This, then, is the end of the story of my second Voyage; and tomorrow, Inshallah! I will tell you what befell me in my third Voyage.

Omar Khayyam

The remarkable impact of the poetry of Omar Khayyam upon the English-speaking peoples, thanks to the gifted translation and adaptation of many of his verses by the Englishman Edward Fitzgerald (1809–1883), has tended to obscure the fact that Omar was a celebrated mathematician. He was born, probably in the sixth or seventh decade of the eleventh century (although the exact year is not known), at Nishapur, one of the principal towns of the Province of Khorasan in Persia. By nature a retiring individual, he devoted himself to the study of astronomy and attained such eminence in that field that he was raised to the post of Astronomer Royal. In this capacity he worked upon a reform of the calendar. He was noted also for a brilliant treatise on algebra. But during his lifetime he was also the author of more than five hundred quatrains of an epigrammatic nature, and it is on these quatrains, or *rubaiyat,* that his fame in the Western world will always depend.

There is no accepted text of these quatrains; and, indeed, it is debatable whether all are to be accredited to Omar Khayyam, but there is no doubt about most of them. In substance the *rubaiyat* comprise: (1) complaints against Fate, or the spirit of necessity; (2) satires on the pious, the learned, and the reputedly good people of the times; (3) love lyrics on the sorrows of separation and the joys of reunion; (4) poems in praise of gardens, flowers, and the springtime; (5) poems of rebellion against the prevailing conceptions of God, Heaven, and Hell, balancing their promise of an afterlife against the certainty or reality of the joys of the moment; and (6) addresses to the Deity, of a strongly mystical nature.

Undoubtedly Omar Khayyam was, even for his day, a freethinker and a liberal, one to live and let live, with a hard core of scientific objectivity in most of his intellectual outlook. There is some evidence to show that his liberalism made it hard for him at Nishapur. In any case, however, it remains a question whether the epicurean nature of some of the quatrains is to be taken literally. The poet preaches the joys of the vine and of the body; he implies, however, the joys of the mind and of the soul as well. At the same time, he is not to be regarded as a pure mystic, for his scientific turn of mind counteracts this tendency.

It is more likely that Omar, a man who adopted the life of the observer and the spectator, was moved to poetic expression of his skepticism, his cynicism, and his regrets at the contemplation of that which is beautiful but which either does not last or is tainted with the commonplace and the thwarting of the ideal. His *rubaiyat* were probably written during the course of a long life, and the conflicting points of view they show— a religiousness on the one hand and a worldliness on the other—may be accounted for on the grounds that his philosophy changed as he grew older. But on the other hand, he may well have had the common failings of a liberal: he may have been a hesitator, one whose practice backslid while his ideals soared aloft. In this respect he is one of the most human and understandable of all poets.

In the essentially contradictory nature of Omar Khayyam's poetry lies one of his greatest sources of appeal. But this dichotomy is not peculiar to him. For example, he admits the problem of evil and then takes to task God, the only real "agent" of evil. Still, God was similarly taken to task by Job in the Old Testament and again in sublime fashion by the poet of Ecclesiastes, who observed that there is one event to all, to him that sacrificeth and to him that sacrificeth not. The author of Job counsels resignation; the poet of Ecclesiastes tells us to make the most of time. Omar Khayyam, in effect, does both, albeit in more flippant and perhaps insolent manner. Even so, Omar wrote many quatrains of deep religious feeling; he cannot be called another Lucretius or another Voltaire, for his faith in a God, whatever His nature and His sense of justice, is unshaken.

The translation of Omar Khayyam's *rubaiyat* by Edward Fitzgerald is admittedly selective; it emphasizes the sybaritic and the rebellious more than did the original and passes lightly over the devotional quatrains. Yet no reader of Omar Khayyam in the original could well deny that Fitzgerald has caught the essence of Omar—his world-weariness, his love of ease and comfort, his skepticism and sophistication, his romantic yearning and passionate regret, his fatalism, his inquisitiveness, and his love of beauty—all couched in phrases that, for all the popular overuse to which they have been put, come close

to the immortal. Omar Khayyam told his friend and pupil, Nizami of Samarkand, "My tomb shall be in a certain place where each breath of the north wind shall shower down roses upon it." His verses have been given imperishable form by Fitzgerald's quatrains, which are the rose petals he desired.

The Rubaiyat

WAKE! For the Sun, who scatter'd into flight
The Stars before him from the Field of Night,
    Drives Night along with them from Heav'n, and strikes
The Sultan's Turret with a Shaft of Light.

Before the Phantom of False Morning died,   5
Methought a Voice within the Tavern cried,
    "When all the Temple is prepared within,
"Why nods the drowsy Worshipper outside?"

And, as the Cock crew, those who stood before
The Tavern shouted—"Open then the Door!   10
    "You know how little while we have to stay,
"And, once departed, may return no more."

Now the New Year reviving old Desires,
The thoughtful Soul to Solitude retires,
    Where the White Hand of Moses on the Bough
Puts out, and Jesus from the Ground suspires.   16

Iram indeed is gone with all his Rose,
And Jamshyd's Sev'n-ring'd Cup where no one knows;
    But still a Ruby kindles in the Vine,
And many a Garden by the Water blows.   20

And David's lips are locked; but in divine
High-piping Pehleví, with "Wine! Wine! Wine!
    "Red Wine!"—the Nightingale cries to the Rose
That sallow cheek of hers to incarnadine.

Come, fill the Cup, and in the fire of Spring   25
Your Winter-garment of Repentance fling:
    The Bird of Time has but a little way
To flutter—and the Bird is on the Wing.

The Rubaiyat. Translated by Edward Fitzgerald.
15. **White Hand of Moses.** Moses, at the command of the Lord, put his hand into his bosom, and he took it out as white as snow. The metaphor is used here for the blooming of flowers in the spring. 16. **Jesus . . . suspires.** The Persians believed Jesus healed by his breath. 17. **Iram,** an ancient Persian garden, now disappeared. 18. **Jamshyd,** a legendary Persian king, whose seven-ringed cup symbolized the seven heavens, the seven seas, etc. 21. **David's . . . locked;** King David's actual language is forgotten. 22. **Pehleví,** the ancient literary language of Persia.

Whether at Nishápúr or Babylon,
Whether the Cup with sweet or bitter run,   30
   The Wine of Life keeps oozing drop by drop,
The Leaves of Life keep falling one by one.

Each Morn a thousand Roses brings, you say;
Yes, but where leaves the Rose of Yesterday?
   And this first Summer month that brings the Rose
Shall take Jamshyd and Kaí-kobád away.   36

Well, let it take them! What have we to do
With Kaí-kobád the Great, or Kai-khosrú?
   Let Zál and Rustum bluster as they will,
Or Hátim call to Supper—heed not you.   40

With me along the strip of Herbage strewn
That just divides the desert from the sown,
   Where name of Slave and Sultan is forgot—
And peace to Mahmúd on his golden Throne!

A Book of Verses underneath the Bough,   45
A Jug of Wine, a Loaf of Bread—and Thou
   Beside me singing in the Wilderness—
Ah, Wilderness were Paradise enow!

Some for the Glories of This World; and some
Sigh for the Prophet's Paradise to come;   50
   Ah, take the Cash, and let the Credit go,
Nor heed the rumble of a distant Drum!

Look to the blowing Rose about us—"Lo,
"Laughing," she says, "into the world I blow,
   "At once the silken tassel of my Purse   55
Tear, and its Treasure on the Garden throw."

And those who husbanded the Golden Grain,
And those who flung it to the winds like Rain,
   Alike to no such aureate Earth are turn'd
As, buried once, Men want dug up again.   60

The Worldly Hope men set their Hearts upon
Turns Ashes—or it prospers; and anon,
   Like Snow upon the Desert's dusty Face,
Lighting a little hour or two—is gone.

Think, in this batter'd Caravanserai   65
Whose Portals are alternate Night and Day,
   How Sultan after Sultan with his Pomp
Abode his destined Hour, and went his way.

29. **Nishápúr,** a town in Persia and Omar's own birthplace.   38.
Kaí-kobád . . . Kai-khosrú. Kaí-kobád, a celebrated Persian hero,
was the founder of an important Persian dynasty; Kai-khosrú has
been tentatively identified with Cyrus the Great of the sixth century B.C. 39. **Zál and Rustum.** Zal was the father of Rustum;
Rustum is perhaps the greatest of Persian epic heroes. 44. **Mahmúd,**
presumably Sultan Mahmud the Great (970?–1030), the Persian
conqueror of the Punjab and Afghanistan. 57. **Golden Grain,** to
be taken here symbolically as "wealth." 65. **Caravanserai,** an inn
where Oriental caravans put up.

Portrait of a physician, by a 16th-century Persian painter.

They say the Lion and the Lizard keep   69
The Courts where Jamshyd gloried and drank deep:
   And Bahrám, that great Hunter—the Wild Ass
Stamps o'er his Head, but cannot break his Sleep.

I sometimes think that never blows so red
The Rose as where some buried Caesar bled;
   That every Hyacinth the Garden wears   75
Dropt in her Lap from some once lovely Head.

And this reviving Herb whose tender Green
Fledges the River-Lip on which we lean—
   Ah, lean upon it lightly! for who knows
From what once lovely Lip it springs unseen!   80

Ah, my Belovéd, fill the Cup that clears
Today of past Regrets and future Fears:

70. **Courts . . . deep,** Persepolis, capital of Jamshyd. 71. **Bahrám,**
a legendary Persian hero who lost his life while hunting a wild ass.

Tomorrow!—Why, Tomorrow I may be
Myself with Yesterday's Sev'n thousand Years.

For some we loved, the loveliest and the best   85
That from his Vintage rolling Time hath prest,
    Have drunk their Cup a Round or two before,
And one by one crept silently to rest.

And we, that now make merry in the Room
They left, and Summer dresses in new bloom,   90
    Ourselves must we beneath the Couch of Earth
Descend—ourselves to make a Couch—for whom?

Ah, make the most of what we yet may spend,
Before we too into the Dust descend;
    Dust into Dust, and under Dust to lie,   95
Sans Wine, sans Song, sans Singer, and—sans End!

Alike for those who for TODAY prepare
And those that after some TOMORROW stare,
    A Muezzin from the Tower of Darkness cries,
"Fools! your Reward is neither Here nor There."

Why, all the Saints and Sages who discuss'd   101
Of the Two Worlds so wisely—they are thrust
    Like foolish Prophets forth; their Words to Scorn
Are scatter'd, and their Mouths are stopt with Dust.

Myself when young did eagerly frequent   105
Doctor and Saint, and heard great argument
    About it and about: but evermore
Came out by the same door where in I went.

With them the seed of Wisdom did I sow,   109
And with mine own hand wrought to make it grow;
    And this was all the Harvest that I reap'd—
"I came like Water, and like Wind I go."

Into this Universe, and *Why* not knowing
Nor *Whence*, like Water willy-nilly flowing;
    And out of it, as Wind along the Waste,   115
I know not *Whither*, willy-nilly blowing.

What, without asking, hither hurried *Whence*?
And, without asking, *Whither* hurried hence!
    Oh, many a Cup of this forbidden Wine
Must drown the memory of that insolence!   120

Up from Earth's Centre through the Seventh Gate
I rose, and on the Throne of Saturn sate,
    And many a Knot unravel'd by the Road;
But not the Master-knot of Human Fate.

There was the Door to which I found no Key;   125
There was the Veil through which I might not see:
    Some little talk awhile of ME and THEE
There was—and then no more of THEE and ME.

Earth could not answer; nor the Seas that mourn
In flowing Purple, of their Lord forlorn;   130
    Nor rolling Heaven, with all his Signs reveal'd
And hidden by the sleeve of Night and Morn.

Then of the THEE IN ME who works behind
The Veil, I lifted up my hands to find
    A Lamp amid the Darkness; and I heard,   135
As from Without—"THE ME WITHIN THEE BLIND!"

Then to the Lip of this poor earthen Urn
I lean'd, the Secret of my Life to learn:
    And Lip to Lip it murmur'd—"While you live,
Drink!—for, once dead, you never shall return."

I think the Vessel, that with fugitive   141
Articulation answer'd, once did live,
    And drink; and Ah! the passive Lip I kiss'd,
How many Kisses might it take—and give!

For I remember stopping by the way   145
To watch a Potter thumping his wet Clay:
    And with its all-obliterated Tongue
It murmur'd—"Gently, Brother, gently, pray!"

And has not such a story from of Old
Down Man's successive generations roll'd   150
    Of such a clod of saturated Earth
Cast by the Maker into Human Mould?

And not a drop that from our Cups we throw
For Earth to drink of, but may steal below
    To quench the fire of Anguish in some Eye   155
There hidden,—far beneath, and long ago.

As then the Tulip for her morning sup
Of Heav'nly Vintage from the soil looks up,
    Do you devoutly do the like, till Heav'n
To Earth invert you—like an empty Cup.   160

Perplext no more with Human or Divine,
Tomorrow's tangle to the winds resign,
    And lose your fingers in the tresses of
The Cypress-slender Minister of Wine.

And if the Wine you drink, the Lip you press,   165
End in what All begins and ends in—Yes;
    Think then you are Today what Yesterday
You were—Tomorrow you shall not be less.

So when that Angel of the darker Drink
At last shall find you by the river-brink   170

99. **Muezzin**, the Mohammedan summoner of the Faithful to Prayer.
119. **forbidden Wine**; because the teachings of Mohammed strictly
forbid the use of alcohol in any form.

131. **Signs**, constellations of the Zodiac.

And, offering his Cup, invite your Soul
Forth to your Lips to quaff—you shall not shrink.

Why, if the Soul can fling the Dust aside,
And naked on the Air of Heaven ride,
   Were't not a Shame—were't not a Shame for him
In this clay carcase crippled to abide?   176

'Tis but a Tent where takes his one day's rest
A Sultan to the realm of Death addrest;
   The Sultan rises, and the dark Ferrásh
Strikes, and prepares it for another Guest.   180

And fear not lest Existence closing your
Account, and mine, should know the like no more;
   The Eternal Sákí from the Bowl has pour'd
Millions of Bubbles like us, and will pour.

When You and I behind the Veil are past,   185
Oh, but the long, long while the World shall last
   Which of our Coming and Departure heeds
As the Sea's self should heed a pebble-cast.

A Moment's Halt—a momentary taste
Of Being from the Well amid the Waste—   190
   And Lo!—the phantom Caravan has reach'd
The Nothing it set out from—Oh, make haste!

Would you that spangle of Existence spend
About THE SECRET—quick about it, Friend!
   A Hair perhaps divides the False and True—   195
And upon what, prithee, may life depend?

A Hair perhaps divides the False and True;
Yes; and a single Alif were the clue—
   Could you but find it—to the Treasure-House,
And peradventure to THE MASTER too;   200

Whose secret Presence, through Creation's veins
Running Quicksilver-like, eludes your pains;
   Taking all shapes from Máh to Máhi; and
They change and perish all—but He remains;

A moment guess'd—then back behind the Fold   205
Immerst of Darkness round the Drama roll'd
   Which, for the Pastime of Eternity,
He doth Himself contrive, enact, behold.

But if in vain, down on the stubborn floor
Of Earth, and up to Heav'n's unopening Door,   210
   You gaze Today, while You are You—how then
Tomorrow, when You shall be You no more?

Waste not your Hour, nor in the vain pursuit
Of This and That endeavor and dispute;
   Better be jocund with the fruitful Grape   215
Than sadden after none, or bitter, Fruit.

You know, my Friends, with what a brave Carouse
I made a Second Marriage in my house;
   Divorced old barren Reason from my Bed,
And took the Daughter of the Vine to Spouse.   220

For "Is" and "Is-not" though with Rule and Line
And "Up-and-down" by Logic I define,
   Of all that one should care to fathom, I
Was never deep in anything but—Wine.

Ah, but my Computations, People say,   225
Reduced the Year to better reckoning?—Nay,
   'Twas only striking from the Calendar
Unborn Tomorrow, and dead Yesterday.

And lately, by the Tavern Door agape,   229
Came shining through the Dusk an Angel Shape
   Bearing a Vessel on his Shoulder; and
He bid me taste of it; and 'twas—the Grape!

The Grape that can with Logic absolute
The Two-and-Seventy jarring Sects confute:
   The Sovereign Alchemist that in a trice   235
Life's leaden metal into Gold transmute:

The mighty Mahmúd, Allah-breathing Lord,
That all the misbelieving and black Horde
   Of Fears and Sorrows that infest the Soul
Scatters before him with his whirlwind Sword.   240

Why, be this Juice the growth of God, who dare
Blaspheme the twisted tendril as a Snare?
   A Blessing, we should use it, should we not?
And if a Curse—why, then, Who set it there?

I must abjure the Balm of Life, I must,   245
Scared by some After-reckoning ta'en on trust,
   Or lured with Hope of some Diviner Drink,
To fill the Cup—when crumbled into Dust!

Oh threats of Hell and Hopes of Paradise!
One thing at least is certain—*This* Life flies;   250
   One thing is certain and the rest is Lies;
The Flower that once has blown forever dies.

Strange, is it not? that of the myriads who
Before us pass'd the door of Darkness through,

225–228. **Computations . . . Yesterday.** Omar, as we have seen,
was a distinguished astronomer noted for his treatise on algebra
and for the reform of the calendar undertaken under the auspices
of Shah Malik of Persia. 234. **Two-and-Seventy . . . Sects,** according to Arabic lore, the number of religious faiths in the world.
237. **Allah-breathing,** worshiping Allah. 252. **blown,** blossomed.

179. **Ferrásh,** a camp-follower and military servant. 183. **Sákí,** a
wine-bearer (see line 401 below). 198. **Alif,** the first letter of the
Arabic alphabet. 203. **Máh to Máhi,** fish to moon.

*Pastoral scene, from a Persian manuscript illumination,
c. 1540.*

Not one returns to tell us of the Road,   255
Which to discover we must travel too.

The Revelations of Devout and Learn'd
Who rose before us, and as Prophets burn'd,
    Are all but Stories, which, awoke from Sleep
They told their comrades, and to Sleep return'd.

I sent my Soul through the Invisible,   261
Some letter of that After-life to spell:
    And by and by my Soul return'd to me,
And answer'd, "I Myself am Heav'n and Hell:"

Heav'n but the Vision of fulfill'd Desire,   265
And Hell the Shadow from a Soul on fire,
    Cast on the Darkness into which Ourselves,
So late emerged from, shall so soon expire.

We are no other than a moving row
Of Magic Shadow-shapes that come and go   270
    Round with the Sun-illumined Lantern held
In Midnight by the Master of the Show;

But helpless Pieces of the Game He plays
Upon this Checker-board of Nights and Days;

Hither and thither moves, and checks, and slays,
And one by one back in the Closet lays.   276

The Ball no question makes of Ayes and Noes,
But Here or There, as strikes the Player, goes;
    And He that toss'd you down into the Field,
He knows about it all—HE knows—HE knows!   280

The Moving Finger writes; and, having writ,
Moves on: nor all your Piety nor Wit
    Shall lure it back to cancel half a Line,
Nor all your Tears wash out a Word of it.

And that inverted Bowl they call the Sky,   285
Whereunder crawling coop'd we live and die,
    Lift not your hands to *It* for help—for It
As impotently moves as you or I.

With Earth's first Clay They did the Last Man
            knead,
And there of the Last Harvest sow'd the Seed: 290
    And the first Morning of Creation wrote
What the Last Dawn of Reckoning shall read.

Yesterday This Day's Madness did prepare;
Tomorrow's Silence, Triumph, or Despair:
    Drink! for you know not whence you came, nor
            why;   295
Drink! for you know not why you go, nor where.

I tell you this—When, started from the Goal,
Over the flaming shoulders of the Foal
    Of Heav'n Parwín and Mushtarí they flung,
In my predestined Plot of Dust and Soul,   300

The Vine had struck a fibre: which about
If clings my Being—let the Dervish flout;
    Of my Base metal may be filed a Key,
That shall unlock the Door he howls without.

And this I know: whether the one True Light   305
Kindle to Love, or Wrath-consume me quite,
    One Flash of It within the Tavern caught
Better than in the Temple lost outright.

What! out of senseless Nothing to provoke
A conscious Something to resent the yoke   310
    Of unpermitted Pleasure, under pain
Of Everlasting Penalties, if broke!

What! from his helpless Creature be repaid
Pure Gold for what he lent him dross-allay'd—
    Sue for a Debt he never did contract,   315
And cannot answer—Oh the sorry trade!

277. **The Ball,** in a game of polo. 298. **the Foal,** the equatorial
constellation of Equulus (little Horse). 299. **Parwín and Mushtarí.**
Parwin refers to the Pleiades; Mushtari is Arabic for the planet
Jupiter. 302. **Dervish,** any Mohammedan zealot.

Oh Thou, who didst with pitfall and with gin
Beset the Road I was to wander in,
    Thou wilt not with Predestined Evil round
Enmesh, and then impute my Fall to Sin!   320

O Thou, who Man of baser Earth didst make,
And ev'n with Paradise devise the Snake:
    For all the Sin wherewith the Face of Man
Is blacken'd—Man's forgiveness give—and take!

As under cover of departing Day   325
Slunk hunger-stricken Ramazán away,
    Once more within the Potter's house alone
I stood, surrounded by the Shapes of Clay.

Shapes of all Sorts and Sizes, great and small,
That stood along the floor and by the wall;   330
    And some loquacious Vessels were; and some
Listen'd perhaps, but never talk'd at all.

Said one among them—"Surely not in vain
My substance of the common Earth was ta'en
    And to this Figure moulded, to be broke,   335
Or trampled back to shapeless Earth again."

Then said a Second—"Ne'er a peevish Boy
Would break the Bowl from which he drank in joy;
    And He that with his hand the Vessel made
Will surely not in after Wrath destroy."   340

After a momentary silence spake
Some Vessel of a more ungainly Make;
    They sneer at me for leaning all awry:
"What! did the Hand then of the Potter shake?"

Whereat some one of the loquacious Lot—   345
I think a Súfi pipkin—waxing hot—
    "All this of Pot and Potter—Tell me, then,
Who is the Potter, pray, and who the Pot?"

"Why," said another, "some there are who tell
Of one who threatens he will toss to Hell   350
    The luckless Pots he marr'd in making—Pish!
He's a Good Fellow, and 't will all be well."

"Well," murmur'd one, "let whoso make or buy,
My Clay with long Oblivion is gone dry:
    But fill me with the old familiar Juice,   355
Methinks I might recover by and by."

So, while the Vessels one by one were speaking,
The little Moon look'd in that all were seeking:

326. **Ramazán,** the Mohammedan fasting month.   346. **Súfi.** See p. 44, Hafiz headnote.

And then they jogg'd each other, "Brother!
    Brother!
Now for the Potter's shoulder-knot a-creaking!"

Ah, with the Grape my fading Life provide,   361
And wash the Body whence the Life has died,
    And lay me, shrouded in the living Leaf,
By some not unfrequented Garden-side.

That ev'n my buried Ashes such a snare   365
Of Vintage shall fling up into the Air
    As not a True-believer passing by
But shall be overtaken unaware.

Indeed the Idols I have loved so long
Have done my credit in this World much wrong:
    Have drown'd my Glory in a shallow Cup,   371
And sold my Reputation for a Song.

Indeed, indeed, Repentance oft before
I swore—but was I sober when I swore?
    And then and then came Spring, and Rose-in-
        hand   375
My threadbare Penitence apieces tore.

And much as Wine has play'd the Infidel,
And robb'd me of my Robe of Honor—Well,
    I wonder often what the Vintners buy
One half so precious as the stuff they sell.   380

Yet ah, that Spring should vanish with the Rose!
That Youth's sweet-scented manuscript should close!
    The Nightingale that in the branches sang,
Ah whence, and whither flown again, who knows!

Would but the Desert of the Fountain yield   385
One glimpse—if dimly, yet indeed, reveal'd,
    To which the fainting Traveller might spring
As springs the trampled herbage of the field!

Would but some wingéd Angel ere too late
Arrest the yet unfolded Roll of Fate,   390
    And make the stern Recorder otherwise
Enregister, or quite obliterate!

Ah, Love! could you and I with Him conspire
To grasp this sorry Scheme of Things entire,
    Would we not shatter it to bits—and then   395
Remould it nearer to the Heart's Desire!

Yon rising Moon that looks for us again—
How oft hereafter will she wax and wane;
    How oft hereafter rising look for us
Through this same Garden—and for *one* in vain!

And when like her, O Sákí, you shall pass   401
Among the Guests Star-scatter'd on the Grass,
   And in your joyous errand reach the spot
Where I made One—turn down an empty Glass!

Hafiz

c. 1300–c. 1388

Friend of Shah and Sultan, religious teacher and mystic, lover of love and worshiper of all that is beautiful in living, Hafiz (Shemsuddin Mohammed) stands as the last of the distinguished group of Persian poets whose preëminence coincides with the intellectual and artistic preëminence of their Moslem world. Hafiz spent his life in Shiraz, Persia, a city as peculiarly identified with him as Nishapur was with Omar Khayyam and Bagdad with Haroun al-Raschid. His life span covered the greater part of the fourteenth century, for he died at a great age in 1388 or very soon thereafter. He was born about the time that Dante wrote *The Divine Comedy* and was a mature writer at the time of Chaucer's birth.

No poet of the Oriental world is more often quoted by Orientals, and none has had such a long-lasting international reputation, although among English-speaking peoples Omar Khayyam is far better known, partly because of Fitzgerald's magnificent English version of Omar's *rubaiyat*. Actually there are many points in common between Hafiz and Omar Khayyam. Both celebrate the joys of the flesh and the joys of the vine, and both imply that these joys are to be received not only in the physical but also in the spiritual sense. But Hafiz, living more than two hundred years after Omar, was clearly caught up in Sufism—the philosophy of a particular mystical sect which Omar Khayyam regarded satirically rather than otherwise. The Sufists preached oneness with God, who was the source of all truth and beauty. It is impossible to read the poetry of Hafiz, as exemplified by *The Divan* (or *Collected Odes*), without sensing sooner or later these Sufistic tendencies; but these tendencies, which show marked affinity with the Platonic writings, are left both vague and diffuse. Perhaps it is this vagueness, which is after all inherent in the very nature of Sufistic teachings, that made Omar Khayyam impatient with the sect; at any rate, his was an instinctively scientific mind, whereas that of Hafiz was by nature transcendental.

There is no doubt, however, that Hafiz was a man of the world as well as a mystic. It is difficult for the Occidental (though not for the Oriental) to comprehend this seeming paradox. None other than the illustrious Sherlock Holmes has borne witness that "there is as much sense in Hafiz as in Horace, and as much knowledge of the world." It was the conqueror Timur (Tamerlane) who sternly reproached Hafiz for having dared to put the eyebrow of the poet's mistress above Tamer-

lane's glory in capturing Shiraz; but Hafiz had the more profound wisdom when he smiled in the assurance that the poet was right. It was Hafiz who expressed the hope that his tomb might be the shrine for all drunkards, very much as Omar Khayyam wished to be identified in death with rose petals and the grape. And in the sense that one can be drunk not only on wine but also on love and on religion—which is precisely the interpretation that Hafiz would put upon the idea of drunkenness—his wish has been fulfilled.

The Divan (Odes)

V

Up, sákí!—let the goblet flow;
   Strew with dust the head of our earthly woe!

Give me thy cup; that, joy-possessed,
I may tear this azure cowl from my breast.

The wise may deem me lost to shame,   5
But no care have I for renown or name.

Bring wine!—how many a witless head
By the wind of pride has with dust been spread!

My bosom's fumes, my sighs so warm,
Have inflamed yon crude and unfeeling swarm.   10

This mad heart's secret, well I know,
Is beyond the thoughts of both high and low.

E'en by that sweetheart charmed am I,
Who once from my heart made sweetness fly.

Who that my Silvern Tree hath seen,   15
Would regard the cypress that decks the green?

> In grief be patient,
>   Night and day,
> Till thy fortune, Hafiz,
>   Thy wish obey.

XII

Oh! where are deeds of virtue and this frail spirit where?
How wide the space that sunders the bounds of Here and There!

The Divan (Odes). Translated by H. Bicknell. Reprinted by permission of P. F. Collier and Son Corporation.
4. **azure cowl,** the cloak of deceit and false humility. Hafiz is here attacking the members of Sheikh Hazan's Order of Dervishes, who were hostile to the poet through most of his career. 10. **yon . . . swarm,** another hostile reference to Sheikh Hazan's Order of Dervishes. 15–16. **Silvern Tree . . . green?** By a silver tree Hafiz is referring to the precious quality of his own way of life, for in many parts of the Orient silver is more highly regarded than gold.

Can toping aught in common with works and wor-
    ship own?
Where is regard for sermons, where is the rebeck's
    tone?

My heart abhors the cloister, and the false cowl its
    sign: 5
Where is the Magian's cloister, and where is his pure
    wine?

'Tis fled: may memory sweetly mind me of union's
    days!
Where is that voice of anger, where those coquettish
    ways?

Can a foe's heart be kindled by the friend's face so
    bright?
Where is a lamp unlighted, and the clear Day-star's
    light?   10

As dust upon thy threshold supplies my eyes with
    balm,
If I forsake thy presence, where can I hope for calm?

Turn from that chin's fair apple; a pit is on the way.
To what, O heart, aspirest thou? Whither thus
    quickly? Say!

    Seek not, O friend, in Hafiz   15
    Patience, nor rest from care;
    Patience and rest—what are they?
    Where is calm slumber? Where?

XLII

'Tis a deep charm which wakes the lover's flame,
Not ruby lip, nor verdant down its name.

Beauty is not the eye, lock, cheek, and mole;
A thousand subtle points the heart control.

XLV

O breeze of morn! where is the place which guards
    my friend from strife?
Where is the abode of that sly Moon who lovers
    robs of life?

The night is dark, the Happy Vale in front of me I
    trace.   3
Where is the fire of Sinai, where is the meeting
    place?

---

4. **rebeck,** an old stringed instrument and ancestor of the violin.
7. **union's days,** that is, the days when the lovers were together.
13. **chin's . . . apple.** A favorite "conceit" of Oriental love poetry
in this era is the belief that a cleft in the chin was a prime indication
of beauty. 3. **Happy Vale.** The Valley of Aiman ("Happiness")
was where God appeared to Moses—metaphorically, then, the abode
of the beloved.

Here jointly are the wine-filled cup, the rose, the
    minstrel; yet   5
While we lack love, no bliss is here: where can my
    Loved be met?

Of the Sheikh's cell my heart has tired, and of the
    convent bare:
Where is my friend, the Christian's child, the vint-
    ner's mansion? Where?

    Hafiz, if o'er the glade of earth
    The autumn blast is borne,   10
    Grieve not, but musing ask thyself:
    "Where has the rose no thorn?"

LXIII

My heart has of the world grown weary and all
    that it can lend:
The shrine of my affection holds no Being but my
    friend.

If e'er for me thy love's sweet garden a fragrant
    breath exhale,
My heart, expansive in its joy, shall bud-like burst
    its veil.

Should I upon love's path advise thee, when now
    a fool I've grown,   5
'Twould be the story of the fool, the pitcher, and
    the stone.

Go! say to the secluded zealot: "Withhold thy
    blame; for know,
I find the Arch of the Mihrab but in an eyebrow's
    bow."

Between the Ka'bah and the wine-house, no differ-
    ence I see:
Whate'er the spot my glance surveys, there equally
    is He.   10

'Tis not for beard, hair, eyebrow only, Kalandarism
    should care:
The Kalandar computes the Path by adding hair to
    hair.

    The Kalandar who gives a hair's head
    An easy path doth tread:
    The Kalandar of genuine stamp,   15
    As Hafiz gives his head.

---

8. **Arch of the Mihrab.** The *mihrab* is the niche in a mosque, facing
which all Mohammedans pray. 9. **Ka'bah,** the Palladium, the
"Holy of Holies," of the Moslem faith, located in the holy city of
Mecca. 11–16. **Kalandarism . . . head.** The Kalenders are an
order of Mohammedan dervishes who wander about and beg. Hafiz
is making the point that the worthless kalendar will observe ex-
ternals by shaving off his beard and by tonsuring but will neglect
his fundamental spiritual duty; the true kalendar, like the poet, will
sacrifice anything, even his head, for the scrupulous observance of
his religious duty.

LXIX

MY HEART desires the face so fair of Farrukh;
It is perturbed as is the hair of Farrukh.

No creature but that lock, that Hindu swart,
Enjoyment from the cheek has sought of Farrukh.

A blackamoor by Fortune blest is he, 5
Placed at the side, and near the knee of Farrukh.

Shy as the aspen is the cypress seen,
Awed by the captivating mien of Farrukh.

Sákí, bring syrtis-tinted wine to tell
Of those narcissi, potent spell of Farrukh. 10

Bent as the archer's bow my frame is now,
From woes continuous as the brow of Farrukh.

E'en Tartar gales which musky odors whirl,
Faint at the amber-breathing curl of Farrukh.

If leans the human heart to any place, 15
Mine has a yearning to the grace of Farrukh.

> That lofty soul
> Shall have my service true,
> That serves, as Hafiz,
> The Hindu of Farrukh. 20

LXXXVII

WHEN beamed thy beauty on creation's morn,
The world was set on fire by love new-born.

Thy cheeks shone bright, yet angels' hearts were
 cold:
Then flashed it fire, and turned to Adam's mould.

The lamp of Reason from this flame had burned, 5
But lightning jealousy the world o'erturned.

The enemy Thy secret sought to gain;
A hand unseen repelled the beast profane.

The die of Fate may render others glad:
My own heart saddens, for its lot is sad. 10

Thy chin's deep pit allures the lofty mind:
The hand would grasp thy locks in twines entwined.

> Hafiz his love-scroll
> To Thyself addressed,
> When he had cancelled 15
> What his heart loved best.

1. **Farrukh,** obviously a beloved.   3. **Hindu swart,** Farrukh's servant.

CXV

LOST Joseph shall return to Kanaan's land—Despair
 not;
Affliction's cell of gloom with flowers shall bloom:
> Despair not.

Sad heart, thy state shall mend; repel despondency;
Thy head confused with pain shall sense regain: 5
> Despair not.

When life's fresh spring returns upon the dais mead,
O night-bird! o'er thy head the rose shall spread.
> Despair not.

Hope on, though things unseen may baffle thy research; 10
Mysterious sports we hail beyond the veil:
> Despair not.

Has the revolving Sphere two days opposed thy
 wish,
Know that the circling Round is changeful found:
> Despair not. 15

If on the Ka' bah bent, thou brave the desert sand,
Though from the acacias' thorns thy foot be torn,
> Despair not.

Heart, should the flood of death life's fabric sweep
 away,
Noah shall steer the Ark o'er billows dark: 20
> Despair not.

Though perilous the stage, though out of sight the
 goal,
Whithersoe'er we wend, there is an end:
> Despair not.

If Love evades our grasp, and rivals press our suit,
God, Lord of every change, surveys the range: 26
> Despair not.

> Hafiz, in thy poor nook—
> Alone, the dark night through—
> Prayer and the Koran's page 30
> Shall grief assuage—
>
> Despair not.

CXXXV

I TRIED my fortune in this city lorn:
From out its whirlpool must my pack be borne.

1. **Lost Joseph.** The Biblical Joseph became in the legendry of the
Near East the symbol of a lover; the story of Joseph and Potiphar's
wife (Zuleika) was considered a deathless romance. 13–14. **Sphere
. . . Round.** The spheres of Heaven in the Ptolemaic system move
daily around the stationary Earth; the Round refers to their astrological influence.

I gnaw my hand, and, heaving sighs of ire,
I light in my rent frame the rose's fire.

Sweet sang the bulbul at the close of day   5
The rose attentive on her leafy spray:

"O heart! be joyful, for thy ruthless Love
Sits down ill-tempered at the sphere above.

"To make the false, harsh world thyself pass o'er,
Ne'er promise falsely and be harsh no more.   10

"If beat misfortune's waves upon heavens roof,
Devout men's fate and gear bide ocean-proof.

> "Hafiz, if lasting
> Were enjoyment's day,
> Jem's throne would never   15
> Have been swept away."

CLXXX

O THOU who art unlearned still, the quest of love
    essay:
Canst thou who hast not trod the path guide others
    on the way?

While in the school of Truth thou stay'st, from
    Master Love to learn,
Endeavor, though a son today, the father's grade to
    earn.

Slumber and food have held thee far from Love's
    exalted good: 5
Wouldst thou attain the goal of love, abstain from
    sleep and food.

If with the rays of love of truth thy heart and soul
    be clear,
By God! thy beauty shall outshine the sun which
    lights the sphere.

Wash from the dross of life thy hands, as the Path's
    men of old,
And winning Love's alchemic power, transmute thy-
    self to gold.   10

On all thy frame, from head to foot, the light of God
    shall shine,
If on the Lord of Glory's path nor head nor foot be
    thine.

An instant plunge into God's sea, nor e'er the truth
    forget
That the Seven Seas' o'erwhelming tide, no hair of
    thine shall wet.

15. Jem, Jamshyd; see notes, pp. 38, 39.   9. Path's men of old,
old and orthodox believers.

If once thy glancing eye repose on the Creator's
    face,   15
Thenceforth among the men who glance shall doubt-
    less be thy place.

When that which thy existence frames all upside-
    down shall be,
Imagine not that up and down shall be the lot of
    thee.

> Hafiz, if ever in thy head
>   Dwell Union's wish serene,   20
> Thou must become the threshold's dust
>   Of men whose sight is keen.

The New Testament

The New Testament evangelical Book of Matthew was probably written somewhere between the years 65 and 68, although some scholars have thought that the passage in Chapter 22:6–7 ("But when the king heard thereof, he was wroth; and he sent forth his armies, and destroyed these murderers, and burned up their city") refers to the destruction of Jerusalem by the Romans in 70. The author of this Gospel was presumably a Greek-speaking or Hellenistic Jewish Christian, who wrote with the definite purpose of confirming others of his race and religious profession in the view that Jesus Christ was the true Messiah, whose coming was prophesied in the Old Testament. This Gospel is therefore much more closely connected than the other three (Mark, Luke, and John) with the traditions of the Old Testament—a fact which appears evident from the very first chapter, with its long genealogy from Abraham to Christ, from the attention given in Matthew to Hebrew prophets and their sayings (which are to be fulfilled in the words and deeds of Christ), and from the constant reference to Christ as the "Son of David."

The source of this Gospel is in part the earlier Book of Mark and in part a lost Gospel, possibly in Aramaic and possibly by the disciple Matthew himself. It contains also, of course, the usual increments of Jewish or Semitic folklore, as well as the permeating atmosphere of Greek and Oriental idealistic philosophies, which can be traced throughout Christian teachings. Although it may be assumed that the author was a Palestinian, it is not certain whether he actually composed the Gospel in Palestine; and localities as far apart as Syria in the north and Alexandria in the south have been suggested for the geographical origin of the work.

One fact, however, is indisputable. The Gospel according to St. Matthew is not only the longest of the four gospels, but it contains also more of the longer discourses of Christ. It seems most likely that these longer discourses represent a culling by the author of various shorter sayings of Christ and the gathering of them into groups of

16. men who glance, lovers.

precepts and admonitions, or, as the product has been rather happily described, into "bouquets of discourse." There are five of these: (1) The Sermon on the Mount (5:1 to 7:27); (2) The Address to the Apostles (10:5–42); (3) The Kingdom of Heaven Parables (13:1–52); (4) On Humility and Forgiveness (18:1–35); and (5) The Apocalyptic Utterances (24:4 to 25:46). In these five great passages, especially in the Sermon on the Mount, lies the quintessence of the Christian ideal of conduct. But no less arresting to the general reader and student are the shrewd grasp of human relationships and the insight into human nature, the poetic didacticism of the parables, the otherworldliness of the kernels of Christian faith, the almost rhapsodic picture of ruin and desolation to be encountered in the Latter Day, and the magnificent human wisdom shown throughout. Apart from these longer discourses, there is portrayed the true personality and life of Christ, from His birth to the unforgettable drama of His Passion and Crucifixion; and although Luke's account of His birth and John's account of His Passion are more moving, neither of these Gospels is more comprehensive in a biographical sense. The impact of all this upon Christian minds since the inception of the Faith need not be dwelt upon here; virtually every chapter of Matthew has contributed to the phraseology and the religious and ethical imagination of the Christian world.

The establishment of the early Christian Church and the part played by Saul of Tarsus, who was converted into the missionary apostle Paul, make up together the most important part of the New Testament Book of Acts. The labors of Paul as the spokesman for Christianity and as the organizer of the Church and queller of factions within the Church are nothing less than monumental; and his various epistles to members of the Church in the many localities of Asia Minor and the Roman world, known as the Pauline Epistles, constitute an extremely influential body of Christian doctrine which does much to explain the structure of modern Christian ecclesiasticism.

Some fifteen years before his death in the year 67, Paul spent more than a year and a half (50–51) in Corinth, Greece, working on the ironing out of a serious factional dispute among the Christians of that city. The result of his efforts was a pair of epistles, in the nature of pastoral letters, to the members of the Church in Corinth, discussing tactfully their points of dispute and stating here and there some of the cardinal tenets of the Christian belief. The first of these two, I Corinthians, written shortly after 50 A.D., is more philosophical than the second, and in the thirteenth and fifteenth chapters reaches perhaps the most eloquent of the many eloquent peaks achieved by Paul in his missionary and administrative career. For the thirteenth chapter, with its noble exaltation of the Love of Mankind, is perhaps the most famous section of the Pauline Epistles; and the fifteenth chapter, with its towering words on immortality, has become an integral part of the Christian burial service, particularly among the many modern Protestant sects.

A twelfth-century manuscript shows St. Matthew writing his gospel, inspired by his traditional symbol, the angel.

The Gospel
ACCORDING TO
Saint Matthew
CHAPTER I

. . . Now the birth of Jesus Christ was on this wise: When as his mother Mary was espoused to Joseph, before they came together, she was found with child of the Holy Ghost.

Then Joseph her husband, being a just man, and not willing to make her a public example, was minded to put her away privily.

But while he thought on these things, behold, the angel of the Lord appeared unto him in a dream, saying, 'Joseph, thou son of David, fear not to take unto thee Mary thy wife; for that which is conceived in her is of the Holy Ghost.

'And she shall bring forth a son, and thou shalt

The Gospel according to Saint Matthew.[A] From the King James Version of the Bible.

call his name JESUS: for he shall save his people from their sins.'

Now all this was done, that it might be fulfilled which was spoken of the Lord by the prophet, saying:

'Behold, a virgin shall be with child, and shall bring forth a son, and they shall call his name Emmanuel, which being interpreted is, God with us.'

Then Joseph, being raised from sleep, did as the angel of the Lord had bidden him, and took unto him his wife:

And knew her not till she had brought forth her firstborn son: and he called his name JESUS.

CHAPTER II

Now when Jesus was born in Bethlehem of Judaea in the days of Herod the king, behold, there came wise men from the east to Jerusalem,

Saying, 'Where is he that is born King of the Jews? for we have seen his star in the east, and are come to worship him.'

When Herod the king had heard these things, he was troubled, and all Jerusalem with him.

And when he had gathered all the chief priests and scribes of the people together, he demanded of them where Christ should be born.

And they said unto him, 'In Bethlehem of Judaea, for thus it is written by the prophet:

"And thou, Bethlehem, in the land of Juda, art not the least among the princes of Juda, for out of thee shall come a Governor, that shall rule my people Israel." '

Then Herod, when he had privily called the wise men, inquired of them diligently what time the star appeared.

And he sent them to Bethlehem, and said, 'Go and search diligently for the young child; and when ye have found him, bring me word again, that I may come and worship him also.'

When they had heard the king, they departed; and, lo, the star, which they saw in the east, went before them, till it came and stood over where the young child was.

When they saw the star, they rejoiced with exceeding great joy.

And when they were come into the house, they saw the young child with Mary his mother, and fell down, and worshipped him; and when they had opened their treasures, they presented unto him gifts: gold, and frankincense, and myrrh.

And being warned of God in a dream that they should not return to Herod, they departed into their own country another way.

1. JESUS, that is, the Savior. 6–8. 'Behold . . . us.' See Isaiah, 7:14 and 9:6. 50. Herod, known as Herod the Great, King of Judaea (appointed by the Roman Senate) from 40 B.C. until his death in 4 B.C. He was known as a servile cringer before Rome, as a builder of cities, and as a despotic and bloody tyrant given to massacres.

And when they were departed, behold, the angel of the Lord appeareth to Joseph in a dream, saying, 'Arise, and take the young child and his mother, and flee into Egypt, and be thou there until I bring thee word, for Herod will seek the young child to destroy him.'

When he arose, he took the young child and his mother by night, and departed into Egypt;

And was there until the death of Herod, that it might be fulfilled which was spoken of the Lord by the prophet, saying: 'Out of Egypt have I called my son.'

Then Herod, when he saw that he was mocked of the wise men, was exceeding wroth, and sent forth, and slew all the children that were in Bethlehem, and in all the coasts thereof, from two years old and under, according to the time which he had diligently inquired of the wise men.

Then was fulfilled that which was spoken by Jeremy the prophet, saying:

'In Rama was there a voice heard, lamentation and weeping, and great mourning; Rachel weeping for her children, and would not be comforted, because they were not.'

But when Herod was dead, behold, an angel of the Lord appeareth in a dream to Joseph in Egypt,

Saying, 'Arise, and take the young child and his mother, and go into the land of Israel, for they are dead which sought the young child's life.'

And he arose, and took the young child and his mother, and came into the land of Israel.

But when he heard that Archelaus did reign in Judaea in the room of his father Herod, he was afraid to go thither; notwithstanding, being warned of God in a dream, he turned aside into the parts of Galilee;

And he came and dwelt in a city called Nazareth, that it might be fulfilled which was spoken by the prophets, 'He shall be called a Nazarene.'

CHAPTER III

In those days came John the Baptist, preaching in the wilderness of Judaea,

And saying, 'Repent ye, for the kingdom of Heaven is at hand.

For this is he that was spoken of by the prophet Esaias, saying, "The voice of one crying in the wilderness, 'Prepare ye the way of the Lord, make his paths straight.' " '

And the same John had his raiment of camel's hair, and a leathern girdle about his loins; and his meat was locusts and wild honey.

Then went out to him Jerusalem, and all Judaea, and all the region about Jordan,

72. Rama. See Jeremiah, 31:15. The name is applied to several places in Palestine and used here to refer to the whole country. 90. Nazarene. See Judges, 13:5 and I Samuel, 1:11. 96–98. "The voice . . . straight." See Isaiah, 11:3.

And were baptized of him in Jordan, confessing their sins.

But when he saw many of the Pharisees and Sadducees come to his baptism, he said unto them, 'O generation of vipers, who hath warned you to flee from the wrath to come?

'Bring forth therefore fruits meet for repentance,

'And think not to say within yourselves, "We have Abraham to our father," for I say unto you, that God is able of these stones to raise up children unto Abraham.

'And now also the axe is laid unto the root of the trees; therefore every tree which bringeth not forth good fruit is hewn down, and cast into the fire.

'I indeed baptize you with water unto repentance, but he that cometh after me is mightier than I, whose shoes I am not worthy to bear; he shall baptize you with the Holy Ghost, and with fire:

'Whose fan is in his hand, and he will thoroughly purge his floor, and gather his wheat into the garner; but he will burn up the chaff with unquenchable fire.'

Then cometh Jesus from Galilee to Jordan unto John, to be baptized of him.

But John forbad him, saying, 'I have need to be baptized of thee, and comest thou to me?'

And Jesus answering said unto him, 'Suffer it to be so now, for thus it becometh us to fulfill all righteousness.' Then he suffered him.

And Jesus, when he was baptized, went up straightway out of the water; and, lo, the heavens were opened unto him, and he saw the Spirit of God descending like a dove, and lighting upon him;

And, lo, a voice from Heaven, saying, 'This is my beloved Son, in whom I am well pleased.'

CHAPTER IV

Then was Jesus led up of the spirit into the wilderness to be tempted of the devil.

And when he had fasted forty days and forty nights, he was afterward a-hungered.

And when the tempter came to him, he said, 'If thou be the Son of God, command that these stones be made bread.'

But he answered and said, 'It is written, "Man shall not live by bread alone, but by every word that proceedeth out of the mouth of God." '

Then the devil taketh him up into the holy city, and setteth him on a pinnacle of the temple,

And saith unto him, 'If thou be the Son of God, cast thyself down, for it is written, "He shall give his angels charge concerning thee; and in their hands they shall bear thee up, lest at any time thou dash thy foot against a stone." '

Jesus said unto him, 'It is written again, "Thou shalt not tempt the Lord thy God." '

Again, the devil taketh him up into an exceeding high mountain, and showeth him all the kingdoms of the world, and the glory of them,

And saith unto him, 'All these things will I give thee, if thou wilt fall down and worship me.'

Then saith Jesus unto him, 'Get thee hence, Satan, for it is written, "Thou shalt worship the Lord thy God, and him only shalt thou serve." '

Then the devil leaveth him, and, behold, angels came and ministered unto him.

Now when Jesus had heard that John was cast into prison, he departed into Galilee;

And leaving Nazareth, he came and dwelt in Capernaum, which is upon the sea coast, in the borders of Zabulon and Nepthalim,

That it might be fulfilled which was spoken by Esaias the prophet, saying:

'The land of Zabulon, and the land of Nepthalim, by the way of the sea, beyond Jordan, Galilee of the Gentiles;

'The people which sat in darkness saw great light; and to them which sat in the region and shadow of death light is sprung up.'

From that time Jesus began to preach, and to say, 'Repent; for the kingdom of heaven is at hand.'

And Jesus walking by the sea of Galilee, saw two brethren, Simon called Peter, and Andrew his brother, casting a net into the sea, for they were fishers.

And he saith unto them, 'Follow me, and I will make you fishers of men.'

And they straightway left their nets, and followed him.

And going on from thence, he saw other two brethren, James the son of Zebedee, and John his brother, in a ship with Zebedee their father, mending their nets; and he called them.

And they immediately left their ship and their father and followed him.

And Jesus went about all Galilee, teaching in their synagogues, and preaching the gospel of the Kingdom, and healing all manner of sickness and all manner of disease among the people.

And his fame went throughout all Syria; and they brought unto him all sick people that were taken with divers diseases and torments, and those which were possessed with devils, and those which were lunatic, and those that had the palsy; and he healed them.

3–4. **Pharisees and Sadducees,** two important sects of Jews in Jerusalem of the time of Christ. The chief contribution of the Pharisees was to make the synagogue the center of social, intellectual, and religious life; they were formalistic and insisted on fundamentalistic links with Hebrew religious traditions, as represented not only by the Old Testament but by the *Talmud* and rabbinical lore. The Sadducees accepted only the written word of the scriptures and not the mass of oral tradition and ritual as well.

69. **Zabulon . . . Nepthalim,** names of two of the original twelve tribes of Israel.

And there followed him great multitudes of people from Galilee, and from Decapolis, and from Jerusalem, and from Judaea, and from beyond Jordan.

CHAPTER V

And seeing the multitudes, he went up into a mountain; and when he was set, his disciples came unto him;

And he opened his mouth, and taught them, saying:

10 'Blessed are the poor in spirit, for theirs is the kingdom of Heaven.

'Blessed are they that mourn, for they shall be comforted.

'Blessed are the meek, for they shall inherit the earth.

'Blessed are they which do hunger and thirst after righteousness, for they shall be filled.

'Blessed are the merciful, for they shall obtain mercy.

20 'Blessed are the pure in heart, for they shall see God.

'Blessed are the peacemakers, for they shall be called the children of God.

'Blessed are they which are persecuted for righteousness' sake, for theirs is the kingdom of Heaven.

'Blessed are ye, when men shall revile you, and persecute you, and shall say all manner of evil against you falsely, for my sake.

'Rejoice, and be exceeding glad, for great is your 30 reward in Heaven, for so persecuted they the prophets which were before you.

'Ye are the salt of the earth, but if the salt have lost his savor, wherewith shall it be salted? It is thenceforth good for nothing, but to be cast out, and to be trodden under foot of men.

'Ye are the light of the world. A city that is set on a hill cannot be hid.

'Neither do men light a candle, and put it under a bushel, but on a candlestick; and it giveth light 40 unto all that are in the house.

'Let your light so shine before men that they may see your good works, and glorify your Father which is in Heaven.

'Think not that I am come to destroy the law, or the prophets; I am not come to destroy, but to fulfill.

'For verily I say unto you, Till Heaven and earth pass, one jot or one tittle shall in no wise pass from the law, till all be fulfilled.

50 'Whosoever therefore shall break one of these least commandments, and shall teach men so, he shall be called the least in the kingdom of Heaven; but whosoever shall do and teach them, the same shall be called great in the Kingdom of Heaven.

'For I say unto you, that except your righteousness shall exceed the righteousness of the scribes and Pharisees, ye shall in no case enter into the kingdom of Heaven.

'Ye have heard that it was said by them of old 60 time, "Thou shalt not kill"; and whosoever shall kill shall be in danger of the judgment:

'But I say unto you, that whosoever is angry with his brother without a cause shall be in danger of the judgment; and whosoever shall say to his brother, "Raca," shall be in danger of the council; but whosoever shall say, "Thou fool," shall be in danger of hell-fire.

'Therefore if thou bring thy gift to the altar, and there rememberest that thy brother hath ought against thee, 70

'Leave there thy gift before the altar, and go thy way; first be reconciled to thy brother, and then come and offer thy gift.

'Agree with thine adversary quickly whiles thou are in the way with him, lest at any time the adversary deliver thee to the judge, and the judge deliver thee to the officer, and thou be cast into prison.

'Verily I say unto thee, thou shalt by no means come out thence, till thou hast paid the uttermost farthing. 80

'Ye have heard that it was said by them of old time, "Thou shalt not commit adultery,"

'But I say unto you, that whosoever looketh on a woman to lust after her hath committed adultery with her already in his heart.

'And if thy right eye offend thee, pluck it out, and cast it from thee, for it is profitable for thee that one of thy members perish, and not that thy whole body should be cast into Hell.

'And if thy right hand offend thee, cut it off, and 90 cast it from thee, for it is profitable for thee that one of thy members should perish, and not that thy whole body should be cast into Hell.

'It hath been said, "Whosoever shall put away his wife, let him give her a writing of divorcement,"

'But I say unto you, that whosoever shall put away his wife, saving for the cause of fornication, causeth her to commit adultery; and whosoever shall marry her that is divorced committeth adultery.

'Again, ye have heard that it hath been said by 100 them of old time, "Thou shalt not forswear thyself, but shalt perform unto the Lord thine oaths,"

'But I say unto you, swear not at all, neither by Heaven, for it is God's throne;

'Nor by the earth, for it is his footstool; neither by Jerusalem, for it is the city of the great King.

2. **Decapolis,** the name of a loose confederation of largely non-Jewish states lying both east and west of the River Jordan. 39. **bushel,** originally a basket or any kind of vessel holding the amount known by the name of the unit.

65. **"Raca,"** vain man.

'Neither shalt thou swear by thy head, because thou canst not make one hair white or black.

'But let your communication be, "Yea, yea; nay, nay!" for whatsoever is more than these cometh of evil.

'Ye have heard that it hath been said, "An eye for an eye, and a tooth for a tooth":

'But I say unto you, that ye resist not evil; but whosoever shall smite thee on thy right cheek, turn
10 to him the other also.

'And if any man will sue thee at the law, and take away thy coat, let him have thy cloak also.

'And whosoever shall compel thee to go a mile, go with him twain.

'Give to him that asketh thee, and from him that would borrow of thee turn thou not away.

'Ye have heard that it hath been said, "Thou shalt love thy neighbor and hate thine enemy."

'But I say unto you, love your enemies, bless them
20 that curse you, do good to them that hate you, and pray for them which despitefully use you, and persecute you,

'That ye may be the children of your Father which is in Heaven, for he maketh his sun to rise on the evil and on the good, and sendeth rain on the just and on the unjust.

'For if ye love them which love you, what reward have ye? Do not even the publicans the same?

'And if ye salute your brethren only, what do ye
30 more than others? Do not even the publicans so?

'Be ye therefore perfect, even as your Father which is in Heaven is perfect.

CHAPTER VI

'Take heed that ye do not your alms before men, to be seen of them; otherwise ye have no reward of your Father which is in Heaven.

'Therefore when thou doest thine alms, do not sound a trumpet before thee, as the hypocrites do in the synagogues and in the streets, that they may have glory of men. Verily I say unto you, they have
40 their reward.

'But when thou doest alms, let not thy left hand know what thy right hand doeth,

'That thine alms may be in secret, and thy Father which seeth in secret himself shall reward thee openly.

'And when thou prayest, thou shalt not be as the hypocrites are, for they love to pray standing in the synagogues and in the corners of the streets, that they may be seen of men. Verily I say unto you,
50 they have their reward.

'But thou, when thou prayest, enter into thy closet, and when thou hast shut thy door, pray to thy Father which is in secret; and thy Father which seeth in secret shall reward thee openly.

'But when ye pray, use not vain repetitions, as the heathen do, for they think that they shall be heard for their much speaking.

'Be not ye therefore like unto them, for your Father knoweth what things ye have need of, before
60 you ask him.

'After this manner therefore pray ye: "Our Father, which art in Heaven, hallowed be thy name.

' "Thy kingdom come. Thy will be done in earth, as it is in Heaven.

' "Give us this day our daily bread,

' "And forgive us our debts, as we forgive our debtors.

' "And lead us not into temptation, but deliver us from evil, for thine is the kingdom and the power
70 and the glory, for ever. Amen."

'For if ye forgive men their trespasses, your heavenly Father will also forgive you;

'But if ye forgive not men their trespasses, neither will your Father forgive your trespasses.

'Moreover, when ye fast, be not, as the hypocrites, of a sad countenance, for they disfigure their faces, that they may appear unto men to fast. Verily I say unto you, they have their reward.

'But thou, when thou fastest, anoint thine head,
80 and wash thy face,

'That thou appear not unto men to fast, but unto thy Father which is in secret; and thy Father, which seeth in secret, shall reward thee openly.

'Lay not up for yourselves treasures upon earth, where moth and rust doth corrupt, and where thieves break through and steal;

'But lay up for yourselves treasures in Heaven, where neither moth nor rust doth corrupt, and where thieves do not break through nor steal.

'For where your treasure is, there will your heart
90 be also.

'The light of the body is the eye; if therefore thine eye be single, thy whole body shall be full of light.

'But if thine eye be evil, thy whole body shall be full of darkness. If therefore the light that is in thee be darkness, how great is that darkness!

'No man can serve two masters, for either he will hate the one and love the other, or else he will hold to the one, and despise the other. Ye cannot serve
100 God and Mammon.

'Therefore I say unto you, take no thought for your life, what ye shall eat, or what ye shall drink; nor yet for your body, what ye shall put on. Is not the life more than meat, and the body than raiment?

'Behold the fowls of the air, for they sow not, neither do they reap, nor gather into barns; yet your heavenly Father feedeth them. Are ye not much better than they?

79–80. **when . . . face;** in other words, go about your outward business in a normal fashion.   100. **Mammon,** a Syriac word used here (and here only) as a personification of riches and material possessions.

'Which of you by taking thought can add one cubit unto his stature?

'And why take ye thought for raiment? Consider the lilies of the field, how they grow; they toil not, neither do they spin;

'And yet I say unto you, that even Solomon in all his glory was not arrayed like one of these.

'Wherefore, if God so clothe the grass of the field, which today is, and tomorrow is cast into the oven, shall he not much more clothe you, O ye of little faith?

'Therefore take no thought, saying, "What shall we eat?" or "What shall we drink?" or "Wherewithal shall we be clothed?"

'(For after all these things do the Gentiles seek;) for your heavenly Father knoweth that ye have need of all these things.

'But seek ye first the kingdom of God, and his righteousness; and all these things shall be added unto you.

'Take therefore no thought for the morrow, for the morrow shall take thought for the things of itself. Sufficient unto the day is the evil thereof.

CHAPTER VII

'Judge not, that ye be not judged.

'For with what judgment ye judge, ye shall be judged; and with what measure ye mete, it shall be measured to you again.

'And why beholdest thou the mote that is in thy brother's eye, but considerest not the beam that is in thine own eye?

'Or how wilt thou say to thy brother, "Let me pull out the mote out of thine eye"; and, behold, a beam is in thine own eye?

'Thou hypocrite, first cast out the beam out of thine own eye; and then shalt thou see clearly to cast out the mote out of thy brother's eye.

'Give not that which is holy unto the dogs, neither cast ye your pearls before swine, lest they trample them under their feet, and turn again and rend you.

'Ask, and it shall be given you; seek, and ye shall find; knock, and it shall be opened unto you.

'For every one that asketh receiveth, and he that seeketh findeth; and to him that knocketh it shall be opened.

'Or what man is there of you, whom if his son ask bread, will he give him a stone?

'Or if he ask a fish, will he give him a serpent?

'If ye then, being evil, know how to give good gifts unto your children, how much more shall your Father which is in Heaven give good things to them that ask him?

2. **cubit,** an ancient measure, from eighteen to twenty inches. 28–29. **mote . . . beam.** A mote is a minute particle or speck of dirt; a beam is theoretically a splinter. Here the two are used virtually interchangeably.

'Therefore all things whatsoever ye would that men should do to you, do ye even so unto them, for this is the law and the prophets.

'Enter ye in at the strait gate, for wide is the gate, and broad is the way that leadeth to destruction, and many there be which go in thereat,

'Because strait is the gate, and narrow is the way, which leadeth unto life, and few there be that find it.

'Beware of false prophets, which come to you in sheep's clothing, but inwardly they are ravening wolves.

'Ye shall know them by their fruits. Do men gather grapes of thorns, or figs of thistles?

'Even so every good tree bringeth forth good fruit, but a corrupt tree bringeth forth evil fruit.

'A good tree cannot bring forth evil fruit, neither can a corrupt tree bring forth good fruit.

'Every tree that bringeth not forth good fruit is hewn down, and cast into the fire.

'Wherefore by their fruits ye shall know them.

'Not every one that saith unto me, "Lord, Lord," shall enter into the kingdom of Heaven, but he that doeth the will of my Father which is in Heaven.

'Many will say to me in that day, "Lord, Lord; have we not prophesied in thy name? and in thy name have cast out devils? and in thy name done many wonderful works?"

'And then will I profess unto them, "I never knew you; depart from me, ye that work iniquity."

'Therefore whosoever heareth these sayings of mine, and doeth them, I will liken him unto a wise man, which built his house upon a rock;

'And the rain descended, and the floods came, and the winds blew, and beat upon that house; and it fell not, for it was founded upon a rock.

'And every one that heareth these sayings of mine, and doeth them not, shall be likened unto a foolish man, which built his house upon the sand.

'And the rain descended, and the floods came, and the winds blew, and beat upon that house; and it fell; and great was the fall of it.'

And it came to pass, when Jesus had ended these sayings, the people were astonished at his doctrine,

For he taught them as one having authority, and not as the scribes.

CHAPTER IX

And he entered into a ship, and passed over, and came into his own city.

And behold, they brought to him a man sick of the palsy, lying on a bed; and Jesus, seeing their faith, said unto the sick of the palsy, 'Son, be of good cheer; thy sins be forgiven thee.'

And behold, certain of the scribes said within themselves, 'This man blasphemeth.'

And Jesus knowing their thoughts said, 'Wherefore think ye evil in your hearts?

'For whether is easier: to say, "Thy sins be forgiven thee?" or to say, "Arise and walk?"

'But that ye may know that the Son of man hath power on earth to forgive sins' (then saith he to the sick of the palsy), "Arise, take up thy bed, and go unto thine house.'

And he arose, and departed to his house.

But when the multitudes saw it, they marvelled, and glorified God, which had given such power unto men.

And as Jesus passed forth from thence, he saw a man named Matthew, sitting at the receipt of custom; and he saith unto him, 'Follow me.' And he arose and followed him.

And it came to pass, as Jesus sat at meat in the house, behold, many publicans and sinners came and sat down with him and his disciples.

And when the Pharisees saw it, they said unto his disciples, 'Why eateth your Master with publicans and sinners?'

But when Jesus heard that, he said unto them, 'They that be whole need not a physician, but they that are sick.

'But go ye and learn what that meaneth, "I will have mercy, and not sacrifice; for I am not come to call the righteous, but sinners to repentance." '

Then came to him the disciples of John, saying, 'Why do we and the Pharisees fast oft, but thy disciples fast not?'

And Jesus said unto them, 'Can children of the bridechamber mourn, as long as the bridegroom is with them? But the days will come, when the bridegroom shall be taken from them, and then shall they fast.

'No man putteth a piece of new cloth unto an old garment, for that which is put in to fill it up taketh from the garment, and the rent is made worse.

'Neither do men put new wine into old bottles, else the bottles break, and the wine runneth out, and the bottles perish; but they put new wine into new bottles, and both are preserved.'

While he spake these things unto them, behold, there came a certain ruler, and worshipped him, saying, 'My daughter is even now dead; but come and lay thy hand upon her, and she shall live.'

And Jesus arose, and followed him, and so did his disciples.

And, behold, a woman, which was diseased with an issue of blood twelve years, came behind him, and touched the hem of his garment,

For she said within herself, 'If I may but touch his garment, I shall be whole.'

But Jesus turned him about, and when he saw her, he said, 'Daughter, be of good comfort; thy faith hath made thee whole.' And the woman was made whole from that hour.

And when Jesus came into the ruler's house, and saw the minstrels and the people making a noise,

He said unto them, 'Give place, for the maid is not dead, but sleepeth.' And they laughed him to scorn.

But when the people were put forth, he went in, and took her by the hand, and the maid arose.

And the fame hereof went abroad into all that land.

And when Jesus departed thence, two blind men followed him, crying, and saying, 'Thou son of David, have mercy on us.'

And when he was come into the house, the blind men came to him; and Jesus said unto them, 'Believe ye that I am able to do this?' They said unto him, 'Yea, Lord.'

Then touched he their eyes, saying, 'According to your faith be it unto you.'

And their eyes were opened, and Jesus straitly charged them, saying, 'See that no man know it.'

But they, when they were departed, spread abroad his fame in all that country.

As they went out, behold, they brought to him a dumb man possessed with a devil.

And when the devil was cast out, the dumb spake; and the multitudes marvelled, saying, 'It was never so seen in Israel.'

But the Pharisees said, 'He casteth out devils through the prince of the devils.'

And Jesus went about all the cities and villages, teaching in their synagogues, and preaching the gospel of the Kingdom, and healing every sickness and every disease among the people.

But when he saw the multitudes, he was moved with compassion on them, because they fainted, and were scattered abroad, as sheep having no shepherd.

Then saith he unto his disciples, 'The harvest truly is plenteous, but the laborers are few;

'Pray ye therefore the Lord of the harvest, that he will send forth laborers into his harvest.'

CHAPTER XII

At that time Jesus went on the sabbath day through the corn, and his disciples were a-hungred, and began to pluck the ears of corn, and to eat.

But when the Pharisees saw it, they said unto him, 'Behold, thy disciples do that which is not lawful to do upon the sabbath day.'

But he said unto them, 'Have ye not read what David did, when he was a-hungred, and they that were with him;

'How he entered into the house of God, and did eat the shewbread, which was not lawful for him to

18. publicans, tax-collectors.

109. shewbread, loaves of unleavened bread shown in the sanctuary.

eat, neither for them which were with them, but only for the priests?

'Or have ye not read in the law, how that on the sabbath days the priests in the temple profane the sabbath, and are blameless?

'But I say unto you, that in this place is one greater than the temple.

'But if ye had known what this meaneth, "I will have mercy, and not sacrifice," ye would not have condemned the guiltless.

'For the Son of man is Lord even of the sabbath day.'

And when he was departed thence, he went into their synagogues;

And behold, there was a man which had his hand withered. And they asked him, saying, 'Is it lawful to heal on the sabbath days?' that they might accuse him.

And he said unto them, 'What man shall there be among you, that shall have one sheep, and if it fall into a pit on the sabbath day, will he not lay hold on it, and lift it out?

'How much then is a man better than a sheep? Wherefore it is lawful to do well on the sabbath days.'

Then saith he to the man, 'Stretch forth thine hand.' And he stretched it forth, and it was restored whole, like as the other.

Then the Pharisees went out and held a council against him, how they might destroy him.

But when Jesus knew it, he withdrew himself from thence; and great multitudes followed him, and he healed them all;

And charged them that they should not make him known,

That it might be fulfilled which was spoken by Esaias the prophet, saying:

'Behold my servant, whom I have chosen; my beloved, in whom my soul is well pleased; I will put my spirit upon him, and he shall show judgment to the Gentiles.

'He shall not strive, nor cry; neither shall any man hear his voice in the streets.

'A bruised reed shall he not break, and smoking flax shall he not quench, till he send forth judgment unto victory.

'And in his name shall the Gentiles trust.'

Then was brought unto him one possessed with a devil, blind, and dumb; and he healed him, insomuch that the blind and dumb both spake and saw.

And all the people were amazed and said, 'Is not this the son of David?'

But when the Pharisees heard it, they said, 'This fellow doth not cast out devils, but by Beelzebub the prince of the devils.'

And Jesus knew their thoughts, and said unto them, 'Every kingdom divided against itself is brought to desolation; and every city or house divided against itself shall not stand;

'And if Satan cast out Satan, he is divided against himself; how shall then his kingdom stand?

'And if I by Beelzebub cast out devils, by whom do your children cast them out? Therefore they shall be your judges.

'But if I cast out devils by the Spirit of God, then the kingdom of God is come unto you.

'Or else how can one enter into a strong man's house, and spoil his goods, except he first bind the strong man? And then he will spoil his house.

'He that is not with me is against me; and he that gathereth not with me scattereth abroad.

'Wherefore I say unto you, all manner of sin and blasphemy shall be forgiven unto men; but the blasphemy against the Holy Ghost shall not be forgiven unto men.

'And whosoever speaketh a word against the Son of man, it shall be forgiven him; but whosoever speaketh against the Holy Ghost, it shall not be forgiven him, neither in this world, neither in the world to come.

'Either make the tree good, and his fruit good; or else make the tree corrupt, and his fruit corrupt, for the tree is known by his fruit.

'O generation of vipers, how can ye, being evil, speak good things? For out of the abundance of the heart the mouth speaketh.

'A good man out of the good treasure of his heart bringeth forth good things; and an evil man out of the evil treasure bringeth forth evil things.

'But I say unto you, that every idle word that men shall speak, they shall give account thereof in the day of judgment.

'For by thy words thou shalt be justified, and by thy words thou shalt be condemned.'

Then certain of the scribes and of the Pharisees answered, saying, 'Master, we would see a sign from thee.'

But he answered and said unto them, 'An evil and adulterous generation seeketh after a sign; and there shall no sign be given to it, but the sign of the prophet Jonas.

'For as Jonas was three days and three nights in the whale's belly, so shall the Son of man be three days and three nights in the heart of the earth.

'The men of Nineveh shall rise in judgment with this generation, and shall condemn it, because they repented at the preaching of Jonas; and behold, a greater than Jonas is here.

'The queen of the south shall rise up in the judgment with this generation, and shall condemn it, for

109. **queen of the south,** the Queen of Sheba, who visited Solomon for counsel and teaching, as told in I Kings, 10:1 ff. and II Chronicles, 9:1 ff.

she came from the uttermost parts of the earth to hear the wisdom of Solomon; and behold, a greater than Solomon is here.

'When the unclean spirit is gone out of a man, he walketh through dry places, seeking rest, and findeth none.

'Then he saith, "I will return into my house from whence I came out," and when he is come, he findeth it empty, swept, and garnished.

'Then goeth he, and taketh with himself seven other spirits more wicked than himself, and they enter in and dwell there; and the last state of that man is worse than the first. Even so shall it be also unto this wicked generation.'

While he yet talked to the people, behold, his mother and his brethren stood without, desiring to speak with him.

Then one said unto him, 'Behold, thy mother and thy brethren stand without, desiring to speak with thee.'

But he answered and said unto him that told him, 'Who is my mother? and who are my brethren?'

And he stretched forth his hand toward his disciples, and said, 'Behold my mother and my brethren?

'For whosoever shall do the will of my Father which is in Heaven, the same is my brother, and sister, and mother.'

CHAPTER XVIII

At the same time came the disciples unto Jesus, saying, 'Who is the greatest in the kingdom of Heaven?'

And Jesus called a little child unto him, and set him in the midst of them,

And said, 'Verily I say unto you, except ye be converted, and become as little children, ye shall not enter into the kingdom of Heaven.

'Whosoever therefore shall humble himself as this little child, the same is greatest in the kingdom of Heaven.

'And whoso shall receive one such little child in my name receiveth me.

'But whoso shall offend one of these little ones which believe in me, it were better for him that a millstone were hanged about his neck, and that he were drowned in the depth of the sea.

'Woe unto the world because of offences! For it must needs be that offences come; but woe to that man by whom the offence cometh!

'Wherefore, if thy hand or thy foot offend thee, cut them off, and cast them from thee; it is better for thee to enter into life halt or maimed, rather than having two hands or two feet to be cast into everlasting fire.

'And if thine eye offend thee, pluck it out, and cast it from thee; it is better for thee to enter into life with one eye, rather than having two eyes to be cast into hell-fire.

'Take heed that ye despise not one of these little ones, for I say unto you, that in Heaven their angels do always behold the face of my Father which is in Heaven.

'For the Son of man is come to save that which was lost.

'How think ye? If a man have a hundred sheep, and one of them be gone astray, doth he not leave the ninety and nine, and goeth into the mountains, and seeketh that which is gone astray?

'And if so be that he find it, verily I say unto you, he rejoiceth more of that sheep, than of the ninety and nine which went not astray.

'Even so it is not the will of your Father which is in Heaven, that one of these little ones should perish.

'Moreover, if thy brother shall trespass against thee, go and tell him his fault between thee and him alone; if he shall hear thee, thou hast gained thy brother.

'But if he will not hear thee, then take with thee one or two more, that in the mouth of two or three witnesses every word may be established.

'And if he shall neglect to hear them, tell it unto the church; but if he neglect to hear the church, let him be unto thee as a heathen man and a publican.

'Verily I say unto you, whatsoever ye shall bind on earth shall be bound in Heaven; and whatsoever ye shall loose on earth shall be loosed in Heaven.

'Again, I say unto you, that if two of you shall agree on earth touching anything that they shall ask, it shall be done for them of my Father which is in Heaven.

'For where two or three are gathered together in my name, there am I in the midst of them.'

Then came Peter to him, and said, 'Lord, how oft shall my brother sin against me, and I forgive him? Till seven times?'

Jesus saith unto him, 'I say not unto thee, until seven times; but, until seventy times seven.

'Therefore is the kingdom of Heaven likened unto a certain king, which would take account of his servants.

'And when he had begun to reckon, one was brought unto him, which owed him ten thousand talents.

'But forasmuch as he had not to pay, his lord commanded him to be sold, and his wife, and children, and all that he had, and payment to be made.

'The servant therefore fell down and worshipped him, saying, "Lord, have patience with me, and I will pay thee all."

'Then the lord of that servant was moved with compassion, and loosed him, and forgave him the debt.

'But the same servant went out, and found one of his fellow-servants which owed him an hundred pence; and he laid hands on him, and took him by the throat, saying, "Pay me that thou owest."

'And his fellow-servant fell down at his feet, and besought him, saying, "Have patience with me, and I will pay thee all."

'And he would not, but went and cast him into prison, till he should pay the debt.

'So when his fellow-servants saw what was done, they were very sorry, and came and told unto their lord all that was done.

'Then his lord, after that he had called him, said unto him, "O thou wicked servant, I forgave thee all that debt, because thou desiredst me;

'"Shouldest not thou also have had compassion on thy fellow-servant . . . ?"'

CHAPTER XXIV

And Jesus went out, and departed from the temple; and his disciples came to him for to show him the buildings of the temple.

And Jesus said unto them, 'See ye not all these things? Verily I say unto you, there shall not be left here one stone upon another, that shall not be thrown down.'

And as he sat upon the Mount of Olives, the disciples came unto him privately, saying, 'Tell us, when shall these things be? And what shall be the sign of thy coming, and of the end of the world?'

And Jesus answered and said unto them, 'Take heed that no man deceive you.

'For many shall come in my name, saying, "I am Christ"; and shall deceive you.

'And ye shall hear of wars and rumors of wars; see that ye be not troubled, for all these things must come to pass, but the end is not yet.

'For nation shall rise against nation, and kingdom against kingdom; and there shall be famines, and pestilences, and earthquakes, in divers places.

'All these are the beginning of sorrows.

'Then shall they deliver you up to be afflicted, and shall kill you; and ye shall be hated of all nations for my name's sake.

'And then shall many be offended, and shall betray one another, and shall hate one another.

'And many false prophets shall rise and shall deceive many.

'And because iniquity shall abound, the love of many shall wax cold.

'But he that shall endure to the end, the same shall be saved.

'And the gospel of the kingdom shall be preached in all the world for a witness unto all nations; and then shall the end come.

'When ye therefore shall see the abomination of desolation, spoken of by Daniel the prophet, stand in the holy place, (whoso readeth, let him understand:)

'Then let them which be in Judaea flee into the mountains;

'Let him which is on the housetop not come down to take anything out of his house;

'Neither let him which is in the field return back to take his clothes.

'And woe unto them that are with child, and to them that give suck in those days!

'But pray ye that your flight be not in the winter, neither on the sabbath day;

'For then shall be great tribulation, such as was not since the beginning of the world to this time, no, nor ever shall be.

'And except those days should be shortened, there should no flesh be saved; but for the elect's sake those days shall be shortened.

'Then if any man shall say unto you, "Lo, here is Christ, or there," believe it not.

'For there shall arise false Christs, and false prophets, and shall show great signs and wonders, insomuch that, if it were possible, they shall deceive the very elect.

'Behold, I have told you before.

'Wherefore if they shall say unto you, "Behold, he is in the desert"; go not forth; "Behold, he is in the secret chambers"; believe it not.

'For as the lightning cometh out of the east, and shineth even unto the west, so shall also the coming of the Son of man be.

'For wheresoever the carcass is, there will the eagles be gathered together.

'Immediately after the tribulation of those days shall the sun be darkened, and the moon shall not give her light, and the stars shall fall from Heaven, and the powers of the heavens shall be shaken;

'And then shall appear the sign of the Son of man in Heaven; and then shall all the tribes of the earth mourn, and they shall see the Son of man coming in the clouds of Heaven with power and great glory.

'And he shall send his angels with a great sound of a trumpet, and they shall gather together his elect from the four winds, from one end of Heaven to the other.

'Now learn a parable of the fig tree. When his branch is yet tender and putteth forth leaves, ye know that summer is nigh;

'So likewise ye, when ye shall see all these things, know that it is near, even at the doors.

'Verily I say unto you, this generation shall not pass, till all these things be fulfilled.

'Heaven and earth shall pass away, but my words shall not pass away.

'But of that day and hour knoweth no man, no, not the angels of Heaven, but my Father only.

'But as the days of Noah were, so shall also the coming of the Son of man be.

'For as in the days before the Flood they were eating and drinking, marrying and giving in marriage, until the day that Noah entered into the Ark,

'And knew not until the Flood came, and took them all away, so shall also the coming of the Son of man be.

'Then shall two be in the field; the one shall be taken, and the other left.

'Two women shall be grinding at the mill; the one shall be taken, and the other left.

'Watch therefore, for ye know not what hour your Lord doth come.

'But know this, that if the good man of the house had known in what watch the thief would come, he would have watched, and would not have suffered his house to be broken up.

'Therefore be ye also ready, for in such an hour as ye think not the Son of man cometh.

'Who then is a faithful and wise servant, whom his lord hath made ruler over his household, to give them meat in due season?

'Blessed is that servant, whom his lord, when he cometh, shall find so doing.

'Verily I say unto you, that he shall make him ruler over all his goods.

'But and if that evil servant shall say in his heart, "My lord delayeth his coming";

'And shall begin to smite his fellow-servants, and to eat and drink with the drunken;

'The lord of that servant shall come in a day when he looketh not for him, and in an hour that he is not aware of,

'And shall cut him asunder, and appoint him his portion with the hypocrites; there shall be weeping and gnashing of teeth.

CHAPTER XXV

'Then shall the kingdom of Heaven be likened unto ten virgins, which took their lamps, and went forth to meet the bridegroom.

'And five of them were wise, and five were foolish.

'They that were foolish took their lamps, and took no oil with them;

'But the wise took oil in their vessels with their lamps.

'While the bridegroom tarried, they all slumbered and slept.

'And at midnight there was a cry made, "Behold, the bridegroom cometh; go ye out to meet him."

'Then all those virgins arose, and trimmed their lamps.

'And the foolish said unto the wise, "Give us of your oil, for our lamps are gone out."

'But the wise answered, saying, "Not so, lest there be not enough for us and you; but go ye rather to them that sell, and buy for yourselves."

'And while they went to buy, the bridegroom came; and they that were ready went in with him to the marriage, and the door was shut.

'Afterward came the other virgins, saying, "Lord, Lord, open to us."

'But he answered and said, "Verily I say unto you, I know you not."

'Watch therefore, for ye know neither the day nor the hour wherein the Son of man cometh.

'For the kingdom of Heaven is as a man travelling into a far country, who called his own servants, and delivered unto them his goods.

'And unto one he gave five talents, to another two, and to another one; and to every man according to his several ability; and straightway took his journey.

'Then he that had received the five talents went and traded the same, and made them other five talents.

'And likewise he that had received two, he also gained other two.

'But he that had received one went and digged in the earth, and hid his lord's money.

'After a long time the lord of those servants cometh, and reckoneth with them.

'And so he that had received five talents came and brought other five talents, saying, "Lord, thou deliveredst unto me five talents; behold, I have gained beside them five talents more."

'His lord said unto him, "Well done, thou good and faithful servant; thou hast been faithful over a few things; I will make thee ruler over many things. Enter thou into the joy of thy lord."

'He also that had received two talents came and said, "Lord, thou deliveredst unto me two talents; behold, I have gained two other talents beside them."

'His lord said unto him, "Well done, good and faithful servant; thou hast been faithful over a few things, I will make thee ruler over many things; enter thou into the joy of thy lord."

'Then he which had received the one talent came and said, "Lord, I knew thee that thou art a hard man, reaping where thou hast not sown, and gathering where thou hast not strawed:

' "And I was afraid, and went and hid thy talent in the earth: lo, there thou hast that is thine."

'His lord answered and said unto him, "Thou wicked and slothful servant, thou knewest that I reap where I sowed not, and gather where I have not strawed;

70. **talents,** an ancient monetary weight of greatly varying value; the Hebraic talent was roughly equal to two thousand dollars.

' "Thou oughtest therefore to have put my money to the exchangers, and then at my coming I should have received mine own with usury.

' "Take therefore the talent from him, and give it unto him which hath ten talents.

' "For unto every one that hath shall be given, and he shall have abundance; but from him that hath not shall be taken away even that which he hath.

' "And cast ye the unprofitable servant into outer darkness; there shall be weeping and gnashing of teeth."

'When the Son of man shall come in his glory, and all the holy angels with him, then shall he sit upon the throne of his glory:

'And before him shall be gathered all nations; and he shall separate them one from another, as a shepherd divideth his sheep from the goats:

'And he shall set the sheep on his right hand, but the goats on the left.

'Then shall the King say unto them on his right hand, "Come, ye blessed of my Father, inherit the kingdom prepared for you from the foundation of the world;

' "For I was a hungred, and ye gave me meat; I was thirsty, and ye gave me drink; I was a stranger, and ye took me in;

' "Naked, and ye clothed me; I was sick, and ye visited me; I was in prison, and ye came unto me."

'Then shall the righteous answer him, saying, "Lord, when saw we thee a hungred, and fed thee? Or thirsty, and gave thee drink?

' "When saw we thee a stranger, and took thee in? Or naked, and clothed thee?

' "Or when saw we thee sick, or in prison, and came unto thee?"

'And the King shall answer and say unto them, "Verily I say unto you, inasmuch as ye have done it unto one of the least of these my brethren, ye have done it unto me."

'Then shall he say also unto them on the left hand, "Depart from me, ye cursed, into everlasting fire, prepared for the devil and his angels,

' "For I was a hungred, and ye gave me no meat; I was thirsty, and ye gave me no drink;

' "I was a stranger, and ye took me not in; naked, and ye clothed me not; sick, and in prison, and ye visited me not."

'Then shall they also answer him, saying, "Lord, when saw we thee a hungred, or athirst, or a stranger, or naked, or sick, or in prison, and did not minister unto thee?"

'Then shall he answer them saying, "Verily I say unto you, inasmuch as ye did it not to one of the least of these, ye did it not to me."

'And these shall go away into everlasting punishment; but the righteous into life eternal.'

CHAPTER XXVI

And it came to pass, when Jesus had finished all these sayings, he said unto his disciples:

'Ye know that after two days is the feast of the Passover, and the Son of man is betrayed to be crucified.'

Then assembled together the chief priests, and the scribes, and the elders of the people, unto the palace of the high priest, who was called Caiaphas,

And consulted that they might take Jesus by subtlety, and kill him.

But they said, 'Not on the feast-day, lest there be an uproar among the people.'

Now when Jesus was in Bethany, in the house of Simon the leper,

There came unto him a woman having an alabaster box of very precious ointment, and poured it on his head, as he sat at meat.

But when his disciples saw it, they had indignation, saying, 'To what purpose is this waste?

'For this ointment might have been sold for much, and given to the poor.'

When Jesus understood it, he said unto them, 'Why trouble ye the woman? For she hath wrought a good work upon me.

'For ye have the poor always with you; but me ye have not always.

'For in that she hath poured this ointment on my body, she did it for my burial.

'Verily I say unto you, wheresoever this gospel shall be preached in the whole world, there shall also this, that this woman hath done, be told for a memorial of her.'

Then one of the twelve, called Judas Iscariot, went unto the chief priests.

And said unto them, 'What will ye give me, and I will deliver him unto you?' And they covenanted with him for thirty pieces of silver.

And from that time he sought opportunity to betray him.

Now the first day of the feast of unleavened bread the disciples came to Jesus, saying unto him, 'Where wilt thou that we prepare for thee to eat the passover?'

And he said, 'Go into the city to such a man, and say unto him, "The Master saith, 'My time is at hand; I will keep the passover at thy house with my disciples.' " '

And the disciples did as Jesus had appointed them; and they made ready the passover.

Now when the even was come, he sat down with the twelve.

And as they did eat, he said, 'Verily I say unto you, that one of you shall betray me.'

And they were exceeding sorrowful, and began

every one of them to say unto him, 'Lord, is it I?'

And he answered and said, 'He that dippeth his hand with me in the dish, the same shall betray me.

'The Son of man goeth as it is written of him; but woe unto that man by whom the Son of man is betrayed! It had been good for that man if he had not been born.'

Then Judas, which betrayed him, answered and said, 'Master, is it I?' He said unto him, 'Thou hast said.'

And as they were eating, Jesus took bread, and blessed it, and brake it, and gave it to the disciples, and said, 'Take; eat. This is my body.'

And he took the cup, and gave thanks, and gave it to them, saying, 'Drink ye all of it;

'For this is my blood of the new testament, which is shed for many for the remission of sins.

'But I say unto you, I will not drink henceforth of this fruit of the vine, until that day when I drink it new with you in my Father's kingdom.'

And when they had sung a hymn, they went out into the Mount of Olives.

Then saith Jesus unto them, 'All ye shall be offended because of me this night; for it is written, "I will smite the shepherd, and the sheep of the flock shall be scattered abroad."

'But after I am risen again, I will go before you into Galilee.'

Peter answered and said unto him, 'Though all men shall be offended because of thee, yet will I never be offended.'

Jesus said unto him, 'Verily I say unto thee, that this night, before the cock crow, thou shalt deny me thrice.'

Peter said unto him, 'Though I should die with thee, yet will I not deny thee.' Likewise also said all the disciples.

Then cometh Jesus with them unto a place called Gethsemane, and saith unto the disciples, 'Sit ye here, while I go and pray yonder.'

And he took with him Peter and the two sons of Zebedee, and began to be sorrowful and very heavy.

Then saith he unto them, 'My soul is exceeding sorrowful, even unto death; tarry ye here, and watch with me.'

And he went a little farther, and fell on his face, and prayed, saying, 'O my Father, if it be possible, let this cup pass from me; nevertheless not as I will, but as thou wilt.'

And he cometh unto the disciples, and findeth them asleep, and saith unto Peter, 'What, could ye not watch with me one hour?

'Watch and pray, that ye enter not into temptation; the spirit indeed is willing, but the flesh is weak.'

He went away again the second time, and prayed,

saying, 'O my Father, if this cup may not pass away from me, except I drink it, thy will be done.'

And he came and found them asleep again, for their eyes were heavy.

And he left them, and went away again, and prayed the third time, saying the same words.

Then cometh he to his disciples, and saith unto them, 'Sleep on now, and take your rest; behold, the hour is at hand, and the Son of man is betrayed into the hands of sinners.

'Rise, let us be going; behold, he is at hand that doth betray me.'

And while he yet spake, lo, Judas, one of the twelve, came, and with him a great multitude with swords and staves, from the chief priests and elders of the people.

Now he that betrayed him gave them a sign, saying, 'Whomsoever I shall kiss, that same is he; hold him fast.'

And forthwith he came to Jesus, and said, 'Hail, master'; and kissed him.

And Jesus said unto him, 'Friend, wherefore art thou come?' Then came they, and laid hands on Jesus, and took him.

And behold, one of them which were with Jesus stretched out his hand, and drew his sword, and struck a servant of the high priest's, and smote off his ear.

Then said Jesus unto him, 'Put up again thy sword into his place, for all they that take the sword shall perish with the sword.

'Thinkest thou that I cannot now pray to thy Father, and he shall presently give me more than twelve legions of angels?

'But how then shall the scriptures be fulfilled, that thus it must be?'

In that same hour said Jesus to the multitudes, 'Are ye come out as against a thief, with swords and staves for to take me? I sat daily with you teaching in the temple, and ye laid no hold on me.'

But all this was done, that the scriptures of the prophets might be fulfilled. Then all the disciples forsook him, and fled.

And they that had laid hold on Jesus led him away to Caiaphas the high priest, where the scribes and the elders were assembled.

But Peter followed him afar off unto the high priest's palace, and went in, and sat with the servants, to see the end.

Now the chief priests, and elders, and all the council, sought false witness against Jesus, to put him to death;

But found none; yea, though many false witnesses came, yet found they none. At the last came two false witnesses

And said, 'This fellow said, "I am able to destroy the temple of God, and to build it in three days."'

And the high priest arose, and said unto him, 'Answerest thou nothing? What is it which these witness against thee?'

But Jesus held his peace. And the high priest answered and said unto him, 'I adjure thee by the living God, that thou tell us whether thou be the Christ, the Son of God.'

Jesus saith unto him, 'Thou hast said; nevertheless I say unto you, hereafter shall ye see the Son of man sitting on the right hand of power, and coming in the clouds of Heaven.'

Then the high priest rent his clothes, saying, 'He hath spoken blasphemy; what further need have we of witnesses? Behold, now ye have heard his blasphemy.

'What think ye?' They answered and said, 'He is guilty of death.'

Then did they spit in his face, and buffeted him; and others smote him with the palms of their hands,

Saying, 'Prophesy unto us, thou Christ. Who is he that smote thee?'

Now Peter sat without in the palace; and a damsel came unto him, saying, 'Thou also wast with Jesus of Galilee.'

But he denied before them all, saying, 'I know not what thou sayest.'

And when he was gone out into the porch, another maid saw him, and said unto them that were there, 'This fellow was also with Jesus of Nazareth.'

And again he denied with an oath, 'I do not know the man.'

And after awhile came unto him they that stood by, and said to Peter, 'Surely thou also art one of them, for thy speech bewrayeth thee.'

Then began he to curse and to swear, saying, 'I know not the man.' And immediately the cock crew.

And Peter remembered the word of Jesus, which said unto him, 'Before the cock crow, thou shalt deny me thrice.' And he went out, and wept bitterly.

CHAPTER XXVII

When the morning was come, all the chief priests and elders of the people took counsel against Jesus to put him to death:

And when they had bound him, they led him away, and delivered him to Pontius Pilate the governor.

Then Judas, which had betrayed him, when he saw that he was condemned, repented himself, and brought again the thirty pieces of silver to the chief priests and elders,

Saying, 'I have sinned in that I have betrayed the innocent blood.' And they said, 'What is that to us? See thou to that.'

And he cast down the pieces of silver in the temple, and departed, and went and hanged himself.

And the chief priests took the silver pieces, and said, 'It is not lawful for to put them into the treasury, because it is the price of blood.'

And they took counsel, and bought with them the potter's field, to bury strangers in.

Wherefore that field was called the Field of Blood, unto this day.

Then was fulfilled that which was spoken by Jeremiah the prophet, saying, 'And they took the thirty pieces of silver, the price of him that was valued, whom they of the children of Israel did value;

'And gave them for the potter's field, as the Lord appointed me.'

And Jesus stood before the governor; and the governor asked him, saying, 'Art thou the King of the Jews?' And Jesus said unto him, 'Thou sayest.'

And when he was accused of the chief priests and elders, he answered nothing.

Then said Pilate unto him, 'Hearest thou not how many things they witness against thee?'

And he answered him to never a word, insomuch that the governor marvelled greatly.

Now at that feast the governor was wont to release unto the people a prisoner, whom they would.

And they had then a notable prisoner, called Barabbas.

Therefore when they were gathered together, Pilate said unto them, 'Whom will ye that I release unto you? Barabbas, or Jesus which is called Christ?'

For he knew that for envy they had delivered him.

When he sat down on the judgment seat, his wife sent unto him, saying, 'Have thou nothing to do with that just man, for I have suffered many things this day in a dream because of him.'

But the chief priests and elders persuaded the multitude that they should ask Barabbas, and destroy Jesus.

The governor answered and said unto them, 'Whether of the twain will ye that I release unto you?' They said, 'Barabbas.'

Pilate saith unto them, 'What shall I do then with Jesus which is called Christ?' They all say unto him, 'Let him be crucified.'

And the governor said, 'Why, what evil hath he done?' But they cried out the more, saying, 'Let him be crucified.'

When Pilate saw that he could prevail nothing, but that rather a tumult was made, he took water and washed his hands before the multitude, saying, 'I am innocent of the blood of this just person; see ye to it.'

Then answered all the people and said, 'His blood be on us, and on our children.'

Then released he Barabbas unto them; and when he had scourged Jesus, he delivered him to be crucified.

Then the soldiers of the governor took Jesus into

the common hall, and gathered unto him the whole band of soldiers.

And they stripped him, and put on him a scarlet robe.

And when they had platted a crown of thorns, they put it upon the head, and a reed in his right hand; and they bowed the knee before him and mocked him, saying, 'Hail! King of the Jews!'

And they spit upon him, and took the reed, and smote him on the head.

And after they had mocked him, they took the robe off from him, and put his own raiment on him, and led him away to crucify him.

And as they came out, they found a man of Cyrene, Simon by name; him they compelled to bear his cross.

And when they were come unto a place called Golgotha, that is to say, a place of a skull,

They gave him vinegar to drink mingled with gall; and when he had tasted thereof, he would not drink.

And they crucified him and parted his garments, casting lots, that it might be fulfilled which was spoken by the prophet, 'They parted my garments among them, and upon my vesture did they cast lots.'

And sitting down they watched him there;

And set up over his head his accusation written, THIS IS JESUS THE KING OF THE JEWS.

Then were there two thieves crucified with him, one on the right hand, and another on the left.

And they that passed by reviled him, wagging their heads,

And saying, 'Thou that destroyedest the temple, and buildest it in three days, save thyself. If thou be the Son of God, come down from the cross.'

Likewise also the chief priests mocking him, with the scribes and elders, said,

'He saved others; himself he cannot save. If he be the King of Israel, let him now come down from the cross, and we will believe him.

'He trusted in God; let him deliver him now, if he will have him; for he said, "I am the Son of God." '

The thieves also, which were crucified with him, cast the same in his teeth.

Now from the sixth hour there was darkness over all the land unto the ninth hour.

And about the ninth hour Jesus cried with a loud voice, saying, 'Eli, Eli, lama sabachthani?', that is to say, 'My God, my God, why hast thou forsaken me?'

Some of them that stood there when they heard that, said, 'This man calleth for Elias.'

And straightway one of them ran, and took a sponge, and filled it with vinegar, and put it on a reed, and gave him to drink.

The rest said, 'Let be, let us see whether Elias will come to save him.'

Jesus, when he had cried again with a loud voice, yielded up the ghost.

And behold, the vail of the temple was rent in twain from the top to the bottom; and the earth did quake; and the rocks rent;

And the graves were opened; and many bodies of the saints which slept arose,

And came out of the graves after his resurrection, and went into the holy city, and appeared unto many.

Now when the centurion, and they that were with him, watching Jesus, saw the earthquake, and those things that were done, they feared greatly, saying, 'Truly this was the Son of God.'

And many women were there beholding afar off, which followed Jesus from Galilee, ministering unto him:

Among which was Mary Magdalene, and Mary the mother of James and Joses, and the mother of Zebedee's children.

When the even was come, there came a rich man of Arimathea, named Joseph, who also himself was Jesus' disciple;

He went to Pilate, and begged the body of Jesus. Then Pilate commanded the body to be delivered.

And when Joseph had taken the body, he wrapped it in a clean linen cloth,

And laid it in his own new tomb, which he had hewn out in the rock; and he rolled a great stone to the door of the sepulchre, and departed.

And there was Mary Magdalene, and the other Mary, sitting over against the sepulchre.

Now the next day, that followed the day of the preparation, the chief priests and Pharisees came together unto Pilate,

Saying, 'Sir, we remember that that deceiver said, while he was yet alive, "After three days I will rise again."

'Command therefore that the sepulchre be made sure until the third day, lest his disciples come by night, and steal him away, and say unto the people, "He is risen from the dead." So the last error shall be worse than the first.'

Pilate said unto them, 'Ye have a watch; go your way, make it as sure as ye can.'

So they went, and made the sepulchre sure, sealing the stone, and setting a watch.

CHAPTER XXVIII

In the end of the sabbath, as it began to dawn toward the first day of the week, came Mary Magdalene and the other Mary to see the sepulchre.

And behold, there was a great earthquake, for the angel of the Lord descended from Heaven, and came and rolled back the stone from the door, and sat upon it.

His countenance was like lightning, and his raiment white as snow;

And for fear of him the keepers did shake, and became as dead men.

And the angel answered and said unto the women, 'Fear not ye, for I know that ye seek Jesus, which was crucified.

'He is not here, for he is risen, as he said. Come, see the place where the Lord lay.

'And go quickly, and tell his disciples that he is risen from the dead; and behold, he goeth before you into Galilee; there shall ye see him. Lo, I have told you.'

And they departed quickly from the sepulchre with fear and great joy, and did run to bring his disciples word.

And as they went to tell the disciples, behold, Jesus met them, saying, 'All hail!' And they came and held him by the feet, and worshipped him.

Then said Jesus unto them, 'Be not afraid; go, tell my brethren that they go into Galilee, and there shall they see me.'

Now when they were going, behold, some of the watch came into the city, and showed unto the chief priests all the things that were done.

And when they were assembled with the elders, and had taken counsel, they gave large money unto the soldiers,

Saying, 'Say ye, his disciples came by night, and stole him away while we slept.

'And if this come to the governor's ears, we will persuade him, and secure you.'

So they took the money, and did as they were taught; and this saying is commonly reported among the Jews until this day.

Then the eleven disciples went away into Galilee, into a mountain where Jesus had appointed them.

And when they saw him, they worshipped him; but some doubted.

And Jesus came and spake unto them, saying, 'All power is given me in Heaven and in earth.

'Go ye therefore, and teach all nations, baptizing them in the name of the Father, and of the Son, and of the Holy Ghost,

'Teaching them to observe all things whatsoever I have commanded you. And lo, I am with you alway, even unto the end of the world. AMEN.'

An Italian mosaic of Saint Peter, c. 600.

First Epistle of Paul to the Corinthians

CHAPTER XIII

THOUGH I speak with the tongues of men and of angels, and have not charity, I am become as sounding brass, or a tinkling cymbal.

And though I have the gift of prophecy, and understand all mysteries, and all knowledge; and though I have all faith, so that I could remove mountains, and have not charity, I am nothing.

And though I bestow all my goods to feed the poor, and though I give my body to be burned, and have not charity, it profiteth me nothing.

Charity suffereth long, and is kind; charity envieth not; charity vaunteth not itself, is not puffed up,

Doth not behave itself unseemly, seeketh not her own, is not easily provoked, thinketh no evil;

Rejoiceth not in iniquity, but rejoiceth in the truth;

Beareth all things, believeth all things, hopeth all things, endureth all things.

Charity never faileth; but whether there be prophecies, they shall fail; whether there be tongues, they shall cease; whether there be knowledge, it shall vanish away.

For we know in part, and we prophesy in part,

But when that which is perfect is come, then that which is in part shall be done away.

When I was a child, I spake as a child, I understood as a child, I thought as a child; but when I became a man, I put away childish things.

For now we see through a glass, darkly; but then face to face. Now I know in part, but then shall I know even as also I am known.

And now abideth faith, hope, charity—these three; but the greatest of these is charity.

CHAPTER XV

Moreover, brethren, I declare unto you the gospel which I preached unto you, which also ye have received, and wherein ye stand;

By which also ye are saved, if ye keep in memory what I preached unto you, unless ye have believed in vain.

For I delivered unto you first of all that which I also received, how that Christ died for our sins according to the scriptures;

First Epistle of Paul to the Corinthians.[8] From the King James Version of the Bible.
69. whether, if.

And that he was buried, and that he rose again the third day according to the scriptures;

And that he was seen of Cephas, then of the twelve;

After that, he was seen of above five hundred brethren at once; of whom the greater part remain unto this present, but some are fallen asleep.

After that, he was seen of James, then of all the apostles.

10 And last of all he was seen of me also, as of one born out of due time.

For I am the least of the apostles, that am not meet to be called an apostle, because I persecuted the church of God.

But by the grace of God I am what I am, and His grace which was bestowed upon me was not in vain; but I labored more abundantly than they all. Yet not I, but the grace of God which was with me.

Therefore whether it were I or they, so we preach,
20 and so ye believed.

Now if Christ be preached that he rose from the dead, how say some among you that there is no resurrection of the dead?

But if there be no resurrection of the dead, then is Christ not risen;

And if Christ be not risen, then is our preaching vain, and your faith is also vain.

Yea, and we are found false witnesses of God, because we have testified of God that he raised up
30 Christ; whom he raised not up, if so be that the dead rise not.

For if the dead rise not, then is not Christ raised;

And if Christ be not raised, your faith is vain; ye are yet in your sins.

Then they also which are fallen asleep in Christ are perished.

If in this life only we have hope in Christ, we are of all men most miserable.

But now is Christ risen from the dead, and be-
40 come the firstfruits of them that slept.

For since by men came death, by man came also the resurrection of the dead.

For as in Adam all die, even so in Christ shall all be made alive.

But every man in his own order: Christ the first-fruits; afterward they that are Christ's at his coming.

Then cometh the end, when he shall have delivered up the kingdom to God, even the Father;
50 when he shall have put down all rule and all authority and power.

For he must reign, till he hath put all enemies under his feet.

The last enemy that shall be destroyed is death.

For he hath put all things under his feet. But when he saith all things are put under him, it is manifest that he is excepted, which did put all things under him.

And when all things shall be subdued unto him, then shall the Son also himself be subject unto him 60 that put all things under him, that God may be all in all.

Else what shall they do which are baptized for the dead, if the dead rise not at all? Why are they then baptized for the dead?

And why stand we in jeopardy every hour?

I protest by your rejoicing which I have in Christ Jesus our Lord, I die daily.

If after the manner of men I have fought with beasts at Ephesus, what advantageth it me, if the 70 dead rise not? Let us eat and drink, for tomorrow we die.

Be not deceived; evil communications corrupt good manners.

Awake to righteousness, and sin not; for some have not the knowledge of God. I speak this to your shame.

But some man will say, 'How are the dead raised up? and with what body do they come?'

Thou fool, that which thou sowest is not quick- 80 ened, except it die;

And that which thou sowest, thou sowest not that body that shall be, but bare grain, it may chance of wheat, or of some other grain;

But God giveth it a body as it hath pleased him, and to every seed his own body.

All flesh is not the same flesh; but there is one kind of flesh of men, another flesh of beasts, another of fishes, and another of birds.

There are also celestial bodies, and bodies ter- 90 restrial; but the glory of the celestial is one, and the glory of the terrestrial is another.

There is one glory of the sun, and another glory of the moon, and another glory of the stars, for one star differeth from another star in glory.

So also is the resurrection of the dead. It is sown in corruption; it is raised in incorruption;

It is sown in dishonor; it is raised in glory; it is sown in weakness; it is raised in power;

It is sown a natural body; it is raised a spiritual 100 body. There is a natural body, and there is a spiritual body.

And so it is written, 'The first man Adam was made a living soul; the last Adam was made a quickening spirit.'

Howbeit that was not first which is spiritual, but that which is natural; and afterward that which is spiritual.

---

3. **Cephas,** Simon, the son of Jonah. **10–11. And last of all . . . time.** See Acts, 9:4. Paul, known as Saul of Tarsus before his conversion, had been a violent anti-Christian. In the ninth chapter of Acts we are told of his conversion by divine intervention.

69–70. **fought . . . Ephesus,** an incident in Paul's career hinted at in II Corinthians, 1:8–9.

The first man is of the earth, earthy; the second man is the Lord from Heaven.

As is the earthy, such are they also that are earthy; and as is the heavenly, such are they also that are heavenly.

And as we have borne the image of the earthy, we shall also bear the image of the heavenly.

Now this I say, brethren, that flesh and blood cannot inherit the kingdom of God; neither doth corruption inherit incorruption.

Behold, I tell you a mystery: We shall not all sleep, but we shall all be changed,

In a moment, in the twinkling of an eye, at the last trumpet. For the trumpet shall sound, and the dead shall be raised incorruptible, and we shall be changed.

For this corruptible must put on incorruption, and this mortal must put on immortality.

So when this corruptible shall have put on incorruption, and this mortal shall have put on immortality, then shall be brought to pass the saying that is written, 'Death is swallowed up in victory.'

O death, where is thy sting? O grave, where is thy victory?

The sting of death is sin; and the strength of sin is the law.

But thanks be to God, which giveth us the victory through our Lord Jesus Christ.

Therefore, my beloved brethren, be ye steadfast, unmoveable, always abounding in the work of the Lord, for as much as ye know that your labor is not in vain in the Lord.

A 15th-century English drawing of a Canterbury bishop.

The Nicaean Creed

The Roman Emperor Constantine the Great in the year 323 defeated the Byzantine tyrant Licinius and thereby assured the Roman state a period of tranquillity. The effect of this victory, considering the sympathy felt by Constantine toward the Christians, was the collapse of opposition to Christianity in any kind of official way within the empire. As is well known, Constantine was himself baptized a few years later on his deathbed and so established the Roman empire as a Christian realm. But in spite of this long-sought victory over its external foes, the Christian Church was in the early fourth century plagued by a fundamental controversy, the first great heresy. This controversy was brought to a head by the stated opinions of Arius, a presbyter under Bishop Alexander of Alexandria, who believed in the essential unity of the Deity rather than in the orthodox Trinity. The resulting conflict was decided officially in 325 by the Council of Nicaea, held in the city of that name in Bithynia, Asia Minor, which denied the teachings of Arius, formulated an official *Credo,* and drove Arius and his followers into banishment, at the same time thrusting into the foreground as a champion of Trinitarian faith a deacon of Alexandria by the name of Athanasius.

This official *Credo,* known as the Nicaean Creed, states the premises on which the orthodox position of the Catholic Church is based.

But Arianism, obviously a forerunner of present-day Unitarianism, persisted for a long time within the Church in spite of the Council of Nicaea; although it had no recognized status, it was particularly attractive to the young and forthright Germanic nations at the time of their conversions to Christianity. It is indeed a beautiful irony of history that Constantine the Great himself should have been baptized by Eusebius of Nicomedia, a powerful Arian spokesman.

The Nicaean Creed

WE BELIEVE in one God, the Father Almighty, Maker of all things, visible and invisible; and in one Lord Jesus Christ, the Son of God, the only begotten of the Father, that is, of the substance of the Father; God of God, light of light, true God of true God; begotten, not made, consubstantial with the Father, by whom all things were made, both in Heaven and in earth; who for us men, and for our salvation, descended, was incarnate, and was made man, and suffered, and rose again the third day; he ascended into Heaven, and shall come to judge the living and the dead; And in the HOLY SPIRIT. But the holy catholic and apostolic Church of God anathematizes those who affirm that there was a time when the Son was not, or that he was not before he was begotten, or that he was made of things not existing; or who say, that the Son of God was of any other substance or essence, or created, or liable to change or conversion.

Thomas à Kempis

c. 1380–1471

Thomas Hammerken was born at Kempen, near Düsseldorf, Germany, whence his monastic name of Thomas à Kempis. A dreamy, shy kind of boy of humble peasant birth, he grew into a retiring young man of pronounced mystical inclinations and, after some education at Deventer, in the Netherlands, he entered the Augustinian Order and went to the monastery at Mount Saint Agnes, near Zwolle, Holland, where his elder brother was prior. He spent all the remaining many years of his life at Mount Saint Agnes, was chosen subprior on two occasions, and ultimately became prior. He was the author of a large number of somewhat pedestrian tracts on the monastic life, and the reputed author of the *Imitatio Christi*, or *Imitation of Christ*, which might have been more properly called "The Following of Christ."

The authorship of this, probably the most famous and influential of all medieval ascetic and monastic writings, is still, however, very much in dispute. The conclusion, in one of the most important of its manuscripts, declares that it was "finished and completed in the year of Our Lord 1441 by the hands of Brother Thomas à Kempis in Mount Saint Agnes near Zwolle." But there are no less than twenty-two manuscripts of the work which can be dated before 1441. In view of the amazing difference in power and inspiration between the *Imitation of Christ* and the other works by Thomas à Kempis, it is altogether likely that he was not the actual author, but rather the redactor or editor of a work by someone else—John

Gersen and Saint Bernard have both been suggested. Yet the *Imitation of Christ* is so characteristic of the temperament of the highly ascetic, self-effacing, and even self-abasing Thomas à Kempis, who could not stay in a room where the conversation was too sprightly, that it may be ascribed to him in spirit if not in actual fact. For no work, not even the writings of the great Scholastics of the twelfth and thirteen centuries, catches more truly the otherworldliness which was so integral a part of the medieval intellect, exhibited here to an almost psychopathological degree. It is notably unscholarly and unacademic, for that matter, but its style is austere and simple; its awareness of the contemporary world is virtually nil and it seems drenched in the flood of divinity. These very qualities, however, have made it a work of great appeal to all minds of an enthusiastically religious nature; it is not remarkable, therefore, that the *Imitation of Christ* should have been translated from its original Latin into all the languages of the Christian world, and that the work should have retained its hold now for nearly five hundred years.

The Imitation of Christ

BOOK II

Here beginneth concerning the admonitions drawing greatly inward.
Of inward conversation

OUR Lord saith that the kingdom of Heaven is within you. Turn thyself to God with all thine heart and forsake this wretched world and thy soul shall find rest.

Learn to despise outward things and to turn thee to inward things and thou shalt see the kingdom come into thee; for the kingdom of God is peace and joy in the Holy Ghost the which is not given to wicked men.

Christ shall come to thee showing thee His consolation if thou make for him within thee a worthy dwelling place; all His glory and honor is within and there is His plesaunce.

His visitation is common and oft with an inward man; with Him is His sweet talking, gracious consolation, much wonderful familiarity.

Ah, thou true soul, array thy soul for thy spouse that He may vouchsafe to come to thee and to dwell in thee; for thus He saith, 'Whoso loveth me shall keep my word and to him we shall come and in him make our dwelling place.' Wherefore give Christ place and as to all other hold them out.

When thou hast Christ, thou art rich and it sufficeth thee; He shall be thy provisor, thy true proc-

10

20

*The Imitation of Christ.*⁸ First English translation, sixteenth century, anonymous.

urator, in all things, so that thou shalt not need to trust in man. Men are soon changed and fail soon; Christ abideth for ever and standeth steadfastly unto the end.

Great trust is not to be put in a mortal and frail man though he be profitable and well beloved; nor great sorrow to be felt though sometimes he withstand thee and is contrary. They that are this day with thee, tomorrow they may be contrary; and in contrary wise they be ofttimes turned as the wind.

Put all thy trust in God; let Him be thy dread; let Him be thy love; He shall answer for thee and do well and as is best.

Thou hast here no dwelling-city and wherever thou be thou art as a stranger and a pilgrim; here gettest thou no rest, unless thou be inwardly one with Christ.

Why lookest thou about here, since this is not the place of thy resting? In heavenly things ought to be thine habitation, and all earthly things are to be considered as in a manner of passing; for all things pass, and thou also with them. Look that thou cleave not to them, lest thou be taken with them and perish.

Let thy thinking be on the high God and let thy prayer be lifted up unto Christ without intermission. If thou canst not behold high celestial things, rest in the passion of Christ and dwell gladly in His holy wounds; for if thou flee devoutly to the wounds and the precious prints of Christ, thou shalt find great comfort in tribulation, nor thou shalt not greatly care for men's despisings, and thou shalt lightly bear backbiting words; for Christ was despised of men in this world, and in His greatest need suffered reproofs, forsaken of His friends and of his known men.

Christ would suffer and be despised; and thou wilt have all men friends and benefactors?

Christ had adversaries, and suffered shrewd speakers; and thou darest complain on any body?

How shall thy patience be crowned if there come no adversity? If thou wilt suffer no contrary, how shalt thou be the friend of Christ? Suffer for Christ and with Christ if thou wilt reign with Christ.

If thou hadst once perfectly entered into the innerness of Jesus and hast savored a little of his burning love, thou wouldst have set naught by thine own profit or harm but rather thou wouldst rejoice of reproof done to thee; for the love of Jesus maketh a man to set naught of himself.

A lover of Jesus and a very inward man and free from inordinate affections may freely turn himself to God and lift himself above himself in spirit and there rest joyously.

The man to whom all things taste as they be, not as they are said or thought to be, he is very wise and taught more by God than by men.

He that can go within and praise things without but little, he seeketh no place, nor abideth for no times to have devout exercises. The inward man soon gathereth himself together, for he never poureth himself out wholly over outward things. Outward labor hindereth him not nor needful occupation of the day, but so as things come, so he giveth himself to them.

He that is well disposed and ordained within, he careth not for the wicked and wonderful conduct and bearing of men.

Just so much is a man hindered and distracted as things are drawn to him.

If it were well with thee and thou wert well purged, all should turn for thee to good and profit.

Many things as yet trouble thee and displease thee, for thou art not yet dead to thyself nor parted from all earthly things; nothing so defouleth and entangleth men's hearts as impure love in created things.

If thou forsake outward comfort, thou shalt be able to behold heavenly things and ofttimes have jubilation within.

Of meek submission

Set not much by this—who is against thee or with thee, but so do and care that God be with thee.

In every thing that thou dost, have a good conscience, and God shall defend thee; for him that God will help no man's overthwartness shall be able to annoy.

If thou canst be still and suffer, thou shalt see without any doubt the help of our Lord; he knoweth the time and manner of helping thee, and therefore thou oughtest to reserve thyself for him.

To God it belongeth to help and to deliver from all confusion.

Ofttimes it availeth to the keeping of greater meekness that other men should know our faults and reprove them.

When a man humbleth himself for his faults, then he appeaseth others lightly and easily maketh satisfaction to them that were displeased.

The meek man God defendeth and delivereth; the meek man He loveth and comforteth; to the meek man He bareth Himself; to the meek man He granteth great grace, and after his humbling He lifteth him in glory; to the meek man He showeth His secrets and draweth him and calleth him sweetly.

The meek man receiving reproofs or wrong or confusion is in peace well enough, for he standeth in God and not in the world.

Account thyself never to have profited till thou feel thee lower than all others.

Of a good peaceable man

Set thyself first in peace, and then shalt thou be able to set others at peace.

A peaceable man availeth more than a great learned man.

A passionate man turneth good into evil and soon believeth evil; a good peaceable man draweth all things to good.

He that is well in peace hath suspicion against no man; he that cannot be content, but is moved, he is shaken with many suspicions; neither can he be in rest nor suffer others to be in rest. Ofttimes he saith that he should not say and leaveth that which were more expedient to do; he considereth what other men ought to do and taketh no heed to his own charge.

Have therefore first zeal to better thyself and then mayst thou have zeal to thy neighbor.

Thou canst well excuse and color thine own deeds, but other men's excuses thou wilt not receive. It were more righteous first to accuse thyself and to excuse thy brother.

If thou wilt be borne, bear thou another.

See how far thou art yet from true charity and meekness the which cannot be wroth, nor have indignation with no man, but only with itself.

It is not a great thing for a man to be conversant with good men and mild men, for that pleaseth all men naturally, and every man gladly hath peace with them that feel as he doth; and such he loveth.

But for a man to live peaceably with hard and overthwart men indisciplined and contrarious is a great grace and a commendable and a manly deed.

There are some that keep themselves at peace and have peace with others also; and there be some also that neither have peace themselves nor suffer others to have peace; to others they be grievous, but most grievous to themselves. And there be that keep their peace in themselves and study to reduce other men to peace.

Nevertheless all our peace in this wretched life is rather to be set in meek suffering than in not feeling what goes contrary.

He that can well suffer shall find most peace; he is an overcomer of himself, lord of the world, the friend of Christ and the heir of Heaven.

Of pure and simple intention

A man is lifted up from earthly things with two wings—they are simplicity and purity; simplicity ought to be in intention; purity in affection. Simplicity intendeth God; purity taketh Him and tasteth Him.

There shall no good deed hinder thee if thou be free within from inordinate affection.

If thou intend not nor seek nothing else but the pleasing of God and the profit of thy neighbor, thou shalt have inward liberty. If thine heart were right, then every creature should be to thee a mirror of life and a book of holy doctrine. There is no creature so little nor so vile but it represents the goodness of God.

If thou wert inward, good and pure, then shouldest thou see all things without impediment and understand them.

A pure heart pierceth Heaven and Hell.

Such as every man is inwardly, so he judgeth outwardly.

If there be any joy in this world, the man of pure heart hath it; and if there be in any place tribulation and anguish, an idle conscience knoweth it best.

Like as iron put in the fire loseth his rust and shall be made bright, so a man turning him wholly to God is freed and taken from sloth and changed into a new man.

When a man beginneth to wax lukewarm, then he dreadeth a little labor and receiveth gladly outward consolation; but when he beginneth perfectly to overcome himself and to go manly in the way of God, then he setteth little by those things that before seemed to him right grievous.

Of consideration of oneself

We ought not to believe ourselves overmuch, for ofttimes grace is lacking in us, and understanding. Little light is in us, and ofttimes we lose that by negligence. And also ofttimes we perceive not how blind we are within.

Ofttimes we do evil, and worse—we excuse it.

Ofttimes we be moved to anger and think that it is zeal.

We reprove small things in others and pass over our own faults that are greater.

We feel and weigh soon enough what we suffer from others; but how much others suffer from us, of this we take no heed.

He that would ponder well and truly his own faults, he should find naught to judge in others grievously. An inward man before all other things taketh care of himself; and he that diligently taketh heed of himself holdeth his peace of others. Thou shalt never be an inward and devout man unless thou keep silence of other men and specially behold thyself. If thou take heed only to God and to thyself, what thou perceivest outside thee shall little move thee.

Where art thou when thou art not present to thyself? And when thou hast run over all things, taking no heed of thyself, what hast thou profited?

If thou wilt have peace and very unity, thou must set all aside and only have thyself before thine eyes; and then thou shalt profit much if thou keep holiday and rest from every temporal care.

Thou shalt greatly fail if thou set great store by any temporal thing. Let nothing be great or high or acceptable to thee but purely God. All things deem as vain comfort that come from any creature—the soul that loveth God, let her despise all things but God alone.

God alone, everlasting and great, without any measure, fulfilling all things; he is the solace of man's soul and true gladness of heart.

Of the gladness of a good conscience

The joy of a good man is the witness of a good conscience; have a good conscience and thou shalt ever have gladness.

A good conscience may bear right many, very many, things and is right glad among adversities; an evil conscience is ever dreadful and out of quiet.

Thou shalt rest sweetly if thine heart reprehend thee not.

Be not glad but when thou hast done well.

Evil men have never true gladness nor never feel inward peace; for, as our Lord saith, there is no peace to wicked men; and if they say, 'we are in peace, there shall none evils come upon us,' believe them not, for the wrath of God shall arise suddenly, and their deeds shall be brought to naught, and their thoughts shall perish.

For a man to rejoice in tribulation is not grievous to him who loves; for so to joy is to joy in the Cross of Christ.

Short is the glory that is given and taken by men; and sorrow followeth ever the glory of the world.

The glory of good men is in their conscience and not in the mouths of men.

The gladness of righteous men is of God and in God; and their joy is of truth.

He that desireth everlasting and true glory setteth no care on that which is temporal; and he that seeketh not temporal glory but despiseth it from his heart, he must needs love heavenly glory. He hath great tranquility of heart that setteth nothing by praisings or blamings.

He whose conscience is clean, he will soon be content and pleased. Thou art not the holier though thou be praised, nor the more vile though thou be blamed or dispraised.

What thou art, that thou art, that God knoweth thee to be and thou canst be said to be no greater.

If thou take heed what thou art within, thou shalt not reck what men say of thee; man looketh on the visage and God on the heart; man considereth the deeds and God praiseth the thoughts.

For a man ever to do well and to think little of himself is token of a meek soul.

For a man not to wish to be comforted by any creature is a token of great purity and of inward trust.

He that seeketh no outward witness for himself, it appeareth openly that he hath committed himself all wholly to God; for, as the apostle saith, he that commendeth himself is not approved, but only he whom God commendeth.

The state of the inner man is to walk with God and to be held by no outward affection.

Of the love of Jesus above all things

Blissful is he that understandeth what it is to love Jesus and to despise himself for Jesus.

It behooveth thee to forsake all things for the loved one, for Jesus would be loved alone above all things: the love of a creature is failing and unstable; the love of Jesus is true and persevering.

He that cleaveth to a creature shall fall with the sliding creature; he that embraceth Jesus shall be made steadfast forever.

Love him and hold him fast as a friend which, when all goeth away, shall not forsake thee nor shall not suffer thee to perish at the end.

From all things thou must be departed some time, whether thou wilt or not. Hold thee with Jesus living and dying and commit thee to His trust, who, all other failing, alone may help thee.

Thy beloved is of such nature that He will admit no stranger, but He alone will have thy heart and there sit as a king on His own throne.

If thou couldest well free thee from every creature, Jesus would gladly dwell with thee.

Thou shalt find almost all lost, whatever trust thou settest in creatures; trust not nor lean not upon a windy reed, for every flesh is grass and all his glory shall fall as the flower of grass.

Thou shalt soon be deceived if thou look only to the outer appearance of men. If thou seek thy solace and thy lucre in others, thou shalt ofttimes find hindrances to thee.

If thou seek Jesus in all things, thou shalt find Jesus; and if thou seek thyself, thou shalt find thyself but—to thine own harm.

A man hurteth himself more, if he seeketh not Jesus, than all the world and all his adversaries can hurt him.

Of the familiar friendship of Jesus

When Jesus is nigh, all goodness is nigh, and nothing seemeth hard; but when Jesus is not nigh, all things are hard.

When Jesus speaketh not within, the comfort is of little price; but if Jesus speak one word, there is found great comfort.

Did not Mary Magdalene rise out of her place wherein she wept, anon as Martha said, 'Our master is nigh and calleth thee'?

Blissful is that man whom, when Jesus cometh, he calleth from tears to the joy of the spirit.

How dry and how hard thou art without Jesus; how unsavory, how vain, if thou covet anything without Jesus; whether is it not more harm than if thou lost all the world?

What may the world avail without Jesus? to be

without Jesus is a grievous Hell, and to be with Jesus is a sweet Paradise.

If Jesus be with thee, there may no enemy hurt thee.

He that findeth Jesus findeth a good treasure; yea, good above all good; and he that loseth Jesus he loseth over much and more than if he lost all the world.

10 It is a great craft for a man to be conversant with Jesus, and to know how to hold Jesus is a great prudence.

Be meek and peaceable, and Jesus shall be with thee; be devout and restful, and Jesus shall abide with thee; thou mayest soon chase out Jesus and lose his grace if thou wilt decline to outer things; and if thou chase out Jesus and lose him, to whom shalt thou flee? and what friend shalt thou seek? Without a friend thou canst not well live, and save Jesus be thy friend before all other, thou shalt be 20 over sorry and over desolate; wherefore thou dost foolishly if thou trust or art glad in any other.

It is more to be chosen for a man to have all the world contrary to him than to have Jesus offended.

Among all therefore that are dear to thee, let Jesus be solely thy darling and thy special friend.

Let all men be loved for Jesus and Jesus for himself.

Only Jesus Christ is singly to be loved, who only is found good and true before all other friends; for 30 Him and in Him let both friends and enemies be dear to thee; and for all them He is to be prayed that they may know Him and love Him.

Desire never to be singularly praised or loved, for that belongeth to God alone, that hath none like Him.

Nor desire not that any man be occupied in his mind about love of thee, nor be not thou occupied about no other love: be pure and free within, without impediment or encumbrance of any creature.

Thou must be bare and bear to God a pure heart 40 if thou wilt taste and see how sweet God is; and verily thereto shalt thou never come unless thou be prevented and nourished with His grace, that all things being voided and left, thou alone be united with Him.

For when the grace of God cometh to a man, then is he mighty to all things; and when it goeth away, then shall he be poor and unmighty and as a man left only to scourgings and beatings and pains.

In these things be not thrown down, nor despair 50 not, but stand simply at the will of God, and suffer all things that come to thee praising our Lord Jesus Christ; for after winter cometh summer, and after even cometh day, and after tempest cometh clearness.

Of lacking of all manner of solace

It is not grievous for a man to set no price as man's solace when God is nigh; but it is great, and right great, for a man to lack both God's solace and man's and for the honor of God gladly to suffer exile of heart and in nothing to seek himself and trust not to his own merit. 60

What great thing is it, when grace comes, that thou be glad and devout? For that hour is desirable to all men: he rideth easily and merrily whom the grace of God beareth.

And what wonder that he feel no burden, who is borne of the Almighty and led of the sovereign leader?

Gladly we take somewhat by way of solace, and hard it is for a man to be drawn out of himself.

Saint Laurence overcame the world with his 70 priest, for he despised all things delectable in the world and for the love of God suffered benignly the high priest Sextus, whom he most loved, to be taken away from him.

The love therefore of the Creator overcame the love of man, and he chose the well-willing of God before man's solace.

So learn thou to forsake for the love of God some dear friend that is necessary to thee, nor bear it heavily when thou art forsaken of thy friend, know- 80 ing that at last we must all depart from each other.

It behooveth a man long time and mightily to strive with himself before a man shall be able perfectly to overcome himself and draw all his affection unto God.

When a man standeth upon himself, he slideth lightly to man's consolations, but the very true lover of Christ and studious follower of virtue slideth not to consolations nor seeketh such sensible sweetness, but rather would suffer for Christ mighty trials and 90 hard labors.

Wherefore, when spiritual consolation is given of God, receive it with great thanks and understand it to be the gift of God and not thy merit.

Be not proud nor rejoice not too much nor presume not vainly; but be the more meek for the gift and the more aware and the more anxious in all thy deeds; for that hour shall pass and temptation shall follow.

And when the consolation is taken away, despair 100 not anon, but with meekness and patience abide the heavenly visitation; for God is mighty enough to give thee greater consolation.

This is no new nor strange thing to them that are expert in the way of God; for ofttimes in great saints and holy prophets hath been this manner of alterna-

70–74. **Saint Laurence . . . him.** The martyred Saint Laurence, a native of Huesca, Spain, went to Rome at an early age and was chosen archdeacon by Pope Sextus II, who intrusted to him the treasures of the Church. Later, in the reign of the Emperor Valerian, Sextus was persecuted, imprisoned, and sentenced to death (258 A.D.), whereupon Laurence addressed to him the words: "Whither goest thou, O my father! without thy son and servant."

tion. Wherefore one, grace being present, said, 'I said in mine abundance I shall never be moved.' And, when grace was absent, he rehearsed what he felt, saying, 'Thou hast turned away, and I was troubled.' Nevertheless among these things he despaired not, but prayed more heartily, saying, 'Lord, to thee shall I cry, and I shall pray to my God.' And then he reported the fruit of his prayer, confessing himself to be heard of God, saying, 'Our Lord hath heard and hath pity on me and is made my helper.' But wherein? 'Thou hast,' he said, 'turned my sorrow into joy, and clothed me with gladness.'

If it were done then with great saints, we, feeble and poor, ought not to despair, if some time we be in fervor and some time in coldness; for the holy spirit goeth and cometh after the well pleasing of His will. Wherefore Job saith, 'Thou visitest Him betimes or in the twilight, and suddenly thou provest Him.'

Upon what, therefore, shall I hope, or in whom shall I trust but in the great mercy of God and only in hope of heavenly grace?

Whether good men be nigh thee or devout brethren or true friends or holy books or fair treatises or sweet songs and melodious hymns; all these help but little, savor but little.

When I am forsaken of grace and left in my poverty, then is there no better remedy than patience and denying of myself in the will of God.

I have found no man so religious or devout that feeleth not some time withdrawing of grace or diminution of fervor. There was never saint so highly ravished or illumined but that later or earlier he was tempted; for he is not high in the contemplation of God who is not tried for God in some tribulation; and tribulation going before is wont to be a token of consolation following. For to them that are proved in temptations is promised heavenly comfort.

'He that overcometh,' saith our Lord, 'I shall give him to eat of the tree of life.' Heavenly comfort is given that a man should be stronger to sustain adversities; temptation also followeth lest man be proud of the gift; the devil sleepeth never and the flesh is not dead.

Wherefore, cease not to array thee to battle, for both on the right hand and on the left are enemies that never cease.

Of thanks for the Grace of God

Why seekest thou rest, since thou are born to labor? Put thee to patience more than to consolations, and to bear the cross more than to gladness.

What secular man is there that would not gladly have spiritual consolations and gladness if he might have it for ever? For spiritual consolations pass all the delights of the world and all fleshly pleasures.

For all the delights of the world, either they are vain or foul, but spiritual delights are jocund and honest, engendered of gentle virtues and infused into pure minds by God.

But no man may use these divine consolations at his own will, for the time of temptation ceaseth not for long.

False liberty and trust in self are much contrary to heavenly visitation.

God doth well in giving grace of consolation, but man doth evil, not giving all to God with thanks; and the gifts of God cannot flow in on us, for we be ungrateful to the giver, and we refund not again all to the original will.

Grace is ever due to him that thinketh worthily, and that shall be taken away from the proud man which is wont to be given to meek men.

I wish not that consolation which shall take away from me compunction, nor do I desire that contemplation which shall bring me into elation, for not every high thing is holy, nor every sweet thing good, nor every desire pure, nor every dear thing acceptable to God.

I receive gladly that grace whereby I am found the more meek, the more anxious, and the more ready to forsake myself.

He that is taught with the gift of grace and learned with the beatings of its withdrawal dare ascribe nothing to himself but rather will acknowledge himself poor and naked.

Give to God that is His, and ascribe to thyself that is thine; give God thanks for His grace and to thyself guilt and pain known to be due to thee for thy guilt.

Put thee ever at the lowest, and the highest shall be given to thee, for the highest cannot stand without the lowest.

The highest saints before God are lowest before themselves, and the more glorious that they be, the more meek they are in themselves.

They that are full of truth and heavenly glory are not desirous of vain glory.

They that are grounded and confirmed in God are not proud;

And they that ascribe all to God whatever good they receive, they seek not glory each of the other but they wish the glory that is only of God; and they desire God to be praised in Himself and in His saints above all things, and to that evermore they tend.

Be thankful, therefore, for a little thing, and thou shalt be worthy to take a greater; let also the least thing be to thee as the greatest, and the least of price as a special gift.

If the dignity of the giver be considered, there shall no gift appear little that is given of the high God; yea, if He give pains and beatings, it ought to be taken gladly, for all is done for our help, whatever he suffereth to come to us.

He that desireth to keep the grace of God, let him be thankful for the grace given and patient when it is taken away; let him pray that it come again, and be aware and meek that he lose it not.

Of the fewness of the lovers of the cross of Christ

Jesus hath many lovers of the kingdom of Heaven but few bearers of the cross; he hath many who desire consolations and few desiring tribulations; he 10 findeth many fellows of the table and few of abstinence.

All desire to joy with Him; but few will suffer any pain for Him.

Many follow Jesus unto the breaking of the bread, but few unto the drinking of the cup of the passion.

Many worship His miracles, but few follow the reproof of the Cross.

Many love Jesus when no adversity happeneth.

Many praise Him and bless Him while they take 20 any consolations from Him; but if Jesus hide Himself and forsake them a little, they fall into a complaining or into over great dejection.

But they that love Jesus for Jesus, and not for any consolations, they bless Him in every tribulation and anguish of heart as in the highest consolation; and if He would never give them consolation, yet would they ever praise Him and ever thank Him.

O how mighty is the pure love of Jesus when it is mingled with no love of self nor profit of self!

30 Whether all they that always seek consolations are not to be called mercenaries and hired men?

Whether are they not proved lovers of themselves and not of Christ who think of their own lucre and profit? where is found one that will serve God freely?

Seldom shall there be any man found so spiritual that will be naked from all worldly things. And who shall find a man very poor in spirit and bare from every creature? his price is from the uttermost 40 coasts.

If a man give all his substance, it is as naught; and if he do great penance, yet it is but little; and if he apprehend all manner of science, yet is he far; and if he have great virtue and right fervent devotion, yet him lacketh much; but one thing is sovereignly necessary to him. What is that? that, all things forsaken, he forsake himself and go wholly out of himself and retain nothing of self-love.

When he hath done all things that he knoweth 50 how to do, let him feel himself to have done naught.

Let him not weigh as great all that may be esteemed great; but let him in truth pronounce himself

39–40. his price . . . coasts, that is, as a gem that is brought from afar (Author's note). 43. science, knowledge.

an unprofitable servant, as the truth saith, 'when ye have done all things that are commanded to you, say that we are unprofitable servants.' For such a one may say with the prophet that 'I am sole and poor' when he beginneth verily to be bare and poor in spirit.

Nevertheless no man is richer, no man is mightier, no man more free than he that can forsake himself 60 and all things and put himself at the lowest.

Of the King's Highway of the cross

This word, 'deny thyself and take thy cross and follow me,' seemeth a hard word to many men; but much harder it shall be to hear this word, 'Go from me, ye cursed people, into the fire everlasting.'

They that gladly hear and follow the word of the cross shall not dread the word of everlasting damnation.

This sign of the cross shall be in Heaven when our Lord shall come to judgment. 70

Then all the servants of the cross that have conformed them to Christ in their life shall come nigh unto Christ the judge with great trust.

Why dreadest thou therefore to take the cross whereby men go to the kingdom?

In the cross is health, in the cross is life, in the cross is protection from enemies, in the cross is infusion of heavenly sweetness, in the cross is strength of mind, in the cross is joy of spirit, in the cross is the sum of virtue, in the cross is perfection 80 of holiness; there is no health of soul nor hope of everlasting life, but in the cross. Take thy cross therefore and follow Jesus, and thou shalt go into life everlasting.

He that bare His own cross is gone before and died for thee on the cross, that thou shouldest bear thy cross and desire to die on the cross; and if thou be fellow in pain, thou shalt be fellow in glory.

Lo, in the cross standeth all things, and in dying lieth all; and there is none other way to life and to 90 very inward peace but the way of the holy cross and of daily mortifying, for if thou be dead with Him, thou shalt also live with Him.

Walk therefore where thou wilt; seek wherever it pleaseth thee, and thou shalt find no higher way above nor surer way beneath than the way of the cross.

Dispose and ordain all things after thy will and thy seeming, and thou shalt not find it anything but a duty to suffer somewhat either willingly or against 100 thy will, and thou shalt ever find the cross.

Thou shalt either suffer sorrow in thy body or tribulation of spirit in the soul.

Sometimes thou shalt be forsaken of God and sometimes thou shalt be stirred by thy neighbor and, what is more, sometimes thou shalt be grievous to thyself.

And yet it shall not lie in thy power to be eased or delivered with no remedy and with no solace; but, while God will, thou must needs suffer and bear.

God willeth that thou shalt learn to suffer tribulation without comfort, for thou shouldest subdue all things to Him and be the meeker for tribulation.

No man so heartily feeleth the passion of Christ as he that suffereth like things.

The cross therefore is ever ready, and over all things it abideth for thee; thou canst not flee it, wherever thou run; and wherever thou come, thou bearest thyself with thee, and ever thou shalt find thyself.

Turn thyself above, turn thyself below, turn thyself outward, turn thyself inward; and in all these thou shalt find the cross; and everywhere it is needful for thee to keep patience, if thou wilt have inward peace and deserve a crown everlasting.

If thou bear the cross gladly, it shall bear thee, and lead thee to a desirable end, where an end shall be of suffering—though it be not here.

If thou bear it against thy will, thou makest for thyself a heavy burden and grievest thyself more; and yet must thou needs sustain it.

If thou put away one cross, doubtless thou shalt find another and peradventure a more grievous one.

Thinkest thou to escape what never mortal man might escape? What saint in this world was without cross and tribulation? Not our Lord Jesus Christ was without sorrow of passion one hour in all his life. The evangelist saith, 'It behooved Christ to suffer and to rise from death and so to enter into his glory.' And how seekest thou another way than the king's highway, the cross way? All Christ's life was a cross and a martyrdom; and thou seekest to thyself rest and joy?

Thou errest, thou goest out of the way if thou seek other thing to thee than tribulation, for all this mortal life is full of miseries and marked all about with crosses; and the higher that a man profiteth in spirit, the higher crosses ofttimes he findeth; for the pain of his exile groweth more through love.

Nevertheless this man, thus pained, is not without some manner of comfort, for he feeleth great fruit to grow to him through the sufferance of his cross; for while he gladly subdueth him thereto, all burden of tribulation is turned into trust of divine consolation; and the more that the flesh is thrown down by affliction, the more the spirit is strengthened by inward grace.

And ofttimes he is so greatly comforted and strengthened that for desire of tribulation and adversity, for love of conformity to the cross of Christ, he would not be without sorrow and tribulation; for the more acceptable he accounteth himself to God, the more and the greater are the pains that he must suffer for God.

This is not man's might, but the grace of Christ, that man doeth so great things in his frail flesh, that through fervor of spirit he can take upon him and love that thing which the flesh ever naturally fleeth and abhorreth.

It is not like man to bear the cross, to love the cross, to chastise the body, to bring it to thralldom, to flee honor, gladly to sustain reproofs and wrongs, to despise himself and to will to be despised, to suffer all manner of adversities with harms and to desire no manner of prosperity in this world.

If thou look to thyself, thou canst do no such thing of thyself; but, if thou trust in our Lord, strength shall be given to thee from Heaven, and the world and the flesh shall be made subject to thy commandment; nor shalt thou dread thine enemy the devil, if thou be armed with faith and marked with the cross.

Put thee therefore forward as a good and true servant of Christ, to bear manly the cross of thy Lord crucified for thee through love. Make thee ready to suffer many contrary things and diverse incommodities in this wretched life; for so he shall be with thee wherever thou be, and so thou shalt find him wherever thou be hid.

It must be so; for there is no remedy of escaping from tribulation of evil men and sorrow—except that thou suffer.

Drink the chalice of our Lord lovingly, if thou desire to be His friend and to have part with Him. Consolations commit thou to God; let Him do therewith as it pleaseth Him.

Put thou thyself forward to suffer tribulations and account them as greatest consolations, for there are no passions of this time worthy to deserve the glory that is to come; yea, though thou mightest suffer all alone.

When thou comest to this, that tribulation is sweet to thee and is savory to thee for Christ, then deem it well with thee, for thou hast found Paradise on earth.

As long as it is grievous to thee to suffer, and thou seekest to flee it, so long shall it be evil with thee, and fleeing after thee, tribulation shall follow thee everywhere.

If thou puttest thee forward, as thou oughtest to do, to suffer and to die, it shall soon be better and thou shalt find peace.

Yea, if thou be ravished into the third heaven with Paul, thou art not yet sure to suffer no contrary

108–109. **Yea, if thou . . . Paul.** There was a tradition that Paul, on the occasion of his martyrdom, was translated immediately into the third Heaven. This is, according to medieval astronomy, the sphere of Venus, or Love. The legend probably grew out of the conception of Paul as the apostle of divine love.

thing: for Jesus said, 'I shall show him how great things he must suffer for my name.'

To suffer, therefore, remaineth to thee if thou wilt love and ever please Him.

Would God that thou wert worthy to suffer any thing for the name of Jesus; how great glory should be to thee, how great exultation to all the saints of Heaven, how great edification of thy neighbor; for all men commend patience, though few will suffer it.

10 Thou shouldest gladly suffer for Christ, since men suffer much more grievous things for the world.

Know for certain that thou must lead a dying life, and the more that a man dieth to himself, the more he beginneth to live to God; there is no man fit to take heavenly things unless he submit himself to bear adversities for Christ.

There is nothing more acceptable to God, nothing more wholesome to thee in this world than gladly to suffer for Christ; and if it lay in thy choice, thou 20 shouldest rather desire to suffer contrary things for Christ than to be refreshed with many consolations, for thou wouldest be more like unto Christ and be more conformed to all saints.

For our merit and the profiting of our estate standeth not in sweetness and consolations, but rather in suffering of grievous things and tribulations; for if there had been any thing more better or more profitable to man than to suffer, Christ would verily have shown it by word and example. But He 30 exhorted all His disciples and all them that desired to follow Him openly to bear the cross, saying, 'Who that will come after me, let him deny himself, and take his cross, and follow me.'

All things therefore being read over and searched, be this the final conclusion, that by many tribulations it behooveth us to enter into the kingdom of Heaven.

Saint Francis of Assisi

c. 1182–1226

Of all the great saints of the Christian Church in the Middle Ages, Saint Francis of Assisi could most properly be called popular. He was the son of a rather well-to-do independent merchant of Assisi, a small town near Perugia, Italy. We have no record of any particular amount of formal education given him, yet he became a great spiritual leader of the people, a man of remarkable personal appeal, which more than seven centuries have not been able to dim. To him all living things, man or beast, were the sacred vessels of God's spirit; yet it is altogether inadequate to think of him as only a gentle, unworldly, devoted soul who preached to the birds and flowers. For it happens that,

although born with mundane comforts at hand, he chose to espouse poverty while still hardly more than an adolescent; and his supreme achievement in life was the founding of the great Order of Franciscan Friars—an order which typifies the very spirit incarnate of the mendicant friars of the later Middle Ages—servants of the Lord and the souls of the people, whose lives were completely dedicated to the triplex vow of poverty, chastity, and obedience.

Saint Francis established this Order, it is believed, in either 1208 or 1209. There were only some half-dozen original members of the group, but the number increased slowly and steadily as the marvelous reputation of the eloquent ascetic of Assisi became known throughout the Christian world. The original center of the Order was a small church near Assisi, known as the Church of Santa Maria degli Angeli, or as the Porziuncula, or simply as The Place. The plan of religious life envisaged by Francis was simple and austere in the extreme, as can be seen from the following:

"Provide neither gold nor silver nor brass in your purses, nor scrip for your journey, neither two coats, nor yet staves . . . Sell all that thou hast, and give to the poor; then thou shalt have treasure in Heaven . . . Fear not because you are small and seem foolish. Have confidence in the Lord who has vanquished the world. Some will receive you. Many proud ones will resist you. Bear all with sweetness and patience. Soon the wise and the noble will be with us. The Lord hath given me to see this . . . Go and preach by two and two. Preach peace and patience; tend the sick and wounded; relieve the distressed; reclaim the erring; bless them which persecute you, and pray for them that despitefully use you."

The strong scriptural influence on Saint Francis is obvious without further comment, for many of the phrases in these instructions are identical with those in the Holy Gospels.

The great initial victory of Saint Francis was the securing of the sanction of the Pope, for the incumbent at that time was none other than the formidable Innocent III, perhaps the most arrogant and absolute in power of any of the medieval popes. Thenceforth the Franciscan Order (often called in English literature the Gray Friars) moved about all over Christendom. In addition, Francis founded an Order of Sisters, known as the Clarisses, or Poor Claras, named after Saint Clara, a woman of Assisi, whom Francis had persuaded to adopt a life of poverty and ascetic devotion and who remained his steadfast friend, even his confidante, throughout her life. Unusual indeed was the third Order of Tertiaries or Brethren of Penitence, which Saint Francis established in 1221. This comprised lay men and women who desired austerity in life but who wished to retain their secular social position and employment. In founding this third Order, Saint Francis demonstrated a shrewdness and an insight into human nature which are quite sufficient by themselves to indicate his effectiveness as a religious leader.

But there are other qualities which show equally well the power of Saint Francis as a spiritual influence.

Saint Francis and a companion, from a painting by Giotto (1276–1337) in the Louvre.

One was his boundless energy; he traveled extensively and was in words and deeds an indefatigable missionary. Tradition has it that he converted the "Sultan of Babylon," although this seems to be apocryphal; but there is no gainsaying the useful work of Saint Francis among Moslems, Hebrews, Levantines, and Byzantines abroad, as well as among sinners at home. Furthermore, his Christian charity was of the most convincing sincerity, as was his essential humanity. The complete antithesis of Chaucer's Friar, he worked willingly among lepers and madmen, among the poor and barren, even preferring them as subjects of his labors to the wealthy and powerful. It is scarcely surprising, then, that he attained something of the preëminence of an epic hero among Christian workers; so many legends gathered about him that it is now virtually impossible, in dealing with the career of Saint Francis, to disentangle fact and fiction.

It has been forgotten also that Saint Francis was a religious poet of great sincerity though of limited poetic accomplishments—an honorable forerunner, however, in the field of religious verse, of the Italian lyricists of the thirteenth century; a well-defined foothill to the towering mountain range of Dante. However, there are many who insist that Saint Francis' poetry is at its best dependent entirely upon his personality and his works of good report.

The *Fioretti di San Francesco*, or *Little Flowers of Saint Francis*, tells the whole story of the saint as it appeared in the popular Italian imagination of the early fourteenth century, about a hundred years after his death. Its authorship is unknown, although Ugolino Brunforte, a member of the Order who died in 1348, is sometimes named in tradition. Actually it is a *Volksbuch*,

or folkbook, of tales about Saint Francis, which remains the most attractive and moving of all medieval biographical writings. The legendary nature of all works relating to the life of Saint Francis is illustrated by the tradition adhering to his death. Saint Francis died in 1226; according to report, his corpse exhibited the same wounds, or marks of wounds, as those suffered by Christ on the Cross. These, the celebrated Stigmata of Saint Francis, were explained by some as marks of wounds self-inflicted during the lifetime of Saint Francis; such an explanation would be entirely credible in the case of one who followed so closely the life of Christ. According to others, of course, they were miraculous indications of the oneness with Christ. In any case, they combined with the saintliness of Saint Francis' character and works to bring about his early canonization (1228). And it is altogether appropriate that such a legend should have arisen, for no man in the long history of Christianity has served better as a living exemplar of the teachings of Christ and His ideals.

The Little Flowers of Saint Francis

CHAPTER X

How Friar Masseo, as if in raillery, said to St. Francis that all the world followed after him; and he replied that that was to the confusion of the world and the grace of God

ONCE while St. Francis dwelt in the place of Porziuncula with Friar Masseo of Marignano, a man of great sanctity, discretion, and grace in speaking of God (wherefore St. Francis loved him much), it came to pass that, one day, when St. Francis was returning from the wood and from prayer, and was already come to the place of egress from the wood, the said Friar Masseo desired to prove how great was his humility and drew nigh unto him and, as if in raillery, said: "Why after thee? why after thee? why after thee?" St. Francis answered: "What is this that thou wouldst say?" Said Friar Masseo: "I say, why doth all the world follow after thee, and why doth every man seem to desire to see thee and to hear thee and to obey thee? Thou art not a man beautiful of body, thou art not greatly learned, thou art not noble; wherefore then should all the world follow after thee?" Hearing this St. Francis rejoiced greatly in spirit, and raising his face to Heaven, stood for a long time with his mind uplifted in God, and thereafter, returning to himself, kneeled down and gave praise and thanks to

The Little Flowers of Saint Francis. Translated by W. Heywood. Reprinted by permission of Methuen and Co., Ltd., Publishers.

God, and then with great fervor of spirit turned to Friar Masseo and said: "Wouldst know why after me? wouldst know why after me? why all the world follows after me? This have I from those eyes of the most high God, which in every place behold the good and the wicked; because these most holy eyes have not seen among sinners any more vile, or more insufficient, or a greater sinner than I am; and since to do that marvelous work which He meaneth to do, He hath not found a viler creature upon earth, therefore hath He chosen me to confound the nobility and the pride and the strength and the beauty and wisdom of the world, to the end that it may know that every virtue and every good thing is of Him and not of the creature, and that no one may be able to glory in His sight; but whosoever shall glory, let him glory in the Lord, to whom is all honor and glory for ever." Then Friar Masseo, at so lowly an answer, spoken with so much fervor, was afraid and knew of a surety that St. Francis was established in humility.

CHAPTER XI

How St. Francis made Friar Masseo turn round and round many times, and thereafter gat him to Siena

One day, while St. Francis journeyed with Friar Masseo, the said Friar Masseo went a little before; and arriving at a certain place where three roads meet which led to Florence, to Siena, and to Arezzo, Friar Masseo said: "Father, by which way must we go?" St. Francis made answer: "By that which God shall will." Said Friar Masseo: "And how shall we be able to know the will of God?" St. Francis answered: "By the sign which I shall show thee. Wherefore I command thee by the duty of holy obedience, that in this place where three roads meet, on the spot where now thy feet are set, thou turn round and round, as children do, and stop not from turning thyself unless I bid thee to do so." Then Friar Masseo began to turn himself round, and so much did he turn that, by reason of the dizziness of the head which is wont to be generated by such turning, he fell divers times to the ground; but, in that St. Francis did not bid him stop, he, desiring to obey faithfully, gat him up again and resumed the said turning. At the last, while he was turning round manfully, St. Francis said: "Stand still, and move not," and he stood; and St. Francis asked him: "Toward which part is thy face set?" Friar Masseo answered: "Toward Siena." St. Francis said: "That is the way whereby God wills that we go." Now, as they went by that way, Friar Masseo marvelled that St. Francis had made him do even as children do, before the worldly folk who were passing by; nevertheless, for the sake of reverence, he

ventured not to say anything to the holy father. As they drew nigh unto Siena, the people of the city heard of the coming of the saint, and went forth to meet him; and for devotion they bare him and his companion even unto the bishop's house, so that they touched no ground with their feet. In that hour certain men of Siena fought together, and already two of them were slain; but when St. Francis arrived there, he preached to them so devoutly and holily that he brought them all to peace and to great unity and concord. For the which thing the Bishop of Siena, hearing of that holy work which St. Francis had done, invited him to his house and lodged him with great honor that day and also that night. And, on the morning of the following day, St. Francis, who, with true humility, in all his actions sought only God's glory, rose up early with his companion and got him thence without the knowledge of the bishop. For which cause the said Friar Masseo went by the way murmuring within himself, and saying: "What is it that this good man hath done? He made me turn round like a child, and to the bishop who hath shown him so much honor he hath spoken never a word nor thanked him;" and it seemed to Friar Masseo that therein St. Francis had borne himself indiscreetly. But afterward, returning to his right mind by Divine inspiration, and reproaching himself in his heart, he said: "Friar Masseo, too proud art thou who judgest Divine works, and thou art worthy of Hell for thy indiscreet pride; for yesterday Friar Francis wrought such holy deeds that if an angel of God had done them they could not have been more marvelous; wherefore, if he should bid thee throw stones, thou oughtest so to do and to obey him; and that which he did upon the way proceeded from Divine inspiration, as is shown by the good result which followed thereupon; in that if he had not made peace between them who fought together, not only would the sword have devoured the bodies of many, even as it had already begun to do, but also the devil would have carried away many souls to Hell; and therefore art thou very foolish and proud who murmurest against that which manifestly proceedeth from the will of God." And all these things which Friar Masseo said in his heart, as he went before, were revealed of God to St. Francis. Wherefore St. Francis drew nigh unto him and spake thus: "Hold fast to those things which now thou thinkest, in that they are good and useful and inspired of God; but the first murmuring which thou madest was blind and vain and proud, and was put in thy mind by the demon." Then Friar Masseo perceived clearly that St. Francis knew the secrets of his heart, and he understood certainly that the spirit of Divine wisdom guided the holy father in all his actions.

CHAPTER XII

How St. Francis laid upon Friar Masseo the service of the gate, of almsgiving, and of the kitchen; and thereafter, at the prayer of the other friars, relieved him of them

St. Francis, desiring to humble Friar Masseo, to the end that he might not become puffed up by reason of the many gifts and graces which God was giving him, but by virtue of humility might increase thereby from virtue to virtue; once when he was dwelling in a solitary place with those true saints, his first companions, among whom was the said Friar Masseo, he spake on a day to Friar Masseo before all his companions, saying: "O Friar Masseo,
10 all these thy companions have the grace of preaching the Word of God to the satisfying of the people; and therefore, to the end that these thy companions may be able to give themselves to contemplation, I will that thou perform the office of the gate and of almsgiving and of the kitchen; and when the other friars shall eat, thou shalt eat without the gate of the Place, so that thou mayest satisfy those who come to the Place with some good words of God or ever they have knocked; thus it will not be
20 necessary for any other to go forth save thee alone; and this do thou for the merit of holy obedience." Thereupon, Friar Masseo drew back his cowl and bowed his head and humbly received this obedience and persevered therein for many days, performing the office of the gate, of almsgiving, and of the kitchen. Wherefore his companions, as men illuminated of God, began to feel great remorse in their hearts, considering that Friar Masseo was a man of great perfection even as they or more so, and upon
30 him was laid all the burthen of the Place and not on them. For which cause they were all moved with one desire and went to beseech the holy father that he would be pleased to distribute among them those offices; inasmuch as their consciences might in no wise bear that Friar Masseo should endure so great labor. Hearing this, St. Francis inclined his ear unto their counsels and consented unto their wish. Calling Friar Masseo, he spake to him after this manner: "Friar Masseo, thy companions desire to share the
40 offices which I have given thee; and therefore I will that they be divided among them." Said Friar Masseo, with great humility and patience: "Father, that which thou layest upon me, whether in whole or in part, I esteem it altogether done of God." Then St. Francis, beholding the charity of those others and the humility of Friar Masseo, preached unto them a marvelous sermon touching most holy humility; teaching them that the greater the gifts and graces which God bestows upon us, the greater
50 should our humility be, because without humility no virtue is acceptable to God. And when he had finished preaching, he distributed the offices with very great love.

CHAPTER XIII

How St. Francis and Friar Masseo placed the bread which they had begged upon a stone hard by a fountain, and St. Francis praised Poverty much. Thereafter, he prayed God and St. Peter and St. Paul, that He would cause him to be enamored of holy Poverty; and how St. Peter and St. Paul appeared to him

The marvelous servant and follower of Christ, Messer St. Francis, to the end that in everything he might conform himself to Christ, who, according to the Gospel, sent His disciples by two and two to all those cities and places whither He Himself was about to go; inasmuch as after the example of Christ
60 he had gathered together twelve companions, sent them through the world to preach by two and two. And, to set them an ensample of true obedience, he himself was the first to go, after the ensample of Christ, who began to do before He began to teach. Wherefore, having assigned to his companions the other regions of the world, he, taking Friar Masseo as his companion, journeyed toward the province of France. And coming one day to a village and being very hungry, they went, according to the Rule,
70 begging bread for the love of God; and St. Francis went through one street and Friar Masseo through another. But because St. Francis was a man too despicable and small of body, and was esteemed a vile mendicant therefor by those who knew him not, he got only some mouthfuls and fragments of dry bread; whereas to Friar Masseo, because he was tall and beautiful of body, were given good pieces and large and in plenty and fresh cut from the loaf. And so when they had finished begging, they met to-
80 gether to eat outside the village in a place where there was a beautiful fountain with a fair large stone beside it, whereupon each of them laid all the bread which he had begged; and when St. Francis saw that Friar Masseo's pieces of bread were more plentiful and better and larger than his, he showed very great joy thereat, and spake after this manner: "O Friar Masseo, we are not worthy of so great treasure;" and when he had repeated these words many times, Friar Masseo replied: "Father, how is
90 it possible to speak of treasure where there is such great poverty and lack of all things needful? Here is neither tablecloth, nor knife, nor trencher, nor porringer, nor house, nor table, nor man-servant, nor maid-servant." Said St. Francis: "And this is

58–59. He himself . . . to go. Here, as elsewhere, it is to be noted how closely St. Francis follows the precepts of Christ.

that which I esteem great treasure, where there is nothing prepared by human industry; but that which there is, is prepared by the Divine Providence, as may be manifestly seen in the bread which we have begged, in this beautiful table of rock and in this clear spring. Wherefore I will that we pray God that He make us to love with our whole heart the so noble treasure of holy Poverty, which hath God to servitor." And when he had said these words and had prayed and partaken for bodily sustenance of these fragments of bread and of that water, they rose up to journey into France; and coming to a church, St. Francis got him behind the altar and betook himself to prayer; and in that prayer he received by Divine visitation such exceeding fervor, the which kindled his soul so mightily to love of holy Poverty, that by the heat of his face and by the unwonted gaping of his mouth it seemed that he breathed forth flames of love. And coming thus enkindled to his companion, he spake to him on this wise: "Ah! Ah! Ah! Friar Masseo, give me thyself"; and so spake he three times; and the third time St. Francis raised Friar Masseo into the air with his breath, and cast him before him a great spear's length. Thereat was Friar Masseo filled with very great wonder; and thereafter, he related to his companions that when St. Francis thus lifted him up and cast him from him with his breath, he experienced such great sweetness of spirit and consolation of the Holy Ghost, that never in his life had he felt the like. And when this was done, St. Francis said: "Companion mine, let us go to St. Peter and St. Paul and pray them that they will teach us and aid us to possess the immeasurable treasure of most holy Poverty; for she is a treasure so surpassing and so Divine that we are not worthy to possess it in our most vile vessels; for this is that celestial virtue whereby all earthly things and transitory are trodden under foot, and every barrier is removed which might hinder the soul from freely uniting itself to the eternal God. This is that virtue which enableth the soul, while yet on earth, to hold converse in Heaven with the angels; this is she, who bare Christ company upon the Cross, with Christ was buried, with Christ was raised again, and with Christ ascended into Heaven; who even in this life grants to the souls which are enamored of her nimbleness to fly to Heaven, seeing that it is she who guards the weapons of true humility and charity. Therefore, pray we the most holy Apostles of Christ, who were perfect lovers of this evangelic pearl, that they may beg this grace for us from our Lord Jesus Christ that, of His most holy pity, He may grant us to be worthy to be true lovers, observers, and humble disciples of most precious, most beloved and evangelic Poverty." And thus discoursing, they came to Rome and entered into the Church of St. Peter; and St. Francis betook

himself to prayer in one corner of the church and Friar Masseo in another; and they abode long time in prayer with great devotion and many tears, until, at the last, the most holy Apostles Peter and Paul appeared to St. Francis in great splendor, and said: "Because thou askest and desirest to observe that which Christ and His Apostles observed, the Lord Jesus Christ sends us to thee to make known unto thee that thy prayer is heard, and that the treasure of most holy Poverty is granted unto thee of God in fullest perfection, to thee and to thy followers. And further we tell thee in His name that whosoever, after thy example, shall perfectly follow this desire, he is assured of the beatitude of life eternal; and thou and all thy followers shall be blessed of God." And when they had thus spoken, they vanished away, leaving St. Francis full of consolation. Thereafter, he rose up from prayer and returned to his companion and asked him if God had revealed aught unto him; and he answered, "No." Then St. Francis told him how the holy Apostles had appeared to him and what they had revealed unto him. Wherefore each of them was fulfilled with joy; and they determined to return to the Val di Spoleto and to leave their journeying into France.

CHAPTER XIV

How while St. Francis and his friars spake of God, He appeared in the midst of them

In the beginning of the Religion, what time St. Francis and his companions were gathered together to speak of Christ, he, in fervor of spirit, commanded one of them that, in the name of God, he should open his mouth and speak of God that which the Holy Ghost inspired him. Now, while the friar was fulfilling that commandment and was discoursing marvelously of God, St. Francis imposed silence upon him and bade another friar speak in like manner. He, yielding obedience and discoursing subtly of God, St. Francis, in like manner, imposed silence upon him, and commanded a third to speak of God, who, in his turn, began to speak so profoundly of the secret things of God that, of a verity, St. Francis knew that he, like the other two, spake through inspiration of the Holy Ghost; and this also was shown by example and by a clear sign: in that, while they were thus speaking, Christ the blessed appeared in the midst of them in the likeness and form of a youth, exceeding beautiful, and, blessing them, fulfilled them all with so much grace and sweetness, that they were all rapt away out of themselves and lay like dead men, wholly insensible to the things of this world. And thereafter, when they had come to themselves, St. Francis said unto them: "My dearest brethren, let us thank God, who hath

83. **Religion,** the way of life prescribed in the Order of the Franciscans.

willed to reveal the treasures of Divine wisdom through the mouths of the simple; for it is God who openeth the mouth of the dumb and maketh the tongues of the simple to talk very wisely."

CHAPTER XV

How St. Clare ate with St. Francis and with the friars, his companions, in Santa Maria degli Angeli

St. Francis, when he abode at Assisi, ofttimes visited St. Clare and gave her holy admonishments; and she having very great longings to eat once with him, and thereto beseeching him many times, he was never willing to give her this consolation; wherefore his companions perceiving the desire of St. Clare, said to St. Francis: "Father, to us it seems that this severity is not in accordance with Divine charity, in that thou hearkenest not to Sister Clare, a virgin so holy and so beloved of God, in so small a matter as is this of eating with thee; and the more so considering that she through thy preaching abandoned the riches and pomps of the world; and, of a surety, if she asked of thee a greater boon than this is, thou oughtest to grant it to thy spiritual offspring." Then St. Francis made answer: "Doth it seem to you that I ought to grant her prayer?" The companions replied: "Yea, father; it is a fitting thing that thou grant her this grace and consolation." Then St. Francis said: "Since it seemeth so to you, it seemeth so also to me. But to the end that she may have the greater consolation, I desire that this meal be eaten in St. Mary of the Angels, because she hath been long shut up in St. Damian, and thus will she have joy in beholding the Place of St. Mary, where she was shorn and made the bride of Jesus Christ; and there will we eat together in the name of God." Accordingly, the day thereunto appointed being come, St. Clare went forth from the convent with one companion, and, accompanied by the companions of St. Francis, came to St. Mary of the Angels, and after she had devoutly saluted the Virgin Mary before her altar, where she had been shorn and veiled, they took her to see the Place until the dinner hour was come. And, in the meantime, St. Francis caused the table to be set upon the bare ground, as he was wont to do. And when the dinner hour was come, St. Francis and St. Clare sat down together, and one of the companions of St. Francis with the companion of St. Clare; and thereafter all the other companions sat them humbly down at the table. And, at the first dish, St. Francis began to speak of God so sweetly, so highly and so marvelously, that abundance of Divine grace descended upon them and they were all rapt in God. And while they were thus rapt, with eyes and hands raised to Heaven, the men of Assisi and of Bettona, and they of the district round about, saw that St. Mary of the Angels, and all the Place, and the wood which was

hard by the Place, were burning fiercely; and it seemed to them that there was a great fire which encompassed the church and the monastery and the wood together; for the which cause the men of Assisi ran down thither with great haste to quench the fire, believing that verily everything was burning. But when they reached the Place, they saw that there was no fire at all, and they went in and found St. Francis and St. Clare and all their company rapt in God through contemplation, and sitting about that lowly board. Whereby they understood of a surety that that had been Divine fire and not material, the which God had made to appear miraculously to show forth and signify the fire of Divine love wherewith were enkindled the souls of those holy friars and holy nuns; wherefore they departed thence with great consolation of heart and holy edification. Then, after a long while, St. Francis and St. Clare, together with the others, returned to themselves and being greatly comforted with spiritual food they gave but little thought to bodily food; and so, that blessed meal being ended, St. Clare, well accompanied, returned to St. Damian; whereof, when they beheld her, the nuns had great joy, in that they feared lest St. Francis should have sent her to rule some other convent, even as he had aforetime sent Sister Agnes, her holy sister, to be abbess of Montecelli in Florence; and St. Francis had once said to St. Clare: "Hold thyself in readiness, that, if need be, I may send thee to some other Place;" whereto she as a daughter of holy obedience had made answer: "Father, I am ready to go whithersoever you shall send me;" and therefore the nuns rejoiced greatly when they received her back again; and from thenceforward St. Clare abode in much consolation.

CHAPTER XVI

How St. Francis received the counsel of St. Clare, and of the holy Friar Sylvester, that he ought by preaching to convert much folk; and how St. Francis founded the Third Order and preached to the birds and made the swallows keep silence

Shortly after his conversion, the humble servant of Christ, St. Francis, having already gathered many companions and received them into the Order, stood in great anxiety and in great doubt as to that which he ought to do; whether to devote himself wholly to prayer or sometimes also to preaching; and touching that matter he desired greatly to know the will of God; and because the holy humility which was in him suffered him not to trust to himself nor to his own prayers, he bethought him to inquire of the Divine will through the prayers of others; wherefore he called Friar Masseo and said: "Go thou to Sister Clare and tell her in my name that, together with certain of the most spiritual of her companions, she should devoutly pray God that He may vouchsafe to show me whether it be better that I give myself to preaching or to prayer alone. And thereafter go to Friar Sylvester and tell him to do the like." Now, in the world, this had been that Messer Sylvester who had seen a cross of gold proceeding out of the mouth of St. Francis, the which was high even unto Heaven and wide even unto the ends of the earth; and this Friar Sylvester was of so great devotion and of so great sanctity that by prayer he prevailed with God and all that he asked was granted him, and ofttimes he talked with God; and therefore St. Francis had great devotion toward him. Friar Masseo departed and, according to the bidding of St. Francis, did his embassage first to St. Clare and thereafter to Friar Sylvester; who, as soon as he had received it, forthwith got himself to prayer, and while he was yet praying he obtained the Divine answer, and turned him to Friar Masseo and said: "Thus doth God bid thee say to Friar Francis: that God hath not called him to this estate for himself alone, but that he may have much fruit of souls, and that many through him may be saved." And when he had heard this, Friar Masseo returned to St. Clare, to know what answer she had received from God; and she replied that she and the other companions had had the selfsame answer from God which Friar Sylvester had had. Therewith Friar Masseo returned to St. Francis; and St. Francis welcomed him with very great charity, washing his feet and setting food before him. And when he had eaten, St. Francis called Masseo into the wood; and there he kneeled down before him, and drew back his cowl, and making a cross of his arms, asked him, "What doth my Lord Jesus Christ bid me do?" Friar Masseo made answer: "To Friar Sylvester as to Sister Clare and to her companion, Christ hath made answer and revealed that His will is that thou go through the world to preach, because He hath not chosen thee for thyself alone but also for the salvation of others." Then St. Francis, when he had had this answer and knew thereby the will of Jesus Christ, rose up with exceeding great fervor and said: "Let us go, in the name of God;" and he took as his companion Friar Masseo and Friar Agnolo, holy men. And going with impetuosity of spirit, taking thought neither of way nor path, they came to a walled place which is called Savurniano; and St. Francis began to preach; but first he bade the swallows which were twittering to keep silence until such time as he should finish preaching; and the swallows obeyed him; and there he preached with so great fervor that for devotion all the men and women of that town were minded to follow him and to abandon the town; but St. Francis suffered them not, saying: "Be not over hasty to depart; and I will ordain that which it behooves you to do for the sal-

vation of your souls;" and then he bethought him to institute the Third Order for the universal salvation of all men; and so, leaving them greatly comforted and with minds turned to repentance, he got him thence and came betwixt Cannaio and Bevagno. And passing on, full of fervor, he lifted up his eyes and saw certain trees hard by the road, whereupon was an almost infinite number of birds; whereat St. Francis marveled, and said to his companions: "Ye shall await me here on the road, and I will go and preach to the birds my sisters;" and he went into the field and began to preach to the birds which were upon the ground; and anon those which were in the trees came to him, and all of them stood still together until St. Francis finished preaching; and even then they departed not until he gave them his blessing; and according to that which Friar Masseo afterward related to Friar James of Massa, when St. Francis went about among them, touching them with his mantle, none of them moved therefor. Now the preaching of St. Francis was on this wise: "My sisters the birds, much are ye beholden unto God your creator, and always and in every place ought ye to praise Him, because He hath given you liberty to fly whithersoever ye will, and hath clothed you on with twofold and threefold raiment. Moreover, He preserved your seed in the Ark of Noah, that your race might not be destroyed. Again, ye are beholden unto Him for the element of the air which He hath appointed for you; furthermore, ye sow not, neither do ye reap; yet God feedeth you and giveth you rivers and fountains wherefrom to drink; He giveth you mountains and valleys for your refuge, and high trees wherein to build your nests; and, in that ye know not how to sew nor spin, God clothed you and your little ones; wherefore doth your Creator love you, seeing that He giveth you so many benefits. Guard yourselves, therefore, my sisters the birds, from the sin of ingratitude and be ye ever mindful to give praise to God." And, as St. Francis spake these words unto them, all those birds began to open their beaks, and to stretch out their necks, and to open their wings, and reverently to bow their heads even unto the ground, and to show by their motions and by their songs that the holy father gave them very great delight; and St. Francis rejoiced with them and was glad and marveled much at so great a multitude of birds, and at the most beautiful diversity of them, and at their attention and fearlessness; for which cause he devoutly praised the Creator in them. Finally, when he had made an end of preaching, St. Francis made over them the sign of the Cross and gave them leave to depart; whereupon all those birds rose into the air with wondrous songs;

59. **Third Order.** See headnote to St. Francis. 62. **Cannaio and Bevagno,** two villages in Perugia near Assisi.

and thereafter, according to the form of the Cross which St. Francis had made over them, they divided themselves into four bands; and one band flew towards the East, and one towards the West, and one towards the South and the fourth towards the North, and each company went singing marvelous songs; signifying thereby that, even as St. Francis, the Standard-bearer of the Cross, had preached to them, and made over them the Sign of the Cross, according whereunto they separated themselves toward the four quarters of the world, so the preaching of the Cross of Christ, renewed by St. Francis, was about to be carried through all the world by him and by his friars; the which friars, like unto the birds, possess nothing of their own in this world but commit their lives wholly to the providence of God.

CHAPTER XVII

How a boy friar, while St. Francis was praying by night, saw Christ and the Virgin Mary and very many other saints hold converse with him

While St. Francis yet lived, a boy very pure and innocent was received into the Order; and he abode in a little Place; wherein the friars, of necessity, slept on rugs. Once St. Francis came to the said Place, and, in the evening, when compline had been said, betook himself to sleep to the end that he might be able to rise up at night and pray, while the other friars slept, as he was wont to do. Now the said boy settled it in his heart to observe carefully the ways of St. Francis, if so be he might know his sanctity and especially that which he did at night when he rose up. Wherefore, that sleep might not betray him, that boy laid down to sleep close to St. Francis and tied his cord to the cord of St. Francis, that he might perceive when he rose up. And of this St. Francis felt nothing. But during the night, in the first watch, while all the other friars slept, he rose up and found his cord thus tied, and he loosed it gently that the boy might not perceive it, and so St. Francis got him alone to the wood which was hard by the Place, and entered into a little cell which was there and betook himself to prayer; and, after a certain time, the boy awoke and finding the cord untied and St. Francis gone away, he rose up and went to seek him; and finding the gate which led into the wood open, he bethought him that St. Francis might have gone thither, and he entered into the wood. And coming nigh unto the place where St. Francis was praying, he began to hear a sound as of many folk talking, and drawing nearer to see and to understand that which he heard, he beheld a wonderful light which encompassed St. Francis round about, and in the midst thereof he saw Christ and the Virgin Mary and St. John the Baptist and the Evangelist and a very great multitude of angels who spake with St. Francis. When he saw and heard this, the boy fell to the ground in a swoon. Thereafter, the mystery of that holy vision being ended, St. Francis, as he returned to the Place, stumbled upon the said boy, lying as if dead; and for compassion he lifted him up and carried him in his arms, even as the good shepherd carrieth his lambs. And then, learning from him how he had beheld the said vision, he commanded him to tell no man as long as he lived. Afterward the boy, increasing in great grace with God and in devotion to St. Francis, became a worthy man in the Order; and after the death of St. Francis, he revealed the said vision to the friars.

CHAPTER XVIII

Of the marvelous chapter which St. Francis held at Santa Maria degli Angeli, where there were more than five thousand friars

Once the faithful servant of Christ, Francis, held a general chapter at Santa Maria degli Angeli, to which chapter were gathered more than five thousand friars; and thither came St. Dominic, head and founder of the Order of Preaching Friars, the which at that time was journeying from Burgundy to Rome. And hearing of the congregation of the chapter which St. Francis was holding in the plain of Santa Maria degli Angeli, he betook himself thither to see the same, with seven friars of his Order. There was then at the said chapter a cardinal who was greatly devoted to St. Francis, who had prophesied to him that he would be Pope, and so thereafter it befell; the which cardinal had come specially from Perugia, where was the court, to Assisi; every day he came to see St. Francis and his friars, and sometimes he sang mass and sometimes he preached to the friars in chapter; and the said cardinal took very great delight and was filled with devotion when he came to visit that holy college. And seeing the friars seated round about Santa Maria, company by company, here forty, there a hundred, and there eighty together, all employed in speaking of God, in prayers, in tears, and in exercises of charity, behaving themselves with so great silence and with such sobriety that no clamor was heard there, nor any disturbance, he marveled to behold so great discipline in so vast a multitude, and, with tears and great devotion, said: "Verily this is the camp of the army of the knights of God!" In all the great multitude no one was heard to tell stories or to jest; but, wherever a company of

21. **compline,** the last service of prayer during the day, held after vespers.

51. **the Evangelist,** the Apostle John. 69–70. **St. Dominic . . . Friars.** Dominic of Calahorra (1170–1221), a Spanish cleric, was the founder of the Order of Dominican Friars (Blackfriars). Their aims were the same as those of the Franciscans but their appeal was more intellectual and less emotional.

friars was gathered together, they either prayed, or said the office, or bewailed their own sins or those of their benefactors, or reasoned of the salvation of souls. In that encampment were booths made of withes and of rushes, separate for each company, according to the diverse provinces of the friars; and therefore that chapter was called the Chapter of the Withes or of the Rushes. Their beds were the bare ground, and some had a little straw; their bolsters were of stone or wood. For which cause, whoever heard or saw them had so great devotion toward them, and such was the fame of their sanctity that, from the court of the Pope, which was then in Perugia, and from other places in the Val di Spoleto, there came many counts, barons, knights and other gentlemen, and many common folk, and cardinals, and bishops and abbots, with many other clerks, to see that so holy and great and humble congregation of so many holy men, the like whereof the world had never; and chiefly they came to see the head and most holy father of that holy folk, who had robbed the world of so fair a prey, and gathered so goodly and devout a flock to follow in the footsteps of the true Shepherd Jesus Christ. All this general chapter, then, being gathered together, the holy father of all and minister-general, St. Francis, in fervor of spirit, expounded the word of God and preached unto them in a loud voice that which the Holy Spirit made him say; and he set forth the argument of his sermon in these words: "My sons, great things have we promised unto God; but greater are the promises of God to us-ward, if we observe these promises which we have made unto Him; and we await with confidence those things which are promised unto us. Short is the pleasure of the world; the pain which follows it is eternal; small is the pain of this life, but the glory of the other life is infinite." And most devoutly preaching upon these words, be comforted and urged the friars to obedience and reverence of Holy Mother Church, and to fraternal love, and to pray God for all men, to have patience in the adversities of the world and temperance in its prosperities, and to hold fast purity and angelic chastity, and to be at peace and concord with God, and with men, and with their own consciences, and to love and observe most holy Poverty. And touching the same he said: "I command you, for the merit of holy obedience, all of you who are here met together, that not one of you take any thought or care of anything to eat or to drink, or of things necessary for the body, but give yourselves wholly to prayer and to praising God; and all the care of your bodies leave ye to Him, for of you He hath peculiar care." And all of them received this commandment with joyful hearts and happy faces; and when St. Francis had finished his sermon, they all with one accord betook themselves to prayer. Wherefore, St. Domi-

nic, who was present while all these things were done, marveled greatly at the commandment of St. Francis, and deemed him indiscreet, being unable to think how so great a multitude could be provided for, without taking any thought of the things necessary for the body. But the Chief Shepherd, Christ the Blessed, willing to show that He careth for His sheep and hath singular love for His poor, presently inspired the inhabitants of Perugia, of Spoleto, of Foligno, of Spello and of Assisi, and of the other places round about, to bring food and drink to that holy congregation. And lo! immediately, from the aforesaid towns came men with pack-animals, horses and carts laden with bread and wine and beans and cheese and other good things to eat, according to that which was necessary for the poor of Christ. Besides this, they brought tablecloths, pitchers, bowls, glasses, and other vessels which were needful for so great a multitude; and blessed was he esteemed who could bring the most, or who could serve most diligently; so that even knights, barons, and other gentlemen, who came to see, waited upon them at table with great humility and devotion. For the which cause, St. Dominic, beholding these things and knowing of a surety that Divine Providence showed forth itself therein, humbly acknowledged that he had wrongly judged St. Francis to have given an indiscreet commandment, and going before him, he kneeled down and humbly confessed his fault, and said: "Verily God hath special care of these holy mendicants, and I knew it not; and from henceforward I promise to observe the holy gospel poverty; and in the name of God do I curse all the friars of my Order who in the said Order shall presume to have private property." Thus was St. Dominic greatly edified by the faith of the most holy Francis, and by the obedience and poverty of so great and ordered an assembly, and by the Divine Providence and by the great abundance of every good thing. In that same chapter, St. Francis was told that many friars wore a mail-shirt next the skin and iron rings whereby many fell sick and died and many were hindered from prayer. Wherefore St. Francis, as a most discreet father, commanded in the name of holy obedience that whosoever had either mail-shirt or iron ring should take it off and place it before him, and they did so; and there were counted more than five hundred iron shirts, and many more rings, both for the arms and for the belly; so that they made a great heap; and St. Francis caused them to be left there. Thereafter, the chapter being ended, St. Francis, exhorting them all to well doing, and teaching them how they ought to keep themselves unspotted from this evil world, sent them back to their provinces, with God's blessing and with his, full of consolation and of spiritual joy.

CHAPTER XIX

How from the vineyard of the priest of Rieti, in whose house St. Francis prayed, the grapes were taken away and gathered by the much folk which came unto him, and how thereafter that priest miraculously made more wine than ever before, even as St. Francis had promised him. And how God revealed to St. Francis that he would have Paradise for his portion

Upon a time, St. Francis being grievously diseased in his eyes, Messer Ugolino, Cardinal Protector of the Order, for the great love which he had toward him, wrote to him that he should go to him at Rieti, where were very excellent physicians for the eyes. Then St. Francis, having received the letter of the Cardinal, betook himself first to St. Damian, where was St. Clare, the most devoted bride of Christ, to give her some consolation; and afterward to go to the cardinal. Now, the night after St. Francis came thither, his eyes became so much worse, that he saw no light at all. Wherefore, in that he could not depart, St. Clare made for him a little cell of reeds, wherein he might the better rest himself. But St. Francis, through the pain of his infirmity and by reason of the multitude of mice, which caused him very great annoyance, was not able on anywise to find rest, either by day or by night. And enduring for much time that pain and tribulation, he began to think and to know that that was a scourge from God for his sins; and he began to thank God with all his heart and with his mouth, and thereafter he cried with a loud voice and said: "My Lord, I am worthy of this and much worse. My Lord Jesus Christ, the Good Shepherd, who showest forth Thy mercy to us sinners through divers pains and bodily afflictions, grant grace and virtue to me, Thy little sheep, that by no infirmity or anguish or pain I may depart from Thee." And, while he was thus praying, there came unto him a voice from Heaven, saying: "Francis, answer Me: if all the earth were gold, and all the seas and fountains and rivers were balm, and all the mountains and hills and rocks were precious stones; and thou shouldst find another treasure more excellent than these things are, even as gold is more excellent than earth, and balm than water, and precious stones than mountains and rocks; and if instead of this infirmity that most excellent treasure were given to thee, wouldst thou not be well content therewith and full of mirth?" St. Francis answered: "Lord, I am not worthy of so precious a treasure." And the voice of God said unto him: "Rejoice, Francis, because that is the treasure of life eternal which I keep for thee, and from this very hour I invest thee therewith, and this infirmity and affliction is the earnest of that blessed treasure." Then St. Francis, full of very great joy at so glorious a promise, called his companion and said: "Let us

go to the Cardinal." And having first consoled St. Clare with holy words, and having humbly taken leave of her, he set out towards Rieti, and when he drew nigh thereto, so great a multitude of people came forth to meet him that he did not wish to enter the city, but betook himself to a church which was distant from the city peradventure two miles. The citizens, knowing that he was in the said church, thronged it round about to look upon him, on such wise that the vineyard of the church was laid waste and all the grapes thereof were carried away; whereat the priest was sore grieved in his heart, and repented him that he had received St. Francis into his church. The thought of the priest being revealed of God to St. Francis, he sent to call him and said unto him: "Most dear father, how many measures of wine doth this vineyard yield thee a year, when it yieldeth its best?" He made answer: "Twelve measures." St. Francis said: "I pray thee, father, bear patiently my sojourning here for certain days, because I find here much repose; and do thou permit every man to take the grapes of this thy vineyard, for the love of God and of me a mendicant; and I promise thee in the name of my Lord Jesus Christ that it shall yield thee this year twenty measures." And this St. Francis did in return for his sojourn there, by reason of the great salvation of souls which was manifestly being wrought among the folk which came thither, of whom many departed drunk with Divine love, and abandoned the world. The priest, trusting to the promise of St. Francis, abandoned his vineyard freely to those who came to him. When, behold a marvel! Albeit the vineyard was wholly wasted and despoiled so that scarcely were there left therein any bunches of grapes; yet when the time of the vintage was come, the priest gathered those few bunches and put them in the winepress and trod upon them; and, according to the promise of St. Francis, drew therefrom twenty measures of excellent wine. By which miracle it was made manifest that, as, by the merits of St. Francis, the vineyard despoiled of grapes abounded in wine, so likewise the Christian people, barren of virtue through their sins, through the merits and doctrine of St. Francis, abounded in the good fruits of repentance.

CHAPTER XX

Of a very beautiful vision which was seen by a young friar, who held the cowl in so great abomination that he was minded to put off the habit and to leave the Order

A young man very noble and dainty entered the Order of St. Francis; the which, after certain days, by the instigation of the demon, began to hold the habit that he wore in such abomination, that it seemed to him that he wore a most base sack; he had a horror of the sleeves, he abominated the cowl, and in the length and roughness of the habit appeared to him an intolerable burden. And his disgust for the Religion ever increasing, he finally resolved to abandon the habit and return to the world. Now he had already accustomed himself, according to that which his master had taught him, whenever he passed before the altar of the convent, wherein was kept the Body of Christ, to kneel with great reverence and to draw back his cowl and with his arms crossed upon his breast to bow himself down. It befell that, on the night on which he was about to depart and leave the Order, it was necessary for him to pass before the altar of the convent, and, according to his custom, he kneeled him down and did reverence. And, anon, he was rapt in spirit and a marvelous vision was showed him by God: for he saw before him an almost infinite number of saints, after the fashion of a procession, two and two, clad in very beautiful and precious vestments of silken stuffs; and their faces and hands shone like the sun, and they moved to the sound of angelic songs and music; among which saints were two more nobly clad and adorned than all the rest; and they were encompassed round about by so bright a light that whosoever looked on them was filled with very great amaze; and, almost at the end of the procession, he saw one adorned with so great glory that he seemed a new-made knight, more honored than his peers. Beholding the aforesaid vision, this young man marveled thereat and knew not what that procession might mean, and he dared not ask but stood dazed with keen delight. Nevertheless, when all the procession had passed by, he took courage and ran after the last of them and with great dread inquired of them, saying: "O most dear ones, I beseech you that it may please you to tell me, who are these so marvelous folk which go in this procession so majestical?" They made answer: "Know, son, that we be all minor friars, who now are coming from Paradise." Whereupon he asked: "Who are those two who are more resplendent than the rest?" They answered: "These be St. Francis and St. Anthony; and he who goeth last, whom thou seest so highly honored, is a holy friar who is newly dead, whom, because he fought valiantly against temptations and persevered even unto the end, we are leading in triumph to the glory of Paradise; and these beautiful silken vestments which we wear, are given us of God in exchange for the rough habits which we wore patiently in the Religion; and the glorious resplendence which thou seest in us, is given us of God for the humility and patience, and for the holy poverty and obedience and chastity which we observed even unto the end. Wherefore, son, deem it not a hard thing to wear the sackcloth of the Religion which bringeth so great a reward; because if, with the sackcloth of St. Francis, for the love of Christ, thou shalt despise the world and mortify the flesh, and shalt fight valiantly against the demon, thou, together with us, shalt have like vestments, brightness and glory." And when these words had been spoken, the young man came to himself, and, comforted by the vision, drove away from him every temptation and confessed his fault before the guardian and the friars: from thenceforward he desired the roughness of penance and of raiment, and ended his life in the Order in great sanctity.

CHAPTER XXI

Of the most holy miracle which St. Francis wrought when he converted the very fierce wolf of Agobio

During the time that St. Francis dwelt in the city of Agobio, there appeared in the territory of Agobio a very great wolf, terrible and fierce, the which not only devoured animals but also men and women, so that all the citizens stood in great fear, because ofttimes he came nigh unto the city; and all men went armed when they went forth from the city, as if they were going to battle; and therewithal they were not able to defend themselves from him, when haply any man encountered him alone; and for dread of this wolf things came to such a pass that no one dared to leave the city. Wherefore, St. Francis, having compassion on the men of the city, was minded to go forth to meet this wolf, albeit the citizens altogether counselled him not to do so; and, making the sign of the cross, he went forth from the city with his companions, putting all his trust in God. And because the others feared to go farther, St. Francis alone took the road toward the place where the wolf was. And lo! while many citizens who had come out to behold this miracle were looking on, the said wolf made at St. Francis with open mouth. Whereupon St. Francis advanced toward him, and making over him the sign of the most holy Cross, called him unto him and spake to him after this manner: "Come hither, friar wolf, I command thee in Christ's name that thou do no harm to me nor to any other." O marvelous thing! Scarcely had St. Francis made the sign of the cross than the terrible wolf instantly closed his mouth and stayed his running; and, in obedience to that command, came, gentle as a lamb, and laid himself down at the feet of St. Francis. Then St. Francis spake unto him thus: "Friar wolf, thou dost much damage in these parts, and thou hast committed great crimes, destroying and slaying the creatures of God without His license; and not only hast thou slain and devoured beasts,

70. **Agobio,** another town of north-central Italy.

but thou hast also had the hardihood to slay men, made in the image of God; for the which cause thou dost merit the gallows as a thief and most iniquitous murderer; and all men cry out against thee and complain, and all this city is thine enemy. But I desire, friar wolf, to make peace between thee and them; to the end that thou mayest no more offend them and that they may forgive thee all thy past offences and neither men nor dogs may pursue thee any more." At these words, the wolf, by movements of his body and tail and eyes, and by bowing his head, showed that he accepted that which St. Francis said and was minded to observe the same. Thereupon St. Francis spake unto him again, saying: "Friar wolf, inasmuch as it seemeth good unto thee to make and keep this peace, I promise thee that, so long as thou shalt live, I will cause thy food to be given thee continually by the men of the city, so that thou shalt no more suffer hunger; for I know full well that whatever of evil thou hast done, thou hast done it through hunger. But seeing that I beg for thee this grace, I desire, friar wolf, that thou shouldst promise me that never from henceforward wilt thou injure any human being or any animal. Dost thou promise me this?" And the wolf, by bowing its head, gave evident token that he promised it. And St. Francis said: "Friar wolf, I desire that thou swear me fealty touching this promise, to the end that I may trust thee utterly." Then St. Francis held forth his hand to receive his fealty, and the wolf lifted up his right fore-foot and put it with friendly confidence in the hand of St. Francis, giving thereby such token of fealty as he was able. Thereupon St. Francis said: "Friar wolf, I command thee in the name of Jesus Christ to come now with me, nothing doubting, and let us go and stablish this peace in the name of God." And the wolf went with him obediently, like a gentle lamb; wherefore the citizens beholding the same marveled greatly. And anon, the fame thereof was noised abroad through all the city, and all the people, men and women, great and small, young and old, thronged to the piazza to see the wolf with St. Francis. And when all the folk were gathered together, St. Francis rose up to preach unto them, saying, among other things, how, by reason of sin, God permits such pestilences; and far more perilous is the fire of Hell, the which must forever torment the damned, than is the fury of a wolf which can only kill the body; how much then are the jaws of Hell to be feared when the jaws of a little beast can hold so great a multitude in fear? "Turn ye then, most dear ones, turn ye to God, and do befitting penance for your sins, and God will save you from the wolf in this present world and from the fire of Hell in that which is to come." And when he had done preach-

ing, St. Francis said: "Hear ye, my brethren. Friar wolf, who is here before you, hath promised and sworn fealty to me, that he will make peace with you and never more offend you in anything; do ye now promise him to give him every day that whereof he hath need; and I become surety unto you for him that he will faithfully observe this covenant of peace." Then all the people with one voice promised to provide him food continually, and St. Francis spake unto the wolf before them all, saying: "And thou, friar wolf, dost thou promise to observe the covenant of peace which thou hast made with this folk, that thou wilt offend neither men nor beasts nor any creature?" And the wolf kneeled him down and bowed his head, and, with gentle movements of his body and tail and ears, showed as far as he was able his determination to keep that covenant wholly. Said St. Francis: "Friar wolf, as thou didst me fealty touching this promise, without the gate, so now I desire that thou do me fealty, before all the people, touching thy promise, and that thou wilt not deceive me concerning my promise and surety which I have given for thee." Then the wolf, lifting up its right foot, put it in the hand of St. Francis. By which act, and by the other acts aforesaid, all the people were fulfilled with so great joy and wonder, alike for devotion toward the saint, and for the strangeness of the miracle, and for the peace with the wolf, that they all began to shout to Heaven, praising and blessing God who had sent them St. Francis, who, by his merits, had freed them from the jaws of the cruel beast. And thereafter, the said wolf lived two years in Agobio, and entered familiarly into the houses, going from door to door, neither doing injury to any one nor receiving any; and he was courteously nourished by the people; and, as he thus went through the town and through the houses, never did any dog bark after him. Finally, after two years, friar wolf died of old age; whereat the citizens lamented much, because as long as they saw him going so gently through their city, they recalled the better the virtue and sanctity of St. Francis.

CHAPTER XXII

How St. Francis tamed the wild turtle-dove

One day, a youth had taken many turtle-doves, and as he was carrying them to sell them, St. Francis, who ever had singular compassion for gentle creatures, chanced to meet him, and looking upon those turtle-doves with compassionate eye, said to the youth: "Good youth, I pray thee give them to me, that birds so gentle, which in the Scriptures are likened unto chaste and humble and faithful souls, come not into the hands of cruel men who would slay them." Whereupon, inspired of God, he forthwith gave them all to St. Francis; and he receiving them in his bosom, began to speak to them sweetly: "O my sisters, simple, innocent, chaste turtle-doves, why do you let yourselves be taken? Now I desire to save you from death and to make nests for you, so that ye may bring forth fruit and multiply, according to the commandments of our Creator." And St. Francis went and made nests for them all, and they resorted thereunto, and began to lay eggs and hatch forth their young, in the presence of the friars; and so tame were they and so familiar with St. Francis and with the other friars that they might have been domestic fowls which had always been fed by them; and never did they depart until St. Francis with his blessing gave them leave to do so. And to the young man, which had given them unto him, St. Francis said: "Son, thou wilt yet be a friar in this Order, and thou wilt serve Jesus Christ with all thy heart;" and so it came to pass, for the said youth became a friar and lived in the Order in great sanctity.

CHAPTER XXIII
How St. Francis set free the friar who was in sin with the demon

Once when St. Francis was praying in the Place of Porziuncula, he saw by Divine revelation, the whole Place encompassed about and besieged by the demons after the fashion of a great army; but none of them could enter into the Place, inasmuch as these friars were of so great sanctity that the demons found none into whom they might enter. But while they thus persisted, it fell upon a day that one of those friars was offended with another, and thought within his heart how he could accuse and avenge himself on him; for the which cause, while yet he cherished this evil thought, the devil, the door being opened, entered into the Place and set himself upon the neck of that friar. Thereupon the compassionate and careful shepherd, who ever watched over his flock, seeing that the wolf had entered in to devour his little sheep, immediately caused that friar to be called to him, and bade him forthwith reveal the poison of hatred conceived against his neighbor, through the which he had come into the hands of the enemy. Wherefore, he, full of fear at seeing himself thus discovered by the holy father, disclosed all the venom and rancor of his heart, and confessed his fault and humbly besought penance and mercy; and when he had so done, and was absolved of his sin, and had received penance, anon, in the presence of St. Francis, the demon departed; and the friar, thus delivered from the hands of the cruel beast, through the loving kindness of the good shepherd, gave thanks to God, and returning, corrected and admonished, to the flock of the holy shepherd, lived afterward in great sanctity.

CHAPTER XXIV
How St. Francis converted the Soldan of Babylon to the faith

St. Francis, urged thereto by zeal for the faith of Christ and by the desire of martyrdom, went once across the seas with his twelve most holy companions, to betake himself straight to the Soldan of Babylon; and being come unto a country of the Saracens, where the passes were guarded by certain cruel men to the end that no Christian who went thereby might be able to escape death; they, as it pleased God, were not slain, but taken, beaten, and bound, and so led into the presence of the Soldan. And being in his presence, St. Francis, taught by the Holy Ghost, preached so divinely of the faith of Christ, that for the faith he even wished to enter into the fire. Wherefore the Soldan began to have very great devotion toward him, alike for the constancy of his faith and for the contempt of the world which he saw in him (inasmuch as he would receive no gift from him, albeit he was exceeding poor), and also for the zeal of martyrdom which he saw in him. From thenceforward the Soldan heard him gladly and prayed him that he would often return to him; granting to him and his companions leave to preach wherever they pleased; and he gave them a token to the end that they might not be offended by any man. Having this leave then, St. Francis sent his chosen companions, two by two, into divers regions of the Saracens to preach the faith of Christ. . . . At last St. Francis, seeing that he could have no more fruit in those parts, prepared, by Divine revelation, to return with all his companions to the land of the faithful; and, having gathered them all together, he returned to the Soldan and took leave of him. Then the Soldan said unto him: "Friar Francis, I would willingly be converted to the faith of Christ, but I fear to be so now, because, if these heard thereof, they would slay both thee and me, with all thy companions; and seeing that thou canst yet do much good and that I have certain matters of great moment to conclude, I would not now bring about thy death and mine; but do thou teach me how I may save myself; I am ready to do that which thou mayest lay upon me." Then St. Francis said: "Sir, I now go from thee; but after I shall be come into my own country and, through the grace of God, shall have ascended into Heaven, after my death, according as it shall please God, I will send thee two of my friars from whom thou mayest receive the holy baptism of Christ, and thou shalt be saved, as my Lord Jesus Christ hath revealed unto me. And do thou, in the meantime, free thyself from every hindrance, to the end that, when the grace of God shall come unto thee, it may find thee prepared to faith and to devotion." And this he promised to do, and so did he. Now when this was done, St. Francis returned with that venerable college of his holy companions; and after certain years, St. Francis by bodily death rendered his soul to God. And the Soldan, falling sick, awaited the fulfillment of the promise of St. Francis, and set guards at certain passes and ordered that, if two friars should appear in the habit of St. Francis, they should immediately be brought to him. At that time, St. Francis appeared to two friars, and commanded them to go without delay to the Soldan to provide for his salvation, according as he had promised him; the which friars set out immediately, and crossing the sea, were led before the Soldan by the aforesaid guard; and when the Soldan saw them, he was exceeding glad and said: "Now know I of a truth that God hath sent me His servants for my salvation, according to the promise which St. Francis made me by Divine revelation." And, when he had been instructed in the faith of Christ and baptised by the said friars, thus born again in Christ, he died of that sickness and his soul was saved through the merits and prayers of St. Francis.

CHAPTER XXV

How St. Francis miraculously healed one who was a leper both in soul and body; and that which the soul said unto him as it went into Heaven

The true disciple of Christ, Messer St. Francis, while he lived in this miserable life, sought with all his strength to follow Christ, the perfect Master; whence it ofttimes befell, through Divine operation, that, in the selfsame hour that he healed men's bodies, their souls were healed by God, even as we read of Christ. And, inasmuch as he not only himself willingly served lepers, but, furthermore, had commanded that the friars of his Order, wheresoever they went or sojourned throughout the world, should serve lepers for the love of Christ, who for our sake willed to be accounted leprous; it came to pass upon a time that, in a certain Place, near to that wherein St. Francis then dwelt, the friars served the lepers and the sick in a hospital; wherein was a leper so impatient and so intolerable and so froward, that every one believed most certainly that he was possessed of the devil, and so in truth he was; for not only did he revile and shamefully belabor whomsoever served him, but (what is far worse) he blasphemously railed upon Christ the blessed and His most holy Mother the Virgin Mary, so that on no wise could any one be found who was able or willing to serve him. And albeit the friars strove to endure patiently the insults and injuries to themselves, that they might increase the merit of patience; nevertheless, because their consciences were

unable to bear those which were uttered against Christ and His Mother, they resolved to abandon the said leper altogether; but they were unwilling to do so until they had duly given notice to St. Francis, who was then dwelling in a Place near at hand. And when they had told him thereof, St. Francis betook himself to this perverse leper, and coming unto him saluted him, saying: "God give thee peace, my dearest brother." The leper made answer: "What peace can I have from God, who hath taken from me peace and every good thing, and hath made me all rotten and stinking?" And St. Francis said: "Son, have patience; for the infirmities of our bodies are given us of God, in this world, for the salvation of our souls, because they are of great merit when they are borne with patience." The sick man answered: "And how can I bear patiently the continual pain which torments me day and night? And not only am I afflicted by my sickness, but yet worse by the friars whom thou gavest me that they might serve me, for they do not serve me as they ought." Then St. Francis, knowing by revelation that this leper was possessed by an evil spirit, departed and betook himself to prayer and devoutly besought God for him. And when he had done praying he returned and spake thus: "Son, I would serve thee myself, since thou art not satisfied with the others." "I am content," said the sick man, "but what canst thou do for me more than the others?" Said St. Francis: "That which thou desirest I will do." Said the leper: "I desire that thou wash me all over, because I stink so greatly that I cannot endure my own self." Then St. Francis forthwith caused water to be heated with many sweet-smelling herbs; thereafter he undressed him and began to wash him with his own hands, while another friar poured on the water; and by Divine miracle, where St. Francis touched him with his holy hands, the leprosy departed and the flesh remained perfectly sound. And even as the flesh began to heal, so the soul began to heal also; wherefore the leper, seeing that he was beginning to be made whole, began to feel great remorse and repentance for his sins, and to weep very bitterly; so that, while the body was cleansed outwardly of the leprosy by washing of water, so the soul was cleansed inwardly of sin by amendment and by tears. And when he was completely cured, both in body and in soul, he humbly confessed his fault and said, weeping aloud: "Woe is me, for I am worthy of Hell for the injuries and revilings which I have done and spoken against the friars, and for my impatience against God and the blasphemies which I have uttered;" wherefore, for fifteen days he continued to weep bitterly for his sins, beseeching mercy of God, and confessing himself wholly to a priest. And St. Francis beholding so clear a miracle, which God had wrought by his hands, gave thanks to God and got him thence, going to countries very far away; because by reason of humility he desired to flee every glory, and in all his works sought only the honor and glory of God and not his own. Afterward, as it pleased God, the said leper, healed in body and soul, after his fifteen days of penance, fell sick of another sickness, and, fortified with the sacraments of the Church, died a holy death; and, as

10 his soul went into Paradise, it appeared in the air to St. Francis, who was praying in a wood, and said unto him: "Knowest thou me?" "Who art thou?" said St. Francis. "I am that leper whom Christ the blessed healed through thy merits, and today I go to eternal life; wherefore I give thanks to God and to thee. Blessed be thy soul and thy body, and blessed thy holy works and words; because through thee many souls shall be saved in the world; and know that there is no day in the world, whereon

20 the holy angels and the other saints thank not God for the holy fruits which thou and thy Order bring forth in divers parts of the world; and therefore do thou take comfort and thank God, abiding always in His benediction." And when he had said these words he went into Heaven; and St. Francis remained much consoled.

Sir Gawain and the Green Knight

A single manuscript in fourteenth-century English literature contains four poems, the resemblances of which one to another are so great that the entire group has been assigned to one author, known simply as the Pearl Poet. Many attempts have been made to identify this author, attempts often showing the greatest ingenuity, but no general agreement has ever been reached, only the belief that there was such a poet, not yet identified, and that he wrote the four poems somewhere around the year 1370.

The Pearl, the first of the four, which has given the poet his mythical name, is a beautiful and elaborate elegy on a little girl. The second and third poems, *Purity (Cleanness)* and *Patience,* are didactic religious poems notable for their generous poetic talent. The last piece, *Sir Gawain and the Green Knight,* however, has been regarded generally as the cream of Middle English metrical romances. It is told with a unity of narrative effect, a vigorous style, a masterly control of suspense, and a highly poetic coloring that are most unusual for the romance, which was inclined to be rather stereotyped. Instead of the usual manifold adventures which befall the hero, there are in this romance only two, and these two are made to depend one upon the other.

These two central incidents, as will be seen, serve as tests for Gawain's character as a knight. One, the beheading incident, tests his physical courage and his fidelity to his word; the other, the incident of the lady in the castle of the Green Knight, makes a trial of Gawain's chastity and moral purpose. The ultimate objective of the romance, therefore, apart from the obvious narrative entertainment, is clearly didactic; *Sir Gawain and the Green Knight,* for that reason, cannot be considered a true example of the chivalric romance, however thoroughly the Pearl Poet may know the usages of chivalric courtesy and conduct. The poem is, rather, a fine and artistic example of the moral romance. But it is to be noted further that Gawain's conduct, exemplary as it is, will not strike the reader as impossibly idealized. He flinches quite naturally under the first terrifying blow of the Green Knight's ax, and he does not emerge unscathed from the ordeal of the bedchamber. The drop of humanity which the Pearl Poet injects into his treatment of Gawain puts him head and shoulders above the mass of moral romance writers in the Middle Ages.

The two incidents are known elsewhere in medieval legendry, but they are combined in this poem only, unless one counts two later romances in Middle English clearly derived from *Sir Gawain and the Green Knight;* that is, *The Green Knight* and *The Turk and Gawain.* The episode of the beheading is paralleled in a medieval Irish romance, *The Feast of Bricriu,* even down to the detail of the three strokes aimed at Gawain in the climactic scene with the Green Knight. The figure of Gawain is a Welsh divinity, and all the important names in the story are also Celtic. Such matters of resemblance suggest a definitely Celtic origin for the story and a possible Celtic ancestry for the Pearl Poet himself, although it is probable that he had as his immediate source a French romance based on Celtic legendry.

At the end of *Sir Gawain and the Green Knight* is the motto, "Honi soit qui mal y pense," made famous by King Edward III, ruler of England during the Pearl Poet's lifetime. Some have seen in this the possibility that the poem was written in honor of some particular knightly order, such as the Order of the Garter, which adopted this French motto. The fifteenth-century derivative romance, *The Green Knight,* actually names the Knights of the Bath, but this Order was not in existence at the time of the Pearl Poet. Some have gone so far as to assume that the green color of the knight and of the girdle is symbolic of spring, and that the poem was a spring poem intended for a celebration of Saint George's Day (April 23), the holiday of the patron saint of the Order of the Garter and of English chivalry in general. Furthermore, the color green is invariably associated in Celtic legendry with the supernatural and magical.

The possibility that *Sir Gawain and the Green Knight* is a Garter poem is, however, something to be inferred but not proved. The presence of the motto may signify merely that the Pearl Poet was a courtier of Edward III. This fact can be reasonably accepted: if he was not a courtier, he was at least acquainted with the court and wrote the poem with his royal sovereign in mind. But all such inferences are playthings for the academic. What is truly important about *Sir Gawain and the Green Knight* is that it is a superb example of the art of the medieval storyteller; it pictures the favorite English chivalric hero, Gawain, in his best and most attractive aspects, before he was debased to make room for the French hero, Lancelot; it is a clear exposition of the ideals of physical and moral integrity demanded of the medieval knight; it combines powerful and vigorous narrative with a deep feeling for nature; it is sophisticated but neither cynical nor oversentimental.

Sir Gawain
and the Green Knight

I

AFTER the siege and assault of Troy after the city had been shattered and burnt to brands and ashes, and the man who had wrought stratagems of treason had been tried for his trickery—the veriest upon earth—it was Aeneas the noble and his exalted family who then vanquished nations and became sovereigns of well nigh all the lands in the Western Isles. So proud Romulus turned to Rome and with great pomp built that city (and named it with his name, which it bears today); Ticius moved to Tuscany and began there his habitation; Langobard in Lombardy raised up homes for himself; and far over the French flood Felix Brutus established on many a shore broad Britain with joy, where wars and waste and wonder by turns have dwelt therein, and often bliss as well as bale have followed one another quickly enow.

And when Britain had been built by this mighty man, brave warriors flourished who loved strife, and many a time they wrought woe. Since that time more wonders have come to pass in this land than in any other of which I have knowledge. But of all the kings of Britain who lived here, Arthur was ever the most gracious, as I have heard tell. And so I desire to make known an adventure that befell in the land (many men consider it a marvel), most surprising even among the many wonders of Arthur's reign. If ye will listen to this lay for a little while, I shall tell it to you straightway, as I heard it told with tongue, and as it has been set forth in story

stout and strong, fixed with true letters, as it has long been known in the land.

King Arthur lay at Camelot of a Christmas tide, with many a splendid lord, the best men in the world. With him in princely fashion was all the mighty brotherhood of the Round Table. There was many a rich revel and careless joy; there folk tourneyed again and again; the noble knights jousted fairly, then repaired to the court to sing carols. For full fifteen days the feast lasted, with all the food and merriment that man could devise, such riotous glee glorious to hear, sounding forth by day, and lovesome dancing by night. There was good fortune everywhere in halls and chambers among lords and ladies, as they most desired. With all the joy in the world they lived there together: the most famous knights in Christendom and the loveliest ladies that ever lived, and the comeliest king that ever held court. For this fair people was in its youth, the happiest under Heaven; their king the greatest on earth; it would be hard now to name so brave a hero in all the land.

The New Year was so recently come that it had barely arrived. The people on the dais were served double that day. The king had come with all his knights into the hall; the ceremony in the chapel had been brought to a close. Loud were the cries raised by clerks and by others; Noel was celebrated anew and named full often. Gallant men hastened to give their gifts—gave them and asked for them both—admired and talked about the gifts one to another. Ladies laughed aloud, even when they were overlooked (and those that received were not wroth, ye may well believe!). All this revelry they kept until meal-time. When they had washed, full worthily they went to their seats; the best knights above, as befitted their rank. Then came Guinevere gay, in royal attire, and sat on the dais amid pomp and pleasure. Of fine silk was the seat; above her a canopy of costly Toulouse, hung with tapestries from Tars that were embroidered and embossed with the fairest of gems that could be bought with money and be proved of value. She was the fairest of all to behold; her gray eyes shone; no man could say truthfully that he ever saw one more beautiful.

But Arthur would not eat till all were served; he was so glad in his joy, even as a child; his desire was for an easy life; he could abide neither to lie long

40
50
60
70
10
20
30

Sir Gawain . . . ᴬ Translated by George K. Anderson.
5. **Aeneas the noble.** It was a medieval tradition that Troy had been taken through the machinations of Aeneas. 8. **Western Isles,** probably "the three islands of Britain" of antiquity—England, with Scotland; the Hebrides; and Ireland—as well as the adjacent islands —Wight, Man, the Orkneys and Shetlands, and probably the Scilly Isles. 11–12. **Ticius . . . Lombardy.** It is likely that Ticius, like Langobard, is the name of a fictitious descendant of Aeneas. Langobard is also the name of the traditional ancestor of the Langobardi, or Lombards. 13. **Felix Brutus,** according to legend, the grandson of Aeneas and the founder of Britain (Brutlond, the land of Brutus).

31. **fixed . . . letters.** This probably signifies, "written in alliterative verse." 33. **Camelot.** This was identified by many medieval writers with Winchester; other possibilities are Colchester, Cadbury (Somersetshire), and Carlisle. But the frequent mention of Logres suggests that Camelot was in the southern portion of England. 36. **Round Table,** a motif of Welsh legendry. The story goes that Arthur's guests once quarreled because of the order in which they had been seated at table. A round table was devised because there could then be no question of "high" or "low." 39. **carols,** in reality dances accompanied by song; originally ring-dances. 71. **Tars,** the usual Middle English form of Tharsia, the old name for Turkestan.

nor to sit; his young blood and impetuous brain so worked upon him. And also another habit was fast upon him, which came from his nobility: he would never eat on such a delightful day until some strange kind of wondrous tale had been recounted, some story of mighty marvel, which he could believe, of his ancestors, or of arms and other adventures; or until some strange knight should ask of him that he might join him in a joust and lay his life in jeopardy, life against life, one against another, as fortune might favor them. This was the king's wont when he was holding court, at every high feast among his noble retinue in the hall. And so, fair of face, he was sitting straight in his seat, making great mirth against the New Year.

Thus the valiant king sat there before the high table, talking of light trifles; there good Gawain was seated by Guinevere, and Agravayne *à la dure main* was sitting on the other side. Both were sons of the King's sister and full courageous knights. Bishop Bawdewyne was at the end of the table; and Ywain, son of Urien, sat eating by himself. These were all worthily served on the dais, and at the lower tables many a valiant retainer. Then in came the first course amid the crackling of trumpets, and many a bright banner waving, the rolling noise of drums with shrill pipes, wild music and melody awakened. Many a heart leaped high at those sounds; dainties were brought forth, full costly meats, abundance of fresh foods, and on so many dishes that it was difficult to find a place before the people to set the silver vessels with their savory viands. Each man took what he liked best; by every two were twelve dishes, good beer and bright wine.

Now I will tell you no more about their table-service, for all can understand that there was no lack of good things. For another sound was heard, and a new wonder that folk might well have left their labor to gaze upon. Scarcely had the hum of the banquet dwindled and the first course been served royally in the court, when there rushed in through the hall-door a terrible knight, the greatest in the world as to stature. From neck to loin he was so square and thickset, and his back and limbs were so long and broad that I think he must have been half giant. Certainly I believe he must have been the tallest of men and the lustiest in size that could ride on horse. His back and breast were sturdy and stout, but his belly and waist were nobly slender; and all his features alike clean-cut. But for his color men stood in wonder, as his semblance appeared clear: he came as a hostile knight, and was green all over.

16–17. **high table;** on a dais at one end of the hall, reserved for the lord of the castle, his family, and his nobles. 19–20. **sons . . . sister.** Gawain is Arthur's nephew. 52–53. **green all over.** Green was a fairy color, hence quite appropriate to this particular knight (see headnote).

This man was, indeed, clad all in green; a green cloak clung to his sides, and a simple mantle over it, worthily lined with fur showing clearly and with cloth full clean. Of bright fur, too, was the hood that was thrown back from his locks and lay on his shoulders. Beautifully trimmed was the hem of his coat, and he wore hose of that same green, fastened neatly to the calves of his leg, and clean spurs attached of bright gold, with silken clasps striped most regally, and neat pads under his legs to protect him from galling. All his vesture, in truth, was of pure green, and the ornaments of his belt and fair stones in his girdle, that were nobly arrayed in neat order about his waist and his saddle, on a silk cloth. It would be too tedious to tell of half the adornments that were woven thereon—birds and insects in gay gauds of green, with gold amid them. There were trappings on the neck of his steed and on the crupper; all the ornaments there were of metal and enamel. The stirrups that he stood in were stained green; and the pommel of his saddle, like the stirrups, gleamed and shone with green jewels. The horse that he rode upon, forsooth, was of that same hue, a steed hard to restrain, strong and powerful, in embroidered bridle, full meet for his rider.

Gaily was this knight attired in green, as was the hair of his fine steed. Fair-flowing hair fell over the knight's shoulders; a beard as great as a bush hung over his breast, which, together with his lordly hair on his head, was clipped round about above his elbows, and half his sleeves were clasped in the same manner as a king's mantle, which encloses the neck. The mane of the horse was curled and twisted with many a knot folded in with gold thread over that fair green; here a twist of hair; there a flash of gold. Both the mane and the tail were tied in like manner and bound around with a band of bright green, decked with precious stones to the very end of the tail, and tied aloft with a very subtle knot. There many bells of shining gold rang out full bright. Such a horse or such a knight to ride him had never been seen before in that hall by man's eye; he flashed like lightning, so that men who looked upon him said it appeared that no man could survive the stroke of the knight.

But the knight had no helmet nor hauberk, no gorget, nor armor to cover his arms, no spear or shield to fend or to smite with. Only in his hand he carried a holly-bough, that is greenest when the groves are bare. In the other hand he bore an ax, huge and monstrous, a cruel battle-weapon if one could but describe it. The head of the ax was a full ell long; the grain of green steel and of gold; the blade burnished bright, with a broad edge, as able to shear as the sharpest of razors. The strong man held it set on a stout staff which was braced with iron down to the edge of the wood, and all engraved with green in cunning work. A lace was wrapped about it, that was looped over the head and then fastened to the handle; attached to it were costly tassels hanging from buttons of bright green full richly bedecked.

The knight rode in through the entrance of the hall, pushing his way up to the dais, fearing no harm. He saluted never a one, but looked over them all. The first word that he uttered was, "Where is the ruler of this company? Gladly would I see that man with my eyes, and speak with him in very truth." On the knights he cast his glance and swaggered up and down, then stopped still and studied them to see who was the most renowned.

Then there was long looking to gaze upon that knight, for every man marveled what it might mean, that a hero and a horse should have such a hue, as green as grown grass and perhaps greener even than green enamel shining on gold. All that stood there gazed upon him and stepped nearer, with all the wonder in the world, to see who he might be. Many a strange sight had they seen, but never such a one as this; therefore the people thought it a phantasm or faerie. Many were afraid to give him answer, and were astounded at his voice; they sat stone-still in a heavy silence through that noble hall; their talking ceased as if they had been struck with slumber. I believe it was not so much for fear as for courtesy; they would let him whom all should defer to speak himself to that knight.

So Arthur beheld this marvel before his high dais; he greeted the stranger in knightly fashion (never was he rash), and said: "Knight, welcome in truth to this place! My name is Arthur, lord of this hall; light down, fair sir, and tarry; we shall know later what thy will is." "Nay, so help me," quoth the knight, "He that sits on high; to stay any time in this dwelling was not my errand. But because the renown of this people has been so exalted, because thy castle and thy warriors are esteemed the best and the bravest to ride on steeds under steel harness, the strongest and worthiest of all mankind and proven of excellence in knightly sports—therefore courtesy has flourished here, as I have heard tell; and that has drawn me hither, forsooth, at this time. Ye may be sure by this branch that I bear here that I come in peace and seek no strife. For if I had come in warlike manner with a band beside me—well, I have a hauberk at home and a helmet also; a shield and a sharp spear, shining bright, and other weapons to wield, as I can vouchsafe. But because I desire no war, my garments are softer! If thou art as bold as all men say, thou wilt grant me by rights the sport that I ask." Arthur answered and said: "Sir courteous knight, if thou cravest a mere battle, thou shalt not fail to fight here!"

"Nay," said the knight, "I seek no fight, in faith; about this bench I see naught but beardless children. If I were enclosed in armor upon a lofty steed, there would be no man here to match me, so weak is their strength. And so I crave in this court a Christmas-game, for it is Yule and New Year, and here are many active men. If any one in this hall considers himself so hardy, be his blood so bold or the brain in his head, that he dare strike one stroke for another, I shall give him as a gift this mighty ax, which is heavy enough for him to handle as he pleases; and I will abide the first blow, unarmed as I sit here. If any man be so fierce as to try what I propose, let him leap swiftly upon me, and take his weapon. I quit claim to it; he may keep it as his own. I shall stand his stroke, firm on this floor. If so, thou shalt grant me the right to deal him another, in faith; and yet I shall give him respite for a year and a day. Now hasten, and let us see whether any one here say aught!"

If he had astonished them at first, now all were more silent than ever—all Arthur's followers in the hall, high and low. The warrior on his steed fixed himself in his saddle, and rolled his red eyes about most violently, bent his beetling brows, glittering green; he twisted his beard about while he waited for whoever would rise. When none would retort to him, he coughed loudly and spoke to them in loud mockery: "What? Is this Arthur's house, whose fame runs through so many realms? Where is your haughtiness and your conquests, your fierceness and your anger and your mighty words? Now the glory and renown of the Round Table has been overturned by the words of one man; for all fear out of dread, and not a blow seen!" With that he laughed so loud that it grieved the king: the blood rushed for shame into his fair face; he was as angry as the blast of winter—so were all that were there. The king so brave by nature stepped near to that stern knight, and said: "Knight, by Heaven, thy request is strange; and since thou hast sought folly, thou must in truth find it! I know of no man here that is afraid of thy big words! Give me now thine ax, in God's name, and I shall grant thy boon which thou hast demanded."

Lightly he leaped at the knight and caught at his hand; then fiercely the knight dismounted. Now Arthur had taken the ax and grasped it by the handle and stoutly brandished it, thinking to strike. The sturdy knight towered over the king, higher than any in the house by a head or more; with grisly cheer he stood there and stroked his beard with immovable countenance, drawing aside his coat, no more frightened or dismayed at the king's threatened blows than if some man on the benches had brought him a draught of wine. Then Gawain, who was sitting by the king, leaned toward him and spoke: "I beseech thee now, of a truth, that this affair be mine."

"Would ye, noble lord," said Gawain to the king, "but bid me rise from this bench and stand by you there, that I without discourtesy may leave the table and not displease my liege-lady, I would come to your counsel before your royal court. For it seems to me not fitting, if the truth be known, when such a demand be raised high in your hall, that you should be desirous of taking it upon yourself, while many men so bold are sitting about on the benches—there are not, I hope, men of more precious courage under the heavens, nor better bodies for fighting when strife is lifted up. I know that I am the weakest of them and the feeblest of understanding; and less would be the loss of my life, if the truth were told. Save that you are my uncle there is little to praise in me; I know no virtue in my body save your blood. And since this business is so strange that it is not seemly for you to assume it, and since I have asked it of you first, grant it to me, and if I speak not in comely fashion, let all this court still be without blame." Then the mighty knights all counseled with one accord that the crowned king withdraw and give Gawain the venture.

Then the king commanded the knight to arise; and he rose up full quickly and fixed him fair. Then he knelt down again before the king and grasped the weapon; the king graciously relinquished it to Gawain, and lifted up his hand and gave him God's blessing and was fain to pray that his heart and his hand should both be valiant. "Keep thyself, nephew," said the king, "and set thyself for one blow; if thou hast heard him aright, I think that thou must abide a blow that he will give thee in return." Gawain advanced against the stranger with the ax in his hand; the stranger boldly awaited him, no whit abashed. Then the knight in green said to Sir Gawain: "Let us renew our agreement ere we proceed further. First I ask thee, Sir Knight, what thy name is; thou must tell me truly, so I may trust it." "In good faith," said the good knight, "Gawain I call myself, who offer thee this buffet, whatsover may befall later. And this time twelvemonth I shall take from thee another, with whatsoever weapon thou wilt, and with none other to help me, none in the world." The other replied: "Sir Gawain, so may I prosper, I am fair and fain to receive the blow that thou shalt direct."

"By God," quoth the Green Knight, "Sir Gawain, it pleases me that I shall take from thy fist what I have asked for here. Thou hast readily rehearsed, correctly indeed, the covenant that I requested of the king; but thou must assure me, knight, by thy troth, that thou shalt seek thyself, wheresoever thou dost believe I am to be found on the earth, and shalt get for thyself such rewards as thou dealest to me today in the presence of this mighty troop." "Where am I to seek thee," asked Gawain; "where is thy home? I know not where thou dwellest, by Him that made me; nor do I know thy court, O knight, nor thy name. But teach me truly thereto, and tell me thy name, and I shall use all my wits to get myself thither. That I swear of a truth, and by my firm troth." "That is enough on the New Year; we need no more," quoth the warrior in green to Gawain the gracious. "If I tell thee truly, after I have received the stroke, and thou hast struck me in all honor, quickly I will tell thee of my house and my home and mine own name; then thou canst ask my business and keep covenant. And if I waste no speech, so much the better for thee, for thou canst stay longer in thy land, and seek no farther. But enough, take now thy grim weapon and let us see how thou canst strike." "Gladly, sir, forsooth," quoth Gawain, stroking his ax.

The Green Knight quickly made him ready on the ground; he bowed his head a little and uncovered his countenance; his long fair locks he laid over his head and let the naked neck show for the ax. Gawain gripped his weapon and gathered it aloft; his left foot he placed forward on the earth, then let the blade fall quickly on the bare neck. The sharp edge shattered the bones of the stranger, bit through the fair skin and sheared it in two, so that the brown-steeled blade ate into the ground. The fair head fell from the neck to earth; many kicked it with their feet as it rolled about; the blood spurted from the body and glistened on the green. Yet the strange warrior never faltered or fell, but stoutly leaped upon sturdy legs, rushed forth and reached out where the warriors were standing, caught up his fair head and lifted it up. Then he turned to his steed, caught the bridle, stepped into the stirrup and mounted; he held his head by the hair with his hand. And he settled himself in his saddle as calmly as if no accident had befallen him there, although he was headless. He turned his horse about—his ugly body bleeding all the while; many were in terror of him and greatly distrusted the covenant.

For he held up his head in his hand, raising the face toward the most valiant king on the dais. And the head raised its eyelids and looked full about and spoke these words with its mouth, as you may now hear: "Look, Gawain, that thou be ready to go as thou didst promise and seek faithfully, O knight, until thou dost find me, as thou didst promise in this hall in the presence of these knights. Take thy way to the Green Chapel, I charge thee, to get such a blow deservedly as thou hast dealt, to be yielded thee promptly next New Year's Morn. Many men know me as the knight of the Green Chapel; therefore, if thou dost ask to find me, thou wilt never fail. So come, or be called recreant and coward!" Then the stranger turned his bridle and rushed out in a gallop, so that sparks flew up from the hooves of his horse. To what land he went, none there could tell any more than they knew whence he had come. And then? The king and Gawain laughed and joked at that Green Knight; yet it assuredly had been a marvel for those knights to behold.

Then King Arthur was astounded at heart, although he let no hint be given of his wonder, but said aloud to the comely queen in fair speech: "Dear lady, be never dismayed today; such a marvel well becomes Christmas-tide, when we lack entertainment, laughing or singing, or fair carols sung by knights and ladies. But now I can turn to my food, for I have seen a miracle I can never forget." He looked at Sir Gawain and quickly said: "Now, sir, hang up thine ax; it has hewn enough." So it was placed above the dais, hanging on the back of a seat, where all men could look upon it as a marvel, and by its true evidence tell of the wonder. Then they bowed them to bench, did these warriors together, the king and the good knight, and brave men served them a double portion of all dainties, as was the share of the most valiant—with all manner of meats and minstrelsy as well. In well-being they spent that day on earth, until it came to an end.

Now bethink thee well, Sir Gawain, that thou delay not to seek the harm-fraught adventure which thou hast taken upon thee.

II

THIS beginning of adventures befell Arthur on the New Year, for he yearned to hear of deeds of glory, though his words were few when he sat at his feasts. But now their hands were filled aplenty with grim work. Gawain was glad to begin the game in the hall, but ye need have no wonder that the end was hard. For though a man be merry in mind when he has had strong drink, a year passes full quickly and never brings again its like; the beginning and the ending accord full seldom. And so this Yule departed, and the year after, and each season in turn followed upon another. After Christmas came crabbed Lent, that tries flesh with fish and simpler foods; then the weather of the world struggles against winter; the cold shrinks away, the clouds uplift themselves; bright pours the rain down in warm showers and falls on the fair fields; flowers peep forth; green are the garments of earth and grove; birds make them ready to build and sing with passion for the solace of soft summer that comes down from the heights. Then bursting blossoms burgeon forth in rich and rank hedgerows, and noble notes enow are heard in the fair woodlands.

After the season of summer with its soft winds, when Zephirus breathes on seeds and grasses—very joyous are the roots that grow thereout—then the moistening dew drips from the leaves, awaiting a blissful glance from the bright sun. But autumn approaches and hardens the seeds, warning them to grow full ripe before winter; in drought he drives the dust in clouds; it whirls aloft over the face of the earth. Angry winds in the heavens wrestle with the sun; leaves drop from the linden and alight on earth; the grass turns gray that once was green. Then all that at first was blooming ripens and rots. So the year passes away into many yesterdays, and winter winds are returned, for which no man need wonder.

When the Michaelmas moon had come with its warnings of winter, Gawain bethought him of his wearisome journey. But he lingered with Arthur until All Souls' Day. And Arthur partook of that feast for the sake of his nephew amid all the rich revel of the Round Table, with knights full courteous and comely ladies. Yet all were in sorrow for the knight Gawain; but nevertheless they spoke of naught but mirth, although many who made there courtly play were joyless. For after the feast, Gawain sadly spoke to his uncle, and mentioned his departure, saying aloud: "Now, liege-lord of my life, I ask your leave. You know the matter of this affair; I need not tell you of the trouble. I am ready unconditionally for the blow; tomorrow I go to seek the man in green, as God will make him known to me." Then gathered together all the best in the castle: Ywain, and Erec, and full many another, Sir Dodinel le Sauvage, the Duke of Clarence, Lancelot, and Lionel, and Lucan the good, Sir Bors and Sir Bedivere, both mighty men, and many other honorable knights, with Mador de la Port. All this company of the court approached the king to counsel the knight, with care in their hearts. In that hall there was much secret grief pressing at their hearts that so worthy a knight as Gawain should go on that adventure, to endure a grievous blow and not be able to return it with his sword. But the knight kept good cheer and said: "Why should I shrink? What can a man do but try his fate, whether stern or pleasant?"

He dwelt there all that day, and arose in the morning and asked for his arms. They were all brought him. First a royal carpet was stretched over the floor, and great was the gold gear that glittered upon it. The valiant knight stepped thereon, and handled his steel. He was dressed in a doublet of precious silk from Tars, and then in a close hood of crafty design that was lined within with a bright-

69. **Michaelmas moon,** the moon which would come to the full about Michaelmas (September 29), hence the harvest moon. 85–90. **Ywain . . . Mador de la Port.** From the standpoint of Middle English romances, the most important of these are Lancelot, Lucan, Bors, and Bedivere. All but Lucan participated in the Quest of the Holy Grail.

Two knights fighting, from a North French sketchbook, c. 1400.

colored fur. Then they set steel shoes upon the knight's feet; his legs they lapped in steel with ornamented greaves and knee-pieces fastened thereto, brightly polished; about his knees they were riveted with knots of gold. Well-fitting cuisses closed with thongs firmly encased his stout and brawny thighs; then the woven corslet of bright steel rings sewn on a fair stuff they fitted upon the knight; and well-burnished braces on both his arms, with good and 10 gay elbow-pieces, and gloves of mail, and all the goodly gear that would help him in his time of trouble. Thus Gawain stood forth in rich coat-of-mail, his gold spurs proudly added, girt with a trusty brand, and a silk girdle about his waist.

When he was clad in arms, his war-harness was costly—the smallest latchet or loop gleamed of gold. And harnessed as he was, he heard mass celebrated, and made his offering at the high altar. Then he came to the king and his companions of the court, 20 took fairly his leave of lords and ladies; and they kissed him and escorted him forth, committing him to Christ. By that time Gringolet was ready, and girded with a saddle that gleamed full gay with its many gold hangings, richly studded anew for that adventure; the bridle was barred about and braced with bright gold thread; the adornment of the neck-piece and of the sweeping saddle-skirts, the crupper and coverture, all matched the saddle-bow; all were bordered with rich, red-gold buttons that glittered 30 and gleamed like the light of the sun. Then Gawain caught up his helmet and hastily kissed it; that helmet was stoutly braced and stuffed within. It towered high on his head, fastened behind with a light linen kerchief over the aventail, embroidered and bedecked with the best of gems and having a broad silken border and designs of birds; preening parrots, turtle-doves, and true-loves so closely interwoven as many a maiden in the town had wrought seven years in the making. The circle atop his

22. **Gringolet,** with Roland's Veillantif perhaps the most famous steed of medieval legendry. The French form Guingalet suggests that he was a white horse (from Welsh *gwen,* "white"). 34. **aventail,** the movable front of the helmet, sometimes called the "beaver."

helmet was of still greater cost; it was a device of 40 diamonds, that were both light and dark.

Then they showed him his shield, that was of bright red, with the pentangle painted thereon in pure gold color. He seized it by the baldric and cast it about his neck; it became the knight wondrous fair. And why the pentangle pertained to that noble knight I purpose to tell you, though it delay my story. It is a sign that Solomon set erewhile, as betokening truth; it has its name because it is a figure that has five points, and each line overlaps 50 and is locked in another; ever it is endless, and the English call it everywhere, so I have heard, "the endless knot." Therefore it was fitting for this knight and for his shining arms; for Gawain was known before God as faithful ever in five and many times five various ways, and as refined gold, void of every impurity, and adorned with all virtue in the assemblage. And so this fresh pentangle he bore on shield and coat, the knight truest of speech and noblest of form. 60

For first he was faultless in his five senses; and the knight had never failed in his five fingers; and all his faith on this earth was in the five wounds that Christ got on the Cross, as the creed tells. And wheresoever this knight was beset in conflict, his earnest thought was in this above all other things: that all his vigor he received from the five joys that the gracious Queen of Heaven had in her Child. For this reason the knight had in the greater part of his shield the image of Our Lady painted, so 70 that, when he looked upon it, his courage could never flag. The fifth five that I find Gawain used were frankness, and fellowship above all; in cleanness and courtesy he was never found wanting; nor in pity that surpasses everything—these virtues five were more firmly wrapped about the hero than about any other. All these, fivefold, forsooth, were linked together in this knight, and each but attached to the other; but they never ended; and were fixed at five points, which never failed. Nor did they ever 80 merge, neither were they ever sundered; everywhere, at all points, they were endless and without a beginning as well. Wherefore on his bright shield this knot was shaped, red-gold upon red; that is the pure pentangle; the people call it so by tradition. Now Sir Gawain was gaily armed; he caught up his lance, and gave them all good-day—he thought, forever.

43. **pentangle,** a five-pointed star, an ancient symbol believed to have the power to repel demons. 48. **Solomon set erewhile.** Solomon's seal consisted of a pentangle circumscribed by a circle. The symbol is still to be found in synagogues and in Freemasonry, which is supposed to have originated in the building of the Temple of Solomon. 67. **five joys.** The five joys of the Virgin Mary were usually considered to be the joys in the Annunciation, the Nativity, the Resurrection, the Ascension, and the Assumption, although the list varied slightly among medieval writers.

He smote his steed with the spurs and sprang on his way, so sternly that he struck fire from the stones. All that saw that seemly sight sighed in their hearts; all folk said truly to each other, in care for that comely knight: "By Christ, it is a pity, that thou, O knight, shouldst be lost, that art of such a pure life! To find his equal in the world, in faith, will not be easy. It would have been wiser to have acted more warily; yonder brave knight should have become a duke; a shining leader of men he is worthy to be, and would have been that more fittingly than cut to pieces or brought low by an elvish man with the pride of arrogance. Whoever knew a king to take such counsel as to put his knights to a venture as a Christmas jest!" Many were the warm tears that were shed when that seemly knight departed from the court that day. But he did not tarry; he went on his way swiftly over many a wild road, as I heard say in the book.

Now the knight was riding through the realm of Logres, Sir Gawain in a good cause, though it seemed to him no sport. Often he lay companionless, alone in the night, nor did he find there the fare that would have been pleasing to him. He had no comrade but his horse, over the woodlands and downs; and there was no one but God with whom he could take counsel. At length he drew full near to North Wales; he kept all the isles of Anglesey on his left and crossed over the fords by the foreland at Holyhead, until he finally passed into the wilderness of Wirral. There dwelt few who loved either God or good men in their hearts. But as Gawain went along, he kept asking folk that he met if they had heard any talk of a green knight anywhere about, or of the Green Chapel. All answered him nay; never in their lives had they seen any such man of such a green hue. Gawain took strange paths over many an impassable height; full often was his mood to change before he could find the Green Chapel.

Many a cliff he climbed over in strange countries; far away from his friends he rode along as a stranger. At every water-ford and stream that the knight passed he found a foe before him, and one so marvelous and so foul and fierce that it behooved Gawain to fight. It would be too tedious to tell the tenth part of all his adventures; so many wonders befell the knight on his journeyings. Sometimes he fought with dragons and with wolves; sometimes with wild men that lived in the stone cliffs; with bulls and bears, and sometimes with boars; with giants of the high moorlands who were wont to attack him. Had he not been doughty and stern and a servant of the Lord, doubtless he had been dead,

for he was often near to being slain. Yet the fighting troubled him not so much; the winter was worse, when cold clear water was shed from the clouds and froze ere it could fall upon the fallow earth. Nearly slain by the sleet he slept in his armor; on more nights than enow on bare rocks, where the cold brook rushed down bubbling from the hillcrest and hung high over his head in hard icicles. Thus in peril and pain and plights full hard, Gawain toiled over the countryside all alone, until Christmas Eve, and on that night he made his prayer to Mary, that she should guide him to some dwelling.

In the morning he rode merrily by a hill into a full deep forest that was fearsome and wild; high hills were on each side of it, and thick woods below them, huge hoary oaks a hundred or more. The hazel and the hawthorn stood there intertwined, with rough ragged moss trailing everywhere and many birds sitting unhappily upon bare twigs, piping piteously for pain of the cold. The knight rode beneath them on Gringolet through many a marsh and quagmire, alone and fearful lest he should not be able to perform the service of our Lord, who on that selfsame night was born of a maiden to allay all our woe. And sighing therefore he said: "I beseech Thee, Lord, and Thee, Mary, that is most mild and precious of mothers, that You grant me some lodging, that I may fittingly hear mass, and Your matins tomorrow. Meekly I ask it and thereto I pray my paternoster and creed." He rode praying and lamenting his misdeeds, blessing himself many times and saying: "May the cross of Christ speed me!"

He had not crossed himself, that knight, more than three times before he was aware of a dwelling in the wood, surrounded by a moat, above a lawn on a hill, enclosed by many a burly oak-tree that grew above the moat. There was a castle, the comeliest that lord ever possessed, built in a meadow with a park about it; a spiked palisade closely driven enclosed the trees for more than two miles. The knight saw the castle from one side, as its lights gleamed through the bright oaks. He seized hold of his helmet in joy, and uttered thanks to Jesus and Saint Julian (both are noble), who had courteously made known to him this abode and had hearkened to his prayer. "Now I beseech You yet," quoth the warrior, "that I may have good lodging!" Then he pricked Gringolet with his gilded heels; he

67. **deep forest . . .** From the direction taken by Gawain in his travels, it would appear that he traveled north or northwest. Wirral in Cheshire, near present Liverpool, was a forest as late as the sixteenth century. It is apparent that Gawain traveled for some time past Wirral; the older theory, therefore, that the castle of the lord and lady near the Green chapel was in Wirral has since been abandoned. It is more likely that the Green Knight lived in Cumberland, not far from Carlisle, where many stories of adventure about Arthur and his knights have collected. 98. **Saint Julian,** the patron saint of travelers and hospitality.

21. **Logres,** the term applied in Welsh legendry to England south of the river Humber. Since the knight's course is northerly, it is to be assumed that Camelot is in the southern portion of England.

rode casually up to the main gate, and came soon to the end of the bridge. The drawbridge had been raised, and the gates were shut fast. The walls were strong; no blast of wind need they fear.

The knight waited on the bank of the deep double ditch that surrounded the place. As he sat on his charger, he saw that the walls were set in the water wondrous deep; and the building towered aloft to a tremendous height. It was of hard hewn stone up to the corbels, which were adorned under the battlements with excellent taste; many fair watchtowers were placed in between with many well-made loopholes. Never had the knight seen a better barbican. Within he could see the high hall and the tower built with thick cornices; fair turrets marvelously high, with carved capitals, cunningly wrought. He could see chalk-white chimneys on the turreted roofs that shone full white. Many pinnacles were scattered everywhere among the battlements, so thick and white that they seemed to be cut out of paper. The noble knight on his steed thought it all fair enow; he wanted to gain the shelter within, to take lodging in that castle, until pleasant Holy-day had passed. He called, and straightway there came a kindly-faced porter, who stood on the wall, and asked the knight-errant in his greeting, what his errand might be.

"Good sir," said Gawain, "wilt thou take my message to the high lord of this house, and crave for me shelter?" "Yea, by Peter," quoth the porter, "truly, I think, O sir knight, you are welcome to stay here while it pleases you." Then the servant went quickly and with him many folk to receive the knight. They let down the great drawbridge, and came forth graciously, and knelt down upon the cold earth, to welcome Gawain as was fitting. They opened for him the broad gate; when it was ready, he bade them rise, and rode over the bridge. Many men held his saddle-horse while he dismounted; and bold men enow then stabled his steed. Knights and squires came down to bring the warrior with honor into the hall. When he raised up his helmet, there were many to take it from his hand and serve the gracious knight; his sword and his shield they also received. Then Gawain greeted full graciously each one of the retinue, and praised there many a proud man in order to honor their prince. In his noble armor they escorted him to the hall, where a fair fire on the hearth was briskly burning. Then the lord of the castle came down from his chambers to meet with ceremony the knight in the hall; he said, "You are welcome to do here as it pleases you. What is here is all your own, to have and wield at your will." "Gramercy," said Gawain, "may Christ it requite

you." As friends that were fain each one embraced the other.

Gawain gazed upon the lord that had greeted him in thus goodly fashion; and thought him a brave warrior who owned the castle—a mighty hero for the nonce, and of high age. Broad and shining was his beard and hued like a beaver; stern and stout was the stride of his stalwart legs. His face was as fierce as fire, but his speech was noble; and he seemed altogether able, so it seemed to Gawain, to be a lord and protector of full valiant men.

The lord led Gawain to a chamber and ordered a retinue to serve his guest in loyal manner. At his bidding came men enow to escort Gawain to a fair bower. There the bedding was royal; the curtains of clean silk and clear gold hems; the counterpanes comely and of fairly embroidered linen. These curtains were run on ropes with red-gold rings; there were tapestries of Toulouse and Tars hung on the walls and carpets underfoot of the same material. There, with many a merry speech, Gawain was relieved of his byrnie and of his bright armor, while alert servants brought him costly garments for him to wear, fair, radiant, and most choice. When he donned these clothes, he saw that they were seemly and fitted him well; the skirts of his mantle flowed gracefully. Truly that hero seemed to outtop all other knights in the fair complexion of his countenance, shining and radiant. It seemed to all that beheld him that Christ had never made a comelier knight. Whatever his origin, they thought that he must be a prince without peer in the field where brave men fight.

Before the fireplace, where a charcoal fire was burning, a chair was placed for Sir Gawain, accoutered with fair cushions and hassocks that were of subtle artistry; and then a simple mantle was offered the knight, of a brown samite, richly embroidered, and lined with skins of ermine, and a hood of the same stuff. So Gawain sat him down in that seemly regal chair and warmed himself first of all, and then his mood lightened. Straightway a table was raised up on trestles, covered with a clean cloth that shone clear white; and there were set on the table salt-cellar and napkin and silver spoons. The knight washed at his will and then sat down before his meat. Men enow served him appropriately with several sweet viands, seasoned well, double portions, as it happened, and several kinds of fishes— some baked in bread, some broiled on the fire, some boiled, some in sauce, savored with spices, with all kinds of subtle devices to please the knight's palate. Gawain called it a feast, full graciously and often, while all the retinue entertained him with gaiety, for they said: "Now take this penance, and it shall be for your amendment." The knight made much mirth of that, for the wine had gone to his head.

10. corbels, the cornice-moldings. 13. barbican, the outer fortification of a castle.

Then they questioned Gawain in most temperate fashion, with skilfully chosen questions put to the knight himself, so that he acknowledged in courteous wise the court whence he had come; that noble Arthur the gracious, who was the rich royal king of the Round Table, considered him one of his own knights; that it was Gawain himself who was sitting in that spot, come there on the Christmas, as chance would have it. When the lord heard that he was entertaining that knight, he laughed aloud; it seemed to him glad news indeed. And all the men in the place made great joy, to be able to appear ready in his presence, for all worth and prowess and pure customs pertained to Gawain's person, and he had ever been praised. Before all men on earth his virtue had been the greatest. Each man said softly to his comrade: "Now we shall see seemly manners and customs and the blameless terms of courtly talk; what charm lies in speech, we can learn without asking, for we have received in our midst the very father of courtesy. God has given us His goodly grace, forsooth, since He has granted us to have a goodly guest like Gawain, when men sit and sing with pleasure and joy of His birth. The true meaning of simple courtesy this knight will now bring us. I think that he who hears him will learn the subtle speech of love."

By that time the dinner was finished and Gawain had risen. It was near nightfall. Chaplains took their way to the chapel; the bells were rung loudly, even as they should be, for the devout evensong of Yule-tide. The lord went thither, and the lady also; she entered into a comely closet; Gawain gaily followed and straightway went thither. The lord caught him by the sleeve and led him to a seat and called him by his name, and told him he was the most welcome person in the world. Gawain thanked him truly, and each saluted the other and sat together in dignity during the time of the service. Then the lady was pleased to look upon the knight; she came forth from her closet with many a fair maiden. But she herself was the fairest of countenance and complexion, of figure and hue and all other charms—even more beautiful than Guinevere, as the knight thought. She passed through the chancel to greet Gawain the gracious; another lady held her by the left hand and was older than she—a dowager, it appeared, with many nobles about her. But the two ladies were unlike in looks; for if the younger was fair, the older was sallow. Rich red was the bloom on the cheeks of the one; rough wrinkled were the cheeks of the other. Kerchiefs with many a lucent pearl adorned the breast and bright throat of the one, and shone more dazzling than snow that falls on the hills. But the other wore on her neck a gorget, wimpling over her pale chin in milk-white folds; her forehead wrapped in silk worked in knots and bordered with trifling decorations. Only the black brows of the dowager were bare, and her two eyes and nose and naked lips—and these were all sour to see and strangely bleared, though one could fairly call her an honorable lady. Her body was short and thick; her buttocks round and broad; far more pleasing to gaze upon was she who walked beside her.

When Gawain saw that gay lady who looked so gracious, he walked towards her, with full permission of the lord. He greeted the elder, bowing full low; but he took the younger lightly in his arms and kissed her in seemly fashion, and spoke to her as became a knight. They hailed him as friend, and he quickly asked to be her servant in truth if it should please her. And so the two ladies escorted him, leading him, while talking, to the hall, before the hearth, and straightway called for spices, which men brought them without stint and right speedily, also good wine to be drunk at this season. The lord sprang to his feet and bade them make merry; he caught off his hood and hung it on a spear, and said he should win the worship thereof who could make most mirth on that Christmas-tide. "And I shall try, by my faith, to contend with the rest, with the help of my friends, before I lose all my raiment!" So with laughing words the lord bestirred him to gladden Sir Gawain that night with games in the hall, until it was time to bid them light the hall. Then Sir Gawain took leave of them and prepared for rest.

On the morrow, when every man calls to mind that Our Lord for our destiny was born to die, joy is breathed into every dwelling in the world for His sake—so it was there on that day amid many delights. Brave men on the dais were dressed in their best, and there was many a feast and many a cunningly cooked dish. The old dowager sat highest; the lord respectfully was seated beside her. Gawain and the gay lady were together, even in the midst of the board, as the feast was worthily served to each man according to his rank. There were meat and mirth and great joy; it would take me too long to speak thereof, and to describe it I could not though I might try. But I know that Gawain and the lovely lady found great pleasure in each other's company through her sweet words and courteous conversation, her gentle talk free from uncleanness, and her vivacious play charming and pure, fit for a prince. Trumpets and drums and merry piping sounded forth; each man hearkened to his minstrel; and they too hearkened to theirs.

High feast they held there that day and the next, and the third day that came in thereafter. The joy on St. John's Day was noble to hear; it was the last of the feast as the folk there intended. The guests

111. **St. John's Day,** December 27.

were to depart on the gray morning; and so they woke early and drank wine, and danced with vigor to the sound of carols. At last, when it was late, they took their leave, each one departing on his way— that was a brave lord! Gawain gave him good-day; the bold lord took him by the hand, and led him to his own chamber, beside the fireplace, and there he thanked him privately for the great honor that Gawain had bestowed upon him in coming to his
10 castle at that high season, and in adorning his home with his fair countenance. "Surely, sir, while I live, I shall be held the better because Gawain has been my guest at God's own feast." "Gramercy, sir," replied Gawain, "in good faith, all yours is the honor. May the High King grant it to you. I am a knight at your will, to do your behest, as I am beholden to you by rights in things both great and small." The lord then endeavored to keep the knight longer; but Gawain answered him that he could nowise tarry.
20   Then the lord asked him full fairly what stern mission had driven him, at that sacred feast, to depart all alone from his king's court so boldly, ere the holiday's holly had been carried from the town. "Forsooth, sir," quoth Gawain, "you say but the truth; it was a lofty mission and a pressing one that drove me from my home, for I myself am summoned to seek a certain place—I know not where in the world to find it. So help me the Lord, I would give all the land in Logres to find it before New Year's
30 Morn. Therefore, sir, I make this request of you here, that you tell me truly, if you ever heard tell of the Green Chapel or where it stands, or of the knight who keeps it, so green of color? There was established by agreement a compact between us; I must meet that man at that appointed place if I can do so; and of that same New Year there lacks little or no time. I would look on that knight, if God but let me, more gladly, by God's Son, than on any fair sight! Therefore, ywis, by your will, it
40 behooves me to go; I have now but barely three days for the business; I had liefer fall doomed than fail in my errand." Then the lord said, laughing: "Now indeed you must stay; for I shall show you that place by the appointed time, that Green Chapel forsooth. So grieve you no longer. You can take your ease, knight, in your bed till the fourth day; then you can ride on the first of the year and come to the appointed place at mid-morn, to do what you like at that time. Dwell here till New Year's Day;
50 then rise and ride thither. We shall set you on your way; it is not two miles hence."
    Then Gawain was full glad, and laughed merrily. "Now I thank you heartily for every thing. Now my quest is achieved; I shall linger here at your service,

39. **ywis,** certainly, indeed.

and do aught else you desire." Then the lord took him and set him beside him; he had the ladies fetched in to please them the better, though they had solace between themselves. The lord for his joy made merry jests, as a man who knew not what to do for his delight. Then he spoke to Gawain, crying 60 aloud: "You have decided to do what I bid you. Will you keep that promise here for the nonce?" "Yea, my lord, forsooth," said Gawain the true, "while I stay in your castle, I shall be obedient to your behests." "Now since you have traveled," said the lord, "from a far-off land, and then watched with me, you have not been refreshed either by rest or by sleep, as I truly perceive. You shall stay in your chamber and lie at your ease tomorrow at mass-tide, and go to meat when you will with my wife. 70 She shall sit with you and console you with her company. Tarry here until I return home; I shall rise early and go a-hunting." To all this Gawain agreed, keeping his word as a gracious man should.
    "Yet further," said the lord, "we shall make a covenant. Whatsoever I win in the wood, it shall be yours; and whatever fortune you achieve, give it to me in exchange. Good friend, let us so exchange, and swear it by oath, whether our fortunes, sir knight, be for better or for worse." "By God," 80 said Gawain the good, "I agree; and whatever it pleases you to propose; I shall do thy bidding." "Bring us the wine-cup; the bargain is made," said the lord of the castle. They laughed each one, they drank and made merry and passed the time of day until night, did these lords and ladies, as it pleased them. Then with gay talk and many a merry jest they arose and stood and spoke softly, kissed full sweetly, and took leave of each other. With many a graceful serving-man and gleaming torches, each 90 knight retired at last to his bed full soft. But before they went to bed they rehearsed the covenant, for the old lord of the castle knew well how to make sport.

III

VERY early before daybreak the folk rose up; the guests who would go called their grooms and made themselves quickly ready; they saddled their steeds and arranged the harness, set the girths in order, and packed up their bags. The knights dressed themselves and came forth arrayed for rid- 100 ing; they leaped lightly to horse, took up their bridles, and each man went on his way as he pleased. The noble lord of the land was not the last to prepare for riding, nor the many men with him. He ate a sop hastily, after he had heard mass. With a blast of the bugle he fared forth to the uplands. Before any daylight shone upon earth, he and his

retine were mounted on their lofty steeds. Then those huntsmen who knew the sport well coupled their hounds, unclosed the kennel-doors, and called them out. Three blasts were blown gaily on the bugle; the hounds bayed at the sound, and made a great racket; and those that were going on the hunt turned and chastised them—at least a hundred hunters, as I have been told. The trackers went to their stations and released the hounds; the forest re-
10 sounded again with their lusty blasts. . . .

[A description of the day-long hunt follows here.]

So the lord of the castle sported on the edge of the linden-woods. But Gawain the good knight lay in his fair bed, resting, till the daylight gleamed on the walls, under a coverlet radiant and closely be-curtained. And as he slipped into slumbering, he heard a soft little noise at his door. So he lifted his head out of the bedclothes and lifted a little the corner of the bedcurtains, and looked out warily to see what it might be. It was the lady, most lovely
20 to behold, that closed the door after her full softly and still, and moved towards the bed. The knight was ashamed and laid him down quickly, pretending to sleep. But she stepped quietly and stole up to his bed, cast up the curtain and crept within, seat-ing herself softly upon the bedside, and stayed there wondrous long, to see when he should awaken. A very long time the knight lay there and considered in his mind what this coming might amount to; he was in great wonder. But finally he said to himself:
30 "It would be more seemly if I asked her in words what she wants here." So he awoke and moved about, and turning towards her unlocked his eyelids, and pretended to marvel, crossing himself with his hand, as if to be safer in speech. The lady, sweet of chin and cheek, looked at him winsomely, her small lips smiling.

"Good morrow, Sir Gawain," said the fair lady, "you are a heavy sleeper, since one can enter hither. Now you are taken unawares, but lest you escape
40 us, I shall bind you in your bed, of that you may be sure." All laughing, the lady thus fell into jesting. "Good morrow, fair lady," said Gawain the blithe, "I will do your will, and that pleases me well. I will yield me promptly and beseech grace; and that will be best, I believe, for I needs must do so!" And so he joked in return with much happy laughter. "But would you, lovely lady, grant me leave; release your prisoner, and pray him to rise. I would get up from this bed and array myself. I should then have more
50 comfort to talk to you better." "Nay, forsooth, fair sir," said that sweet one, "you shall not rise from your bed; I shall direct you better. I shall keep you

8. **trackers,** keepers of the hounds.

here even longer, and then talk with my knight which I have captured. For I know well, of a surety, Sir Gawain the noble—whom all the world wor-ships, wheresoever you ride—your honor and cour-tesy have been graciously praised among lords and ladies and all that are alive. And now you are here, ywis, and we are alone. My lord and his men are far off; other servants in their beds, and my maidens
60 also; the door is drawn and fastened with a strong bolt. And since I have in this house him whom ev-eryone likes, I shall take good care of my time in speech, as long as it lasts. You are welcome to my body, at the wish of your will; it is proper for me, out of courtesy, to be your servant; so will I be."

"In good faith," quoth Gawain, "it seems unfitting for me—though I am not what you were speaking of—to attain to such an honor as you have just
70 mentioned. I am an unworthy man; I know it my-self. By God, I should be glad, if it seemed good to you, to please you with words or with service; verily, it would be pure joy!" "In good faith, Sir Gawain," quoth the fair lady, "the prowess and worth that pleases all other women—if I lacked it, or set it at naught, it were sad courtesy! But there are ladies enow that had liefer now hold a knight in their power, as I hold you here, to dally with the charm of your courteous words, to show them comfort and lighten their cares, than much of the treasure or gold
80 that they possess. But as I love that same Lord who rules the heavens, I have through His grace gotten wholly in my hands that which they all desire." She that was so fair of face made him good cheer; and he with modest speech answered all her sallies.

"Madam," said the happy knight, "Mary requite you, for I have found, in good faith, your frankness noble. Other folk have shown me much courtesy, in truth, but the honor that they have shown me for my poor deserts seems foolish; what is important is
90 the worship of yourself, who know naught but good." "By Mary," said the lady, "it seems to me otherwise; for were I worth all the riches of women alive, and had all the weal of the world in my power, and if I should bargain and choose to get me a lord, then, for the virtues that I have seen in you, Sir Gawain, of beauty, and mildness, and blithe sem-blance, or have heard of you and consider true—no man in the world would be chosen rather than you!" "Certes, my lady," replied Gawain, "you could have
100 chosen a better; but I am proud of the value that you put on me, and humbly as servant I acknowl-edge you my sovereign, and am become your knight. Christ requite you." So they talked of many things until mid-morn passed; and ever the lady made as if she loved him, and the knight was cautious and turned the talk aside. Though she were the most radiant of women, the one most in his mind, yet he

would show the less love in his bearing, because of the adventure that he sought so near at hand—the blow that must confound him and yet must needs be done. The lady then took her leave, and Sir Gawain straightway granted it.

She gave him good-day, and with a laughing glance; but as she stood before him, she astonished him with full stern words: "Now He that speeds fair speech reward you for this disport! But that you are Gawain I sorely mistrust!" "Wherefore?" asked the knight, and repeated the question, afraid lest he had failed somehow in his courtesy. But the lady blessed him, and spoke thus: "As good as Gawain is held among men, with courtesy so pure enclosed within him, he could not easily have tarried so long with a lady without asking a kiss out of courtesy, or some token or trifle at the end of the story." Then said Gawain: "Surely; let it be as you will; I shall kiss under orders, as befits a knight who fears lest he displease you. So ask it no more." She came near at those words, and caught him in her arms, bent down in her beauty and kissed the knight. Then they fairly commended each other to Christ; she went out of the door without any sound; and he hastened to rise forthwith. He called to his chamberlain and chose his garments and went forth, when he was ready, blithely to mass. Then he went to his meal that had been graciously kept for him, and made merry with mirth all day until the moon was rising. Never was a knight more fairly lodged; he sat between the two worthy ladies, the older and the younger; in merriment and comfort.

Meanwhile the lord of the castle was occupied with his sport, hunting in holt and heath and chasing the hinds. Such a number he slew, before the sun declined, of does and other deer, that it was a wonder. Then happily they returned in a group at last, and quickly made a quarry of all the killed deer. . . . Boldly they sounded the bugle that broke up the hunt; their hounds bayed. Then they took their trussed booty home, blowing stoutly many a stirring measure. Before daylight was done, the troop were all within the comely castle, where Gawain abode quietly. Amid the warmth of a kindled fire, the lord had come home, and Gawain met him with all the joy in the world.

Then the lord had all his retainers gathered together in the hall; and both the happy ladies joined them with their maidens. Before all that folk in the hall he had the venison brought in, and called to Gawain in jest and counted to him all the tails of the beasts and showed him the glistening fat shorn from the ribs. "How does this sport please you? Have I not won praise? Have I not earned hearty thanks for my craft in the hunt?" "Yea, assuredly,"

38. **quarry,** a collection of game slain during the hunt.

answered Gawain, "here is the fairest game that I have seen these seven years in the winter season." "And all I give to you, Gawain," said the lord, "for by the terms of our agreement you can claim it as your own." "That is true," said the knight, "I say the same to you, and this I have honorably won within these walls; and with as good will I yield it to you." So he clasped the lord's neck within his arms, and kissed him as courteously as he might. "Take here my booty; I gained no more. I vouchsafe it wholly, though it were greater than this." "It is good," quoth the fair lord, "gramercy therefore. So be it; but were it not better that you tell me where you won this booty, and if it were by your own wit?" "That was not our covenant," replied Gawain, "ask me no more; for you have taken what belongs to you; you can look for no more." They laughed and made them blithe and spoke low to each other; straightway they went to a supper of fresh dainties enow.

And later they sat by the hearth in the chamber. Men bore them excellent wine more than once. And still in their jesting they agreed on the morrow to carry out the same compact that they had made before; for chance might bring it about that their gains might be different; but what new things they won they would exchange when they met at night in the presence of the court—such was their covenant. The night-drink was served amid merriment; and in friendly wise they took leave of each other at last, and each knight prepared himself for bed. Scarcely had the cock crowed and cackled but thrice before the lord of the castle had left his bed and each of his followers. The meal was served and mass heard quickly; the retainers turned once more to the wood, to begin the hunt before day broke. Hunters and horns sounded forth as they passed over the meadows; the hounds uncoupled ran racing among the thorny brakes.

Straightway they struck a scent in a field; the huntsmen cheered on the hounds that had first come upon it; wild shouts were cast forth in a noisy din. The hounds heard it and hastened up and fell fast to the chase, forty at once. Then such a yelping clamor of packing hounds arose that the very rocks rang out; hunters urged them on with horn and mouth. All came together beside a pool in the woods, before a rugged crag; in a knot, by a cliff, at the side of a bluff. There rough boulders had tumbled in jagged heaps. The huntsmen fared to the finding and looked about them; the men surrounded the rocky crag, till they knew for certain that the beast they had uncovered with their bloodhounds was within their circle. Then they beat about the bushes and bade him spring up. Suddenly he rushed fiercely across the path of the men, a most marvelous boar. Long since he had grown old and departed from his herd. Surely he was the greatest of wild swine-kind; and every time he grunted, he caused trouble to many, for he thrust three to earth at the first rush, and then raced forth with great speed, without further injury. Then they hallooed loudly and cried out "Hay! Hay!" and put their horns to their mouth to blow the recheat. Great was the rout of men and of hounds that rushed with boast and noise after the boar to make the kill. Long he stood at bay, however, and maimed the pack of hounds pressing upon him, hurting them so badly that they most mournfully yowled and yelled.

The men then turned to shooting; they aimed their arrows at him and hit him often enow; but the arrow-heads were blunted by the strength of his shield-like hide, and the barbs would not bite on his brow, for the smooth shafts splintered in pieces, and the arrow-head fell back wherever it struck. But when the blows of their mighty strokes began to hurt him, then, mad from strife, he rushed upon the huntsmen once more, hurting them sorely wherever he attacked, so that many waxed fearful and drew back a little. But the lord on a swift horse darted after him; like the brave man he was, he swung over the meadow, blowing his horn. He recheated and rode through thick underbrush, ever pursuing this wild boar until the sun sank low.

All the day the huntsmen spent in this wise, while our gracious knight lay in his bed, Gawain the noble, at home in rich gear so fair of hue. The lady did not forget, but came in to greet him; full early she was at his side to cheer his mood.

She came to the curtain and looked at the knight. And Gawain welcomed her fittingly at that time, and she yielded him good morrow, with eager and ready words. Softly she sat down at his side, and laughed much, and with a lovesome look spoke to him thus: "Sir, if you be Gawain, it is a wonder to me—a man that is so turned to God and does not bother with the courtesies of companionship; and if one teaches you how to recognize these courtesies, you cast them forthwith from your mind. You have forgotten promptly what I showed you yesterday, by all the truest tokens of which I have knowledge." "What is that?" asked the knight. "I know, forsooth, nothing of all this; if what you say is true, the blame is all mine." "And yet I taught you of kissing," said the beautiful lady; "wherever a fair face is shown him, it becomes every knight quickly to claim courtly usage." "My dear," said the strong knight, "do away that speech, for that I dare not do, lest I be denied. If I were refused, surely I would be in the wrong if I still proffered a kiss." "My faith," said the sweet woman, "you cannot be denied; you are strong enough to force it with your strength, if it pleased you—if, perchance, any were so churlish as to deny you." "Yea, by God," said Gawain, "your speech is fair; but threats are not profitable in the land where I live; nor any gift that is not given with good will. I am at your command, to kiss you when you please; you may take them when you wish and leave them when it seems the best time." The lady then bent down and kissed his face in comely wise. Much talk they made there of the woes and charms of secret love.

"I would know from you, sir knight," said the noble lady, "if you will not be angry, what the reason may be that you, so young and so active, as you are at this moment, so courteous and so knightly, as you are known abroad, and choicest of all chivalry and most praised of all in the faithful joys of love and the science of arms—I know not. For to tell all the troubles of a true knight is the beginning, the title, and the text of all works: how ladies for their loyal loves have risked their very lives and endured for their loved one doleful hours; and how their lovers avenged them by their valor and eased all their care and brought bliss into the bower and raptures all their own. Now you are a knight, fairest of renown in your age; your words and your worship have gone everywhere. Yet I have sat by your side two separate times, and never have I heard you utter any words that pertained to love, small or great. And you, that are so courteous and careful of your promises, should be willing to show a young thing like me some token of true love's craft. Why are you so unlearned who have all men's praise? Is it that you deem me too foolish to listen to your teaching? For shame! I came hither single, and sit beside you to learn from you some skill; come, teach me of your knowledge while my lord is away."

"In good faith," replied Gawain, "God requite you! Good glee is a great thing; and a wondrous pleasure it is to me that such a beautiful one as you should come hither and bother yourself with so poor a man and pretend that he is your knight with such a sweet countenance; truly it brings me heart's ease! But to take the task upon myself to expound true love, to turn to the stories of love and tales of arms and relate them to you who, I know well, have more skill in the sweet art than a hundred such as I am or ever shall be on earth where I live—truly, my sweet, it would be manifold folly! I would gladly do your desires as best I can, as I am bound to do, and evermore I will be servant to you, so may God save me!" Thus she tried the knight and tempted him oft to have won him to wrong, whatever else her purpose. But he defended himself so well that no fault appeared and no evil on either side—naught but happiness and jest. They laughed and joked forsooth;

7. **recheat.** Originally the recheat was sounded to call back the hounds from a wrong scent, but later, as used here, to call them to the hunters or to urge them on.

at last she kissed him, that fair one, and then took her leave and went her way.

Then Gawain bestirred him and rose to mass; and then their dinner was prepared and richly served. The knight amused himself all day with the ladies. But the lord of the castle meanwhile rushed over the land in pursuit of the wild boar that went hurtling through the brush and biting the best of his hounds in two. Finally the beast stopped at bay; the bow-men caught up with him and made him, in spite of himself, take to flight again. Many an arrow flew through the air, when those folk gathered. But even the bravest of them the boar made to spring back, until at last he was so wearied that he could run no longer, but with all the haste possible, he hid in a hole in a mound by a rock where the brook ran by. He got the mound over his back and began to dig; the froth foamed at his mouth and dismayed the hunters. He gnashed his white tusks, while the bold hunters that stood near him all exhausted came on toward him. But none yet dared come too near him for fear of harm. He had hurt many before, which all thought was a pity; all the more they were afraid of him and his rending tusks; he was both coura-geous and frenzied.

But the lord of the castle came up and reined in his steed. Seeing the boar at bay and his men near by, he alighted and left his courser, snatched out his bright brand, and strode forth boldly. Quickly he stalked through the brook to where the fierce creature was standing. The wild beast caught sight of the man with the weapon in his hand. He set his bristles high and snorted so violently that many feared for the lord, lest the monster should crush him. The boar made a lunge at the man; and both knight and swine were thrown in a heap full in the water. But the boar had the worst of it, for the man took good aim when they first met, and plunged the sharp blade fair in the pit of the animal's stomach, driving it up to the hilt, so that the boar's heart was shivered, and snarling he gave up the ghost and was swept down to the water. A hundred hounds leaped upon him and chewed him famously; the hunters dragged him to the bank, and the dogs completed his death.

Then came a notable blowing of many a famous horn, the hallooing of huntsmen on the heights, the baying of the best of hounds, as their masters urged them on—those who were the chief hunters in that dangerous chase. Then a man who was wise in woodcraft began to flay the boar. First he hewed off the head and set it aloft and then rent the shaggy hide along the backbone, snatched out the entrails and burnt them in a fire, later rewarding his hounds with bread mixed therewith. Next he broke out the muscles from the bright broad flanks and removed the heart and lights, as was fit and proper. Then he bound the two sides of the beast all whole together and hung the carcass bravely on a stiff, strong pole. And then with this boar they came marching home; the boar's head was borne before the huntsman himself—he who had destroyed it in the brook, through the force of his hand so strong. It seemed long to that lord before he caught sight of Gawain in the hall; he called, and Gawain came towards him to receive his reward.

In jesting manner the lord laughed full loud and merry, when he saw Sir Gawain; with kind words he spoke to him. The good ladies were summoned, and the retinue gathered; he showed them the boar's flanks and told them the tale of its largeness and length and fierceness also, and of the fight the wild swine offered in the wood where he had fled. The other knight commended his deeds in comely wise and praised them as great feats and well proving his courage. For such a brawny beast, bold Gawain said, nor such flanks of a boar he had never seen before. Then they felt of the huge head, and the gracious knight praised it, and courteously spoke it so that the lord of the castle might hear. "Now, Ga-wain," quoth that good man, "this game is all yours, by a nice covenant and a firm, as you very well know." "That is true," said Gawain, "of a surety; all I have won I shall give back to you, by my troth." He took the lord about the neck and gave him gra-cious kisses, two of them. "Now we are even," said Gawain, "for this time, in all the covenants that we sealed by law, since I came hither." The lord said, "By Saint Giles; you are the best that I know; you will be rich in a short time if you drive such bar-gains!"

Then they set up the tables on trestles, cast cloths over them; a clear light shone over the walls, for men had set waxen torches whereby they might serve in the hall. Much noise and laughter rose up therein, about the fire and over the floor, in all manner wise. At the supper and after there were many lovely songs, lays of Christmas-tide and new carols, with all the mirth that a man could imagine. And ever our fair knight sat beside the lady; such a semblant of love she made to Gawain, with still demure coun-tenance to please that stalwart man, that Gawain was all wonder and wroth with himself. But he would not out of courtesy proffer her aught in re-turn, but treated her in all deference, howsoever she might try to twist the words awry. When they had played in the hall as long as it was their will, she called them all to the inner chamber; they turned to the hearth.

And there they drank and dallied and discoursed

98. lays of Christmas-tide, probably motets, or songs for many voices, sung while the priest was proceeding to the altar. It is from these medieval songs that the modern Christmas carol has been derived. The carols mentioned here were dancing-songs.

anew, conversing on a like covenant for the day of New Year's Eve. But Gawain craved leave to depart on the morrow, for it was near to term-time, when he should meet his appointment with the Green Knight. The lord forbade him to go and constrained him to linger and said, "As I am a truthful man, I swear by my troth, that thou shalt reach the Green Chapel and do thy task, sir knight, at the daybreak of the New Year, long before prime. So lie in thy
10 tower, and take thine ease; I shall hunt in the wood and keep the covenant to exchange with thee my winnings, such as I may bring back hither. For I have tried thee twice, and I find thee faithful; now tomorrow will be the third time and the best. Let us make merry while we can, and think of naught but joy. A man can always find misfortune when he so desires!" This Gawain agreed to in courtesy; therefore he tarried. Sweet drink was brought to him, and then they were all lighted to bed. Sir
20 Gawain lay and slept still and soft all night long; the lord of the castle kept to his woodcraft—full early he was all ready.

After mass he and his men had a morsel or two to eat. Fair was the morning, as he called for his mount. All the hunters on horse followed after him: fairly accoutered were their steeds before the hall-gates. Very fair shone the earth to which the frost still clung; all streaked with red the majestic sun rose on a rack of clouds; soft and clear were the
30 clouds in the heavens. The huntsmen scattered by the wood-side; the rocks beneath the boughs of hanging trees echoed to the voice of the hunting-horn. Some came upon the scent of the wily fox, carried often across the path, true to the beast's tricks. A hound cried out thereat; the hunter called to him; his fellows joined him, panting hard; they ran forth in a rabble, as was their habit. The fox flitted before them; they espied him straightway; and as they caught sight of him they followed him
40 fast, driving after him savagely with a horrid noise. And the fox tricked and turned through many a rough copse; crossed over and stopped to listen in hedge-rows. Finally he leaped a little ditch near one of those hedges and then stole forth quietly by a rugged path, thinking to escape by his wiles from the wood—and from the hounds. Then he came, ere he knew it, to a skilful tracker; indeed, three men at one rush pressed upon the gray little beast together. He drew back quickly and stoutly leaped
50 to one side; in the utmost anguish he turned back to the wood.

Then was it a pleasure indeed to listen to the hounds, when all the hunters had met together in counsel. Such a tumult they made when they caught sight of him once more, as if all the clustering cliffs had crashed down at once. Here the fox was hal-looed, when the huntsmen met him; loud was he

cried upon with snarling yells. Often was he threatened and called a thief, and ever there were hounds at his tail, so that he could not linger; often was he 60 run at, when he darted out of covert, and often forced back again. But Reynard was wily, and led them low and high, the lord and his huntsmen; now over the hills, now down, over, and under.

Meanwhile gracious Gawain at home slept most wholesomely, beneath comely coverlets on that cold morning. But the lady for love cared not to sleep, and thus spoil the purpose that was set in her heart. She rose up early, and hurried to Gawain, in a lovely mantle that reached to the ground, furred fine with 70 costly furs, well cared for. No gems wore she on her hair, but the precious stones were all bordering her head-dress, in clusters of twenty. Her beautiful face and her throat she showed all bare, and her breast bare, and her back as well. She came through the chamber door, and closed it after her. Opening a window, she called to Gawain, and thus readily greeted him with cheerful sweet words: "Ah, man, how canst thou sleep, on this morning so clear?" He was in a deep drowse; nevertheless he did hear her. 80

In a fierce fitful slumber that knight was disturbed, as a man often is in the morning from many bold thoughts. He was dreaming of the destiny that should next day prepare his fate at the Green Chapel, when he was to meet the Green Knight and must abide his buffet without further fight. But when comely Sir Gawain had recovered his wits and awakened from his dreams, he answered the lady in haste. She came towards him laughing in sweet loving manner, bent over his fair face, and featly 90 did kiss him. He welcomed her fondly, with fair good cheer. He saw her so glorious and beautifully attired, so faultless of feature, and so fine of complexion that welling joy warmed his heart. With gentle smiles they fell into mirthful speech, and all was bliss and gaiety and joy that passed between them. They uttered sweet words and exchanged much happiness. Truly, great peril was there for both of them, unless the knight was ware of it!

For the princely Gawain was so hard borne down; 100 so tense was his feeling, that it behooved him by need either to take her love on the spot or hatefully refuse it. He cared for his courtesy, lest he be deemed craven, and even more for his honor if he should sin and be a traitor to the lord of the castle. "God forbid!" said the knight, "that shall never happen!" With laughter in love, he turned aside all the special speeches that came from her mouth. Said the lady to the knight: "You should be blamed, if you do not love the life that lies next to you, above all the 110 creatures in the world wounded as she is in heart, unless you have a mistress or true-love that pleases you better, and unless you have pledged faith to that lady, fixed so firm that you will not loosen it. Indeed, that is what I believe. Now I pray you, tell me this truly. For all the love in the world, do not keep the truth a secret, out of guile." The knight replied, "By Saint John," and softly smiled. "In faith, I possess not such a one, nor will I possess one for a time."

"That," said the lady, "is the worst thing you could have said; but at least I have been answered, though it is a vexation to me. Now kiss me in courtly wise, and I shall go hence; I can but mourn and weep as a maiden who loves much." Sighing she bent down and gave him a seemly kiss; and then left his embrace and said as she stood beside him: "Now, dear, at our parting give me at least this comfort; yield me some sort of gift, thy glove mayhap, that I may remember the man and lessen my mourning." "Now truly," replied Gawain, "I would that I had here the most precious thing I owned, that I might give it you for your love. Forsooth, you have deserved far more reward, and rightly, than I could ever give. But alas, I would then be giving you a keepsake of a love that profitted little or nothing. Indeed, it would not be honorable to give you at this time my glove for a recompense, a glove of Gawain, as I am here on an errand the strangest in the world and have with me no retainers bearing bags brimful of precious things. That displeases me greatly, lady, at this time. But every man must fare as he is taken, even for sorrow or ill." "Nay, gracious knight of high honor," said that lovely lawn-clad lady, "though I have naught of yours, yet you shall have something of mine."

She caught up a rich ring worked in red gold with a staring gem standing out of it, that cast beams as dazzling as the bright sun; know ye well, it was of immense worth. But the knight refused it and said forthwith: "I will have no gifts even for good, fair lady, at this time. I have none to offer you, and I will take none." She prayed him eagerly to receive it, and he denied her prayer, and swore firmly by his truth that he would not take it. And she was grieved that he refused it and spoke thus: "If you refuse my ring because it seems to you too costly and you do not wish to be obligated to me, I shall at least give you my girdle that will be a lesser gift." She loosened a lace here and there, which encircled her waist, fastened at her side under the bright mantle. The girdle was of green silk and decorated with gold thread worked about by the fingers; this she offered to the knight and blithely besought him to take it though it were unworthy. But he denied that he would accept in any wise either gold or gift, before God sent him grace to achieve the adventure that he had undertaken there. "And so, I pray you, do not be displeased, and let the matter go, for I cannot at all grant your request. I am dearly beholden to you because of your beauty, and will ever be your true servant in hot and cold alike."

"Well, do you refuse this silken piece," then asked the lady, "because it is too simple, as it well seems? Indeed, it seems little, and therefore of less value. But whoever knew the virtues that are hidden therein would appraise it more highly, peradventure. For whatever man is wrapped in this green lace, while he has it tied about him, no hero under the heavens could hew him down; he could not be slain or struck to earth." Truly then Gawain thought, when he pondered in his heart, that it would be a jewel in the jeopardy which had been decreed him when he went to the Green Chapel to receive his blow; might he escape unslain, this were a noble stratagem! So he endured her chiding and suffered her to speak. She carried the girdle to him and offered it to him again. He accepted it, and she handed it over with a good will, and besought him for her sake never to reveal it, but to conceal it faithfully from the lord of the castle. The knight agreed that no wight should know it, for certain, but the two of them. He thanked her again and again, earnestly, with heart and mind. By that time the lady had kissed the gracious knight three times.

Then she took her leave and left him there, for she could not get more pleasure from the knight. When she had gone, Sir Gawain got him ready, rose, and arrayed himself in rich attire, caught up the love-lace which the lady had bestowed upon him, and hid it loyally where he might find it again. Then he took his way fairly to the chapel; there he privily approached a priest and prayed him to forgive his life and teach him better how his soul might be saved when he should go hence. There he was sweetly shriven and confessed his misdeeds both more and less, and besought mercy, and called on the priest for absolution. And he was assoiled in certainty and was made as pure as if Doomsday had been appointed for that morning. And after that he made merry among the noble ladies, with comely carols and all kinds of mirth (as he never had done but that one day with such bliss) even till dark night. Each man had great and marvelous respect for him there and said, of a truth, that he had never been thus joyful before that time, since he had come hither.

Now let Gawain linger in the castle where love had befallen him. But the lord was still abroad, leading his huntsmen. He had destroyed the fox that he had followed long. As he rushed over a spinney to catch sight of the rascal (for he heard the hounds hastening in that direction), Reynard came running through a bushy grove, and all the rabble of hounds in a rush at his heels. The knight saw the wild animal and bided his time, and snatched out his bright sword and struck at the beast. He shrank from the

106. spinney, a thorny hedge.

blow and tried to retreat, but a hound seized him before he could reach safety, and they all fell upon him right at the horse's feet and worried him to death with a horrid noise. The lord quickly alighted and caught the fox, raising him quickly out of the mouth of a dog, and holding him high aloft, hallooed loudly. Many a brave hound bayed in return; the hunters all hurried thither with many a horn, re-cheating aright till they caught sight of their lord. By that time his whole noble retinue had assembled; all that had bugles blew at one and the same time; and those that had no horns hallooed—it was the merriest meet that men ever heard, and the noisiest uproar that was lifted up in jest for Reynard's soul. The hounds had their reward; their heads were stroked and patted; and then they took Reynard and stripped off his coat.

So then they turned homeward, for it was nearly night, blowing most loudly on their mighty horns. The lord at last alighted at his beloved castle; he found fire on the hearth and the knight beside it, Sir Gawain the good, who was fain withal and was having much joy out of love for the ladies. He wore a robe of blue that reached to the earth; his surcoat fitted him well and was beautifully furred; and his hood of the same material hung down to his shoulders, blended with fine linen all about. He met the good lord in the middle of the floor and greeted him in all mirth and said fairly: "Now I shall be the first to fulfill our covenant which we made most happily when there was no lack of wine." So he embraced the lord of the castle and kissed him thrice, as carefully and soberly as he could. "By Christ," said the lord, "you had great fortune in the obtaining of this bargain, if the exchange be good!" "Yea, of the exchange no matter," said the other knight, "since what I owe has been openly paid." "Marry," quoth the lord, "mine is behind, for I have hunted all this day and have got naught but this foul fox-skin— the devil take it—for it is very poor to pay for such precious things as you have given me here—three such kisses so fair!" "Enough!" replied Sir Gawain, "I thank you, by the rood!" Then the lord told him, as they were standing there, how the fox was slain.

With mirth and minstrelsy and dainties at their will, with laughing of the ladies and jests along the board, they made as merry as any men could. Gawain and the good lord were both as high-spirited as if the band had gone mad or become over-drunk. Both the men and the retainers joked and jested until the time came when they should depart, when the knights must retire to their beds. Then Gawain the noble humbly took his leave of the lord and thanked him fairly: "For all this happy sojourn that I have had here at this high feast, may the great King repay your worship! I yield myself here as one of yours, if it so please you; now I must needs,

as you know, move on the morrow; and you will give me, as you promised, a man to show me the way to the Green Chapel, where God will suffer me to partake on New Year's Day of the destiny decreed me." "In good faith," said the noble lord, "with a good will; all that I ever promised you I shall ful-fill with good intent." So he assigned Gawain a serv-ant to set him on his way, and to lead him over the downs, that he might have no trouble in riding through the woods and passing most speedily through the groves. Gawain thanked the lord for the honor he had done him; then the knight took leave of the two noble ladies; with sorrow he kissed them and spoke to them and begged them to have his sincere thanks for everything. And they gave him back a like reply; they commended him to Christ with many cold sighs.

Then Gawain departed from the company in cour-tesy; each man that he met he thanked for his serv-ice and his comfort and his many little pains that he had made for Gawain's sake, to treat him well. And each man was as sorry to part from him as if he had dwelt in the castle forever. Then the servants led him with torches to his chamber and he happily laid down on the bed, to be at rest. Whether he slept soundly I dare not say, for he had much to think about on the morrow, if he would turn his thoughts thereto. Let him lie there still; he was near what he had sought. Now if you will be still a while, I shall tell you what happened.

IV

Now New Year's Day drew nigh, and the night passed; the day put the darkness to flight, as the Lord had commanded. But stormy weather awak-ened the world that day; clouds hurled sharp cold down on the earth, hard enow from the north for those who lacked clothing. The snow lay about in heaps and nipped the wild animals of the wood; the howling wind swooped down from on high and piled each valley full of great drifts. Gawain, ly-ing in bed, listened to the storm; though he closed his eyes, full little he had slept; he knew the voice of every cock that had crowed. Quickly he rose ere day broke, for there was light from a lamp that burned in his chamber. He called to his chamberlain, who speedily answered him, and bade him fetch his byrnie and saddle his steed. The chamberlain arose and brought the knight's armor, and got Gawain ready in knightly fashion. First he put on his clothes to protect him from the cold, and then his armor that was nobly cared for, his coat of mail and his hauberk, burnished and shining. The rust had been polished away from the ringed mail on his rich byrnie. All was as fresh as at first, and Gawain was fain to thank the chamberlain, for each piece of armor was wiped well and clean—it was the gayest armor from here to Greece. Gawain then called for his steed.

Meanwhile he cast upon himself the proudest garments; his coat with the badge of famous deeds, adorned with precious stones on velvet, the borders worked and embroidered and lined fairly with costly furs. Nor did he forget the girdle, the lady's gift; that, you may be sure, he did not leave behind, for the good it might do him. When he had belted his sword over his round and smooth waist, he wrapped the love-token doubly about him, closely and sweetly folded over his loins, a girdle of green silk that became him very well on the background of royal red cloth, that was gorgeous to behold. But the knight wore the girdle not for its value in treasure or for the glory of its pendants, although they were polished, and although glittering gold-thread gleamed brightly on the ends, but rather to save himself, when it was necessary for him to suffer, to await destruction without fighting back, to guard him against brand or knife. With that the hero, all ready, marched forth quickly, thanking full often the renowned retinue of the lord of the castle.

Then Gringolet the great and strong was ready; he had been lodged with care in a safe place; that proud horse was in good condition for his journey. The knight went up to him and looked on Gringolet's coat, and said soberly to himself, swearing by his truth: "There is a band in this castle that think upon honor; joy may they have, and the lord who maintains them; the dear lady, may love befall her all her life long. Since they for charity cherish a guest and hold honor in their hands, may the Lord, who holds the heavens on high, requite them and all of you! And if I might lead my life anywhere on earth, I would bring you full reward in truth if I could." Then he stepped to the stirrup and bestrode the horse; his servant handed him his shield, and he laid it on his shoulder. He struck Gringolet with his golden spurs, and the steed started to prance on the stones and abide still no longer. His servant was mounted on horse then, bearing Gawain's spear and lance. "This castle I commend to Christ; may He give it ever good chance!"

The drawbridge was let down and the broad gates unbarred and opened on both sides. The knight crossed himself and passed beyond the limits of the castle. He praised the porter, who knelt before the knight, and gave him good-day and commended him to God, that he should pray for Gawain. Then he went on his way, alone with his man, who should show him where to turn to come to that place of woe where he was to receive that rueful blow. They passed by banks and trees with bare boughs; they climbed along cliffs, where the cold clung fast. Naught fell from the heavens, but it was ugly un-

derfoot; mist hovered over the moorlands and dissolved on the mountains. Every hill wore a hat and a huge cloak of haze; the brooks boiled and foamed between their banks, dashed sparkling against the shores where they shelved downwards. Exceeding lonesome was the road as they passed through the wood, until it was the time when the sun should rise on that day of the New Year. They found themselves on a very high hill, covered over with the whitest of snow. The servant riding beside Gawain bade his master halt.

"Well, I have brought you hither, sir knight, this time; and now you are not far from that noted place that you have sought and inquired for so particularly. But I will tell you in truth, since I know you, and you are a knight in the world that I greatly love, that if you follow my counsel you would fare the better. The place to which you proceed is esteemed full perilous. There dwells a creature in that desolation, the worst on earth, for he is brave and stern and loves to strike, and he is greater in size than any man in the world, and his body bigger than those of the best four in Arthur's house or of Hector himself or of any other. He brings it to pass at the Green Chapel that no man can go by that place, be he never so proud in his arms, that this creature does not strike him dead with a blow from his hand. For he is a man without pity and practices no mercy; for be it churl or chaplain that ride by the Chapel, monk or mass-priest, or any other man, it is as pleasant for him to slay them as to pass alive himself. Therefore I say to you, as truly as you are sitting in that saddle, that if you go there, you will be killed. I can counsel you truly, knight, though you had twenty lives to spend. He has lived here full long, and has brought about much violence. Against his terrible blows you cannot defend yourself.

"Therefore, good Sir Gawain, let that man alone, and depart some other way, for the sake of Christ. Turn home by some other land, where Christ may speed you; and I shall hie me home again, and promise you, moreover, that I shall swear by God and all His good saints—so help me God and all the saints—oaths enow that I shall faithfully conceal it and never tell tale that you ever took to flight, for fear of the man I described to you."

"Gramercy," quoth Gawain, and said in ill humor, "Good fortune for the man who wishes me good; I believe well that thou wouldst conceal my shame loyally! But though thou didst keep my secret ever so truly, and I passed by here, and took to flight out of fear, in the manner you spoke of, I should be a

81. **Hector himself.** The manuscript reads *Hestor*, a reading which occurs in several French romances, but refers without doubt to the great Trojan hero, one of the Nine Worthies of the World.

coward knight and could never be forgiven. Therefore I will go on to the Chapel, whatever chance may befall, and tell that fellow there whatever tale I please, be it for weal or for woe, or as fate will be pleased to have it. Though he be a strong knave to control or rule by the rod, still the Lord knows full well how to save His servants."

"Marry," said the retainer, "since thou talkest so much and will take this danger upon thyself, and since it pleases thee to lose thy life, I shall not stop thee. Take here thy helmet on thy head and thy spear in thy hand, and ride down this very path by yonder rocks till thou hast come to the bottom of this rugged valley; then look about a little on thy left hand, and thou shalt see in a grove the very Chapel, and the burly warrior that guards it. Now farewell in God's name, noble Gawain; I would not go with thee for all the gold in the ground, nor bear thee fellowship further on foot through this woodland." With that the man in the wood turned his bridle, hit his horse over his heel as hard as he could, leapt quickly over the land, and left the knight there alone. "By God's self," quoth Gawain, "I shall neither wail nor groan aloud; I am full obedient to God's will, and I have committed myself to Him."

Then he spurred on Gringolet, and followed the path, which inclined down through the woods to the edge of a grove. He rode through the rough land right down to the valley, and then looked about him. It was wild country; he saw no sign of a resting-place anywhere about, nothing but towering banks on both sides and rough craggy rocks with jagged stones strewn about. The clouds seemed to him grazed by the cliffs. Then he halted, reining in his horse for the moment, and changed his gaze now and again, to find the Green Chapel. He saw no such Chapel in any direction, and it seemed strange to him. Then he saw as it were on a rise near by, a little round mound by a bank, near a stream—near the ford of a stream, indeed, that rushed past. The brook bubbled away as if it were boiling. The knight reined his steed and came to the mound, gracefully dismounted, and fastened the reins to a linden-branch and tied his noble horse likewise. Then he turned to the mound and walked about it, debating within himself what it might be. It had an opening in the end and on each side, and was overgrown everywhere with clumps of grass; it was all hollow within, as an old cave, or the crevice of an old crag. He could not tell what it was. "Ah," said the gentle knight, "can this be the Green Chapel? Here the devil may pray his matins at midnight!"

"Now truly," continued Gawain, "it is desolate here. This is an ugly oratory overgrown with herbs; indeed a fitting place for the man clad in green to perform his devotions in devil's worship. In my five wits I feel that it is the fiend that has appointed for me this meeting that he may destroy me here. This is a chapel of mischance, ill fortune befall it; it is the cursedest kirk that ever I came upon!" With his high helmet on his head and his lance in his hand, he wandered up the wall of the rude rocky dwelling. Then he heard from that hill, aloft in a towering rock beyond the brook and above the bank, a wondrous fierce noise. Lo! it echoed about the cliffs so loud that it seemed wild enough to cleave the rocks—as if one were grinding a scythe upon a grindstone. Lo! it whirred and grated like water on a mill-wheel; truly, it rumbled and rang out that it was terrible to hear. Then, "By God!" exclaimed Gawain, "that gear is being prepared, so I think, for the use of the warrior who is to meet me here according to our agreement. But let God do his will. Well, it helps me not a whit even though I lose my life. But no mere sound shall affright me."

Then the brave knight called aloud: "Who dwells in this place, let him hold discourse with me. For now brave Gawain has come hither; if any man would have anything of him now, let him get his business done now or never." "Stay," answered one on the bank above Gawain's head, "and thou shalt have all in haste that I promised thee." Yet for a while the loud noise went on with its jarring sound of whetting before the man appeared. Then he descended from a craggy boulder; he had come out of a cave in the rock, out of some obscure corner, and now stepped forth brandishing a wicked weapon—a Danish ax new burnished, with which to give a mighty blow. The powerful blade bent back in line with the handle; it had been freshly sharpened on a grindstone and was at least four feet wide, no less, and bound to the handle with thongs that shone bright. And the warrior in green was attired as at first as to complexion and limbs, locks, and beard, save that now he walked fair on the ground. He set the handle to the ground and stalked along. When he came to the brookside, he would not wade through, but vaulted over with the help of his ax, and strode along with vigor, fierce and angry in the snow-covered field that stretched far around them. Sir Gawain met the Green Knight without any kind of obeisance; the other said, "Now, fair sir, one may trust thee to keep an agreement."

"Gawain," said the Green Knight, "may God protect thee! Truly thou art welcome, knight, to my place; and thou hast timed thy travel as well as a true man could; and thou knowest the covenant drawn up between us: at this time twelvemonth thou wouldst take what befell thee; and I should

89. **Danish ax,** the long-bladed battle-ax without the spike at the end of the shaft, so called because it was a favorite weapon of the Norse Vikings.

on this New Year quickly repay thee. Now we are in this valley verily alone; here are no henchmen to separate us; we may meet as we please. Take thy helmet off thy head, and receive here thy reward; make no more talk now than I offered thee when thou didst strike off my head with one blow." "Nay, by God," replied Gawain, "who didst give me soul; I shall not murmur in ill-will for any mischief that shall be my lot; now settle thyself for the stroke, and I shall stand still and cast no refusal in thy teeth, but let thee do as thou wilt." He stretched forth his neck and bowed, showing his bright skin all bare, and made as if he did not fear, for he would not tremble out of dread.

Then the knight in green got him ready and gathered up the grim weapon to smite Gawain; with all the power in his body he lifted it on high with a mighty feint to slay him. Had the blow fallen as violently as he seemed to intend, Gawain would have been dead from the stroke, doughty as he may have been. But our bold knight caught a glimpse of that ax as it came swishing downward to destroy him there on the hill, and he flinched a little from that sharp iron, moving his shoulders slightly. The Green Knight let the blow swerve and withheld the ax, and then reproved Gawain with many haughty words: "Thou art not Gawain," said the warrior, "who is esteemed so good, who never waxed timid before any band on either hill or dale; and now thou dost shrink for fear before thou dost feel any hurt. Such cowardice I never knew in that knight. Nor did I shrink nor flee, sir knight, when thou didst swing thy stroke over me, nor did I cast any trifling objection in the way there in King Arthur's court. My head rolled at my feet, and yet I never fled. And thou, ere any harm has befallen thee, art fearful in heart; wherefore I ought to be called the better knight." Said Gawain then: "I flinched once, but I will not do so again; but if my head drops down on the stones, I shall not be able to restore it.

"But, sir knight, by thy faith, hasten and bring me to the point; deal out to me my destiny, and do it out of hand; for I will stand thee a stroke and start no more until thine ax has struck me. Here is my troth!" "Have at thee then," said the Green Knight, and heaved the ax aloft and looked as fierce and grim as if he were beside himself. He aimed a mighty blow, but did not cut Gawain; he held quickly his hand before the weapon could hurt him. Gawain bravely awaited it, and did not flinch in any part of him, but stood as still as a stone or rather the stock of a tree that is fixed in rocky ground with a hundred roots. Then the Green Knight spoke in merry tones: "So now that thou hast thy heart whole, it behooves me to hit. Hold up thy noble hood, that Arthur gave thee, and keep thy neck with this blow,

if perchance it survive!" But Gawain in full wrathful anger spoke thus: "Why smite further, thou fierce man; thou hast threatened too long. I believe that thine own heart has grown timid." "Forsooth," retorted the Green Knight, "so boldly thou hast spoken; I will no longer hold back thine adventure. Here it is right now!" So he spread his legs far apart to strike and frowned horribly with lips and brow; it was no marvel that it pleased him little who hoped for no rescue.

Lightly he lifted his ax and let it fall fair, with the cutting edge of the blade against the bare neck. But though he swung mightily, he hurt him no more than before, but nicked him slightly on the side, so that he broke the skin. The sharp blade bit through the flesh and the swelling muscle, so that the bright blood ran over his shoulders and dropped on the ground. And when the knight saw the blood flow on the snow, he sprang forth, swift of foot, more than a spear's length, quickly seized his helmet and set it on his head, threw the fair shield in front of his shoulders, snatched out his bright sword, and spoke fiercely (never since he had been born of his mother had he been so joyous): "Cease, knight, of thy blows; give me no more. I have received a blow in this place without combat; and if thou dost yield me any more, I shall readily repay you and yield you back still more forbidding blows; thou mayest be sure of that! But one stroke is my lot here; the covenant we shaped just so in Arthur's hall. Therefore, sir knight, halt!"

The Green Knight drew off and rested on his ax, setting the shaft on earth, and leaning against the blade. He looked at Sir Gawain, who was in a clearing, and saw how that doughty warrior stood there fearless, armed, and dangerous; in his heart he was pleased. Then in a loud voice he addressed Gawain gaily, and said to the knight in a mighty rumble: "Bold warrior, be not so wroth in the field; no man here has offered thee wrong, nor will do so, except according to the covenant drawn up at the king's court. I promised thee a stroke, and thou hast received it—consider thyself well paid. I release thee of all other claims. If I had been active, peradventure I could have dealt thee a buffet more harshly and have stirred thee to frenzy. First I menaced thee jestingly with a feigned blow, and did not rend thee with a gash or a wound which in justice I should offer thee according to the covenant that we bound on that first night, and that thou faithfully didst hold in keeping with thy faith and troth. All thy gains thou didst yield me, as a good man should. The second blow, sir knight, I gave thee for that morn. Thou didst kiss my lovely wife; those kisses thou didst give to me. For both those days I offered thee here but two more feints without harm to thee: true man, true return—he need fear no harm. But the third day thou didst fail me, and therefore hadst thou the real blow, though slight.

"For it is my weed that thou art wearing, that same woven girdle; my own wife wove it; I know it well forsooth. Now I know thy kisses, and thy virtues as well, and the wooing of my wife—I brought it all about. I sent her to try thee; in truth I think that thou art the most faultless knight that ever walked on earth. As a pearl among white peas is of more value than they, so is Gawain, in good faith, beside other knights. But yet thou wert lacking in a little, sir, and wert wanting in loyalty; but that was not for any base intrigue or lustful wooing, but because you loved your life. So I blame you the less." Gawain stood for a great while in silent thought, so grieved and angry he trembled within; all the blood from his breast poured into his face, and he shrank back for very shame at what the Green Knight had said. The first words that Gawain spoke were: "Cursed be cowardice and covetousness alike! In you both are villainy and vice that destroy virtue." Then he caught at the knot and loosened the twist and angrily hurled the belt at the Green Knight himself: "Lo! there is the breaking of faith, evil befall it! For fear of thy blow, cowardice taught me to be reconciled with covetousness, to forsake my own nature, which is the generosity and loyalty that pertain to knights. Now I am faulty and false and have been afraid from the beginning; from treachery and untruth come both sorrow and care! I acknowledge to thee once again, sir knight, I have done wrong. Do then thy will; hereafter I shall be more wary."

Then the Green Knight laughed and spoke in friendly manner: "I believe it is all whole now, the hurt that I had. Thou art so cleanly confessed and hast acknowledged thy sins and hast borne open penance through the edge of my weapon, that I esteem thee cleansed of that fault and pure and clean withal as if thou hadst never done ill since the time thou wast born. And I give thee, sir knight, this girdle all gold-hemmed; for it is green like my raiment, Sir Gawain. You can think upon this contest when thou goest forth among great princes of worth; it shall be a pure token of the adventure of the Green Chapel, as it befell among chivalrous knights. And in this New Year you shall come back to my castle, and we shall revel for the remnant of this high season in mirth and joy." And the Green Knight invited Gawain further and said: "We shall make peace between you and my wife, I ween, for she was your bitter enemy."

"Nay, forsooth," said Gawain, and seized his helmet and doffed it courteously as he thanked the Green Knight, "I have sojourned ill, but may bliss betide you, and may He that dispenses all honor reward you fittingly. Commend me to that noble lady, your comely wife, both to her and to that other lady,

both honored, who have thus cleverly beguiled their knight with their trick. But it is no wonder if a man be made a fool of and be brought to sorrow through the wiles of a woman. For so was Adam beguiled by one, and Solomon by a great many, and Samson also—Delilah dealt him his doom—and David thereafter was deluded by Bathsheba and suffered much woe. All these were brought to disaster by women's wiles; if a knight could love them well and believe them not, it were a great gain! And these were of old the noblest that lived for a time in all worldly prosperity, preëminent among all in the kingdoms of this earth, and all bemused by love, all beguiled by women with whom they had dealings. And so if I have now been deceived, I may well be excused.

"But as for your girdle," said Gawain, "God be with you! I will accept it with pleasure, not for the gain of the gold, nor for the silk or the samite, nor for the costly pendants, neither for weal nor for worship nor for pride of workmanship; but as a sign of my fault I shall often look upon it. When I ride in pomp, I shall see it as a rebuke to myself for the sin and faintness of crabbed flesh—how likely it is to entice to the desire for evil. And thus when pride shall spur me on in prowess of arms, the sight of this lovely girdle will humble my heart. But one thing I would ask of you, if it displease you not: since you are lord of yonder land, where I have dwelt with you in happiness (may the Lord who upholds the heavens and sits on the high throne ever keep it for you)—what, indeed, is your rightful name? Pray tell me, and I will ask no more." "That I shall truly," said the Green Knight. "I am called Bernlak de Hautdesert in this my home. Morgan le Fay dwells in my house, and through the power and knowledge of clerkly works, well learned in craft, she, the pupil of Merlin, has taken many. For she has long since been the paramour of the excellent magician Merlin, who knows all the knights in Arthur's court. Morgain the goddess is she called therefore; none has so great haughtiness of spirit that she cannot tame him.

"She sent me in this manner to your joyous hall, to test the pride, if there be pride, that comes from the great renown of the Round Table. She taught me this marvel to take away your wits and to grieve Guinevere and frighten her to death with the fear of the man who spoke in ghostly fashion before the high dais, with his head in his hand. That is she at my home, the dowager lady; she is even thine aunt, Arthur's half-sister, the daughter of the Duchess of Tintagel, on whom great Uther begat Arthur, who

96–97. **Morgain the goddess,** sister of Arthur, and an evil figure in Arthurian legend. Her hatred of Guenevere is due to the fact that Morgain had an affair which Guenevere discovered and made known. 107–108. **Duchess . . . Arthur.** Uther Pendragon had fallen in love with Ygerne, Duchess of Tintagel and wife of Gorlois. Gorlois died in battle, and, helped by Merlin, Uther visited Ygerne in the guise of her husband. The child of this union was Arthur.

now is so famous. Therefore I ask thee, sir knight, to come to thine aunt; make merry in my house; my retinue loves thee; and I myself, sir knight, by my faith, I wish thee as well as any man under Heaven, because of thy great devotion to faith." But Gawain shook his head in refusal; he would not return. They embraced and kissed and commended each other to the Prince of Paradise, and parted right there on the cold ground. Gawain on his fair steed turned away boldly to King Arthur's castle; and the knight in bright green turned whither he would.

Through many a wild path now rode Gawain on Gringolet—Gawain who had thus won grace of his life. Often he lodged in a house, and often outside, and had many adventures by the way and vanquished many men, things that I do not intend to recount in this tale. The wound in his neck healed; he bore the shining belt about him; the badge of his fault he wore as a baldric bound at his side, knotted under his left arm, in token of the fact that he had been found remiss; and so he came to Arthur's court, a knight strong and whole. Joy was lifted up in that castle when great Arthur knew that Gawain had come, for he deemed it gain. The king kissed the knight, and the queen also, and many another trusty knight who hurried up to greet him. They asked him of his adventure, and he told them all the wondrous happenings—the chance of the chapel, the actions of the Green Knight, the love of the lady, and last of all the girdle. He showed them the scar in his bare neck that he had won from the hands of the Green Knight as a reproach for his lack of loyalty. He suffered torment when he had to tell of that last adventure; he groaned aloud for very grief and shame; the blood rushed into his face in chagrin, but he told of his humiliation.

"Lo, my lords and ladies," said knight Gawain, and handled the girdle, "this is the bond of the blame that I bear on my neck; this is the offense and the loss that I have got for myself, the cowardice and the covetousness that I felt there; this is the token of my disloyalty, in which I was taken; and I must needs wear this as long as I live. For none can hide his fault, but some mishap will reveal it; for if it once has clung to thee, it will never be severed from thee." The king comforted Gawain, and all the court as well, laughing loudly at the whole story. With general accord the lords and the ladies who belonged to the Round Table agreed that each knight of the brotherhood should wear a baldric, a band of bright green as a badge, following Gawain's example. And with this was the renown of the Round Table

52–53. **Round Table in accord.** As suggested in the headnote above, *Sir Gawain and the Green Knight* may have been written in honor of the Knights of the Garter, though the Garter, so far as is known, never used a green collar or band as a badge. The decision of the Round Table here certainly suggests the founding of some order, but the evidence as to a particular one is so vague as to be unconvincing.

in accord; and he was honored ever after who wore the badge, as the best book of romance tells the tale.

Thus the adventure of Gawain and the Green Knight befell in Arthur's day, as the book of Brutus bears witness. For since Brutus, that brave knight, first came hither, after the siege and assault of Troy had ceased, forsooth,

> Many adventures herebefore
> Have fallen such as this;
> He that the crown of thorns once bore
> Now bring us to His bliss!
>
> AMEN.

Honi Soit Qui Mal Y Pense.

The Song of Roland

In the year 777 some Saracens of Spain, irked by what they considered their unrewarded fealty to the Caliph of Cordova, and impressed by the great power and liberality of the King of the Franks, later the Emperor of the Romans, came to Charlemagne at Paderborn and offered to transfer their allegiance to him. In order to make the best of the opportunity thus offered to spread his influence and the influence of Christianity south of the Pyrenees, Charlemagne in the next year (778), still a young man, advanced into Spain as far south as the river Ebro. His imperialistic aims satisfied for the time, he returned to France. On his way back through the Pyrenees, his rear guard was attacked and destroyed by a raiding force of Basque mountaineers, known in the old chronicles as Gascons. To quote the contemporary biographer of Charlemagne, one Einhard: "In the struggle that ensued, the Gascons cut them off to a man; they then plundered the baggage, and dispersed with all speed in every direction under the cover of approaching night . . . Eggihard, the King's steward; Anselm, Count Palatine; and Roland, Governor of the March of Brittany, with very many others, fell in this engagement. This ill turn could not be avenged for the nonce, because the enemy scattered so widely after carrying out their plan that not the least clue could be had to their whereabouts."

So much for history. But the inscrutable process of hero making has decreed that Eggihard and Anselm, who doubtless fought most valiantly, have been forgotten, whereas Roland has become a great epic champion. Perhaps the fact that he came from Brittany had something to do with the development; perhaps his personality was in any case more memorable; perhaps it was merely that he was blessed with more articulate friends and publicity agents. At any rate, Roland became in the following centuries the subject of more than one French epic lay, or *cantilene*. These epic lays were circulated in oral tradition, taking on with the passing of time various increments and elaborations from the mouths of successive bards, until they combined to give an extended account of the hero's progress. At this point the assembled lays about Roland were brought into an artistic whole by some interested individual, probably a cleric, who no doubt gave them literary embellishment and a more orderly arrangement than they had possessed while in oral tradition. The resulting epic poem now constituted a *chanson de geste*, a form of aristocratic narrative in verse which flourished during the ninth, tenth, and eleventh centuries in France and adjacent parts.

The Song of Roland, most celebrated of the *chansons de geste*, probably came into being in its present form during the latter half of the eleventh century. Tradition has it that the Norman Taillefer sang it at the Battle of Hastings in 1066; but whether this was the epic we now have, or some earlier form thereof, is not known. At any rate, reference is made in *The Song of Roland* to England's being subject to Charlemagne; while this was never historically true, it might have been suggested by the contemporary Norman Conquest of England by William, Duke of Normandy. The poem consistently refers to Jerusalem as being in heathen hands, whence the assumption that it was composed before the First Crusade established the Christian Kingdom of Jerusalem in 1099.

There is no question, however, about the significance of *The Song of Roland* as a national epic. Its glorification and idealization of "sweet France" can never leave the reader in doubt as to its patriotic viewpoint. Roland is in all respects a complete exemplar of the epic hero. He is physically overwhelming; courageous to the point of contempt for his adversary; intensely loyal to his comrades-at-arms, his king, his country, and his God; proud in his achievements past and present; jealous of the reputation of his great sphere of activity; a bulwark to all who need him in an emergency; a champion of champions. He has been exalted above everyone else in the poem. Charlemagne, also exalted, is nevertheless made vaguely glorious and venerable in a fictitious old age conferred upon him; his true radiance shines in his mighty *comitatus*, or knightly retinue: Roland, Oliver, the fighting Archbishop Turpin, and the Twelve Peers.

The general absence of any significant female characters or of any important love elements is remarkable; it stamps the poem as distinct from a medieval romance. Although Roland is affianced to Aude, Oliver's sister, she is a mere concession to feudal perpetuity and conveniently dies at once when she hears of Roland's demise. The society in *The Song of Roland* is military and feudal; the action is largely a series of personal encounters on the battlefield. The tone of the poem is that of aggressive, intolerant medieval Christianity; such chivalrousness as it possesses is directed only toward those who profess the Christian faith. Most noteworthy is, therefore, the formidable power of Archbishop Turpin of Rheims, who survives the disaster of Roncevals longer than any Frank except Roland himself. And Roland, be it observed, does not fall by the blows of Saracen warriors; he wounds himself mortally in blowing the ivory horn to summon aid from Charlemagne—something he should have done long before but which in his epic pride he postponed

until too late. Such is his tragic flaw, if flaw there must be in an epic hero. But his fame is secure; no other heroes of medieval epic or romance, with the exceptions of Lancelot, Gawain, and Siegfried, have had a more lasting international renown.

The Song of Roland

[Charlemagne has made himself master of all Spain, except for Saragossa, whose king, Marsila, vows vengeance upon the Franks. Marsila sends envoys to Charlemagne, ostensibly to sue for peace, but actually to give Marsila opportunity for a treacherous assault on the Franks. Charlemagne offers Marsila peace—the price being Marsila's conversion to Christianity. At the suggestion of the great champion Roland, Charlemagne sends his terms to Marsila by Count Ganelon, stepfather of Roland. Ganelon, envious of Roland and his select comrades, the Twelve Peers of Charlemagne, and feeling that he has been sent through Roland's machinations upon an unnecessarily dangerous mission, plots with Marsila to fall upon the rear guard of Charlemagne's army, commanded by Roland, while it is passing through the vale of Roncevals. The dire event is consummated; Roland and his group are attacked while Charles is too far forward to be of any immediate use.]

THEN Oliver goes up into a high mountain, and looks away to the right, all down a grassy valley, and sees the host of the heathen coming on, and he called to Roland, his comrade, saying: "From the side of Spain I see a great light coming, thousands of white hauberks and thousands of gleaming helms. They will fall upon our Franks with great wrath. Ganelon the felon has done this treason, and he it was adjudged us to the rear guard, before the Emperor." "Peace, Oliver," saith Count Roland, "he is my mother's husband, speak thou no ill of him."   10

Oliver has fared up the mountain, and from the summit thereof he sees all the kingdom of Spain and the great host of the Saracens. Wondrous is the shine of helmets studded with gold, of shields and broidered hauberks, of lances and gonfanons. The battles are without number, and no man may give count thereof, so great is the multitude. Oliver was all astonied at the sight; he got him down the hill as best he might, and came to the Franks, and gave   20 them his tidings.

"I have seen the paynims," said Oliver; "never was so great a multitude seen of living men. Those of the vanguard are upon a hundred thousand, all

The Song of Roland ▲ Translated by Isabella Butler. Reprinted by permission of and arrangement with Houghton Mifflin Company, the authorized publishers.
16. **gonfanons,** battle standards, sometimes known as gonfalons.

armed with shields and helmets, and clad in white hauberks; right straight are the shafts of their lances, and bright the points thereof. Such a battle we shall have as was never before seen of man. Ye lords of France, may God give you might! and stand ye firm that we be not overcome." "Foul fall him who flees!" then say the Franks, "for no peril of death will we fail thee."

"Great is the host of the heathen," saith Oliver, "and few is our fellowship. Roland, fair comrade, I pray thee sound thy horn of ivory that Charles may hear it and return again with all his host." "That were but folly," quoth Roland, "and thereby would I lose all fame in sweet France. Rather will I strike good blows and great with Durendal, that the blade thereof shall be blooded even unto the hilt. Woe worth the paynims that they come into the passes! I pledge thee my faith, short life shall be theirs."

"Roland, comrade, blow now thy horn of ivory, and Charles shall hear it, and bring hither his army again, and the King and his barons shall succor us." But Roland answers him, saying: "Now God forfend that through me my kinsman be brought to shame, or aught of dishonor befall fair France. But first I will lay on with Durendal, the good sword that is girded here at my side, and thou shalt see the blade thereof all reddened. Woe worth the paynims when they gathered their hosts! I pledge me they shall all be given over to death."

"Roland, comrade, blow thy horn of ivory, that Charles may hear it as he passes the mountains, and I pledge me the Franks will return hither again." But Roland saith: "Now God forfend it be said of any living man that I sounded my horn for dread of paynims. Nay, that reproach shall never fall upon my kindred. But when I am in the stour I will smite seven hundred blows, or mayhap a thousand, and thou shalt see the blade of Durendal all crimson. The Franks are goodly men, and they will lay on right valiantly, nor shall those of Spain have any surety from death."

Saith Oliver, "I see no shame herein. I have seen the Saracens of Spain; they cover the hills and the valleys, the heaths and the plains. Great are the hosts of this hostile folk, and ours is but a little fellowship." And Roland makes answer: "My desire is the greater thereby. May God and His most holy angels forfend that France should lose aught of worship through me. Liefer had I die than bring dishonor upon me. The Emperor loves us for dealing stout blows."

Roland is brave, and Oliver is wise; and both are good men of their hands; once armed and a-horse-back, rather would they die than flee the battle. Hardy are the Counts and high their speech. The felon paynims ride on in great wrath. Saith Oliver:

36. **stour**, the onset of battle.

"Roland, prithee look. They are close upon us, but Charles is afar off. Thou wouldst not deign to sound thy horn of ivory; but were the King here we should suffer no hurt. Look up towards the passes of Aspre and thou shalt see the woeful rear guard; they who are of it will do no more service henceforth." But Roland answers him: "Speak not so cowardly. Cursed be the heart that turns coward in the breast! Hold we the field, and ours be the buffets and the slaughter."

When Roland sees that the battle is close upon them, he waxes fiercer than lion or leopard. He calls to the Franks, and he saith to Oliver: "Comrade, friend, say not so. When the Emperor left us his Franks, he set apart such a twenty thousand of men that, certes, among them is no coward. For his liege lord a man ought to suffer all hardship, and endure great heat and great cold, and give both his blood and his body. Lay on with thy lance, and I will smite with Durendal, my good sword that the King gave me. If I die here, may he to whom it shall fall say, 'This was the sword of a goodly vassal.'"

Nigh at hand is Archbishop Turpin; he now spurs his horse to the crest of a knoll, and speaks to the Franks, and this is his sermon: "Lords, barons, Charles left us here, and it is a man's devoir to die for his King. Now help ye to uphold Christianity. Certes, ye shall have a battle, for here before you are the Saracens. Confess your sins and pray God's mercy, and that your souls may be saved I will absolve you. If ye are slain, ye will be holy martyrs, and ye shall have seats in the higher Paradise." The Franks light off their horses and kneel down, and the Archbishop blesses them, and for a penance bids them that they lay on with their swords.

The Franks get upon their feet, freed and absolved from sin; and the Archbishop blesses them in the name of God. Then they mounted their swift horses, and armed themselves after the manner of knights, and made them ready for battle. Count Roland calls to Oliver, saying: "Sir comrade, rightly thou saidst Ganelon hath betrayed us all, and hath received gold and silver and goods therefor; but the Emperor will well revenge us. King Marsila hath bought and sold us, but he shall pay for it with the sword."

Roland rides through the passes of Spain on Veillantif, his good horse and swift. He is clad in his harness; right well it becomes him, and as he rides he brandishes his spear, turning its point towards Heaven; and to its top is bound a gonfanon of pure

78. **Archbishop Turpin**, the reputed author of a history of the reign of Charlemagne. Turpin may have been the name of an authentic Frankish warrior confused with Tilpin, Archbishop of Rheims, who did not participate in the battle of Roncevals. 102. **Veillantif.** Compare Gawain and his great steed Gringolet. The celebrated swords named—Roland's Durendal, Oliver's Hauteclere, and Turpin's Almace—are also to be compared to the Arthurian Excalibur.

white, whereof the golden fringes fall down even unto his hands. Well fashioned is his body, and his face fair and laughing; close behind him rides his comrade; and all the Franks claim him as their champion. Full haughtily he looks on the Saracens, but gently and mildly on the Franks, and he speaks to them courteously, saying: "Lords, barons, ride on softly. The paynims come seeking destruction, and this day we shall have plunder so goodly and great

10 that no King of France hath ever taken any of so great price." At these words the two hosts come together.

Saith Oliver: "I have no mind for more words. Thou wouldst not deign to sound thy horn of ivory, and no help shalt thou get from Charles; naught he knows of our case, nor is the wrong his, the baron's. They who are beyond the mountains are no wise to blame. Now ride on with what might ye may. Lords, barons, hold ye the field! And in God's name I pray

20 you bethink you both how to deal good blows and how to take them. And let us not forget the device of our King." At these words all the Franks cried out together, and whosoever may have heard that cry of Montjoy must call to mind valor and worth. Then they rode forward—God! how proudly—spurring their horses for the more speed, and fell a-smiting—how else should they do? But no whit adread were the Saracens. And lo you! Franks and paynims come together in battle.

30 The nephew of Marsila, who was called Aelroth, rides before all his host, and foul are his words to our Franks: "Ye Frankish felons, today ye shall do battle with us. He who should have been your surety has betrayed you; mad is the King who left you behind in the passes. Today shall fair France lose her fame, and the right arm of Charles shall be smitten off from his body." When Roland hears this, God! how great is his wrath. He spurs as fast as his horse may run, and with all the might he hath he

40 smites Aelroth, and breaks his shield, and rends apart his hauberk, that he cleaves his breast and breaks the bone, and severs the spine from the back; with his lance he drives out the soul from the body, for so fierce is the blow that Aelroth wavers, and with all the force of his lance Roland hurls him from his horse dead, his neck broken in two parts. Yet Roland still chides him, saying: "Out, coward! Charles is not mad, nor loves he treason. He did well and knightly to leave us in the passes. Today

50 shall France lose naught of her fame. Franks, lay on! Ours is the first blow. Right is with us, and these swine are in the wrong."

Among the paynims is a Duke, Falsaron by name,

A French warrior of the Carolingian period.

who was brother to King Marsila, and held the land of Dathan and Abiram; there is no more shameless felon on all the earth; so wide is his forehead that the space between his eyes measures a full half foot. When he sees his nephew slain, he is full of dole, and he drives through the press as swift as he may, and cries aloud the paynim war-cry. Great is 60 his hatred of the Franks. "Today shall fair France lose her fame!" Oliver hears him and is passing wroth; with his golden spurs he pricks on his horse and rides upon him like a true baron; he breaks the shield, tears asunder the hauberk, and drives his lance into the body up to the flaps of his pennon, and with the might of his blow hurls him dead from the saddle. He looks to earth where lies the felon, and speaks him haughtily: "Coward, naught care I for thy threats. Lay on, Franks, certes, we shall over- 70 come them." And he cries out Montjoy, the war-cry of Charles.

A King there is, Corsablis by name; he is of Barbary, a far-off land, and he spoke to the Saracens, saying: "We shall win a fair day on these Franks, for few is their fellowship. And such as be here shall prove themselves of small avail, nor shall one be saved alive for Charles; the day has come whereon they must die." Archbishop Turpin hears him right well, and to no man under Heaven has he ever 80 borne such hate; with his spurs of fine gold he pricks on his horse, and rides upon the King with great might, cleaves his shield and rends his hauberk, and

24. **Montjoy.** The obscure etymology of this war cry is partially cleared up in the final section (Book III) of *The Song of Roland.* The word seems to be a corruption of "mon joie," an ungrammatical form of "ma joie"—"my joy."

55–58. **shameless felon . . . foot.** It is an old medieval belief that moral turpitude is reflected in a grotesque physical appearance. 58. **nephew.** It is a commonplace of the Western epic that the relationship of nephew to uncle is the closest possible tie, for fathers and sons might be hostile to one another.

thrusts his great lance into his body, and so drives home the blow that sorely the King wavers, and with all the force of his lance Turpin hurls him dead into the path. He looks on the ground where he sees the glutton lie, nor doth he withhold him from speech, but saith: "Coward and heathen, thou hast lied! Charles, my liege lord, is ever our surety, and our Franks have no mind to flee; and we shall have a care that thy comrades go not far hence; yea, and a second death must ye suffer, Lay on, ye Franks, let no man forget himself! This first blow is ours, thanks be to God." And he cries out Montjoy, to hold the field.

And Gerin smites Malprimis de Brigal, that his good shield no whit avails; he shatters the jewelled boss thereof, and half of it falls to earth; he pierces the hauberk to the flesh, and drives his good lance into the body; the paynim falls down in a heap, and his soul is carried away by Satan.

And Gerier, the comrade of Gerin, smites the Emir, and shatters his shield and unmails his hauberk, and thrusts his good lance into his heart; so great is the blow his lance drives through the body, and with all the force of the shaft he throws him to the ground dead. "Ours is a goodly battle," quoth Oliver.

Samson the Duke rides upon the Almaçur, and breaks his shield all flowered and set with gold, nor doth his good hauberk give him any surety, but Samson pierces him through heart and liver and lungs, and fells him dead, whether any one grieves for him or no. Saith the Archbishop, "That was knightly stricken."

And Anseis urges on his horse and encounters with Turgis of Tortosa, cleaves his shield below the golden boss, rends asunder his twofold hauberk, and sets the point of his good lance in his body, and thrusts so well that the iron passes sheer through him, that the might of the blow hurls him to the ground dead. "That was the buffet of a man of good prowess," saith Roland.

And Engelier, the Gascon of Bordeaux, spurs his horse, slackens his rein, and encounters with Escremis of Valtierra, breaks and carves the shield from his shoulder, rends apart the ventail of his hauberk, and smites him in his breast between his two collarbones, and with the might of the blow hurls him from the saddle, saying: "Ye are all given over to destruction."

And Oton smites the paynim Esturgant upon the leathern front of his shield, marring all the blue and white thereof, breaks through the sides of his hauberk, and drives his good spear and sharp into his body, and casts him from his swift horse, dead. "Naught may save thee," saith Oliver thereat.

27. **Almaçur,** an honorary title bestowed upon a Saracen chieftain, from the Arabic *al mansur,* "the victorious."

And Berengier rides on Estramaris, shatters his shield, rends asunder his hauberk, and drives his stout lance into his body, and smites him dead amid a thousand Saracens. Of the Twelve Peers ten are now slain and but two are still living men, to wit, Chernuble and Count Margaris.

Margaris is a right valiant knight, strong and goodly, swift and keen; he spurs his horse and rides on Oliver, breaks his shield below the boss of pure gold, that the lance passed along his side, but by God's help, it did not pierce the body; the shaft grazes him but doth not overthrow him, and Margaris drives on, in that he has no hindrance, and sounds his horn to call his men about him.

Now the battle waxes passing great on both sides. Count Roland spares himself no whit, but smites with his lance as long as the shaft holds, but by fifteen blows it is broken and lost; thereupon he draws out Durendal his good sword, all naked, spurs his horse and rides on Chernuble, breaks his helm whereon the carbuncles blaze, cleaves his mail-coif and the hair of his head so that the sword cuts through eyes and face, and the white hauberk of fine mail, and all the body to the fork of the legs, sheer into the saddle of beaten gold, nor did the sword stint till it had entered the horse and cleft the backbone, never staying for joint, that man and horse fell dead upon the thick grass. Thereupon Roland cried: "Coward, woe worth the day thou camest hither! no help shalt thou get from Mahmoud; nor by such swine as thou shalt today's battle be achieved."

Count Roland rides through the press; in his hand he hath Durendal, right good for hacking and hewing, and doth great damage upon the Saracens. Lo, how he hurls one dead upon another, and the bright blood flows out on the field. All reddened are his hauberk and his arms, and the neck and shoulders of his good horse. Nor doth Oliver hold back from the battle; the Twelve Peers do not shame themselves, and all the Franks smite and slay, that the paynims perish or fall swooning. Then saith the Archbishop, "Our barons do passing well," and he cries out Montjoy, the war-cry of Charles.

Oliver drives through the stour; his lance is broken and naught is left him but the truncheon; yet he smites the paynim Malsaron that his shield patterned with gold and flowers is broken, and his two eyes fly out from his head, and his brains fall at his feet; among seven hundred of his fellows Oliver smites him dead. Then he slew Turgin and Esturgus, and

60. **Twelve Peers,** here the Saracen champions; the French poet has evidently assigned the Saracen leader a *comitatus* of twelve nobles exactly similar to that which surrounded Charlemagne. The Twelve Peers of France are perhaps the most famous of the set *comitatus* groups in European legendry. 77. **mail-coif,** a skull-cap worn under the mail hood, which in turn lay beneath the helmet. 96. **Twelve Peers,** in this case clearly the twelve of France.

thereby broke his lance that it splintered even unto the pommel. Thereat Roland saith: "Comrade, what dost thou? I have no mind for a staff in so great battle, rather a man hath need of iron and steel. Where is thy sword Halteclere?" "I may not draw it," Oliver answered him. "So keen am I to smite."

But now the lord Oliver hath drawn his good sword, even as his comrade had besought him, and hath shown it to him in knightly wise; and therewith
10 he smites the paynim Justin de Val Ferrée that he severs his head in twain, cuts through his broidered hauberk and his body, through his good saddle set with gold, and severs the backbone of his steed, that man and horse fall dead on the field before him. Then said Roland: "Now I hold you as my brother, and 'tis for such buffets the Emperor loves us." And on all sides they cry out Montjoy.

Count Gerin rides his horse Sorel, and Gerier, his comrade, rides Passecerf; both slacken rein, and
20 spurring mightily set upon the paynim Timosel; one smites him on the shield, and the other on the hauberk, that both their lances break in his body; and he falls dead in the field. I wot not, nor have I ever heard man say, which of the twain was the more swift. Then Esperveris, son of Borel, died at the hand of Engelier of Bordeaux. And the Archbishop slew Siglorel, that enchanter who of old had passed down into Hell, led thither by the spells of Jupiter. "Of him we are well rid," quoth Turpin.
30 And Roland answered him: "Yea, the coward is overthrown. Oliver, my brother, such buffets please me right well."

Meantime the battle waxes passing hard, and both Franks and paynims deal such blows that it is wonder to see; here they smite, and there they make what defence they may; and many a lance is broken and reddened, and there is great rending of pennons and ensigns. Many a good Frank loses his youth, and will never again see wife or mother, or the men of
40 France who await him in the passes. Charles the Great weeps for them, and makes great sorrow; but what avails it? No help shall they get therefrom. An ill turn Ganelon did them the day he sold his own kindred in Saragossa. Thereafter he lost both life and limb therefor; in the council at Aix, he was condemned to hang, and with him upon thirty of his kindred to whom death left no hope.

Dread and sore is the battle. Roland and Oliver lay on valiantly, and the Archbishop deals more than
50 a thousand buffets, nor are the Twelve Peers backward, and all the Franks smite as a man. The paynims are slain by hundreds and thousands, whosoever

does not flee has no surety from death, but will he, nill he, must take his end. But the Franks lose their goodliest arms; lances adorned with gold, and trenchant spears, and gonfanons red and white and blue, and the blades of their good swords are broken, and thereto they lose many a valiant knight. Never again shall they see father or kindred, or Charles their liege lord who abides for them in the passes.   60

Meantime, in France, a wondrous tempest broke forth, a mighty storm of wind and lightning, with rain and hail out of all measure, and bolts of thunder that fell ever and again; and verily therewith came a quaking of the earth that ran through all the land from Saint Michael of the Peril, even unto Xanten, and from Besançon to the port of Guitsand; and there was not a dwelling whose walls were not rent asunder. And at noon fell a shadow of great darkness, nor was there any light save as the heavens   70
opened. They that saw these things were sore afraid, and many a one said: "This is the Day of Judgment, and the end of the world is at hand." But they were deceived, and knew not whereof they spoke; it was the great mourning for the death of Roland.

Meantime the Franks smote manfully and with good courage, and the paynims were slain by thousands and by multitudes; of a hundred thousand not two may survive. Then said the Archbishop: "Our Franks are of good prowess, no man under Heaven   80
hath better; it is written in the annals of France that valiant they are for our Emperor." And the Franks fare through the field seeking their fellows, and weeping from dole and pity for their kin, in all love and kindness. But even now King Marsila is upon them with his great host.

Count Roland is a knight of much worship, so likewise are Oliver and the Twelve Peers, and all the Franks are good warriors. By their great might they have made such slaughter of paynims that of a   90
hundred thousand only one hath escaped, Margaris, to wit. Blame him not that he fled, for in his body he bore the wounds of four lances. Back he fared in haste towards Spain, and came to Marsila and gave him tidings. And in a loud voice he cried: "Good King of Spain, now ride on with all speed, the Franks are weary and spent with the smiting and

53–54. **will he, nill he,** the modern "willy-nilly." 61. **Meantime, in France.** . . . The ensuing effective section is an illustration of the extremely common folklore motif which associates the passing of a hero with storm, earthquake, or some perturbation of nature. 66–67. **Saint Michael . . . Guitsand.** The monastery of Mont Saint Michel, off the coast of France at the boundary line of Brittany and Normandy, was founded in the ninth century as Saint Michael "in periculo maris," or "of the peril of the sea." Xanten, a town in the northeastern area of the French domain, in present Cleves, is not mentioned in some manuscripts, which give the reading Senz, a town not precisely identifiable. Besançon is an important city in extreme central eastern France of today. Guitsand, or Wissant, was a famous medieval Flemish port. 72–73. **"This is . . . hand."** It was a widespread belief in Western Christendom that the world was to come to an end in the year 1000.

28–29. **spells of Jupiter.** To the medieval Christian writer Jupiter was merely a pagan god, and that was enough to give him a claim on the Saracens' worship. 44–46. **Thereafter . . . to hang.** Actually, however, the later passages explain that Ganelon, having been arrested by Charles and his knights, was first humiliated and then executed by being torn to pieces by horses.

slaying of our Saracens; they have lost their lances and spears, and a good half of their men, and those who yet live are weakened, and the more part of them maimed and bleeding, nor have they more arms wherewith to help themselves."

Marsila comes on down the valley with the mighty host that he has assembled; full twenty battles the King has arrayed. There is a great shining of helmets, set with gold and precious stones, and of shields and of broidered hauberks. Trumpets to the number of seven thousand sound the onset, and the din thereof runs far and wide. Then saith Roland: "Oliver, comrade and brother, Ganelon the felon has sworn our death. The treason is manifest, and great vengeance shall the Emperor take therefor. The battle will be sore and great, such a one as was never before fought of man. I will smite with Durendal my sword, and do thou, comrade, lay on with Halteclere. Through many lands have we carried them, and with them have we conquered many a battle; no ill song must be sung of them."

When the Franks see how great is the multitude of the paynims, that on all sides they cover the field, they call upon Roland, and Oliver, and the Twelve Peers, that they may be their defence. Then the Archbishop tells them his mind, saying: "Lords, barons, put from you all cowardly thoughts; and in God's name I pray you give not back. Better it were that we die in battle than that men of worship should speak foully of us in their songs. Certain it is we shall straightway take our end, nor shall we from today be living men; yet there is a thing I can promise you, blessed Paradise shall be opened to you, and ye shall take your place among the innocent." At his words, the Franks take heart, and every man cries out Montjoy.

Wily and cunning is King Marsila, and he saith to the paynims: "Now set your trust in me; this Roland is of wondrous might, and he who would overcome him must strive his uttermost; in two encounters he will not be vanquished, methinks; and if not, we will give him three. Then Charles the King shall lose his glory, and shall see France fall into dishonor. Ten battles shall abide here with me, and the remaining ten shall set upon the Franks." Then to Grandonie he gave a broidered banner that it might be a sign unto the rest, and gave over to him the commandment.

King Marsila abides on the mountain, and Grandonie comes on down the valley. By three golden nails he has made fast his gonfanon; and he cries aloud: "Now ride on, ye barons!" And for the more goodly noise he bids them sound a thousand trumpets. Say the Franks: "God our Father, what shall we do? Woe worth the day we saw Count Ganelon! he hath sold us by foul treason. Now help us, ye Twelve Peers!" But the first to answer them is the Archbishop, saying: "Good knights, this day great honor shall be yours, for God will give you crowns and flowers in Paradise among the glorious; but therein the coward shall not enter." And the Franks make answer: "We will lay on as one man, and though we die we will not betray him." Then they spur on with their golden spurs to smite the miscreant felons.

Among the paynims is a Saracen of Saragossa; lord he is of half the city, and Climborin he hight; never will he flee from any living man. He it was who swore fellowship with Count Ganelon, kissed him in all friendship upon the lips, and gave him his helm and his carbuncle. And he hath sworn to bring the Great Land to shame, and to strip the Emperor of his crown. He rides his horse whom he calls Barbamusche, that is swifter than falcon or swallow; and slackening his rein, he spurs mightily, and rides upon Engelier of Gascony that neither shield nor byrnie may save him, but he drives the head of his lance into his body, thrusting so manfully that the point thereof passes through to the other side, and with all the might of his lance hurls him in the field dead. Thereafter he cries: "These folk are good to slay!" But the Franks say: "Alack, that so good a knight should take his end."

And Count Roland speaks to Oliver, saying: "Sir comrade, now is Engelier slain, nor have we any knight of more valor." And the Count answers him, saying: "Now God grant me to avenge him." He pricks on his horse with spurs of pure gold, and he grasps Halteclere—already is the blade thereof reddened—and with all his strength he smites the paynim; he drives the blow home that the Saracen falls; and the devils carry away his soul. Then Oliver slew Duke Alphaien, and cut off the head of Escababi, and unhorsed seven Arabs—never again shall they do battle. Then said Roland: "Wroth is my comrade, and now at my side he wins great worship; for such blows Charles holds us the more dear." And he cried aloud: "To battle, knights, to battle!"

Hard by is the paynim Valdabrun, that had stood godfather to King Marsila; on the sea he is lord of four hundred dromonds, and well honored of all shipmen. He it was who aforetime took Jerusalem by treason, violated the Temple of Solomon, and slew the Patriarch before the baptismal fonts. And he had sworn fellowship with Ganelon, and had given him a sword and a thousand mangons. He rides a horse called Gramimond, swifter than any

102. **dromonds,** large and swift sea-going galleys.   103–105. **He it was . . . fonts.** According to the chronicler Adhemar of Chabannes, Jews and Saracens in the year 1010 sacked the Church of the Holy Sepulchre in Jerusalem and killed the Patriarch. France of the militant eleventh century doubtless accepted this story. Actually, however, the raid was led by a fanatical Caliph, did not destroy the Church, and happened over two centuries after the battle of Roncevals.

falcon; he spurs him well with his sharp spurs, and rides upon Samson the mighty Duke, breaks his shield, and rends his hauberk, and drives the flaps of his gonfanon into his body, and with all the force of his lance, hurls him from the saddle dead. "Lay on, paynims, for hardily we shall overthrow them!" But the Franks say: "God, woe worth the good baron!"

When Roland sees that Samson is dead, ye may guess he is sore stricken; he spurs his horse and lets him run as fast as he may; in his hand he holds Durendal, of greater worth than is pure gold, and with all the might he hath, he smites the paynim on the helm set with gold and gems, and cuts through head and hauberk and body, and through the good saddle set with gold and jewels, deep into the back of the horse, and slays both him and his rider, whosoever has dole or joy thereof. Cry the paynims: "That was a woeful blow for us." Then quoth Roland: "No love have I for any one of you, for yours is the pride and the iniquity."

Among the paynims is an African, Malquiant, son of King Malcud; his armor is all of the beaten gold, and brighter than all the rest it shines to Heaven. His horse, which he calls Salt-Perdut, is so swift that he has not his fellow in any four-footed beast. And now Malquiant rode on Anseis, and smote him full on the shield that its scarlet and blue were hewn away, and he rent the sides of his hauberk, and drove his lance into his body, both point and shaft. Dead is the Count and done are his life-days. Thereat cry the Franks: "Alack for thee, good baron!"

Through the press rides Turpin the Archbishop —never did another priest say mass who did with his own strength so great deeds of arms—and he saith to the paynim: "Now may God bring all evil upon thee! for thou hast slain one for whom my heart is sore stricken." Then he set his good horse at a gallop, and smote Malquiant on his shield of Toledo, that he fell dead upon the green grass.

Hard by is the paynim Grandonie, son of Capuel, King of Cappadocia; he rides a horse called Marmorie, swifter than any bird that flies; he now slackens rein, and spurring well, thrusts mightily upon Gerin, breaks his crimson shield that it falls from his shoulder, and rends all asunder his hauberk, and thereafter drives all his blue gonfanon into his body that he falls dead beside a great rock. Then he slays Gerier, Gerin's comrade, and Berengier, and Guyon of Saint-Antonie; and thereafter he smote Austor, the mighty Duke that held Valence and the land along the Rhône, and felled him dead that the paynims had great joy thereof. But the Franks cry: "How many of ours are stricken."

Roland holds his ruddied sword in his hand; he has heard the Franks make lament, and so great is his sorrow that his heart is nigh to bursting, and he saith to the paynims: "Now may God bring all evil upon thee! Methinks thou shalt pay me dear for him thou hast slain." And he spurs his horse, which springs forward eagerly; and let whoso will pay the price, the two knights join battle.

Grandonie was a man of good prowess, of much valor and hardiness, and amid the way he encounters with Roland, and albeit before that time he had never set eyes upon him, he none the less knew him of a certainty by his look and countenance; and he could not but be sore adread at the sight, and fain would he have fled, but he could not. The Count smites him mightily, so that he rends all his helm down to the nasal, cleaves through nose and mouth and teeth, through the hauberk of fine mail, and all the body, splits the silver sides from off the golden saddle, and cuts deep into the back of the horse, that both he and the rider are slain beyond help. Thereat those of Spain make great lament, but the Franks cry: "That was well stricken of our captain."

Wondrous and fierce is the battle; the Franks lay on in their wrath and their might, that hands and sides and bones fall to earth, and garments are rent off to the very flesh, and the blood runs down to the green grass. The paynims cry: "We may not longer endure. May the curse of Mahmoud fall upon the Great Land, for its folk have not their fellows for hardiness." And there was not a man but cried out: "Marsila! haste, O King, for we are in sore need of thy help."

Wondrous and great is the battle. And still the Franks smite with their burnished lances. There is great dolor of folk, and many a man is slain and maimed and bleeding, and one lies on another, or on his back, or face down. The Saracens may not longer endure, but howsoever unwillingly they must give back. And eagerly the Franks pursue after them.

Marsila sees the slaughter of his people, and lets sound his horns and bussynes, and gets to horse with all his vassal host. In the foremost front rides the Saracen Abisme, the basest knight of his fellowship, all compact of evil and villainy. He believes not in God the son of Mary; and he is black as melted pitch. Dearer than all the gold of Galicia he loves treachery and murder, nor did any man ever see him laugh or take disport. But he is a good man of arms, and bold to rashness, wherefore he is well beloved of the felon King Marsila, and to him it is given to bear the Dragon, around which the paynims gather. The Archbishop hath small love for Abisme, and so soon as he sees him, he is all desirous to smite him, and quietly, within himself, he saith: "This Saracen seems a misbelieving felon; I had liefer die than not set upon him to slay him; never shall I love coward or cowardice."

97. bussynes, an old French trumpet.

Whereupon the Archbishop begins the battle. He rides the horse that he won from Grossaille, a King whom he slew in Denmark; the good steed is swift and keen, featly fashioned of foot, and flat of leg; short in the thigh and large of croupe, long of flank and high of back; his tail is white and yellow his mane, his head is the color of the fawn, and small are his ears; of all four-footed beasts none may outstrip him. The Archbishop spurs mightily, and will not fail to meet with Abisme and smite him on his shield, a very marvel, set with gems,—topaz and amethysts, and precious crystals, and blazing carbuncles; the gift it was of Galafré the Amiral, who had received it of a devil in Val-Metas. Now Turpin smites it and spares it not, so that after his buffet it has not the worth of a doit. And he pierces Abisme through the body, and hurls him dead in the open field. And the Franks say: "That was a good deed of arms; in the hands of our Archbishop safe is the crozier."

And Count Roland speaks to Oliver, saying: "Sir comrade, what say ye, is not the Archbishop a right good knight, that there is no better under Heaven? For well he knows how to smite with lance and spear." "Now let us aid him," the Count makes answer. And at these words the Franks go into battle again; great are the blows and grievous the slaughter, and great is the dolor of the Christians.

The Franks have lost much of their arms, yet still there are a good four hundred of naked swords, with which they smite and hew on shining helmets. God! how many a head is cleft in twain; and there is great rending of hauberks and unmailing of byrnies; and they smite off feet and hands and heads. The paynims cry: "These Franks sore mishandle us; whoso doth not defend himself hath no care for his life." King Marsila hears them make lament, and saith in his wrath: "Terra Major, now may Mahmoud destroy thee, for thy folk hath discomfited mine, and hath destroyed and spoiled me of many cities which Carles of the white beard now holds; he hath conquered Rome and Apulia and Calabria, Constantinople, and Saxony the wide, liefer had I die than flee before him. Paynims, now lay on that the Franks may have no surety. If Roland dies, Charles loses the life of his body; if he lives, we shall all take our end."

The felon paynims again smite with their lances upon shields and bright helmets; so great is the shock of iron and steel that the flame springs out towards Heaven; and lo, how the blood and brains run down! Great is the dolor and grief of Roland when he sees so many good knights take their end; he calls to remembrance the land of France, and his uncle, Charlemagne the good King, and he cannot help but be heavy.

Yet still he thrust through the press and did not leave from smiting. In his hand he held Durendal, his good sword, and rent hauberks, and broke helmets, and pierced hands and heads and trunks that he threw a hundred paynims to ground, they who had held themselves for good men of arms.

And on his side the lord Oliver drove forward, smiting great blows; in his hand he held Halteclere, his good and trusty sword that had not its fellow under Heaven, save only Durendal, and with it he fought valorously; all stained he was with blood even to his arms. "God!" saith Roland, "that is a goodly baron. O gentle Count, all courage and all loyalty, this day our friendship must have an end, for today, though great, woe we twain must part! Never again shall we see the Emperor; never again shall there be such lamentation in fair France. The Frankish folk will pray for us, and in holy churches orisons will be offered; certes, our souls will come into Paradise." Oliver slackens rein and spurs his horse, and in the thick of the press comes nigh unto Roland, and one saith unto the other: "Comrade, keep near me; so long as death spares me I will never fail thee."

Would ye had seen Roland and Oliver hack and hew with their swords, and the Archbishop smite with his lance! We can reckon those that fell by their hands, for the number thereof is written in charter and record; the Geste says more than four thousand. In four encounters all went well with the Franks, but the fifth was sore and grievous to them, for in this all their knights were slain save only sixty, spared by God's mercy. Before they die they will sell their lives dear.

When Count Roland is ware of the great slaughter of his men, he turns to Oliver, saying: "Sir comrade, as God may save thee, see how many a good man of arms lies on the ground; we may well have pity on sweet France, the fair, that must now be desolate of such barons. Ah, King and friend, would thou wert here! Oliver, my brother, what shall we do? How shall we send him tidings?" "Nay, I know not how to seek him," saith Oliver; "but liefer had I die than bring dishonor upon me."

Then saith Roland: "I will sound my horn of ivory, and Charles, as he passes the mountains, will hear it; and I pledge thee my faith the Franks will return again." Then saith Oliver: "Therein would be great shame for thee, and dishonor for all thy kindred, a reproach that would last all the days of their life. Thou wouldst not sound it when I bid thee, and now thou shalt not by my counsel. And if thou dost sound it, it will not be hardily, for now

16. doit, a penny.   38. Terra Major. The "Great Land," mentioned several times in the course of the poem, refers to Charlemagne's empire as a whole.

85. Geste; that is, the Latin chronicles.

both thy arms are stained with blood." "Yea," the Count answers him, "I have dealt some goodly blows."

Then saith Roland: "Sore is our battle; I will blow a blast, and Charles the King will hear it." "That would not be knightly," saith Oliver; "when I bid thee, comrade, thou didst disdain it. Had the King been here, we had not suffered this damage; but they who are afar off are free from all reproach. By this my beard, an I see again my sister, Aude the Fair, never shalt thou lie in her arms."

Then saith Roland: "Wherefore art thou wroth with me?" And Oliver answers him, saying: "Comrade, thou thyself art to blame. Wise courage is not madness, and measure is better than rashness. Through thy folly these Franks have come to their death; nevermore shall Charles the King have service at their hands. Hadst thou taken my counsel, my liege lord had been here, and this battle had been ended, and King Marsila had been taken or slain. Woe worth thy prowess, Roland! Henceforth Charles shall get no help of thee; never till God's Judgment Day shall there be such another man; but thou must die, and France shall be shamed thereby. And this day our loyal fellowship shall have an end; before this evening grievously shall we be parted."

The Archbishop, hearing them dispute together, spurs his horse with his spurs of pure gold, and comes unto them, and rebukes them, saying: "Sir Roland, and thou, Sir Oliver, in God's name I pray you, let be this strife. Little help shall we now have of thy horn; and yet it were better to sound it; if the King come, he will revenge us, and the paynims shall not go hence rejoicing. Our Franks will light off their horses, and find us dead and maimed, and they will lay us on biers, on the backs of sumpters, and will weep for us with dole and pity; and they will bury us in the courts of churches, that our bones may not be eaten by wolves and swine and dogs." "Sir, thou speakest well and truly," quoth Roland.

And therewith he sets his ivory horn to his lips, grasps it well and blows it with all the might he hath. High are the hills, and the sound echoes far, and for thirty full leagues they hear it resound. Charles and all his host hear it, and the King saith: "Our men are at battle." But Count Ganelon denies it, saying: "Had any other said so, we had deemed it great falsehood."

With dolor and pain, and in sore torment, Count Roland blows his horn of ivory, that the bright blood springs out of his mouth, and the temples of his brain are broken. Mighty is the blast of the horn, and Charles, passing the mountains, hears it; and Naymes hears it, and all the Franks listen and hear. Then saith the King: "I hear the horn of Roland; never would he sound it, an he were not at battle." But Ganelon answers him, saying: "Battle is there

none; thou art old and white and hoary, and thy words are those of a child. Well thou knowest the great pride of Roland—a marvel is it that God hath suffered it thus long. Aforetime he took Noples against thy commandment, and when the Saracens came out of the city and set upon Roland the good knight (he slew them with Durendal his sword), thereafter with water he washed away the blood which stained the meadow, that none might know of what he had done. And for a single hare he will blow his horn all day long; and now he but boasts among his fellows, for there is no folk on earth would dare do him battle. I prithee ride on. Why tarry we? The Great Land still lies far before us."

Count Roland's mouth has burst out a-bleeding, and the temples of his brain are broken. In dolor and pain he sounds his horn of ivory; but Charles hears it and the Franks hear it. Saith the King: "Long drawn is the blast of that horn." "Yea," Naymes answers, "for in sore need is the baron who blows it. Certes, our men are at battle; and he who now dissembles hath betrayed Roland. Take your arms and cry your war-cry, and succor the men of your house. Dost thou not hear Roland's call?"

The Emperor has commanded that his trumpets be sounded, and now the Franks light down from their horses and arm themselves with hauberks and helms and swords adorned with gold; fair are their shields, and goodly and great their lances, and their gonfanons are scarlet and white and blue. Then all the barons of the host get them to horse, and spur through the passes; and each saith to other: "An we may but see Roland a living man, we will strike good blows at his side." But what avails it? For they have abode too long.

Clear is the evening as was the day, and all their armor glistens in the sun, and there is great shining of hauberks, and helms, and shields painted with flowers, and lances, and gilded gonfanons. The Emperor rides on in wrath, and the Franks are full of care and foreboding; and not a man but weeps full sore and hath great fear for Roland. Then the King let take Count Ganelon, and gave him over to the cooks of his household; and he called Besgon their chief, saying: "Guard him well, as beseems a felon who hath betrayed my house." Besgon took him, and set a watch about him of a hundred of his fellows of the kitchen, both best and worst. They plucked out the hairs of Ganelon's beard and moustache, and each one dealt him four blows with his fist, and hardily they beat him with rods and staves; then they put about his neck a chain, and bound him even as they would a bear, and in derision they set him upon a sumpter. So they guard him until they return him unto Charles.

61. **Noples**, a good example of one of the unknown Spanish towns so often mentioned in *The Song of Roland*.

A Carolingian coin showing the head of Charlemagne.

High are the hills and great and dark, deep the valleys, and swift the waters. To answer Roland's horn all the trumpets are sounded, both rear and van. The Emperor rides on in wrath, and the Franks are full of care and foreboding; there is not a man but weepeth and maketh sore lament, praying to God that he spare Roland until they come unto the field, that at his side they may deal good blows. But what avails it? They have tarried too long, and may
10 not come in time.

Charles the King rides on in great wrath, and over his hauberk is spread his white beard. And all the barons of France spur mightily, not one but is full of wrath and grief that he is not with Roland the captain who is at battle with the Saracens of Spain. If he be wounded, what hope that one soul be left alive? God! what a sixty he still hath in his fellowship; no king or captain ever had better.

Roland looks abroad over hill and heath and sees
20 the great multitude of the Frankish dead, and he weeps for them as beseems a gentle knight, saying: "Lords and barons, now may God have mercy upon you, and grant Paradise to all your souls, that ye may rest among the blessed flowers. Man never saw better men of arms that ye were. Long and well, year in and year out, have ye served me, and many wide lands have ye won for the glory of Charles. Was it to such an end that he nourished you? O France, fair land, today art thou made
30 desolate by rude slaughter. Ye Frankish barons, I see you die through me, yet can I do naught to save you or defend you. May God, who knows no lie, aid you! Oliver, brother, I must not fail thee; yet I shall die of grief, an I be not slain by the sword. Sir comrade, let us get us into battle."

So Count Roland falls a-smiting again. He holds Durendal in his hand, and lays on right valiantly, so that he cleaves in twain Faldron de Pui, and slays four and twenty of the most worshipful of the
40 paynims. Never shall you see a man more desirous to revenge himself. And even as the hart flies before the hounds, so flee the heathen from before Roland. "Thou dost rightly," then said the Archbishop; "such valor well beseems a knight who bears arms and sits a good horse; in battle such a one should be fell and mighty, or he is not worth four deniers, and it behooves him to turn monk and get him into a monastery to pray the livelong day for our sins." And Roland answered him, saying: "Smite and spare not." And at these words the Franks go into
50 battle again; but great is the slaughter of the Christians.

That man who knows he shall get no mercy defends himself savagely in battle. Wherefore the Franks are fierce as lions. Marsila like a true baron sits his horse Gaignon; he spurs him well and rides on Bevon—lord he was of Beaune and Dijon—and breaks his shield, and rends his hauberk, that without other hurt he smites him dead to ground. And
60 thereafter he slew Ivon and Ivory, and with them Gerard the Old of Roussillon. Now nigh at hand is Count Roland, and he saith to the paynim: "May the Lord God bring thee to mishap! And because thou hast wrongfully slain my comrades, thou shalt thyself get a buffet before we twain dispart, and this day thou shalt learn the name of my sword." And therewith he rides upon him like a true baron, and smites off his right hand, and thereafter he takes off the head of Jurfaleu the Fair, the son of King Marsila. Thereat the paynims cry: "Now help us,
70 Mahound! O ye our gods, revenge us upon Charles! He has sent out against us into our marches men so fierce that though they die they will not give back." And one saith to another: "Let us fly." At these words a hundred thousand turn and flee, and let whosoever will call them, they will not return again.

King Marsila has lost his right hand; and now he throws his shield on earth, and pricks on his horse with his sharp spurs, and with slackened rein, flees away towards Spain. Upon twenty thousand Sara-
80 cens follow after him, nor is there one among them who is not maimed or hurt of body, and they say one to another; "The nephew of Charles has won the field."

But alack, what avails it? For though Marsila be fled, his uncle the Caliph yet abides, he who ruled Aferne, Carthage, Garmalie, and Ethiopia, a cursed land; under his lordship he has the black folk; great are their noses and large their ears, and they are with him to the number of fifty thousand. And now
90 they come up in pride and wrath, and cry aloud the war-cry of the paynims. Then saith Roland: "Now must we needs be slain, and well I know we have but a little space to live; but cursed be he who does not sell himself right dear. Lay on, lords, with your burnished swords, and debate both life and death; let not sweet France be brought to shame

46. **deniers**, pennies.

through us. When Charles, my liege lord, shall come into this field, he will see such slaughter of the Saracens, that he shall find fifteen of them dead over against each man of ours, and he will not fail to bless us."

When Roland sees the cursed folk whose skin is blacker than any ink, and who have naught of white about them save their teeth, he saith: "Now I know in very sooth that we shall die this day. Lay on, lords, and yet again I bid thee, smite." "Now foul fall him who lags behind," quoth Oliver. And at this word the Franks haste into the fray.

Now when the paynims see how few are the Franks, they have great pride and joy thereof; and one saith to another: "Certes, the Emperor is in the wrong." The Caliph bestrides a sorrel horse; he pricks him on with his spurs of gold, and smites Oliver from behind, amid the back, so that he drives the mails of his white hauberk into his body, and his lance passes out through his breast. "Now hast thou got a good buffet," quoth the Caliph. "On an ill day Charles the Great left thee in the passes; much wrong hath he done us, yet he shall not boast thereof, for on thee alone have I well revenged us."

Oliver feels that he is wounded unto death; in his hand he holds Halteclere; bright was its blade, and with it he smites the Caliph on his golden pointed helmet, that its flowers and gems fall to earth, and he cleaves the head even unto the teeth, and with the force of the blow smote him dead to earth, and said: "Foul fall thee, paynim! *Say not that I am come to my death through Charles;* and neither to thy wife, nor any other dame, shalt thou ever boast in the land from which thou art come, that thou hast taken from me so much as one farthing's worth, or hast done any hurt to me or to others." And thereafter he called to Roland for succor.

Oliver feels that he is wounded unto death; never will he have his fill of vengeance. In the thick of the press he smites valiantly, cleaving lances and embossed shields, and feet and hands and flanks and shoulders. Whoever saw him thus dismember the Saracens, and hurl one dead upon another, must call to mind true valiance; nor did he forget the war-cry of Charles, but loud and clear he cries out Montjoy! And he calls to Roland, his friend and peer: "Sir comrade, come stand thou beside me. In great dolor shall we twain soon be disparted."

Roland looks Oliver in the face; pale it is and livid and all discolored; the bright blood flows down from amid his body and falls in streams to the ground. "God!" saith the Count, "now I know not what to do. Sir comrade, woe worth thy valor! Never shall the world see again a man of thy might. Alas, fair France, today art thou stripped of goodly vassals, and fallen and undone. The Emperor will suffer great loss thereby." And so speaking he swoons upon his horse.

Lo! Roland has swooned as he sits his horse, and Oliver is wounded unto death; so much has he bled that his sight is darkened, and he can no longer distinguish any living man whether far off or near at hand; and now, as he meets his comrade, he smites him upon the helm set with gold and gems, and cleaves it down to the nasal, but does not come unto the head. At the blow Roland looks up at him, and asks him full softly and gently: "Comrade, dost thou this wittingly? I am Roland, who so loves thee. Never yet hast thou mistrusted me." Then saith Oliver: "Now I hear thee speak, but I cannot see thee; may the Lord God guard thee. I have struck thee, but I pray thy pardon." "Thou hast done me no hurt," Roland answers him; "I pardon thee before God, as here and now." So speaking each leans forward towards other, and lo! in such friendship they are disparted.

Oliver feels the anguish of death come upon him; his two eyes turn in his head; and his hearing goes from him, and all sight. He lights down from his horse and lies upon the ground, and again and again he confesses his sins; he holds out his clasped hands towards Heaven and prays God that He grant him Paradise, and he blesses Charles and sweet France, and Roland, his comrade, above all men. Then his heart fails him, and his head sinks upon his breast, and he lies stretched at all his length upon the ground. Dead is the Count and gone from hence. Roland weeps for him and is sore troubled; never on the earth shall ye see a man so sorrowful.

When Count Roland sees his friend lie prone and dead, facing the East, gently he begins to lament him: "Sir comrade, woe worth thy hardiness! We twain have held together for years and days; never didst thou me wrong or I thee. Since thou art dead, alack that I yet live." So speaking, the Count swoons as he sits Veillantif his steed, but his golden spurs hold him firm, and let him go where he will, he cannot fall.

So soon as Roland comes to his senses, and is restored from his swoon, he is ware of the great slaughter about him. Slain are the Franks; he has lost them all save only Gualter del Hum and the Archbishop. Gualter has come down from the mountains where he fought hardily with those of Spain; the paynims conquered, and his men are slain, and howsoever unwillingly, he must perforce flee down into the valley and call upon Roland for succor. "O gentle Count, brave captain, where art thou? For where thou art, I have no fear. It is I, Gualter, who conquered Maelgut, I the nephew of Droon the old, the hoary, I whom thou wert wont to love for my hardihood. Now my shield is pierced, and the shaft of my lance is broken, and my hauberk rent and unmailed; I have the wounds of eight lances in my body, and I must die, but dear have I sold myself."

So he saith, and Roland hears him, and spurs his horse and rides towards him.

"Sir Gualter," then saith Roland, "thou hast, as I know, done battle with the paynims, and thou art a hardy and valiant warrior. A thousand good knights thou didst take with thee; my men they were, and now I would ask them of thee again; give them over to me, for sore is my need." But Gualter makes answer: "Never again shall ye see one of them alive. I left them on the dolorous field. We encountered a great host of Saracens, Turks and Armenians, Persians, and men of Canaan and of Lude, warriors of the best, mounted on swift Arabian horses. And we fought a battle so fierce that never a paynim shall boast thereof; sixty thousand lie dead and bleeding; and we, on our part, lost all our Franks, but vengeance we took therefor with our swords of steel. Rent and torn is my hauberk, and deadly wounds I have in side and flank, and from all my body flows out the bright blood, and takes from me my strength; certes, my time is nigh spent. Thy man am I, and I look to thee as protector. Blame me not, that I fled." "Nay, I blame thee no whit," quoth Count Roland. "But now do thou aid me, so long as thou art a living man."

Full sorrowful is Roland and of great wrath; he falls a-smiting in the thick of the press, and of those of Spain he cast twenty to the ground dead, and Gualter slew six, and the Archbishop five. Then say the paynims: "Fierce and fell are these men. Take ye heed, lords, that they go not hence alive. He who doth not set upon them is traitor, and recreant he who lets them go hence." Then the hue and cry begins again, and from all sides they close about the three Franks.

Count Roland is a full noble warrior, and a right good knight is Gualter del Hum; the Archbishop is of good valor and well tried; not one would leave aught to his fellows, and together, in the thick of the press, they smite the paynims. A thousand Saracens get them to foot, and there are still forty thousand on horseback, yet in sooth they dare not come nigh unto the three, but they hurl upon them lances and spears, arrows and darts and sharp javelins. In the first storm they slew Gualter, and sundered the shield of Turpin of Rheims, broke his helmet and wounded him in his head, and rent and tore his hauberk that he was pierced in the body by four spears; and his horse was slain under him. The Archbishop falls; great is the pity thereof.

But so soon as Turpin of Rheims finds himself beaten down to earth with the wounds of four lances in his body, he right speedily gets him afoot again; he looks toward Roland, and hastes to him, and saith: "I am nowise vanquished; no good vassal yields him so long as he is a living man." And he draws Almace, his sword of brown steel, and in the thick of the press he deals well more than a thousand buffets. Afterwards Charles bore witness that Turpin spared himself no whit, for around him they found four hundred dead, some wounded, some cut in twain amid the body, and some whose heads had been smitten off; so saith the Geste and he who was on the field, the valiant Saint Gilles, for whom God wrought miracles; he it was who wrote the annals of the monastery of Laon. And he who knows not this, knows naught of the matter.

Count Roland fights right nobly, but all his body is a-sweat and burning hot, and in his head he hath great pain and torment, for when he sounded his horn, he rent his temples. But he would fain know that Charles were coming, and he takes his horn of ivory, and feebly he sounds it. The Emperor stops to listen: "Lords," he saith, "now has great woe come upon us; this day shall we lose Roland my nephew; I wot from the blast of his horn that he is nigh to death. Let him who would reach the field ride fast. Now sound ye all the trumpets of the host." Then they blew sixty thousand, so loud that the mountains resound and the valleys give answer. The paynims hear them and have no will to laugh, but one saith to another; "We shall have ado with Charles anon."

Say the paynims: "The Emperor is returning; we hear the trumpets of France; if Charles come hither, we shall suffer sore loss. Yet if Roland live, our war will begin again, and we shall lose Spain our land." Then four hundred, armed in their helmets, and of the best of those on the field, gather together, and on Roland they make onset fierce and sore. Now is the Count hard bestead.

When Count Roland sees them draw near he waxes hardy and fierce and terrible; never will he yield as long as he is a living man. He sits his horse Veillantif, and spurs him well with his spurs of fine gold, and rides into the stour upon them all; and at his side is Archbishop Turpin. And the Saracens say one to another: "Now save yourselves, friends. We have heard the trumpets of France; Charles the mighty King is returning."

Count Roland never loved the cowardly, or the proud, or the wicked, or any knight who was not a good vassal, and now he calls to Archbishop Turpin, saying: "Lord! thou art on foot and I am a-horseback, for thy love I would make halt, and together we will take the good and the ill; I will not leave thee for any living man; the blows of Almace and of Durendal shall give back this assault to the paynims." Then saith the Archbishop: "A traitor is he who doth not smite; Charles is returning, and well will he revenge us."

64–66. **the valiant Saint Gilles . . . Laon.** Saint Giles (Aegidius) was not mentioned in the chronicles as present with Charlemagne's army as it came upon the battlefield of Roncevals; perhaps the poet meant that Saint Giles was present in spirit only.

"In an evil hour," say the paynims, "were we born; woeful is the day that has dawned for us! We have lost our lords and our peers. Charles the valiant cometh hither again with his great host; we hear the clear trumpets of those of France, and great is the noise of their cry of Montjoy. Count Roland is of such might he cannot be vanquished by any mortal man. Let us hurl our missiles upon him, and then leave him." Even so they did; and cast upon him many a dart and javelin, and spears and lances and feathered arrows. They broke and rent the shield of Roland, tore open and unmailed his hauberk, but did not pierce his body; but Veillantif was wounded in thirty places, and fell from under the Count, dead. Then the paynims flee, and leave him; Count Roland is left alone and on foot.

The paynims flee in anger and wrath, and in all haste they fare toward Spain. Count Roland did not pursue after them, for he has lost his steed Veillantif, and whether he will or no, is left on foot. He went to the help of Archbishop Turpin, and unlaced his golden helm from his head, and took off his white hauberk of fine mail, and he tore his tunic into strips and with the pieces bound his great wounds. Then he gathers him in his arms, and lays him down full softly upon the green grass, and gently he beseeches him: "O gracious baron, I pray thy leave. Our comrades whom we so loved are slain, and it is not meet to leave them thus. I would go seek and find them, and range them before thee." "Go and return again," quoth the Archbishop. "Thank God, this field is thine and mine."

Roland turns away and fares on alone through the field; he searches the valleys and the hills; and there he found Ivon and Ivory, and Gerier his comrade, and he found Engelier the Gascon, and Berengier, and Oton, and he found Anseis and Samson, and Gerard the Old of Rousillon. One by one he hath taken up the barons, and hath come with them unto the Archbishop, and places them in rank before him. The Archbishop cannot help but weep; he raises his hand and gives them benediction, and thereafter saith: "Alas for you, lords! May God the Glorious receive your souls, and bring them into Paradise among the blessed flowers. And now my own death torments me sore; never again shall I see the great Emperor."

Again Roland turned away to search the field; and when he found Oliver his comrade, he gathered him close against his breast, and as best he might returned again unto the Archbishop, and laid his comrade upon a shield beside the others; and the Archbishop absolved and blessed him. Then their sorrow and pity broke forth again, and Roland saith: "Oliver, fair comrade, thou wert son of the great Duke Reinier, who held the marches of Rivier and Genoa; for the breaking of lances or the piercing of shields, for vanquishing and affrighting the proud, for upholding and counselling the good, never in any land was there a better knight."

When Roland sees the peers, and Oliver whom he so loved, lying dead, pity takes him and he begins to weep; and his face is all discolored; so great is his grief he cannot stand upright, but will he, nill he, falls to the ground in a swoon. Saith the Archbishop: "Alack for thee, good baron!"

When the Archbishop sees Roland swoon, he has such dole as he has never known before. He stretches out his hand and takes the horn of ivory, for in Roncevals there is a swift streamlet, and he would go to it to bring of its water to Roland. Slowly and falteringly he sets forth, but so weak is he that he cannot walk; his strength has gone from him; too much blood has he lost, and before a man might cross an acre his heart faileth, and he falls forward upon his face, and the anguish of death comes upon him.

When Count Roland recovers from his swoon, he gets upon his feet with great torment; he looks up and he looks down, and beyond his comrades, on the green grass, he sees that goodly baron, the Archbishop, appointed of God in His stead. Turpin saith his *mea culpa*, and looks up, and stretches out his two hands towards Heaven, and prays God that He may grant him Paradise. And so he dies, the warrior of Charles. Long had he waged strong war against the paynims, both by his mighty battling and his goodly sermons. May God grant him His holy benison.

Count Roland sees the Archbishop upon the ground; his bowels have fallen out of his body, and his brains are oozing out of his forehead; Roland takes his fair, white hands and crosses them upon his breast between his two collar-bones; and lifting up his voice, he mourns for him, after the manner of his people: "Ah, gentle man, knight of high parentage, now I commend thee to the heavenly Glory; never will there be a man who shall serve Him more willingly; never since the day of the apostles hath there been such a prophet to uphold the law, and win the hearts of men; may thy soul suffer no dole or torment, but may the doors of Paradise be opened to thee."

Now Roland feels that death is near him, and his brains flow out at his ears; he prays to the Lord God for his peers, that He will receive them, and he prays to the Angel Gabriel for himself. That he may be free from all reproach, he takes his horn of ivory in the one hand, and Durendal, his sword, in the other, and farther than a cross-bow can cast an arrow, through a cornfield he goeth on towards Spain. At the crest of a hill, beneath two fair trees, are four stairs of marble; there he falls down on the green grass in a swoon, for death is close upon him.

High are the hills, and very tall are the trees; the four stones are of shining marble; and there Count Roland swoons upon the green grass. Meantime a Saracen is watching him; he has stained his face and his body with blood, and feigning death, he lies still among his fellows; but now he springs to his feet and hastens forward. Fair he was, and strong, and of good courage; and in his pride he breaks out into mighty wrath, and seizes upon Roland, both him and his arms, and he cries: "Now is the nephew of Charles overthrown. This his sword will I carry into Arabia." But at his touch the Count recovered his senses.

Roland feels that his sword hath been taken from him; he opens his eyes, and saith: "Certes, thou art not one of our men." He holds his horn of ivory, which he never lets out of his grasp, and he smites the Saracen upon the helm, which was studded with gold and gems, and he breaks steel and head and bones, so that his two eyes start out, and he falls down dead at his feet. Then saith Roland: "Coward, what made thee so bold as to lay hands upon me, whether right or wrong? No man shall hear it but shall hold thee a fool. Now is my horn of ivory broken in the bell, and its gold and its crystals have fallen."

Now Roland feels that his sight is gone from him. With much striving he gets upon his feet; the color has gone from his face; before him lies a brown stone, and in his sorrow and wrath he smites ten blows upon it. The sword grates upon the rock, but neither breaks nor splinters; and the Count saith: "Holy Mary, help me now! Ah, Durendal, alas for your goodness! *Now am I near to death, and have no more need of you.* Many a fight in the field have I won with you; many a wide land have I conquered with you, lands now ruled by Charles with the white beard. May the man who would flee before another never possess you. For many a day have you been held by a right good lord; never will there be such another in France the free."

Roland smote upon the block of *hard stone,* and the steel grates, but neither breaks nor splinters. And when he sees that he can in nowise break it, he laments, saying: "O Durendal, how fair and bright thou art, in the sunlight how thou flashest and shinest! Charles was once in the Valley of Moriane, when God commanded him by one of His angels that he should give thee to a chieftain Count; then the great and noble King girded thee upon me; and with thee I won for him Anjou and Bretagne, and I conquered Poitou and Maine for him, and for him I conquered Normandy the free, and Provence, and Aquitaine; and Lombardy, and all of Romagna; and I conquered for him Bavaria, and Flanders, and Bulgaria, and all of Poland; Constantinople, which now pays him fealty, and Saxony, where he may

work his will. And I conquered for him Wales, and Scotland, and Ireland, and England, which he holds as his demesne. Many lands and countries have I won with thee, lands which Charles of the white beard rules. And now am I heavy of heart because of this my sword; rather would I die than that it should fall into the hands of the paynims. Lord God our Father, let not this shame fall upon France."

And again Roland smote upon the brown stone, and beyond all telling shattered it; the sword grates, but springs back again into the air and is neither dinted nor broken. And when the Count sees that he may in nowise break it, he laments, saying: "O Durendal, how fair and holy a thing thou art! In thy golden hilt is many a relic—a tooth of Saint Peter, and some of the blood of Saint Basil, and hairs from the head of my lord, Saint Denis, and a bit of the raiment of the Virgin Mary. It is not meet that thou fall into the hands of the paynims; only Christians should wield thee. May no coward ever possess thee! Many wide lands have I conquered with thee, lands which Charles of the white beard rules; and thereby is the Emperor great and mighty."

Now Roland feels that death has come upon him, and that it creeps down from his head to his heart. In all haste he fares under a pine tree, and hath cast himself down upon his face on the green grass. Under him he laid his sword and his horn of ivory; and he turned his face toward the paynim folk, for he would that Charles and all his men should say that the gentle Count had died a conqueror. Speedily and full often he confesses his sins, and in atonement he offers his glove to God.

Roland lies on a high peak looking towards Spain; he feels that his time is spent, and with one hand he beats upon his breast: "O God, I have sinned; forgive me through Thy might the wrongs, both great and small, which I have done from the day I was born even to this day on which I was smitten." With his right hand he holds out his glove to God; and lo! the angels of Heaven come down to him.

Count Roland lay under the pine tree; he has turned his face toward Spain, and he begins to call many things to remembrance—all the lands he had won by his valor, and sweet France, and the men of his lineage, and Charles, his liege lord, who had brought him up in his household; and he cannot help but weep. But he would not wholly forget himself, and again he confesses his sins and begs forgiveness of God: "Our Father, who art truth, who raised up Lazarus from the dead, and who defended Daniel from the lions, save Thou my soul from the perils to which it is brought through the sins I

58–60. **And . . . demesne.** Charlemagne never conquered Britain, of course; but William the Conqueror's successful expedition may have led the poet to transfer this feat to Roland. 90. **offers . . . God.** To hand the glove to someone was to submit to him.

wrought in my life-days." With his right hand he offers his glove to God, and Saint Gabriel has taken it from his hand. Then his head sinks on his arm, and with clasped hands he hath gone to his end. And God sent him His cherubim, and Saint Michael of the Seas, and with them went Saint Gabriel, and they carried the soul of the Count into Paradise.

Knight's tournament costume of the fifteenth century in France.

The Nibelungenlied

In what is now Austria there was written about the middle of the twelfth century an epic poem which has ever since been recognized as the German contribution to the literature of the national epic. *The Nibelungenlied* is actually a blending of more than one ancient Germanic saga into one medieval epic poem of German feudal aristocracy. The poem falls clearly into two parts: the first part, culminating in the death and burial of Siegfried, is based upon the celebrated *Volsungasaga* of Scandinavian legendry; the second, recounting the story of Kriemhild's revenge for the killing of her husband, Siegfried, is derived chiefly from the only slightly less renowned *Dietrich Saga* of Continental origin. The *Volsungasaga,* except for a passing reference in the Anglo-Saxon epic *Beowulf* of the eighth or ninth century, is first told in the *Poetic* or *Elder Edda* of the Scandinavian countries, dating from some time near 900. An independent Norse version survives from about 1200;

this is a long epic poem based upon the account in the *Poetic Edda.* The *Prose* or *Younger Edda* of about 1230, however, contains an epitome of the Norse version of the saga, which is extremely useful as a means of understanding some of the details in *The Nibelungenlied.*

Even in this epitome the early deeds of Sigurd (Siegfried) are given more fully than in *The Nibelungenlied.* Indeed, the German poem seems to know very little about these, for it presents Siegfried as a warrior of great, established reputation, with a few legendary and mythical attributes (particularly his cloak of invisibility, his fabulous physical strength, and his spot of vulnerability), who wins Brunhild for King Gunther and then falls through the treacherous acts of Brunhild, Gunther, and Hagen. The intimacy between Siegfried and Brunhild implied in the Norse version has been somewhat diluted in *The Nibelungenlied,* and Brunhild herself tends to fade out of the story.

The entire second part of *The Nibelungenlied,* which follows the burial of Siegfried, has drawn upon an extensive amount of material from other Germanic legends, notably, as has been said, from the *Dietrich Saga.* It is concerned primarily with Kriemhild, widow of Siegfried and later wife of King Etzel (the Hun Attila of history). Kriemhild corresponds to Gudrun in the Norse versions; her name has evidently been suggested by that of the Norse Gudrun's mother—an interesting example of simple "contamination" of details in different versions of what was originally the same story. Kriemhild plans and achieves a notable revenge upon the slayers of Siegfried, although she loses her own life in doing so. Since, in *The Nibelungenlied,* Gunther and Hagen thrive and prosper after Siegfried's murder, it is necessary for Kriemhild to revenge herself against them rather than against her second husband Etzel (the Norse Atli), as Gudrun did in the *Volsungasaga.* In any event, the poem ends in a grand slaughter.

Certain characters in *The Nibelungenlied* are based upon historical personages: King Gunther of the Burgundians was defeated and killed by the Huns in the year 437, although the famous Attila (Etzel or Atli) was not actually involved in this battle. Dietrich of Bern is Theodoric the Great, the Ostrogothic conqueror of Italy, who lived from 475 to 526. The natural implication is that other characters have a historical basis; such an implication arises in the study of any epic. But the four other chief characters in the poem—Siegfried, Brunhild, Kriemhild, and Hagen—are not at present identifiable with any specific historical figures; theirs seems to be clearly a legendary origin, and in the cases of Siegfried and Brunhild there is every reason to suppose that they belong to Germanic mythology.

At any rate *The Nibelungenlied* is more important as fiction than as fact. It glows on almost every page with the glamor and pomp of medieval feudal aristocracy, yet this encrustation of feudalism is not in the slightest degree worthy of the chivalric age. No more savage succession of incidents will be found in the entire field of the epic. If, as some maintain, this is not only the great epic of Germany but in its widest sense the epic of the Germanic people as well, it implies a certain amount of brutality in the Germanic imagination. Not a character in the story, save perhaps Dietrich of Bern—a wayfarer from another saga—is in any way attractive. Treachery, cruelty, childishness, vindictive bloodthirstiness of motive, greed, and a kind of cosmic destructiveness fill the lines of the whole poem. Here is none of the knightly fealty of the Frankish Roland, nor the sober steadiness and loyalty of the "English" Scandinavian Beowulf (either of whom would be a more admirable representative of the Germanic race). The same moral strictures can be expressed in regard to the Norse saga, of course; but in the Norse saga there is little of the pride and circumstance of what is presumed to be medieval Christian chivalric feudalism, and therefore there is more excuse for its having the qualities we deplore in *The Nibelungenlied*. For, despite the medieval atmosphere of *The Nibelungenlied*, the gore-caked warriors at King Etzel's castle are not fighting paynim infidels as Roland was or monstrous incarnations of evil as was Beowulf. It is, rather, internecine warfare of the crudest kind, although described in extremely talented narrative verse.

The Nibelungenlied

ADVENTURE 2. *Of Siegfried*

In the Netherlands there grew the child of a noble king (his father had for name, Siegmund, his mother Siegelind), in a mighty castle, known far and wide, in the lowlands of the Rhine: Xanten, men called it. Of this hero I sing, how fair he grew. Free he was of every blemish. Strong and famous he later became, this valiant man. Ho! what great worship he won in this world! Siegfried hight this good and doughty knight. Full many kingdoms did he put to the test through his warlike mood. Through his strength of body he rode into many lands. Ho! what bold warriors he after found in the Burgundian land! Mickle wonders might one tell of Siegfried in his prime, in youthful days; what honors he received and how fair of body he. The most stately women held him in their love; with the zeal which was his due men trained him. But of himself what virtues he attained! Truly his father's lands were honored, that he was found in all things of such right lordly mind. Now was he become of age that he might ride to court. Gladly the people saw him, many a maid wished that his desire might ever bear him hither. Enow gazed on him with favor; of this

the prince was well aware. Full seldom was the youth allowed to ride without a guard of knights. Siegmund and Siegelind bade deck him out in brave attire. The older knights who were acquaint with courtly custom, had him in their care. Well therefore might he win both folk and land.

Now he was of the strength that he bare weapons well. Whatever he needed thereto, this he had enow. With purpose he began to woo fair ladies; these bold Siegfried courted well in proper wise. Then bade Siegmund have cried to all his men, that he would hold a feasting with his loving kindred. The tidings thereof men brought into the lands of other kings. To the many strangers and the home-folk he gave steeds and armor. Wheresoever any was found who, because of his birth, should become a knight, these noble youths were summoned to the land for the feasting. Here with the youthful prince they gained the knightly sword. Wonders might one tell of this great feast; Siegmund and Siegelind wist well how to gain great worship with their gifts, of which their hands dealt out great store. Wherefore one beheld many a stranger riding to their realm. Four hundred sword-thanes were to be put on knightly garb with Siegfried. Many a fair maid was aught but idle with the work, for he was beloved of them all. Many precious stones the ladies inlaid on the gold, which together with the edging they would work upon the dress of the proud young warriors, for this must be done.

The host bade make benches for the many valiant men, for the midsummer festival, at which Siegfried should gain the name of knight. Then full many a noble knight and many a high-born squire did hie them to the minster. Right were the elders in that they served the young, as had been done to them afore. Pastimes they had and hope of much good cheer. To the honor of God a mass was sung; then there rose from the people full great a press, as the youths were made knights in courtly wise, with such great honors as might not ever lightly be again. Then they ran to where they found saddled many a steed. In Siegmund's court the hurtling waxed so fierce that both palace and hall were heard to ring; the high-mettled warriors clashed with mighty sound. From young and old one heard many a shock, so that the splintering of the shafts reëchoed to the clouds. Truncheons were seen flying out before the palace from the hand of many a knight. This was done with zeal. At length the host bade cease the

---

The Nibelungenlied ᴬ Translated by Daniel Shumway. Reprinted by permission of and arrangement with Houghton Mifflin Company, the authorized publishers.
The Nibelungenlied means the song or lay of the Nibelungs. These were a legendary Germanic people whose name is believed to mean "Children of the Mist." 2. **Siegmund,** originally the hero of an independent legend, as told in the *Volsungasaga* of Norse tradition. 5. **Xanten,** Santen, a town in Germany near Düsseldorf.

47. **sword-thanes,** young squires who were eligible for the knighthood. 55. **midsummer festival,** the summer solstice (about June 21), originally a pagan German festival which the medieval church brought into agreement with St. John's Eve (June 23), a day celebrated by merry-making and bonfires. 66. **hurtling,** a form of jousting, featuring head-on clashes of armed knights. 67. **palace,** as used in medieval romances, a large hall standing alone and used for audiences and receptions. 71. **Truncheons,** originally, as here, fragments of lances or spears.

A tournament, as sketched in a late fifteenth-century German manuscript.

tourney and the steeds were led away. Upon the turf one saw all to-shivered many a mighty buckler and great store of precious stones from the bright spangles of the shields. Through the hurtling this did hap.

Then the guests of the host betook them to where men bade them sit. With good cheer they refreshed them and with the very best of wine, of which one bare full plenty. To the strangers and the home-folk was shown worship enow. Through much pastime they had throughout the day, many of the strolling folk forsware all rest. They served for the largess, which men found there richly, whereby Siegmund's whole land was decked with praise. Then bade the king enfeoff Siegfried, the youth, with land and castles, as he himself had done. Much his hand bestowed upon the sword-companions. The journey liked them well, that to this land they were come. The feasting lasted until the seventh day. Siegelind, the noble queen, for the love of her son, dealt out ruddy gold in time-honored wise. Full well she wot how to make him beloved of the folk. Scarce could a poor man be found among the strolling mimes. Steeds and raiment were scattered by their hand, as if they were to live not one more day. I trow that never did serving folk use such great bounty. With worshipful honors the company departed hence. Of the mighty barons the tale doth tell that they desired the youth unto their lord, but of this the stately knight, Sir Siegfried, listed naught. Forasmuch as both Siegmund and Siegelind were still alive, the dear child of them twain wished not to wear a crown, but fain would he become a lord against all the deeds of force within his lands, whereof the bold and daring knight was sore adread.

[So Siegfried, hearing reports of the beauty of Kriemhild, goes to Worms, seat of King Gunther of Burgundy.

He makes a tremendous impression and fights successfully against the Saxons, winning the favor of his Kriemhild, to whom he is ultimately married. Meanwhile Gunther has become enamored of the peerless princess Brunhild of Isenland; he manages to win her theoretically, but in the contest to establish his right to this Amazon-at-arms, he is obliged to call upon the most spectacular Siegfried. Siegfried, relying upon a cloak of invisibility, substitutes for Gunther in a spear-throwing contest. And later, though married to Kriemhild, he helps Gunther once more in a more intimate way. Gunther is unable to consummate his marriage with Brunhild, but Siegfried subdues her. Unfortunately for all, he takes from the hand of Brunhild a ring, the famous Ring of the Nibelungs, and gives it to his wife, Kriemhild. At first all goes well; then—]

ADVENTURE 14. *How the queens reviled each other*

On a day before the vesper tide a great turmoil arose, which many knights made in the court, where they plied their knightly sports for pastime's sake, and a great throng of men and women hasted there to gaze. The royal queens had sat them down together and talked of two worshipful knights.

Then spake the fair Kriemhild: 'I have a husband who by right should rule over all these kingdoms.'

Quoth Lady Brunhild: 'How might that be? If none other lived but he and thou, then might these kingdoms own his sway, but the while Gunther liveth, this may never hap.'

Kriemhild replied: 'Now dost thou see, how he standeth, how right royally he walketh before the knights, as the moon doth before the stars? Therefore must I needs be merry of mood.'

Said Lady Brunhild: 'However stately be thy husband, howso worthy and fair, yet must thou grant the palm to Knight Gunther, the noble brother of thine. Know of a truth, he must be placed above all kings.'

Then Kriemhild spake again: 'So doughty is my husband, that I have not lauded him without good cause. His worship is great in many things. Dost thou believe it, Brunhild, he is easily Gunther's peer.'

'Forsooth thou must not take it amiss of me, Kriemhild, for I have not spoken thus without good reason. I heard them both aver, when I saw them first of all, and the king was victor against me in the games, and when he won my love in such knightly wise, that he was liegeman to the king, and Siegfried himself declared the same. I hold him therefore as my vassal, sith I heard him speak thus himself.'

Then spake fair Kriemhild: 'Ill had I then sped. How could my noble brothers have so wrought, that I should be a mere vassal's bride? Therefore I do beseech thee, Brunhild, in friendly wise, that for my sake thou kindly leave off this speech.'

'I'll not leave it off,' quoth the king's wife. 'Why

should I give up so many a knight, who with the warrior doth owe us service?'

Kriemhild, the passing fair, waxed wroth out of wit. 'Thou must forego that he ever do you a vassal's service; he is worthier than my brother Gunther, the full noble man. Thou must retract what I have heard thee say. Certes, it wondereth me, sith he be thy vassal and thou hast so much power over us twain, why he hath rendered thee no tribute so long a time.
10 By right I should be spared thy overweening pride.'

'Thou bearest thee too high,' spake the king's wife. 'I would fain see whether men will hold thee in such high honor as they do me.'

The ladies both grew wonderly wroth of mood. Then spake the Lady Kriemhild: 'This must now hap. Sith thou hast declared my husband for thy liegeman, now must the men of the two kings perceive today whether I durst walk before the queen to church. Thou must see today that I am noble and
20 free and that my husband is worthier than thine; nor will I myself be taxed therewith. Thou shalt mark today how thy liegewoman goeth to court before the knights of the Burgundian land. I myself shall be more worshipful than any queen was known to be, who ever wore a crown.' Great hate enow rose then betwixt the ladies.

Then Brunhild answered: 'Wilt thou not be a liegewoman of mine, so must thou sunder thee with thy ladies from my train when that we go to church.'
30 To this Kriemhild replied: 'In faith that shall be done.'

'Now array you, my maids,' spake Siegfried's wife. 'I must be here without reproach. Let this be seen today, and ye do have rich weeds. Brunhild shall fain deny what she hath here averred.'

They needed not much bidding, but sought rich robes and many a dame and maid attired her well. Then the wife of the noble king went forth with her train. Fair Kriemhild, too, was well arrayed and
40 three and forty maidens with her, whom she had brought hither to the Rhine. They wore bright vesture wrought in Araby, and thus the fair-fashioned maids betook them to the minster. All Siegfried's men awaited them before the house. The folk had marvel whence it chanced that the queens were seen thus sundered, so that they did not walk together as afore. From this did many a warrior later suffer dire distress. Here before the minster stood Gunther's wife, while many a good knight had pastime with
50 the comely dames whom they there espied.

Then came the Lady Kriemhild with a large and noble train. Whatever kind of clothes the daughters of noble knights have ever worn, these were but the wind against her retinue. She was so rich in goods, that what the wives of thirty kings could not purvey, that Kriemhild did. An one would wish to, yet he could not aver that men had ever seen such costly

dresses as at this time her fair-fashioned maidens wore. Kriemhild had not done it, save to anger Brunhild. They met before the spacious minster. 60 Through her great hate the mistress of the house in evil wise bade Kriemhild stand: 'Forsooth no vassaless should ever walk before the queen.'

Then spake the fair Kriemhild (angry was her mood): 'Couldst thou have held thy peace, 'twere well for thee. Thou hast disgraced thee and the fair body of thine. How might a vassal's leman ever be the wife of any king?'

'Whom callest thou here leman?' spake the queen.

'That call I thee,' quoth Kriemhild. 'Thy fair per- 70 son was first caressed by Siegfried, my dear husband. Certes, it was not my brother who won thy maidhood. Whither could thy wits have wandered? It was an evil trick. Wherefore didst thou let him love thee, sith he be thy vassal? I hear thee make plaint without good cause,' quoth Kriemhild.

'I' faith,' spake then Brunhild, 'Gunther shall hear of this.'

'What is that to me?' said Kriemhild. 'Thy pride hath bewrayed thee. With words thou hast claimed 80 me for thy service. Know, by my troth, it will ever grieve me, for I shall be no more thy faithful friend.'

Then Brunhild wept. Kriemhild delayed no longer, but entered the minster with her train before the queen. Thus there rose great hatred, from which bright eyes grew dim and moist.

Whatso men did or sang to God's service there, the time seemed far too long for Brunhild, for she was sad of heart and mood. Many a brave knight and a good must later rue this day. Brunhild with 90 her ladies now went forth and stopped before the minster. Her thought: 'Kriemhild must tell me more of what this word-shrewd woman hath so loudly charged me. Hath Siegfried made boast of this, 'twill cost his life.'

Now the noble Kriemhild came with many a valiant liegeman. Lady Brunhild spake: 'Stand still a while. Ye have declared me for a leman; that must ye let be seen. Know, that through thy speech, I have fared full ill.' 100

Then spake the Lady Kriemhild: 'Ye should have let me pass. I'll prove it by the ring of gold I have upon my hand, and which my lover brought me when he first lay at your side.'

Brunhild had never seen so ill a day. She spake: 'This costly hoop of gold was stolen from me, and hath been hid full long a time from me in evil wise. I'll find out yet who hath ta'en it from me.'

Both ladies now had fallen into grievous wrath.

Kriemhild replied: 'I'll not be called a thief. Thou 110 hadst done better to have held thy peace, an thou hold thine honor dear. I'll prove it by the girdle

67. leman, paramour or mistress.

which I wear about my waist, that I lie not. Certes, my Siegfried became thy lord.'

She wore the cord of silk of Nineveh, set with precious stones; in sooth 't was fair enow. When Brunhild spied it, she began to weep. Gunther and all the Burgundian men must needs now learn of this.

Then spake the queen: 'Bid the prince of the Rhineland come hither. I will let him hear how his sister hath mocked me. She saith here openly that I be Siegfried's wife.'

The king came with knights, and when he saw his love a-weeping, how gently he spake: 'Pray tell me, dear lady, who hath done you aught?'

She answered to the king: 'I must stand unhappy; thy sister would fain part me from all mine honors. I make here plaint to thee, she doth aver that Siegfried, her husband, hath had me as his leman.'

Quoth King Gunther: 'Then hath she done ill.'

'She weareth here my girdle, which I have lost, and my ring of ruddy gold. It doth repent me sore that I was ever born, unless be thou clearest me of this passing great shame; for that I'll serve thee ever.'

King Gunther spake: 'Have him come hither. He must let us hear if he hath made boast of this, or he must make denial, the hero of Netherland.' One bade fetch at once Kriemhild's love.

When Siegfried saw the angry dames (he wist not of the tale), how quickly that he spake: 'I fain would know why these ladies weep, or for what cause the king hath had me fetched.'

Then King Gunther spake: 'It doth rue me sore, forsooth. My Lady Brunhild hath told me here a tale, that thou hast boasted thou wast the first to clasp her lovely body in thine arms; this Lady Kriemhild, thy wife, doth say.'

Then spake Lord Siegfried: 'An she hath told this tale, she shall rue it sore, or ever I turn back, and I'll clear me with solemn oaths in front of all thy men, that I have not told her this.'

Quoth the king of the Rhineland: 'Let that be seen. The oath thou dost offer, and let it now be given, shall free thee of all false charges.'

They bade the proud Burgundians form a ring. Siegfried, the bold, stretched out his hand for the oath; then spake the mighty king: 'Thy great innocence is so well known to me, that I will free thee of that of which my sister doth accuse thee and say, thou hast never done this thing.'

Siegfried replied: 'If it boot my lady aught to have thus saddened Brunhild, that will surely cause me boundless grief.'

Then the lusty knights and good gazed one upon the other. 'One should so train women,' spake again Siegfried, the knight, 'that they leave haughty words unsaid. Forbid it to thy wife, and I'll do the same to mine. In truth, I do shame me of her great discourtesie.'

Many fair ladies were parted by the speech. Brunhild mourned so sore, that it moved King Gunther's men to pity. Then came Hagen of Troneg to his sovran lady. He found her weeping, and asked what grief she had. She told him then the tale. On the spot he vowed that Kriemhild's lord should rue it sore, or he would nevermore be glad. Ortwin and Gernot joined their parley and these heroes counseled Siegfried's death. Gieselher, the son of the noble Uta, came hither too. When he heard the talk, he spake full true: 'Ye trusty knights, wherefore do ye this? Siegfried hath not merited forsooth such hate, that he should therefore lose his life. Certes, women oft grow angry over little things.'

'Shall we then raise cuckolds?' answered Hagen; 'such good knights would gain from that but little honor. Because he hath boasted of my liege lady, I will rather die, an it cost him not his life.'

Then spake the king himself: 'He hath shown us naught but love and honor, so let him live. What booteth it, if I now should hate the knight? He was ever faithful to us, and that right willingly.'

Knight Ortwin of Metz then spake: 'His great prowess shall not in sooth avail him aught. If my lord permit, I'll do him every evil.'

So without cause the heroes had declared a feud against him. In this none followed, save that Hagen counseled all time Knight Gunther that if Siegfried no longer lived, then many knightly lands would own his sway. At this the king grew sad, so they let it rest.

Jousting was seen once more. Ho! what stout shafts they splintered before the minster in the presence of Siegfried's wife, even down to the hall! Enow of Gunther's men were now in wrath. The king spake: 'Let be this murderous rage; he is born to our honor and to our joy. Then, too, the wonderly bold man is so fierce of strength, that none durst match him, if he marked it.'

'No, not he,' spake Hagen then. 'Ye may well keep still; I trow to bring it to pass in secret, that he rue Brunhild's tears. Certes, Hagen hath broken with him for all time.'

Then spake King Gunther: 'How might that chance?'

3. **silk of Nineveh.** Oriental materials were introduced into Europe extensively at the time of the Crusades, although the name given them did not necessarily correspond to their place of origin. Here "Nineveh" merely indicates a general locality in the Near East.

63. **Troneg,** the corrupted name of an ancient Roman colony, Colonia Trajana, on the Lower Rhine. Hagen would therefore seem to be a Frank rather than a Burgundian. 67–68. **Ortwin and Gernot.** Ortwin is merely another knight in the story, but Gernot (Godomar, Gutthormr) is described in the first Adventure as the brother of Gunther and Kriemhild. 69. **Gieselher,** the youngest brother of Kriemhild and Gunther. 70. **Uta,** the mother of Kriemhild.

To this Hagen made answer: 'I'll let you hear. We'll bid messengers, that be not known to any here, ride into our land, to declare war upon us openly. Then do ye say before your guests that ye and your men will take the field. When that is done, he will vow to serve you then, and from this he shall lose his life, an I learn the tale from the bold knight's wife.'

The king followed his liegeman in evil wise. These ¹⁰ chosen knights gan plan great faithlessness, or ever any one was ware. From two women's quarreling full many a hero lost his life.

ADVENTURE 15. *How Siegfried was betrayed*

Upon the fourth morning two and thirty men were seen to ride to court and the tale was brought to mighty Gunther that war had been declared. The very direst woes befell fair women from a lie. They gained leave to come before the king and say that they were Liudeger's men, whom Siegfried's hand had conquered afore and had brought as hostages to ²⁰ Gunther's land. He greeted then the messengers and bade them go and seat them. One among them spake: 'My lord, pray let us stand till we have told the message we do bear you. This know, ye have of a truth many a mother's son as foe. Liudegast and Liudeger, whom ye one time gave grievous sores, declare a feud against you and are minded to ride with an army to this land.' The king waxed wroth when he heard this tale.

Men bade lead the perjurers to their lodgings. ³⁰ How might Siegfried, or any else against whom they plotted, ware himself against their wiles? This later brought great sorrow to them all. The king walked whispering with his friends; Hagen of Troneg never let him rest. Enow of the king's liegemen would fain have parted the strife, but Hagen would not give up his plan. On a day Siegfried found them whispering. The hero of Netherland gan ask: 'How go the king and his men so sadly? I'll help avenge it, hath any done you aught.'

⁴⁰ Then spake King Gunther: 'I am rightly sad. Liudegast and Liudeger have challenged me to war; they are minded to ride openly into my land.'

At this the bold knight said: 'Siegfried's hand shall hinder that with zeal, as beseemeth all your honors. I'll do yet to these knights as I did before; I'll lay waste their lands, or ever I turn again. Be my head your pledge of this. Ye and your warriors shall stay at home and let me ride to meet them with those I have. I'll let you see how fain I serve you. ⁵⁰ This know, through me it shall go evil with your foes.'

'Well is me of these tidings,' spake then the king, as though he were glad in earnest of this aid. With guile the faithless man bowed low.

Quoth Lord Siegfried: 'Ye shall have small care.' Then they made ready for the journey hence with the men-at-arms. This was done for Siegfried and his men to see. He, too, bade those of Netherland get them ready. Siegfried's warriors sought out warlike weeds. Then the stalwart Siegfried spake: 'My father ⁶ Siegmund, ye must stay here. We shall return in short space hither to the Rhine, and God give us luck. Ye must here make merry with the king.'

They tied fast their banners, as though they would away, and there were enow of Gunther's men who wist not wherefore this was done. Great rout of men was seen at Siegfried's side. They bound their helmets and their breastplates upon the steeds, and many a stout knight made ready to quit the land. Then Hagen of Troneg went to find Kriemhild and ⁷ asked for leave, sith they would void the land.

'Now well is me,' spake Kriemhild, 'that I have won a husband who dare protect so well my loving kinsfolk, as my Lord Siegfried doth here. Therefore,' spake the queen, 'will I be glad of heart. Dear friend Hagen, think on that, that I do serve you gladly and never yet did bear you hate. Requite this now to me in my dear husband. Let him not suffer, if I have done to Brunhild aught. I since have rued it,' spake the noble wife. 'Moreover, he since hath beaten me ⁸ black and blue; the brave hero and a good hath well avenged that ever I spake what grieved her heart.'

'Ye'll be friends once more after some days, Kriemhild, dear lady, pray tell me how I may serve you in your husband Siegfried. Liefer will I do this for you than for any else.'

'I should be without all fear,' quoth the noble dame, 'that any one would take his life in the fray, if he would not follow his overweening mood; then the bold knight and a good were safe.'

'Lady,' spake then Hagen, 'an ye do think that ⁹ men might wound him, pray let me know with what manner of arts I can prevent this. On foot, on horse, will I ever be his guard.'

She spake: 'Thou art my kinsman and I am thine. I'll commend to thee trustingly the dear lover of mine, that thou mayst guard him well, mine own dear husband.' She made him acquaint with tales which had been better left unsaid. She spake: 'My husband is brave and strong enow. When he slew ¹⁰ the dragon on the hill, the lusty warrior bathed him of a truth in the blood, so that since then no weapon ever cut him in the fray. Yet am I in fear, whenever he standeth in the fight and many javelins are cast by heroes' hands, that I may lose this dear husband

---

18–20. **Siegfried's hand . . . land.** This deed of Siegfried is narrated in Adventure Four, and is the only prominent military feat of the hero to be told in detail in *The Nibelungenlied.*

100–101. **When . . . dragon.** This, because of the Wagnerian influence, is the best known of Siegfried's achievements. It occupies a central position in the career of the hero as told in the *Volsungasaga.*

of mine. Alas, how oft I suffer sore for Siegfried's sake! Dear kinsman, in the hope that thou wilt hold thy troth with me, I'll tell thee where men may wound the dear lord of mine. I let thee hear this, 't is done in faith. When the hot blood gushed from the dragon's wounds and the bold hero and a good bathed him therein, a broad linden leaf did fall betwixt his shoulder blades. Therefore am I sore afraid that men may cut him there.'

Then spake Hagen of Troneg: 'Sew a small mark upon his coat, whereby I may know where I must guard him, when we stand in battle.'

She weened to save her knight, but 't was done unto his death. She spake: 'With fine silk I'll sew a secret cross upon his vesture. There, knight, thy hand must guard my husband, when the strife is on and he standeth in the battle before his foes.'

'That will I well, dear my lady,' Hagen then replied.

The lady weened that it would boot him aught, but Kriemhild's husband was thereby betrayed. Hagen then took leave; merrily he hied him hence. The king's liegeman was blithe of mood. I ween that nevermore will warrior give such false counsel, as was done by him when Kriemhild trusted in his troth.

Next morning Siegfried with a thousand of his men rode merrily forth. He weened he should avenge the grievance of his kinsmen. Hagen rode so near him that he could eye his clothes. When he saw the sign, he sent in secret twain of his men, who should tell another tale; that Gunther's land should still have peace and that Liudeger had sent them to the king. How loth Siegfried now rode home again, or ever he had avenged his kinsmen's wrongs! Gunther's men could hardly turn him back. He rode then to the king; the host gan thank him. 'Now God requite you of your will, friend Siegfried, that ye do so willingly what I bid you. For this I'll ever serve you, as I rightly should. I trust you more than all my friends. Now that we be rid of this foray, I am minded to ride a-hunting for bears and boars to the Vosges forest, as I have done oft-time.' That Hagen, the faithless knight, had counseled. 'Let it be told to all my guests, that we ride betimes. Those that would hunt with me must make them ready. If any choose to stay at home to court the ladies, that liketh me as well.'

Then spake Sir Siegfried in lordly wise: 'An ye would a-hunting, I'd fain go with you. Pray lend me a huntsman and some brach, and I will ride to the pines.'

'Will ye have but one?' spake the king anon. 'I'll lend you, an ye will, four men to whom both wood

51. **brach,** a hunting dog; later it was applied to the female of the species only.

and paths be known where the game is wont to go, and who will not let you miss the camp.'

Then rode the full lusty warrior to his wife, whilst Hagen quickly told the king how he thought to trap the doughty knight. A man should never use such faithlessness.

ADVENTURE 16. *How Siegfried was slain*

Gunther and Hagen, the passing bold knights, faithlessly let cry a-hunting in the woods, that with sharp spears they would hunt boars and bears and bison. What might be braver? With them rode Siegfried in lordly guise; many kinds of victual did they take along. At a cool spring he later lost his life, the which Brunhild, King Gunther's wife, had counseled. The bold knight then went to where he found Kriemhild. His costly hunting garb and those of his fellowship were already bound upon the sumpters, for they would cross the Rhine. Never could Kriemhild have been more sorrowful. He kissed his love upon her mouth. 'God let me see thee, lady, still in health and grant that thine eyes may see me too. Thou shalt have pastime with thy loving kinsmen. I may not stay at home.'

Then she thought of the tale she had told to Hagen, though she durst not say a whit. The noble queen began to rue that she was ever born. Lord Siegfried's wife wept out of measure. She spake to the knight: 'Let be your hunting. I had an evil dream last night, how two wild boars did chase you across the heath; then flowers grew red. I have in truth great cause to weep so sore. I be much adread of sundry plans and whether we have not misserved some who might bear us hostile hate. Tarry here, dear my lord, that I counsel by my troth.'

He spake: 'Dear love, I'll come back in a few short days. I wot not here of people who bear me aught of hate. Each and all of thy kinsmen be my friends, nor have I deserved it other of the knights.'

'No, no, Sir Siegfried; in truth I fear thy fall. I had last night an evil dream, how two mountains fell upon thee. I saw thee nevermore. It doth cut me to the heart, that thou wilt part from me.'

In his arms he clasped his courteous wife and kissed her tenderly. Then in a short space he took his leave and parted hence. Alas, she never saw him in health again.

Then they rode from thence into a deep wood for pastime's sake. Many bold knights did follow Gunther and his men, but Gernot and Gieselher stayed at home. Many laden sumpters were sent before them across the Rhine, the which bare for the hunting fellowship bread and wine, meat and fish, and great store of other things, which so mighty a king might rightly have. They bade the proud huntsmen and bold halt before a green wood over against the courses of the game, upon a passing broad glade where they should hunt. The king was told that Siegfried, too, was come. The hunting fellowship now took their stand on every side. Then the bold knight, the sturdy Siegfried, asked: 'Ye heroes bold and brave, who shall lead us to the game within the wood?'

'Let us part,' spake Hagen, 'ere we begin the chase. Thereby my lords and I may know who be the best hunter on this woodland journey. Let us 10 divide the folk and hounds and let each turn whithersoever he list. He who doth hunt the best shall have our thanks.' Short time the huntsmen bided by another after that.

Then spake Lord Siegfried: 'I need no dogs save one brach that hath been trained that he can tell the track of the beasts through the pine woods.' Quoth Kriemhild's husband: 'We'll find the game.'

Then an old huntsman took a good sleuth-hound and in a short space brought the lord to where many 20 beasts were found. Whatso rose from its lair the comrades hunted as good hunters still are wont to do. Whatever the brach started, bold Siegfried, the hero of Netherland, slew with his hand. His horse did run so hard that none escaped him. In the chase he gained the prize above them all. Doughty enow he was in all things. The beast which he slew with his hands was the first, a mighty boar; after which he found full soon a monstrous lion. When the brach started this from its lair, he shot it with his 30 bow, in which he had placed a full sharp arrow. After the shot the lion ran the space of but three bounds. The hunting fellowship gave Siegfried thanks. Thereafter he speedily slew a bison and an elk, four strong ure-oxen, and a savage shelk. His horse bare him so swiftly that naught escaped him, nor could hart or hind avoid him. Then the sleuth hound found a mighty boar; when he began to flee, at once there came the master of the hunt and encountered him upon his path. Wrathfully the boar 40 did run against the valiant hero, but Kriemhild's husband slew him with his sword. Another huntsman might not have done this deed so lightly. When he had felled him, they leashed the sleuth-hound; his rich booty was soon well known to the Burgundian men.

Then spake his huntsman: 'Sir Siegfried, if might so be, let us leave a deal of the beasts alive. Ye'll empty both our hills and woods today.'

At this the brave knight and a bold gan smile. 50 Then the calls of men and the baying of hounds were heard on every side; so great was the noise that both hill and pine woods echoed with the sound. The huntsmen had let loose full four and twenty packs.

Then passing many beasts must needs lose their lives. Each man weened to bring it to pass that men should give him the prize of the hunt; that might not be, for the stalwart Siegfried was already standing by the fire. The chase was over, and yet not quite. Those who would to the campfire brought with them thither hides of many beasts and game in 60 plenty. Ho! how much the king's meiny bare then to the kitchen!

Then bade the king announce to the huntsmen that he would dismount. A horn was blown full loud just once, that all might know that one might find the noble prince in camp. Spake then one of Siegfried's huntsmen: 'My lord, I heard by the blast of a horn that we must now hie to the quarters; I'll now give answer.'

Thus by many blasts of horns they asked about the 70 hunters. Then spake Sir Siegfried: 'Now let us leave the pine wood!' His steed bare him smoothly and with him they hasted hence. With their rout they started up a savage beast; a wild bear it was. Quoth then the knight to those behind: 'I'll give our fellowship a little pastime. Let loose the brach. Forsooth I spy a bear which shall journey with us to the camp. Flee he never so fast, he shall not escape us.'

The brach was loosed, the bear sprang hence; Kriemhild's husband would fain overtake him. He 80 reached a thicket, where none could follow. The mighty beast weened now to escape from the hunter with his life, but the proud knight and a good leaped from his steed and began to chase him. The bear was helpless and could not flee away. At once the hero caught it and bound it quickly with not a wound, so that it might neither scratch nor bite the men. The doughty knight then tied it to his saddle and horsed him quickly. Through his overweening mood the bold warrior and a good brought it to the 90 camp-fire as a pastime. In what lordly wise he rode to the quarters! Mickle was his boar-spear, strong and broad. A dainty sword hung downward to his spurs. The lord bare also a fair horn of ruddy gold. Never heard I tale of better hunting weeds. One saw him wear a coat of black and silky cloth and a hat of sable: rich enow it was. Ho! what costly bands he wore upon his quiver! A panther's skin was drawn over it for the sake of its sweet fragrance. He bare a bow, which any but the hero must needs draw 100 back with a windlass, an he would bend it. His vesture was befurred with otter skin from head to toe. From the bright fur shone out on both sides of the bold master of the hunt many a bar of gold. Balmung he also bare, a good broad sword, that was

61. **meiny,** retinue. 98–99. **panther's skin . . . fragrance.** According to medieval legend, the panther's breath was so sweet as to enable it to lure its prey through that alone, and the fragrance permeated its whole body. 102. **otter.** It is not known whether this means the familiar fish-otter or a mythical faun-like beast. 105. **Balmung,** the famous sword of Siegfried.

28. **lion;** a good example of embroidery with the fabulous to which the medieval romancer often resorted. 34. **ure-oxen,** the aurochs or European bison, now extinct in Europe, although specimens may be found in Siberia. **shelk,** a giant deer, possibly akin to the moose.

so sharp that it never failed when 'twas wielded 'gainst a helmet; its edge was good. In high spirits was the lordly huntsman. Sith I must tell you all the tale, his costly quiver was full of goodly darts, the heads a full hand's breadth, on golden shafts. What he pierced therewith must needs die soon.

Thus the noble knight rode hence in hunter's garb. Gunther's men espied him coming and ran out to meet him and took his horse in charge. On his sad-10 dle he carried a large bear and a strong. When he had dismounted, he loosed the bonds from feet and snout. Those of the pack bayed loudly, that spied the bear. The beast would to the woods; the serving folk had fear. Dazed by the din, the bear made for the kitchen. Ho! how he drove the scullions from the fire! Many a kettle was upset and many a firebrand scattered. Ho! what good victual men found lying in the ashes! Then the lordings and their liegemen sprang from their seats. The bear grew furious and 20 the king bade loose the pack that lay enleashed. Had all sped well, they would have had a merry day. No longer the doughty men delayed, but ran for the bear with bows and pikes. There was such press of dogs that none might shoot, but from the people's shouts the whole hill rang. The bear began to flee before the dogs; none could follow him but Kriem-hild's husband, who caught and slew him with his sword. Then they bore the bear again to the fire. Those that saw it, averred he was a mighty man.

30 Men bade now the proud hunting fellowship seat them at the tables. Upon a fair mead there sate a goodly company. Ho! what rich viands they bare there to the noble huntsmen! The butlers who should bring the wine delayed; else might never heroes have been better served. Had they not been so falsely minded, then had the knights been free of every blame.

Now the Lord Siegfried spake: 'Me wondereth, since men do give us such great store from the 40 kitchen, why the butlers bring us not the wine. Un-less men purvey the hunters better, I'll be no more your hunting-fellow. I have well deserved that they regard me, too.'

The king addressed him from his seat with guile: 'We fain would do your remedy of what we lack. It is Hagen's fault, who is willed to let us die of thirst.'

Then spake Hagen: 'Dear my lord, I weened that the hunt should be in the Spessart wood, therefore sent I thither the wine. Though we may not drink 50 today, how well will I avoid this in the future!'

At this Lord Siegfried spake: 'Small thanks ye'll get for that. One should have brought me hither seven sumpter loads of mead and mulled wine. If

that might not be, then men should have placed our benches nearer to the Rhine.'

Then spake Hagen of Troneg: 'Ye noble knights and bold, I wot nearby a good spring. Let us go thither, that ye wax not wroth.'

To the danger of many a knight was this counsel 60 given. The pangs of thirst now plagued the warrior Siegfried. He bade the tables be borne away the sooner, for he would go to the spring in the moun-tains. With false intent the counsel was then given by the knights. They bade the game which Sieg-fried's hand had slain, be carried home on wains. Whoever saw it gave him great laud. Hagen of Troneg now foully broke his troth to Siegfried. When they would hence to the broad linden, he spake: 'It hath oft been told me, that none can keep pace with Kriemhild's husband when he be minded for to race. 70 Ho! if he would only let us see it here!'

Bold Siegfried from Netherland then answered: 'Ye can well test that, an ye will run a race with me to the spring. When that is done, we can give the prize to him who winneth.'

'So let us try it then,' quoth Hagen, the knight.

Spake the sturdy Siegfried; 'Then will I lay me down on the greensward at your feet.'

How lief it was to Gunther, when he heard these words! Then the bold knight spake again: 'I'll tell 80 you more. I'll take with me all my trappings, my spear and shield and all my hunting garb.' Around him he quickly girded his quiver and his sword.

Then they drew the clothes from off their limbs; men saw them stand in two white shifts. Like two wild panthers through the clover they ran, but men spied bold Siegfried first at the spring. In all things he bare away the prize from many a man. Quickly he ungirt his sword and laid aside his quiver and leaned the stout spear against a linden bough. The 90 lordly stranger stood now by the flowing spring. Passing great was Siegfried's courtesie. He laid down his shield where the spring gushed forth, but the hero drank not, albeit he thirsted sore, until the king had drunk, who gave him evil thanks. Cool, clear, and good was the spring. Gunther stooped down then to the flowing stream, and when he had drunken straightened up again. Bold Siegfried would fain also have done the same, but now he paid for his courtesie. Hagen bare quite away from him both 100 bow and sword and bounded then to where he found the spear; then he looked for the mark on bold Sieg-fried's coat. As Lord Siegfried drank above the spring, he pierced him through the cross, so that his heart's blood spurted from the wounds almost on Hagen's clothes. Nevermore will hero do so foul a

48. **Spessart wood,** a forest about fifty miles east of Worms, consid-erably farther than an ordinary day's hunt would carry the knights. 53. **mulled wine,** a claret mixed with spices and herbs and allowed to clear.

77–78. **'Then will I . . . feet.'** Siegfried arrogantly suggests this in order to enhance his assumed victory over Hagen. In other words, Hagen will start from a standing position while Siegfried will first have to rise to his feet. Hagen had not requested this handicap.

deed. Hagen left the spear a-sticking in his heart and fled more madly than he ever in the world had run from any man.

When Lord Siegfried felt the mighty wound, up from the spring he started in a rage. From betwixt his shoulder blades a long spear-shaft towered. He weened to find his bow or his sword, and then had Hagen been repaid as he deserved. But when the sorely wounded hero found no trace of his sword, then had he naught else but his shield. This he snatched from the spring and ran at Hagen; nor could King Gunther's man escape him. Albeit he was wounded unto death, yet he smote so mightily that a plenty of precious stones were shaken from the shield. The shield itself burst quite apart. Fain would the lordly stranger have avenged him. Now was Hagen fallen to the ground at his hands, and from the force of the blow the glade rang loudly. Had he had a sword in hand, then had it been Hagen's death, so sore enraged was the wounded man. Forsooth he had good cause thereof. His hue grew pale, he could not stand; his strength of body melted quite away, for in bright colors he bore the signs of death. Thereafter he was bewailed by fair dames enow.

Kriemhild's husband fell now among the flowers. Fast from his wounds blood was seen to gush. He began to rail, as indeed he had great cause, at those who had planned this treacherous death. The deadly wounded spake: 'Forsooth, ye evil cowards, what avail my services now that ye have slain me? This is my reward that I was always faithful to you. Alas, ye have acted ill against your kinsmen. Those of them who are born in after days will be disgraced. Ye have avenged your wrath too sore upon me. With shame shall ye be parted from all good warriors!'

The knights all ran to where he lay slain. For enow of them it was a hapless day. He was bewailed by those who had aught of loyalty, and this the brave and lusty knight had well deserved. The king of the Burgundians bemoaned his death. Quoth the deadly wounded: 'There is no need that he should weep who hath done the damage; he doth merit mickle blame. It had been better left undone.'

Then spake the fierce Hagen: 'Forsooth I wot not what ye now bewail. All our fear and all our woe have now an end. We shall find scant few who dare withstand us now. Well is me, that to his rule I have put an end.'

'Ye may lightly boast you,' Siegfried then replied. 'Had I wist your murderous bent, I had well guarded my life against you. None doth rue me so sore as Lady Kriemhild, my wife. Now may God have pity that I ever had a son to whom the reproach will be made in after days, that his kindred have slain a man with murderous intent. If I might,' so spake Siegfried, 'I should rightly make complaint of this.'

Piteously the deadly wounded spake again: 'Noble king, if ye will keep your troth to any in the world, then let my dear love be commended to your grace and let it avail her that she be your sister. For the sake of your princely courtesie, protect her faithfully. My father and my men must wait long time for me. Never was woman sorer wounded in a loving friend.'

The flowers on every side were wet with blood. With death he struggled, but not for long, sith the sword of death had cut him all too sorely. Then the lusty warrior and a brave could speak no more.

When the lordings saw that the knight was dead, they laid him on a shield of ruddy gold and took counsel how they might conceal that Hagen had done the deed. Enow of them spake: 'Ill hath it gone with us. Ye must all aver alike that robbers slew Kriemhild's husband as he rode alone a-hunting through the pine wood.'

Then Hagen of Troneg spake: 'I'll bring him home; I care not if it be known to her, for she hath saddened Brunhild's heart. Little doth it trouble me however much she weep.'

ADVENTURE 17. *How Kriemhild mourned her husband and how he was buried*

Then they waited for the night and crossed the Rhine. Never had heroes hunted worse. Noble maids bewept the game they slew. Forsooth many good warriors must needs atone for this in after days. Now ye may hear a tale of great overweening and dire revenge. Hagen bade carry Siegfried of the Nibelungland, thus dead, before the bower where Kriemhild lodged. He bade place him stealthily against the door, that she might find him when she went forth before the break of day to matins, which Lady Kriemhild full seldom missed through sleep.

Men rang the minster bells according to their custom. Lady Kriemhild, the fair, now waked her many maids and bade them bring a light and her vesture, too. Then came a chamberlain and found Siegfried there. He saw him red with blood, his clothes all wet. He wist not it was his lord, but with the light in his hand he hasted to the bower and through this Lady Kriemhild learned the baneful tale. As she would set out with her ladies for the minster, the chamberlain spake: 'Pray stay your feet, there doth lie before the chamber a knight, slain unto death.'

Kriemhild gan make passing sore wail, or ever she heard aright that it was her husband. She began to think of Hagen's question, of how he might protect him. Then first she suffered dole; she renounced all pleasure at his death. To the earth she sank, not a word she spake, and here they found lying the hapless fair. Passing great grew Kriemhild's woe. After her faint, she shrieked, that all the chamber rang. Then her meiny said: 'Perchance it is a stranger knight.'

The blood gushed from her mouth, from dole of heart; she spake: 'Tis Siegfried, mine own dear husband. Brunhild hath counseled this and Hagen hath done the deed.'

The lady bade them lead her to where the hero lay. With her white hand she raised his head, and though it was red with blood, she knew him soon. There lay the hero of the Nibelungland in piteous guise. The gracious queen cried sadly: 'Oh, woe is me of my sorrow! Thy shield is not carved with swords; thou liest murdered here. Wist I who hath done the deed, I'd ever plot his death.'

All her maids made mourn and wailed with their dear lady, for they grieved full sore for their noble lord whom they had lost. Hagen had cruelly avenged the wrath of Brunhild.

Then spake the grief-stricken dame: 'Go now and wake with haste all Siegfried's men. Tell Siegmund also of my grief, mayhap he'll help me bewail brave Siegfried.'

A messenger ran quickly to where lay Siegfried's warriors from the Nibelungland, and with his baleful tidings stole their joy. They could scarcely believe it, till they heard the weeping. Right soon the messenger came to where the king did lie. Siegmund, the lord, was not asleep. I trow his heart did tell him what had happed. Never again might he see his dear son alive.

'Awake, Sir Siegmund! Kriemhild, my lady, bade me go to fetch you. A wrong hath been done her that doth cut her to the heart, more than all other ills. Ye must help her mourn, for much it doth concern you.'

Siegmund sat up; he spake: 'What are fair Kriemhild's ills, of which thou tellest me?'

Weeping the messenger spake: 'I cannot hide them from you; alas, bold Siegfried of Netherland is slain.'

Quoth Siegmund: 'For my sake let be this jesting and such evil tales, that thou shouldst tell any that he be dead, for I might never bewail him fully before my death.'

'If ye will believe naught of what ye hear me say, then ye may hear yourself Kriemhild and all her maids bewailing Siegfried's death.'

Siegmund then was sore affrighted, as indeed he had great need. He and a hundred of his men sprang from their beds and grasped with their hands their long sharp swords. In sorrow they ran toward the sound of wail. Then came a thousand men-at-arms, bold Siegfried's men. When they heard the ladies wail so pitifully, some first grew ware that they should dress them. Forsooth they lost their wits

for very sorrow. Great heaviness was buried in their hearts.

Then King Siegmund came to where he found Kriemhild. He spake: 'Alas for the journey hither to this land! Who hath so foully bereft me of my child and you of your husband among such good friends?'

'Oh, if I knew him,' spake the noble wife, 'neither my heart nor soul would ever wish him well. I would plan such ill against him that his kin must ever weep because of me.'

Around the prince Lord Siegmund threw his arms. So great grew the sorrow of his kin, that the palace, the hall, and the town of Worms resounded from the mighty wail and weeping. None might now comfort Siegfried's wife. They stripped off the clothes from his fair body; they washed his wounds and laid him on the bier. Woe were his people from their mighty grief. Then spake his warriors from the Nibelungland: 'Our hands be ever ready to avenge him; he liveth in this castle who hath done the deed.'

All of Siegfried's men hasted then to arms. These chosen knights came with their shields, eleven hundred men-at-arms, whom Lord Siegfried had in his troop. He would fain avenge the death of his son, as indeed he had great need. They wist not to whom they should address their strife, unless it be to Gunther and his men, with whom Lord Siegfried had ridden to the hunt.

Kriemhild saw them armed, which rued her sore. However great her grief and how dire her need, yet she did so mightily fear the death of the Nibelungs at the hands of her brothers' liegemen, that she tried to hinder it. In kindly wise she warned them, as kinsmen do to loving kin. The grief-stricken woman spake: 'My Lord Siegmund, what will ye do? Ye wot naught aright; forsooth King Gunther hath so many valiant men, ye will all be lost, and ye would encounter these knights.'

With their shields uncovered, the men stood eager for the fight. The noble queen both begged and bade that the lusty knights avoid it. When they would not give it over, sorely it grieved her. She spake: 'Lord Siegmund, ye must let it be until more fitting time, then I'll avenge my husband with you. An I receive proof who hath bereft me of him, I'll do him scathe. There be too many haughty warriors by the Rhine, wherefore I will not counsel you to fight. They have full well thirty men to each of ours. Now God speed them, as they deserve of us. Stay ye here and bear with me my dole. When it beginneth to dawn, help me, ye lusty knights, to coffin the dear husband of mine.'

Quoth the knights: 'That shall be done.'

None might tell you all the marvel of knights and

ladies, how they were heard to wail, so that even in the town men marked the sound of weeping. The noble burghers hasted hither. With the guests they wept, for they, too, were sore aggrieved. None had told them of any guilt of Siegfried, or for what cause the noble warrior lost his life. The wives of the worthy burghers wept with the ladies of the court. Men bade smiths haste to work a coffin of silver and gold, mickle and strong, and make it firm with strips of good hard steel. Sad of heart were all the folk.

The night was gone, men said the day was dawning. Then the noble lady bade them bear Lord Siegfried, her loved husband, to the minster. Whatever friends he had there were seen weeping as they went. Many bells were ringing as they brought him to the church. On every side one heard the chant of many priests. Then came King Gunther with his men and grim Hagen also toward the sound of wail. He spake: 'Alas for thy wrongs, dear sister, that we may not be free from this great scathe. We must ever lament for Siegfried's death.'

'That ye do without cause,' spake the sorrow-laden wife. 'Were this loath to you, it never would have happed. I may well aver, ye thought not on me, when I thus was parted from my dear husband. Would to God,' quoth Kriemhild, 'that it had happed to me.'

Firmly they made denial. Kriemhild gan speak: 'Whoso declareth him guiltless, let him show that now. He must walk to the bier before all the folk; thereby one may know the truth eftsoon.'

This is a great marvel, which oft doth hap: whenever the blood-stained murderer is seen to stand by the dead, the latter's wounds do bleed, as indeed happed here, whereby one saw the guilt was Hagen's. The wounds bled sore, as they had done at first. Much greater grew the weeping of those who wailed afore.

Then spake King Gunther: 'I'd have you know that robbers slew him; Hagen did not do the deed.'

'I know these robbers well,' quoth she. 'Now may God yet let his friends avenge it. Certes, Gunther and Hagen, 'twas done by you.'

Siegfried's knights were now bent on strife. Then Kriemhild spake again: 'Now share with me this grief.'

Gernot, her brother, and young Gieselher, these twain now came to where they found him dead. They mourned him truly with the others; Kriemhild's men wept inly. Now should mass be sung, so on every side, men, wives, and children did hie them to the minster. Even those who might lightly bear his loss, wept then for Siegfried. Gernot and Gieselher spake: 'Sister mine, now comfort thee after this

33–35. **whenever . . . bleed.** This is an age-old superstition, as defined in the text.

death, as needs must be. We'll try to make it up to thee, the while we live.'

Yet none in the world might give her comfort. His coffin was ready well towards midday. From the bier whereon he lay they raised him. The lady would not have that he be buried, so that all the folk had mickle trouble. In a rich cloth of silk they wound the dead. I ween, men found none there that did not weep. Uta, the noble dame, and all her meiny mourned bitterly the stately man. When it was noised abroad that men sang in the minster and had encoffined him, then rose a great press of folk. What offerings they made for his soul's sake! He had good friends enow among these foes. Poor Kriemhild spake to her chamberlains: 'Ye must now be put to trouble for my sake, ye who wished him well and be my friends. For Siegfried's soul shall ye deal out his gold.'

No child, however small, that had its wits, but must go to service, or ever he was buried. Better than a hundred masses were sung that day. Great throng were there of Siegfried's friends.

When that mass was sung, the folk went hence. Then Lady Kriemhild spake: 'Pray let me not hold vigil over the chosen knight this night alone. With him all my joys have come to fall. I will let him lie in state three days and nights, until I sate me with my dear lord. What if God doth bid that death should take me too. Then had ended well the grief of me, poor Kriemhild.'

The people of the town returned now to their lodgings. She begged the priests and monks and all his retinue, that served the knight, to stay. They spent full evil nights and toilsome days; many a man remained without all food and drink. For those who would partake, it was made known that men would give them to the full. This Sir Siegmund purveyed. Then were the Nibelungs made acquaint with mickle toil. During the three days, as we hear tell, those who knew how to sing, were made to bear a deal of work. What offerings men brought them! Those who were very poor, grew rich enow. Whatever of poor men there were, the which had naught, these were bid go to mass with gold from Siegfried's treasure chamber. Since he might not live, many thousand marks of gold were given for his soul. She dealt out well-tilled lands, wherever cloisters and pious folk were found. Enow of gold and silver was given to the poor. By her deeds she showed that she did love him fondly.

Upon the third morning at time of mass, the broad churchyard by the minster was full of weeping country folk. They served him after death, as one should do to loving kin. In the four days, as hath been told, full thirty thousand marks or better still were given to the poor for his soul's sake. Yet his great beauty and his life lay low. When God had been

served and the chants were ended, many people
fought against monstrous grief. Men bade bear him
from the minster to the grave. Those were seen to
weep and wail who missed him most. With loud
laments the people followed hence; none was merry,
neither wife nor man. They sang and read a service
before they buried him. Ho, what good priests were
present at his burial! Ere Siegfried's wife was come
to the grave, her faithful heart was wrung with
10 grief, so that they must needs oft sprinkle her with
water from the spring. Her pain was passing great;
a mickle wonder it was that she ever lived. Many a
lady helped her in her plaint.

Then spake the queen: 'Ye men of Siegfried, by
your loyalty must ye prove your love to me. Let me
receive this little favor after all my woe, that I may
see once more his comely head.'

She begged so long, with grief's strong will, that
they must needs break open the lordly casket. Then
20 men brought the lady to where he lay. With her
white hand she raised his fair head and kissed the
noble knight and good, thus dead. Tears of blood
her bright eyes wept from grief. Then there happed
a piteous parting. Men bare her hence, she could
not walk, and soon they found the high-born lady
lying senseless. Fain would the lovely fair have died
of grief.

When they had now buried the noble lord, those
who were come with him from the Nibelungland
30 were seen to suffer from unmeasured grief. Men
found Siegmund full seldom merry then. There were
those that for three days would neither eat nor drink
for passing grief. Yet might they not so waste away
their bodies, but that they recovered from their
sorrows, as still happeneth oft enow.

*A German prince in tourney costume, the early fifteenth
century.*

Aucassin and Nicolete

Some time near the middle of the twelfth century a gifted Frenchman composed *Aucassin
and Nicolete*. Nothing is known about him, however, except through surmise. He appears to have been a man of
popular rather than of clerical mold, entirely secular in
his outlook, a man of delightful fancy and delicately satirical expression, but thoroughly in love with love, albeit
with a somewhat middle-aged tolerance. The tale of the
two naïve young lovers he told in the so-called *chante-
fable* form, with alternating prose and verse sections to
the narrative, garnished with interspersed lyrics. This
form is known in early literature from Scotland to India
and the Far East, but *Aucassin and Nicolete* is the
unique surviving example of the type from medieval
France, and it is quite possible that the poet was seeking
(and seeking successfully) a fresh form of narrative for
the sake of variety.

The name of the hero, Aucassin, which could be a
French form of an Arabic Al-Kassim, as well as the fact
that Nicolete is by birth a Saracen princess, suggests
that the story was of Oriental origin. Indeed, the theme
of the separation and reuniting of devoted lovers is commonplace in Mediterranean and Oriental tales. The matter is academic, however, and immaterial for the general
reader, for the story of two young lovers who in their
simple, sensuous, and passionate way refuse to remain
separated is a universal one. What is more important is
the manner in which the poet treats this familiar material.

The knightly young hero, Aucassin, is so bemused
by love that he neglects his knightly duties and talks
back to his father when reminded of them; and his
ideas about Paradise and Hell are refreshingly frank and
unecclesiastical. There is more than a hint, in fact, that
the poet is satirizing not only the institution of knighthood but also the narrow insistence of the more evangelical members of the clergy that the world to come is
more important than the world that is. On the contrary,
in *Aucassin and Nicolete* the world that is strikes one as
a thoroughly charming place for the noble and the beloved. Although there are sieges and stours, they are
touched upon but lightly and then in jocose fashion;
although there is humanitarian sympathy for the loathly
churl whom Aucassin meets, the poet solves the problem
quickly. More significant are the rose-covered lodge of
Nicolete in the woods, the charming picture of Nicolete
in flight from Biaucaire, the ride of Aucassin and Nicolete
to Torelore, and the final reunion of the lovers. The
bizarre episode of Torelore anticipates the fantastic satire
of Rabelais written centuries later. But whether the purpose of the poet is satirical or merely imaginative, the
result is nothing if not entertaining, affording a delightful
contrast to the more serious and rugged specimens of
courtly narrative of which the age was full.

Aucassin and Nicolete

Tis of Aucassin and Nicolete.
Who would list to the good lay,
Gladness of the captive grey?
'Tis how two young lovers met,
Aucassin and Nicolete,
Of the pains the lover bore
And the sorrows he outwore,
For the goodness and the grace
Of his love, so fair of face.

10 Sweet the song, the story sweet.
There is no man hearkens it,
No man living 'neath the sun,
So outwearied, so fordone,
Sick and woful, worn and sad,
But is healed, but is glad
'Tis so sweet.

So say they, speak they, tell they the Tale:
How the Count Bougars de Valence made war
on Count Garin de Biaucaire, war so great, and so
20 marvellous, and so mortal that never a day dawned,
but always he was there, by the gates and walls, and
barriers of the town with a hundred knights, and ten
thousand men at arms, horsemen and footmen; so
burned he the Count's land, and spoiled his country,
and slew his men. Now the Count Garin de Biaucaire was old and frail, and his good days were gone
over. No heir had he, neither son nor daughter, save
one young man only; such an one as I shall tell you.
Aucassin was the name of the damoiseau; fair was
30 he, goodly, and great, and feately fashioned of his
body, and limbs. His hair was yellow, in little curls,
his eyes blue and laughing, his face beautiful and
shapely, his nose high and well set, and so richly
seen was he in all things good that in him was none
evil at all. But so suddenly overtaken was he of
Love, who is a great master, that he would not, of
his will, be dubbed knight, nor take arms, nor follow
tourneys, nor do whatsoever him beseemed. Therefore his father and mother said to him:
40 "Son, go take thine arms, mount thy horse, and
hold thy land, and help thy men, for if they see thee
among them, more stoutly will they keep in battle
their lives and lands and thine and mine."
"Father," said Aucassin, "I marvel that you will

be speaking. Never may God give me aught of my
desire if I be made knight, or mount my horse, or
face stour and battle wherein knights smite and are
smitten again, unless thou give me Nicolete, my true
love, that I love so well."
"Son," said the father, "this may not be. Let Nico- 50
lete go, a slave girl she is, out of a strange land, and
the captain of this town bought her of the Saracens,
and carried her hither, and hath reared her and let
christen the maid, and took her for his daughter in
God, and one day will find a young man for her,
to win her bread honorably. Herein hast thou naught
to make or mend, but if a wife thou wilt have, I
will give thee the daughter of a King, or a Count.
There is no man so rich in France, but if thou desire
his daughter, thou shalt have her." 60
"Faith! my father," said Aucassin, "tell me where
is the place so high in all the world, that Nicolete,
my sweet lady and love, would not grace it well? If
she were Empress of Constantinople or of Germany,
or Queen of France or England, it were little enough
for her; so gentle is she and courteous and debonaire
and compact of all good qualities."

Here singeth one:

Aucassin was of Biaucaire,
Of a goodly castle there,
But from Nicolete the fair 70
None might win his heart away,
Though his father, many a day,
And his mother said him nay,
"Ha! fond child, what wouldest thou?
Nicolete is glad enow!
Was from Carthage cast away,
Paynims sold her on a day!
Wouldst thou win a lady fair,
Choose a maid of high degree, 80
Such an one is meet for thee."
"Nay, of these have I no care,
Nicolete is debonaire,
Her body sweet and the face of her
Take my heart as in a snare,
Loyal love is but her share
That is so sweet."

Then speak, they, say they, tell they the Tale:
When the Count Garin de Biaucaire knew that
he would not avail to withdraw Aucassin his son 90
from the love of Nicolete, he went to the Captain
of the city, who was his man, and spake to him,
saying:
"Sir Count; away with Nicolete thy daughter in
God; cursed be the land whence she was brought

Aucassin and Nicolete. Translated by Andrew Lang.
19. **Biaucaire.** The setting of this poem is in general the lower Rhone
Valley in southern France. Beaucaire is about fifteen miles from the
mouth of the Rhone; Valence, mentioned in the preceding line, is
some sixty miles farther up the river. 29. **damoiseau,** a young unmarried man of superior birth.

47. **stour,** the onset of battle. 54. **christen the maid.** In *Aucassin
and Nicolete* the traditional course is reversed, for it is much more
common in medieval romances for a hero to be of Saracen birth and
then to be converted and baptized. A Saracen heroine is not unknown,
however.

into this country, for by reason of her do I lose Aucassin, that will neither be dubbed knight, nor do aught of the things that fall to him to be done. And wit ye well," he said, "that if I might have her at my will, I would burn her in a fire, and yourself might well be sore adread."

"Sir," said the Captain, "this is grievous to me that he comes and goes and hath speech with her. I had bought the maiden at mine own charges, and nour-ished her, and baptized, and made her my daughter in God. Yea, I would have given her to a young man that should win her bread honorably. With this had Aucassin thy son naught to make or mend. But, sith it is thy will and thy pleasure, I will send her into that land, and that country, where never will he see her with his eyes."

"Have a heed to thyself," said the Count Garin, "thence might great evil come on thee."

So parted they each from other. Now the Captain was a right rich man; so had he a rich palace with a garden in face of it; in an upper chamber thereof he let place Nicolete, with one old woman to keep her company, and in that chamber put bread and meat and wine and such things as were needed. Then he let seal the door, that none might come in or go forth, save that there was one window, over against the garden, and strait enough, wherethrough came to them a little air.

Here singeth one:

Nicolete, as ye heard tell
Prisoned is within a cell
That is painted wondrously
With colors of a far country,
And the window of marble wrought,
There the maiden stood in thought,
With straight brows and yellow hair,
Never saw ye fairer fair!
On the wood she gazed below,
And she saw the roses blow,
Heard the birds sing loud and low,
Therefore spoke she wofully:
"Ah me, wherefore do I lie
Here in prison wrongfully;
Aucassin, my love, my knight,
Am I not thy heart's delight,
Thou that lovest me aright!
'Tis for thee that I must dwell
In the vaulted chamber cell,
Hard beset and all alone!
By our Lady Mary's Son
Here no longer will I wonn,
    If I may flee!"

Then speak they, say they, tell they the Tale:

Nicolete was in prison, as ye have heard soothly, in the chamber. And the noise and bruit of it went through all the country and all the land, how that Nicolete was lost. Some said she had fled the coun-try, and some that the Count Garin de Biaucaire had let slay her. Whosoever had joy thereof, Aucas-sin had none, so he went to the Captain of the town and spoke to him, saying:

"Sir Captain, what hast thou made of Nicolete, my sweet lady and love, the thing that best I love in all the world? Hast thou carried her off or rav-ished her away from me? Know well that if I die of it, the price shall be demanded of thee, and that will be well done, for it shall be even as if thou hadst slain me with thy two hands, for thou hast taken from me the thing that in this world I loved the best."

"Fair Sir," said the Captain, "let these things be. Nicolete is a captive that I did bring from a strange country. Yea, I bought her at my own charges of the Saracens, and I bred her up and baptized her, and made her my daughter in God. And I have cherished her, and one of these days I would have given her a young man, to win her bread honorably. With this hast thou naught to make, but do thou take the daughter of a King or a Count. Nay more, what wouldst thou deem thee to have gained, hadst thou made her thy leman, and taken her to thy bed? Plentiful lack of comfort hadst thou got thereby, for in Hell would thy soul have lain while the world en-dures, and into Paradise wouldst thou have entered never."

"In Paradise what have I to win? Therein I seek not to enter, but only to have Nicolete, my sweet lady that I love so well. For into Paradise go none but such folk as I shall tell thee now: thither go these same old priests, and halt old men and maimed, who all day and night cower continually before the altars, and in the crypts; and such folk as wear old amices and old clouted frocks, and naked folk and shoeless, and covered with sores, perishing of hunger and thirst, and of cold, and of little ease. These be they that go into Paradise; with them have I naught to make. But into Hell would I fain go; for into Hell fare the goodly clerks, and goodly knights that fall in tourneys and great wars, and stout men at arms, and all men noble. With these would I liefly go. And thither pass the sweet ladies and courteous that have two lovers, or three, and their lords also thereto. Thither goes the gold, and the silver, and cloth of vair, and cloth of gris, and harpers, and makers, and the prince of this world. With these I would gladly go, let me but have with me Nicolete, my sweetest lady."

86. "In Paradise . . ." This passage, probably the most celebrated in *Aucassin and Nicolete*, is an excellent corrective to the prevailing concept of the Middle Ages as altogether priest-ridden. 93. **amices,** vestments consisting of a rectangular piece of fine white linen on which a small cross is embroidered. **clouted,** ragged. 104. **vair . . . gris,** two kinds of fur; vair is believed to have been used only by the nobility and may have been ermine; gris was presumably less costly, and, as the name implies, gray in color.

"Certes," quoth the Captain, "in vain wilt thou speak thereof, for never shalt thou see her; and if thou hadst word with her, and thy father knew it, he would let burn in a fire both her and me, and thyself might well be sore adread."

"That is even what irketh me," quoth Aucassin. So he went from the Captain sorrowing.

Here singeth one:

Aucassin did so depart
10 Much in dole and heavy at heart
For his love so bright and dear,
None might bring him any cheer,
None might give good words to hear,
To the palace doth he fare,
Climbeth up the palace-stair,
Passeth to a chamber there,
Thus great sorrow doth he bear
For his lady and love so fair.

"Nicolete, how fair art thou,
20 Sweet thy foot-fall, sweet thine eyes,
Sweet the mirth of thy replies,
Sweet thy laughter, sweet thy face,
Sweet thy lips and sweet thy brow,
And the touch of thine embrace,
All for thee I sorrow now,
Captive in an evil place,
Whence I ne'er may go my ways,
   Sister, sweet friend!"

So say they, speak they, tell they the Tale:
30 While Aucassin was in the chamber sorrowing for Nicolete his love, even then the Count Bougars de Valence, that had his war to wage, forgot it no whit, but had called up his horsemen and his footmen, so made he for the castle to storm it. And the cry of battle arose, and the din, and knights and men at arms, busked them, and ran to walls and gates to hold the keep. And the townsfolk mounted to the battlements, and cast down bolts and pikes. Then while the assault was great; even at its height, the
40 Count Garin de Biaucaire came into the chamber where Aucassin was making lament, sorrowing for Nicolete, his sweet lady that he loved so well.

"Ha! son," quoth he, "how caitiff art thou, and cowardly, that canst see men assail thy goodliest castle and strongest. Know thou that if thou lose it, thou losest all. Son, go to, take arms, and mount thy horse, and defend thy land, and help thy men, and fare into the stour. Thou needst not smite nor be smitten. If they do but see thee among them, better
50 will they guard their substance, and their lives, and thy land and mine. And thou art so great, and hardy of thy hands, that well mightst thou do this thing, and to do it is thy devoir."

"Father," said Aucassin, "what is this thou sayest

The siege of a medieval city, from a manuscript history.

now? God grant me never aught of my desire, if I be dubbed knight, or mount steed, or go into the stour where knights do smite and are smitten, if thou givest me not Nicolete, my sweet lady, whom I love so well."

"Son," quoth his father, "this may never be; rather 60 would I be quite disinherited and lose all that is mine, than that thou shouldst have her to thy wife, or to love *par amours*."

So he turned him about. But when Aucassin saw him going, he called to him again, saying,

"Father, go to now; I will make with thee fair covenant."

"What covenant, fair son?"

"I will take up arms, and go into the stour, on this covenant, that, if God bring me back sound and 70 safe, thou wilt let me see Nicolete my sweet lady, even so long that I may have of her two words or three, and one kiss."

"That will I grant," said his father.

At this was Aucassin glad.

Here one singeth:

Of the kiss heard Aucassin
That returning he shall win.
None so glad would he have been 80
Of a myriad marks of gold
Of a hundred thousand told.
Called for raiment brave of steel,
Then they clad him, head to heel,
Twyfold hauberk doth he don,
Firmly braced the helmet on.
Girt the sword with hilt of gold,

63. *par amours*, as a paramour or mistress.

Horse doth mount, and lance doth wield,
Looks to stirrups and to shield,
Wondrous brave he rode to field.
Dreaming of his lady dear
Setteth spurs to the destrere,
Rideth forward without fear,
Through the gate and forth away
    To the fray.

So speak they, say they, tell they the Tale:

10   Aucassin was armed and mounted as ye have heard tell. God! how goodly sat the shield on his shoulder, the helm on his head, and the baldric on his left haunch! And the damoiseau was tall, fair, featly fashioned, and hardy of his hands, and the horse whereon he rode swift and keen, and straight had he spurred him forth of the gate. Now believe ye not that his mind was on kine, nor cattle of the booty, nor thought he how he might strike a knight, nor be stricken again; nor no such thing. Nay, no 20 memory had Aucassin of aught of these; rather, he so dreamed of Nicolete, his sweet lady, that he dropped his reins, forgetting all there was to do, and his horse that had felt the spur, bore him into the press and hurled him among the foe, and they laid hands on him all about, and took him captive, and seized away his spear and shield, and straight-way they led him off a prisoner, and were even now discoursing of what death he should die.

   And when Aucassin heard them,

30   "Ha! God," said he, "sweet Saviour. Be these my deadly enemies that have taken me, and will soon cut off my head? And once my head is off, no more shall I speak with Nicolete, my sweet lady that I love so well. Natheless have I here a good sword, and sit a good horse unwearied. If now I keep not my head for her sake, God help her never, if she love me more!"

   The damoiseau was tall and strong, and the horse whereon he sat was right eager. And he laid hand 40 to sword, and fell a-smiting to right and left, and smote through helm and nasal, and arm and clenched hand, making a murder about him, like a wild boar when hounds fall on him in the forest, even till he struck down ten knights, and seven he hurt, and straightway he hurled out of the press, and rode back again at full speed, sword in hand. The Count Bougars de Valence heard say they were about hanging Aucassin, his enemy, so he came into that place, and Aucassin was ware of him, and gat 50 his sword into his hand, and lashed at his helm with such a stroke that he drove it down on his head, and he being stunned, fell grovelling. And Aucassin laid hands on him, and caught him by the nasal of his helmet, and gave him to his father.

"Father," quoth Aucassin, "lo, here is your mortal foe, who hath so warred you with all malengin. Full twenty years did this war endure, and might not be ended by man."

"Fair son," said his father, "thy feats of youth shouldst thou do, and not seek after folly." 60

"Father," saith Aucassin, "sermon me no sermons, but fulfill my covenant."

"Ha! what covenant, fair son?"

"What, father, hast thou forgotten it? By mine own head, whosoever forgets, will I not forget it, so much it hath me at heart. Didst thou not covenant with me when I took up arms, and went into the stour, that if God brought me back safe and sound, thou wouldst let me see Nicolete, my sweet lady, ever so long that I may have of her two words or 70 three, and one kiss? So didst thou covenant, and my mind is that thou keep thy word."

"I!" quoth the father, "God forsake me when I keep this covenant! Nay, if she were here, I would let burn her in the fire, and thyself shouldst be sore adread."

"Is this thy last word?" quoth Aucassin.

"So help me God," quoth his father, "yea!"

"Certes," quoth Aucassin, "this is a sorry thing, meseems, when a man of thine age lies!" 80

"Count of Valence," quoth Aucassin, "I took thee?"

"In sooth, Sir, thou didst," saith the Count.

"Give me thy hand," saith Aucassin.

"Sir, with good will."

So he set his hand in the other's.

"Now givest thou me thy word," saith Aucassin, "that never whilst thou art living man wilt thou avail to do my father dishonor, or harm him in body, or in goods, but do it thou wilt?" 90

"Sir, in God's name," saith he, "mock me not, but put me to my ransom; ye cannot ask of me gold nor silver, horses nor palfreys, vair nor gris, hawks nor hounds, but I will give you them."

"What," quoth Aucassin, "Ha! knowest thou not it was I that took thee?"

"Yea, sir," quoth the Count Bougars.

"God help me never, but I will make thy head fly from thy shoulders, if thou makest not troth," said Aucassin. 100

"In God's name," said he, "I make what promise thou wilt."

So they did the oath, and Aucassin let mount him on a horse, and took another and so led him back till he was in all safety.

Here one singeth:

When the Count Garin doth know
That his child would ne'er forego

41. nasal, nose-guard.

56. malengin, evil intent.

Love of her that loved him so,
Nicolete, the bright of brow,
In a dungeon deep below
Childe Aucassin did he throw.
Even there the Childe must dwell
In a dun-walled marble-cell.
There he waileth in his woe
Crying thus as ye shall know.

"Nicolete, thou lily white,
10 My sweet lady, bright of brow,
Sweeter than the grape art thou,
Sweeter than sack posset good
In a cup of maple wood!
Was it not but yesterday
That a palmer came this way,
Out of Limousin came he,
And at ease he might not be,
For a passion him possessed
That upon his bed he lay,
20 Lay and tossed and knew not rest
In his pain discomforted.
But thou camest by the bed,
Where he tossed amid his pain,
Holding high thy sweeping train,
And thy kirtle of ermine,
And thy smock of linen fine,
Then these fair white limbs of thine,
Did he look on, and it fell
That the palmer straight was well,
30 Straight was hale—and comforted,
And he rose up from his bed,
And went back to his own place,
Sound and strong, and full of face!
My sweet lady, lily white,
Sweet thy footfall, sweet thine eyes,
And the mirth of thy replies.
Sweet thy laughter, sweet thy face,
Sweet thy lips and sweet thy brow,
And the touch of thine embrace.
40 Who but doth in thee delight?
I for love of thee am bound
In this dungeon under ground,
All for loving thee must lie
Here where loud on thee I cry,
Here for loving thee must die
          For thee, my love."

Then say they, speak they, tell they the Tale:
    Aucassin was cast into prison as ye have heard
tell, and Nicolete, of her part, was in the chamber.
50 Now it was summer time, the month of May, when
days are warm, and long, and clear, and the night
still and serene. Nicolete lay one night on her bed,
and saw the moon shine clear through a window,
yea, and heard the nightingale sing in the garden,
so she minded her of Aucassin her lover, whom she
loved so well. Then fell she to thoughts of Count
Garin de Biaucaire, that hated her to the death;
therefore deemed she that there she would no longer
abide, for that, if she were told of, and the Count
knew whereas she lay, an ill death would he make 60
her die. Now she knew that the old woman slept
who held her company. Then she arose, and clad
her in a mantle of silk she had by her, very goodly,
and took napkins, and sheets of the bed, and knotted
one to the other, and made therewith a cord as long
as she might, so knitted it to a pillar in the window,
and let herself slip down into the garden, then
caught up her raiment in both hands, behind and
before, and kilted up her kirtle, because of the dew
that she saw lying deep on the grass, and so went 70
her way down through the garden.
    Her locks were yellow and curled, her eyes blue
and smiling, her face feately fashioned, the nose high
and fairly set, the lips more red than cherry or rose
in time of summer, her teeth white and small; her
breasts so firm that they bore up the folds of her
bodice as they had been two apples; so slim was she
in the waist that your two hands might have clipped
her, and the daisy flowers that brake beneath her
as she went tip-toe, and that bent above her instep, 80
seemed black against her feet, so white was the
maiden. She came to the postern-gate, and unbarred
it, and went out through the streets of Biaucaire,
keeping always on the shadowy side, for the moon
was shining right clear, and so wandered she till she
came to the tower where her lover lay. The tower
was flanked with buttresses, and she cowered under
one of them, wrapped in her mantle. Then thrust
she her head through a crevice of the tower that
was old and worn, and so heard she Aucassin wail- 90
ing within, and making dole and lament for the
sweet lady he loved so well. And when she had
listened to him, she began to say;
    Here one singeth:

Nicolete the bright of brow
On a pillar leanest thou,
All Aucassin's wail dost hear
For his love that is so dear,
Then thou spakest, shrill and clear,
"Gentle knight withouten fear, 100
Little good befalleth thee,
Little help of sigh or tear,
Ne'er shalt thou have joy of me.
Never shalt thou win me; still
Am I held in evil will
Of thy father and thy kin,
Therefore must I cross the sea,
And another land must win."
Then she cut her curls of gold,

76–77. **breasts . . . apples.** "*Nois gauges* in the original. But 'wal-
nuts' sound inadequate." (Translator's note.)

AUCASSIN AND NICOLETE

Cast them in the dungeon bold,
Aucassin doth clasp them there,
Kissed the curls that were so fair,
Them doth in his bosom bear,
Then he wept, even as of old,
   All for his love!

Then say they, speak they, tell they the Tale:
   When Aucassin heard Nicolete say that she would
pass into a far country, he was all in wrath.
10 "Fair sweet friend," quoth he, "thou shalt not go,
for then wouldst thou be my death. And the first
man that saw thee and had the might withal, would
take thee straightway into his bed to be his leman.
And once thou camest into a man's bed, and that
bed not mine, wit ye well that I would not tarry till
I had found a knife to pierce my heart and slay
myself. Nay, verily, wait so long I would not; but
would hurl myself on it so soon as I could find a
wall, or a black stone, thereon would I dash my head
20 so mightily that the eyes would start and my brain
burst. Rather would I die even such a death than
know thou hadst lain in a man's bed, and that bed
not mine."
   "Aucassin," she said, "I trow thou lovest me not
so much as thou sayest, but I love thee more than
thou lovest me."
   "Ah, fair sweet friend," said Aucassin, "it may not
be that thou shouldst love me even as I love thee.
Woman may not love man as man loves woman,
30 for a woman's love lies in the glance of her eye, and
the bud of her breast, and her foot's tip-toe; but the
love of man is in his heart planted, whence it can
never issue forth and pass away."
   Now while Aucassin and Nicolete held this parley
together, the town's guards came down a street, with
swords drawn beneath their cloaks, for the Count
Garin had charged them that if they could take her
they should slay her. But the sentinel that was on
the tower saw them coming, and heard them speak-
40 ing of Nicolete as they went, and threatening to slay
her.
   "God!" quoth he, "this were great pity to slay so
fair a maid! Right great charity it were if I could
say aught to her, and they perceive it not, and she
should be on her guard against them, for if they slay
her, then were Aucassin, my damoiseau, dead, and
that were great pity."
   Here one singeth:

Valiant was the sentinel,
50 Courteous, kind, and practised well,
So a song did sing and tell

51. **song did sing.** This warning song of the sentinel belongs to the
tradition of the *aubade,* or "dawn-song," a French courtly lyric poem
lamenting the necessity for lovers to separate but urging them to do
so in the face of danger, usually from an oncoming husband.

Of the peril that befell.
"Maiden fair that lingerest here,
Gentle maid of merry cheer,
Hair of gold, and eyes as clear
As the water in a mere,
Thou, meseems, hast spoken word
To thy lover and thy lord,
That would die for thee, his dear;
Now beware the ill accord, 60
Of the cloaked men of the sword,
These have sworn and keep their word,
They will put thee to the sword
   Save thou take heed!"

Then speak they, say they, tell they the Tale:
   "Ha!" quoth Nicolete, "be the soul of thy father
and the soul of thy mother in the rest of Paradise,
so fairly and courteously hast thou spoken me!
Please God, I will be right ware of them, God keep
me out of their hands." 70
   So she shrank under her mantle into the shadow
of the pillar till they had passed by, and then took
she farewell of Aucassin, and so fared till she came
unto the castle wall. Now that wall was wasted and
broken, and some deal mended, so she clomb
thereon till she came between wall and fosse, and
so looked down, and saw that the fosse was deep
and steep, whereat she was sore adread.
   "Ah God," saith she, "sweet Saviour! If I let myself fall hence, I shall break my neck, and if here I 80
abide, tomorrow they will take me, and burn me in
a fire. Yet liefer would I perish here than that
tomorrow the folk should stare on me for a gazing-
stock."
   Then she crossed herself, and so let herself slip
into the fosse, and when she had come to the
bottom, her fair feet, and fair hands that had not
custom thereof, were bruised and frayed, and the
blood springing from a dozen places, yet felt she
no pain nor hurt, by reason of the great dread 90
wherein she went. But if she were in cumber to win
there, in worse was she to win out. But she deemed
that there to abide was of none avail, and she found
a pike sharpened, that they of the city had thrown
out to keep the hold. Therewith made she one stepping place after another, till, with much travail, she
climbed the wall. Now the forest lay within two
crossbow shots, and the forest was of thirty leagues
this way and that. Therein also were wild beasts,
and beasts serpentine, and she feared that if she 100
entered there, they would slay her. But anon she
deemed that if men found her there they would hale
her back into the town to burn her.
   Here one singeth:

Nicolete, the fair of face,
Climbed upon the coping-stone,

II : 143

There made she lament and moan,
Calling on our Lord alone
For His mercy and His grace.

"Father, king of Majesty,
Listen, for I nothing know
Where to flee or whither go.
If within the wood I fare,
Lo, the wolves will slay me there,
Boars and lions terrible,
10 Many in the wild wood dwell,
But if I abide the day,
Surely worse will come of it,
Surely will the fire be lit
That shall burn my body away,
Jesus, lord of Majesty,
Better seemeth it to me,
That within the wood I fare,
Though the wolves devour me there
Than within the town to go,
20   Never be it so!"

Then speak they, say they, tell they the Tale:
   Nicolete made great moan, as ye have heard; then
commended she herself to God, and anon fared till
she came unto the forest. But to go deep into it she
dared not, by reason of the wild beasts, and beasts
serpentine. Anon crept she into a little thicket, where
sleep came upon her, and she slept till prime next
day, when the shepherds issued forth from the town
and drove their beasts between wood and water.
30 Anon came they all into one place by a fair fountain
which was on the fringe of the forest; thereby spread
they a mantle, and thereon set bread. So while they
were eating, Nicolete wakened, with the sound of
the singing birds, and the shepherds, and she went
unto them, saying, "Fair boys, our Lord keep you!"
   "God bless thee," quoth he that had more words
to his tongue than the rest.
   "Fair boys," quoth she, "know ye Aucassin, the
son of Count Garin de Biaucaire?"
40   "Yea, well we know him."
   "So may God help you, fair boys," quoth she,
"tell him there is a beast in this forest, and bid him
come chase it, and if he can take it, he would not
give one limb thereof for a hundred marks of gold,
nay, for five hundred, nor for any ransom."
   Then looked they on her, and saw her so fair that
they were all astonied.
   "Will I tell him thereof?" quoth he that had more
words to his tongue than the rest, "foul fall him who
50 speaks of the thing or tells him the tidings. These
are but visions ye tell of, for there is no beast so
great in this forest, stag, nor lion, nor boar, that
one of his limbs is worth more than two deniers, or
three at the most, and ye speak of such great ransom. Foul fall him that believes your word, and

him that telleth Aucassin. Ye be a Fairy, and we
have no liking for your company; nay, hold on your
road."
   "Nay, fair boys," quoth she, "nay, ye will do my
bidding. For this beast is so mighty of medicine that 60
thereby will Aucassin be healed of his torment. And
lo! I have five sols in my purse, take them, and tell
him; for within three days must he come hunting it
hither, and if within three days he find it not, never
will he be healed of his torment."
   "My faith," quoth he, "the money will we take,
and if he come hither we will tell him, but seek
him we will not."
   "In God's name," quoth she; and so took farewell
of the shepherds, and went her way. 70
   Here singeth one:

Nicolete the bright of brow
From the shepherds doth she pass
All below the blossomed bough
Where an ancient way there was,
Overgrown and choked with grass,
Till she found the cross-roads where
Seven paths do all way fare,
Then she deemeth she will try,
Should her lover pass thereby,
If he love her loyally. 80
So she gathered white lilies,
Oak-leaf, that in green wood is,
Leaves of many a branch I wis,
Therewith built a lodge of green,
Goodlier was never seen,
Swore by God who may not lie,
"If my love the lodge should spy,
He will rest awhile thereby
If he love me loyally." 90
Thus his faith she seemed to try,
"Or I love him not, not I,
           Nor he loves me!"

Then speak they, say they, tell they the Tale:
   Nicolete built her lodge of boughs, as ye have
heard, right fair and feteously, and wove it well,
within and without, of flowers and leaves. So lay
she hard by the lodge in a deep coppice to know
what Aucassin will do. And the cry and the bruit
went abroad through all the country and all the land, 100
that Nicolete was lost. Some told that she had fled,
and some that the Count Garin had let slay her.
Whosoever had joy thereof, no joy had Aucassin.
And the Count Garin, his father, had taken him out
of prison, and had sent for the knights of that land,
and the ladies, and let make a right great feast, for
the comforting of Aucassin his son. Now at the
high time of the feast, was Aucassin leaning from a

62. sols, sous, the modern French coin; its value in the twelfth century is altogether problematical.   96. feteously, neatly.

gallery, all woful and discomforted. Whatsoever men might devise of mirth, Aucassin had no joy thereof, nor no desire, for he saw not her that he loved. Then a knight looked on him, and came to him, and said:

"Aucassin, of that sickness of thine have I been sick, and good counsel will I give thee, if thou wilt hearken to me—"

"Sir," said Aucassin, "gramercy, good counsel would I fain hear."

"Mount thy horse," quoth he, "and go take thy pastime in yonder forest; there wilt thou see the good flowers and grass, and hear the sweet birds sing. Perchance thou shalt hear some word, whereby thou shalt be the better."

"Sir," quoth Aucassin, "gramercy; that will I do."

He passed out of the hall, and went down the stairs, and came to the stable where his horse was. He let saddle and bridle him, and mounted, and rode forth from the castle, and wandered till he came to the forest, so rode till he came to the fountain and found the shepherds at the point of noon. And they had a mantle stretched on the grass, and were eating bread, and making great joy.

Here one singeth:

There were gathered shepherds all,
Martin, Esmerie, and Hal,
Aubrey, Robin, great and small.
Saith the one, "Good fellows all,
God keep Aucassin the fair,
And the maid with yellow hair,
Bright of brown and eyes of vair.
She that gave us gold to ware,
Cakes therewith to buy, ye know,
Goodly knives and sheaths also,
Flutes to play, and pipes to blow,
    May God him heal!"

Here speak they, say they, tell they the Tale:

When Aucassin heard the shepherds, anon he bethought him of Nicolete, his sweet lady whom he loved so well, and he deemed that she had passed thereby; then set he spurs to his horse, and so came to the shepherds.

"Fair boys, God be with you."

"God bless you," quoth he that had more words to his tongue than the rest.

"Fair boys," quoth Aucassin, "say the song again that anon ye sang."

"Say it again we will not," quoth he that had more words to his tongue than the rest, "foul fall him who will sing it again for you, fair sir!"

"Fair boys," quoth Aucassin, "know ye me not?"

"Yea, we know well that you are Aucassin, our damoiseau, natheless we be not your men, but the Count's."

"Fair boys, yet sing it again, I pray you."

"Hearken! by the Holy Heart," quoth he, "wherefore should I sing it for you, if it likes me not? Lo, there is no such rich man in this country, saving the body of Garin the Count, that dare drive forth my oxen, or my cows, or my sheep, if he finds them in his fields, or his corn, lest he lose his eyes for it, and wherefore should I sing for you, if it likes me not?"

"God be your aid, fair boys, sing it ye will, and take ye these ten sols I have here in a purse."

"Sir, the money will we take, but never a note will I sing, for I have given my oath; but I will tell thee a plain tale, if thou wilt."

"By God," saith Aucassin, "I love a plain tale better than naught."

"Sir, we were in this place, a little time agone, between prime and tierce, and were eating our bread by this fountain, even as now we do, and a maid came past, the fairest thing in the world, whereby we deemed that she should be a fay, and all the wood shone round about her. Anon she gave us of that she had, whereby we made covenant with her, that if ye came hither we would bid you hunt in the forest, wherein is such a beast that, an ye might take him, ye would not give one limb of him for five hundred marks of silver, nor for no ransom; for this beast is so mighty of medicine, that, an ye could take him, ye should be healed of your torment, and within three days must ye take him, and if ye take him not then, never will ye look on him. So chase ye the beast, an ye will, or an ye will let be, for my promise have I kept with her."

"Fair boys," quoth Aucassin, "ye have said enough. God grant me to find this quarry."

Here one singeth:

Aucassin when he had heard,
Sore within his heart was stirred,
Left the shepherds on that word,
Far into the forest spurred,
Rode into the wood; and fleet
Fled his horse through paths of it,
Three words spoke he of his sweet,
"Nicolete the fair, the dear,
'Tis for thee I follow here
Track of boar, nor slot of deer,
But thy sweet body and eyes so clear,
All thy mirth and merry cheer,
That my very heart have slain,
So please God to me maintain
I shall see my love again,
    Sweet sister, friend!"

Then speak they, say they, tell they the Tale:

Aucassin fared through the forest from path to path after Nicolete, and his horse bore him furiously. Think ye not that the thorns him spared, nor the briars, nay, not so, but tore his raiment, that scarce a knot might be tied with the soundest part thereof, and the blood sprang from his arms, and flanks, and legs, in forty places, or thirty, so that behind the Childe men might follow on the track of his blood in the grass. But so much he went in thoughts of Nicolete, his lady sweet, that he felt no pain nor torment, and all the day hurled through the forest in this fashion nor heard no word of her. And when he saw Vespers draw nigh, he began to weep for that he found her not. All down an old road, and grassgrown, he fared, when anon, looking along the way before him, he saw such an one as I shall tell you. Tall was he, and great of growth, laidly and marvellous to look upon; his head huge, and black as charcoal, and more than the breadth of a hand between his two eyes, and great cheeks, and a big nose and broad, big nostrils and ugly, and thick lips redder than a collop, and great teeth yellow and ugly, and he was shod with hosen and shoon of bull's hide, bound with cords of bark over the knee, and all about him a great cloak twyfold, and he leaned on a grievous cudgel, and Aucassin came unto him, and was afraid when he beheld him.

"Fair brother, God aid thee."

"God bless you," quoth he.

"As God he helpeth thee, what makest thou here?"

"What is that to thee?"

"Nay, naught, naught," saith Aucassin, "I ask but out of courtesy."

"But for whom weepest thou," quoth he, "and makest such heavy lament? Certes, were I as rich a man as thou, the whole world should not make me weep."

"Ha, know you me?" saith Aucassin.

"Yea, I know well that ye be Aucassin, the son of the Count, and if ye tell me for why ye weep, then will I tell you what I make here."

"Certes," quoth Aucassin, "I will tell you right gladly. Hither came I this morning to hunt in this forest; and with me a white hound, the fairest in the world; him have I lost, and for him I weep."

"By the Heart our Lord bore in His breast," quoth he, "are ye weeping for a stinking hound? Foul fall him that holds thee high henceforth! for there is no such rich man in the land, but if thy father asked it of him, he would give thee ten, or fifteen, or twenty, and be the gladder for it. But I have cause to weep and make dole."

"Wherefore so, brother?"

"Sir, I will tell thee. I was hireling to a rich villain, and drove his plough; four oxen had he. But three days since came on me great misadventure, whereby I lost the best of mine oxen, Roger, the best of my team. Him go I seeking, and have neither eaten nor drunken these three days, nor may I go to the town, lest they cast me into prison, seeing that I have not wherewithal to pay. Out of all the wealth of the world have I no more than ye see on my body. A poor mother bore me, that had no more but one wretched bed; this have they taken from under her, and she lies in the very straw. This ails me more than mine own case, for wealth comes and goes; if now I have lost, another time will I gain, and will pay for mine ox whenas I may; never for that will I weep. But you weep for a stinking hound. Foul fall whoso thinks well of thee!"

"Certes thou art a good comforter, brother, blessed be thou! And of what price was thine ox?"

"Sir, they ask me twenty sols for him, whereof I cannot abate one doit."

"Nay, then," quoth Aucassin, "take these twenty sols I have in my purse, and pay for thine ox."

"Sir," saith he, "gramercy. And God give thee to find that thou seekest."

So they parted each from other, and Aucassin rode on; the night was fair and still, and so long he went that he came to the lodge of boughs, that Nicolete had builded and woven within and without, over and under, with flowers, and it was the fairest lodge that might be seen. When Aucassin was ware of it, he stopped suddenly, and the light of the moon fell therein.

"God!" quoth Aucassin, "here was Nicolete, my sweet lady, and this lodge builded she with her fair hands. For the sweetness of it, and for love of her, will I alight, and rest here this night long."

He drew forth his foot from the stirrup to alight, and the steed was great and tall. He dreamed so much on Nicolete his right sweet lady, that he slipped on a stone, and drove his shoulder out of its place. Then knew he that he was hurt sore; natheless he bore him with what force he might, and fastened with the other hand the mare's son to a thorn. Then turned he on his side, and crept backwise into the lodge of boughs. And he looked through a gap in the lodge and saw the stars in Heaven, and one that was brighter than the rest; so began he to say:

Here one singeth:

"Star, that I from far behold,
Star, the Moon calls to her fold,
Nicolete with thee doth dwell,
My sweet love with locks of gold,
God would have her dwell afar,
Dwell with him for evening star,
Would to God, whate'er befall,
Would that with her I might dwell.

---

4. **Childe,** young knight.   13. **Tall was he** . . . The man represented here is the loathly (laidly) churl, who is a convention of medieval legend. To be noted here is his forthrightness in the presence of Aucassin (matched by that of the shepherds some lines above) and particularly his tender regard for his mother, since sentimentality about mothers was not a common feature of medieval literature.
18. **collop,** a large piece of meat for stewing.

I would clip her close and strait;
Nay, were I of much estate,
Some king's son desirable,
Worthy she to be my mate,
Me to kiss and clip me well,
  Sister, sweet friend!"

So speak they, say they, tell they the Tale:

When Nicolete heard Aucassin, right so came she unto him, for she was not far away. She passed 10 within the lodge, and threw her arms about his neck, and clipped and kissed him.

"Fair sweet friend, welcome be thou."

"And thou, fair sweet love, be thou welcome."

So either kissed and clipped the other, and fair joy was between them.

"Ha! sweet love," quoth Aucassin, "but now was I sore hurt, and my shoulder wried, but I take no force of it, nor have no hurt therefrom since I have thee."

20 Right so felt she his shoulder and found it was wried from its place. And she so handled it with her white hands, and so wrought in her surgery, that by God's will who loveth lovers, it went back into its place. Then took she flowers, and fresh grass, and leaves green, and bound these herbs on the hurt with a strip of her smock, and he was all healed.

"Aucassin," saith she, "fair sweet love, take counsel what thou wilt do. If thy father let search this 30 forest tomorrow, and men find me here, they will slay me, come to thee what will."

"Certes, fair sweet love, therefore should I sorrow heavily, but, an if I may, never shall they take thee."

Anon got he on his horse, and his lady before him, kissing and clipping her, and so rode they at adventure.

Here one singeth:

Aucassin the frank, the fair,
40 Aucassin of the yellow hair,
Gentle knight, and true lover,
From the forest doth he fare,
Holds his love before him there,
Kissing cheek, and chin, and eyes,
But she spoke in sober wise,
"Aucassin, true love and fair,
To what land do we repair?"
Sweet my love, I take no care,
Thou art with me everywhere!
50 So they pass the woods and downs,
Pass the villages and towns,
Hills and dales and open land,
Came at dawn to the sea sand,
Lighted down upon the strand,
  Beside the sea.

1. **clip,** embrace.

Then say they, speak they, tell they the Tale:

Aucassin lighted down and his love, as ye have heard sing. He held his horse by the bridle, and his lady by the hands; so they went along the sea shore, and on the sea they saw a ship, and he called unto 60 the sailors, and they came to him. Then held he such speech with them, that he and his lady were brought aboard that ship, and when they were on the high sea, behold a mighty wind and tyrannous arose, marvellous and great, and drove them from land to land, till they came unto a strange country, and won the haven of the castle of Torelore. Then asked they what this land might be, and men told them that it was the country of the King of Torelore. Then he asked what manner of man was he, and 70 was there war afoot, and men said,

"Yea, and mighty!"

Therewith took he farewell of the merchants, and they commended him to God. Anon Aucassin mounted his horse, with his sword girt, and his lady before him, and rode at adventure till he was come to the castle. Then asked he where the King was, and they said that he was in childbed.

"Then where is his wife?"

And they told him she was with the army, and 80 had led with her all the force of that country.

Now when Aucassin heard that saying, he made great marvel, and came into the castle, and lighted down, he and his lady, and his lady held his horse. Right so went he up into the castle, with his sword girt, and fared hither and thither till he came to the chamber where the King was lying.

Here one singeth:

Aucassin the courteous knight
To the chamber went forthright, 90
To the bed with linen dight
Even where the King was laid.
There he stood by him and said:
"Fool, what makest thou here abed?"
Quoth the King: "I am brought to bed
Of a fair son, and anon
When my month is over and gone,
And my healing fairly done,
To the Minster will I fare
And will do my churching there, 100
As my father did repair,
Then will sally forth to war,
Then will drive my foes afar
  From my countrie!"

Then speak they, say they, tell they the Tale:

When Aucassin heard the King speak on this wise,

78. **he was in childbed.** This is an old folklore motif, known as the Couvade, that a man lay in childbirth while his wife assumed his manly and military duties. "The feigned lying-in of the father may have been either a recognition of paternity . . . or may have been caused by the belief that the health of the father at the time of a child's birth affected that of the child . . ." (Translator's note.)

he took all the sheets that covered him, and threw them all abroad about the chamber. Then saw he behind him a cudgel, and caught it into his hand, and turned, and took the King, and beat him till he was well-nigh dead.

"Ha, fair sir," quoth the King, "what would you with me? Art thou beside thyself, that beatest me in mine own house?"

10 "By God's heart," quoth Aucassin, "thou ill son of an ill wench, I will slay thee if thou swear not that never shall any man in all thy land lie in of child henceforth for ever."

So he did that oath, and when he had done it,

"Sir," said Aucassin, "bring me now where thy wife is with the army."

"Sir, with good will," quoth the King.

He mounted his horse, and Aucassin got on his own, and Nicolete abode in the Queen's chamber.
20 Anon rode Aucassin and the King even till they came to that place where the Queen was, and lo! men were warring with baked apples, and with eggs, and with fresh cheeses, and Aucassin began to look on them, and made great marvel.

Here one singeth:

Aucassin his horse doth stay,
From the saddle watched the fray,
All the stour and fierce array;
Right fresh cheeses carried they,
Apples baked, and mushrooms gray,
30 Whoso splasheth most the ford
He is master called and lord.
Aucassin doth gaze awhile,
Then began to laugh and smile
  And made game.

Then speak they, say they, tell they the Tale:
When Aucassin beheld these marvels, he came to the King, and said: "Sir, be these thine enemies?"

"Yea, Sir," quoth the King.

"And will ye that I should avenge you of them?"
40 "Yea," quoth he, "with all my heart."

Then Aucassin put hand to sword, and hurled among them, and began to smite to the right hand and the left, and slew many of them. And when the King saw that he slew them, he caught at his bridle and said,

"Ha, fair sir! Slay them not in such wise."

"How?" quoth Aucassin. "Will ye not that I should avenge you of them?"

"Sir," quoth the King, "overmuch already hast
50 thou avenged me. It is nowise our custom to slay each other."

Anon turned they and fled. Then the King and Aucassin betook them again to the castle of Torelore, and the folk of that land counselled the King to put Aucassin forth, and keep Nicolete for his son's wife, for that she seemed a lady high of lineage.

And Nicolete heard them, and had no joy of it, so began to say:

Here singeth one:

Thus she spoke, the bright of brow: 60
"Lord of Torelore and king,
Thy folk deem me a light thing.
When my love doth me embrace,
Fair he finds me, in good case,
Then am I in such derray, 65
Neither harp, nor lyre, nor lay,
Dance nor game, nor rebeck-play
  Were so sweet."

Then speak they, say they, tell they the Tale:
Aucassin dwelt in the castle of Torelore, in great 70 ease and great delight, for that he had with him Nicolete his sweet love, whom he loved so well. Now while he was in such pleasure and such delight, came a troop of Saracens by sea, and laid siege to the castle and took it by main strength. Anon took they the substance that was therein and carried off the men and maidens captives. They seized Nicolete and Aucassin, and bound Aucassin hand and foot, and cast him into one ship, and Nicolete into another. Then rose there a mighty 80 wind over sea, and scattered the ships. Now that ship wherein was Aucassin went wandering on the sea, till it came to the castle of Biaucaire, and the folk of the country ran together to wreck her, and there found they Aucassin, and they knew him again. So when they of Biaucaire saw their damoiseau, they made great joy of him, for Aucassin had dwelt full three years in the castle of Torelore, and his father and mother were dead. So the people took him to the castle of Biaucaire, and there were they all his 90 men. And he held the land in peace.

Here singeth one:

Lo ye, Aucassin hath gone
To Biaucaire that is his own,
Dwelleth there in joy and ease
And the kingdom is at peace.
Swears he by the Majesty
Of our Lord that is most high,
Rather would he they should die
All his kin and parentry, 100
So that Nicolete were nigh.

"Ah sweet love, and fair of brow,
I know not where to seek thee now,
God made never that countrie,
Not by land, and not by sea,
Where I would not search for thee,
  If that might be!"

65. derray, distraction.

Then speak they, say they, tell they the Tale:

Now leave we Aucassin, and speak we of Nicolete. The ship wherein she was cast pertained to the King of Carthage, and he was her father, and she had twelve brothers, all princes or kings. When they beheld Nicolete, how fair she was, they did her great worship, and made much joy of her, and many times asked her who she was, for surely seemed she a lady of noble line and high parentry. But she might not tell them of her lineage, for she was but a child when men stole her away. So sailed they till they won the City of Carthage, and when Nicolete saw the walls of the castle, and the countryside, she knew that there had she been nourished and thence stolen away, being but a child. Yet was she not so young a child but that well she knew she had been daughter of the King of Carthage; and of her nurture in that city.

Here singeth one:

Nicolete the good and true
To the land hath come anew,
Sees the palaces and walls,
And the houses and the halls!
Then she spoke and said, "Alas!
That of birth so great I was,
Cousin of the Amiral
And the very child of him
Carthage counts King of Paynim,
Wild folk hold me here withal;
Nay, Aucassin, love of thee,
Gentle knight, and true, and free,
Burns and wastes the heart of me.
Ah, God grant it of His grace,
That thou hold me, and embrace,
That thou kiss me on the face,
    Love and lord!"

Then speak they, say they, tell they the Tale:

When the King of Carthage heard Nicolete speak in this wise, he cast his arms about her neck.

"Fair sweet love," saith he, "tell me who thou art, and be not adread of me."

"Sir," said she, "I am daughter to the King of Carthage, and was taken, being then a little child, it is now fifteen years gone."

When all they of the court heard her speak thus, they knew well that she spoke sooth: so made they great joy of her, and led her to the castle in great honor, as the King's daughter. And they would have given her to her lord a King of Paynim, but she had no mind to marry. There dwelt she three days or four. And she considered by what means she might seek for Aucassin. Then she got her a viol, and learned to play on it, till they would have married her on a day to a great King of Paynim, and she stole forth by night, and came to the sea-port, and dwelt with a poor woman thereby. Then took she

This French donjon *was built in the twelfth century at Château-Gaillard by Richard Coeur de Lion. Since restored.*

a certain herb, and therewith smeared her head and her face, till she was all brown and stained. And she let make coat, and mantle, and smock, and hose, and attired herself as if she had been a harper. So she took the viol and went to a mariner, and so wrought on him that he took her aboard his vessel. Then hoisted they sail, and fared on the high seas even till they came to the land of Provence. And Nicolete went forth and took the viol, and went playing through all that country, even till she came to the castle of Biaucaire, where Aucassin lay.

Here singeth one:

At Biaucaire below the tower
Sat Aucassin, on an hour,
Heard the bird, and watched the flower,
With his barons him beside,
Then came on him in that tide,
The sweet influence of love
And the memory thereof;
Thought of Nicolete the fair,
And the dainty face of her
He had loved so many years,
Then was he in dule and tears!
Even then came Nicolete,
On the stair a foot she set,
And she drew the viol-bow
Through the strings and chanted so:
"Listen, lords and knights, to me,

Lords of high or low degree,
To my story list will ye,
All of Aucassin and her
That was Nicolete the fair?
And their love was long to tell,
Deep woods through he sought her well;
Paynims took them on a day
In Torelore and bound they lay.
Of Aucassin naught know we,
10 But fair Nicolete the free
Now in Carthage doth she dwell,
There her father loves her well,
Who is king of that countrie.
Her a husband hath he found,
Paynim lord that serves Mahound!
Ne'er with him the maid will go,
For she loves a damoiseau,
Aucassin, that ye may know,
Swears to God that never mo
20 With a lover will she go
Save with him she loveth so
        In long desire."

So speak they, say they, tell they the Tale:
When Aucassin heard Nicolete speak in this wise,
he was right joyful, and drew her on one side, and
spoke, saying:
"Sweet fair friend, know ye nothing of this Nicolete, of whom ye have thus sung?"
"Yea, Sir, I know her for the noblest creature, and
30 the most gentle, and the best that ever was born on
earth. She is daughter to the King of Carthage, that
took her there where Aucassin was taken, and
brought her into the City of Carthage, till he knew
that verily she was his own daughter, whereon he
made right great mirth. Anon wished he to give her
for her lord one of the greatest kings of all Spain,
but she would rather let herself be hanged or
burned than take any lord, how great soever."
"Ha! fair sweet friend," quoth the Count Aucassin,
40 "if thou wilt go into that land again, and bid her
come and speak to me, I will give thee of my substance, more than thou wouldst dare to ask or take.
And know ye, that for the sake of her, I have no
will to take a wife, howsoever high her lineage. So
wait I for her, and never will I have a wife, but her
only. And if I knew where to find her, no need
would I have to seek her."
"Sir," quoth she, "if ye promise me that, I will
go in quest of her for your sake, and for hers, that
50 I love much."
So he swore to her, and anon let give her twenty
livres, and she departed from him, and he wept for
the sweetness of Nicolete. And when she saw him
weeping, she said:
"Sir, trouble not thyself so much withal. For in a

little while shall I have brought her into this city,
and ye shall see her."
When Aucassin heard that, he was right glad
thereof. And she departed from him, and went into
the city to the house of the Captain's wife, for the 60
Captain her father in God was dead. So she dwelt
there, and told all her tale; and the Captain's wife
knew her, and knew well that she was Nicolete that
herself had nourished. Then she let wash and bathe
her, and there rested she eight full days. Then took
she an herb that was named *Eyebright* and anointed
herself therewith, and was as fair as ever she had
been all the days of her life. Then she clothed herself in rich robes of silk whereof the lady had great
store, and then sat herself in the chamber on a 70
silken coverlet, and called the lady and bade her go
and bring Aucassin her love, and she did even so.
And when she came to the Palace she found Aucassin
weeping, and making lament for Nicolete his love,
for that she delayed so long. And the lady spoke
unto him and said:
"Aucassin, sorrow no more, but come thou on
with me, and I will show thee the thing in the world
that thou lovest best; even Nicolete thy dear love,
who from far lands hath come to seek of thee." And 80
Aucassin was right glad.
Here singeth one:

When Aucassin heareth now
That his lady bright of brow
Dwelleth in his own countrie,
Never man was glad as he.
To her castle doth he hie
With the lady speedily,
Passeth to her chamber high, 90
Findeth Nicolete thereby.
Of her true love found again
Never maid was half so fain.
Straight she leaped upon her feet;
When his love he saw at last,
Arms about her did he cast,
Kissed her often, kissed her sweet,
Kissed her lips and brows and eyes.
Thus all night do they devise,
Even till the morning white.
Then Aucassin wedded her, 100
Made her Lady of Biaucaire.
Many years abode they there,
Many years in shade or sun,
In great gladness and delight.
Ne'er hath Aucassin regret
Nor his lady Nicolete.
Now my story all is done,
        Said and sung!

66. *Eyebright.* ". . . a fanciful rendering of *Esclaire*." (Translator's note.)

The Minnesingers

When the great vogue of chivalric literature spread from France into Germany, it had for its representatives and missionaries in Germany the talented and numerous group of poets known ever since as the Minnesingers, or singers of courtly love. These poets flourished in the twelfth and thirteenth centuries, and the peak of their achievement was reached close to the year 1200. Although for a time they remained relatively independent of the metrical forms developed by the French courtly poets and troubadours, in spirit they were dedicated to the established traditions of *courtoisie*. Their work was sometimes epic in spirit, as in the fine medieval chivalric romances composed by Wolfram von Eschenbach and Gottfried von Strassburg, but it was more often lyrical. The emotion universally expressed was that of an admiring, worshipful love, addressed nearly always to a married woman or to one who had already been spoken for. The poet was customarily of the lesser nobility, and his patroness was above him in station; consequently much of this love poetry was both fulsome and artificial. In some instances the passion expressed was Platonic, in others altogether carnal; but in every case the lady was placed upon a pedestal from which she could either gaze scornfully or beam amiably upon the poet, depending upon circumstances.

Later the subject matter of these poems acquired greater range, and their forms became experimental. More than a few came to contain political or satirical implications; some were even antireligious and discreetly hostile to the tyrannies of feudalism. But the majority were usually assignable to one of a handful of types. There was, for instance, the *Spruch*, a poem in a single strophe of pure lyric outburst or of philosophical utterance. More commonly, however, the poems were in three strophes—or at least of a threefold structure—in which the first two strophes served to state and develop the theme, and the last, the so-called *Abgesang*, gave the conclusion and allowed the poet to take his leave in a manner appropriate to the court. Of this sort was the *Tagelied*, the blood-cousin of the French *aubade*, which lamented the call of the sentinel or warder who warned the lovers of the approach of daylight and danger. The *Leiche*, or lays, were more extensively narrative and were often virtually religious odes in essence. Many of the individual Minnesingers were known chiefly for writing Crusaders' Hymns, which were obviously religious in both a militant and chivalric manner. Apart from the chivalric romances like Wolfram von Eschenbach's *Parzival* or Gottfried von Strassburg's *Tristan*, which are not, strictly speaking, to be classed among the *Minnelieder*, there were many ballads of somewhat popular cast. By and large, however, the poetry of the Minnesingers is to be referred most properly to the great library of amoristic

poetry, of which, it must be insisted, shades and variations are innumerable. It is a mistake to think of this poetry as a matter of formula alone, and it is equally erroneous to demand the strict categorization of each and every one of these poems as *Sprüche, Tagelieder, Leiche,* or Crusader Hymns.

These poems were probably first delivered orally in open court, the poet himself singing the verses to a melody (the *Weise*), accompanying himself on a small harp or a lute. Their vogue in the courtly society of central Europe during the later Middle Ages was enormous; the more successful entertainers among the Minnesingers became personally so celebrated as to assume in later years a legendary status which often had no correspondence to fact. Good examples of such treatment are the cases of Tannhäuser and Walther von der Vogelweide, the latter of whom, all things considered, is the finest lyric poet of the group. Medieval European literature owes much to the Minnesingers. Leaving aside the matter of their obvious talents, we can see in them ample testimony to the perennial existence of love poetry and an excellent check upon the point of view that medieval lyricism was inspired only by religious or political considerations.

The Minnesingers

O LADY, long have I been fain
　To set my love on thee,
And made good use of all I was:
Thou hast ennobled me.
May all that I from thee have won　　　　5
To my advantage tell;
And if it ends as it begun,
You have done all things well.

—*Dietmar von Aist*

TO MY lady's bower I crept
　By the watchers unsuspected.
"Sir, the bounds you have o'erstepped!
You surprise me unprotected."
"Lady, now committed is the sin."　　　　5
"Tell me, Sir, what bringeth you my bower within?"
　　"Once again to swear the truth:
I for love of you am dying."
"Out upon thee, foolish youth!
Save the effort of thy sighing."　　　　10
"You will kill me sweet, if so you gird."
"Sigh a thousand years, you never shall be heard."
　　"And is this my recompense:
Chiding in such cruel fashion?"

The Minnesingers [8] Translated by Jethro Bithell. From *The Minnesingers* by Jethro Bithell, published by Longmans Green and Co., Ltd.
4. **Thou . . . me.** This is the basic idea of all chivalric love poetry, or, in the terms of the Minnesingers, the *Minnedienst*, or service of love.

"Sir, you have but little sense, 15
Wantonly to stir my passion."
"Mistress, my existence you have blighted."
"You're an arrant fool to love me uninvited."
 "Could I other than adore you
When I looked upon your beauty?" 20
"You insult me! I implore you
To respect my wifely duty."
"To insult you never came into my mind."
"You would boast of my dishonor, were I kind."
 "I am faithful and discreet; 25
My deserts you still have scanted."
"I forbid you to entreat
Favors that can ne'er be granted."
"Of love's long servitude is this the fee?"
"Others may accord you what you seek of me." 30
 "Then my singing must remain,
And true service, unrewarded?"
"Nay, your pains were not in vain:
Guerdon good shall be accorded."
"I entreat you, make your meaning plain!" 35
"You are happier now and nobler in the grain."
    —Albrecht von Johannsdorf

W HAT sweetness into that old word *woman*
   grew!
How soothing is it both to speak and hear!
There is no other word rings half so true;
It is the seal of noble things and dear.
Not even he thou lovest, none on earth, 5
O woman, praises thee to thy full worth.
Thou dost enrich the soul
Of all: and shall I lack my dole?
    —Reinmar von Hagenau

W ILL you take this wilding wreath?"
   I murmured to a maiden fair,
"To grace the dance on the heath
When you wear it on your shining hair,
If I had many a precious jewel, 5
Yourself should wear them all
In one bright coronal—
Believe it, dearest maid, and be not cruel!

 You are so exquisite,
I culled the garland but for you: 10
Think not too mean of it.
I know where flowers of brightest hue

Are growing in the distant heather:
Birds are singing
Where they are springing— 15
There let us go to gather them together!"

 She took the gift; and said
Her thanks in maiden's manner, shy.
Her cheeks grew red
Like roses that by lilies lie. 20
She veiled her eyes as she were frightened;
The curtsy that she made
My trouble all repaid.
And was that all? Ye shall not be enlightened.

 Methought as then so fain 25
My mind had never been before:
The trees did rain
Their blossoms down upon us more and more.
Then laughed I so my sides were shaken—
Such joy it seemed 30
The while I dreamed;
And then it dawned and I was forced to awaken.

 And thus it did arise
The girls I meet these summer days
I peep into their eyes 35
Hoping my dream-maiden meet my gaze.
Is she dancing here with you, I wonder?
Lassie, just bend back
Your bonnet brim! Alack!
Could I but find her out my garland under!
    —Walther von der Vogelweide

W HATEVER be my faults, one quality
   I have been fain from childhood's days to
   keep:
I can join in not unseemly jollity,
And I am loth to laugh when others weep.
For others' sake I grieve: 5
For others' sake I sorrow;
Though sorrow to me cleave,
What matter? joy I borrow.
As others are, so will I be,
That they grow not tired of me. 10
Some there are with no compassion
For others' pains; let them be treated in like fashion.
 In the good old days, when love and honor ruled,
My youthful songs were ever smooth and cheery:
But now that love and honor are befooled, 15
My songs, alas! are rugged grown and dreary.
According as things be,
The real poet sings:
Not till boorishness shall flee
Will I sing of courtly things. 20

29. **"Of . . . fee."** This is a commonplace of all chivalric love-poetry, even down to the Renaissance. 1. **What . . . grew . . .** This little poem, a typical example of the Minnesingers' *Spruch*, was considered by Walther von der Vogelweide as Reinmar's masterpiece. Few of the Minnesingers' poems can summarize so well the essential spirit of the genre. 1. **"Will . . . wreath."** This is classed as a dancing song of the sort made famous by Reinmar von Hagenau. It is also, however, a dream song; none of the Minnesingers was capable of more beautiful lyric effects in this typical medieval medium.

39. **Your . . . brim.** Large hats were at the time especially the fashion in Austria, the home of Walther von der Vogelweide.

Joy will return and a day for song;
Happy who can wait so long.
If you will only take my word,
I know the way and when a poet should be heard.
    For a bare greeting I did praise the ladies,   25
And took it as the payment of my praise:
But now I wait in vain till my song paid is—
Let another laud, if any lady pays.
Since I no more can earn
With all my songs their smile,   30
A proud man I will turn
My back on them the while:
Which signifies: "As thou to me,
Lady, so am I to thee."
Grateful ladies, not the crowd   35
My song shall praise: what profit me the overproud?
    I will tell you of my common harm and shame—
Ladies compare with scant discrimination.
For them the good and bad men are the same:
So the good men are debased from their high sta-
        tion.   40
When dames again shall learn
To sort the men, that they
Be sorted in their turn,
Love will the more repay.
What were bad, and what were good,   45
If none distinguish could?
Noble ladies, pray you think:
If women all are equal, then your worth will sink.
                  —*Walther von der Vogelweide*

WHO slays the lion, who slays the dragon?
    He that can leave the cork in the flagon.
He that from passion's storm and strife
Can pilot his soul to a quiet life.
Virtue false, and hypocrite shame,   5
May shine awhile, like the candle's flame,
That flickers, splutters, dies out quick,
Smothered on its own muddy wick.
                  —*Walther von der Vogelweide*

WENT a maid fair to behold
    To the warder on the castle wall:
"Warder, be thou glad and bold!
If any creep, when shadows fall,
To thee, then whisper: 'Who goes there?'   5
But with a humble voice and low.
If 'yes' be answer, have no care:
That he is welcome, thou mayst know;
To the bower-window guide my lord:
Our châtelaine should well reward."   10

    In the wall's shadow, very soon,
The well-beloved holds his breath:

1. **Who . . . dragon,** another fine example of the *Spruch.*
1. **Went . . . behold,** an elaborate example of the *Tageslied.*

Keen is the warder on his boon,
And, "Who is there?" he whispereth.
"It is I who am Love's paladin: 15
Keep thou thy watch upon thy tower."
"I will not stay to guide you in!
You are of courtesy the flower."
Soon to the bower the knight was led:
He kissed the lady's lips so red.   20

    "The sun is at the heaven's brim,"
Sang a warder o'er the window-sill:
"Who sleepeth long, the worse for him;
I warn you with a right good will.
And I am innocent of all   25
If aught should hap to lovers twain.
No man the darkness can recall:
The morning star is bright again
Over the cradle of the day.
Thou trusty knight, up and away."   30

    Tears filled the gentle lady's eyes,
When such shrill song her dreams awoke:
"My knight, it dawns, thou must arise!"
In frightened loveliness she spoke.
"Let me be dearest unto thee,   35
As thou to me my dearest art,
And, as I hold thy heart with me,
I grudge thee not to hold my heart.
To the highest God I thee confide;
O woe that thou must leave my side!"   40

    With many a rich and tender word
He comforts her who fills his soul;
Such speech as is of lovers heard
Comes quick from love beyond control.
Sweet interchange of agonies,   45
With many a kiss and long delay;
Her heart did break a way to his,
As closely in his arms she lay.
After joys come often woes:
From her embrace the hero goes.
                  —*The Burgrave of Lüenz*

THE BALLAD
OF SIR TANNHÄUSER

NOW I begin another song,
    Of Tannhäuser for to tell,
And of his leman, fair Venus,
With whom he long did dwell.

    Tannhäuser was, as men do say,   5
A goodly knight of pride.

The Ballad of Sir Tannhäuser, a good example of the ballad which
was attached to the name of a prominent Minnesinger. It serves as
a basis for Wagner's famous opera.

He has wended his way to the women gay,
Through the mountain side.

"Sir Tannhäuser, I love thee still!
Thou sworest here to one; 10
To love thy fill in the hollow hill,
And never to get thee gone."

"Now I were loth to swear such oath:
I give you back the lie.
And if it were not you who spoke, 15
Then he should surely die."

"Sir Tannhäuser, hold thy tongue!
Yet shalt thou with me tarry;
And one of these my maidens young
I give thee now to marry." 20

"If another wife I take to me
Than her I love so well,
Then may I everlastingly
Burn in the fire of Hell!"

"Thou speakest of the fire of Hell, 25
Which never yet hath burned thee!
Bethink thee of my red, red mouth
And that I never spurned thee."

"O what avails your red, red mouth,
That I have come to hate? 30
Let me be gone from thee, sweet Venus,
Ere that it be too late."

"Tannhäuser, wouldst thou fain depart?
Thou shalt not go from me!
O stay with me here, my Tannhäuser dear, 35
In ravishment and glee."

"O I am growing thin and wan,
And ready for my shroud.
Let me e'en hie before I die,
All by thy body proud." 40

"Sir Tannhäuser, speak no more!
Your mind is all distraught.
But in my bower we'll go for an hour,
If love can help you aught."

"The love of your limbs is a loathsome snare! 45
I am persuaded well,
Beneath your hair and skin so fair
You are a fiend from Hell!"

"Sir Tannhäuser, thy words are ill,
And ye are bold to chide! 50
In this my hill ye must tarry still,
And dear those words abide."

"Whate'er you say, I will not stay,
I may no longer bide!
Sweet Mother of God, now help me away 55
From this evil witch's side!"

"Now will I give you leave to fare;
And only this I pray you!
To sing my praises everywhere.
The graybeard will not stay you." 60

Tannhäuser from the hill is boun,
In ruth and yet in hope.
"I will to Rome, the holy town;
My trust is in the Pope.

"Now I set out with heart so stout, 65
And Jesus' guidance crave,
Unto a Pope is Urban hight,
If haply he will save.

"Sir Pope, thou ghostly Father of mine,
My sins lie hard on me! 70
But since I truly do repine,
Let me confess to thee.

"I lingered for a long, long year
With Venus, a fair lady,
And now I seek some penance here, 75
That I my God may see."

The Pope he has a staff so stout,
The dry bough of a tree:
"Lo, when this staff shall green and sprout,
Thy sins are forgiven thee." 80

"Though I lived no more than short, short year,
To suffer away my sin,
I thought my penance to endure,
God's mercy for to win."

He has gone forth from the city gates, 85
In grief and agony.
"Mary Mother, Thou pure Virgin,
Since Thou wilt none of me,

"Then I will to the mountain go,
And ever there remain, 90
Since God has sent me to my sweet
Lady love again."

"O welcome, thou good Tannhäuser,
Whom I have missed so sore!

60. **"The graybeard . . . you."** The graybeard is taken to refer to one Eckhart, a sentinel who was stationed at the entrance to the Venusberg, the unsanctified abode of Venus.

O welcome now, my dearest lord,   95
Never to leave me more!"

And ere the third day was gone by,
The staff began to green,
And messengers rode to every land
Where Tannhäuser had been seen.   100

But he was in the mountain den,
With his sweet love to be;
And Urban that fourth Pope is damned
To all eternity.

—*Author Unknown*

LIFE AND DEATH OF THE NOBLE BRENNENBERGER

FIT I

IN VIENNA town at the Austrian court
A thousand tongues are ringing
With what the Brennenberger hath
To the noble Duchess been singing.

"O Brennenberger, dear vassal of mine,   5
Art thou indeed in earnest,
To sing there is no lady so fair
Whithersoever thou turnest?"

"Yea, lady, the fairest of women are you!
These fables that men weave   10
Of the beauty of the Queen of France
I never can believe."

"Yet will I rest not till this skein
Of lies some man unravels.
Take thou my gold, and jewels sheen,   15
And get thee on thy travels.

"And when thou seest the Queen of France,
Be judge between us twain:
And she who winneth beauty's prize,
Shall pay thee for thy pain."   20

"O lady, if ill news I bring,
I lose my hopes of Heaven;
But I am sure I shall tell you a tale
With a merry heart and steven."

FIT II

Now he has come to Paris town,   25
With jewels and with gold;

Life and Death of the Noble Brennenberger. Brennenberger was
a Minnesinger of repute but of mediocre talent. This poem probably
was of the fifteenth century and popular not at court but among the
people.

And there to the innkeeper's wife
He hath his purpose told.

"Sit in a huckster-woman's weeds,
The castle-gate before,   30
And cry, when the Queen comes forth to church:
'Come buy my jewels' store!' "

Now he became a huckster-wife,
And spread his wares to view;
And it was bruited at the Court,   35
And when the fair Queen knew,

She called her page, and charged him so:
"Before my face go summon—
With stealth and care, lest the King should know—
This wealthy huckster-woman."   40

The huckster came into the Queen's bright bower;
She could not trust her eyes.
"God sain you, most noble Queen," she said;
"Your noble ladies likewise."   44

The Queen she took her by the hand,
With snow-white hands and tender;
She bought her bracelets, she bought her rings;
There was no end of the splendor.

Now this went on till the evening came,
The huckster was in sorrow: 50
"Where shall I lie this night?" she said;
"Good store is left for tomorrow."

Brennenberger thought: "I would I were at home;
I am not made of stone.
If you vouchsafe, most noble Queen,   55
I fain would sleep alone."

The Queen spoke out: "That may not be;
Thou must be bedded meetly.
For thy necklaces and rings of price
We must with honor treat thee.   60

"Now I have here twelve maidens dear:
Lie with the youngest together;
Lie close and warm, and fear no harm
From this inclement weather."

It was about the time of Yule,   65
The longest nights of the year:
Brennenberg lay with the youngest maid,
He lay in dule and fear.

Sore dismayed by the gentle maid,
His elbow out he bent;   70

43. **sain,** bless.

*The costume worn by noble women in
the second half of the fifteenth century.*

Had he not called upon the Saints,
The Devil him had shent.

FIT III

The huckster rose at break of day;
She was in evil plight;
Twelve days the Queen there kept her pent,   75
With another maid each night.

The thirteenth day out spoke the Queen:
"With all my maids ye lay;
Now lie with me this last night of all,
We will part at the break of day."   80

He was afeared of such rich meed,
His face did blood-red burn!
"Most noble Queen, O let it wait
Till I again return.

"I will return with richer wares,   85
Which, if they you delight—
And O, if the King, your noble Lord,
Should come to you at night!"

"The King comes not to me at night;
He is to me a stranger.   90
The King has shunned me ever so long,
Thy honor will be in no danger.

"And warders three in my service stand,
Of his approach to warn:

We will of knights and heroes talk,   95
Until the break of morn."

Brennenberg was in sore distress:
"With the Queen so close to me,
She is so fair, it would be my death;
Worsted I should be.   100

"And if I harmed the lady fair,
I should forever rue;
Hers of Austria is my heart,
I will to her be true."

FIT IV

And when they went to bed that night,   105
They sought for the huckster in vain;
Brennenberg never rested an hour,
Till he came to Vienna again.

"Brennenberg, thou dear vassal of mine,
How hath it gone with thee, say?"   110
"O lady, ill and well, and I
Twelve days a prisoner lay.

"Twelve nights with tender virgins twelve;
A youth distressed was I!
And the last night of all the Queen herself   115
Desired with me to lie.

"My huckster's heart was ill bestead,
This had I not withstood;
I slunk out of the city-gate,
And fled as fast as I could."   120

"Alas, that ever I counselled thee
On her to cast thine eyes!
But say, my love, to whom wouldst thou
Adjudge all beauty's prize?"

"O lady, she is Heaven on earth,   125
None can be peer to her;
Her face was like a sun; it seemed
As if in Heaven I were."

"And if thou deemest her fairer than I,
Sing thou thy songs to her;   130
Go back to France again forthwith,
To be her servitor."

"Nay, noble lady, I say not so,
You dwell in my heart's core;
I know no fairer woman than you,   135
For whom I suffer sore."

"Yet didst thou say, a fairer dame
Thine eyes did never see."

"Yea, verily; it must have been
Her beauty blinded me.   140

"Yet you have fairer neck and chin,
And nobler is your mien;
But after you no woman is
So lovely as the Queen.   144

"And if she were twenty times fairer than you,
You is it I would praise;
For to you belong my heart and mind,
To you belong my lays."

FIT V

Now had the noble Brennenberg
Sung song on song abounding   150
In praises of his mistress high,
From land to land resounding.

The Duke he was an angry man,
And to suspicion prone:
"Ye woo my wife so much, ye yet   155
May with your life atone."

He hired three murderers with red gold,
That never pity knew;
They tore his heart hot out of his breast,
And mocked him while they slew.   160

At eve the cook, in a golden dish,
Did serve it, spiced sweet:
And her red mouth did eat the heart,
That but for her had beat.

"And do ye know what now you ate,   165
The larks baked in the pie?"
"I do not know, it tasted sweet,
And fain to know were I."

"It was the heart of Brennenberg,
Who often you delighted;   170
He brought you ever much joy and glee;
So is false love requited."

The Duchess waxed as pale as death,
As pale as death waxed she:
"And if I have eaten the heart of the knight,   175
Who brought me joy and glee,

"Thereafter I will drain a draught,
Such draught I straight will drain,
That food or drink shall nevermore
Pass my lips again."   180

Then did the noble Duchess rise,
And to her chamber go:

"Mary, Queen of Heaven, to thee
I cry my anguished woe.

"I must forever grieve for him;   185
For my sake he was killed;
My anguish for his guiltless death
Can but by death be stilled.

"Thou knowest, he never came so near
That he might me embrace;   190
And he had rather, for noble fear,
Fled a hundred miles from my face.

"To thee I cry, my heart is sore;
I die in agony;
For Thy Son's Passion's sake, give thou   195
Eternal peace to me."

Merciful Mary lifted her up,
And in her bosom cherished;
The Duke was put to the Empire's ban,
And soon repentant perished.
                                        —*Author Unknown*

HIDDEN lovers' woes
    Thou wert wont to sing ere dawn arose:
Bitter parting after raptured meeting.
Whosoever love and lady's greeting
So received that he was torn   5
From her breast by fear of men,
Thou wouldst sing him counsel, when
Shone the star of morn.
Warder, sing it now no more, lay by thy bugle-horn!

He to whom is given   10
Not to be from love by morning riven—
Whom the watchers think not to beleaguer,
Hath no need to be alert and eager
To avert the peril rife
In the day; his rest is pure,   15
Nor a warder makes secure
His unhappy life.
Love so sweet bestows in all men's sight his own
        true wife!
                              —*Wolfram von Eschenbach*

Dante Alighieri

1265–1321

The Middle Ages culminate in Dante's *Commedia*. Produced as Europe stood on the brink of a new era, this magnificent epic poem summarized nine hundred years in the evolution of Christian thought and chivalric idealism. It is shot through with an affectionate awareness of pagan antiquity, but its world is still the neat, enclosed, assured world of medieval theology, not the new world of limitless space and conflicting creeds that the Renaissance was soon to usher in.

The vast scope of Dante's masterpiece and its elaborate and intricate plan reflect the towering intellect, immense erudition, and lofty poetic vision of the man. We might assume from his learning and intense mysticism that Dante was a scholarly recluse of monkish inclinations, but nothing could be further from the truth. Only the accident of exile from his native Florence forced him into retirement from the life of action and power to which he first aspired. His family was ancient but impoverished, and had adhered to the Guelph party against the Ghibellines in the city's bitter political strife. In the rivalry of the Pope and the Holy Roman Emperor for control of the states of Italy, the Guelphs held that the Pope was supreme in both the temporal and spiritual spheres, and hence that the Emperor was his vassal. But the Ghibellines contended that the Emperor was responsible only to God and hence that he was supreme in the temporal sphere as the Pope was in the spiritual. For half a century the political power shifted from one party to the other through violent contest, but in 1289 the Ghibellines were decisively defeated at Campaldino, where young Dante served gallantly in the Guelph cavalry.

The Guelphs, now in control, soon split into two new factions—the aristocratic Blacks, who continued the Guelph support of papal authority, and the more democratic Whites, who revived some of the policies of the Ghibellines. Favoring the Whites' position, Dante served as one of the six Priors who ruled Florence in 1300, so that when the city fell to the Blacks two years later, he and other newly appointed officials were exiled and threatened with a sentence of death by fire if they returned. Thus began Dante's years of wandering through various Italian cities—Verona, Lunigiana, Lucca, Ravenna—where he made his living as a tutor and political adviser in the households of great lords. He expounded his political convictions in a Latin treatise, *De Monarchia*, setting forth the Ghibelline contention for the division of supreme power in the temporal and spiritual realms between the Emperor and the Pope. He pictured a unification of the Italian states under the peaceful rule of the Emperor, and argued for it earnestly again in the *Commedia*. But his idealistic vision was never to materialize. Although he was nostalgic for Florence in his later years, he indignantly refused to return under the humiliating conditions that he pay a fine to the state and do penance for his opposition to the Pope. At the time of his death he was at Ravenna under the protection of Guido da Polenta, a nephew of Francesca da Rimini, whose tragic love story he had told in Canto V of the *Inferno*.

Dante married Gemma Donati, of an aristocratic family, to whom he was probably betrothed in childhood. She bore him four children, but played no part in his emotional life, as far as we know from his works. It was another woman that he idealized as his symbol of romantic love, a shadowy figure in his works whom he called simply Beatrice but whom his biographer Boccaccio identified as Bice Portinari, the daughter of a prominent Florentine and eventually the wife of another, Simone de' Bardi. More important than her actual life is her life in Dante's imagination, which he set forth in brief introductions to a series of exquisite sonnets and other love poems written in 1292 as the *Vita Nuova* (New Life). According to his account, "at the beginning of her ninth year, the Glorious Lady of my mind, who was called Beatrice by many who knew not what to call her, appeared to me, and I near the end of my ninth year saw her. She appeared to me clothed in a most noble color, a modest and becoming crimson, and she was girt and adorned in such wise as befitted her very youthful age. At that instant I say truly that the spirit of life, which dwells in the most secret chamber of the heart, began to tremble with such violence that it appeared fearfully in the least pulses, and, trembling, said these words: 'Behold a god stronger than I, who coming shall rule over me!'" So began Dante's intense idealization of Beatrice, which eventually exalted her to the symbol of divine revelation in the *Commedia*. Their acquaintance seems to have been slight and confined to large social gatherings; indeed, she may never have known of his worship, because he made efforts to shield it so as to protect her reputation. Some critics see in her simply the ideal of Platonic love, a love convention that Dante inherited from older poets, especially Guido Guinicelli, his immediate master. Following this tradition, Dante's passion for Beatrice is the path to virtue and an understanding of God's love. After her early death, what personality she had for Dante in the *Vita Nuova* was gradually lost, and she became in the *Commedia* little more than the sweet embodiment of a theological idea.

But it was for her that he wrote the *Commedia*, as he had predicted he would in the closing lines of the *Vita Nuova*. He had completed seven cantos of the hundred at the time of his banishment in 1302 and apparently finished the work just before his death. Through the years he did not deviate from the mammoth plan that he had first worked out for it. Into it he poured all of the spiritual experience of his life, all of the knowledge and philosophy of his time, so that the modern reader may approach the work on at least three levels of interpretation.

On the most obvious and literal of these levels, the *Commedia* is the narrative of a journey that Dante made in a vision through hell, purgatory, and paradise, the three realms of departed spirits, which he projects in highly specific terms. Dante's conception of the universe amplified and particularized the orthodox view of the medieval Church, but he had certainly no notion that all of the geography was literally as his imagination pictured it. Several conflicting theories of the universe were current in late antiquity, but the medieval Church accepted the geocentric theory of Ptolemy because it harmonized best with Biblical tradition and Christian doctrine. If God created man as the climax of creation, it was only reasonable to suppose that the earth man inhabited was at the center of the universe.

Dante pictured the earth as a sphere floating in space, whose northern hemisphere consisted primarily of land extending from Gibraltar in the west to the Ganges in the east with the holy city of Jerusalem in its center. Beneath this inhabited hemisphere is hell, a vast pit in the shape of a funnel or inverted cone, having its apex at the center of the earth. When Satan and the rebellious angels were driven from heaven, they fell to earth, which opened this great pit to receive them. Hell has nine circles, corresponding to the seriousness of the sins of the damned souls, at the lowest of which is Satan himself, frozen forever in ice. In the center of the southern hemisphere of water, directly opposite Jerusalem, is the island mountain of Purgatory, with the Garden of Eden, the earthly paradise, at its top. On the nine ledges on its side repenting souls purify themselves for eventual worthiness of the pristine state of Eden and the actual Paradise above. Paradise consists of nine concentric circles of heavens revolving about the earth and corresponding to the moon, the sun, the planets, and the stars. Enclosing them all is the Empyrean, the motionless heaven where God and the Virgin Mary reside. It is this long way that Dante in his vision travels through the days immediately preceding and following Easter in 1300, a holy year of Papal Jubilee.

On a second plane, the *Commedia* is the spiritual autobiography of Dante himself, stripped of references to his external experiences. His parents, his wife, his children, his years of wandering find no place here, but his spiritual struggle and the divine inspiration of Beatrice are clearly set forth in symbolic terms. He informs us more than once of the evil habits into which he fell in the decade after Beatrice's death. At last at 35, a mid-point in his career, Dante finds himself lost in the dark forest of worldly sin and prevented from escaping to the hill of salvation by the three beasts of ambition, pride, and physical desire. But Beatrice as the symbol of revelation sees his plight from her abode in heaven and sends him human understanding in the form of his beloved Virgil to lead him out of the evil of hell to the purification of purgatory. He is made aware of the sins of hell one by one and then of the penances that bring him to salvation. But human understanding can lead him only to the threshold of redemption, and so Virgil, the sorrowful pagan, must leave Dante at the gate of Eden to return to his fellow heathen in Limbo. At this point revelation embodied in Beatrice appears to conduct him to the ecstasy of paradise. Human reason has guided him out of sin to temporal happiness, but the higher judgments of God he can understand only through revelation (Beatrice), grace (St. Lucy), and divine mercy (The Virgin Mary). With this assistance he at last achieves the vision of God.

But Dante's experience is every Christian's experience, and on a third level the *Commedia* is, like *Pilgrim's Progress*, a gigantic allegory of the life of a Christian in this world. Hell is the error into which every man falls, a grotesque panorama of the ugliness in human nature. In the hopelessness of the sad souls there we see the depths of sin and despair into which man may fall. Purgatory points the way to salvation through repentance and penance. It is a happy place, though tinged with melancholy, as the contrite souls renounce their unworthy past with a joyful knowledge of the infinite happiness beyond. Paradise is the climax of human bliss, as the Christian exults in the surety of salvation and a sense of his spiritual perfection. This is the triumph of his better self aided by God's revelation and mercy. Dante called his work *Commedia* to signify that it is not a tragedy, nor composed in a tragic style, but a story with a happy ending, the spiritual salvation that God holds out to every man.*

This account of the *Commedia* will suggest that it is built on layers of symbols. More baffling to the understanding than the allegory are the numerical symbols that reflect Dante's complete absorption in the medieval outlook. The mystical number that honeycombs the *Commedia* is three, the most common of all in an age that saw God in three persons, the blessed Trinity. The epic describes three great realms in three long books. Each of these books has thirty-three cantos, which with one introductory canto add up to a round one hundred. Three beasts stand in the way of Dante's salvation, and three guides lead him to it. Three ladies intercede for him. Even the metrical form of the poem embodies the mystical number, because Dante developed for the *Commedia* the *terza rima*, whereby units of three lines of iambic pentameter are rhymed *aba, bcb*, etc. On the other hand, nine is the number that Dante associates with Beatrice, since her root is the Trinity as the root of nine is three. No feature of the poem is more remote from us than this medieval notion of the mystical properties of numbers.

Indeed, a reader in our century must overlook many medieval trappings in Dante to get at his perennial message for all mankind. His view of the universe is patently obsolete in an age that calls our earth a lesser planet revolving around a lesser sun in an infinite universe. The pagans of antiquity often seem closer to us in their intellectual sophistication than the sober Florentine hedged in by severe restrictions of knowledge and point of view. But the limits of his knowledge should not obscure the universal meaning of his work on other planes. His exquisite flights of poetry must touch even the most skeptical reader. His vigorous narrative, as in the account of the giants and demons, is first-rate storytelling. The humanity of the man shines through his warm account of Virgil. And his vision itself is ultimately the vision of every thoughtful, well-intentioned human being, whatever his creed may be. However much we may accept intellectually the insignificance of our planet, it is still all of the universe that really concerns us, and on the surface of this planet nothing is more important to us than the spiritual life of man. Few can be so completely absorbed in material affairs as to lose sight of their aspi-

---

* The term "Divine" was added to its title two hundred years after Dante's time and gives it a highly misleading slant.

ration toward a worthier life. Many poets and thinkers have pointed the way, but none more compellingly than Dante.

The Divine Comedy

HELL

CANTO I. *The Dark Wood: Virgil*

IN THE middle of the journey of our life I came to myself in a dark wood where the straight way was lost. Ah! how hard a thing it is to tell what a wild, and rough, and stubborn wood this was, which in my thought renews the fear! So bitter is it, that scarcely more is death: but to treat of the good that I there found, I will relate the other things that I discerned. I cannot rightly tell how I entered it, so full of sleep was I about the moment that I left the
10 true way. But after I had reached the foot of a Hill there, where that valley ended, which had pierced my heart with fear, I looked up and saw its shoulders already clothed with the rays of the Planet that leads men straight on every road. Then the fear was somewhat calmed, which had continued in the lake of my heart the night that I passed so piteously. And as he, who with panting breath has escaped from the deep sea to the shore, turns to the dangerous water and gazes: so my mind, which still was fleeing, turned
20 back to see the pass that no one ever left alive.

After I had rested my wearied body a short while, I took the way again along the desert strand. And behold, almost at the commencement of the steep, a Leopard, light and very nimble, which was covered with spotted hair. And it went not from before my face; nay, so impeded my way, that I had often turned to go back. The time was at the beginning of the morning; and the sun was mounting up with those stars, which were with him when
30 Divine Love first moved those fair things: so that the hour of time and the sweet season caused me to have good hope of that animal with the gay skin; yet not so, but that I feared at the sight, which appeared to me, of a Lion. He seemed coming upon me with head erect, and furious hunger; so that the air seemed to have fear thereat; and a She-wolf, that looked full of all cravings in her leanness; and has ere now made many live in sorrow. She brought such

heaviness upon me with the terror of her aspect, that I lost the hope of ascending. And as one who is eager 40 in gaining, and, when the time arrives that makes him lose, weeps and afflicts himself in all his thoughts: such that restless beast made me, which coming against me, by little and little drove me back to where the Sun is silent.

Whilst I was rushing downwards, there appeared before my eyes one who seemed hoarse from long silence. When I saw him in the great desert, I cried: "Have pity on me, whate'er thou be, whether shade or veritable man!" He answered me: "Not man, a 50 man I once was; and my parents were Lombards, and both of Mantua by country. I was born *sub Julio,* though it was late; and lived at Rome under the good Augustus, in the time of the false and lying Gods. A poet I was; and sang of that just son of Anchises, who came from Troy after proud Ilium was burnt. But thou, why returnest thou to such disquiet? why ascendest not the delectable mountain, which is the beginning and the cause of all gladness?"

"Art thou then that Virgil, and that fountain 60 which pours abroad so rich a stream of speech?" I answered him, with bashful front. "O glory, and light of other poets! May the long zeal avail me, and the great love, that made me search thy volume. Thou art my master and my author; thou alone art he from whom I took the good style that hath done me honour. See the beast from which I turned back; help me from her, thou famous sage; for she makes my veins and pulses tremble."

"Thou must take another road," he answered, 70 when he saw me weeping, "if thou desirest to escape from this wild place: because this beast, for which thou criest, lets not men pass her way; but so entangles that she slays them; and has a nature so perverse and vicious, that she never satiates her craving appetite; and after feeding, she is hungrier than before. . . . Wherefore I think and discern this for thy best, that thou follow me; and I will be thy guide, and lead thee hence through an eternal place, where thou shalt hear the hopeless shrieks, shalt see the 80 ancient spirits in pain, so that each calls for a second death; and then thou shalt see those who are contented in the fire: for they hope to come, whensoever it be, amongst the blessed; then to these, if thou desirest to ascend, there shall be a spirit worthier than I to guide thee; with her will I leave thee at my parting: for that Emperor who reigns above, because I was rebellious to his law, wills not that I come into his city. In all parts he rules and there holds sway; there is his city, and his high seat: 90 O happy whom he chooses for it!"

*The Divine Comedy*ᴬ Translated by J. A. Carlyle, Thomas Okey, and Philip H. Wicksteed. From *The Divine Comedy* by Dante, published by E. P. Dutton and Co., Inc., New York. By permission of E. P. Dutton and Co., Inc. and J. M. Dent and Sons.

1. In the middle . . . life. The poem opens on the night before Good Friday, 1300, when Dante was 35. 10. a Hill, the Hill of Salvation in the Bible. 13. Planet, the sun. 24. Leopard. The leopard, the lion, and the she-wolf represent worldly pleasure, pride, and avarice.

52. born *sub Julio.* Virgil, Dante's guide through Hell and Purgatory, represents the highest wisdom of man. He was born in the time of Julius Caesar. 85. a spirit, Beatrice, who represents heavenly wisdom.

And I to him: "Poet, I beseech thee by that God whom thou knowest not: in order that I may escape this ill and worse, lead me where thou now hast said, so that I may see the Gate of St. Peter, and those whom thou makest so sad." Then he moved; and I kept on behind him.

CANTO II. *Virgil's Explanation and Promise*

The day was departing, and the brown air taking the animals, that are on earth, from their toils; and I, one alone, was preparing myself to bear the war
10 both of the journey and the pity, which memory, that errs not, shall relate. O Muses, O high Genius, now help me! O Memory, that hast inscribed what I saw, here will be shown thy nobleness.

I began: "Poet, who guidest me, look if there be worth in me sufficient, before thou trust me to the arduous passage. Thou sayest that the father of Sylvius, while subject to corruption, went to the immortal world, and was there in body. But if the Adversary of all evil was propitious to him, con-
20 sidering the high effect, and who and what should come from him, it seems not unfitting to an understanding mind: for in the empyreal heaven, he was chosen to be the father of generous Rome, and of her Empire; both these, to say the truth, were established for the holy place, where the Successor of the greatest Peter sits. . . . But I, why go? or who permits it? I am not Æneas, am not Paul; neither myself nor others deem me worthy of it. Wherefore, if I resign myself to go, I fear my going may prove
30 foolish; thou art wise, and understandest better than I speak." And as one who unwills what he willed, and with new thoughts changes his purpose, so that he wholly quits the thing commenced, such I made myself on that dim coast: for with thinking I wasted the enterprise, that had been so quick in its commencement.

"If I have rightly understood thy words," replied that shade of the Magnanimous, "thy soul is smit with coward fear, which oftentimes encumbers men,
40 so that it turns them back from honoured enterprise; as false seeing does a startled beast. To free thee from this dread, I will tell thee why I came, and what I heard in the first moment when I took pity of thee. I was amongst them who are in suspense and a Lady, so fair and blessed that I prayed her to command, called me. Her eyes shone brighter than the stars; and she began soft and gentle to tell me with angelic voice, in her language: 'O courteous Mantuan Spirit, whose fame still lasts in the world, and

will last as long as Time! my friend, and not the 50 friend of fortune, is so impeded in his way upon the desert shore, that he has turned back for terror; and I fear he may already be so far astray, that I have risen too late for his relief, from what I heard of him in Heaven. Now go, and with thy ornate speech, and with what is necessary for his escape, help him so, that I may be consoled thereby. I am Beatrice who send thee; I come from a place where I desire to return; love moved me, that makes me speak. When I shall be before my Lord, I oft will praise thee to 60 him.'

"She was silent then, and I began: 'So grateful to me is thy command, that my obeying, were it done already, seems tardy; it needs not that thou more explain to me thy wish. But tell me the cause, why thou forbearest not to descend into this centre here below from the spacious place, to which thou burnest to return.'

"'Since thou desirest to know thus far, I will tell thee briefly,' she replied, 'why I fear not to come 70 within this place. Those things alone are to be feared that have the power of hurting; the others not, which are not fearful. I am made such by God, in his grace, that your misery does not touch me; nor the flame of this burning assail me. There is a noble Lady in Heaven who has such pity of this hindrance, for which I send thee, that she breaks the sharp judgment there on high. She called Lucia, in her request, and said: "Now thy faithful one has need of thee; and I commend him to thee." Lucia, enemy of all 80 cruelty, arose and came to the place where I was sitting with the ancient Rachel. She said: "Beatrice, true praise of God; why helpest thou not him who loved thee so, that for thee he left the vulgar crowd? Hearest not thou the misery of his plaint? Seest thou not the death which combats him upon the river over which the sea has no boast?" None on earth were ever swift to seek their good, or flee their hurt, as I, after these words were uttered, to come down from my blessed seat; confiding in thy noble speech, 90 which honours thee, and them who have heard it.'

"After saying this to me, she turned away her bright eyes weeping; by which she made me hasten more to come; and thus I came to thee, as she desired; took thee from before that savage beast, which bereft thee of the short way to the beautiful mountain. What is it then? why, why haltest thou? why lodgest in thy heart such coward fear? why art thou not bold and free, when three such blessed Ladies care for thee in the court of Heaven, and my words 100 promise thee so much good?"

As flowerets, by the nightly chillness bended down

---

4. **Gate of St. Peter,** the Gate of Purgatory. 16–17. **father of Sylvius,** Aeneas. 44. **amongst them . . . suspense,** among the virtuous pagans in Limbo, where Beatrice came to him.

75–76. **noble Lady in Heaven,** the Virgin Mary, representing Divine Mercy. 78. **Lucia,** St. Lucy, representing Illuminating Grace. 82. **Rachel;** Rachel represents the Contemplative Life.

and closed, erect themselves all open on their stems when the sun whitens them: thus I did, with my fainting courage; and so much good daring ran into my heart, that I began as one set free: "O compassionate she, who succoured me! and courteous thou, who quickly didst obey the true words that she gave thee! Thou hast disposed my heart with such desire to go, by what thou sayest, that I have returned to my first purpose. Now go, for both have one will;
10 thou guide, thou lord and master." Thus I spake to him; and he moving, I entered on the arduous and savage way.

CANTO III. *The Gate of Hell, Ante-hell, and Acheron*

"Through me is the way into the doleful city; through me the way into the eternal pain; through me the way among the people lost. Justice moved my High Maker; Divine Power made me, Wisdom Supreme, and Primal Love. Before me were no things created, but eternal; and eternal I endure: leave all hope, ye that enter." These words, of colour
20 obscure, saw I written above a gate; whereat I: "Master, their meaning to me is hard."

And he to me, as one experienced: "Here must all distrust be left; all cowardice must here be dead. We are come to the place where I told thee thou shouldst see the wretched people, who have lost the good of the intellect." And placing his hand on mine, with a cheerful countenance that comforted me, he led me into the secret things.

Here sighs, plaints, and deep wailings resounded
30 through the starless air: it made me weep at first. Strange tongues, horrible outcries, words of pain, tones of anger, voices deep and hoarse, and sounds of hands amongst them, made a tumult, which turns itself unceasing in that air for ever dyed, as sand when it eddies in a whirlwind. And I, my head begirt with horror, said: "Master, what is this that I hear? and who are these that seem so overcome with pain?"

And he to me: "This miserable mode the dreary
40 souls of those sustain, who lived without blame, and without praise. They are mixed with that caitiff choir of the angels, who were not rebellious, nor were faithful to God; but were for themselves. Heaven chased them forth to keep its beauty from impair; and the deep Hell receives them not, for the wicked would have some glory over them."

And I: "Master, what is so grievous to them, that makes them lament thus bitterly?" He answered: "I will tell it to thee very briefly. These have no hope
50 of death; and their blind life is so mean, that they are envious of every other lot. Report of them the world permits not to exist; Mercy and Justice disdains them: let us not speak of them; but look, and pass."

And I, who looked, saw an ensign, which whirling ran so quickly that it seemed to scorn all pause; and behind it came so long a train of people, that I should never have believed death had undone so many. Forthwith I understood and felt assured, that this was the crew of caitiffs, hateful to God and to 60 his enemies. These unfortunates, who never were alive, were naked, and sorely goaded by hornets and by wasps that were there. These made their faces stream with blood, which mixed with tears was gathered at their feet by loathsome worms.

And then, as I looked onwards, I saw people on the Shore of a great River: whereat I said: "Master, now grant that I may know who these are; and what usage makes them seem so ready to pass over, as I discern by the faint light." And he to me: "The 70 things shall be known to thee, when we stay our steps upon the joyless strand of Acheron." Then, with eyes ashamed and downcast, fearing my words might have offended him, I kept myself from speaking till we reached the stream. And lo! an old man, white with ancient hair, comes towards us in a bark, shouting: "Woe to you, depraved spirits! hope not ever to see Heaven: I come to lead you to the other shore; into the eternal darkness; into fire and into ice. And thou who art there, alive, depart 80 thee from these who are dead." But when he saw that I departed not, he said: "By other ways, by other ferries, not here, shalt thou pass over: a lighter boat must carry thee."

And my guide to him: "Charon, vex not thyself: thus it is willed there, where what is willed can be done; and ask no more." Then the woolly cheeks were quiet of the steersman on the livid marsh, who round his eyes had wheels of flame. But those spirits, who were foreworn and naked, changed colour and 90 chattered with their teeth, soon as they heard the bitter words. They blasphemed God and their parents; the human kind; the place, the time, and origin of their seed, and of their birth. Then all of them together, sorely weeping, drew to the accursed shore, which awaits every man that fears not God. Charon the demon, with eyes of glowing coal, beckoning them, collects them all; smites with his oar whoever lingers. As the leaves of autumn fall off one after the other, till the branch sees all its spoils upon 100 the ground: so one by one the evil seed of Adam cast themselves from that shore at signals, as the bird at its call. Thus they depart on the brown water; and ere they have landed on the other shore, again a fresh crowd collects on this.

45–46. **for the wicked . . . over them,** because the wicked could at least make up their minds.

55. **an ensign;** this represents the uncertainty of these souls.

"My son," said the courteous Master, "those who die under God's wrath, all assemble here from every country; and they are prompt to pass the river, for Divine Justice spurs them so, that fear is changed into desire. By this way no good spirit ever passes; and hence, if Charon complains of thee, thou easily now mayest know the import of his words." When he had ended, the dusky champaign trembled so violently, that the remembrance of my terror bathes me still with sweat. The tearful ground gave out wind, which flashed forth a crimson light that conquered all my senses; and I fell, like one who is seized with sleep.

CANTO IV. *Circle I, Limbo: the unbaptized and the virtuous heathen*

A heavy thunder broke the deep sleep in my head; so that I started like one who is awaked by force; and, having risen erect, I moved my rested eyes around, and looked steadfastly to know the place in which I was. True is it, that I found myself upon the brink of the dolorous Valley of the Abyss, which gathers thunder of endless wailings. It was so dark, profound, and cloudy, that, with fixing my look upon the bottom, I there discerned nothing.

"Now let us descend into the blind world here below," began the Poet all pale; "I will be first, and thou shalt be second." And I, who had remarked his colour, said: "How shall I come, when thou fearest, who are wont to be my strength in doubt?" And he to me: "The anguish of the people who are here below, on my face depaints that pity, which thou takest for fear. Let us go; for the length of way impels us."

Thus he entered, and made me enter, into the first circle that girds the abyss. Here there was no plaint, that could be heard, except of sighs, which caused the eternal air to tremble; and this arose from the sadness, without torment, of the crowds that were many and great, both of children, and of women and men.

The good Master to me: "Thou askest not what spirits are these thou seest? I wish thee to know, before thou goest farther, that they sinned not; and though they have merit, it suffices not: for they had not Baptism, which is the portal of the faith that thou believest; and seeing they were before Christianity, they worshipped not God aright; and of these am I myself. For such defects, and for no other fault, are we lost; and only in so far afflicted, that without hope we live in desire." Great sadness took me at the heart on hearing this; because I knew men of much worth, who in that Limbo were suspense. . . .

Our way was not yet far since my slumber, when I saw a fire, which conquered a hemisphere of the darkness. We were still a little distant from it; yet not so distant, that I did not in part discern what honourable people occupied that place. "O thou, that honourest every science and art; who are these, who have such honour, that it separates them from the manner of the rest?" And he to me: "The honoured name, which sounds of them, up in that life of thine, gains favours in heaven which thus advances them."

Meanwhile a voice was heard by me: "Honour the great Poet! His shade returns that was departed." After the voice had paused, and was silent, I saw four great shadows come to us; they had an aspect neither sad nor joyful. The good Master began to speak: "Mark him with that sword in hand, who comes before the three as their lord: that is Homer, the sovereign Poet; the next who comes is Horace the satirist; Ovid is the third, and the last is Lucan. Because each agrees with me in the name, which the one voice sounded, they do me honour: and therein they do well." Thus I saw assembled the goodly school of those lords of highest song, which, like an eagle, soars above the rest.

After they had talked a space together, they turned to me with a sign of salutation; and my Master smiled thereat. And greatly more besides they honoured me for they made me of their number, so that I was a sixth amid such intelligences. Thus we went onwards to the light, speaking things which it is well to pass in silence, as it was well to speak there where I was.

We came to the foot of a Noble Castle, seven times circled with lofty Walls, defended round by a fair Rivulet. This we passed as solid land; through seven gates I entered with those sages; we reached a meadow of fresh verdure. On it were people with eyes slow and grave, of great authority in their appearance; they spoke seldom, with mild voices. Thus we retired on one of the sides, into a place open, luminous, and high, so that they could all be seen.

There direct, upon the green enamel, were shown to me the great spirits, so that I glory within myself for having seen them. I saw Electra with many companions: amongst whom I knew both Hector and Æneas; Cæsar armed, with the falcon eyes. I saw Camilla and Penthesilea on the other hand, and saw the Latian King, sitting with Lavinia his daughter. I saw that Brutus who expelled the Tarquin.

When I raised my eyelids a little higher, I saw the Master of those that know, sitting amid a philosophic family. All regard him; all do him honour; here I saw Socrates and Plato, who before the rest stand nearest to him; Democritus, who ascribes the world to chance: Diogenes, Anaxagoras, and Thales; Emped-

70. **Lucan,** Roman poet (39–65 A.D.), author of the heroic poem, *Pharsalia.* 95. **Electra,** the mother of Dardanus, the founder of Troy. Caesar, as descendant of Aeneas, belongs in the Trojan company. 102. **Master . . . that know,** Aristotle.

ocles, Heraclitus, and Zeno; and I saw the good collector of the qualities, Discorides I mean; and saw Orpheus, Tully, Linus, and Seneca the moralist; Euclid the geometer, and Ptolemæus; Hippocrates, Avicenna, and Galen; Averroës, who made the great comment. I may not paint them all in full: for the long theme so chases me, that many times the word comes short of the reality.

The company of six diminishes to two; by another road the sage guide leads me, out of the quiet, into the trembling air; and I come to a part where there is naught that shines.

CANTO V. *Circle II: the carnal sinners*

Thus I descended from the first circle down into the second, which encompasses less space, and so much greater pain, that it stings to wailing. There Minos sits horrific, and grins: examines the crimes upon the entrance; judges, and sends according as he girds himself. I say, that when the ill-born spirit comes before him, it confesses all; and that sin-discerner sees what place in hell is for it, and with his tail makes as many circles round himself as the degrees he will have it to descend. Always before him stands a crowd of them; they go each in its turn to judgment; they tell, and hear; and then are whirled down.

"O thou who comest to the abode of pain!" said Minos to me, when he saw me leaving the act of that great office; "look how thou enterest, and in whom thou trustest; let not the wideness of the entrancy deceive thee." And my guide to him: "Why criest thou too? Hinder not his fated going; thus it is willed there where what is willed can be done: and ask no more."

Now begin the doleful notes to reach me; now am I come where much lamenting strikes me. I came into a place void of all light, which bellows like the sea in tempest, when it is combated by warring winds. The hellish storm, which never rests, leads the spirits with its sweep; whirling, and smiting it vexes them. When they arrive before the ruin, there the shrieks, the moanings, and the lamentation; there they blaspheme the divine power. I learnt that to such torment are doomed the carnal sinners, who subject reason to lust. And as their wings bear along the starlings, at the cold season, in large and crowded troop: so that blast, the evil spirits; hither, thither, down, up, it leads them. No hope ever comforts them, not of rest but even of less pain. And as the cranes go chanting their lays, making a long streak of themselves in the air: so I saw the shadows come, uttering wails, borne by that strife of winds.

Whereat I said: "Master, who are those people, whom the black air thus lashes?" "The first of these concerning whom thou seekest to know," he then replied, "was Empress of many tongues. With the vice of luxury she was so broken, that she made lust and law alike in her decree, to take away the blame she had incurred. She is Semiramis, of whom we read that she succeeded Ninus, and was his spouse; she held the land which the Soldan rules. That other is she who slew herself in love, and broke faith to the ashes of Sichæus; next comes luxurious Cleopatra. Helena see, for whom so long a time of ill revolved; and see the great Achilles, who fought at last with love; see Paris, Tristan"; and more than a thousand shades he showed to me, and pointing with his finger, named to me those whom love had parted from our life.

After I had heard my teacher name the olden dames and cavaliers, pity came over me, and I was as if bewildered. I began: "Poet, willingly would I speak with those two that go together, and seem so light upon the wind." And he to me: "Thou shalt see when they are nearer to us; and do thou then entreat them by that love, which leads them; and they will come."

Soon as the wind bends them to us, I raised my voice: "O wearied souls! come to speak with us, if none denies it." As doves called by desire, with raised and steady wings come through the air to their loved nest, borne by their will: so those spirits issued from the band where Dido is, coming to us through the malignant air; such was the force of my affectuous cry.

"O living creature, gracious and benign; that goest through the black air, visiting us who stained the earth with blood: if the King of the Universe were our friend, we would pray him for thy peace; seeing that thou hast pity of our perverse misfortune. Of that which it pleases thee to hear and to speak, we will hear and speak with you, whilst the wind, as now, is silent for us. The town, where I was born, sits on the shore, where Po descends to rest with his attendant streams. Love, which is quickly caught in gentle heart, took him with the fair body of which I was bereft; and the manner still afflicts me. Love, which to no loved one permits excuse for loving, took me so strongly with delight in him, that, as thou seest, even now it leaves me not. Love led us to one death; Caïna waits for him who quenched our life." These words from them were offered to us.

After I had heard those wounded souls, I bowed my face, and held it low until the Poet said to me: "What art thou thinking of?" When I answered, I

61–62. **she . . . Sichaeus,** Dido. 72. **those two,** Paolo and Francesca, the famous lovers. Francesca of Ravenna, married for political reasons to the deformed Gianciotto of Rimini, accepted the love of his younger brother, Paolo, and was killed with her lover by the outraged husband. 100. **Caïna,** the section of the ninth hell reserved for those who had killed relatives, as Cain his brother Abel.

began: "Ah me! what sweet thoughts, what longing led them to the woeful pass!" Then I turned again to them; and I spoke, and began: "Francesca, thy torments make me weep with grief and pity. But tell me: in the time of the sweet sighs, by what and how love granted you to know the dubious desires?"

And she to me: "There is no greater pain than to recall a happy time in wretchedness; and this thy teacher knows. But if thou hast such desire to learn the first root of our love, I will do like one who weeps and tells. One day, for pastime, we read of Lancelot, how love constrained him; we were alone, and without all suspicion. Several times that reading urged our eyes to meet, and changed the colour of our faces; but one moment alone it was that overcame us. When we read how the fond smile was kissed by such a lover, he, who shall never be divided from me, kissed my mouth all trembling: the book, and he who wrote it, was a Galeotto. That day we read in it no farther." Whilst the one spirit thus spake, the other wept so, that I fainted with pity, as if I had been dying; and fell, as a dead body falls.

CANTO VI. *Circle III: the gluttons*

On sense returning, which closed itself before the pity of the two kinsfolk that stunned me all with sadness, I discern new torments, and new tormented souls, whithersoever I move, and turn, and gaze. I am in the Third Circle, that of the eternal, accursed, cold, and heavy rain; its law and quality is never new. Large hail, and turbid water, and snow, pour down through the darksome air; the ground, on which it falls, emits a putrid smell. Cerberus, a monster fierce and strange, with three throats, barks dog-like over those that are immersed in it. His eyes are red, his beard greasy and black, his belly wide, and clawed his hands; he clutches the spirits, flays, and piecemeal rends them. The rain makes them howl like dogs; with one side they screen the other; they often turn themselves, the impious wretches.

When Cerberus, the great Worm, perceived us, he opened his mouths and showed his tusks: no limb of him kept still. My Guide, spreading his palms, took up earth; and, with full fists, cast it into his ravening gullets. As the dog, that barking craves, and grows quiet when he bites his food, for he strains and battles only to devour it: so did those squalid visages of Cerberus, the Demon, who thunders on the spirits so, that they would fain be deaf. We passed over the shadows whom the heavy rain subdues; and placed our soles upon their emptiness, which seems a body. . . .

Thus passed we through the filthy mixture of the shadows and the rain, with paces slow, touching a

19. a Galeotto, a pander.

little on the future life. Wherefore I said: "Master, shall these torments increase after the great Sentence, or grow less, or remain as burning?" And he to me: "Return to thy science, which has it, that the more a thing is perfect, the more it feels pleasure and likewise pain. Though these accursed people never attain to true perfection, yet they look to be nearer it after than before."

We went round along that road, speaking much more than I repeat; we reached the point where the descent begins; here found we Plutus, the great enemy.

CANTO VII. *Circle IV: Misers and Prodigals; Circle V, Styx: the angry and sullen*

"Pape Satan! pape Satan, aleppe!" began Plutus, with clucking voice; and that gentle Sage, who knew all, said, comforting me: "Let not thy fear hurt thee: for, whatever power he have, he shall not hinder thee from descending this rock." Then he turned himself to that inflated visage, and said: "Peace, cursed Wolf! consume thyself internally with thy greedy rage. Not without cause is our journey to the deep: it is willed on high." As sails, swelled by the wind, fall entangled when the mast breaks: so fell that cruel monster to the ground. Thus we descended into the fourth concavity, taking in more of the dismal bank, which shuts up all the evil of the universe.

Ah, Justice Divine! who shall tell in few the many fresh pains and travails that I saw? and why does guilt of ours thus waste us? As does the surge, there above Charybdis, that breaks itself against the surge wherewith it meets: so have the people here to counter-dance. Here saw I too many more than elsewhere, both on the one side and on the other, with loud howlings, rolling weights by force of chests; they smote against each other, and then each wheeled round just there, rolling aback, shouting "Why holdest thou?" and "Why throwest thou away?" Thus they returned along the gloomy circle, on either hand, to the opposite point, again shouting at each other their reproachful measure. Then every one, when he had reached it, turned through his half-circle towards the other joust. And I, who felt my heart as it were stung, said: "My Master, now show me what people these are, and whether all those tonsured on our left were of the clergy."

And he to me: "In their first life, all were so squint-eyed in mind, that they made no expenditure in it with moderation. Most clearly do their voices

63. **Plutus.** Dante probably meant Pluto, the god of the underworld, rather than Plutus, the god of wealth. 65. "**Pape . . . aleppe!**" The meaning of the words is unknown. 82. **Charybdis,** the whirlpool encountered by Odysseus (Odyssey, XI).

bark out this, when they come to the two points of the circle, where contrary guilt divides them. These were Priests, that have not hairy covering on their heads, and Popes and Cardinals, in whom avarice does its utmost."

And I: "Master, among this set, I surely ought to recognize some that were defiled by these evils." And he to me: "Vain thoughts combinest thou: their undiscerning life, which made them sordid, now makes them too obscure for any recognition. To all eternity they shall continue butting one another; these shall arise from their graves with closed fists; and these with hair shorn off. Ill-giving, and ill-keeping, has deprived them of the bright world, and put them to this conflict; what a conflict it is, I adorn no words to tell. But thou, my Son, mayest now see the brief mockery of the goods that are committed unto Fortune, for which the human kind contend with one another. For all the gold that is beneath the moon, or ever was, could not give rest to a single one of these weary souls."

"Master," I said to him, "now tell me also: this Fortune, of which thou hintest to me; what is she, that has the good things of the world thus within her clutches?" And he to me: "O foolish creatures, how great is this ignorance that falls upon ye! Now I wish thee to receive my judgment of her. He whose wisdom is transcendent over all, made the heavens and gave them guides, so that every part shines to every part, equally distributing the light; in like manner, for worldly splendours, he ordained a general minister and guide, to change betimes the vain possession, from people to people, and from one kindred to another, beyond the hindrance of human wisdom: hence one people commands, another languishes; obeying her sentence, which is hidden like the serpent in the grass. Your knowledge cannot understand her: she provides, judges, and maintains her kingdom, as the other Gods do theirs. Her permutations have no truce; necessity makes her be swift; thus he comes oft who doth a change obtain. This is she, who is so much reviled, even by those who ought to praise her, when blaming her wrongfully, and with evil words. . . . But let us now descend to greater misery; already every star is falling, that was ascending when I set out, and to stay too long is not permitted."

We crossed the circle, to the other bank, near a fount, that boils and pours down through a cleft, which it has formed. The water was darker far than perse; and we, accompanying the dusky waves, entered down by a strange path. This dreary streamlet makes a Marsh, that is named Styx, when it has descended to the foot of the grey malignant shores. And I, who stood intent on looking, saw muddy people in that bog, all naked and with a look of anger. They were smiting each other, not with hands only, but with head, and with chest, and with feet; maiming one another with their teeth, piece by piece.

The kind Master said: "Son, now see the souls of those whom anger overcame; and also I would have thee to believe for certain, that there are people underneath the water, who sob, and make it bubble at the surface; as thy eye may tell thee, whichever way it turns. Fixed in the slime, they say: 'Sullen were we in the sweet air, that is gladdened by the Sun, carrying lazy smoke within our hearts; now lie we sullen here in the black mire.' This hymn they gurgle in their throats, for they cannot speak it in full words."

Thus, between the dry bank and the putrid fen, we compassed a large arc of that loathly slough, with eyes turned towards those that swallow of its filth; we came to the foot of a tower at last.

CANTO VIII. *The Entrance to the City of Dis: the fallen angels*

I say continuing, that, long before we reached the foot of the high tower, our eyes went upwards to its summit, because of two flamelets, that we saw put there, and another from far give signal back, so far that the eye could scarcely catch it. And I turned to the Sea of all intelligence; I said: "What says this? and what replies yon other fire? And who are they that made it?" And he to me: "Over the squalid waves, already thou mayest discern what is expected, if the vapour of the fen conceal it not from thee."

Never did cord impel from itself an arrow, that ran through the air so quickly, as a little bark which I saw come towards us then through the water, under the guidance of a single steersman, who cried: "Now art thou arrived, fell spirit?" "Phlegyas, Phlegyas," said my Lord, "this time thou criest in vain; thou shalt not have us longer than while we pass the wash." As one who listens to some great deceit which has been done to him, and then sore resents it: such grew Phlegyas in his gathered rage. My Guide descended into the skiff, and then made me enter after him; and not till I was in, did it seem laden. Soon as my Guide and I were in the boat, its ancient prow went on, cutting the water. . . .

The kind Master said: "Now, Son, the city that is named of Dis draws nigh, with its grave citizens, with its great company." And I: "Master, already I discern its mosques, distinctly there within the valley, red as if they had come out of fire." And to me he said: "The eternal fire, which causes them to glow within, shows them red, as thou seest, in this low Hell."

74. **a tower**; from which signals are sent to Phlegyas, the ferryman, to indicate that passengers await the ferry across the marsh.

We now arrived in the deep fosses, which moat that joyless city; the walls seemed to me as if they were of iron. Not before making a long circuit, did we come to a place where the boatman loudly cried to us: "Go out: here is the entrance." Above the gates I saw more than a thousand spirits, rained from the Heavens, who angrily exclaimed: "Who is that, who, without death, goes through the kingdom of the dead?" And my sage Master made a sign of wishing to speak with them in secret. Then they somewhat shut up their great disdain, and said: "Come thou alone; and let that one go, who has entered so daringly into this kingdom. Let him return alone his foolish way; try, if he can: for thou shalt stay here, that hast escorted him through so dark a country."

Judge, Reader, if I was discouraged at the sound of the accursed words: for I believed not that I ever should return hither. "O my loved Guide, who more than seven times hast restored me to safety, and rescued from deep peril that stood before me, leave me not so undone," I said, "and if to go farther be denied us, let us retrace our steps together rapidly." And that Lord, who had led me thither, said to me: "Fear not, for our passage none can take from us: by Such has it been given to us. But thou, wait here for me; and comfort and feed thy wearied spirit with good hope: for I will not forsake thee in the low world."

Thus the gentle Father goes, and leaves me here, and I remain in doubt: for yes and no contend within my head. I could not hear that which was offered to them; but he had not long stood with them, when they all, vying with one another, rushed in again. These our adversaries closed the gates on the breast of my Lord who remained without; and turned to me with slow steps. He had his eyes upon the ground, and his eyebrows shorn of all boldness, and said with sighs: "Who hath denied me the doleful houses?" And to me he said: "Thou, be not dismayed, though I get angry: for I will master the trial, whatever be contrived for hindrance." . . .

CANTOS IX–X. *Circle VI, the City of Dis: the heretics*

And more he said, but I have it not in memory: for my eye had drawn me wholly to the high tower with glowing summit, where all at once had risen up three Hellish Furies, stained with blood; who had the limbs and attitude of women, and were girt with greenest hydras; for hair, they had little serpents and cerastes, wherewith their horrid temples were bound. And he, knowing well the handmaids of the Queen of everlasting lamentation, said to me: "Mark

the fierce Erinnyes! This is Megæra on the left hand; she, that weeps upon the right, is Alecto; Tisiphone is in the middle"; and therewith he was silent. With her claws each was rending her breast; they were smiting themselves with their palms, and crying so loudly, that I pressed close to the Poet for fear. "Let Medusa come, that we may change him into stone," they all said, looking downwards.

"Turn thee backwards, and keep thy eyes closed: for if the Gorgon show herself, and thou shouldst see her, there would be no returning up again." Thus said the Master, and he himself turned me, and trusted not to my hands, but closed me also with his own.

And now there came, upon the turbid waves, a crash of fearful sound, at which the shores both trembled; a sound as of a wind, impetuous for the adverse heats, which smites the forest without any stay; shatters off the boughs, beats down, and sweeps away; dusty in front, it goes superb, and makes the wild beasts and the shepherds flee. He loosed my eyes, and said: "Now turn thy nerve of vision on that ancient foam, there where the smoke is harshest." As frogs, before their enemy the serpent, run all asunder through the water, till each squats upon the bottom: so I saw more than a thousand ruined spirits flee before one, who passed the Stygian ferry with soles unwet. He waved that gross air from his countenance, often moving his left hand before him; and only of that trouble seemed he weary.

Well did I perceive that he was a Messenger of Heaven; and I turned to the Master; and he made a sign that I should stand quiet, and bow down to him. Ah, how full he seemed to me of indignation! He reached the gate, and with a wand opened it: for there was no resistance. "O outcasts of Heaven! race despised!" began he, upon the horrid threshold, "why dwells this insolence in you? Why spurn ye at that Will, whose object never can be frustated, and which often has increased your pain?" . . . Then he returned by the filthy way, and spake no word to us; but looked like one whom other care urges and incites than that of those who stand before him.

And we moved our feet towards the city, secure after the sacred words. We entered into it without any strife; and I, who was desirous to behold the condition which such a fortress encloses, as soon as I was in, sent my eyes around; and saw, on either hand, a spacious plain full of sorrow and of evil torment. . . . The sepulchres make all the place uneven: so did they here on every side, only the manner here was bitterer: for amongst the tombs were scattered flames, whereby they were made all over so glowing-hot, that iron more hot no craft requires.

5–7. **Above the gates . . . Heavens**; at the time that Satan fell from Heaven. 49–50. **the Queen,** Proserpine, Queen of the Underworld.

56–57. **Let Medusa come . . . stone.** The terrible head of the Gorgon Medusa would turn its beholder to stone.

Their covers were all raised up; and out of them proceeded moans so grievous, that they seemed indeed the moans of spirits sad and wounded.

And I: "Master, what are these people who, buried within those chests, make themselves heard by their painful sighs?" And he to me: "Here are the Arch-heretics with their followers of every sect; and much more, than thou thinkest, the tombs are laden. Like with like is buried here; and the monuments are more and less hot." Then, after turning to the right hand, we passed between the tortures and the high battlements.

Now by a secret path, between the city-wall and the torments, my Master goes on, and I behind him. "O Virtue supreme! who through the impious circles thus wheelest me, as it pleases thee," I began; "speak to me, and satisfy my wishes. Might these people, who lie within the sepulchres, be seen? the covers are all raised, and none keeps guard." And he to me: "All shall be closed up, when, from Jehosaphat, they return here with the bodies which they have left above. In this part are entombed with Epicurus all his followers, who make the soul die with the body." . . .

CANTO XII. *Circle VII, the River Phlegethon: tyrants and murderers*

The place to which we came, in order to descend the bank, was alpine, and such, from what was there besides, that every eye would shun it, for from the summit of the mountain, whence it moved, to the plain, the rock is shattered so, that it might give some passage to one that were above: such of that rocky steep was the descent. . . . Thus we took our way downwards on the ruin of those stones, which often moved beneath my feet, from the unusual weight.

I went musing, and he said: ". . . Fix thy eyes upon the valley: for the river of blood draws nigh, in which boils every one who by violence injures others." O blind cupidity both wicked and foolish, which so incites us in the short life, and then, in the eternal, steeps us so bitterly!

I saw a wide fosse bent arcwise, as embracing all the plain, according to what my Guide had told me; and between it and the foot of the bank were Centaurs, running one behind the other, armed with arrows, as they were wont on earth to go in hunting. Perceiving us descend, they all stood still; and from the band three came forth with bows and javelins chosen first. And one of them cried from far: "To what torment come ye, ye that descend the coast? Tell from thence; if not, I draw the bow."

22-24. **In this part . . . body.** See Lucretius, *Of the Nature of Things*, Book III.

My Master said: "Our answer we will make to Chiron, there near at hand; unhappily thy will was always thus rash." Then he touched me and said: "This is Nessus, who died for the fair Dejanira, and of himself took vengeance for himself; he in the middle, who is looking down upon his breast, is the great Chiron, he who nursed Achilles; that other is Pholus, who was so full of rage. Around the foss they go by thousands, piercing with their arrows whatever spirit wrenches itself out of the blood farther than its guilt has allotted for it."

We drew near those rapid beasts; Chiron took an arrow, and with the notch put back his beard upon his jaws. When he had uncovered his great mouth, he said to his companions: "Have ye perceived that the one behind moves what he touches? The feet of the dead are not wont to do so." And my good Guide, who was already at the breast of him, where the two natures are consorted, replied: "Indeed he is alive, and solitary thus have I to show him the dark valley; necessity brings him to it, and not sport. From singing Alleluiah, came She who gave me this new office; he is no robber, nor I a thievish spirit. But by that virtue through which I move my steps on such a wild way, give us some one of thine whom we may follow, that he may show us where the ford is, and carry over him upon his back, for he is not a spirit to go through the air." Chiron bent round on his right breast, and said to Nessus: "Turn, and guide them then; and if another troop encounter you, keep it off."

We moved onwards with our trusty guide, along the border of the purple boiling, wherein the boiled were making loud shrieks. I saw people down in it even to the eyebrows; and the great Centaur said: "These are tyrants who took to blood and plunder. Here they lament their merciless offences; here is Alexander; and fierce Dionysius, who made Sicily have years of woe.". . .

A little farther on, the Centaur paused beside a people which, as far as the throat, seemed to issue from that boiling stream. . . . Then some I saw, who kept the head and likewise all the chest out of the river; and of these I recognized many. Thus more and more that blood grew shallow, until it cooked the feet only; and here was our passage through the fosse. "As thou seest the boiling stream, on this side, continually diminish," said the Centaur, "so I would have thee to believe that, on this other, it lowers its bottom more and more, till it comes again to where tyranny is doomed to mourn." . . .

CANTO XIII. *Circle VII, the Wood of the Harpies: the suicides*

Nessus had not yet reached the other side, when we moved into a wood, which by no path was marked. Not green the foliage, but of colour dusky; not smooth the branches, but gnarled and warped; apples none were there, but withered sticks with poison. . . . Here the unseemly Harpies make their nests. . . . Wide wings they have, and necks and faces human, feet with claws, and their large belly feathered; they make rueful cries on the strange trees. The kind Master began to say to me: "Before thou goest farther, know that thou art in the second

10 round; and shalt be, until thou comest to the horrid sand. Therefore look well, and thou shalt see things which would take away belief from my speech."

Already I heard wailings uttered on every side, and saw no one to make them: wherefore I, all bewildered, stood still. I think he thought that I was thinking so many voices came, amongst those stumps, from people who hid themselves on our account. Therefore the Master said: "If thou breakest off any little shoot from one of these plants, the

20 thoughts, which thou hast, will all become defective."

Then I stretched my hand a little forward, and plucked a branchlet from a great thorn; and the trunk of it cried, "Why dost thou rend me?" And when it had grown dark with blood, it again began to cry: "Why dost thou tear me? hast thou no breath of pity? Men we were, and now are turned to trees: truly thy hand should be more merciful, had we been souls of serpents." As a green brand, that is

30 burning at one end, at the other drops, and hisses with the wind which is escaping: so from that broken splint, words and blood came forth together: whereat I let fall the top, and stood like one who is afraid. . . .

The Poet then said to me: "Since he is silent, lose not the hour; but speak, and ask him, if thou wouldst know more." Whereat I to him: "Do thou ask him farther, respecting what thou thinkest will satisfy me; for I could not, such pity is upon my heart."

40 He therefore resumed: "So may the man do freely for thee what thy words entreat him, O imprisoned spirit, please thee tell us farther, how the soul gets bound up in these knots; and tell us, if thou mayest, whether any ever frees itself from such members." Then the trunk blew strongly, and soon that wind was changed into these words: "Briefly shall you be answered. When the fierce spirit quits the body, from which it has torn itself, Minos sends it to the seventh gulf. It falls into the wood, and no place is

50 chosen for it; but wherever fortune flings it, there it sprouts, like grain of spelt; shoots up to a sapling, and to a savage plant; the Harpies, feeding then upon its leaves, give pain, and to the pain an outlet. Like the others, we shall go for our spoils, but not to the end that any may be clothed with them again: for it is not just that a man have what he takes from himself. Hither shall we drag them, and through the

mournful wood our bodies shall be suspended, each on the thorny tree of its tormented shade." . . .

CANTO XIV. *Circle VII, the Burning Sands: blasphemers, sodomists, and usurers*

The love of my native place constraining me, I 60 gathered up the scattered leaves; and gave them back to him, who was already hoarse. Then we came to the limit, where the second round is separated from the third, and where is seen a fearful device of justice. To make the new things clear, I say we reached a plain which from its bed repels all plants. The dolorous wood is a garland to it round about, as to the wood the dismal fosse; here we stayed our steps close to its very edge.

I saw many herds of naked souls, who were all 70 lamenting very miserably; and there seemed imposed upon them a diverse law. Some were lying supine upon the ground; some sitting all crouched up; and others roaming incessantly. Those that moved about were much more numerous; and those that were lying in the torment were fewer, but uttered louder cries of pain. Over all the great sand, falling slowly, rained dilated flakes of fire, like those of snow in Alps without a wind . . . so fell the eternal heat, by which the sand was kindled, like 80 tinder under flint and steel, redoubling the pain. Ever restless was the dance of miserable hands, now here, now there, shaking off the fresh burning.

I began: "Master, thou who conquerest all things, save the hard Demons, that came forth against us at the entrance of the gate, who is that great spirit, who seems to care not for the fire, and lies disdainful and contorted, so that the rain seems not to ripen him?" And he himself, remarking that I asked my Guide concerning him, exclaimed: "What I was liv- 90 ing, that am I dead." . . .

Then my Guide spake with a force such as I had not heard before: "O Capaneus! in that thy pride remains unquenched, thou art punished more: no torture, except thy own raving, would be pain proportioned to thy fury." Then to me he turned with gentler lip, saying: "That was the one of the seven kings who laid siege to Thebes; and he held, and seems to hold, God in defiance and prize him lightly; but, as I told him, his revilings are ornaments that 100 well befit his breast. Now follow me, and see thou place not yet thy feet upon the burning sand; but always keep them back close to the wood."

In silence we came to where there gushes forth from the wood a little rivulet, the redness of which still makes me shudder. . . . Its bottom and both its shelving banks were petrified, and also the margins near it: whereby I discerned that our passage lay there. . . . Then he said: "Now it is time to quit the wood; see that thou follow me; the margins which are not burning, form a path and over them all fire is quenched." . . .

CANTOS XVI–XVII. *The Descent to Circle VIII*

I followed him; and we had gone but little, when the sound of the water was so near us, that in speaking we should scarce have heard each other. . . . I had a cord girt round me; and with it I thought some time to catch the Leopard of the painted skin. After I had quite unloosed it from me, as my Guide commanded me, I held it out to him coiled and wound up. Then he bent himself toward the right side, and threw it, some distance from the edge, down into that steep abyss. "Surely," said I within myself, "something new must answer this new signal, which my Master thus follows with his eye." Ah! how cautious ought men to be with those who see not only the deed, but with their sense look through into the thoughts! He said to me: "What I expect will soon come up; and what thy thought dreams of, soon must be discovered to thy view."

Always to that truth which has an air of falsehood, a man should close his lips, so far as he is able, for, though blameless, he incurs reproach; but here keep silent I cannot; and, Reader, I swear to thee, by the notes of this my Comedy—so may they not be void of lasting favour—that I saw, through that air gross and dark, come swimming upwards, a figure marvellous to every steadfast heart; like as he returns, who on a time goes down to loose the anchor, which grapples a rock or other thing that in the sea is hid, who spreads the arms and gathers up the feet.

"Behold the savage beast with the pointed tail, that passes mountains, and breaks through walls and weapons; behold him that pollutes the whole world." Thus began my Guide to speak to me; and beckoned him to come ashore, near the end of our rocky path; and that uncleanly image of Fraud came onward, and landed his head and bust, but drew not his tail upon the bank. His face was the face of a just man, so mild an aspect had it outwardly; and the rest was all a reptile's body. He had two paws, hairy to the armpits; the back and the breast, and both the flanks, were painted with knots and circlets. . . . In the void glanced all his tail, twisting upwards the venomed fork, which, as in scorpions, armed the point.

My Guide said: "Now must we bend our way a little, to that wicked brute which couches there." Then we descended on the right, and made ten paces towards the edge, that we might quite avoid the sand and flames. . . . I found my Guide, who had already mounted on the haunch of the dreadful animal; and he said to me: "Now be stout and bold! Now by such stairs must we descend; mount thou in front: for I wish to be in the middle, that the tail may not do hurt to thee."

As one who has the shivering of the quartan so near, that he has his nails already pale and trembles all, still keeping the shade, such I became when these words were uttered; but his threats excited in me shame, which makes a servant brave in presence of a worthy master. I placed myself on those huge shoulders; I wished to say, only the voice came not as I thought: "See that thou embrace me." But he, who at other times assisted me in other difficulties, soon as I mounted, clasped me with his arms, and held me up; then he said: "Geryon, now move thee! be thy circles large, and gradual thy descent: think of the unusual burden that thou hast."

As the bark goes from its station backwards, backwards, so the monster took himself from thence; and when he felt himself quite loose, there where his breast had been he turned his tail, and stretching moved it, like an eel, and with his paws gathered the air to him. Greater fear there was not, I believe, . . . than was mine, when I saw myself in the air on all sides, and saw extinguished every sight, save of the beast. He goes on swimming slowly, slowly; wheels and descends; but I perceive it not, otherwise than by a wind upon my face and from below. Already, on the right hand, I heard the whirlpool make a hideous roaring under us; whereat, with eyes downwards, my head I stretched.

Then was I more timorous as regards dismounting: for I saw fires and heard lamentings, so that I cower all trembling. And then I saw—for I had not seen it before—the sinking and the wheeling, through the great evils which drew near on diverse sides. As the falcon, that has been long upon his wings—that, without seeing bird or lure, makes the falconer cry, "Ah, ah! thou stoopest"—descends weary; then swiftly moves himself with many a circle, and far from his master sets himself disdainful and sullen: so at the bottom Geryon set us, close to the foot of the ragged rock; and, from our weight relieved, he bounded off like an arrow from the string.

CANTOS XVIII–XX. *Circle VIII, Malebolge: the fraudulent*

There is a place in Hell called Malebolge, all of stone, and of an iron colour, like the barrier which winds round it. Right in the middle of the malignant

---

8. **Leopard of the painted skin.** A monk's severe life would destroy the thirst for worldly pleasure. 27. **a figure,** Geryon, the monster guarding Circle VIII.

98. **Malebolge,** Italian for "evil pouches," since there are ten pouches or regions in Circle VIII.

field yawns a well exceeding wide and deep, whose structure I shall tell in its own place. The border therefore that remains, between the well and the foot of the high rocky bank, is round; and it has its bottom divided into ten valleys. As is the form that ground presents, where to defend the walls successive ditches begird a castle: such image these made here; and as, from the thresholds of the fortress, there are bridges to the outward bank: so from the basis of the rock proceeded cliffs that crossed the embankments and the ditches, down to the well which truncates and collects them. In this place, shaken from the back of Geryon, we found ourselves; and the Poet kept to the left, and I moved behind.

On the right hand I saw new misery, new torments, and new tormentors, wherewith the first chasm was filled. In its bottom the sinners were naked; on our side of the middle they came facing us; and, on the other side, along with us, but with larger steps. . . . On this side, on that, along the hideous stone, I saw horned Demons with large scourges, who smote them fiercely from behind. Ah! how they made them lift their legs at the first strokes! truly none waited for the second or the third. . . . We had already come to where the narrow pathway crosses the second bank, and makes of it a buttress for another arch. Here we heard people whining in the other chasm, and puffing with mouth and nostrils, and knocking on themselves with their palms. The banks were crusted over with a mould from the vapour below, which concretes upon them, which did battle with the eyes and with the nose. The bottom is so deep, that we could see it nowhere without mounting to the ridge of the arch, where the cliff stands highest. We got upon it; and thence in the ditch beneath, I saw a people dipped in excrement, that seemed as it had flowed from human privies. . . .

And through the circular valley I saw a people coming silent and weeping, at the pace which the Litanies make in this world. When my sight descended lower on them, each seemed wondrously distorted, between the chin and the commencement of the chest: for the face was turned towards the loins; and they had to come backward, for to look before them was denied. Perhaps by force of palsy some have been thus quite distorted; but I have not seen, nor do believe it to be so. Reader, so God grant thee to take profit of thy reading, now think for thyself how I could keep my visage dry, when near at hand I saw our image so contorted, that the weeping of the eyes bathed the hinder parts at their division? Certainly I wept, leaning on one of the rocks of the hard cliff, so that my Escort said to me: "Art thou,

1–2. a well . . . its own place, Circle IX.

too, like the other fools? Here pity lives when it is altogether dead. Who more impious than he that sorrows at God's judgment?" . . .

CANTOS XXI–XXII. *Encounter with the Demons*

Thus from bridge to bridge we came, with other talk which my Comedy cares not to recite; and held the summit, when we stood still to see the other cleft of Malebolge and the other vain lamentings; and I found it marvellously dark. As in the arsenal of the Venetians boils the clammy pitch in winter, to caulk their damaged ships, which they cannot navigate; and, instead thereof, one builds his ship anew, one plugs the ribs of that which hath made many voyages; some hammer at the prow, some at the stern; some make oars, and some twist ropes; one mends the jib, and one the mainsail: so, not by fire but by art Divine, a dense pitch boiled down there, and overglued the banks on every side. It I saw; but saw naught therein, except the bubbles which the boiling raised, and the heaving and compressed subsiding of the whole.

Whilst I was gazing fixedly down on it, my Guide, saying, "Take care, take care!" drew me to him from the place where I was standing. Then I turned round, like one who longs to see what he must shun, and who is dashed with sudden fear, so that he puts not off his flight to look; and behind us I saw a black Demon come running up the cliff. Ah, how ferocious was his aspect! and how bitter he seemed to me in gesture, with his wings outspread, and light of foot! His shoulders that were sharp and high, a sinner with both haunches laded; and of each foot he held the sinew grasped. . . . Down he threw him, then wheeled along the flinty cliff; and never was mastiff loosed with such a haste to follow thief. The sinner plunged in, and came up again writhing convolved; but the Demons, who were under cover of the bridge, cried: "Unless thou wishest to make trial of our drags, come not out above the pitch." Then they struck him with more than a hundred prongs, and said: "Covered thou must dance thee here; so that, if thou canst, thou mayest pilfer privately." Not otherwise do the cooks make their vassals dip the flesh into the middle of the boiler with their hooks, to hinder it from floating.

The kind Master said to me: "That it may not be seen that thou art here, cower down behind a jag, so that thou mayest have some screen for thyself; and whatever outrage may be done to me, fear not thou: for I know these matters, having once before been in the like affray." Then he passed beyond the head of the bridge; and when he arrived on the sixth bank, it was needful for him to have a steadfast front. With that fury and that storm, wherewith the dogs rush forth upon the poor man who where he stops suddenly seeks alms, rushed those Demons from beneath the bridge, and turned against him all their crooks; but he cried: "Be none of ye outrageous! Before ye touch me with your forks, let one of you come forth to hear me, and then take counsel about hooking me."

All cried: "Let Malacoda go"; thereat one moved himself, the other standing firm, and came to him, saying: "What will this avail him?" "Dost thou expect, Malacoda," said my Master, "to find I have come here, secure already against all your hindrances, without will Divine and fate propitious? Let me pass on: for it is willed in Heaven that I show another this savage way." Then was his pride so fallen, that he let the hook drop at his feet, and said to the others: "Now strike him not!"

And my Guide to me: "O thou that sittest cowering, cowering amongst the great splinters of the bridge, securely now return to me!" Whereat I moved, and quickly came to him; and the Devils all pressed forward, so that I feared they might not hold the compact. . . . I drew near my Guide with my whole body, and turned not away my eyes from the look of them, which was not good. They lowered their drag-hooks, and kept saying to one another: "Shall I touch him on the rump?" and answering: "Yes, see thou nick it for him."

But that Demon, who was speaking with my Guide, turned instant round, and said: "Quiet, quiet, Scarmiglione!" Then he said to us: "To go farther by this cliff will not be possible: for the sixth arch lies all in fragments at the bottom; and if it please you still to go onward, go along this ridge: near at hand is another cliff which forms a path. . . . Thitherward I send some of these my men, to look if anyone be out airing himself; go with them, for they will not be treacherous. Draw forward, Alichino and Calcabrina," he then began to say, "and thou, Cagnazzo; and let Barbariccia lead the ten. Let Libicocco come besides, and Draghignazzo, tusked Ciriatto, and Graffiacane, and Farfarello, and furious Rubicante. Search around the boiling glue; be these two safe as far as the other crag, which all unbroken goes across the dens."

"Oh me! Master, what is this that I see?" said I; "ah, without escort let us go alone, if thou knowest the way; for as to me, I seek it not! If thou beest so wary, as thou art wont, dost thou not see how they grind their teeth, and with their brows threaten mischief to us?" And he to me: "I would not have thee be afraid; let them grind on at their will: for they do it at the boiled wretches." . . .

We went with the ten Demons: ah, hideous company! but, "In church with saints, and with guzzlers in the tavern." Yet my intent was on the pitch, to see each habit of the chasm and of the people that were burning in it. As dolphins, when with the arch of the back they make sign to mariners that they may prepare to save their ship: so now and then, to ease the punishment, some sinner showed his back and hid in less time than it lightens. And as at the edge of the water of a ditch, the frogs stand only with their muzzles out, so that they hide their feet and other bulk: thus stood on every hand the sinners; but as Barbariccia approached, they instantly retired beneath the seething.

I saw, and my heart still shudders thereat, one linger so, as it will happen that one frog remains while the other spouts away; And Graffiacane, who was nearest to him, hooked his pitchy locks and hauled him up, so that to me he seemed an otter. I already knew the name of everyone, so well I noted them as they were chosen, and when they called each other, listened how. "O Rubicante, see thou plant thy clutches on him, and flay him!" shouted together all the accursed crew.

And I: "Master, learn if thou canst, who is that piteous wight, fallen into the hand of his adversaries." My Guide drew close to his side and asked him whence he came; and he replied: "I was born in the kingdom of Navarre. My mother placed me as a servant of a lord; for she had borne me to a ribald waster of himself and of his substance. Then I was domestic with the good king Thibault; here I set myself to doing barratry, of which I render reckoning in this heat."

And Ciriatto, from whose mouth on either side came forth a tusk as from a hog, made him feel how one of them did rip. Amongst evil cats the mouse had come; but Barbariccia locked him in his arms, and said: "Stand off whilst I enfork him!" . . . And Libicocco cried: "Too much have we endured!" and with the hook seized his arm, and mangling carried off a part of brawn. Draghignazzo, he too, wished to have a catch at the legs below; whereat their Decurion wheeled around with evil aspect. . . .

O Reader, thou shalt hear new sport! All turned their eyes toward the other side, he first who had been most unripe for doing it. The Navarrese chose well his time; planted his soles upon the ground, and in an instant leapt and from their purpose freed himself. Thereat each was stung with guilt; but he most who had been cause of the mistake; he therefore started forth, and shouted: "Thou'rt caught!" But little it availed him; for wings could not outspeed the terror the sinner went under; and he, flying, raised up his breast: not otherwise the duck suddenly dives down, when the falcon approaches, and he returns up angry and defeated.

Calcabrina, furious at the trick, kept flying after him, desirous that the sinner might escape, to have a quarrel. And, when the barrator had disappeared, he turned his talons on his fellow, and was clutched with him above the ditch. But the other was indeed a sparrowhawk to claw him well; and both dropt down into the middle of the boiling pond. The heat at once unclutched them; but rise they could not, their wings were so beglued. Barbariccia with the rest lamenting, made four of them fly over to the other coast with all their drags; and most rapidly on this side, on that, they descended to the stand; they stretched their hooks towards the limed pair, who were already scalded within the crust; and we left them thus embroiled. . . .

CANTOS XXIV–XXV. *The Punishment of Thieves*

When we reached the shattered bridge, my Guide turned to me with that sweet aspect which I saw first at the foot of the mountain. He opened his arms after having chosen some plan within himself, first looking well at the ruin, and took hold of me. And as one who works, and calculates, always seeming to provide beforehand: so, lifting me up towards the top of one big block, he looked out another splinter, saying: "Now clamber over that, but try first if it will carry thee."

It was no way for one clad with cloak of lead: for scarcely we, he light and I pushed on, could mount up from jag to jag. And were it not on that precinct the ascent was shorter than on the other, I know not about him, but I certainly had been defeated. But as Malebolge all hangs towards the entrance of the lowest well, the site of every valley imports that one side rises and the other descends; we, however, came at length to the point from which the last stone breaks off. The breath was so exhausted from my lungs, when I was up, that I could no farther; nay, seated me at my first arrival.

"Now it behoves thee thus to free thyself from sloth," said the Master: "for sitting on down, or under coverlet, men come not into fame; without which whoso consumes his life, leaves such vestige of himself on earth, as smoke in air or foam in water; and therefore rise! conquer thy panting with the soul, that conquers every battle, if with its heavy body it sinks not down. A longer ladder must be climbed: to have quitted these is not enough; if thou understandest me, now act so that it may profit thee." I then rose, showing myself better furnished with breath than I felt, and said: "Go on; for I am strong and confident." We took our way up the cliff, which was rugged, narrow, and difficult, and greatly steeper than the former. . . .

We went down the bridge, at the head where it joins with the eighth bank; and then the chasm was manifest to me: and I saw within it a fearful throng of serpents, and of so strange a look, that even now the recollection scares my blood. . . . Amid this cruel and most dismal swarm were people running, naked and terrified, without hope of lurking hole or heliotrope. They had their hands tied behind with serpents; these through their loins fixed the tail and the head, and were coiled in knots before.

And lo! at one, who was near our shore, sprang up a serpent, which transfixed him there where the neck is bound upon the shoulders. Neither "O" nor "I" was ever written so quickly as he took fire, and burnt, and dropt down all changed to ashes; and after he was thus dissolved upon the ground, the powder reunited of itself and at once resumed the former shape: thus by great sages 'tis confest the Phœnix dies, and then is born again, when it approaches the five-hundredth year; in its life it eats no herb or grain, but only tears of incense and amomum; and nard and myrrh are its last swathings. And as one who falls, and knows not how, through force of Demon which drags him to the ground, or of other obstruction that fetters men; who, when he rises, looks fixedly round him, all bewildered by the great anguish he has undergone, and looking sighs: such was the sinner when he rose. Power of God! O how severe, that showers such blows in vengeance! . . .

Under us there came three spirits, whom neither I nor my Guide perceived, until they cried: "Who are ye?" Our story therefore paused and we then gave heed to them alone. . . .

Whilst I kept gazing on them, lo! a serpent with six feet darts up in front of one, and fastens itself all upon him. With its middle feet it clasped his belly, with the anterior it seized his arms; then fixed its teeth in both his cheeks. The hinder feet it stretched along his thighs; and put its tail between the two, and bent it upwards on his loins behind. Ivy was never so rooted to a tree, as round the other's limbs the hideous monster entwined its own; then they stuck together, as if they had been of heated wax, and mingled their colours; neither the one, nor the other, now seemed what it was at first: as up before the flame on paper, goes a brown colour which is not yet black, and the white dies away.

The other two looked on, and each cried: "O me! Agnello, how thou changest! lo, thou art already neither two nor one!" The two heads had now become one, when two shapes appeared to us mixed in one face, where both were lost. Two arms were made of the four lists; the thighs with the legs, the belly, and the chest, became such members as were never seen. The former shape was all extinct in them: both, and neither the perverse image seemed; and such it went away with languid step.

As the lizard, beneath the mighty scourge of the canicular days, going from hedge to hedge, appears

---

56. **heliotrope,** a stone, supposed to make its wearer invisible.

a flash of lightning, if it cross the way: so, coming towards the bowels of the other two, appeared a little reptile burning with rage, livid and black as peppercorn. And it pierced that part, in one of them, at which we first receive our nourishment; then fell down stretched out before him. The pierced thief gazed on it but said nothing; nay, with his feet motionless, yawned only as if sleep or fever had come upon him. He eyed the reptile, the reptile him; the
10 one from his wound, the other from its mouth, smoked violently, and their smoke met. . . .

They mutually responded in such a way, that the reptile cleft its tail into a fork, and the wounded spirit drew his steps together. The legs and the thighs along with them so stuck to one another, that soon their juncture left no mark that was discernible. The cloven tail assumed the figure that was lost in the other; and its skin grew soft, the other's hard. I saw the arms enter at the armpits, and the two feet
20 of the brute, which were short, lengthen themselves as much as those arms were shortened. Then the two hinder feet, twisted together, became the member which man conceals; and the wretch from his had two thrust forth.

Whilst the smoke with a new colour veils them both, and generates on one part hair, and strips it from another, the one rose upright, and prostrate the other fell, not therefore turning the impious lights, under which they mutually exchanged visages. He
30 that was erect, drew his towards the temples; and from the too much matter that went thither, ears came out of the smooth cheeks; that which went not back, but was retained, of its superfluity formed a nose, and enlarged the lips to a fit size. He that lay prone, thrusts forward his sharpened visage, and draws back his ears into the head, as the snail does its horns; and his tongue, which was before united and apt for speech, cleaves itself; and in the other the forked tongue recloses; and the smoke now rests.
40 The soul that had become a brute, fled hissing along the valley, and after it the other talking and sputtering. . . .

CANTOS XXVI–XXVII. *The Meeting with Odysseus*

We departed thence; and, by the stairs which the curbstones had made for us to descend before, my Guide remounted and drew me up; and pursuing our solitary way among the jags and branches of the cliff, the foot without the hand sped not. I sorrowed then, and sorrow now again when I direct my memory to what I saw; and curb my genius more
50 than I am wont, lest it run where Virtue guides it not; so that, if kindly star or something better have given to me the good, I may not grudge myself that gift.

As many fireflies as the peasant who is resting on the hill—at the time that he who lights the world least hides his face from us, when the fly yields to the gnat—sees down along the valley, there perchance where he gathers grapes and tills: with flames thus numerous the eighth chasm was all gleaming, as I perceived, so soon as I came to where
60 the bottom showed itself, and every flame steals a sinner. I stood upon the bridge, having risen so to look, that if I had not caught a rock, I should have fallen down without being pushed. And the Guide, who saw me thus attent, said: "Within those fires are the spirits; each swathes himself with that which burns him."

"Master," I replied, "from hearing thee I feel more certain; but had already discerned it to be so, and already wished to say to thee: who is in that fire,
70 which comes so parted at the top, as if it rose from the pyre where Eteocles with his brother was placed?"

He answered me: "Within it there Ulysses is tortured, and Diomed; and thus they run together in punishment, as erst in wrath." . . . "If they within those sparks can speak," said I, "Master! I pray thee much, and repray that my prayer may equal a thousand, deny me not to wait until the horned flame comes hither; thou seest how with desire I
80 bend me towards it." And he to me: "Thy request is worthy of much praise, and therefore I accept it; but do thou refrain thy tongue. Let me speak: for I have conceived what thou wishest; and they, perhaps, because they were Greeks, might disdain thy words."

After the flame had come where time and place seemed fitting to my Guide, I heard him speak in this manner: "O ye, two in one fire! if I merited of you whilst I lived, if I merited of you much or little,
90 when on earth I wrote the High Verses, move ye not; but let the one of you tell where he, having lost himself, went to die."

The greater horn of the ancient flame began to shake itself, murmuring, just like a flame that struggles with the wind. Then carrying to and fro the top, as if it were the tongue that spake, threw forth a voice, and said: "When I departed from Circe, who beyond a year detained me there near Gaeta, ere Æneas thus had named it, neither fondness for my
100 son, nor reverence for my aged father, nor the due love that should have cheered Penelope, could conquer in me the ardour that I had to gain experience of the world, and of human vice and worth; I put forth on the deep open sea, with but one ship, and with that small company, which had not deserted me. Both the shores I saw as far as Spain, far as Mo-

72. Eteocles with his brother, the sons of Oedipus, parted on their funeral pyre as they were opposed in life.

rocco; and saw Sardinia and the other isles which that sea bathes round.

"I and my companions were old and tardy, when we came to that narrow pass, where Hercules assigned his landmarks to hinder man from venturing farther; on the right hand, I left Seville; on the other, had already left Ceuta. 'O brothers!' I said, 'who

through a hundred thousand dangers have reached the West, deny not, to this the brief vigil of your senses that remains, experience of the unpeopled world behind the Sun. Consider your origin: ye were not formed to live like brutes, but to follow virtue and knowledge.'

"With this brief speech I made my companions so

10

The complex structures of Dante's Hell and Purgatory are shown in the above diagrams. Hell, the Inferno, extends from the surface of the earth to its center in nine concentric circles diminishing in circumference to the abode of Satan. Purgatory Dante pictures as an island mountain rising to the Earthly Paradise of Eden at its summit.

eager for the voyage, that I could hardly then have checked them; and, turning the poop towards morning, we of our oars made wings for the foolish flight, always gaining on the left. Night already saw the other pole, with all its stars; and ours so low, that it rose not from the ocean floor. Five times the light beneath the Moon had been rekindled and quenched as oft, since we had entered on the arduous passage, when there appeared to us a Mountain, dim with distance; and to me it seemed the highest I had ever seen.

"We joyed, and soon our joy was turned to grief: for a tempest rose from the new land, and struck the forepart of our ship. Three times it made her whirl round with all the waters; at the fourth, made the poop rise up and prow go down, as pleased Another, till the sea was closed above us."

The flame was now erect and quiet, having ceased to speak, and now went away from us with license of the sweet Poet. . . .

CANTO XXXI. *The Meeting with the Giants*

We turned our back to the wretched valley, up by the bank that girds it round, crossing without any speech. Here was less than night and less than day, so that my sight went little way before me; but I heard a high horn sound so loudly, that it would have made any thunder weak; which directed my eyes, that followed its course against itself, all to one place: after the dolorous rout, when Charlemain had lost the holy emprise, Roland did not sound with his so terribly. Short while had I kept my head turned in that direction, when I seemed to see many lofty towers; whereat I: "Master! say, what town is this?"

And he to me: "Because thou traversest the darkness too far off, it follows that thou errest in thy imagining. Thou shalt see right well, if thou arrivest there, how much the sense at distance is deceived: therefore spur thee somewhat more." Then lovingly he took me by the hand, and said: "Ere we go farther, that the reality may seem less strange to thee, know, they are not towers, but Giants; and are in the well, around its bank, from the navel downwards all of them."

As when a mist is vanishing, the eye by little and little reshapes that which the air-crowding vapour hides; so whilst piercing through that gross and darksome air, more and more approaching towards the brink, error fled from me, and my fear increased. For as on its round wall Montereggione crowns itself with towers: so with half their bodies, the horrible giants whom Jove from heaven still threatens when he thunders, turreted the bank which compasses the pit.

And already I discerned the face of one, the shoulders and the breast, and great part of the belly, and down along his sides both arms. Nature certainly, when she left off the art of making animals like these, did very well, in taking away such executioners from Mars; and if she repents her not of Elephants and Whales, whoso subtly looks, therein regards her as more just and prudent: for where the instrument of the mind is joined to evil will and potency, men can make no defence against it. His face seemed to me as long and large as the pine of St. Peter's at Rome, and his other bones were in proportion to it; so that the bank, which was an apron from his middle downwards, showed us certainly so much of him above, that three Frieslanders had vainly boasted to have reached his hair: for downwards from the place where a man buckles on his mantle, I saw thirty large spans of him.

"Rafel mai amech zabi almi," began to shout the savage mouth, for which no sweeter psalmody was fit. And towards him my Guide: "Stupid soul! keep to thy horn; and vent thyself with that, when rage or other passion touches thee. Search on thy neck, and thou wilt find the belt that holds it tied, O soul confused, and see the horn itself that girdles thy huge breast." Then he said to me: "He accuses himself; this is Nimrod, through whose ill thought one language is not still used in the world. Let us leave him standing, and not speak in vain: for every language is to him as to others his which no one understands.". . .

We then proceeded farther on, and reached Antæus, who full five ells, besides the head, forth issued from the cavern. "O thou! who in the fateful valley, which made Scipio heir of glory when Hannibal retreated with his hosts, didst take of old a thousand lions for thy prey; and through whom, hadst thou been at the high war of thy brethren, it seem yet to be believed that the sons of earth had conquered; set us down—and be not shy to do it— where the cold locks up Cocytus.". . . Thus spake the Master; and he in haste stretched forth the hands, whence Hercules of old did feel great stress, and took my Guide. Virgil, when he felt their grasp, said to me: "Come here, that I may take thee"; then of himself and me he made one bundle. . . . It was so terrible a moment, that I should have wished to go by other road; but gently on the deep, which swallows Lucifer with Judas, he set us down; nor lingered there thus bent, but raised himself as in a ship the mast. . . .

9. a Mountain, Purgatory. 49. Montereggione, a castle near Siena.

80–81. Nimrod . . . in the world; Nimrod supposedly built the Tower of Babel. 94. where the cold . . . Cocytus; Circle IX.

CANTOS XXXII–XXXIII. *Circle IX: the traitors*

When we were down in the dark pit, under the Giant's feet, much lower, and I still was gazing at the high wall, I heard a voice say to me: "Look how thou passest: take care that with thy soles thou tread not on the heads of thy weary wretched brothers." Whereat I turned myself, and saw before me and beneath my feet a lake, which through frost had the semblance of glass and not of water. . . . And as the frog to croak, sits with his muzzle out of the water, when the peasant-woman oft dreams that she is gleaning: so, livid, up to where the hue of shame appears, the doleful shades were in the ice, sounding with their teeth like storks. Each held his face turned downwards; by the mouth their cold, and by the eyes the sorrow of their hearts is testified amongst them. . . .

I saw two frozen in one hole so closely, that the one head was a cap to the other; and as bread is chewed for hunger, so the uppermost put his teeth into the other there where the brain joins with the nape. "O thou! who by such brutal token showest thy hate on him whom thou devourest, tell me why," I said; "on this condition, that if thou with reason complainest of him, I, knowing who ye are and his offence, may yet repay thee in the world above, if that, wherewith I speak, be not dried up."

From the fell repast that sinner raised his mouth, wiping it upon the hair of the head he had laid waste behind. Then he began: "Thou willest that I renew desperate grief, which wrings my heart, even at the very thought, before I tell thereof. But if my words are to be a seed, that may bear fruit of infamy to the traitor whom I gnaw, thou shalt see me speak and weep at the same time. I know not who thou mayest be, nor by what mode thou hast come down here; but, when I hear thee, in truth thou seemest to me a Florentine.

"Thou hast to know that I was Count Ugolino, and this the Archbishop Ruggieri; now I will tell thee why I am such a neighbour to him. That by the effect of his ill devices I, confiding in him, was taken and thereafter put to death, it is not necessary to say. But that which thou canst not have learnt, that is, how cruel was my death, thou shalt hear and know if he has offended me.

"A narrow hole within the mew, which from me has the title of Famine, and in which others yet must be shut up, had through its opening already shown me several moons, when I slept the evil sleep that rent for me the curtain of the future. This man seemed to me lord and master, chasing the wolf and his whelps, upon the mountain for which the Pisans cannot see Lucca. . . . After short course, the father and his sons seemed to me weary; and methought I saw their flanks torn by the sharp teeth.

"When I awoke before the dawn, I heard my sons who were with me, weeping in their sleep, and asking for bread. Thou art right cruel, if thou dost not grieve already at the thought of what my heart foreboded; and if thou weepest not, at what art thou used to weep? They were now awake, and the hour approaching at which our food used to be brought us, and each was anxious from his dream, and below I heard the outlet of the horrible tower locked up: whereat I looked into the faces of my sons, without uttering a word. I did not weep: so stony grew I within; they wept; and my little Anselm said: 'Thou lookest so, father, what ails thee?' But I shed no tear, nor answered all that day, nor the next night, till another sun came forth upon the world.

"When a small ray was sent into the doleful prison, and I discerned in their four faces the aspect of my own, I bit on both my hands for grief. And they, thinking that I did it from desire of eating, of a sudden rose up, and said: 'Father, it will give us much less pain, if thou wilt eat of us: thou didst put upon us this miserable flesh, and do thou strip it off.' Then I calmed myself, in order not to make them more unhappy; that day and the next we all were mute. Ah, hard earth! why didst thou not open?

"When we had come to the fourth day, Gaddo threw himself stretched out at my feet, saying: 'My father! why don't you help me?' There he died; and even as thou seest me, saw I the three fall one by one, between the fifth day and the sixth: whence I betook me, already blind, to groping over each, and for three days called them, after they were dead; then fasting had more power than grief." When he had spoken this, with eyes distorted he seized the miserable skull again with his teeth, which as a dog's were strong upon the bone. . . .

CANTO XXXIV. *Satan*

"*Vexilla regis prodeunt inferni* towards us: therefore look in front of thee," my Master said, "if thou discernest him." As, when a thick mist breathes, or when the night comes on our hemisphere, a mill, which the wind turns, appears at distance: such an edifice did I now seem to see; and, for the wind, shrunk back behind my Guide, because no other shed was there. Already I had come (and with fear I put it into verse) where the souls were wholly covered, and shone through like straw in glass. Some are ly-

88. **then fasting . . . than grief.** This cryptic clause means that Ugolino died of hunger, not that hunger forced him to eat the bodies. 92. "*Vexilla regis prodeunt inferni*," "The standards of the King of Hell advance"—from an old Latin hymn.

ing; some stand upright, this on its head, and that upon its soles; another, like a bow, bends face to feet.

When we had proceeded on so far, that it pleased my Guide to show to me the Creature which was once so fair, he took himself from before me, and made me stop, saying: "Lo Dis! and lo the place where it behoves thee arm thyself with fortitude." How icy chill and hoarse I then became, ask not, O Reader! for I write it not, because all speech would fail to tell. I did not die, and did not remain alive; now think for thyself, if thou hast any grain of ingenuity, what I became, deprived of both death and life.

The Emperor of the dolorous realm, from mid breast stood forth out of the ice; and I in size am liker to a giant, than the giants are to his arms: mark now how great that whole must be, which corresponds to such a part. If he was once as beautiful as he is ugly now, and lifted up his brows against his Maker, well may all affliction come from him. Oh how great a marvel seemed it to me, when I saw three faces on his head! The one in front, and it was fiery red; the others were two, that were adjoined to this, above the very middle of each shoulder; and they were joined at his crest; and the right seemed between white and yellow; the left was such to look on, as they who come from where the Nile descends. Under each there issued forth two mighty wings, of size befitting such a bird: sea-sails I never saw so broad. No plumes had they; but were in form and texture like a bat's: and he was flapping them, so that three winds went forth from him. Thereby Cocytus all was frozen; with six eyes he wept, and down three chins gushed tears and bloody foam.

In every mouth he champed a sinner with his teeth, like a brake; so that he thus kept three of them in torment. To the one in front, the biting was nought, compared with the tearing: for at times the back of him remained quite stript of skin. "That soul up there, which suffers greatest punishment," said the Master, "is Judas Iscariot, he who has his head within, and outside plies his legs. Of the other two, who have their heads beneath, that one, who hangs from the black visage, is Brutus: see how he writhes himself, and utters not a word; and the other is Cassius, who seems so stark of limb. But night is re-ascending; and now must we depart: for we have seen the whole."

As he desired, I clasped his neck; and he took opportunity of time and place; and when the wings were opened far, applied him to the shaggy sides, and then from shag to shag descended down, between the tangled hair and frozen crusts. When we

had come to where the thigh revolves just on the swelling of the haunch, my Guide with labour and with difficulty turned his head where he had had his feet before, and grappled on the hair, as one who mounts; so that I thought we were returning into Hell again. "Hold thee fast! for by such stairs," said my Guide, panting like a man forspent, "must we depart from so much ill."

Thereafter through the opening of a rock he issued forth, and put me on its brim to sit; then towards me he stretched his wary step. I raised my eyes, and thought to see Lucifer as I had left him; and saw him with the legs turned upwards; and the gross people who see not what that point is which I had passed, let them judge if I grew perplexed then. "Rise up!" said the Master, "upon thy feet: the way is long, and difficult the road." . . . The Guide and I entered by that hidden road, to return into the bright world; and, without caring for any rest, we mounted up, he first and I second, so far that I distinguished through a round opening the beauteous things which Heaven bears; and thence we issued out, again to see the Stars.

PURGATORY

CANTO I. *The Shore of the Island of Purgatory*

To COURSE o'er better waters now hoists sail the little bark of my wit, leaving behind her a sea so cruel. And I will sing of that second realm, where the human spirit is purged and becomes worthy to ascend to Heaven. . . .

Sweet hue of orient sapphire which was gathering on the clear forehead of the sky, pure even to the first circle, to mine eyes restored delight, soon as I issued forth from the dead air which had afflicted eyes and heart. . . . I saw near me an old man solitary, worthy of such great reverence in his mien, that no son owes more to a father. Long he wore his beard and mingled with white hair, like unto his locks of which a double list fell on his breast. The rays of the four holy lights adorned his face so with brightness, that I beheld him as were the sun before him.

"Who are ye that against the dark stream have fled the eternal prison?" said he, moving those venerable plumes. "Who hath guided you? or who was a lamp unto you issuing forth from the deep night that ever maketh black the infernal vale? Are the laws of the pit thus broken, or is there some new counsel changed in Heaven that being damned ye come to my rocks?"

46–47. . . . the other is Cassius. As Judas betrayed the founder of Christianity, Brutus and Cassius betrayed the founder of the Roman empire.

83–84. Sweet hue . . . the sky; it is dawn of Easter Sunday. 87. an old man. Cato of Utica (95–46 B.C.), the stern Roman statesman who committed suicide rather than surrender to Caesar, is the guardian of Purgatory.

Then did my Leader lay hold on me, and with words, and with hand, and with signs, made reverent my knees and brow. Then answered him: "Of myself I came not. A lady came down from Heaven through whose prayers I succoured this man with my company. But since it is thy will that more be unfolded of our state, how it truly is, my will it cannot be that thou be denied. He hath ne'er seen the last hour, but by his madness was so near to it, that very short time
10 there was to turn. Even as I said, I was sent to him to rescue him, and no other way there was but this along which I have set me. I have shown him all the guilty people, and now do purpose showing those spirits that purge them under thy charge. How I have brought him, 'twere long to tell thee: Virtue descends from on high which aids me to guide him to see thee and to hear thee. Now may it please thee to be gracious unto his coming: he seeketh freedom, which is so precious, as he knows who giveth up life
20 for her. Thou knowest it; since for her sake death was not bitter to thee in Utica, where thou leftest the raiment which at the great day shall be so bright.". . .

"Go then," said he, "and look that thou gird this man with a smooth rush, and that thou bathe his face so that all filth may thence be wiped away: for 'twere not meet with eye obscured by any mist to go before the first minister of those that are of Paradise. This little isle all round about the very base, there,
30 where the wave beats it, bears rushes on the soft mud. No other plant that would put forth leaf or harden can live there, because it yields not to the buffetings. Then be not this way your return; the sun, which now is rising, will show you how to take the mount at an easier ascent." So he vanished; and I uplifted me without speaking, and drew me all back to my Leader, and directed mine eyes to him. He began: "Son, follow thou my steps: turn we back, for this way the plain slopes down to its low
40 bounds."

The dawn was vanquishing the breath of morn which fled before her, so that from afar I recognized the trembling of the sea. We paced along the lonely plain, as one who returns to his lost road, and, till he reach it, seems to go in vain. When we came there where the dew is striving with the sun, being at a place where, in the cool air, slowly it is scattered; both hands outspread, gently my Master laid upon the sweet grass; wherefore I who was ware of his
50 purpose, raised towards him my tear-stained cheeks: there made he all revealed my hue which Hell had hidden. We came then on to the desert shore, that never saw man navigate its waters who thereafter knew return. There he girded me even as it pleased Another: O marvel! that such as he plucked the lowly plant, even such did it forthwith spring up again, there whence he tore it. . . .

CANTO II. *The Meeting with Casella*

We were alongside the ocean yet, like folk who ponder o'er their road, who in heart do go and in body stay; and lo, as on the approach of morn, 60 through the dense mists Mars burns red, low in the West o'er the ocean-floor; such to me appeared—so may I see it again!—a light coming o'er the sea so swiftly, that no flight is equal to its motion; from which, when I had a while withdrawn mine eyes to question my Leader, I saw it brighter and bigger grown. Then on each side of it appeared to me a something white; and from beneath it, little by little, another whiteness came forth.

My Master yet did speak no word, until the first 70 whitenesses appeared as wings; then, when well he knew the pilot, he cried: "Bend, bend thy knees; behold the Angel of God: fold thy hands: henceforth shalt thou see such ministers. Look how he scorns all human instruments, so that oar he wills not, nor other sail than his wings, between shores so distant. See how he has them heavenward turned, plying the air with eternal plumes, that are not mewed like mortal hair."

Then as more and more towards us came the bird 80 divine, brighter yet he appeared, wherefore mine eye endured him not near: but I bent it down, and he came on to the shore with a vessel so swift and light that the waters nowise drew it in. On the stern stood the celestial pilot, such, that blessedness seemed writ upon him, and more than a hundred spirits sat within. *In exitu Israel de Ægypto,* sang they all together with one voice, with what of that psalm is thereafter written. Then made he to them the sign of Holy Cross, whereat they all flung them 90 on the strand and quick even as he came he went his way.

The throng that remained there seemed strange to the place, gazing around like one who assayeth new things. On every side the sun, who with his arrows bright had chased the Goat from midst of heaven, was shooting forth the day, when the new people lifted up their faces towards us, saying to us: "If ye know show us the way to go to the mount." And Virgil answered: "Ye think perchance that we 100 have experience of this place, but we are strangers even as ye are. We came but now, a little while before you, by other way which was so rough and hard, that the climbing now will seem but play to us."

The souls who had observed me by my breathing that I was yet alive, marvelling grew pale; and as to a messenger, who bears the olive, the folk draw nigh to hear the news, and none shows himself shy at trampling; so on my face those souls did fix their gaze, fortunate every one, well nigh forgetting to go 110 and make them fair.

88–89. that psalm, Psalm 114.

I saw one of them draw forward to embrace me with such great affection, that he moved me to do the like. O shades empty save in outward show! thrice behind it my hands I clasped, and as often returned with them to my breast. With wonder methinks I coloured me, whereat the shade smiled and drew back, and I, following it, flung me forward. Gently it bade me pause: then knew I who it was, and did pray him that he would stay a while to speak
10 to me. He answered me: "Even as I loved thee in the mortal body so do I love thee freed; therefore I stay: but wherefore goest thou?"

"Casella mine, to return here once again where I am, make I this journey," said I, "but if a new law take not from thee memory or skill in that song of love which was wont to calm my every desire, may it please thee therewith to solace awhile my soul, that, with its mortal form journeying here, is sore distressed." "*Love that in my mind discourseth to*
20 *me*," began he then so sweetly, that the sweetness yet within me sounds.

My Master and I and that people who were with him, seemed so glad as if to aught else the mind of no one of them gave heed. We were all fixed and intent upon his notes; and lo the old man venerable, crying: "What is this, ye laggard spirits? what negligence, what tarrying is this? Haste to the mount and strip you of the slough, that lets not God be manifest to you." As doves when gathering wheat or tares, all
30 assembled at their repast, quiet and showing not their wonted pride, if aught be seen whereof they have fear, straightway let stay their food, because they are assailed by greater care; so saw I that new company leave the singing, and go towards the hillside, like one who goes, but knoweth not where he may come forth; nor was our parting less quick. . . .

CANTOS III–VIII. *Ante-Purgatory and the Valley of the Princes: the late repentants*

On the left hand appeared to me a throng of souls, who moved their feet towards us, and yet seemed not *to advance,* so slow they came. "Master," said I,
40 "lift up thine eyes, behold there one who will give us counsel; if of thyself thou mayest have it not." He looked at them, and with gladsome mien answered: "Go we thither, for slowly they come, and do thou confirm thy hope, sweet son.". . .

As sheep come forth from the pen, in ones, in twos, in threes, and the others stand all timid, casting eye and nose to earth, and what the first one doeth, the others do also, huddling up to her if she stand still, silly and quiet, and know not why, so saw I then

the head of that happy flock move to come on, mod-
50 est in countenance, in movement dignified. . . . He began: "Whoever thou art, thus while going turn thy face, give heed if e'er thou sawest me yonder."

I turned me to him, and steadfastly did look: golden-haired was he, and fair, and of noble mien; but one of his eyebrows a cut had cleft. When I humbly had disclaimed ever to have seen him, he said: "Now look"; and he showed me a wound above his breast. Then smiling said: "I am Manfred, grand-
60 son of Empress Constance; wherefore I pray thee, that when thou returnest, thou go to my fair daughter, parent of the glory of Sicily and of Aragon, and tell her sooth, if other tale be told. After I had my body pierced by two mortal stabs, I gave me up weeping to him who willingly doth pardon. Horrible were my transgressions; but infinite goodness hath such wide arms that it accepteth all that turn to it. . . .

"True is it, that he who dies in contumacy of Holy Church, even though at the last he repent, needs
70 must stay outside this bank thirtyfold for all the time that he hath lived in his presumption, if such decree be not shortened by holy prayers. Look now, if thou canst make me glad, by revealing to my good Constance how thou hast seen me, and also this ban: for here, through those yonder, much advancement comes.". . .

And I: "My Lord, go we with greater haste; for already I grow not weary as before, and look, the hill-
80 side doth now a shadow cast." "We with this day will onward go," answered he, "so far as yet we may; but the fact is other than thou deemest. Ere thou art above, him shalt thou see return that now is being hidden by the slope, so that thou makest not his rays to break. But see there a soul which, placed alone, solitary, looketh towards us; it will point out to us the quickest way."

We came to it: O Lombard soul, how wast thou haughty and disdainful, and in the movement of
90 thine eyes majestic and slow! Naught it said to us, but allowed us to go on, watching only after the fashion of a lion when he couches. Yet did Virgil draw on towards it, praying that it would show to us the best ascent; and that spirit answered not his demand, but of our country and of our life did ask us. And the sweet Leader began: "Mantua,". . . and the shade, all rapt in self, leapt towards him from the place where first it was, saying: "O Mantuan, I am Sordello of thy city." And one embraced
100 the other. . . .

After the greetings dignified and glad had been repeated three and four times, Sordello drew him back, and said: "Who art thou?". . .

13. Casella, a musician friend of Dante, who probably set to music the poem *Love that in my mind discourseth to me,* included by Dante in his *Convito.*

59. **Manfred,** (c. 1231–1266), usurping king of Sicily, was excommunicated and died in battle.   99. **Sordello,** a medieval Italian poet.

"I am Virgil; and for no other sin did I lose heaven than for not having faith": thus answered then my Leader. As one who seeth suddenly a thing before him whereat he marvels, who believes, and believes not, saying: "It is, it is not"; such seemed he, and forthwith bent his brow, and humbly turned back towards my Leader, and embraced him where the inferior clasps.

"O glory of the Latins," said he, "by whom our tongue showed forth all its power, O eternal praise of the place whence I sprang, what merit or what favour showeth thee to me? If I am worthy to hear thy words, tell me if thou comest from Hell, and from what cloister."

"Through all the circles of the woeful realm," answered he him, "came I here. A virtue from heaven moved me, and with it I come. Not for doing, but for not doing, have I lost the vision of the high Sun, whom thou desirest, and who too late by me was known. Down there is a place not sad with torments, but with darkness alone, where the lamentations sound not as wailings, but as sighs. There do I abide with the innocent babes, bitten by the fangs of death, ere they were exempt from human sin. There dwell I with those who clad them not with the three holy virtues, and without offence knew the others and followed them all. But if thou knowest and canst, give us some sign whereby we may most quickly come there where Purgatory has right beginning."

He answered: "No fixed place is set for us: 'tis permitted to me to go up and around; so far as I may go, as guide I place me beside thee. But see now how the day is declining, and ascend by night we cannot; therefore 'tis well to think of some fair resting-place. Here are souls on the right apart; if thou allow it I will lead thee to them, and not without joy will they be known to thee.". . .

There, seated on the grass and on the flowers, singing *Salve Regina,* saw I souls who because of the valley were not seen from without. "Ere the little sun now sinks to his nest," began the Mantuan who had led us aside, "desire not that I guide you among them. From this terrace ye will better know the acts and faces of them all, than if received among them down in the hollow.". . .

I saw that noble army thereafter silently gaze upward, as if in expectancy, pale and lowly; and I saw two angels come forth from on high and descend below with two flaming swords, broken short and deprived of their points. Green, as tender leaves just born, was their raiment, which they trailed behind, fanned and smitten by green wings. One came and alighted a little above us, and the other descended on the opposite bank, so that the people were contained in the middle. Clearly I discerned the fair hair of them; but in their faces the eye was dazed, like a faculty which by excess is confounded. "Both come from Mary's bosom," said Sordello, "as guard of the vale, because of the serpent that straightway will come."

Whereat I, who knew not by what way, turned me around, and placed me all icy cold close to the trusty shoulders. . . . And Night, in the place where we were, had made two of the steps wherewith she climbs, and the third was already down-stooping its wings; when I, who with me had somewhat of Adam, vanquished by sleep, sank down on the grass.

CANTO IX. *The Gate of St. Peter*

At the hour when the swallow begins her sad lays nigh unto the morn, perchance in memory of her former woes, and when our mind, more of a wanderer from the flesh and less prisoned by thoughts, in its visions is almost prophetic; in a dream methought I saw an eagle poised in the sky, with plumes of gold, with wings outspread, and intent to swoop. . . . Then meseemed that, having wheeled awhile, terrible as lightning, he descended and snatched me up far as the fiery sphere. There it seemed that he and I did burn, and the visionary flame so scorched that needs was my slumber broken. . . . I startled, soon as sleep fled from my face, and I grew pale even as a man who freezes with terror.

Alone beside me was my Comfort, and the sun was already more than two hours high, and mine eyes were turned to the sea. "Have no fear," said my Lord, "make thee secure, for we are at a good spot: hold not back, but put out all thy strength. Thou art now arrived at Purgatory; see there the rampart that compasseth it around; see the entrance there where it seems cleft. Erewhile, in the dawn which precedes the day, when thy soul was sleeping within thee upon the flowers wherewith down below is adorned, came a lady and said: 'I am Lucy, let me take this man who sleepeth, so will I prosper him on his way.' Sordello remained and the other noble forms. She took thee, and as day was bright, came on upward, and I followed in her track. Here she placed thee, and first her fair eyes did show to me that open entrance; then she and sleep together went away." As doth a man who in dread is reassured, and who changes his fear to comfort after the truth is revealed to him, I changed me; and when my Leader saw me

---

40–41. **souls who . . . from without**; these are the kings who neglected duty for selfish war or luxury. 50. **swords, broken . . . ;** to symbolize justice tempered with mercy.

65–67. **two of the steps . . . wings**; it was the third hour of night. 78–81. **There it seemed . . . broken**; the dream symbolized moral purification. 94. **Lucy,** symbol of Illuminating Grace. See Inferno II.

freed from care, he moved up by the rampart, and I following, towards the height.

Reader, well thou seest how I exalt my subject, therefore marvel thou not if with greater art I sustain it. We drew nigh, and were at a place, whence there where first appeared to me a break just like a fissure which divides a wall, I espied a gate, and three steps beneath to go to it, of divers colours, and a warder who as yet spake no word. And as more I 10 opened mine eyes there, I saw him seated upon the topmost step, such in his countenance that I endured him not; and in his hand he held a naked sword which reflected the rays so towards us, that I directed mine eyes to it oft in vain.

"Tell, there where ye stand, what would ye?" he began to say; "where is the escort? Beware lest coming upward be to your hurt!" "A heavenly lady who well knows these things," my Master answered him, "even now did say to us: 'Go ye thither, there is the 20 gate.'" "And may she speed your steps to good," again began the courteous door-keeper; "come then forward to our stairs."

There where we came, at the first step, was white marble so polished and smooth that I mirrored me therein as I appear. The second darker was then perse, of a stone, rugged and calcined, cracked in its length and in its breadth. The third, which is massy above, seemed to me of porphyry so flaming red as blood that spurts from a vein. Upon this God's angel 30 held both his feet, sitting upon the threshold, which seemed to me adamantine stone. Up by the three steps, with my good will, my Leader brought me, saying: "Humbly ask that the bolt be loosed." Devoutly I flung me at the holy feet; for mercy I craved that he would open to me; but first on my breast thrice I smote me.

Seven P's upon my forehead he described with the point of his sword and: "Do thou wash these wounds when thou art within," he said. Ashes, or earth 40 which is dug out dry, would be of one colour with his vesture, and from beneath it he drew forth two keys. One was of gold and the other was of silver; first with the white and then with the yellow he did so to the gate that I was satisfied. "Whensoever one of these keys fails so that it turns not aright in the lock," said he to us, "this passage opens not. More precious is one, but the other requires exceeding art and wit ere it unlocks, because it is the one which unties the knot. From Peter I hold them; and he 50 told me to err rather in opening, than in keeping it locked, if only the people fell prostrate at my feet."

Then he pushed the door of the sacred portal, saying: "Enter, but I make you ware that he who look-

eth behind returns outside again.". . . I turned me intent for the first sound, and *Te Deum laudamus* meseemed to hear in a voice mingled with sweet music. Just such impression gave me that which I heard, as we are wont to receive when people are singing with an organ, and now the words are clear, and now are not. 60

CANTO X–XII. *Terrace I: Pride vs. Humility*

When we were within the threshold of the gate, which the evil love of souls disuses, because it makes the crooked way seem straight, by the ringing sound I heard it was shut again; and had I turned mine eyes to it what would have been a fitting excuse for the fault? We climbed through a cleft rock, which was moving on one side and on the other, even as a wave that recedes and approaches. "Here we must use a little skill," began my Leader, "in keeping close, now hither now thither, to the side that is 70 receding." And this made our steps so scant, that the waning orb of the moon regained its bed to sink again to rest ere we were forth from that needle's eye. But when we were free and on the open above, where the mount is set back, I wearied and both uncertain of our way, we stood still on a level place more solitary than roads through deserts. From its edge where it borders on the void, to the foot of the high bank which sheer ascends, a human body would measure in thrice; and so far as mine eye 80 could wing its flight, now on the left now on the right side, such this cornice appeared to me.

Thereon our feet had not yet moved, when I discerned that circling bank (which, being upright, lacked means of ascent) to be of pure white marble, and adorned with sculptures so that not only Polycletus, but Nature there would be put to shame. The angel that came to earth with the decree of peace wept for since many a year, which opened heaven from its long ban, before us appeared so vividly 90 graven there in gentle mien, that it seemed not an image which is dumb. One would have sworn that he was saying: *Ave*, for there she was fashioned who turned the key to open the supreme love. . . .

While I was rejoicing to look on the images of humilities so great and for their Craftsman's sake precious to see, "Lo here," murmured the Poet, "much people, but few they make their steps; these will send us on to the high stairs." Mine eyes, that were intent on gazing to see new things whereof 100 they are fain, were not slow in turning towards him. I would not, reader, that thou be scared from a good purpose through hearing how God wills that the

---

8–9. **a warder,** the angel-confessor with his sword of divine justice. 37. **Seven P's,** the seven deadly sins (peccata), corresponding to the seven terraces of Purgatory where they are expiated.

86–87. **Polycletus,** ancient Greek sculptor. 93–94. **she . . . who turned the key,** the Angel of the Annunciation.

debt be paid. Heed not the form of the pain; think what followeth, think that at worst beyond the great judgment it cannot go.

I began: "Master, that which I see moving towards us seems not persons to me, yet I know not what, so wanders my sight." And he to me: "The grievous state of their torment doubles them down to earth so that mine eyes at first thereat were at strife. But look steadily there and disentwine with thy sight what is coming beneath those stones; already thou canst discern how each one beats his breast."

O ye proud Christians, wretched and weary, who, sick in mental vision, put trust in backward steps, perceive ye not that we are worms, born to form the angelic butterfly that flieth to judgment without defence? Why doth your mind soar on high, since ye are as 'twere imperfect insects, even as the grub in which full form is wanting? As to support ceiling or roof is sometimes seen for corbel a figure joining knees to breast, which of unreality begetteth real discomfort in him who beholds it; in such wise saw I these when I gave good heed. True it is that more and less were they contracted, according as they had more or less upon them, and he who had most patience in his bearing, weeping seemed to say: "I can no more.". . .

Already more of the mount was circled by us, and of the sun's path much more spent, than the mind, not set free, esteemed; when he, whoever in front of me alert was going, began: "Lift up thy head, this is no time to go thus engrossed. See there an angel who is making ready to come towards us; look how the sixth handmaiden is returning from the day's service. Adorn with reverence thy bearing and thy face, so that it may delight him to send us upward; think that this day never dawns again." Right well was I used to his monitions never to lose time, so that in that matter he could not speak to me darkly.

To us came the beauteous creature, robed in white, and in his countenance, such as a tremulous star at morn appears. His arms he opened and then outspread his wings; he said: "Come; here nigh are the steps, and easily now is ascent made." To this announcement few be they who come. O human folk, born to fly upward, why at a breath of wind thus fall ye down? He led us where the rock was cut; there he beat his wings upon my forehead, then did promise me my journey secure. . . . While we were turning there our persons, "Beati pauperes spiritu" voices so sweetly sang, that no speech would tell it. Ah! how different are these openings from those in Hell! for here we enter through songs, and down there through fierce wailings.

40. the beauteous creature, the Angel of Humility. 50. "Beati pauperes spiritu," "Blessed are the poor in spirit." (Matthew 5:3)

Now were we mounting up by the sacred steps, and meseemed I was exceeding lighter, than meseemed before on the flat; wherefore I: "Master, say, what heavy thing has been lifted from me, that scarce any toil is perceived by me in journeying?" He answered: "When the P's which have remained still nearly extinguished on thy face, shall, like the one, be wholly rased out, thy feet shall be so vanquished by good will, that not only will they feel it no toil, but it shall be a delight to them to be urged upward." Then did I, like those who go with something on their head unknown to them, save that another's signs make them suspect; wherefore the hand lends its aid to make certain, and searches, and finds, and fulfils that office which cannot be furnished by the sight; and with the fingers of my right hand outspread, I found but six the letters, which he with the keys had cut upon me over the temples: whereat my Leader looking did smile.

CANTOS XIII–XV. *Terrace II: Envy vs. Fraternal Love*

We were at the top of the stairway where a second time the mount is cut away which, by our ascent, frees us from evil. . . . As far as here counts for a mile, so far there had we already gone, in short time, by reason of our ready will; and, flying towards us were heard, but not seen, spirits, speaking courteous invitations to the table of love. . . .

"O Father," said I, "what voices are these?" and as I was asking, lo one of them saying: "Love them from whom ye have suffered evil." And the good Master: "This circle doth scourge the sin of envy, and therefore the cords of the whip are drawn from love. . . . But fix thine eyes through the air full steadily, and thou shalt see people sitting down in front of us, and each one along the cliff is seated."

Then wider than before mine eyes I opened; I looked before me, and saw shades with cloaks not different from the hue of the stone. And after we were a little further forward, I heard a cry: "Mary, pray for us"; a cry: "Michael, and Peter, and all Saints." I believe not that on earth there goeth this day a man so hardened, who were not pierced with compassion at what I then saw; for when I had reached so nigh to them that their features came distinctly to me, heavy grief was running from mine eyes.

With coarse haircloth they seemed to me covered, and one was supporting the other with the shoulder, and all were supported by the bank. Even so the blind, to whom means are lacking, sit at Pardons begging for their needs; and one sinks his head upon the other, so that pity may quickly be awakened in others, not only by the sound of their words, but by their appearance which pleads not less. And as to the blind the sun profits not, so to the shades there where I was now speaking, heaven's light will not be bounteous of itself; for all their eyelids an iron wire pierces and stitches up, even as is done to a wild hawk because it abideth not still. . . .

As when a ray of light leaps from the water or from the mirror to the opposite direction, ascending at an angle similar to that at which it descends, and departs as far from the line of the falling stone in an equal space, even as experiment and science shows, so I seemed to be smitten by reflected light in front of me, wherefore mine eyes were swift to flee. "What is that, sweet Father, from which I cannot screen my sight so that it may avail me," said I, "and seems to be moving towards us?"

"Marvel thou not if the heavenly household yet dazes thee," he answered me, " 'tis a messenger that cometh to invite us to ascend. Soon will it be that to behold these things shall not be grievous to thee, but shall be a joy to thee, as great as nature hath fitted thee to feel." When we had reached the blessed angel, with gladsome voice, he said: "Enter here to a stairway far less steep than the others." We were mounting, already departed thence, and *"Beati misericordes"* was sung behind, and "Rejoice thou that overcomest.". . .

CANTOS XV–XVII. *Terrace III: Anger vs. Meekness*

We were journeying on through the evening, straining our eyes forward, as far as we could, against the evening and shining rays; and lo, little by little, a smoke, dark as night, rolling towards us, nor any room was there to escape from it. This reft us of sight and the pure air. Gloom of hell and of a night bereft of every planet under a meagre sky, darkened by cloud as much as it can be, made not to my sight so thick a veil, nor of a pile so harsh to the feel, as that smoke which there covered us; for it suffered not the eye to stay open: wherefore my wise and trusty Escort closed up to me, and offered me his shoulder. Even as a blind man goeth behind his guide in order not to stray, and not to butt against aught that may do him hurt, or perchance kill him, so went I through the bitter and foul air, listening to my Leader who was saying ever: "Look that thou be not cut off from me."

I heard voices, and each one seemed to pray for peace and for mercy, to the Lamb of God that taketh away sins. Only *"Agnus Dei"* were their beginnings; one word was with them all, and one measure; so that full concord seemed to be among them. "Are those spirits, Master, that I hear?" said I. And he

to me: "Thou apprehendest truly, and they are untying the knot of anger."

"Now who art thou that cleavest our smoke, and speakest of us even as if thou didst still measure time by calends?" Thus by a voice was said.

And I: "Hide not from me who thou wast before death, but tell it me, and tell me if I am going aright for the pass; and thy words shall be our escort." "A Lombard was I and was called Mark; I had knowledge of the world, and loved that worth at which now every one hath unbent his bow; for mounting up thou goest aright." Thus answered he, and added: "I pray thee that thou pray for me, when thou art above."

And I to him: "By my faith I bind me to thee to do that which thou askest of me, but I am bursting within at a doubt, if I free me not from it. First 'twas simple, and now is made double by thy discourse, which makes certain to me, both here and elsewhere, that whereto I couple it. The world is indeed so wholly desert of every virtue, even as thy words sound to me, and heavy and covered with sin; but I pray that thou point the cause out to me, so that I may see it, and that I may show it to others; for one places it in the heavens and another here below."

A deep sigh, which grief compressed to "Alas!" he first gave forth, and then began: "Brother, the world is blind, and verily thou comest from it. Ye who are living refer every cause up to the heavens alone, even as if they swept all with them of necessity. Were it thus, Free Will in you would be destroyed, and it were not just to have joy for good and mourning for evil. The heavens set your impulses in motion; I say not all, but suppose I said it, a light is given you to know good and evil, and Free Will, which, if it endure the strain in its first battlings with the heavens, at length gains the whole victory, if it be well nurtured. Ye lie subject, in your freedom, to a greater power and to a better nature; and that creates in you mind which the heavens have not in their charge.

"Therefore, if the world to-day goeth astray, in you is the cause, in you be it sought, and I now will be a true scout to thee therein. From his hands who fondly loves her ere she is in being, there issues, after the fashion of a little child that sports, now weeping, now laughing, the simple, tender soul, who knoweth naught save that, sprung from a joyous maker, willingly she turneth to that which delights her. First she tastes the savour of a trifling good; there she is beguiled and runneth after it, if guide or curb turn not her love aside. Wherefore 'twas needful to put law as a curb, needful to have a ruler who might discern at least the tower of the true city.

21–22. **the blessed angel,** the Angel of Fraternal Love.   25. *"Beati misericordes,"* "Blessed are the merciful." (Matthew 5:7)

59. **Mark,** Marco Lombardo, a learned courtier of thirteenth-century Venice.

"Laws there are, but who putteth his hand to them? None. . . . Wherefore the people, that see their guide aiming only at that good whereof he is greedy, feed on that and ask no further. Clearly canst thou see that evil leadership is the cause which hath made the world sinful, and not nature that may be corrupted within you. Rome, that made the good world, was wont to have two suns, which made plain to sight the one road and the other; that of the world, and that of God. One hath quenched the other; and the sword is joined to the crook; and the one together with the other must perforce go ill; because, being joined, one feareth not the other. . . .

"God be with you, for no further I come with you. See the light, that beams through the smoke, now waxing bright; the angel is there, and it behooves me to depart ere I am seen of him." So turned he back and no more would hear me. . . .

I turned me to see where I was, when a voice which removed me from every other intent, said: "Here one ascends"; and it gave my desire to behold who it was that spake, such eagerness as never rests until it sees face to face. But, as at the sun which oppresses our sight, and veils his form by excess, so my virtue there was failing me. "This is a divine spirit, that directs us to the way of ascent without our prayer, and conceals itself with its own light.". . . Thus spake my Leader, and I with him did turn our footsteps to a stairway; and soon as I was at the first step, near me I felt as 'twere the stroke of a wing, and my face fanned, and heard one say: *"Beati pacifici* who are without evil wrath."

CANTOS XVII–XIX. *Terrace IV: Sloth vs. Diligence*

Now were the last rays whereafter night followeth so far risen above us that the stars were appearing on many sides. . . . The moon, almost retarded to midnight, made the stars appear more thin to us, fashioned like a bucket all burning; wherefore I, who had garnered clear and plain reasons to my questionings, stood like one who is rambling drowsily.

But this drowsiness was taken from me on a sudden, by people who behind our backs had already come round to us. . . . Soon were they upon us, because all that great throng was moving at a run; and two in front were shouting in tears. "Haste! Haste! let no time be lost through little love," cried the others afterwards, "that striving to do well may renew grace.". . . We are so filled with desire to speed us, that stay we cannot; therefore forgive, if thou hold our penance for rudeness.". . .

Then, when those shades were so far parted from us, that they could be seen no more, a new thought was set within me, wherefrom many and divers others sprang; and so from one to another I rambled, that I closed mine eyes for very wandering, and thought I transmuted into dream. . . . There came to me in a dream, a stuttering woman, with eyes asquint, and crooked on her feet, with maimed hands, and of sallow hue. I gazed upon her; and as the sun comforteth the cold limbs which night weighs down, so my look made ready her tongue, and then set her full straight in short time, and her pallid face even as love wills did colour. When she had her tongue thus loosed, she began to sing, so that with difficulty should I have turned my attention from her.

"I am," she sang, "I am the sweet Siren, who leads mariners astray in mid-sea, so full am I of pleasantness to hear. I turned Ulysses from his wandering way with my song, and whoso liveth with me rarely departs, so wholly do I satisfy him." Her mouth was not yet shut, when a lady appeared holy and alert alongside me, to put her to confusion. "O Virgil, Virgil, who is this?" angrily she said; and he came with eyes ever fixed on that honest one. He seized the other, and, rending her clothes, laid her open in front and showed me her belly; that awakened me with the stench which issued therefrom.

I turned my eyes, and the good Virgil said: "At least three calls have I uttered to thee; arise and come, find we the opening by which thou mayst enter." Up I lifted me, and all the circles of the holy mount were now filled with the high day, and we journeyed with the new sun at our backs. Following him, I was bearing my brow like one that hath it burdened with thought, who makes of himself half an arch of a bridge, when I heard: "Come, here is the pass," spoken in a tone so gentle and kind as is not heard in this mortal confine. With outspread wings which swanlike seemed, he who thus spoke to us did turn us upward, between the two walls of the hard stone. He stirred his pinions then, and fanned us, affirming *qui lugent* to be blessed, for they shall have their souls rich in consolation.

CANTOS XIX–XXI. *Terrace V: Avarice vs. Liberality*

When I was in the open, on the fifth circle, I saw people about it who wept, lying on the ground all turned downwards. *"Adhæsit pavimento anima mea,"* I heard them say with such deep sighs that hardly

7–10. **Rome . . . that of God.** The clearest statement of Dante's view of temporal and spiritual power. 30–32. **near me . . . "Beati pacifici.** The Angel of Meekness said, "Blessed are the peace-makers." (Matthew 5:9)

75–78. **He seized . . . therefrom.** Dante's dream of the Siren contrasts the superficial attractiveness and the essential loathsomeness of the three sins of sense that follow. 92–93. **He stirred . . . qui lugent.** The Angel of Diligence said, "Blessed are they that mourn." (Matthew 5:4) 97. *"Adhaesit pavimento anima mea,"* "My spirit cleaveth unto the dust." (Psalms 119: 25)

were the words understood. "O chosen of God, whose sufferings both justice and hope make less hard, direct us towards the high ascents." "If ye come secure from lying prostrate, and desire to find the way most quickly, let your right hands be ever to the outside." Thus prayed the poet, and thus a little in front of us was answer made; wherefore I noted what else was concealed in the words, and turned mine eyes then to my Lord; whereat he gave
10 assent with glad sign to what the look of my desire was craving.

When I could do with me according to my own mind, I drew forward above that creature whose words before made me take note, saying: "Spirit, in whom weeping matures that without which one cannot turn to God, stay a while for me thy greater care. Who thou wast, and why ye have your backs turned upward, tell me, and if thou wouldst that I obtain aught for thee yonder, whence living I set
20 forth."

And he to me: "Wherefore heaven turneth our backs to itself shalt thou know; but first, *scias quod ego fui successor Petri.* Between Sestri and Chiaveri flows down a fair river, and from its name the title of my race takes origin. One month, and little more, I learned how the great mantle weighs on him who keeps it from the mire, so that all other burdens seem feathers. My conversion, ah me! was late; but when I was made Pastor of Rome, so I discovered
30 the life which is false. I saw that there the heart was not at rest, nor could one mount higher in that life; wherefore love of this was kindled within me. Up to that moment, I was a soul wretched and parted from God, wholly avaricious; now, as thou seest, here am I punished for it.

"What avarice works, here is declared in the purgation of the down-turned souls, and no more bitter penalty hath the mount. Even as our eye, fixed on earthly things, did not lift itself on high, so
40 here justice hath sunk it to earth. As avarice quenched our love for every good, wherefore our works were lost, so justice here doth hold us fast, bound and seized by feet and hands; and so long as it shall be the pleasure of the just Lord, so long shall we lie here motionless and outstretched."

I had kneeled down, and was about to speak; but as I began, and he perceived my reverence merely by listening, "What reason," he said, "thus bent thee down?" And I to him: "Because of your dignity
50 my conscience smote me for standing." "Make straight thy legs, uplift thee, brother," he answered; "err not, a fellow-servant am I with thee and with the others unto one Power. . . . Now get thee hence; I desire not that thou stay longer, for thy

tarrying disturbs my weeping, whereby I mature that which thou didst say.". . .

A shade appeared to us, and came on behind us, gazing at its feet on the prostrate crowd, nor did we perceive it until it first spake, saying: "My brothers, God give you peace." Quickly we turned us, and 60 Virgil gave back to him the sign that is fitting thereto. Then began: "May the true court, which binds me in eternal exile, bring thee in peace to the council of the blest." "How," said he, and meantime we went sturdily, "if ye are shades that God deigns not above, who hath escorted you so far by his stairs?"

And my Teacher: "If thou lookest at the marks which this man bears, and which the angel outlines, clearly wilt thou see 'tis meet he reign with the 70 good. But since she who spins day and night, had not yet drawn for him the fibre which Clotho charges and packs on the distaff for each one, his spirit, which is thy sister and mine, coming up, could not come along, because it sees not after our fashion: wherefore I was brought forth from Hell's wide jaws to guide him, and I will guide him onward, so far as my school can lead him.". . .

Answered that spirit, "I was yonder, great in fame, but not yet with faith. So sweet was the music 80 of my words, that me, a Toulousian, Rome drew to herself, where I did merit a crown of myrtle for my brow. Statius folk yonder still do name me; I sang of Thebes, and then of the great Achilles; but I fell by the way with the second burden. The sparks, which warmed me, from the divine flame whence more than a thousand have been kindled, were the seeds of my poetic fire: of the Æneid I speak, which was a mother to me, and was to me a nurse in poesy; without it I had not stayed the weight of a drachm. 90 And to have lived yonder, when Virgil was alive, I would consent to one sun more than I owe to my coming forth from exile."

These words turned Virgil to me with a look that silently said: "Be silent." But the virtue which wills is not all powerful; for laughter and tears follow so closely the passion from which each springs, that they least obey the will in the most truthful. I did but smile, like one who makes a sign: whereat the shade was silent and looked at me in the eyes, where 100 most the soul is fixed.

And he said: "So may such great toil achieve its end; wherefore did thy face but now display to me a flash of laughter?" Now am I caught on either side; one makes me keep silence, the other conjures me to speak; wherefore I sigh and am understood by my Master, and he said to me, "Have no fear of

3–6. "If ye come . . . the outside." The words are spoken by a pope, Adrian V, who later identifies himself.

57. A shade, the Roman poet Statius, author of the *Thebaid*, allegedly converted to Christianity. Hence he represents the human wisdom of Virgil enlightened by the Christianity that Virgil never knew. 72. Clotho, the fate who prepared the thread of life.

speaking, but speak, and tell him that which he asketh with so great desire."

Wherefore I: "Perchance thou dost marvel, O ancient spirit, at the laugh I gave, but I desire that yet greater wonder seize thee. He who guideth mine eyes on high, is that Virgil from whom thou drewest power to sing of men and gods. If thou didst believe other cause for my laughter, set it aside as untrue, and believe it was those words which thou spakest of him."

Already was he stooping to embrace my Teacher's feet; but he said: "Brother, do not so, for thou art a shade and a shade thou seest." And he, rising: "Now canst thou comprehend the measure of the love which warms me toward thee, when I forget our nothingness, and treat shades as a solid thing."

CANTOS XXII–XXIV. *Terrace VI: Gluttony vs. Temperance*

Already was the angel left behind us, the angel that had turned us to the sixth circle, having erased a scar from my face, and had said to us that those who have their desire to righteousness were blessed, and his words accomplished that with *sitiunt*, and naught else. And I, lighter than by the other passages, went on so that without any toil I was following the fleet spirits upward. . . . They journeyed on in front, and I, solitary, behind; and I hearkened to their discourse which gave me understanding in poesy. . . .

Even as musing wayfarers do, who on overtaking strange folk by the way, turn round to them and stay not, so behind us, moving more quickly, coming, and passing by, a throng of spirits, silent and devout, was gazing upon us in wonder. Dark and hollow-eyed was each one, pallid of face, and so wasted away that the skin took form from the bones. . . . Who, not knowing the reason, would believe that the scent of fruit and that of water had thus wrought, by begetting desire?

Already I was in astonishment at what thus famishes them, because of the reason not yet manifest, of their leanness, and of their sad scurf, when lo, from the hollow of the head a shade turned its eyes to me and fixedly did gaze; then cried aloud: "What grace is this to me?" Never had I recognized him by the face, but in his voice, was revealed to me, that which was blotted out in his countenance. This spark rekindled within me all my knowledge of the changed features, and I recognized the face of Forese.

"Ah stare not," he prayed, "at the dry leprosy which discolours my skin, nor at any default of flesh that I may have, but tell me sooth of thyself, and who those two spirits are that there make thy escort; abide thou not without speaking to me." "Thy face," answered I him, "which in death I wept for once, gives me now not less grief, even unto tears, seeing it so disfigured. Therefore tell me, in God's name, what strips you so; make me not talk while I am marvelling, for ill can he speak who is full of other desire."

And he to me: "From the eternal counsel virtue descends into the water, and into the tree left behind, whereby I thus do waste away. All this people, who weeping sing, sanctify themselves again in hunger and thirst, for having followed appetite to excess. The scent which issues from the fruit, and from the spray that is diffused over the green, kindles within us a desire to eat and to drink. . . . But pray, brother, look that thou hide thee no longer from me; thou seest that not only I, but all this people are gazing where thou veilest the sun."

Wherefore I to him: "If thou bring back to mind what thou hast been with me and what I have been with thee, the present memory will still be grievous. From that life he who goeth before me did turn me, the other day."

Neither did our speech make the going, nor the going, more slow; but, talking we went bravely on, even as a ship driven by a fair wind. And the shades, that seemed things twice dead, drew in wonderment at me through the pits of their eyes, aware of my being alive. . . . Thus we passed close against one of the two margins, hearing sins of gluttony, once followed by woeful gains. Then, spread out along the solitary way, full a thousand paces and more bore us onward, each in contemplation without a word.

"What go ye thus pondering on, ye lone three," a sudden voice did say; wherefore I startled as frightened and timid beasts do. I raised my head to see who it was, and never in a furnace were glasses or metals seen so glowing and red, as I saw one who said: "If it please you to mount upward, here must a turn be given; hence goeth he who desires to go for peace." His countenance had bereft me of sight; wherefore I turned me back to my Teachers, like one who goeth according as he listens. And as the May breeze, herald of the dawn, stirs and breathes forth sweetness, all impregnate with grass and with flowers, such a wind felt I give on the middle of my brow, and right well I felt the pinions move which wafted ambrosial fragrance to my senses; and I heard say: "Blessed are they who are illumined by

---

19–22. **and had said . . . naught else.** The Angel of Justice said, "Blessed are they which do thirst after righteousness." (Matthew 5:6)   48. **Forese,** Forese Donati, a friend of Dante.

74. **From that life he . . . did turn me . . .** ; clear indication that Dante had fallen into actual dissipation after the death of Beatrice.
88. **a sudden voice,** the voice of the Angel of Temperance.

so much grace, that the love of taste kindleth not too great desire in their breasts, and who hunger always so far as is just.". . .

[Cantos XXV–XXVI, describing the journey through Terrace VII: Lust vs. Chastity, are omitted.]

CANTO XXVII. *The Steps to Eden, the Earthly Paradise*

The day was passing away when God's glad angel appeared to us. Outside the flames on the bank he was standing and singing *"Beati mundo corde"* in a voice more piercing far than ours. Then: "No farther may ye go, O hallowed souls, if first the fire bite not; enter therein and to the singing beyond 10 be not deaf," he said to us when we were nigh to him; wherefore I became when I heard him, such as one who is laid in the grave. I bent forward over my clasped hands, gazing at the fire, and vividly imagining human bodies once seen burnt.

The kindly escorts turned them toward me, and Virgil said to me: "My son, here may be torment but not death. Remember thee, remember thee, . . . and if on Geryon I guided thee safely, what shall I do now nearer to God? Of a surety believe, that if 20 within the womb of these flames thou didst abide full a thousand years, they could not make thee bald of one hair; and if perchance thou thinkest that I beguile thee, get thee toward them, and get credence with thy hands on the hem of thy garments. Put away now, put away all fear; turn thee hither, and onward come securely." And I, yet rooted, and with accusing conscience.

When he saw me stand yet rooted and stubborn, troubled a little he said: "Now look, my son, 'twixt 30 Beatrice and thee is this wall." As at Thisbe's name Pyramus opened his eyes at the point of death, and gazed at her, when the mulberry became red, so, my stubbornness being softened, I turned me to my wise Leader on hearing the name which ever springs up in my mind. Whereupon he shook his head, and said: "What? do we desire to stay this side?" then smiled as one does to a child that is won by an apple.

Then he entered into the fire in front of me, pray-40 ing Statius that he would come behind; who for a long way before had separated us. When I was within, I would have flung me into molten glass to cool me, so immeasurable there was the burning. My sweet Father, to encourage me, went on discoursing ever of Beatrice, saying: "Already I seem to behold her eyes." A voice guided us, which was singing on the other side, and we, intent only on it, came forth, there where the ascent began. . . .

Straight the way mounted through the rock, toward such a quarter, that in front of me I stayed the 50 rays of sun who already was low. And of few steps made we assay, when I and my sages perceived that the sun had set behind us, because of the shadow which had vanished. And ere the horizon in all its stupendous range had become of one hue, and night held all her dominion, each of us made a bed of a step; for the law of the mount took from us the power, rather than the desire, to ascend. . . . Little of the outside could there be seen, but through that little I saw the stars brighter and bigger than 60 their wont. As I was thus ruminating, and thus gazing at them, sleep fell on me, sleep which oft doth know the news ere the fact come to pass. . . .

And now, at the brightness ere dayspring born, which rises the gratefuler to wayfarers as on their return they lodge less far from home, the shades of night were fleeing on every side, and my sleep with them; wherefore I arose, seeing the great Masters already risen. "That sweet fruit whereof the care of mortals goeth in search on so many boughs, this day 70 shall give thy hungerings peace." Words such as these did Virgil use to me, and never have there been gifts that were equal in sweetness to these. So greatly did desire upon desire come over me to be above, that at every step after I felt my pinions grow for the flight.

When the stairway was all sped beneath us, and we were upon the topmost step, on me did Virgil fix his eyes, and said: "Son, the temporal fire and the eternal, hast thou seen, and art come to a place 80 where I, of myself, discern no further. Here have I brought thee with wit and with art; now take thy pleasure for guide; forth art thou from the steep ways, forth art from the narrow. Behold there the sun that shineth on thy brow; behold the tender grass, the flowers, and the shrubs, which the ground here of itself alone brings forth. While the glad fair eyes are coming, which weeping made me come to thee, thou canst sit thee down and canst go among them. No more expect my word, nor my sign. Free, 90 upright, and whole, is thy will, and 'twere a fault not to act according to its prompting; wherefore I do crown and mitre thee over thyself."

CANTO XXVIII. *Eden, the Earthly Paradise*

Now eager to search within and around the divine forest dense and verdant, which to mine eyes was tempering the new day, without waiting more I left the mountain-side, crossing the plain with lingering

---

6–7. *"Beati mundo corde."* The Angel of Chastity said, "Blessed are the pure in heart." (Matthew 5:8)

90. **No more expect my word.** . . . Virgil the pagan, who can never enter Eden or Paradise, has brought Dante as far as human wisdom alone can do. Beatrice, symbolizing revelation, will be his new guide.

step, over the ground which gives forth fragrance on every side. A sweet breeze, itself invariable, was striking on my brow with no greater force than a gentle wind, before which the branches, responsively trembling, were all bending toward that quarter, where the holy mount casts its first shadow. . . .

And lo, a stream took from me further passage which, toward the left with its little waves, bent the grass which sprang forth on its bank. All the waters 10 which here are purest, would seem to have some mixture in them, compared with that, which hideth nought; albeit full darkly it flows beneath the everlasting shade, which never lets sun, nor moon, beam there.

With feet I halted and with mine eyes did pass beyond the rivulet, to gaze upon the great diversity of the tender blossoms; and there to me appeared, even as on a sudden something appears which, through amazement, sets all other thought astray, a 20 lady solitary, who went along singing, and culling flower after flower, wherewith all her path was painted. "Pray, fair lady, who at love's beams dost warm thee, if I may believe outward looks, which are wont to be a witness of the heart, may it please thee to draw forward," said I to her, "towards this stream, so far that I may understand what thou singest.". . .

As a lady who is dancing turns her round with feet close to the ground and to each other, and 30 hardly putteth foot before foot, she turned toward me upon the red and upon the yellow flowerets, not otherwise than a virgin that droppeth her modest eyes; and made my prayers satisfied, drawing so near that the sweet sound reached me with its meaning. Soon as she was there, where the grass is already bathed by the waves of the fair river, she vouchsafed to raise her eyes to me. I do not believe that so bright a light shone forth under the eyelids of Venus, pierced by her son, against all his 40 wont. . . .

"New-comers are ye," she began, "and perchance, because I am smiling in this place, chosen for nest of the human race, some doubt doth hold you marvelling. . . . I will tell from what cause that arises which makes thee marvel, and I will purge away the mist that offends thee. The highest Good, who himself alone doth please, made man good and for goodness, and gave this place to him as an earnest of eternal peace. Through his default, small time he 50 sojourned here; through his default, for tears and sweat he exchanged honest laughter and sweet play. . . .

"The water which thou seest wells not from a spring that is fed by moisture which cold condenses, like a river that gains and loses volume, but issues from a fount, constant and sure, which regains by God's will, so much as it pours forth freely on either side. On this side it descends with a virtue which takes from men the memory of sin; on the other it restores the memory of every good deed. On this 60 side Lethe, as on the other Eunoë 'tis called, and works not except first it is tasted on this side and on that. This exceedeth all other savours; and albeit thy thirst may be full sated, even tho' I reveal no more to thee, I will give thee yet a corollary as a grace; nor do I think that my words will be less precious to thee if they extend beyond my promise to thee. They who in olden times sang of the golden age and its happy state, perchance dreamed in Parnassus of this place. Here the root of man's race was innocent; 70 here spring is everlasting, and every kind of fruit; this is the nectar whereof each one tells." Then did I turn me right back to my poets, and saw that with smiles they had heard the last interpretation. . . .

CANTOS XXX–XXXI. *The Meeting with Beatrice*

As the saints at the last trump shall rise ready each one from his tomb, with re-clad voice singing Halleluiah, such on the divine chariot rose up a hundred ministers and messengers of life eternal. . . . Ere now have I seen, at dawn of day, the eastern part all rosy red, and the rest of heaven adorned 80 with fair clear sky, and the face of the sun rise shadowed, so that by the tempering of the mists the eye long time endured him: so within a cloud of flowers, which rose from the angelic hands and fell down again within and without, olive-crowned over a white veil, a lady appeared to me, clad, under a green mantle, with hue of living flame. And my spirit, that now so long a time had passed, since, trembling in her presence, it had been broken down with awe, without having further knowledge by 90 mine eyes through hidden virtue which went out from her, felt the mighty power of ancient love.

Soon as on my sight the lofty virtue smote, which already had pierced me ere I was out of my boyhood, I turned me to the left with the trust with which the little child runs to his mother when he is frightened or when he is afflicted, to say to Virgil: "Less than a drachm of blood is left in me that trembleth not; I recognize the tokens of the ancient flame." But Virgil had left us bereft of himself, Vir- 100 gil sweetest Father, Virgil to whom for my weal I gave me up; nor did all that our ancient mother lost, avail to keep my dew-washed cheeks from turning dark again with tears. "Dante, for that Virgil

---

5. **toward that quarter** . . . , the west. 7. **a stream,** Lethe, whose waters brought forgetfulness of the past. 19–20. **a lady,** Matilda, symbolizing the original purity of Eden.

102. **our ancient mother,** Eve.

goeth away, weep not yet, weep not yet, for thou must weep for other sword."

Even as an admiral, who at stern and at bow, comes to see the folk that man the other ships, and heartens them to brave deeds, so on the left side of the car, when I turned me at sound of my name, which of necessity here is recorded, I saw the lady, who first appeared to me veiled beneath the angelic festival, directing her eyes to me on this side the stream. Albeit the veil which fell from her head, crowned with Minerva's leaves, did not let her appear manifest, queenlike, in bearing yet stern, she continued, like one who speaks and holdeth back the hottest words till the last: "Look at me well; verily am I, verily am I Beatrice. How didst thou deign to draw nigh the mount? knewest thou not that here man is happy?"

Mine eyes drooped down to the clear fount; but beholding me therein, I drew them back to the grass, so great a shame weighed down my brow. So doth the mother seem stern to her child, as she seemed to me; for the savour of harsh pity tasteth of bitterness. She was silent, and straightway the angels sang. . . . But when I heard in their sweet harmonies their compassion on me, more than if they had said "Lady, why dost thou so shame him?" The ice which had closed about my heart became breath and water, and with anguish through mouth and eyes issued from my breast.

She, standing yet fixed on the said side of the car, then turned her words to the pitying angels thus: . . . "This man was such in his new life potentially, that every good talent would have made wondrous increase in him. But so much the more rank and wild the ground becomes with evil seed and untilled, the more it hath of good strength of soil. Some time I sustained him with my countenance; showing my youthful eyes to him I led him with me turned to the right goal. So soon as I was on the threshold of my second age, and I changed life, he forsook me, and gave him to others. When I was risen from flesh to spirit, and beauty and virtue were increased within me, I was less precious and less pleasing to him; and he did turn his steps by a way not true, pursuing false visions of good, that pay back no promise entire. Nor did it avail me to gain inspirations, with which in dream and otherwise, I called him back; so little recked he of them. so low sank he, that all means for his salvation were already short, save showing him the lost people. For this I visited the portal of the dead, and to him who has guided him up hither, weeping my prayers were borne. God's high decree would be broken, if Lethe were passed, and such viands were tasted, without some scot of penitence that may shed tears."

"O thou that art yon side the sacred stream," her speech directing with the point towards me, which

even with the edge had seemed sharp to me, she began again, continuing without delay, "say, say, if this is true; to such accusation thy confession must be joined.". . . Confusion and fear, together mingled, drove forth from my mouth a "Yea" such that to understand it the eyes were needed. As a crossbow breaks, when shot at too great tension, both its string and bow, and with less force the bolt hits the mark, so burst I under this heavy charge, pouring forth a torrent of tears and sighs, and my voice died away in its passage. . . . And she: "If thou wert silent, or if thou hadst denied what thou confessest, not less noted were thy fault; by such a judge 'tis known. But when self-accusation of sin bursts from the cheeks in our Court, the grindstone is turned back against the edge. . . . Put away the seed of weeping.". . . Then when my heart restored to me the sense of outward things, the lady whom I had found alone I saw above me; and she said: "Hold me! Hold me!" She had drawn me into the river up to my neck, and, pulling me after her, went along over the water light as a shuttle. . . . The fair lady opened her arms, clasped my head, and dipped me where I must needs swallow of the water; then drew me forth, and led me bathed within the dance of the four fair ones, and each did cover me with her arm.

"Here we are nymphs and in heaven are stars; ere Beatrice descended to the world we were ordained to her for her handmaids. We will lead thee to her eyes; but the three on the other side who deeper gaze, will sharpen thine eyes to the joyous light that is within." Thus singing they began; and then did lead me with them up to the breast of the griffin, where Beatrice stood turned towards us. . . . O glory of living eternal, who that so pale hath grown beneath the shade of Parnassus, or hath drunk at its well, that would not seem to have mind encumbered, on trying to render thee as thou appearedest, when in the free air thou didst disclose thee, where heaven in its harmony shadows thee forth?

Then she placed them all seven in front of her, and, merely by her nod, motioned behind her, me and the Lady and the Sage who had stayed. . . . Both more refulgent, and with slower steps, the sun was holding the meridian circle, which varies hither and thither as positions vary, when did halt, even as he halts who goes for escort before folk, if he finds aught that is strange or the traces thereof, those seven ladies at the margin of a pale shadow, such as beneath green leaves and dark boughs, the Alp casts over its cool streams. In front of them I seemed to behold Euphrates and Tigris welling up from one spring, and parting like friends that linger. "O light,

72. **the grindstone is turned . . .** ; and blunts the sword of justice. 82–83. **the four fair ones,** the four cardinal virtues—prudence, justice, temperance, and fortitude. 87. **the three on the other side,** the three theological virtues—faith, hope, and charity.

O glory of human kind, what water is this that here pours forth from one source, and self from self doth wend away?"

At such prayer was said to me: "Pray Matilda that she tell it thee"; and here made answer, as he doth who frees him from blame, the fair Lady: "This and other things have been told him by me, and sure am I that Lethe's water hid them not from him." And Beatrice: "Haply a greater care that oft bereaves of memory hath dimmed his mind's eyes. But behold Eunoë, which there flows on; lead him to it, and as thou art wont, requicken his fainting virtue."

As a gentle soul that maketh no excuse, but makes her will of the will of another, soon as it is disclosed by outward sign, so the fair Lady, after I was taken by her, set forth, and to Statius with queenly mien did say: "Come with him." If, reader, I had greater space for writing, I would sing, at least in part, of the sweet draught which never would have sated me; but forasmuch as all the pages ordained for this second canticle are filled, the curb of art no further lets me go. I came back from the most holy waves, born again, even as new trees renewed with new foliage, pure and ready to mount to the stars.

PARADISE

CANTOS I–VI. *Sphere I, the Moon: breakers of vows; Sphere II, Mercury: seekers of fame*

O YE who in your little skiff longing to hear, have followed on my keel that singeth on its way, turn to revisit your own shores; commit you not to the open sea; for perchance, losing me, ye would be left astray. The water which I take was never coursed before; Minerva bloweth, Apollo guideth me, and the nine Muses point me to the Bears. . . .

Beatrice was gazing upward, and I on her; and perchance in such space as an arrow stays and flies and is discharged from the nocking point, I saw me arrived where a wondrous thing drew my sight to it; and therefore she from whom my doing might not be hidden turning to me as much in joy as beauty, "Direct thy mind to God in gratitude," she said, "who hath united us with the first star." Meseemed a cloud enveloped us, shining, dense, firm and polished, like diamond smitten by the sun. Within itself the eternal pearl received us, as water doth receive a ray of light, though still itself uncleft. . . .

But there appeared to me a sight which so straitly held me to itself, to look upon it, that I bethought me not of my confession. In such guise as, from glasses transparent and polished, or from waters clear and tranquil, not so deep that the bottom is darkened, come back the notes of our faces, so faint that a pearl on a white brow cometh not slowlier upon our pupils; so did I behold many a countenance, eager to speak; wherefore I fell into the counter error of that which kindled love between the man and fountain.

No sooner was I aware of them, than, thinking them reflected images, I turned round my eyes to see of whom they were; and I saw naught, and turned them forward again straight on the light of my sweet guide, whose sacred eyes glowed as she smiled. "Wonder not that I smile," she said, "in presence of thy child-like thought, since it trusts not its foot upon the truth, but turneth thee after its wont, to vacancy. True substances are they which thou beholdest, relegated here for failure of their vows. Wherefore speak with them, and listen and believe; for the true light which satisfieth them, suffereth them not to turn their feet aside from it."

And I to the shade who seemed most to long for converse turned me and began, as one whom too great longing doth confound: "O well-created spirit, who in the rays of eternal life dost feel the sweetness which, save tasted, may ne'er be understood; it were acceptable to me, wouldst thou content me with thy name and with your lot." Whereat she, eager and with smiling eyes: "Our love doth no more bar the gate to a just wish, than doth that love which would have all its court like to itself. In the world I was a virgin sister; and if thy memory be rightly searched, my greater beauty will not hide me from thee, but thou wilt know me again for Piccarda, who, placed here with these other blessed ones, am blessed in the sphere that moveth slowest. Our affections, which are aflame only in the pleasure of the Holy Spirit, rejoice to be informed after his order. And this lot, which seemeth so far down, therefore is given us because our vows were slighted, and on some certain side were not filled in.". . .

Thus did she speak to me, and then began to sing *Ave Maria*, and vanished as she sang, like to a heavy thing through the deep water. My sight, which followed her far as it might, when it had lost her turned to the target of a greater longing, and bent itself all upon Beatrice; but she so flashed upon my look, that at the first my sight endured it not; and this made me the slower with my questioning. . . .

So Beatrice began this chant, and, as one who interrupteth not his speech, continued thus the sacred progress: "The greatest gift God of his largess

---

31–32. **the Bears,** the constellation of the Bears, since Dante now leaves the earth to rise through the nine revolving heavens. 40. **the first star,** the moon.

53–54. **the counter error.** . . . Dante mistook the real spirits for reflections, unlike Narcissus, who fell in love with his own reflection in the water.

made at the creation, and the most conformed to his own excellence, and which he most prizeth, was the will's liberty, wherewith creatures intelligent, both all and only, were and are endowed. . . . Ye Christians, be more sedate in moving, not like a feather unto every wind; nor think that every water cleanseth you. Ye have the Old and the New Testament and the shepherd of the Church to guide you; let this suffice you, unto your salvation. If sorry greed proclaim aught else to you, be men, not senseless sheep, lest the Jew in your midst should scoff at you. Do not ye as the lamb who leaves his mother's milk, silly and wanton, fighting with himself for his disport." Her ceasing and her transmuted semblance enjoined silence on my eager wit, which already had new questionings before it.

And even as an arrow which smiteth the targe ere the cord be still, so fled we to the second realm. . . . As in a fish-pool still and clear, the fishes draw to aught that so droppeth from without as to make them deem it somewhat they may feed on, so did I see more than a thousand splendours draw towards us, and in each one was heard: . . . "This little star adorneth her with good spirits who were active that honour and that fame might come to them; and when hereon desire, thus swerving, leaneth, needs must the rays of the true love mount upward with less life. But in the commeasuring of our rewards to our desert is part of our joy, because we see them neither less nor more. Whereby the living justice so sweeteneth our affection that it may ne'er be warped to any malice. Divers voices upon earth make sweet harmony, and so the divers seats in our life render sweet harmony amongst these wheels.". . .

CANTOS VIII–XIV. *Sphere III, Venus: lovers; Sphere IV, the Sun: religious teachers*

The world was wont to think in its peril that the fair Cyprian rayed down mad love, rolled in the third epicycle; and from her from whom I take my start, they took the name of the star which courts the sun, now from the nape, now from the brow. I had no sense of rising into her, but my Lady gave me full faith that I was there, because I saw her grow more beautiful. And as we see a spark within a flame, and as a voice within a voice may be distinguished, if one stayeth firm, and the other cometh and goeth; so in that light itself I perceived other torches moving in a circle more and less swift, after the measure, I suppose, of their eternal vision. . . . And within those who most in front appeared, Hosannah sounded in such wise that never since have I been free from longing to re-hear it.

Then one drew himself more nigh to us, and alone began: "All we are ready at thy will, that thou mayst have thy joy of us. We roll with those celestial Princes in one circle and in one circling and in one thirst, to whom thou from the world didst sometime say: *Ye who by understanding give the third heaven motion,* and so full of love are we that, to pleasure thee, a space of quiet shall be no less sweet to us. . . . Here we not repent, but smile; not at the sin, which cometh not again to mind, but at the Worth that ordered and provided. Here gaze we on the Art that beautifieth its so great effect, and here discern the Good which bringeth back the world below unto the world above.". . .

Now stay thee, reader, on thy bench, back thinking on this foretaste, wouldst thou have good joyance ere that thou be weary. I have set before thee; now feed thou thyself, for that matter whereof I have made me scribe, now wresteth to itself my total care. The greatest minister of Nature, who with the worth of heaven stampeth the world, and with his light measureth the time for us, united with that part now called to mind, was circling on the spirals whereon he doth present him ever earlier. And I was with him; but of my ascent I was no more aware than is a man, ere his first thought, aware that it is coming. 'Tis Beatrice who leadeth thus from good to better, so instantly that her act doth not expatiate through time. How shining in itself must that needs be which in the sun, whereinto I had entered, itself revealeth not by hue, but light! . . . Such, there, was the fourth household of the exalted Father who ever satisfieth it, showing how he doth breathe, and how beget.

And Beatrice began: "Give thanks, give thanks to the sun of the Angels, who of his grace hath to this sun of sense exalted thee." Never was heart of mortal so disposed unto devotion, and so keen to give itself to God with all its will, as to those words was I; and so wholly was my love committed unto him, it eclipsed Beatrice in oblivion. Her it displeased not; but she so smiled thereat, the splendour of her laughing eyes parted my erst united mind amongst things multiform.

Then saw I many a glow, living and conquering, make of us a centre, and of themselves a crown; sweeter in voice than shining in appearance. . . . When, so singing, those burning suns had circled round us thrice, like stars neighbouring the fixed poles, they seemed as ladies, not from the dance released, but pausing, silent, listening till they catch the notes renewed. And within one I heard begin: . . ."Thou wouldst know with what plants this garland is enflowered, which amorously doth circle

35–36. **the fair Cyprian,** Venus. 45–46. **other torches.** The spirits in Paradise are no longer represented with human features.

70. **greatest minister of Nature,** the sun. 74. **. . . doth present him ever earlier;** that is, from midwinter to midsummer.

round the beauteous lady who strengtheneth thee for heaven. I was of the lambs of the sacred flock that Dominic leadeth upon the way where is good fattening if there be no straying. This, who most neighboureth me upon the right, brother and master was to me, and he was Albert of Cologne, I Thomas of Aquino. . . .

"The providence which governeth the world,— with counsel wherein every creature's gaze must stay, defeated, e'er it reach the bottom,—in order that the spouse of him, who with loud cries espoused her with the blessed blood, might go toward her delight, secure within herself and faithfuller to him, two Princes did ordain on her behalf, who on this side and that should be for guides. The one was all seraphic in his ardour, the other by his wisdom was on earth a splendour of cherubic light. Of one will I discourse, because of both the two he speaketh who doth either praise, which so he will; for to one end their works. . . .

"Not yet was he far distant from his rising when he began to make the earth to feel from his great power a certain strengthening; for in his youth for such a lady did he rush into war against his father, to whom, as unto death, not one unbars the gate of his good pleasure; and in the spiritual court that had rule over him, and in his father's presence he was united to her, and then from day to day loved her more strongly. She, reft of her first husband, a thousand and a hundred years and more, despised, obscure, even till he stood without invitation. . . . But, lest I should proceed too covertly, Francis and Poverty as these two lovers now accept in speech outspread. Their harmony and joyous semblance, made love and wonder and tender looks the cause of sacred thoughts; so that the venerable Bernard first cast off his sandals and ran to follow so great peace, and as he ran him thought him all too slow. . . .

"Thence took his way, this father and this master, together with his lady, and with the household already binding on the humble cord; nor abjectness of heart weighed down his brow, that he was Pietro Bernadone's son, nor that he seemed so marvellous despised. But royally his stern intent to Innocent revealed he, and from him had the first imprint upon his Order. . . . And when, in thirst of martyrdom, in the proud presence of the Soldan, he preached Christ and his followers; and because he found the folk too crude against conversion,—not to stay in vain,—returned to gather fruit from the Italian herbage. . . . When it pleased him who for such good ordained him, to draw him up to his reward

6–7. **Albert of Cologne, Thomas of Aquino,** Albertus Magnus and Thomas Aquinas, the great theologians. 15–16. **The one . . . the other. . . .** St. Francis and St. Dominic, founders of holy orders emphasizing love and knowledge respectively. 17. **Of one;** St. Francis. 29. **her first husband,** Jesus. 41. **the humble cord,** the rope girdle of the Franciscans.

which he had earned in making himself lowly, to his brethren; as to his right heirs, his dearest lady he commended, and bade that they should love her faithfully; and from her bosom the illustrious soul willed to depart, turning to its own realm, and for its body would no other bier. Think now what he was, who was a worthy colleague to maintain the bark of Peter in deep sea towards the right sign! And such was our patriarch; wherefore who followeth him as he commandeth, thou must perceive, loadeth him with good wares.". . .

Into my mind this thought dropped sudden, just as the glorious life of Thomas held its peace, because of the resemblance that sprang from his discourse, and then from Beatrice's, whom to begin thus after him it pleased: "This man hath need, and telleth it you not, neither with voice, nor as yet with his thought, to track another truth unto its root. Tell if the light wherewith your being blossometh, eternally will cleave to you as now, and if it doth remain, tell how, when ye grow visible again, it may not grieve your vision.". . .

And I heard in the divinest light of the smaller circle an unassuming voice, perchance such as the Angel's unto Mary, answering: "Whenas the garment of the glorified and sainted flesh shall be resumed, our person shall be more acceptable by being all complete. Whereby shall grow that which the highest Good giveth to us of unearned light, light which enableth us him to see; wherefore the vision must needs wax, and wax the ardour which is kindled by it, and wax the ray which goeth forth from it. But like the coal which giveth forth the flame, and by its living glow o'ercometh it, so that its own appearance is maintained, so shall this glow which doth already swathe us, be conquered in appearance by the flesh which yet and yet the earth o'ercovereth; nor shall such light have power to baffle us, for the organs of the body shall be strong to all that may delight us." So swift and eager to cry *Amen*, meseemed, was the one and the other chorus, that verily they showed desire for their dead bodies. . . .

CANTOS XIV–XVIII. *Sphere V, Mars: holy warriors*

Therefrom my eyes regained their power to uplift them, and I saw me transported, only with my Lady, to more exalted weal. Surely did I perceive that I was more uplifted by the enkindled smile of the star which seemed to me more ruddy than his wont. . . . for with such shining, and so ruddy, within two rays, splendours appeared to me, that I ex-

58. **. . . would no other bier;** than the earth. 76. **an unassuming voice,** Solomon.

claimed: "O God! who thus dost glorify them!" As, pricked out with less and greater lights, between the poles of the universe the Milky Way so gleameth white as to set very sages questioning, so did those rays, star-decked, make in the depth of Mars the venerable sign which crossing quadrant lines make in a circle. . . .

From horn to horn, from summit unto base, were moving lights that sparkled mightily in meeting one another and in passing. . . . And as viol and harp tuned in harmony of many cords, make sweet chiming to one by whom the notes are not apprehended, so from the lights that there appeared to me was gathered on the cross a strain that rapt me albeit I followed not the hymn. Well I discerned it was of lofty praise, for there came to me "Rise thou up and conquer," as to who understandeth not, but heareth. And so was I enamoured there, that up till then there had been naught that me had bound with so sweet chains.

As through the tranquil and pure skies darteth, from time to time, a sudden flame setting a-moving eyes that erst were steady, seeming a star that changeth place, save that from where it kindleth no star is lost, and that itself endureth but a little; such from the horn that stretcheth to the right unto that cross's foot, darted a star of the constellation that is there a-glow; nor did the gem depart from off its riband, but coursed along the radial line, like fire burning behind alabaster. With such-like tenderness Anchises' shade proffered itself, if our greatest Muse deserveth credit, when in Elysium he perceived his son. "Oh blood of mine! oh grace of God poured o'er thee! to whom, was ever twice, as unto thee, heaven's gate thrown open?". . . Then said he "He from whom thy kindred hath its name, and who a hundred years and more hath circled round the Mount on the first terrace, was son to me, and thy grandfather's father; meet it is, that with thy works thou shouldst abate his long-stretched toil for him. Florence, within the ancient circling wherefrom she still receiveth tierce and nones, abode in peace, sober and chaste. . . . To so reposeful and so fair a life among the citizens, to so faithful cityhood, to so sweet abode, Mary—with deep wailings summoned—gave me; and, in your ancient Baptistery, at once a Christian I became and Cacciaguida. Moronto was my brother and Eliseo; my wife came to me from Po valley, and from her was thy surname derived. Then followed I the Emperor Conrad, who girt me with his knighthood, so much by valiant work did I advance me in his grace. In his train I marched against the infamy of that Law whose people doth usurp, shame to the pastors,

what is yours by right. There by that foul folk was I unswathed of the deceitful world, whose love befouleth many a soul, and came from martyrdom unto this peace."

Ah puny blood-nobility of ours! If thou makest folk glory in thee here below, where our affections sicken, it shall be marvel to me never more; for there, where appetite is unwarped, I mean in heaven, I gloried me therein. Yet verily thou art a mantle that soon shrinketh, so that, if day by day there be nought added, time goeth round with the shears. . . . I began: "Ye are my father, ye give me full boldness to speak, ye so uplift me, that I am more than I. . . . Thou dost see contingent things, or ere themselves exist, gazing upon the point whereto all times are present; whilst I was companioned by Virgil along the mount which cureth souls, and down-going through the world defunct, heavy words were said to me anent my future life; albeit I feel me squarely set against the blows of fortune; wherefore my will were well content to hear what the disaster drawing nigh to me; for the arrow seen before cometh less rudely." So spake I unto that same light which had before addressed me, and, as Beatrice willed, was my wish confessed.

In no dark sayings, such as limed the foolish folk of old, before the Lamb of God who taketh sins away, was slain, but in clear words, and with precise discourse, answered that love paternal, hidden and revealed by his own smile: ". . . Thou shalt abandon everything beloved most dearly; this is the arrow which the bow of exile shall first shoot. Thou shalt make trial of how salt doth taste another's bread, and how hard the path to descend and mount upon another's stair. And that which most shall weigh thy shoulders down, shall be the vicious and ill company with which thou shalt fall down into this vale, for all ungrateful, all mad and impious shall they become against thee; but, soon after, their temples and not thine shall redden for it. . . . Yet would I not have thee envious of thy neighbours, since thy life shall be prolonged far beyond falling of the penalty upon their perfidies."

When by his silence the sacred soul showed he had finished setting of the woof across the warp I had held out in readiness to him, I began, as he who longeth in doubt for counsel from one who seeth and willeth straight, and loveth: "Well do I see, my father, how time cometh spurring toward me to give me such a buffet as is heaviest to whoso most abandoneth himself; wherefore with foresight it were well to arm me, that if the dearest place be reft from me, I lose not all the rest by reason of my songs.". . .

The light wherein was smiling my treasure which I there had found, first coruscated as at the sun's rays doth a golden mirror; then answered: "Con-

23. a star, Cacciaguida, an ancestor of Dante.   42. tierce and nones, the canonical hours, sounded from the belfry of the Badia church.

Spheres of Paradise

science darkened, or by its own or by another's shame, will in truth feel thy utterance grating. But none the less, every lie set aside, make thy entire vision manifest, and let them scratch wherever is the scab; for if thy voice be grievous at first taste, yet vital nutriment shall it leave thereafter when digested. This cry of thine shall do as doth the wind, which smiteth most upon the loftiest summits; and this shall be no little argument of honour. Therefore 10 have been displayed to thee, in these wheels, upon the mount, and in the dolorous vale, only souls known to fame; for the soul of him who heareth resteth not nor fixeth faith by an example which hath its root unknown and hidden, nor other unconspicuous argument.". . .

As here sometimes we read the affection in the countenance, if it be so great that all the mind is taken up by it, so in the flaming of the sacred glow to which I turned me, I recognized the will in him yet further somewhat to discourse with me. He be- 20 gan: "In this fifth range of the tree which liveth from the summit, and ever beareth fruit, and never sheddeth leaf, are spirits blessed, who below, ere they came unto heaven, were of a great name, so that every Muse would be enriched by them. Wherefore gaze upon the horns of the cross; he whom I shall name shall there do the act which in a cloud its swift flame doth."

I saw a light drawn along the cross at the naming of Joshua, as it was done; nor was the word known 30 to me ere the fact. And at the name of the lofty Maccabee I saw another move, wheeling, and glad-

ness was the lash unto the top. Thus for Charlemagne and for Orlando two more were followed by my keen regard, as the eye followeth its falcon flying. . . . Thereon amongst the other lights, moving and mingling, the soul which had discoursed to me showed me his artist quality among heaven's singers. I turned to my right side to see in Beatrice my duty, whether by speech or gesture indicated, and I saw her eyes so clear, so joyous, that her semblance sur-
10 passed all former usage and the last.

CANTOS XVIII–XX. *Sphere VI, Jupiter:*
righteous rulers

As by feeling more delight in doing well, man from day to day perceiveth that his virtue gaineth ground; so did I perceive that my circling round together with the heaven had increased its arc, seeing this miracle yet more adorned. And such change as cometh in short passage of time over a fair dame, when her countenance unburdeneth shame's burden, was presented to my eyes, when I turned me, because of the white glow of the temperate sixth star
20 which had received me into it. I saw in that torch of Jove the sparkling of the love which was therein signalling to my eyes our speech. . . .

As at the smiting of burnt brands there rise innumerable sparks, wherefrom the foolish ones use to draw augury, meseemed there rose thence more than thousand lights, and mounted some much, some little, even as the sun which kindleth them, ordained them; and when each one had stilled it in its place, an eagle's head and neck I saw presented
30 by that pricked-out fire. . . . With outstretched wings appeared before me the fair image which those enwoven souls, rejoicing in their sweet fruition, made. Each one appeared as a ruby whereon the sun's ray should burn, enkindled so as to re-cast it on mine eyes. And that which I must now retrace, nor ever voice conveyed, nor ink did write, nor ere by fantasy was comprehended; for I saw and eke I heard the beak discourse and utter in its voice both *I* and *Mine*, when in conception it was *We* and *Our*.
40 And it began: "In that I was just and duteous am I here exalted to this glory which suffereth not itself to be surpassed by longing; and upon earth have I left a memory, so fashioned that there the evil folk commend it, though they follow not the tale." So do we feel one glow from many coals as from those many loves there issued forth one only sound out of that image.

Whereon straightway I: "O perpetual flowers of the eternal gladness, ye who make all your odours

seem to me but one, solve, as ye breathe, the great 50 fast which long hath held me hungering, because on earth I found no food for it. Well do I know that if the divine justice maketh any other realm of heaven its mirror, yours apprehendeth it without a veil. Ye know how eager I prepare me to hearken; ye know what is that question which hath been to me a fast of so long date.". . .

Then it began: "Thou didst say: 'A man is born upon the bank of Indus and there is none to tell of Christ, nor none to read, nor none to write; and all 60 his volitions and his deeds are good so far as human reason seeth, sinless in life or in discourse. He dieth unbaptized and without faith; where is that justice which condemneth him? where is his fault, in that he not believes?' Now who art thou who wouldst sit upon the seat to judge at a thousand miles away with the short sight that carries but a span? Truly to him who goeth subtly to work with me, were not the Scripture over you, there were marvellous ground for questioning. O animals of earth, minds 70 gross! the primal Will, good in itself, never departed from its own self which is the highest good. All is just which doth harmonize with it; no created good draweth it to itself, but it by raying forth giveth rise to it. . . . To this realm ne'er rose one who believed not in Christ, neither before nor after he was nailed unto the tree. But see, many cry Christ, Christ, who at the judgment shall be far less near to him than such as know not Christ.". . . So by this divine image to clear my curtailed vision was given 80 me sweet medicine. . . .

CANTOS XXI–XXII. *Sphere VII, Saturn:*
the contemplatives

Already were mine eyes fixed on my Lady's countenance again, and my mind with them, from all other intent removed; and she smiled not, but: "Were I to smile," she began, "thou wouldst be such as was Semele, when she turned to ashes; for my beauty, which, along the steps of the eternal palace kindleth more, as thou hast seen, the higher the ascent, were it not tempered, so doth glow as that 90 thy mortal power, at its flash, would be like foliage that the thunder shattereth. We have arisen to the seventh splendour, which, underneath the bosom of the glowing Lion, downrayeth now mingling with its power. Fix thy mind after thine eyes, and make of them mirrors to the figure which in this mirror shall be shown unto thee.". . . .

I saw a ladder erected upward so far that my sight might not follow it. I saw, moreover, descend upon the steps so many splendours that methought

14. had increased its arc; because they were now farther from the earth. 19. temperate sixth star. Jupiter is temperate between hot Mars and cold Saturn. 29. an eagle's head and neck. The eagle is the symbol of justice.

86. Semele . . . ashes. Jove's undisguised presence turned Semele to ashes.

every light which shineth in the heaven had been thence poured down. And as, after their nature's way, the daws at the beginning of the day set out in company to warm their chilled feathers; then some go off without return, others come again to whence they started, and others make a wheeling sojourn; such fashion, meseemed, was in that sparkling which came in company, soon as it smote upon a certain step, and the one which abode nighest to us became

10 so bright that in my thought I said: "I do perceive the love which thou art signalling unto me. But she from whom I wait the how and when of speech and silence, pauses, and therefore I, counter to my desire, do well not to demand."

Whereat she, who saw my silence in his sight who seeth all, said to me: "Loose thy warm desire." And I began: "My merit maketh me not worthy of thy response, but for her sake who granteth me to make request, O blessed life, who abidest hidden in thy

20 gladness, make known to me the cause which so nigh to me hath placed thee; and say, wherefore in this wheel the sweet symphony of Paradise keepeth silence, which below throughout the others soundeth so devoutly."

"Thou hast the hearing, as the sight, of mortals," he answered me; "wherefore here is no song for that same reason for which Beatrice hath not smiled. Down by the steps of the sacred ladder I so far descended only to do thee joyance with speech and

30 with the light which mantleth me; nor was it greater love that made me swifter; for more and so much love up there doth burn, as the flashing maketh plain to thee; but the deep love which holdeth us prompt servants of the counsel which governeth the world, maketh assignment here as thou observest. . . . I, Peter of Damian, was. Little of mortal life was left to me when I was called and drawn unto the hat which doth but change from bad receptacle to worse. Now the modern pastors must needs be but-

40 tressed on this side and on that, and have one to lead them on, so heavy are they, and one to hoist behind. With their mantles they o'erspread their palfreys, so that two beasts travel beneath one hide; O patience, that so much endureth!"

At this voice I saw more flames from step to step descend and whirl, and every whirl made them more beauteous. Around this one they came and stayed themselves and raised a cry of so deep sound that here it may not find similitude; nor did I understand

50 it, so vanquished me the thunder. . . . The assembly drew close; then like a whirlwind was all gathered upward. The sweet Lady thrust me after them, only with a sign, up by that ladder, so did her power overcome my nature; nor ever here below, where we

9. the one, Peter of Damian (d. 1072), a stern cardinal who attacked the loose morals of monks in his day.

mount and descend by nature's law, was so swift motion as might compare unto my wing.

"Thou art so nigh to the supreme weal," began Beatrice, "that thou shouldst have thine eyes clear and keen. And therefore, ere thou further wend thereinto, look down and see how great a universe 60 I have already put beneath thy feet; so that thy heart, rejoicing to its utmost, may be presented to the throng triumphant which cometh glad through this sphered ether." With my sight I turned back through all and every of the seven spheres, and saw this globe such that I smiled at its sorry semblance; and that counsel I approve as best which holdeth it for least; and he whose thoughts are turned elsewhither may be called truly upright. . . . And all the seven were displayed to me, how great they are 70 and swift, and how distant each from other in repair. . . .

CANTOS XXIII–XXVII. *Sphere VIII, the Fixed Stars: the redeemed*

As the bird amidst the loved foliage who hath brooded on the nest of her sweet offspring through the night which hideth things from us, who, to look upon their longed-for aspect and to find the food wherewith to feed them, wherein her heavy toils are pleasant to her, foreruns the time, upon the open spray, and with glowing love awaiteth the sun, fixedly gazing for the dawn to rise; so was my Lady 80 standing, erect and eager, turned toward the region beneath which the sun showeth least speed; so that, as I looked on her in her suspense and longing, I became like him who, desiring, would fain have other than he hath, and payeth him with hope. But short the space 'twixt one and the other *when*, of fixing my attent I mean, and of seeing the heaven grow brilliant more and more. And Beatrice said: "Behold the hosts of Christ's triumph, and all the fruit gathered by the circling of these spheres.". . . 90

I saw, thousands of lamps surmounting, one sun which all and each enkindled, as doth our own the things we see above; and through the living light outglowed the shining substance so bright upon my vision that it endured it not. O Beatrice, sweet guide and dear! She said to me: "That which o'ercometh thee is power against which nought hath defence. Therein is the wisdom and the might which oped the pathways betwixt heaven and earth, for which there erst had been so long desire." Even as fire is un- 100 barred from the cloud, because it so dilateth that it hath not space within, and counter to its nature dasheth down to earth, so my mind, grown greater 'mid these feasts, forth issued from itself, and what it then became knoweth not to recall. . . .

"Open thine eyes and look on what I am; thou hast seen things by which thou art made mighty to sustain my smile." I was as one who cometh to himself from a forgotten vision, and doth strive in vain to bring it back unto his mind, when I heard this proffer, worthy of so great gratitude, as never to be blotted from the book that doth record the past. . . . As under the sun's ray, which issueth pure through a broken cloud, ere now mine eyes have seen a meadow full of flowers, when themselves covered by the shade; so beheld I many a throng of splendours, glowed on from above by ardent rays, beholding not the source whence came the glowings. O benign power which dost so imprint them! thou hadst thyself uplifted to yield place there for mine eyes that lacked in power. The name of the beauteous flower which I ever invoke, morning and evening, drew all my mind together to look upon the greatest flame.

And when on both mine eyes had been depicted the quality and greatness of the living star which conquereth up there, e'en as down here it conquered, from within the heaven descended a torch circle-formed, in fashion of a crown, and girt her and wheeled round her. Whatever melody soundeth sweetest here below, and most doth draw the soul unto itself, would seem a rent cloud thundering, compared unto the sound of that lyre whereby was crowned the beauteous sapphire by which the brightest heaven is ensapphired. "I am the angelic love who circles the lofty gladness that doth breathe from out the womb which was the hostelry of our desire; and I will circle, Lady of heaven, until thou followest thy son, and dost make yet more divine the supreme sphere in that thou enterest it."

Thus the circling melody impressed itself, and all the other lights made sound the name of Mary. . . . And as the infant who toward his mother stretcheth up his arms when he hath had the milk, because his mind flameth forth even into outward gesture; so each one of these glowings up-stretched with its flame, so that the deep love which they had for Mary was made plain to me. Then they stayed there within my sight, singing *O Queen of heaven* so sweetly that ne'er hath parted from me the delight. . . .

"O fellowship elect to the great supper of the blessed Lamb, who feedeth you in such fashion that your desire ever is fulfilled; if by the grace of God this man foretasteth of that which falleth from your table ere death prescribe the time to him, give heed to his unmeasured yearning and bedew him somewhat: ye drink ever of the fountain whence floweth that on which his thought is fixed." Thus Beatrice: and those glad souls made themselves spheres upon fixed poles, outflaming mightily like unto comets. And even as wheels in harmony of clock-work so turn that the first, to whoso noteth it, seemeth still,

and the last to fly, so did these carols with their differing whirl, or swift or slow, make me deem of their riches.

Should it e'er come to pass that the sacred poem to which both heaven and earth so have set hand, that it hath made me lean through many a year, should overcome the cruelty which doth bar me forth from the fair sheepfold wherein I used to sleep, a lamb, foe to the wolves which war upon it; with changed voice now, and with changed fleece shall I return, a poet, and at the font of my baptism shall I assume the chaplet; because into the Faith which maketh souls known of God, 'twas there I entered; and afterward Peter, for its sake, circled thus my brow. . . .

All Paradise took up the strain, "To the Father, to the Son, to the Holy Spirit, glory!" so that the sweet song intoxicated me. Meseemed I was beholding a smile of the universe; wherefore my intoxication entered both by hearing and by sight. O joy! O gladness unspeakable! O life compact of love and peace! O wealth secure that hath no longing!

CANTO XXVII–XXIX. *Sphere IX, Primum Mobile: the angels*

My enamoured mind, which held amorous converse ever with my Lady, burned more than ever to bring back my eyes to her; and whatsoever food nature or art e'er made, to catch the eyes and so possess the mind, be it in human flesh, be it in pictures, if all united, would seem nought towards the divine delight which glowed upon me when that I turned me to her smiling face. And the power of which that look made largest to me, from the fair nest of Leda plucked me forth, and into the swiftest heaven thrust me. Its parts most living and exalted are so uniform that I know not to tell which Beatrice chose for my position.

But she, who saw my longing, smiling began—so glad that God seemed joying in her countenance—"The nature of the universe which stilleth the centre and moveth all the rest around, hence doth begin as from its starting point. And this heaven hath no other *where* than the divine mind wherein is kindled the love which rolleth it and the power which it sheddeth. Light and love grasp it in one circle, as doth it the others, and this engirdment he only who doth gird it understandeth. Its movement by no other is marked out; but by it all the rest are measured, as ten by half and fifth. And how Time in this same vessel hath its roots, and in the rest its leaves, may now be manifest to thee.". . .

57. these **carols**; in the old sense of groups of singing dancers.   87–88. from the . . . Leda, the constellation of the Twins, Castor and Pollux, children of Leda and Jupiter.

A point I saw which rayed forth light so keen, needs must the vision that it flameth on be closed because of its strong poignancy; and whatever star from here appeareth smallest, were seen a moon neighboured with it, as star with star is neighboured. Perhaps as close as the halo seemeth to gird the luminary that doth paint it, whenso the vapour which supporteth it is thickest, at such interval around the point there wheeled a circle of fire so rapidly it had surpassed the motion which doth swiftest gird the universe; and this was by a second girt around, that by a third, and the third by a fourth, by a fifth the fourth, then by a sixth the fifth. Thereafter followed the seventh, already in its stretch so far outspread that were the messenger of Juno made complete, it were too strait to hold it. And so the eighth and ninth; and each one moved slower according as in number it was more remote from unity; and that one had the clearest flame, from which the pure spark was least distant; because, I take it, it sinketh deepest into the truth thereof.

My Lady, who beheld me in toil of deep suspense, said: "From that point doth hang heaven and all nature. Look on that circle which is most conjoint thereto, and know its movement is so swift by reason of the enkindled love whereby 'tis pierced. The first circles have revealed to thee the Seraphs and the Cherubs. So swift they follow their withies that they may liken them unto the point as most they may; and they may in measure as they are sublime in vision. Those other loves which course around them are named Thrones of the divine aspect, because they brought to its completion the first ternary. And thou shouldst know that all have their delight in measure as their sight sinketh more deep into the truth wherein every intellect is stilled. . . . The second ternary which thus flowereth in this eternal spring. . . . In that hierarchy are the three divinities, first Dominations, and then Virtues; the third order is of Powers. Then in the two last-save-one upleapings, Principalities and Archangels whirl; the last consisteth all of Angelic sports.

"These orders all gaze upward, and downward have such conquering might that toward God all are drawn and all draw. . . . These substances, since first they gathered joy from the face of God, have never turned their vision from it wherefrom nought is concealed; wherefore their sight is never intercepted by a fresh object, and so behoveth not to call aught back to memory because thought hath been cleft. . . . See now the height and breadth of the eternal worth, since it hath made itself so many mirrors wherein it breaketh, remaining in itself one as before."

CANTOS XXX–XXXIII. *Sphere X, the Empyrean: the Saints, the Virgin, and God*

Love constrained me to turn with mine eyes to Beatrice. If that which up till here is said of her were all compressed into one act of praise 'twould be too slight to serve this present turn. The beauty I beheld transcendeth measure, not only past our reach, but surely I believe that only he who made it enjoyeth it complete. At this pass I yield me vanquished more than e'er yet was overborne by his theme's thrust comic or tragic poet. For as the Sun in sight that most trembleth, so the remembrance of the sweet smile sheareth my memory of its very self. From the first day when in this life I saw her face, until this sight, my song hath ne'er been cut off from the track.

But now needs must my tracking cease from following her beauty further forth in poesy, as at his utmost reach must every artist. Such as I leave her for a mightier proclamation than of my trumpet, which draweth its arduous subject to a close, with alert leader's voice and gesture, did she again begin: "We have issued forth from the greatest body into the heaven which is pure light, light intellectual fullcharged with love, love of true good full-charged with gladness, gladness which transcendeth every sweetness. Here shalt thou see the one and the other soldiery of Paradise, and the one in those aspects which thou shalt see at the last judgment."

As a sudden flash of lightning which so shattereth the visual spirits as to rob the eye of power to realize e'en strongest objects; so there shone around me a living light, leaving me swathed in such a web of its glow that naught appeared to me. "Ever doth the love which stilleth heaven, receive into itself with such like salutation, duly to fit the taper for its flame." So soon as these brief words came into me I felt me to surmount my proper power; and kindled me with such new-given sight that there is no such brightness unalloyed that mine eyes might not hold their own with it.

And I saw a light, in river form, glow tawny betwixt banks painted with marvellous spring. From out this river issued living sparks, and dropped on every side into the blossoms, like rubies set in gold. Then as inebriated with the odours they plunged themselves again into the marvellous swirl, and as one entered issued forth another. "The lofty wish that now doth burn and press thee to have more

1. **A point.** The point is God, and the nine circles are the nine orders of angels, corresponding to the nine heavens that Dante has come through. 15–16. **messenger of Juno,** Iris, the rainbow. 33. **the first ternary;** that is, the first of the three groups of angelic orders.

79–80. **the one and . . . Paradise,** the redeemed and the angels.

knowledge of the things thou seest, pleaseth me more the more it swelleth. But of this water needs thou first must drink, ere so great thirst in thee be slaked." So spoke mine eyes' sun unto me; then added: "The river and the topaz-gems that enter and go forth, and the smiling of the grasses are the shadowy prefaces of their reality. Not that such things are harsh as in themselves; but on thy side is the defect, in that thy sight not yet exalteth it so high."

Never doth child so sudden rush with face turned to the milk, if he awake far later than his wont, as then did I, to make yet better mirrors of mine eyes, down bending to the wave which floweth that we may better us. And no sooner drank of it mine eyelids' rim than into roundness seemed to change its length. Then—as folk under masks seem other than before, if they do off the semblance not their own wherein they hid them,—so changed before me into ampler joyance the flowers and the sparks, so that I saw both the two courts of heaven manifested.

O splendour of God whereby I saw the lofty triumph of the truthful realm, give me the power to tell how I beheld it. A light there is up yonder which maketh the Creator visible unto the creature, who only in beholding him hath its own peace; and it so far outstretcheth circle-wise that its circumference would be too loose a girdle for the sun. All its appearance is composed of rays reflected from the top of the First Moved, which draweth thence its life and potency. And as a hill-side reflect itself in water at its foot, as if to look upon its own adornment when it is rich in grasses and in flowers, so, mounting o'er the light, around, around, casting reflection in more than thousand ranks I saw all that of us hath won return up yonder.

And if the lowest step gathereth so large a light within itself, what then the amplitude of the rose's outmost petals? My sight in the breath and height lost itself not, but grasped the scope and nature of that joyance. Near and far addeth not nor subtracteth there, for where God governeth without medium the law of nature hath no relevance. Within the yellow of the eternal rose, which doth expand, rank upon rank, and reeketh perfume of praise unto the Sun that maketh spring for ever, me—as who doth hold his peace yet fain would speak—Beatrice drew, and said: "Behold how great the white-robed concourse! See how large our city sweepeth! See our thrones so filled that but few folk are now awaited there.". . .

In form, then, of a white rose displayed itself to me that sacred soldiery which in his blood Christ made his spouse; but the other, which as it flieth seeth and doth sing his glory who enamoureth it, and the excellence which hath made it what it is, like to a swarm of bees which doth one while plunge into the flowers and another while wend back to where its toil is turned to sweetness, ever descended into the great flower adorned with so many leaves, and reascended thence to where its love doth ceaseless make sojourn. They had their faces all of living flame, and wings of gold, and the rest so white that never snow reacheth such limit. When they descended into the flower, from rank to rank they proffered of the peace and of the ardour which they acquired as they fanned their sides, nor did the interposing of so great a flying multitude, betwixt the flower and that which was above, impede the vision nor the splendour; for the divine light so penetrateth through the universe, in measure of its worthiness, that nought hath power to oppose it. . . .

As the pilgrim who doth draw fresh life in the temple of his vow as he gazeth, and already hopeth to tell again how it be placed, so, traversing the living light, I led mine eyes along the ranks, now up, now down, and now round circling. I saw countenances suasive of love, adorned by another's light and their own smile, and gestures graced with every dignity. The general form of Paradise my glance had already taken in, in its entirety, and on no part as yet had my sight paused; and I turned me with rekindled will to question my Lady concerning things whereanent my mind was in suspense.

One thing I purposed, and another answered me; I thought to see Beatrice, and I saw an elder clad like the folk in glory. His eyes and cheeks were overpoured with benign gladness, in kindly gesture as befits a tender father. And: "Where is she?" all sudden I exclaimed; whereunto he: "To bring thy desire to its goal Beatrice moved me from my place; and if thou look up to the circle third from the highest rank, thou shalt re-behold her, on the throne her merits have assigned to her."

Without answering I lifted up mine eyes and saw her, making to herself a crown as she reflected from her the eternal rays. From that region which thundereth most high, no mortal eye is so far distant, though plunged most deep within the sea, as there from Beatrice was my sight; but that wrought not upon me, for her image descended not to me mingled with any medium. "O Lady, in whom my hope hath vigour, and who for my salvation didst endure to leave in Hell thy footprints; of all the things which I have seen I recognize the grace and might, by thy power and by thine excellence. Thou hast drawn me from a slave to liberty by all those paths, by all those methods by which thou hadst the power so to do. Preserve thy munificence in me, so that my soul which thou hast made sound, may unloose it from the body, pleasing unto thee." So did I pray;

87. **an elder,** St. Bernard, symbolizing intuition.

and she, so distant as she seemed, smiled and looked on me, then turned her to the eternal fountain.

And the holy elder said: "That thou mayest consummate thy journey perfectly—whereto prayer and holy love dispatched me,—fly with thine eyes throughout this garden; for gazing on it will equip thy glance better to mount through the divine ray."
. . . I lifted up mine eyes, and as at morn the oriental regions of the horizon overcome that where the sun declineth, so, as from the valley rising to the mountain; with mine eyes I saw a region at the boundary surpass all the remaining ridge in light.
. . . And at that mid point, with out-stretched wings, I saw more than a thousand Angels making festival, each one distinct in glow and art. I saw there, smiling to their sports and to their songs, a beauty which was gladness in the eyes of all the other saints. And had I equal wealth in speech as in conception, yet dared I not attempt the smallest part of her delightsomeness. Bernard, when he saw mine eyes fixed and eager towards the glowing source of his own glow, turned his eyes to her, with so much love that he made mine more ardent to regaze.

With his Love fixed on his Delight, that contemplating saint took the free office of the teacher on him, and began these sacred words: "Virgin Mother, daughter of thy son, lowly and uplifted more than any creature, fixed goal of the eternal counsel, thou art she who didst human nature so ennoble that its own Maker scorned not to become its making. In thy womb was lit again the love under whose warmth in the eternal peace this flower hath thus unfolded. Here art thou unto us the meridian torch of love and there below with mortals art a living spring of hope. Lady, thou art so great and hast such worth, that if there be who would have grace yet betaketh not himself to thee, his longing seeketh to fly without wings. Thy kindliness not only succoureth whoso requesteth, but doth oftentimes freely forerun request. In thee is tenderness, in thee is pity, in thee munificence, in thee united whatever in created being is of excellence. Now he who from the deepest pool of the universe even to here hath seen the spirit lives one after one imploreth thee, of grace, for so much power as to be able to uplift his eyes more high towards final bliss.". . .

And I, who to the goal of all my longings was drawing nigh, even as was meet the ardour of the yearning quenched within me. Bernard gave me the sign and smiled to me that I should look on high, but I already of myself was such as he would have me; because my sight, becoming purged, now more and more was entering through the ray of the deep light which in itself is true. . . . And so I was the bolder, as I mind me, so long to sustain it as to unite my glance with the Worth infinite.

16. a beauty, the Virgin Mary.   56. the Worth infinite, God.

O grace abounding, wherein I presumed to fix my look on the eternal light so long that I consumed my sight thereon! Within its depths I saw ingathered, bound by love in one volume, the scattered leaves of all the universe; substance and accidents and their relations, as though together fused, after such fashion that what I tell of is one simple flame. The universal form of this complex I think that I beheld, because more largely, as I say this, I feel that I rejoice. . . .

Thus all suspended did my mind gaze fixed, immovable, intent, ever enkindled by its gazing. Such at that light doth man become that to turn thence to any other sight could not by possibility be ever yielded. For the good, which is the object of the will, is therein wholly gathered, and outside it that same thing is defective which therein is perfect. . . . In the profound and shining being of the deep light appeared to me three circles, of three colours and one magnitude; one by the second as Iris by Iris seemed reflected, and the third seemed a fire breathed equally from one and from the other. Oh but how scant the utterance, and how faint, to my conceit! and it, to what I saw, is such that it sufficeth not to call it little.

O Light eternal who only in thyself abidest, only thyself dost understand, and to thyself, self-understood self-understanding, turnest love and smiling! That circling which appeared in thee to be conceived as a reflected light, by mine eyes scanned some little, in itself, of its own colour, seemed to be painted with our effigy, and thereat my sight was all committed to it. As the geometer who all sets himself to measure the circle and who findeth not, think as he may, the principle he lacketh; such was I at this new-seen spectacle; I would perceive how the image consorteth with the circle, and how it settleth there; but not for this were my proper wings, save that my mind was smitten by a flash wherein its will came to it. To the high fantasy here power failed; but already my desire and will were rolled—even as a wheel that moveth equally—by the Love that moves the sun and the other stars.

Geoffrey Chaucer

c. 1340–1400

The greatest English poet of the Middle Ages was born in London, the son of a wine-merchant, sometime between the years 1340 and 1343. Entering the service of the nobility at the court of Edward III of England, Chaucer spent his life as a busy and efficient servant of the Crown. His formal education was apparently limited to some legal studies, but we cannot be sure even of that detail, and the general fact remains that we know as little about Chaucer's life as we do about Shakespeare's, and far less than we know about Dante's. There is no doubt, however, that Chaucer was all his life a man of letters, for he gives clear evidence of being a widely, though not phenomenally, read man, seizing every possible opportunity which presented itself to cultivate literature, if only as an avocation. This is one of the two inescapable facts which every reader of Chaucer must bear in mind at all times.

The other fact is Chaucer's professional career at court just mentioned, which accounts for his unquestionably courtly or aristocratic attitude toward humanity and his equally objective view of life as a whole. His abilities as a servant of his government were evidently noteworthy; his tasks ranged from administration, such as a comptrollership of customs and a supervisorship of royal works and forests, to ambassadorial duties, the latter often involving such delicate matters as the negotiation of a royal marriage, although the details of these embassies, probably secret at the time, are necessarily obscure today. There is ample evidence, however, that Chaucer was all his life a successful man in worldly affairs, regardless of the various ups and downs which would be inevitable at the court of a Plantagenet king of England. (The reign of Richard II, from 1377 to 1399, is particularly notorious as a period of intrigue and counter-intrigue in royal feudal society.) It is scarcely likely that Chaucer was ever seriously in want, although he was of course dependent upon royal favor; and while it is true that we know little of his life during the decade of the 1390's, at which time he wrote some of his most distinguished works, it is not to be supposed that he was then much less fortunate in circumstances than he had been before. His death took place in 1400.

For most general purposes, it is best to concentrate on Chaucer as a man of affairs who wrote as an avocation, for if we do this, we do much to explain Chaucer's work. Being a success and a courtier at one and the same time, Chaucer developed an independence of outlook, an obvious social snobbishness, a typical superior spectator's point of view, which, combined with his truly remarkable human insight, made him one of the most effective reporters of society who ever lived. By instinct Chaucer's major interest lay in humanity alive and breathing, not in philosophical abstractions or mystical visions of the Other World. As a philosopher, indeed, Chaucer is negligible; aside from the Platonic philosophy of Boethius, whose magnum opus, De Philosophiae Consolatione (c. 520), he translated somewhere in the early 1380's, he has no regard for sheer dialectics. If a knotty intellectual or spiritual problem poses itself, Chaucer is inclined to leave it to the "clerkes," for he seems always to imply that the world is served best by personal integrity, a fidelity to principles, and in addition by a practical viewpoint and a rational approach to living, since he believes that it is useless to kick against the pricks and essential to co-operate with the inevitable. The important thing for him, it would seem, is to take life as one finds it.

Such an idea is no different from that held by millions of people both before and after Chaucer's time, and so we must look farther to see what makes Chaucer's empirical attitude so unusual as to place him in the very top rank of interpreters of life. The reason for this is not far to seek. For one thing, Chaucer has an uncanny gift of putting an individual in his place, in his proper pigeonhole, neatly wrapped up; his talents for decisive portraiture, especially on a small canvas, have never been surpassed. Moreover, he is a superbly direct and economical storyteller; some of his masterpieces of narrative, such as The Pardoner's Tale, can literally be said to contain not a single waste word or phrase. His inescapable sense of humor—a gift most rare among famous writers—can be either kindly or malicious, but in either case it cannot long be suppressed; it is, in its most characteristic vein, of a deft, Puckish type. Still, Chaucer can wage stern warfare upon the social parasite, the hypocrite, and the pretender to knowledge not possessed; then his battery of satire is formidable.

In his earlier career—that is, until the middle of the 1380's—Chaucer's poetry was rather derivative. He wrote short lyrics, some of them of much grace and finish, in the manner of the contemporary courtly poets of France like Deschamps, Machaut, and Froissart. He was, in a manner typical of the Middle Ages, prone to allegory—explicit, as in the case of The Book of the Duchess (c. 1370), or implicit, as in the case of The Parliament of Fowls (c. 1380)—and very much under the influence of the thirteenth-century French allegorical romance, the Roman de la Rose. It was in Troilus and Criseyde (c. 1385–86), however, that Chaucer's genius reached full stature. This long narrative poem, beautifully integrated in structure, has all the requirements of a modern novel except possibly for its poetic form. The characterization of its major figures is complex, subtle, and completely human; only the hero, Troilus, who is anchored in the tradition of the chivalric knight, strikes the present-day reader as "medieval," and even Troilus can be recognized as a human being. This work alone, a study of a triangular situation which affects nearly all men and women at some time in their lives, would have been sufficient to make Chaucer a great writer in the judgment of posterity. It is, incidentally, the only long work that Chaucer ever completed.

As for the famous Canterbury Tales, it was probably written over a considerable number of years. Some of these tales were probably composed early in Chaucer's career and then were incorporated into the collection. The Second Nun's Tale or The Prioress's Tale are examples. Others, like The Knight's Tale, probably existed in some early form and then were revised before they were included among The Canterbury Tales. Most of them, however, sprang full-fledged from the author with no previous incarnation. Conservative estimates date different parts of The Canterbury Tales anywhere from 1386 to 1398; Chaucer may even have been working on them at the time of his death in 1400. It is unnecessary to discuss at any length either these multifarious tales or the brilliant *Prologue*, the most celebrated of all Chaucerian pieces, except to remark that as a gallery of portraits of medieval types of society as well as of individual men and women, it is absolutely unrivaled in medieval literature. The tales told by these characters are all appropriate to the tellers. They cover every type of medieval literature with the exception of the drama. They are arranged, by means of the plausible, realistic, and dramatic framework of the Canterbury Pilgrimage, in a delightfully informal way. Although a few are grouped by the fact that they discuss various aspects of married life (the so-called Marriage Group), and others are connected as part of a quarrel between members of the company, there is no overall plan of arrangement in evidence, as is the case with most other medieval story collections. Incomplete as Chaucer's design may be, it only serves to illustrate his characteristically frank acceptance of life as he finds it—as it is instead of as it ought to be.

The Canterbury Tales

PROLOGUE

WHAN that Aprille with his shoures soote *
The droghte of Marche hath percéd to the roote,
And bathed every veyne in swich licour,
Of which vertu engendred is the flour;
Whan Zephirus eek with his swete breeth   5
Inspiréd hath in every holt and heeth
The tendre croppes, and the yonge sonne
Hath in the Ram his halfe cours y-ronne,
And smale fowles maken melodye,
That slepen al the night with open yë,   10

The Canterbury Tales. Text prepared by George K. Anderson, with the exception of *The Reeve's Tale*, which is from the Tyrwhitt edition revised in the light of present-day Chaucerian scholarship.
* In *The Canterbury Tales* Chaucer makes use chiefly (1) of the iambic pentameter riming couplet and (2) of the seven-line iambic pentameter stanza (riming *a b a b b c c*), known as the Chaucerian stanza or Rime Royal. The iambic pentameter couplet is the "heroic" or "closed" couplet of neo-classical fame, except that the writers of the seventeenth and eighteenth centuries preferred to "close" it to a greater degree; that is, to bring the thought to a more definite conclusion at the end of the second line.
1. **soote,** sweet. 3. **swich,** such. **licour,** "moisture," not "liquor." 4. **vertu,** power, efficacy, magical influence. **flour,** flower. 5. **eek,** also. 6. **holt and heeth.** A *holt* is a cultivated tract, or plantation; *heeth* is the modern *heath.* No doubt the combining of these two words in such a phrase is to be attributed in part to the popularity of alliterative formulas in Middle English poetry—a popularity which is in some degree found in all English literature. 7. **sonne,** sun—"young" in the sense that it is early in the year. The medieval calendar started the year at the vernal equinox in March rather than on the first of January. 8. **Ram,** the constellation of Aries, one of the constellations of the zodiac, along the path of the sun. Aries is the spot on the celestial map at which the sun is located at the time of the vernal equinox; hence it is the first constellation of the year. There are twelve such zodiacal constellations.

(So priketh hem nature in hir corages),
Than longen folk to goon on pilgrimages
(And palmers for to seken straunge strondes)
To ferne halwes, couthe in sondry londes;
And specially, from every shires ende   15
Of Engelond, to Caunterbury they wende,
The holy blisful martir for to seke,
That hem hath holpen, whan that they were seke.
    Bifel that, in that sesoun on a day,
In Southwerk at the Tabard as I lay   20
Redy to wenden on my pilgrimage
To Caunterbury with ful devout corage,
At night was come in-to that hostelrye
Wel nyne and twenty in a companye,
Of sondry folk, by aventure y-falle   25
In felawshipe, and pilgrims were they alle,
That toward Caunterbury wolden ryde;
The chambres and the stables weren wyde,
And wel we weren esed atte beste.
And shortly, whan the sonne was to reste,   30
So hadde I spoken with hem everichon,
That I was of hir felawshipe anon,
And made forward erly for to ryse,
To take our wey, ther as I yow devyse.
    But natheles, whyl I have tyme and space,   35
Ere that I ferther in this tale pace,
Me thinketh it acordaunt to resoun,

11. **hem,** them. The modern forms of the third person plural pronoun probably to be traced to the Norse, were beginning to come into general use during Chaucer's lifetime (note *they* in l. 18), but they had not yet been accepted for the oblique cases. So *hem* for *them,* *hir(e)* for *their.* **corages.** This word may be either singular or plural, and its meanings are many. The modern meaning of "courage" is usually the last to be thought of in Middle English literature. "Disposition," "temperament," "sexual desire," "will" are some of the more common meanings. Here the sense of the line can be construed thus: "the small birds make melody; Nature so prompts them (priketh hem) in their desires or instincts." 13. **strondes,** strands, shores. 14. **ferne halwes,** distant shrines or hallowed places. **couthe,** famous, well-known. 17. **The holy . . . seke.** The "holy martyr" is Thomas à Becket, Archbishop of Canterbury, slain during the course of a Church and Crown dispute during the reign of Henry II of England. His assassination took place in 1170, and he was canonized in 1173. His position in the quarrel with Henry could be interpreted by the commoners as in their favor, and he was immensely popular after his death; his tomb became the most famous shrine in medieval England. 18. **seke,** sick. Note that this actually forms an identical rime with *seke* (seek) in the preceding line. Identical rimes of this sort were not only not avoided as unharmonious and inadequate, but were even sought at times. 20. **Southwerk,** the bustling suburb of London, on the south bank of the Thames River, the beginning of the Canterbury road. **the Tabard.** A *tabard* was a short, sleeveless coat, and was here the "sign" of the inn. 22. **corage.** See note to l. 11. "Full devout will" would be the modern equivalent. 25. **y-falle,** befallen, taken place—here, happened along. The prefix *y-* is frequently found on past participles in Middle English; it is a development of the older form *ge-*, which students of Modern German would at once recognize. 29. **esed,** entertained, set at ease. **atte beste,** at the best, in the best possible way. 31. **everichon,** every (each) one. 33. **forward,** agreement. 34. **ther . . . devyse,** where I describe it to you. In Chaucer *ther* and *wher* are virtually interchangeable. 36. **pace,** pass. 37. **acordaunt to resoun,** according to right, in keeping with the right thing to do. Note the meaning of the Modern French *raison.* But the word may here have the meaning of "order," "arrangement."

To telle yow al the condicioun
Of ech of hem, so as it semed me,
And whiche they weren, and of what degree;   40
And eek in what array that they were inne:
And at a knight than wol I first biginne.

A KNIGHT ther was, and that a worthy man,
That fro the tyme that he first bigan
To ryden out, he loved chivalrye,   45
Trouthe and honour, fredom and curteisye.
Ful worthy was he in his lordes werre,
And therto hadde he riden (no man ferre)
As wel in cristendom as hethenesse,
And ever honoured for his worthinesse.   50
    At Alisaundre he was, whan it was wonne;
Ful ofte tyme he hadde the bord bigonne
Aboven alle naciouns in Pruce.
In Lettow hadde he reysed and in Ruce,
No cristen man so ofte of his degree.   55
In Gernade at the sege eek hadde he be
Of Algezir, and riden in Belmarye.
At Lyeys was he, and at Satalye,
Whan they were wonne; and in the Grete See
At many a noble aryve hadde he be.   60
At mortal batailles hadde he been fiftene,
And foughten for our feith at Tramissene
In listes thryes, and ay slayn his foo.
This ilke worthy knight hadde been also

Sometyme with the lord of Palatye,   65
Ageyn another hethen in Turkye:
And everemore he hadde a sovereyn prys,
And though that he were worthy, he was wys,
And of his port as meek as is a mayde.
He nevere yet no vileinye ne sayde   70
In al his lyf, un-to no maner wight.
He was a verray parfit gentil knight.
But for to tellen yow of his array,
His hors were goode, but he was nat gay.
Of fustian he weréd a gipoun   75
Al bismoteréd with his habergeoun,
For he was late y-come from his viage,
And wente for to doon his pilgrimage.
    With him there was his sone, a yong SQUYER,
A lovyere, and a lusty bacheler,   80
With lokkes crulle, as they were leyd in presse.
Of twenty yeer of age he was, I gesse.
Of his stature he was of evene lengthe,
And wonderly deliver, and greet of strengthe.
And he had been somtyme in chivachye,   85
In Flaundres, in Artoys, and Picardye,
And born him wel, as of so litel space,
In hope to stonden in his lady grace.
Embrouded was he, as it were a mede
Al ful of fresshe floures, whyte and rede.   90
Singinge he was, or floytinge, al the day;
He was as fresh as is the month of May.
Short was his goune, with sleves longe and wyde.
Wel coude he sitte on hors, and faire ryde.
He coude songes make and wel endyte,   95
Juste and eek daunce, and wel purtreye and wryte.
So hote he lovede, that by nightertale
He sleep namore than doth a nightingale.
Curteys he was, lowly, and servisable,

---

47. **worthy.** See also l. 43. Here, as elsewhere in Chaucer, the word has a much stronger meaning (with no connotation of condescension) than in Modern English. **werre,** war. 48. **ferre,** farther. 51. ff. **Alisaundre,** etc. The knight, as a soldier of fortune and a mercenary, is a veteran of many wars of the fourteenth century. His service is the feudal service to his immediate lord, whose political interests were doubtless many; and the Knight could often change his lord. (Compare the issue in the Danish ballad, *Niels Ebbeson*, p. 11:252.) 52. **hadde . . . bigonne.** "To begin the board" was to sit at the head of the table, the obvious place of honor. 53. **Pruce,** Prussia. The line means undoubtedly that the Knight was a member of the Teutonic Order of Knights, one of the great chivalric associations of the Middle Ages, and a powerful preserver of the old Germanic warrior spirit; it looks forward to the Prussian military tradition. 54. **Lettow,** Lithuania. The Lithuanians were converted to Christianity in 1386, largely through the instrumentality of the Teutonic Order of Knights. If the date of this conversion meant the earliest possible time at which the Knight could have returned to England, this would be a valuable detail in dating the *Prologue*. The conversion, however, was preceded by much campaigning, and the evidence may not be very convincing. **reysed,** made expeditions (compare the German *reisen*). **Ruce,** Russia. The Teutonic Order was a strong buffer between Western Christendom and pagan nations in the East, particularly the Tartars, who had made several incursions into Russia during the Middle Ages. 56–57. **Gernade,** Granada, Spain. **sege . . . Algezir,** modern Algeciras, captured by the English under the Earl of Derby in 1344. **Belmarye,** Benmarin, Morocco. There were several raids upon the Moorish inhabitants during the forties, sixties, and eighties of the fourteenth century; it is consequently impossible to tell in which the Knight was involved. 58. **Lyeys,** Lyas in Armenia, harried by Pierre de Lusignan (see note to l. 65) in 1367. **Satalye,** Atalia, on the coast of Asia Minor, captured by Pierre de Lusignan in 1361. 59. **Grete See,** the Mediterranean. 62. **Tramissene,** Tlemcen in Algeria; as in the case of *Belmarye* in l. 57, the allusion is too vague to help us much; there was fighting along the Moroccan and Algerian coasts all through the middle of the fourteenth century. 64. **ilke,** same.

65. **Palatye,** probably the Turkish *Balat;* the "lord of Palatye" was, then, a heathen allied to Pierre de Lusignan—further evidence of the difference between the chivalric adventurer like Pierre in the dying days of knighthood, and the chivalric idealist of the medieval romances; or perhaps it is merely the difference between fact and romance. But it is difficult to imagine Lancelot or Roland fighting on the same side as a Saracen. 67. **sovereyn prys,** noble or sovereign worth. 68. **though that he . . . wys,** though he was brave, he was prudent. 69. **port,** bearing, behavior. 72. **verray parfit,** "true and perfect," not "very perfect." 74. **hors.** This word was in Old English a neuter noun (compare the Modern German *Kind,* "child," or *Weib,* "woman"), and as such had no ending in the plural, as here. 75. **fustian,** a thick cotton cloth. **gipoun,** a tunic. 76. **bismoteréd,** smutted, marked with dirt. **habergeoun,** hauberk, coat of mail. 77. **viage,** voyage, expedition. 79. SQUYER, a young candidate for knighthood. In *The Canterbury Tales* the squire is the type of the young courtly lover. 81. **crulle,** curled. 84. **deliver,** active, agile. 85. **chivachye,** cavalry-raids. 87. **as . . . space,** considering the small opportunity, or short period of time the Squire had been training for knighthood. 88. **lady.** Many Old English feminine nouns had no ending in the genitive case, so *lady* instead of *lady's.* 89. **Embrouded,** decorated with embroidery; but it is altogether possible that Chaucer is thinking of the young man's pink-and-white complexion. **mede,** meadow. 91. **floytinge,** playing the flute. 95. **make,** write in poetry. **endyte,** compose, in particular, the words of a song (as differentiated from *make*). 96. **Juste,** joust (in a tournament). **purtreye,** draw pictures. 97. **nightertale,** nighttime.

And carf biforn his fader at the table.　　　100
　A YEMAN hadde he, and servaunts namo
At that tyme, for him liste ryde so;
And he was clad in cote and hood of grene;
A sheef of pecok-arwes brighte and kene
Under his belt he bar ful thriftily;　　　105
(Wel coude he dresse his takel yemanly:
His arwes drouped noght with fetheres lowe),
And in his hand he bar a mighty bowe.
A not-heed hadde he, with a broun visage.
Of wode-craft wel coude he al the usage.　　　110
Upon his arm he bar a gay bracer,
And by his syde a swerd and a bokeler,
And on that other syde a gay daggere,
Harneised wel and sharp as point of spere;
A Cristofre on his brest of silver shene.　　　115
An horn he bar, the bawdrik was of grene;
A forster was he, soothly, as I gesse.
　Ther was also a Nonne, a PRIORESSE,
That of hir smyling was ful simple and coy,
Hir gretteste ooth was but by seÿnt Loy;　　　120
And she was cleped madame Eglentyne.
Ful wel she song the service divyne,
Entuned in hir nose ful semely;
And Frensh she spak ful faire and fetisly,
After the scole of Stratford atte Bowe,　　　125
For Frensh of Paris was to hir unknowe.
At mete wel y-taught was she with-alle;
She leet no morsel from hir lippes falle,
Ne wette hir fingres in hir sauce depe.
Wel coude she carie a morsel, and wel kepe,　　　130
That no drope ne fille up-on hir brest.
In curteisye was set ful muche hir lest.
Hir over lippe wyped she so clene,
That in hir coppe was no ferthing sene
Of grece, whan she dronken hadde hir draughte.
Ful semely after hir mete she raughte,　　　136
And sikerly she was of greet disport,
And ful plesaunt, and amiable of port,

And peyned hir to countrefete chere
Of court, and been estatlich of manere,　　　140
And to ben holden digne of reverence.
But, for to speken of hir conscience,
She was so charitable and so pitous,
She wolde wepe, if that she sawe a mous
Caught in a trappe, if it were deed or bledde.　　　145
Of smale houndes had she, that she fedde
With rosted flesh, or milk and wastel breed.
But sore weep she if oon of hem were deed,
Or if men smoot it with a yerde smerte:
And al was conscience and tendre herte.　　　150
Ful semely hir wimpel pinched was;
Hir nose tretys; hir eyen greye as glas;
Hir mouth ful smal, and ther-to softe and reed;
But sikerly she hadde a fair forheed;
It was almost a spanne brood, I trowe;　　　155
For, hardily, she was nat undergrowe.
Ful fetis was hir cloke, as I was war.
Of smal coral aboute hir arm she bar
A peire of bedes, gauded al with grene;
And ther-on heng a broche of gold ful shene,　　　160
On which ther was first write a crowned A,
And after, *Amor vincit omnia.*
　Another NONNE with hir hadde she,
That was hir chapeleyne, and PREESTES three.
　A MONK ther was, a fair for the maistrye,　　　165
An out-rydere, that lovede venerye;
A manly man, to been an abbot able.
Ful many a deyntee hors hadde he in stable:
And, whan he rood men mighte his brydel here
Ginglen in a whistling wynd as clere,　　　170
And eek as loude as doth the chapel-belle
Ther as this lord was keper of the celle.
The reule of seint Maure or of seint Beneit,

139–140. countrefete . . . court, a satirical thrust at the elegant manners of the Prioress, and possibly her aping of courtly custom. The word *countrefete*, unlike our modern *counterfeit*, does not suggest dishonesty or insincerity or falseness, rather mere imitation.　141. digne, worthy; cf. Latin *dignus.*　142. conscience, sensibility, tender feelings.　143. pitous, having pity, tender-hearted.　147. wastel breed, a fine white wheat-bread.　149. yerde, rod, stick. The *smerte* immediately following is the adverb *smartly.*　151. pinched, pleated, fluted.　152. tretys, well-formed.　156. hardily, surely, certainly, without need for hesitation.　159. peire of bedes, apparently a rosary, although *peire* is still obscure. gauded, covered with large beads.　161. crowned A, evidently a large *A* surmounted by a crown. To some this is a reference to Queen Anne, first wife of Richard II, and hence a means of dating the *Prologue*, since Anne died in 1394.　162. *Amor . . . omnia,* "Love conquers all"—proverbial.　164. chapeleyne, a secretary and personal assistant. PREESTES three. Possibly this is an error on Chaucer's part; three nun's priests would bring the total of Canterbury pilgrims up to 31, instead of the 29 mentioned in l. 24.　165. for the maistrye, for the mastery (of all others), hence "surpassing all others"; then loosely as an adverb, "extremely," and finally as a weak pleonastic phrase, "all right."　166. out-rydere, a monk who had the duty of inspecting the estates of the monastery, which were often of considerable extent.　168. deyntee, from the Latin *dignus;* here, "worthy," "fine."　172. celle, a subordinate monastery.　173. seint Maure or of seint Beneit. St. Benedict was the founder of monasticism in Western Europe. St. Maurus was his follower.

100. carf . . . table. It was a regular duty of a squire to do the carving before a meal.　101. YEMAN, yeoman. Strictly speaking, he should be ranked in military service below the Squire (because he as a mere freeman would have no pretensions to chivalric knighthood), but above the groom. namo, no more.　102. him liste, it pleased him to.　106. takel, tackle; that is, equipment.　109. not-heed, head with hair cropped short or shaved.　111. bracer, an arm-guard worn just above the wrist to protect the archer from the impact of the string.　114. Harneised, armored, sheathed.　115. Cristofre, an emblem or image of Saint Christopher, the patron saint of foresters, whose protection he desired.　116. bawdrik, baldric, the cord or belt by which the horn was attached to its owner.　117. forster, a forester.　119. simple, naïve, unsophisticated. coy, quiet.　120. seÿnt Loy, St. Eloi, St. Eligius, chosen here partly for the sake of the rime, partly for the ladylike sound of the name, and possibly for some other reasons which are now obscure.　121. cleped, called.　124. fetisly, neatly, accurately.　125. Stratford atte Bowe, a nunnery of St. Leonard's in Bromley, Middlesex. The implication is, therefore, clear: the Prioress spoke the kind of French one would hear in a nunnery-*cum*-finishing-school of medieval England, not the true French of Paris.　132. lest, pleasure, joy.　134. ferthing, bit, trace.　136. raughte, reached.　137. sikerly, surely, certainly.

By-cause that it was old and som-del streit,
This ilke monk leet olde thinges pace,   175
And held after the newe world the space.
He yaf nat of that text a pulled hen,
That seith, that hunters been nat holy men;
Ne that a monk, whan he is cloisterlees,
Is lykned til a fish that is waterlees;   180
This is to seyn, a monk out of his cloystre.
But thilke text heeld he nat worth an oystre.
And I seyde his opinion was good.
What sholde he studie, and make hymselven wood,
Upon a book in cloystre alwey to poure,   185
Or swynken with his handes, and laboure,
As Austyn bit? How shal the world be served?
Lat Austyn have his swynk to him reserved.
Therfore he was a prikasour aright;
Grehoundes he hadde, as swift as fowel in flight;   190
Of prikyng and of huntyng for the hare   191
Was al his lust, for no cost wolde he spare.
I seigh his sleves y-purfiled at the hond
With grys, and that the fyneste of a lond;
And, for to festne his hood under his chyn,   195
He hadde of gold y-wroght a ful curious pyn:
A love-knotte in the gretter ende ther was.
His heed was balled, that shoon as any glas,
And eek his face, as it hadde been anoynt.
He was a lord ful fat and in good poynt;   200
Hise eyen stepe, and rollynge in his heed,
That stemed as a forneys of a leed;
His botes souple, his hors in greet estat.
Now certeinly he was a fair prelat;
He was nat pale as a for-pyned goost.   205
A fat swan loved he best of any roost.
His palfrey was as broun as is a berye.
    A FRERE ther was, a wantown and a merye,
A limitour, a ful solempne man.
In alle the ordres foure is noon that can   210
So muche of daliaunce and fair langage.

He hadde maad ful many a mariage
Of yonge wommen, at his owne cost.
Un-to his ordre he was a noble post.
Ful wel biloved and famulier was he   215
With frankeleyns over-al in his contree,
And eek with worthy wommen of the toun:
For he had power of confessioun,
As seyde him-self, more than a curat,
For of his ordre he was licentiat.   220
Ful swetely herde he confessioun,
And plesaunt was his absolucioun;
He was an esy man to yeve penaunce
Ther as he wiste to han a good pitaunce;
For unto a povre ordre for to yive   225
Is signe that a man is wel y-shrive.
For if he yaf, he dorste make avaunt,
He wiste that a man was repentaunt.
For many a man so hard is of his herte,
He may nat wepe al-thogh him sore smerte.   230
Therfore, in stede of weping and preyeres,
Men moot yeve silver to the povre freres.
His tipet was ay farsed ful of knyves
And pinnes, for to yeven faire wyves.
And certeinly he hadde a mery note;   235
Wel coude he singe and pleyen on a rote.
Of yeddinges he bar utterly the prys.
His nekke whyt was as the flour-de-lys;
There-to he strong was as a champioun.
He knew the tavernes wel in every toun,   240
And everich hostiler and tappestere
Bet than a lazar or a beggestere;
For un-to swich a worthy man as he
Acorded nat, as by his facultee,
To have with seke lazars aqueyntaunce.   245
It is nat honest, it may nat avaunce
For to delen with no swich poraille,
But al with riche and sellers of vitaille.
And over-al, ther as profit sholde aryse,
Curteys he was, and lowly of servyse.   250
Ther nas no man nowher so vertuous.
He was the beste beggere in his hous;
For thogh a widwe hadde noght a sho,

174. **som-del streit,** somewhat strict.   176. **the space.** This phrase is probably purely adverbial, and can be translated "meanwhile," "for the time (he held after the new ways)."   177. **yaf,** gave. **pulled hen,** plucked hen, another one of the endless symbols of the time for worthlessness.   180. **til,** to.   184. **What,** why? **wood,** mad, out of his wits.   187. **Austyn bit.** Austyn is the shortened form of Augustine, the great Church Father (354–430). *Bit* is the third person singular present indicative of *bid,* a contracted form of *biddeth.*   188. **swynk,** labor.   189. **prikasour,** a hunter on horseback.   191. **prikyng,** tracking an animal by its footprints (pricks).   193. **seigh,** saw. **y-purfiled,** trimmed at the edges.   194. **grys,** an expensive gray fur, possibly of squirrel.   197. **love-knotte,** cloth or brooch in an intertwined pattern.   200. **in good poynt,** *en bon point,* in good condition, but implying plumpness or even fatness.   202. **stemed . . . leed,** glistened or gleamed like a furnace or fire under a cauldron—a somewhat strained simile.   203. **greet estat,** fine condition.   205. **for-pyned,** tormented, wasted by torture.   208. **wantown,** gay. This description of the Friar, however, is full of sly insinuations, and the probability that he was "wanton" in the later Elizabethan sense of "sexually irregular" is more than likely to be inferred here.   209. **limitour,** a friar licensed, in return for a rental, to beg within assigned limits. **solempne,** formal, even pompous.   210. **ordres foure,** Dominicans, Franciscans, Carmelites, and Augustinians.   211. **daliaunce,** social conversation, chat; but again, the word veers here into the chivalric and modern use of the term to mean "love-caresses."

212–213. **mariage . . . cost,** he found husbands or dowries, at his own expense, for women whom he himself had seduced with embarrassing results.   214. **post,** pillar; compare the modern "pillar of the church." Note the bitter sarcasm of this line.   216. **frankeleyns,** landholders of free but not of noble birth. **over-al,** everywhere.   220. **licentiat.** The Friar had received from his Order a license to hear confession and to give absolution and penance. This practice led to considerable rivalry between mendicant friars and parish priests. The friars were often accused of making shrift altogether too easy if their palms had been acceptably greased.   223. **yeve,** give.   224. **pitaunce,** allowance, especially of food, to religious folk.   227. **make avaunt,** boast.   233. **tipet,** cape. **farsed,** stuck through, stuffed.   236. **rote,** a stringed instrument.   237. **yeddinges,** songs or ballads, originally in alliterative verse. By Chaucer's time, however, the term had been generalized to refer to any type of ballad or song.   241. **hostiler,** inn-keeper. **tappestere,** female tapster, barmaid.   242. **lazar,** leper. **beggestere,** female beggar or tramp.   246. **honest,** a good thing. **avaunce,** be helpful, advance one—apparently intransitive here.   247. **poraille,** poor folk, trash.   248. **vitaille,** victuals.   253. **sho,** shoe.

So plesaunt was his *"In principio,"*
Yet wolde he have a ferthing, er he wente.   255
His purchas was wel bettre than his rente.
And rage he coude, as it were right a whelpe.
In love-dayes ther coude he muchel helpe.
For ther he was nat lyk a cloisterer,
With a thredbar cope as is a povre scoler,   260
But he was lyk a maister or a pope.
Of double worsted was his semi-cope,
That rounded as a belle out of the presse.
Somwhat he lipsed, for his wantownesse,
To make his English swete up-on his tonge;   265
And in his harping, whan that he had songe,
His eyen twinkled in his heed aright,
As doon the sterres in the frosty night.
This worthy limitour was cleped Huberd.

A MARCHANT was ther with a forked berd,   270
In mottelee, and hye on horse he sat,
Up-on his heed a Flaundrish bever hat;
His botes clasped faire and fetisly.
His resons he spak ful solempnely,
Souninge alway th'encrees of his winning.   275
He wolde the see were kept for any thing
Bitwixe Middelburgh and Orewelle.
Wel coude he in eschaunge sheeldes selle.
This worthy man ful wel his wit bisette;
Ther wiste no wight that he was in dette,   280
So estatly was he of his governaunce,
With his bargaynes, and with his chevisaunce.
For sothe he was a worthy man with-alle,
But sooth to seyn, I noot how men him calle.

A CLERK ther was of Oxenford also,   285
That un-to logik hadde longe y-go.

As lene was his hors as is a rake,
And he nas nat right fat, I undertake;
But loked holwe, and ther-to soberly.
Ful thredbar was his overest courtepy;   290
For he had geten him yet no benefyce,
Ne was so worldly for to have offyce.
For him was lever have at his beddes heed
Twenty bokes, clad in blak or reed,
Of Aristotle and his philosophye,   295
Than robes riche, or fithele, or gay sautrye.
But al be that he was a philosophre,
Yet hadde he but litel gold in cofre;
But al that he mighte of his freendes hente,
On bokes and on lerninge he it spente,   300
And bisily gan for the soules preye
Of hem that yaf him wher-with to scoleye.
Of studie took he most cure and most hede.
Noght o word spak he more than was nede,
And that was seyd in forme and reverence,   305
And short and quik, and ful of hy sentence.
Souninge in moral vertu was his speche,
And gladly wolde he lerne, and gladly teche.

A SERGEANT OF THE LAWE, war and wys,
That often hadde been at the parvys,   310
Ther was also, ful riche of excellence.
Discreet he was, and of greet reverence:
He semed swich, his wordes weren so wyse,
Iustyce he was ful often in assyse,
By patente and by pleyn commissioun;   315
For his science, and for his heigh renoun
Of fees and robes hadde he many oon.
So greet a purchasour was nowher noon.
Al was fee simple to him in effect,

254. *"In principio,"* "in the beginning (was the Word, etc.)"—John 1: 1. These opening words of the Gospel of John were believed to have special saving, almost magical, value.   256. **His purchas . . . his rente.** What he picked up on the side (his *purchas*) amounted to more than his lawful income (his *rente*). The term *purchas* seems always to have had a somewhat sinister connotation in Middle English, applying particularly to what one comes by illegally.   257. **as it . . . whelpe,** as if he were a pup or cub. The line is unquestionably contemptuous.   258. **love-dayes,** special days set aside for the arbitration of all disputes; the clergy usually took a firm hand in the proceedings.   260. **cope,** cape, cloak.   262. **semi-cope,** short over-cloak or cape.   264. **lipsed,** lisped.   271. **mottelee,** motley, cloth with a figured design, often of more than one color. The material was frequently used for distinctive liveries among the different guildsmen.   275. **Souninge,** pertaining to, in keeping with, proclaiming. **th'encrees,** the increase or profit.   277. **Middelburgh and Orewelle.** Middelburgh is a port on the island of Walcheren on the coast of the Low Countries; Orewelle is the old port of Orwell, near Harwich, almost directly opposite Middelburgh. Here would be, in other words, a direct line for the wool trade between England and the Low Countries. Obviously, then, the Merchant would want this sea path kept free from pirates and smugglers at all costs.   278. **sheeldes,** the French *écu.* This selling of *écus* to Englishmen for profit was distinctly illegal, according to a statute of King Edward III.   279. **bisette,** used.   281. **governaunce,** demeanor. **estatly,** stately, dignified. In other words, the Merchant put up an impressive front.   282. **chevisaunce,** a term referring to borrowing and lending; it was used also loosely for any illicit income, particularly from usury. Such is its meaning here, for the Merchant is a slippery individual.   284. **noot,** *ne* plus *woot,* I know not.   286. **y-go,** gone. Here the verb is to be construed with *un-to* in the same line. "To go to logic" would mean "to study logic."

290. **courtepy,** short-coat.   291. **geten . . . benefyce,** been given no religious office. The Clerk, be it noted, is a man of clerical training preparing for the priesthood.   293. **him was lever,** he would rather.   295. **Aristotle . . . philosophye.** The amount of Aristotle's work available to the Middle Ages through Latin channels to Englishmen could easily have filled twenty volumes, but it is not sensible to assume that Chaucer meant his statement to be taken literally. Indeed, Aristotle was often a convenient name to represent all the sages of antiquity.   296. **fithele,** fiddle, violin. **sautrye,** a zither-like stringed instrument, psaltery.   299. **hente,** get, seize, acquire.   302. **to scoleye,** to go to school, to receive learning.   303. **cure,** care.   306. **hy sentence,** lofty thoughts, sentiments, or meaning.   309. SERGEANT OF THE LAWE, a legal servant of the Crown, chosen from barristers of at least sixteen years' experience. Those who were not chosen to serve as judges of the King's courts or of the Exchequer went about on circuit as justices of the assizes. In short, The Man of Law is a jurist rather than a practicing lawyer. **war and wys,** a common alliterative formula: discreet and prudent.   310. **parvys,** the porch of old St. Paul's Church in London, where members of the legal profession were accustomed to consult with their clients.   315. **patente,** letters patent from the King, making the appointment as judge. **pleyn commissioun,** the more common certificates of appointment made in the form of letters sealed and addressed to the appointee, giving him full jurisdiction.   316. **science,** knowledge (of the law). The Sergeant of the Law should certainly be considered among the heads of his profession.   318. **purchasour.** Note again the implication of this word, in reference to l. 256. But on its face value, we can take this to mean, "Such a getter never was."   319. **Al . . . in effect,** all things were in effect fee simple to him. In other words, he always got property in unrestricted possession, with a clear title (fee simple).

His purchasing mighte nat been infect. 320
No-wher so bisy a man as he ther nas,
And yet he semed bisier than he was.
In termes hadde he caas and domes alle,
That from the tyme of King William were falle.
Thereto he coude endyte, and make a thing, 325
Ther coude no wight pinche at his wryting;
And every statut coude he pleyn by rote
He rood but hoomly in a medlee cote
Girt with a ceint of silk, with barres smale;
Of his array telle I no lenger tale. 330

A FRANKELEYN was in his companye;
Whyt was his berd, as is the dayesye.
Of his complexioun he was sangwyn.
Wel loved he by the morwe a sop in wyn.
To liven in delyt was ever his wone, 335
For he was Epicurus owne sone,
That heeld opinioun, that pleyn delyt
Was verraily felicitee parfyt.
An housholdere, and that a greet, was he;
Seynt Iulian he was in his contree. 340
His breed, his ale, was alwey after oon;
A bettre envyned man was nowher noon.
With-oute bake mete was never his hous,
Of fish and flesh, and that so plentevous,
It snewed in his hous of mete and drinke, 345
Of alle deyntees that men coude thinke.
After the sondry sesons of the yeer,
So chaunged he his mete and his soper.
Ful many a fat partrich hadde he in mewe,
And many a breem and many a luce in stewe. 350
Wo was his cook, but-if his sauce were
Poynaunt and sharp, and redy al his gere

His table dormant in his halle alway
Stood redy covered al the longe day.
At sessiouns ther was he lord and sire; 355
Ful ofte tyme he was knight of the shire.
An anlas and a gipser al of silk
Heng at his girdel, whyt as morne milk.
A shirreve hadde he been, and a countour;
Was nowher such a worthy vavasour. 360

AN HABERDASSHER and a CARPENTER,
A WEBBE, a DYERE, and a TAPICER,
Were with us eek, clothed in o liveree,
Of a solempne and greet fraternitee,
Ful fresh and newe hir gere apyked was; 365
Hir knyves were y-chaped noght with bras,
But al with silver, wroght ful clene and weel.
Hir girdles and hir pouches every-deel.
Wel semed ech of hem a fair burgeys,
To sitten in a yeldhalle on a deys. 370
Everich, for the wisdom that he can,
Was shaply for to been an alderman.
For catel hadde they y-nogh and rente,
And eek hir wyves wolde it wel assente;
And elles certein were they to blame. 375
It is ful fair to been y-clept "ma dame,"
And goon to vigilyës al bifore,
And have a mantel royalliche y-bore.

A COOK they hadde with hem for the nones,
To boille chiknes with the mary-bones, 380
And poudre-marchant tart, and galingale.
Wel coude he knowe a draughte of London ale.
He coude roste, and sethe, and broille, and frye,
Maken mortreux, and wel bake a pye.
But greet harm was it, as it thoughte me, 385

320. **purchasing . . . infect,** no defect (*nat . . . infect*) could be found in his title to his possessions. 323. **caas and domes,** cases and judgments. He knew statutes and court decisions (common law) as well. Nouns ending in *s*, like *caas*, if of foreign origin, were in many instances not given plural endings. 324. **King William,** William the Conqueror (William I of England), whose passion for orderly codification of the law resulted in the famous Doomsday Book. 325. **endyte,** to write out a legal document (see note to l. 95). 326. **pinche,** object to, cavil at. 327. **coude,** knew. **by rote,** on basic principles. 328. **medlee,** cloth of mixed weave and often of many colors. The official robes of the Sergeant of Law had the colors brown and green. 329. **ceint,** girdle, sash. 330. **telle . . . tale,** I shall not tell a longer story. 333. **sangwyn,** etc. According to the older conception of the human body, before Harvey's discovery of the circulation of the blood in 1610, there were four component *humours:* blood, phlegm, bile, and black bile. These humours were held in a kind of harmony or balance, known as the *complexioun.* But all *complexiouns* showed a tendency on the part of some particular *humour* to dominate, with the result that we hear of sanguine, phlegmatic, bilious, and melancholy *complexiouns* or temperaments, according as to whether blood, phlegm, bile, or black bile predominated. The Franklin, then, was of sanguine complexion or temperament: blood predominated in his make-up; he was ruddy, cheerful, and a hearty liver. 334. **sop in wyn,** bread soaked in wine. 335. **wone,** habit, custom. 336. **Epicurus owne sone.** In other words, he was an epicure. 340. **Seynt Iulian . . . contree.** St. Julian was the patron saint of hospitality. 342. **bettre envyned,** with a better stock of wine. 348. **So chaunged . . . soper,** so did he vary his meals and his supper. 349. **mewe,** the coop or pen for birds. 350. **breem,** bream, a fish with arched back. **luce,** a luce, a pickerel. **stewe,** fish-pool. 351. **but-if,** unless. 352. **gere,** equipment, furnishings.

353. **table dormant,** a table fixed in the floor, instead of movable, intended for unexpected guests. This would be in keeping with the Franklin's noted hospitality. 355. **sessiouns,** sessions of the local courts, which were presided over by local justices of the peace, of which the Franklin was one. 356. **knight of the shire,** member of Parliament for his county. 357. **anlas,** a short, two-edged knife or dagger, sometimes referred to as an *anlace.* **gipser,** purse or pouch. 359. **shirreve,** sheriff, king's administrator in a county or shire. **countour.** This term is very vague; it might mean "accountant," or it might be a "sergeant at law" (see note to l. 309). From the mention of the Franklin's position as sheriff, it would seem that the sergeant at law is denoted here. 360. **vavasour,** a substantial landholder, not of the nobility. 362. **WEBBE,** weaver. **TAPICER,** a tapestry-maker. 365. **apyked,** adorned. 366. **y-chaped,** capped; that is, the tops of the handles of the knives were crowned with a metal piece. 368. **every-deel,** every bit, entirely. 369. **burgeys,** burgess, townsman, citizen. 370. **yeldhalle,** guild-hall. **deys,** dais, raised platform. In all town councils the mayor and his aldermen sat on the dais; the common councilors on the floor. 372. **shaply,** fitted. 373. **catel,** property in general, rather than cattle in particular. 377. **vigilyës.** Each guild had a certain day in the year dedicated to it, usually the saint's day of its patron saint. The *vigilyë* was the celebration held on the eve of the feast-day. 378. **y-bore,** carried, borne. 379. **for the nones,** for that one time, for the occasion, but often a rather meaningless expletive like the modern "all right." "They had a cook with them for the occasion," however, makes fairly good sense as it stands. 380. **mary-bones,** marrow-bones. 381. **poudre-marchant tart,** a tart made with a heavy coating of a sweetish flavoring-powder. **galingale,** the extract of sweet cyperus. 384. **mortreux.** The *x* was probably pronounced as an *s.* This was a thick soup or stew.

That on his shine a mormal hadde he;
For blankmanger, that made he with the beste.

A SHIPMAN was ther, woning fer by weste:
For aught I woot, he was of Dertemouthe.
He rood up-on a rouncy as he couthe,   390
In a gowne of falding to the knee.
A daggere hanging on a laas hadde he
Aboute his nekke under his arm adoun.
The hote somer had maad his hewe al broun;
And, certeinly, he was a good felawe.   395
Ful many a draughte of wyn had he y-drawe
From Burdeux-ward, whyl that the chapman sleep.
Of nyce conscience took he no keep.
If that he faught, and hadde the hyer hond,
By water he sente hem hoom to every lond.   400
But of his craft to rekene wel his tydes,
His stremes and his daungers him bisydes,
His herberwe and his mone, his lodemenage,
Ther nas noon swich from Hulle to Cartage.
Hardy he was, and wys to undertake;   405
With many a tempest hadde his berd been shake.
He knew wel alle the havenes, as they were,
From Gootlond to the cape of Finistere,
And every cryke in Britayne and in Spayne;
His barge y-cleped was the Maudelayne.   410

With us ther was a DOCTOUR OF PHISYK,
In al this worlde ne was ther noon him lyk
To speke of phisik and of surgerye;
For he was grounded in astronomye.
He kepte his pacient a ful greet del   415
In houres, by his magik naturel.

Wel coude he fortunen the ascendent
Of his images for his pacient.
He knew the cause of everich maladye,
Were it of hoot or cold, or moiste, or drye,   420
And where engendred, and of what humour;
He was a verray parfit practisour.
The cause y-knowe, and of his harm the roote,
Anon he yaf the seke man his boote.
Ful redy hadde he his apothecaries,   425
To sende him drogges, and his letuaries,
For ech of hem made other for to winne;
Hir frendschipe nas nat newe to biginne.
Wel knew he th'olde Esculapius,
And Deiscorides, and eek Rufus,   430
Old Ypocras, Haly, and Galien;
Serapion, Razis, and Avicen;
Averrois, Damascien, and Constantyn;
Bernard, and Gatesden, and Gilbertyn.
Of his diete mesurable was he,   435
For it was of no superfluitee,
But of greet norissing and digestible.
His studie was but litel on the bible.
In sangwin and in pers he clad was al,
Lyned with taffata and with sendal;   440
And yet he was but esy of dispence;
He kepte that he wan in pestilence.
For gold in phisik is a cordial,
Therfor he lovede gold in special.

A good WYF was ther of bisyde BATHE,   445
But she was som-del deef, and that was scathe.

386. **mormal**, an ulcer, a running sore. 387. **blankmanger**, creamed meat stewed with rice, eggs, sugar, and sometimes nuts; not the modern "blanc-mange." 388. SHIPMAN, a seafaring man, but here the captain of a ship. **woning**, dwelling. 390. **rouncy**. This word, strangely enough, appears in the equivocal meanings of (1) a broken-down nag, and (2) a good strong horse. The reader can take his choice. **as he couthe**, as best he knew how; the sailor would not be expected to ride like a knight. 391. **falding**, a coarse woolen cloth. 392. **laas**, a string or cord; compare the modern shoe*lace*. 397. **whyl . . . sleep**, while the merchant napped. The Shipman stole much of the wine which he was carrying for a merchant; he extracted, in other words, some of the cargo which had been entrusted to him. 398. **nyce conscience**, foolish scruples or tender feelings. 400. **By water . . . every lond**. Presumably the Shipman could turn to piracy and sink his victim's ship or drown his prisoners. 402. **daungers**, here a kind of generic term for which tides, currents, moons, and compass-bearings would be specific details; in short, factors governing his business of navigation. The word *daunger* in Middle English is always close to its Latin source, the verb *dominare*, to rule or control. 403. **herberwe**, lodgings as applied to a shipman, his harbor or anchorage. **lodemenage**, pilotage. 404. **Cartage**, not ancient Carthage, but one of the Spanish ports, Cartagena. 408. **Gootlond**, the island of Gothland, off the coast of Sweden in the Baltic. **Finistere**, the westernmost point in the Iberian Peninsula, in Spain. 414. **astronomye**. The science which the scholars of the Middle Ages called astronomy is nearer what we would call today the pseudoscience of astrology than modern astronomy, inasmuch as all natural phenomena observable in the heavens were supposed to have direct bearing upon the lives of men. Even a physician, therefore, would in the Middle Ages have to be cognizant of the natural laws of astronomy, as they were then understood. 415–416. **kepte . . . In houres . . . magik naturel.** The physician watched his patient for the times most advantageous to his treatment. "Magik naturel" is what we would today term the doctor's scientific medical knowledge.

417. **fortunen**, place in a favorable position. **ascendent**, that degree of the ecliptic (the celestial path of the sun) which is rising at any given time. It would have to lie in one of the twelve constellations (signs) of the zodiac, since the zodiacal constellations are those through which the ecliptic runs. The Physician, then, was skillful at picking ascendants that showed a favorable grouping of beneficent planets and constellations, and an arrangement of malefic constellations and planets at points where they would do the least harm to the patient. 418. **images**, either representations of the patient in wax or clay figures, or talismans representing the different signs of the zodiac, which any astrological chart will furnish to the modern reader. By exposing these images to the firmament when there was a favorable ascendant, the Physician was supposed to work wonders with the patient's condition. 420. **hoot . . . drye**. There were four elementary "qualities," consisting of contrary attributes, which in combinations produced the four elements: (1) cold and dry (Earth); (2) hot and moist (Air); (3) cold and moist (Water); (4) hot and dry (Fire). 421. **humour**. See note to l. 333. The humours were similarly produced by the combination of contrary attributes: (1) hot and moist (Blood); (2) cold and moist (Phlegm); (3) hot and dry (Bile); (4) cold and dry (Black Bile). This conception goes back to Hippocrates and Galen. 424. **boote**, remedy. 426. **letuaries**, electuaries, remedies. 429–434. **Esculapius . . . Gilbertyn**. This is a noteworthy list of the great names in medicine prior to and contemporaneous with Chaucer. 435. **mesurable**, moderate. 439. **sangwin**, a cloth of blood-red color. **pers**, a cloth of Persian blue or azure. 440. **sendal**, a thin kind of silk. 441. **esy of dispence**, slow (easy-going) about spending. 442. **pestilence**, not necessarily the Black Death, although such an allusion is certainly possible here, but simply any kind of epidemic. 443. **gold . . . cordial**. Gold in solution, *aurum potabile*, was a sovereign remedy for desperate diseases, but the word "cordial" means specifically a heart stimulant, and Chaucer may therefore imply that gold in his profession was a heart-warming thing to the Physician, perhaps more heart-warming than his Hippocratic oath called for. 446. **som-del**, somewhat. **scathe**, a pity.

Of clooth-making she hadde swiche an haunt,
She passed hem of Ypres and of Gaunt.
In al the parisshe wyf ne was ther noon
That to th' offring bifore hir sholde goon;   450
And if ther dide, certeyn, so wrooth was she,
That she was out of alle charitee.
Hir coverchiefs ful fyne were of ground;
I dorste swere they weyeden ten pound
That on a Sonday were upon hir heed.   455
Hir hosen weren of fyn scarlet reed.
Ful streite y-teyd, and shoos ful moiste and newe.
Bold was hir face, and fair, and reed of hewe.
She was a worthy womman al hir lyve,
Housbondes at chirche-dore she hadde fyve,   460
Withouten other companye in youthe;
But thereof nedeth nat to speke as nouthe.
And thryes hadde she been at Jerusalem;
She hadde passed many a straunge streem;
At Rome she hadde been, and at Boloigne,   465
In Galice at seint Jame, and at Coloigne.
She coude muche of wandring by the weye:
Gat-tothed was she, soothly for to seye.
Up-on an amblere esily she sat,
Y-wimpled wel, and on hir heed an hat   470
As brood as is a bokeler or a targe;
A foot-mantel aboute hir hipes large,
And on hir feet a paire of spores sharpe.
In felawschip wel coude she laughe and carpe.
Of remedyes of love she knew perchaunce,   475
For she coude of that art the olde daunce.

    A good man was ther of religioun,
And was a povre PERSOUN of a toun;
But riche he was of holy thoght and werk.
He was also a lerned man, a clerk,   480
That Cristes gospel trewely wolde preche;
His parisshens devoutly wolde he teche.
Benigne he was, and wonder diligent,
And in adversitee ful pacient;
And swich he was y-preved ofte sythes.   485
Ful looth were him to cursen for his tythes,

But rather wolde he yeven, out of doute,
Un-to his povre parisshens aboute
Of his offring, and eek of his substaunce.
He coude in litel thing han suffisaunce.   490
Wyd was his parisshe, and houses fer a-sonder,
But he ne lafte nat, for reyn ne thonder,
In siknes nor in meschief, to visyte
The ferreste in his parisshe, muche and lyte,
Up-on his feet, and in his hand a staf.   495
This noble ensample to his sheep he yaf,
That first he wroghte, and afterward he taughte;
Out of the gospel he tho wordes caughte;
And this figure he added eek ther-to,
That if gold ruste, what shal yren do?   500
For if a preest be foul, on whom we truste,
No wonder is a lewed man to ruste;
And shame it is, if a preest take keep,
A shiten shepherde and a clene sheep.
Wel oghte a preest ensample for to yive,   505
By his clennesse, how that his sheep shold live.
He sette nat his benefice to hyre,
And leet his sheep encombred in the myre,
And ran to London, un-to seÿnt Poules,
To seken him a chaunterie for soules,   510
Or with a bretherhed to been withholde;
But dwelte at hoom, and kepte wel his folde,
So that the wolf ne made it nat miscarie;
He was a shepherde and no mercenarie.
And though he holy were, and vertuous,   515
He was to sinful man nat despitous,
Ne of his speche daungerous ne digne,
But in his teching discreet and benigne.
To drawen folk to heven by fairnesse
By good ensample, was his bisinesse: 520
But it were any persone obstinat,
What so he were, of heigh or lowe estat,
Him wolde he snibben sharply for the nones.
A bettre preest, I trowe that nowher noon is.
He wayted after no pompe and reverence,   525
Ne maked him a spyced conscience,
But Cristes lore, and his apostles twelve,
He taughte, but first he folwed it him-selve.

447. **swiche an haunt,** such a skill or practice. 448. **Ypres . . .
Gaunt.** Ypres and Ghent were two important centers of the Flemish
textile trade. 453. **coverchiefs,** kerchiefs, head-scarves. **ground,**
texture. 454–455. **they weyeden . . . hir heed.** Women of fashion
in England during the late fourteenth and early fifteenth centuries
wore extremely elaborate and heavy headdress. 462. **as nouthe,** as
now, at this moment. 466. **seint Jame,** etc. The places mentioned
in reference to the pilgrimages of the Wife of Bath were the choicest
shrines in the Western world of the time. *Seint Jame* is the shrine
of Saint James of Compostella in Spain. 468. **Gat-tothed,** with teeth
set far apart, "gap-toothed" or "gate-toothed." The medieval mind
associated this characteristic with sensuality. 469. **amblere,** an
ambling or easy-paced horse. 471. **targe,** a large round shield. 472.
foot-mantel, an outer riding-skirt. 474. **carpe,** discourse greatly.
475. **remedyes of love,** cures for love; the conduct of the suitor and
of the rejected lover, and the discussion of all other features of lovemaking, so far as the Middle Ages went, were to be found in Ovid's
Ars Amoris, one section of which, the *Remedia Amoris,* was devoted
to the question of remedies. 478. **PERSOUN,** parson, parish priest.
482. **parisshens,** parishioners. 485. **y-preved,** proved. **ofte sythes,**
oftentimes, many times. 486. **cursen,** to curse in the sense of ex-
communicate for nonpayment of tithes.

493. **meschief,** misfortune. 494. **ferreste,** farthest, most remote.
muche and lyte, high and low (in social rank). 500. **if gold . . .
yren do?** This expression is proverbial, particularly in the medieval
French didactic romances. 502. **lewed,** ignorant, unlearned; hence,
a layman. The modern meaning, highly specialized in a moral sense,
is comparatively recent. 507. **sette . . . to hyre,** he did not rent
his churchly office to someone else, while he went up to London, etc.
510. **chaunterie,** a provision whereby a priest was to sing a daily
mass for the repose of a soul. There were many such at St. Paul's in
London, whither the more self-seeking clergymen tried to go, but
after 1391 only minor canons of the Cathedral were allowed to sing
chantries, and the abuse diminished. 511. **a bretherhed . . . withholde,** to be retained by a guild as a chaplain—an additional source of
income for a worldly priest. 513. **wolf,** "the world, the flesh, and the
Devil." 516. **despitous,** spiteful and contemptuous. 517. **daungerous,** arrogant, arbitrary (see note to l. 402). **digne,** haughty. 523.
snibben, snub, chide, rebuke. **for the nones,** here loosely used; an
expletive, "all right." See note to l. 379. 526. **spyced conscience,**
oversweetened feelings.

With him ther was a PLOWMAN, was his brother,
That hadde y-lad of dong ful many a fother,   530
A trewe swinker and a good was he,
Livinge in pees and parfit charitee.
God loved he best with al his hole herte
At alle tymes, thogh him gamed or smerte,
And thanne his neighebour right as him-selve.   535
He wolde thresshe, and ther-to dyke and delve,
For Cristes sake, for every povre wight,
Withouten hyre, if it lay in his might.
His tythes payed he full faire and wel,
Bothe of his propre swink and his catel.   540
In a tabard he rood upon a mere.
    Ther was also a Reve and a Millere,
A Somnour and a Pardoner also,
A Maunciple, and my-self; ther were namo.
    The MILLER was a stout carl, for the nones,   545
Ful big he was of braun, and eek of bones;
That proved wel, for over-al ther he cam,
At wrastling he wolde have alwey the ram.
He was short-sholdred, brood, a thikke knarre,
Ther nas no dore that he nolde heve of harre,   550
Or breke it, at a renning, with his heed.
His berd as any sowe or fox was reed,
And ther-to brood, as though it were a spade.
Up-on the cop right of his nose he hade
A werte, and ther-on stood a tuft of heres,   555
Reed as the bristles of a sowes eres;
His nose-thirles blake were and wyde.
A swerd and bokeler bar he by his syde;
His mouth as greet was as a greet forneys.

He was a janglere and a goliardeys,   560
And that was most of sinne and harlotryes.
Wel coude he stelen corn, and tollen thryes,
And yet he hadde a thombe of gold, pardee.
A whyt cote and blew hood wered he.
A baggepype wel coude he blowe and sowne,   565
And therwithal he broghte us out of towne.
    A gentil MAUNCIPLE was ther of a temple,
Of which achatours mighte take exemple
For to be wyse in bying of vitaille.
For whether that he payde, or took by taille,   570
Algate he wayted so in his achat,
That he was ay biforn and in good stat.
Now is nat that of God a ful fair grace,
That swich a lewed mannes wit shal pace
The wisdom of an heep of lerned men?   575
Of maistres hadde he mo than thryes ten,
That were of lawe expert and curious;
Of which ther were a doseyn in that hous
Worthy to been stiwardes of rente and lond
Of any lord that is in Engelond,   580
To make him live by his propre good,
In honour dettelees, but he were wood,
Or live as scarsly as him list desire;
And able for to helpen al a shire
In any cas that mighte falle or happe;   585
And yit this maunciple sette hir aller cappe.
    The REVE was a sclendre colerik man,
His berd was shave as ny as ever he can.
His heer was by his eres round y-shorn.
His top was dokked lyk a preest biforn.   590
Ful longe were his legges, and ful lene,
Y-lyk a staf, ther was no calf y-sene.
Wel coude he kepe a gerner and a binne;
Ther was noon auditor coude on him winne.
Wel wist he, by the droghte, and by the reyn,   595
The yeldyng of his seed, and of his greyn.

530. **y-lad**, led, pulled. **fother**, load. 531. **swinker**, laborer. 533–535. **God loved . . . neighebour . . . him-selve.** This "eleventh" commandment is found expressed most completely in Matthew, 22: 37–39. 534. **him gamed or smerte**, he was pleased to or was reluctant to. Note the impersonal construction, extremely common in Middle English. The general effect of the clause is "under all circumstances." 536. **dyke**, dig, make a ditch. The phrase dyke and delve is an alliterative formula, both words meaning almost the same thing. 541. **tabard.** See note to l. 20. 542. **Reve.** This official's duties were many and vague. If the steward (or seneschal) was the manager of a feudal estate, his immediate subordinate would be the bailiff, who would enforce the statutes of the estate and collect taxes, etc. The Reeve was apparently subordinate to the bailiff, but in some cases he was superior, as in the case of Chaucer's Reeve. 543. **Somnour**, an officer of the ecclesiastical courts; in effect, a policeman for all offenses involving a breach of ecclesiastical law (rather than civil law). **Pardoner.** Pardoners were distributors of papal indulgences, sometimes for money. In many instances, pardoners were not even ordained clergymen, and were itinerant and irresponsible in consequence. Their capacity for dishonesty is vouched for unanimously by the writers of the time. Some, however, like Chaucer's Pardoner, were even allowed to preach. 544. **Maunciple**, the purchasing agent for a college of law or any similar institution, such as an Inn of Court or a college at Oxford or Cambridge; note *The Reeve's Tale*, p. II:216, l. 73. **namo**, no more. 545. **carl**, fellow, churl. **for the nones.** See note to l. 523. 548. **wrastling . . . the ram.** At country fairs, wrastling was one of the favorite diversions. The prize for the winner of a contest was often some livestock, such as a ram or goat. 549. **knarre**, literally, a knot of wood; hence, a tough individual. There may be a trace of our contemptuous *blockhead* present in the meaning of the word. 550. **of harre**, from the hinge. Note the original sense of *of*. 551. **renning.** The Miller could break down any door by running at it with his head in the role of battering ram. 554. **cop**, top. 557. **nose-thirles**, nostrils.

560. **janglere**, a chatterbox, one who talks incessantly and to little purpose. **goliardeys**, a retailer of smutty stories. By Chaucer's time the word had come to signify merely a coarse buffoon. 562. **tollen thryes**, take toll three times; that is, charge excessively. 563. **a thombe of gold**, referring to the skill of the Miller in testing the fineness of flour with his thumb, thereby learning its value. English bakers still know how to do this. There was an old proverb, "An honest miller has a thumb of gold," indicating that the miller's thumb, thus used honestly, was worth money to him. On the other hand, taken satirically, this proverb might indicate that there was no such thing as an honest miller. 565. **sowne**, sound forth, play. 567. **MAUNCIPLE.** See note to l. 544. **temple**, possibly the Inner or Middle Temple near the Strand in London, occupied in Chaucer's time by societies of lawyers. 568. **achatours**, buyers, caterers. 570. **took by taille**, took by tally, took on credit. The "tally" was a stick on which the amount of the debt was notched. 571. **Algate**, always, any way, in any case. **achat**, purchase, buying. 572. **in good stat**, in good financial standing. 577. **curious**, having care for, diligent, skillful. 586. **sette hir aller cappe**, "set the cap of them all," a slang expression of the time for "made fools of them all." 587. **colerik**, choleric, one in whom the humour *choler* (bile) predominated; see notes to ll. 333 and 421. Such a man would be "hot and dry"—the lean, sallow, wiry, nervous type. 590. **dokked**, docked, shorn. This was a sign of his servile station, one relic of which is the old practice of shaving the heads of convicts. 593. **gerner**, garner, granary. 594. **on him winne**, get any profit with him around.

His lordes sheep, his neet, his dayerye,
His swyn, his hors, his stoor, and his pultrye,
Was hoolly in this reves governing,
And by his covenaunt yaf the rekening, 600
Sin that his lord was twenty yeer of age;
Ther coude no man bringe him in arrerage.
Ther nas baillif, ne herde, ne other hyne,
That he ne knew his sleighte and his covyne,
They were adrad of him, as of the deeth. 605
His woning was ful fair up-on an heeth,
With grene treës shadwed was his place.
He coude bettre than his lord purchace.
Ful riche he was astored prively,
His lord wel coude he plesen subtilly, 610
To yeve and lene him of his owne good,
And have a thank, and yet a cote, and hood.
In youthe he lerned hadde a good mister;
He was a wel good wrighte, a carpenter.
This reve sat up-on a ful good stot, 615
That was al pomely grey, and highte Scot.
A long surcote of pers up-on he hade,
And by his syde he bar a rusty blade.
Of Northfolk was this reve, of which I telle,
Bisyde a toun men clepen Baldeswelle. 620
Tukked he was, as is a frere, aboute,
And ever he rood the hindreste of our route.

A Somnour was ther with us in that place,
That hadde a fyr-reed cherubinnes face,
For sawceflem he was, with eyen narwe. 625
As hoot he was, and lecherous, as a sparwe;
With scalled browes blake, and piled berd;
Of his visage children were aferd.
Ther nas quik-silver, litarge, ne brimstoon,
Boras, ceruce, ne oille of tartre noon, 630
Ne oynement that wolde clense and byte,

That him mighte helpen of his whelkes whyte,
Ne of the knobbes sittinge on his chekes.
Wel loved he garleek, oynons, and eek lekes,
And for to drinken strong wyn, reed as blood. 635
Thanne wolde he speke, and crye as he were wood.
And whan that he wel dronken hadde the wyn,
Than wolde he speke no word but Latyn.
A fewe termes hadde he, two or thre,
That he had lerned out of som decree; 640
No wonder is, he herde it al the day;
And eek ye knowen wel, how that a jay
Can clepen "Watte," as well as can the pope.
But who-so coude in other thing him grope,
Thanne hadde he spent al his philosophye; 645
Ay "Questio quid iuris" wolde he crye.
He was a gentil harlot and a kynde;
A bettre felawe sholde men noght fynde.
He wolde suffre, for a quart of wyn,
A good felawe to have his concubyn 650
A twelf-month, and excuse him atte fulle;
And prively a finch eek coude he pulle.
And if he fond o-wher a good felawe,
He wolde techen him to have non awe,
In swich cas, of the erchedeknes curs, 655
But-if a mannes soule were in his purs;
For in his purs he sholde y-punisshed be.
"Purs is the erchedeknes helle," seyde he.
But wel I woot he lyed right in dede;
Of cursing oghte ech gilty man him drede— 660
For curs wol slee, right as assoilling saveth—
And also war him of a significavit.
In daunger hadde he at his owne gyse
The yonge girles of the diocyse,
And knew hir counseil, and was al hir reed. 665
A gerland hadde he set up-on his heed,
As greet as it were for an ale-stake;
A bokeler hadde he maad him of a cake.

With him ther rood a gentil Pardoner
Of Rouncival, his freend and his compeer, 670
That streight was comen fro the court of Rome.

---

597. **neet,** domestic animals, but usually specifying cattle. 598. **stoor,** general possessions, but possibly specialized to livestock. 601. **Sin,** since. 602. **bringe . . . arrerage,** no man could catch him in arrears; his books were always up to the minute. 603. **herde,** herdsman, shepherd. **hyne,** servant. 604. **covyne,** etc. The Reeve knew all their tricks (*sleights*) and their deceits (*covyne*). 605. **adrad,** afraid of, in dread of. **the deeth.** With the definite article before it, this word usually signifies in Middle English plague or pestilence. 606. **woning,** dwelling. 609. **astored,** provided for. 613. **mister,** trade, profession; see the French *métier.* 615. **stot,** stallion. 616. **pomely,** dappled, with spots like an apple; note the French *pomme.* **highte,** was called. 617. **surcote,** outer coat, overcoat. 620. **Baldeswelle,** Bawdswell in northern Norfolkshire, the property of the Pembroke family, whom Chaucer may have once served as deputy. The specific locality mentioned leads us to suspect that here, as often in other instances, Chaucer had a real person in mind for the prototype of the Reeve, but the matter is still speculative. 621. **Tukked,** with his coat hitched up and held with a girdle. 622. **hindreste,** farthest behind, the last in line. Since the Reeve later has a violent quarrel with the Miller, who led the way playing his bagpipe (note l. 566), it is significant that the two men are as far apart as possible. 625. **sawceflem,** pimpled, erupted. The Summoner was suffering from a skin disease akin to leprosy. 627. **scalled,** scaly, scabby. **piled,** scanty, moth-eaten, with hair falling out in patches. 629. **litarge,** the protoxide of lead used in an ointment. The remedies mentioned in these lines were the stock remedies for skin diseases during the Middle Ages; some of them, the mercury and sulphur particularly, still are of value. 630. **ceruce,** white lead.

632. **whelkes,** pustules, blotches. 643. **"Watte,"** the diminutive of Walter. Parrots were evidently taught to call out (*clepen*) "Watte!" instead of our traditional "Polly!" 644. **grope,** question, test. 646. **"Questio quid iuris,"** "the question is, what (part) of the law (applies)?"—apparently a familiar piece of legalistic jargon. 647. **harlot,** rascal, not necessarily limited to the female of the species. 651. **atte fulle,** at the full, fully; the same formation as *atte beste* (see note to l. 29). 652. **prively . . . pulle,** secretly . . . pluck a finch, a slang phrase of highly indecent nature. 653. **o-wher,** anywhere. 661. **assoilling,** absolution. 662. **significavit,** the first word in the writ which sent a person to prison following excommunication, the gravest penalty which an ecclesiastical court could impose. 663. **daunger.** Here, as is usual in Chaucer, the meaning is "power," "control." **at his owne gyse,** at his own discretion. 664. **girles,** young people of either sex, not young females only. 667. **ale-stake.** As a sign, every inn had a stake projecting horizontally over the door, on which was suspended a hoop (or *gerland,* l. 666) decorated with ivy leaves—a symbol of festivity. The Summoner's wreath of flowers was not unusual among church people on special occasions, such as an ecclesiastical procession or a pilgrimage. 670. **Rouncival,** the hospital of the Blessed Mary of Rouncivale, near Charing Cross, London. **compeer,** comrade.

Ful loude he song, "Com hider, love, to me."
This somnour bar to him a stif burdoun,
Was nevere trompe of half so greet a soun.
This pardoner hadde heer as yelow as wex,   675
But smothe it heng, as doth a strike of flex;
By ounces henge his lokkes that he hadde,
And there-with he his shuldres overspradde;
But thinne it lay, by colpons oon and oon;
But hood, for jolitee, ne wered he noon,   680
For it was trussed up in his walet.
Him thoughte, he rood al of the newe jet;
Dischevele, save his cappe, he rood al bare.
Swiche glaringe eyen hadde he as an hare.
A vernicle hadde he sowed on his cappe.   685
His walet lay biforn him in his lappe,
Bret-ful of pardoun come from Rome al hoot.
A voys he hadde as smal as hath a goot.
No berd hadde he, ne never sholde have.
As smothe it was as it were late y-shave;   690
I trowe he were a gelding or a mare.
But of his craft, fro Berwik into Ware,
Ne was ther swich another pardoner.
For in his male he hadde a pilwe-beer,
Which that, he seyde, was our lady veyl: 695
He seyde, he hadde a gobet of the seyl
That seynt Peter hadde, whan that he wente
Up-on the see, til Jesu Crist him hente.
He hadde a croys of latoun, ful of stones,
And in a glas he hadde pigges bones.   700
But with thise relikes, whan that he fond
A povre person dwelling up-on lond,
Up-on a day he gat him more moneye
Than that the person gat in monthes tweye.
And thus with feyned flaterye and japes,   705
He made the person and the peple his apes.
But trewely to tellen, atte laste,
He was in chirche a noble ecclesiaste.
Wel coude he rede a lessoun or a storie,
But alderbest he song an offertorie;   710
For wel he wiste, whan that song was songe,

He moste preche, and wel affyle his tonge,
To winne silver, as he ful wel coude;
Therefore he song so meriely and loude.
    Now have I told you shortly, in a clause,   715
Th'estat, th'array, the nombre, and eek the cause
Why that assembled was this companye
In Southwerk, at this gentil hostelrye,
That highte the Tabard, faste by the Belle.
But now is tyme to yow for to telle   720
How that we baren us that ilke night,
Whan we were in that hostelrye alight.
And after wol I telle of our viage,
And al the remenaunt of our pilgrimage.
But first I pray yow, of your curteisye,   725
That ye n'arette it nat my vileinye,
Though that I pleynly speke in this matere,
To telle yow hir wordes and hir chere;
Ne thogh I speke hir wordes proprely.
For this ye knowen al-so wel as I,   730
Who-so shal telle a tale after a man,
He moot reherce, as ny as ever he can,
Everich a word, if it be in his charge,
Al speke he never so rudeliche and large;
Or elles he moot telle his tale untrewe,   735
Or feyne thing, or finde wordes newe.
He may nat spare, al-though he were his brother;
He moot as wel seye o word as another.
Crist spak him-self ful brode in holy writ,
And wel ye woot, no vileinye is it.   740
Eek Plato seith, who-so that can him rede,
The wordes mote be cosin to the dede.
Also I prey yow to foryeve it me,
Al have I nat set folk in hir degree
Here in this tale, as that they sholde stonde;   745
My wit is short, ye may wel understonde.
    Greet chere made our hoste us everichon,
And to the soper sette he us anon;
And served us with vitaille at the beste.

672. "Com . . . to me," probably the first line of a current popular song.   673. stif burdoun, a stout "burden," or basic ground-melody (bass).   676. strike, a bunch (of flax).   677. ounces, small tufts or bunches.   679. colpons, shreds, strips.   681. trussed up, packed up, stuffed.   682. al of the newe jet, all in the new manner or style. 685. vernicle, a little "veronica," a copy of the handkerchief which tradition says St. Veronica lent to Christ during the march to Calvary, and which was said to bear the imprint of His face.   687. Bret-ful, brimful.   692. Berwik into Ware. Berwik is undoubtedly Berwick, at the mouth of the River Tweed in Northumberland, the town at the northeastern extremity of England. Ware is in Hertfordshire and is hardly the southernmost town of importance in England. Chaucer merely wishes to say that there was not another Pardoner like him in all England.   694. male, bag. pilwe-beer, pillow-case. 696. gobet, piece, fragment.   698. hente, caught. The episode referred to is to be found in Matthew, 14: 22–33.   699. croys of latoun, a cross of latten, an alloy of copper and zinc.   702–704. person, parson. This is a direct reference to the friction that arose between parish priests and mendicant friars and pardoners; see note to l. 220.   705. japes, japes, jests, jokes.   707. atte laste, at the last, finally; see *atte beste* (l. 29) and *atte fulle* (l. 651).   710. alderbest, best of all; for *alder-* (*aller-*) see note to l. 586.

712. affyle, file, smooth off and sharpen.   719. the Tabard . . . the Belle. For *the Tabard* and its general location in Southwark, see note to l. 20; *the Belle* has not been identified certainly, although several inns by that name have been located in Southwark—none, however, authentically dated before 1600.   726. n'arette, etc., do not impute or ascribe. Chaucer's disclaimer of responsibility here is extremely interesting, since he is deliberately telling the reader or listener of his intention to be as realistic as a true reporter should be.   734. Al, although. The inverted word order in a clause introduced by a concessive conjunction (*Al speke he* instead of *Al he speke*) is characteristic of Chaucer's syntax.   735. moot, must.   741. Plato. The great Greek philosopher (p. 1:258) and his works were probably known to Chaucer not through the original work, but through Latin derivatives, such as Boethius' *Consolation of Philosophy*.   747. our hoste. The Host, whose description begins with this line, is certainly one of the most important figures in the Canterbury pilgrimage, although he appears only in the framework of *The Canterbury Tales*. He serves as interlocutor and as master of ceremonies, and his reactions to the different stories seem to have been intended by Chaucer as the reactions of a typical English fourteenth-century middle-class *burgeys*. His identity with Henry or Harry Bailly, an actual innkeeper of Southwark, who appears in historical documents, has been reasonably well established. Undoubtedly he is the most "historical" member of the pilgrimage except Chaucer himself. everichon, every one.

Strong was the wyn, and wel to drinke us leste. 750
A semely man our hoste was with-alle
For to han been a marshal in an halle;
A large man he was with eyen stepe,
A fairer burgeys was ther noon in Chepe:
Bold of his speche, and wys, and wel y-taught, 755
And of manhood him lakkede right naught.
Eek thereto he was right a mery man,
And after soper pleyen he bigan,
And spak of mirthe amonges othere thinges,
Whan that we hadde maad our rekeninges; 760
And seyde thus: "Now, lordinges, trewely,
Ye ben to me right welcome hertely:
For by my trouthe, if that I shal nat lye,
I ne saugh this yeer so mery a companye
At ones in this herberwe as is now. 765
Fayn wolde I doon yow mirthe, wiste I how.
And of a mirthe I am right now bithoght,
To doon yow ese, and it shal coste noght.

"Ye goon to Caunterbury; God yow spede,
The blisful martir quyte yow your mede. 770
And wel I woot, as ye goon by the weye,
Ye shapen yow to talen and to pleye;
For trewely, confort ne mirthe is noon
To ryde by the weye doumb as a stoon;
And therfore wol I maken yow disport, 775
As I seyde erst, and doon yow som confort.
And if yow lyketh alle, by oon assent,
Now for to stonden at my jugement,
And for to werken as I shal yow seye,
To-morwe, whan ye ryden by the weye, 780
Now, by my fader soule, that is deed,
But ye be merye, I wol yeve yow myn heed.
Hold up your hond, withouten more speche."

Our counseil was nat longe for to seche;
Us thoughte it was noght worth to make it wys, 785
And graunted him withouten more avys,
And bad him seye his verdit, as him leste.
"Lordinges," quod he, "now herkneth for the
            beste;
But tak it not, I prey yow, in desdeyn;
This is the poynt, to speken short and pleyn, 790
That ech of yow, to shorte with your weye,
In this viage, shal telle tales tweye,
To Caunterbury-ward, I mene it so,
And hom-ward he shal tellen othere two,

Of aventures that whylom han bifalle. 795
And which of yow that bereth him best of alle,
That is to seyn, that telleth in this cas
Tales of best sentence and most solas,
Shal have a soper at our aller cost
Here in this place, sitting by this post, 800
Whan that we come agayn fro Caunterbury.
And for to make yow the more mery,
I wol my-selven gladly with yow ryde,
Right at myn owne cost, and be your gyde.
And who-so wol my jugement withseye 805
Shal paye al that we spenden by the weye.
And if ye vouche-sauf that it be so,
Tel me anon, with-outen wordes mo,
And I wol erly shape me therfore."

This thing was graunted, and our othes swore
With ful glad herte, and preyden him also 811
That he wold vouche-sauf for to do so,
And that he wolde been our governour,
And of our tales juge and reportour,
And sette a soper at a certeyn prys; 815
And we wold reuled been at his devys,
In heigh and lowe; and thus, by oon assent,
We been acorded to his jugement
And ther-up-on the wyn was fet anoon;
We dronken, and to reste wente echon, 820
With-outen any lenger taryinge.

A-morwe, whan that day bigan to springe,
Up roos our host, and was our aller cok,
And gadrede us togidre, alle in a flok,
And forth we riden, a litel more than pas, 825
Un-to the watering of seint Thomas.
And there our host bigan his hors areste,
And seyde; "Lordinges, herkneth if yow leste.
Ye woot your forward, and I it yow recorde.
If even-song and morwe-song acorde, 830
Lat se now who shal telle the firste tale.
As ever mote I drinke wyn or ale,
Who-so be rebel to my jugement
Shal paye for al that by the weye is spent.
Now draweth cut, er that we ferrer twinne, 835
He which that hath the shortest shal beginne.
Sire knight," quod he, "my maister and my lord,
Now draweth cut, for that is myn acord.
Cometh neer," quod he, "my lady prioresse;
And ye, sir clerk, lat be your shamfastnesse, 840
Ne studieth noght; ley hond to, every man."
    Anon to drawen every wight bigan,

750. **us leste,** it pleased us. 752. **marshal in an halle;** that is, the Host was imposing enough in personality to have been a marshal in any assembly of people. 754. **Chepe,** Cheapside, one of the principal London streets of the time. 758. **pleyen,** a very vague word, not as definite even as our modern *play.* Here the meaning is simply "waxed merry," "disported himself," "joked," etc. 765. **At ones,** at one time. **herberwe,** inn. 770. **quyte,** requite, reward. **mede,** meed, reward. 772. **shapen,** plan. **talen,** talk and tell stories. 776. **erst,** first, before. 781. **fader soule.** *Fader* (father) is often undeclined in Middle English. 785. **make it wys,** to play the wise man, to deliberate. 786. **avys,** consideration, argument. 787. **verdit,** verdict, decision. **him leste,** he wished. 789. **in desdeyn,** in contempt. 794. **tellen othere two.** This would call for four stories from each pilgrim. Chaucer never completed this design.

795. **whylom,** formerly. 798. **solas,** amusement, entertainment. 799. **our aller cost,** at the expense of us all. (On *aller* or *alder,* see note to l. 586.) 805. **withseye,** deny, gainsay. 813. **governour,** guide and leader. 814. **reportour,** commentator or referee. 816. **at his devys,** at his discretion. 817. **heigh and lowe,** in high and low, in every respect. 819. **fet,** fetched. 823. **our aller cok,** cock for all of us, our reveille. 825. **more than pas,** at a trot. 826. **watering of seint Thomas,** a brook at the second milestone out of London on the old Kent road. 829. **forward,** agreement. 835. **ferrer twinne,** get farther away (from London). 840. **shamfastnesse,** not our shamefacedness, but rather shyness, bashfulness, overmodesty.

And shortly for to tellen, as it was,
Were it by aventure, or sort, or cas,
The sothe is this, the cut fil to the knight,   845
Of which ful blythe and glad was every wight;
And telle he moste his tale, as was resoun,
By forward and by composicioun,
As ye han herd; what nedeth wordes mo?
And whan this gode man saugh it was so,   850
As he that wys was and obedient
To kepe his forward by his free assent,
He seyde: "Sin I shal beginne the game,
What, welcome be the cut, a Goddes name!
Now lat us ryde, and herkneth what I seye."   855
  And with that word we riden forth our weye;
And he bigan with right a mery chere
His tale anon, and seyde in this manere.

THE REEVE'S TALE

The medieval *fabliau*, the nature of which has already
been outlined, appears in more than one form. But it is
clear that the handling of this type of fiction must be
either strictly popular or strictly literary, in the academic
sense of the word. It is not easy to find written records
of this, the secular tale of masculine amusement, for the
medieval Church would not look with lenity upon the
mundane stories of husbands deceived, mere practical
jokes, or blasphemous *divertissements*. A few collections
of such narrative material have come down to us, chiefly
through the French. Nevertheless, the student will be
better informed and edified by an artistic treatment of
the *fabliau* as it is told by Geoffrey Chaucer than by its
more popular and vulgar representatives. *The Reeve's
Tale* illustrates all the characteristics of the *fabliau*—the
theme of the biter bit, the sex motif, the horseplay, the
rough realism and humor of the age.

The Knight, as we will see, is the first of the Canterbury pilgrims to tell a tale; his choice is a long and
eminently correct romance. Although the pilgrims as a
group applaud his effort, the Miller, who is drunk, inter-
rupts to tell a tale of scabrous adventure involving a
carpenter, his young wife, a star boarder in their house,
and a lecherous clerk of the local parish. Since the
carpenter husband is the butt of this brilliant *fabliau*,
Chaucer's Reeve, who was once a carpenter (see 1. 614
of the *Prologue* to *The Canterbury Tales*), takes issue
with the Miller, and in retaliation tells the following
tale, almost as brilliant as that of the Miller. Especially
noteworthy in *The Reeve's Tale* is the use of the northern
Middle English dialect for the purposes of local color—

the first good example of this in English literature, for
the two young students at Cambridge come from the
north of England. The situations arising in this tale are
altogether typical of the *fabliau*.

THE REEVE'S TALE

AT TROMPINGTON, not fer fro Cantebrigge,
    Ther goth a brook, and over that a brigge,
Upon the whiche brook there stent a melle:
And this is veray sothe, that I you telle.
A miller was ther dwelling many a day,   5
As any peacok he was proude and gay:
Pipen he coude, and fishe, and nettes bete,
And turnen cuppes, and wrastlen wel, and shete.
Ay by his belt he bare a long panade,
And of a swerd ful trenchant was the blade.   10
A joly popper bare he in his pouche;
Ther nas no man for peril dorst him touche.
A Shefeld thwitel bare he in his hose.
Round was his face, and camuse was his nose.
As piled as an ape was his skull.   15
He was a market-beter at the full.
Ther dorste no wight hond upon him legge,
That he ne swore he shuld anon abegge.
  A thefe he was forsooth, of corn and mele,
And that a slye, and usant for to stele.   20
His name was hoten deinous Simekin.
A wif he hadde, comen of noble kin:
The persoun of the toun hire fader was.
With hire he yaf ful many a panne of bras,
For that Simkin shuld in his blood allye.   25
She was yfostered in a nonnerie:
For Simkin wolde no wif, as he sayde,
But she were wel ynourished, and a mayde,
To saven his estat of yemanrie:
And she was proud, and pert as is a pie.   30
A ful faire fight was it upon hem two.
On holy dayes beforne hire wolde he go
With his tipet ybounde about his hed;
And she came after in a gite of red,
And Simkin hadde hosen of the same.   35
Ther dorste no wight clepen hire but dame:

3. **stent,** stands. 7. **bete,** mend, repair. 8. **turnen cuppes,** make
wooden cups in a lathe. 9. **panade,** cutlass. Note that the miller,
for a supposedly orderly citizen, was armed to the teeth. 11. **popper,**
a short dagger, probably the same as the bodkin (bodekin) of l. 40.
13. **Shefeld thwitel,** a whittling-knife from Sheffield, then, as now,
noted for its cutlery. 14. **camuse,** pug-nosed; his daughter had
the same characteristic (l. 54). 15. **piled,** here "bald" rather than
"moth-eaten." 16. **market-beter,** one who frequents markets and
fairs, generally to no good purpose. 17. **legge,** lay. 18. **abegge,**
pay for it. 19. **corn,** the customary English meaning of grain in
general. 20. **usant,** accustomed to, in the habit of. 21. **hoten,**
called. **deinous,** haughty and spiteful. It is something of a fixed
epithet like *hende* for Nicholas in *The Miller's Tale*, a regular nick-
name, which in many instances produced family surnames in later
years. 23. **persoun,** parish priest. 29. **estat of yemanrie,** status of a
free yeoman; the snobbishness of Simkin and his wife is a particular
motive for bringing them low. 30. **pie,** magpie. 34. **gite,** dress,
robe (?).

844. **aventure . . . cas.** There is no clear distinction here in the use
of these three nouns, although they originally had separate meanings.
All seem to be synonymous with *luck* or *chance*. 845. **cut . . .
knight.** The Knight, as a representative of chivalric society, is treated
by Chaucer with the greatest respect. In the mind of its author,
The Knight's Tale was the obvious choice to begin the collection of
stories. 848. **By forward . . . composicioun,** according to the agreement and the arrangement. 850. **saugh,** saw. 854. **What,** an old
interjection, approximately the equivalent of our *Lo!* or *Well!* **a
Goddes name!** in God's name! The weakened form of *on* (*in*) appears
as *a*.

Was non so hardy, that went by the way,
That with hire dorste rage or ones play,
But if he wold be slain of Simekin
With panade, or with knif, or bodekin.   40
(For jalous folk ben perilous evermo:
Algate they wold hir wives wenden so).
And eke for she was somdel smoterlich,
She was as digne as water in a dich,
And also ful of hoker and of bismare.   45
Hire thoughte that a ladie shuld hire spare,
What for hire kinrede, and hire nortelrie,
That she had lerned in the nonnerie.

A doughter hadden they betwix hem two
Of twenty yere, withouten any mo,   50
Saving a child that was of half yere age;
In cradle it lay, and was a propre page.
This wenche thikke and wel ygrowen was,
With camuse nose, and eyen grey as glas;
With buttokes brode, and brestes round and hie;   55
But right faire was hire here, I wol nat lie.

The person of the toun, for she was faire,
In purpos was to maken hire his haire
Both of his catel, and of his mesuage,
And strange he made it of hire mariage.   60
His purpos was for to bestowe hire hie
Into som worthy blood of ancestrie.
For holy chirches good mote ben despended
On holy chirches blood that is descended.
Therfore he wolde his holy blood honoure,   65
Though that he holy chirche shuld devoure.

Gret soken hath this miller, out of doute,
With whete and malt, of all the land aboute;
And namely ther was a gret college
Men clepe the Soler Hall at Cantebregge,   70
Ther was hir whete and eke hir malt yground.
And on a day it happed in a stound,
Sike lay the manciple on a maladie,
Men wenden wisly that he shulde die.
For which this miller stale both mele and corn   75
An hundred times more than beforn.
For ther beforn he stale but curteisly,
But now he was a thefe outrageously.
For which the wardein chidde and made fare,
But therof set the miller not a tare;   80
He craked bost, and swore it nas not so.

Than were ther yonge poure scoleres two,
That dwelten in the halle of which I say;
Testif they were, and lusty for to play;
And only for hir mirth and revelrie   85
Upon the wardein besily they crie,
To yeve hem leve but a litel stound
To gon to mille, and seen hir corn yground:
And hardily they dorsten lay hir nekke,
The miller shuld not stele hem half a pekke   90
Of corn by sleighte, ne by force hem reve.

And at the last the wardein yave hem leve.
John highte that oon, and Alein highte that other,
Of o toun were they born, that highte Strother,
Fer in the North, I can not tellen where.   95

This Alein maketh redy all his gere,
And on a hors the sak he cast anon:
Forth goth Alein the clerk, and also John,
With good swerd and with bokeler by hir side.
John knew the way, him neded not no guide,   100
And at the mille the sak adoun he laith.

Alein spake first: "All haile, Simond, in faith,
How fares thy faire doughter, and thy wif?"

"Alein, welcome," quod Simkin, "by my lif,
And John also: how now, what do ye here?"   105

"By God, Simond," quod John, "nede has na pere.
Him behoves serve himself that has na swain,
Or elles he is a fool, as clerkes sain.
Our manciple, I hope he wol be ded,
Swa werkes ay the wanges in his hed;   110
And therfore is I come, and eke Alein,
To grind our corn and cary it hame agein;
I pray you, spede us hethen that ye may."

"It shal be don," quod Simkin, "by my fay.
What wol ye don while that it is in hand?"   115

"By God, right by the hopper wol I stand,"
Quod John, "and seen how that the corn gas in.
Yet saw I never by my fader kin,
How that the hopper wagges til and fra."

Alein answered: "John, and wolt thou swa?   120
Than wol I be benethe, by my croun,
And see how that the mele falles adoun
In til the trogh, that shal be my disport:
For, John, in faith I may ben of your sort;
I is as ill a miller as ar ye."   125

This miller smiled at hir nicetee,
And thought, "All this nis don but for a wile.
They wenen that no man may hem bigile,
But by my thrift, yet shal I blere hir eie,
For all the sleighte in hir philosophie.   130

---

38. **rage,** make over her amorously. 42. **wenden,** thought, supposed. 43. **smoterlich,** besmirched in reputation because of her illegitimacy (l. 23). 44. **digne . . . dich,** as worthy as ditch water. 45. **hoker,** scorn, snobbishness. **bismare,** shrewishness, abusiveness. 46. **spare,** overlook (her illegitimacy). 52. **page,** little boy. 59. **mesuage,** or *mansuage,* dwelling; see the modern *manse.* 60. **strange . . . mariage,** made difficulties about marrying the girl. 63. **mote,** must. 67. **soken,** toll, receipts. 69. **namely,** particularly, specifically. 70. **the Soler Hall,** King's Hall at Cambridge, founded by Edward III in 1337, and later merged with Trinity College, Cambridge; the early name was apparently derived from a solarium in the building. 72. **stound,** occasion, hour. 73. **manciple,** the purchasing agent of the college. 79. **wardein,** the warden or head of the institution. **made fare,** made some trouble (unsuccessfully). 81. **craked bost,** boasted loudly and with coarse wit.

84. **Testif,** headstrong, impulsive. 89. **lay,** wager, bet. 94. **Strother.** There is no longer a town by this name in England, but the name belongs to an old family of Northumberland. In any event, it is to be assumed that the two young men are both from the north of England, for Chaucer puts into their mouths an unmistakable northern dialect. Incidentally, this is the first effective use of dialect in English literature for the purpose of portraying local color. 106. **nede has na pere,** necessity has no equal. 109. **hope,** expect. 110. **werkes ay the wanges,** his molars ache so. 113. **hethen,** hence. 123. **disport,** recreation or diversion. 129. **blere hir eie,** cheat them.

The more queinte krakkes that they make,
The more wol I stele whan that I take.
In stede of flour yet wol I yeve hem bren.
The gretest clerkes ben not the wisest men,
As whilom to the wolf thus spake the mare;   135
Of all hir art ne count I not a tare."

Out at the dore he goth ful prively,
Whan that he saw his time softely.
He loketh up and doun, til he hath found
The clerkes hors, ther as he stood ybound   140
Behind the mille, under a levesell;
And to the hors he goth him faire and well,
And stripeth of the bridel right anon.
And whan the hors was lous, he gan to gon
Toward the fen, ther wilde mares renne,   145
And forth, with "wehee," thurgh thick and thinne.
This miller goth again, no word he said,
But doth his note, and with these clerkes plaid,
Till that hir corn was faire and wel yground.
And whan the mele is sacked and ybound,   150
This John goth out, and fint his hors away,
And gan to crie, "Harow and Wala wa!
Our hors is lost; Alein, for Goddes banes,
Step on thy feet; come of, man, al at anes!
Alas! our wardein has his palfrey lorn!"   155

This Alein al forgat both mele and corn;
Al was out of his mind his husbandrie:
"What! whilke way is he gon?" he gan to crie.

The wif came leping inward at a renne;
She sayd: "Alas! youre hors goth to the fenne   160
With wilde mares, as fast as he may go.
Unthank come on his hand that bond him so,
And he that better shuld have knit the rein."

"Alas!" quod John, "Alein, for Cristes pein,
Lay doun thy swerd, and I shal min alswa.   165
I is ful wight, God wat, as is a ra.
By Goddes saule, he shal not scape us bathe.
Why ne had thou put the capel in the lathe?
Ill haile, Alein, by God! thou is a fonne!"

These sely clerkes han ful fast yronne   170
Toward the fen, bothe Alein and eke John;
And whan the miller saw that they were gon,
He half a bushel of hir flour hath take,
And bad his wif go knede it in a cake.
He sayd: "I trow, the clerkes were aferde.   175
Yet can a miller make a clerkes berde,

For all his art. Ye, let hem gon hir wey.
Lo! wher they gon! Ye, let the children play;
They get him not so lightly, by my croun!"

These sely clerkes rennen up and doun   180
With "Kepe, kepe! stand, stand! jossa! warderere!
Ga whistle thou, and I shal kepe him here."
But shortly, til that it was veray night,
They coude not, though they did all hir might,
Hir capel catch; he ran alway so fast: 185
Til in a diche they caught him at the last.

Wery and wet, as bestes in the rain,
Cometh sely John, and with him cometh Alein.
"Alas!" quod John, "the day that I was borne!
Now are we driven til hething and til scorne.   190
Our corn is stolne, men wol us fonnes calle,
Both the wardein, and eke our felawes alle,
And namely the miller, wala wa!"

Thus plaineth John, as he goth by the way
Toward the mille, and Bayard in his hond.   195
The miller sitting by the fire he fond,
For it was night, and forther might they nought,
But for the love of God they him besought
Of herberwe and of ese, as for hir peny.

The miller saide agen, "If ther be any,   200
Swiche as it is, yet shull ye have your part.
Myn hous is streit, but ye have lerned art;
Ye can by arguments maken a place
A mile brode, of twenty foot of space.
Lat see now if this place may suffice,   205
Or make it roume with speche, as if your gise."
"Now, Simond," said this John, "by Seint Cuthberd,
Ay is thou mery, and that is faire answerd.
I have herd say, man sal take of twa thinges,
Slike as he findes, or slike as he bringes.   210
But specially I pray thee, hoste dere,
Gar us have mete and drinke, and make us chere,
And we sal paien trewely at the full;
With empty hand, men may na haukes tull.
Lo! here our silver, redy for to spend."   215

This miller to the toun his doughter send
For ale and bred, and rosted hem a goos,
And bond hir hors, he shuld no more go loos:
And in his owen chambre hem made a bedde,
With shetes and with chalons faire yspredde,   220
Nat from his owen bed ten foot or twelve:
His doughter had a bed all by hire selve,
Right in the same chambre by and by:
It mighte be no bet, and cause why?

131. **queinte krakkes**, subtly arrogant remarks. 133. **bren**, bran. 135. **wolf . . . mare.** In the old beast fables of the Middle Ages, the Wolf once wished to buy the Mare's foal, and was told by her that the price was written on her hind foot, and that if he had learning enough, he could come and read it. When the unwary Wolf went to look, he received a kick that knocked him out completely. The Fox, who, as usual, had brought about this disaster to the Wolf, hypocritically remarked that clerks are not always the wisest men. 141. **levesell**, an arbor formed of branches or foliage. 144. **lous**, loose. 148. **note**, job. 154. **at anes**, at once, in a hurry. 159. **renne**, run. 162. **Unthank . . . hand**, "Bad luck come to his hand who, etc." 166. **I . . . ra**, "I am as fast, God knows, as a roe." 167. **bathe**, both. 168. **capel**, a sturdy horse. **lathe**, barn. 169. **fonne**, fool. 176. **make . . . berde**, cheat, make a fool of.

181. **jossa!** from an Old French cry of direction, "Down here!" **warderere**, "Look out for the rear!" 190. **hething**, scorn, contempt. 193. **namely**, particularly, especially. 199. **herberwe**, lodging. 202. **streit**, narrow and small. 206. **roume**, roomy, spacious. **gise**, manner, practice. 207. **Cuthberd**, St. Cuthbert, Bishop of Lindisfarne in Northumbria, who died in 686. It is appropriate that John, as a man from that part of England, should swear by a Northumbrian saint. 209–210. **man sal take . . . he bringes**, "A man must take one of two things—what he finds or what he brings." In other words, a man must put up with what he can get. 214. **tull**, lure, entice. 220. **chalons**, blankets.

Ther was no roumer herberwe in the place. 225
They soupen, and they speken of solace,
And drinken ever strong ale at the best.
Abouten midnight wente they to rest.
    Wel hath this miller vernished his hed,
Ful pale he was, for dronken, and nought red. 230
He yexeth, and he speketh thurgh the nose,
As he were on the quakke, or on the pose.
To bed he goth, and with him goth his wif;
As any jay she light was and jolif,
So was hire joly whistle wel ywette. 235
The cradel at hire beddes feet was sette,
To rokken, and to yeve the child to souke.
And whan that dronken was all in the crouke,
To bedde went the doughter right anon,
To bedde goth Alein, and also John. 240
Ther nas no more; it nedeth hem no dwale.
This miller hath so wisly bibbed ale,
That as an hors he snorteth in his slepe,
Ne of his tail behind he toke no kepe.
His wif bare him a burdon, a ful strong; 245
Men might hir routing heren a furlong.
The wenche routeth eke *par compagnie*.
    Alein the clerk, that herd this melodie,
He poketh John, and sayde: "Slepest thou?
Herdest thou ever slike a sang er now? 250
Lo! whilke a complin is ymell hem alle.
A wilde fire upon hir bodies falle!
Wha herkned ever slike a ferly thing?
Ye, they sall have the flour of yvel ending.
This lange night ther tides me no reste. 255
But yet na fors; all sal be for the beste.
For John," sayd he, "as ever mote I thrive,
If that I may, yon wenche wol I swive.
Som esement has lawe yshapen us.
For John, ther is a lawe that saieth thus, 260
That if a man in o point be agreved,
That in another he sal be releved.
Our corn is stolen, sothly it is na nay,
And we han had an yvel fit today.
And sin I sal have nan amendement 265
Again my losse, I wol have an esement;
By Goddes saule, it sal nan other be!"
    This John answered: "Alein, avise thee!
The miller is a perilous man," he sayde.
"And if that he out of his slepe abrayde, 270
He mighte don us bathe a vilanie."
Alein answered: "I count him nat a flye!"
And up he rist, and by the wenche he crepte.

This wenche lay upright, and faste slepte,
Til he so nigh was, or she might espie, 275
That it had ben to late for to crie.
And, shortly for to say, they were at on.
Now play, Alein, for I wol speke of John.
    This John lith still a furlong way or two,
And to himself he maketh routh and wo: 280
"Alas!" quod he, "this is a wikked jape;
Now may I say that I is but an ape.
Yet has my felaw somwhat for his harme;
He has the millers doughter in his arme;
He auntred him, and hath his nedes spedde, 285
And I lie as a draf-sak in my bedde;
And whan this jape is told another day,
I sal be halden a daffe or a cokenay;
I wol arise, and auntre it, by my fay;
Unhardy is unsely, thus men say." 290
    And up he rose, and softely he wente
Unto the cradel, and in his hand it hente,
And bare it soft unto his beddes fete.
Sone after this the wif hir routing lete,
And gan awake, and went hire out to pisse, 295
And came again, and gan the cradel misse,
And groped here and ther, but she fond non.
"Alas!" quod she, "I had almost misgon.
I had almost gon to the clerkes bedde.
Ey! *benedicite!* than had I foule yspedde." 300
And forth she goth, til she the cradel fond.
She gropeth alway forther with hire hond,
And fond the bed, and thoughte nat but good,
Because that the cradel by it stood,
And niste wher she was, for it was derk, 305
But faire and wel she crepte in by the clerk,
And lith ful still, and wold han caught a slepe.
Within a while this John the clerk up lepe,
And on this goode wif he layeth on sore;
So mery a fit ne had she nat ful yore. 310
He priketh hard and depe, as he were mad.
    This joly life han these two clerkes lad,
Til that the thridde cok began to sing.
Alein wex werie in the morwening,
For he had swonken all the longe night, 315
And sayd: "Farewel, Malkin, my swete wight.

229. **vernished his hed,** "varnished his head," become drunk. 231. **yexeth,** hiccoughs. 232. **quakke,** asthma. **on the pose,** suffering from a head cold. 235. **whistle wel ywette,** well drunk. The expression "to wet one's whistle" is still found in Modern English. 238. **crouke,** crock, jug, pitcher. 241. **dwale,** sedative, sleeping-potion. 245. **burdon,** refrain. 246. **routing,** snoring. 247. *par compagnie,* in concert. 250. **slike,** such (northern form). 252. **wilde fire,** the vicious skin disease known as erysipelas. 253. **ferly,** weird and fearsome. 255. **tides,** betides, happens to. 256. **na fors,** no matter. 258. **swive,** have intercourse with. 270. **abrayde,** started up.

274. **upright,** straight on her back. 277. **at on,** agreed. 279. **a furlong way or two,** the time it would take one to go a furlong, or an eighth of a mile. 285. **auntred,** ventured, risked. 286. **draf-sak,** a sack full of draff or chaff. 288. **daffe,** fool. **cokenay.** There was an old folk belief that all imperfect eggs were laid by the cock rather than by the hen. Hence a *cokenay* or "cock's egg," is the equivalent of a half-formed creature, an effeminate weakling. In addition, it carries the idea of freakishness. The term, as the slang term for the inhabitants of a certain part of London, *cockney,* is of modern development; see the *New English Dictionary.* 290. **Unhardy is unsely;** that is, the coward has no luck; nothing ventured, nothing gained. 294. **lete,** stopped, ceased. 300. *benedicite!* This mild oath, "Bless us!" is usually pronounced in three syllables, as if spelled *bencite.* 310. **nat ful yore,** not for a long time past. 313. **thridde cok.** In British folklore, the first cockcrow comes shortly after midnight, the second about three in the morning, and the third between five and six A.M.

The day is come, I may no longer bide,
But evermo, wherso I go or ride,
I is thin awen clerk, so have I hele."
"Now, dere lemman," quod she, "go, farewele;   320
But or thou go, o thing I wol thee telle.
Whan that thou wendest homeward by the melle,
Right at the entree of the dore behinde
Thou shalt a cake of half a bushel finde,
That was ymaked of thin owen mele,   325
Which that I halpe my fader for to stele.
And, good lemman, God thee save and kepe."
And with that word she gan almost to wepe.
      Alein uprist and thought, "Er that it dawe
I wol go crepen in by my felawe";   330
And fond the cradel at his hand anon.
"By God," thought he, "all wrang I have misgon;
My hed is tottie of my swink tonight,
That maketh me that I go nat aright.
I wot wel by the cradel I have misgo;   335
Here lith the miller and his wif also."
And forth he goth, a twenty divel way
Unto the bed, ther as the miller lay.
He wend have cropen by his felaw John,
And by the miller in he crept anon,   340
And caught him by the nekke, and gan him shake,
And sayd: "Thou John, thou swinesshed, awake!
For Cristes saule, and here a noble game,
For, by that lord that called is Seint Jame,
As I have thries as in this shorte night   345
Swived the millers doughter bolt upright,
While thou hast as a coward ben agast."
      "Ye, false harlot," quod the miller, "hast?
A, false traitour, false clerk," quod he,
"Thou shalt be ded, by Goddes dignitee,   350
Who dorste be so bold to disparage
My doughter, that is come of swiche linage."
And by the throte-bolle he caught Alein,
And he him hent despitously again,
And on the nose he smote him with his fist;   355
Doun ran the blody streme upon his brest;
And in the flore, with nose and mouth tobroke,
They walwe, as done two pigges in a poke.
And up they gon, and doun again anon,
Til that the miller sporned at a ston,   360
And doun he fell backward upon his wif,
That wiste nothing of this nice strif;
For she was fall aslepe a litel wight
With John the clerk, that waked had all night;
And with the fall out of hire slepe she brayde.   365
"Helpe, holy crois of Bromeholme!" she sayde,

"*In manus tuas*, Lord, to thee I calle.
Awake, Simond, the fend is on me falle;
Myn herte is broken; helpe! I nam but ded!
Ther lith on up my wombe and up myn hed.   370
Helpe, Simkin, for the false clerkes fighte!"
This John sterte up as fast as ever he might,
And graspeth by the walles to and fro
To find a staf, and she sterte up also,
And knew the estres bet than did this John,   375
And by the wall she toke a staf anon;
And saw a litel shemering of a light,
For at an hole in shone the mone bright,
And by that light she saw hem bothe two,
But sikerly she niste who was who,   380
But as she saw a white thing in hire eye.
And whan she gan this white thing espie,
She wend the clerk had wered a volupere;
And with the staf she drow ay nere and nere,
And wend han hit this Alein atte fulle,   385
And smote the miller on the piled skulle,
That doun he goth, and cried, "Harrow! I die!"
Thise clerkes bete him wel, and let him lie,
And greithen hem, and take hir hors anon,
And eke hir mele, and on hir way they gon;   390
And at the mille dore eke they toke hir cake
Of half a bushel flour, ful wel ybake.
      Thus is the proude miller wel ybete,
And hath ylost the grinding of the whete,
And payed for the souper every del   395
Of Alein and of John, that bete him wel;
His wif is swived, and his doughter als;
Lo! swiche it is a miller to be fals.
And therfore this proverbe is sayd ful soth:
Him thar not winnen wel that evil doth;   400
A gilour shal himself begiled be;
And God that siteth hie in magestee
Save all this compagnie, grete and smale.
Thus have I quit the miller in my tale.

THE FRANKLIN'S TALE

The Franklin's Tale is generally accepted as the concluding tale in the so-called Marriage Group of *The Canterbury Tales;* this is an old designation for a handful
of stories which are designed to illustrate divergent
points of view about the problem of who should rule
in the married state. Perhaps Chaucer had no such group
actually in mind, and the Marriage Group may be, as
some scholars would have it, a myth; but if so, it is a
convenient myth, because it seems obvious enough that

320. **lemman,** sweetheart, beloved. 322. **melle,** mill. 333. **tottie,**
dizzy, muddled. 337. **twenty divel way,** with extremely bad luck.
342. **swinesshed,** pig's head. 346. **bolt upright;** see note to l. 274.
bolt; that is, "like a bolt," calls attention to the extreme rectilinear
quality of the girl's position. 352. **come . . . linage;** that is, descended from the parish priest. 353. **throte-bolle,** Adam's apple.
360. **sporned,** kicked, stumbled. 366. **Bromeholme,** a celebrated
shrine in Norfolk, alleged to have housed a piece of the Cross of
Christ.

367. *In manus tuas,* "into Thy hands (I commend my spirit)," a
formula to be recited by all those who stand in the imminence of
death. 370. **wombe,** belly. 375. **estres,** interior. 383. **volupere,**
night-cap. 384. **nere and nere,** nearer and nearer. 389. **greithen,**
dressed themselves and prepared to return. 400. **thar,** need. The
meaning of the proverb is, "He need not expect good who does evil."
401. **gilour,** beguiler, deceiver. The idea of a deceiver deceived is one
of the cardinal points in the medieval *fabliau.* 404. **quit,** repaid with
satisfaction.

there *are* different stories in the collection which serve as *exempla*—if the term is admissible in this case—of different attitudes toward marriage.

Assuming the reality of the Marriage Group as a talking point, we note that the Wife of Bath begins the forum (in the long, extremely brilliant and satirical *Prologue* to *The Wife of Bath's Tale*) by expressing her violent prejudices in favor of a wife's complete supremacy over the husband. The Clerk implies, at least, the directly opposite position, and his tale of Griselda converts the wife into a figurative door mat for a domineering husband. The Merchant is sour and disillusioned on the whole subject of matrimony, and the Squire is wildly romantic. But the Franklin wishes at least to present the tempered outlook that marriage is successful only when it rests upon mutual respect and when the partners are both persons of "gentilesse" who are true to their obligations and responsibilities. Unfortunately Chaucer, as a medievalist, makes his colors too much black and white in this story; in any event it is the complex, realistic, human experience of *The Wife of Bath's Prologue* and *The Merchant's Tale* that raises these pieces above the others in the Marriage Group; and as between the Wife of Bath and the Merchant, further human experience shows that the Wife of Bath will always win.

But *The Franklin's Tale* has another special point of interest. In the *Prologue* to this tale Chaucer indicates that the story is based upon an old Breton *lai*. The *lai* was a type of short, imaginative chivalric romance which seems to be best represented by the brilliant little narratives of Marie de France (c. 1200). In spite of the assertion in lines 1–6 of this *Prologue*, there is little historical evidence that these *lais* were ever composed in the Breton tongue, although there may well have been Celtic Breton tales corresponding to the type. Indeed, in the color and imagination displayed in these Breton *lais*—which were in French or English—there is ample suggestion of the Celtic spirit. It is probable that Chaucer imitated the type in *The Franklin's Tale*, either from the *lais* of Marie de France herself or, more probably, from those of her imitators and followers, who were many during the thirteenth and fourteenth centuries. Whatever its source, however, *The Franklin's Tale* is a pleasant story of generosity and moral sanity, entirely appropriate to the Franklin, the sanguine, hospitable, kindly *bon vivant* of wealth and social standing.

THE PROLOGUE
OF THE FRANKELEYNS TALE

THISE olde gentil Britons in hir dayes
Of diverse aventures maden layes,
Rymeyed in hir firste Briton tonge;
Which layes with hir instruments they songe,
Or elles redden hem for hir plesaunce;   5
And oon of hem have I in remembraunce,

1. gentil, aristocratic, cultivated. hir, their. 3. Rymeyed, put into rime. Briton, here, as in l. 1, "Breton."

Which I shal seyn with good wil as I can.
But, sires, by-cause I am a burel man,
At my biginning first I yow biseche
Have me excused of my rude speche;   10
I lerned never rethoryk certeyn;
Thing that I speke, it moot be bare and pleyn.
I sleep never on the mount of Pernaso,
Ne lerned Marcus Tullius Cithero,
Colours ne knowe I none, with-outen drede,   15
But swiche colours as growen in the mede,
Or elles swiche as men dye or peynte.
Colours of rethoryk ben me to queynte;
My spirit feleth noght of swich matere.
But if yow list, my tale shul ye here.   20

THE FRANKELEYNS TALE

In Armorik, that called is Britayne,
Ther was a knight that loved and dide his payne
To serve a lady in his beste wyse;
And many a labour, many a greet empryse
He for his lady wroghte, er she were wonne.   25
For she was oon the faireste under sonne,
And eek therto come of so heigh kinrede,
That wel unnethes dorste this knight, for drede,
Telle hir his wo, his peyne, and his distresse.
But atte laste, she, for his worthinesse,   30
And namely for his meke obeysaunce,
Hath swich a pitee caught of his penaunce,
That prively she fil of his accord
To take him for hir housbonde and hir lord,
Of swich lordshipe as men han over hir wyves;   35
And for to lede the more in blisse hir lyves,
Of his free wil he swoor hir as a knight,
That never in al his lyf he, day ne night,
Ne sholde upon him take no maistrye
Agayn hir wil, ne kythe hir jalousye,   40
But hir obeye, and folwe hir wil in al
As any lovere to his lady shal;
Save that the name of soveraynetee,
That wolde he have for shame of his degree.

8. burel. Burel, or borel, was a coarse woolen cloth; hence *burel man* was one who wore burel, a humble, ignorant layman; compare our modern "homespun," with its connotations. The deprecating tone of the Franklin's *Prologue* is something of a commonplace, not only in *The Canterbury Tales* but also in medieval literature generally. It is hardly in keeping with the high-flown sentiments of *The Franklin's Tale*. 13. Pernaso, Parnassus, the mountain in Greece on which the Muses were traditionally supposed to dwell. Note the apparently Italian form of the word here. This is actually due to a following by Chaucer of the ablative form of the Latin, because he is here quoting from the Latin satirist, Persius (34–62). 14. Cithero, Cicero. 15. Colours, rhetorical figures. drede, doubt. 18. queynte, subtle, complicated. 21. Armorik, Armorica, the ancient name for Brittany. Britayne, Brittany. 25. were, might be (the subjunctive mood). 26. oon the faireste. The preposition *of*, necessary in the Modern English construction, was not used in Early English, although the modern idiom was beginning to appear in Chaucer; see l. 224. 28. unnethes, without ease, with difficulty, uneath (arch.). 30. atte laste, the early form of Modern English *at last*. 31. namely, particularly. 33. fil . . . accord, agreed with him. 39. maistrye, mastery, assumption of power over. 40. kythe, make known, show. 44. shame . . . degree, respect for his social position and rank as a husband.

She thanked him, and with ful greet humblesse
She seyde, "Sire, sith of your gentillesse   46
Ye profre me to have so large a reyne,
Ne wolde never God bitwixe us tweyne,
As in my gilt, were outher werre or stryf.
Sir, I wol be your humble trewe wyf,   50
Have heer my trouthe, til that myn herte breste."
Thus been they bothe in quiete and in reste.

For o thing, sires, saufly dar I seye,
That frendes everich other moot obeye,
If they wol longe holden companye.   55
Love wol nat ben constreyned by maistrye;
Whan maistrie comth, the god of love anon
Beteth hise winges, and farewel! he is gon!
Love is a thing as any spirit free;
Wommen of kinde desiren libertee,   60
And nat to ben constreyned as a thral;
And so don men, if I soth seyen shal.
Loke who that is most pacient in love,
He is at his avantage al above.
Pacience is an heigh vertu certeyn;   65
For it venquisseth, as thise clerkes seyn,
Thinges that rigour sholde never atteyne.
For every word men may nat chyde or pleyne.
Lerneth to suffre, or elles, so moot I goon,
Ye shul it lerne, wher-so ye wole or noon.   70
For in this world, certein, ther no wight is,
That he ne dooth or seith som-tyme amis.
Ire, siknesse, or constellacioun,
Wyn, wo, or chaunginge of complexioun
Causeth ful ofte to doon amis or speken.   75
On every wrong a man may nat be wreken;
After the tyme, moste be temperaunce
To every wight that can on governaunce.
And therfore hath thise wyse worthy knight,
To live in ese, suffrance hir bihight,   80
And she to him ful wisly gan to swere
That never sholde ther be defaute in here.

Heer may men seen an humble wys accord;
Thus hath she take hir servaunt and hir lord,
Servant in love, and lord in mariage;   85
Than was he bothe in lordship and servage;

Servage? nay, but in lordshipe above,
Sith he hath bothe his lady and his love;
His lady, certes, and his wyf also,
The which that lawe of love acordeth to,   90
And whan he was in this prosperitee,
Hoom with his wyf he gooth to his contree,
Nat fer fro Penmark, ther his dwelling was,
Wher-as he liveth in blisse and in solas.

Who coude telle, but he had wedded be,   95
The joye, the ese, and the prosperitee
That is bitwixe an housbonde and his wyf?
A yeer and more lasted this blisful lyf,
Til that the knight of which I speke of thus,
That of Kayrrud was cleped Arveragus,   100
Shoop him to goon, and dwelle a yeer or tweyne
In Engelond, that cleped was eek Briteyne,
To seke in armes worship and honour;
For al his lust he sette in swich labour;
And dwelled ther two yeer, the book seith thus.   105

Now wol I stinte of this Arveragus,
And speken I wole of Dorigene his wyf,
That loveth hir housbonde as hir hertes lyf.
For his absence wepeth she and syketh,
As doon thise noble wyves whan hem lyketh.   110
She moorneth, waketh, wayleth, fasteth, pleyneth;
Desyr of his presence hir so distreyneth,
That al this wyde world she sette at noght.
Hir frendes, whiche that knewe hir hevy thoghte,
Conforten hir in al that ever they may;   115
They prechen hir, they telle hir night and day,
That causelees she sleeth hir-self, allas!
And every confort possible in this cas
They doon to hir with al hir bisinesse,
Al for to make hir leve hir hevinesse.   120

By proces, as ye knowen everichoon,
Men may so longe graven in a stoon,
Til som figure ther-inne emprented be.
So longe han they conforted hir, til she
Receyved hath, by hope and by resoun,   125
Th' emprenting of hir consolacioun,
Thurgh which hir grete sorwe gan aswage;
She may nat alwey duren in swich rage.

And eek Arveragus, in al this care,
Hath sent hir lettres hoom of his welfare,   130
And that he wol come hastily agayn
Or elles hadde this sorwe hir herte slayn.

---

48. **God.** There is a curious blend of Christian and pagan deities in this tale. But the Christian God appears only in oaths and asseverations, such as might occur anywhere in Middle English speech; the pagan divinities, on the other hand, are appealed to as important factors in the story. 49. **As . . . gilt,** through my fault. **werre,** war. The entire sentence beginning with l. 48 might be translated: "Would God there may never be war or strife between us through my fault." 53. **saufly,** safely. 60. **of kinde,** by nature. 64. **He . . . avantage,** he has an advantage. 69. **suffre,** tolerate, be tolerant. **so . . . goon,** a mild asseveration, "as I can walk," "as I live and breathe," etc. 70. **wher-so ye . . . noon,** whether you will or not. 73. **constellacioun.** This has reference to the influence of heavenly bodies and their celestial positions on human affairs. 74. **complexioun,** the harmony or balance of the humours in the body; see the *Prologue* to *The Canterbury Tales,* p. 11:209, l. 421 and note; also *The Nun's Priest's Tale,* l. 104 and note. 76. **wreken,** avenged. 77. **After the tyme,** according to the time and situation. 78. **can on governaunce,** knows how to control himself. 80. **bihight,** promised. 86. **servage,** service, used here in the sense of chivalric love.

93. **Penmark,** Pedmark in some of the manuscripts. It was probably Penmarch, a commune in the southwestern portion of the Department of Finisterre, France. This section of the Brittany peninsula is still noted for its dangerously rocky coast. 95. **he,** he who. 100. **Kayrrud,** the modern Breton Kerru, the name of several places in Brittany. None of these, however, exactly fits the geographical situation indicated here. 101. **Shoop,** shaped, planned. 104. **lust,** pleasure. 105. **book,** the obscure source of Chaucer's tale. Perhaps he has made up this book out of whole cloth in order to give his story the "authority" which the medieval public loved. 109. **syketh,** sighs. 111. **waketh,** either "lies awake" or "watches"; probably both meanings are intended. 112. **distreyneth,** afflicts. 121. **proces,** due course. 128. **duren,** endure. **rage,** distemper, abnormal state.

Hir frendes sawe hir sorwe gan to slake,
And preyede hir on knees, for Goddes sake,
To come and romen hir in companye, 135
Awey to dryve hir derke fantasye.
And finally, she graunted that requeste;
For wel she saugh that it was for the beste.

Now stood hir castel faste by the see,
And often with hir freendes walketh she 140
Hir to disporte up-on the bank an heigh,
Wher-as she many a ship and barge seigh
Seilinge hir cours, wher-as hem liste go;
But than was that a parcel of hir wo.
For to hir-self ful ofte "allas!" seith she, 145
"Is ther no ship, of so manye as I see,
Wol bringen hom my lord? than were myn herte
Al warisshed of his bittre peynes smerte."

Another tyme ther wolde she sitte and thinke,
And caste hir eyen dounward fro the brinke. 150
But whan she saugh the grisly rokkes blake,
For verray fere so wolde hir herte quake,
That on hir feet she might hir noght sustene.
Than wolde she sitte adoun upon the grene,
And pitously into the see biholde, 155
And seyn right thus, with sorweful sykes colde:
"Eterne God, that thurgh thy purveyaunce
Ledest the world by certein governaunce,
In ydel, as men seyn, ys no-thing make;
But, Lord, thise grisly feendly rokkes blake, 160
That semen rather a foul confusioun
Of werk than any fair creacioun
Of swich a parfit wys God and a stable,
Why han ye wroght this werk unresonable?
For by this werk, south, north, ne west, ne est, 165
Ther nis y-fostred man, ne brid, ne beest;
It dooth no good, to my wit, but anoyeth.
See ye nat, Lord, how mankinde it destroyeth?
An hundred thousand bodies of mankinde
Han rokkes slayn, al be they nat in minde, 170
Which mankinde is so fair part of thy werk
That thou it madest lyk to thyn owene merk.
Than semed it ye hadde a greet chiertee
Toward mankinde; but how than may it be
That ye swiche menes make it to destroyen, 175
Whiche menes do no good, but ever anoyen?
I woot wel clerkes wol seyn, as hem leste,
By arguments, that al is for the beste,
Though I ne can the causes nat y-knowe.
But thilke God, that made wind to blowe, 180
As kepe my lord! this my conclusioun;
To clerkes lete I al disputisoun.
But wolde God that alle thise rokkes blake

Were sonken in-to Helle for his sake!
Thise rokkes sleen myn herte for the fere." 185
Thus wolde she seyn, with many a pitous tere.

Hir freendes sawe that it was no disport
To romen by the see, but disconfort;
And shopen for to pleyen somwher elles.
They leden hir by riveres and by welles, 190
And eek in othere places delitables;
They dauncen, and they pleyen at ches and tables.

So on a day, right in the morwe-tyde,
Un-to a gardin that was ther bisyde,
In which that they had maad hir ordinaunce 195
Of vitaille and of other purveyaunce,
They goon and pleye hem al the longe day.
And this was on the sixte morwe of May,
Which May had peynted with his softe shoures
This gardin ful of leves and of floures; 200
And craft of mannes hand so curiously
Arrayed hadde this gardin, trewely,
That never was ther gardin of swich prys,
But-if it were the verray paradys.
Th'odour of floures and the fresshe sighte 205
Wolde han maad any herte for to lighte
That ever was born, but-if to gret siknesse,
Or to gret sorwe helde it in distresse;
So ful it was of beautee with plesaunce.
At after-diner gonne they to daunce, 210
And singe also, save Dorigen allone,
Which made alwey hir compleint and hir mone;
For she ne saugh him on the daunce go,
That was hir housbonde and hir love also.
But nathelees she moste a tyme abyde, 215
And with good hope lete hir sorwe slyde.

Up-on this daunce, amonges othere men,
Daunced a squyer biforen Dorigen,
That fressher was and jolyer of array,
As to my doom, than is the monthe of May. 220
He singeth, daunceth, passinge any man
That is or was, sith that the world bigan.
Ther-with he was, if men sholde him discryve,
Oon of the beste faringe man on-lyve;
Yong, strong, right vertuous, and riche and wys, 225
And wel biloved, and holden in gret prys.
And shortly, if the sothe I tellen shal,
Unwiting of this Dorigen at al,
This lusty squyer, servant to Venus,
Which that y-cleped was Aurelius, 230
Had loved hir best of any creature
Two yeer and more, as was his aventure,
But never dorste he telle hir his grevaunce;

135. **romen,** walk about, wander. 142. **seigh,** saw (v.). 148. **warisshed,** cured. 156. **sykes,** sighs. 157. **purveyaunce,** Providence, foresight. 159. **In ydel,** in vain, to no purpose. 173. **chiertee,** love. 177. **as hem leste,** as it pleases them, as they will. 180. **thilke,** that same. 182. **lete,** leave. The sentiment of this line is typical of Chaucer when a knotty problem of human thought or conduct presents itself.

190. **welles,** springs, fountains. 191. **delitables,** delectable, delightful. The -s is an indication that the word was originally a French adjective, agreeing in number and form with the noun it modified. 192. **tables,** backgammon. 195. **ordinaunce,** arrangements. 196. **purveyaunce,** provisions. 201. **curiously,** carefully, with skill and pains. 204. **But-if,** unless. 210. **after-diner,** the period of relaxation following the midday meal. 219–220. **That fressher . . . May.** Compare the description of the Squire as given in the *Prologue* to *The Canterbury Tales*, ll. 91–92. 232. **aventure,** chance.

With-outen coppe he drank al his penaunce.
He was despeyred, no-thing dorste he seye,   235
Save in his songes somwhat wolde he wreye
His wo, as in a general compleyning;
He seyde he lovede, and was biloved nothing.
Of swich matere made he manye layes,
Songes, compleintes, roundels, virelayes,   240
How that he dorste nat his sorwe telle,
But languisseth, as a furie dooth in Helle;
And dye he moste, he seyde, as dide Ekko
For Narcisus, that dorste nat telle hir wo.
In other manere than ye here me seye,   245
Ne dorste he nat to hir his wo biwreye;
Save that, paraventure, som-tyme at daunces,
Ther yonge folk kepen hir observaunces,
It may wel be he loked on hir face
In swich a wyse, as man that asketh grace;   250
But no-thing wiste she of his entente.

Nathelees, it happed, er they thennes wente,
By-cause that he was hir neighebour,
And was a man of worship and honour,
And hadde y-knowen him of tyme yore,   255
They fille in speche; and forth more and more
Un-to his purpos drough Aurelius,
And whan he saugh his tyme, he seyde thus:
   "Madame," quod he, "by God that this world made,
So that I wiste it mighte your herte glade,   260
I wolde, that day that your Arveragus
Wente over the see, that I, Aurelius,
Had went ther never I sholde have come agayn;
For wel I woot my service is in vayn.
My guerdon is but bresting of myn herte;   265
Madame, reweth upon my peynes smerte;
For with a word ye may me sleen or save,
Heer at your feet God wolde that I were grave!
I ne have as now no leyser more to seye;
Have mercy, swete, or ye wol do me deye!"   270
   She gan to loke up-on Aurelius:
"Is this your wil," quod she, "and sey ye thus?
Never erst," quod she, "ne wiste I what ye mente.
But now, Aurelie, I knowe your entente,
By thilke God that yaf me soule and lyf,   275
Ne shal I never been untrewe wyf
In word ne werk, as fer as I have wit:
I wol ben his to whom that I am knit;

---

234. **With-outen coppe.** This rather obscure expression, *without a cup,* seems to mean either "under difficulties" or possibly "in full draught," "in abundance." 236. **wreye**, reveal. 238. **nothing**, not at all. 240. **compleintes . . . virelayes**, names of common French courtly lyrical forms of the period. Chaucer wrote several of these in his earlier career. The *compleinte* is a lament expressing the sorrows of unrequited love. The *roundel* was a rather rigid form for a short lyric of love or nature. The *virelay* was a poem characterized by the presence of only two sets of rime in the rime-scheme. 243-244. **Ekko . . . Narcisus.** According to the old classical legend, the nymph Echo was madly in love with the beautiful youth Narcissus, but he was so absorbed in the contemplation of his own beauty that he paid no attention to Echo. She pined away until she became nothing but a voice, and Narcissus was transformed into a flower. 248. **observaunces**, customary social attentions and duties.

257. **drough**, drew. 263. **ther**, where. 268. **grave**, buried. 273. **erst**, before.

Tak this for fynal answer as of me."
But after that in pley thus seyde she: 280
    "Aurelie," quod she, "by heighe God above,
Yet wolde I graunte yow to been your love,
Sin I yow see so pitously complayne;
Loke what day that, endelong Britayne,
Ye remoeve alle the rokkes, stoon by stoon,   285
That they ne lette ship ne boot to goon—
I seye, whan ye han maad the coost so clene
Of rokkes, that ther nis no stoon y-sene,
Than wol I love yow best of any man;
Have heer my trouthe in al that ever I can."   290
"Is ther non other grace in yow?" quod he.
"No, by that Lord," quod she, "that maked me!
For wel I woot that it shal never bityde.
Lat swiche folies out of your herte slyde.
What deyntee sholde a man han in his lyf   295
For to go love another mannes wyf,
That hath hir body whan so that him lyketh?"
    Aurelius ful ofte sore syketh;
Wo was Aurelie, whan that he this herde,
And with a sorweful herte he thus answerde: 300
    "Madame," quod he, "this were an inpossible!
Than moost I dye of sodein deth horrible."
And with that word he turned him anoon.
Tho come hir othere freendes many oon,
And in the aleyes romeden up and doun,   305
And no-thing wiste of this conclusioun,
But sodeinly bigonne revel newe
Til that the brighte sonne lost his hewe:
For th'orisonte hath reft the sonne his light;
This is as muche to seye as it was night.   310
And hoom they goon in joye and in solas,
Save only wrecche Aurelius, allas!
He to his hous is goon with sorweful herte;
He seeth he may nat fro his deeth asterte.
Him semed that he felte his herte colde;   315
Up to the hevene his handes he gan holde,
And on his knowes bare he sette him doun,
And in his raving seyde his orisoun.
For verray wo out of his wit he breyde.
He niste what he spak, but thus he seyde;   320
With pitous herte his pleynt hath he bigonne
Un-to the goddes, and first un-to the sonne:
    He seyde, "Appollo, god and governour
Of every plaunte, herbe, tree and flour,
That yevest, after thy declinacioun,   325

To ech of hem his tyme and his sesoun,
As thyn herberwe chaungeth lowe or hye,
Lord Phebus, cast thy merciable yë
On wrecche Aurelie, which that am but lorn.
Lo, lord! my lady hath my deeth y-sworn   330
With-oute gilt, but thy benignitee
Upon my dedly herte have som pitee!
For wel I woot, lord Phebus, if yow lest,
Ye may me helpen, save my lady, best.
Now voucheth sauf that I may yow devyse   335
How that I may been holpe and in what wyse.
    "Your blisful suster, Lucina the shene,
That of the see is chief goddesse and quene,
Though Neptunus have deitee in the see,
Yet emperesse aboven him is she;   340
Ye knowen wel, lord, that right as hir desyr
Is to be quiked and lightned of your fyr,
For which she folweth yow ful bisily,
Right so the see desyreth naturelly
To folwen hir, as she that is goddesse   345
Bothe in the see and riveres more and lesse.
Wherfore, lord Phebus, this is my requeste—
Do this miracle, or do myn herte breste—
That now, next at this opposicioun,
Which in the signe shal be of the Leoun,   350
As preyeth hir so greet a flood to bringe,
That fyve fadme at the leeste it overspringe
The hyeste rokke in Armorik Britayne;
And lat this flood endure yeres tweyne;
Than certes to my lady may I seye: 355
'Holdeth your heste, the rokkes been aweye.'
    "Lord Phebus, dooth this miracle for me;
Preye hir she go no faster cours than ye;
I seye, preyeth your suster that she go
No faster cours than ye thise yeres two.   360
Than shal she been evene atte fulle alway,
And spring-flood laste bothe night and day.
And, but she vouche-sauf in swiche manere
To graunte me my sovereyn lady dere,
Prey hir to sinken every rok adoun   365
In-to hir owene derke regioun
Under the ground, ther Pluto dwelleth inne,
Or never-mo shal I my lady winne.
Thy temple in Delphos wol I barefoot seke;

327. **herberwe,** lodging, dwelling-place. 335. **voucheth sauf,** vouchsafe. **devyse,** describe. 337. **Lucina,** Diana in her aspect of goddess
of the Moon, which governs the tides. **shene,** beautiful, fair. 342.
quiked, made alive, quickened. 348. **do . . . breste,** make my
heart break. 349. **opposicioun,** when the moon and the sun are on
opposite sides of the earth, all three bodies being approximately in
line. This is the occasion of full moon, which, with the time of new
moon, is the period of highest tides on the earth. 350. **the Leoun,**
Leo, one of the major constellations of the zodiac. The sun is in this
constellation during most of July, and the constellation is "favorable" to the sun; it is, therefore, one of the sun's "mansions."
351. **As,** a pleonastic particle that can be omitted entirely from the
translation of the line. 356. **heste,** promise. 367. **Pluto,** in classical
mythology, the god of the underworld and the ruler of Hades. 369.
Delphos, Delphi, a town in Phocis, Greece, near the base of Mount
Parnassus, the seat of a famous shrine sacred to Apollo. The priestess
of this shrine had the power of effective though ambiguous prophecy.

284. **endelong,** all along. 286. **lette,** hinder, prevent. 295. **deyntee,**
dignity, honor. 302. **dye . . . horrible.** The lover tormented by an
unrequited and unsatisfied love was likely to fall into a wasting sickness, which would inevitably prove fatal unless the beloved should
relent. This conception of love-sickness (*care-bed*) is a commonplace
in all medieval romances of chivalric nature (see *Aucassin and
Nicolete*). 305. **aleyes,** pathways or walks. 309. **th'orisonte,** the
horizon. 314. **asterte,** escape. 317. **knowes,** knees. 319. **breyde,**
started up. 320. **niste,** knew not. 323. **Appollo.** Apollo is here invoked as the god of vegetation and hence regeneration (see, however,
note to l. 48). As such, he was also god of the sun (*Phebus*, l. 328)
and is considered as the solar body in the next line. 325. **declinacioun,** the distance of the sun north or south of the celestial equator.

Lord Phebus, see the teres on my cheke,   370
And of my peyne have som compassioun."
And with that word in swowne he fil adoun,
And longe tyme he lay forth in a traunce.
   His brother, which that knew of his penaunce,
Up caughte him and to bedde he hath him broght.
Dispeyred in this torment and this thoght   376
Lete I this woful creature lye;
Chese he, for me, whether he wol live or dye.
   Arveragus, with hele and greet honour,
As he that was of chivalrye the flour,   380
Is comen hoom, and othere worthy men.
O blisful artow now, thou Dorigen,
That hast thy lusty housbonde in thyne armes,
The fresshe knight, the worthy man of armes
That loveth thee, as his owene hertes lyf.   385
No-thing list him to been imaginatyf
If any wight had spoke, whyl he was oute,
To hire of love; he hadde of it no doute.
He noght entendeth to no swich matere,
But daunceth, justeth, maketh hir good chere;   390
And thus in joye and blisse I lete hem dwelle,
And of the syke Aurelius wol I telle.
   In langour and in torment furious
Two yeer and more lay wrecche Aurelius,
Er any foot he mighte on erthe goon;   395
Ne confort in this tyme hadde he noon,
Save of his brother, which that was a clerk;
He knew of al this wo and al this werk.
For to non other creature certeyn
Of this matere he dorste no word seyn.   400
Under his brest he bar it more secree
Than ever dide Pamphilus for Galathee.
His brest was hool, with-oute for to sene,
But in his herte ay was the arwe kene.
And wel ye knowe that of a sursanure   405
In surgerye is perilous the cure,
But men mighte touche the arwe, or come therby.
His brother weep and wayled prively,
Til atte laste him fil in remembraunce,
That whyl he was at Orliens in Fraunce,   410
As yonge clerkes, that been likerous
To reden artes that been curious,
Seken in every halke and every herne
Particuler sciences for to lerne,
He him remembred that, upon a day,   415
At Orliens in studie a book he say

Of magik naturel, which his felawe,
That was that tyme a bacheler of lawe,
Al were he ther to lerne another craft,
Had prively upon his desk y-laft;   420
Which book spak muchel of the operaciouns,
Touchinge the eighte and twenty mansiouns
That longen to the mone, and swich folye,
As in our dayes is nat worth a flye;
For holy chirches feith, in our bileve,   425
Ne suffreth noon illusion us to greve.
And whan this book was in his remembraunce,
Anon for joye his herte gan to daunce,
And to him-self he seyde prively,
"My brother shal be warisshed hastily;   430
For I am siker that ther be sciences,
By whiche men make diverse apparences
Swiche as thise subtile tregetoures pleye.
For ofte at festes have I wel herd saye,
That tregetours, with-inne an halle large,   435
Have maad come in a water and a barge,
And in the halle rowen up and doun.
Somtyme hath semed come a grim leoun;
And somtyme floures springe as in a mede;
Somtyme a vyne, and grapes whyte and rede;   440
Somtyme a castel, al of lym and stoon;
And whan hem lyked, voyded it anoon.
Thus semed it to every mannes sighte.
   "Now than conclude I thus, that if I mighte
At Orliens som old felawe y-finde,   445
That hadde this mones mansions in minde,
Or other magik naturel above,
He shulde wel make my brother han his love.
For with an apparence a clerk may make
To mannes sighte, that alle the rokkes blake   450
Of Britaigne weren y-voyded everichon,
And shippes by the brinke comen and gon,
And in swich forme endure a day or two;
Than were my brother warisshed of his wo.
Than moste she nedes holden hir biheste,   455
Or elles he shal shame hir atte leste."
   What sholde I make a lenger tale of this?
Un-to his brotheres bed he comen is,
And swich confort he yaf him for to gon
To Orliens, that he up stirte anon,   460
And on his wey forthward thanne is he fare,
In hope for to ben lissed of his care.
   Whan they were come almost to that citee,
But-if it were a two furlong or three,

378. **Chese,** let him choose. 379. **hele,** health, well-being. 386. **to been imaginatyf,** to imagine things. 388. **doute,** fear, suspicion. 402. **Pamphilus for Galathee.** Pamphilus was the hero of a medieval Latin poem, *De Amore,* well known in Chaucer's time. He was in love with the beautiful Galatea. 404. **arwe,** arrow. 405. **sursanure,** in medieval medicine, the name given to a deep wound which had healed superficially but not beneath the surface. 407. **But,** unless. 410. **Orliens,** Orleans, the seat of a famous old French university, which had something of a reputation in the Middle Ages as the seat of scientific learning; to the popular mind this suggested that it was the home of practitioners of magic, black as well as white. 411. **likerous,** avid for, eager for, lusting after. 413. **halke . . . herne,** nook and corner.

417. **magik naturel.** "Natural magic" was generally what we should call today scientific information, knowledge, and procedure; it is virtually the same as "white magic" and hence is diametrically opposed to "black magic," or necromancy. At the same time, it should be remarked that the magician's feat of making the rocks disappear from the coast of Brittany is more necromancy than otherwise. 422. **eighte and twenty mansiouns.** The twenty-eight mansions of the moon were the positions of the moon at noon on each of the twenty-eight days of the lunar month. 423. **longen,** belong. 433. **tregetoures,** jugglers, magicians, sleight-of-hand men. 451. **y-voyded,** removed. 462. **lissed,** relieved. 464. **But-if,** except for.

A yong clerk rominge by him-self they mette, 465
Which that in Latin thriftily hem grette,
And after that he seyde a wonder thing:
"I knowe," quod he, "the cause of your coming";
And er they ferther any fote wente,
He tolde hem al that was in hir entente. 470
  This Briton clerk him asked of felawes
The whiche that he had knowe in olde dawes;
And he answerde him that they dede were,
For which he weep ful ofte many a tere.
  Doun of his hors Aurelius lighte anon, 475
And forth with this magicien is goon
Hoom to his hous, and made hem wel at ese.
Hem lakked no vitaille that mighte hem plese;
So wel arrayed hous as ther was oon
Aurelius in his lyf saugh never noon. 480
  He shewed him, er he wente to sopeer,
Forestes, parkes ful of wilde deer;
Ther saugh he hertes with hir hornes hye,
The gretteste that ever were seyn with yë. 484
He saugh of hem an hondred slayn with houndes,
And somme with arwes blede of bittre woundes.
He saugh, whan voided were thise wilde deer,
Thise fauconers upon a fair river,
That with hir haukes han the heron slayn.
Tho saugh he knightes justing in a playn; 490
And after this, he dide him swich plesaunce,
That he him shewed his lady on a daunce
On which him-self he daunced, as him thoughte.
And whan this maister, that this magik wroughte,
Saugh it was tyme, he clapte his handes two, 495
And farewel! al our revel was ago.
And yet remoeved they never out of the hous,
Whyl they saugh al this sighte merveillous,
But in his studie, ther-as his bookes be,
They seten stille, and no wight but they three. 500
  To him this maister called his squyer,
And seyde him thus: "Is redy our soper?
Almost an houre it is, I undertake,
Sith I yow bad our soper for to make,
Whan that thise worthy men wenten with me 505
In-to my studie, ther-as my bookes be."
  "Sire," quod this squyer, "whan it lyketh yow,
It is al redy, though ye wol right now."
"Go we than soupe," quod he, "as for the beste;
This amorous folk som-tyme mote han reste." 510
  At after-soper fille they in tretee,
What somme sholde this maistres guerdon be,
To remoeven alle the rokkes of Britayne,

466. **thriftily,** heartily and suitably. 472. **dawes,** days. 483. **hertes,** harts, deer. 496. **And farewel! . . . ago.** Compare the speech by Prospero in Shakespeare's *The Tempest,* iv, i, 148 ff., beginning "Our revels now are ended." There are other echoes of lines from Chaucer in lines by Shakespeare, which suggest to some that Shakespeare knew the work of Chaucer to some extent, which is altogether likely, for that matter; but such echoes are also explained by two men of poetic ability expressing the same idea in the same felicitous words though altogether independently. 511. **after-soper,** the period of relaxation immediately following the evening meal.

And eek from Gerounde to the mouth of Sayne.
  He made it straunge, and swoor, so God him
    save, 515
Lasse than a thousand pound he wolde nat have,
Ne gladly for that somme he wolde nat goon.
  Aurelius, with blisful herte anoon,
Answerde thus, "Fy on a thousand pound!
This wyde world, which that men saye is round,
I wolde it yeve, if I were lord of it. 521
This bargayn is ful drive, for we ben knit.
Ye shal be payed trewely, by my trouthe!
But loketh now, for no necligence or slouthe,
Ye tarie us heer no lenger than to-morwe." 525
  "Nay," quod this clerk, "have heer my feith to
    borwe."
  To bedde is goon Aurelius whan him leste,
And wel ny al that night he hadde his reste;
What for his labour and his hope of blisse,
His woful herte of penaunce hadde a lisse. 530
  Upon the morwe, whan that it was day,
To Britaigne toke they the righte way,
Aurelius, and this magicien bisyde,
And been descended ther they wolde abide;
And this was, as the bookes me remembre, 535
The colde frosty seson of Decembre.
  Phebus wex old, and hewed lyk latoun,
That in his hote declinacioun
Shoon as the burned gold with stremes brighte;
But now in Capricorn adoun he lighte, 540
Wher-as he shoon ful pale, I dar wel seyn.
The bittre frostes, with the sleet and reyn,
Destroyed hath the grene in every yerd.
Janus sit by the fyr, with double berd,
And drinketh of his bugle-horn the wyn, 545
Biforn him stant braun of the tusked swyn,
And "Nowel!" cryeth every lusty man.
  Aurelius, in al that ever he can,
Doth to his maister chere and reverence,

514. **Gerounde . . . Sayne.** The river Seine in France, on which the city of Paris is situated, needs no comment beyond the fact that it empties into the western end (extended) of the English Channel. The *Gerounde* is the Garonne, the large river of western France on which Bordeaux is located; it empties into the Bay of Biscay. The stretch of coast between the mouths of these two rivers would include all of northwestern maritime France. 515. **made it straunge,** found or made difficulties. 520. **This wyde world . . . round.** Note the reference to the roundness of the earth, which is often met with in the learned literature of the fourteenth century, a century and a half before Columbus or Magellan. 526. **borwe,** pledge, promise. 530. **lisse,** stop, cessation. 534. **descended,** that is, from their horses. 537. **latoun,** latten, an alloy of copper and zinc. 538. **declinacioun.** See note to l. 325. But here the reference is to the fact that in December the sun was south of the celestial equator, in the zodiacal constellation of Capricornus (l. 540). There was an erroneous idea that the farther south one went, even below the equator, the hotter it became. 544. **Janus,** an old Roman solar god, who watched both the rising and the setting sun, and hence was regarded as having two faces looking in opposite directions (note the *double berd*). He has given his name to the month of January. 546. **braun,** brawn, roasted flesh of the boar. This entire passage, lines 536–547, is a striking English medieval scene, and one of the happiest of such descriptive touches in English literature.

And preyeth him to doon his diligence 550
To bringen him out of his peynes smerte,
Or with a swerd that he wolde slitte his herte.

    This subtil clerk swich routhe had of this man,
That night and day he spedde him that he can,
To wayte a tyme of his conclusioun; 555
This is to seye, to make illusioun,
By swich an apparence or jogelrye
(I ne can no termes of astrologye),
That she and every wight sholde wene and seye,
That of Britaigne the rokkes were aweye, 560
Or elles they were sonken under grounde.
So atte laste he hath his tyme y-founde
To maken his japes and his wrecchednesse
Of swich a supersticious cursednesse.
His tables Toletanes forth he broght, 565
Ful wel corrected, ne ther lakked noght,
Neither his collect ne his expans yeres,
Ne his rotes ne his othere geres,
As been his centres and his arguments,
And his proporcionels convenients 570
For his equacions in every thing.
And, by his eighte spere in his wirking,
He knew ful wel how fer Alnath was shove
Fro the heed of thilke fixe Aries above

That in the ninthe speere considered is; 575
Ful subtilly he calculed al this.

    Whan he had founde his firste mansioun,
He knew the remenant by proporcioun;
And knew the arysing of his mone weel,
And in whos face, and terme, and everydeel; 580
And knew ful weel the mones mansioun
Acordaunt to his operacioun,
And knew also his othere observaunces
For swiche illusiouns and swiche meschaunces
As hethen folk used in thilke dayes; 585
For which no lenger maked he delayes,
But thurgh his magyk, for a wyke or tweye,
It semed that alle the rokkes were aweye.

    Aurelius, which that yet despeired is
Wher he shal han his love or fare amis, 590
Awaiteth night and day on this miracle;
And whan he knew that ther was noon obstacle,
That voided were thise rokkes everichon,
Doun to his maistres feet he fil anon,
And seyde, "I, woful wrecche, Aurelius, 595
Thanke yow, lord, and lady myn Venus,
That me han holpen fro my cares colde."
And to the temple his wey forth hath he holde,
Wher-as he knew he sholde his lady see.
And whan he saugh his tyme, anon-right he, 600
With dredful herte and with ful humble chere,
Salewed hath his soveryn lady dere:

    "My righte lady," quod this woful man,
"Whom I most drede and love as I best can,
And lothest were of al this world displese, 605
Nere it that I for yow have swich disese,
That I moste dyen heer at your foot anon,
Noght wolde I telle how me is wo bigon;
But certes outher moste I dye or pleyne;
Ye slee me giltelees for verray peyne. 610
But of my deeth, thogh that ye have no routhe,
Avyseth yow, er that ye breke your trouthe.
Repenteth yow, for thilke God above,
Er ye me sleen by-cause that I yow love.
For, madame, wel ye woot what ye han hight; 615
Nat that I chalange any thing of right
Of yow my sovereyn lady, but your grace;
But in a gardin yond, at swich a place,
Ye woot right wel what ye bihighten me;
And in myn hand your trouthe plighten ye 620
To love me best, God woot, ye seyde so,

555. **wayte,** watch for. 558. **can,** know. Perhaps the Franklin knew no astronomical terms, although he does pretty well in the ensuing lines, but Chaucer was a master of the science and actually wrote a textbook on the use of an astronomical instrument, the astrolabe. 563. **japes . . . wrecchednesse,** wretched tricks; an interesting example of the old rhetorical figure of hendiadys. The Franklin, as a good orthodox Christian, is occasionally distressed by the suggestion that there should be a belief in magic. 565. **tables Toletanes,** Toledo tables, astronomical tables drawn up under the supervision of King Alphonso X of Castile, and based upon the position of the city of Toledo, Spain; they date from the thirteenth century. 567. **collect . . . yeres.** *Collect yeres* are the computations of the changes in a planet's position over a long period of time—from twenty to three thousand years; *expans yeres* computed the changes in a planet's position for single years and short periods up to twenty years. 568. **rotes,** roots, data for a given year which must serve as the basis for computations. **geres,** gear, equipment for computation. 569. **centres . . . arguments.** *Centres* refers to the small brass projection on an astrolabe, the instrument then used for ascertaining the astronomical position of a fixed star. *Arguments* denotes the mathematical material from which other mathematical material is to be deduced, or on which its calculation depends. 570. **proporcionels convenients,** tables of proportional parts, as in a modern table of logarithms, to be used for computing the changes in a planet's position during the fractions of a year. For the *-s* on *convenients*, see note to l. 191. 572. **eighte spere.** According to Ptolemaic astronomy, there were seven concentric spheres which rotated around the earth, one to each of the seven planets (Sun, Moon, Mercury, Venus, Mars, Jupiter, and Saturn). The eighth sphere, beyond that of Saturn, was the sphere of the fixed stars. 573. **Alnath,** the chief star in the zodiacal constellation of Aries, the Ram. 574. **Aries** is called fixed (*fixe*) because it was in Aries that the vernal equinox was located; that is, the sun was in that constellation when it crossed the celestial equator in March coming northward and bringing spring. For several centuries after Chaucer's time the year began officially not on January 1 but on March 21. The vernal equinox was the starting point for all measurements of the positions of celestial bodies; it still is in respect to right ascension and azimuth. It was, in short, a focal point in the heavens and was believed to attach the eighth sphere of the fixed stars to the vague ninth sphere, or Primum Mobile, which made the entire works go round; hence the reference in l. 575.

577. **firste mansioun,** the first mansion of the moon (see note to l. 422) was named Alnath, after the brightest star in Aries. 578. **by proporcioun,** that is, by the use of his *proporcionels convenients* of l. 570. 580. **face, and terme.** Each constellation (sign) of the zodiac, to which was assigned thirty degrees along the celestial equator, was for purposes of calculation divided into three equal parts of ten degrees each (*faces*). Fractions of these equal parts were called *termes*. Each *face* and *terme* of a constellation had, of course, a particular relation to one or more of the planets. 585. **thilke,** those (same). Note the rather contemptuous tone of the Franklin in these lines. 601. **dredful,** timid, full of fear. 604. **drede,** respect; literally, fear. 606. **disese,** lack of comfort and ease. 609. **outher,** either. 615. **high,** promised. 619. **bihighten,** promised.

Al be that I unworthy be therto.
Madame, I spake it for the honour of yow,
More than to save myn hertes lyf right now;
I have do so as ye comanded me;   625
And if ye vouche-sauf, ye may go see.
Doth as yow list, have your biheste in minde,
For quik or deed, right ther ye shul me finde;
In yow lyth al, to do me live or deye;—
But wel I woot the rokkes been aweye!"   630
    He taketh his leve, and she astonied stood,
In al hir face nas a drope of blood;
She wende never han come in swich a trappe:
"Allas!" quod she, "that ever this sholde happe!
For wende I never, by possibilitee,   635
That swich a monstre or merveille mighte be!
It is agayns the process of nature."
And hoom she gooth a sorweful creature.
For verray fere unnethe may she go,
She wepeth, wailleth, al a day or two,   640
And swowneth, that it routhe was to see;
But why it was, to no wight tolde she;
For out of toune was goon Arveragus.
But to hir-self she spak, and seyde thus,
With face pale and with ful sorweful chere,   645
In hir compleynt, as ye shul after here:
    "Allas," quod she, "on thee, Fortune, I pleyne,
That unwar wrapped hast me in thy cheyne;
For which, t'escape, woot I no socour
Save only deeth or elles dishonour;   650
Oon of thise two bihoveth me to chese.
But nathelees, yet have I lever lese
My lyf than of my body have a shame,
Or knowe my-selven fals, or lese my name,
And with my deth I may be quit, y-wis.   655
Hath ther nat many a noble wyf, er this,
And many a mayde y-slayn hir-self, allas!
Rather than with hir body doon trespas?
    "Yis, certes, lo, thise stories beren witnesse;
Whan thretty tyraunts, ful of cursednesse,   660
Had slayn Phidoun in Athenes, atte feste,
They comanded his doghtres for t'areste,
And bringen hem biforn hem in despyt
Al naked, to fulfille hir foul delyt,
And in hir fadres blood they made hem daunce   665
Upon the pavement, God yeve hem mischaunce!
For which thise woful maydens, ful of drede,
Rather than they wolde lese hir maydenhede,
They prively ben stirt into a welle,
And dreynte hem-selven, as the bokes telle.   670
    "They of Messene lete enquere and seke

Of Lacedomie fifty maydens eke,
On whiche they wolden doon hir lecherye;
But was ther noon of al that companye
That she nas slayn, and with a good entente   675
Chees rather for to dye than assente
To been oppressed of hir maydenhede.
Why sholde I thanne to dye been in drede?
    "Lo, eek, the tiraunt Aristoclides
That loved a mayden, heet Stimphalides,   680
Whan that hir fader slayn was on a night,
Un-to Dianes temple goth she right,
And hente the image in hir handes two,
Fro which image wolde she never go.
No wight ne mighte hir handes of it arace,   685
Til she was slayn right in the selve place.
Now sith that maydens hadden swich despyt
To been defouled with mannes foul delyt,
Wel oghte a wyf rather hir-selven slee
Than be defouled, as it thinketh me.   690
    "What shal I seyn of Hasdrubales wyf,
That at Cartage birafte hir-self hir lyf?
For whan she saugh that Romayns wan the toun,
She took hir children alle, and skipte adoun
In-to the fyr, and chees rather to dye   695
Than any Romayn dide hir vileinye.
    "Hath nat Lucresse y-slayn hir-self, allas!
At Rome, whanne she oppressed was
Of Tarquin, for hir thoughte it was a shame
To liven when she hadde lost hir name?   700
    "The sevene maydens of Milesie also
Han slayn hem-self, for verray drede and wo,
Rather than folk of Gaule hem sholde oppresse.
Mo than a thousand stories, as I gesse,
Coude I now telle as touchinge this matere.   705
    "Whan Habradate was slayn, his wyf so dere
Hirselven slow, and leet hir blood to glyde
In Habradates woundes depe and wyde,
And seyde, 'my body, at the leeste way,
Ther shal no wight defoulen, if I may,'   710
    "What sholde I mo ensamples heer-of sayn,
Sith that so manye han hem-selven slayn
Well rather than they wolde defouled be?
I wol conclude, that it is bet for me
To sleen my-self, than been defouled thus.   715
I wol be trewe un-to Arveragus,
Or rather sleen my-self in som manere,

627. biheste, promise. 633. wende, weened, thought, expected.
639. unnethe, uneath, with difficulty. 660. thretty tyraunts. The
following lines (670–748), characteristic of Chaucer's annoying tendency to parade his knowledge of classical or other "authorities," cite
a number of *exempla* of women who died for the sake of their chastity.
They are taken from the *Epistle of St. Jerome against Jovinian*, a
work which Chaucer evidently knew very well. 669. stirt, leaped,
jumped. 670. dreynte, drowned. 671. Messene, the city of Mes-
senia, in ancient Greece.

672. Lacedomie, Lacedemonia, Sparta, in Greece. 677. oppressed,
threatened. 679. Aristoclides, tyrant of Orchomenos in Arcadia,
Greece. 680. heet, called, named. 683. hente, seized. 685. arace,
tear away. 687. sith, since. 691. Hasdrubales wyf. Hasdrubal was
a leader of the Carthaginians in the Third Punic War. Historically,
Hasdrubal eventually surrendered to Scipio Africanus, and his wife,
upbraiding him for cowardice, killed herself and her children. 697.
Lucresse, Lucretia, in ancient Roman history the wife of Collatinus,
was raped by Tarquinius Sextus. She later killed herself; and public
opinion was so aroused against the Tarquins that they were expelled,
and the Roman republic was founded. 701. Milesie, Miletus, a city
in Asia Minor. It was sacked by the Gauls in 276 B.C. 706. Habra-
date, Abradates, King of the Susi, a tribe who once constituted a part
of the mighty Persian empire.

As dide Demociones doghter dere,
By-cause that she wolde nat defouled be.
    "O Cedasus! it is ful greet pitee,   720
To reden how thy doghtren deyde, allas!
That slowe hem-selven for swich maner cas.
    "As greet a pitee was it, or wel more,
The Theban mayden, that for Nichanore
Hir-selven slow, right for swich maner wo.   725
    "Another Theban mayden dide right so;
For oon of Macedoine hadde hir oppressed,
She with hir deeth hir maydenhede redressed.
    "What shal I seye of Nicerates wyf,
That for swich cas birafte hir-self hir lyf?   730
    "How trewe eek was to Alcebiades
His love, that rather for to dyen chees
Than for to suffre his body unburied be!
Lo, which a wyf was Alceste," quod she.
    "What seith Omer of gode Penalopee?   735
Al Grece knoweth of hir chastitee.
    "Pardee, of Laodomya is writen thus,
That whan at Troye was slayn Protheselaus,
No lenger wolde she live after his day.
    "The same of noble Porcia telle I may;   740
With-oute Brutus coude she nat live,
To whom she hadde al hool hir herte yive.
    "The parfit wyfhood of Arthemesye
Honoured is thurgh al the Barbarye.
    "O Teüta, queen! thy wyfly chastitee   745
To alle wyves may a mirour be.
The same thing I seye of Bilia,
Of Rodogone, and eek Valeria."

718. **Demociones doghter.** Demotion, a member of the famous court of the Areopagus at Athens, had a daughter who, when she heard of the death of the man she was engaged to marry, killed herself because she felt that she was married only to this man. 720. **Cedasus.** The two daughters of Scedasus of Boeotia, Greece, were violated, and killed themselves rather than face dishonor. 724. **Nichanore,** an officer of Alexander the Great at the capture of Thebes (336 B.C.). **Another Theban mayden** (l. 726) has reference to the same circumstances. 729. **Nicerates wyf.** Nicerates of Athens was put to death by the Thirty Tyrants (see l. 660), and his wife killed herself lest she fall into their hands. 731. **Alcebiades.** The mistress of Alcibiades, leader of the Athenians in the Peloponnesian War, was Timandra. 734. **Alceste.** Alcestis was the wife of Admetus, King of Pherae in Thessaly, Greece. She consented to die in his place in order to prolong his life. Later Hercules brought her back from Hades. 735. **Penalopee.** Penelope, wife of Odysseus (Ulysses) in *The Odyssey*, fended off innumerable suitors until the return of her husband after his wanderings. She did not, however, sacrifice herself in death, yet she has always been a symbol of conjugal fidelity. 737. **Laodomya.** Protesilaus was reputedly the first Greek to fall in the Trojan War. 740. **Porcia.** The story of Portia is no doubt familiar from Shakespeare and his *Julius Caesar.* When her husband, Brutus, departed from Rome in the civil war following the assassination of Caesar, Portia committed suicide by swallowing live coals. 743. **Arthemesye,** Artemisia, wife of King Mausolus of Caria, Asia Minor; it was he whose magnificent tomb has given us the word *mausoleum.* 745. **Teuta,** a queen of Illyria, along the eastern coast of the Adriatic Sea. She was noted for her chastity. 747. **Bilia,** wife of Duellius, a famous Roman naval commander who won a victory over the Carthaginians in 260 B.C. 748. **Rodogone,** daughter of Emperor Darius of Persia. When her nurse tried to persuade her to a second marriage, she killed her. **Valeria,** wife of Servius, the ancient king of Rome; she refused to marry a second time.

    Thus pleyned Dorigene a day or tweye,
Purposinge ever that she wolde deye.   750
    But natholees, upon the thridde night,
Hom cam Arveragus, this worthy knight,
And asked hir why that she weep so sore.
And she gan wepen ever lenger the more.
    "Allas!" quod she, "that ever was I born!   755
Thus have I seyd," quod she, "thus have I sworn—"
And told him al as ye han herd bifore;
It nedeth nat reherce it yow na-more.
    This housbond with glad chere, in freendly
        wyse,
Answerde and seyde as I shal yow devyse: 760
"Is ther oght elles, Dorigen, but this?"
    "Nay, nay," quod she, "God help me so, as wis;
This is to muche, and it were Goddes wille."
    "Ye, wif," quod he, "lat slepen that is stille;
It may be wel, paraventure, yet to-day   765
Ye shul your trouthe holden, by my fay!
For God so wisly have mercy on me,
I hadde wel lever y-stiked for to be,
For verray love which that I to yow have,
But-if ye sholde your trouthe kepe and save.   770
Trouthe is the hyeste thing that man may kepe."
But with that word he brast anon to wepe,
And seyde, "I yow forbede, up peyne of deeth,
That never, whyl thee lasteth lyf ne breeth,
To no wight tel thou of this aventure.   775
As I may best, I wol my wo endure,
Ne make no contenance of hevinesse,
That folk of yow may demen harm or gesse."
    And forth he cleped a squyer and a mayde:
"Goth forth anon with Dorigen," he sayde,   780
"And bringeth hir to swich a place anon."
They take hir leve, and on hir wey they gon;
But they ne wiste why she thider wente.
He nolde no wight tellen his entente.
    Paraventure an heep of yow, y-wis,   785
Wol holden him a lewed man in this,
That he wol putte his wyf in jupartye;
Herkneth the tale, er ye up-on hir crye.
She may have bettre fortune than yow semeth;
And whan that ye han herd the tale, demeth.   790
    This squyer, which that highte Aurelius,
On Dorigen that was so amorous,
Of aventure happed hir to mete
Amidde the toun, right in the quikkest strete,
As she was boun to goon the wey forthright   795
Toward the gardin ther-as she had hight.
And he was to the gardinward also;
For wel he spyed, whan she wolde go

754. **lenger the more,** the longer the more. 762. **as wis,** as (is) certain. 763. **and,** even if. 764. **stille,** quiet. The phrase is the equivalent of the old "let sleeping dogs lie." 768. **lever y-stiked,** rather be stabbed. 773. **up peyne of,** on pain of. 779. **cleped,** called. 786. **lewed,** ignorant, foolish. 787. **jupartye,** jeopardy. 790. **demeth,** judge (the imperative of the verb). 794. **quikkest,** liveliest, busiest.

Out of hir hous to any maner place.
But thus they mette, of aventure or grace; 800
And he saleweth hir with glad entente
And asked of hir whiderward she wente.

And she answerde, half as she were mad,
"Unto the gardin, as myn housbond bad,
My trouthe for to holde, allas! allas!" 805

Aurelius gan wondren on this cas,
And in his herte had greet compassioun
Of hir and of hir lamentacioun,
And of Arveragus, the worthy knight,
That bad hir holden al that she had hight, 810
So looth him was his wyf sholde breke hir trouthe;
And in his herte he caught of this greet routhe,
Consideringe the beste on every syde,
That fro his lust yet were him lever abyde
Than doon so heigh a cherlish wrecchednesse 815
Agayns franchyse and alle gentillesse;
For which in fewe wordes seyde he thus:

"Madame, seyth to your lord Arveragus,
That sith I see his grete gentillesse
To yow, and eek I see wel your distresse, 820
That him were lever han shame (and that were routhe)
Than ye to me sholde breke thus your trouthe,
I have wel lever ever to suffre wo
Than I departe the love bitwix yow two.
I yow relesse, madame, in-to your hond 825
Quit every surement and every bond,
That ye han maad to me as heer-biforn,
Sith thilke tyme which that ye were born.
My trouthe I plighte, I shal yow never repreve
Of no biheste, and here I take my leve, 830
As of the treweste and the beste wyf
That ever yet I knew in al my lyf.
But every wyf be-war of hir biheste,
On Dorigene remembreth atte leste.
Thus can a squyer doon a gentil dede, 835
As well as can a knight, with-outen drede."

She thonketh him up-on hir knees al bare,
And hoom un-to hir housbond is she fare,
And tolde him al as ye han herd me sayd;
And be ye siker, he was so weel apayd, 840
That it were inpossible me to wryte;
What sholde I lenger of this cas endyte?

Arveragus and Dorigene his wyf
In sovereyn blisse leden forth hir lyf.
Never eft ne was ther angre hem bitwene; 845
He cherisseth hir as though she were a quene;
And she was to him trewe for evermore.
Of thise two folk ye gete of me na-more.

Aurelius, that his cost hath al forlorn,
Curseth the tyme that ever he was born; 850

"Allas!" quod he, "allas! that I bihighte
Of pured gold a thousand pound of wighte
Un-to this philosophre! how shal I do?
I see na-more but that I am fordo.
Myn heritage moot I nedes selle, 855
And been a begger; heer may I nat dwelle,
And shamen al my kinrede in this place,
But I of him may gete bettre grace.
But nathelees, I wol of him assaye,
At certeyn dayes, yeer by yeer, to paye, 860
And thanke him of his grete curteisye;
My trouthe wol I kepe, I wol nat lye."

With herte soor he gooth un-to his cofre,
And broghte gold un-to this philosophre,
The value of fyve hundred pound, I gesse, 865
And him bisecheth, of his gentillesse,
To graunte him dayes of the remenaunt,
And seyde, "Maister, I dar wel make avaunt,
I failled never of my trouthe as yit;
For sikerly my dette shal be quit 870
Towardes yow, how-ever that I fare
To goon a-begged in my kirtle bare.
But wolde ye vouche-sauf, up-on seurtee,
Two yeer or three for to respyten me,
Than were I wel; for elles moot I selle . 875
Myn heritage; ther is na-more to telle."

This philosophre sobrely answerde,
And seyde thus, whan he thise wordes herde:
"Have I nat holden covenant un-to thee?"
"Yes, certes, wel and trewely," quod he. 880
"Hastow nat had thy lady as thee lyketh?"
"No, no," quod he, and sorwefully he syketh.
"What was the cause? tel me if thou can."
Aurelius his tale anon bigan,
And tolde him al, as ye han herd bifore; 885
It nedeth nat to yow reherce it more.

He seide, "Arveragus, of gentillesse,
Had lever dye in sorwe and in distresse
Than that his wyf were of hir trouthe fals."
The sorwe of Dorigen he tolde him als, 890
How looth hir was to been a wikked wyf,
And that she lever had lost that day hir lyf,
And that hir trouthe she swoor, thurgh innocence:
"She never erst herde speke of apparence;
That made me han of hir so greet pitee, 895
And right as frely as he sente hir me,
As frely sente I hir to him ageyn.
This al and som, ther is na-more to seyn."

This philosophre answerde, "Leve brother,
Everich of yow dide gentilly til other. 900
Thou art a squyer, and he is a knight;
But God forbede, for His blisful might,
But-if a clerk coude doon a gentil dede
As wel as any of yow, it is no drede!

"Sire, I relesse thee thy thousand pound, 905

---

800. **of aventure or grace**, by chance or by (God's) grace. 811. **him**; that is, Arveragus. 816. **franchyse**, nobleness. 826. **surement**, surety. 842. **endyte**, write. 849. **forlorn**, completely lost.

852. **pured**, refined. **wighte**, weight. 853. **philosophre**, wise man, magician. 872. **a-begged**, a-begging.

As thou right now were cropen out of the ground,
Ne never er now ne haddest knowen me.
For, sire, I wol nat take a peny of thee
For al my craft, ne noght for my travaille.
Thou hast y-payed wel for my vitaille; 910
It is y-nogh, and farewel, have good day!"
And took his hors, and forth he gooth his way.

     Lordinges, this question wolde I aske now,
Which was the moste free, as thinketh yow?
Now telleth me, er that ye ferther wende. 915
I can na-more, my tale is at an ende.

THE NUN'S PRIEST'S TALE

    There were three priests mentioned in the *Prologue*
as convoying the Prioress and her companion (the Second Nun), but only one of these three is ever mentioned
again. He is the narrator of the vigorous *exemplum* on
flattery—and other things—presented in the form of a
beast-story. But the most effective quality of *The Nun's
Priest's Tale* is its satire—on husbands, on wives, on
husbands and wives together, on people who believe in
dreams, on people who do not believe in dreams, on the
medieval weakness for quoting authorities. The bumbling
Chantecleer and his sprightly favorite wife, Pertelote, are
portrayed with unfailing good humor, and the end of the
story rises to a full frenzy of mock-heroic action.

THE NUN'S PRIEST'S TALE

A POVRE widwe, somdel stape in age,
   Was whylom dwelling in a narwe cotage,
Bisyde a grove, stonding in a dale.
This widwe, of which I telle yow my tale,
Sin thilke day that she was last a wyf, 5
In pacience ladde a ful simple lyf,
For litel was hir catel and hir rente;
By housbondrye, of such as God hir sente,
She fond hir-self, and eek hir doghtren two.
Three large sowes hadde she, and namo, 10
Three kyn, and eek a sheep that highte Malle.
Ful sooty was hir bour, and eek hir halle,
In which she eet ful many a sclendre meel.
Of poynaunt sauce hir neded never a deel.
No deyntee morsel passed thurgh hir throte; 15
Hir dyete was accordant to hir cote.

Repleccioun ne made hir nevere syk;
Attempree dyete was al hir phisyk,
And exercyse, and hertes suffisaunce.
The goute lette hir no-thing for to daunce, 20
N'apoplexye shente nat hir heed;
No wyn ne drank she, neither whyt ne reed;
Hir bord was served most with whyt and blak,
Milk and broun breed, in which she fond no lak,
Seynd bacoun, and somtyme an ey or tweye, 25
For she was as it were a maner deye.

  A yerd she hadde, enclosed al aboute
With stikkes, and a drye dich with-oute,
In which she hadde a cok, hight Chauntecleer,
In al the land of crowing nas his peer. 30
His vois was merier than the merye orgon
On messe dayes that in the chirche gon;
Wel sikerer was his crowing in his logge,
Than is a clokke, or an abbey orlogge.
By nature knew he ech ascencioun 35
Of equinoxial in thilke toun;
For whan degrees fiftene were ascended,
Thanne crew he, that it mighte nat ben amended.
His comb was redder than the fyn coral,
And batailed as it were a castel-wal. 40
His bile was blak, and as the jeet it shoon;
Lyk asur were his legges, and his toon;
His nayles whytter than the lilie flour,
And lyk the burned gold was his colour.
This gentil cok hadde in his governaunce 45
Sevenne hennes, for to doon al his pleasaunce,
Whiche were his sustres and his paramours,
And wonder lyk to him, as of colours.
Of whiche the faireste hewed on hir throte
Was cleped faire damoysele Pertelote. 50
Curteys she was, discreet, and debonaire,
And compaignable, and bar hir-self so faire,
Sin thilke day that she was seven night old,
That trewely she hath the herte in hold
Of Chauntecleer loken in every lith, 55
He loved hir so, that wel him was therwith.
But such a joye was it to here hem singe,
Whan that the brighte sonne gan to springe,

906. **As thou . . . ground,** as if you had just crawled out of the
ground; that is, as if I had just seen you for the first time. 914–
916. **Which . . . ende.** The closing question is a common device
in medieval courtly fiction, and has here the additional point of
sharpening the marriage problem for the concluding tale in what most
Chaucerians call the "marriage group" in *The Canterbury Tales.*
1. **stape,** "stepped," advanced. 7. **catel . . . rente.** *Catel* is any
kind of property (note our modern chattel); *rente* is simply income.
9. **fond,** provided for. **doghtren,** daughters. 11. **kyn,** kine, cows.
16. **dyete . . . cote,** her diet was in keeping with her garments.

17. **Repleccioun,** repletion, overeating. 18. **Attempree,** temperate.
moderate. 20. **goute lette,** etc., the gout did not prevent her from
dancing. 21. **shente,** injured, harmed. 23. **whyt and blak,** light
and dark ale. 25. **Seynd,** singed, crisped. **ey,** egg. 26. **deye,** dairy-
man or dairywoman; note the modern English surname Day. 30.
nas, "ne" and "was," was not. 32. **messe dayes,** feast-days, church
holidays. 33. **sikerer,** more certain, more dependable. 34. **orlogge,**
horologe, large clock. 35–36. **ascencioun . . . equinoxial.** The *equinoxial* is the great circle made in the heavens by the extended plane of
the earth's equator. It makes a complete revolution in twenty-four
hours; consequently fifteen degrees would pass, or "ascend,"
every hour. In short, Chauntecleer knew by instinct every
hour of the day when it came around, and proclaimed by crowing
the arrival of each new hour. 38. **it . . . amended,** it could not be
improved upon. 40. **batailed,** with battlements (the cock's wattles).
41. **jeet,** jet. 42. **toon,** toes. This word has both the *n*-plural and
the *s*-plural in Chaucer's English; see l. 509 below. 45. **governaunce,**
control, power. 51. **debonaire,** meek. 54. **in hold,** in her grasp,
in her possession. 55. **loken,** locked. **lith,** limb.

In swete accord, "my lief is faren in londe."
For thilke tyme, as I have understonde,   60
Bestes and briddes coude speke and singe.

And so bifel, that in a dawenynge,
As Chauntecleer among his wyves alle
Sat on his perche, that was in the halle,
And next him sat this faire Pertelote,   65
This Chauntecleer gan gronen in his throte,
As man that in his dreem is drecched sore.
And whan that Pertelote thus herde him rore,
She was agast, and seyde, "O herte dere,
What eyleth yow, to grone in this manere?   70
Ye been a verray sleper, fy for shame!"
And he answerde and seyde thus, "Madame,
I pray yow, that ye take it nat a-grief:
By God, me mette I was in swich meschief
Right now, that yet myn herte is sore afright.   75
Now God," quod he, "my swevene recche aright,
And keep my body out of foul prisoun!
Me mette, how that I romed up and doun
Withinne our yerde, wher-as I saugh a beste,
Was lyk an hound, and wolde han maad areste   80
Upon my body, and wolde han had me deed.
His colour was bitwixe yelwe and reed;
And tipped was his tail, and bothe his eres,
With blak, unlyk the remenant of his heres;
His snowte smal, with glowinge eyen tweye.   85
Yet of his look for fere almost I deye;
This caused me my groning, douteles.

"Avoy!" quod she, "fy on yow, herteles!
Allas!" quod she, "for, by that God above,
Now han ye lost myn herte and al my love;   90
I can nat love a coward, by my feith.
For certes, what so any womman seith,
We alle desyren, if it mighte be,
To han housbonds hardy, wyse, and free,
And secree, and no nigard, ne no fool,   95
Ne him that is agast of every tool,
Ne noon avauntour, by that God above!
How dorste ye seyn for shame unto your love,
That any thing mighte make yow aferd?
Have ye no mannes herte, and han a berd?   100

Allas! and conne ye been agast of swevenis?
No-thing, God wot, but vanitee, in sweven is.
Swevenes engendren of replecciouns
And ofte of fume, and of complecciouns,
Whan humours been to habundant in a wight.   105
Certes this dreem, which ye han met to-night,
Cometh of the grete superfluitee
Of youre rede *colera*, pardee,
Which causeth folk to dremen in here dremes
Of arwes, and of fyr with rede lemes,   110
Of grete bestes, that they wol hem byte,
Of contek, and of whelpes grete and lyte;
Right as the humour of malencolye
Causeth ful many a man, in sleep, to crye,
For fere of blake beres, or boles blake,   115
Or elles, blake develes wole hem take.
Of othere humours coude I telle also,
That werken many a man in sleep ful wo;
But I wol passe as lightly as I can.

"Lo Catoun, which that was so wys a man,   120
Seyde he nat thus, ne do no fors of dremes?
Now, sire," quod she, "whan we flee fro the bemes,
For goddes love, as tak som laxatyf;
Up peril of my soule, and of my lyf,
I counseille yow the beste, I wol nat lye,   125
That both of colere, and of malencolye
Ye purge yow; and for ye shul nat tarie,
Though in this toun is noon apotecarie,
I shal my-self to herbes techen yow,
That shul ben for your hele, and for your prow;   130
And in our yerd tho herbes shal I fynde,
The whiche han of hir propretee, by kynde,
To purgen yow binethe, and eek above.
Forget not this, for goddes owene love!
Ye been ful colerik of compleccioun.   135
Ware the sonne in his ascencioun
Ne fynde yow nat repleet of humours hote;

60–61. **For thilke . . . singe,** "For in that same time . . . birds and beasts could speak and sing"—the usual trick of the writer of fables, who thereby colors his satire with the harmless tints of unreality. 67. **drecched,** troubled, afflicted. 73. **a-grief,** amiss. 74. **me mette,** "it met me"—a common circumlocution for "dreamt." 76. **swevene,** dream. **recche,** interpret. Chaucer in his works frequently shows us his interest in dreams, and although the careful reader will probably decide that Chaucer believed in the physiological explanation of dreams (as does Dame Pertelote in this story), it still is true that he gives plenty of space to the premonitory element which is dear to the common people. In reference to this premonitory element, *The Nun's Priest's Tale* is an interesting commentary upon the medieval attitude toward dreams, in that the two main characters, Chauntecleer and Pertelote, represent in a sense the two fundamentally different approaches to the question of dreams. 87. **douteles,** doubtless, "never fear." 88. **"Avoy!"** "Fie!", an expression of contemptuous reproach. **herteles,** "heartless" in the sense of "lacking courage or heart." 97. **avauntour,** "boaster," "braggart," which often connotes cowardice and indiscretion.

101–102. **swevenis . . . sweven is.** Identical rimes, common enough in modern humorous verse, are not considered out of place in serious verse of the Middle Ages. See note to l. 18 of the *Prologue to The Canterbury Tales.* 103. **engendren,** have their source in, come about from. 104. **fume,** air or gas on the stomach. **complecciouns,** the combination and balance of the four "humours" of the body; see the *Prologue to The Canterbury Tales* (p. II:203), and note to l. 333. 106. **Certes,** surely, certainly. 108. **rede colera.** The *colera* would be the bile. The belief was held in medical quarters that a serious overbalance of one humour in respect to the others would give a corresponding tinge to all objects seen by the patient. Too much bile was supposed to make all things appear red; note in this connection ll. 113 ff. below. 110. **lemes,** flames. 112. **contek,** conflict. 115. **boles,** bulls. 120. **Catoun,** Dionysius Cato, the name given to the unknown author of a Latin work, probably of about the fourth century, called the *Dionysii Catonis Disticha de Moribus ad Filium,* "The Couplets of Dionysius Cato to his Son on the Subject of Morals." The collection was extremely popular in the Middle Ages and well illustrates the incurable Anglo-Saxon predilection for didactic epigrams—pithy statements of the laws underlying human nature. 121. **do no fors of,** make no account of, attach no importance to. 123. **as,** a superfluous particle here; translate, if at all, as "now (go)". 124. **Up,** upon, on. 126. **colere,** choler, bile. **malencolye,** another humour, "black bile." 130. **hele,** health. **prow,** benefit, profit. 132. **by kynde,** by nature.

And if it do, I dar wel leye a grote,
That ye shul have a fevere terciane,
Or an agu, that may be youre bane.   140
A day or two ye shul have digestyves
Of wormes er ye take your laxatyves,
Of lauriol, centaure, and fumetere,
Or elles of ellebor, that groweth there,
Of catapuce, or of gaytres beryis,   145
Of erbe yve, growing in our yerd, that mery is;
Pekke hem up right as they growe, and ete hem in.
Be mery, housbond, for your fader kyn!
Dredeth no dreem; I can say yow namore."
"Madame," quod he, "*graunt mercy* of your lore.
But natheless, as touching daun Catoun,   151
That hath of wisdom such a gret renoun,
Though that he had no dremes for to drede,
By God, men may in olde bokes rede
Of many a man, more of auctoritee   155
Than ever Catoun was, so mote I thee,
That al the revers seyn of this sentence,
And han wel founden by experience,
That dremes ben significaciouns,
As wel of joye as tribulaciouns   160
That folk enduren in this lyf present.
Ther nedeth make of this noon argument;
The verray preve sheweth it in dede.
"Oon of the gretteste auctours that men rede
Seith thus, that whylom two felawes wente   165
On pilgrimage, in a ful good entente;
And happed so, thay came into a toun,
Wher as ther was swich congregacioun
Of peple, and eek so streit of herbergage,
That they ne founde as muche as o cotage,   170
In which they bothe mighte y-logged be.
Wherfor thay mosten, of necessitee,
As for that night, departen compaignye;
And ech of hem goth to his hostelrye,
And took his logging as it wolde falle.   175
That oon of hem was logged in a stalle,

Fer in a yerd, with oxen of the plough;
That other man was logged wel y-nough,
As was his aventure, or his fortune,
That us governeth alle as in commune.   180
"And so bifel, that, long er it were day,
This man mette in his bed, ther as he lay,
How that his felawe gan up-on him calle,
And seyde, 'Allas! for in an oxes stalle
This night I shal be mordred ther I lye.   185
Now help me, dere brother, er I dye;
In alle haste com to me,' he sayde.
This man out of his sleep for fere abrayde;
But whan that he was wakned of his sleep,
He turned him, and took of this no keep;   190
Him thoughte his dreem nas but a vanitee.
Thus twyës in his sleping dremed he.
And atte thridde tyme yet his felawe
Cam, as him thoughte, and seide, 'I am now slawe,
Bihold my blody woundes, depe and wyde!   195
Arys up erly in the morwe-tyde,
And at the west gate of the toun,' quod he,
'A carte ful of donge ther shaltow see,
In which my body is hid ful prively;
Do thilke carte aresten boldely.   200
My gold caused my mordre, sooth to sayn';
And tolde him every poynt how he was slayn,
With a ful pitous face, pale of hewe.
And truste wel, his dreem he fond ful trewe;
For on the morwe, as sone as it was day,   205
To his felawes in he took the way;
And whan that he cam to this oxes stalle,
After his felawe he bigan to calle.
"The hostiler answerde him anon,
And seyde, 'Sire, your felawe is agon,   210
As sone as day he wente out of the toun.'
This man gan fallen in suspecioun,
Remembring on his dremes that he mette,
And forth he goth, no lenger wolde he lette,
Unto the west gate of the toun, and fond   215
A dong-carte, as it were to donge lond,
That was arrayed in that same wyse
As ye han herd the dede man devyse;
And with an hardy herte he gan to crye
Vengeaunce and justice of this felonye: 220
'My felawe mordred is this same night,

138. leye a grote, wager a groat. A groat was a Low German coin from the trading ports of Holland and North Germany, notably from Bremen, worth about four silver pennies. 139. fevere terciane, a tertian fever, one that recurs every third day. The medieval authorities attributed the disease to a superabundance of bile or black bile; it would seem to be, according to present-day diagnosis, a malarial infection. 140. youre bane. The original meaning of *bane* is "slayer," "killer." 143–146. lauriol . . . erbe yve. The drugs mentioned in this list include the common cathartics in use during the Middle Ages. *Lauriol* is the spurge-laurel. *centaure*, the century plant, a common remedy for pain in the abdomen. *fumetere*, fumitory. *ellebor*, hellebore. *catapuce*, the caperberry. *gaytres beryis*, berries of the dogwood. *erbe yve*, ground ivy. 151. daun. Here, as elsewhere, the shortened form of the Latin *dominus* ("lord") is used as a title of respect. (Note the Spanish *Don*.) *Daun Catoun* is therefore Lord Cato. So Tennyson in his *Palace of Art* speaks of Dan Chaucer, and there is also the familiar Dan Cupid. 156. so mote I thee, a mild asseveration meaning literally "so may I prosper." 157. sentence, statement, opinion. 163. verray preve, etc., "the true test (of the statement) proves it in fact." 166. ful good entente, the best of intentions. 169. streit, "narrow"; here used in the sense of "crowded." herbergage, lodgings. 173. departen, part (company).

182. ther as, where. 188. abrayde, started up. The word is used for any kind of violent motion. 191. Him thoughte, not "he thought" but "it seemed to him," an impersonal construction. The same is true of the more common "methinks," which means "it seems to me." This is not the verb "to think," but the verb seen in the German *es dünkt mir* ("it seems to me"). nas, "ne" plus "was," therefore "was not." The construction with *but* means simply: "It seemed to him that his dream was nothing but a foolish thing." 194. slawe, slain. 203. pitous, pitiful, awakening pity. 206. in, inn. 214. lette, literally "hinder" (compare the legal phrase "without let or hindrance" or a "let" ball in tennis); then the meaning here of "linger," "loiter." 216. to donge lond, to cover land with dung. Raw sewage was carried outside the city gates and dumped. 218. devyse, describe.

And in this carte he lyth gapinge upright.
I crye out on the ministres,' quod he,
'That sholden kepe and reulen this citee;
Harrow! allas! her lyth my felawe slayn!'   225
What sholde I more un-to this tale sayn?
The peple out-sterte, and caste the cart to grounde,
And in the middel of the dong they founde
The dede man, that mordred was al newe.

"O blisful God, that art so just and trewe!   230
Lo, how that thou biwreyest mordre alway!
Mordre wol out, that se we day by day.
Mordre is so wlatsom and abhominable
To God, that is so just and resonable,
That he ne wol nat suffre it heled be;   235
Though it abyde a yeer, or two, or three,
Mordre wol out, this my conclusioun.
And right anoon, ministres of that toun
Han hent the carter, and so sore him pyned,
And eek the hostiler so sore engyned,   240
That thay biknewe hir wikkednesse anoon,
And were an-hanged by the nekke-boon.

"Here may men seen that dremes been to drede.
And certes, in the same book I rede,
Right in the nexte chapitre after this,   245
(I gabbe nat, so have I joye or blis,)
Two men that wolde han passed over see,
For certeyn cause, in-to a fer contree,
If that the wind ne hadde been contrarie,
That made hem in a citee for to tarie,   250
That stood ful mery upon an haven-syde.
But on a day, agayn the even-tyde,
The wind gan chaunge, and blew right as hem leste.
Jolif and glad they wente un-to hir reste,
And casten hem ful erly for to saille;   255
But to that oo man fel a greet mervaille.
That oon of hem, in sleping as he lay,
Him mette a wonder dreem, agayn the day;
Him thoughte a man stood by his beddes syde,
And him comaunded, that he sholde abyde,   260
And seyde him thus, 'If thou to-morwe wende,

Thou shalt be dreynt; my tale is at an ende.'
He wook, and tolde his felawe what he mette,
And preyde him his viage for to lette;
As for that day, he preyde him to abyde.   265
His felawe, that lay by his beddes syde,
Gan for to laughe, and scorned him ful faste.
'No dreem,' quod he, 'may so myn herte agaste,
That I wol lette for to do my thinges.
I sette not a straw by thy dreminges,   270
For swevenes been but vanitees and japes.
Men dreme al-day of owles or of apes,
And eek of many a mase therwithal;
Men dreme of thing that never was ne shal.
But sith I see that thou wolt heer abyde,   275
And thus for-sleuthen wilfully thy tyde,
God wot it reweth me; and have good day.'
And thus he took his leve, and wente his way.
But er that he hadde halfe his cours y-seyled,
Noot I nat why, ne what mischaunce it eyled,   280
But casuelly the shippes botme rente,
And ship and man under the water wente
In sighte of othere shippes it byside,
That with hem seyled at the same tyde.
And therfor, faire Pertelote so dere,   285
By swiche ensamples olde maistow lere,
That no man sholde been to recchelees
Of dremes, for I sey thee, doutelees,
That many a dreem ful sore is for to drede.

"Lo, in the lyf of seint Kenelm, I rede,   290
That was Kenulphus sone, the noble king
Of Mercenrike, how Kenelm mette a thing;
A lyte er he was mordred, on a day,
His mordre in his avisioun he say.
His norice him expounded every del   295
His sweven, and bad him for to kepe him wel
For traisoun; but he nas but seven yeer old,
And therfore litel tale hath he told
Of any dreem, so holy was his herte.

222. **upright.** This word does not necessarily refer to a vertical or perpendicular position, as in Modern English, so much as to straightness or rigidity of posture. One can lie "upright" in Middle English, meaning to lie straight, stretched out in a horizontal position. One can also stand "upright." The murdered man here was lying stretched out and gaping up at the light of day. 225. **Harrow! allas!** The two cries of distress are usually found in combination. The first, *Harrow!*, may originally have had some relation to the idea of "raking," "harrowing," hence "distressing" (we can still speak of a "harrowing" experience), but no doubt the original meaning had long since faded. 231. **biwreyest,** uncoverest, makest known. 233. **wlatsom,** disgusting, horrible. 235. **heled,** concealed. 239. **hent,** seized. **pyned,** tortured (to force a confession). 240. **engyned,** put on the rack or some other instrument of torture. 241. **biknewe,** acknowledged, confessed. 242. **an-hanged,** hanged. 246. **gabbe,** speak idly. It is amusing to see how consistently Chaucer has portrayed Chauntecleer as the pompous, self-important husband. 252. **agayn,** toward, just before. 254. **Jolif,** jolly, merry, with the Old French *-if* suffix still seen in "active," "pensive," etc. 255. **hem,** them. 256. **oo,** one.

262. **dreynt,** drowned. 264. **lette,** put off; see note to l. 214 above. 271. **vanitees and japes,** follies and jokes. 273. **mase,** confusion, bewilderment. 274. **shal,** shall (be). 275. **sith,** since. 276. **for-sleuthen,** waste in sloth. **tyde,** time; see the alliterative formula, "time and tide," or combinations like "Yuletide," "Christmastide," "Eventide," etc. 277. **it reweth me,** "it rues me," "I am sorry"—still another in the long list of Middle English impersonal constructions. 281. **casuelly,** by accident. 287. **recchelees,** not caring for, not heeding. 290. **seint Kenelm,** etc. The story is told in one of the many collections of medieval English saints' lives. Kenulphus (Cenwulf), mentioned in the next line, had a son Kenelm (Cenhelm). Kenulphus was King of Mercia, one of the important Anglo-Saxon kingdoms in England before King Alfred (d. 901); he died in 821. The boy Kenelm was but seven years of age at the time, and was put under the care of his aunt, who conspired to murder him. Before his death the child dreamt that he climbed into a lofty tree; one of his friends came and cut it down, whereupon the boy flew to Heaven as a bird. As a symbol of martyred childhood and innocence, Kenelm was later canonized. 294. **avisioun,** vision, dream. **say,** saw. 295. **norice,** nurse. 298. **tale,** importance, account. **told,** ascribed, attributed.

By God, I hadde lever than my sherte 300
That ye had rad his legende, as have I.
Dame Pertelote, I sey yow trewely,
Macrobeus, that writ th'avisioun
In Affrike of the worthy Cipioun,
Affermeth dremes, and seith that they been 305
Warning of thinges that men after seen.
　"And forther-more, I pray yow loketh wel
In th'olde testament, of Daniel,
If he held dremes any vanitee.
Reed eek of Joseph, and ther shul ye see 310
Wher dremes ben somtyme (I set nat alle)
Warning of thinges that shul after falle.
Loke of Egipt the king, daun Pharao,
His bakere and his boteler also,
Wher they ne felte noon effect in dremes. 315
Who-so wol seken actes of sondry remes,
May rede of dremes many a wonder thing.
　"Lo Cresus, which that was of Lyde king,
Mette he nat that he sat upon a tree;
Which signified he sholde anhanged be? 320
Lo heer Andromacha, Ectores wyf,
That day that Ector sholde lese his lyf,
She dremed on the same night biforn,
How that the lyf of Ector sholde be lorn,
If thilke day he wente in-to bataille; 325
She warned him, but it mighte nat availle;
He wente for to fighte nathelees,
But he was slayn anoon of Achilles.
But thilke tale is al to long to telle,
And eek it is ny day, I may nat dwelle. 330

Shortly I seye, as for conclusioun,
That I shal han of this avisoun
Adversitee; and I seye forther-more,
That I ne telle of laxatyves no store,
For they ben venimous, I woot it wel; 335
I hem defye, I love hem nevere a del.
　"Now let us speke of mirthe, and stinte al this;
Madame Pertelote, so have I blis,
Of o thing God hath sent me large grace;
For whan I see the beautee of your face, 340
Ye ben so scarlet-reed about youre yën,
It maketh al my drede for to dyen;
For, also siker as In principio,
Mulier est hominis confusio;
Madame, the sentence of this Latin is— 345
Womman is mannes joye and al his blis.
For whan I feele anight your softe syde,
Al be it that I may nat on yow ryde,
For that oure perche is maad so narwe, allas!
I am so ful of joye and of solas 350
That I defye bothe sweven and dreem."
And with that word he fley doun fro the beem,
For it was day, and eek his hennes alle;
And with a chuk he gan hem for to calle,
For he had founde a corn, lay in the yerd. 355
Royal he was, he was namore aferd;
He fethered Pertelote twenty tyme,
And trad as ofte, er that it was pryme.
He loketh as it were a grim leoun,
And on his toos he rometh up and doun, 360
Him deyned not to sette his foot to grounde.
He chukketh, whan he hath a corn y-founde,
And to him rennen thanne his wyves alle.
Thus royal, as a prince is in his halle,
Leve I this Chauntecleer in his pasture; 365
And after wol I telle his aventure.
　Whan that the month in which the world bigan,
That highte March, whan God first maked man,
Was complet, and [y]-passed were also,
Sin March bigan, thritty dayes and two, 370
Bifel that Chauntecleer, in al his pryde,
His seven wyves walking by his syde,
Caste up his eyen to the brighte sonne,
That in the signe of Taurus hadde y-ronne

300. **lever,** "liefer," rather. 303. **Macrobeus,** the "authority" on dreams during the Middle Ages. His accredited importance is hardly fair to another greater writer, Cicero, who, by the way, is probably "oon of the grettste auctours" of l. 164 above, since the story of the murdered traveler is found in Cicero's *De Divinatione*. Macrobeus, a Latin writer of about the fifth century, made an elaborate commentary to that section of Cicero's *De Republica* known as the *Somnium Scipionis* or "Dream of Scipio," in which commentary there appears a discussion of the various kinds of dreams and their applica-'ion to human life. It is worth noting that Macrobeus is certainly .he leading champion of the "portentous" or "premonitory" interpretation of dreams as opposed to the physiological interpretation (see note to l. 76 above). 308. **Daniel,** the Old Testament prophet. The passage in the Bible relevant to this line is Daniel, 7:1, 1 ff. 310. **Joseph.** The manner in which Joseph interpreted dreams is told in Genesis 37:40–41. The marshaling of authorities (Macrobeus, Daniel, Joseph, and the classical folk) is absolutely typical of the method of reasoning in the Middle Ages. 311. **Wher,** whether. Chauntecleer is, after all, a citizen of the late fourteenth century in Europe, which produces its Chaucer and its Mandeville. The little caution that he assumes here is symptomatic of the growing caution of the age in asserting all statements of authority as truth; this tendency is a definite indication of the coming of the Renaissance. 316. **remes,** realms. 318. **Cresus.** The story is told in *The Romance of the Rose*. Croesus, King of Lydia (603–546 B.C.) was defeated and killed by Cyrus the Great (d. 529 B.C.). 321. **Andromacha,** Andromache, the wife of Hector in Homer's *Iliad*. There is nothing in Homer about her dream; it is a fiction of the medieval authors in the development of the Legend of Troy. 322. **lese,** lose. 324. **lorn,** lost.

335. **venimous,** venomous, poisonous. 337. **stinte,** stop, cease. 343. **siker,** sure, surely. **In principio,** the beginning of the first verse of the Gospel of John or of the Book of Genesis. 344. **Mulier . . . confusio,** "woman is man's confusion," more or less of a proverb of the time. 355. **corn,** grain (of any kind). 359. **leoun,** lion. 370. **bigan,** passed, went by (not "began"). In other words, this means thirty-two days after March 31, which would be May 2–3. 374. **signe of Taurus,** the second of the twelve Signs of the Zodiac, constellations through which the sun must pass in its annual journey through the heavens. The sun would be in Taurus from about April 20 to May 20. The reference in the next line to the "twenty-one or more degrees" would put the date of Chauntecleer's adventure later than May 3; in other words Chaucer's astronomical data is a little out of line, a most unusual error for him.

Twenty degrees and oon, and somwhat more; 375
And knew by kynde and by noon other lore,
That it was pryme, and crew with blisful stevene.
"The sonne," he sayde, "is clomben up on hevene
Fourty degrees and oon, and more, y-wis.
Madame Pertelote, my worldes blis, 380
Herkneth thise blisful briddes how they singe,
And see the fresshe floures how they springe;
Ful is myn hert of revel and solas."
But sodeinly him fil a sorweful cas;
For ever the latter ende of joye is wo. 385
God woot that worldly joye is sone ago;
And if a rethor coude faire endyte,
He in a cronique saufly mighte it write,
As for a sovereyn notabilitee.
Now every wys man, lat him herkne me; 390
This storie is al-so trewe, I undertake,
As is the book of Launcelot de Lake,
That wommen holde in ful gret reverence.
Now wol I torne agayn to my sentence.
    A col-fox, ful of sly iniquitee, 395
That in the grove hadde woned yeres three,
By heigh imaginacioun forn-cast,
The same night thurgh-out the hegges brast
Into the yerd, ther Chauntecleer the faire
Was wont, and eek his wyves, to repaire; 400
And in a bed of wortes stille he lay,
Til it was passed undern of the day,
Wayting his tyme on Chauntecleer to falle
As gladly doon thise homicydes alle,
That in awayt liggen to mordre men. 405
O false mordrer lurking in thy den!
O newe Scariot, newe Genilon!
False dissimilour, O Greek Sinon
That broghtest Troye al outrely to sorwe!

O Chauntecleer, acursed be that morwe, 410
That thou into that yerd flough fro the bemes!
Thou were ful wel y-warnéd by thy dremes,
That thilke day was perilous to thee.
But what that God forwoot mot nedes be,
After the opinioun of certeyn clerkis. 415
Witnesse on him, that any perfit clerk is,
That in scole is gret altercacioun
In this matere, and greet disputisoun,
And hath ben of an hundred thousand men.
But I ne can not bulte it to the bren, 420
As can the holy doctour Augustyn,
Or Boëce, or the bishop Bradwardyn,
Whether that Goddes worthy forwiting
Streyneth me nedely for to doon a thing,
(Nedely clepe I simple necessitee); 425
Or elles, if free choys be graunted me
To do that same thing, or do it noght,
Though God forwoot it, er that it was wroght;
Or if his witing streyneth nevere a del
But by necessitee condicionel. 430
I wol not han to do of swich matere;
My tale is of a cok, as ye may here,
That took his counseil of his wyf, with sorwe,
To walken in the yerd upon that morwe
That he had met the dreem, that I yow tolde. 435
Wommennes counseils been ful ofte colde;
Wommannes counseil broghte us first to wo,
And made Adam fro paradys to go,
Ther-as he was ful mery, and wel at ese.—
But for I noot, to whom it mighte displese, 440
If I counseil of wommen wolde blame,
Passe over, for I seyde it in my game.
Rede auctours, wher they trete of swich matere,
And what thay seyn of wommen ye may here.
Thise been the cokkes wordes, and nat myne; 445

376. **by kynde**, by nature, by instinct. 377. **pryme**, the first hour of the day (6 A.M.), or roughly, from 6 to 9 in the morning. **stevene**, voice. 379. **y-wis**, indeed, in truth, surely. Forty-one degrees would be almost halfway to the zenith. In May this would be shortly after nine o'clock in the morning. 381. **briddes**, birds. 384. **sorweful cas**, sad event. 386. **ago**, gone. 387. **rethor**, rhetorician. 389. **sovereyn**, mighty superior. 392. **Launcelot de Lake**, the great chivalric hero of the Arthurian saga; the reference here is probably to the French romance (book) of the thirteenth century, which was the source of all English treatments of this non-English hero. 396. **woned**, dwelt. 397. **heigh imaginacioun forn-cast**, by divine foreknowledge (*imaginacioun*) foreordained. 398. **brast**, burst. 401. **wortes**, herbs. 402. **undern**, early morning. The usual hour conveyed by this term is nine o'clock in the morning, but it is quite possible that, as in the case of *pryme* (see note to l. 377 above), the word expresses a two- or three-hour period following the precise original hour. On this analogy, *undern* could mean anywhere from nine o'clock in the morning until noon. 405. **liggen**, lie. 407. **Scariot**, Judas Iscariot, the disciple who betrayed Christ; see Matthew, 26:14–25 and 47–56. **Genilon**, Ganelon, the traitor in *The Song of Roland* (p. II:110), who betrayed Roland's command to the Saracens. 408. **Sinon**, the man who persuaded the Trojans to admit the Wooden Horse to Troy, by which stratagem the city was captured. The story was probably familiar to medieval readers through Virgil's *Aeneid*, Book II (p. I:375).

411. **flough**, flew. 414. **forwoot**, foreknows, has foreknowledge of; see note to l. 397 above. The question of Providence vs. Free Will was one of the favorite points of discussion among medieval theologians and philosophers. 418. **disputisoun**, argument, dispute. 420. **bulte . . . bren**, "sift it to the bran," "analyze the question thoroughly and leave nothing behind but immaterial or irrelevant facts." Chaucer's attitude, here as elsewhere, is that of the casual spectator and observer whenever weighty or insoluble problems of philosophy happen to get in his way. 421. **Augustyn**, St. Augustine of Hippo, the Church Father (354–430), who was the great representative of orthodox doctrine. 422. **Boëce**, Boethius (480?–524), whose *Consolation of Philosophy* was the great book on philosophy in the Middle Ages. **bishop Bradwardyn**, lecturer at Oxford and Archbishop of Canterbury at the time of his death in 1349. His treatment of the problem was conservative and orthodox—he relied chiefly upon Providence. 424. **Streyneth**, constrains, forces. **nedely**, of necessity, by necessity. 425. **clepe**, call. 430. **necessitee condicionel**, necessity conditioned by God's foreknowledge as contrasted to simple necessity, whereby a thing happens because it must happen. 440. **noot**, "ne" plus "woot," therefore "know not." 442. **game**, joke, sport. 443. **auctours**, authors and authorities. Once more there appears the medieval love of authority (*magister dixit*) motif; see note to l. 310 above.

I can noon harm of no womman divyne.
   Faire in the sond, to bathe hir merily,
Lyth Pertelote, and alle hir sustres by,
Agayn the sonne; and Chauntecleer so free
Song merier than the mermayde in the see;   450
For Phisiologus seith sikerly,
How that they singen wel and merily.
And so bifel that, as he caste his yë,
Among the wortes, on a boterflyë,
He was war of this fox that lay ful lowe.   455
No-thing ne liste him thanne for to crowe,
But cryde anon, "cok, cok," and up he sterte,
As man that was affrayed in his herte.
For naturelly a beest desyreth flee
Fro his contrarie, if he may it see,   460
Though he never erst had seyn it with his yë.
   This Chauntecleer, whan he gan him espyë,
He wolde han fled, but that the fox anon
Seyde, "Gentil sire, allas! wher wol ye gon?
Be ye affrayed of me that am your freend?   465
Now certes, I were worse than a feend,
If I to yow wolde harm or vileinye.
I am nat come your counseil for t'espye;
But trewely, the cause of my cominge
Was only for to herkne how that ye singe.   470
For trewely ye have as mery a stevene,
As eny aungel hath, that is in hevene;
Therwith ye han in musik more felinge
Than hadde Boëce, or any that can singe.
My lord your fader (God his soule blesse!),   475
And eek your moder, of hir gentilesse,
Han in myn hous y-been, to my gret ese;
And certes, sire, ful fayn wolde I yow plese.
But for men speke of singing, I wol saye,
So mote I brouke wel myn eyen tweye,   480

Save yow, I herde never man so singe,
As dide your fader in the morweninge;
Certes, it was of herte, al that he song.
And for to make his voys the more strong,
He wolde so peyne him, that with both his yën   485
He moste winke, so loude he wolde cryen,
And stonden on his tiptoon ther-with-al,
And strecche forth his nekke long and smal.
And eek he was of swich discrecioun,
That ther nas no man in no regioun   490
That him in song or wisdom mighte passe.
I have wel rad in daun Burnel the Asse,
Among his vers, how that there was a cok,
For that a preestes sone yaf him a knok
Upon his leg, whyl he was yong and nyce,   495
He made him for to lese his benefyce.
But certeyn, ther nis no comparisoun
Bitwix the wisdom and discrecioun
Of youre fader, and of his subtiltee.
Now singeth, sire, for seinte Charitee,   500
Let see, conne ye your fader countrefete?"
This Chauntecleer his winges gan to bete,
As man that coude his tresoun nat espye,
So was he ravisshed with his flaterye.
   Allas! ye lordes, many a fals flatour   505
Is in your courtes, and many a losengeour,
That plesen yow wel more, by my feith,
Than he that soothfastnesse unto yow seith.
Redeth Ecclesiaste of flaterye;
Beth war, ye lordes, of hir trecherye.   510
   This Chauntecleer stood hye up-on his toos,
Strecching his nekke, and heeld his eyen cloos,
And gan to crowe loude for the nones;
And daun Russel the fox sterte up at ones,
And by the gargat hente Chauntecleer,   515
And on his bak toward the wode him beer,
For yet ne was ther no man that him sewed.
O destinee, that mayst nat been eschewed!

446. **I . . . devyne,** "I can guess (or imagine) no harm of any woman," probably to be taken as sarcastic. The double negative, a feature of Early English, is purely for emphasis. In no case do two negatives cancel each other out to make a positive. 451. **Phisiologus . . . sikerly.** *Sikerly* means *certainly.* The *Physiologus* is the Latin Physiologus or Bestiary, a collection of verses treating of the habits of certain animals and drawing therefrom moral lessons of Christian import. 460. **contrarie,** opposite (sb.). According to medieval belief, every creature had another creature that was its contrary, toward which it felt a natural dislike or fear (dog to cat, snake to bird, etc.). 461. **erst,** before, first. The antipathy would be instinctive. 474. **Boëce.** Boethius (see note to l. 422 above) was also an authority on the music of his time. 476. **gentilesse.** The word *gentilesse*, a combination in sense of "gentleness" and "gentility," has a variety of meanings, which, when blended together, come close to producing the ideal of chivalry either for man or for woman. Nobility or aristocracy of birth, nobility of character according to the Christian or knightly codes, courtesy, good breeding, delicacy, tact, and even slenderness of body—all come at one time or another under this one word *gentilesse.* But most important of all considerations here is the matter of innate virtuous qualities. In consequence, no one translation of the word can fit any one occurrence thereof, and the reader must choose for himself. 480. **So . . . brouke,** another extremely mild oath, of the same kind as "So mote I thee" of l. 156 above, "as I may enjoy my eyes!"

486. **winke,** to close the eyes, not to blink them momentarily, as in Modern English. 488. **smal,** narrow, slender. 492. **daun Burnel the Asse.** There was an Anglo-Latin poem of the twelfth century, satirical in nature, by Nigel Wireker, called *Burnellus, seu Speculum Stultorum* (Burnell, or the Mirror of Fools). A young man named Gundulfus was annoyed by a cock, and upon throwing a stone broke the bird's leg. Later Gundulfus was to be ordained, but the injured cock delayed his crowing, so that Gundulfus overslept and lost his benefice, or church living. 495. **nyce.** As usual before the seventeenth century, this word means here "ignorant," "foolish." 501. **countrefete,** imitate and match. This word does not have in Middle English the suggestion of falseness or criminality that it has assumed in Modern English. 505. **flatour,** flatterer. 506. **losengeour,** flatterer. 508. **soothfastnesse,** truth. 509. **Ecclesiaste of flaterye.** The reference is to the Apocryphal Book of Ecclesiasticus, not to the Poetic Book of Ecclesiastes in the Old Testament. The specific passages in Ecclesiasticus, which are too long to quote here, are to chapters 12: 10 ff. and 27: 26. 514. **Russel.** This, in the medieval Beast Epic, was the name of one of the sons of Reynard the Fox. 515. **gargat,** throat, **hente,** seized. 517. **sewed,** pursued, followed.

Allas, that Chauntecleer fleigh fro the bemes!
Allas, his wyf ne roghte nat of dremes! 520
And on a Friday fil al this meschaunce.
O Venus, that art goddesse of plesaunce,
Sin that thy servant was this Chauntecleer,
And in thy service dide al his poweer,
More for delyt, than world to multiplye, 525
Why woldestow suffre him on thy day to dye?
O Gaufred, dere mayster soverayn,
That, whan thy worthy king Richard was slayn
With shot, compleynedest his deth so sore,
Why ne hadde I now thy sentence and thy lore, 530
The Friday for to chide, as diden ye?
(For on a Friday soothly slayn was he.)
Than wolde I shewe yow how that I coude pleyne
For Chauntecleres drede, and for his peyne.

Certes, swich cry ne lamentacioun 535
Was never of ladies maad, whan Ilioun
Was wonne, and Pirrus with his streite swerd,
Whan he hadde hent king Priam by the berd,
And slayn him (as saith us *Eneydos*),
As maden alle the hennes in the clos, 540
Whan they had seyn of Chauntecleer the sighte.
But sovereynly dame Pertelote shrighte,
Ful louder than dide Hasdrubales wyf,
Whan that hir housbond hadde lost his lyf,
And that the Romayns hadde brend Cartage; 545
She was so ful of torment and of rage,
That wilfully into the fyr she sterte,
And brende hir-selven with a stedfast herte.
O woful hennes, right so cryden ye,
As, whan that Nero brende the citee 550
Of Rome, cryden senatoures wyves,
For that hir housbondes losten alle hir lyves;
Withouten gilt this Nero hath hem slayn.
Now wol I torne to my tale agayn:

This sely widwe, and eek hir doghtres two, 555
Herden thise hennes crye and maken wo,
And out at dores sterten they anoon,
And syen the fox toward the grove goon,
And bar upon his bak the cok away;

And cryden, "Out! harrow! and weylaway! 560
Ha, ha, the fox!" and after him they ran,
And eek with staves many another man;
Ran Colle our dogge, and Talbot, and Gerland,
And Malkin, with a distaf in hir hand;
Ran cow and calf, and eek the verray hogges 565
So were they fered for berking of the dogges
And shouting of the men and wimmen eke,
They ronne so, hem thoughte hir herte breke.
They yolleden as feendes doon in helle;
The dokes cryden as men wolde hem quelle; 570
The gees for fere flowen over the trees;
Out of the hyve cam the swarm of bees;
So hidous was the noyse, a! *benedicite!*
Certes, he Jakke Straw, and his meynee,
Ne made never shoutes half so shrille, 575
Whan that they wolden any Fleming kille,
As thilke day was maad upon the fox.
Of bras thay broghten bemes, and of box,
Of horn, of boon, in whiche they blewe and pouped,
And therwithal thay shryked and they houped; 580
It seemed as that heven sholde falle.
Now, gode men, I pray yow herkneth alle!

Lo, how fortune turneth sodeinly
The hope and pryde eek of hir enemy!
This cok, that lay upon the foxes bak, 585
In al his drede, un-to the fox he spak,
And seyde, "Sire, if that I were as ye,
Yet sholde I seyn (as wis God helpe me):
'Turneth agayn, ye proude cherles alle!
A verray pestilence up-on yow falle! 590
Now am I come un-to this wodes syde,
Maugree your heed, the cok shal heer abyde;
I wol him ete in feith, and that anon.'"
The fox answerde, "In feith, it shal be don"—
And as he spak that word, al sodeinly 595
This cok brak from his mouth deliverly,
And heighe up-on a tree he fleigh anon.
And whan the fox saugh that he was y-gon,
"Allas!" quod he, "O Chauntecleer, allas!
I have to yow," quod he, "y-doon trespas, 600
In-as-muche as I maked yow aferd,
Whan I yow hente, and broghte out of the yerd;
But, sire, I dide it in no wikke entente;
Com doun, and I shal telle yow what I mente.

---

520. **roghte**, recked, heeded, took account of. 527. **Gaufred**, Geoffrey de Vinsauf, a writer on the art of poetry. His great work, the *Poetria Nova*, appeared shortly after the death of Richard I (the Lion-Heart) of England, near 1200. Geoffrey's model for an elegy consists of some lines of lament on the death of Richard. 532. **on a Friday**. Friday has been a traditionally unlucky day because it has been associated with the goddess of love (Venus, Freya), who is notoriously fickle and changeable. The death of the Saviour on Friday has stimulated the supersitition most powerfully. 533. **pleyne**, complain, lament for. 539. **Eneydos**, Virgil's *Aeneid* (p. 1:369). 540. **clos**, close (sb.), yard. 542. **sovereynly**, more than anyone else. **shrighte**, shrieked. 543–545. **louder . . . Cartage**. Hasdrubal was ruler of Carthage when the Romans sacked it (146 B.C.). **brend**, burned. 546. **rage**, not "wrath" or "anger" in our modern sense, but "madness." 550. **Nero . . . citee**, a reference to the disastrous fire at Rome during the reign of Nero (37–68) in the year 64. Nero was popularly supposed to have set the fire himself, but modern historians disbelieve the story. 555. **sely**, good.

565. **verray hogges**, even the hogs. 570. **dokes**, ducks. **quelle**, kill. 574. **Jakke Straw . . . meynee**, Jack Straw and his followers. This passage is virtually the only one in Chaucer's works having reference to an important event in England during his lifetime. The Peasants' Revolt of 1381 was featured by rioting against the Flemish (Flemings) who had settled in London and adjacent parts to pursue their occupation of weaving, at which they were expert. The competition with native workers offered by the Flemish in the textile industry was the chief reason for the bad feeling toward them on the part of the English. 578. **bemes**, trumpets, horns. **box**, box-wood; there were wooden as well as metal trumpets. 579. **pouped**, puffed. 580. **houped**, whooped. 592. **Maugree your heed**, "in spite of your head," "in spite of you." 596. **deliverly**, quickly. 603. **wikke**, wicked, evil.

I shal seye sooth to yow, God help me so."   605
"Nay than," quod he, "I shrewe us bothe two,
And first I shrewe my-self, bothe blood and bones,
If thou bigyle me ofter than ones.
Thou shalt namore, thurgh thy flaterye
Do me to singe and winke with myn yë.   610
For he that winketh, whan he sholde see,
Al wilfully, God lat him never thee!"
"Nay," quod the fox, "but God yive him mes-
      chaunce,
That is so undiscreet of governaunce,
That jangleth whan he sholde holde his pees."   615
      Lo, swich it is for to be recchelees,
And necligent, and truste on flaterye.
But ye that holden this tale a folye,
As of a fox, or of a cok and hen,
Taketh the moralitee, good men.   620
For seint Paul seith, that al that writen is,
To our doctryne it is y-write, y-wis.
Taketh the fruyt, and lat the chaf be stille.
      Now, gode God, if that it be Thy wille,
As seith my Lord, so make us alle good men;   625
And bringe us to His heighe blisse. Amen.

THE PARDONER'S TALE

The Pardoner, hypocrite, swindler, winebibber, and eunuch, is a repulsive figure among the Canterbury pilgrims. In his portrait he appeared as an unattractive physical specimen, but he obviously had a personality of some kind beyond the average, for he boasts of his success as an orator and a wielder of words. His tale bears him out on that point, for it is one of the most effective pieces of writing in all medieval literature—powerful, dramatic, economical to the point of terseness, unforgettable.

The pilgrims pause beside the road, and the Pardoner, asked for a story, requests that he be allowed some liquid refreshment first. Warmed by his drink, he proceeds to a remarkable prologue in which he exposes himself and all the frauds and deceits which he practices upon the populace, what with his pig's bones and rags which he palms off as holy relics. He then launches upon his moral tale, which is in reality a medieval sermon on the evils of avarice and self-indulgence. Imbedded in the sermon is the characteristic *exemplum*—in this case *The Pardoner's Tale* itself. At the conclusion the Pardoner shamelessly bids the pilgrims step up and take out spiritual insurance against the perils of their expedition by

buying some of his relics; with equal shamelessness he bids the Host to be the first to acquiesce, for he has considered the Host's inveterate swearing and profanity to be a heinous sin. Unfortunately the Host is too much of a fighter, and the result is disastrous for the Pardoner, who retires in disorder.

It is not known where Chaucer got this particular version, but the story itself has been traced to the Orient. The setting of the pestilence must have been suggested to Chaucer and his contemporaries by the Black Death and all its horrors; indeed, *The Pardoner's Tale* is unusual for Chaucer, in that it makes an allusion, however remote, to events of contemporary or near-contemporary interest. The terse style and rushing pace of the narrative, in combination with the impressive dramatic force, make the tale one of the most remarkable of Chaucer's achievements.

THE PROLOGUE
OF THE PARDONER'S TALE

LORDYNGES (quod he), in chirches whan I
      preche,
I peyne me to han an hauteyn speche,
And rynge it out as round as gooth a belle,
For I kan al by rote that I telle.
My theme is alwey oon and ever was,   5
"Radix malorum est Cupiditas."
      First I pronounce whennes that I come,
And thanne my bulles shewe I, alle and some;
Oure lige lordes seel on my patente,
That shewe I first, my body to warente,   10
That no man be so boold, ne preest ne clerk,
Me to destourbe of Cristes hooly werk.
And after that thanne telle I forth my tales,
Bulles of popes and of cardynales,
Of patriarkes and bishopes I shewe,   15
And in Latyn I speke a wordes fewe,
To saffron with my predicacioun,
And for to stire hem to devocioun.
Thanne shew I forth my longe cristal stones,
Ycrammed ful of cloutes and of bones;   20
Relikes been they, as wenen they echoon.
Thanne have I in latoun a sholder-boon
Which that was of an hooly Jewes sheepe.
"Goode men," I seye, "taak of my wordes keepe:

606. **shrewe**, curse. 612. **God . . . thee**, "God let him never prosper," a malediction parallel to the "So mote I thee" of l. 156 above. 614. **governaunce**, self-control, behavior. 615. **jangleth**, chatter, babble. 616. **recchelees**, reckless, careless. 621–622. **seint Paul . . . y-write.** "For whatever things were written aforetime were written for our learning." (Romans, 15: 4). The doctrine is implicit in all medieval literature until an idea of art for art's sake began to emerge in the Rennaissance.

2. **hauteyn**, exalted, eloquent. 6. **"Radix . . . Cupiditas."**, "The root of evil is greed." 8. **bulles**, bulls not from the Pope, in all probability, but rather from the local bishop (the *lige lorde* in l. 9 below), although, since the Pardoner's pardons had come hot from Rome (see *Prologue to The Canterbury Tales*, p. 11:213, l. 687), the Pope may be actually the source. 9. **patente**, an "open" document conferring the rights and privileges of the Pardoner. 10. **warente**, guarantee, safeguard. 17. **saffron . . . predicacioun**, to color my sermon; saffron is a yellow dye newly brought to Europe from the Middle East. 19. **cristal stones**, hollow glass cases for the preservation of relics. 20. **cloutes**, rags. 22. **latoun**, an alloy of copper and zinc. 23. **hooly Jewes sheepe**, the sheep of a Jewish patriarch of the Old Testament; Jews after the incarnation of Christ would never be called holy in the Middle Ages.

If that this boon be wasshe in any welle, 25
If cow, or calf, or sheep, or oxe swelle,
That any worm hath ete, or worm ystonge,
Taak water of that welle, and wassh his tonge,
And it is hool anon; and forthermoor,
Of pokkes and of scabbe and every soor 30
Shal every sheepe be hool that of this welle
Drynketh a draughte; taak kepe eek what I telle,
If that the goode man that the beestes oweth,
Wol every wyke, er that the cok hym croweth,
Fastynge, drinken of this welle a draughte, 35
As thilke hooly Jew oure eldres taughte,
Hise beestes and his stoor shal multiplie.
And, sire, also it heeleth jalousie;
For though a man be falle in jalous rage,
Lat maken with this water his potage, 40
And nevere shal he moore his wyf mistriste,
Though he the soothe of hir defaute wiste,
Al had she taken preestes two or thre.
    Heere is a miteyn, eek, that ye may see:
He that his hand wol putte in this mitayn, 45
He shal have multipliyng of his grayn
What he hath sowen, be it whete or otes,
So that he offre pens, or elles grotes.
Goode men and wommen, o thyng warne I yow,
If any wight be in this chirche now, 50
That hath doon synne horrible, that he
Dar nat for shame of it yshryven be,
Or any womman, be she yong or old,
That hath ymaad hir housbonde cokewold,
Swich folk shal have no power ne no grace 55
To offren to my relikes in this place.
And who so fyndeth hym out of swich fame,
He wol come up and offre, on Goddes name,
And I assoille him, by the auctoritee
Which that by bulle ygraunted was to me." 60
    By this gaude have I wonne, yeer by yeer,
An hundred mark, sith I was pardoner.
I stonde lyk a clerk in my pulpet,
And whan the lewed peple is doun yset,
I preche so, as ye han herd bifoore, 65
And telle an hundred false japes moore.
Thanne peyne I me to strecche forth the nekke,
And est and west upon the peple I bekke,
As doth a dowve sittyng on a berne.
Myne handes and my tonge goon so yerne 70
That it is joye to se my bisynesse.
Of avarice and of swich cursednesse
Is al my prechyng, for to make hem free
To yeven hir pens; and namely unto me!

For myn entente is nat but for to wynne, 75
And no thyng for correccioun of synne.
I rekke nevere, whan that they been beryed,
Though that hir soules goon a-blakeberyed,
For certes, many a predicacioun
Comth ofte tyme of yvel entencioun. 80
Som for plesance of folk, and flaterye,
To ben avaunced by ypocrisye,
And som for veyne glorie, and som for hate.
For whan I dar noon oother weyes debate,
Thanne wol I stynge hym with my tonge smerte 85
In prechyng, so that he shal not asterte
To been defamed falsely, if that he
Hath trespased to my bretheren, or to me.
For though I telle noght his propre name,
Men shal wel knowe that it is the same 90
By signes, and by othere circumstances.
Thus quyte I folk that doon us displesances,
Thus spitte I out my venym, under hewe
Of hoolynesse, to semen hooly and trewe.
    But shortly, myn entente I wol devyse; 95
I preche of no thyng but for coveityse.
Therfore my theme is yet, and evere was,
"*Radix malorum est Cupiditas.*"
Thus kan I preche agayn that same vice
Which that I use, and that is avarice. 100
But though myself be gilty in that synne,
Yet kan I maken oother folk to twynne
From avarice, and soore to repente;
But that is nat my principal entente.
I preche no thyng but for coveitise; 105
Of this mateere it oghte ynogh suffise.
Thanne telle I hem ensamples many oon
Of olde stories longe tyme agoon,
For lewed peple loven tales olde;
Swiche thynges kan they wel reporte and holde.
What? trowe ye, the whiles I may preche, 111
And wynne gold and silver for I teche,
That I wol lyve in poverte wilfully?
Nay, nay, I thoghte it nevere, trewely.
For I wol preche and begge in sondry landes, 115
I wol nat do no labour with myne handes,
Ne make baskettes, and lyve thereby,
Because I wol nat beggen ydelly.
I wol non of the apostles counterfete;
I wol have money, wolle, chese, and whete, 120
Al were it yeven of the povrest page,
Or of the povrest widwe in a village,
Al sholde hir children sterve for famyne.
Nay! I wol drinke licour of the vyne,
And have a joly wenche in every toun. 125

25. **welle,** water-spring. 33. **oweth,** owns, possesses. 34. **wyke,**
week. 37. **stoor,** possessions. 42. **defaute,** fault, offense. 43. **Al,**
although. 44. **miteyn,** mitten, glove. 48. **So that,** provided that.
58. **offre,** make his offering. 61. **gaude,** trickery. 62. **mark.** The
mark was in Chaucer's time about the equivalent of fourteen shillings.
64. **lewed,** laymen, or perhaps also in the secondary sense of ignorant
folk. 66. **japes,** tricks. 68. **bekke,** nod, glance. 69. **dowve,** dove,
pigeon. 70. **yerne,** eagerly, quickly.

76. **no thyng,** not at all. 77–78. I . . . **a-blakeberyed,** "after they
have been buried, I don't care if their souls go a-blackberrying (that
is, wandering off)." 82. **avaunced,** advanced. 96. **for,** concerning,
in reference to. 102. **twynne,** part from. 113. **poverte wilfully?**
Willful, or voluntary, poverty is that kind assumed by the holy
Orders. 119. **counterfete,** imitate, emulate. 121. **page,** little boy.

But herkneth, lordings, in conclusioun;
Your lyking is that I shal telle a tale.
Now have I dronke a draughte of corny ale,
By God, I hope I shal yow telle a thing
That shal, by resoun, been at your lyking. 130
For, thogh myself be a ful vicious man,
A moral tale yet I yow telle can,
Which I am wont to preche, for to winne.
Now holde your pees, my tale I wol beginne.

THE PARDONER'S TALE

In Flaundres whylom was a companye 135
Of yonge folk, that haunteden folye,
As ryot, hasard, stewes, and tavernes,
Wher-as, with harpes, lutes, and giternes,
They daunce and pleye at dees bothe day and
  night,
And ete also and drinken over hir might, 140
Thurgh which they doon the devel sacrifyse
With-in that develes temple, in curséd wyse,
By superfluitee abhominable;
Hir othes been so grete and so dampnable,
That it is grisly for to here hem swere; 145
Our blisséd Lordes body they to-tere;
Hem thoughte that Jewes rente hym noght ynough,
And ech of hem at otheres synne lough.
And right anon thanne comen tombesteres,
Fetys and smale, and yonge frutesteres, 150
Syngeres with harpes, baudes, wafereres,
Whiche been the verray develes officeres
To kyndle and blowe the fyr of lecherye,
That is annexed unto glotonye.
The hooly writ take I to my witnesse, 155
That luxurie is in wyn and dronkenesse.
  Lo, how that dronken Looth unkyndely
Lay by hise doghtres two unwityngly;
So dronke he was, he nyste what he wroghte.
Herodes, whoso wel the stories soghte, 160
Whan he of wyn was repleet at his feeste,

Right at his owene table he yaf his heeste
To sleen the Baptist John, ful giltelees.
Senec seith a good word, doutelees;
He seith, he kan no difference fynde 165
Bitwix a man that is out of his mynde,
And a man which that is dronkelewe,
But that woodnesse fallen in a shrewe
Persevereth lenger than dooth dronkenesse.
O glotonye, ful of cursednesse! 170
O cause first of oure confusioun!
O original of oure dampnacioun
Til Crist hadde boght us with his blood agayn!
Lo, how deere, shortly for to sayn,
Aboght was thilke cursed vileynye! 175
Corrupt was al this world for glotonye!
Adam oure fader, and his wyf also,
Fro Paradys to labour and to wo
Were dryven for that vice, it is no drede;
For whil that Adam fasted, as I rede, 180
He was in Paradys, and whan that he
Eet of the fruyt deffended on the tree,
Anon he was out-cast to wo and peyne.
O glotonye, on thee wel oghte us pleyne!
O, wiste a man how manye maladyes 185
Folwen of excesse and of glotonyes,
He wolde been the moore mesurable
Of his diete, sittynge at his table.
Allas! the shorte throte, the tendre mouth
Maketh that est and west and north and south 190
In erthe, in eir, in water, man to swynke
To gete a glotoun deyntee mete and drynke!
Of this matiere, O Paul! wel kanstow trete,
"Mete unto wombe and wombe eek unto mete
Shal God destroyen bothe," as Paulus seith. 195
Allas, a foul thyng is it, by my feith!
To seye this word, and fouler is the dede,
Whan man so drinketh of the whyte and rede,
That of his throte he maketh his privee,
Thurgh thilke cursed superfluitee. 200
  The apostel weping seith ful pitously,
"Ther walken many of whiche yow told have I,
I seye it now weping with pitous voys,
That they been enemys of Cristes croys,
Of whiche the ende is deeth, wombe is her god." 205
O wombe! O bely! O stinking cod,
Fulfild of donge and of corrupcioun!
At either ende of thee foul is the soun.

128. **corny ale**, ale with plenty of grain or body to it. 130. **by resoun**, rightfully. 137. **hasard**, gambling, games of chance. 138. **giternes**, citherns, small stringed instruments. 139. **dees**, dice. 140. **over hir might**, beyond their powers, with disastrous effect. 146. **to-tere**, a reference to the "tearing" or "rending" of Christ's body through ill-advised oaths like "By God's bones," "By God's blood!" God in all such oaths is Christ. 148. **lough**, laugh. 149. **tombesteres**, female tumblers, dancing-girls. 150. **frutesteres**, women who sell fruit; they were traditionally prostitutes. 151. **wafereres**, sellers of cakes and wafers, pastry and confectionery. 153–154. **lecherye . . . glotonye**. These two of the Seven Deadly Sins were nearly always bracketed in the medieval treatment of sin. 155–156. **The hooly writ . . . dronkenesse**. "And be not drunk with wine, wherein is excess."—Ephesians, 5:18; "Wine is a mocker, strong drink is raging; and whosoever is deceived thereby is not wise."—Proverbs, 20:1. 157. **dronken Looth**. The story of Lot's incest is told in Genesis, 19:30–36. **unkyndely**, unnaturally. 160. **Herodes**. The basis for the stories about Herod, Herodias, the daughter of Herodias (Salome), and John the Baptist is in Matthew, 14:3–12, and Mark, 6:17–29.

162. **yaf his heeste**, gave his commands. 164. **Senec**, Seneca (3 B.C.– 65 A.D.), the Roman philosopher and writer of tragedies. 168. **woodnesse**, madness, insanity. 173. **boght**, bought and paid for, redeemed. 182. **deffended**, forbidden. For the story, see Genesis, 3. 191. **swynke**, labor. 195. **as Paulus seith**: "Meats for the belly (*wombe*), and the belly for meats; but God shall destroy both it and them."—I Corinthians, 6:13. 202–205. **"Ther walken . . . her god."** "For many walk, of whom I have told you often, and now tell you even weeping, that they are the enemies of the cross of Christ; whose end is destruction, whose God is their belly," etc.—Philippians, 3:18–19. 206. **cod**, gut, stomach, intestines. 207. **Fulfild**, filled full.

How greet labour and cost is thee to finde!
Thise cokes, how they stampe, and streyne, and
    grinde,   210
And turnen substance into accident,
To fulfille al thy likerous talent!
Out of the harde bones knokke they
The mary, for they caste noght a-wey
That may go thurgh the golet softe and swote; 215
Of spicerye of leef, and bark, and rote
Shal been his sauce y-maked by delyt,
To make him yet a newer appetyt.
But certes, he that haunteth swich delyces
Is deed, whyl that he liveth in tho vyces. 220
    A lecherous thing is wyn, and dronkenesse
Is ful of stryving and of wrecchednesse.
O dronke man, disfigured is thy face,
Sour is thy breeth, foul artow to embrace,
And thurgh thy dronke nose semeth the soun 225
As though thou seydest ay "Sampsoun, Sampsoun!"
And yet, God wot, Sampsoun drank never no wyn.
Thou fallest, as it were a stiked swyn;
Thy tonge is lost, and al thyn honest cure;
For dronkenesse is verray sepulture 230
Of mannes wit and his discrecioun.
In whom that drinke hath dominacioun,
He can no conseil kepe, it is no drede.
Now kepe yow fro the whyte and fro the rede,
And namely, fro the white wyn of Lepe, 235
That is to selle in Fysshstrete, or in Chepe.
This wyn of Spaigne crepeth subtilly
In othere wynes, growynge faste by,
Of which ther ryseth swich fumositee,
That whan a man hath dronken draughtes three 240
And weneth that he be at hoom in Chepe,
He is in Spaigne, right at the toune of Lepe,
Nat at the Rochele, ne at Burdeux toun,
And thanne wol he seye "Sampsoun, Sampsoun!"
But herkneth, lordes, o word, I yow preye, 245
That alle the sovereyn actes, dar I seye,
Of victories in the Olde Testament,
Thurgh verray God that is omnipotent,
Were doon in abstinence and in preyere.
Looketh the Bible, and ther ye may it leere. 250
Looke, Attilla, the grete conquerour,

Deyde in his sleepe, with shame and dishonour,
Bledynge ay at his nose in dronkenesse.
A capitayn sholde lyve in sobrenesse;
And over al this avyseth yow right wel, 255
What was comaunded unto Lamuel,
Nat Samuel, but Lamuel, seye I;
Redeth the Bible and fynde it expresly,
Of wyne-yevyng to hem that han justise.
Namoore of this, for it may wel suffise. 260
    And now that I have spoken of glotonye,
Now wol I yow deffenden hasardrye.
Hasard is verray moder of lesynges,
And of deceite and cursed forswerynges,
Blasphemyng of Crist, manslaughtre and wast also 265
Of catel and of tyme, and forthermo
It is repreeve and contrarie of honour
For to ben holde a commune hasardour.
And ever the hyer he is of estaat,
The more is he holden desolaat. 270
If that a prince useth hasardrye,
In alle governaunce and policye
He is, as by commune opinioun,
Y-holde the lasse in reputacioun.
    Stilbon, that was a wys embassadour, 275
Was sent to Corinthe, in ful greet honour,
Fro Lacedomie, to make hir alliaunce.
And whan he cam, him happede, par chaunce,
That alle the grettest that were of that lond,
Pleyinge atte hasard he hem fond. 280
For which, as sone as it mighte be,
He stal him hoom agayn to his contree,
And seyde, "ther wol I nat lese my name;
N' I wol nat take on me so greet defame,
Yow for to allye un-to none hasardours. 285
Sendeth othere wyse embassadours;
For, by my trouthe, me were lever dye,
Than I yow sholde to hasardours allye.
For ye that been so glorious in honours
Shul nat allyen yow with hasardours 290
As by my wil, ne as by my tretee."
This wyse philosophre thus seyde he.
    Loke eek that, to the king Demetrius
The king of Parthes, as the book seith us,
Sente him a paire of dees of gold in scorn, 295
For he hadde used hasard ther-biforn;
For which he heeld his glorie or his renoun
At no value or reputacioun.
Lordes may finden other maner pley

209. **How greet . . . finde!** How great a labor and cost it is to provide for (*finde*) thee! 211. **substance into accident.** In a sense peculiar to medieval philosophy, the "substance" of a thing is its real essence; the "accident" comprises the external qualities (color, weight, shape, etc.). The cooks, then, must take an edible and labor to change its "accident" in such a way as to tickle the palate afresh. 212. **likerous talent,** lecherous or gluttonous appetite. 214. **mary,** marrow. 229. **honest cure,** care for one's honor, self-respect. 235. **Lepe,** a town near Cadiz, Spain. 236. **Fysshstrete . . . Chepe.** Fishstreet was a very busy mercantile street near London Bridge. Chaucer's father had been a wine-dealer in the immediate vicinity of Fishstreet. *Chepe,* Cheapside, was another. 239. **fumositee,** fumes, gas. 243. **the Rochele,** La Rochelle, France. **Burdeux toun,** Bordeaux, France. 251. **Attilla,** Attila, the great leader of the Huns, whose disastrous inroads into Western Europe threatened the foundations of Occidental culture, died in 453, according to story, as a result of overdissipation on his wedding night.

256. **Lamuel,** Lemuel. Note the words of Lemuel in Proverbs, 30, notably the passage beginning in verse 4 on the evils of strong drink. 264. **deceite and cursed forswerynges,** swearing falsely, taking "the name of the Lord thy God in vain." 267. **repreeve and contrarie of honour,** a shame and a foe to honor. 270. **holden desolaat,** considered debased. 275. **Stilbon,** etc. The story is told in a late Greek chronicle, but the ambassador's name there was *Chilon.* 293. **Demetrius,** etc. This story is taken from the same source as that of Stilbon's legend (see preceding note); we are uncertain as to which of several kings by the name of Demetrius the incident treats.

Honeste y-nough to dryve the day awey.   300
    Now wol I speke of othes false and grete
A word or two, as olde bokes trete.
Gret sweryng is a thyng abhominable
And fals sweryng is yet moore reprevable.
The heighe God forbad sweryng at al,   305
Witnesse on Mathew; but in special
Of sweryng seith the hooly Jeremye,
"Thou shalt seye sooth thýne othes, and nat lye,
And swere in doom, and eek in rightwisnesse,"
But ydel sweryng is a cursednesse.   310
Bihoold and se, that in the firste table
Of heighe Goddes heestes honurable
How that the seconde heeste of Hym is this:
"Take nat my name in ydel or amys."
Lo, rather He forbedeth swich sweryng   315
Than homycide, or any cursed thyng!
I seye, that as by ordre thus it stondeth,
This knowen that Hise heestes understondeth
How that the seconde heeste of God is that.
And forther-over I wol thee telle al plat,   320
That vengeance shal nat parten from his hous
That of hise othes is to outrageous—
"By Goddes precious herte and by His nayles,
And by the blood of Crist that is in Hayles,
Sevene is my chaunce and thyn is cynk and treye.   325
By Goddes armes, if thou falsly pleye,
This dagger shal thurghout thyn herte go!"
This fruyt cometh of the bicched bones two,
Forsweryng, ire, falsnesse, homycide!
Now for the love of Crist, that for us dyde,   330
Lete youre othes bothe grete and smale.
But, sires, now wol I telle forth my tale.

————

    Thise ryotoures three, of whiche I telle,
Longe erst er pryme rong of any belle,
Were set hem in a taverne for to drinke;   335
And as they satte, they herde a belle clinke
Biforn a cors was caried to his grave;
That oon of hem gan callen to his knave,
    "Go bet," quod he, "and axe redily,

<hr>

306. **Witnesse on Mathew.** "Swear not at all; neither by Heaven, for
it is God's throne."—Matthew, 5:34. 308–309. **"Thou . . . rightwisnesse,"** see Jeremiah, 4:2. 320. **plat,** flatly. 322. **outrageous,**
immoderate, raging, excessive. 324. **in Hayles,** etc. Some of Christ's
blood, shed at the time of the Crucifixion, was believed to be contained in a vessel at the noted shrine in Hayles, Gloucestershire.
325. **Sevene . . . treye.** This is a clear reference to the game of
hazard, which has a close resemblance to the modern game of craps.
The man throwing the dice chooses a number—any number from five
to nine, but usually seven. "If he then throws either seven or eleven,
he wins; if he throws aces or deuce-ace or twelve, he loses. If he throws
some other number, that number is called the caster's chance and he
goes on throwing until either his 'main' or his 'chance' turns up. In
the first case he loses; in the second he wins." **cynk,** the number five;
treye, the number three. 328. **bicched bones,** the perfect description of a pair of dice. 334. **pryme,** the first hour of the day; later, the
period between six and nine in the morning; see *The Nun's Priest's
Tale* (p. II:236, l. 377 and note). 339. **"Go bet,"** a hunting term: the
call to the hounds.

What cors is this that passeth heer forby;   340
And look that thou reporte his name wel."
    "Sir," quod this boy, "it nedeth never-a-del.
It was me told, er ye cam heer, two houres;
He was, pardee, an old felawe of youres;
And sodeynly he was y-slayn to-night,   345
For-dronke, as he sat on his bench upright;
Ther cam a privee theef, men clepeth Deeth,
That in this contree al the peple sleeth,
And with his spere he smoot his herte atwo,
And wente his wey with-outen wordes mo.   350
He hath a thousand slayn this pestilence:
And, maister, er ye come in his presence,
Me thinketh that it were necessarie
For to be war of swich an adversarie:
Beth redy for to mete him evermore.   355
Thus taughte me my dame, I sey namore."
    "By seinte Marie," seyde this taverner,
"The child seith sooth, for he hath slayn this yeer,
Henne over a myle, within a greet village,
Both man and womman, child and hyne and page.
I trowe his habitacioun be there;   361
To been avyséd greet wisdom it were,
Er that he dide a man a dishonour."
    "Ye, Goddes armes," quod this ryotour,
"Is it swich peril with him for to mete?   365
I shal him seke by wey and eek by strete,
I make avow to Goddes digne bones!
Herkneth, felawes, we three been al ones;
Lat ech of us holde up his hond til other,
And ech of us bicomen otheres brother,   370
And we wol sleen this false traytour Deeth;
He shal be slayn, which that so many sleeth,
By Goddes dignitee, er it be night."
    Togidres han thise three her trouthes plight,
To live and dyen ech of hem for other,   375
As though he were his owene y-boren brother.
And up they sterte al dronken, in this rage,
And forth they goon towardes that village,
Of which the taverner had spoke biforn;
And many a grisly ooth than han they sworn,   380
And Cristes blesséd body they to-rente—
Deeth shal be deed, if that they may him hente!
    Whan they han goon nat fully half a myle,
Right as they wolde han troden over a style,
An old man and a povre with hem mette.   385
This olde man ful mekely hem grette,
And seyde thus, "Now, lordes, God yow see!"
    The proudest of thise ryotoures three

<hr>

342. **ʒever-a-del,** never a bit, not at all. 346. **For-dronke,** very
drunk. 347. **privee,** secret, stealthy. 359. **Henne,** hence, from here.
360. **hyne,** servant; specifically, a farm laborer. **page,** boy. 362.
avyséd, forewarned. 367. **digne,** worthy, honorable. 368. **al ones,**
all of one mind. 373. **dignitee,** worthiness, honor. 387. **God yow
see!** It should be noted that the name of the Deity is not capitalized
in a Chaucer text, unless some modern editor has done it. The phrase
means literally, "God see you!"; that is, "God behold you!" or "God
protect you!"

Answerde agayn, "What? carl, with sory grace,
Why artow al forwrappéd save thy face? 390
Why livestow so longe in so greet age?"
This olde man gan loke in his visage,
And seyde thus, "For I ne can nat finde
A man, though that I walkéd into Inde,
Neither in citee nor in no village, 395
That wolde chaunge his youthe for myn age;
And therefore moot I han myn age stille,
As longe time as it is Goddes wille.
Ne deeth, allas! ne wol nat han my lyf;
Thus walke I, lyk a resteles caityf, 400
And on the ground, which is my modres gate,
I knokke with my staf, bothe erly and late,
And seye, 'Leve moder, leet me in!
Lo, how I vanish, flesh, and blood, and skin!
Allas! whan shul my bones been at reste? 405
Moder, with yow wolde I chaunge my cheste,
That in my chambre longe tyme hath be,
Ye! for an heyre clowt to wrappe me!'
But yet to me she wol nat do that grace,
For which ful pale and welkéd is my face. 410
"But, sirs, to yow it is no curteisye
To speken to an old man vileinye,
But he trespasse in worde, or elles in dede.
In holy writ ye may your-self wel rede,
'Agayns an old man, hoor upon his heed, 415
Ye sholde aryse'; wherefor I yeve yow reed,
Ne dooth un-to an old man noon harm now,
Na-more than ye wolde men dide to yow
In age, if that ye so longe abyde;
And God be with yow, wher ye go or ryde. 420
I moot go thider as I have to go."
"Nay, olde cherl, by God, thou shalt nat so,"
Seyde this other hasardour anon;
"Thou partest nat so lightly, by seint John!
Thou spak right now of thilke traitour Deeth, 425
That in this contree alle our frendes sleeth.
Have heer my trouthe, as thou art his aspye,
Tel wher he is, or thou shalt it abye,
By God, and by the holy sacrament!
For soothly thou art oon of his assent, 430
To sleen us yonge folk, thou false theef!"
"Now, sirs," quod he, "if that yow be so leef
To finde Deeth, turne up this crokéd wey,
For in that grove I lafte him, by my fey,
Under a tree, and ther he wol abyde; 435
Nat for your boost he wol him no-thing hyde.
See ye that ook? right ther ye shul him finde.
God save yow, that boghte agayn mankinde,
And yow amende!"—thus seyde this olde man.

And everich of thise ryotoures ran, 440
Til he cam to that tree, and ther they founde
Of florins fyne of golde y-coynéd rounde
Wel ny an eighte busshels, as hem thoughte.
No lenger thanne after Deeth they soughte,
But ech of hem so glad was of that sighte, 445
For that the florins been so faire and brighte,
That doun they sette hem by this precious hord.
The worste of hem he spak the firste word.
"Brethren," quod he, "tak kepe what I seye;
My wit is greet, though that I bourde and pleye. 450
This tresor hath Fortune un-to us yiven,
In mirthe and jolitee our lyf to liven,
And lightly as it comth, so wol we spende.
Ey! Goddes precious dignitee! who wende
Today, that we sholde han so faire a grace? 455
But mighte this gold be caried fro this place
Hoom to myn hous, or elles un-to youres—
For wel ye woot that al this gold is oures—
Than were we in heigh felicitee.
But trewely, by daye it may nat be; 460
Men wolde seyn that we were theves stronge,
And for our owene tresor doon us honge.
This tresor moste y-caried be by nighte
As wysly and as slyly as it mighte.
Wherfore I rede that cut among us alle 465
Be drawe, and lat se wher the cut wol falle;
And he that hath the cut with herte blythe
Shal renne to the toune, and that ful swythe,
And bringe us breed and wyn ful prively.
And two of us shul kepen subtilly 470
This tresor wel; and, if he wol nat tarie,
Whan it is night, we wol this tresor carie
By oon assent, wher-as us thinketh best."
That oon of hem the cut broughte in his fest,
And bade hem drawe, and loke wher it wol falle; 475
And it fil on the yongeste of hem alle;
And forth toward the toun he wente anon.
And al-so sone as that he was gon,
That oon of hem spak thus un-to that other,
"Thou knowest wel thou art my sworne brother, 480
Thy profit wol I telle thee anon.
Thou woost wel that our felawe is agon;
And heer is gold, and that ful greet plentee,
That shal departed been among us three.
But natheles, if I can shape it so 485
That it departed were among us two,
Hadde I nat doon a frendes torn to thee?"
That other answerde, "I noot how that may be:
He woot how that the gold is with us tweye,

389. carl, churl, old fellow—a term of disrespect. 390. forwrappéd, excessively wrapped up. 408. heyre clowt, a hair shirt, the garment for repentants. 410. welkéd, withered. 415–416. 'Agayns an old man . . . aryse.' "Thou shalt rise up before the hoary head, and honor the face of the old man."—Leviticus, 19:32. 420. go, walk. 428. abye, pay for it. 432. leef, lief, glad, eager.

450. bourde, jest, joke. 454. wende, (would have) weened, supposed, expected. 462. doon us honge, make us hang, have us hanged. 465–466. cut . . . drawe, lots be drawn. 468. swythe, quickly; the word is a general intensifying adverb. 474. fest, fist. The lot was chosen, presumably, by plucking grass—the shortest blade determined the choice. 476. fil on, fell to. 479. other. The original meaning of this word was always *second*; it was the regular ordinal numeral for *two*. 484. departed, divided, shared. 487. frendes torn, a friendly turn.

What shal we doon, what shal we to him seye?" 490
    "Shal it be conseil?" seyde the firste shrewe,
"And I shal tellen thee, in wordes fewe,
What we shal doon, and bringe it wel aboute."
    "I graunte," quod that other, "out of doute,
That, by my trouthe, I wol thee nat biwreye." 495
    "Now," quod the firste, "thou woost wel we be
        tweye,
And two of us shul strenger be than oon.
Look whan that he is set, and right anoon
Arys, as though thou woldest with him pleye;
And I shal ryve him thurgh the sydes tweye 500
Whyl that thou strogelest with him as in game,
And with thy dagger look thou do the same;
And than shal al this gold departed be,
My dere freend, bitwixen me and thee;
Than may we bothe our lustes al fulfille, 505
And pleye at dees right at our owene wille."
And thus accorded been thise shrewes tweye
To sleen the thridde, as ye han herd me seye.
    This yongest, which that wente un-to the toun,
Ful ofte in herte he rolleth up and doun
The beautee of thise florins newe and brighte. 510
"O lord!" quod he, "if so were that I mighte
Have al this tresor to my-self allone,
Ther is no man that liveth under the trone
Of God, that sholde live so mery as I!" 515
And atte laste the feend, our enemy,
Putte in his thought that he shold poyson beye,
With which he mighte sleen his felawes tweye;
For-why the feend fond him in swich lyvinge,
That he had leve him to sorwe bringe, 520
For this was outrely his fulle entente
To sleen hem bothe, and never to repente.
And forth he gooth, no lenger wold he tarie,
Into the toun, un-to a pothecarie,
And preyéd him, that he him wolde selle 525
Some poyson, that he mighte his rattes quelle,
And eek ther was a polcat in his hawe,
That, as he seyde, his capouns hadde y-slawe,
And fayn he wolde wreke him, if he mighte,
On vermin, that destroyéd him by nighte. 530
    The pothecarie answerde, "and thou shalt have
A thing that, al-so God my soule save,
In al this world ther nis no creature,
That ete or dronke hath of this confiture
Noght but the mountance of a corn of whete, 535
That he ne shal his lyf anon forlete;
Ye, sterve he shal, and that in lasse whyle
Than thou wolt goon a paas nat but a myle;

491. conseil, a secret. 495. biwreye, betray. 519. For-why, because. 520. leve, leave, permission. God permitted the Devil to bring this man to sorrow. The idea lies back of Job, 1:12 and 2:6. 526. quelle, kill. 527. hawe, yard; the original meaning is *hedge* or *fence*. 528. y-slawe, slain. 529. wreke him, avenge himself. 534. confiture, concoction, mixture; the apothecary is obviously being ironical. 535. mountance, amount. 536. forlete, leave, abandon, give up. 537. sterve, die (from any cause); not specifically our modern *starve*.

This poyson is so strong and violent."
    This curséd man hath in his hond y-hent 540
This poyson in a box, and sith he ran
In-to the nexte strete, un-to a man,
And borwed [of] him large botels three;
And in the two his poyson pouréd he;
The thridde he kepte clene for his drinke. 545
For all the night he shoop him for to swinke
In caryinge of the gold out of that place.
And whan this ryotour, with sory grace,
Had filled with wyn his grete botels three,
To his felawes agayn repaireth he. 550
    What nedeth it to sermone of it more?
For right as they had cast his deeth bifore,
Right so they han him slayn, and that anon.
And whan that this was doon thus spak that oon,
"Now lat us sitte and drinke, and make us merie, 555
And afterward we wol his body berie."
And with that word it happéd him, par cas,
To take the botel ther the poyson was,
And drank, and yaf his felawe drinke also,
For which anon they storven bothe two. 560
    But certes, I suppose that Avicen
Wroot nevere in no canoun, ne in no fen,
Mo wonder signes of empoisonyng
Than hadde thise wrecches two, er hir endyng.
Thus ended been thise homycides two, 565
And eek the false empoysoner also.
    O cursed synne ful of cursednesse!
O traytours homycide! O wikkednesse!
O glotonye, luxurie, and hasardrye!
Thou blasphemour of Crist, with vileynye, 570
And othes grete, of usage and of pride,
Allas, mankynde! how may it bitide
That to thy Creatour which that the wroghte,
And with His precious herte-blood thee boghte,
Thou art so fals and so unkynde, allas! 575
Now, goode men, God foryeve yow youre trespas,
And ware yow fro the synne of avarice;
Myn hooly pardoun may yow alle warice,
So that ye offre nobles or sterlynges,
Or elles silver broches, spoones, rynges; 580
Boweth youre heed under this hooly bulle,
Com up, ye wyves, offreth of youre wolle;
Youre names I entre heer in my rolle anon,
Into the blisse of hevene shul ye gon.
I yow assoille by myn heigh power, 585
Yow that wol offre, as clene and eek as cleer

541. sith, afterwards. 551. nedeth . . . sermone, why is it necessary to make a sermon? 557. par cas, by chance. 560. storven, died. 561. Avicen, Avicenna, the famous Arab philosopher and physician of the eleventh century, particularly famous for his studies of toxicology; cf. the *Prologue* to *The Canterbury Tales*, p. II:209, l. 432. 562. fen, chapter, book; canoun signifies the chapter heading. 568. traytours, a possessive form serving as an adjective, *traitorous*. 575. unkynde, unnatural, monstrous. 578. warice, cure. 579. So that, provided that. nobles or sterlynges. The *noble* was a coin first used in the fourteenth century, worth six shillings eight pence; the *sterlyng* was probably a silver penny rather than the pound sterling.

As ye were born—and lo, sires, thus I preche;
And Jesu Crist, that is oure soules leche,
So graunte yow His pardoun to receyve,
For that is best, I wol yow nat deceyve.   590

    But sires, o word forgat I in my tale,
I have relikes and pardoun in my male
As faire as any man in Engelond,
Whiche were me yeven by the popes hond.
If any of yow wole, of devocioun,   595
Offren and han myn absolucioun,
Com forth anon, and kneleth heere adoun,
And mekely receyveth my pardoun,
Or elles taketh pardoun as ye wende,
Al newe and fressh at every miles ende,   600
So that ye offren alwey newe and newe
Nobles or pens, whiche that be goode and trewe.
It is an honour to everich that is heer,
That ye mowe have a suffisant pardoneer
Tassoille yow, in contree as ye ryde,   605
For aventures whiche that may bityde.
Paraventure ther may fallen oon or two
Doun of his hors, and breke his nekke atwo.
Look, which a seuretee is it to yow alle
That I am in youre felaweship yfalle,   610
That may assoille yow, bothe moore and lasse,
Whan that the soule shal fro the body passe.
I rede that oure Hoost heere shal bigynne,
For he is moost envoluped in synne.
Com forth, sire Hoost, and offre first anon,   615
And thou shalt kisse my relikes everychon,
Ye, for a grote, unbokele anon thy purs—

    "Nay, nay," quod he, "thanne have I Cristes curs!"
"Lat be," quod he, "it shal nat be, so theech,
Thou woldest make me kisse thyn olde breech,   620
And swere it were a relyk of a seint,
Though it were with thy fundement depeint!
But, by the croys which that Seint Eleyne fond,
I wolde I hadde thy coillons in myn hond
In stide of relikes or of seintuarie.   625
Lat kutte hem of, I wol thee helpe hem carie;
They shul be shryned in an hogges toord!"

    This pardoner answerde nat a word;

---

592. **male,** bag; see *Prologue* to *The Canterbury Tales,* p. ii:213, l. 694
and note. 602. **pens,** pence, pennies. 605. **Tassoille,** to absolve; the
elision here is of the preposition *to.* 613–614. **oure Hoost . . . en-**
voluped in synne. It is clear that the Host is one of those men who can
hardly open his mouth without uttering some sort of profanity. The
Pardoner is obviously objecting to this habit in the Host, which certainly cuts across the lines of the homily which he has just completed;
see especially ll. 169–170. That the Pardoner may be completely
hypocritical in his objection is beside the point. But the Host seems
to sense insincerity in the Pardoner, which is probably the chief reason for his rage. 619. **so theech,** "so may I prosper!"—a rather mild
asseveration, considering the general ferocity of the Host's retort.
The southern form of the first personal pronoun, *ich,* has been
suffixed to the verb *thee(n),* "to prosper." 622. **with thy fundement**
depeint! daubed with thy excrement! 623. **croys . . . fond.** St.
Helen, the mother of Constantine the Great, was believed to have
been the finder of the True Cross. 624. **coillons,** cullions, testicles.
626. **of,** off.

So wrooth he was, no word ne wolde he seye.
    "Now," quod our host, "I wol no lenger pleye   630
With thee, ne with noon other angry man."
But right anon the worthy Knight bigan,
Whan that he saugh that al the peple lough,
"Na-more of this, for it is right y-nough;
Sir Pardoner, be glad and mery of chere;   635
And ye, sir Host, that been to me so dere,
I prey yow that ye kisse the Pardoner.
And Pardoner, I prey thee, drawe thee neer.
And, as we diden, lat us laughe and pleye."
Anon they kiste, and riden forth hir weye.

British and Danish Popular Ballads

The term "popular ballad" has been applied to
narrative songs which originated among the
people rather than at the courts of kings or in the parlors
of the aristocratic and educated. The process of making
such ballads is many centuries old, and may take place at
any time where a state of general illiteracy obtains. The
ballads of Denmark, England, and Scotland—to take the
three most famous collections—lived in oral tradition for
hundreds of years. Some of them were brought to the
New World by emigrants. They can be found today in
many of the less sophisticated communities in the United
States. They are a part of the spontaneous heritage of
Western Europe. But, as has been noted again and again,
to commit these ballads to writing has a curiously blight-
ing effect upon them. To appreciate the full value of a
popular ballad, one must hear it sung by an authentic
ballad singer.

    The first great modern assemblage of these ballads
was the repository of Danish ballads assembled by Svend
Grundtvig, the publication of which was begun in 1853.
This served as a model for the impressive collection of
English and Scottish popular ballads published under
the editorship of Francis J. Child in the 1860's and
stamped in definitive style in his great five-volume edition of 1882–1898. Child gathered over three hundred
of these ballads. The Danish ballads collected are somewhat fewer in number, but statistics mean little here, for
there must be hundreds of ballads, even those of modern
vintage, which have never found their way into the
pages of Grundtvig or Child. Many of these ballads have
an origin in the later Middle Ages, though scarcely before. The great majority of them, however, were not
written down until the sixteenth and seventeenth centuries; in Britain, for example, less than a dozen survive
in a form older than that of the celebrated Percy Manuscript of about 1650. The most ancient English ballad is

Judas (Child #23), which survives from the thirteenth century; the next extant ballad was not written down until the middle of the fifteenth century. Most of the Robin Hood ballads, most famous of all, exist in a text from well past 1500. And yet the Middle English vision-satire, *Piers Plowman*, originating in the latter half of the fourteenth century, makes a reference to the "rimes of Robin Hood" so casual that it is possible to assume the currency of Robin Hood ballads long before 1350. Besides, many of the stock situations in the popular ballads belong to the province of Germanic and Celtic folklore and as such know not the limits of time.

The problem of the authorship of the popular ballads has vexed scholars since Bishop Percy wrote his memorable preface to his *Reliques of Ancient English Poetry* (1765). Since that time three main schools of thought have emerged: (1) the ballads were composed by individual authors; (2) the ballads were composed by a community as a whole (communal authorship); (3) the ballads were composed by an individual who made, as George Lyman Kittredge so aptly observed, "an improvisation in the presence of a sympathetic company which may even, at times, participate in the process."

It is essential for us to realize that there are two distinct types of popular ballad, which we may designate as the folk ballad and the minstrel ballad. The *folk ballad*, much the older type, is characterized by much dialogue; refrains of marked rhythmic or choral value; and repetition, at least of a single word or phrase, and usually of a more subtle nature called "incremental repetition," by which the story is made to "hitch along" through small variations on a repetitive element. The true folk ballad is notably objective; the very presence of the words "I" or "my," except in direct discourse, should render it suspect as a folk ballad. There is also a minimum of descriptive or atmospheric material; the folk ballad, indeed, is further characterized by notable simplicity of thought, situation, and metrical style. The importance of the repetitive elements, the implication of a chorus or a dance in the refrain material, the strong suggestion of possible dramatic or mimetic interpretation in the interchanging dialogue—all this lends weight to the argument that the folk ballad is in some sense a communal affair. One or more individuals could have composed the narrative portions, and even acted out the story, while the community group, assembled for some special occasion, could have roared the refrain, perhaps dancing as they did so. In fact, such a process is familiar to any folklorist who observes similar gatherings in the present age. Knowing as we do that improvisation was not regarded as out of the ordinary on the part of any intelligent person of earlier times, we may well accept the theory that several members had a hand in the composition of the main body of the folk ballad. Their number would be small, however, because one must reckon always with the obvious fact that every gathering has its few guiding spirits. Song is to be assumed for the ballad; choral dancing may have entered into it as well; indeed, the choreographic element seems to have been especially prominent in the early Danish ballads.

On the other hand, a number of ballads show no traces of the many peculiar characteristics of the folk ballad, or exhibit at most only feeble, imitative suggestions of these. They proceed to the business of the story after a brief, "Come, all ye, and listen" formula; and they possess often a special "literary" flavor, such as comes from a description of the countryside or an analysis of the thoughts and feelings of the characters in the story. In other words, they are more subjective than the folk ballads; and to say that they are subjective implies an individual originator and an individual only. Such ballads we call *minstrel ballads*. The minstrel was simply a bard of the people, and as such he had to possess a keen insight into the tastes of the people and had to have at his command an extensive repertory of popular song. Perhaps he may have had some experience at the court of a nobleman and in that way have become familiar with romance materials. This possibility would explain how some of the minstrel ballads have to do with shreds of medieval romances. In the British collection there are even a few Arthurian ballads. The minstrel could be responsible for the creation of Robin Hood, that great popular hero of epic proportions; he might be fighting in the armies of My Lords Douglas and Percy and so create the ballads of border warfare; he might participate in the assassination of Count Gert by Niels Ebbeson. But however much he might imitate the manner and even the language and style of the older folk ballad—even to the point of throwing in a few rhythmic devices in the form of meaningless words and a few faint echoes of incremental repetition—still his work was entirely his own. He was the author of the entire ballad. To put *Edward* or *Sir Luno and the Mermaid* beside *Robin Hood's Death and Burial* is to see at once the basal differences between the two types, the folk ballad and the minstrel ballad. Moreover, some of the Danish ballads, according to the researches of Grundtvig and Olrik, originated from the pens of lords and ladies of Denmark during the sixteenth and seventeenth centuries, just as some of the English ballads came from writers of established reputation in England from the Renaissance to the present time.

It is possible, then, to argue that the folk ballad was composed by individuals with the assistance of the community in varying degrees; the minstrel ballad, on the other hand, is the work of an individual who is catering to the tastes of the people and conforming in a measure to the style of the older folk ballad. The theory of Grimm that the community as a whole was responsible for a ballad ("das Volk dichtet") has been generally discredited; taken literally it would be impossible. But the community was certainly the fertile soil in which the folk ballad could grow, and in that sense at least, "communal authorship" has meaning.

The subject matter of the popular ballad was, of course, extremely varied. The ballads in their older aspects dealt with mortals of a dateless age, when contact with the supernatural was not considered in the least miraculous. They are rich in folklore and the expression of folkways, but they may give their attention wholly to tragic family or clan relationships (cf. *Edward* and

Young Engel. Historical ballads of all kinds, as well as ballads of the outlaw, are of the minstrel ballad variety (cf. the Robin Hood ballad and *Niels Ebbeson*).

It has been pointed out that musical settings are the rule for all ballads. Many of these melodies have been recovered, but many others are lost forever. Careful usage, however, should limit the term "ballad" to *narrative* rather than *lyric* verse set to music, although in the "coronach," or song of lamentation, it is often difficult to tell whether the narrative or the lyric predominates (cf. *Bonnie George Campbell*). Similarly, the ballad often veers toward the didactic or satirical in that ancient type called the "riddle" ballad (cf. *Riddles Wisely Expounded*). Finally, there is to be recognized a burlesque or farcical type of ballad (cf. *The Bride of Ribe*), which is usually of later date, and which moves all the way from slapstick and horseplay to a fairly sophisticated type of humor.

Because the ballad was the unwritten product of peasant and commoner, it was not considered highly by scholars and critics of literature until the interest in antiquities that was a feature of the later eighteenth century resulted in the printing of as many of these ancient songs as were accessible. But it should be remembered that ballads appeared in print almost as soon as the art of printing became current; these were usually put out in the form of single sheets, or broadsides, and often in cheap little pamphlets, or "chap-books." The romantic writers of the late eighteenth and early nineteenth century, such as Burger, Goethe, Schiller, Burns, and Scott, undertook many imitations of the ballad. The nineteenth-century writers all over Europe emulated them most industriously and often brilliantly. But none of the imitations of the folk ballad have been quite so effective as the better examples of the original type—the simple and grim domestic tragedy of *Edward*, like the naïve and gripping course of many a folk tune, is virtually impossible for the sophisticate to render with equal sincerity and appeal.

Riddles Wisely Expounded

(BRITISH)

The riddle or enigma is of frequent occurrence in all folk literatures. It is extremely ancient and remarkably vital; riddle tales, of which this ballad is an illustration, can still be found, in much the same form as the following, among primitive European and Asiatic peoples. It should be observed that one person has to guess another person's riddle, with a severe penalty, usually death, in case he fails.

In this ballad appears also the theme of the devil in the shape of a man, come down to try a human being, who will be carried away to Hell unless he or she survives the test by answering the riddle. This device was often used in the Middle Ages for didactic purposes.

THERE was a knicht riding frae the east,
   Sing the Cather banks, the bonnie brume,
Wha had been wooing at monie a place,
   And ye may beguile a young thing sune.

He came unto a widow's door,   5
And speired whare her three dochters were.

The auldest ane's to a washing gane,
The second's to a baking gane.

The youngest ane's to a wedding gane,
And it will be nicht or she be hame.   10

He set him doun upon a stane,
Till thir three lasses came tripping hame.

The auldest ane's to the bed making,
And the second ane's to the sheet spreading.

The youngest ane's was bauld and bricht,   15
And she was to lye with this unco knicht.

"Gin ye will answer me questions ten,
The morn ye sall be made my ain.

"O what is heigher nor the tree?
And what is deeper nor the sea?   20

"Or what is heavier nor the lead?
And what is better nor the breid?

"O what is whiter nor the milk?
Or what is safter nor the silk?

"Or what is sharper nor a thorn?   25
Or what is louder nor a horn?

"Or what is greener nor the grass?
Or what is waur nor a woman was?"

"O Heaven is higher nor the tree,
And Hell is deeper nor the sea.   30

"O sin is heavier nor the lead,
The blessing's better nor the bread.

2. **Sing . . . brume.** This is the characteristic refrain, made up of words chosen for sound rather than sense, although if we could trace the ballad back far enough the significance of the lines might be plainer. The localities appearing in these refrains are definite ones, such as the Cather banks, and suggest the possible place of origin of the ballad. On the other hand it would be simple for some ballad minstrel to transfer a rhythmical refrain from one ballad to another. This line is repeated as the second line of each ensuing stanza. **And . . . sune** (l. 4) is the fourth and final line of each stanza. Again, it is a refrain, but this time it serves as a kind of motif to sound the theme of the whole ballad. *Sune* is modern "soon." 6. **speired,** asked; still common in Anglo-Scottish. 10. **or,** ere, before. 12. **thir,** these. 15. **bauld,** bold, sharp, brisk. 16. **unco knicht,** the devil. 18. **sall,** shall. 22. **breid,** bread. 28. **waur,** worse.

"The snaw is whiter nor the milk,
And the down is safter nor the silk.

"Hunger is sharper nor a thorn, 35
And shame is louder nor a horn.

"Poison is greener nor the grass,
And Clootie's waur nor a woman was."

As sune as she the fiend did name,
He flew away in a blazing flame.

Edward

(BRITISH)

This fine folk ballad should be studied not only for its story, a characteristic tragedy of the "domestic relations" group of ballads, but also for its structure. The tale is told in typical hitching, though highly dramatic, fashion through the skillful use of incremental repetition. Refrains like "Edward, Edward" or "Mither, Mither," which are not incremental, are spoken of as "parallel repetition."

WHY dois your brand sae drap wi bluid,
                    Edward, Edward,
Why dois your brand sae drap wi bluid,
    And why sae sad gang yee O?"
"O I hae killed my hauke sae guid, 5
                    Mither, mither,
O I hae killed my hauke sae guid,
    And I had nae mair bot hee O."

"Your haukis bluid was nevir sae reid,
                    Edward, Edward, 10
Your haukis bluid was nevir sae reid,
    My dear son I tell thee O."
"O I hae killed my reid-roan steid,
                    Mither, mither,
O I hae killed my reid-roan steid, 15
    That erst was sae fair and frie O."

"Your steid was auld, and ye hae gat mair,
                    Edward, Edward,
Your steid was auld, and ye hae gat mair,
    Sum other dule ye drie O." 20
"O I hae killed my fadir deir,
                    Mither, mither,
O I hae killed my fadir deir,
    Alas, and wae is mee O!"

"And whatten penance wul ye drie for that, 25
                    Edward, Edward?

And whatten penance wul ye drie for that?
    My deir son, now tell me O."
"Ile set my feit in yonder boat,
                    Mither, mither, 30
Ile set my feit in yonder boat,
    And Ile fare ovir the sea O."

"And what wul ye doe wi your towirs and your ha,
                    Edward, Edward?
And what wul ye doe wi your towirs and your ha, 35
    That were sae fair to see O?"
"Ile let them stand tul they doun fa,
                    Mither, mither,
Ile let them stand tul they doun fa,
    For here nevir mair maun I bee O." 40

"And what wul ye leive to your bairns and your wife,
                    Edward, Edward?
And what wul ye leive to your bairns and your wife,
    Whan ye gang ovir the sea O?"
"The warldis room, late them beg thrae life, 45
                    Mither, mither,
The warldis room, late them beg thrae life,
    For thame nevir mair wul I see O."

"And what wul ye leive to your ain mither deir,
                    Edward, Edward? 50
And what wul ye leive to your ain mither deir,
    My deir son, now tell me O."
"The curse of Hell fram me sall ye beir,
                    Mither, mither,
The curse of Hell fram me sall ye beir, 55
    Sic counseils ye gave to me O."

Aage and Else

(DANISH)

This ballad deals with one of the most common themes of the supernatural ballads—the love of a dead man for a mortal woman. In most versions, as typified for example by the British *Sweet William's Ghost*, the mortal woman rides off with her dead lover and is carried irretrievably to the grave and damnation. In *Aage and Else* the dead lover averts this melancholy end for his mortal sweetheart by bidding her at the last minute look up to the stars. The theme of these ballads is known in folklore simply as the theme of the Demon Lover; but, from the many excellent German versions of the ballad, culminating in the *Lenore* of Gottfried Bürger (1748–1794)—much the most famous "literary" treatment of the subject—it is sometimes known as the "Lenore" theme. The demon lover, to be sure, may not cause the maiden's death, but

38. **Clootie,** the devil. A cloot is the half-hoof of a cloven-footed animal.
8. **mair,** more. 9. **reid,** red. 16. **erst,** once. 20. **dule,** sorrow, anguish. **drie,** suffer. 25. **whatten,** what a?—what kind of?

29. **feit,** feet. 33. **ha,** hall. This "satirical legacy," as it is called, is a feature of popular literature. 37. **fa,** fall. 45. **thrae,** through.

at least does irreparable damage to her soul. The same is true of the obverse of this tale—the love of a mortal man for a supernatural woman, illustrated by the Tann-häuser ballad (p. II:153) and in English literature by the ballad of *Thomas Rymer*.

Three maidens sit in a bower,
Two broider with gold,
The third she weeps her own true-love
Under darksome mould,
For her troth to him was plighted.   5

It was the knight Sir Aage
That rode by land and lea,
He loved the lady Elselil,
So fair was she.

He wooed the lady Elselil   10
With gifts and gold,
On Monday thereafter
He lay in the mould.

Sore wept the lady Elselil
With wellaway,   15
That heard the knight Sir Aage,
Low where he lay.

Up stood the knight Sir Aage,
His coffin black he bore,
With mickle toil and trouble   20
He sought her door.

He knocked there with his coffin,
No cloak had he:
"Rise up, thou lady Elselil,
Open to me!"   25

Up spake the lady Elselil,
With tears spake she:
"Canst thou name the name of Jesu
I'll open to thee!"

"Rise up, thou lady Elselil,   30
Open thy door!
I can name the name of Jesu
As ever I could of yore."

Up stood the lady Elselil
In dule and dread.   35
So opened she the bower door,
Let in the dead.

She took her golden comb
To smooth his hair,
For every lock she ordered   40
Down fell a tear.

"Now lithe and list, Sir Aage,
Dearest love mine,
How goes it under murk and mould
In grave of thine?"   45

"So goes it under darksome mould
Where I am laid,
As in the happy realm of Heaven,
Therefore be glad."

"Lithe and list, Sir Aage,   50
Dearest love mine,
Fain would I lie 'neath murk and mould
In grave of thine."

"So goes it under darksome mould
There where I rest,   55
As in the blackest depths of Hell!
Cross thou thy breast.

"For every tear thou lettest fall
In mournful mood,
Adown into my grave doth drip   60
A drop of blood.

"Up above my head
The green grass grows,
Down about my feet
The dark worm goes.   65

"But when a song thou singest
All in delight,
Then all my darksome grave is hung
With roses red and white.

"Now in the darksome entry   70
The black cocks crow,
And all the doors are opening,
Forth must I go.

"And now the white cock croweth
In the high hall,   75
To earth I now betake me
With dead men all.

"Now croweth on the high-loft
The cock so red,
And I must back to earth again   80
With all the dead."

Aage and Else. Translated by E. M. Smith-Dampier. From *Book of Danish Ballads*, edited by Axel Obrick, published by Princeton University Press, 1939. Reprinted by permission of the American-Scandinavian Foundation.

8. Elselil. The suffix "-lil" implies that Else was both fair and small.
14–16. Sore wept . . . heard. It is a common belief in folklore that when someone weeps for a dead person, the corpse will not lie easily in the grave. Note ll. 58–62 below.

71. The black cocks . . . For the general significance of cocks in this situation, see *The Wife of Usher's Well*, note to l. 33; but the color combination of black, white (l. 74), and red (l. 79) is suggestive of the old tricolor of the Germanic or Teutonic Knights of the Middle Ages—white for purity, black for death, and red for courage.

Up stood the knight Sir Aage,
His coffin took once more,
Forth fared he to the kirkyard
With travail sore.   85

Up stood the lady Elselil,
In mournful mood,
To follow him, her own true-love,
Through the greenwood.

And when they came to the kirkyard   90
With toil and care,
Wan it grew and faded,
His goodly golden hair.

"Behold now up in Heaven
The stars so bright!   95
There mayst thou see full surely
How goes the night."

She saw the stars a-shining
In Heaven so blue
Down in the earth the dead man sank   100
Or e'er she knew.

Home went the lady Elselil
With care so cold,
And when a moon was over
Lay she in the mould.

Thomas Rymer

(BRITISH)

TRUE Thomas lay oer yon grassy bank,
  And he beheld a ladie gay,
A lady that was brisk and bold,
  Come riding oer the fernie brae.

Her skirt was of the grass-green silk,   5
  Her mantel of the velvet fine,
And ilka tett of her horse's mane
  Hung fifty silver bells and nine.

True Thomas he took off his hat,
  And bowed him low down till his knee: 10
"All hail, thou mighty Queen of Heaven!
  For your peer on earth I never did see."

"O no, O no, True Thomas," she says,
  "That name does not belong to me;
I am but the queen of fair Elfland,   15
  And I'm come here for to visit thee.

7. **ilka tett**, each lock; the preposition "from" should be read before *ilka*. 16. **I'm come . . . visit thee.** In the present version there is here a gap in the ballad, but other versions indicate that at this point the lady granted Thomas her love.

"But ye maun go wi me now, Thomas,
  True Thomas, ye maun go wi me,
For ye maun serve me seven years,
  Thro weel or wae as may chance to be."   20

She turned about her milk-white steed,
  And took True Thomas up behind,
And aye wheneer her bridle rang,
  The steed flew swifter than the wind.

For forty days and forty nights   25
  He wade through red blude to the knee,
And he saw neither sun nor moon,
  But heard the roaring of the sea.

O they rade on, and further on,
  Until they came to a garden green: 30
"Light down, light down, ye ladie free,
  Some of that fruit let me pull to thee."

"O no, O no, True Thomas," she says,
  "That fruit maun not be touched by thee,
For a' the plagues that are in Hell   35
  Light on the fruit of this countrie.

"But I have a loaf here in my lap,
  Likewise a bottle of claret wine,
And now ere we go farther on,
  We'll rest a while, and ye may dine."   40

When he had eaten and drunk his fill,
  "Lay down your head upon my knee,"
The lady said, "ere we climb yon hill,
  And I will show you fairlies three.

"O see not ye yon narrow road,   45
  So thick beset wi thorns and briers?
That is the path of righteousness,
  Tho after it but few enquires.

"And see not ye that braid braid road,
  That lies across yon lillie leven?   50
That is the path of wickedness,
  Tho some call it the road to Heaven.

"And see not ye that bonny road,
  Which winds about the fernie brae?
That is the road to fair Elfland,   55
  Where you and I this night maun gae.

"But Thomas, ye maun hold your tongue,
  Whatever you may hear or see,
For gin ae word you should chance to speak,
  You will neer get back to your ain countrie."   60

19. **serve me seven years.** Thomas must serve the traditional period of apprenticeship, so to speak. 44. **fairlies,** wonders, marvels. 50. **lillie leven,** lovely glades.

He has gotten a coat of the even cloth,
And a pair of shoes of velvet green,
And till seven years were past and gone
True Thomas on earth was never seen.

Sir Patrick Spens

(BRITISH)

In spite of the fine atmospheric quality of this ballad, which bespeaks a gifted minstrel author whose talents resemble those of a poet like Coleridge, this is probably to be classed as a historical ballad. It is believed that Sir Patrick Spens, himself difficult to identify, was lost at sea while returning from the expedition which conducted Margaret, daughter of King Alexander III of Scotland, to her husband, King Eric of Norway. The marriage took place in 1281.

THE king sits in Dunfermline toune
    Drinking the blude-red wine:
"O whar will I get guid sailor,
    To sail this schip of mine?"

Up and spak an eldern knicht,   5
    Sat at the kings richt kne:
"Sir Patrich Spens is the best sailor
    That sails upon the se."

The king has written a braid letter,
    And signed it wi his hand,   10
And sent it to Sir Patrick Spens,
    Was walking on the sand.

The first line that Sir Patrick red,
    A loud lauch lauched he;
The next line that Sir Patrick red,   15
    The teir blinded his ee.

"O wha is this has don this deid,
    This ill deid don to me,
To send me out this time o' the yeir,
    To sail upon the se!   20

"Mak haste, mak haste, my mirry men all,
    Our guid schip sails the morne:"
"O say na sae, my master deir,
    For I feir a deadlie storme.

"Late late yestreen I saw the new moone,   25
    Wi the auld moone in his arme,
And I feir, I feir, my deir master,
    That we will cum to harme."

64. **True Thomas . . . seen;** because of his breaking bread, drinking wine, and having intercourse with the fairy queen.
9. **braid letter,** a letter written on a long or broad sheet. 25–26. **Late . . . arme.** The bad omen in such a sight lay in the fact that the new moon was seen *late* in the evening.

O our Scots nobles wer richt laith
    To weet their cork-heild schoone;   30
But lang owre a' the play wer playd,
    Their hats they swam aboone.

O lang, lang may their ladies sit,
    Wi their fans into their hand,
Or eir they se Sir Patrick Spens   35
    Cum sailing to the land.

O lang, lang may the ladies stand,
    Wi their gold kems in their hair,
Waiting for their ain deir lords,
    For they'll se thame na mair.   40

Haf owre, haf owre to Aberdour,
    It's fiftie fadom de ip,
And thair lies guid Sir Patrick Spens,
    Wi the Scots lords at his feit.

Niels Ebbeson

(DANISH)

In the year 1340 in Denmark, King Christian had died, the young prince Valdemar was absent from the country, and the unscrupulous barons of Holstein were making merry in the North Jutland section of Denmark. A certain Niels Ebbeson, a Danish patriot of whom little is known beyond his major feat, got the help of a group of like-minded citizens, and on a raiding expedition directed against Count Gert, or Gerhardt, assassinated the count and thus disposed of one of the most obnoxious of these tyrannous barons. Niels Ebbeson as a result became a popular hero of major dimensions, and the balladry about him has some of the outlaw flavor that characterizes the approximately contemporary Robin Hood ballads; at any rate, there is in these ballads the same championing of the people against the aristocracy.

THE Count to Denmark took his way,
    And would not be gainsaid,
What though the spaeman told him true
That there should he lie dead.

Was none could cross his wilful mind   5
His fate to put to test,
Yeoman and boor, and knight and squire,
Must have him for their guest.

29. **laith,** loath. 30. **cork-heild schoone,** shoes with heels of cork, much affected by the nobility. 31. **owre, ere,** before. 32. **hats . . . aboone.** Their hats were floating above their bodies. 35. **Or eir, ere** ever. 41. **Haf . . . Aberdour,** halfway on the return journey to Aberdour (Aberdeen); that is, halfway home.
Niels Ebbeson. Translated by E. M. Smith-Dampier. From *Book of Danish Ballads,* edited by Axel Obrick, published by Princeton University Press, 1939. Reprinted by permission of the American-Scandinavian Foundation.
3. **spaeman,** fortune-teller.

The Count has called Niels Ebbeson
To come and meet with him,   10
And peace should reign whilst the hour endured,
With truce for life and limb.

The Count he met Niels Ebbeson
Northward beside the sea:
"Now be thou welcome, Niels Ebbeson,   15
Right welcome unto me!

"Blithe is thy cheer, Niels Ebbeson,
Retainer dear of mine!
Now what is the mind of the Northern Jutes,
And what of kinsfolk thine?"   20

"Yea, kinsfolk enow are mine, I trow,
And my wife hath kin also,
And all of them shall do thy will
If they thy will may know."

"Niels Ebbeson, thou art a valiant man,   25
And a man of wit beside,
And canst thou not ride straightforward
The long way round thou'lt ride.

"Now lithe and listen, Niels Ebbeson,
Wilt thou mine errand speed,   30
Then say how many swains hast thou
Will stand by thee at need?"

"Some five and forty swains have I,
Such as they well may be,
And are they many or are they few   35
Right dear they are to me."

"And hast thou five and forty carles,
Well art thou served, I ween—
But last night wert thou in Sir Bugge's hold
With a hundred mail-clad men!"   40

Niels Ebbeson he stamped his foot,
And straight made answer high:
"Is any man here, or knight or knave,
That dares maintain that lie?

"Is any man here, or knight or knave,   45
Who dares that lie maintain,
Never a foot will I retreat
Till I answer him back again!"

"Now lithe and list, Niels Ebbeson,
Of this we'll make an end,   50
Go, ask of him, Sir Bugge,
If he will be my friend.

"Sir Bugge and Povl Glob the young
To do my will did swear,
And Sir Anders Frost is one with them,   55
And foremost in counsel there.

"Yea, more have sworn to do my will
That now would work me woe,
So hear and heed Sir Bugge's rede,
And see how the thing will go!"   60

"Oh, nought know I of Sir Bugge's mind,
What he may say or do,
But Anders has kept his troth with thee
As all men will tell thee true.

"Anders hath kept his faith with thee,   65
As all men will tell thee true,
But would he take leave of thy service
Such leave is a free man's due.

"For this is the Danish custom,
And hath been since days of yore,   70
If a swain would change his service
He should have leave therefor."

Up and spake Lord Gert the Count
That liked his words right ill:
"Nay, never a vassal may leave his Lord   75
Save with his Lord's good will."

"Oh, none is bound with a holy vow
Save a monk to his cowl of grey!
Let chieftains come and chieftains go,
Men serve them as best they may."   80

"Overbold is his speech, Niels Ebbeson,
That bandies words with me!
Or thou shalt depart from Denmark,
Or I'll hang thee to a tree!"

"And must I depart from Denmark,   85
From wife's and bairns' embrace,
Oh, thou shalt call it a luckless hour
That e'er thou sawest my face!"

"Get hence, get hence, Niels Ebbeson,
And let thy prating be,   90
Or I will do what well I may
And break my truce with thee!"

"Oh, ne'er hast thou seen me so sore afraid
As to tremble for curse and ban,
Look well to thyself, Count Gert, I say,   95
And defend thy head like a man!"

69–72. **For this . . . therefor.** This is a reference to the ancient Danish Law of Commutation, which gave every retainer the right to take his leave every year and find service with another lord. It is a difference of opinion between Niels and Count Gert on this question which precipitates the action of the ballad.

29. lithe, listen.

"Niels Ebbeson, thy words are hard,
As oft ere this was shown,
But I will hold truce with thee today,
E'en till the sun goes down."   100

Niels Ebbeson waved his lily-white hand,
And turned his steed on the shore:
"Farewell, Count Gert, with all thy men!
Soon shall we meet once more!"

Niels Ebbeson he fled full fast,   105
Nor spur was fain to spare,
And the Count held back with all his men,
Was none durst follow there.

It was he, Niels Ebbeson,
That home to hold did win,   110
And it was his own dear lady
Went forth to lead him in.

"Now lithe thou and listen, wife, I pray,
Some counsel give to me,
For the Count will make me an outlawed man,   115
Or hang me on gallows-tree!"

"What counsel can I give to thee
That have but a woman's wit?
The worst of rede were here the best,
Could we but light on it.   120

"The worst of rede were here the best,
All in this evil hour,
The Count to slay whilst yet we may,
Or burn him in his bower.

"Now take thy steeds to the smithy,   125
(This is my counsel true),
And turn their shoon the backward way
When they are shod anew.

"Turn thou their shoon the backward way,
So the foeman thy track shall miss,   130
And take heed and tell to no man
That a woman taught thee this!"

Up and spake Niels Ebbeson,
Unto his men spake he:
"Now which of you will follow,   135
And which take leave of me?

"Let him that now will follow
Reach forth his hand to me,
And he that now will take his leave
Speak up right speedily!"   140

Up they stood, his Danish squires,
And answered their lord so free:

"Now all of us will follow
And risk our lives for thee!"

Now up they rode to Ladywood,   145
And there their steeds did bind,
And into Randers Town they went,
Count Gert to seek and find.

And when to Randers Bridge he came
He spake to his squires anew: 150
"Now let him take his leave and go
Who will not stand me true!"

Up and spake the little lad Trust,
The truest of them all:
"Now give me leave, my master,   155
And saddle and steed withal."

He gave him leave, his master,
And saddle and steed withal,
And or ever the day was over
He served him best of all.   160

It was he, Niels Ebbeson,
Through cloak that smote the door:
"Rise up, rise up, Lord Gert the Count,
For thou must sleep no more!

"Stand up, Lord Gert the Count,   165
And lend to me thine ear!
Duke Henrik's messenger am I,
And he hath sent me here.

"Rise up, Lord Gert the Count,
Nor longer lay thee down!   170
Kolding is beleaguered
And burnt is Ribe Town."

"And dost thou tell me tidings true,
Then good are they to hear!
Free in my hold whilst yet we live   175
Thou shalt have steed and gear."

Oh, they have opened wide the door
More of that news to know,
And it was he, Niels Ebbeson,
To the Count's bedside did go.   180

"Now thou and I, Niels Ebbeson,
Can league us far and wide,
Word will we send to Duke Henrik,
And Sir Klaus his friend beside."

Up and spake the swarthy swain: 185
"Now waste no further word!
Let be, let be thy tedious tale,
And hearken to the sword!"

They've seized him, Gert the Count,
  All by his golden hair,   190
Body from head they've sundered
  Over his bedside there.

Now when the Count was done to death
  All on the drums they beat,
Forth fared he, Niels Ebbeson,   195
  And hastened down the street.

It was he, Niels Ebbeson,
  That fain would flee away,
But Sir Ove Haas he barred the road,
  And strove to say him nay.   200

"Now lithe and listen, Sir Ove Haas,
  And seek not to hinder me,
For thou art wed to my kinswoman,
  As well is known to thee."

"Yea, he that has wed thy kinswoman   205
  Is kin to thee, I trow,
But thou hast slain my Lord this day,
  And thou shalt not pass me now!"

Niels Ebbeson he drew his blade,
  He would not flee the strife,   210
Sir Ove and many a German foe
  Must there lay down their life.

It was he, Niels Ebbeson,
  To Randers Bridge did ride,
And the little page that took his leave   215
  Was standing there beside.

Over the bridge rode Niels Ebbeson,
  For his foes came like the wind,
And it was the little foot-page
  Broke down the bridge behind.   220

Niels Ebbeson rode to Noringsris,
  And fast he spurred his steed,
Sore, good sooth, was his anguish,
  And sorer still his need.

She sheltered him, an old good-wife,   225
  Of loaves that had but two,
And she's given one to Niels Ebbeson,
  Because Count Gert he slew.

The Wife
of Usher's Well

(BRITISH)

Like *Aage and Else* or the British *Sweet William's
Ghost*, this ballad typifies the common theme of the

return of the dead, or the revenant, but the ghosts in *The
Wife of Usher's Well* are benevolent ghosts. This particular ballad has had a very long and complicated history
and still exists among English-speaking peoples in the
United States. In fact, in the American version, *The Blue
and the Gray*, a widow has three sons, killed respectively
in the Mexican, the Civil, and the Spanish Wars (!), who
return to visit her.

THERE lived a wife at Usher's well,
  And a wealthy wife was she;
She had three stout and stalwart sons,
  And sent them o'er the sea.

They hadna been a week from her,   5
  A week but barely ane,
When word came to the carline wife
  That her three sons were gane.

They hadna been a week from her,
  A week but barely three,   10
When word came to the carline wife
  That her sons she'd never see.

"I wish the wind may never cease,
  Nor fashes in the flood,
Till my three sons come hame to me   15
  In earthly flesh and blood!"

It fell about the Martinmas,
  When nights are lang and mirk,
The carline's wife's three sons came hame,
  And their hats were o' the birk.   20

It neither grew in syke nor ditch,
  Nor yet in ony sheugh;
But at the gates o' Paradise
  That birk grew fair enugh.

"Blow up the fire, my maidens!   25
  Bring water from the well!
For a' my house shall feast this night,
  Since my three sons are well."

And she has made to them a bed,
  She's made it large and wide;   30
And she's ta'en her mantle her about,
  Sat down at the bedside.

Up then crew the red, red cock,
  And up and crew the gray;

7. **carline wife,** old woman. 14. **fashes,** trouble, turbulence. 17.
Martinmas, the feast of St. Martin which fell on November 11. 20.
hats . . . birk, hats of birch. There is an old tradition that a man
returning from the dead wears some form of vegetation on his head
to prevent the wind on earth from having power over him. The
herbs of Paradise are his protection. 21. **syke,** trench. 22. **sheugh,**
furrow. 33. **Up then crew . . . cock.** The dead arose from their
graves at midnight and remained above ground until the cock
crowed.

The eldest to the youngest said, 35
"'Tis time we were away."

The cock he hadna crawed but once,
And clapped his wings at a',
When the youngest to the eldest said,
"Brother, we must awa'." 40

"The cock doth craw, the day doth daw,
The channerin' worm doth chide;
Gin we be missed out o' our place,
A sair pain we maun bide."

"Lie still, lie still but a little wee while, 45
Lie still but if we may;
Gin my mother should miss us when she wakes,
She'll go mad ere it be day."

"Fare ye weel, my mother dear!
Fareweel to barn and byre! 50
And fare ye weel, the bonny lass
That kindles my mother's fire."

Bonny Barbara Allan

(BRITISH)

Here is the familiar old theme of "lovesickness," this time carried to a fatal conclusion. The maiden, resenting a slight, real or fancied, spurns the suddenly enamored lover. He takes to his bed ("care-bed") and dies the wasting death of a rejected lover. The maiden then dies in sympathy. Few ballads in the entire Child collection have had a greater vitality in America.

IT WAS in and about the Martinmas time,
  When the green leaves were a-falling,
That Sir John Graeme, in the West Country,
  Fell in love with Barbara Allan.

He sent his man down through the town, 5
  To the place where she was dwelling;
"O haste and come to my master dear,
  Gin ye be Barbara Allan."

O hooly, hooly rose she up,
  To the place where he was lying, 10
And when she drew the curtain by,
  "Young man, I think you're dying."

"O it's I'm sick, and very, very sick,
  And 'tis a' for Barbara Allan;"
"O 'tis better for me ye's never be, 15
  Tho your heart's blood were a-spilling."

38. at a', at all. The phrase apparently means that the cock had crowed but once and had not yet flapped his wings. 42. channerin', devouring. 50. byre, a shed for cattle.
9. hooly, slowly and softly.

He turned his face unto the wall,
  And death was with him dealing:
"Adieu, adieu, my dear friends all,
  And be kind to Barbara Allan." 20

"O dinna ye mind, young man," said she,
  "When ye was in the tavern a-drinking,
That ye made the healths gae round and round,
  And slighted Barbara Allan?"

And slowly, slowly raise she up, 25
  And slowly, slowly left him,
And sighing said, she could not stay,
  Since death of life had reft him.

She had not gane but a mile or twa,
  When she heard the dead-bell ringing, 30
And every jow that the dead-bell geid,
  It cryed "Woe to Barbara Allan!"

"O mother, mother, make my bed!
  O make it soft and narrow!
My love has died for me today, 35
  I'll die for him tomorrow."

The Bride of Ribe

(DANISH)

This ballad represents the tradition of the shrewish, churlish woman, so formidable to mankind that neither saint nor devil can control her. A similar representative in British balladry is *The Farmer's Curst Wife*.

THERE dwelt a man in Ribe Town
  So rich and full of pride,
He gave his daughter a silken sark
Was fifteen fathoms wide.
She swept the dew from all the earth. 5

And fifteen tailors sewed the sark
That were of great renown,
And some dwelt up in Ribe
If they dwelt not in Ribe Town.

And fifteen maids of good repute 10
That sark must wash and dry,
And some got cramp in every limb,
While some lay down to die.

21. mind, remember. 31. jow, stroke of a bell. geid, gave (from "gived").
The Bride of Ribe. Translated by E. M. Smith-Dampier. From *Book of Danish Ballads*, edited by Axel Obrick, published by Princeton University Press, 1939. Reprinted by permission of the American-Scandinavian Foundation.
3. sark, here a blouse rather than a coat of mail.

And fifteen were the carpenters
That hung it out to air,   15
Some broke their arms and some their legs,
And some lay sick a year.

And now the bride went forth to kirk
All wrappen in cloak of skin,
Full fifteen fathom must they unfurl   20
Ere she could enter in.

And when she entered in the kirk
Loud did she rage and roar
She struck adown the holy Cross
That stood therein of yore.   25

A penny was all the bridal-fee
That she in pouch did find,
She threw one deacon off his legs,
And struck another blind.

Before the altar stood the priest,   30
And by Saint Knud he cried:
"No bridal can be hallowed here
Till ye remove the bride!"

With nose in air that maiden fair
From kirk returned again,   35
And all the kine in field that fed
Went galloping home again.

And when she sat at bridal feast
She laughed both loud and high:
"A penny we spent and to kirk we went,   40
As nobody can deny!"

Robin Hood's Death and Burial

(BRITISH)

As Child, the great authority on the British popular ballads, has so aptly observed, "Robin Hood is absolutely a creation of the ballad-muse." Attempts to associate Robin Hood, most celebrated of all ballad characters, with a historical personage have thus far failed completely. Nor is it possible to get far with the theory that he is a medieval popularization of Woden, the god of the Germanic peoples. Instead, he is a fictitious yeoman, idealized, with a kingly courtesy and courage, the defender of the poor and the champion of womanhood, the avowed enemy of the organized Church. But he is devout and reverent to the Virgin. He is an epic figure in the greenwood; his followers—Little John, Scarlet, and Friar Tuck—are analogous to the retainers of Roland or Beowulf or even to the knights of King Arthur, but they are nevertheless as much yeomen as Robin Hood himself.

The most extensive and withal the best treatment of the entire career of Robin Hood is *A Gest of Robyn Hode*, a long minstrel ballad of the later Middle English or early Modern English period. So close does the *Gest* come to an epic that it might be called a heroic epic, except that Robin Hood was not created by any poet of the court. Later isolated ballads make Robin Hood less impressive than his associates; he suffers a debasement comparable to that suffered by King Arthur or Charlemagne. But *Robin Hood's Death and Burial* shows the hero still in a heroic light.

The betrayal of Robin Hood by his cousin is reminiscent of the tragic "domestic relations" ballad, in which one relative either kills another or does him a great wrong.

WHEN Robin Hood and Little John
        Down a down a down a down
Went oer yon bank of broom,
        Said Robin Hood bold to Little John,
We have shot for many a pound.   5
        Hey down a down a down a down!

But I am not able to shoot one shot more,
        My broad arrows will not flee;
But I have a cousin lives down below,
        Please God, she will bleed me.   10

Now Robin he is to fair Kirkly gone,
        As fast as he can win;
But before he came there, as we do hear,
        He was taken very ill.

And when he came to fair Kirkly Hall,   15
        He knocked all at the ring,
But none was so ready as his cousin herself
        For to let Bold Robin in.

"Will you please to sit down, cousin Robin," she said,
        "And drink some beer with me?"   20
"No, I will neither eat nor drink,
        Till I am blooded by thee."

"Well, I have a room, cousin Robin," she said,
        "Which you did never see,
And if you please to walk therein,   25
        You blooded by me shall be."

She took him by the lily-white hand,
        And led him to a private room,
And there she blooded bold Robin Hood,
        While one drop of blood would run down.   30

2. **Down . . . down.** The refrain, the second line of each stanza, is repeated to make the sixth and last line of most of the stanzas, though not of the second and third stanzas from the end.   2. **broom,** the broom-plant.   8. **broad arrows,** arrows with a forked or barbed head.   11. **Kirkly,** Kirklees, not clearly identified. Some of the versions mention Bricklies (in Yorkshire) and others Bricklies (in Scotland).

She blooded him in a vein of the arm,
   And locked him up in the room;
There did he bleed all the live-long day,
   Until the next day at noon.

He then bethought him of a casement there,   35
   Thinking for to get down;
But was so weak he could not leap,
   He could not get him down.

He then bethought him of his bugle-horn,
   Which hung low down to his knee;   40
He set his horn upon his mouth,
   And blew out weak blasts three.

Then Little John, when hearing him,
   As he sat under a tree,
"I fear my master is now near dead,   45
   He blows so wearily."

Then Little John to fair Kirkly is gone,
   As fast as he can dree;
But when he came to Kirkly Hall,
   He broke locks two or three;   50

Until he came bold Robin to see,
   Then he fell on his knee;
"A boon, a boon," cries Little John,
   "Master, I beg of thee."

"What is that boon," said Robin Hood,   55
   "Little John, thou begs of me?"
"It is to burn fair Kirkly Hall,
   And all their nunnery."

"Now nay, now nay," quoth Robin Hood,
   "That boon I'll not grant thee;   60
I never hurt woman in all my life,
   Nor men in woman's company.

"I never hurt fair maid in all my time,
   Nor at mine end shall it be;
But give me my bent bow in my hand,   65
   And a broad arrow I'll let flee,
And where this arrow is taken up,
   There shall my grave digged be.

"Lay me a green sod under my head,
   And another at my feet;   70
And lay my bent bow by my side,
   Which was my music sweet;
And make my grave of gravel and green,
   Which is most right and meet.

"Let me have length and breadth enough,   75
   With a green sod under my head;

48. **dree,** literally "endure," to be interpreted here as "be able."
Contrast the word here with *drie* in *Edward,* l. 25 and note.

Then they may say, when I am dead
   'Here lies bold Robin Hood.' "

These words they readily granted him,
   Which did bold Robin Hood please;   80
And there they buried bold Robin Hood,
   Within the fair Kirkleys.

Bonnie George Campbell

(SCOTTISH)

This ballad is a characteristic example of the Scottish
coronach, or ballad of lamentation.

Hie upon Hielands,
   And laigh upon Tay,
Bonnie George Campbell
   Rode out on a day.

He saddled, he bridled,   5
   And gallant rode he,
And hame cam his guid horse,
   But never cam he.

Out cam his mother dear,
   Greeting fu sair,   10
And out cam his bonnie bryde,
   Riving her hair.

"The meadow lies green,
   The corn is unshorn,
But Bonnie George Campbell   15
   Will never return."

Saddled and bridled
   And booted rode he,
A plume in his helmet,
   A sword at his knee.   20

But toom cam his saddle,
   All bloody to see,
Oh, hame cam his guid horse,
   But never cam he!

Young Engel

(DANISH)

Although *Young Engel* has generally been classified
by Danish scholars as historical, its central situation—
that of the interrupted elopement—is essentially a com-

2. **laigh,** low.
Young Engel. Translated by E. M. Smith-Dampier. From *Book of
Danish Ballads,* edited by Axel Obrick, published by Princeton University Press, 1939. Reprinted by permission of the American-Scandinavian Foundation.

monplace motif in the "domestic relation" type of ballad. The couple, in this situation, will be pursued by
angry relatives bent on punishing the man in the case.

I T WAS the swain young Engel
   That was both free and fair,
Up did he ride in the countryside
And seized a maiden there.
Will the day ne'er be dawning?   5

Now Malfred hight the maiden,
Was honest as the day,
And on the night of their luckless flight
In greenwood wild they lay.

It was the swain young Engel   10
At midnight did awake,
And of his dream so dreary
To her he up and spake:

"A wolf methought was on me,
A wolf so grim and grey,   15
That tore my heart with bloody teeth
E'en when I waking lay."

"Small marvel if thus thou dreamest,
Nor doth thy dream deceive,
When thou by force hast taken me   20
Lacking my kinsfolk's leave."

In he came, the little foot-page,
And stood beside the board,
Both swift of wit and sharp of tongue,
He well could speak his word.   25

"Now hearken thou, young Engel,
And be for flight well boun,
For Gode Lovmand and his host
By four ways come to town!"

"Oh, not for four I tremble,   30
Nor do I fear for five,
I reck not of Gode Lovmand,
Nor any man alive!"

"Nay, more of five the number,
And a greater tale than ten!   35
Here cometh Gode Lovmand
With an hundred weaponed men."

It was the swain young Engel
That kissed his fair lady:
"If aught thou know'st of counsel   40
In God's name counsel me!"

"Now call thy squires together
To saddle each his steed,

And seek we the kirk of Our Lady
So long as endures our need!"   45

And now round the kirk of Our Lady
Was laid a leaguer close,
And ever Gode Lovmand
Was foremost among the foes.

Up spake the mother of Malfred   50
Of mood so grim and cold:
"An ye fire the kirk of Saint Mary
Ye can build it again for gold.

"Now cast we our gold and silver
Till it brims o'er a lordly cup;   55
An ye level the kirk of Our Lady,
I trow ye can build it up!"

Oh, they fired the kirk of Saint Mary,
And fast the flames leapt on,
And 'twas the lady Malfred   60
Must needs grow pale and wan.

Now heat like a fiery furnace
Did in the kirkyard glow,
But 'twas hotter within the walls, I ween,
When the lead dripped down below.   65

Up spake the swain young Engel
That was so bold of mood:
"Now let us slay our coursers
And cool us in their blood!"

Up spake the little horse-boy   70
That loved the steeds so free:
"Slay rather the lady Malfred,
More worthy of death is she!"

It was the swain young Engel
That took her in his arm: 75
"Thou art not worthy death, dear love,
And none shall do thee harm!"

Oh, they've set her on a shining shield
To lift her with glaive and spear,
They've hoisted her out of the kirk-window,   80
A-weeping full many a tear.

With many a tear young Malfred
Did through the kirkyard fare,
Blackened were all her garments
And burnt her golden hair.   85

Sore wept the lady Malfred
Came in the meads so green:
"Now burneth the kirk of Our Lady,
And a gallant swain therein!"

'Twas so soon thereafter,   90
Ere harvest time was done,
The lady sought her bower,
And bore so fair a son.

Born was he at even,
And christened the selfsame night;   95
They gave him the name of his father,
And fostered him while they might.

She fostered him seven winters,
And ever these words did say:
"My brother slew thy father,   100
And this must thou learn today."

She fostered him for a winter,
And for nine winters yet:
"My brother slew thy father,
And never shalt thou forget!"   105

And now her son, young Engel,
Unto his kinsfolk saith:
"Fain would I seek my father's foes
All to avenge his death."

It was Gode Lovmand   110
Sat drinking at the board,
And in he came, the little page,
So ready with his word.

"Now hearken, Gode Lovmand,
Ye may to flight be boun,   115
Here come young Engel and his men
By four ways to the town!

"Young Engel and his merry men
Upon the town advance,
And wrathful is his mood, I ween,   120
So high he shakes his lance."

"To Thing and meeting-place afar
My way I oft have won,
But the name of this young Engel
Was spoken of by none!"   125

It was Gode Lovmand
That clapped his cheek so white:
"Now canst thou give me counsel,
Then counsel thou me aright!"

"And if thou ask me counsel   130
This will I give to thee,
Seek we our stone-built tower
So long as need there be.

"The doors are all of the lead so grey,
And the walls of marble stone,   135

And a wondrous lot will be ours, I wot,
If ever that hold be won!"

And now that stone-built tower
On four sides they beset,
And 'twas the swain young Engel   140
That would be foremost yet.

It was Gode Lovmand
From loophole looked below:
"Who be ye that come hither
To make so proud a show?"   145

Up spake the swain young Engel,
Decked all in scarlet gear:
"Engel the name men call me,
Son of thy sister dear."

Up spake Gode Lovmand   150
All with a darkening brow:
"Of that needs little boasting,
For a bastard bairn wert thou!"

"And was I born of love, Godsooth,
The better is my breed!   155
And I have gold and liegemen bold,
And many a gallant steed.

"And was I but a bastard bairn
The fault was thine, I trow,
Yet am I lord of lands so broad,   160
With towers and holds enow."

It was the swain young Engel
Would sooner fight than fly;
He fired the stone-built tower
Till the flames leapt to the sky.   165

It was the swain young Engel
That would not ride his way,
Till he saw the stone-built tower
Lie low in ashes grey.

It was the swain young Engel   170
That clapped his lily-white hands,
When he saw his father's slayer
Lie dead 'mid burning brands.

It was the swain young Engel
Did home to hold repair,   175
And met by the gate his mother
Wrapped in her cloak of vair.

"Now greetings, greetings, mother dear,
Let all thy sorrow be!
My father's death have I avenged,   180
And bring the news to thee."

It was the lady Malfred
Wrung hands in dule and pain:
"I had one daily sorrow,
And thou hast made it twain!"   185

It was the swain young Engel
That turned and rode away:
"Strange are the ways of women,
And that for sooth I say!"

Now lieth Gode Lovmand   190
All under darksome mould,
But Engel serves before the King
For goods and red, red gold.

Sir Luno
and the Mermaid

(DANISH)

As in the ballad of *Riddles Wisely Expounded,* we are
dealing here with the case of a mortal who, confronted
by a supernatural creature and threatened with disaster,
is able to save himself by solving a riddle or reading a
secret message (a *rune*).

SIR Luno built him a ship so great
That ne'er on sea did sail its mate.
So they gained their red, red gold all up in Green-
        land.

A ship so great
That ne'er on sea did sail its mate.   5
On either side the red gold shone,
And Our Lady's name was written thereon.

The red gold shone,
Our Lady's name was written thereon.
On stem and stern did the red gold flame,   10
And thereon was written Our Saviour's name.

Did the red gold flame,
And thereon was written Our Saviour's name.
Of silk so fine the sails were spread,
And pied with stripes of blue and red.   15

The sails were spread,
And pied with stripes of blue and red.
The yards were all of silver white,
And with red gold the mast was dight.

Of silver white,   20
And with red gold the mast was dight.

Sir Luno and the Mermaid. Translated by E. M. Smith-Dampier.
From *Book of Danish Ballads*, edited by Axel Obrick, published by
Princeton University Press, 1939. Reprinted by permission of the
American-Scandinavian Foundation.

Down to the strand they bore
Both anchor stout and oar.

They bore
Both anchor stout and oar.   25
Swiftly Sir Luno sailed the sea,
And there met a Mermaid, and grim was she.

Sailed the sea,
And there met a Mermaid, and grim was she.
"Turn back now, Sir Luno, and get thee gone,   30
Or thy ship will I straightway change to stone!

"Get thee gone,
Or thy ship will I straightway change to stone!"
"Ne'er shalt thou live to see the day
When for a Mermaid I turned from my way.   35

"To see the day
When for a Mermaid I turned from my way."
With the first blue billow the Mermaid sent,
Both mast and yard were asunder rent.

The Mermaid sent,   40
Both mast and yard were asunder rent.
With the second she sent against the boat
The silken sail on the sea did float.

Against the boat,
The silken sail on the sea did float.   45
Up spake the steersman and said this word:
"Is there no man who knoweth the runes aboard?"

Said this word:
"Is there no man who knoweth the runes aboard?"
Up spake Sir Luno, the well-born knight: 50
"'Tis I that can rist the runes aright."

The well-born knight:
"'Tis I that can rist the runes aright."
On a linden-twig did he rist the spell,
And there as a stone must the Mermaid dwell.   55

Rist the spell,
And there as a stone must the Mermaid dwell.
He risted the runes on a linden-bough,
And bound the Mermaid with power enow.

On a linden-bough,   60
And bound the Mermaid with power enow.
"Sir Luno, Sir Luno, now loose thou me!
Seven barrels of silver I'll give to thee.

"Loose thou me,
Seven barrels of silver I'll give to thee,   65
And another of gold will I bestow
Wilt thou have mercy and let me go.

"Will I bestow,
Wilt thou have mercy and let me go."
"Sit thou a stone and starve for aye,   70
I'll loose thee not till the Judgment Day!

"Starve for aye,
I'll loose thee not till the Judgment Day.
Tell all who come hither by sea or land
Thou wert bound by Sir Luno's lily-white hand.   75

"By sea or land,
Thou wert bound by Sir Luno's lily-white hand."
He sailed back to Greenland, that knight so bold,
And there sits the Mermaid, a stone so cold.

Kemp Owyne

(BRITISH)

The common folklore themes here are (1) the "loathly
lady" and (2) the magic transformation. Perhaps it could
be said that one grows out of the other. The lady is made
hideous through the working of magic, but can be released from her spell through the courage and love of a
mortal who is willing to kiss her even in her hideous
form. There is, moreover, a test of the knight's physical
courage and endurance. On the magic ring, for example,
see *Hind Horn.*

HER mother died when she was young,
    Which gave her cause to make great moan;
Her father married the warst woman
    That ever lived in Christendom.

She served her with foot and hand,   5
    In every thing that she could dee,
Till once, in an unlucky time,
    She threw her in ower Craigy's sea.

Says, "Lie you there, dove Isabel,
    And all my sorrows lie with thee;   10
Till Kemp Owyne come ower the sea,
    And borrow you with kisses three,
Let all the world do what they will,
    Oh, borrowed shall you never be!"

Her breath grew strang, her hair grew lang,   15
    And twisted thrice about the tree,
And all the people, far and near,
    Thought that a savage beast was she.

These news did come to Kemp Owyne,
    Where he lived, far beyond the sea;   20
He hasted him to Craigy's sea,
    And on the savage beast looked he.

Her breath was strang, her hair was lang,
    And twisted was about the tree,
And with a swing she came about: 25
    "Come to Craigy's sea, and kiss with me.

"Here is a royal belt," she cried,
    "That I have found in the green sea;
And while your body it is on,
    Drawn shall your blood never be;   30
But if you touch me, tail or fin,
    I vow my belt your death shall be."

He stepped in, gave her a kiss,
    The royal belt he brought him wi;
Her breath was strang, her hair was lang,   35
    And twisted twice about the tree,
And with a swing she came about:
    "Come to Craigy's sea, and kiss with me.

"Here is a royal ring," she said,
    "That I have found in the green sea;   40
And while your finger it is on,
    Drawn shall your blood never be;
But if you touch me, tail or fin,
    I swear my ring your death shall be."

He stepped in, gave her a kiss,   45
    The royal ring he brought him wi;
Her breath was strang, her hair was lang,
    And twisted ance about the tree,
And with a swing she came about:
    "Come to Craigy's sea, and kiss with me.   50

"Here is a royal brand," she said,
    "That I have found in the green sea;
And while your body it is on,
    Drawn shall your blood never be;
But if you touch me, tail or fin,   55
    I swear my brand your death shall be."

He stepped in, gave her a kiss,
    The royal brand he brought him wi;
Her breath was sweet, her hair grew short,
    And twisted nane about the tree,   60
And smilingly she came about,
    As fair a woman as fair could be.

6. **dee,** do. 8. **Craigy's sea.** Although this body of water has not been
identified, there is known a Craigie Wood, a hill south of Perth,
Scotland, on the shores of the River Tay. Possibly, then, Craigy's
Sea is the Tay itself.   9. **dove,** a helpless or innocent young woman.
11. **Kemp Owyne.** A *kemp* is a champion fighting man. *Owyne* is very
likely the Owain of the Arthurian romance-cycles; if so, there is
here another instance of a figure taken from the chivalric romances
appearing in a popular ballad.   12. **borrow,** ransom, release.

27, 39, 51. **belt . . . ring . . . brand.** These three acouterments are
the commonest talismans against wounds. One would have been
enough, but three kisses are necessary to redeem the loathly lady,
and so three talismans come into the story. For the magic ring in
another use, see *Hind Horn,* line 9 ff.

Johnie Armstrong

(BRITISH)

The Armstrongs were a powerful Scottish family living near the Border, for many centuries the debatable land between England and Scotland. John Armstrong, the hero of this ballad, appears about 1525. He was an independent nobleman, paying little respect either to the English or to the Scots, and consequently making frequent border raids on both. Finally, in 1530, King James V of Scotland got possession of John Armstrong and had him executed. The suggestion here is that James captured Armstrong through treachery, but such suggestions are frequently made in outlaw ballads, where the sympathy is always with the outlaw.

THERE dwelt a man in faire Westmerland,
  Ionne Armstrong men did him call,
He had nither lands nor rents coming in,
  Yet he kept eight score men in his hall.

He had horse and harness for them all,   5
  Goodly steeds were all milke-white;
O the golden bands an about their necks,
  And their weapons, they were all alike.

Newes then was brought unto the king
  That there was sicke a won as hee,   10
That lived lyke a bold outlaw,
  And robbed all the north country.

The king he writt an a letter then,
  A letter which was large and long;
He signed it with his owne hand,   15
  And he promised to doe him no wrong.

When this letter came Ionne untill,
  His heart it was as blythe as birds on the tree:
"Never was I sent for before any king,
  My father, my grandfather, nor none but mee.   20

"And if wee goe the king before,
  I would we went most orderly;
Every man of you shall have his scarlet cloak,
  Laced with silver laces three.

"Every one of you shall have his velvett coat,   25
  Laced with sillver lace so white;
O the golden bands an about your necks,
  Black hatts, white feathers, all alyke."

1. **Westmerland**, Westmoreland, the county in northwest England.
7. **an**, a superfluous word, inserted to fill out the meter. 10. **sicke a won**, such a one. 17. **untill**, unto. The preposition is put after the word in many instances.

By the morrow morninge by ten of the clock,
  Towards Edenburough gon was hee,   30
And with him all his eight score men;
  Good Lord, it was a goodly sight for to see!

When Ionne came befower the king,
  He fell downe on his knee:
"O pardon, my soveraine leige," he said,   35
  "O pardon my eight score men and mee!"

"Thou shalt have no pardon, thou traytor strong,
  For thy eight score men nor thee;
For tomorrow morning by ten of the clock,
  Both thou and them shall hang on the gallow-
    tree."   40
But Ionne looked over his left shoulder,
  Good Lord, what a grievious look looked hee!
Saying, "Asking grace of a graceles face—
  Why there is none for you nor me."

But Ionne had a bright sword by his side,   45
  And it was made of the mettle so free,
That had not the king stept his foot aside,
  He had smitten his head from his faire boddë.

Saying, "Fight on, my merry men all,
  And see that none of you be taine;   50
For rather then men shall say we were hanged,
  Let them report how we were slaine."

Then, God wot, faire Eddenburrough rose,
  And so besett poore Ionne rounde,
That fowerscore and tenn of Ionnes best men   55
  Lay gasping all upon the ground.

Then like a mad man Ionne laid about,
  And like a mad man then fought hee,
Until a falce Scot came Ionne behinde,
  And runn him through the faire boddee.   60

Saying, "Fight on, my merry men all,
  And see that none of you be taine;
For I will stand by and bleed but awhile,
  And then will I come and fight againe."

Newes then was brought to young Ionne Arm-
    strong,   65
  As he stood by his nurse's knee,
Who vowed if ere he lived for to be a man,
  O the treacherous Scots revenged hee'd be.

59. **falce Scot**. It is a commonplace of the outlaw ballads to have the death of the outlaw encompassed by "treachery" of some sort.
65. **young Ionne Armstrong**, the little son of the outlaw.

REBIRTH
AND
DISCOVERY

1350 TO 1650

Lorenzo de' Medici, patron of art and letters and ruthless Renaissance ruler, by the sculptor Verrocchio.

T HE Middle Ages reached their climax in the thirteenth century, when all the faith and spirituality of Christian Europe, united in the fold of a common Church, expressed themselves in lofty masterpieces of literature and Gothic building. It was the century of Albertus Magnus, Thomas Aquinas, Roger Bacon, and Duns Scotus, of St. Francis and St. Dominic, of the Minnesingers and *Roman de la Rose* and the Dante of *La Vita Nuova*. In the hundred years that followed, the medieval synthesis began to disintegrate under the pressure of new forces in the life of Europe, and with the fifteenth century a new era supplanted it. The change did not come quickly nor to all countries at the same time. The first focal point of the new movement was the Italian city of Florence in the mid-fourteenth century, and from there it spread to the rest of Italy, Germany, and France in the next hundred years. The new movement did not affect England and Spain significantly until the sixteenth century, and it was still animating Spain as late as the mid-seventeenth century, when the rest of western Europe had already passed beyond it.

As this period cannot be exactly dated, so it cannot be briefly defined. For some historians it is simply an elaborate transition from the Middle Ages to modern times without a special name or integrity of its own. But for the classical French of the eighteenth century it had come to seem the time of Renaissance, or rebirth, after the long night of the Middle Ages, the time when ancient learning, literature, and architecture were rediscovered and the continuity of antiquity and modern times was re-

established. By rights, the term Renaissance should be confined to the art and philosophy of the period, though even here it carries with it a classical prejudice against the hardy culture of the later Middle Ages. But no more accurate term has risen to identify this whole age, and we fall back on it because the distinctness of the period in literature cannot be denied.

The great cultural activity of the thirteenth century brought with it no radical changes in the intellectual outlook or social life of Europe. It simply carried to their most articulate and striking expression the forces of the medieval Church and Scholasticism, of feudalism and chivalry, which had prevailed for centuries. But the Renaissance brought a basic change in men's attitude toward themselves and the world. A new spirit gradually permeated every phase of life—a spirit of exploration and adventure that pushed back the limits of the physical and intellectual world in which medieval men had lived. Little by little, men became aware of a new interest in themselves and in the world around them. They awoke from the medieval dream of a snug universe centered upon man and neatly ordered to enable him to work out his destiny in this life and in the life to come. They opened their eyes to a challenging new reality which intoxicated the youthful pioneers but sobered the Montaignes and the Francis Bacons at the end of the period. Yet all felt a new excitement in the actual things of everyday experience and the actual life they were sharing, and they found among the ancient Romans and Greeks kindred spirits who had felt the same curiosity centuries before.

If antiquity was reborn in this age, it was not because it had been unknown to the Middle Ages, but because a gigantic barrier of spiritual concentration and intellectual orthodoxy stood between the medieval mind and the ancient classics. This wall gradually crumbled in the atmosphere of cosmopolitanism and sophistication that the fourteenth and fifteenth centuries ushered in. Independent thinking and self-expression invited back the Greeks of ancient Athens and their belief in the freedom of the individual. Eventually we will see that literature was exchanging one authority for another, but the new tyranny of the classics did not become complete until the age beyond the Renaissance. This is a time of creative adventure and discovery in all the realms of mind and spirit.

COMMERCE AND COSMOPOLITANISM

No phase of the Renaissance—economic, political, social, religious, or artistic—can be understood apart from the total complex of changes that were converting the medieval world into the modern world. But the starting point would seem to be the sphere of trade and finance. In the Middle Ages, Christian Europe had lapsed into a purely agricultural economy, cut off from trade as it was by Arab conquests to the east and south and by Norse piracy to the west and north. The powerful middle class of Roman days gradually disappeared as the sources of wealth dried up. With it went the large cities and the ready communication over open roads so essential to commerce. The cosmopolitanism of ancient times vanished with the cities, and the map of Europe broke up into a myriad of little self-contained feudal cells, where the money economy of antiquity was replaced by the simple barter of a still older day. Land, labor on the land, and the produce of the land were the chief forms of wealth under the feudal system, and the provincial conservatism of rural life condemned education as useless and new ideas as heresy.

The coastal towns of northern Italy, Venice and Genoa especially, best survived the decay of commerce, and, when trade with the East was resumed in the eleventh century through the decline of Arab power and the early Crusades, Italian merchants were the first to establish sea routes in the eastern Mediterranean and land routes to the Low Countries in the north. Italy was the natural center for the exchange of Oriental luxuries for raw materials from the primitive northern lands, and in time the Italian cities developed export industries, fashioning products of their own out of the goods they handled. Venice and Genoa grew rapidly in size, wealth, and political power, and eventually accumulated eastern empires to insure unhampered trade monopolies. In the thirteenth century a third city, Florence, rose to challenge the commercial position of Venice and Genoa as well as to lead the intellectual movement of the Renaissance.

Wealth flowed into the Italian cities and attracted population away from the land, so that in the thirteenth century feudalism disappeared in northern Italy, taking with it the rural provincialism of medieval society. The barter system was replaced by gold coins, especially the Venetian ducat and Florentine florin, which became the standard media of exchange. Modern capitalism was born as the great merchants invested their earnings from trade in well-organized industries, such as the Florentine textile manufacture, and competed with each other in building vast fortunes. Despite the formal prohibition of the church, moneylending and banking flourished, and the great Florentine houses, such as the Bardi, the Peruzzi, and later the Medici, not only established agencies beyond Italy in the Low Countries, France, and England, but handled the Pope's finances as well. When cities north of the Alps began to challenge the preëminence of Italy in commerce, a great financial center arose in the south-German city of Augsburg, and with it the wealthiest of all the Renaissance banking houses, the Fuggers, who built a huge fortune on mine exploitation. Farther north the Low Countries, and especially Antwerp, enjoyed enormous prosperity. But the vigorous Italian cities retained their economic leadership of Europe until the late fifteenth century.

One might well ask why the great nations along the Atlantic seaboard, England, France, and Spain, allowed the small city-states of northern Italy, southern Germany, and the Low Countries to monopolize this lucrative trade for three centuries. In the western lands feudalism had achieved a more complete domination of economic life than in the Italian states, so that they were not so immediately respon-

"The Banker and His Wife," by a Flemish painter, Matsys.

lantic powers in an effort to gain commercial advantages over the Italians and Germans. Portugal pioneered, and her great hero, Vasco da Gama, found a new and cheaper route to India around Africa in 1498, shortly after the Ottoman Turks conquered the Byzantine Empire and absorbed the colonies of Venice in the eastern Mediterranean. Meanwhile, Spain had financed the expedition of Columbus and Pinzón to find a third route to India, which instead opened up the Americas to Spanish galleons. Magellan's circumnavigation of the globe in 1519–1522 proved the distinctness of the Americas from India and challenged the Renaissance imagination with the undreamed-of size of the earth. The Netherlands were quick to turn their attention from the eastern overland route to the western sea. Antwerp and all of Flanders declined under Spanish rule in the sixteenth century, while the Dutch of the northern Netherlands freed themselves from Spain and, at the expense of the Portuguese, carved out an empire in the East Indies around 1600. England too entered the race and supplanted Portugal in India. More important, however, was her colonization of the Atlantic seaboard of North America in the seventeenth century, where she soon came in conflict with Dutch and even Swedish colonies and with French settlements farther north.

So geographical discovery led to a commercial revolution as the big nations of the Atlantic seaboard scrambled to exploit the new worlds overseas. The economic movement that brought fabulous prosperity to the Italian cities in the fourteenth century shifted westward in the sixteenth. A new capitalism of national proportions outstripped the power of city-states, and their decline was insured when Spain and France made Italy a battleground of empire. In the shifting fortunes of central and western Europe during the Renaissance we may see one explanation of why the Italian cities, Florence, Venice, and Rome, led the early and middle periods of the Renaissance in literature and art, while France, England, and Spain dominated its last century.

sive to the revival of trade. Moreover, all three were involved in costly wars that consumed their attention and energy—England and France in the Hundred Years' War (1339–1453) that devastated France; England in the civil Wars of the Roses (1455–1485); Spain in the long struggle to oust the Moors. But most important was their remote geographical situation at a time when the chief trade was with the East, and Italy was the natural center of exchange.

The geographical discoveries of the fifteenth century that opened up the Americas and Africa to exploitation shifted the center of commerce from the Mediterranean to the Atlantic seaboard and brought a rapid decline in the prosperity of Italy and the south-German cities. The explorations that led to these discoveries were sponsored by the At-

MONARCHY AND NATIONALISM

THE agricultural economy of the Middle Ages with its barter of goods and services worked against the power of national sovereigns and in favor of the barons living in close contact with their retainers on feudal estates. Without a money economy the kings could not readily collect taxes, and without the power of wealth they could not force their rule on the nation as a whole. The self-sufficient and virtually independent estates that dotted the map of Europe discouraged the rise of national feel-

ing among the people as well as any strong national rule.

But the revival of trade in the late Middle Ages restored the money economy of the ancient world, and there emerged a powerful merchant class, which, in order to pursue its farflung trading, demanded a more stable government than the petty feudal rulers could provide with their limited resources. Money enabled the national sovereign to collect taxes, develop a national army, and assert a personal rule **over** his country as a whole. The merchants readily supported the power of the throne in return for a stable national law and uniform conditions of trade throughout the land. But the national monarchies of the Renaissance rose out of bitter civil struggles in which the kings finally destroyed the power of feudal nobles and the entire system of feudalism.

ITALY. In Italy, the first area to feel the force of the Renaissance, special conditions produced a peculiar political evolution. During the thirteenth and fourteenth centuries the Italian cities in the north formed part of the Holy Roman Empire, the international agglomeration of many little states that was theoretically ruled by a German royal house. There was no native king of Italy in the Middle Ages comparable to the feudal kings of England and France. Consequently, when the authority of the emperors declined in Italy in the thirteenth and fourteenth centuries, the Italian city-states were bent on securing independence from imperial rule rather than union under an Italian sovereign. The growth of their wealth through commerce owed nothing to the protection of a king, and they used it to strengthen their independence. The presence in Italy of the Church and the Pope also discouraged a national spirit, since the Church was an international force and the Pope laid claim to being an international ruler, who was therefore in frequent conflict with the Emperor. Moreover, the temporal rule of the Pope over large states of his own in central Italy discouraged the unification of the northern, central, and southern sections of the peninsula.

Except for the southern Kingdom of Naples, Italy was cut up into numerous small states, each focused on a large city—Venice, Genoa, Pisa, Florence, Milan, Bologna—which controlled its politics and sought through ultimately disastrous little wars to extend its power over its neighbors. The turbulent political history of the oligarchic city-states during this period recalls the tumultuous careers of the Greek cities of antiquity. This internal strife interfered with the commercial prosperity of the states and led the ruling classes in the fourteenth century to sacrifice their power to despots who would guarantee peace and orderly government for a period of years. Since the dictator was often a *condottiere,* or leader of an army of mercenary soldiers, he might continue his rule indefinitely and bequeath it to a member of his family. Thus remarkable dynasties of despots were established in several Italian states and eventually took on the magnificence of royalty in other countries. The famous Medici rule of Florence was founded by Cosimo de' Medici in 1434 and produced in his grandson, Lorenzo the Magnificent (1449–1492), the greatest patron of scholarship, art, and literature in Renaissance Italy. Men did not inquire into the morality of dictatorship but assumed the pragmatic view that any means, however dishonest or inhumane, was justified if it achieved the end of increasing the prosperity and power of the state. This cynical, if realistic, view of state dictatorship was brilliantly enunciated by Machiavelli in his treatise, *The Prince.* Yet, though it might carry the states to remarkable prosperity in the fourteenth century, this sordid philosophy destroyed patriotism and the citizen's sense of responsibility for the welfare of the state, so that in the sixteenth the states were an easy prey to the imperialistic designs of France and Spain.

GERMANY. Germany too failed to achieve unification under a national monarchy, and for somewhat similar reasons. The many small German states were theoretically united under the Holy Roman Emperor, but since he was elected by seven local rulers called Electors, his office until 1438 lacked the dynastic continuity of the kingships of France and England and did not inspire ambitions to effective monarchy. Moreover, the Holy Roman Emperor was usually more interested in pursuing his international claims or advancing his family holdings than in unifying the German states. The decline of the Empire in the thirteenth century enfeebled central government still further. Nevertheless, some states were gradually consolidated in clusters, as the powerful ones absorbed the weaker, so that several large states emerged from the medieval confusion, although there were still over three hundred states until the nineteenth century. There undoubtedly was national feeling in Germany of the Renaissance, but it expressed itself in the religious Reformation of Luther rather than in a national monarchy, and was thereafter weakened by the religious differences engendered by the Reformation.

ENGLAND. It was in the countries along the Atlantic seaboard that the great monarchies of the Renaissance developed. The time was the fifteenth century, when the little Italian states were enjoying their last period of commercial supremacy. England was the first to evolve a strong central government, perhaps because the power of the king had been stronger in England since the days of William the Conqueror (1028–1087) than in France and elsewhere. The greater power of the king explains why England was the first to achieve a strong monarchy; the importance of the parliament of nobles, church dignitaries, and commoners explains why the English monarchy was never so absolute as the French. When the authority of the king weakened, as in the fourteenth century, the national parliament rather than individual nobles assumed his powers. Yet the fifteenth century brought a civil struggle in which the nobles supporting the rival houses of Lancaster and York fought the War of the Roses (1455–1485) to decide the kingship and in the process dissipated their own authority and paved the way for a dynasty of strong monarchs, who temporarily eclipsed the power of parliament.

After a long period of war and devastation the populace welcomed the firm rule of the Tudors. Henry VII established the line in 1485 and quickly shaped the national monarchy that England was to become. But it was the last of the dynasty, Queen Elizabeth (who reigned from 1558 to 1603), that brought its greatest glory and presided over the Golden Age of the English Renaissance. Personal loyalty to Elizabeth was strong throughout her long and enlightened reign, and as a result her great authority was seldom questioned. Loyalty to the crown inspired national feeling as well, and the chronicle plays of Shakespeare, re-creating the past history of England, are evidence of the patriotic fervor that made England a world power under Elizabeth.

FRANCE. The rise of national monarchy in France was at first inhibited by the claim of the English kings to huge sections of the land. In the Hundred Years' War (1339–1453) the English, using new methods of warfare unknown to the backward French, won brilliant victories at Crécy, Poitiers, and Agincourt and even secured the aid of the Dukes of Burgundy, the most powerful of the feudal nobles in France, against the French king. But in 1429 a naïve peasant girl, Joan of Arc, inspired by what she thought to be divine voices, rallied the French and led an army herself to relieve the siege of Orleans and restore the prestige of the French crown. Soon after, the English evacuated nearly all of France and left that unhappy country to fifty years of slow revival. The process of unifying France as a strong nation was begun by Louis XI, the ugly but able king from 1461 to 1483 who finally established the authority of the French crown over Burgundy. But his successors interrupted French recovery by four expensive and unsuccessful wars with Spain for control of Italy. In the later sixteenth century these were followed by eight civil wars, most of which turned on the religious antagonism of Catholic extremists and the Protestant Huguenots.

Not until the accession of Henry IV, the first Bourbon, in 1589, did France settle down to repair its ravaged land, develop domestic prosperity, and enter competition with the other powers for empires abroad. Henry brought peace and wealth to France by making himself absolute over the nobles and the rival religious factions, and thus laid the foundation of the unlimited monarchy that ruled France for two centuries. The nobility challenged the royal power twice during the seventeenth century, but in the reign of Louis XIV (1661–1715) the monarchy justified its absolute authority over every phase of national life by an efficient domestic policy, successful wars abroad that made France the most powerful nation in Europe, and a stimulation of culture that gave France her Golden Age of art and literature.

SPAIN. Early in the eighth century the Arabs of the East had extended their power from northern Africa over virtually all of the Iberian peninsula (which contains modern Spain and Portugal). The history of this region for the seven centuries that followed is chiefly the gradual liberation of the land from the Moslems by the dogged persistence of the Christians in pushing them ever farther south toward Gibraltar. By the twelfth century the Moslems controlled merely the southern third, and four powerful feudal states had emerged in the north—Portugal, Leon, Castile, and Aragon. In the thirteenth century the Moslems were reduced to the kingdom of Granada, and Castile had absorbed Leon to become the largest state in the peninsula. The marriage of King Ferdinand of Aragon and Queen Isabella of Castile in 1469 and their conquest of Granada in 1492 completed the political unification. But little Portugal remained an independent kingdom, except for a brief Spanish conquest, and in the late fifteenth and early sixteenth centuries amassed a fantastic empire in South America, Africa, and Asia. Her national poet, Camoëns, preserved the glory of her great century in his magnificent epic, The Lusiads (1572), which told in heroic fashion of the voyage of Vasco da Gama around Africa to India in 1498.

The long struggle with the Moslems gave Spain a unique national fervor in the Renaissance that blended with the Christian ardor of her holy wars. Catholic mysticism was nowhere so intense as in the land of St. John of the Cross and St. Teresa. Spain led the Catholic Reformation with the militant zeal of the Jesuits under Ignatius Loyola and the heresy hunts of the Inquisition. When the national monarchy appeared under Ferdinand and Isabella, the absolute authority of the Spanish monarchs was enforced for several generations by their profound piety, so that the Spaniard's devotion to "dios y el rey" (God and the king) was centered in his Most Catholic Majesty. Ferdinand's grandson, Charles I, became Holy Roman Emperor as Charles V and ruled (1516–1558), not simply the Spanish empire, but the Hapsburg territories in Germany and the Low Countries as well. Throughout his vast realm he thought of himself as the chosen defender of Catholic Christianity against Moslems, Jews, and Protestants. Under his son, Philip II, emperor from 1558 to 1598, religious zeal and absolute rule reached their climax on the Spanish throne. The imperialistic exploitation of America, upon which Spain had been engaged for half a century, was blended with a religious crusade to convert the heathen natives. Spain amassed a great empire in the Americas during the sixteenth century, and their plundered wealth made

Renaissance Europe 1559

S. Fleishman

her for a short time the leading power in Europe. To this period of her imperial splendor (1500–1650) belongs her Golden Age of art and letters.

NATIONALISM AND INTERNATIONALISM. The rise of aggressive national states and the decline of chivalry, with its idealistic codes of warfare, destroyed for a time the moral basis of international law as the new nations competed in a ruthless struggle for empire. War took on a new horror with more deadly weapons, and respect for treaties and moral obligations declined. The Hundred Years' War ended without a treaty. The English crown actually sanctioned piracy against Spain on the high seas. But humanitarian forces gradually came to demand a regulation of warfare, and even the grasping monarchies began to realize that they all stood to gain from some recognized control of their savage competition.

The Dutch jurist, Hugo Grotius, experiencing the horrors of the Thirty Years' War, provided the first set of rules for an international law in his *Rights of War and Peace* (1625). Assuming that the very nature of man, which had naturally evolved a system of law for his civil life, demanded a similar natural code among nations, Grotius argued that kings should deal with each other as ordinary men are bound by moral law to do, neither stealing nor assaulting nor violating contract. Wars are justified, he insisted, only as a means of enforcing law or punishing international criminals. The work of Grotius did not lead to any moral revolution in the practice of nations, nor have we yet achieved the international law that this idealist prefigured. But he gave voice to the perennial longing of modern man for a curb on the repeated horrors of war that nationalism has brought with it.

FROM KNIGHT TO COURTIER

ALTHOUGH the social changes of the Renaissance did not take place evenly in all of the emerging nations, the general pattern of change was almost universal. Medieval society had been dominated by two powerful classes: the clergy, who controlled the spiritual and intellectual forces of Europe under a divinely inspired authority, and the knightly class of feudal nobles, who controlled the temporal sphere under an international code of chivalry. Both classes gave a universal cast to medieval society and opposed the power of national government, as it was nominally embodied in national sovereigns. The middle class of artisans and shopkeepers was small and only in the towns enjoyed a life apart from the feudal system. The peasant foundation of medieval society was a submerged majority, conservative, illiterate, and inarticulate.

The Renaissance was to see almost everywhere a shift of power from clergy and nobility to absolute national monarchs and a new middle class of wealthy merchants. The clergy, of course, continued its power within the spiritual realm, but the scope of its authority declined sharply, as the Church ceased to embrace the totality of men's lives and the new national churches, whether Catholic in Spain and France or Protestant in Germany and England, became independent, relatively or completely, from the power of Rome. The new economic and social interests of a worldly society challenged religion's enveloping control of men's minds, and the new nationalism weakened everywhere the international power of the Church. As a result, the literature of the Renaissance was to be predominantly secular.

The feudal nobility suffered a decline close to extermination. In a word, the haughty medieval knight became the dependent courtier of the Renaissance. As international commerce revived and national monarchy emerged, the feudal noble discovered that society had no longer a place for him. For centuries he had held his power by monopolizing the art of war. In an age of simple and unorganized military tactics the medieval knight, resplendent on horseback with his flashing armor, deadly lance, and trusty sword, was the supreme embodiment of military glory and protection to his vassals, who in time of danger could crowd within the impregnable walls of their liege lord's stone castle. But the new use of gunpowder in the fourteenth century destroyed the invulnerable strength of these strongholds, and the invention of effective infantry weapons raised the prestige of the common foot-soldier over the knight on horseback. In vain did the knights increase the thickness of their armor against the crossbow and longbow, for the cumbersome weight merely forced them to take the defensive. The doom of the individual knight, fighting picturesquely rather than effectively by the code of chivalry, was sealed when the Italian cities began to employ mercenary armies, drilled to coordinated action by professional soldiers. National armies, fighting for king and country, supplanted the chaotic feudal aggregations, and nobles, if they continued to fight, did so as warriors of the king.

Moreover, the rise of a money economy overturned the barter economy of feudalism and fixed rents and pay for services. Peasants were freed from their anchorage to the land and might even assert their independence of their noble masters by aban doning work on the farm for the new industries of the cities. Ill-equipped by training to cope with the new money economy, the nobles often squandered their resources on new luxuries and then relied on shrewd moneylenders, to whom they gradually lost their estates.

Thus, necessity or the superior sophistication of urban life might lead them to move to the capital, where they lacked roots and were forced to depend on the king for support through sinecures, pensions, and positions in the army, ministry, or church. The king welcomed them, at first because their dependence on the crown made them impotent to oppose it, later because of their ornamental value, since an aristocratic court formed a glamorous setting for the royal presence. Indeed, the actual refinement of the nobility increased greatly as they moved from their isolated country estates to the brilliant capital. The medieval knight, whose exalted code of courtesy did not free him from coarseness and brutality, evolved at the capital into the polished courtier who sought to make himself worthy of his king and the ladies by his charming manners, intellectual culture, sharp wit, and skill with the rapier to defend his personal honor. The code of chivalry did not die with feudalism; it was adapted to the new conditions of the royal court, from which it was to descend to us in our concept of the gentleman, with his romantic deference to women and his personal ideals of loyalty, truth to his word, generosity, and courtesy. Castiglione's *Book of the Courtier* (1514) epitomized the ideal gentleman of the Renaissance, but we must suspect that the usual courtier fell short of the perfect combination of good breeding, character, and intellect that he described. Nevertheless, the polished literature of the Renaissance resulted from the patronage of this aristocracy and was often written by gifted members of such a court. Spenser's *Faerie Queene* and the exquisite lyrics of Ronsard reflect the immaculate ideals for which the courtier stood.

Although the snobbish nobility disdained the money-making of the middle class, it could not indefinitely remain aloof from the wealthy merchants. In some of the Italian cities the two classes eventually cooperated in politics and fell together as the upper class. In England the tradition of primogeniture converted younger sons into commoners and often forced them into trade to support themselves, so that the separation between the nobility and the upper bourgeoisie was never so rigid there as in France and Spain. But the wealthy merchants suffered from a sense of social inferiority and imitated the manners and code of the aristocracy rather than developing new standards of their own. Hence, though they often achieved a culture equal to that of the nobility and patronized art and learning munificently, they created no separate literary tradition. We must wait until the eighteenth century for a socially conscious literature of a militant middle class. Still lower classes, the petty bourgeoisie and the commoners of farm and city, exerted no influence on art and letters, and when they appeared as characters, for example in Shakespeare's Roman rabble in *Julius Caesar* or his artisans in *A Midsummer-Night's Dream,* they were usually ridiculed as dull buffoons. But Lope de Vega's picture of a proud and self-respecting Spanish peasantry in *The Sheep Well* assures us that even at this early time the proletariat of Europe was developing a consciousness of its human rights.

HUMANISM AND THE NEW LEARNING

THE economic, social, and political changes of the Renaissance produced a profound revolution in European thought and culture. Although the feudal courts had developed a secular literature in the twelfth and thirteenth centuries, the learning of the Middle Ages was entirely in the hands of the clergy, and architecture, sculpture, and painting were generally commissioned by the Church and involved a religious purpose or religious subject matter. As the growth of private wealth in the fourteenth century produced generous private patrons, learning and art took on a secular character such as Europe had not known since the Silver Age of Rome. The horizon of this secular culture broadened immensely as it lost the provincial outlook of the feudal estates and came to reflect the cosmopolitanism of the new cities, born of commercial contact with far corners of the world. As it expanded in space, so it reached backward in time and found a new inspiration in the rediscovery of ancient Greece and Rome and a way of life that excited the exploring imagination of the Renaissance.

A knowledge of antiquity and ancient philosophy and literature had never died completely, though it nearly expired in the darkest of the Dark Ages. Because of his *Fourth Eclogue,* Virgil survived as a prophet of Christ's coming and the *Aeneid* was religiously interpreted as a parable of man's search for perfection and peace. Ovid's love poetry was incorporated in the courtly love tradition, and other Latin poets were dimly known. Homer and Aristotle were read only in Latin epitomes. The Greek language and hence its literature were practically forgotten in the West, and not only the classical drama but the very concept of acting and the stage were lost. Even the few ancients who struggled through were largely misunderstood, because the religious mind of the Middle Ages, bound up in mystical symbols and lacking historical perspective, interposed a barrier of Christian theology between itself and the ancient past. Achilles and Aeneas became chivalrous knights with armor and lance, and the Hades of Virgil was transformed into a Christian hell. Hence the "renaissance" of the ancients was not simply a recovery of the ancient classics from oblivion. It was the rebirth of an understanding of the ancients in their own terms, freed from the veil of medieval mysticism. Only the revival of secular culture made possible this new perspective divorced from theology and symbolism.*

The bond between secular culture and the revival of the classics was important to both. If the poets and philosophers of Greece and Rome had to wait for lay scholars to rediscover them, they repaid their benefactors by showing them a new way of life that was basically opposed to the dogma of medieval Christianity. The Church had taught that, because of the fall of Adam, human nature is fundamentally bad, and that within man there is an endless conflict between the flesh and the spirit. The good Christian, recognizing the evil of the flesh, would renounce this world and the enjoyment of life in which the body delights. For the surest salvation of his soul, he would choose the life of the ascetic. But the Greeks had believed precisely the opposite. Aspiring toward an ideal of general perfection, they had sought a rounded development of all human faculties—body, mind, and spirit. The joy of this life was their compensation for grim death to come. Platonists, Stoics, and Epicureans differed widely in their views of how this life should be lived, but they were united in insisting on the dignity of all phases of human nature and in prescribing for a life in this world. In rediscovering the ancients, the Humanistic scholars rediscovered what they thought of as the dignity of man and the ancients' belief in the general perfectability of human nature. It was Leonardo Bruni (1370–1444) who named this new, dynamic learning Humanism after Cicero's *humanitas,* a term for the education that exalts the full worth of man— those liberal arts, literature and philosophy, which are called the humanities to this day.

Rallying behind Terence's claim that "nothing human is alien to me," the Humanists renounced asceticism and eagerly embraced the world and its pleas-

ures, emancipating the body as well as the spirit. Accepting the Greek view of a well-rounded life, the Renaissance produced the fantastic versatility of a Leonardo da Vinci, a Michelangelo, and a Cellini. As the new learning inspired a new way of life, nominal Christians embraced the worldliness of epicureans and stoics, and the liberation of the flesh from the restraints of Christian morality led in time to license and depravity, especially in the Italian cities of the sixteenth century. But such excesses do not concern us here; the rediscovery of "human nature" through the rediscovery of the ancient classics revolutionized the Renaissance outlook on the world and reshaped education and literature.

Although the beginnings of Humanism cannot be exactly dated, Petrarch of fourteenth-century Florence is usually thought of as the first scholar and writer of the new type. A secular man of letters, he divided his life between the enthusiastic unearthing and study of ancient manuscripts and the pursuit of literary fame. His example inspired his friend Boccaccio to turn from the earthy storytelling of the *Decameron* to classical scholarship. The physical gusto running through Boccaccio's hundred tales also implies the new freedom with which the Renaissance man expressed himself. From a wandering Greek scholar of Constantinople Boccaccio learned Greek and labored at translating Homer. His studies predicted the Greek Renaissance in Italy, which dates from the lectures of Emanuel Chrysoloras at Florence in 1397–1400 and the Platonic Academy founded by Cosimo de' Medici. Most of the Italian Humanists, such as Lorenzo Valla and Marsilio Ficino, belong to scholarship rather than literature, but Pico della Mirandola gave eloquent voice to their ideals in his *Oration on the Dignity of Man.*

Humanism was an international movement which, because of the freemasonry of scholars, found its way to the northern countries before other phases of the Renaissance. It was greatly accelerated by the invention of printing in the fifteenth century, which freed learning from dependence on scribes for the laborious reproduction of manuscripts, rapidly increased the circulation of book knowledge, and destroyed the Church monopoly of libraries. Significantly, the new learning did not reach Germany, France, and England until the second half of the fifteenth century, the first era of the printing press.

Of all the continental Humanists who carried the movement through its golden century (1450–1550), none was better known nor more universally esteemed than the wise and gentle Dutch scholar who called himself Desiderius Erasmus. This restless seeker after knowledge moved from one end of western Europe to the other and was greeted everywhere as the bearer of a new enlightenment. He at first entered a monastery but soon rebelled against the

---

* The term "Revival of Learning" is so ambiguous that it is omitted from this discussion of Humanism. The first revival of learning took place in the twelfth and thirteenth centuries when the first European universities were founded, but the term is generally applied to the revival of classical scholarship in the fourteenth and fifteenth centuries and hence carries with it, like the term "Renaissance," a classical prejudice against the Middle Ages.

austere discipline and the empty formalism of the monk's activities, though he retained deep religious convictions throughout his life and remained loyal to Catholicism after the Protestant Reformation. His classical studies made him crusade against the narrow horizon of the medieval Church, but his mild and peaceful spirit argued for reform from within. The treatises of Erasmus cover a wide variety of Humanist interests—the enlightened use of the classics, the art of writing, the stupidity of the monastic life, the moral education of a Christian king. But the best known of all his works is the delightful satire on human foibles called *The Praise of Folly*, supposedly delivered by a female personification of folly itself, who argues that, for all his blundering, man should follow his human impulses unafraid and guide himself by the natural discipline of moderation.

Humanism began in the universities but soon spread to the court, where the new learning and the new outlook on life became part of the courtier's education. Indeed, it worked a revolution in Renaissance schooling during the sixteenth century as the control of teaching passed from ecclesiastical to lay hands and the subject matter and objectives of the curriculum were completely reoriented. The most boisterous statement of the Renaissance revolt against the medieval disciplines appears in the *Gargantua and Pantagruel* of Rabelais. In famous sections of his extravaganza the emancipated Frenchman satirizes the useless pedantry of the old methods and demands a new type of education designed to produce, not a bookish scholar, but a well-rounded man (or woman). In Ponacrates' instruction of Gargantua, we see the pedagogy that Rabelais had in mind—the emphasis upon the matter rather than the form of knowledge, the constant application of book learning to the world of nature, and the cultivation of all sides of human personality. This Renaissance faith in the trustworthiness of human nature and instinct is revealed in the motto of Rabelais' utopian Abbey of Theleme—"Do what you want to." Only trust men to follow their natural inclinations, he believed, and they will reach inevitably a healthy and worthy goal.

A generation later the last great Renaissance thinker about education, Montaigne, extended Rabelais's radicalism to an attack upon the new tyranny of the ancient classics which had supplanted the medieval tyranny of church rule. Surveying the effects of Humanism, both good and bad, he decided that the ancients had emancipated men from one discipline only to enslave them to another. Attacking knowledge as an end in itself, he insisted that the only end of learning is to contribute to man's understanding of himself and his success in leading a useful, moderate, and upright life. Admittedly Humanism had its evil effects, not the least of which was the pedantic encouragement of literature in Latin at the expense of the vernacular tongues. But its influence endured in European and American education down to the beginning of our century, and the English schools have hardly yet abandoned the idea that the Greek and Latin classics are the cornerstone of a liberal education.

REFORMATION AND COUNTER-REFORMATION

THE various changes that formed the Renaissance were not slow in affecting the status of the Church and the medieval Christianity that had bound all of Europe in one empire of the spirit. The ascetic ideal of the medieval Church and its strictures against moneylending and finance were out of harmony with the economic ambitions of the aggressive and powerful merchant aristocracy, which pursued luxury and worldly culture with a new sophistication. The secularization of learning and art which they sponsored challenged the domination of men's minds and spirits that the Church had enjoyed for a thousand years. Humanism as a movement developed partially within and partially outside the Church, but its objectives ran counter to medieval Christianity at every point. It set a revival of pagan philosophy against a declining Scholasticism; it set the Greek ideal against the ascetic ideal of the medieval churchman; it preferred classical Latin over Church Latin; it sought to emancipate the individual from the dogma and discipline of the Middle Ages that had stifled personality within a general mold.

The growth of national monarchies opposed the claims of the papacy to international temporal power. At its height in the late Middle Ages the Church had conceived of Christendom as a single realm ruled by the Pope, who had the God-given right to depose kings and choose their successors, determine the boundaries of their lands, and appoint a clergy to function within these lands. This clergy should owe its loyalty to Rome, be immune to taxation by the king, and be required to send tribute to the Pope from the kings' realms. Under feudalism the papacy had gradually codified this theory of its temporal power and used it successfully against the rival Holy Roman Emperor. But the new kings of the Renaissance wielded a growing authority that was to force the papacy to relinquish its international claims and content itself with governing the

Papal States. The decisive contest was that between Pope Boniface VIII and King Philip IV of France in which the king met the Pope's sentence of deposition and excommunication by moving the papacy from Rome to Avignon, where for seventy-three years (1305–1378) it functioned under the close supervision of the French throne. The papacy never recovered its temporal prestige after this so-called Babylonian Captivity and the Great Schism (1378–1415) that followed, during which rival popes attacked each other from Avignon and Rome. In the following century most Christian countries asserted their new nationalism against papal power in one way or another: Portugal, Spain, and France secured virtually independent administration for their national churches and so remained loyal to Rome. Northern Germany, Switzerland, Holland, England, and the Scandinavian states seceded entirely in the Protestant Reformation.

In some respects the Reformation movement of the sixteenth century was a continuation of the Renaissance; in others it had the character of a countermovement. In so far as the Renaissance attacked the empty ceremonies and sterile scholasticism of the medieval Church, it was in line with the religious revival. Erasmus, the greatest of the Humanists, was also the greatest harbinger of the Reformation. In his *The Praise of Folly* he denounced the ignorance of the religious orders, the greed and vulgarity of the lower ecclesiastics, and the lack of piety and humility among cardinals and popes. The Reformation, too, was one expression of the new national feeling that resulted from the political unification of Renaissance states. Most important, it reflected the new importance of the layman in Renaissance life, since it took the Bible out of Church Latin into vernacular tongues where every man might read it, encouraged lay interpretation of the Bible against church monopoly of enlightenment, removed education from the hands of the clergy, and sanctified a new middle-class morality that exalted over monastic asceticism the virtues of thrift and hard work for profit.

On the other hand, the intellectual enlightenment of the Renaissance had already saturated the papacy by the sixteenth century. The popes of this period were often classical scholars and patrons of art and humanistic learning, who had strayed far from the simple piety of the medieval Church into secular cosmopolitanism and pagan morality. Increasingly Italian in outlook, the papacy fell into the enlightened depravity of the Italian aristocracy, and reached its nadir in a succession of five popes between 1471 and 1521, notorious for their worldliness, political ambition, avarice, and, in some cases, lust. The infamous Alexander VI was a Borgia; the cultured Leo X was of the Medici. The Italian Renaissance had cap-

Pope Julius II (1503–1513), by Raphael. He patronized artists and beautified Rome while ruling with much skill.

tivated the papacy, and the dissolute papal circles infuriated many northern churchmen and led them to support separation from Rome when the papal court seemed beyond spiritual regeneration. Many Italian ecclesiastics deplored the declining prestige of the papacy and its failure in spiritual leadership. Girolamo Savonarola (1452–1498) inspired the degenerate city of Florence to a brief spiritual revival with his impassioned eloquence and his bold denunciation of the worldliness of Rome, but Pope Alexander VI had him convicted of heresy and executed.

The Reformation of Luther and Calvin was preceded by numerous forerunners of the Protestant movement, which the Church dismissed as heresies. The Waldensians who followed Peter Waldo (fl. 1170) in southern France, the Lollards who rallied around John Wycliffe (d. 1384) in England, and the Hussites who supported John Huss (d. 1415) in Bohemia were national sects aiming at reform of the Church, but all were persecuted out of existence. Something like accident made the German monk Martin Luther the founder of an enduring Protestantism, for his original purpose in nailing his 95 Theses to the door of the Wittenberg Church in 1517 was simply to attack the sale of papal indulgences in Germany which Leo X was authorizing in order to raise funds for building St. Peter's in Rome. But conditions were right for the establishment of a national church in the German states, and when Luther found himself pushed by papal persecution into the leadership of an independent church, he had the protection of many German princes and the support of militant German peasants. With the formulation of the Augsburg Confession in 1530 the Lutheran Church was established as the official Protestant Church in most German states (and eventually Scandinavia), though some states, especially in the west and south, remained loyal to Catholicism, and others turned to Calvinism. In his later years Luther's outlook hardened into a dogmatic provincialism and prevented an international union of Lutheranism with the Swiss reform movement of the same period.

The Lutheran creed established the general Protestant pattern by insisting on the direct and personal relationship of every Christian soul to God without any intermediary of church or priest. Thus with one stroke it tried to sweep away the huge hierarchy of the Roman Church and destroy the separateness of the priestly caste, committed to celibacy and a special religious life. Every human vocation was dignified, and the workman at his bench, the merchant in the market place, and the mother in her home achieved a status before God equal to the minister's in the community church. In a word, Luther secularized the church as he nationalized it.

Similar movements were not slow in getting under way in other countries. John Calvin (1509–1564), a French refugee, set the character of Swiss Protestantism in the direction of rigorous puritanism and fiery intolerance during his twenty-year rule in Geneva. This narrow, austere view of religious reform raised the Bible as a stern master over men's lives and worked against the broad intellectuality and worldly enlightenment of the Renaissance. Calvin's influence shaped the Huguenot movement in France and strongly influenced the strict codes of the English Puritans and Scotch Covenanters in the following century. The Dutch Republic and some German states accepted this form of Protestantism.

England secured a national church separate from Rome in 1534, when Henry VIII forced his parliament to declare him head of the Church in England because the Pope refused to recognize his divorce from his first queen. But Henry was thoroughly orthodox in his religious views and persecuted heretics and Protestants as vigorously as any Catholic sovereign. Hence, although the Catholic church still sought to gain control of England from the national Anglican church through the reign of James II (1685–1688), the real Protestant movement centered in the stern Puritan group which strove to convert the Anglican church into a Calvinist church by purging church ritual of Roman splendor and national life of worldliness and luxury. Though persecuted by Queen Elizabeth and James I, the Puritans increased their numbers and staged a successful revolution in 1642–1649; they ruled England under Oliver Cromwell for the following ten years, and gave English literature one of its greatest poets—John Milton. Transplanted to the New England colonies of North America, Puritanism exerted an enduring influence on American life and produced a brilliant school of stern divines, of whom Jonathan Edwards the elder was probably the most eloquent. His sermon, *Sinners in the Hands of an Angry God*, terrified his congregation with its grisly warning of divine vengeance.

The Protestant Reformation quickly inspired a Counter-Reformation in the Roman Church, as a reawakened Catholic world recognized the abuses within its hierarchy and set about reviving the pious and militant spirit of medieval Christianity. Catholic Spain took the lead in this vigorous movement and contributed the Jesuit army of Ignatius Loyola (1491–1556) to the Church's war against the heathens and the Protestants. The Council of Trent (1545–1563), which brought representatives from the whole Catholic world to a council of war, produced some reform of ecclesiastical government but in general reinforced the conservative theology and church practice of the Middle Ages. Its lack of a conciliatory attitude toward the Protestants strengthened the breach between northern and southern Europe, so that, by the end of the Renaissance, the unified medieval Church had split into four major churches—Catholic, Lutheran, Calvinist, and Anglican—with a growing background of minor sects.

THE RISE OF MODERN SCIENCE

HUMANISM had only an indirect influence on the religious reformation and almost none on the birth of modern science. Its concern was with the cultural life of man, his individuality and integrity as a human being; it found in ancient literature no stimulus to explore the world by scientific method. Yet the age of the Renaissance saw the first major discoveries of modern science and ended with the articulation of the experimental method that was to expand man's knowledge of his world immeasurably in the next period.

At first sight the later Middle Ages seem much more important to science than does the Renaissance. Beginning in the second half of the eleventh century, a stream of scientific knowledge born of the ancient Greeks, translated into Arabic terms, and combined with the Arabic discoveries of Avicenna and Averroës found its way into Europe via the cultural contacts of the Moslem and Christian worlds in Sicily and Spain. In the thirteenth century it inspired Albertus Magnus and especially Roger Bacon to an enlightened study of the natural sciences, chemistry, physics, and geography. Bacon used the experimental method to reach natural explanations of natural phenomena, such as rainbows and earthquakes, and to understand the magnifying properties of convex lenses and the explosive propensities of gunpowder. But he was as much philosopher as scientist, and susceptible to the superstitions and mysticism of his day. His attacks on the inane activities of the later Scholastics won him the suspicion of his fellow churchmen and twenty years' confinement for the novelty of his ideas. Later generations thought of him as a wizard in league with the devil, and the Church classified him with the magicians and alchemists as a practitioner of forbidden arts. In general, the outlook of the Middle Ages could not comprehend science any more than classical literature, and outlawed new discoveries as a threat to Aristotle and the absolute truth of Christian theology.

The new intellectual horizon of the Renaissance was bound to touch science in time. As medieval restraints on speculation were thrust aside, the biological approach to the world for which Aristotle stood was challenged by a new mathematical interpretation inspired by Plato and the Pythagoreans. Aristotle's conception of a limited universe of concentric spheres was gradually supplanted by the idea of an infinite universe animated by interrelated forces which could be understood only by the application of mathematics. The most brilliant argument for this theory was pronounced by Giordano Bruno. Accepting the new Copernican astronomy, this fiery monk argued that there are innumerable worlds extending into infinity, but that all the phenomena of the universe gain coherence and order by the unifying animation of God.

The conception of an infinite universe paralleled the rise of modern astronomy. Although ancient astronomers had debated whether the earth or the sun was the center of our universe, the geocentric theory of the Alexandrian Ptolemy was accepted by the medieval Church because the idea of an immovable earth around which moved the planets, moon, sun, and stars confirmed the Christian conception of man as the climax of creation and the chief concern of God. Several astronomers of the Renaissance questioned the geocentric theory, but it remained for Nicolaus Copernicus, a Pole, to publish a formal challenge in his *Revolutions of the Heavenly Bodies*

(1543). He long delayed announcement of his heliocentric theory, fearing church persecution as a heretic, but even ecclesiastical condemnation could not prevent the spread of his theory and its acceptance under his name as the starting point of modern astronomy. The Italian Galileo Galilei (1564–1642) strengthened the Copernican theory by perfecting the first useful telescope and proved by observing the spots on the sun's surface that it turned on its axis.

Other modern sciences got their start during the Renaissance. The amazing Leonardo da Vinci began a study of human anatomy and the mathematics of perspective, partially to improve his painting and sculpture, partially out of an enlightened interest in pure science. Andreas Vesalius, a Flemish physician, applied the experimental method to anatomy and produced in 1543 a revolutionary study of the human body. Georg Agricola, a German scholar, founded modern metallurgy and mineralogy.

Clearly, the scientific method was being used by Galileo, Vesalius, and Agricola and had even been identified in part by Roger Bacon, Leonardo da Vinci, and others. But though the metaphysical speculation of ancient science might give way to actual observation and experiment, Renaissance science was still obsessed by the notion of final causes and the supernatural significance of natural facts. In part, it was motivated by the practical urge to gain mastery over nature, even to exploit it as alchemy had tried to do; in part, by the view of nature as the key to human destiny, inherited from

A study of the muscles of torso and legs by Leonardo da Vinci shows his scientific approach to anatomy.

astrology. It remained for Francis Bacon, the English chancellor of James I, to formulate a scientific method freed from medieval objectives and prejudices and to lend to it the weight of his learning and his political prestige. In the *Novum Organum* (1620) Bacon denounced the deductive method of Aristotle, long used by the Scholastics, because it ignored the facts of observation except when they confirmed a preconceived truth or a priori statement. He argued that knowledge must originate in the careful observation of natural facts and unprejudiced experiment with them. The scientist must begin with what is, not with what he has been told there is or what he believes there should be. Neither bookish authority, nor our own speculation, nor any prejudice must stand in the way of our objective observation of nature. Bacon summarized the progress of scientific method to the end of the Renaissance and led to the greater achievements of Descartes and Newton in the next generation.

RENAISSANCE BELLES-LETTRES

ALL of the dynamic forces of Renaissance life are reflected in the magnificent literature of this extravagant period. As the preoccupation of medieval man with theology and Scholastic metaphysics dissolved under the pressure of new intellectual forces, literature lost its absorption in the problems of Christian salvation, its didactic purpose, and its obsession with symbols and allegory. The Middle Ages had had its secular literature in the chivalric romances and commoners' fabliaux, but they were appendages to the religious writings of the time and further illustrated the cultural synthesis of medieval life within the ideology of the Church. A broad secular literature that eagerly returned to nature and exalted every phase of human life was reborn with Boccaccio and Rabelais, as Renaissance man grew inquisitive about his present world and set out in eager pursuit of new experience. Urges long checked by the universal orthodoxy gained free expression under the new sanction of pagan philosophy.

The lay spirit of Renaissance literature is reflected in its passionate individualism. Personality emerged from its long regimentation in the ranks of the theologians and Scholastics, the troubadours and trouvères, the Minnesingers and Mastersingers. The emancipation of the intellect and senses from official sanctions invited divergent responses to the world. As Platonism inspired a new realization of personality in a vast new realm of experience, men developed a consuming interest in themselves, and literature grew subjective and varied in attitude. Autobiography reappeared in Benvenuto Cellini; biography in the hands of Vasari and Pérez de Guzmán reflected the new curiosity about people as individuals. The conventional love poetry of the troubadours took on a personal realism in Petrarch and Ronsard. The familiar essay was reborn as a medium of self-revelation with Montaigne.

Humanism, through exalting the dignity of man, stimulated this new individualism and inspired literature in other directions as well. As ancient classics were rediscovered, old types of literature—the epic, the pastoral, the satire, tragedy, and comedy—reappeared as fresh areas for men of letters. The polished Latin of Cicero and Seneca made men ashamed of the vagaries of Church Latin and the crudities of the vernacular tongues, and a new passion for form and style sprang up. But these fruits of Humanism were mixed blessings. The scorn that Renaissance writers came to feel for all the achievements of the Middle Ages led to a slavish imitation of the classics by which they hoped to regain finesse and dignity. Gradually what had begun as a healthy stimulus from the ancient past became an oppressive deterrent to any deviation from classical models. Latin prosody was forced upon vernacular verse which, in the case of English and German, might be founded on a totally different principle. Form as an end in itself all but swamped the substance of literature. In a misguided application of Ciceronian rhetoric, prose was subjected to artificial laws and led to the excesses of Góngorism in Spain and Euphuism in England.

Most unfortunate of all was the snobbish preference of the Humanists for Latin composition, that interrupted for a century the development of vernacular literatures. The achievements of Dante, Petrarch, and Boccaccio in the vigorous Italian speech of the fourteenth century were contemptuously set aside in the fashionable worship of Virgil and Cicero, and not until the sixteenth did Italian poetry revive with Ariosto and Tasso. The Humanists as an international aristocracy of scholars thought of Latin as the one enduring medium of expression and the only tongue capable of the supreme elegance of the Augustan Romans. The vast Renaissance literature in Latin is little read today, for we have a prejudice against its artificial refinement quite as great as the Humanists' prejudice against the vernacular. Petrarch, Boccaccio, Politian, Sannazaro, Vida, Erasmus, Calvin, More, and Bacon cast what they thought to be their greatest works in Latin, and as late as the time of Milton and Addison the fashion had not died out. But the social and political forces of the Renaissance ultimately worked in favor of the vernacular tongues. The wealthy middle class that patronized men of letters could seldom enjoy Latin prose and verse. The ladies of the courts who became an increasing power in the shaping of taste rarely understood Latin. And the rise of national monarchies undermined the international brotherhood of letters and encouraged the growth of national schools of literature in Italian, French, English, and Spanish as cultural aspects of national life began to emerge.

THE RENAISSANCE THEATER

THOUGH the transition from the medieval to the Renaissance theater was very gradual, so that provincial productions of the religious folk plays were still common in Shakespeare's early years, the true Renaissance stage can be dated from the first modern performances of ancient Roman comedies soon after 1450 and the discovery of a treatise by the Augustan architect, Vitruvius, containing an account of ancient stage arrangements. Italy was naturally the first center of this development, and threaters in strict imitation of the supposed classical models were soon built in Ferrara, Rome, and Florence, though the influence of the medieval stage filled in the gaps in the ancient record. The historic Teatro Olimpico, planned by Palladio in 1580 and completed four years later, still stands in Vicenzo as a monument to the classical tradition of the Renaissance theater. With its semi-elliptical arrangement of seats, its orchestra space between the stage and spectators, its long, narrow, rectangular stage, and its elaborate proscenium and sculptured doorways facing the audience, it is a faithful imitation of a Roman theater. But the Italians also pioneered in spectacular scenery and stage effects, extraordinary lighting devices and machines to represent thunder and lightning or even the fiery destruction of whole cities. Lacking great original playwrights at this time, the Italian theater was to assert its originality in striking productions.

France, always friendly to the classical tradition, followed Italy in careful imitation of the ancient, but in Spain and England different theatrical conditions produced a much freer theater and drama. In contrast to the elaborate staging and conventional playwriting of Italy and France, these two countries developed a magnificent literary drama with far simpler productions. The folk plays of the Middle Ages exerted a powerful influence on the more democratic theater of London and especially Madrid, so that there was not here the great cleavage between the aristocrats' neo-classical stage and the plebians' *commedia dell' arte* that appeared in Florence, Rome, and Paris. And like other Renaissance movements, the influence of the ancients on the drama came later to Spain and England. The year 1576 saw the opening of the first public playhouse in London, while the first in Madrid came three years later.

Until the closing of the London theaters in 1642, the theatrical histories of the two capitals were to run parallel courses.

In both countries court shows had been presented for some years before the first public theaters were built. The earliest actors in these graceful entertainments were choir-boys and courtly gentlemen, and in England even after the establishment of professional acting companies, boys continued to play the women's roles. In Spain there was no such taboo against women on the stage, and it has been conjectured that their refining influence encouraged the early development of the graceful cloak and sword *comedias* of Lope de Vega. Still, the glory of the English and Spanish stages of the Renaissance lay always in the plays themselves, the masterworks of Marlowe and Shakespeare, Lope de Vega and Calderón, which gained boldness and power from the very freedom offered by the simple stages on which they were performed.

James Burbage built the first public theater in London (called merely *The Theater*) in 1576, on a site beyond the limits of the city proper so as to avoid the interference of the municipal authorities, who still viewed the shows with disapproval and suspicion. Indeed, theater folk long continued to be frowned on in the more sober quarters, especially by the church, with a prejudice that linked their calling with the buffoonery and bohemianism of medieval showmen. But Queen Elizabeth's enthusiastic support of the stage and the cultured background of numerous figures in the Elizabethan theater were fast diminishing this prejudice. Shakespeare was typical of the respectable burghers who now found their way into the theater and, in his case, retired from it to a country house and even a coat of arms. In Spain too, though the stage was even more popular and more democratic, its leading personages were often highly respected. This was in part because the Spanish theaters were generally operated for the benefit of hospitals and other charitable institutions, which conferred a moral vindication on those who worked in them. In England, on the other hand, actors depended on the personal patronage of the king or queen and members of the nobility.

In both countries the repertory system of production prevailed, though popular plays might run for a number of nights in a row. Since the plays were written for permanent companies, the playwrights had to bear in mind the personnel of the companies and necessarily developed stock parts to suit the special talents of the leading actors. This was particularly true in Spain, where Lope de Vega established the type characters to be used by his successors for over half a century. But even Shakespeare's dramatic output shows a clear relationship to the changing personnel of his company.

The costuming of actors was far from being so realistic as in our day. Greek and Roman characters, such as Timon of Athens and Julius Caesar, wore a conventionalized ancient costume, and Eastern characters such as Othello had their distinctive dress. So would such special characters as lawyers, pedants, ancient deities, ghosts, animals, and those with marked physical traits, like the obese Falstaff.

But such characters as Hamlet, who had no distinctive appearance, always wore the ordinary dress of the actors' time, regardless of the period in which they were supposed to have lived. This convention the audience accepted without question. Indeed, in the early period of this drama a company lacking the means for realistic staging might further tax the imagination of the audience through merely indicating by signboards what the various objects on the stage were supposed to represent. Reared on a realistic stage and cinema tradition, we must prod our lazy imaginations today to appreciate the meaning of the dramatic occasion for a Renaissance audience. Above all, it was the poetry of the great dramatists declaimed by lordly actors that the audiences crowded the theaters of Spain and England in 1600 to hear.

NATIONAL SCHOOLS OF THOUGHT

ITALY. In the fourteenth century Italy regained the leadership of European literature from France with a magnificent triumvirate of writers. Though all three were of the Florentine school and flourished within a period of about sixty years (1293–1353), Dante is in spirit the culmination of the Middle Ages, while Petrarch and Boccaccio transform medieval literary forms with a new awareness of the world that points to the Renaissance and modern times.

Petrarch, variously called "the Father of the Renaissance," "the first Humanist," and "the first modern man," was born Francesco Petracco but Latinized his surname to Petrarca to express his devotion to the new study of classical antiquity which he in large measure initiated. His reverence for the literary form of Roman authors led him to turn from vernacular writing to the imitation of Cicero in his Latin letters and Virgil in his Latin epic, *Africa*, which won him the homage of the learned world. But his many Latin works are unread today, and his popular reputation rests on a slender volume of Italian love poems with which he celebrated his idealistic love for Laura, an acquaintance of his youth. Though inspired by the troubadour tradition of Dante's *Vita Nuova*, Petrarch's exquisite sonnets breathe a new humanity and psychological insight into a medieval convention.

His close friend Boccaccio had a similar experience. In his youth he penned elegant sonnets to a faithless lady whom he called Fiammetta and produced his masterpiece, the *Decameron*, a collection of one hundred lively prose tales. Occasionally pathetic or even tragic, more often humorous, frequently satiric and bawdy, these vigorous tales spring from the earth and revitalize medieval story types with the new freedom of the Renaissance. As

a complement to Dante, they bring us down from the eternal worlds of the *Commedia* to the world of everyday reality. But Boccaccio's friendship with the learned Petrarch turned his attention from the salon and the market place to the library, to Latin and Greek scholarship and a reverent study of Dante. Immersed in Humanistic endeavors he came to consider it an indiscretion of his youth that he wrote the first great monument of Italian prose and one of the most influential works in all literature.

After 1350 the passion of the Humanists for classical Latin virtually submerged vernacular literature in Italy for about a hundred years. The fifteenth century saw the spread of Humanism from an embattled cult to a broad movement saturating the Roman church as well as the lay society in which it began. The rediscovery and reinterpretation of ancient literature now occupied the leading minds of the land, who came to view Italian as a vulgar medium of the unenlightened. A reversal of taste in later centuries was to discredit these elegant imitators of Virgil, Ovid, and Catullus, but the best of them did not deserve the general oblivion that has overtaken the school. By the second half of the fifteenth century the scholarly labors of the Italian Humanists were largely completed, and both Latin and vernacular literature showed the effect of a new philosophical outlook absorbed from the ancient classics, a revival of Neoplatonic idealism fused with Christian doctrine. Florence remained the center of literary activity, especially because of the Platonic Academy founded there by Cosimo de' Medici as an intellectual center of the Humanists. His grandson, Lorenzo the Magnificent (1448–1492), continued his patronage of art and letters and attracted to Florence a brilliant assemblage of talents, such as Ficino and Pico della Mirandola, the Platonic phi-

Wealthy Italians of the Renaissance encouraged all the arts, including interior decoration. The Ducal Palace at Gubbio, Italy, contained this room which in its splendid carving and ornamentation typifies the period.

losophers, and Poliziano the poet. Lorenzo was himself an excellent poet who admired Petrarch and the older Italian school and began a movement for the revival of vernacular literature. His influence more than any other accounts for the remarkable flowering of Italian poetry in the sixteenth century.

The favorite literary form in this revival was the romantic epic, a long poem which treated the traditional material of medieval romance on a grand scale with the sophisticated outlook of the new age. The influence of Virgil is strong in this form. As deliberate imitations of a popular type, these literary epics were admittedly artificial, and yet their courtly idealism and polished style gave them a subtle charm for their urbane public. Ariosto's romantic epic, *Orlando Furioso* (Insane Roland), of which he published forty cantos in 1516 and others in later years, weaves into a loose pattern a number of chivalric tales of Christian-Moslem struggle in the days of

Charlemagne, but the love stories of the knights, such as Roland's hapless passion for the fickle Angelica that drives him insane, dominate the lively action. Epitomizing the romantic idealism and courtly sophistication of the later Renaissance in Italy, this popular poem remains readable for its sprightly narrative and colorful style.

Ariosto's literary twin, Torquato Tasso, continued the tradition of the romantic epic in the second half of the sixteenth century. Precocious but morbidly sensitive, he completed his great romantic epic, *Jerusalem Delivered*, by the age of thirty-one but betrayed already the mental instability that was to harass his later years, destroy his genius, and lead him at last to a madhouse. Modeled on Virgil, Tasso's pious epic of the First Crusade is now remembered for its charming pagan heroines, Armida, Clorinda, Erminia, and their disrupting amours with the Christian knights. Thoroughly romantic by nature, the poet is at his best in his tender interpretations of courtly love affairs, while his routine treatment of battles and religious themes reveals the synthetic character of the Renaissance epic. We will meet it in the delicate pages of Spenser's *Faerie Queene.*

Italian prose of the Renaissance was long impeded by imitation of classical Latin style. Involved sentence construction, heavy diction, and studied figures of speech raised a wall of rhetoric between author and audience. But the sixteenth century saw some improvement in the direction of greater freedom and clarity. Niccolò Machiavelli, the outstanding political theorist of the age, was also its most influential prose stylist. Typical of Renaissance Italy in his dazzling versatility and his frankly amoral attitude toward life, he gave a brilliant picture of cuckoldry in his excellent comedy, *Mandragola,* and an equally cynical, if realistic, defense of political expediency in his famous treatise, *The Prince.* Though *The Prince* made his name forever a symbol of sinister statecraft, the vigorous prose of the little book has made it also an enduring work of literature.

The romantic counterpart of the realistic Machiavelli was that perfect courtier, Baldassare Castiglione, whose delightful dialogue, *The Courtier,* prescribed for Renaissance social life as *The Prince* had done for its politics. Castiglione's model gentleman is the master of courtesy and refined conversation who makes an art of good manners and whose classical learning has taught him the Ciceronian virtue of *humanitas.* As the Renaissance adaptation of medieval chivalry, this ideal penetrated to such remote lands as England, where Sir Philip Sidney deliberately embodied it in his own life and Spenser illustrated it in the courteous knights of his *Faerie Queene.* Closer to the typical Italian courtier of the Renaissance, however, was that reckless rascal, Benvenuto Cellini (1500–71), whose swaggering *Autobiography* is the most popular work of Renaissance prose. Sculptor, engraver, and goldsmith by profession, he crammed his turbulent life with political intrigue, free-style lovemaking, and incessant quarrels that often led to bloodshed, and wrote of his adventures with brazen exaggeration and an utter indifference to conventional morality. This last great work of the Italian Renaissance summarizes the whole brilliant but ultimately extravagant age.

FRANCE. The Renaissance reached France at least a century after its arrival in Italy. The fourteenth century of Petrarch and Boccaccio was a dismal desert in French history when the Hundred Years' War with England laid waste the land and literature reached its lowest ebb. The proud leadership of France in medieval culture was lost in a period of painful transition from feudalism to national monarchy. Just when the Renaissance spirit

from Italy began to revitalize French culture it is difficult to say. But the slow process of revival may be conveniently dated from the end of the Hundred Years' War in 1453 and the final expulsion of the English from French soil. In the decade that followed there appeared in the exhausted capital of Paris a colorful vagabond poet, François Villon, whose reckless career in crime and literature expressed both the disorderly state of post-war France and the new spirit of adventure that was about to infect the intellectual life of the rejuvenated country. The beautiful lyrics tossed off by this colorful scamp in his spare moments look backward to a medieval school of Provençal poetry, but in his contempt for authority and tradition, his instinctive love of freedom, Villon is the forerunner of Rabelais and the harbinger of the French Renaissance.

With the sixteenth century the movement got unmistakably under way. The French invasions of Italy under Charles VIII and his successors suddenly revealed the new learning and culture to French noblemen, who enthusiastically imported ideas and art works to stimulate a great national revival. Erasmus had taught in Paris and Louvain, but France was to develop a great Humanist of her own in Guillaume Budé. The court of the new monarchs of France became the great center of literary patronage and remained such well into the eighteenth century. Poetry was the first type to reflect the new spirit, and in the transitional career of Clement Marot, who threw off both the conventional poetic forms and the traditional religious views, we see a new burst of freedom in literature.

In the next generation the influence of Italy and the ancients in French poetry became pronounced in the militant circle of seven poets who called themselves the Pleiades after the constellation that had given a name also to seven ancient Greek poets. In the manifesto of this school Joachim du Bellay declared that their purpose was to elevate the French language by borrowings from Latin and Greek so that it should become a fit medium for a literature based on ancient models. The Pleiades' deep respect for the ancients brought a new finish to French poetry but led as well to a servile imitation that ultimately strangled inspiration. The greatest of them, Pierre de Ronsard, combined a Humanist's devotion to the classics with a deep love of natural beauty, so that, while his imitations of Pindar, Horace, and Ovid seem studied and cold today, his nature poems and love songs to Hélène and Marie retain a freshness and charm unique in this school.

But it was in prose that the French best expressed the Renaissance spirit of intellectual emancipation and self-scrutiny. The movement had two phases that are clearly summarized in the personalities of Rabelais in the first half of the sixteenth century and

Montaigne in the second. François Rabelais, as reckless and merry a figure as Villon before him, became the literary spokesman for revolt against church domination of man's intellectual life. Since his radical views brought him into constant danger of persecution by churchmen, Rabelais conceived the scheme of presenting his attack upon medievalism within a rough-and-tumble narrative about two giants, *Gargantua and Pantagruel,* father and son. This merry mélange is an unpredictable extravaganza of vulgar humor, realistic pictures of social types, obscure learning, and shrewd sense. Rabelais had the boundless faith of the early Renaissance in the goodness and perfectability of human nature, the new-found hope that, once freed from the discipline of the medieval church, it would naturally find its way to right behavior and glorious achievement.

Michel de Montaigne belonged to the dying years of the Renaissance, when these high hopes were sinking into disillusionment and skepticism. The more knowledge Montaigne accumulated, the less he felt he knew about human nature and himself as a specimen of it. Distrusting the reason that had given confidence to so many before him, he returned repeatedly after his studies to the question, "What do I know?" Skeptical of Rabelais's trust in the instincts and questioning the value of the Humanists' learning, he fell back upon a plan of life within the established order as the most sensible after all. Despite his doubts, Montaigne was one of the great sages of all time, and the charm of his intimate style in his *Essays* makes him the most readable prose writer of the French Renaissance.

E NGLAND . The English Renaissance followed the French by about fifty years. Although Chaucer in the fourteenth century had been personally inspired by Boccaccio, the new spirit did not reach English learning and literature until the arrival of the scholars William Grocyn and John Colet at Oxford and Erasmus at Cambridge shortly before 1500. The reign of Henry VIII (1509–1547), a magnificent, ruthless prince on the Italian model, saw a strong national monarchy in England and the establishment of a national church, both of which encouraged the development of a national literature. The first fruit of these influences was Sir Thomas More's *Utopia* (1516), a political romance in Latin reminiscent of Plato's *Republic,* which described an ideal state operated by the laws of reason. Like Rabelais's abbey, More's *Utopia* revealed the ardent hopes of the Renaissance for a better world to come from man's new-found freedom, and prepared the way for Bacon's *New Atlantis* a century later.

The English poets who first felt the challenge of the Italian Renaissance were Wyatt and Surrey. Sir Thomas Wyatt, a favorite of Henry VIII, visited Italy in his youth and was inspired by the love sonnets of Petrarch to write some of his own, frankly imitative but still sincere, and probably the first English poems in sonnet form. The Earl of Surrey, another favorite of Henry until he was suspected of treason and executed, also traveled in Italy and wrote sonnets, but with a new rhyme scheme more appealing to the English ear, which was adopted by many later poets, especially Shakespeare, and became known as the English sonnet. Surrey also introduced blank verse into England, a form that was to be quickly accepted as the most appropriate for serious drama and narrative poetry.

The English Renaissance reached its climax in the reign of Elizabeth (1558–1603), the proud and determined, yet masterful and enlightened daughter of Henry VIII, who realized her father's dream of a strong England ruled by a strong sovereign. Herself a mistress of learning in many languages, Elizabeth approved of her poets' imitation of ancient classics and Italian writers, but encouraged as well a national drama freed from the classical restraints that ruled the Italian and French theater. The genius that her patronage unearthed among her subjects produced a golden age comparable only to the fifth century B.C. in Athens.

Most of the new writers were gentleman amateurs, cultured courtiers like Spenser and Sidney, who wrote to please their fancies and their friends rather than to earn a living by publication. Often addressed hopefully to powerful patrons, their works might be rewarded by gifts or preferment. The court atmosphere in which this literature flourished is reflected in the extravagant style, the classical allusions, the elaborate "conceits" of language, the colorful and bizarre vocabulary better adapted to verse than to prose. Romantic in outlook, it idealizes rather than mirrors the society for which it was written.

The beginnings made by Wyatt and Surrey flowered in a magnificent school of courtly lyric poets. A sudden burst of song rang through the Elizabethan court and countryside. The sonnet, whether in the Italian form of Petrarch or the English form of Surrey, became the vehicle of the love sentiments of Sidney, Spenser, Daniel, Drayton, Shakespeare, and others. Eventually, John Donne showed in his *Holy Sonnets* that it could be used for subjects other than love and pointed the way to its later popularity as a medium of poetic reflection. The exalted woman-worship of the Elizabethan sonneteers gave way to a whimsical view of woman in Donne's love songs, where his satiric and even perverse attitude toward the sex is reflected in cynical irony. Robert Herrick added a playful, pagan quality to his treatment of love and rounded out the Renaissance tradition with some of the most graceful and melodious poems in the language.

Narrative verse of the English Renaissance also

Francis I of France, like Henry VIII of England, was one of the strong monarchs of the national states emerging during the Renaissance period. He is here portrayed by the well-known painter of the French nobility, François Clouet. The painting, done in oil on a panel, is now in the Uffizi Gallery, Florence. It is sometimes ascribed to Jean Clouet.

owed much to the ancients and the new Italian school. Edmund Spenser, the greatest Elizabethan poet, became saturated with Platonic philosophy during his years at Cambridge, and imitated the pastorals of the Greek Theocritus, the Roman Virgil, and the Italian Sannazaro in his *Shepheardes Calender*. On the model of Ariosto, Spenser's masterpiece, *The Faerie Queene*, is a romantic epic each of whose books was to represent one of the twelve virtues of Aristotle in the career of a knight who embodied it. The archaic style of the long poem suggests a strong inspiration as well from older English literature, especially Chaucer. This exquisite work, so delightful in small doses, so tiresome in long draughts, is a Renaissance epitome of chivalry interpreted with the new awareness that the ancients had brought.

But the supreme glory of Elizabethan literature is its drama. In no other country of Europe had the medieval theater of mystery and miracle plays been more popular, and when the Renaissance grafted the secular tradition of the ancients upon the lively Christian tradition, English playwrights experimented with imitations of Plautan comedy and Senecan tragedy. As English drama matured in Elizabethan London, one group of playwrights who had been well schooled in classical tradition continued to demand that modern drama model itself strictly on the ancients. Ben Jonson, a brilliant scholar despite his brief schooling, spent his life in the thick of critical controversy and illustrated his theory of a classical drama in dull, regular tragedies, such as *Sejanus*, and brilliant comedies, such as *Volpone*.

Fortunately the tradition of classical imitation was never so widespread in England as in Italy and France, and a popular tradition of dramatic freedom competed with it throughout the Renaissance, blissfully ignoring the Aristotelian unities and other conventions of the ancient stage. The brilliant but ill-fated Christopher Marlowe (1564–1593), one of the so-called University Wits, reflected his own reckless life in tavern and court in a series of epic plays about unrestrained men misled by extravagant ambition. The boundless energy and aspiration of the Renaissance motivate Tamburlaine and Doctor Faustus in their thirst for power, the Jew of Malta in his lust for money. Loosely constructed and often rhetorical in style, Marlowe's tragedies are also full of poetic fire and titanic force, so that they speak for that school of Elizabethan playwrights who gained confidence from the classics to throw off classical restraints.

William Shakespeare avoided the critical controversy of Jonson and his camp, but allowed no ancient conventions to hamper the full and natural expression of his genius. Inconspicuous in the society of his day, mediocre as a professional actor, he was still the great master of Elizabethan drama, whose reputation has since become second to none in world literature. His life was modest and unexciting; during the twenty years that he spent in London its most important events were the thirty-seven plays by which he gained fame and sufficient fortune to retire to a comfortable home in his native town of Stratford-on-Avon. A quiet and conventional man, he revealed his passionate nature and masterful study of human character only in his plays, his exquisite sonnets, and charming minor poems. His forte in the structure of his plays was not originality; he borrowed all but two of his plots from earlier works and followed the patterns of construction used by other playwrights of his time. His greatness lay in his rich versatility, ranging from the fairyland of *A Midsummer-Night's Dream* to the city streets of *The Comedy of Errors*, from the romantic treatment of love in *Romeo and Juliet* to a cynical contempt for it in *Troilus and Cressida*, from the study of a passionate man of action in *Coriolanus* to the sympathetic portrayal of an introvert bound down by thought in *Hamlet*, perhaps his greatest creation of all. Regardless of his mood or his material, Shakespeare was everywhere a poet with a poet's mastery of language. The profusion of imagery, the lavish use of verbal color, and the restless vigor of his style spring from the extravagant energy of the Renaissance period and yet reveal the unique mind of England's greatest writer.

In comparison with its verse, whether lyric or dramatic, the prose of the English Renaissance is a poor thing, cluttered up with Latin pedantry or ornate figures of speech that reveal the contempt of its courtly practitioners for a natural prose inspired by everyday speech. Fired by the example of Castiglione's *Courtier*, John Lyly sought in his prose romance, *Euphues, or the Anatomy of Wit* (1579), to instruct his readers in courtly language and developed an affected style of elaborately balanced constructions easy for them to imitate. Although it contributed to the refinement of Renaissance prose, the gross artificiality of "euphuistic" style, as it came to be called, perpetuated the misguided notion that prose should have as exact laws as verse and be somehow poetic rather than "prosaic." Support for this came from the ancients, especially Cicero; and the Italians from Boccaccio down had favored ponderous constructions and elegant ornament.

Best loved of all English prose works in this period were the wise and witty *Essays* written by the philosopher-statesman, Sir Francis Bacon. Though his more ambitious works are unfortunately composed in the heavy manner of *The Advancement of Learning* or even the scholarly Latin of the *Novum Organum*, Bacon used a clear-cut, epigrammatic style in his little essays that accounts in very large measure for their perennial popularity as practical guides to conduct.

Toward the end of the Renaissance the religious Reformation exerted a powerful influence on English letters through the nonconformist sect of Puritans. During Elizabeth's reign these extremists suffered legal restrictions because they disapproved of the queen's conception of the royal power, but by 1640 they had increased their numbers to the point where they precipitated a civil war and established a national government of their own under Oliver Cromwell.

The literature of the seventeenth century reflected the religious war of the time, with a militant Puritan school alongside their opponents, the Cavaliers. Drama declined under Puritan opposition to its Royalist outlook and supposed immorality, and with the closing of the theaters by the Puritan Parliament in 1642 playwriting went underground for nearly twenty years. Yet the Puritans produced two great literary spokesmen for their cause in John Bunyan and John Milton. Bunyan was a humble craftsman whose reading was confined to the Bible. His zeal in preaching Puritan doctrine during the Commonwealth led, with the restoration of the monarchy in 1660, to his imprisonment for twelve years. In Bedford jail Bunyan searched his soul to discover his sins and conceived the mission of preaching to a larger audience through personal confessions and allegorical revelations in print. His masterpiece, *The Pilgrim's Progress from this World to that Which is to Come* (1678–1679), is a simple but compelling tale of the spiritual trials of a well-intentioned Christian. This great Protestant allegory appeals to children with its tale of giants and warrior knights and to adults with its underlying symbolism of Christian doctrine. Long popular only with the middle and lower classes, it is written in a direct and vigorous prose that finally influenced the style of more polite literature.

But the supreme Puritan master was John Milton, one of the world's great poets. Unlike Bunyan, Milton was an aristocrat, with a Humanist's familiarity with the ancients reflected in the classical allusions that stud his verse. His early works, such as the masque *Comus* and the pastoral elegy *Lycidas*, show clearly his contact with the Italian Renaissance. During the Cromwell regime Milton forsook poetry for service to the state, but with the restoration of the monarchy he retired into poverty as a still unregenerate rebel, now totally blind. His last years were sustained by the composition of his masterpiece, *Paradise Lost* (1667), and the Christian tragedy in Greek form, *Samson Agonistes* (1671). The epic majesty of the first of these and its sublime vision of the celestial heights make it one of the world's classics of poetry. But in the latter we come

closer to Milton himself, spiritually isolated by the Royalist Restoration, in the defiant character of the blind Samson, destroying the alien and sinful Philistines with his own death. The Puritan Reformation was not killed in England by political defeat, but in Milton's last years it was being blended with other social forces to produce a new era in intellectual history. By 1660 the movement of Renaissance and Reformation had run its course, and Milton's work is a final summary of its achievements.

SPAIN. Spain had her Golden Age during the Renaissance, when Spanish seadogs sailed the Spanish Main, and far-flung colonies poured their riches into the imperial coffers of Charles v and Philip ii. Humanism arrived early in the sixteenth century, but the study of Latin and Greek classics was never so important here as in Italy and was more successfully harmonized with traditional Christianity in Catholic Spain than in the rest of Europe. It coincided with the religious Reformation in Germany and Switzerland, a movement that only strengthened the orthodox faith in Spain and inspired the Catholic Counter-Reformation of the Jesuits. Hence the resurrection of the ancients reinforced the authority of Aristotle in philosophy and science, and revived Plato in the Christian tradition of Plotinus rather than in the pagan spirit of the Medici Platonic Academy.

But the influence of the new outlook was clearer and stronger in less austere quarters. In Spain the idealistic tradition of medieval chivalry had lingered longer than in other lands, so that as late as 1508 there was first published the most popular of all its chivalric romances, *Amadis of Gaul*. The Christian knight riding through the countryside in quest of wrongs to right, defending his honor and his lady's with his trusty lance, still challenged the Spanish imagination as a living symbol, whereas in Italy and England he had become picturesquely archaic beside the new figure of the Renaissance courtier. Yet even in Spain social conditions were changing, and it remained for a Spaniard, Miguel de Cervantes, to write the great satire of chivalry that finally exposed the inadequacy of its idealism in a changing world. It was the time of Montaigne, when the self-assurance and high hopes of the early Humanists were also dissolving in a new skepticism. As Montaigne applied the devastating test of reason to the claims of Pico and Rabelais, Cervantes applied it to the outmoded social codes of feudalism.

Cervantes began *Don Quixote* as a literary satire of chivalric romance, but as he wrote, the character of his Knight of the Woeful Countenance, so well-intentioned in his noble enterprise, so ignominiously frustrated at every point by a coarse and heartless reality, became a pathetic figure pursuing his high mission on the open road. He became the embodi-

An example of Spanish religious painting is this work by El Greco, "Crucifixion," with a view of Toledo in the background. The elongation and somber atmosphere are characteristic of El Greco.

ment of human aspiration after justice and noble conduct, and in his repeated defeats Cervantes represented the tragic compromise with his better nature that the world forces on every man. Cervantes himself had learned this lesson through a lifetime of defeat and tragedy. The unchecked idealism of the Don is contrasted with the earthy realism of his peasant-squire, Sancho, the voice of common sense through his endless adages and folk wisdom. *Don Quixote* can be read as a comic novel of an absurd old man tilting with windmills and flocks of sheep, but like all really great comedies it carries as well a profound comment on human nature and human society.

Don Quixote sounded the death knell of chivalric romance, but the romantic idealism that it unmasked was too ingrained in Spanish temperament and the whole Renaissance movement not to withstand this exposure. It gives the characteristic flavor to the great school of drama that flourished in this *siglo del oro,* or "golden century," as the Spaniards call the period 1554–1681. Like the English, the Spanish drama of the period ignored the classical code of Aristotle and developed a free form of its own that would allow full range to the romantic imagination of a passionate people. The Spanish *comedia* was not necessarily a comedy, but rather a play that combined serious and comic elements within its three-act structure, usually with a happy ending. Humorous comments on the romantic affairs of the gallant and his lady were generally entrusted to a clownish servant or peasant called the *gracioso,* spokesman for the realistic common sense with which the Spaniards have always tempered their flamboyant romanticism. The *comedias* are classified according to subject matter: historical, religious, mythological, pastoral, and so forth, but all reveal the Renaissance Spaniards' unquestioning devotion to *dios, el rey, y mi dama* (God, the king, and my lady). The fanatical insistence on personal honor that makes every character, from the king to the lowliest peasant, ever ready to defend it gives a high-strung quality to Spanish drama. Although the school flourished at the time of the Elizabethans (1590–1660), its plays seem superficial and repetitious in comparison with Shakespeare and betray the fantastic speed with which Lope de Vega and Calderón turned them out.

Lope led an extravagant and tumultuous life as reckless student, soldier with the Spanish Armada, boastful libertine and faithless husband, finally an unconventional priest. Yet he found time to surpass all other authors in productivity. Despite his careless haste, Lope's endless imagination gave great variety to his dramas and their lively action and brilliant poetic style compensate in part for their shallow thinking and conventionalized characters. *The Sheep Well* is a startling play of proletarian revolt in which Lope's favorite types—the tyrannical feudal lord, the proud peasant and burgher, the noble king, the romantic lovers, and the witty *gracioso*—all appear. Behind its violent conflict lies the war of Renaissance monarchy on the feudal system, and the robust nationalism that animated the playwright in this great period of Spanish power.

Pedro Calderón de la Barca, who preserved the glory of the Spanish Renaissance through the midseventeenth century, followed the example of Lope the pioneer in his two hundred *comedias,* using the same themes and sometimes the same plots. A devoutly religious man, he specialized in such religious studies as *The Devotion to the Cross* and gave us in *Life Is a Dream* the only famous philosophical play of the Spanish Renaissance. With the death of Calderón and the rapid decline of the Spanish empire, Spain virtually disappeared from world literature for two hundred years. The Renaissance had already been dead for half a century in France, which was leading Europe into a new era.

The Wandering Scholars

The Wandering Scholars, or *vagantes,* are our link between medieval Church learning and the Humanism of the Renaissance. In France, Germany, and England of the twelfth and thirteenth centuries they formed a distinct order dedicated to the revival of pagan learning and, especially, pagan morality in the very midst of the Christian renascence. Uninterested in church careers as they were, these young men lacked the economic protection of the church and wandered from university to university, homeless and generally penniless, more familiar with low taverns than with lecture halls. With a strong sense of brotherhood born of their contempt for churchmen and laymen alike, they came to constitute an informal guild with a mythical patron called "Bishop Golias," a Rabelaisian character whom they jokingly thought of as their father and master. He was generally pictured as a reckless foe of the Pope, frankly devoted to free love and riotous living. Hence the wandering scholars were the "Goliards," and their lusty Latin songs in praise of wine, women, and poetry are the so-called Goliardic verse.

As found in the manuscript of the *Carmina Burana,* these student songs are anonymous and reveal no individual personalities but a single type of scholar-tramp singing the pleasures of this world, preferring Ovid to the churchmen, and wine and lovemaking in the springtime to musty scholarship. Sober clerics are frequently the butt of their satire. The pleasures of the country, the beauties of woods and pasture lands in May, flood these poems with a wholesome air from out-of-doors, and the love described is lusty and sensual. Unlike formal classical verse based on long and short syllables, the best of these rollicking stanzas give a new melody to Latin through recurrent accents and ingenious rhymes in tune with English prosody. At least one of them, *Gaudeamus Igitur,* has survived on the Continent as a universal student song.

A Song of the Open Road

We in our wandering,
Blithesome and squandering,
Tara, tantara, teino!

Eat to satiety,
Drink with propriety;   5
Tara, tantara, teino!

Laugh till our sides we split,

A Song of the Open Road. Translated by John Addington Symonds.

Rags on our hides we fit;
Tara, tantara, teino!

Jesting eternally,   10
Quaffing infernally:
Tara, tantara, teino!

Craft's in the bone of us,
Fear 'tis unknown of us:
Tara, tantara, teino!   15

When we're in neediness,
Thieve we with greediness:
Tara, tantara, teino!

Brother catholical,
Man apostolical,   20
Tara, tantara, teino!

Say what you will have done,
What you ask 'twill be done!
Tara, tantara, teino! . . .

License and vanity   25
Pamper insanity:
Tara, tantara, teino!

As the Pope bade us do,
Brother to brother's true:
Tara, tantara, teino!   30

Brother, best friend, adieu!
Now, I must part from you!
Tara, tantara, teino!

When will our meeting be?
Glad shall our greeting be!   35
Tara, tantara, teino!

Vows valedictory
Now have the victory;
Tara, tantara, teino!

Clasped on each other's breast,   40
Brother to brother pressed,
Tara, tantara, teino!

The Confessions of Golias

Boiling in my spirit's veins
With fierce indignation,
From my bitterness of soul
Springs self-revelation:
Framed am I of flimsy stuff,   5
Fit for levitation,

The Confessions of Golias. Translated by John Addington Symonds.

Like a thin leaf which the wind
    Scatters from its station. . . .

Down the broad road do I run,
    As the way of youth is;   10
Snare myself in sin, and ne'er
    Think where faith and truth is,
Eager far for pleasure more
    Than soul's health, the sooth is,
For this flesh of mine I care,   15
    Seek not ruth where ruth is.

Prelate, most discreet of priests,
    Grant me absolution!
Dear's the death whereof I die,
    Sweet my dissolution;   20
For my heart is wounded by
    Beauty's soft suffusion;
All the girls I come not nigh,
    Mine are in illusion.

'Tis most arduous to make   25
    Nature's self surrender;
Seeing girls, to blush and be
    Purity's defender!
We young men our longings ne'er
    Shall to stern law render,   30
Or preserve our fancies from
    Bodies smooth and tender. . . .

In the second place I own
    To the vice of gaming:
Cold indeed outside I seem,   35
    Yet my soul is flaming:
But when once the dice-box hath
    Stripped me to my shaming,
Make I songs and verses fit
    For the world's acclaiming.   40

In the third place, I will speak
    Of the tavern's pleasure;
For I never found nor find
    There the least displeasure;
Nor shall find it till I greet   45
    Angels without measure,
Singing requiems for the souls
    In eternal leisure.

In the public-house to die
    Is my resolution;   50
Let wine to my lips be nigh
    At life's dissolution:
That will make the angels cry,
    With glad elocution,
"Grant this toper, God on high,   55
    Grace and absolution!" . . .

Nature gives to every man
    Gifts as she is willing;

I compose my verses when
    Good wine I am swilling,   60
Wine the best for jolly guest
    Jolly hosts are filling;
From such wine rare fancies fine
    Flow like dews distilling.

Such my verse is wont to be   65
    As the wine I swallow;
No ripe thoughts enliven me
    While my stomach's hollow;
Hungry wits on hungry lips
    Like a shadow follow,   70
But when once I'm in my cups,
    I can beat Apollo. . . .

There are poets, worthy men,
    Shrink from public places,
And in lurking-hole or den   75
    Hide their pallid faces;
There they study, sweat, and woo
    Pallas and the Graces,
But bring nothing forth to view
    Worth the girls' embraces.   80

Fasting, thristing, toil the bards,
    Swift years flying o'er them;
Shun the strife of open life,
    Tumults of the forum;
They, to sing some deathless thing,   85
    Lest the world ignore them,
Die the death, expend their breath,
    Drowned in dull decorum. . . .

I have uttered openly
    All I knew that shamed me,   90
And have spued the poison forth
    That so long defamed me;
Of my old ways I repent,
    New life hath reclaimed me;
God beholds the heart—'twas man   95
    Viewed the face and blamed me.

The Invitation to Youth

TAKE your pleasure, dance and play,
    Each with other while ye may:
Youth is nimble, full of grace;
Age is lame, of tardy pace.

We the wars of love should wage,   5
Who are yet of tender age;

The Invitation to Youth. Translated by John Addington Symonds.
78. **Pallas**, Athena.

'Neath the tents of Venus dwell
All the joys that youth loves well.

Young men kindle heart's desire;
You may liken them to fire: 10
Old men frighten love away
With cold frost and dry decay.

There's No Lust
Like to Poetry

SWEET in goodly fellowship
    Tastes red wine and rare O!
But to kiss a girl's ripe lip
    Is a gift more fair O!
Yet a gift more sweet, more fine,   5
    Is the lyre of Maro!
While these three good gifts were mine,
    I'd not change with Pharaoh.

Bacchus wakes within my breast
    Love and love's desire,   10
Venus comes and stirs the blessed
    Rage of Phoebus' fire;
Deathless honour is our due
    From the laurelled sire:
Woe should I turn traitor to   15
    Wine and love and lyre!

Should a tyrant rise and say,
    "Give up wine!" I'd do it;
"Love no girls!" I would obey,
    Though my heart should rue it.   20
"Dash thy lyre!" suppose he saith,
    Naught should bring me to it;
"Yield thy lyre or die!" my breath,
    Dying, should thrill through it!

Gaudeamus Igitur

LET us live, then, and be glad,
    While young life's before us!
After youthful pastime had,
After old age hard and sad,
Earth will slumber o'er us.   5

Where are they who in this world,
    Ere we kept, were keeping?
Go ye to the gods above;
Go to hell; inquire thereof:
They are not; they're sleeping.   10

There's No Lust Like to Poetry. Translated by John Addington
Symonds.
6. **Maro**, Virgil. 12. **Phoebus**, Apollo.
Gaudeamus Igitur. Translated by John Addington Symonds.

Brief is life, and brevity
    Briefly shall be ended:
        Death comes like a whirlwind strong,
        Bears us with his blast along;
    None shall be defended.   15

Live this university,
    Men that learning nourish;
        Live each member of the same,
        Long live all that bear its name;
    Let them ever flourish!   20

Live the commonwealth also,
    And the men that guide it!
        Live our town in strength and health,
        Founders, patrons, by whose wealth
    We are here provided!   25

Live all girls! A health to you,
    Melting maids and beauteous!
        Live the wives and women too,
        Gentle, loving, tender, true,
    Good, industrious, duteous!   30

Perish cares that pule and pine!
    Perish envious blamers!
        Die the Devil, thine and mine!
        Die the starch-necked Philistine!
    Scoffers and defamers!

Pico della Mirandola

1463–1494

The new discovery by the Humanists of the
beauty and perfectability of human nature is
nowhere more enthusiastically expressed than in Pico's
Oration on the Dignity of Man. Pico della Mirandola,
the youngest son of a petty Italian prince, was a child
prodigy, who was already at sixteen an eager student at
the University of Ferrara. His thirst for learning exposed
him to the Aristotelian tradition and the oriental tradition of Averroës at Padua, the Platonic tradition in
Lorenzo de' Medici's Platonic Academy at Florence, and
the scholastic tradition of the Middle Ages at Paris. From
the four he attempted to synthesize a philosophy that
reconciled the ancient schools of Plato and Aristotle with
a revitalized Christianity. But his passion for Humanism
brought him into a dangerous conflict with the Church
when two of his major works were declared heretical by
the Pope. His early death from a fever at the age of
thirty cut short his masterpiece, the *Symphonia Platonis
et Aristotelis,* and probably saved him from more serious
embroilment with Rome.

His famous *Oration on the Dignity of Man* proclaims
the worth of human nature in an almost unconscious

revolt against the humility of Christian ethics. With his divine gift of reason, man gains a self-reliance that can carry him to the heights of intellectual achievement. The free, confident spirit of this Humanistic document predicts the more earthy emancipation of Rabelais and his Abbey of Theleme.

Of the Dignity of Man

I HAVE read in the records of the Arabians, worshipful Fathers, that Abdala the Saracen, when questioned as to what on this stage of the world, as it were, should be considered most worthy of wonder, replied: "There is nothing to be seen more wonderful than Man," with which opinion the saying of Hermes Trismegistus agrees: "A great miracle, Asclepius, is Man." But when I weighed the reason for these maxims, the many excellences reported of human nature by many men did not satisfy me—that Man is the intermediary between creatures, the intimate of the gods, king of the lower beings, by the acuteness of his senses, by the discernment of his reason and the light of his intelligence the interpreter of nature, the interval between fixed eternity and fleeting time, and (as the Persians say), the bond, nay rather the marriage-song of the world, on David's testimony but little lower than the angels. Admittedly great though these be, they are not the principal reasons, that is to say, those which may rightfully claim for themselves the privilege of the highest admiration. For why should we not admire more the angels themselves and the blessed choirs of Heaven? At last, it seems to me, I have come to understand why Man is the most fortunate of beings, and consequently worthy of all admiration, and what precisely is that rank which is his lot in the universal chain of Being, and which is to be envied not only by brutes but even by the stars, by minds more than earthly. It is a matter past faith, and a wondrous one. Why should it not be? For on this very account Man is rightly both called a great miracle, and judged a wonderful being indeed.

But hear, Fathers, exactly what is this rank, and, as kindly auditors, conformably to your cultivation, forbear to punish me for this work. God the Father, the Supreme Architect, had already built this earthly home we behold of his Godhead, as his most sacred temple, by the laws of his mysterious wisdom. The

supercelestial region He had adorned with intelligences, the heavenly spheres He had quickened with eternal souls, and the excrementary and filthy parts of the lower world He had filled with a multitude of creatures of every kind. But when the work was finished the Artist kept wishing that there were someone to ponder the rationality of so great a work, to love its beauty, and to wonder at its vastness. Therefore when everything was done (as Moses and Timaeus bear witness) He finally took thought concerning the creation of Man. But there was not among his archetypes that from which He could fashion a new offspring, nor was there in his treasure-houses anything He might bestow on his new son as an inheritance, nor was there in the courts of all the world a place where the latter might sit as contemplator of the universe. All was now complete, all things had been assigned to the highest, the middle, and the lowest orders. But in its final creation it was not the part of the Father's power to fail as though exhausted. It was not the part of his wisdom to waver in a case of need through poverty of counsel. It was not the intention of his kindly love that he who was to praise God's divine generosity in regard to others, should be compelled to condemn it in regard to himself.

At last the Best of Artisans ordained that that creature to whom he had been able to give nothing proper to himself should have joint possession of whatever had been the peculiar characteristics of the different creatures. He therefore accorded to Man the function of a form not set apart, and a place in the middle of the world, and addressed him thus: "I have given thee neither a fixed abode nor a form that is thine alone nor any function peculiar to thyself, Adam, to the end that, according to thy longing and according to thy judgment, thou mayest have and possess that abode, that form, and those functions which thou thyself shalt desire. The nature of all other things is limited and constrained within the bounds of laws prescribed by me: thou, coerced by no necessity, shalt ordain for thyself the limits of thy nature in accordance with thine own free will, in whose hand I have placed thee. I have set thee at the world's center, that thou mayest from thence more easily observe whatever is in the world. I have made thee neither of heaven nor of earth, neither mortal nor immortal, so that thou mayest with greater freedom of choice and with more honor, as though the maker and moulder of thyself, fashion thyself in whatever shape thou shalt prefer. Thou shalt have the power to degenerate into the lower forms of life, which are animal; thou shalt have the power, out of thy soul's judgment, to be reborn into the higher forms of life, which are divine."

Of the Dignity of Man.^A Translated by Elizabeth L. Forbes. Reprinted from the *Journal of the History of Ideas*, III (1942), by permission of the editors.
2. **Abdala the Saracen,** a learned and pious Moor. 7. **Hermes Trismegistus,** the assumed author of a body of ancient Egyptian Neoplatonic literature, including the dialogue *Asclepius* (ref. I, 294). 18-19. **but little . . . angels.** Psalms, 8:5.

49. **Timaeus,** a Pythagorean philosopher, to whom Plato credits in *Timaeus* an account of the origin of man.

O supreme generosity of God the Father, O highest and most marvellous felicity of Man! to whom it is granted to have that which he chooses, to be that which he wills. Beasts as soon as they are born (so says Lucilius) bring with them from their mother's womb that which they will possess for ever; spiritual beings, either from the beginning or soon thereafter, become what they are to be for ever and ever. On Man when he came into life the Father conferred the seeds of all good and the germs of every form of life. Whatever seeds each man cultivates, those seeds will grow to maturity and bear in him their own fruit. If they be vegetative, he will be like a plant. If sensual, he will become brutish. If rational, he will issue as a heavenly being. If intellectual, he will be an angel and the son of God. And if, happy in the lot of no created thing, he withdraws into the center of his own unity, his spirit made one with God in the solitary darkness of God who is set above all things, he shall surpass them all. Who will not admire this our chameleon? Or who could more greatly admire aught else whatever? It is Man who Asclepius of Athens, arguing from his mutability of character and from his self-transforming nature, on just grounds says was symbolized by Proteus in the mysteries. Hence those metamorphoses renowned among the Hebrews and the Pythagoreans. . . .

Are there any who would not admire Man, who is, in the sacred writings of Moses and the Christains, not without reason described sometimes by the name of "all flesh," sometimes by that of "every creature," in as much as he himself moulds, fashions, and changes himself into the form of all flesh and into the character of every creature? For this reason the Persian Euanthes, in describing the Chaldaean religion, writes that Man has no semblance that is inborn and his very own, but many that are external and foreign to him; whence this saying of the Chaldaeans: "Hanorish tharah sharinas," that is, Man is a being of varied, manifold, and inconstant nature. But to what end is this so? To the end that, after we have been born to this condition, we may understand that we may become that which we will to be. We should have especial care to this, that it should never be said against us, that although born to a privileged position, we failed to recognize it and became like unto wild animals and senseless beasts of burden; but that rather the saying of Asaph the Prophet should apply: "Ye are all angels and sons of the Most High"; and that we may not by abusing

5. **Lucilius,** Roman satirist of second century B.C., here quoted in Nonius Marcellus, *De Compendiosa Doctrina* (Lindsay edition, I, 109). 23. **Asclepius of Athens,** supposed author of a Greek dialogue between Hermes and himself on God, Man, and the World. 25. **Proteus,** the legendary Greek prophetic sea god, capable of changing his form at will. 48-49. **Asaph the Prophet,** the Hebrew musician, to whom many of the Psalms are traditionally attributed, as here: Psalms 82:6.

the most indulgent generosity of the Father, that freedom of choice He has given, make for ourselves something harmful out of what is salutary. Let a certain holy ambition invade our souls, so that, not content with the mediocre, we shall pant after the highest, and (since we may if we wish) toil with all our strength to follow it.

Desiderius Erasmus

1466–1536

The best known of the Humanists was a Hollander by birth, but he thought of Latin as his natural tongue. He Latinized and Hellenized his Dutch name Gerhard into Desiderius Erasmus, and during a long life traveled restlessly back and forth through the scholarly circles of France, England, Italy, the Netherlands, and Switzerland, spreading the gospel of the new learning to a host of eager pupils. His love of literature appeared early in youth, but the death of both his parents before he had completed his schooling forced him into training for the priesthood. Though he became learned in theology, he was unhappy under the severe discipline of a monastic life, so that when his reputation for classical scholarship brought him wealthy English pupils in Paris, he was glad to accept patronage from one of them, Lord Mountjoy, and to make the first (1499–1500) of three visits to England.

At Oxford he found a kindred spirit in John Colet, the English Humanist, and he was later to number Linacre, Grocyn, Sir Thomas More, and even Henry VIII among his good friends. He taught Greek and theology at Oxford for a time, but refused to settle permanently in England, as his friends desired. He was by turns in Paris, Padua, Venice, Rome, Louvain, and Basel and everywhere won patrons, friends, and disciples through his charming manners, stimulating conversation, and enlightened scholarship. Although he severely criticized church dogma and the arrogant ignorance of churchmen of his day, he generally retained the good will of the Church and at the time of Luther's split with Rome refused to declare himself for or against the Reformation. Protestants criticized him for not joining a movement that his critical writings had done much to bring about, but he was true to himself in his neutrality.

Erasmus was a pillar of common sense in an era of warring creeds. Although he was opposed to the elaborate theology of Catholicism, he was no friendlier toward the new theology of the Reformation. His urbane rationalism kept him aloof from party strife; his was a detached and independent spirit, interested primarily in the spread of learning, both classical and Christian, and in the liberation of mankind from superstition and entrenched tradition. Strongly interested in ethical problems, he worked for a rational Christianity, freed from dogma and mystical faith and enlightened by the clear common sense of the ancients, especially the stoic Romans. This innate conservatism made him look backward to a revived antiquity and a Christianity revived on what he thought of as the original message of the great teacher, Jesus. Resolute in his opposition to the medieval world, he advocated a fusion of two older schools of thought in a new intellectual outlook, liberal with the tolerance born of knowledge.

But his horizon was limited by the characteristic outlook of the Humanists. Indifferent to the new art, opposed to the new science, skeptical of the Reformation, he could not point the way to a new horizon. Although he wrote much about religion and churchmen, he was at heart a literary scholar, whose contacts with the civilized Horace and Cicero of ancient Rome were most congenial with his own rational temperament. Like Voltaire over two centuries later, he was for his age the symbol of intellectual enlightenment, wittily attacking ignorance and dogmatism as he found them exalted in the Middle Ages.

The most famous work of Erasmus, *The Praise of Folly,* was written in the house of Sir Thomas More, to which he had come from Italy in 1509 upon learning of the accession of Henry VIII, his friend and expected patron. This brilliant satire, probably inspired by the *Ship of Fools* (1494) of the German Humanist, Sebastian Brant, is a witty attack on stupidity and corruption in both secular and religious circles, ironically disguised as a praise of ignorance and evil from the lips of Folly herself. Scholars and men of letters, philosophers and men of the Church, popes and kings are all tainted with her touch. The criticism of simony and other ecclesiastical abuses aroused churchmen to indignation, and Erasmus' satire undoubtedly influenced Luther and other spokesmen for the Reformation. But his purpose was merely reform within the establishment, and his work shares with that of Horace and Juvenal the attitude of the armchair observer of the follies committed by men when they are not guided by the cool light of reason.

The Praise of Folly

FOLLY SPEAKS

Aᴛ what rate soever the world talks of me (for I am not ignorant what an ill report Folly hath got, even among the most foolish), yet that I am that She, that only She, whose deity recreates both gods and men, even this is a sufficient argument, that I no sooner stepped up to speak to this full assembly than all your faces put on a kind of new and unwonted pleasantness. So suddenly have you cleared your brows and with so frolic and hearty
10 a laughter given me your applause that in truth, as many of you as I behold on every side of me seem

*The Praise of Folly.*ᴬ Translation by John Wilson, revised.

to me no less than Homer's gods drunk with nectar and nepenthe; whereas before you sat as lumpish and pensive as if you had come from consulting an oracle. And as it usually happens when the sun begins to show his beams, or when after a sharp winter the spring breathes afresh on the earth, all things immediately get a new face, new color, and recover a certain kind of youth again: in like manner, by but beholding me, you have in an instant gotten another 20 king of countenance; and so what the otherwise great rhetoricians with their tedious and long-studied orations can hardly effect, to wit, to remove the trouble of the mind, I have done at once with my single look. . . .

And therefore, I think it high time to look down a little on the earth, wherein you'll find nothing frolic or fortunate that it owes not to me. So provident has that great parent of mankind, Nature, been that there should not be anything without its mixture and, 30 as it were, seasoning of folly. For since according to the definition of the Stoics, wisdom is nothing else than to be governed by reason, and on the contrary folly to be given up to the will of our passions; that the life of man might not be altogether disconsolate and hard to bear, of how much more passion than reason has Jupiter composed us? Besides, he has confined reason to a narrow corner of the brain and left all the rest of the body to our passions; as also set up against this one two masterless tyrants—anger, 40 that possesses the region of the heart, and consequently the very fountain of life, the heart itself, and lust, that stretches its empire everywhere. Against which double force how powerful reason is, let common experience declare, inasmuch as she, which yet is all she can do, may call out to us till she be hoarse again and tell us the rules of honesty and virtue, while they give up the reins to their governor and make a hideous clamor, till at last being wearied, he suffer himself to be carried whither they please to 50 hurry him.

But forasmuch as such as are born to the business of the world have some little sprinklings of reason more than the rest, yet that they may the better manage it, even in this as well as in other things, they call me to counsel; and I give them such as is worthy of myself, to wit, that they take to them a wife—a silly thing, God wot, and foolish, yet wanton and pleasant, by which means the roughness of the masculine temper is seasoned and sweetened by her 60 folly. For in that Plato seems to doubt under which genus he should put woman, to wit that of rational creatures or brutes, he intended nothing else than to show the apparent folly of the sex. For if perhaps any of them goes about to be thought wiser than the rest, what else does she do but play the fool twice, as if a man should teach a cow to dance, a thing quite against nature. For as it doubles the crime if anyone should put a disguise upon nature, or endeavor to bring her to that which she will in no wise bear, according to that proverb of the Greeks, "An ape is an ape, though clad in scarlet;" so a woman is a woman still, that is to say foolish, let her put on whatever vizard she please. . . .

THE FOLLY OF FRIENDSHIP AND MARRIAGE

But perhaps there are some that neglect this way of pleasure and rest satisfied in the enjoyment of their friends, calling friendship the most desirable of
10 all things, more necessary than air, fire, or water, so delectable that he that shall take it out of the world had as good put out the sun, and so commendable that not even the philosophers themselves doubted to reckon it among their chiefest good. But what if I show you that I am both the beginning and end of this so great good also? And now tell me if to wink, slip over, be blind at, or deceived in the vices of our friends, nay, to admire and esteem them for virtues, be not at least the next degree to folly? What is it
20 when one kisses his mistress's freckled neck, another the wart on her nose? When a father shall swear his squint-eyed child is more lovely than Venus? What is this, I say, but mere folly? And so, perhaps you'll cry, it is; and yet it is this only that joins friend together and continues them so joined. . . .

And what has been said of friendship may more reasonably be presumed of matrimony, which in truth is no other than an inseparable conjunction of life. Good God! What divorces, or what not worse
30 than that, would daily happen, were not the converse between a man and his wife supported and cherished by flattery, apishness, gentleness, ignorance, dissembling—certain retainers of mine also! How few marriages should we have if the husband should but examine thoroughly how many tricks his pretty little mop of modesty has played before she was married! And how fewer of them would hold together, did not most of the wife's actions escape the husband's knowledge through his neglect or sot-
40 tishness! And for this also you are beholden to me, by whose means it is that the husband is pleasant to his wife, the wife to her husband, and the house kept in quiet. A man is laughed at when, seeing his wife weeping, he licks up her tears. But how much happier is it to be thus deceived than by being troubled with jealousy, not only to torment himself, but set all things in a hubbub!

In fine, I am so necessary to the making of all society and manner of life both delightful and last-
50 ing that neither would the people long endure their governors, nor the servant his master, nor the master his footman, nor the pupil his tutor, nor one friend another, nor the wife her husband, nor the usurer the borrower, nor a soldier his commander, nor one

One of the most famous pictures of Erasmus of Rotterdam is this engraving by Albrecht Dürer made in 1526.

companion another, unless all of them had their interchangeable failings, one while flattering, another while prudently conniving, and generally sweetening one another with some small relish of folly. . . .

SOLDIERS AND PHILOSOPHERS

Is not war the very root and matter of all famed enterprises? And yet what more foolish than to undertake it for I know not what trifles, especially when both parties are sure to lose more than they get by the bargain? For of those that are slain, not a word of them; and for the rest, when both sides are closely engaged and the trumpets make an ugly noise, what use are those wise men, I pray, that are so exhausted with study that their thin cold blood has scarcely any spirits left? No, it must be those blunt fat fellows that by how much the more they exceed in courage fall short in understanding. Unless perhaps one had rather choose Demosthenes for a soldier, who threw away his arms and betook him to his heels ere he had scarce seen his enemy; as ill a soldier, as happy an orator.

But counsel, you will say, is not of least concern in matters of war. In a general I grant it, but this thing of warring is no part of philosophy, but managed by parasites, panders, thieves, cut-throats, plowmen, sots, spendthrifts, and such other dregs of mankind, not philosophers; who how unapt they are even for common converse, let Socrates, whom the oracle of Apollo judged "the wisest of all men living," be witness; who stepping up to speak in public was forced to come down again well laughed at for his pains. Though yet in this he was not altogether a fool, because he refused the appellation of wise, and returning it to the oracle, delivered his opinion that a wise man should abstain from meddling with public business; unless perhaps he should have rather admonished us to beware of wisdom if we intended to be reckoned among the number of men, there being nothing but his wisdom that first accused and afterwards sentenced him to the drinking of his poisoned cup. For while as you find him in Aristophanes philosophizing about clouds and ideas, measuring how far a flea could leap, and admiring that so small a creature as a fly should make so great a buzz, he meddled not with anything that concerned common life. . . .

Invite a wise man to a feast and he'll spoil the company, either with morose silence or troublesome disputes. Take him out to a dance and you'll swear a cow would have done it better. Bring him to the theater and his very looks are enough to spoil all, till like Cato he take an occasion of withdrawing rather than put off his supercilious gravity. Let him fall into discourse and he shall make more sudden stops than if he had a wolf before him. Let him buy or sell or, in short, go about any of those things without which there is no living in this world, and you'll say this piece of wisdom were rather a stock than a man, of so little use is he to himself, country, or friends; and all because he is wholly ignorant of common things and lives a course of life quite different from the people. . . .

WITHOUT FOLLY, WISDOM WOULD LEAD TO SUICIDE

Suppose a man in some lofty tower, and that he could look round him, as the poets say Jupiter was now and then wont. To how many misfortunes would he find the life of man subject! How miserable, to say no worse, our birth, how difficult our education; to how many wrongs our childhood exposed, to what pains our youth; how unsupportable our old age and grievous our unavoidable death, as also what troops of diseases beset us, how many casualties hang over our heads, how many troubles invade us, and how little there is that is not steeped in gall. To say nothing of those evils that one man brings upon another, as poverty, imprisonment, infamy, dishonesty, racks, snares, treachery, reproaches, actions, deceits—but I'm got into as endless a work as numbering the sands. For what offenses mankind have deserved these things, or what

angry god compelled them to be born into such miseries is not my present business. Yet he that shall diligently examine it with himself, would he not, think you, kill himself?

But I, partly through ignorance, partly unadvisedness, and sometimes through forgetfulness of evil, do now and then so sprinkle pleasure with the hopes of good, and sweeten men up in their greatest misfortunes that they are not willing to leave this life, even when according to the account of the destinies this life has left them; and by how much the less reason they have to live, by so much the more they desire it; so far are they from being sensible of the least wearisomeness of life. Of my gift it is that you have so many old Nestors everywhere, that have scarce left them the shape of a man: stutterers, dotards, toothless, gray-haired, bald—or rather, to use the words of Aristophanes, nasty, miserable, shriveled, bald, toothless, and wanting their baubles—yet so delighted with life and to be thought young that one dyes his gray hair, another covers his baldness with a periwig, another gets a set of new teeth, another falls desperately in love with a young wench and keeps more flickering about her than a young man would have been ashamed of. For to see such an old crooked piece, with one foot in the grave, to marry a plump young wench, and that too without a portion, is so common that men almost expect to be commended for it. But the best sport of all is to see our old women, even dead with age, and such skeletons that one would think they had stolen out of their graves, and ever mumbling in their mouths, "Life is sweet;" and as old as they are, still catterwauling, daily plastering their faces, scarcely ever from the glass, gossiping, dancing, and writing love letters. These things are laughed at as foolish, as indeed they are; yet they please themselves, live merrily, swim in pleasure, and in a word are happy, by my courtesy. But I would have them to whom these things seem ridiculous consider whether it be not better to live so pleasant a life in such kind of follies than, as the proverb goes, "to take a halter and hang themselves." Besides, though these things may be subject to censure, it concerns not my fools in the least, in as much as they take no notice of it, or if they do, they easily neglect it. If a stone fall upon a man's head, that's evil indeed; but dishonesty, infamy, villainy, ill reports carry no more hurt in them than a man is sensible of, and if a man have no sense of them, they are no longer evils. What are you the worse if the people hiss at you, so long as you applaud yourself? And that a man be able to do so, he must owe it only to folly.

FOOLS ARE NOT UNHAPPY

But methinks I hear the philosophers opposing it and saying it is a miserable thing for a man to be foolish, to err, mistake, and know nothing truly. Nay rather, this is to be a man. And why they should call it miserable, I see no reason; forasmuch as we are so born, so bred, so instructed, such is the common condition of us all. And nothing can be called miserable that suits with its kind, unless perhaps you'll think a man such because he can neither fly with birds, nor walk on all fours with beasts, and is not armed with horns as a bull. For by the same reason he would call the warlike horse unfortunate because he understood not grammar, nor ate cheesecakes; and the bull miserable because he'd make so ill a wrestler. And therefore, as a horse that has no skill in grammar is not miserable, no more is man in this respect, for that they agree with his nature. . . .

When fools have passed over this life with a great deal of pleasantness and without so much as the least fear or sense of death, they go straight forth into the Elysian Field to recreate their pious and careless souls with such sports as they used here. Let's proceed then and compare the condition of your wise men with that of this fool. Fancy to me now some example of wisdom you'd set up against him, one that had spent his childhood and youth in learning the sciences and lost the sweetest part of his life in watchings, cares, studies, and for the remaining part of it never so much as tasted the least of pleasure, ever sparing, poor, sad, sour, unjust and rigorous to himself, and troublesome and hateful to others; broken with paleness, leanness, craziness, sore eyes, and an old age and death contracted before their time (though yet, what matter is it when he dies who never lived?); and such is the picture of this great wise man. . . .

THE SUPERSTITIOUS

There is no doubt that that kind of men are wholly ours who love to hear or tell feigned miracles and strange lies, and are never weary of any tale, though never so long, if it be of ghosts, spirits, goblins, devils, or the like; which the farther they are from truth, the more readily they are believed and the more do they tickle their itching ears. And these serve not only to pass away time, but bring profit, especially to mass priests and pardoners. And next to these are they who have gotten a foolish but pleasant persuasion that if they can but see a wooden or painted Polypheme Christopher, they shall not die that day, or do but salute a carved Barbara in the usual set form, that they shall return safe from battle, or make their application to Erasmus on certain days with some small wax candles and proper prayers, that they shall quickly be rich. Or what should I say of them that hug themselves with their

46. **Polypheme Christopher.** Since St. Christopher, the patron saint of travelers, was painted with only one eye showing, Erasmus likens him to the Cyclops.

counterfeit pardons, that have measured purgatory by an hour glass and can without the least mistake demonstrate its ages, years, months, days, hours, minutes, and seconds, as it were in a mathematical table? Or what of those who, having confidence in certain magical charms and short prayers invented by some pious imposter, either for his soul's health or profit's sake, promise to themselves everything: wealth, honor, pleasure, plenty, good health, long life, lively old age, and the next place to Christ in the other world, which yet they desire may not happen too soon, that is to say before the pleasures of this life have left them?

And now suppose some merchant, soldier, or judge, out of so many rapines, parts with some small piece of money. He straight conceives all that sink of his whole life quite cleansed; so many perjuries, so many lusts, so many debaucheries, so many contentions, so many murders, so many deceits, so many breaches of trust, so many treacheries bought off that they may begin upon a new score. But what is more foolish than those, or rather more happy, who daily reciting those seven verses of the Psalms promise to themselves more than the top of felicity? And these are so foolish that I am half ashamed of them myself, and yet they are approved, and that not only by the common people but even the professors of religion. And what, are not they also almost the same where several countries avouch to themselves their peculiar saint, and as every one of them has his particular gift, so also his particular form of worship? As, one is good for the toothache, another for groaning women, a third for stolen goods, a fourth for making a voyage prosperous, and a fifth to cure sheep of the rot; and so of the rest, for it would be too tedious to run over all. And some there are that are good for more things than one, but chiefly the Virgin Mother, to whom the common people do in a manner attribute more than to the Son. . . .

But why do I launch into this ocean of superstitions? Had I a hundred tongues, as many mouths, and a voice never so strong, yet were I not able to run over the several sorts of fools or all the names of folly, so thick do they swarm everywhere. And yet our priests make no scruple to receive and cherish them, as proper instruments of profit, whereas if some scurvy wise fellow should step up and speak things as they are, as, To live well is the way to die well; The best way to get quit of sin is to add to the money thou givest, the hatred of sin, tears, watchings, prayers, fastings, and amendment of life; Such or such a saint will favor thee if thou imitatest his life—these, I say, and the like should this wise man chat to the people, from what happiness into how great troubles would he draw them?

Of this college also are they who in their lifetime appoint with what solemnity they'll be buried, and particularly set down how many torches, how many mourners, how many singers, how many almsmen they will have at it; as if any sense of it could come to them, or that it were a shame to them that their corpse were not honorably interred. . . .

THE SAD THING IS NOT TO BE DECEIVED

But it is a sad thing, they say, to be mistaken. Nay rather, he is most miserable that is not so. For they are quite beside the mark that place the happiness of men in things themselves, since it only depends upon opinion. . . .

And now at how cheap a rate is this happiness purchased! Forasmuch as to the thing itself a man's whole endeavor is required, be it never so inconsiderable, but the opinion of it is easily taken up, which yet conduces as much or more to happiness. For suppose a man were eating rotten stockfish, the very smell of which would choke another, and yet believed it a dish for the gods, what difference is there as to his happiness? Whereas, on the contrary, if another's stomach should turn at a sturgeon, wherein, I pray, is he happier than the other? If a man have a crooked, ill-favored wife, who yet in his eye may stand in competition with Venus, is it not the same as if she were truly beautiful? Or if seeing an ugly, ill-painted piece, he should admire the work as believing it some great master's hand, were he not much happier, think you, than they that buy such things at vast rates and yet perhaps reap less pleasure from them than the other? I know one of my name that gave his new married wife some counterfeit jewels and, as he was a pleasant droll, persuaded her that they were not only right, but of an inestimable price; and what difference, I pray, to her, that was as well-pleased and contented with the glass and kept it as warily as if it had been a treasure? In the meantime the husband saved his money and had this advantage of her folly, that he obliged her as much as if he had bought them at a great rate. Or what difference, think you, between those in Plato's imaginary cave that stand gaping at the shadows and figures of things, so they please themselves and have no need to wish, and that wise man who, being got loose from them, sees things truly as they are? So then there is no difference, or, if there be, the fools have the advantage: first, in that their happiness costs them least, that is to say, only some small persuasion; next, that they enjoy it in common. And the possession of no good can be delightful without a companion. . . .

SCHOLARS AND AUTHORS

Of the same batch are they that hunt after immortality of fame by setting out books. They that write learnedly to the understanding of a few schol-ars seem to me rather to be pitied than happy, as persons that are ever tormenting themselves, adding, changing, putting in, blotting out, revising, reprinting, showing it to friends, and nine years in correcting, yet never fully satisfied. At so great a rate do they purchase this vain reward, praise, and that too of a very few, with so many watchings, so much sweat, so much vexation and loss of sleep, the most precious of all things. Add to this the waste of health, spoil of complexion, weakness of eyes or blindness, poverty, envy, abstinence from pleasure, over-hasty old age, untimely death, and the like; so highly does this wise man value the approbation of one or two blear-eyed fellows. . . .

But they are the wiser that put out other men's works for their own, and transfer that glory which others with great pains have obtained to themselves, relying on this, that they conceive, though it should so happen that their theft be never so plainly detected, that yet they should enjoy the pleasure of it for the present. And it is worth one's while to consider how they please themselves when they are applauded by the common people, pointed at in a crowd: "This is that excellent person.". . .

But the most pleasant of all is to see them praise one another with reciprocal epistles, verses, and encomiums; fools their fellow-fools, and dunces their brother dunces. And sometimes too they pick out their antagonist and think to raise themselves a fame by writing one against the other, while the giddy multitude are so long divided as to whether of the two they shall determine the victory, till each goes off conqueror and, as if he had done some great action, fancies himself a triumph. And now wise men laugh at these things as foolish, as indeed they are. Who denies it? Yet in the meantime, such is my kindness to them, they live a merry life; while yet those learned men, though they laugh their fill and reap the benefit of the others' folly, cannot without ingratitude deny that even they too are not a little beholden to me themselves.

LAWYERS

And among them our advocates challenge the first place, nor is there any sort of people that please themselves like them; for while they daily quote you a thousand cases as it were in a breath, no matter how little to the purpose, and heap glosses upon glosses and opinions on the neck of opinions, they bring it at last to this pass, that that study of all other seems the most difficult. Add to these our logicians and sophisters, a generation of men more prattling than an echo, and the worst of them able to outchat a hundred of the best-picked gossips. And yet their condition would be much better were they only full of words and not so given to scolding that they must obstinately hack and hew one another about a matter of nothing and make such a sputter about terms and words till they have quite lost the sense. And yet they are so happy in the good opinion of themselves that as soon as they are furnished with two or three syllogisms, they dare boldly enter the lists against any man upon any point, as not doubting to run him down with noise, though the opponent were another Stentor. . . .

MONKS

And next these come those that commonly call
10 themselves the religious and monks, most false in both titles when both a great part of them are farthest from religion and no men swarm thicker in all places than themselves. Nor can I think of anything that could be more miserable, did not I support them so many several ways. For whereas all men detest them to that height that they take it for ill luck to meet one of them by chance, yet such is their happiness that they flatter themselves. For first, they reckon it one of the main points of piety if they are
20 so illiterate that they can't so much as read. And then when they run over their offices, which they carry about them, rather by tale than understanding, they believe the gods more than ordinarily pleased with their braying. And some there are among them that put off their trumperies at vast rates, yet rove up and down for the bread they eat; nay, there is scarce an inn, wagon, or ship into which they intrude not, to the no small damage of the commonwealth of beggars. And yet, like pleasant fellows,
30 with all this vileness, ignorance, rudeness, and impudence, they represent to us, for so they call it, the lives of the apostles. Yet what is more pleasant than that they do all things by rule and, as it were, a kind of mathematics, the least swerving from which were a crime beyond forgiveness; as, how many knots their shoes must be tied with, of what color everything is, what distinction of habits, of what stuff made, how many straws broad their girdles and of what fashion, how many bushels wide their cowl,
40 how many fingers long their hair, and how many hours sleep; which exact equality, how disproportionable it is among such variety of bodies and tempers, who is there that does not perceive it? And yet by reason of these fooleries, they not only set slight by others, but each different order, men otherwise professing apostolical charity, despise one another, and for the different wearing of a habit, or that it is of darker color, they put all things in combustion. And among these there are some so rigidly religious
50 that their upper garment is hair-cloth, their inner of the finest linen; and, on the contrary, others wear linen without and hair next their skins. Others, again, are as afraid to touch money as poison, and yet neither forbear wine nor dallying with women.

21. **their offices,** the canonical hours.

In a word, it is their only care that none of them come near one another in their manner of living, nor do they endeavor how they may be like Christ, but how they may differ among themselves.

And another great happiness they conceive in their names, while they call themselves Cordeliers, and 60 among these too some are Colletes, some Minors, some Minims, some Crossed; and again, these are Benedictines, those Bernardines; these Carmelites, those Augustines; these Williamites, and those Jacobines; as if it were not worth the while to be called Christians. And of these, a great part build so much on their ceremonies and petty traditions of men that they think one heaven is too poor a reward for so great merit, little dreaming that the time will come when Christ, not regarding any of these trifles, will 70 call them to account for His precept of charity. . . . Christ, interrupting them in their vanities, which otherwise were endless, will ask them, "Whence this new kind of Jews? I acknowledge one commandment, which is truly mine, of which alone I hear nothing. I promised, it is true, my Father's heritage, and that without parables, not to cowls, odd prayers, and fasting, but to the duties of faith and charity. Nor can I acknowledge them that least acknowledge their faults. They that would seem holier than my- 80 self, let them if they list possess to themselves those three hundred sixty-five heavens of Basilides the Heretic's invention, or command them whose foolish traditions they have preferred before my precepts, to erect them a new one." When they shall hear these things and see common ordinary persons preferred before them, with what countenance, think you, will they behold one another? In the meantime they are happy in their hopes, and for this also they are beholden to me. . . . 90

THE CHRISTIAN RELIGION
IS AKIN TO FOLLY

But not to run too far in that which is infinite. To speak briefly, all the Christian religion seems to have a kind of alliance with folly, and in no respect to have any accord with wisdom. Of which if you ask proof, consider first that boys, old men, women, and fools are more delighted with religious and sacred things than others, and to that purpose are ever next the altars; and this they do by mere impulse of nature. And in the next place, you see that those first founders of it were plain, simple persons 100 and most bitter enemies of learning. Lastly, there are no sort of fools that seem more out of the way than are those whom the zeal of the Christian religion has

61. **Colletes,** the order founded by St. Coleta. **Minors,** an order founded by St. Francis of Assisi.
62. **Minims,** an order founded by St. Francis of Paola. **Crossed,** an English order of monks with crosses on their garments. 82. **Basilides,** a heretic of the second century.

once swallowed up, so that they waste their estates, neglect injuries, suffer themselves to be cheated, put no difference between friends and enemies, abhor pleasure, are crammed with poverty, watchings, tears, labors, and reproaches, loathe life, and wish death above all things. In short, they seem senseless to common understanding, as if their minds lived elsewhere and not in their own bodies; which, what else is it than to be mad? . . .

10 Which yet will be more clear if I briefly show you that that great reward they so much fancy is nothing else but a kind of madness. And therefore suppose that Plato dreamed of something like it when he called the madness of lovers the most happy condition of all others. For he that's violently in love lives not in his own body, but in the thing he loves; and by how much the farther he runs from himself into another, by so much the greater is his pleasure. And then, when the mind strives to rove from 20 its body and does not rightly use its own organs, without doubt you may say it is downright madness and not to be mistaken, or otherwise what's the meaning of those common sayings, "Nobody home," "Come to yourself," "He's his own self again"? Besides, the more perfect and true his love is, the more pleasant is his madness. And therefore, what is that life hereafter, after which these holy minds so pantingly breathe, like to be? To wit, the spirit shall swallow up the body, as conqueror and more dura-30 ble, and this it shall do with the greater ease because heretofore in its lifetime it had cleansed and thinned it into such another nothing as itself. And then the spirit again shall be wonderfully swallowed up by that highest mind, as being more powerful than its infinite parts, so that the whole man is to be out of himself nor to be otherwise happy in any respect but that, being stripped of himself, he shall have some ineffable portion in that chiefest good that draws all things into itself. And this happiness, 40 though it is only then perfected when souls being joined to their former bodies shall be made immortal, yet forasmuch as the life of holy men is nothing but a continued meditation and, as it were, shadow of that life, it so happens that at length they have some taste or relish of it; which, though it be but as the smallest drop in comparison with that fountain of eternal happiness, yet it far surpasses all worldly delight, though all the pleasures of all mankind were all joined together. So much better are things spir-50 itual than things corporeal, and things invisible than things visible; which doubtless is that which the Prophet promises: "The eye hath not seen, nor the ear heard, nor has it entered into the heart of man to consider what God has provided for them that love Him."

52–55. "The eye hath not . . . that love Him." I Corinthians 2:9.

And therefore they that are sensible of it, and few there are to whom this happens, suffer a kind of thing little differing from madness, for they utter many things that do not hang together, and that too not after the manner of men, but make a kind 60 of sound which they neither heed themselves, nor is it understood by others, and change the whole figure of their countenance, one while jocund, another while dejected, now weeping, then laughing, and again sighing. And when they come to themselves, they tell you they know not where they have been, whether in the body or out of the body, or sleeping; nor do they remember what they have heard, seen, spoken, or done, and only know this, as it were in a mist or dream, that they were the most happy while 70 they were so out of their wits. And therefore they are sorry they are come to themselves again, and desire nothing more than this kind of madness, to be perpetually mad. And this is a small taste of that future happiness.

But I forget myself and run beyond my bounds. Though yet, if I seem to have spoken anything more boldly or impertinently than I ought, be pleased to consider that not only Folly but a woman said it, remembering in the meantime that Greek proverb, 80 "Sometimes a fool may speak a word in season," unless perhaps you'll say this concerns not women. I see you expect an epilogue, but give me leave to tell you you are much mistaken if you think I remember anything of what I have said, having foolishly bolted out such a hodge-podge of words. It is an old proverb, "I hate one that remembers what's done over the cup." This is a new one of my own making: I hate a man that remembers what he hears. Where-fore farewell, clap your hands, live and drink lustily, 90 my most excellent disciples of folly.

Giovanni Boccaccio

1313–1375

The fame of the *Decameron* as a collection of racy stories has given Boccaccio an undeserved notoriety in popular fancy and has obscured his powerful role in shaping Italian Humanism and the early Renaissance. The renowned hundred tales, though they remain his chief contribution to world letters, were an incident of his middle years of which he was not proud in later life. Historians remember him today as the founder of the Greek revival and the serious classical scholar who carried forward the pioneer work of his friend, Petrarch.

Boccaccio's life breaks into two quite distinct periods around his meeting with Petrarch in 1351. His scapegrace youth in the social whirl of Naples belongs to literature. His serious later life as Latin writer and professor belongs to Humanistic scholarship. The illegitimate son of a Florentine merchant by his Parisian mistress, Giovanni was brought to Florence in his childhood at a time when that magnificent city had just begun her leadership in European literature. His father intended him for a business career and apprenticed him to another merchant for six years, despite the boy's total lack of interest in trade. Ignoring Giovanni's passionate desire to write poetry, his father next forced him to study canon law for six years as a means to financial security. A bitter friction developed between father and son, and young Boccaccio neglected his law studies to perfect himself in the poet's craft.

A fit subject for his verses appeared around 1338, when his law studies took him to the gay and dissolute city of Naples, then a center of Italian culture under the enlightened King Robert of Anjou. Immediately infatuated with the brilliant social life of the city, Boccaccio soon fell in love with a beautiful siren named Maria d' Aquino, supposedly the natural daughter of King Robert himself and then the wife of a gentleman of the town. It was not his first affair and certainly not hers. Indeed, so sensual and earthy were both the lovers that Boccaccio's efforts to exalt their relationship to the heights of ideality suggest that he was frankly imitating Dante (with his Beatrice) and Petrarch (with his Laura). Fiammetta, as he called Maria, is transformed by his sonnets into the impossible vision of feminine loveliness long familiar in the verse of the troubadours. Actually, she was a jaded product of a worldly society, who could hardly have been faithful for long to her hot-blooded suitor, but she apparently inspired in him the closest thing to overpowering love of which his nature was capable.

For her he wrote a series of impassioned romances, *Il Filocolo, Teseide, Il Filostrato,* and *La Fiammetta,* in the last of which she appears as heroine, telling how her lover betrayed her (although the case was actually reversed). Even after she had forsaken him, she remained the ideal love of his life and the cause of much spiritual anguish. To her he directed exquisite love poems not far below the sonnets of Petrarch. She was still in his mind as he began the *Decameron* and figures as one of the characters in the frame tale of that work. The memory of his agonized love declined only after he completed the *Decameron* (c. 1353), began his close friendship with Petrarch, and entered upon the second period of his career.

Petrarch, enveloped in the Latin spirit of Humanism, dismissed the Italian *Decameron* as a skit, and Boccaccio's humble admiration for his new master led him to turn from it to the study of antiquity. His great service to the Renaissance lay in his revival of Greek studies. With the aid of a crude, ill-tempered Greek named Leontius Pilatus, he made a prose translation of Homer into Italian and thus restored the ancient master to the modern world. Nor were the industrious studies of his later years confined to the ancients. His deep appreciation of Dante led him to write the earliest life of the medieval poet and to hold the first chair of Dante study in any university. Yet the sedate and learned Boccaccio

of his later years, pursuing his researches in poverty, is a sad substitute for the robust, enthusiastic youth who lived a natural, passionate life in the world. Sustained in time of gloom by his friendship for Petrarch, he still shared his master's belief that he had wasted his youth in living and literature and had squandered his talents on what was actually his masterpiece. This sincere, kindly, and self-effacing man survived his friend by only a year, dying on December 21, 1375.

As its Greek title suggests, the *Decameron* (written 1348–1353) is an account of a ten-day sojourn in the countryside near Florence of ten young people, seven ladies and three gentlemen, to avoid the plague that actually ravaged that city and much of Europe in 1348. Three fifths of the population of Florence had died of it, including Petrarch's Laura and probably Fiammetta, though Boccaccio represents his beloved as one of the gay company who dispelled their memory of the harrowing scenes in the city by banqueting, dancing, playing games, and telling stories. As in the case of the *Arabian Nights* and Chaucer's *Canterbury Tales,* this frame tale is merely a device for bringing together a hundred prose stories which are supposedly told by the ten young people on their ten days in the country. Unlike Chaucer's delightful pilgrims, Boccaccio's storytellers are not individualized or interesting in themselves. But the hundred tales which he collected from many sources introduce a wide variety of characters in situations both serious and gay, both moral and ribald. Though the cynicism bred of his youth in Naples reveals itself in these ribald yarns of faithless wives and unholy churchmen, Boccaccio was not favoring immorality or attacking the church, but holding up the glass, like Erasmus, to human folly and lust. As Dante's *Commedia* toured the world to come, the Decameron explored in frankest terms the world that we know in the flesh. The animal spirits and lusty exuberance underlying it predict the emancipation of human instincts in the Renaissance and the new absorption with man as he is rather than man as he should be. The elegant style, inspired by a study of Cicero's Latin constructions, made this the first great monument of Italian prose and a model throughout the Renaissance.

Decameron

THE THREE RINGS

SALADIN was so brave and great a man, that he had raised himself from an inconsiderable person to be Sultan of Babylon, and had gained many victories over both the Saracen and Christian princes. This monarch having in divers wars, and by many extraordinary expenses, run through all his treasure,

Decameron. An old translation revised by various scholars. Reprinted by permission of Pocket Books, Inc.
The Three Rings. This story was used by Lessing as a plea for tolerance in his play, *Nathan the Wise.*

Melchifedech giudeo con una nouella di tre anella, ceffa un gran perico·
lo da'l Saladino apparecchiatogli.   Nouella   III.

Oi che commēlata da tutti la nouella di Neiphile, ella fi
p   tacque, come alla Reina piacque, Philomena cofi comincio·
a parlare. La nouella di Neiphile detta mi ritorna a me·
moria il dubbiofo cafo gia auenuto ad un giudeo, percio che gia·
& di Dio & della uerita della noſtra fede è affai bene ſtato detto, il
diſcendere hoggimai a glia auenimēti & a gliatti de glihuomini nō
fi douria diſdire, a narrarui quella uerro, laquale udita forfe piu caute
diuerrete nelle rifpoſte alle quiſtioni, che fatte ui foſero. Voi douete
Amorofe compagne fapere che fi come la fciocchezza fpeſe uolte tra·
he altrui di felice ſtato, & mette in grandiſſima miferia, cofi il fenno·
di grandiſſimi pericoli trahe il fauio & ponlo in grande & in fi·
curo ripofo. Et che uero fia, che la fciocchezza di buono ſtato in mife·
ria alcun conduca, per molti exempli fi uede, liquali non fia al pre·
fente noſtra cura di raccontare, hauendo riguardo, che tutto'l di mil·
le exempli n'appaiano manifeſti. Ma che il fenno di confolation fia
cagione, come promifi, per una nouelletta moſterro brieuemente.
Il Saladino, il ualore del qual fu tante, che non folamente di piccolo
huomo!

---

some urgent occasion fell out, that he wanted a large sum of money. Not knowing which way he might raise enough to answer his necessities, he at last called to mind a rich Jew of Alexandria, named Melchizedech, who lent out money on interest. Him he believed to have wherewithal to serve him; but then he was so covetous that he would never do it willingly, and he was unwilling to force him. But as necessity has no law, after much thinking which way the matter might best be effected, he at last resolved to use force under some colour of reason. He therefore sent for and received him in a most gracious manner, and making him sit down, he thus addressed him: "Honest man, I hear from divers persons that thou art very wise, and knowing in religious matters; wherefore I would gladly know from thee which religion thou judgest to be the true one—the Jewish, the Mahometan, or the Christian?" The Jew (truly a wise man) found that Saladin had a mind to trap him; and perceiving that he must gain his point should he prefer any one religion, after considering a little how best to avoid the snare, his invention at last supplied him with the following answer:—

"The question which your highness has proposed is very curious; and, that I may give you my sentiments, I must beg leave to tell a short story. I remember often to have heard of a great and rich man, who, among his most rare and precious jewels, had a ring of exceeding great beauty and value; and being proud of possessing a thing of such worth, and desirous that it should continue for ever in his family, he declared, by will, that to whichsoever of his sons he should give this ring, him he designed for his heir, and that he should be respected as the head of the family. That son to whom the ring was given made the same law with respect to his descendants, and the ring passed from one to another in a long succession, till it came to a person who had three sons, all virtuous and dutiful to their father, and all equally beloved by him. And the young men, knowing what depended upon the ring, and ambitious of superiority, began to entreat their father, who was now growing old, every one for himself, that he would give the ring to him. The good man, equally fond of all, was at a loss which to prefer; and as he had promised all, and being willing to satisfy all, privately got an artist to make two others, which were so like the first that he himself scarcely knew the true one, and at his death gave one privately to each of his sons. They afterwards all claimed the honour and estate, each disputing them with his brothers, and producing his ring; and the rings were found so much alike that the true one could not be distinguished. To law then they went, which should succeed, nor is that yet decided. And thus it has happened, my lord, with regard to the three laws given by God the Father to the three peoples concerning which you proposed your question: every one believes he is the true heir of God, has His law, and obeys His commandments; but which is in the right is uncertain in like manner as of the rings."

Saladin perceived that Melchizedech had escaped the net which was spread for him: he therefore resolved to discover his necessity to him, to see if he would lend him money, telling him at the same time what he designed to have done, had not his discreet answer prevented him. The Jew freely supplied him with what he wanted; Saladin afterwards paid him with a great deal of honour, made him large presents, besides maintaining him nobly at his court, and was his friend as long as he lived.

DON FEDERIGO'S FALCON

At Florence dwelt a young gentleman named Federigo, son of Filippo Alberighi, who, in feats of arms and gentility, surpassed all the youth in Tuscany. This gentleman, as usually happens, fell in love with a lady called Madam Giovanna, one of the most agreeable women in Florence, and, to gain her affection, used to be continually making tilts, balls, and such diversions; lavishing away his money in rich presents, and everything that was extravagant. But she, as careful of her honour as she was fair, made no account either of what he did for her sake or of himself. Living in this manner, his wealth soon began to waste, till at last he had nothing left but a very small farm, the income of which was a most slender maintenance, and a single hawk, one of the best in the world. Yet loving his mistress still more than ever, and finding he could subsist no longer in the city in the manner he would choose to

Don Federigo's Falcon. This famous tale of devotion and self-sacrifice was used by many later authors—La Fontaine, Lope de Vega, Longfellow, and Tennyson.

live, he retired to his farm, where he went out a-fowling, as often as the weather would permit, and bore his distress patiently, and without ever making his necessity known to anybody.

Now, one day it happened that, as he was reduced to the last extremity, this lady's husband, who was very rich, chanced to fall sick, and, feeling the approach of death, made his will, leaving all his substance to an only son, who was almost grown up; and, if he should die without issue, he then ordered that it should revert to his lady, whom he was extremely fond of; and when he had disposed thus of his fortune he died. She now, being left a widow, retired, as our ladies usually do during the summer season, to a house of hers in the country, near to that of Federigo, whence it happened that her son soon became acquainted with him, and they used to divert themselves together with dogs and hawks, when he, having often seen Federigo's hawk fly, and being strangely taken with it, was desirous of having it, though the other valued it to that degree that he knew not how to ask for it. This being so, the lad soon fell sick, which gave his mother great concern, as he was her only child: and she ceased not to attend on and comfort him, often requesting him, if there were any particular thing which he fancied, to let her know it, and promising to procure it for him if it were possible. The young gentleman, after many offers of this kind, at last said, "Madam, if you could contrive for me to have Federigo's hawk, I believe that I should soon be well." She was in some suspense at this, and began to consider how best to act. She knew that Federigo had long entertained a liking for her, without the least encouragement on her part; therefore she said to herself, "How can I send or go to ask for this hawk, which I hear is the very best of the kind, and what alone maintains him in the world? Or how can I offer to take away from a gentleman all the pleasure that he has in life?" Being in this perplexity, though she was very sure of having it for the asking, she stood without making any reply; till at last the love of her son so far prevailed that she resolved at all events to make him easy, and not send, but go herself, to bring it. She then replied, "Son, set your heart at rest, and think only of your recovery; for I promise you that the first thing I do to-morrow morning will be to ask for it, and bring it to you." This afforded him such joy that he immediately showed signs of amendment.

The next morning she went, by way of a walk, with another lady in company, to Federigo's little cottage to inquire for him. At that time, as it was too early to go out upon his diversion, he was at work in his garden. Hearing therefore that his mistress inquired for him at the door, he ran thither, surprised and full of joy; whilst she, with a great

"Man with a Falcon." A painting by Titian.

deal of complaisance, went to meet him; and, after the usual compliments, she said, "Good morning, Federigo; I come to give you some recompense for the trouble you have formerly taken on my account, when your love carried you beyond reasonable bounds: it is in this wise,—I mean to dine with you in a homely way, with this lady, my friend." He replied, with a great deal of humility, "Madam, I do not remember ever to have received any hurt or loss

10 by your means, but rather so much good that if I were worth anything at any time it was due to your singular merit and the love I had for you; and most assuredly this courteous visit is more welcome to me than if I had all that I have wasted returned to me to spend over again; but you are come to a very poor host." With these words he showed her into his house, seeming much out of countenance, and from thence they went into the garden, when, having no company for her, he said, "Madam, as I have nobody

20 else, please to admit this honest woman, a labourer's wife, to be with you, whilst I set forth the table."

He, although his poverty was extreme, was never so sensible of his having been extravagant as now; but finding nothing to entertain the lady with, for whose sake he had treated thousands, he was in the utmost perplexity, cursing his evil fortune and running up and down like one out of his wits. At length, having neither money nor anything he could pawn, and being willing to treat her as honourably as he

30 could, at the same time that he would not make his case known, even so much as to his own labourer,

he espied his hawk upon the perch, which he seized, and finding it very fat, judged it might make a dish not unworthy of such a lady. Without further thought, then, he twisted its neck, and gave it to a girl to truss and roast carefully, whilst he laid the cloth and the napkins, having a small quantity of linen yet left; and then he returned, with a smile on his countenance, into the garden, telling her that what little dinner he was able to provide was now 40 ready. She and her friend, therefore, entered and sat down with him, he serving them all the time with great respect, when they ate the hawk. After dinner was over, and they had sat chattering a little together, she thought it a fit time to tell her errand, and she spoke to him courteously in this manner:—

"Sir, if you call to mind your past life, and my resolution, which perhaps you may call cruelty, I doubt not but you will wonder at my presumption, when you know what I am come for: if you had 50 children of your own, whereby you might understand how strong our natural affection is towards them, I am very sure you would excuse me. But, though you have none, I who have am bound by the natural laws of maternity, the force of which is greater than my own will, and indeed my duty: I am therefore constrained to request a thing of you which I know you value extremely, as you have no other comfort or diversion left in the extremity of your fortunes; I mean your hawk, which my son has 60 taken such a fancy to that unless I bring him back with me I very much fear that he will die of his disorder. Therefore I entreat you, not for any regard you have for me (for in that respect you are no way obliged to me), but for that generosity with which you have always distinguished yourself, that you would please to let me have him, by which means you will save my child's life, and lay him under perpetual obligations."

Federigo, hearing the lady's request, and know- 70 ing it was out of his power to serve her, began to weep before he was able to make a word of reply. This she first thought was his great concern to part with his favourite bird, and she was about to say that she would not accept it; but she restrained herself, and awaited his reply when he should become more composed. At last he said, "Madam, ever since I have fixed my affections upon you, Fortune has still been contrary to me in many things, and I have often complained of her treatment; but her former 80 harshness has been light and easy compared with what I now endure, which banishes all my peace of mind. You are here to visit me in this my poor mansion, whither in my prosperity you would never deign to come; you also entreat a small present from me, which it is no way in my power to give, as I am going briefly to tell you. As soon as I was acquainted with the great favour you designed me, I thought it proper, considering your superior merit and excellency, to treat you, according to my ability, with something more choice and valuable than is usually given to other persons, when, calling to mind my hawk, which you now request, and his goodness, I judged him a fit repast for you, and you have had him served roasted on your dish. Nor could I have thought him better bestowed, had you not now desired him in a different manner, which is such a grief to me that I shall never be at peace as long as I live;" and upon saying this he produced his feathers, feet, and beak. She began now to blame him for killing such a bird to entertain any woman with, inwardly praising the greatness of his soul, which poverty had no power to abase. Thus, having no farther hopes of obtaining the hawk, she thanked him for the respect and good-will he had showed towards her, and returned full of concern to her son, who, either out of grief for the disappointment or through the violence of his disorder, died within a few days.

She continued sorrowful for some time; but, being left rich and young, her brothers were very pressing with her to marry again; and, though this were against her inclinations, yet, finding them still importunate, and remembering Federigo's great worth and the late instance of his generosity in killing such a bird for her entertainment, she said, "I should rather choose to continue as I am; but, since it is your desire that I take a husband, I will have none save Federigo degli Alberighi." They smiled contemptuously at this, and said, "You simple woman! what are you talking of? He is not worth one farthing in the world." She replied, "I believe it, brothers, to be as you say; but know that I would sooner have a man that stands in need of riches, than riches without a man." They, hearing her resolution, and well knowing his generous temper, gave her to him with all her wealth; and he, seeing himself possessed of a lady whom he had so dearly loved, and such a large fortune, lived in all true happiness with her, and was a better manager of his affairs for the time to come.

FRIAR ONION AND THE RELICS OF THE ANGEL GABRIEL

FOLLOWING your footsteps, I shall show you with what a sudden shift a certain friar, of the order of Saint Antony, most artfully avoided the disgrace which two arch young fellows had prepared for him: and if, to make my story more complete, I spin it out a little in length, I hope it will not be disagreeable, as the sun is yet in the midst of heaven.

Certaldo, as you have all heard, is a village in the vale of Elsa, dependent on the state of Florence;

and, though small, was formerly inhabited by many gentlemen and people of substance. Thither a certain friar, known as Friar Onion, of the order of Saint Antony, used to go once a year, as he found pretty good pickings, to receive the contributions of many simple people, and met with great encouragement always—perhaps not through any devotion so much as his name, for that country was famous for the best onions in all Tuscany. Now this friar had a little low person, was red-haired and of a merry countenance, as artful a knave too as any in the world: add to this that, though he was no scholar, yet was he so prompt and voluble of tongue that such as knew him not would not only have considered him as some great orator, but have compared him even to Tully or Quintillian, and yet was he a common gossip-acquaintance to the whole neighborhood.

Coming thither, therefore, in the month of August, according to custom, one Sunday morning, when all the honest people were met together in the principal church to hear mass, as soon as he saw a fit opportunity, he stepped forward and said:—

"Gentlemen and ladies, you know it has been a commendable custom with you to send every year, to the poor brethren of our lord baron Saint Antony, both of your corn and other provisions, some more and some less, according to your several abilities and devotions, to the end that our blessed Saint Antony should be more careful of your oxen, sheep, asses, swine, and other cattle. Moreover, you are accustomed to pay, such especially as have their names registered in our fraternity, those small dues which are paid only once a year, to collect which I am now sent by my superior, namely, our lord abbot. Therefore, with the blessing of God, after twelve o'clock, as soon as you shall hear the bells ring, you may all come to the church-door, when I shall preach a sermon as usual, and you shall all kiss the cross: and, besides this, as I know you all to be devoted to our lord Saint Antony, I intend to show you by special grace a very fair and holy relic, which I myself brought from the Holy Land, that is to say, one of the feathers of the Angel Gabriel, which he dropped at the Annunciation in the Virgin's chamber at Nazareth;" and, having made this speech, he returned to mass.

Whilst he was haranguing upon this subject, there were two arch fellows in the church, one named Giovanni del Bragoniera, and the other Biagio Pizzini, who, after they had laughed together at the father's relics, although they were his friends and acquaintance, resolved to play him a trick with regard to this feather; and, understanding that he was to dine that day with a friend, as soon as they thought he might be set down at table they went to the inn where he lodged, where Biagio was to keep his man in talk, whilst Giovanni ransacked his wallet to steal this feather, that they might see what he would then say to the people.

Now the friar had a lad called by many nicknames —Guccio Balena, Guccio Imbratta, and sometimes Guccio Porco; and even the celebrated Lipotopo could hardly have caricatured his figure; but Father Onion used frequently to say in jest, "My rascal has in him nine qualities, if any one of which belonged either to Solomon, Aristotle, or Seneca, it would baffle and confound all their philosophy, and all their virtue. You may suppose then what sort of creature he must be that has nine such, without either philosophy or virtue to counterbalance." Being asked what those nine qualities were, and having put them into a kind of rhyme, he answered,

"Forgetfulness, lying, and lewdness;
Filching, facing, and nastiness;
Sloth, gracelessness, and worthlessness.

Besides these, he has also many others, and one in particular I cannot help laughing at, which is, that he is for taking a wife and a lodging wherever he goes; and, having a great black greasy beard, he is persuaded that all women must fall in love with him; or, should they take no notice of him, he will burst his belt in running after them. But yet he is a notable fellow to me in one respect, that if anybody has a secret to communicate, he will come in for his share of it; and, should any one ask me a question, he is so fearful that I should not know how to make an answer that he will be sure to say Yes or No before me, just as he thinks most proper."

But to return to our story. This worthy fellow Friar Onion left at the inn, with a particular charge to see that nobody meddled with anything belonging to him, especially his wallet, because the holy relics were contained therein. But the man, whose inclinations stood more for the kitchen than the birds for the branches, and especially if he knew some serving-maid were there, as soon as his master was gone went down thither, where he found a fat, dirty, big-breasted wench, with a face of the Baronci stamp, greasy and grimy, as attractive to him as carrion to a vulture. So, leaving his master's door open, and his things scattered about, and falling into discourse with her, he sat down by the fireside, though it was in August, whilst she was busy in cooking, and began to tell her he was a gentleman who was worth an incredible sum of money, and owed as much more; that he could do and say wonders; and (without considering that his own hat was all over grease and dirt, that his jacket was nothing but a thousand different patches, that his breeches were torn throughout, and his shoes all to pieces) he talked as finely as if he had been some lord, saying that he would buy her new clothes, and take her out of service, and that she should partake of his present posses-

sions, as well as future fortunes, with a great deal more of that kind of stuff, mere froth and wind.

The two young fellows, finding him thus engaged, were very well satisfied, supposing half their work to be done; and, leaving them together, they went upstairs into the friar's chamber, which, thanks to the servant, was open, when the first thing they saw was the wallet: this they opened, and found a cabinet wrapped up in some foldings of fine taffeta, in which was a parroquet's feather, which they supposed to be the same that he had promised to show the people; and surely at that time it was easy enough to impose upon them in that manner, for the vices which have since come from Egypt, and overspread all Italy, had not yet reached them; the ancient simplicity still prevailed, nor was there a person that, so far from seeing, had ever heard of such a thing as a parrot. Not a little pleased at meeting with this feather, they took it away, and, that the box should not be empty, put some coals therein, which they saw lying in a corner of the chamber; and wrapping it up again as before, and making all safe, they walked off, waiting to see how he would behave when he found the coals instead of the feather. The people that were at church, being told that they were to see the Angel Gabriel's feather, went home and acquainted all their neighbours, and the news ran from one to another, so that the moment dinner was over they all crowded to the town, in such manner that every part was full, waiting for the sight.

Accordingly, Friar Onion, having eaten a good dinner and swallowed his wine, and taken his nap, understanding now that there were great multitudes expecting him, sent to the servant to come away with his wallet, and ring to church. The fellow, though loth to leave his mistress and the fireside, did as he ordered him, and fell to chiming the bells. As soon then as the people were all assembled, the friar, not perceiving that anything had been meddled with, entered upon his discourse, running over a thousand things proper to his purpose; and being come to the showing of the feather, he began with a solemn confession, and lighting up two torches, and gently unwrapping the silken cover, having first pulled off his cap, he took out the box, and, making some short ejaculations to the praise and honour of the Angel Gabriel and of that relic, he opened it, when, seeing it full of coals, he could not help secretly blaming himself for leaving such a fellow in trust, who, he imagined, had been imposed upon by somebody or other; but yet, without so much as changing colour, or showing the least concern, he lifted up his eyes and hands to heaven, and said, "O God, blessed for ever be Thy power and might!" Then shutting the box, he turned again to the people, and added—

"Gentlemen and ladies, you must all understand

that, being very young, I was sent by my superior to those parts where the sun first appears, with an express command to inquire into the nature of porcelain, which, though it cost but little in making, affords more profit to others than it does to us. For this purpose I embarked at Venice, and went through the town of Greece; I proceeded thence on horseback through the kingdom of Garbo, and through Baldacca; afterwards I came to Parione, and so to Sardinia. But wherefore need I mention to you all these places? I coasted on still, till I passed the straits of Saint George, into Truffia, and then into Buffia, which are countries much inhabited, and with great people. From thence into the land of Menzogna, where I found many of our order, as well as of other religious, who avoid all labour and trouble, for Heaven's sake, taking no care for other people's sufferings, when their own interest is promoted thereby, and where they spend only uncoined money. Thence I went to the land of Abruzzi, where the men and women go on pattens over the mountains, clothing the swine in their own guts, and in the neighbouring country they carried bread in their staves, and wine in satchels. Parting from thence, I came to the mountains of Bacchus, where the waters all run down hill. Last of all, I arrived in India Pastinaca; where, I swear to you, by the habit I wear, that I saw serpents fly, a thing incredible to such as have never seen it: but, if you doubt the truth of this, ask Maso del Saggio, a great merchant, whom I found cracking nuts, and selling the shells by retail. Nevertheless, not being able to find what I went to look for, and being to pass from thence by water, I returned to the Holy Land, where, in the year of summer, a loaf of cold bread is worth fourpence, and the hot is given away for nothing. There I found the venerable father Blame-me-not-pray, the patriarch of Jerusalem, who, out of reverence to my habit, and love to our lord baron Saint Antony, would have me see all the holy relics which he had in keeping, and which were so many, that were I to recount them, I should never come to an end; but yet, not to leave you altogether disconsolate, I shall mention a few. First, then, he showed me a finger of the Holy Ghost, as whole and perfect as ever; next the muzzle of that seraph which appeared to Saint Francis; with one of the nails of a cherub; also a rib of the Verbum Caro, fastened to one of the windows; some fragments of the vestments of the Holy Catholic Faith; and a few rays of that star which appeared to the three kings who came out of the East; a phial also of Saint Michael's sweat, when he fought with the devil; the jaw-bone of Saint Lazarus, and many others. And because I gave him two of the plains of Mount Morello, in the vulgar edition, and some chapters of Del Caprezio, which he had been long searching after, he let me partake

of his relics. And, first, he gave me a tooth of the Holy Cross; and a little bottle filled with some of the sound of those bells which hung in the Temple of Solomon; a feather also of the Angel Gabriel, as I have told you; with a wooden patten, which the good Saint Gherardo da Villa Magna used to wear in his travels, and which I have lately given to Gherardo di Bonsi, at Florence, who holds it in great veneration. He farther gave me some of the coals on which our blessed martyr, Saint Laurence, was broiled, all which I devoutly received, and do now possess. It is true, my superior would not suffer me to make them public till he was assured that they were genuine; but being now convinced of it by sundry miracles, as well as by letters received from the patriarch, he has given me leave to show them; and these, for fear of trusting any one with them, I always carry with me. Indeed, I have the angel's feather, for its better preservation, in a wooden box, and I have Saint Laurence's coals in another, and these boxes are so like each other, that I have often mistaken them; and so it has happened now, for instead of that with the feather, I have brought the one which contains the coals. This I would not have you call an error; no, I am well assured it was Heaven's particular will, now I call to mind that two days hence is the feast of Saint Laurence. Therefore it was ordered that I should show you the most holy coals on which he was broiled, extinguished by the moisture of his holy body, to kindle in your hearts that true devotion which you ought to have towards him, and not the feather. Approach then, my blessed children, with reverence, and uncover your heads with all due devotion, whilst you behold them. But first I must acquaint you, that whoever is marked with these coals with the sign of the cross may live secure for one whole year that, unless he feel it, no fire shall have any power over him."

So, singing a hymn to the praise of Saint Laurence, he opened the box and showed the coals, which the simple multitude beheld with the utmost zeal and astonishment, and crowded about him with larger offerings than usual, entreating to be signed by them. Then taking the coals in his hand, he began to mark all their white mantles, fine jackets, and veils, with the largest crosses that could be made upon them, affirming that what was consumed of the coals in this manner grew again in the box, as he had frequently experienced. Thus having crossed all the people of Certaldo to his own great benefit, by this dexterous device, he laughed in his sleeve at those who had designed to have made a jest of him. And they being present at his discourse, and hearing this sudden shift of his, and how he had set it off to the multitude, were ready to die with laughter. After the people were all departed, they went and told him, with all the pleasure in the world, what they had done, and returned him his feather, which served him the following year to as good purpose as the coals had done that day.

THE CRADLE

IN the plain of Mugnone, not long since, lived an honest man who kept a little inn for the entertainment of travellers, serving them with meat and drink for their money, but seldom lodging any, unless they were his particular acquaintance. Now, he had a wife, a good comely woman, by whom he had two children, the one an infant, not yet weaned, and the other a pretty girl of about fifteen or sixteen years of age, but unmarried, who had taken the fancy of a young gentleman of our city, one who used to travel much that way; whilst she, proud of such a lover, and endeavouring, by her agreeable carriage, to preserve his good opinion, soon felt the same liking for him: which love of theirs would several times have taken effect, to the desire of both, had not Pinuccio—for that was the young gentleman's name—carefully avoided it, for her credit as well as his own. Till at last, his love growing every day more fervent, he resolved, in order to gain his point, to lie all night at her father's house, judging that the matter might then be effected without any one's privity. Accordingly he let into the secret a friend of his, named Adriano, who had been acquainted with his love; so they hired a couple of horses one evening, and having their portmanteaus behind them, filled with things of no moment, they set out from Florence, and, after taking a circuit, came, as it grew late, to the plain of Mugnone; then turning their horses, as if they had come from Romagna, they rode on to this cottage, and knocking at the door, the landlord, who was always very diligent in waiting upon his guests, immediately went and opened it. Pinuccio then accosted him, and said, "Honest landlord, we must beg the favour of a night's lodging, for we had designed to reach Florence, but have so mistaken that it is now much too late, as you see." The host replied, "Sir, you know very well how ill I can accommodate such gentlemen as yourselves; but, as you are come in at an unseasonable hour, and there is no time for your travelling any farther, I will entertain you as well as I can." So they dismounted, and went into the house, having first taken care of their horses; and, as they had provision along with them, they sat down and invited their host to sup with them.

Now there was only one little chamber in the house, which had three beds in it—namely, two at one end, and the third at the other, opposite to them, with just room to go between. The least bad

The Cradle. This amusing *falliau* was used by Chaucer for his *Reeve's Tale.*

and incommodious of the three the landlord ordered to be prepared for these two gentlemen, and put them to bed. A little time afterwards, neither of them being asleep, though they pretended it, he made his daughter lie in one of the beds that remained, and he and his wife went into the other, whilst she set the cradle with the child by her bedside. Things being so disposed, and Pinuccio having made an exact observation of every particular, as soon as he thought it a proper time, and that every one was asleep, he arose, and went softly to the bed of the daughter, and lay down beside her, she, though very fearful, receiving him joyfully, and so they took what pastime they pleased. In the meantime, a cat happened to throw something down in the house, which awakened the wife, who, fearing it was something else, got up in the dark, and went to find the cause of the noise. Adriano now rose by chance, upon a particular occasion, and finding the cradle in his way, he removed it, without any design, nearer to his own bed, and, having done what he rose for, went to bed again, without putting the cradle in its place. The good woman, finding what was thrown down to be of no moment, never troubled herself to strike a light, to see farther about it, but having driven away the cat, returned to the bed where her husband lay; and, not finding the cradle, "Bless me," she said to herself, "I had like to have made a strange mistake, and gone to bed to my guests!" Going farther then, and finding the cradle, which stood by Adriano, she stepped into bed to him, thinking it had been her husband. He was awake, and treated her very kindly, without saying a word all the time to undeceive her.

At length Pinuccio, fearing lest he should fall asleep, and so be surprised with his mistress, after having made the best use of his time, left her to return to his own bed, when meeting with the cradle, and supposing that was the host's bed, he went farther, and stepped into the host's bed indeed, who immediately awoke. Pinuccio, thinking it was his friend, said to him, "Surely, nothing was ever so sweet as Niccolosa; never man was so blessed as I have been with her; I can assure you that since I left you I have been well employed." The host, hearing this, and not liking it over well, said first to himself, "What the devil does this man mean?" Afterwards, being more passionate than wise, he cried out, "Thou art the greatest of villains to use me in that manner; but I vow to God I will pay thee for it." Pinuccio, who was none of the sharpest men in the world, seeing his mistake, without ever thinking how to amend it, as he might have done, replied, "You pay me? What can you do?" The hostess, imagining that she had been with her husband, said to Adriano, "Alas! dost thou hear our guests? What do they talk of?" He replied, with a laugh, "Let them talk as they will, and be hanged; they drank too much, I suppose, last night."

The woman now distinguishing her husband's voice, and hearing Adriano, soon knew where she was, and with whom. Therefore she very wisely got up, without saying a word, and removed the cradle, though there was no light in the chamber, as near as she could guess to her daughter's bed, and crept in to her; when, seeming as if she had been awakened by her husband's noise, she called out to him, to know what was the matter with him and the gentleman. The husband replied, "Do not you hear what he says he has been doing to-night with our daughter?" "He lies in his throat," quoth she; "for he was never in bed with her; it was I, and I assure you I have never closed my eyes since; you are a great fool to think otherwise. You drink to that degree in the evening that you rave all night long, and walk up and down, without knowing anything of the matter, and think you do wonders; it is a pity that you do not break your neck. But what is Pinuccio doing there? why is he not in his own bed?" Adriano, on the other side, perceiving that the good woman had found a very artful evasion both for herself and daughter, said, "Pinuccio, I have told you a hundred times that you should never lie out of your own house; for that great failing of yours, of walking in your sleep and telling your dreams for truth, will be of ill consequence to you some time or other. Come here, then, to your own bed." The landlord hearing what his wife said, and what Adriano had just been speaking, began to think Pinuccio was really dreaming; so he got up and shook him by the shoulders to rouse him, saying, "Awake, and get thee to thine own bed."

Pinuccio, understanding what had passed, began now to ramble in his talk, like a man that was half asleep and dreaming, with which our host made himself vastly merry. At last when daylight came he seemed to awake, after much ado; and, calling to Adriano, he said, "Is it day? what do you wake me for?" "Yes, it is," quoth he; "pray come hither." Then, pretending to be very sleepy, he got up at last, and went to Adriano. And in the morning the landlord laughed very heartily, and was full of jokes about him and his dreams. So they passed from one merry subject to another, whilst their horses were getting ready, and their portmanteaus trussed up, when, taking the host's parting cup, they mounted and went to Florence, no less pleased with the manner in which the thing had happened than the way in which it had been effected.

Afterwards Pinuccio found other means of being with Niccolosa, who still affirmed to her mother that he had been asleep; whilst she, remembering how well she had fared with Adriano, thought herself the only person that had been awake on that occasion.

François Rabelais

c. 1495–1553

The Humanist emancipation of the natural man reaches its climax in the turbulent career, lawless writings, and militant individualism of Rabelais. His life story is one of continuous rebellion against the intellectual restraints of the Middle Ages, as he had known them through church schooling and a restless preparation for the clergy. The youngest son of an apothecary (or possibly an innkeeper), he chose a church career as almost the only one open to a poor boy with a keen desire for education. But his years at the Franciscan monastery of Fontenoy le Comte, where the monks, following the example of St. Francis, frowned upon learning as incompatible with humility, gave him a savage hatred of the order, and he was severely punished for secretly pursuing classical studies, especially Greek. When a powerful friend persuaded the Pope to transfer him to the more liberal Benedictine order, he still chafed under the monastic discipline and eventually freed himself from it entirely to become a secular priest.

His private studies went beyond the ancient classics to medicine, so that after six weeks of official work at the University of Montpellier he secured his medical degree in 1530 and became a lecturer on anatomy. Two years later he published Latin translations of the Greek textbooks on medicine by Hippocrates and Galen. But he neglected his duties on the medical faculty and was dismissed for absence without leave when he accompanied his friend, Jean du Bellay, on a political mission to Rome. He served as city physician in both Lyons and Metz, but apparently was dismissed from both jobs for irresponsibility and had to seek financial aid from Du Bellay, his patron. Eventually, perhaps because he needed funds to support an illegitimate son, he became a parish priest at Meudon, but he was as negligent here as he had been in his medical positions. Rabelais was much too reckless and carefree to submit to professional routine. Throughout his life he demanded complete freedom to pursue his whims and current enthusiasms. No other writer illustrates so well the lusty individualism of the Renaissance. He is said to have made his will in the form of a joke: "I possess nothing; the rest I give to the poor." He died drunk, and his last words were "Draw the curtain; the farce is ended."

But the legend of the great scoffer and laugher that has given the word "rabelaisian" to our language springs from his one important literary work, the huge extravaganza called *Gargantua and Pantagruel*, which he scribbled at odd hours during two stays at Montpellier, perhaps to repay the printer with a broadly popular book for his losses on the translations of Hippocrates and Galen. The result is a unique work, a kind of nonsense novel which half conceals its satire of medieval institutions, especially ecclesiastical education, monastic orders, and feudal wars, under a cloak of ribald fun and personal eccentricity. Like *Tristram Shandy* in a later age, it gushes forth the pranks and prejudices of a literary scalawag, without plan or even connected story. Although it purports to tell the lives of two great giants, father and son, the Pantagruel part was written before the first part, and the careers of the two genial monsters are merely a framework for Rabelais's whimsical learning, playful hoaxes, lists of nonsensical epithets, coarse profanity, parodies, and biting satire. Everything that interested this intense and reckless fellow turns up in his rambling narrative, linked together by a free association of ideas on the conversational level.

Certain characters stand out—the kindly Gargantua, inspired by a gigantic character in French Arthurian story, the benign Grandgousier who is forced into a senseless war with the foolishly arrogant Picrochole, the fighting Friar John of the Choppers, and the cunning, debauched buffoon Panurge, whose search for enlightenment about marriage is the chief theme of the last section. Through all the reckless humor of the piece runs Rabelais's boundless faith in human nature. It lies behind his satiric attack on the stultifying discipline of medieval education and motivates his account of the Abbey of Theleme, an ideal monastery devoted to Humanistic learning, where, instead of the usual monastic restrictions, the only rule is "Do what you want to." Read as a whole, *Gargantua and Pantagruel* is too strong and heaping a dish for modern taste, but the great passages conceal in rollicking, hearty fun a roughly noble plea for the dignity of man.

Gargantua and Pantagruel

BOOK ONE

THE AUTHOR'S PROLOGUE

Most noble and illustrious drinkers, and you thrice precious pockified blades, (for to you, and none else do I dedicate my writings,) Alcibiades, in that dialogue of Plato's, which is entitled, *The Banquet,* whilst he was setting forth the praises of his schoolmaster, Socrates, (without all question the prince of philosophers,) amongst other discourses to that purpose said, that he resembled the Sileni. Sileni of old were little boxes, like those we now may see in the shops of apothecaries, painted on the outside with wanton toyish figures, as harpies, satyrs, bridled geese, horned hares, saddled ducks, flying goats, thiller harts, and other such counterfeited pictures, at pleasure, to excite people unto laughter, as Silenus himself, who was the foster-father of good Bacchus, was wont to do; but

*Gargantua and Pantagruel.*ᴬ Translated by Sir Thomas Urquhart.

within those capricious caskets called Sileni, were carefully preserved and kept many rich and fine drugs, such as balm, ambergreese, amomon, musk, civet, with several kinds of precious stones, and other things of great price. Just such another thing was Socrates: for to have eyed his outside, and esteemed of him by his exterior appearance, you would not have given the peel of an onion for him, so deformed he was in body, and ridiculous in his gesture. He had a sharp pointed nose, with the look of a bull, and countenance of a fool; he was in his carriage simple, boorish in his apparel, in fortune poor, unhappy in his wives, unfit for all offices in the commonwealth, always laughing, tippling, and merry, carousing to every one, with continual gibes and jeers, the better by those means to conceal his divine knowledge. Now, opening this box you would have found within it a heavenly and inestimable drug, a more than human understanding, an admirable virtue, matchless learning, invincible courage, inimitable sobriety, certain contentment of mind, perfect assurance, and an incredible disregard of all that for which men commonly do so much watch, run, sail, fight, travel, toil, and turmoil themselves.

Whereunto (in your opinion) doth this little flourish of a preamble tend? For so much as you, my good disciples, and some other jolly fools of ease and leisure, reading the pleasant titles of some books, of our invention, as Gargantua, Pantagruel, Whippot, the Dignity of Codpieces, of Pease and Bacon, with a commentary, &c., are too ready to judge, that there is nothing in them but jests, mockeries, lascivious discourse, and recreative lies; because the outside (which is the title) is usually, without any farther inquiry, entertained with scoffing and derision. But truly it is very unbeseeming to make so slight account of the works of men, seeing yourselves avouch that it is not the habit that makes the monk, many being monasterially accoutred, who inwardly are nothing less than monachal; and that there are of those that wear Spanish caps, who have but little of the valour of Spaniards in them. Therefore is it, that you must open the book, and seriously consider of the matter treated in it. Then shall you find that it containeth things of far higher value than the box did promise; that is to say, that the subject thereof is not so foolish, as by the title at the first sight it would appear to be.

And put the case, that in the literal sense you meet with purposes merry and solacious enough, and consequently very correspondent to their inscriptions, yet must not you stop there as at the melody of the charming Syrens, but endeavour to interpret that in a sublimer sense, which possibly you intended to have spoken in the jollity of your heart. Did you ever pick the lock of a cupboard to steal a bottle of wine out of it? Tell me truly, and, if you did, call to mind the countenance which then you had. Or, did you ever see a dog with a marrow-bone in his mouth,—the beast of all others, says Plato, lib. 2, de Republica, the most philosophical? If you have seen him, you might have remarked with what devotion and circumspectness he wards and watcheth it: with what care he keeps it: how fervently he holds it: how prudently he gobbets it: with what affection he breaks it: and with what diligence he sucks it. To what end all this? What moveth him to take all these pains? What are the hopes of his labour? What doth he expect to reap thereby? Nothing but a little marrow. True it is, that this little is more savoury and delicious than the great quantities of other sorts of meat, because the marrow, (as Galen testifieth, 3, facult. nat. and 11, de usu partium) is a nourishment most perfectly elaboured by nature.

In imitation of this dog, it becomes you to be wise to smell, feel, and have in estimation, these fair, goodly books, stuffed with high conceptions, which though seemingly easy in the pursuit, are in the cope and encounter somewhat difficult. And then, like him, you must, by a sedulous lecture, and frequent meditation, break the bone, and suck out the marrow; that is, my allegorical sense, or the things I to myself propose to be signified by these Pythagorical symbols; with assured hope, that in so doing, you will at last attain to be both well-advised and valiant by the reading of them: for, in the perusal of this treatise, you shall find another kind of taste, and a doctrine of a more profound and abstruse consideration, which will disclose unto you the most glorious doctrines and dreadful mysteries, as well in what concerneth our religion, as matters of the public state and life economical.

Do you believe, upon your conscience, that Homer, whilst he was couching his Iliads and Odysses, had any thought upon those allegories, which Plutarch, Heraclides, Ponticus, Eustathius, Cornutus, squeezed out of him, and which Politian filched again from them? If you trust it, with neither hand nor foot do you come near to my opinion, which judgeth them to have been as little dreamed of by Homer, as the gospel sacraments were by Ovid, in his Metamorphosis; though a certain gulligut friar, and true bacon-picker would have undertaken to prove it, if, perhaps, he had met with as very fools as himself, and as the proverb says, "a lid worthy of such a kettle."

If you give any credit thereto, why do not you the same to these jovial new Chronicles of mine? Albeit, when I did dictate them, I thought thereof no more than you, who possibly were drinking the whilst, as I was. For in the composing of this lordly book, I never lost nor bestowed any more, nor any other time, than what was appointed to serve me for taking of my bodily refection, that is, whilst I was eating and drinking. And, indeed, that is the fittest and most proper hour, wherein to write these high matters and deep sentences: as Homer knew very well, the paragon of all philologues, and Ennius, the father of the Latin poets, as Horace calls him, although a certain sneaking jobbernol alleged that his verses smelled more of the wine than oil.

So saith a Turlupin or a new start-up grub of my books; but a turd for him. The fragrant odour of the wine, oh! how much more dainty, pleasant, laughing, celestial, and delicious it is, than that smell of oil! and I will glory as much when it is said of me, that I have spent more on wine than oil, as did Demosthenes, when it was told him, that his expense on oil was greater than on wine. I truly hold it for an honour and praise to be called and reputed a frolic Gaulter and a Robin Goodfellow; for under this name am I welcome in all choice companies of Pantagruelists. It was upbraided to Demosthenes, by an envious, surly knave, that his Orations did smell like the sarpler, or wrapper of a foul and filthy oil vessel. For this cause interpret you all my deeds and sayings, in the perfectest sense; reverence the cheese-like brain that feeds you with these faire billevezees, and trifling jollities, and do what lies in you to keep me always merry. Be frolic now, my lads, cheer up your hearts, and joyfully read the rest, with all the ease of your body and profit of your reins. But hearken, joltheads, you viedazes, or dickens take ye, remember to drink a health to me for the favour again, and I will pledge you instantly, Tout ares-metys.

CHAPTER VII

After what manner Gargantua had his name given him, and how he tippled, bibbed, and curried the can

The good man Grangousier, drinking and making merry with the rest, heard the horrible noise which his son had made as he entered into the light of this world, when he cried out, Some drink, some drink, some drink; whereupon he said in French, Que *grand tu as* et souple le gousier! that is to say, How great and nimble a throat thou hast. Which the company hearing said, that verily the child ought to be called Gargantua; because it was the first word that after his birth his father had spoke, in imitation,

---

16. **Galen,** the Greek physician and philosopher (131–201).   40. **Ponticus,** a philosopher of the first century B.C., author of a treatise on Homer.   **Eustathius,** twelfth-century author of a commentary on Homer.   **Cornutus,** a Stoic philosopher of the first century A.D.   41. **Politian,** Angelo Poliziano (1454–1494), the Italian humanist.

66. **Turlupin,** French for a bad punster.   75. **Gaulter,** good companion.   89–90. **Tout ares-metys,** at once.

and at the example, of the ancient Hebrews; whereunto he condescended, and his mother was very well pleased therewith. In the mean while, to quiet the child, they gave him to drink a tirelarigot, that is, till his throat was like to crack with it; then was he carried to the font, and there baptized, according to the manner of good Christians.

Immediately thereafter were appointed for him seventeen thousand nine hundred and thirteen cows
10 of the towns of Pautille and Brehemond, to furnish him with milk in ordinary, for it was impossible to find a nurse sufficient for him in all the country; considering the great quantity of milk that was requisite for his nourishment; although there were not wanting some doctors of the opinion of Scotus, who affirmed that his own mother gave him suck, and that she could draw out of her breasts one thousand four hundred two pipes, and nine pails of milk at every time.

20 Which indeed is not probable, and this point hath been found duggishly scandalous and offensive to tender ears, for that it savoured a little of heresy. Thus was he·handled for one year and ten months; after which time, by the advice of physicians, they began to carry him, and then was made for him a fine little cart drawn with oxen, of the invention of Jan Denio, wherein they led him hither and thither with great joy; and he was worth the seeing, for he was a fine boy, had a burly physiognomy, and almost
30 ten chins. . . . If he happened to be vexed, angry, displeased, or sorry, if he did fret, if he did weep, if he did cry, and what grievous quarter soever he kept, in bringing him some drink, he would be instantly pacified, reseated in his own temper, in a good humour again, and as still and quiet as ever. One of his governesses told me (swearing by her fig), how he was so accustomed to this kind of way, that, at the sound of pints and flagons, he would on a sudden fall into an ecstasy, as if he had then tasted
40 of the joys of paradise; so that they, upon consideration of this, his divine complexion, would every morning, to cheer him up, play with a knife upon the glasses, on the bottles with their stopples, and on the pottle-pots with their lids and covers, at the sound whereof he became gay, did leap for joy, would loll and rock himself in the cradle, then nod with his head, monocordising with his fingers, and barytonising with his tail.

CHAPTER XII

Of Gargantua's Wooden Horses

Afterwards, that he might be all his lifetime a good
50 rider, they made to him a fair great horse of wood, which he did make leap, curvet, yerk out behind,

15. **Scotus,** the Scottish scholastic theologian of the thirteenth century.

and skip forward, all at a time: to pace, trot, rack, gallop, amble, to play the hobby, the hackney gelding: go the gate of the camel, and of the wild ass. He made him also change his colour of hair, as the Monks of Coultibo (according to the variety of their holidays) use to do their clothes, from bay brown, to sorrel, daple-grey, mouse-dun, deer-colour, roan, cow-colour, gin-gioline, skued colour, piebald, and the colour of the savage elk. 60

Himself of a huge big post made a hunting nag, and another for daily service of the beam of a winepress: and of a great oak made up a mule, with a foot-cloth, for his chamber. Besides this, he had ten or twelve spare horses, and seven horses for post; and all these were lodged in his own chamber, close by his bed-side. One day the Lord of Breadinbag came to visit his father in great bravery, and with a gallant train: and at the same time, to see him, came likewise the Duke of Freemeale, and the Earl of 70 Wetgullet. The house truly for so many guests at once was somewhat narrow, but especially the stables; whereupon the steward and harbinger of the said Lord Breadinbag, to know if there were any other empty stable in the house, came to Gargantua, a little young lad, and secretly asked him where the stables of the great horses were, thinking that children would be ready to tell all. Then he led them up along the stairs of the castle, passing by the second hall unto a broad great gallery, by which they en- 80 tered into a large tower, and as they were going up at another pair of stairs, said the harbinger to the steward,—This child deceives us, for the stables are never on the top of the house. You may be mistaken, said the steward, for I know some places at Lyons, at the Basmette, at Chaisnon, and elsewhere, which have their stables at the very tops of the houses; so it may be, that behind the house there is a way to come to this ascent. But I will question with him further. Then said he to Gargantua, my pretty little 90 boy, whither do you lead us? To the stable, said he, of my great horses. We are almost come to it, we have but three stairs to go up at. Then leading them along another great hall, he brought them into his chamber, and, closing the door, said unto them, this is the stable you ask for, this is my gennet, this is my gelding, this is my courser, and this is my hackney, and laid on them with a great lever. I will bestow upon you, said he, this Frizeland horse, I had him from Francfort, yet will I give him you; for he is a 100 pretty little nag, and will go very well, with a tessel of goshawks, half a dozen of spaniels, and a brace of grey-hounds: thus are you king of the hares and partridges for all this winter. By St. John, said they, now we are paid, he hath gleeked us to some pur-

86–87. **which have . . . of the houses;** because here houses were built against the side of a steep hill.

pose, bobbed we are now for ever. I deny it, said he, he was not here above three days. Judge you now, whether they had most cause, either to hide their heads for shame, or to laugh at the jest. As they were going down again thus amazed, he asked them, will you have a whimwham? What is that, said they? It is, said he, five turds to make you a muzzle. To-day, said the steward, though we happen to be roasted, we shall not be burnt, for we are pretty well quipped and larded in my opinion. O my jolly dapper boy, thou has given us a gudgeon, I hope to see thee pope before I die. I think so, said he, myself; and then shall you be a puppy, and this gentle popinjay a perfect papelard, that is, dissembler. . . . Cocksbod, said the steward, we have met with a prater. Farewell, master tatler, God keep you, so goodly are the words which you come out with, and so fresh in your mouth, that it had need to be salted.

Thus going down in great haste, under the arch of the stairs they let fall the great lever, which he had put upon their backs; whereupon Gargantua said, what a devil! you are, it seems, but bad horsemen, that suffer your bilder to fail you, when you need him most. If you were to go from hence to Cahusac, whether had you rather ride on a gosling, or lead a sow in a leash? I had rather drink, said the harbinger. With this they entered into the lower hall, where the company was, and relating to them this new story, they made them laugh like a swarm of flies.

CHAPTER XVI

How Gargantua was sent to Paris, and of the huge Great Mare that he rode on; how she destroyed the Ox-Flies of the Beauce

In the same season Fayoles, the fourth King of Numidia, sent out of the country of Africa to Grangousier, the most hideous great mare that ever was seen, and of the strangest form, for you know well enough how it is said, that Africa always is productive of some new thing. She was as big as six elephants, and had her feet cloven into fingers, like Julius Cæsar's horse, with slouch-hanging ears, like the goats in Languedoc, and a little horn on her buttock. She was of a burnt sorel hue, with a little mixture of daple grey spots, but above all she had a horrible tail; for it was little more or less, than every whit as great as the steeple-pillar of St. Mark, besides Langes: and squared as that is, with tuffs,

and ennicroches or hair-plaits wrought within one another, no otherwise than as the beards are upon the ears of corn.

If you wonder at this, wonder rather at the tails of the Scythian rams, which weighed above thirty pounds each, and of the Surian sheep, who need, if Tenaud say true, a little cart at their heels to bear up their tail, it is so long and heavy. Your female lechers in the plain countries have no such tails. And she was brought by sea in three carricks and a brigantine into the harbour of Olone in Thalmondois. When Grangousier saw her, "Here is," said he "what is fit to carry my son to Paris. So now, in the name of God, all will be well. He will in times coming be a great scholar. If it were not, my masters, for the beasts, we should live like clerks. The next morning, after they drunk, you must understand, they took their journey; Gargantua, his pedagogue Ponocrates, and his train, and with them Eudemon the young page. And because the weather was fair and temperate, his father caused to be made for him a pair of dun boots; Babin calls them buskins. Thus did they merrily pass their time in travelling on their high way, always making good cheer, and were very pleasant till they came a little above Orleans, in which place there was a forest of five-and-thirty leagues long, and seventeen in breadth, or thereabouts. This forest was most horribly fertile and copious in dorflies, hornets, and wasps, so that it was a very purgatory for the poor mares, asses, and horses. But Gargantua's mare did avenge herself handsomely of all the outrages therein committed upon beasts of her kind, and that by a trick whereof they had no suspicion. For as soon as ever they were entered into the said forest, and that the wasps had given the assault, she drew out and unsheathed her tail, and therewith skirmishing, did so sweep them, that she overthrew all the wood alongst and athwart, here and there, this way and that way, longwise and sidewise, over and under, and felled every where the wood with as much ease, as the mower doth the grass, in such sort that never since hath there been there, neither wood, nor dorflies: for all the country was thereby reduced to a plain champagne field. Which Gargantua took great pleasure to behold, and said to his company no more but this, "Je trouve beau ce," I find this pretty; whereupon that country hath been ever since that time called Beauce. But all the breakfast the mare got that day, was but a little yawning and gaping, in memory whereof the gentlemen of Beauce do as yet to this day break their fast with gaping, which they find to be very good, and do spit the better for it. At last they came to Paris, where Gargantua refreshed himself two or three

---

1–2. **I deny it . . . days.** An idiomatic rejoinder, badly translated here. 32. **Fayoles.** Rabelais facetiously uses the names of his friends and acquaintances for his characters. 45. **Langes,** an old brick tower beside the Loire River.

52. **Tenaud;** who wrote of a trip to Cairo. 96. **Beauce;** the name is actually of ancient origin.

days, making very merry with his folks, and inquiring what men of learning there were then in the city, and what wine they drank there.

CHAPTER XVII

How Gargantua paid his welcome to the Parisians, and how he took away the great Bells of Our Lady's Church

Some few days after that they had refreshed themselves, he went to see the city, and was beheld of every body there with great admiration; for the people of Paris are so sottish, so badot, so foolish and fond by nature, that a juggler, a carrier of indulgences, a sumpter-horse, or mule with cymbals, or tinkling bells, a blind fiddler in the middle of a cross lane, shall draw a greater confluence of people together, than an Evangelical preacher. And they pressed so hard upon him, that he was constrained to rest himself upon the towers of Our Lady's Church. . . .

This done, he considered the great bells, which were in the said towers, and made them sound very harmoniously. Which whilst he was doing, it came into his mind, that they would serve very well for tingling Tantans, and ringing Campanels, to hang about his mare's neck, when she should be sent back to his father, as he intended to do, loaded with Brie cheese, and fresh herring. And indeed he forthwith carried them to his lodging. . . .

All the city was risen up in sedition, they being, as you know, upon any slight occasion, so ready to uproars and insurrections, that foreign nations wonder at the patience of the kings of France who do not by good justice restrain them from such tumultuous courses, seeing the manifold inconveniences which thence arise from day to day. Would to God, I knew the shop wherein are forged these divisions and factious combinations, that I might bring them to light in the confraternities of my parish! Believe for a truth, that the place wherein the people gathered together, were thus sulphured, hopurymated, and moiled, was called Nesle, where then was, but now is no more, the Oracle of Leucetia. There was the case proposed, and the inconvenience showed of the transporting of the bells. After they had well ergoted pro and con, they concluded in baralipton, that they should send the oldest and most sufficient of the faculty unto Gargantua, to signify unto him the great and horrible prejudice they sustain'd by the want of those bells. And notwithstanding the good reasons given in by some of the university, why this charge was fitter for an orator than a sophister, there was chosen for this purpose our Master Janotus de Bragmardo.

CHAPTER XVIII

How Janotus de Bragmardo was sent to Gargantua, to recover the Great Bells

Master Janotus, with his hair cut round like a dish à la Cæsarine, in his most antic accoutrement liripipionated with a graduate's hood, and, having sufficiently antidoted his stomach with oven marmalades, that is, bread and holy water of the cellar, transported himself to the lodging of Gargantua, driving before him three red muzzled beadles, and dragging after him five or six artless masters, all thoroughly bedraggled with the mire of the streets. At their entry Ponocrates met them, who was afraid, seeing them so disguised, and thought they had been some maskers out of their wits, which moved him to inquire of one of the said artless masters of the company, what this mummery meant? It was answered him, that they desired to have their bells restored to them. As soon as Ponocrates heard that, he ran in all haste to carry the news unto Gargantua, that he might be ready to answer them, and speedily resolve what was to be done. Gargantua being advertised hereof, called apart his schoolmaster Ponocrates, Philotimus steward of his house, Gymnastes his esquire, and Eudemon, and very summarily conferred with them, both of what he should do, and what answer he should give. They were all of opinion that they should bring them unto the goblet-office, which is the buttery, and there make them drink like roysters, and line their jackets soundly. And that this cougher might not be puft up with vain glory, by thinking the bells were restored at his request, they sent, whilst he was chopining and plying the pot, for the major of the city, the rector of the faculty, and the vicar of the church, unto whom they resolved to deliver the bells, before the sophister had propounded his commission. After that, in their hearing, he should pronounce his gallant oration, which was done; and they being come, the sophister was brought in full hall, and began as followeth, in coughing.

CHAPTER XIX

The Oration of Master Janotus de Bragmardo, for the recovery of the Bells

Hem, hem, gud-day, sirs, gud-day. Et vobis, my masters. It were but reason that you should restore to us our bells; for we have great need of them. Hem, hem, aihfuhash. We have often-times heretofore refused good money for them of those of London, in Cahors, yea and those of Bourdeaux in Brie, who would have bought them for the substantific quality of the elementary complexion, which is intronificated in the terrestreity of their quidditative nature, to extraneize the blasting mists, and whirlwinds upon our vines, indeed not ours, but these round about us. For if we lose the piot and liquor of the grape, we lose all, both sense and law. If you restore them unto us at my request, I shall gain it by six baskets full of sausages, and a fine pair of breeches, which will do my legs a great deal of good, or else they will not keep their promise to me. Ho by gob, Domine, a pair of breeches is good, et vir sapiens non abhorrebit eam. Ha, ha, a pair of breeches is not so easily got; I have experience of it myself. Consider, Domine, I have been these eighteen days in matagrabolising this brave speech. Reddite quæ sunt Cæsaris, Cæsari, et quæ sunt Dei, Deo. Ibi jacet lepus. By my faith, Domine, if you will sup with me in cameris, by cox body, charitatis, nos faciemus bonum cherubin. Ego occidi unum porcum, et ego habet bonum vino: but of good wine we cannot make bad Latin. Well, de parte Dei date nobis bellas nostras. Hold, I give you in the name of the faculty a Sermones de Utino, that utinam you will give us our bells. Vultis etiam pardonos? Per diem vos habebitis, et nihil payabitis.

O Sir, Domine, bellagivaminor nobis; verily, est bonum urbis. They are useful to everybody. If they fit your mare well, so do they do our faculty; quæ comparata est jumentis insipientibus, et similis facta est eis, Psalmo nescio quo. Yet did I quote it in my note-book, et est unum bonum Achilles, a good defending argument. Hem, hem, hem, haikhash! For I prove unto you that you should give me them. Ego sic argumentor. Omnis bella bellabilis in bellerio bellando, bellans bellativo, bellare facit, bellabiliter bellantes. Parisius habet bellas. Ergo gluc. Ha, ha, ha. This is spoken to some purpose. It is in tertio primæ, in Darii, or elsewhere. By my soul, I have seen the time that I could play the devil in arguing, but now I am much failed, and henceforward want nothing but a cup of good wine, a good bed, my back to the fire, my belly to the table, and a good deep dish. Hei, Domine, I beseech you, in nomine Patris, Filii, et Spiritûs Sancti, Amen, to restore unto us our bells: and God keep you from evil, and our Lady from health, qui vivit et regnat per omnia secula seculorum, Amen. Hem, hashchehhawksash, qzrchremhemhash.

Verum enim vero, quandoquidem, dubio procul. Edepol, quoniam, ita certe, meus deus fidius; a town without bells is like a blind man without a staff, an ass without a crupper, and a cow without cymbals. Therefore be assured, until you have restored them unto us, we will never leave crying after you, like a blind man that hath lost his staff, braying like an ass without a crupper, and making a noise like a cow without cymbals. A certain Latinisator, dwelling near the hospital, said once, producing the authority of one Taponus,—I lie, it was one Pontanus the secular poet,—who wished those bells had been made of feathers, and the clapper of a foxtail, to the end that they might have begot a chronicle in the bowels of his brain, when he was about the composing of his carminiformal lines. But nac petetin petetac, tic, torche lorgne, or rot kipipur kipipot put pantse malf, he was declared an heretic. We make them as of wax. And no more saith the depondent. Valete et plaudite. Calepinus recensui.

CHAPTER XX

How the Sophister carried away his cloth

The sophister had no sooner ended, but Ponocrates and Eudemon burst out into a laughing so heartily, that they had almost split with it, and given up the ghost, in rendering their souls to God: even just as Crassus did, seeing a lubberly ass eat thistles; and as Philemon, who, for seeing an ass eat those figs which were provided for his own dinner, died with force of laughing. Together with them Master Janotus fell a-laughing too as fast as he could, in which mood of laughing they continued so long, that their eyes did water by the vehement concussion of the substance of the brain, by which these lachrymal humidities, being prest out, glided through the optic nerves, and so to the full represented Democritus Heraclitising, and Heraclitus Democritising.

When they had done laughing, Gargantua consulted with the prime of his retinue, what should be done. There Ponocrates was of opinion, that they should make this fair orator drink again; and seeing he had showed them more pastime, and made them laugh more than a natural fool could have done, that they should give him ten baskets full of sausages, mentioned in his pleasant speech, with a pair of hose, three hundred great billets of logwood, five and twenty hogsheads of wine, a good large down bed, and a deep capacious dish, which he said were necessary for his old age. All this was done as they did appoint. . . .

CHAPTER XXI

The Study of Gargantua, according to the discipline of his School-masters and Sophisters

The first day being thus spent, and the bells put up again in their own place, the citizens of Paris, in acknowledgment of this courtesy, offered to maintain and feed his mare as long as he pleased, which Gar-

72-73. **Crassus, Philemon,** a Roman politician and an Athenian playwright, both remembered in incidents of laughing. 81-82. **Democritus . . . Democritising.** Democritus was called the laughing philosopher and Heraclitus the weeping philosopher.

gantua took in good part, and they sent her to graze in the forest of Biere. I think she is not there now. This done, he with all his heart submitted his study to the discretion of Ponocrates; who for the beginning appointed that he should do as he was accustomed, to the end he might understand by what means, in so long time, his old masters had made him so sottish and ignorant. He disposed therefore of his time in such fashion, that ordinarily he did awake between eight and nine a clock, whether it was day or not, for so had his ancient governors ordained, alleging that which David saith, *Vanum est vobis ante lucem surgere*. Then did he tumble and toss, wag his legs, and wallow in the bed some time, the better to stir up and rouse his vital spirits, and appareled himself according to the season: but willingly he would wear a great long gown of thick frieze, furred with fox skins. Afterwards he combed his head with an Alman comb, which is the four fingers and the thumb. For his preceptor said, that to comb himself other ways, to wash and make himself neat, was to lose time in this world. Then he dunged, pist, spued, belched, cracked, yawned, spitted, coughed, yexed, sneezed, and snotted himself like an arch-deacon, and to suppress the dew and bad air, went to breakfast, having some good fried tripe, fair rashers on the coals, excellent gammons of bacon, store of fine minced meat, and a great deal of sippit brewis, made-up of the fat of the beef-pot, laid upon bread, cheese, and chopped parsley stewed together. Ponocrates showed him, that he ought not eat so soon after rising out of his bed, unless he had performed some exercise beforehand. Gargantua answered, what! have not I sufficiently well exercised myself? I have wallowed and rolled myself six or seven turns in my bed, before I rose. Is not that enough? Pope Alexander did so, by the advice of a Jew his physician, and lived till his dying day in despite of his enemies. My first masters have used me to it, saying that to breakfast made a good memory, and therefore they drank first. I am very well after it, and dine but the better. And Master Tubal, who was the first licenciate at Paris, told me, that it was not enough to run a pace, but to set forth betimes: so doth not the total welfare of our humanity depend upon perpetual drinking in a ribble rabble, like ducks, but on drinking early in the morning; *unde versus*,

> To rise betimes is no good hour,
> To drink betimes is better sure.

After he had thoroughly broke his fast, he went to church, and they carried him in a great basket, a huge impantoufled or thick covered breviary, weighing, what in grease, clasps, parchment, and cover, little more or less than eleven hundred and six pounds. There he heard six and twenty or thirty masses. This while, to the same place came his orison-mutterer impaletocked, or lapped up about the chin, like a tufted whoop, and his breath antidoted with the store of the vine-tree-sirup. With him he mumbled all his kiriels, and dunsicals breborions, which he so curiously thumbed and fingered, that there fell not so much as one grain to the ground. As he went from the church, they brought him, upon a dray drawn with oxen, a confused heap of pater-nosters and aves of Sanct Claude, every one of them being of the bigness of a hat-block; and thus walking through the cloisters, galleries or garden, he said more in turning them over, than sixteen hermits would have done. Then did he study some paltry half hour with his eyes fixed upon his book; but as the comic saith, his mind was in the kitchen. He sat down at table; and because he was naturally phlegmatic, he began his meal with some dozens of gammons, dried neat's tongues, hard rows of mullet, called botargos, andouilles, or sausages, and such other forerunners of wine. In the mean while, four of his folks did cast into his mouth one after another continually mustard by whole shovels full. Immediately after that, he drank a horrible draught of white-wine for the ease of his kidneys. When that was done, he ate according to the season meat agreeable to his appetite, and then left off eating when his belly began to strout, and was like to crack for fulness. As for his drinking, he had neither end nor rule. For he was wont to say that the limits and bounds of drinking were, when the cork of the shoes of him that drinketh swelleth up half a foot high.

CHAPTER XXIII

How Gargantua was instructed by Ponocrates, and in such sort disciplinated, that he lost not one hour of the day

When Ponocrates knew Gargantua's vicious manner of living, he resolved to bring him up in another kind; but for a while he bore with him, considering that nature cannot endure such a change, without great violence. Therefore to begin his work the better, he requested a learned physician of that time, called Master Theodorus, seriously to perpend, if it were possible, how to bring Gargantua unto a better course. The said physician purged him canonically with Anticyrian-hellebore, by which medicine he cleansed all the alteration, and perverse habitude of his brain. By this means also Ponocrates made him forget all that he had learned under his ancient preceptors, as Timotheus did to his disciples, who had

---

12–13. **Vanum . . . surgere,** "It is vain for you to get up before daylight." (Psalms 127:2) 37–38. **a Jew his physician,** Bonnet de Lates, physician to Alexander VI.

61. **kiriels,** kyrie eleison, litanies. 102. **Timotheus,** the Greek musician of the fourth century B.C.

been instructed under other musicians. To do this better, they brought him into the company of learned men, which were there, in whose imitation he had a great desire and affection to study otherwise, and to improve his parts. Afterwards he put himself into such a road and way of studying that he lost not any one hour in the day, but employed all his time in learning, and honest knowledge. Gargantua awak'd them about four o'clock in the morning. Whilst they were in rubbing of him, there was read unto him some chapter of the Holy Scripture aloud and clearly, with a pronunciation fit for the matter, and hereunto was appointed a young page born in Basché, named Anagnostes. According to the purpose and argument of that lesson, he oftentimes gave himself to worship, adore, pray, and send up his supplications to that good God, whose word did show his majesty and marvellous judgment. Then went he into the secret places to make excretion of his natural digestions. There his master repeated what had been read, expounding unto him the most obscure and difficult points. In returning, they considered the face of the sky, if it was such as they had observed it the night before, and into what signs the sun was entering, as also the moon for that day. This done, he was appareled, combed, curled, trimmed and perfumed, during which time they repeated to him the lessons of the day before. He himself said them by heart, and upon them would ground some practical cases concerning the estate of man, which he would prosecute sometimes two or three hours, but ordinarily they ceased as soon as he was fully clothed. Then for three good hours he had a lecture read unto him. This done, they went forth, still conferring of the substance of the lecture, either unto a field near the university called the Brack, or unto the meadows where they played at the ball, the long-tennis, and at the pile trigone, most gallantly exercising their bodies, as formerly they had done their minds. All their play was but in liberty, for they left off when they pleased, and that was commonly when they did sweat over all their body, or were otherwise weary. Then were they very well wiped and rubbed, shifted their shirts, and walking soberly, went to see if dinner was ready. Whilst they stayed for that, they did clearly and eloquently pronounce some sentences that they had retained of the lecture. In the meantime Master Appetite came, and then very orderly sat they down at table. At the beginning of the meal, there was read some pleasant history of the warlike actions of former times, until he had taken a glass of wine. Then, if they thought good, they continued reading, or began to discourse merrily together; speaking first of the virtue, propriety, efficacy and nature of all that was served in at that table; of bread, of wine, of water, of salt, of

38. pile trigone, a ball game for three players.

fleshes, fishes, fruits, herbs, roots, and of their dressing. By means whereof, he learned in a little time all the passages competent for this, that were to be found in Pliny, Athenæus, Dioscorides, Julius Pollux, Galen, Porphyrius, Oppian, Polybius, Heliodorus, Aristotle, Ælian, and others. Whilst they talked of these things, many times, to be the more certain, they caused the very books to be brought to the table, and so well and perfectly did he in his memory retain the things above said, that in that time there was not a physician that knew half so much as he did. Afterwards they conferred of the lessons read in the morning, and, ending their repast with some conserve or marmalade of quinces, he picked his teeth with mastic tooth-pickers, washed his hands and eyes with fair fresh water, and gave thanks unto God in some fine canticks, made in praise of the divine bounty and munificence. This done, they brought in cards, not to play, but to learn a thousand pretty tricks, and new inventions, which were all grounded upon arithmetic. By this means he fell in love with that numerical science, and every day after dinner and supper he passed his time in it as pleasantly, as he was wont to do at cards and dice: so that at last he understood so well both the theory and practical part thereof, that Tunstal the Englishman, who had written very largely of that purpose, confessed that verily in comparison of him he had no skill at all. And not only in that, but in the other mathematical sciences, as geometry, astronomy, music, &c. For in waiting on the concoction, and attending the digestion of his food, they made a thousand pretty instruments and geometrical figures, and did in some measure practice the astronomical canons.

After this they recreated themselves with singing musically, in four or five parts, or upon a set theme or ground at random, as it best pleased them. In matter of musical instruments, he learned to play upon the lute, the virginals, the harp, the Allman flute with nine holes, the violin, and the sackbut. This hour thus spent, and digestion finished, he did purge his body of natural excrements, then betook himself to his principal study for three hours together, or more, as well to repeat his matutinal lectures, as to proceed in the book wherein he was, as also to write handsomely, to draw and form the antique and Roman letters. This being done, they went out of their house, and with them a young gentleman of Touraine, named the Esquire Gymnast, who taught him the art of riding. Changing then his clothes, he rode a Naples courser, Dutch roussin, a Spanish gennet, a barbed or trapped steed, then a light fleet horse, unto whom he gave a hundred carieres, made him go the high saults, bounding in the air, free a ditch with a skip, leap over a stile or

82–83. Tunstal the Englishman, sixteenth-century churchman.

pale, turn short in a ring both to the right and left hand. There he broke not his lance; for it is the greatest foolery in the world to say, I have broken ten lances at tilts or in fight. A carpenter can do even as much. But it is a glorious and praiseworthy action, with one lance to break and overthrow ten enemies. Therefore with a sharp, stiff, strong, and well-steeled lance, would he usually force up a door, pierce a harness, beat down a tree, carry away the ring, lift up a cuirassier saddle, with the mail-coat and gauntlet. All this he did in complete arms from head to foot. As for the prancing flourishes, and smacking popisms, for the better cherishing of the horse, commonly used in riding, none did them better than he. The voltiger of Ferrara was but as an ape compared to him. He was singularly skilful in leaping nimbly from one horse to another without putting foot to ground, and these horses were called desultories. He could likewise from either side, with a lance in his hand, leap on horseback without stirrups, and rule the horse at his pleasure without a bridle, for such things are useful in military engagements. Another day he exercised the battle-axe, which he so dexterously wielded, both in the nimble, strong, and smooth management of that weapon, and that in all the feats practiceable by it, that he passed knight of arms in the field, and at all essays.

Then tossed he the pike, played with the two-handed sword, with the back sword, with the Spanish tuck, the dagger, poniard, armed, unarmed, with a buckler, with a cloak, with a target. Then would he hunt the hart, the roebuck, the bear, the fallow deer, the wild boar, the hare, the pheasant, the partridge and the bustard. He played at the balloon, and made it bound in the air, both with fist and foot. He wrestled, ran, jumped, not at three steps and a leap, called the hops, nor at clochepied, called the hare's leap, nor yet at the Almanes; for, said Gymnast, these jumps are for the wars altogether unprofitable, and of no use: but at one leap he would skip over a ditch, spring over a hedge, mount six paces upon a wall, ramp and grapple after this fashion up against a window, of the full height of a lance. He did swim in deep waters on his belly, on his back, sideways, with all his body, with his feet only, with one hand in the air, wherein he held a book, crossing thus the breadth of the River Seine, without wetting, and dragging along his cloak with his teeth, as did Julius Cæsar; then with the help of one hand he entered forcibly into a boat, from whence he cast himself again headlong into the water, sounded the depths, hollowed the rocks, and plunged into the pits and gulfs. Then turned he the boat about, governed it, led it swiftly or slowly with the stream and against the stream, stopped it in his

15. **Ferrara,** Cesare Fieschi of Ferrara, a celebrated horseman (*voltigeur*).

course, guided it with one hand, and with the other laid hard about him with a huge great oar, hoisted the sail, hied up along the mast by the shrouds, ran upon the edge of the decks, set the compass in order, tackled the bowlines, and steered the helm. Coming out of the water, he ran furiously up against a hill, and with the same alacrity and swiftness ran down again. He climbed up trees like a cat, leaped from the one to the other like a squirrel. He did pull down the great boughs and branches, like another Milo; then with two sharp well-steeled daggers, and two tried bodkins, would he run up by the wall to the very top of a house like a rat; then suddenly come down from the top to the bottom with such an even composition of members, that by the fall he would catch no harm.

He did cast the dart, throw the bar, put the stone, practise the javelin, the boar spear or partisan, and the halbert. He broke the strongest bows in drawing, bended against his breast the greatest cross-bows of steel, took his aim by the eye with the hand-gun, and shot well, traversed and planted the cannon, shot at but-marks, at the papgay from below upwards, or to a height from above downwards, or to a descent; then before him sidewise, and behind him, like the Parthians. They tied a cable-rope to the top of a high tower, by one end whereof hanging near the ground he wrought himself with his hands to the very top; then upon the same tract came down so sturdily and firm that you could not on a plain meadow have run with more assurance. They set up a great pole fixed upon two trees. There would he hang by his hands, and with them alone, his feet touching at nothing, would go back and fore along the aforesaid rope with so great swiftness, that hardly could one overtake him with running; and then, to exercise his breast and lungs, he would shout like all the devils in hell. I heard him once call Eudemon from St. Victor's gate to Montmartre. Stentor never had such a voice at the siege of Troy. Then for the strengthening of his nerves or sinews, they made him two great sows of lead, each of them weighing eight thousand and seven hundred quintals, which they called Alteres. Those he took up from the ground, in each hand one, then lifted them up over his head, and held them so without stirring three quarters of an hour or more, which was an inimitable force. He fought at barriers with the stoutest and most vigorous champions; and when it came to the cope, he stood so sturdily on his feet, that he abandoned himself unto the strongest, in case they could remove him from his place, as Milo was wont to do of old. In whose imitation likewise

65. **Milo,** the Greek athlete, famous for his feats of strength. 78. **papgay,** a popinjay, or target in the form of a parrot. 95. **Stentor,** the herald with the loud voice, from whose name the English "stentorian" is derived. 99. **Alteres,** weights like dumbbells.

he held a pomegranate in his hand, to give it unto him that could take it from him. The time being thus bestowed, and himself rubbed, cleansed, wiped, and refreshed with other clothes, he returned fair and softly; and passing through certain meadows, or other grassy places, beheld the trees and plants, comparing them with what is written of them in the books of the ancients, such as Theophrast, Dioscorides, Marinus, Pliny, Nicander, Macer, and Galen, and carried home to the house great handfuls of them, whereof a young page called Rizotomos had charge; together with little mattocks, pickaxes, grubbing hooks, cabbies, pruning knives, and other instruments requisite for herborising. Being come to their lodging, whilst supper was making ready, they repeated certain passages of that which had been read, and then sat down at table. Here remark, that his dinner was sober and thrifty, for he did then eat only to prevent the gnawings of his stomach, but his supper was copious and large; for he took then as much as was fit to maintain and nourish him; which indeed is the true diet prescribed by the art of good and sound physic, although a rabble of loggerheaded physicians, muzzled in the brabbling shop of sophisters, counsel the contrary. During that repast was continued the lesson read at dinner as long as they thought good: the rest was spent in good discourse, learned and profitable. After that they had given thanks, he set himself to sing vocally, and play upon harmonious instruments, or otherwise passed his time at some pretty sports, made with cards and dice, or in practising the feats of legerdemain with cups and balls. There they staid some nights in frolicking thus, and making themselves merry till it was time to go to bed; and on other nights they would go make visits unto learned men, or to such as had been travellers in strange and remote countries. When it was full night before they retired themselves, they went unto the most open place of the house to see the face of the sky, and there beheld the comets, if any were, as likewise the figures, situations, aspects, oppositions and conjunctions of both the fixed stars and planets.

Then with his master did he briefly recapitulate, after the manner of the Pythagoreans, that which he had read, seen, learned, done and understood in the whole course of that day.

Then prayed they unto God the Creator, in falling down before him, and strengthening their faith towards him, and glorifying him for his boundless bounty; and, giving thanks unto him for the time that was past, they recommended themselves to his divine clemency for the future. Which being done, they went to bed, and betook themselves to their repose and rest.

[Gargantua is called home by his father.]

CHAPTER XXXVIII

How Gargantua did eat up six Pilgrims in a sallad

The story requireth, that we relate that which happened unto six pilgrims, who came from Sebastian near to Nantes: and who for shelter that night had hid themselves in the garden upon the chichling peas, among the cabbages and lettuces. Gargantua finding himself somewhat dry, asked whether they could get any lettuce to make him a sallad; and hearing that there were the greatest and fairest in the country, for they were as great as plum-trees, or as walnut-trees, he would go thither himself, and brought thence in his hand what he thought good, and withal carried away the six pilgrims, who were in so great fear, that they did not dare to speak nor cough. Washing them, therefore, first at the fountain, the pilgrims said one to another softly, What shall we do? We are almost drowned here amongst these lettuce, shall we speak? But if we speak he will kill us. And, as they were thus deliberating what to do, Gargantua put them with the lettuce into a platter of the house, as large as the huge tun of the White Friars of the Cistertian order; which done, with oil, vinegar, and salt, he ate them up, to refresh himself a little before supper, and had already swallowed up five of the pilgrims, the sixth being in the platter, totally hid under a lettuce, except his bourbon or staff that appeared, and nothing else. Which Grangousier seeing, said to Gargantua, I think that is the horn of a shell snail, do not eat it. Why not, said Gargantua, they are good all this month: which he no sooner said, but, drawing up the staff, and therewith taking up the pilgrim, he ate him very well, then drank a terrible draught of excellent white wine. The pilgrims, thus devoured, made shift to save themselves as well as they could, by drawing their bodies out of the reach of the grinders of his teeth, but could not escape from thinking they had been put in the lowest dungeon of a prison. And when Gargantua whiffed the great draught, they thought to have drowned in his mouth, and the flood of wine had almost carried them away into the gulf of his stomach. Nevertheless, skipping with their bourbons, as St. Michael's palmers use to do, they sheltered themselves from the danger of that inundation under the banks of his teeth. But one of them by chance, groping or sounding the country with his staff, to try whether they were in safety or no, struck hard against the cleft of a hollow tooth, and hit the mandibulary sinew or nerve of the jaw, which put Gargantua to very great pain, so that he began to cry

75–76. **as large as . . . Cistertian order.** The friars' great tun allegedly had a capacity of 300 hogsheads. 97. **as St. Michael's palmers use to do;** pilgrims to Mont St. Michel had to leap over the quicksands between the mount and the coast.

for the rage that he felt. To ease himself therefore of his smarting ache, he called for his tooth-picker, and rubbing towards a young walnut-tree, where they lay skulking, unnestled you my gentlemen pilgrims.

For he caught one by the legs, another by the scrip, another by the pocket, another by the scarf, another by the band of the breeches, and the poor fellow that had hurt him with the bourbon, him he hooked to him by the codpiece, which snatch never-
10 theless did him a great deal of good, for it pierced unto him a pocky botch he had in the groin, which grievously tormented him ever since they were past Ancenis. The pilgrims thus dislodged, ran away thwart the plain a pretty fast pace, and the pain ceased, even just at the time when by Eudemon he was called to supper. . . .

CHAPTER XXXIX

How the Monk was feasted by Gargantua, and of the jovial discourse they had at supper

There was then in the abbey a claustral monk, called Friar John of the funnels and gobbets, in French, des Entommeures, young, gallant, frisk,
20 lusty, nimbly, quick, active, bold, adventurous, reso- lute, tall, lean, wide-mouthed, long-nosed, a fair

A caricature of Friar John with his breviary. From the "Droll Dreams of Pantagruel" published in Paris in 1565.

despatcher of morning prayers, unbridler of masses, and runner over vigils; and, to conclude summarily in a word, a right monk, if ever there was any, since the monking world monked a monkery: for the rest, a clerk even to the teeth in matter of breviary. . . .

Then Gargantua desired that he might be pres- ently sent for, to the end that with him they might consult of what was to be done. Whereupon, by a joint consent, his steward went for him, and brought 30 him along merrily, with his staff of the cross, upon Grangousier's mule. When he was come, a thousand huggings, a thousand embracements, a thousand good days were given. Ha, Friar John, my friend, Friar John, my brave cousin, Friar John from the devil! Let me clip thee, my heart, about the neck; to me an armsful. I must gripe thee, my ballock, till thy back crack with it. Come, my cod, let me coll thee till I kill thee. And Friar John, the gladdest man in the world, never was man made welcomer, never 40 was any more courteously and graciously received than Friar John. Come, come, said Gargantua, a stool here close by me at this end. I am content, said the monk, seeing you will have it so. Some water, page; fill, my boy, fill, it is to refresh my liver. Give me some, child, to gargle my throat withal. Deposita cappà, said Gymnast, let us pull off this frock. Ho, by G——, gentlemen, said the monk, there is a chapter in Statutis Ordinis, which opposeth my laying of it down. Pish! said Gymnast, a fig for your chapter! 50 This frock breaks both your shoulders, put it off. My friend, said the monk, let me alone with it; for, by G——, I'll drink the better that it is on. It makes all my body jocund. If I should lay it aside, the waggish pages would cut to themselves garters out of it as I was once served at Coulaines. And, which is worse, I shall lose my appetite. But if in this habit I sit down at table, I will drink, by G——, both to thee and to thy horse, and so, courage, frolic, God save the com- pany! I have already supped, yet will I eat never a 60 whit the less for that: for I have a paved stomach, as hollow as a butt of malvasie, or St. Benedictus' boot, and always open like a lawyer's pouch. Of all fishes, but the tench, take the wing of a partridge, or the thigh of a nun. Doth not he die like a good fel- low that dies with a stiff catso? Our prior loves ex- ceedingly the white of a capon. In that, said Gymnast, he doth not resemble the foxes: for of the capons, hens, and pullets, which they carry away, they never eat the white. Why, said the monk? Be- 70 cause, said Gymnast, they have no cooks to dress them; and, if they be not competently made ready, they remain red and not white; the redness of meats being a token that they have not got enough of the fire, whether by boiling, roasting, or otherwise, ex- cept shrimps, lobsters, crabs, and cray-fishes, which

46–47. **Deposita cappà**, a rubric in the ritual, indicating where the priest should take off his cope.

are cardinalised with boiling. By God's feast-gazers, said the monk, the porter of our abbey, then, hath not his head well boiled, for his eyes are as red as a mazer made of an alder-tree. The thigh of this leveret is good for those that have the gout. . . .

Diavolo, is there no more must? No more sweet wine? Germinavit radix Jesse. Je renie ma vie, j'enrage de soif; I renounce my life, I rage for thirst. This wine is none of the worst. What wine drink you at Paris? I give myself to the devil, if I did not once keep open house at Paris for all comers six months together. Do you know Friar Claud of the High Kilderkins? Oh the good fellow that he is! But I do not know what fly hath stung him of late, he is become so hard a student. For my part, I study not at all. In our abbey we never study for fear of the mumps, which disease in horses is called the mourning in the chine. Our late abbot was wont to say, that it is a monstrous thing to see a learned monk. By G—, master, my friend. Magis magnos clericos non sunt magis magnos sapientes. You never saw so many hares as there are this year. I could not any where come by a gosshawk, nor tassel of falcon. My Lord Belloniere promised me a lanner, but he wrote to me not long ago, that he was become pursy. The partridges will so multiply henceforth, that they will go near to eat up our ears. I take no delight in the stalking-horse; for I catch such cold, that I am like to founder myself at that sport. If I do not run, toil, travel, and trot about, I am not well at ease. True it is, that in leaping over the hedges and bushes, my frock leaves always some of its wool behind it. I have recovered a dainty greyhound; I give him to the devil, if he suffer a hare to escape him. A groom was leading him to my Lord Huntlittle, and I robbed him of him. Did I ill? No, Friar John, said Gymnast, no, by all the devils that are, no! So, said the monk, do I attest these same devils so long as they last, or rather, virtue G—, what could that gouty limpard have done with so fine a dog? By the body of G—, he is better pleased, when one presents him with a good yoke of oxen. How now, said Ponocrates, you swear, Friar John; it is only, said the monk, but to grace and adorn my speech. They are colours of a Ciceronian rhetoric.

CHAPTER XL

Why Monks are the outcasts of the World

By the faith of a Christian, said Eudemon, I do wonderfully dote, and enter in a great ecstasy, when I consider the honesty and good fellowship of this monk; for he makes us here all merry. How is it, then, that they exclude the monks from all good companies, calling them feast-troublers, marrers of

One of the monks who, according to Rabelais, are always to be found in the kitchen. From "Droll Dreams."

mirth, and disturbers of all civil conversation, as the bees drive away the drones from their hives? Ignavum fucos pecus, said Maro, à præsepibus arcent. Hereunto, answered Gargantua, there is nothing so true, as that the frock and cowl draw to them the opprobries, injuries, and maledictions of the world, just as the wind called Cecias, attracts the clouds. . . . If you conceive, how an ape in a family is always mocked, and provokingly incensed, you shall easily apprehend how monks are shunned of all men, both young and old. The ape keeps not the house as a dog doth; he draws not in the plough as the ox; he yields neither milk nor wool as the sheep; he carrieth no burthen as a horse doth. That which he doth, is only to conskite, spoil, and defile all, which is the cause wherefore he hath of men mocks, frumperies and bastonadoes.

After the same manner a monk; I mean those lither, idle, lazy monks, doth not labour and work, as do the peasant and artificer; doth not ward and defend the country, as doth the man-of-war; cureth not the sick and diseased, as the physician doth; doth neither preach nor teach, as do the Evangelical doctors and school-masters; doth not import commodities and things necessary for the commonwealth, as

28. **stalking-horse,** catching birds with nets.

53–54. **Ignavum . . . arcent.** The preceding clause translates this quotation from Virgil (*Georgics*, IV, 168). 58. **the wind called Cecias,** the northeast wind.

the merchant doth. Therefore is it, that by and of all men they are hooted at, hated and abhorred. Yea, but, said Grangousier, they pray to God for us. Nothing less, answered Gargantua. True it is, that with a tingle tangle jangling of bells they trouble and disquiet all their neighbours about them. Right, said the monk; a mass, a matin, a vesper well rung is half said. They mumble out great store of legends and psalms, by them not at all understood: they say many pater-nosters, interlarded with Ave-Maries, without thinking upon, or apprehending the meaning of what it is they say, which truly I call mocking of God, and not prayers. But so help them God, as they pray for us, and not for being afraid to lose their victuals, their manchets, and good fat pottage. All true Christians, of all estates and conditions, in all places, and at all times, send up their prayers to God, and the Mediator prayeth and intercedeth for them, and God is gracious to them. Now such a one is our good Friar John, therefore every man desireth to have him in his company. He is no bigot or hypocrite, he is not torn and divided betwixt reality and appearance, no wretch of a rugged and peevish disposition, but honest, jovial, resolute, and a good fellow. He travels, he labours, he defends the oppressed, comforts the afflicted, helps the needy, and keeps the close of the abbey. Nay, said the monk, I do a great deal more than that; for, whilst we are despatching our matins and anniversaries in the quire, I make withal some cross-bow strings, polish glass-bottles and bolts; I twist lines and weave purse nets, wherein to catch coneys. I am never idle. But now, hither come, some drink, some drink here! Bring the fruit. These chesnuts are of the wood of Estrox, and with good new wine are able to make you a fine cracker and composer of bum-sonnets. You are not as yet, it seems, well-moistened in this house with the sweet wine and must. By G——, I drink to all men freely, and at all fords like a proctor, or promoter's horse. Friar John, said Gymnast, take away the snot that hangs at your nose. Ha, ha, said the monk, am not I in danger of drowning, seeing I am in water even to the nose? No, no, Quare? Quia, though some water come out from thence, there never goes in any; for it is well antidoted with pot-proof armour, and sirrup of the vine-leaf. . . .

CHAPTER LII

How Gargantua caused to be built for the Monk the Abbey of Theleme

Gargantua would have made the monk Abbot of Sevillé, but he refused it. He would have given him the Abbey of Bourgueil, or of Sanct Florent, which was better, or both, if it pleased him; but the monk gave him a very peremptory answer, that he would never take upon him the charge nor government of monks. For how shall I be able, said he, to rule over others, that have not full power and command of myself? If you think I have done you, or may hereafter do you any acceptable service, give me leave to found an abbey after my own mind and fancy. The motion pleased Gargantua very well, who thereupon offered him all the country of Theleme by the River of Loire, till within two leagues of the great forest of Port-Huaut. The monk then requested Gargantua to institute his religious order contrary to all others. First then, said Gargantua, you must not build a wall about your convent, for all other abbeys are strongly walled and mured about. See, said the monk, and not without cause, where there is mur before, and mur behind, there is store of murmur, envy, and mutual conspiracy. Moreover, seeing there are certain convents in the world, whereof the custom is, if any women come in, I mean chaste and honest women, they immediately sweep the ground which they had trod upon; therefore was it ordained, that if any man or woman, entered into religious orders, should by chance come within this new abbey, all the rooms should be thoroughly washed and cleansed through which they had passed. And because in all other monasteries and nunneries all is compassed, limited, and regulated by hours, it was decreed that in this new structure there should be neither clock nor dial, but that according to the opportunities and incident occasions, all their hours should be disposed of; for, said Gargantua, the greatest loss of time that I know, is to count the hours. What good comes of it? Nor can there be any greater dotage in the world than for one to guide and direct his courses by the sound of a bell, and not by his own judgment and discretion.

Item, Because at that time they put no women into nunneries, but such as were either purblind, blinkards, lame, crooked, ill-favoured, mis-shapen, fools, senseless, spoiled, or corrupt; nor encloistered any men, but those that were either sickly, subject to defluxions, ill-bred louts, simple sots, or peevish trouble-houses. But to the purpose, said the monk. A woman that is neither fair nor good, to what use serves she? To make a nun of, said Gargantua. Yea, said the monk, to make shirts and smocks. Therefore was it ordained, that into this religious order should be admitted no women that were not fair, well-featured, and of a sweet disposition; nor men that were not comely, personable, and well conditioned.

Item, Because in the convents of women, men come not but underhand, privily, and by stealth; it was therefore enacted, that in this house there shall be no women in case there be not men, nor men in case there be not women.

Item, Because both men and women, that are received into religious orders after the expiring of their noviciat or probation year, were constrained and forced perpetually to stay there all the days of their life; it was therefore ordered, that all whatever, men or women, admitted within this abbey, should have full leave to depart with peace and contentment, whensoever it should seem good to them so to do.

Item, for that the religious men and women did ordinarily make three vows, to wit, those of chastity, poverty, and obedience; it was therefore constituted
10 and appointed, that in this convent they might be honourably married, that they might be rich, and live at liberty. In regard of the legitimate time of the persons to be initiated, and years under and above which they were not capable of reception, the women were to be admitted from ten till fifteen, and the men from twelve till eighteen.

CHAPTER LIV

The Inscription set upon the great Gate of Theleme

Here enter not vile bigots, hypocrites,
Externally devoted apes, base snites,
Puft up, wry-necked beasts, worse than the Huns,
20 Or Ostrogots, forerunners of baboons:
Cursed snakes, dissembling varlets, seeming sancts,
Slipshop caffards, beggars pretending wants,
Fat chuffcats, smell-feast knockers, doltish gulls,
Out-strouting cluster-fists, contentious bulls,
Fomenters of divisions and debates,
Elsewhere, not here, make sale of your deceits.
    Your filthy trumperies
    Stuffed with pernicious lies,
      (Not worth a bubble)
30   Would only trouble
    Our earthly paradise,
    Your filthy trumperies.

Here enter not attorneys, barristers,
Nor bridle-champing law-practitioners;
Clerks, commissaries, scribes, nor pharisees,
Wilful disturbers of the people's ease:
Judges, destroyers, with an unjust breath,
Of honest men, like dogs, ev'n unto death.
Your salary is at the gibbet-foot:
40 Go drink there! for we do not here fly out
On those excessive courses, which may draw
A waiting on your courts by suits in law.
    Law-suits, debates, and wrangling
    Hence are exil'd, and jangling.
    Here we are very
    Frolic and merry,
    And free from all entangling,
    Law-suits, debates, and wrangling.

Here enter not base pinching usurers,
50 Pelf-lickers, everlasting gatherers.
Gold-graspers, coin-gripers, gulpers of mists,

With harpy-griping claws, who, though your chests
Vasts sums of money should to you afford,
Would ne'ertheless add more unto that hoard,
And yet not be content,—you clunchfists dastards,
Insatiable fiends, and Pluto's bastards,
Greedy devourers, chichy sneakbill rogues,
Hell-mastiffs gnaw your bones, you rav'nous dogs,
    You beastly-looking fellows,
    Reason doth plainly tell us,   60
      That we should not
      To you allot
    Room here, but at the gallows,
    You beastly-looking fellows.

Here enter not fond makers of demurs
In love adventures, peevish jealous curs,
Sad pensive dotards, raisers of garboyles,
Hags, goblins, ghosts, firebrands of household broils,
Nor drunkards, liars, cowards, cheaters, clowns,
Thieves, cannibals, faces o'ercast with frowns,   70
Nor lazy slugs, envious, covetous,
Nor blockish, cruel, nor too credulous,—
Here mangy, pocky folks shall have no place,
No ugly lusks, nor persons of disgrace.
    Grace, honour, praise, delight,
    Here sojourn day and night.
      Sound bodies lin'd
      With a good mind,
    Do here pursue with might
    Grace, honour, praise, delight.   80

Here enter you, and welcome from our hearts,
All noble sparks, endow'd with gallant parts.
This is the glorious place, which bravely shall
Afford wherewith to entertain you all.
Were you a thousand, here you shall not want
For anything: for what you'll ask we'll grant.
Stay here you lively, jovial, handsome, brisk,
Gay, witty, frolic, cheerful, merry, frisk,
Spruce, jocund, courteous, furtherers of trades,
And in a word, all worthy, gentle blades.   90
    Blades of heroic breasts
    Shall taste here of the feasts,
      Both privily
      And civilly
    Of the celestial guests,
    Blades of heroic breasts.

Here enter you, pure, honest, faithful, true,
Expounders of the Scriptures old and new.
Whose glosses do not blind our reason, but
Make it to see the clearer, and who shut   100
Its passages from hatred, avarice,
Pride, factions, covenants, and all sort of vice.
Come, settle here a charitable faith,
Which neighbourly affection nourisheth.
And whose light chaseth all corrupters hence,

Of the blest word, from the aforesaid sense.
> The Holy Sacred Word,
> May it always afford
> > T' us all in common,
> > Both man and woman,
> A spiritual shield and sword,
> The Holy Sacred Word.

Here enter you all ladies of high birth,
Delicious, stately, charming, full of mirth,
10 Ingenious, lovely, miniard, proper, fair,
Magnetic, graceful, splendid, pleasant, rare,
Obliging, sprightly, virtuous, young, solacious,
Kind, neat, quick, feat, bright, compt, ripe, choice,
> dear, precious.
Alluring, courtly, comely, fine, complete.
Wise, personable, ravishing, and sweet,
Come joys enjoy. The Lord celestial
Hath given enough, wherewith to please us all.
> Gold give us, God forgive us,
20 > And from all woes relieve us;
> > That we the treasure
> > May reap of pleasure,
> And shun whate'er is grievous,
> Gold give us, God forgive us.

CHAPTER LVII

*How the Thelemites were governed, and of their
manner of living*

All their life was spent not in laws, statutes, or rules,
but according to their own free will and pleasure.
They rose out of their beds when they thought
good: they did eat, drink, labour, sleep, when they
had a mind to it, and were disposed for it. None did
30 awake them, none did offer to constrain them to eat,
drink, nor to do any other thing; for so had Gargantua established it. In all their rule, and strictest
tie of their order, there was but this one clause to
be observed,

DO WHAT THOU WILT.

Because men that are free, well-born, well-bred,
and conversant in honest companies, have naturally
an instinct and spur that prompteth them unto virtuous actions, and withdraws them from vice, which is
40 called honour. Those same men, when by base subjection and constraint they are brought under and
kept down, turn aside from that noble disposition,
by which they formerly were inclined to virtue, to
shake off and break that bond of servitude, wherein
they are so tyrannously enslaved; for it is agreeable
with the nature of man to long after things forbidden, and to desire what is denied us.

By this liberty they entered into a very laudable
emulation, to do all of them what they saw did
50 please one. If any of the gallants or ladies should

say, Let us drink, they would all drink. If any one of
them said, Let us play, they all played. If one said,
Let us go a walking into the fields, they went all. If
it were to go a hawking or a hunting, the ladies
mounted upon dainty well-paced nags, seated in a
stately palfrey saddle, carried on their lovely fists,
miniardly begloved every one of them, either a spar-
hawk, or a laneret, or a merlin, and the young gallants carried the other kinds of hawks. So nobly
were they taught, that there was neither he nor she 60
amongst them, but could read, write, sing, play upon
several musical instruments, speak five or six several
languages, and composed in them all very quaintly,
both in verse and prose. Never were seen so valiant
knights, so noble and worthy, so dexterous and skilful both on foot and a horseback, more brisk and
lively, more nimble and quick, or better handling
all manner of weapons than were there. Never were
seen ladies so proper and handsome, so miniard and
dainty, less forward, or more ready with their hand, 70
and with their needle, in every honest and free action belonging to that sex, than were there. For this
reason, when the time came, that any man of the
said abbey, either at the request of his parents, or
for some other cause, had a mind to go out of it, he
carried along with him one of the ladies, namely her
whom he had before that chosen for his mistress,
and they were married together. And if they had
formerly in Theleme lived in good devotion and
amity, they did continue therein and increase it to a 80
greater height in their state of matrimony: and did
entertain that mutual love till the very last day of
their life, in no less vigour and fervency, than at the
very day of their wedding.

Michel de Montaigne

1533–1592

The robust optimism of Rabelais and the early
Renaissance gave way in Montaigne to a rational skepticism of the perfectability of human nature
and the value of learning as such in the achievement of
self-knowledge. Actually, Montaigne was one of the most
learned men of his time and interlarded his essays with
quotations from his vast reading in the ancient classics.
But these ideas of others he had so thoroughly digested
that he used them only to illustrate his own thinking
and never as the sources of wisdom and hope that they
were for the typical Humanists. In a quite different way,
Montaigne is as much an individualist as Rabelais, and
his quiet skepticism reflects the deep-seated independence of his mind as much as it does the fading hopes of
the later Renaissance.

His temperament is revealed in his gentle life. The
careful education that his father gave him began that

quest for self-knowledge that was the whole aim and end of his career. Montaigne's father, a self-made man whom his son adored as the summary of all the abilities and virtues that he himself lacked, reared his nine children in a palatial château near the thriving city of Bordeaux according to a careful plan that expressed his own wise if also eccentric views on education. Michel, the eldest, had peasant godparents in order that he might not lose touch with the simple life of earthy folk. Corporal punishment was outlawed as injurious to children's nervous systems, and they were awakened in the morning by chamber music rather than by the alarming sound of a gong. A German tutor who knew no French taught them Latin in infancy, so that when Michel went off to school at six he spoke Latin much better than his native tongue. His seven years at the Collège de Guyenne in Bordeaux made him an accomplished classical scholar.

Montaigne was educated as a lawyer, and his father's position as mayor of Bordeaux assured him a thriving practice. But public life did not appeal to him, and after two years in Paris seeking an important post he retired from a political scene dominated by the savage struggle of Catholics and Protestant Huguenots that signalized the coming of the Reformation to France. The bloody Massacre of St. Bartholomew's Day in 1572, in which thousands of Huguenots were butchered, shocked his peaceful nature and enforced his design to seclude himself in his château, which his father's death had left him. After eight years of retirement there he published in 1580 the first two volumes of his *Essays* and then ventured forth on a tourist's trip through Switzerland, Germany, and Italy, during which he kept a careful journal of his observations. Upon his return he served as an able mayor of Bordeaux between 1581 and 1585, but his last years were spent in complete retirement on his estate, pursuing his studies in his magnificent library and revising and augmenting his *Essays*. Although he was happily married in 1565 to an efficient and self-effacing woman and had six daughters by her, he never overcame the sexual wanderlust of his youth and was whimsically devoted in later years to a Parisian girl, Marie de Gournay, thirty-four years younger than himself, who was happy to be called his "adopted daughter." However, the great inspiration of his life was not a woman but the friend of his youth, Étienne de la Boetie, a brilliant lawyer and classical scholar whom Montaigne met in 1559 and whose untimely death four years later cut short an intense friendship. In his fervent essay on *Friendship* Montaigne proclaimed the satisfying nature of their relationship and its enduring effect on his life.

Montaigne's reputation as philosopher and man of letters rests on his three books of *Essays* (published 1580–1595) in which he virtually created a modern literary form to embody his unique role in literature. As a genial skeptic who could discuss human problems better than he could reach conclusions about them, he thought of the essay as a discursive and tentative statement of his personal opinions about such varied subjects as education, social customs, cannibalism, idleness, drunkenness, honesty, old age, repentance, vanity—to mention the titles of only a few of the ninety-three. His prose style is intimate and informal, according to the literary standards of his day, and reading one of his essays is like listening to his wise, witty, and rambling conversation before a warm fire in the great library of his château.

Yet from the seemingly haphazard pages of the essays emerges a consistent intellectual attitude, if not a formal philosophy. Montaigne is the symbol of the open mind. Lacking the cocksure faith in man's reason assisted by learning that animated Rabelais, he was content to end each discussion with a shrug of the shoulders and his favorite phrase, "Que sçais-je?" ("What do I know?") The objective of all his thinking was to know himself as a specimen of mankind, and upon this study he focused the experiences of his classical education, his public service, his many friendships, his travels in foreign lands, and his years in his library. But knowledge led him at last to agnosticism and the belief that he could do no better in the end than to accept the life that he knew, with all its defects. This amiable note of resignation before the status quo completes a cycle of Renaissance thought and prepares the way for a new kind of rationalism in the next age.

The Author to the Reader

READER, thou hast here an honest book; it doth at the outset forewarn thee that, in contriving the same, I have proposed to myself no other than a domestic and private end: I have had no consideration at all either to thy service or to my glory. My powers are not capable of any such design. I have dedicated it to the particular commodity of my kinsfolk and friends, so that, having lost me (which they must do shortly), they may therein recover some traits of my conditions and humours, and by that means preserve more whole, and more life-like, the knowledge they had of me. Had my intention been to seek the world's favour, I should surely have adorned myself with borrowed beauties: I desire therein to be viewed as I appear in mine own genuine, simple, and ordinary manner, without study and artifice: for it is myself I paint. My defects are therein to be read to the life, and my imperfections and my natural form, so far as public reverence hath permitted me. If I had lived among those nations, which (they say) yet dwell under the sweet liberty of nature's primitive laws, I assure thee I would most willingly have painted myself quite fully and quite naked. Thus, reader, myself am the matter of my book: there's no reason thou shouldst employ thy leisure about so frivolous and vain a subject. Therefore, farewell.

The Author to the Reader. Translated by Charles Cotton.
7. **commodity,** advantage.

Of Democritus
and Heraclitus

THE judgment is an utensil proper for all subjects, and will have an oar in everything: which is the reason that in these Essays I take hold of all occasions where, though it happen to be a subject I do not very well understand, I try however, sounding it at a distance, and finding it too deep for my stature, I keep me on the shore; and this knowledge that a man can proceed no further is one effect of its virtue, yea, one of those of which it is most proud. One while in an idle and frivolous subject, I try to find out matter whereof to compose a body, and then to prop and support it; another while, I employ it in a noble subject, one that has been tossed and tumbled by a thousand hands, wherein a man can scarce possibly introduce anything of his own, the way being so beaten on every side that he must of necessity walk in the steps of another. In such a case, 'tis the work of the judgment to take the way that seems best, and of a thousand paths, to determine that this or that is the best. I leave the choice of my arguments to fortune, and take that she first presents to me; they are all alike to me. I never design to go through any of them; for I never see all of anything: neither do they who so largely promise to show it others. Of a hundred members and faces that everything has, I take one, onewhile to look it over only, another while to ripple up the skin, and sometimes to pinch it to the bones. I give a stab, not so wide but as deep as I can, and am for the most part tempted to take it in hand by some new light I discover in it. Did I know myself less, I might perhaps venture to handle something or other to the bottom, and to be deceived in my own inability; but sprinkling here one word and there another, patterns cut from several pieces and scattered without design and without engaging myself too far, I am not responsible for them, or obliged to keep close to my subject, without varying at my own liberty and pleasure, and giving up myself to doubt and uncertainty, and to my own governing method, ignorance.

All motion discovers us: the very same soul of Caesar, that made itself so conspicuous in marshalling and commanding the battle of Pharsalia, was also seen as solicitous and busy in the softer affairs of love and leisure. A man makes a judgment of a horse, not only by seeing him when he is showing off his paces, but by his very walk, nay, and by seeing him stand in the stable.

Amongst the functions of the soul, there are some of a lower and meaner form; he who does not see her in those inferior offices as well as in those of nobler note, never fully discovers her; and, peradventure, she is best shown where she moves her simpler pace. The winds of passions take most hold of her in her highest flights; and the rather by reason that she wholly applies herself to, and exercises her whole virtue upon, every particular subject, and never handles more than one thing at a time, and that not according to it, but according to herself. Things in respect to themselves have, peradventure, their weight, measures, and conditions; but when we once take them into us, the soul forms them as she pleases. Death is terrible to Cicero, coveted by Cato, indifferent to Socrates. Health, conscience, authority, knowledge, riches, beauty, and their contraries all strip themselves at their entering into us, and receive a new robe, and of another fashion, from the soul; and of what colour, brown, bright, green, dark, and of what quality, sharp, sweet, deep, or superficial, as best pleases each of them, for they are not agreed upon any common standard of forms, rules, or proceedings; every one is a queen in her own dominions. Let us, therefore, no more excuse ourselves upon the external qualities of things; it belongs to us to give ourselves an account of them. Our good or ill has no other dependence but on ourselves. 'Tis there that our offerings and our vows are due, and to fortune: she has no power over our manners; on the contrary, they draw and make her follow in their train, and cast her in their own mould. Why should not I judge of Alexander at table, ranting and drinking at the prodigious rate he sometimes used to do? Or, if he played at chess? what string of his soul was not touched by this idle and childish game? I hate and avoid it, because it is not play enough, that it is too grave and serious a diversion, and I am ashamed to lay out as much thought and study upon it as would serve to much better uses. He did not more pump his brains about his glorious expedition into the Indies, nor than another in unravelling a passage upon which depends the safety of mankind. To what a degree does this ridiculous diversion molest the soul, when all her faculties are summoned together upon this trivial account! and how fair an opportunity she herein gives every one to know and to make a right judgment of himself? I do not more thoroughly sift myself in any other posture than this: what passion are we exempted from in it? Anger, spite, malice, impatience, and a vehement desire of getting the better in a concern wherein it were more excusable to be ambitious of being over-

Of Democritus and Heraclitus. Translated by Charles Cotton.

75. **excuse ourselves upon,** release ourselves from considering.

come; for to be eminent, to excel above the common rate in frivolous things, nowise befits a man of honour. What I say in this example may be said in all others. Every particle, every employment of man manifests him equally with any other.

Democritus and Heraclitus were two philosophers, of whom the first, finding human condition ridiculous and vain, never appeared abroad but with a jeering and laughing countenance; whereas Heraclitus commiserating that same condition of ours, appeared always with a sorrowful look, and tears in his eyes: "The one always, when he stepped over his threshold, laughed at the world, the other always wept." I am clearly for the first humour; not because it is more pleasant to laugh than to weep, but because it expresses more contempt and condemnation than the other, and I think we can never be despised according to our full desert. Compassion and bewailing seem to imply some esteem of and value for the thing bemoaned; whereas the things we laugh at are by that expressed to be of no moment. I do not think that we are so unhappy as we are vain, or have in us so much malice as folly; we are not so full of mischief as inanity; nor so miserable as we are vile and mean. And therefore Diogenes, who passed away his time in rolling himself in his tub, and made nothing of the great Alexander esteeming us no better than flies, or bladders puffed up with wind, was a sharper and more penetrating, and, consequently in my opinion, a juster judge than Timon, surnamed the Man-hater; for what a man hates he lays to heart. This last was an enemy to all mankind, who passionately desired our ruin and avoided our conversation as dangerous, proceeding from wicked and depraved natures: the other valued us so little that we could neither trouble nor infect him by our example; and left us to herd one with another, not out of fear, but from contempt of our society: concluding us as incapable of doing good as ill.

Of the same strain was Statilius' answer, when Brutus courted him into the conspiracy against Caesar; he was satisfied that the enterprise was just, but he did not think mankind worthy of a wise man's concern; according to the doctrine of Hegesias, who said, that a wise man ought to do nothing but for himself, forasmuch as he only was worthy of it: and to the saying of Theodorus, that it was not reasonable a wise man should hazard himself for his country, and endanger wisdom for a company of fools. Our condition is as ridiculous as risible.

12–13. "The one always . . . always wept." Juvenal, *Satires*, x, 28. 31. **Timon**, of Athens, the noted misanthrope. 43–45. **he was satisfied . . . concern;** quoted in Plutarch's *Life of Brutus*, chapter 12. 45. **Hegesias,** Cyrenaic philosopher, here quoted in Diogenes Laertius, ii, 95. 48. **Theodorus,** another Cyrenaic, here quoted in Diogenes Laertius, ii, 98.

Of the Education of Children

. . . A FRIEND of mine the other day told me that I should a little farther have extended my discourse on the education of children. Now, madam, if I had any sufficiency in this subject, I could not possibly better employ it than to present my best instructions to the little gentleman that threatens you shortly with a happy birth (for you are too generous to begin otherwise than with a male); for having had so great a hand in the treaty of your marriage, I have a certain particular right and interest in the greatness and prosperity of the issue that shall spring from it; besides that, your having had the best of my services so long in possession sufficiently obliges me to desire the honour and advantage of all wherein you shall be concerned. But, in truth, all I understand as to that particular is only this, that the greatest and most important difficulty of human science is the education of children. For as in agriculture, the husbandry that is to precede planting, as also planting itself, is certain, plain, and well known; but after that which is planted comes to life, there is a great deal more to be done, more art to be used, more care to be taken, and much more difficulty to cultivate and bring it to perfection: so it is with men; it is no hard matter to get children; but after they are born, then begins the trouble, solicitude, and care rightly to train, principle, and bring them up. The symptoms of their inclinations in that tender age are so obscure and the promises so uncertain and fallacious that it is very hard to establish any solid judgment or conjecture upon them. Look at Cimon, for example, and Themistocles, and a thousand others, who very much deceived the expectation men had for them. Cubs of bears and puppies readily discover their natural inclination; but men so soon as ever they are grown up, applying themselves to certain habits, engaging themselves in certain opinions, and conforming themselves to particular laws and customs, easily alter, or at least disguise, their true and real disposition; and yet it is hard to force the propension of nature. Whence it comes to pass that, for not having chosen the right course, we often take very great pains and consume a good part of our time in training up children to things for which, by their natural constitution, they are totally unfit. In this difficulty, nevertheless, I am clearly of opinion that they ought to be elemented in the best and most advantageous studies,

*Of the Education of Children.*ᴬ Translated by Charles Cotton.
54. **madam,** the Comtesse de Gurson, to whom the essay is dedicated.
83. **Cimon, Themistocles,** Greek commanders of the fifth century B.C.

without taking too much notice of, or being too superstitious in, those light prognostics they give of themselves in their tender years, and to which Plato in his "Republic" gives, methinks, too much authority.

Madam, science is a very great ornament, and a thing of marvellous use, especially in persons raised to that degree of fortune in which you are. And, in truth, in persons of mean and low condition it cannot perform its true and genuine office, being naturally more prompt to assist in the conduct of war, in the government of peoples, in negotiating the leagues and friendships of princes and foreign nations, than in forming a syllogism in logic, in pleading a process in law, or in prescribing a dose of pills in physic. . . .

For a boy of quality, then, who pretends to letters not upon the account of profit (for so mean an object as that is unworthy of the grace and favour of the Muses, and moreover, in it a man directs his service to and depends upon others), nor so much for outward ornament, as for his own proper and peculiar use, and to furnish and enrich himself within, having rather a desire to come out an accomplished cavalier than a mere scholar or learned man; for such a one, I say, I would also have his friends solicitous to find him out a tutor who has rather a well-made than a well-filled head; seeking, indeed, both the one and the other, but rather of the two to prefer manners and judgment to mere learning, and that this man should exercise his charge after a new method.

'Tis the custom of pedagogues to be eternally thundering in their pupil's ears, as they were pouring into a funnel, whilst the business of the pupil is only to repeat what the others have said. Now I would have a tutor to correct this error, and that at the very first he should, according to the capacity he has to deal with, put it to the test, permitting his pupil himself to taste things and of himself to discern and choose them, sometimes opening the way to him, and sometimes leaving him to open it for himself; that is, I would not have him alone to invent and speak, but that he should also hear his pupil speak in turn. Socrates, and since him Arcesilaus, made first their scholars speak, and then they spoke to them. "The authority of those who teach, is very often an impediment to those who desire to learn." It is good to make him, like a young horse, trot before him, that he may judge of his going and how much he is to abate of his own speed to accommodate himself to the vigour and capacity of the other. For want of which due proportion we spoil all; which also to know how to adjust, and to keep within an exact and due measure, is one of the hardest things I know, and 'tis the effect of a high and well-tempered soul to know how to condescend to such puerile motions and to govern and direct them. I walk firmer and more secure up hill than down.

Such as, according to our common way of teaching, undertake with one and the same lesson and the same measure of direction to instruct several boys of differing and unequal capacities are infinitely mistaken; and 'tis no wonder if in a whole multitude of scholars there are not found above two or three who bring away any good account of their time and discipline. Let the master not only examine him about the grammatical construction of the bare words of his lesson, but about the sense and substance of them, and let him judge of the profit he has made, not by the testimony of his memory, but by that of his life. Let him make him put what he has learned into a hundred several forms, and accommodate it to so many several subjects, to see if he yet rightly comprehends it, and has made it his own, taking instruction of his progress by the pedagogic institutions of Plato. 'Tis a sign of crudity and indigestion to disgorge what we eat in the same condition it was swallowed; the stomach has not performed its office unless it has altered the form and condition of what was committed to it to concoct. Our minds work only upon trust when bound and compelled to follow the appetite of another's fancy, enslaved and captivated under the authority of another's instruction. We have been so subjected to the trammel that we have no free nor natural pace of our own; our own vigour and liberty are extinct and gone: "They are ever in wardship.". . .

Let him make him examine and thoroughly sift everything he reads, and lodge nothing in his fancy upon simple authority and upon trust. Aristotle's principles will then be no more principles to him than those of Epicurus and the Stoics. Let this diversity of opinions be propounded to, and laid before him; he will himself choose, if he be able; if not, he will remain in doubt.

"I love to doubt, as well as to know."

For, if he embrace the opinions of Xenophon and Plato by his own reason, they will no more be theirs, but become his own. Who follows another follows nothing, finds nothing, nay, is inquisitive after nothing. "We are under no king; let each look to himself." Let him, at least, know that he knows. It will be necessary that he imbibe their knowledge, not that he be corrupted with their precepts; and no matter if he forget where he had his learning, provided he know how to apply it to his own use. Truth

45–46. Arcesilaus, Arcesilas of Pitane (c. 315–240 B.C.), founder of the Second Academy in Athens. 47–49. "The authority . . . to learn." Cicero, De Natura Deorum, i, 5.

88. "They are . . . wardship." Seneca, Epistles, 33. 97. "I love . . . to know." Dante, Inferno, xi, 93. 102–103. "We are . . . himself." Seneca, Epistles, 33.

and reason are common to every one and are no more his who spake them first than his who speaks them after. 'Tis no more according to Plato than according to me, since both he and I equally see and understand them. Bees cull their several sweets from this flower and that blossom, here and there where they find them, but themselves afterwards make the honey, which is all and purely their own, and no more thyme and marjoram. So the several fragments he borrows from others, he will transform and shuffle together to compile a work that shall be absolutely his own; that is to say, his judgment: his instruction, labour, and study tend to cover whence he got the materials that have assisted him, but only to produce what he has himself done with them. Men that live upon pillage and borrowing expose their purchases and buildings to every one's view: but do not proclaim how they came by the money. We do not see the fees and perquisites of a gentleman of the long robe; but we see the alliances wherewith he fortifies himself and his family, and the titles and honours he has obtained for him and his. No man divulges his revenue; or at least, which way it comes in: but every one publishes his acquisitions. The advantages of our study are to become better and more wise. 'Tis, says Epicharmus, the understanding that sees and hears, 'tis the understanding that improves and reigns; all other faculties are blind, and deaf, and without soul. And certainly we render it timorous and servile in not allowing it the liberty and privilege to do anything of itself. Whoever asked his pupil what he thought of grammar and rhetoric, or of such and such a sentence of Cicero? Our masters stick them, full feathered, in our memories, and there establish them like oracles, of which the letters and syllables are of the substance of the thing.

To know by rote is no knowledge, and signifies no more but only to retain what one has intrusted to our memory. That which a man rightly knows and understands, he is the free disposer of at his own full liberty, without any regard to the author from whence he had it or fumbling over the leaves of his book. A mere bookish learning is a poor, paltry learning; it may serve for ornament, but there is yet no foundation for any superstructure to be built upon it, according to the opinion of Plato, who says that constancy, faith, and sincerity are the true philosophy, and the other sciences, that are directed to other ends, mere adulterate paint. I could wish that Paluel or Pompey, those two noted dancers of my time, could have taught us to cut capers by only seeing them do it, without stirring from our places,

as these men pretend to inform the understanding without ever setting it to work; or that we could learn to ride, handle a pike, touch a lute, or sing without the trouble of practice, as these attempt to make us judge and speak well without exercising us in judging or speaking. Now in this initiation of our studies and in their progress, whatsoever presents itself before us is book sufficient; a roguish trick of a page, a sottish mistake of a servant, a jest at the table are so many new subjects.

And for this reason, conversation with men is of very great use and travel into foreign countries; not to bring back (as most of our young monsieurs do) an account only of how many paces Santa Rotonda is in circuit; or of the richness of Signora Livia's petticoats; or, as some others, how much Nero's face, in a statue in such an old ruin, is longer and broader than that made for him on some medal; but to be able chiefly to give an account of the humours, manners, customs, and laws of those nations where he has been, and that we may whet and sharpen our wits by rubbing them against those of others. I would that a boy should be sent abroad very young, and first, so as to kill two birds with one stone, into those neighbouring nations whose language is most differing from our own, and to which, if it be not formed betimes, the tongue will grow too stiff to bend.

And also 'tis the general opinion of all that a child should not be brought up in his mother's lap. Mothers are too tender, and their natural affection is apt to make the most discreet of them all so overfond that they can neither find in their hearts to give them due correction for the faults they commit, nor suffer them to be inured to hardships and hazards, as they ought to be. They will not endure to see them return all dust and sweat from their exercise, to drink cold drink when they art hot, nor see them mount an unruly horse, nor take a foil in hand against a rude fencer, or so much as to discharge a carbine. And yet there is no remedy; whoever will breed a boy to be good for anything when he comes to be a man must by no means spare him when young and must very often transgress the rules of physic:— "Let him live in the open air, and ever in movement about something." It is not enough to fortify his soul; you are also to make his sinews strong; for the soul will be oppressed if not assisted by the members and would have too hard a task to discharge two offices alone. I know very well to my cost how much mine groans under the burden from being accommodated with a body so tender and indisposed as eternally leans and presses upon her; and often in reading perceive that our masters in their writings make examples pass for magnanimity and fortitude of mind, which really are rather toughness of skin

26. **Epicharmus**, a Greek comic poet of the fifth century B.C., also considered a philosopher because a philosophical poem, probably by another writer, was published under his name.

67. **Santa Rotonda**, the Pantheon of Rome. 97–98. **"Let him live . . . something."** Horace, *Odes*, II, 3, 5.

and hardness of bones; for I have seen men, women, and children naturally born of so hard and insensible a constitution of body that a sound cudgelling has been less to them than a flirt with a finger would have been to me, and that would neither cry out, wince, nor shrink for a good swinging beating; and when wrestlers counterfeit the philosophers in patience, 'tis rather strength of nerves than stoutness of heart. Now to be inured to undergo labour is to be accustomed to endure pain: "Labour hardens us against pain." A boy is to be broken in to the toil and roughness of exercise, so as to be trained up to the pain and suffering of dislocations, cholics, cauteries, and even imprisonment and the rack itself; for he may come, by misfortune, to be reduced to the worst of these, which (as this world goes) is sometimes inflicted on the good as well as the bad. As for proof, in our present civil war whoever draws his sword against the laws threatens the honestest men with the whip and the halter.

And, moreover, by living at home, the authority of this governor, which ought to be sovereign over the boy he has received into his charge, is often checked and hindered by the presence of parents; to which may also be added that the respect the whole family pay him as their master's son, and the knowledge he has of the estate and greatness he is heir to are, in my opinion, no small inconveniences in these tender years.

And yet, even in this conversing with men I spoke of but now, I have observed this vice, that instead of gathering observations from others we make it our whole business to lay ourselves upon them, and are more concerned how to expose and set out our own commodities than how to increase our stock by acquiring new. Silence, therefore, and modesty are very advantageous qualities in conversation. One should, therefore, train up this boy to be sparing and a husband of his knowledge when he has acquired it; and to forbear taking exceptions at or reproving every idle saying or ridiculous story that is said or told in his presence; for it is a very unbecoming rudeness to carp at everything that is not agreeable to our own palate. Let him be satisfied with correcting himself and not seem to condemn everything in another he would not do himself, nor dispute it as against common customs. "Let him be wise without ostentation, without envy." Let him avoid these vain and uncivil images of authority, this childish ambition of coveting to appear better bred and more accomplished than he really will, by such carriage, discover himself to be. And, as if opportunities of interrupting and reprehending were not to be omitted, to desire thence to derive the reputation

of something more than ordinary. For as it becomes none but great poets to make use of the poetical licence, so it is intolerable for any but men of great and illustrious souls to assume privilege above the authority of custom; "If Socrates and Aristippus have transgressed the rules of good conduct or custom, let him not imagine that he is licensed to do the same; for it was by great and sovereign virtues that they obtained this privilege." Let him be instructed not to engage in discourse or dispute but with a champion worthy of him, and even there not to make use of all the little subtleties that may seem pat for his purpose, but only such arguments as may best serve him. Let him be taught to be curious in the election and choice of his reasons, to abominate impertinence, and, consequently, to affect brevity; but, above all, let him be lessoned to acquiesce and submit to truth so soon as ever he shall discover it, whether in his opponent's argument or upon better consideration of his own, for he shall never be preferred to the chair for a mere clatter of words and syllogisms and is no further engaged to any argument whatever than as he shall in his own judgment approve it: nor yet is arguing a trade, where the liberty of recantation and getting off upon better thoughts are to be sold for ready money: "Neither is there any necessity upon him that he should defend all things that are recommended to and enjoined him."

If his governor be of my humour, he will form his will to be a very good and loyal subject to his prince, very affectionate to his person and very stout in his quarrel; but withal he will cool in him the desire of having any other tie to his service than public duty. Besides several other inconveniences that are inconsistent with the liberty every honest man ought to have, a man's judgment, being bribed and prepossessed by these particular obligations, is either blinded and less free to exercise its function or blemished with ingratitude and indiscretion. A man that is purely a courtier can neither have power nor will to speak or think otherwise than favourably and well of a master, who, amongst so many millions of other subjects, has picked out him with his own hand to nourish and advance. This favour, and the profit flowing from it, must needs, and not without some show of reason, corrupt his freedom and dazzle him; and we commonly see these people speak in another kind of phrase than is ordinarily spoken by others of the same nation, though what they say in that courtly language is not much to be believed.

Let his conscience and virtue be eminently manifest in his speaking and have only reason for their guide. Make him understand that to acknowledge the error he shall discover in his own argument,

---

10-11. "Labour . . . pain." Cicero, *Tusculan Disputations*, II, 15. 18. **present civil war**, the Huguenot wars in France. 47-48. "**Let him . . . envy.**" Seneca, *Moral Epistles*, 103.

59-63. "**If Socrates . . . this privilege.**" Cicero, *Offices*, I, 41. 80-83. "**Neither is . . . enjoined him.**" Cicero, *Acad.*, II, 3.

though only found out by himself, is an effect of judgment and sincerity, which are the principal things he is to seek after; that obstinacy and contention are common qualities, most appearing in mean souls; that to revise and correct himself, to forsake an unjust argument in the height and heat of dispute, are rare, great, and philosophical qualities. Let him be advised, being in company, to have his eye and ear in every corner; for I find that the places of greatest honour are commonly seized upon by men that have least in them and that the greatest fortunes are seldom accompanied with the ablest parts. I have been present when, whilst they at the upper end of the chamber have been only commending the beauty of the arras, or the flavour of the wine, many things that have been very finely said at the lower end of the table have been lost and thrown away. Let him examine every man's talent; a peasant, a bricklayer, a passenger: one may learn something from every one of these in their several capacities, and something will be picked out of their discourse whereof some use may be made at one time or another; nay, even the folly and impertinence of others will contribute to his instruction. By observing the graces and manners of all he sees, he will create to himself an emulation of the good and a contempt of the bad.

Let an honest curiosity be suggested to his fancy of being inquisitive after everything; whatever there is singular and rare near the place where he is, let him go and see it; a fine house, a noble fountain, an eminent man, the place where a battle has been anciently fought, the passages of Caesar and Charlemagne: "What country is bound in frost, what land is friable with heat, what wind serves fairest for Italy." Let him inquire into the manners, revenues, and alliances of princes, things in themselves very pleasant to learn, and very useful to know.

In this conversing with men, I mean also, and principally, those who only live in the records of history; he shall, by reading those books, converse with the great and heroic souls of the best ages. 'Tis an idle and vain study to those who make it so by doing it after a negligent manner, but to those who do it with care and observation, 'tis a study of inestimable fruit and value; and the only study, as Plato reports, that the Lacedaemonians reserved to themselves. What profit shall he not reap as to the business of men by reading the lives of Plutarch? But, withal, let my governor remember to what end his instructions are principally directed, and that he do not so much imprint in his pupil's memory the date of the ruin of Carthage as the manners of Hannibal and Scipio; nor so much where Marcellus died as why it was unworthy of his duty that he died

there. Let him not teach him so much the narrative parts of history as to judge them; the reading of them, in my opinion, is a thing that of all others we apply ourselves unto with the most differing measure. I have read a hundred things in Livy that another has not, or not taken notice of at least; and Plutarch has read a hundred more there than ever I could find, or than, peradventure, that author ever wrote. To some it is merely a grammar study, to others the very anatomy of philosophy, by which the most abstruse parts of our human nature penetrate. There are in Plutarch many long discourses very worthy to be carefully read and observed, for he is, in my opinion, of all others the greatest master in that kind of writing; but there are a thousand others which he has only touched and glanced upon, where he only points with his finger to direct us which way we may go if we will, and contents himself sometimes with giving only one brisk hit in the nicest article of the question, whence we are to grope out the rest. As, for example, where he says that the inhabitants of Asia came to be vassals to one only, for not having been able to pronounce one syllable, which is No. Which saying of his gave perhaps matter and occasion to LaBoetie to write his "Voluntary Servitude." Only to see him pick out a light action in a man's life, or a mere word that does not seem to amount even to that, is itself a whole discourse. 'Tis to our prejudice that men of understanding should so immoderately affect brevity; no doubt their reputation is the better by it, but in the meantime we are the worse. Plutarch had rather we should applaud his judgment than commend his knowledge, and had rather leave us with an appetite to read more than glutted with that we have already read. He knew very well that a man may say too much even upon the best subjects, and that Alexandridas justly reproached him who made very good but too long speeches to the Ephori, when he said: "O stranger! thou speakest the things thou shouldst speak, but not as thou shouldst speak them." Such as have lean and spare bodies stuff themselves out with clothes; so they who are defective in matter endeavour to make amends with words.

Human understanding is marvellously enlightened by daily conversation with men, for we are, otherwise, compressed and heaped up in ourselves and have our sight limited to the length of our own noses. One asking Socrates of what country he was, he did not make answer, of Athens, but of the world; he whose imagination was fuller and wider, em-

34–36. "What country . . . for Italy." Propertius, IV, 3, 39.

76. where he says. . . . In his *Essay on False Shame.* 80. **LaBoetie,** Montaigne's close friend, Étienne de la Boetie, whom he praises in his essay on friendship. 94–96. **"O stranger . . . speak them."** Plutarch's *Apothegms of the Lacedaemonians.* 104–105. **One asking Socrates . . . of the world.** Cicero, *Tusculan Disputations,* V, 37.

braced the whole world for his country, and extended his society and friendship to all mankind; not as we do, who look no further than our feet. When the vines of my village are nipped with the frost, my parish priest presently concludes that the indignation of God is gone out against all the human race and that the cannibals have already got the pip. Who is it that, seeing the havoc of these civil wars of ours, does not cry out that the machine of the world
10 is near dissolution and that the day of judgment is at hand; without considering that many worse things have been seen and that, in the meantime, people are very merry in a thousand other parts of the earth for all this? For my part, considering the licence and impunity that always attend such commotions, I wonder they are so moderate and that there is no more mischief done. To him who feels the hailstones patter about his ears, the whole hemisphere appears to be in storm and tempest; like the
20 ridiculous Savoyard who said very gravely that, if that simple king of France could have managed his fortune as he should have done, he might in time have come to have been steward of the household to the duke his master: the fellow could not, in his shallow imagination, conceive that there could be anything greater than a Duke of Savoy. And, in truth, we are all of us, insensibly, in this error, an error of a very great weight and very pernicious consequence. But whoever shall represent to his
30 fancy, as in a picture, that great image of our mother Nature in her full majesty and lustre, whoever in her face shall read so general and so constant a variety, whoever shall observe himself in that figure, and not himself but a whole kingdom, no bigger than the least touch or prick of a pencil in comparison of the whole, that man alone is able to value things according to their true estimate and grandeur.

This great world which some do yet multiply as several species under one genus, is the mirror wherein
40 we are to behold ourselves, to be able to know ourselves as we ought to do in the true bias. In short, I would have this to be the book my young gentleman should study with the most attention. So many humours, so many sects, so many judgments, opinions, laws, and customs teach us to judge aright of our own and inform our understanding to discover its imperfection and natural infirmity, which is no trivial speculation. So many mutations of states and kingdoms and so many turns and revolutions of pub-
50 lic fortune will make us wise enough to make no great wonder of our own. So many great names, so many famous victories and conquests drowned and swallowed in oblivion render our hopes ridiculous of eternising our names by the taking of half-a-score of light horse, or a henroost, which only derives its memory from its ruin. The pride and arrogance of so many foreign pomps and ceremonies, the tumorous

majesty of so many courts and grandeurs accustom and fortify our sight without astonishment or wink-
60 ing to behold the lustre of our own; so many millions of men, buried before us, encourage us not to fear to go seek such good company in the other world: and so of all the rest. Pythagoras was wont to say that our life resembles the great and populous assembly of the Olympic games, wherein some exercise the body, that they may carry away the glory of the prize, others bring merchandise to sell for profit; there are, also some (and those none of the worst sort) who pursue no other advantage than
70 only to look on, and consider how and why everything is done, and to be spectators of the lives of other men, thereby the better to judge of and regulate their own.

To examples may fitly be applied all the profitable discourses of philosophy, to which all human actions, as to their best rule, ought to be especially directed: a scholar shall be taught to know—"Learn what it is right to wish; what is the true use of coined money; how much it becomes us to give in liberality to our country and our dear relations; whom and
80 what the Deity commanded thee to be; and in what part of the human system thou art placed; what we are and to what purpose engendered"; what it is to know, and what to be ignorant; what ought to be the end and design of study; what valor, temperance, and justice are; the difference betwixt ambition and avarice, servitude and subjection, licence and liberty; by what token a man may know true and solid contentment; how far death, affliction, and disgrace are to be apprehended: "And how you may shun or sus-
90 tain every hardship"; by what secret springs we move and the reason of our various agitations and irresolutions: for, methinks, the first doctrine with which one should season his understanding ought to be that which regulates his manners and his sense; that teaches him to know himself and how both well to die and well to live. Amongst the liberal sciences, let us begin with that which makes us free; not that they do not all serve in some measure to the instruction and use of life, as all other things in some sort
100 also do; but let us make choice of that which directly and professedly serves to that end. If we are once able to restrain the offices of human life within their just and natural limits, we shall find that most of the sciences in use are of no great use to us, and even in those that are, that there are many very unnecessary cavities and dilations which we had better let alone, and following Socrates' direction, limit the course of our studies to those things only where is a true and real utility: "Dare to be wise; begin: he

63. **Pythagoras . . . say.** Cicero, *Tusculan Disputations*, v, 3. 77–83. **"Learn what . . . purpose engendered."** Persius, III, 69. 90–91. **"And how . . . hardship."** Virgil, *Aeneid*, III, 459. 110. **"Dare to be wise. . . ."** Horace, *Epistles*, I, 2, 40.

who defers the hour of living well is like the clown, waiting till the river shall have flowed out; but the river still runs on, and will run on, with constant course, to ages without end." 'Tis a great foolery to teach our children—"What influence Pisces have, or the sign of angry Leo, or Capricorn laving in the Hesperian wave."

Anaximenes writing to Pythagoras, "To what purpose," said he, "should I trouble myself in searching out the secrets of the stars, having death or slavery continually before my eyes?" For the kings of Persia were at that time preparing to invade his country. Every one ought to say thus, "Being assaulted as I am by ambition, avarice, temerity, superstition, and having within so many other enemies of life, shall I go cudgel my brains about the world's revolutions?"

After having taught him what will make him more wise and good, you may then entertain him with the elements of logic, physics, geometry, rhetoric, and the science which he shall then himself most incline to, his judgment being beforehand formed and fit to choose, he will quickly make his own. The way of instructing him ought to be sometimes by discourse and sometimes by reading; sometimes his governor shall put the author himself, which he shall think most proper for him, into his hands, and sometimes only the marrow and substance of it; and if himself be not conversant enough in books to turn to all the fine discourses the books contain for his purpose, there may some man of learning be joined to him that upon every occasion shall supply him with what he stands in need of, to furnish it to his pupil. And who can doubt but that this way of teaching is much more easy and natural than that of Gaza, in which the precepts are so intricate and so harsh and the words so vain, lean, and insignificant that there is no hold to be taken of them, nothing that quickens and elevates the wit and fancy, whereas here the mind has what to feed upon and to digest. This fruit, therefore, is not only without comparison much more fair and beautiful, but will also be much more early ripe.

'Tis a thousand pities that matters should be at such a pass in this age of ours that philosophy, even with men of understanding, should be looked upon as a vain and fantastic name, a thing of no use, no value, either in opinion or effect, of which I think those egotisms and petty sophistries, by prepossessing the avenues to it, are the cause. And people are much to blame to represent it to children for a thing of so difficult access and with such a frowning, grim, and formidable aspect. Who is it that has disguised it thus with this false, pale, and ghostly countenance?

There is nothing more airy, more gay, more frolic, and, I had like to have said, more wanton. She preaches nothing but feasting and jollity; a melancholic, anxious look shows that she does not inhabit there. Demetrius the grammarian finding in the temple of Delphos a knot of philosophers set chatting together, said to them, "Either I am much deceived, or by your cheerful and pleasant countenances, you are engaged in no very deep discourse." To which one of them, Heracleon the Megarean, replied: "'Tis for such as are puzzled about inquiring whether the future tense of the verb βάλλω be spelt with a double λ, or that hunt after the derivation of the comparatives χείρον and βέλτιον, and the superlatives χείριστον and βέλτιστον, to knit their brows whilst discoursing of their science: but as to philosophical discourses, they always divert and cheer up those that entertain them, and never deject them or make them sad." "You may discern the torments of mind lurking in a sick body; you may discern its joys: each habit the face assumes from the mind."

The soul that lodges philosophy ought to be of such a constitution of health as to render the body in like manner healthful too; she ought to make her tranquillity and satisfaction shine so as to appear without, and her contentment ought to fashion the outward behaviour to her own mould and consequently to fortify it with a graceful confidence, an active and joyous carriage, and a serene and contented countenance. The most manifest sign of wisdom is a continual cheerfulness; her state is like that of things in the regions above the moon, always clear and serene. 'Tis Baroco and Baralipton that render their disciples so dirty and illfavoured, and not she; they do not so much as know her but by hearsay. What! It is she that calms and appeases the storms and tempests of the soul, and who teaches famine and fevers to laugh and sing; and that, not by certain imaginary epicycles, but by natural and manifest reasons. She has virtue for her end; which is not, as the schoolmen say, situate upon the summit of a perpendicular, rugged, inaccessible precipice. Such as have approached her find her, quite on the contrary, to be seated in a fair, fruitful, and flourishing plain, from whence she easily discovers all things below; to which place anyone may, however, arrive if he know but the way, through shady, green, and sweetly flourishing avenues, by a pleasant, easy, and smooth descent, like that of the celestial vault. 'Tis for not having frequented this supreme, this beautiful, triumphant, and amiable, this equally delicious and courageous virtue, this so professed and implacable enemy to anxiety, sorrow, fear, and constraint, who, having nature for her guide, has fortune

5-7. "What influence . . . wave." Propertius, IV, 1, 89. 8-11. Anaximenes . . . before my eyes?" according to Diogenes Laertius, II, 4. 35. Gaza, Theodore Gaza, rector of the Academy of Ferrara.

72-75. "You may discern . . . mind." Juvenal, IX, 18. 87. Baroco and Baralipton, two terms of old scholastic logic.

and pleasure for her companions, that they have gone according to their own weak imagination and created this ridiculous, this sorrowful, querulous, despiteful, threatening, terrible image of it to themselves and others, and placed it upon a rock apart, amongst thorns and brambles, and made of it a hobgoblin to affright people.

But the governor that I would have, that is such a one as knows it to be his duty to possess his pupil with as much or more affection than reverence to virtue, will be able to inform him that the poets have evermore accommodated themselves to the public humour, and make him sensible that the gods have planted more toil and sweat in the avenues of the cabinets of Venus than in those of Minerva. And when he shall once find him begin to apprehend and shall represent to him a Bradamante or an Angelica for a mistress, a natural, active, generous, and not a viragoish, but a manly beauty, in comparison of a soft, delicate, artificial, simpering, and affected form; the one in the habit of a heroic youth, wearing a glittering helmet, the other tricked up in curls and ribbons like a wanton minx; he will then look upon his own affection as brave and masculine when he shall choose quite contrary to that effeminate shepherd of Phrygia.

Such a tutor will make a pupil digest this new lesson, that the height and value of true virtue consists in the facility, utility, and pleasure of its exercise; so far from difficulty that boys as well as men and the innocent as well as the subtle may make it their own: it is by order, and not by force, that it is to be acquired. Socrates, her first minion, is so averse to all manner of violence, as totally to throw it aside, to slip into the more natural facility of her own progress. 'Tis the nursing mother of all human pleasures, who in rendering them just, renders them also pure and permanent; in moderating them, keeps them in breath and appetite; in interdicting those which she herself refuses, whets our desire to those that she allows; and, like a kind and liberal mother, abundantly allows all that nature requires, even to satiety, if not to lassitude: unless we mean to say that the regimen which stops the toper before he has drunk himself drunk, the glutton before he has eaten to a surfeit, and the lecher before he has got the pox is an enemy to pleasure. If the ordinary fortune fail, she does without it and forms another, wholly her own, not so fickle and unsteady as the other. She can be rich, be potent and wise, and knows how to lie upon soft perfumed beds: she loves life, beauty, glory, and health; but her proper and peculiar office is to know how to regulate the use of all these good things, and how to lose them without concern: an office much more noble than troublesome, and with-

out which the whole course of life is unnatural, turbulent, and deformed, and there it is indeed, that men may justly represent those monsters upon rocks and precipices.

If this pupil shall happen to be of so contrary a disposition that he had rather hear a tale of a tub than the true narrative of some noble expedition or some wise and learned discourse; who at the beat of drum that excites the youthful ardour of his companions leaves that to follow another that calls to a morris dance or the bears; who would not wish, and find it more delightful and more excellent, to return all dust and sweat victorious from a battle than from tennis or from a ball, with the prize of those exercises; I see no other remedy but that he be bound prentice in some good town to learn to make minced pies, though he were the son of a duke; according to Plato's precept that children are to be placed out and disposed of, not according to the wealth, qualities, or condition of the father, but according to the faculties and the capacity of their own souls.

Since philosophy is that which instructs us to live, and that infancy has there its lessons as well as other ages, why is it not communicated to children betimes? "The clay is moist and soft: now, now make haste, and form the pitcher on the rapid wheel."

They begin to teach us to live when we have almost done living. A hundred students have got the pox before they have come to read Aristotle's lecture on temperance. Cicero said that though he should live two men's ages, he should never find leisure to study the lyric poets; and I find these sophisters yet more deplorably unprofitable. The boy we would breed has a great deal less time to spare; he owes but the first fifteen or sixteen years of his life to education; the remainder is due to action. Let us, therefore, employ that short time in necessary instruction. Away with the thorny subtleties of dialectics; they are abuses, things by which our lives can never be amended. Take the plain philosophical discourses, learn how rightly to choose, and then rightly to apply them; they are more easy to be understood than one of Boccaccio's novels; a child from nurse is much more capable of them than of learning to read or to write. Philosophy has discourses proper for childhood as well as for the decrepit age of men.

I am of Plutarch's mind that Aristotle did not so much trouble his great disciple with the knack of forming syllogisms or with the elements of geometry as with infusing into him good precepts concerning valor, prowess, magnanimity, temperance, and the contempt of fear; and with this ammunition sent him,

17. a Bradamante or an Angelica, heroines of Ariosto's *Orlando Furioso*. 25–26. that effeminate . . . Phrygia, Paris of Troy.

66. the bears; a reference to bear-baiting, an ugly sport of the time. 81–83. "The clay . . . wheel." Persius, III, 23.   105. his great disciple, Alexander the Great.

whilst yet a boy, with no more than thirty thousand foot, four thousand horse, and but forty-two thousand crowns to subjugate the empire of the whole earth. For the other arts and sciences, he says, Alexander highly indeed commended their excellence and charm and had them in very great honour and esteem, but not ravished with them to that degree as to be tempted to affect the practice of them in his own person. "Young men and old men derive hence 10 a certain end to the mind, and stores for miserable grey hairs."

Epicurus, in the beginning of his letter to Meniceus, says, "That neither the youngest should refuse to philosophize nor the oldest grow weary of it." Who does otherwise seems tacitly to imply that either the time of living happily is not yet come or that it is already past. And yet, for all that, I would not have this pupil of ours imprisoned and made a slave to his book; nor would I have him given up 20 to the morosity and melancholic humour of a sour, ill-natured pedant; I would not have his spirit cowed and subdued by applying him to the rack and tormenting him, as some do, fourteen or fifteen hours a day and so make a packhorse of him. Neither should I think it good when, by reason of a solitary and melancholic complexion, he is discovered to be overmuch addicted to his book, to nourish that humour in him; for that renders him unfit for civil conversation, and diverts him from better employ- 30 ments. And how many have I seen in my time totally brutified by an immoderate thirst after knowledge? Carneades was so besotted with it that he would not find time so much as to comb his head or to pare his nails. Neither would I have his generous manners spoiled and corrupted by the incivility and barbarism of those of another. The French wisdom was anciently turned into proverb: "Early, but of no continuance." And, in truth, we yet see that nothing can be more ingenious and pleasing than the chil- 40 dren of France; but they ordinarily deceive the hope and expectation that have been conceived of them; and grown up to be men, have nothing extraordinary or worth taking notice of: I have heard men of good understanding say, these colleges of ours to which we send our young people (and of which we have but too many) make them such animals as they are.

But to our little monsieur, a closet, a garden, the table, his bed, solitude and company, morning and 50 evening, all hours shall be the same, and all places to him a study; for philosophy, who, as the formatrix of judgment and manners, shall be his principal lesson, has that privilege to have a hand in everything. The orator Isocrates, being at a feast entreated to

A portrait of Michel de Montaigne ascribed to the French school of Corneille de Lyon.

speak of his art, all the company were satisfied with and commended his answer: "It is not now a time," said he, "to do what I can do; and that which it is now time to do, I cannot do." For to make orations and rhetorical disputes in a company met together to laugh and make good cheer had been very un- 60 seasonable and improper, and as much might have been said of all the other sciences. But as to what concerns philosophy, that part of it at least that treats of man and of his offices and duties, it has been the common opinion of all wise men that, out of respect to the sweetness of her conversation, she is ever to be admitted in all sports and entertainments. And Plato, having invited her to his feast, we see after how gentle and obliging a manner, accommodated both to time and place, she entertained 70 the company, though in a discourse of the highest and most important nature. "It profits poor and rich alike, but, neglected, equally hurts old and young." By this method of instruction, my young pupil will be much more and better employed than his fellows of the college are. But as the steps we take in walking to and fro in a gallery, though three times as many, do not tire a man so much as those we em-

9–11. "Young men . . . grey hairs." Persius, v, 64. 12–14. Epicurus . . . weary of it." Diogenes Laertius, x, 122. 32–34. Carneades . . . pare his nails. Idem, IV, 62.

56–58. "It is not . . . I cannot do." Plutarch, *Symposium*, I, 1. 72–73. "It profits . . . old and young." Horace, *Epistles*, I, 1, 25.

ploy in a formal journey, so our lesson, as it were ac-
cidentally occurring without any set obligation of
time or place and falling naturally into every action,
will insensibly insinuate itself. By which means our
very exercises and recreations, running, wrestling,
music, dancing, hunting, riding, and fencing, will
prove to be a good part of our study. I would have
his outward fashion and mien and the disposition of
his limbs formed at the same time with his mind. 'Tis
10 not a soul, 'tis not a body that we are training up,
but a man, and we ought not to divide him. And, as
Plato says, we are not to fashion one without the
other, but make them draw together like two horses
harnessed to a coach. By which saying of his, does
he not seem to allow more time for, and to take more
care of, exercises for the body, and to hold that the
mind, in a good proportion, does her business at the
same time too?

As to the rest, this method of education ought to
20 be carried on with a severe sweetness, quite contrary to the practice of our pedants, who, instead of
tempting and alluring children to letters by apt and
gentle ways, do in truth present nothing before them
but rods and ferules, horror and cruelty. Away with
this violence! away with this compulsion! than
which, I certainly believe nothing more dulls and
degenerates a well-descended nature. If you would
have him apprehend shame and chastizement, do
not harden him to them: inure him to heat and cold,
30 to wind and sun, and to dangers that he ought to
despise; wean him from all effeminacy and delicacy
in clothes and lodging, eating and drinking; accustom him to everything, that he may not be a Sir
Paris, a carpet-knight, but a sinewy, hardy, and vigorous young man. I have ever, from a child to the
age wherein I now am, been of this opinion, and am
still constant to it. But amongst other things, the
strict government of most of our colleges has evermore displeased me; peradventure they might have
40 erred less perniciously on the indulgent side. 'Tis a
real house of correction of imprisoned youth. They
are made debauched by being punished before they
are so. Do but come in when they are about their
lesson and you shall hear nothing but the outcries of
boys under execution, with the thundering noise of
their pedagogues drunk with fury. A very pretty way
this, to tempt these tender and timorous souls to
love their book, with a furious countenance and a
rod in hand! A cursed and pernicious way of pro-
50 ceeding! Besides what Quintilian has very well observed, that this imperious authority is often attended by very dangerous consequences, and particularly our way of chastising. How much more
decent would it be to see their classes strewed with
green leaves and fine flowers than with the bloody
stumps of birch and willows? Were it left to my ordering, I should paint the school with the pictures of

joy and gladness; Flora and the Graces, as the philosopher Speusippus did his. Where their profit is,
let them there have their pleasure too. Such viands 60
as are proper and wholesome for children should be
sweetened with sugar, and such as are dangerous to
them embittered with gall. 'Tis marvellous to see
how solicitous Plato is in his *Laws* concerning the
gaiety and diversion of the youth of his city, and
how much and often he enlarges upon their races,
sports, songs, leaps, and dances: of which, he says,
that antiquity has given the ordering and patronage
particularly to the gods themselves, to Apollo, Minerva, and the Muses. He insists long upon, and is 70
very particular in, giving innumerable precepts for
exercises; but as to the lettered sciences, says very
little, and only seems particularly to recommend
poetry upon the account of music.

All singularity in our manners and conditions is to
be avoided as inconsistent with civil society. Who
would not be astonished at so strange a constitution
as that of Demophoon, steward to Alexander the
Great, who sweated in the shade, and shivered in
the sun? I have seen those who have run from the 80
smell of a mellow apple with greater precipitation
than from a harquebuss shot; others afraid of a
mouse; others vomit at the sight of cream; others
ready to swoon at the making of a feather bed; Ger-
manicus could neither endure the sight nor the crowing of a cock. I will not deny but that there may,
peradventure, be some occult cause and natural aver-
sion in these cases; but, in my opinion, a man might
conquer it if he took it in time. Precept has in this
wrought so effectually upon me, though not without 90
some pains on my part, I confess, that beer excepted,
my appetite accommodates itself indifferently to all
sorts of diet.

Young bodies are supple; one should, therefore, in
that age bend and ply them to all fashions and customs: and provided a man can contain the appetite
and the will within their due limits, let a young man,
in God's name, be rendered fit for all nations and all
companies, even to debauchery and excess, if need
be; that is, where he shall do it out of complacency 100
to the customs of the place. Let him be able to do
everything, but love to do nothing but what is good.
The philosophers themselves do not justify Cal-
listhenes for forfeiting the favour of his master Alexander the Great by refusing to pledge him a cup of
wine. Let him laugh, play, wench, with his prince:
nay, I would have him, even in his debauches, too
hard for the rest of the company and to excel his
companions in ability and vigour, and that he may
not give over doing it, either through defect of power 110
or knowledge how to do it, but for want of will.

58–59. **as the philosopher Speusippus did his**; according to Diogenes
Laertius. IV, 1.

"There is a vast difference betwixt forbearing to sin and not knowing how to sin." I thought I passed a compliment upon a lord, as free from those excesses as any man in France, by asking him before a great deal of very good company how many times in his life he had been drunk in Germany in the time of his being there about his majesty's affairs; which he also took as it was intended, and made answer, "Three times;" and withal, told us the whole story of his debauches. I know some who, for want of this faculty, have found a great inconvenience in negotiating with that nation. I have often with great admiration reflected upon the wonderful constitution of Alcibiades, who so easily could transform himself to so various fashions without any prejudice to his health; one while outdoing the Persian pomp and luxury, and another, the Lacedaemonian austerity and frugality; as reformed in Sparta, as voluptuous in Ionia. "Every complexion of life, every station and circumstance, well became Aristippus." I would have my pupil to be such a one: "I should admire him who, with patience bearing a patched garment, bears well a changed fortune, acting both parts equally well." These are my lessons, and he who puts them in practice shall reap more advantage than he who has had them read to him only, and so only knows them. If you see him, you hear him; if you hear him, you see him. God forbid, says one in Plato, that to philosophize were only to read a great many books and to learn the arts. "They have proceeded to this discipline of living well, which of all arts is the greatest, by their lives rather than by their reading." Leo, prince of the Phliasians, asking Heraclides Ponticus of what art or science he made profession; "I know," said he, "neither art nor science, but I am a philosopher." One reproaching Diogenes that, being ignorant, he should pretend to philosophy, "I therefore," answered he, "pretend to it with so much the more reason." Hegesias entreated that he would read a certain book to him; "You are pleasant," said he; "you choose those figs that are true and natural and not those that are painted; why do you not also choose exercises which are naturally true rather than those written?"

The lad will not so much get his lesson by heart as he will practise it: he will repeat it in his actions. We shall discover if there be prudence in his exercises, if there be sincerity and justice in his deportment, if there be grace and judgment in his speaking, if there be constancy in his sickness, if there be modesty in his mirth, temperance in his pleasures,

order in his domestic economy, indifference in his palate, whether what he eats or drinks be flesh or fish, wine or water. "Who considers his own discipline, not as a vain ostentation of science, but as a law and rule of life; and who obeys his own decrees, and the laws he has prescribed to himself." The conduct of our lives is the true mirror of our doctrine. Zeuxidamus, to one who asked him why the Lacedaemonians did not commit their constitutions of chivalry to writing and deliver them to their young men to read, made answer that it was because they would inure them to action and not amuse them with words. With such a one, after fifteen or sixteen years' study, compare one of our college Latinists, who has thrown away so much time in nothing but learning to speak. The world is nothing but babble; and I hardly ever yet saw that man who did not rather prate too much than speak too little. And yet half of our age is embezzled this way: we are kept four or five years to learn words only, and to tack them together into clauses; as many more to form them into a long discourse, divided into four or five parts; and other five years at least to learn succinctly to mix and interweave them after a subtle and intricate manner: let us leave all this to those who make a profession of it. . . .

Let but our pupil be well furnished with things, words will follow but too fast; he will pull them after him if they do not voluntarily follow. I have observed some to make excuses that they cannot express themselves and pretend to have their fancies full of a great many very fine things which yet, for want of eloquence, they cannot utter; 'tis a mere shift, and nothing else. Will you know what I think of it? I think they are nothing but shadows of some imperfect images and conceptions that they know not what to make of within, nor consequently bring out. They do not yet themselves understand what they would be at, and if you but observe how they haggle and stammer upon the point of parturition, you will soon conclude that their labour is not to delivery, but about conception, and that they are but licking their formless embryo. For my part, I hold, and Socrates commands it, that whoever has in his mind a sprightly and clear imagination will express it well enough in one kind of tongue or another, and, if he be dumb, by signs. "Once a thing is conceived in the mind, the words to express it soon present themselves."

And as another as poetically says in his prose, "When things are once in the mind, the words offer themselves readily:" and this other, "The things themselves force words to express them." He knows

1–2. "There is a vast . . . sin." Seneca, *Epistles*, 90. 19–20. "Every complexion . . . Aristippus." Horace, *Epistles*, XVII, 23. 21–24. "I should . . . well." Idem, 25. 30–32. "They have proceeded . . . reading." Cicero, *Tusculan Disputations*, IV, 3. 35–36. "I know," said he. . . . According to Cotton, Pythagoras (and not Heraclides) made this answer. 40–44. "You are pleasant . . . written?" Diogenes Laertius, VI, 48.

54–57. "Who considers . . . to himself." Cicero, *Tusculan Disputations*, II, 4. 59. Zeuxidamus, a king of Sparta. 98–100. "Once a thing . . . themselves." Horace, *Art of Poetry*, v, 311. 102–103. "When things . . . readily." Seneca, *Controvers.*, III, proem. 103–104. "The things . . . them." Cicero, *De Finibus*, III, 5.

nothing of ablative, conjunctive, substantive, or grammar, no more than his lackey or a fishwife of the Petit Pont; and yet these will give you a bellyful of talk, if you will hear them, and peradventure shall trip as little in their language as the best masters of art in France. He knows no rhetoric, nor how in a preface to bribe the benevolence of the courteous reader; neither does he care to know it. Indeed, all this fine decoration of painting is easily effaced by the lustre of a simple and blunt truth: these fine flourishes serve only to amuse the vulgar, of themselves incapable of more solid and nutritive diet, as Aper very evidently demonstrates in Tacitus. The ambassadors of Samos, prepared with a long and elegant oration, came to Cleomenes, King of Sparta, to incite him to a war against the tyrant Polycrates; who, after he had heard their harangue with great gravity and patience, gave them this answer: "As to the exordium, I remember it not, nor consequently the middle of your speech; and for what concerns your conclusion, I will not do what you desire:" a very pretty answer this, methinks, and a pack of learned orators most sweetly gravelled. And what did the other man say? The Athenians were to choose one of two architects for a very great building they had designed; of these, the first, a pert, affected fellow, offered his service in a long premeditated discourse upon the subject of the work in hand, and by his oratory inclined the voices of the people in his favour; but the other in three words; "O, Athenians, what this man says, I will do." Let it go before or come after, a good sentence or a thing well said is always in season; if it neither suit well with what went before, nor has much coherence with what follows after, it is good in itself. I am none of those who think that good rhyme makes a good poem. Let him make short long and long short if he will, 'tis no great matter; if there be invention and the wit and judgment have well performed their offices, I will say, here's a good poet, but an ill rhymer —"of delicate humour, but of rugged versification." Let a man, says Horace, divest his work of all method and measure, "take away certain rhythms and measures, and change the order of the words, putting that which should be first last, and the last first, still these misplaced members have all the elements of poetry," he will never the more lose himself for that; the very pieces will be fine by themselves. Menander's answer had this meaning, who being reproved by a friend, the time drawing on at which he had promised a comedy, that he had not

yet fallen in hand with it; "It is made and ready," said he, "all but the verses." Having contrived the subject and disposed the scenes in his fancy, he took little care for the rest. Since Ronsard and Du Bellay have given reputation to our French poesy, every little dabbler, for aught I see, swells his words as high and makes his cadences very near as harmonious as they. "More sound than sense." For the vulgar, there were never so many poetasters as now; but though they find it no hard matter to imitate their rhyme, they yet fall infinitely short of imitating the rich descriptions of the one and the delicate invention of the other of these masters. . . .

Words are to serve and to follow a man's purpose; and let Gascon come in play where French will not do. I would have things so excelling and so wholly possessing the imagination of him that hears that he should have something else to do than to think of words. The way of speaking that I love is natural and plain, the same in writing as in speaking, and a sinewy and muscular way of expressing a man's self, short and pithy, not so elegant and artificial as prompt and vehement; rather hard than wearisome; free from affectation; irregular, incontinuous, and bold; where every piece makes up an entire body; not like a pedant, a preacher, or a pleader, but rather a soldier-like style, as Suetonius calls that of Julius Caesar; and yet I see no reason why he should call it so. I have ever been ready to imitate the negligent garb, which is yet observable amongst the young men of our time, to wear my cloak on one shoulder, my cap on one side, a stocking in disorder, which seems to express a kind of haughty disdain of these exotic ornaments and a contempt of the artificial; but I find this negligence of much better use in the form of speaking. All affectation, particularly in the French gaiety and freedom, is ungraceful in a courtier, and in a monarchy every gentleman ought to be fashioned according to the court model; for which reason, an easy and natural negligence does well. I no more like a web where the knots and seams are to be seen than a fine figure, so delicate that a man may tell all the bones and veins. "Let the language that is dedicated to truth be plain and unaffected. . . . For who studies to speak too accurately, that does not at the same time design to perplex his auditory?" That eloquence prejudices the subject it would advance, that wholly attracts us to itself. And as in our outward habit, 'tis a ridiculous effeminacy to distinguish ourselves by a particular and unusual garb or fashion; so in language, to study new phrases and to affect words that are not of current use proceeds from a puerile and scholastic ambition. May I be bound to speak no other language than what is

10–13. these fine flourishes . . . in Tacitus. Tacitus, De Causis Corrputae Eloquentiae. 18–21. "As to the exordium . . . you desire." Plutarch, Apothegms of the Lacedaemonians. 30–31. "O, Athenians . . . will do." Plutarch, Instructions to Statesmen, 4. 41. "of delicate humour . . . versification." Horace, Satires, IV, 8. 43–47. "take away . . . elements of poetry." Horace, Satires, I, 4, 58.

59. "More sound than sense." Seneca, Epistles, 40. 94–98. "Let the language . . . his auditory?" Seneca, Epistles, 40 and 57.

spoken in the market-places of Paris! Aristophanes the grammarian was quite out when he reprehended Epicurus for his plain way of delivering himself, and the design of his oratory, which was only perspicuity of speech. The imitation of words, by its own facility, immediately disperses itself through a whole people; but the imitation of inventing and fitly applying those words is of a slower progress. The generality of readers, for having found a like robe, very mistakenly imagine they have the same body and inside too, whereas force and sinews are never to be borrowed; the gloss and outward ornament, that is, words and elocution, may. Most of those I converse with speak the same language I here write; but whether they think the same thoughts I cannot say. The Athenians, says Plato, study fullness and elegancy of speaking; the Lacedaemonians affect brevity, and those of Crete aim more at the fecundity of conception than the fertility of speech; and these are the best. Zeno used to say that he had two sorts of disciples, one that he called φιλολόγως curious to learn things, and these were his favourites; the other, λογοφίλως that cared for nothing but words. Not that fine speaking is not a very good and commendable quality; but not so excellent and so necessary as some would make it; and I am scandalized that our whole life should be spent in nothing else. I would first understand my own language and that of my neighbours, with whom most of my business and conversation lies.

No doubt but Greek and Latin are very great ornaments, and of very great use, but we buy them too dear. I will here discover one way, which has been experimented in my own person, by which they are to be had better cheap, and such may make use of it as will. My late father, having made the most precise inquiry that any man could possibly make amongst men of the greatest learning and judgment, of an exact method of education, was by them cautioned of this inconvenience then in use, and made to believe that the tedious time we applied to the learning of the tongues of them who had them for nothing was the sole cause we could not arrive to the grandeur of soul and perfection of knowledge of the ancient Greeks and Romans. I do not, however, believe that to be the only cause. However, the expedient my father found out for this was that in my infancy, and before I began to speak, he committed me to the care of a German, who since died a famous physician in France, totally ignorant of our language, but very fluent, and a great critic in Latin. This man, whom he had fetched out of his own country, and whom he entertained with a great salary for this only end, had me continually with

him: to him there were also joined two others, of inferior learning, to attend me and to relieve him; who all of them spoke to me in no other language but Latin. As to the rest of his family, it was an inviolable rule that neither himself, nor my mother, man nor maid, should speak anything in my company but such Latin words as every one had learned only to gabble with me. It is not to be imagined how great an advantage this proved to the whole family; my father and my mother by this means learned Latin enough to understand it perfectly well and to speak it to such a degree as was sufficient for any necessary use; as also those of the servants did who were most frequently with me. In short we Latined it at such a rate, that it overflowed to all the neighbouring villages, where there yet remain, that have established themselves by custom, several Latin appellations of artisans and their tools. As for what concerns myself, I was above six years of age before I understood either French or Perigordin, any more than Arabic; and without art, book, grammar, or precept, whipping, or the expense of a tear, I had, by that time, learned to speak as pure Latin as my master himself, for I had no means of mixing it up with any other. . . .

As to Greek, of which I have but a mere smattering, my father also designed to have it taught me by a device, but a new one, and by way of sport; tossing our declensions to and fro, after the manner of those who, by certain games at tables and chess, learn geometry and arithmetic. For he, amongst other rules, had been advised to make me relish science and duty by an unforced will and of my own voluntary motion and to educate my soul in all liberty and delight without any severity or constraint; which he was an observer of to such a degree, even of superstition, if I may say so, that some being of opinion that it troubles and disturbs the brains of children suddenly to wake them in the morning and to snatch them violently and over-hastily from sleep (wherein they are much more profoundly involved than we), he caused me to be wakened by the sound of some musical instrument and was never unprovided of a musician for that purpose. By this example you may judge of the rest, this alone being sufficient to recommend both the prudence and the affection of so good a father, who is not to be blamed if he did not reap fruits answerable to so exquisite a culture. Of this, two things were the cause: first, a sterile and improper soil; for, though I was a strong and healthful constitution, and of a disposition tolerably sweet and tractable, yet I was, withal, so heavy, idle, and indisposed that they could not rouse me from my sloth, not even to get me out to play. What I saw, I saw clearly enough, and under this heavy complexion nourished a bold imagination and opinions above my age. I had a slow wit, that

1–5. **Aristophanes . . . perspicuity of speech.** As reported by Diogenes Laertius, x, 13. 16. **The Athenians, says Plato. . . .** Idem.

would go no faster than it was led; a tardy understanding, a languishing invention, and, above all, incredible defect of memory; so that it is no wonder if from all these nothing considerable could be extracted. Secondly, like those who, impatient of a long and steady cure, submit to all sorts of prescriptions and recipes, the good man being extremely timorous of any way failing in a thing he had so wholly set his heart upon, suffered himself at last to be overruled by the common opinions, which always follow their leader as a flight of cranes, and complying with the method of the time, having no more those persons he had brought out of Italy and who had given him the first model of education about him, he sent me at six years of age to the College of Guienne, at that time the best and most flourishing in France. And there it was not possible to add anything to the care he had to provide me the most able tutors, with all other circumstances of education, reserving also several particular rules contrary to the college practice; but so it was, that with all these precautions it was a college still. My Latin immediately grew corrupt, of which also by discontinuance I have since lost all manner of use; so that this new way of education served me to no other end than only at my first coming to prefer me to the first forms; for at thirteen years old, that I came out of the college, I had run through my whole course (as they call it), and, in truth, without any manner of advantage that I can honestly brag of in all this time. . . .

To return to my subject, there is nothing like alluring the appetite and affections; otherwise you make nothing but so many asses laden with books; by dint of the lash, you give them their pocketful of learning to keep; whereas, to do well, you should not only lodge it with them, but make them espouse it.

Of Age

I CANNOT allow of the way in which we settle for ourselves the duration of our life. I see that the sages contract it very much in comparison of the common opinion: "What," said the younger Cato to those who would stay his hand from killing himself, "am I now of an age to be reproached that I go out of the world too soon?" And yet he was but eight-and-forty years old. He thought that to be a mature and advanced age, considering how few arrive unto it. And such as, soothing their thoughts with I know not what course of nature, promise to themselves some years beyond it, could they be privileged from the infinite number of accidents to which we are by a natural subjection exposed, they might have some reason so to do. What an idle con-

Of Age. Translated by Charles Cotton.

ceit is it to expect to die of a decay of strength, which is the effect of extremest age, and to propose to ourselves no shorter lease of life than that, considering it is a kind of death of all others the most rare and very seldom seen? We call that only a natural death; as if it were contrary to nature to see a man break his neck with a fall, be drowned in shipwreck, be snatched away with a pleurisy or the plague, and as if our ordinary condition did not expose us to these inconveniences. Let us no longer flatter ourselves with these fine words; we ought rather, peradventure, to call that natural which is general, common, and universal.

To die of old age is a death rare, extraordinary, and singular, and, therefore, so much less natural than the others; 'tis the last and extremest sort of dying: and the more remote, the less to be hoped for. It is, indeed, the bourn beyond which we are not to pass, and which the law of nature has set as a limit not to be exceeded; but it is, withal, a privilege she is rarely seen to give us to last till then. 'Tis a lease she only signs by particular favour, and it may be to one only in the space of two or three ages, and then with a pass to boot, to carry him through all the traverses and difficulties she has strewed in the way of this long career. And therefore my opinion is that when once forty years we should consider it as an age to which very few arrive. For seeing that men do not usually proceed so far, it is a sign that we are pretty well advanced; and since we have exceeded the ordinary bounds, which is the just measure of life, we ought not to expect to go much further; having escaped so many precipices of death, whereinto we have seen so many other men fall, we should acknowledge that so extraordinary a fortune as that which has hitherto rescued us from those eminent perils and kept us alive beyond the ordinary term of living is not likely to continue long.

'Tis a fault in our very laws to maintain this error. These say that a man is not capable of managing his own estate till he be five-and-twenty years old, whereas he will have much ado to manage his life so long. Augustus cut off five years from the ancient Roman standard, and declared that thirty years old was sufficient for a judge. Servius Tullius superseded the knights of above seven-and-forty years of age from the fatigues of war; Augustus dismissed them at forty-five; though methinks it seems a little unreasonable that men should be sent to the fireside till five-and-fifty or sixty years of age. I should be of opinion that our vocation and employment should be as far as possible extended for the public good: I find the fault on the other side, that they do not employ us early enough. This emperor was arbiter of the whole world at nineteen, and yet would have a man to be thirty before he could be fit to determine a dispute about a gutter.

For my part, I believe our souls are adult at twenty as much as they are ever likely to be, and as capable then as ever. A soul that has not by that time given evident earnest of its force and virtue will never after come to proof. The natural qualities and virtues produce what they have of vigorous and fine within that term or never. "If the thorn does not prick at its birth, 'twill hardly ever prick at all," as they say in Dauphiné.

Of all the great human actions I ever heard or read of, of what sort soever, I have observed, both in former ages and our own, more were performed before the age of thirty than after; and this ofttimes in the very lives of the same men. May I not confidently instance in those of Hannibal and his great concurrent Scipio? The better half of their lives they lived upon the glory they had acquired in their youth; great men after, 'tis true, in comparison of others; but by no means in comparison of themselves. As to my own particular, I do certainly believe that since that age, both my understanding and my constitution have rather decayed than improved, and retired rather than advanced. 'Tis possible that with those who make the best use of their time, knowledge and experience may increase with their years; but vivacity, promptitude, steadiness, and other pieces of us, of much greater importance and much more essentially our own, languish and decay. "When once the body's shaken by the violence of time, blood and vigour ebbing away, the judgment then also halts, the tongue trips, and the mind dotes." Sometimes the body first submits to age, sometimes the mind, and I have seen enough who have got a weakness in their brains before either in their legs or stomach; and by how much the more it is a disease of no great pain to the sufferer, and of obscure symptoms, so much greater is the danger. For this reason it is that I complain of our laws, not that they keep us too long to our work, but that they set us to work too late. For the frailty of life considered, and to how many ordinary and natural rocks it is exposed, one ought not to give up so large a portion of it to childhood, idleness, and apprenticeship.

That We
Taste Nothing Pure

THE imbecility of our condition is such that things cannot, in their natural simplicity and purity, fall into our use; the elements that we enjoy are changed, and so 'tis with metals; and gold must be debased with some other matter to fit it for our

29–32. "When once . . . the mind dotes." Lucretius, iii, 452. *That We Taste Nothing Pure.* Translated by Charles Cotton.

service. Neither has virtue, so simple as that which Aristo, Pyrrho, and also the Stoics, made the End of life; nor the Cyrenaic and Aristippic pleasure, been without mixture useful to it. Of the pleasure and goods that we enjoy, there is not one exempt from some mixture of ill and inconvenience: "In the very source of our pleasure, there is something that is bitter, and that vexes even the flowers." Our extremest pleasure has some air of groaning and complaining in it; would you not say that it is dying of pain? Nay, when we frame the image of it in its full excellence, we stuff it with sickly and painful epithets and qualities, languor, softness, feebleness, faintness, *morbidezza*: a great testimony of their consanguinity and consubstantiality. The most profound joy has more of severity than gaiety in it. The highest and fullest contentment offers more of the grave than of the merry; "Even felicity, unless it moderate itself, oppresses." Pleasure chews and grinds us; according to the old Greek verse, which says that the gods sell us all the goods they give us; that is to say, that they give us nothing pure and perfect, and that we do not purchase but at the price of some evil.

Labour and pleasure, very unlike in nature, associate, nevertheless, by I know not what natural conjunction. Socrates says, that some god tried to mix in one mass and to confound pain and pleasure, but not being able to do it, he bethought him at least, to couple them by the tail. Metrodorus said that in sorrow there is some mixture of pleasure. I know not whether or no he intended anything else by that saying; but for my part, I am of opinion that there is design, consent, and complacency in giving a man's self up to melancholy. I say, that besides ambition, which may also have a stroke in the business, there is some shadow of delight and delicacy which smiles upon and flatters us even in the very lap of melancholy. Are there not some constitutions that feed upon it? "'Tis a certain kind of pleasure to weep." And one Attalus in Seneca says that the memory of our lost friends is as grateful to us, as bitterness in wine, when too old, is to the palate— "Boy, when you pour out old Falernian wine, the bitterest put into my bowl"—and as apples that have a sweet tartness.

Nature discovers this confusion to us; painters hold that the same motions and screwings of the

51. **Aristo,** Stoic philosopher, fl. 260 B.C. **Pyrrho,** founder of the Sceptic school (fourth century B.C.). 52. **Cyrenaic,** the Hedonic school of Aristippus of Cyrene, which made pleasure the end of human life. 55–57. "In the . . . flowers." Lucretius, iv, 1130. 63. *morbidezza,* softness. 67–68. "Even felicity . . . oppresses." Seneca, *Epistles,* 74. 68–69. Pleasure . . . Greek verse. Epicharmus, in Xenophon's *Memorabilia,* ii, 1, 20. 76. Socrates says. . . . *Phaedo,* ii, 1, 20. 79. **Metrodorus said.** . . . A disciple of Democritus in the Atomistic school, here quoted by Seneca in *Epistles,* 99. 89–90. "'Tis a certain . . . to weep." Ovid, *Tristia,* iv, 3, 27. 90. **one Attalus in Seneca says.** . . . *Epistles,* 70.

face that serve for weeping, serve for laughter too; and indeed, before the one or the other be finished, do but observe the painter's manner of handling, and you will be in doubt to which of the two the design tends; and the extreme of laughter does at last bring tears. "No evil is without its compensation."

When I imagine man abounding with all the conveniences that are to be desired (let us put the case that all his members were always seized with a pleasure like that of generation, in its most excessive height), I feel him melting under the weight of his delight, and see him utterly unable to support so pure, so continual, and so universal a pleasure. Indeed, he is running away whilst he is there, and naturally makes haste to escape, as from a place where he cannot stand firm, and where he is afraid of sinking.

When I religiously confess myself to myself, I find that the best virtue I have has in it some tincture of vice; and I am afraid that Plato, in his purest virtue (I, who am as sincere and loyal a lover of virtue of that stamp as any other whatever) if he had listened and laid his ear close to himself, and he did so no doubt, would have heard some jarring sound of human mixture, but faint and only perceptible to himself. Man is wholly and throughout but patch and motley. Even the laws of justice themselves cannot subsist without mixture of injustice; insomuch that Plato says, they undertake to cut off the hydra's head, who pretend to clear the law of all inconveniences. "Every great example has in it some mixture of injustice, which recompenses the wrong done to particular men by the public utility," says Tacitus.

It is likewise true that for the use of life and the service of public commerce, there may be some excesses in the purity and perspicacity of our minds; that penetrating light has in it too much of sublety and curiosity: we must a little stupefy and blunt them to render them more obedient to example and practice, and a little veil and obscure them, the better to proportion them to this dark and earthy life. And therefore common and less speculative souls are found to be more proper for and more successful in the management of affairs; and the elevated and exquisite opinions of philosophy unfit for business. This sharp vivacity of soul, and the supple and restless volubility attending it, disturb our negotiations. We are to manage human enterprises more superficially and roughly, and leave a great part to fortune; it is not necessary to examine

affairs with so much subtlety and so deep: a man loses himself in the consideration of so many contrary lustres, and so many various forms; "Whilst they considered of things so indifferent in themselves, they were astonished, and knew not what to do."

'Tis what the ancients say of Simonides, that by reason his imagination suggested to him, upon the question King Hiero had put to him (to answer which he had had many days to meditate in), several sharp and subtle considerations, whilst he doubted which was the most likely, he totally despaired of the truth.

He who dives into and in his inquisition comprehends all circumstances and consequences, hinders his election: a little engine well-handled is sufficient for executions, whether of less or greater weight. The best managers are those who can worst give account how they are so; while the greatest talkers, for the most part, do nothing to purpose. I know one of this sort of men, and a most excellent discourser upon all sorts of good husbandry, who has miserably let a hundred thousand livres yearly revenue slip through his hands. I know another who talks, who better advises than any man of his counsel, and there is not in the world a fairer show of soul and understanding than he has; nevertheless, when he comes to the test, his servants find him quite another thing; not to make any mention of his misfortunes.

Of Three Commerces

W E must not rivet ourselves so fast to our humours and complexions: our chiefest sufficiency is to know how to apply ourselves to divers employments. 'Tis to be, but not to live, to keep a man's self tied and bound by necessity to one only course; those are the bravest souls that have in them the most variety and pliancy. Of this here is an honourable testimony of the elder Cato: "His parts were so pliable to all uses that a man would think he had been born only for precisely that which he was at any time doing." Had I liberty to set myself forth after my own mode, there is no graceful fashion to which I would be so fixed as not to be able to disengage myself from it; life is an unequal, irregular, and multiform motion. 'Tis not to be a friend to one's self, much less a master—'tis to be a slave, incessantly to be led by the nose by

6–7. "No evil . . . compensation." Seneca, *Epistles*, 69.   30. Plato says. . . . *Republic*, iv, 5.   31. the hydra, the many-headed water-serpent in Greek mythology on whom two heads would grow as fast as one was cut off.   35. . . . says Tacitus. *Annals*, xiv, 44.

55–58. "Whilst they . . . what to do." Livy, xxxii, 20.   60–61. the question . . . to him. According to Cicero (*De Natura Deorum*, i, 22), King Hiero of Syracuse asked the Greek lyric poet Simonides (556–c. 468 B.C.) what God was.
Of Three Commerces.ᴬ Translated by Charles Cotton.
89. the elder Cato. . . , the Roman statesman (234–149 B.C.) as quoted by Livy, xxxix, 49.

one's self, and to be so fixed in one's previous in-clinations that one cannot turn aside nor writhe one's neck out of the collar. I say this now in this part of my life, wherein I find I cannot easily disengage myself from the importunity of my soul, which can-not ordinarily amuse itself but in things of limited range, nor employ itself otherwise than entirely and with all its force; upon the lightest subject offered it swells and stretches it to that degree as therein to employ its utmost power; wherefore, its idleness is to me a very painful labour, and very prejudicial to my health. Most men's minds require foreign matter to exercise and enliven them; mine has rather need of it to sit still and repose itself. "The vices of sloth are to be shaken off by business," for its chiefest and hardest study is to study itself. Books are to it a sort of employment that debauch it from its study. Upon the first thoughts that possess it, it begins to bustle and make trial of its vigour in all directions, exer-cises its power of handling, now making trial of force, now fortifying, moderating, and ranging itself by the way of grace and order. It has of its own wherewith to rouse its faculties: nature has given to it, as to all others, matter enough of its own to make advantage of, and subjects proper enough where it may either invent or judge.

Meditation is a powerful and full study to such as can effectually taste and employ themselves; I had rather fashion my soul than furnish it. There is no employment, either more weak or more strong, than that of entertaining a man's own thoughts, according as the soul is; the greatest men make it their whole business; "To whom to live is to think." Nature has therefore favoured it with this privilege, that there is nothing we can do so long, nor any action to which we more frequently and with greater facility addict ourselves. 'Tis the business of the gods, says Aristotle, and from which both their beatitude and ours proceed.

The principal use of reading to me is that by vari-ous objects it rouses my reason and employs my judgment, not my memory. Few conversations de-tain me without force and effort; it is true that beauty and elegance of speech take as much or more with me than the weight and depth of the subject; and forasmuch as I am apt to be sleepy in all other communication and give but the rind of my atten-tion, it often falls out that in such poor and pitiful discourses, mere chatter, I either make drowsy, un-meaning answers, unbecoming a child, and ridicu-lous, or more foolishly and rudely still, maintain an obstinate silence. I have a pensive way that with-draws me into myself, and, with that, a heavy and childish ignorance of many very ordinary things, by

which two qualities I have earned this, that men may truly relate five or six as ridiculous tales of me as of any other man whatever.

But, to proceed in my subject, this difficult com-plexion of mine renders me very nice in my conver-sation with men, whom I must cull and pick out for my purpose; and unfits me for common society. We live and negotiate with the people; if their conversa-tion be troublesome to us, if we disdain to apply ourselves to mean and vulgar souls (and the mean and vulgar are often as regular as those of the finest thread, and all wisdom is folly that does not accom-modate itself to the common ignorance), we must no more intermeddle either with other men's affairs or our own; for business, both public and private, has to do with these people. The least forced and most natural motions of the soul are the most beauti-ful; the best employments, those that are least strained. Good God! how good an office does wis-dom to those whose desires it limits to their power! that is the most useful knowledge: "what a man can," was ever the sentence Socrates was so much in love with. A motto of great substance.

We must moderate and adapt our desires to the nearest and easiest to be acquired things. Is it not a foolish humour of mine to separate myself from a thousand to whom my fortune has conjoined me, and without whom I cannot live, and cleave to one or two who are out of my intercourse; or rather a fantastic desire of a thing that I cannot obtain? My gentle and easy manners, enemies of all sourness and harshness, may easily enough have secured me from envy and animosities; to be beloved, I do not say, but never any man gave less occasion of being hated; but the coldness of my conversation has, reasonably enough, deprived me of the goodwill of many, who are to be excused if they interpret it in another and worse sense.

I am very capable of contracting and maintaining rare and exquisite friendships; for, by reason that I so greedily seize upon such acquaintance as fit my liking, I throw myself with such violence upon them that I hardly fail to stick, and to make an impression where I hit; as I have often made happy proof. In ordinary friendships I am somewhat cold and shy, for my motion is not natural, if not with full sail; besides which, my fortune having in my youth given me a relish for one sole and perfect friendship has, in truth, created in me a kind of distaste to others, and too much imprinted in my fancy that it is a beast of company, as the ancient said, but not of the herd. And also I have a natural difficulty of communicating myself by halves, with the modifica-tions and the servile and jealous prudence required in the conversation of numerous and imperfect

14-15. "The vices . . . by business," Seneca, *Epistles*, 56. 33. "To whom . . . to think." Cicero, *Tusculan Disputations*, v, 38. 38. . . . says Aristotle; *Nicomachean Ethics*, x, 8.

105. . . . as the ancient said, Plutarch, *On the Plurality of Friends*, c, 2.

friendships: and we are principally enjoined to these in this age of ours, when we cannot talk of the world but either with danger or falsehood. . . .

There are some particular natures that are private and retired: my natural way is proper for communication, and apt to lay me open; I am all without and in sight, born for society and friendship. The solitude that I love myself and recommend to others is chiefly no other than to withdraw my thoughts and affections into myself; to restrain and check, not my steps, but my own cares and desires, resigning all foreign solicitude, and mortally avoiding servitude and obligation, and not so much the crowd of men, as the crowd of business. Local solitude, to say the truth, rather gives me more room, and sets me more at large; I more readily throw myself upon affairs of state and the world when I am alone. At the Louvre and in the bustle of the court, I fold myself within my own skin; the crowd thrusts me upon myself; and I never entertain myself so wantonly, with so much licence, or so especially, as in places of respect and ceremonious prudence: our follies do not make me laugh, but our wisdom does. I am naturally no enemy to a court life; I have therein passed a good part of my own, and am of a humour cheerfully to frequent great company, provided it be by intervals and at my own time: but this softness of judgment whereof I speak ties me perforce to solitude. Even at home, amidst a numerous family, and in a house sufficiently frequented, I see people enough, but rarely such with whom I delight to converse; and I there reserve both for myself and others an unusual liberty: there is in my house no such thing as ceremony, ushering or waiting upon people down to the coach, and such other troublesome ceremonies as our courtesy enjoins (O servile and importunate custom!) Every one there governs himself according to his own method; let who will speak his thoughts, I sit mute, meditating and shut up in my closet, without any offence to my guests.

The men whose society and familiarity I covet are those they call sincere and able men; and the image of these makes me disrelish the rest. It is, if rightly taken, the rarest of our forms, and a form that we chiefly owe to nature. The end of this commerce is simply privacy, frequentation, and conference, the exercise of souls, without other fruit. In our discourse, all subjects are alike to me; yet there be neither weight nor depth, 'tis all one: there is yet grace and pertinency; all there is tinted with a mature and constant judgment, and mixed with goodness, freedom, gaiety, and friendship. 'Tis not only in talking of the affairs of kings and state that our wits discover their force and beauty, but every whit as much in private conferences. I understand my men even by their silence and smiles; and better

discover them, perhaps, at table than in the council. Hippomachus said very well, "that he could know the good wrestlers by only seeing them walk in the street." If learning pleased to step into our talk, it shall not be rejected, not magisterial, imperious, and importunate, as it commonly is, but suffragan and docile itself. We there only seek to pass away our time; when we have a mind to be instructed and preached to, we will go seek this in its throne. Please let it humble itself to us for the nonce; for, useful and profitable as it is, I imagine that at need we may manage well enough without it and do our business without its assistance. A well-descended soul, and practised in the conversation of men, will of herself render herself sufficiently agreeable; art is nothing but the counterpart and register of what such souls produce.

The conversation also of beautiful and well-bred women is for me a sweet commerce: "For we also have eyes that are versed in the matter." If the soul has not therein so much to enjoy as in the first, the bodily senses, which participate more of this, bring it to a proportion near to, though in my opinion not equal to, the other. But 'tis a commerce wherein a man must stand a little upon his guard, especially those of a warm temperament such as mine. I there scalded myself in my youth, and suffered all the torments that poets say are to befall those who precipitate themselves into love without order and judgment: it is true that the whipping has made me wiser since: "Whoever of the Grecian fleet has escaped the Capharean rocks ever takes care to steer from those of the Euboean sea." 'Tis folly to fix all a man's thoughts upon it and to engage in it with a furious and indiscreet affection; but, on the other hand, to engage there without love and without inclination, like comedians to play a common part, without putting anything to it of his own but words, is indeed to provide for his safety, but, withal, after as cowardly a manner as he who should abandon his honour, profit, or pleasure for fear of ordinary danger; for it is certain that from such a practice they who set it on foot can expect no fruit that can please or satisfy a noble soul. A man must have, in good earnest, desired that which he, in good earnest, expects to have a pleasure in enjoying; I say, though fortune should unjustly favour their dissimulation; which often falls out, because there is none of the sex, let her be as ugly as the devil, who does not think herself well worthy to be beloved, and who does not prefer herself before other women, either for her youth, the colour of her hair, or her graceful motion (for there are no more women universally and throughout ugly than there are women univer-

59–61. Hippomachus said . . . in the street." Plutarch, *Life of Dion*, c, 1.   76–77. "For we also . . . in the matter." Cicero, *Paradox*, v, 2.   88–90. "Whoever . . . sea." Ovid, *Tristia*, i, 1, 83.

sally and throughout beautiful). Consequently, there is not one who does not easily suffer herself to be overcome by the first vow that is made to serve her. Now from this common and ordinary treachery of the men of the present day, that must fall out which we already experimentally see, either that they rally together and separate themselves by themselves to evade us or else form their discipline by the example we give them, play their parts of the farce as we do ours, and give themselves up to the sport, without passion, care, or love: "Incapable of attachment, insensible to that of others:" believing, according to the persuasion of Lysias in Plato, that they may with more utility and convenience surrender themselves up to us the less we love them; where it will fall out, as in comedies, that the people will have as much pleasure or more than the comedians. For my part, I no more acknowledge a Venus without a Cupid than a mother without issue: they are things that mutually lend and owe their essence to one another. . . .

As one who does not desire that men should think me better than I am, I will here say this as to the errors of my youth. Not only from the danger of impairing my health (and yet I could not be so careful but that I had two light mischances), but moreover upon the account of contempt, I have seldom given myself up to common and mercenary embraces. I would heighten the pleasure by the difficulty, by desire, and a certain kind of glory: and was of Tiberius's mind, who in his amours was as much taken with modesty and birth as any other quality; and of the courtesan Flora's humour, who never prostituted herself to less than a dictator, a consul, or a censor, and took pleasure in the dignity of her lovers. Doubtless pearls and gold tissue, titles and train, add something to it.

As to the rest, I had a great esteem for wit, provided the person was not exceptionable; for, to confess the truth, if the one or the other of these two attractions must of necessity be wanting, I should rather have quitted that of the understanding, that has its use in better things; but in the subject of love, a subject principally relating to the senses of seeing and touching, something may be done without the graces of the mind: without the graces of the body, nothing. Beauty is the true prerogative of women, and so peculiarly their own that ours, though naturally requiring another sort of feature, is never in its lustre but when youthful and beardless, a sort of confused image of theirs. 'Tis said, that such as serve the Grand Signior upon the account of beauty, who are an infinite number, are,

at the latest, dismissed at two and twenty years of age. Reason, prudence, and the offices of friendship are better found amongst men, and therefore it is that they govern the affairs of the world.

These two commerces are fortuitous and depending upon others: the one is troublesome by its rarity, the other withers with age, so that they could never have been sufficient for the business of my life. That of books, which is the third, is much more certain, and much more our own. It yields all other advantages to the two first; but has the constancy and facility of its service for its own share. It goes side by side with me in my whole course, and everywhere is assisting me: it comforts me in my old age and solitude; it eases me of a troublesome weight of idleness, and delivers me at all hours from company that I dislike: it blunts the point of griefs, if they are not extreme and have not got an entire possession of my soul. To divert myself from a troublesome fancy, 'tis but to run to my books; they presently fix me to them and drive the other out of my thoughts and do not mutiny at seeing that I have only recourse to them for want of other more real, natural, and lively commodities; they always receive me with the same kindness. He may well go a foot, they say, who leads his horse in his hand; and our James, king of Naples and Sicily, who, handsome, young, and healthy, caused himself to be carried about on a barrow, extended upon a pitiful mattress in a poor robe of grey cloth and a cap of the same, but attended withal by a royal train of litters, led horses of all sorts, gentlemen and officers, did yet herein represent a tender and unsteady authority: "The sick man is not to be pitied, who has his cure in his sleeve." In the experience and practice of this maxim, which is a very true one, consists all the benefit I reap from books; and yet I make as little use of them, almost, as those who know them not. I enjoy them as a miser doth his money, in knowing that I may enjoy them when I please: my mind is satisfied with this right of possession. I never travel without books, either in peace or war; and yet sometimes I pass over several days, and sometimes months, without looking on them. I will read by-and-by, say I to myself, or to-morrow, or when I please; and in the interim, time steals away without any inconvenience. For it is not to be imagined to what degree I please myself and rest content in this consideration that I have them by me to divert myself with them when I am so disposed and to call to mind what a refreshment they are to my life. 'Tis the best viaticum I have yet found out for this human journey, and I very much pity those men of understanding who are unprovided of it. I rather accept of any other sort of diversion, how light soever, because this can never fail me.

When at home, I a little more frequent my library,

11-12. "Incapable . . . of others." Tacitus, *Annals*, xiii, 45. 13. . . . the persuasion of Lycias in Plato; in the *Phaedo*. 31. of Tiberius's mind . . . ; the Roman emperor (42 B.C.-37 A.D.), as quoted by Tacitus (*Annals*, vi, 1).

whence I overlook at once all the concerns of my family. 'Tis situated at the entrance into my house, and I thence see under me my garden, court, and base-court, and almost all parts of the building. There I turn over now one book, and then another, on various subjects without method or design. One while I meditate, another I record and dictate, as I walk to and fro, such whimsies as these I present to you here. 'Tis in the third storey of a tower, of which the ground room is my chapel, the second storey a chamber with a withdrawing-room and closet, where I often lie, to be more retired; and above is a great wardrobe. This formerly was the most useless part of the house. I there pass away both most of the days of my life and most of the hours of those days. In the night I am never there. There is by the side of it a cabinet handsome enough, with a fireplace very commodiously contrived, and plenty of light: and were I not more afraid of the trouble than the expense—the trouble that frights me from all business—I could very easily adjoin on either side, and on the same floor, a gallery of an hundred paces long and twelve broad, having found walls already raised for some other design to the requisite height. Every place of retirement requires a walk: my thoughts sleep if I sit still; my fancy does not go by itself, as when my legs move it: and all those who study without a book are in the same condition. The figure of my study is round, and there is no more open wall than what is taken up by my table and my chair, so that the remaining parts of the circle present me a view of all my books at once, ranged upon five rows of shelves round about me. It has three noble and free prospects, and is sixteen paces in diameter. I am not so continually there in winter; for my house is built upon an eminence, and no part of it is so much exposed to the wind and weather as this, which pleases me the better, as being of more difficult access and a little remote, as well upon the account of exercise, as also being there more retired from the crowd. 'Tis there that I am in my kingdom, and there I endeavour to make myself an absolute monarch, and to sequester this one corner from all society, conjugal, filial, and civil; elsewhere I have but verbal authority only, and of a confused essence. That man, in my opinion, is very miserable who has not at home where to be by himself, where to entertain himself alone, or to conceal himself from others. Ambition sufficiently plagues her proselytes by keeping them always in show, like the statue of a public square: "A great fortune is a great slavery." They cannot so much as be private in the water-closet. I have thought nothing so severe in the austerity of life that our monks affect as what I have observed in some of their com-

51–52. **"A great fortune . . . great slavery."** Seneca, *De Consolatione ad Polybium,* c, 26.

munities; namely, by rule to have a perpetual society of place, and numerous persons present in every action whatever; and think it much more supportable to be always alone than never to be so.

If anyone shall tell me that it is to undervalue the muses, to make use of them only for sport and to pass away the time, I shall tell him that he does not know so well as I the value of the sport, the pleasure, and the pastime; I can hardly forbear to add that all other end is ridiculous. I live from hand to mouth, and, with reverence be it spoken, I only live for myself; there all my designs terminate. I studied, when young, for ostentation; since, to make myself a little wiser; and now for my diversion, but never for any profit. A vain and prodigal humour I had after this sort of furniture, not only for the supplying my own need, but, moreover, for ornament and outward show, I have since quite cured myself of.

Books have many charming qualities to such as know how to choose them; but every good has its ill. 'Tis a pleasure that is not pure and clean, no more than others: it has its inconveniences, and great ones too. The soul indeed is exercised therein, but the body, the care of which I must withal never neglect, remains in the meantime without action and grows heavy and sombre. I know no excess more prejudicial to me, nor more to be avoided in this my declining age.

These have been my three favourite and particular occupations; I speak not of those I owe to the world by civil obligation.

Miguel de Cervantes
1547–1616

The political and social revolution of the Renaissance that destroyed medieval feudalism disposed as well of the fearless Christian knight on his faithful steed roaming the countryside as the heroic avenger of wrongs. By the sixteenth century knighthood and the code of chivalry were becoming quaint anachronisms in a world of powerful monarchies and wars with gunpowder. They survived as sweet conventions at the courts of the new-style kings, but even here they were attacked by rational observers as ludicrously out of step with the times. Chief among these realists was the Spaniard Cervantes, who began his *Don Quixote* as a satire on chivalric romances but developed it as a timeless commentary on the pathetic aspirations of mankind toward an impossible ideal.

The life of Cervantes was so filled with misfortune and frustration that he may well have presented himself sardonically in the good Don whose noblest ambitions led him to grotesque failure in the unsympathetic world in which he was forced to live. Born as the second son of an itinerant surgeon of Alcalá de Henares, Cervantes later tried to disguise his humble origin by styling himself *hidalgo,* or "gentleman." His desultory education reflected the repeated migrations of his family from one city to another in central Spain. By 1571 he had enlisted as a common soldier, and, at the Battle of Lepanto in the Mediterranean off Greece, he lost the use of his left hand, so that he was styled thereafter "El Manco de Lepanto" (the one-handed man of Lepanto). In 1575 he set out from Italy on leave for Spain, but his ship was captured by Barbary pirates and he endured five years of slavery in Algiers before his repeated efforts to escape were rewarded with a ransom from a religious order.

Back in Spain, he turned to literature to support himself, but his plays, poems, and pastoral romance *Galatea* of this period (1582–1587) had no great success. In desperation he applied to the king for a government post, which turned out to be the uncongenial job of commissary to the Armada. Often destitute, he was several times in prison for debt or for careless bookkeeping in his official position. Down to the age of fifty-seven, he had published no work of enduring worth and had reason to consider himself an abject failure. But in 1605 he issued his resounding masterpiece, *Don Quixote,* which he had conceived in prison and worked at from time to time for five years. His reputation (but not his fortune) was made overnight, and all Spaniards who could read, from King Philip III down, laughed at the droll adventures of the Knight of the Woeful Countenance.

But the book was immediately pirated by unscrupulous publishers, and as Cervantes was at work on a second part in 1614 a mysterious "Avellaneda" beat him to it with a spurious sequel. This imposture may have led him not only to rush his own sequel to completion but to make it superior in art and depth of thought to the first part. The ill-mannered preface of "Avellaneda" maliciously taunted Cervantes with his infirmities, poverty, and loneliness, and these comments were all too true. He lived out his days as a poor but famous author and saw his daughter involved in ugly scandals. His later works —the charming *Exemplary Novels* and especially the conventional *Labors of Persiles and Sigismunda*—reveal his gallant spirit but his weariness of a life that had brought unending hardship. He died on April 23, 1616, the very day on which Shakespeare died in England.

Begun as a parody of the absurdities of romance, *Don Quixote* matured into a thoughtful study of human nature in humorous terms. Like all great comedy, it went beyond the laughter of burlesque to a profound observation about man's efforts to adjust himself to his environment. At the start the Don is a ludicrous figure, a middle-aged bachelor grown insane through reading too much *Amadis of Gaul* and other high-flown romances, who sets out on his bony nag, Rozinante, with his rusty lance to play the medieval knight-errant, righting wrongs in the name of his lady, Dulcinea del Toboso, who proves to be no more than a coarse country wench. All the commonplace things in his path are transfigured by his demented imagination into objects of romance—a wag-

gish innkeeper into a great lord of knights, a windmill into a giant enemy, sheep into an army, and a barber's basin into the helmet of Mambrino. Despite his rebuffs and the derision of those about him, the idealism of the Don remains undiminished.

In time Cervantes came to see in the high-minded lunatic the longing of us all for something nobler than reality. Most of us escape ridicule because we compromise our hopes and finer instincts with conditions as we find them. It is the melancholy message of Cervantes' novel that the idealist who dares to practice what he believes appears to be a fool in a cynical world. Society demands that he should not lose touch with reality and never live so nobly as he would like to live. A prosy foil to the poetic knight is his earthy squire, Sancho Panza, who left home and followed the would-be knight, in part to avoid the dull routine of his peasant existence, in part to gain wealth and power as governor of the island that the Don promised him. The buffoon with his endless proverbs and naïve faith in his master also grows in our esteem, especially when he displays a homely wisdom in managing the affairs of his supposed island. If the Don has his head in the clouds, Sancho has his eyes to the ground, and his very lack of imagination leads him into delusions no less serious than the Don's. Each carries a necessary ingredient of human nature to grotesque extremes. Both idealism and realism are essential to a sound view of life.

But this philosophy is merely implicit in *Don Quixote.* On the surface it is an uproarious comic novel, full of humorous characters and absurd situations. With the pen of a meticulous realist Cervantes brings to life the countryside of La Mancha, its landlords and scullery-maids, its puppet-showmen and talkative barbers, its friendly priests and gracious noblemen. The droll style of the book conveys the infectious mirth in the author's heart as he developed his laughable and yet sympathetic pair of heroes.

THE LIFE AND ACHIEVEMENTS OF

THE RENOWNED

Don Quixote de la Mancha

PART I

The quality and manner of life of the renowned Don Quixote de la Mancha.

A T a certain village in La Mancha, which I shall not name, there lived not long ago one of those old-fashioned gentlemen who are never without a lance upon a rack, an old target, a lean horse, and a greyhound. His diet consisted more of beef than mutton; and with minced meat on most nights,

*Don Quixote de la Mancha.*⁴ Translated by Peter Motteux.

Don Quixote and Sancho Panza, from the title page of the 1605 edition of Don Quixote *printed in Lisbon.*

lentils on Fridays, griefs and groans on Saturdays, and a pigeon extraordinary on Sundays, he consumed three quarters of his revenue: the rest was laid out in a plush coat, velvet breeches, with slippers of the same, for holidays; and a suit of the very best home-spun cloth, which he bestowed on himself for working days. His whole family was a housekeeper something turned of forty, a niece not twenty, and a man that served him in the house and in the field, and

10 could saddle a horse, and handle the pruning-hook. The master himself was nigh fifty years of age, of a hale and strong complexion, lean-bodied, and thin-faced, an early riser, and a lover of hunting. Some say his surname was Quixada, or Quesada (for authors differ in this particular): however, we may reasonably conjecture he was called Quixana (*i.e.* lanthorn-jaws) though this concerns us but little, provided we keep strictly to the truth in every point of this history.

20 You must know then, that when our gentleman had nothing to do (which was almost all the year round), he passed his time in reading books of knight-errantry; which he did with that application and delight, that at last he in a manner wholly left off his country sports, and even the care of his estate; nay, he grew so strangely besotted with those amusements, that he sold many acres of arable land to purchase books of that kind; by which means he collected as many of them as were to be had. . . .

30 He would often dispute with the curate of the parish, a man of learning, that had taken his degrees at Ciguenza, who was the better knight, Palmerin of England, or Amadis de Gaul? but master Nicholas, the barber of the same town, would say, that none of them could compare with the Knight of the Sun; and that if any one came near him, it was certainly Don Galaor, the brother of Amadis de Gaul; for he

was a man of a most commodious temper, neither was he so cynical, nor such a puling whining lover as his brother; and as for courage, he was not a jot 40 behind him.

In fine, he gave himself up so wholly to the reading of romances, that a-nights he would pore on until it was day, and a-days he would read on until it was night; and thus, by sleeping little and reading much, the moisture of his brain was exhausted to that degree, that at last he lost the use of his reason. A world of disorderly notions, picked out of his books, crowded into his imagination; and now his head was full of nothing but enchantments, quarrels, 50 battles, challenges, wounds, complaints, amours, torments, and abundance of stuff and impossibilities; insomuch, that all the fables and fantastical tales which he read seemed to him now as true as the most authentic histories. . . .

Having thus lost his understanding, he unluckily stumbled upon the oddest fancy that ever entered into a madman's brain; for now he thought it convenient and necessary, as well for the increase of his own honour, as the service of the public, to turn 60 knight-errant, and roam through the whole world, armed *cap-à-pie* and mounted on his steed, in quest of adventures; that thus imitating those knights-errant of whom he had read, and following their course of life, redressing all manner of grievances, and exposing himself to danger on all occasions, at last, after a happy conclusion of his enterprises, he might purchase everlasting honour and renown. Transported with these agreeable delusions, the poor gentleman already grasped in imagination the im- 70 perial sceptre of Trapizonda; and, hurried away by his mighty expectations, he prepared with all expedition to take the field.

The first thing he did was to scour a suit of armour that had belonged to his great-grandfather, and had lain time out of mind carelessly rusting in a corner; but, when he had cleaned and repaired it as well as he could, he perceived there was a material piece wanting; for instead of a complete helmet, there was only a single head-piece: however, his 80 industry supplied that defect; for, with some pasteboard, he made a kind of half-beaver, or vizor, which being fitted to the head-piece, made it look like an entire helmet. Then, to know whether it was cutlass-proof, he drew his sword, and tried its edge upon the pasteboard vizor; but, with the first stroke, he unluckily undid in a moment what he had been a whole week a-doing. He did not like its being broke with so much ease, and therefore to secure it from the like accident, he made it anew, and fenced it 90 with thin plates of iron, which he fixed in the inside of it so artificially, that at last he had reason to be satisfied with the solidity of the work; and so, without any experiment, he resolved it should pass to all intents and purposes for a full and sufficient helmet.

The next moment he went to view his horse, whose bones stuck out like the corners of a Spanish Real; however, his master thought, that neither Alexander's Bucephalus, nor the Cid's Babieca could be compared with him. He was four days considering what name to give him; for, as he argued with himself, there was no reason that a horse bestrid by so famous a knight, and withal so excellent in himself, should not be distinguished by a particular name; and therefore he studied to give him such a one as should demonstrate as well what kind of horse he had been before his master was a knight-errant, as what he was now; thinking it but just, since the owner had changed his profession, that the horse should also change his title, and be dignified with another; a sonorous word, such a one as should fill the mouth, and seem consonant with the quality and profession of his master. And thus after many names which he devised, rejected, changed, liked, disliked, and pitched upon again, he concluded to call him Rozinante; a name, in his opinion, lofty sounding, and significant of what he had been before, and also of what he was now; in a word, a horse before or above all the vulgar breed of horses in the world.

When he had thus given his horse a name so much to his satisfaction, he thought of choosing one for himself; and having seriously pondered on the matter eight whole days more, at last he determined to call himself Don Quixote. Whence the author of this most authentic history draws this inference, that his name was Quixada, and not Quesada, as others obstinately pretend. And observing that the valiant Amadis, not satisfied with the bare appellation of Amadis, added to it the name of his country, that it might grow more famous by his exploits, and styled himself Amadis de Gaul; so he, like a true lover of his native soil, resolved to call himself Don Quixote de la Mancha; which addition, to his thinking, denoted very plainly his parentage and country, and consequently would fix a lasting honour on that part of the world.

And now, his armour being scoured, his headpiece improved to a helmet, his horse and himself new-named, he perceived he wanted nothing but a lady, on whom he might bestow the empire of his heart; for he was sensible that a knight-errant without a mistress was a tree without either fruit or leaves, and a body without a soul. "Should I," said he to himself, "by good or ill fortune chance to encounter some giant, as it is common in knight-errantry, and happen to lay him prostrate on the ground, transfixed with my lance, or cleft in two, or, in short, overcome and have him at my mercy, would

it not be proper to have some lady to whom I may send him as a trophy of my valour? That, when he comes into her presence, throwing himself at her feet, he may thus make his humble submission: 'Lady, I am the giant Caraculiambro, lord of the island of Malindrania, vanquished in single combat by that never-deservedly-enough-extolled knight-errant Don Quixote de la Mancha, who has commanded me to cast myself most humbly at your feet, that it may please your honour to dispose of me according to your will.'" Oh! how elevated was the Knight with the conceit of this imaginary submission of the giant; especially having bethought himself of a person on whom he might confer the title of mistress! which, it is believed, happened thus. Near the place where he lived dwelt a good likely country lass, for whom he had formerly had a sort of an inclination, though it is believed she never heard of it, nor regarded it in the least. Her name was Aldonza Lorenzo, and this was she whom he thought he might entitle to the sovereignty of his heart: upon which he studied to find her out a new name, that might have some affinity with her old one, and yet at the same time sound somewhat like that of a princess, or lady of quality: so at last he resolved to call her Dulcinea, with the addition of del Toboso, from the place where she was born; a name, in his opinion, sweet, harmonious, extraordinary, and no less significative than the others which he had devised.

Of Don Quixote's First Sally

These preparations being made, he found his designs ripe for action, and thought it now a crime to deny himself any longer to the injured world, that wanted such a deliverer; the more when he considered what grievances he was to redress, what wrongs and injuries to remove, what abuses to correct, and what duties to discharge. So one morning before day, in the greatest heat of July, without acquainting any one with his design, with all the secrecy imaginable, he armed himself cap-à-pie, laced on his ill-contrived helmet, braced on his target, grasped his lance, mounted Rozinante, and at the private door of his back-yard sallied out into the fields, wonderfully pleased to see with how much ease he had succeeded in the beginning of his enterprise. But he had not gone far ere a terrible thought alarmed him, a thought that had like to have made him renounce his great undertaking; for now it came into his mind that the honour of knighthood had not yet been conferred upon him, and therefore, according to the laws of chivalry, he neither could nor ought to appear in arms against any professed knight: nay, he also considered, that though he were already knighted, it would become him to wear white armour, and not to adorn his shield with any

---

22–25. Rozinante . . . in the world. *Rozin* means a common horse; *ante* before.

device, till he had deserved one by some extraordinary demonstration of his valour.

These thoughts staggered his resolution; but his folly prevailing more than any reason, he resolved to be dubbed a knight by the first he should meet, after the example of several others, who, as his distracting romances informed him, had formerly done the like. . . . He travelled all that day; and, towards the evening, he and his horse being heartily tired, and almost famished, Don Quixote looking about him in hopes to discover some castle, or at least some shepherd's cottage, there to repose and refresh himself; at last, near the road which he kept, he espied an inn, as welcome a sight to his longing eyes, as if he had discovered a star directing him to the gate, nay, to the palace of his redemption. Thereupon hastening towards the inn with all the speed he could, he got thither just at the close of the evening. There stood by chance at the inn-door, two young female adventurers, alias common wenches, who were going to Sevil with some carriers, that happened to take up their lodgings there that very evening; and, as whatever our knight-errant saw, thought, or imagined, was all of a romantic cast, and appeared to him altogether after the manner of the books that had perverted his imagination, he no sooner saw the inn, but he fancied it to be a castle fenced with four towers and lofty pinnacles, glittering with silver, together with a deep moat, drawbridge, and all those other appurtenances peculiar to such kind of places.

Therefore when he came near it, he stopped a while at a distance from the gate, expecting that some dwarf would appear on the battlements, and sound his trumpet to give notice of the arrival of a knight; but finding that nobody came, and that Rozinante was for making the best of his way to the stable, he advanced to the inn-door, where, spying the two young doxies, they seemed to him two beautiful damsels, or graceful ladies, taking the benefit of the fresh air at the gate of the castle. It happened also at the very moment, that a swine-herd, getting together his hogs from the stubble-field, winded his horn; and Don Quixote presently imagined this was the wished-for signal, which some dwarf gave to notify his approach; therefore, with the greatest joy in the world he rode up to the inn. The wenches, affrighted at the approach of a man cased in iron, and armed with a lance and target, were for running into their lodging; but Don Quixote, perceiving their fear by their flight, lifted up the pasteboard beaver of his helmet, and discovering his withered, dusty face, with comely grace and grave delivery accosted them in this manner. "I beseech ye, ladies, do not fly, nor fear the least offence: the order of knighthood, which I profess, does not permit me to countenance or offer injuries to any one in the universe,

and least of all to virgins of such high rank as your presence denotes."

The wenches looked earnestly upon him, endeavouring to get a glimpse of his face, which his ill-contrived beaver partly hid; but when they heard themselves styled virgins, a thing so out of the way of their profession, they could not forbear laughing outright; which Don Quixote resented as a great affront. "Give me leave to tell ye, ladies," cried he, "that modesty and civility are very becoming in the fair sex; whereas laughter without ground is the highest piece of indiscretion: however," added he, "I do not presume to say this to offend you, or incur your displeasure; no, ladies, I assure you I have no other design but to do you service." This uncommon way of expression, joined to the Knight's scurvy figure, increased their mirth; which incensed him to that degree, that this might have carried things to an extremity, had not the innkeeper luckily appeared at that juncture. He was a man whose burden of fat inclined him to peace and quietness, yet when he had observed such a strange disguise of human shape, in his old armour and equipage, he could hardly forbear keeping the wenches company in their laughter; but, having the fear of such a warlike appearance before his eyes, he resolved to give him good words, and therefore accosted him civilly: "Sir Knight," said he, "if your worship be disposed to alight, you will fail of nothing here but of a bed; as for all other accommodations, you may be supplied to your mind." Don Quixote observing the humility of the governor of the castle (for such the innkeeper and inn seemed to him), "Senior Castellano," said he, "the least thing in the world suffices me; for arms are the only things I value, and combat is my bed of repose."

The innkeeper . . . made him this reply: "At this rate, Sir Knight, your bed might be a pavement, and your rest to be still awake; you may then safely alight, and I dare assure you, you can hardly miss being kept awake all the year long in this house, much less one single night." With that he went and held Don Quixote's stirrup, who having not broke his fast that day, dismounted with no small trouble or difficulty. He immediately desired the governor (that is, the innkeeper), to take especial care of his steed, assuring him that there was not a better in the universe; upon which the innkeeper viewed him narrowly, but could not think him to be half so good as Don Quixote said: however, having set him up in the stable, he came back to the Knight to see what he wanted, and found him pulling off his armour by the help of the good natured wenches, who had already reconciled themselves to him; but, though they had eased him of his corslet and back-plate, they could

89. Senior Castellano; that is, governor of a castle.

by no means undo his gorget, nor take off his ill-contrived beaver, which he had tied so fast with green ribbons, that it was impossible to get it off without cutting them; now he would by no means permit that, and so was forced to keep on his helmet all night, which was one of the most pleasant sights in the world; and while his armour was being taken off by the two kind lasses, imagining them to be persons of quality, and ladies of that castle, he very gratefully made them the following compliment: "O Rozinante! for that is my horse's name, ladies, and mine Don Quixote de la Mancha; I never thought to have discovered it, till some feats of arms, achieved by me in your service, had made me better known to your ladyships; but necessity has extorted the secret from me before its time; yet a day will come, when you shall command, and I obey, and then the valour of my arm shall evince the reality of my zeal to serve your ladyships."

The two females, who were not used to such rhetorical speeches, could make no answer to this; they only asked him whether he would eat any-thing? "That I will with all my heart," cried Don Quixote, "whatever it be, for I am of opinion, noth-ing can come to me more seasonably." Now, as ill-luck would have it, it happened to be Friday, and there was nothing to be had at the inn but some pieces of fish, which is called Abadexo in Castile, Bacalloa in Andalusia, Curadillo in some places, and in others Truchuela or Little Trout, though, after all, it is but Poor Jack: so they asked him whether he could eat any of that Truchuela, because they had no other fish to give him. Don Quixote, imagining they meant a small trout, told them, that, provided there were more than one, it was the same thing to him, "for," continued he, "it is all one to me whether I am paid a piece of eight in one single piece, or in eight small reals, which are worth as much: besides, it is probable these small trouts may be like veal, which is finer meat than beef; or like the kid, which is better than the goat. In short, let it be what it will, so it comes quickly, for the weight of armour and the fatigue of travel are not to be supported without recruiting food." Thereupon they laid the cloth at the inn-door, for the benefit of the fresh air, and the landlord brought him a piece of that salt fish, but ill-watered and as ill-dressed; and, as for the bread, it was as mouldy and brown as the Knight's armour: but it would have made one laugh to have seen him eat; for, having his helmet on, with his beaver lifted up, it was impossible for him to feed himself with-out help, so that one of those ladies had that office; but there was no giving him drink that way, and he must have gone without it, had not the innkeeper bored a cane, and setting one end of it to his mouth,

poured the wine in at the other; all which the Knight suffered patiently, because he would not cut the ribbons that fastened his helmet. . . . The only thing that vexed him was, that he was not dubbed a knight; for he fancied he could not lawfully under-take any adventure till he had received the order of knighthood.

An account of the pleasant method taken by Don Quixote to be dubbed a Knight.

Don Quixote's mind being disturbed with that thought, he abridged even his short supper; and as soon as he had done, he called his host, then shut him and himself up in the stable, and falling at his feet, "I will never rise from this place," cried he, "most valorous knight, till you have graciously vouchsafed to grant me a boon, which I will now beg of you, and which will redound to your honour and the good of mankind." The landlord, strangely at a loss to find his guest at his feet, and talking at this rate, endeavoured to make him rise, but all in vain till he had promised to grant him what he asked. "I expected no less from your great magnif-icence, noble sir," replied Don Quixote, "and there-fore I make bold to tell you, that the boon which I beg, and you generously condescend to grant me, is, that tomorrow you will be pleased to bestow the honour of knighthood upon me. This night I will watch my armour in the chapel of your castle, and then in the morning you shall gratify me, as I pas-sionately desire that I may be duly qualified to seek out adventures in every corner of the universe, to relieve the distressed, according to the laws of chiv-alry, and the inclinations of knights-errant like my-self." The innkeeper, who, as I said, was a sharp fellow, and had already a shrewd suspicion of the disorder in his guest's understanding, was fully con-vinced of it when he heard him talk after this man-ner; and, to make sport that night, resolved to hu-mour him in his desires. . . .

He said that his castle at present had no chapel, where the Knight might keep his vigil of arms, it being pulled down in order to be new-built; but that he knew they might lawfully be watched in any other place in a case of necessity, and therefore he might do it that night in the court-yard of the castle; and in the morning (God willing) all the necessary ceremonies should be performed, so that he might assure himself he should be dubbed a knight, nay, as much a knight as any one in the world could be. He then asked Don Quixote, whether he had any money? "Not a cross," replied the Knight, "for I never read in any history of chivalry that any knight-errant ever carried money about him." "You are mistaken," cried the innkeeper; "for admit the his-tories are silent in this matter, the authors thinking it needless to mention things so evidently necessary as money and clean shirts, yet there is no reason to believe the knights went without either; and you may rest assured that all the knights-errant, of whom so many histories are full, had their purses well lined to supply themselves with necessaries, and carried also with them some shirts, and a small box of salves to heal their wounds; for they had not the conveniency of surgeons to cure them every time they fought in fields and deserts, unless they were so happy as to have some sage or magician for their friend, to give them present assistance, sending them some damsel or dwarf through the air in a cloud, with a small bottle of water of so great a virtue, that they no sooner tasted a drop of it, but their wounds were as perfectly cured as if they had never received any. . . . I must therefore advise you," continued he, "nay, I might even charge and command you, as you are shortly to be my son in chivalry, never from this time forwards to ride without money, nor without the other necessaries of which I spoke to you, which you will find very beneficial when you least expect it." Don Quixote promised to perform very punctually all his injunctions; and so they disposed everything in order to his watching his arms in a great yard that adjoined to the inn. To which purpose the Knight, having got them all together, laid them in a cistern close by a well in that yard; then, bracing his target and grasping his lance, just as it grew dark, he began to walk about by the horse-trough with a graceful deportment. . . .

While he was thus employed, one of the carriers who lodged in the inn came out to water his mules, which he could not do without removing the arms out of the trough. With that Don Quixote, who saw him make towards him, cried out to him aloud, "O thou, whoever thou art, rash knight, that prepares to lay thy hands on the arms of the most valorous knight-errant that ever wore a sword, take heed; do not audaciously attempt to profane them with a touch, lest instant death be the too-sure reward of thy temerity." But the carrier never regarded these dreadful threats; and, laying hold on the armour by the straps, without any more ado threw it a good way from him; though it had been better for him to have let it alone: for Don Quixote no sooner saw this, but lifting up his eyes to heaven, and addressing his thoughts, as it seemed, to his lady Dulcinea, "Assist me, lady," cried he, "in the first opportunity that offers itself to your faithful slave; nor let your favour and protection be denied me in this first trial of my valour!" Repeating such like ejaculations, he let slip his target, and lifting up his lance with both his hands, he gave the carrier such a terrible knock on his inconsiderate pate with his lance, that he laid him at his feet in a woeful condition; and, had he backed that blow with another, the fellow would

certainly have had no need of a surgeon. This done, Don Quixote took up his armour, laid it again in the horse-trough, and then walked on, backwards and forwards, with as great unconcern as he did at first.

Soon after another carrier, not knowing what had happened, came also to water his mules, while the first yet lay on the ground in a trance; but, as he offered to clear the trough of the armour, Don Quixote, without speaking a word or imploring any one's assistance, once more dropped his target, lifted up his lance, and then let it fall so heavily on the fellow's pate, that, without damaging his lance, he broke the carrier's head in three or four places. His outcry soon alarmed and brought thither all the people in the inn, and the landlord among the rest; which Don Quixote perceiving, "Thou queen of beauty," cried he, bracing on his shield, and drawing his sword, "thou courage and vigour of my weakened heart, now is the time when thou must enliven thy adventurous slave with the beams of thy greatness, while this moment he is engaging in so terrible an adventure!" With this, in his opinion, he found himself supplied with such an addition of courage, that, had all the carriers in the world at once attacked him, he would undoubtedly have faced them all.

On the other side, the carriers enraged to see their comrades thus used, though they were afraid to come near, gave the Knight such a volley of stones, that he was forced to shelter himself as well as he could under the covert of his target, without daring to go far from the horse-trough, lest he should seem to abandon his arms. The innkeeper called to the carriers as loud as he could to let him alone; that he had told them already that he was mad, and consequently the law would acquit him, though he should kill them. Don Quixote also made yet more noise, calling them false and treacherous villains, and the lord of the castle a base, inhospitable, and discourteous knight, for suffering a knight-errant to be so abused. "I would make thee know," cried he, "what a perfidious wretch thou art, had I but received the order of knighthood; but for you, base, ignominious rabble! fling on, do your worst; come on, draw nearer if you dare, and receive the reward of your indiscretion and insolence." This he spoke with so much spirit and undauntedness, that he struck a terror into all his assailants; so that, partly through fear and partly through the innkeeper's persuasions, they gave over flinging stones at him; and he, on his side, permitted the enemy to carry off their wounded, and then returned to the guard of his arms as calm and composed as before. . . .

Upon this the innkeeper, lest the Knight should proceed to such extremities, fetched the book in which he used to set down the carrier's accounts for straw and barley; and having brought with him the two kind females, already mentioned, and a boy that held a piece of lighted candle in his hand, he ordered Don Quixote to kneel: then reading in his manual, as if he had been repeating some pious oration, in the midst of his devotion, he lifted up his hand, and gave him a good blow on the neck, and then a gentle slap on the back with the flat of his sword, still mumbling some words between his teeth in the tone of a prayer. After this he ordered one of the wenches to gird the sword about the Knight's waist; which she did with much solemnity, and, I may add, discretion, considering how hard a thing it was to forbear laughing at every circumstance of the ceremony. It is true, the thoughts of the Knight's late prowess did not a little contribute to the suppression of their mirth. As she girded on his sword, "Heaven," cried the kind lady, "make your worship a lucky knight, and prosper you wherever you go." Don Quixote desired to know her name, that he might understand to whom he was indebted for the favour she had bestowed upon him, and also make her partaker of the honour he was to acquire by the strength of his arm. To which the lady answered with all humility, that her name was Tolosa, a cobbler's daughter, that kept a stall among the little shops of Sanchobinaya at Toledo; and that, whenever he pleased to command her, she would be his humble servant. Don Quixote begged of her to do him the favour to add hereafter the title of Lady to her name, and for his sake to be called from that time the Lady Tolosa; which she promised to do. Her companion, having buckled on his spurs, occasioned a like conference between them; and, when he had asked her name, she told him she went by the name of Miller, being the daughter of an honest miller of Antequera. Our new Knight entreated her also to style herself the Lady Miller, making her new offers of service. These extraordinary ceremonies (the like never seen before) being thus hurried over in a kind of post-haste, having immediately saddled his Rozinante, and being mounted, he embraced the innkeeper, and returned him so many thanks at so extravagant a rate, for the obligation he had laid upon him in dubbing him a knight, that it is impossible to give a true relation of them all: to which the innkeeper, in haste to get rid of him, returned as rhetorical, though shorter answers; and, without stopping his horse for the reckoning, was glad with all his heart to see him go. . . .

Being highly pleased with himself and what had happened, imagining he had given a most fortunate and noble beginning to his feats of arms, as he went on towards his village, "O most beautiful of beauties," said he with a low voice, "Dulcinea del Toboso! well mayest thou deem thyself most happy, since it was thy good fortune to captivate and hold a willing slave to thy pleasure, so valorous and renowned a knight as is, and ever shall be, Don Quixote de la Mancha.". . . Just as he had said this, he found himself at a place where four roads met. The curate and the barber of the village, both of them Don Quixote's intimate acquaintance, happened to be there at that juncture. Then did they ask the Don a thousand questions, but to every one he made no other answer, but that they should give him something to eat, and then leave him to his repose, a thing which was to him of the greatest importance. . . .

Don Quixote's second sally in quest of adventures.

Full fifteen days did our knight remain quietly at home, without betraying the least sign of his desire to renew his rambling; during which time there passed a great deal of pleasant discourse between him and his two friends, the curate and the barber; while he maintained, that there was nothing the world stood so much in need of as knights-errant; wherefore he was resolved to revive the order. In which disputes Mr. Curate sometimes contradicted him, and sometimes submitted; for had he not now and then given way to his fancies, there would have been no conversing with him.

In the mean time, Don Quixote earnestly solicited one of his neighbours, a country labourer, and a good honest fellow, if we may call a poor man honest, for he was poor indeed, poor in purse, and poor in brains; and, in short, the knight talked so long to him, plied him with so many arguments, and made him so many fair promises, that at last the poor silly clown consented to go along with him, and become his squire. Among other inducements to entice him to do it willingly, Don Quixote forgot not to tell him, that it was likely such an adventure would present itself, as might secure him the conquest of some island, in the time he might be picking up a straw or two, and then the squire might promise himself to be made governor of the place. Allured with these large promises, and many others, Sancho Pança (for that was the name of the fellow) forsook his wife and children to be his neighbour's squire.

This done, Don Quixote made it his business to furnish himself with money; for which purpose, selling one house, mortgaging another, and losing by all, he at last got a pretty good sum together. He also borrowed a target of a friend, and having patched up his headpiece and beaver as well as he could, he gave his squire notice of the day and hour when he intended to set out, that he might also furnish himself with what he thought necessary; but, above all, he charged him to provide himself with a wallet; which Sancho promised him to do, telling him he would also take his ass along with him, which, being a very good one, might be a great ease to him, for he was not used to travel much a-foot. The mentioning of the ass made the noble knight pause a while; he mused, and pondered whether he had ever read of any knight-errant whose squire used to ride upon an ass; but he could not remember any precedent for it: however, he gave him leave at last to bring his ass, hoping to mount him more honourably with the first opportunity, by unhorsing the next discourteous knight he should meet. He also furnished himself with shirts, and as many other necessaries as he could conveniently carry, according to the innkeeper's injunctions. Which being done, Sancho Pança, without bidding either his wife or children good-bye; and Don Quixote, without taking any more notice of his housekeeper or of his niece, stole out of the village one night, not so much as suspected by anybody, and made such haste, that by break of day they thought themselves out of reach, should they happen to be pursued. As for Sancho Pança, he rode like a patriarch, with his canvas knapsack, or wallet, and his leathern bottle, having a huge desire to see himself governor of the island, which his master had promised him. . . .

As they jogged on, "I beseech your worship, Sir Knight-errant," quoth Sancho to his master, "be sure you do not forget what you promised me about the island; for, I dare say, I shall make shift to govern it, let it be never so big." "You must know, friend Sancho," replied Don Quixote, "that it has been the constant practice of knights-errant, in former ages, to make their squires governors of the islands or kingdoms they conquered: now, I am not only resolved to keep up that laudable custom, but even to improve it, and outdo my predecessors in generosity: for whereas sometimes, or rather most commonly, other knights delayed rewarding their squires till they were grown old, and worn out with service, bad days, worse nights, and all manner of hard duty, and then put them off with some title, either of Count, or at least Marquis of some valley or province of great or small extent; now, if thou and I do but live, it may happen, that before we have passed six days together, I may conquer some kingdom, having many other kingdoms annexed to its imperial crown; and this would fall out most luckily for thee; and then would I presently crown thee king of one of them. Nor do thou imagine this to be a mighty matter; for so strange accidents and revolutions, so sudden and so unforeseen, attend the profession of chivalry, that I might easily give thee a great deal more than I have promised." "Why, should this come to pass," quoth Sancho Pança, "and I be made a king by some such miracle as your worship says, then happy-be-lucky, my Whither-d'ye-go Mary Gutierrez would be at least a queen, and my children infantas and princes, if it like your worship." "Who doubts of that?" cried Don Quixote. "I doubt of it," replied Sancho; "for I cannot help believing, that though it should rain kingdoms down upon the face of the earth, not one of them would fit well upon Mary Gutierrez's head; for, I must needs tell you, she is not worth two brass jacks to make a queen of: no, Countess would be better for her, if it please you; and that too, God help her, will be as much as she can handsomely manage." "Recommend the matter to providence," returned Don Quixote, "it will be sure to give what is most expedient for thee."

Of the good success which the valorous Don Quixote had in the most terrifying and never-to-be-imagined adventure of the wind-mills.

As they were thus discoursing, they discovered some thirty or forty wind-mills that are in that plain; and, as soon as the knight had spied them, "Fortune," cried he, "directs our affairs better than we ourselves could have wished: look yonder, friend Sancho, there are at least thirty outrageous giants, whom I intend to encounter; and, having deprived them of life, we will begin to enrich ourselves with their spoils: for they are lawful prize; and the extirpation of that cursed brood will be an acceptable service to Heaven." "What giants?" quoth Sancho Pança. "Those whom thou seest yonder," answered Don Quixote, "with their long-extended arms; some of that detested race have arms of so immense a size, that sometimes they reach two leagues in length." "Pray, look better, sir," quoth Sancho; "those things yonder are no giants, but wind-mills, and the arms you fancy, are their sails, which, being whirled about by the wind, make the mill go." "It is a sign," cried Don Quixote, "thou art but little acquainted with adventures. I tell thee they are giants; and therefore, if thou art afraid, go aside and say thy prayers, for I am resolved to engage in a dreadful, unequal combat against them all."

This said, he clapped spurs to his horse Rozinante, without giving ear to his squire Sancho, who bawled out to him, and assured him that they were windmills, and no giants. But he was so fully possessed with a strong conceit of the contrary, that he did not so much as hear his squire's outcry, nor was he sensible of what they were, although he was already very near them; far from that. "Stand, cowards," cried he as loud as he could; "stand your ground, ignoble creatures, and fly not basely from a single knight, who dares encounter you all." At the same time the wind rising, the mill-sails began to move, which, when Don Quixote spied, "Base miscreants," cried he, "though you move more arms than the giant Briareus, you shall pay for your arrogance." He most devoutly recommended himself to his lady Dulcinea, imploring her assistance in this perilous adventure; and so, covering himself with his shield, and couching his lance, he rushed with Rozinante's utmost speed upon the first windmill he could come at, and, running his lance into the sail, the wind whirled

Don Quixote's battle with the windmills as pictured by the famous nineteenth-century illustrator, Gustave Doré.

about with such swiftness, that the rapidity of the motion presently broke the lance into shivers, and hurled away both knight and horse along with it, till down he fell, rolling a good way off in the field.

Sancho Pança ran as fast as his ass could drive to help his master, whom he found lying, and not able to stir, such a blow he and Rozinante had received. "Mercy on me!" cried Sancho, "did I not give your worship fair warning? did not I tell you they were windmills, and that nobody could think otherwise, unless he had also wind-mills in his head?" "Peace, friend Sancho," replied Don Quixote: "there is nothing so subject to the inconstancy of fortune as war. I am verily persuaded, that cursed necromancer Freston has transformed these giants into wind-mills, to deprive me of the honour of the victory; such is his inveterate malice against me; but, in the end, all his pernicious wiles and stratagems shall prove ineffectual against the prevailing edge of my sword." "Amen, say I," replied Sancho. . . .

After many bitter Ohs, and screwed faces, Sancho laid Don Quixote on the ass, tied Rozinante to its tail, and then, leading the ass by the halter, he took the nearest way he could guess to the high road; to which he luckily came before he had travelled a short league, and then he discovered an inn; which,

in spite of all he could say, Don Quixote was pleased to mistake for a castle. Sancho swore bloodily it was an inn, and his master was as positive of the contrary. In short, their dispute lasted so long, that before they could decide it they reached the inn-door, where Sancho straight went in, with all his train, without troubling himself any further about the matter.

What happened to Don Quixote in the inn which he took for a castle.

The innkeeper, seeing Don Quixote lying quite athwart the ass, asked Sancho what ailed him? Sancho answered, it was nothing, only his master had got a fall from the top of a rock to the bottom, and had bruised his sides a little. The innkeeper had a wife very different from the common sort of hostesses, for she was of a charitable nature, and very compassionate of her neighbour's affliction; which made her immediately take care of Don Quixote, and call her daughter (a good handsome girl) to set her helping hand to his cure. One of the servants in the inn was an Asturian wench, a broad-faced, flat-headed, saddle-nosed dowdy, blind of one eye, and the other almost out. However, the activity of her body supplied all other defects. She was not above three feet high from her heels to her head; and her shoulders, which somewhat loaded her, as having too much flesh upon them, made her look downwards oftener than she could have wished. This charming original likewise assisted the mistress and the daughter; and, with the latter, helped to make the Knight's bed, and a sorry one it was; the room where it stood was an old gambling cock-loft, which by manifold signs seemed to have been, in the days of yore, a repository for chopped straw. Somewhat further, in a corner of that garret, a carrier had his lodging; and, though his bed was nothing but the pannels and coverings of his mules, it was much better than that of Don Quixote, which only consisted of four rough-hewn boards laid upon two uneven tressels, a flock-bed, that, for thinness, might well have passed for a quilt, and was full of knobs and bunches, which, had they not peeped out through many a hole, and shown themselves to be of wool, might well have been taken for stones. The rest of that extraordinary bed's furniture was a pair of sheets, which rather seemed to be of leather than of linen-cloth, and a coverlet whose every individual thread you might have told, and never have missed one in the tale.

In this ungracious bed was the Knight laid to rest his belaboured carcase, and presently the hostess and her daughter anointed and plastered him all over, while Maritornes (for that was the name of the Asturian wench) held the candle. The hostess, while she greased him, wondering to see him so bruised all over: "I fancy," said she, "those bumps look much more like a dry beating than a fall." "It was no dry beating, mistress, I promise you," quoth Sancho, "but the rock had I know not how many cragged ends and knobs, whereof every one gave my master a token of his kindness. . . ." "How do you call this same gentleman?" quoth Maritornes. "He is Don Quixote de la Mancha," replied Sancho; "and he is a knight-errant, and one of the primest and stoutest that ever the sun shined on." "A knight-errant," cried the wench, "pray, what is that?" "Heyday!" cried Sancho, "does the wench know no more of the world than that comes to? Why, a knight-errant is a thing which in two words you see well cudgelled, and then an emperor. To-day there is not a more wretched thing upon the earth, and yet to-morrow he will have you two or three kingdoms to give away to his squire." "How comes it to pass, then," quoth the landlady, "that thou, who art this great person's squire, hast not yet got thee at least an earldom?" "Fair and softly goes far," replied Sancho; "why, we have not been a month in our gears, so that we have not yet encountered any adventure worth the naming; besides, many a time we look for one thing, and light on another. But if my lord Don Quixote happens to get well again, and I escape remaining a cripple, I will not take the best title in the land for what I am sure will fall to my share."

Here Don Quixote, who had listened with great attention to all these discourses, raised himself up in his bed with much ado, and taking the hostess in a most obliging manner by the hand, "Believe me," said he, "beautiful lady, you may well esteem it a happiness that you have now the opportunity to entertain my person in your castle. Self praise is unworthy a man of honour, and therefore I shall say no more of myself, but my squire will inform you who I am; only thus much let me add, that I will eternally preserve your kindness in the treasury of my remembrance, and study all occasions to testify my gratitude: and I wish," continued he, "the Powers above had so disposed my fate, that I were not already love's devoted slave, and captivated by the charms of the disdainful beauty who engrosses all my softer thoughts; for then would I be proud to sacrifice my liberty to this beautiful damsel." The hostess, her daughter, and the kind-hearted Maritornes stared on one another, quite at a loss for the meaning of this high-flown language, which they understood full as well as if it had been Greek. Yet, conceiving these were words of compliment and courtship, they looked upon him, and admired him as a man of another world: and so, having made him such returns as innkeeper's breeding could afford, they left him to his rest; only Maritornes stayed to rub down Sancho, who wanted her help no less than his master.

Now you must know, that the carrier and she had agreed to pass the night together; and she had given

him her word that, as soon as all the people in the inn were in bed, she would be sure to come to him, and be at his service. And it is said of this good-natured thing, that whenever she had passed her word in such cases, she was sure to make it good, though she had made the promise in the midst of a wood, and without any witness at all: for she stood much upon her gentility, though she undervalued herself so far as to serve in an inn; often saying, that nothing but crosses and necessity could have made her stoop to it.

Don Quixote's hard, scanty, beggarly, miserable bed was the first of the four in that wretched apartment; next to that was Sancho's kennel, which consisted of nothing but a bed-mat and a coverlet, that rather seemed shorn canvas than a rug. Beyond these two beds was that of the carrier, made, as we have said, of the pannels and furniture of two of the best of twelve mules which he kept, every one of them goodly beasts, and in special good case; for he was one of the richest muleteers of Arevalo. . . . After the carrier had visited his mules, and given them their second course, he laid himself down upon his pannels, in expectation of the most punctual Maritornes's kind visit. . . .

And now was every soul in the inn gone to bed, nor any light to be seen, except that of a lamp which hung in the middle of the gate-way. This general tranquillity setting Don Quixote's thoughts at work, offered to his imagination one of the most absurd follies that ever crept into a distempered brain from the perusal of romantic whimsies. Now he fancied himself to be in a famous castle (for, as we have already said, all the inns he lodged in seemed no less than castles to him) and that the innkeeper's daughter (consequently daughter to the lord of the castle) strangely captivated with his graceful presence and gallantry, had promised him the pleasure of her embraces, as soon as her father and mother were gone to rest. This chimera disturbed him, as if it had been a real truth; so that he began to be mightily perplexed, reflecting on the danger to which his honour was exposed. But at last his virtue overcame the powerful temptation, and he firmly resolved not to be guilty of the least infidelity to his lady Dulcinea del Toboso, though Queen Guinever herself, with her trusty Matron Quintaniona, should join to decoy him into the alluring snare.

While these wild imaginations worked in his brain, the gentle Maritornes was mindful of her assignation, and with soft and wary steps, bare-foot, and in her smock, with her hair gathered up in a fustian coif, stole into the room, and felt about for her beloved carrier's bed: but scarce had she got to the door, when Don Quixote, whose ears were on the

80. their second course; of fodders.

scout, was sensible that something was coming in: and therefore, having raised himself in his bed, sore and wrapped up in plasters as he was, he stretched out his arms to receive his fancied damsel, and caught hold of Maritornes by the wrist, as she was, with her arms stretched, groping her way to her paramour; he pulled her to him, and made her sit down by his bed's side, she not daring to speak a word all the while. Now, as he imagined her to be the lord of the castle's daughter, her smock, which was of the coarsest canvas, seemed to him of the finest holland; and the glass beads about her wrist, precious oriental pearls; her hair, that was almost as rough as a horse's mane, he took to be soft flowing threads of bright curling gold; and her breath, that had a stronger hogo than stale venison, was to him a grateful compound of the most fragrant perfumes of Arabia. In short, flattering imagination transformed her into the likeness of those romantic beauties, one of whom, as he remembered to have read, came to pay a private visit to a wounded knight, with whom she was desperately in love; and the poor gentleman's obstinate folly had so infatuated his outward sense, that his feeling and his smell could not in the least undeceive him, and he thought he had no less than a balmy Venus in his arms, while he hugged a fulsome bundle of deformities, that would have turned any man's stomach but a sharp-set carrier's.

Therefore clasping her still closer, with a soft and amorous whisper: "Oh! thou most lovely temptation," cried he; "oh! that I now might but pay a warm acknowledgment for the mighty blessing which your extravagant goodness would lavish on me; yes, most beautiful charmer, I would give an empire to purchase your more desirable embraces: but fortune, madam, fortune, that tyrant of my life, that unrelenting enemy to the truly deserving, has maliciously hurried and riveted me to this bed, where I lie so bruised and macerated, that, though I were eager to gratify your desires, I should at this dear unhappy minute be doomed to impotence; nay, to that unlucky bar fate has added a yet more invincible obstacle; I mean my plighted faith to the unrivalled Dulcinea del Toboso, the sole mistress of my wishes, and absolute sovereign of my heart. Oh! did not this oppose my present happiness, I could never be so dull and insensible a knight, as to lose the benefit of this extraordinary favour which you have now condescended to offer me."

Poor Maritornes all this while sweated for fear and anxiety, to find herself thus locked in the Knight's arms; and without either understanding, or willing to understand his florid excuses, she did what she could to get from him, and sheer off without speaking a word. On the other side, the carrier, whose lewd thoughts kept him awake, having heard his trusty Lady when she first came in, and listened ever since to the Knight's discourse, began to be afraid that she had made some other assignation; and so, without any more ado he crept softly to Don Quixote's bed, where he listened a while to hear what would be the end of all this talk, which he could not understand. But perceiving at last, by the struggling of his faithful Maritornes, that it was none of her fault, and that the Knight strove to detain her against her will, he could by no means bear his familiarity; and therefore, taking it in mighty dudgeon, he up with his fist, and hit the enamoured Knight such a swinging blow on the jaws, that his face was all over blood in a moment. And, not satisfied with this, he got on the top of the Knight, and with his splay-feet betrampled him as if he had been trampling a hay-mow. With that the bed, whose foundations were none of the best, sunk under the additional load of the carrier, and fell with such a noise, that it waked the innkeeper, who presently suspects it to be one of Maritornes's nightly skirmishes; and therefore, having called her aloud, and finding that she did not answer, he lighted a lamp, and made to the place where he heard the bustle. The wench, who heard him coming, knowing him to be of a passionate nature, was scared out of her wits, and fled for shelter to Sancho's sty, where he lay snoring to some tune: there she pigged in, and slunk under the coverlet, where she lay snug, and trussed up as round as an egg.

Presently her master came in, in a mighty heat: "Where is this damned whore?" cried he. "I dare say, this is one of her pranks." By this, Sancho awaked; and feeling that unusual lump, which almost overlaid him, he took it to be the night-mare, and began to lay about him with his fists, and thumped the wench so unmercifully, that at last flesh and blood were no longer able to bear it; and, forgetting the danger she was in, and her dear reputation, she paid him back his thumps as fast as her fists could lay them on, and soon roused the drowsy squire out of his sluggishness, whether he would or no: who, finding himself thus pommelled by he did not know who, bustled up in his nest, and catching hold of Maritornes, they began the most pleasant skirmish in the world. When the carrier perceiving, by the light of the innkeeper's lamp, the dismal condition that his dear mistress was in, presently took her part; and leaving the knight, whom he had more than sufficiently mauled, flew at the squire, and paid him confoundedly. On the other hand, the innkeeper, who took the wench to be the cause of all this hurly-burly, cuffed and kicked, and kicked and cuffed her over and over again: and so there was a strange multiplication of fisticuffs and drubbings. The carrier pommelled Sancho, Sancho mauled the wench, the wench belaboured the squire, and the innkeeper thrashed her again: and all of them laid on with such expedition, that you would have thought they had been afraid of losing time. But the jest was, that in the heat of the fray the lamp went out, so that being now in the dark, they plied one another at a venture: they struck and tore, all went to rack, while nails and fists flew about without mercy.

There happened to lodge that night in the inn one of the officers belonging to that society which they call the old holy brotherhood of Toledo, whose chief office is to look after thieves and robbers. Being waked with the heavy bustle, he presently jumped out of his bed, and, with his short staff in one hand, and a tin-box with his commission in it in the other, he groped out his way; and, having entered the room in the dark, cried out, "I charge ye all to keep the peace: I am an officer of the holy brotherhood." The first he popped his hand upon happened to be the poor battered knight, who lay upon his back at his full length, without any feeling, upon the ruins of his bed. The officer, having caught him by the beard, presently cried out, "I charge you to aid and assist me:" but finding he could not stir, though he gripped him hard, he presently imagined him to be dead, and murdered by the rest in the room. With that he bawled out to have the gates of the inn shut. "Here is a man murdered," cried he; "look that nobody makes his escape." These words struck all the combatants with such a terror, that as soon as they reached their ears, they gave over, and left the argument undecided. Away stole the innkeeper to his own room, the carrier to his pannels, and the wench to her kennel; only the unfortunate knight, and his as unfortunate squire, remained where they lay, not being able to stir; while the officer, having let go Don Quixote's beard, went out for a light, in order to apprehend the supposed murderers: but the innkeeper having wisely put out the lamp in the gate-way, as he sneaked out of the room, the officer was obliged to repair to the kitchen-chimney, where, with much ado, puffing and blowing a long while amidst the embers, he at last made shift to get a light.

A further account of the innumerable hardships which the brave Don Quixote, and his worthy squire Sancho, underwent in the inn, which the knight unluckily took for a castle.

Don Quixote, who by this time was come to himself, began to call Sancho with the same lamentable tone as the day before. "Sancho," cried he, "friend Sancho! art thou asleep? art thou asleep, friend Sancho?" "Sleep!" replied Sancho, mightily out of humour, "may Old Nick rock my cradle then: why, how the devil should I sleep, when all the imps of hell have been tormenting me to-night?" "Nay, thou art in the right," answered Don Quixote, "for either I have no skill in these matters, or this castle is enchanted. Hear what I say to thee, but first swear thou wilt never reveal it till after my death." "I swear

it," quoth Sancho. "I am thus cautious," said Don Quixote, "because I hate to take away the reputation of any person." "Why," quoth Sancho, "I tell you again, I swear never to speak a word of the matter while you live; and I wish I may be at liberty to talk on it to-morrow." "Why!" cried Don Quixote, "have I done thee so much wrong, Sancho, that you would have me die so soon?" "Nay, it is not for that neither," quoth Sancho; "because I cannot abide to keep things long, for fear they should grow mouldy." "Well, let it be as thou pleasest," said Don Quixote: "for I dare trust greater concerns to thy courtesy and affection. In short, know, that this very night there happened to me one of the strangest adventures that can be imagined; for the daughter of the lord of this castle came to me, who is one of the most engaging and most beautiful damsels that ever nature has been proud to boast of: what could I not tell thee of the charms of her shape and face, and the perfections of her mind! what could I not add of other hidden beauties, which I condemn to silence and oblivion, lest I endanger my allegiance and fidelity to my lady Dulcinea del Toboso! I will only tell thee, that the Heavens, envying the inestimable happiness which fortune had thrown into my hand; or rather, because this castle is enchanted, it happened, that in the midst of the most tender and passionate discourses that passed between us, the profane hand of some mighty giant, which I could not see, nor imagine whence it came, hit me such a dreadful blow on the jaws, that they are still embrued with blood; after which the discourteous wretch, presuming on my present weakness, did so barbarously bruise me, that I feel myself in a worse condition now than I did yesterday, after the carriers had so roughly handled me for Rozinante's incontinency: from which I conjecture, that the treasure of this damsel's beauty is guarded by some enchanted Moor, and not reserved for me."

"Nor for me neither," quoth Sancho; "for I have been rib-roasted by above four hundred Moors, who have hammered my bones. But, sir, pray tell me, do you call this such a pleasant adventure, when we are so lamentably pounded after it? And yet your hap may well be accounted better than mine, seeing you have hugged that fair maiden in your arms. But I, what have I had, I pray you, but the heaviest blows that ever fell on a poor man's shoulders? Woe is me and the mother that bore me, for I neither am, nor ever mean to be a knight-errant; and yet, of all the misadventures, the greater part falls still to my lot." "What, hast thou been beaten as well as I?" said Don Quixote. "What a plague," cried Sancho, "have not I been telling you so all this while!" "Come, never let it trouble thee, friend Sancho," replied Don Quixote; "for I will immediately make the precious balsam, that will cure thee in the twinkling of an eye."

By this time the officer, having lighted his lamp, came into the room, to see who it was that was murdered. Sancho seeing him enter in his shirt, a napkin wrapped about his head like a turban, and the lamp in his hand, he being also an ugly ill-looked fellow: "Sir," quoth the squire to his master, "pray see whether this be not the enchanted Moor, that is come again to have the other bout with me, and try whether he has not left some place unbruised for him now to maul as much as the rest." "It cannot be the Moor," replied Don Quixote; "for persons enchanted are to be seen by nobody." "If they do not suffer themselves to be seen," quoth Sancho, "at least they suffer themselves to be felt: if not, let my carcase bear witness." "So might mine," cried Don Quixote: "yet this is no sufficient reason to prove, that what we see is the enchanted Moor."

While they were thus arguing, the officer advanced, and wondered to hear two men talk so calmly to one another there: yet finding the unfortunate knight lying in the same deplorable posture as he left him, stretched out like a corpse, bloody, bruised and beplastered, and not able to stir himself, "How is it, honest fellow," quoth he to the champion, "how do you find yourself?" "Were I your fellow," replied Don Quixote, "I would have a little more manners than you have, you blockhead, you; is that your way of approaching knights-errant in this country?" The officer could not bear such a reprimand from one who made so scurvy a figure, and lifting up the lamp, oil and all, hit Don Quixote such a blow on the head with it, that he had reason to fear he had made work for the surgeon, and therefore stole presently out of the room, under the protection of the night. "Well, sir," quoth Sancho, "do you think now it was the enchanted Moor, or no? For my part, I think he keeps the treasure you talk of for others, and reserves only kicks, cuffs, thumps and knocks for your worship and myself." "I am now convinced," answered Don Quixote; "therefore let us waive that resentment of these injuries, which we might otherwise justly show; for considering these enchanters can make themselves invisible when they please, it is needless to think of revenge. But I pray thee rise, if thou canst, Sancho, and desire the governor of the castle to send me some oil, salt, wine and rosemary, that I may make my healing balsam; for truly I want it extremely, so fast the blood flows out of the wound which the phantasm gave me just now."

Sancho then got up as fast as his aching bones would let him, and with much ado made shift to crawl out of the room to look for the innkeeper, and stumbling by the way on the officer, who stood hearkening to know what mischief he had done. "Sir," quoth he to him, "for heaven's sake, do so much as help us to a little oil, salt, wine and rosemary, to make a medicine for one of the best knights-errant that ever trod one shoe of leather, who lies yonder grievously wounded by the enchanted Moor of this inn." The officer hearing him talk at that rate, took him to be one out of his wits; and it beginning to be daylight, he opened the inn-door, and told the innkeeper what Sancho wanted. The host presently provided the desired ingredients, and Sancho crept back with them to his master, whom he found holding his head and sadly complaining of the pain which he felt there; though, after all, the lamp had done him no more harm than only raising of two huge bumps; for that which he fancied to be blood was only sweat, and the oil of the lamp, that had liquored his hair and face.

The knight took all the ingredients, and having mixed them together, he had them set over the fire, and there kept them boiling till he thought they were enough. That done, he asked for a vial to put this precious liquor in: but there being none to be got, the innkeeper presented him with an old earthen jug, and Don Quixote was forced to be contented with that. Then he mumbled over the pot above fourscore *paternosters,* and as many *ave-marias, salve reginas,* and *credos,* making the sign of the Cross at every word, by way of benediction. At which ceremony Sancho, the innkeeper, and the officer were present; for, as for the carrier, he was gone to look after his mules, and took no manner of notice of what was passed. This blessed medicine being made, Don Quixote resolved to make an immediate experiment of it on himself; and to that purpose he took off a good draught of the overplus, which the pot would not hold: but he had scarce gulped it down, when it set him a-vomiting so violently, that you would have thought he would have cast up his heart, liver, and guts; and his reaching and straining put him into such a sweat that he desired to be covered up warm, and left to his repose. With that they left him, and he slept three whole hours; and then waking, found himself so wonderfully eased, that he made no question but he had now the right balsam of Fierabrass; and therefore he thought he might safely undertake all the most dangerous adventures in the world, without the least hazard of his person.

Sancho, encouraged by the wonderful effect of the balsam on his master, begged that he would be pleased to give him leave to sip up what was left in the pot, which was no small quantity; and the Don having consented, honest Sancho lifted it up with both his hands, and, with a strong faith and better will, poured every drop down his throat. Now the man's stomach not being so nice as his master's, the drench did not set him a-vomiting after that manner, but caused such a wambling in his stomach, such a bitter loathing, kecking, and reaching, and such grinding pangs, with cold sweats and swoonings, that he verily believed his last hour was come, and in the midst of his agony gave both the balsam and him that made it to the Devil. "Friend," said Don Quixote, seeing him in that condition, "I begin to think all this pain befalls thee, only because thou hast not received the order of knighthood; for, it is my opinion, this balsam ought to be used by no man that is not a professed knight." "What a plague did you mean then by letting me drink it?" quoth Sancho. "A murrain on me and all my generation, why did not you tell me this before?" . . . This dreadful hurricane lasted about two hours; and then, too, instead of finding himself as free from pain as his master, he felt himself as feeble, and so far spent, that he was not able to stand.

But Don Quixote, as we have said, found himself in an excellent temper; and his active soul loathing an inglorious repose, he presently was impatient to depart to perform the duties of his adventurous profession: for he thought those moments that were trifled away in amusements or other concerns, only a blank in life; and all delays a depriving distressed persons, and the world in general, of his needed assistance. The confidence which he reposed in his balsam, heightened, if possible, his resolution; and thus, carried away by his eager thoughts, he saddled Rozinante himself, and then put the pannel upon the ass, and his squire upon the pannel, after he had helped him to huddle on his clothes: that done, he mounted his steed; and, having spied a javelin that stood in a corner, he seized and appropriated it to himself, to supply the want of his lance. Above twenty people that were in the inn stood spectators of all these transactions; and among the rest the innkeeper's daughter, from whom Don Quixote had not power to withdraw his eyes, breathing out at every glance a deep sigh from the very bottom of his heart; which those who had seen him so mortified the night before, took to proceed from the pain of his bruises.

And now, being ready to set forwards, he called for the master of the house, and with a grave delivery: "My Lord Governor," cried he, "the favours I have received in your castle are so great and extraordinary, that they bind my grateful soul to an eternal acknowledgment: therefore that I may be so happy as to discharge part of the obligation, think if there be ever a proud mortal breathing on whom you desire to be revenged for some affront or other injury, and acquaint me with it now, and by my order of knighthood which binds me to protect the weak, relieve the oppressed, and punish the bad, I promise you I will take effectual care, that you shall have ample satisfaction to the utmost of your wishes." "Sir Knight," answered the innkeeper, with an austere gravity, "I shall not need your assistance to revenge any wrong that may have been offered to

my person; for I would have you to understand, that I am able to do myself justice, whenever any man presumes to do me wrong: therefore all the satisfaction I desire is, that you will pay your reckoning for horse meat and man's meat, and all your expenses in my inn." "How!" cried Don Quixote, "is this an inn?" "Yes," answered the host, "and one of the most noted, and of the best repute upon the road." "How strangely have I been mistaken then!" cried Don Quixote; "upon my honour I took it for a castle, and a considerable one too: but, if it be an inn, and not a castle, all I have to say is, that you must excuse me from paying anything; for I would by no means break the laws which we knights-errant are bound to observe: nor was it ever known, that they ever paid in any inn whatsoever; for this is the least recompense that can be allowed them for the intolerable labours they endure day and night, winter and summer, on foot and on horseback, pinched with hunger, choked with thirst, and exposed to all the injuries of the air, and all the inconveniences in the world." "I have nothing to do with all this," cried the innkeeper: "pay your reckoning, and do not trouble me with your foolish stories of a cock and a bull: I cannot afford to keep house at that rate." "Thou art both a fool and a knave of an innkeeper," replied Don Quixote: and with that, clapping spurs to Rozinante, and brandishing his javelin at his host, he rode out of the inn without any opposition, and got a good way from it, without so much as once looking behind him to see whether his squire came after him.

The Knight being marched off, there remained only the squire, who was stopped for the reckoning. However, he swore bloodily he would not pay a cross; for the self-same law that acquitted the Knight acquitted the squire. This put the innkeeper into a great passion, and made him threaten Sancho very hard, telling him, if he would not pay him by fair means, he would have him laid by the heels that moment. . . . The innkeeper kept his wallet for the reckoning; but the poor squire was so dismayed, and in such haste to be gone, that he never missed it. . . .

Of the discourse between the knight and the squire, with other matters worth relating.

Sancho overtook his master, but so pale, so dead-hearted, and so mortified, that he was hardly able to sit on his ass. "My dear Sancho," said Don Quixote, seeing him in that condition, "I am now fully convinced that this castle, or inn, is enchanted; for what could they be that made themselves such barbarous sport with thee, but spirits and people of the other world? And I the rather believe this, seeing, that when I looked over the wall, I saw thee thus abused, I strove to get over it, but could not stir, nor by any means alight from Rozinante. For, by my honour, could I either have got over the wall or dismounted, I would have revenged thee so effectually on those discourteous wretches, that they should never have forgot the severity of their punishment, though for once I had infringed the laws of chivalry; which, as I have often informed thee, do not permit any knight to lay hands on one that is not knighted, unless it be in his own defence, and in case of great necessity." "Nay," quoth Sancho, "I would have paid them home myself, whether knight or no knight, but it was not in my power; and yet I dare say, those that made themselves so merry with my carcase were neither spirits nor enchanted folks, as you will have it, but mere flesh and blood as we be." . . .

Thus they went on discoursing, when Don Quixote, perceiving a thick cloud of dust arise right before them in the road: "The day is come," said he, turning to his squire, "the day is come, Sancho, that shall usher in the happiness which fortune has reserved for me: this day shall the strength of my arm be signalized by such exploits as shall be transmitted even to the latest posterity. Seest thou that cloud of dust, Sancho? It is raised by a prodigious army marching this way, and composed of an infinite number of nations." "Why then, at this rate," quoth Sancho, "there should be two armies; for yonder is as great a dust on the other side." With that Don Quixote looked, and was transported with joy at the sight, firmly believing that two vast armies were ready to engage each other in that plain. For his imagination was so crowded with those battles, enchantments, surprising adventures, amorous thoughts, and other whimsies which he had read of in romances, that his strong fancy changed everything he saw into what he desired to see; and thus he could not conceive that the dust was only raised by two large flocks of sheep that were going the same road from different parts, and could not be discerned till they were very near. He was so positive that they were two armies that Sancho firmly believed him at last. "Well, sir," quoth the squire, "what are we to do, I beseech you?" "What shall we do," replied Don Quixote, "but assist the weaker and the injured side? For know, Sancho, that the army which now moves toward us is commanded by the great Alifanfaron, emperor of the vast island of Taprobana: the other that advances behind us is his enemy, the king of the Garamantians, Pentapolin with the naked arm; so called, because he always enters into battle with his right arm bare." . . .

Sancho listened to this romantic muster-roll as mute as a fish, with amazement; all that he could do was to turn his head on this side and the other side, to see if he could discern the knights whom his master named. But at length, not being able to discover any: "Why," cried he, "you had as good tell me it snows; the devil of any knight, giant, or man can I see, of all those you talk of now; who knows but all this may be witchcraft and spirits, like yesternight?" "How," replied Don Quixote, "dost thou not hear their horses neigh, their trumpets sound, and their drums beat?" "Not I," quoth Sancho, "I prick up my ears like a sow in the beans, and yet I can hear nothing but the bleating of sheep." Sancho might justly say so indeed, for by this time the two flocks were got very near them. "Thy fear disturbs thy senses," said Don Quixote, "and hinders thee from hearing and seeing right: but it is no matter; withdraw to some place of safety, since thou art so terrified; for I alone am sufficient to give the victory to that side which I shall favour with my assistance." With that he couched his lance, clapped spurs on Rozinante, and rushed like a thunder-bolt from the hillock into the plain. Sancho bawled after him as loud as he could: "Hold, sir," cried Sancho, "for Heaven's sake come back. What do you mean? As sure as I am a sinner, those you are going to maul are nothing but poor harmless sheep. Come back, I say. Woe be to him that begot me! Are you mad, sir? There are no giants, no knights, no cats, no asparagus gardens, no golden quarters, nor what-do-you-call-thems. Does the Devil possess you? You are leaping over the hedge before you come at the stile. You are taking the wrong sow by the ear. Oh, that I was ever born to see this day!"

But Don Quixote, still riding on, deaf and lost to good advice, outroared his expostulating squire. "Courage, brave knights," cried he: "march up, fall on all you who fight under the standard of the valiant Pentapolin with the naked arm: follow me, and you shall see how easily I will revenge him on that infidel Alifanfaron of Taprobana;" and, so saying, he charged the squadron of sheep with that gallantry and resolution, that he pierced, broke, and put it to flight in an instant, charging through and through, not without a great slaughter of his mortal enemies, whom he laid at his feet, biting the ground and wallowing in their blood. The shepherds seeing their sheep go to rack, called out to him; till, finding fair means ineffectual, they unloosed their slings, and began to ply him with stones as big as their fists. But the champion, disdaining such a distant war, spite of their showers of stones, rushed among the routed sheep, trampling both the living and the slain in a most terrible manner, impatient to meet the general of the enemy, and end the war at once. "Where, where art thou," cried he, "proud Alifanfaron? Appear! see here a single knight who seeks thee everywhere, to try now, hand to hand, the boasted force of thy strenuous arm, and deprive thee of life, as a due punishment for the unjust war which thou hast audaciously waged with the valiant Penta-polin." Just as he had said this, while the stones flew about his ears, one unluckily fell upon his small ribs, and had like to have buried two of the shortest deep in the middle of his body. The Knight thought himself slain, or at least desperately wounded; and, therefore, calling to mind his precious balsam, and pulling out his earthen jug, he clapped it to his mouth: but, before he had swallowed a sufficient dose, souse comes another of those bitter almonds that spoiled his draught, and hit him so pat upon the jug, hand and teeth, that it broke the first, maimed the second, and struck out three or four of the last. These two blows were so violent, that the boisterous Knight falling from his horse, lay upon the ground as quiet as the slain; so that the shepherds fearing he was killed, got their flock together with all speed, and carrying away their dead, which were no less than seven sheep, they made what haste they could out of harm's way, without looking any further into the matter.

All this while Sancho stood upon the hill, mortified upon the sight of his mad adventure. There he stamped, swore, and banned his master to the bottomless pit; he tore his beard for madness, and cursed the moment he first knew him: but seeing him at last knocked down, and settled, the shepherds being scampered, he thought he might venture to come down; and found him in a very ill plight, though not altogether senseless. "Ah! master," quoth he, "this comes of not taking my counsel. Did I not tell you it was a flock of sheep, and no army?" "Friend Sancho," replied Don Quixote, "know it is an easy matter for necromancers to change the shapes of things as they please: thus that malicious enchanter, who is my inveterate enemy, to deprive me of the glory which he saw me ready to acquire, while I was reaping a full harvest of laurels, transformed in a moment the routed squadrons into sheep. If thou wilt not believe me, Sancho, yet do one thing for my sake: do but take thy ass, and follow those supposed sheep at a distance, and I dare engage thou shalt soon see them resume their former shapes, and appear such as I described them. But stay, do not go yet, for I want thy assistance: draw near, and see how many cheek-teeth and others I want; for, by the dreadful pain in my jaws and gums, I fear there is a total dilapidation in my mouth."

With that the Knight opened his mouth as wide as he could, while the squire gaped to tell his grinders, with his snout almost in his chops; but just in that fatal moment the balsam that lay wambling and fretting in Don Quixote's stomach, came up with an unlucky hickup; and, with the same violence that the powder flies out of a gun, all that he had in his stomach discharged itself upon the beard, face, eyes, and mouth of the officious squire. "Santa Maria," cried poor Sancho, "what will become of me! my master is a dead man! he is vomiting his very heart's blood!" but he had hardly said this, when the colour, smell, and taste soon undeceived him; and finding it to be his master's loathsome drench, it caused such a sudden rumbling in his maw, that before he could turn his head he unladed the whole cargo of his stomach full in his master's face, and put him in as delicate a pickle as he was himself. Sancho having thus paid him in his own coin, half-blinded as he was, ran to his ass, to take out something to clean himself and his master: but when he came to look for his wallet, and found it missing, not remembering till then that he had unhappily left it in the inn, he was ready to run quite out of his wits. He stormed and stamped, and cursed him worse than before, and resolved with himself to let his master go to the Devil, and even trudge home by himself, though he was sure to lose his wages, and his hopes of being governor of the promised island.

Thereupon Don Quixote got up with much ado, and clapping his left hand before mouth, that the rest of his loose teeth might not drop out, he laid his right hand on Rozinante's bridle; (for such was the good nature of the creature, that he had not budged a foot from his master) then it crept along to squire Sancho, that stood lolling on his ass's pannel, with his face in the hollow of both his hands, in a doleful, moody, melancholy fit. "Friend Sancho," said he, seeing him thus abandoned to sorrow, "learn of me, that one man is no more than another, if he do no more than what another does. All these storms and hurricanes are but arguments of the approaching calm: better success will soon follow our past calamities; good and bad fortune have their vicissitudes; and it is a maxim, that nothing violent can last long; and therefore we may well promise ourselves a speedy change in our fortune, since our afflictions have extended their reign beyond the usual stint; besides, thou oughtest not to afflict thyself so much for misfortunes, of which thou hast no share, but what friendship and humanity bid thee take." "How," quoth Sancho, "have I no other share in them? Did not the wallet, and all that was in it, which I have lost, belong to the son of my mother?" "How," asked Don Quixote, "hast thou lost thy wallet?" "I do not know," said Sancho, "whether it is lost or no, but I am sure I cannot tell what is become of it." "Nay, then," replied Don Quixote, "I find we must fast today." "Ay, marry must we," quoth Sancho, "unless you take care to gather in these fields some of those roots and herbs which I have heard you say you know, and which use to help such unlucky knights-errant as yourself at a dead lift."

"For all that," cried Don Quixote, "I would rather have at this time a good luncheon of bread, or a cake and two pilchards heads, than all the roots and simples in Dioscorides's herbal, and Doctor Laguna's supplement and commentary: I pray thee, therefore, get upon thy ass, good Sancho, and follow me once more; for God's providence, that relieves every creature, will not fail us, especially since we are about a work so much to His service; thou seest He even provides for the little flying insects in the air, the wormlings in the earth, and the spawnlings in the water; and, in His infinite mercy, He makes His sun shine on the righteous and on the unjust, and rains upon the good and the bad." "Many words will not fill a bushel," quoth Sancho, interrupting him; "you would make a better preacher than a knight-errant, or I am plaguedly out." "Knights-errant," replied Don Quixote, "ought to know all things; there have been such in former ages, that have delivered as ingenious and learned a sermon or oration at the head of an army, as if they had taken their degrees at the University of Paris: from which we may infer, that the lance never dulled the pen, nor the pen the lance." "Well then," quoth Sancho, "for once let it be as you would have it; let us even leave this unlucky place, and seek out a lodging; where, I pray God, there may be neither blankets, nor blanket-heavers, nor hobgoblins, nor enchanted Moors; for, before I will be hampered as I have been, may I be cursed with bell, book and candle, if I do not give the trade to the Devil." . . .

How Don Quixote set free many miserable creatures, who were carrying, much against their wills, to a place they did not like.

Cid Hamet Benengeli, an Arabian and Manchegan author, relates in this most grave, high-sounding, minute, soft, and humorous history, that after this discourse between the renowned Don Quixote and his squire, Sancho Pança, the Knight lifting up his eyes, saw about twelve men a-foot, trudging in the road, all in a row, one behind another, like beads upon a string, being linked together by the neck to a huge iron chain, and manacled besides. They were guarded by two horsemen, armed with carabines, and two men a-foot, with swords and javelins. As soon as Sancho spied them, "Look ye, sir," cried he, "here is a gang of wretches hurried away by main force to serve the king in the galleys." "How!" replied Don Quixote, "is it possible the king will force anybody?" "I do not say so," answered Sancho; "I mean these are rogues whom the law has sentenced for their misdeeds, to row in the king's galleys." "However," replied Don Quixote, "they are forced, because they do not go of their own free will." "Sure enough," quoth Sancho. "If it be so," said Don Quixote, "they come within the verge of my office, which is to hinder violence and oppression, and succour all people in misery." "Ay, sir," quoth Sancho, "but neither the king nor law offer any violence to such wicked wretches, they have but their deserts." By this the chain of slaves came up, when Don Quixote, in very civil terms, desired the guards to inform him why these poor people were led along in that manner? "Sir," answered one of the horsemen, "they are criminals condemned to serve the king in his galleys. That is all that I have to say to you, and you need inquire no further." "Nevertheless, sir," replied Don Quixote, "I have a great desire to know in few words the cause of their misfortune, and I will esteem it an extraordinary favour, if you will let me have that satisfaction." "We have here the copies and certificates of their several sentences," said the other horseman, "but we cannot stand to pull them out and read them now; you may draw near and examine the men yourself: I suppose they themselves will tell you why they are condemned; for they are such honest people, they are not ashamed to boast of their rogueries."

With this permission, which Don Quixote would have taken of himself had they denied it him, he rode up to the chain, and asked the first, for what crimes he was in these miserable circumstances? The galley-slave answered him, that it was for being in love. "What, only for being in love!" cried Don Quixote; "were all those that are in love to be thus used, I myself might have been long since in the galleys." "Ay, but," replied the slave, "my love was not of that sort which you conjecture: I was so desperately in love with a basket of linen, and embraced it so close, that had not the judge taken it from me by force, I would not have parted with it willingly. In short, I was taken in the fact, and so there was no need to put me to the rack, it was proved so plain upon me. So I was committed, tried, condemned, had the gentle lash; and besides that, was sent, for three years, to be an element-dasher, and there is an end of the business." "An element-dasher!" cried Don Quixote, "what do you mean by that?" "A galley-slave," answered the criminal, who was a young fellow, about four-and-twenty years old, and said he was born at Piedra-Hita.

Then Don Quixote examined the second, but he was so sad and desponding, that he would make no answer; however, the first rogue informed the Knight of his affairs. "Sir," said he, "this canary-bird keeps us company for having sung too much." "Is it possible!" cried Don Quixote; "are men sent to the galleys for singing?" "Ay, Mary are they," quoth the arch rogue; "for there is nothing worse than to sing in anguish." "How!" cried Don Quixote, "that contradicts the saying, 'Sing away sorrow, cast away care.'" "Ay, but with us the case is different," replied the slave, "he that sings in disaster, weeps all his

Sancho sits patiently on his mule while Don Quixote harangues the prisoners. A Gustave Doré illustration.

life after.'" "This is a riddle which I cannot un-fold," cried Don Quixote. "Sir," said one of the guards, "singing in anguish, among these jail-birds, means to confess upon the rack: this fellow was put to the torture, and confessed his crime, which was stealing of cattle; and because he squeaked, or sung, as they call it, he was condemned to the galleys for six years, besides an hundred jerks with a cat-o'-nine-tails that have whisked and powdered his shoul-10 ders already. Now the reason why he goes thus mopish and out of sorts, is only because his com-rogues jeer and laugh at him continually for not having had the courage to deny: as if it had not been as easy for him to say No as Yes; or, as if a fellow, taken up on suspicion, were not a lucky rogue, when there is no positive evidence can come in against him but his own tongue; and in my opinion they are somewhat in the right." "I think so too," said Don Quixote.

20 Thence addressing himself to the third, "And you," said he, "what have you done?" "Sir," answered the fellow, readily and pleasantly enough, "I must mow the great meadow for five years together, for want of twice five ducats." "I will give twenty with all my heart," said Don Quixote, "to deliver thee from that misery." "Thank you for nothing," quoth

the slave; "it is just like the proverb, 'After meat comes mustard'; or, like money to a starving man at sea, when there are no victuals to be bought with it. Had I had the twenty ducats you offer me before I 30 was tried, to have greased the clerk's [or recorder's] fist, and have whetted my lawyer's wit, I might have been now at Toledo in the market-place of Zocodover, and not have been thus led along like a dog in a string." . . .

With that the officer held up his staff to strike him; but Don Quixote stepped between them, and desired him not to do it, and to consider, that the slave was the more to be excused for being too free of his tongue, since he had never another member 40 at liberty. Then addressing himself to all the slaves, "My dearest brethren," cried he, "I find, by what I gather from your own words, that though you de-serve punishment for the several crimes of which you stand convicted, yet you suffer execution of the sentence by constraint, and merely because you cannot help it. Now, as Heaven has sent me into the world to relieve the distressed, and free suffering weakness from the tyranny of oppression, according to the duty of my profession of knight-errantry, these 50 considerations induce me to take you under my pro-tection—but, because it is the part of a prudent man not to use violence where fair means may be effectual, I desire you, gentlemen of the guard, to release these poor men, there being people enough to serve his majesty in their places; for it is a hard case to make slaves of men whom God and nature made free; and you have the less reason to use these wretches with severity, seeing they never did you any wrong. Let them answer for their sins in the other world: Heaven is just, you know, and will be sure to punish the wicked, as it will certainly reward the good. Consider besides, gentlemen, that it is neither a Christian-like, nor an honourable action, for men to be the butchers and tormentors of one another; particularly, when no advantage can arise from it. I choose to desire this of you, with so much mildness, and in so peaceable a manner, gentlemen, that I may have occasion to pay you a thankful acknowledgment, if you will be pleased to grant so reasonable a request: but, if you provoke me by refusal, I must be obliged to tell ye, that this lance, and this sword, guided by this invincible arm, shall force you to yield that to my valour which you deny to my civil entreaties."

"A very good jest indeed," cried the officer, "what a devil makes you dote at such a rate? Would you have us set at liberty the king's prisoners, as if we had authority to do it, or you to command it? Go, go about your business, good Sir Errant, and set your basin right upon your empty pate; and pray do not meddle any further in what does not concern you, for those who will play with cats must expect to be scratched."

"Thou art a cat, and rat, and a coward also," cried Don Quixote; and with that he attacked the officer with such a sudden and surprising fury, that before he had any time to put himself into a posture of defence, he struck him down dangerously wounded with his lance, and as fortune had ordered it, this happened to be the horseman who was armed with a carbine. His companions stood astonished at such a bold action, but at last fell upon the champion with their swords and darts, which might have proved fatal to him, had not the slaves laid hold of this opportunity to break the chain, in order to regain their liberty: for, the guards perceiving their endeavours to get loose, thought it more material to prevent them, than to be fighting a madman. But as he pressed them vigorously on one side, and the slaves were opposing them and freeing themselves on the other, the hurly-burly was so great, and the guards so perplexed, that they did nothing to the purpose. . . .

They betook themselves to their heels, leaving Don Quixote and the criminals masters of the field. Sancho, who was always for taking care of the main chance, was not at all pleased with this victory; for he guessed that the guards who were fled would raise a hue and cry, and soon be at their heels with the whole posse of the holy brotherhood, and lay them up for a rescue and rebellion. This made him advise his master to get out of the way as fast as he could, and hide himself in the neighbouring mountains. "I hear you," answered Don Quixote to this motion of his squire, "and I know what I have to do." Then calling to him all the slaves, who by this time had uncased the keeper to his skin, they gathered about him to know his pleasure, and he spoke to them in this manner. "It is the part of generous spirits to have a grateful sense of the benefits they receive, no crime being more odious than ingratitude. You see, gentlemen, what I have done for your sakes, and you cannot but be sensible how highly you are obliged to me. Now all the recompense I require is only, that every one of you, loaded with that chain from which I have freed your necks, do instantly repair to the city of Toboso; and there, presenting yourselves before the Lady Dulcinea del Toboso, tell her, that her faithful votary, the Knight of the Woeful Countenance, commanded you to wait on her, and assure her of his profound veneration. Then you shall give her an exact account of every particular relating to this famous achievement, by which you once more taste the sweets of liberty; which done, I give you leave to seek your fortunes where you please."

To this the ringleader and master-thief, Gines de Passamonte, made answer for all the rest. "What you would have us do," said he, "our noble deliverer, is absolutely impracticable and impossible; for we dare not be seen all together for the world. We must rather part, and skulk some one way, some another, and lie snug in creeks and corners underground, for fear of those damned manhounds that will be after us with a hue and cry; therefore all we can, and ought to do in this case, is to change this compliment and homage which you would have us pay to the Lady Dulcinea del Toboso, into a certain number of Ave Marias and Creeds, which we will say for your worship's benefit; and this may be done by night or by day, walking or standing, and in war as well as in peace: but to imagine we will return to our flesh-pots of Egypt; that is to say, take up our chains again, and lug them the Devil knows where, is as unreasonable as to think it is night now at ten o'clock in the morning. 'Sdeath, to expect this from us, is to expect pears from an elm-tree." "Now, by my sword," replied Don Quixote, "Sir Ginesello de Parapilla, or whatever be your name, you yourself, alone, shall go to Toboso, like a dog that has scalded his tail, with the whole chain about your shoulders." Gines, who was naturally very choleric, judging, by Don Quixote's extravagance in freeing them, that he was not very wise, winked on his companions, who, like men that understood signs, presently fell back to the right and left, and pelted Don Quixote with such a shower of stones, that all his dexterity to cover himself with his shield was now ineffectual, and poor Rozinante no more obeyed the spur, than if he had been only the statue of a horse. As for Sancho, he got behind his ass, and there sheltered himself from the volleys of flints that threatened his bones, while his master was so battered, that in a little time he was thrown out of his saddle to the ground. He was 10 no sooner down, but the student leaped on him, took off his basin from his head, gave him three or four thumps on the shoulders with it, and then gave it so many knocks against the stones, that he almost broke it to pieces. After this, they stripped him of his upper coat, and had robbed him of his hose too, but that his greaves hindered them. They also eased Sancho of his upper coat, and left him in his doublet: then, having divided the spoils, they shifted every one for himself, thinking more how to avoid being taken up, 20 and linked again in the chain, than of trudging with it to my Lady Dulcinea del Toboso. . . . The Knight and the squire continued their journey for the city of Toboso.

PART II

Don Quixote's success in his journey to visit the Lady Dulcinea del Toboso

"Friend Sancho," said Don Quixote, "I find the approaching night will overtake us ere we can reach Toboso, where, before I enter upon any expedition, I am resolved to pay my vows, receive my benediction, and take my leave of the peerless Dulcinea; being assured after that of happy events, in the most 30 dangerous adventures; for nothing in this world inspires a knight-errant with so much valour as the smiles and favourable aspects of his mistress." "I am of your mind," quoth Sancho; "but I am afraid, sir, you will hardly come at her, to speak with her, at least not meet her in a place where she may give you her blessing, unless she throw it you over the mud-wall of the yard, where I first saw her." "Mudwall, dost thou say!" cried Don Quixote. "Mistaken fool, that wall could have no existence but in thy 40 muddy understanding: it is a mere creature of thy dirty fancy; for that never-duly-celebrated paragon of beauty and gentility was then undoubtedly in some court, in some stately gallery, or walk, or as it is properly called, in a sumptuous and royal palace." "It may be so," said Sancho, "though, so far as I can remember, it seemed to me neither better nor worse than a mud-wall." "It is no matter," replied the Knight, "let us go thither; I will visit my dear Dulcinea; let me but see her, though it be over a mud- 50 wall, through a chink of a cottage, or the pales of a garden, at a lattice, or anywhere; which way soever

the least beam from her bright eyes reaches mine, it will so enlighten my mind, so fortify my heart, and invigorate every faculty of my being, that no mortal will be able to rival me in prudence and valour.". . .

At last, towards evening the next day, they discovered the goodly city of Toboso, which revived the Knight's spirits wonderfully, but had a quite contrary effect on his squire, because he did not know the house where Dulcinea lived, no more than his mas- 60 ter. So that the one was mad till he saw her, and the other very melancholic and disturbed in mind, because he had never seen her; nor did he know what to do, should his master send him to Toboso. . . . When Don Quixote was retired into the wood or forest, or rather into the grove of oaks near the grand Toboso, he ordered Sancho to go to the city, and not to return to his presence till he had had audience of his lady; beseeching her that it might please her to be seen by her captive knight, and vouchsafe to be- 70 stow her benediction on him, that by the virtue of that blessing he might hope for a prosperous event in all his onsets and perilous attempts and adventures. Sancho undertook the charge, engaging him as successful a return of this as of his former message.

"Go then, child," said the Knight, ". . . thy own better stars, not mine, attend thee; and meet with a more prosperous event, than that which in this doleful desert, tossed between hopes and fears, I dare 80 expect." "I will go, sir," quoth Sancho, "and I will be back in a trice: meanwhile cheer up, I beseech you; come, sir, comfort that little heart of yours, no bigger than a hazelnut! Do not be cast down, I say; remember the old saying, 'Faint heart never won fair lady': where there is no hook, to be sure there will hang no bacon: the hare leaps out of the bush where we least look for her." "Well, Sancho," said the Knight, "thou hast a rare talent in applying thy proverbs; Heaven give thee better success in thy designs!" This 90 said, Sancho turned his back, and switching his Dapple, left the Don on horseback, leaning on his lance, and resting on his stirrups, full of melancholy and confused imaginations. Let us leave him too, to go along with Sancho, who was no less uneasy in his mind.

No sooner was he got out of the grove, but turning about, and perceiving his master quite out of sight, he dismounted, and laying himself down at the foot of a tree, thus began to hold a parley with himself. 100 "Well, there is a remedy for all things but death, which will be sure to lay us flat one time or other. This master of mine, by a thousand tokens I have seen, is a downright madman, and I think I come within an inch of him; nay, I am the greatest cod's-head of the two, to serve and follow him as I do, if the proverb be not a liar, 'Show me thy company, I will tell thee what thou art'; and the other old saw,

'Birds of a feather flock together.' Now then my master being mad, and so very mad as to mistake sometimes one thing for another, black for white, and white for black; as when he took the windmills for giants and the flocks of sheep for armies, and much more to the same tune; I guess it will be no hard matter to pass upon him the first country wench I shall meet with, for the Lady Dulcinea. If he will not believe it, I will swear it; if he swear again, I will outswear him; if he be positive, I will be more positive than he; and stand to it, and out-face him in it, come what will of it: so that when he finds I will not flinch, he will either resolve never to send me more of his sleeveless errands, seeing what a lame account I bring him, or he will think some one of those wicked wizards, who, he says, owes him a grudge, has transmogrified her into some other shape out of spite." This happy contrivance helped to compose Sancho's mind, and now he looked on his grand affair to be as good as done. Having therefore stayed till the evening, that his master might think he had employed so much time in going and coming, things fell out very luckily for him; for as he arose to mount his Dapple, he spied three country wenches coming towards him from Toboso, upon three young asses. . . .

Sancho thereupon made all the haste he could to get to his master, and found him breathing out a thousand sighs and amorous lamentations. "Well, my Sancho," said the Knight, immediately upon his approach, "what news? Are we to mark this day with a white or a black stone?" "Even mark it rather with red oker," answered Sancho, "as they do church chairs, that everybody may know who they belong to." "Why then," said Don Quixote, "I suppose thou bringest good news?" "Ay, marry do I," quoth Sancho, "you have no more to do but to clap spurs to Rozinante, and get into the open fields, and you will see my Lady Dulcinea del Toboso, with a brace of her damsels, coming to see your worship." "Blessed heavens!" cried Don Quixote, "what art thou saying, my dear Sancho? Take heed, and do not presume to beguile my real grief with a delusive joy." "Adsookers! sir," said Sancho, "what should I get by putting a trick upon you, and being found out the next moment? Seeing is believing all the world over. Come, sir, put on, put on, and you will see our Lady Princess coming, dressed up and bedecked like her own sweet self indeed. Her damsels and she are all one spark of gold; all pearls, all diamonds, all rubies, all cloth of gold above ten inches high. Their hair spread over their shoulders like so many sunbeams, and dangling and dancing in the wind; and what is more, they ride upon three flea-bitten gambling hags; there is not a piece of horse-flesh can match them in three kingdoms." " 'Ambling nags' thou meanest, Sancho," said Don Quixote. " 'Ambling

hags' or 'ambling nags,' " quoth Sancho, "there is no such difference methinks; but be they what they will, I am sure, I never set eyes on finer creatures than those that ride upon their backs, especially my Lady Dulcinea; it would make one swoon away but to look upon her." "Let us move, then, my Sancho," said Don Quixote: "and as a gratification for these unexpected happy tidings, I freely bestow on thee the best spoils the next adventure we meet with shall afford; and if that content thee not, take the colts which my three mares thou knowest of, are now ready to foal on our town common." "Thank you for the colts," said Sancho; "but as for the spoils, I am not sure they will be worth anything."

They were now got out of the wood, and discovered the three country lasses at a small distance. Don Quixote casting his eyes towards Toboso, and seeing nobody on the road but the three wenches, was strangely troubled in mind, and turning to Sancho, asked him, whether the princess and her damsels were come out of the city when he left them. "Out of the city," cried Sancho, "why, where are your eyes? are they in your heels, in the name of wonder, that you cannot see them coming towards us, shining as bright as the sun at noon-day?" "I see nothing," returned Don Quixote, "but three wenches upon as many asses." "Now Heaven deliver me from the Devil," quoth Sancho. "Is it possible your worship should mistake three what-d'ye-call-ems, three ambling nags I mean, as white as driven snow, for three ragged ass colts? Body of me! I will even pull off my beard by the roots, if it be so." "Take it from me, friend Sancho," said the Knight, "they are either he or she asses, as sure as I am Don Quixote, and thou Sancho Pança; at least, they appear to be such." "Come, sir," quoth the squire, "do not talk at that rate, but snuff your eyes, and go pay your homage to the mistress of your soul; for she is near at hand"; and so saying, Sancho hastens up to the three country wenches, and alighting from Dapple, took hold of one of the asses by the halter, and falling on his knees, "Queen, and princess, and duchess of beauty," quoth he, "if it please your Haughtiness, and Greatness, vouchsafe to take into your good grace and liking, yonder Knight, your prisoner and captive, who is turned of a sudden into cold marble stone, and struck all of a heap, to see himself before your High and Mightiness. I am Sancho Pança, his squire, and he himself the wandering weather-beaten knight, Don Quixote de la Mancha, otherwise called the Knight of the Woeful Figure." By this time, Don Quixote, having placed himself down on his knees by Sancho, gazed with dubious and disconsolate eyes on the creature, whom Sancho called Queen and Lady; and perceiving her to be no more than a plain country wench, so far from being well-favoured, that she was blubber-cheeked, and flat-nosed, he was lost in astonishment, and could not utter one word. On the other side, the wenches were no less surprised, to see themselves stopped by two men in such different outsides, and on their knees.

But at last she whose ass was held by Sancho took courage, and broke silence in an angry tone. "Come," cried she, "get out of our way with a murrain, and let us go about our business; for we are in haste." "O Princess! and universal Lady of Toboso," answered Sancho, "why does not that great heart of yours melt, to see the post and pillar of knight-errantry fall down before your high and mighty presence?" "Heyday," quoth another of the females, hearing this, "what is here to do? Look how your small gentry come to jeer and flout poor country girls, as if we could not give them as good as they bring. Go, get about your business, and let us go about ours, and speed you well." "Rise, Sancho," said Don Quixote, hearing this, "for I am now convinced, that my malicious stars, not yet satisfied with my past misfortunes, still shed their baleful influence, and have barred all the passages that could convey relief to my miserable soul, in this frail habitation of animated clay. O! thou extremity of all that is valuable, masterpiece of all human perfection, and only comfort of this afflicted heart, thy adorer; though now a spiteful enchanter persecutes me, and fascinates my sight, hiding with mists and cataracts from me, and me alone, those peerless beauties under the foul disguise of rustic deformity, if he has not transformed thy faithful Knight into some ugly shape to make me loathsome to thy sight, look on me with a smiling amorous eye; and in the submission and genuflexion which I pay to thy beauty, even under the fatal cloud that obscures it, read the humility with which my soul adores thee." "Tittle-tattle," quoth the country wench, "spare your breath to cool your porridge, and rid me of your idle gibberish. Get you on, sir, and let us go; and we shall think it a kindness."

This said, Sancho made way for her, and let her pass, overjoyed his plot had succeeded so well. The imaginary Dulcinea was not sooner at liberty, but punching her ass with the end of a staff which she had in her hand, she began to scour along the plain: but the angry beast not being used to such smart instigations, fell a-kicking and wincing at such a rate, that down came my Lady Dulcinea. Presently Don Quixote ran to help her up, and Sancho to re-settle and gird her pack-saddle, that hung under the ass's belly. Which being done, the Knight very courteously was going to take his enchanted mistress in his arms, to set her on her saddle; but she being now got on her legs, took a run, and clapping her hands upon the ass's crupper, at one jump leaped into her pannel, as swift as a hawk, and there she sat with her legs astride like a man. "By the lord Harry!" quoth Sancho, "our lady mistress is as nimble as an eel. Let me be hanged, if I do not think she might teach the best jockey in Cordova or Mexico to mount a horse-back. At one jump she was vaulted into the saddle, and, without spurs, makes her nag smoke it away like a greyhound; her damsels are notable whipsters too; adad! they do not come much short of her, for they fly like the wind." Indeed, he said true, for when Dulcinea was once mounted, they both made after her full speed, without so much as looking behind them for above half a league. Don Quixote followed them as far as he could with his eyes; and when they were quite out of sight, turning to his squire, "Now, Sancho," saith he, "what thinkest thou of this matter? Are not these base enchanters inexorable? How extensive is their spite, thus to deprive me of the happiness of seeing the object of my wishes in her natural shape and glory? Sure I was doomed to be an example of misfortunes, and the mark against which those caitiffs are employed to shoot all the arrows of their hatred. Note, Sancho, that these traitors were not content to turn and transform my Dulcinea, but they must do it into the vile and deformed resemblance of that country wench; nay, they even took from her that sweet scent of flagrant flowers and amber, those grateful odours, so essential to ladies of her rank; for, to tell the truth, when I went to help her upon her nag, as thou callest it (for to me it seemed nothing but an ass), such a whiff, such a rank hogo of raw garlic invaded my nostrils, as had like to have overcome me, and put me into a convulsion." "O ye vile wretches!" cried Sancho. "O ye wicked and ill-minded enchanters! O that I might but once see the whole nest of ye threaded together on one string, and hung up a-smoking by the gills like so many pilchards!" . . .

Where you will find set forth the highest and utmost proof that the great Don Quixote ever gave, or could give of his incredible courage, with the successful issue of the adventure of the lions.

While they were in this conversation, they were overtaken by a gentleman, mounted on a very fine flea-bitten mare. He had on a riding-coat of fine green cloth, faced with murry-coloured velvet, and a hunter's cap of the same. The furniture of his mare was country-like, and after the jennet-fashion, and also murry and green. By his side hung a Moorish scimitar, in a large belt of green and gold. His buskins were of the same work with his belt: his spurs were not gilt, but burnished so well with a certain green varnish, that they looked better to suit with the rest of his equipage, than if they had been of pure gold. As he came up with them, he very civilly saluted them, and clapping spurs to his mare, began to leave them behind. Thereupon Don Quixote called to him: "Sir," cried he, "if you are not in too much haste, we should be glad of the favour of your company, so far as you travel this road." "Indeed," answered the gentleman, "I had not thus rid by you, but that I am afraid your horse may prove unruly with my mare." "If that be all," quoth Sancho, "you may hold in your mare; for our horse here is the honestest and soberest horse in the world; he is not in the least given to do any naughty thing on such occasions. Once upon a time indeed he happened to forget himself, and go astray; but then he, and I, and my master rued for it, with a vengeance. I tell you again, sir, you may safely stay if you please, for if your mare were to be served up to him in a dish, I will lay my life he would not so much as touch her." Upon this the traveller stopped his mare, and did not a little gaze at the figure and countenance of our Knight, who rode without his helmet, which, like a wallet, hung at the saddle-bow of Sancho's ass. If the gentleman in green gazed on Don Quixote, Don Quixote looked no less upon him, judging him to be some man of consequence. His age seemed about fifty; he had some grey hairs, a sharp look, and a grave, yet pleasing aspect. In short, his mien and appearance spoke him a man of quality. When he looked on Don Quixote, he thought he had never beheld before such a strange appearance of a man. He could not but admire at the lankness of his horse; he considered then the long-backed, raw-boned thing that bestrid him; his wan, meagre face, his air, his gravity, his arms, and equipage; such a figure as, perhaps, had not been seen in that country time out of mind. . . .

Don Quixote lifting up his eyes, perceived a wagon on the road, set round with little flags, that appeared to be the king's colours; and believing it to be some new adventure, he called out to Sancho to bring him his helmet. "Give me that helmet, friend," said the Knight, "for if I understand anything of adventures I descry one yonder that obliges me to arm." The gentleman in green hearing this, looked about to see what was the matter, but could perceive nothing but a wagon, which made towards them, and by the little flags about it, he judged it to be one of the King's carriages, and so he told Don Quixote. But his head was too much possessed with notions of adventures to give any credit to what the gentleman said.

The knight-errant having put on the helmet, fixed himself well in the stirrups, tried whether his sword were loose enough in his scabbard, and rested his lance. "Now," cried he, "come what will come; here am I, who dare encounter the Devil himself in *propria persona!*" By this time the wagon was come up with them, attended only by the carter, mounted on

54. *propria persona!* in his own person.

one of the mules, and another man that sat on the fore part of the wagon. Don Quixote making up to them, "Whither go ye, friends?" said he. "What wagon is this? What do you convey in it? And what is the meaning of these colours?" "The wagon is mine," answered the wagoner; "I have there two brave lions, which the General of Oran is sending to the King our master, and these colours are to let people understand that what goes here belongs to him." "And are the lions large?" inquired Don Quixote. "Very large," answered the man in the fore part of the wagon; "there never came bigger from Africa into Spain. I am their keeper," added he, "and have had charge of several others, but I never saw the like of these before. In the foremost cage is a he-lion, and in the other behind, a lioness. By this time they are cruel hungry, for they have not eaten to-day; therefore pray, good sir, ride out of the way, for we must make haste to get to the place where we intend to feed them." "What!" said Don Quixote, with a scornful smile, "lion-whelps against me! Against me those puny beasts! And at this time of day? Well, I will make those gentlemen, that sent their lions this way, know whether I am a man to be scared with lions. Get off, honest fellow; and since you are the keeper, open their cages, and let them both out; for maugre and in despite of those enchanters that have sent them to try me, I will make the creatures know, in the midst of this very field. who Don Quixote de la Mancha is." . . .

"Good sir," cried the wagoner, seeing this strange apparition in armour so resolute, "for mercy's sake do but let me take out our mules first, and get out of harm's way with them as fast as I can, before the lions get out; for if they should once set upon the poor beasts, I should be undone for ever; for alas! that cart and they are all I have in the world to get a living with." "Thou man of little faith," said Don Quixote, "take them out quickly then, and go with them where thou wilt; though thou shalt presently see that thy precaution was needless, and thou mightest have spared thy pains." The wagoner upon this made all the haste he could to take out his mules, while the keeper cried out as loud as he was able, "Bear witness all ye that are here present, that it is against my will I am forced to open the cages and let loose the lions; and that I protest to this gentleman here, that he shall be answerable for all the mischief and damage they may do; together with the loss of my salary and fees. And now, sirs, shift for yourselves as fast as you can before I open the cages: for, as for myself, I know the lions will do me no harm." The gentleman tried to dissuade Don Quixote from doing so mad a thing, telling him, that he tempted Heaven, in exposing himself without reason to so great a danger. To this Don Quixote made no other answer, but that he knew what he had to do. "Consider, however, what you do," replied the gentleman, "for it is most certain that you are very much mistaken." "Well, sir," said Don Quixote, "if you care not to be spectator of an action, which you think is like to be tragical, even set spurs to your mare, and provide for your safety."

Sancho came up to his master with tears in his eyes, and begged him not to go about this fearful undertaking, to which the adventure of the wind-mills, and all the brunts he had ever borne in his life, were but children's play. "Good your worship," cried he, "do but mind, here is no enchantment in the case, nor anything like it. Alack-a-day! sir, I peeped even now through the grates of the cage, and I am sure I saw the claw of a true lion, and such a claw as makes me think the lion that owns it must be as big as a mountain." "Alas, poor fellow!" said Don Quix-ote, "thy fear will make him as big as half the world. Retire, Sancho, and leave me, and if I chance to fall here, thou knowest our old agreement; repair to Dulcinea, I say no more." To this he added some ex-pressions, which cut off all hopes of his giving over his mad design. The gentleman in the green would have opposed him, but considering the other was much better armed, and that it was not prudence to encounter a madman, he even took the opportunity while Don Quixote was storming at the keeper, to march off with his mare, as Sancho did with Dapple, and the carter with his mules, every one making the best of their way to get as far as they could from the wagon, before the lions were let loose. Poor Sancho at the same time made sad lamentations for his mas-ter's death; for he gave him up for lost, not question-ing but the lions had already got him into their clutches. He cursed his ill-fortune, and the hour he came again to his service; but for all his wailing and lamenting, he punched on poor Dapple, to get as far as he could from the lions. The keeper, perceiving the persons who fled to be at a good distance, fell to arguing and entreating Don Quixote as he had done before. But the Knight told him again, that all his reasons and entreaties were but in vain, and bid him say no more, but immediately dispatch. Now while the keeper took time to open the foremost cage, Don Quixote stood debating with himself, whether he had best make his attack on foot or on horseback; and upon mature deliberation, he resolved to do it on foot, lest Rozinante, not used to lions, should be put into disorder. Accordingly he quitted his horse, threw aside his lance, grasped his shield, and drew his sword; then advancing with a deliberate motion, and an undaunted heart, he posted himself just be-fore the door of the cage, commending himself to Heaven, and afterwards to his Lady Dulcinea. . . .

The keeper observing the posture Don Quixote had put himself in, and that it was not possible for him to prevent letting out the lions, without incur-ring the resentment of the desperate knight, set the door of the foremost cage quite open; where, as I have said, the male lion lay, who appeared of a mon-strous bigness, and of a hideous frightful aspect. The first thing he did was to roll and turn himself round in his cage; in the next place he stretched out one of his paws, put forth his claws, and roused himself. After that he gaped and yawned for a good while, and showed his dreadful fangs, and then thrust out half a yard of a broad tongue, and with it licked the dust out of his eyes and face. Having done this, he thrust his head out of his cage, and stared about with his eyes that looked like two live coals of fire; a sight and motion enough to have struck terror into temer-ity itself. But Don Quixote only regarded it with at-tention, wishing his grim adversary would leap out of his hold, and come within his reach, that he might exercise his valour, and cut the monster piecemeal. To this height of extravagance had his folly trans-ported him; but the generous lion, more gentle than arrogant, taking no notice of his vapouring and bra-vadoes, after he had looked about him awhile, turned his tail, and showing Don Quixote his posteriors, very contentedly lay down again in his apartment.

Don Quixote seeing this, commanded the keeper to rouse him with his pole, and force him out whether he would or no. "Not I, indeed, sir," an-swered the keeper; "I dare not do it for my life; for, if I provoke him, I am sure to be the first he will tear to pieces. Let me advise you, sir, to be satisfied with your day's work. It is as much as the bravest he that wears a head can pretend to do. Then pray go no further, I beseech you: the door stands open, the lion is at his choice, whether he will come out or no. You have waited for him, you see he does not care to look you in the face, and since he did not come out at the first, I dare engage he will not stir out this day. You have shown enough the greatness of your courage. No man is obliged to do more than chal-lenge his enemy, and wait for him in the field. If he comes not, that is his own fault, and the scandal is his, as the honour is the challenger's." "It is true," replied Don Quixote. "Come, shut the cage door, honest friend, and give me a certificate under thy hand, in the amplest form thou canst devise, of what thou hast seen me perform; how thou didst open the cage for the lion; how I expected his coming, and he did not come out. How, upon his not coming out then, I stayed his own time, and instead of meeting me, he turned tail and lay down. I am obliged to do no more. So, enchantments avaunt! and Heaven pros-per truth, justice, and knight-errantry! Shut the door, as I bid thee, while I make signs to those that ran away from us, and get them to come back, that they may have an account of this exploit from thy own mouth." The keeper obeyed, and Don Quixote clap-ping on the point of his lance the handkerchief, with which he had wiped off the curds from his face, waved it in the air, and called as loud as he was able to the fugitives, who fled nevertheless, looking behind them all the way, and trooped on in a body with the gentleman in green at the head of them.

At last, Sancho observed the signal of the white flag, and calling out to the rest, "Hold," cried he, "my master calls us; I will be hanged if he has not got the better of the lions." At this they all faced about, and perceived Don Quixote flourishing his ensign; whereupon recovering a little from their fright, they leisurely rode back, till they could plainly distinguish Don Quixote's voice; and then they came up to the wagon. As soon as they were come near it, "Come on, friend," said he to the carter; "put thy mules into the wagon again, and pursue thy journey; and Sancho, do thou give him two ducats for the lion-keeper and himself, to make them amends for the time I have detained them." "Ay, that I will with all my heart," quoth Sancho; "but what is become of the lions? Are they dead or alive?" Then the keeper very formally related the whole action, not failing to exaggerate, to the best of his skill, Don Quixote's courage; how at his sight alone the lion was so terrified, that he neither would nor durst quit his stronghold, though for that end his cage door was kept open for a considerable time; and how at length, upon his remonstrating to the knight, who would have had the lion forced out, that it was presuming too much upon Heaven, he had permitted, though with great reluctancy, that the lion should be shut up again. "Well, Sancho," said Don Quixote to his squire, "what dost thou think of this? Can enchantment prevail over true fortitude? No, these magicians may perhaps rob me of success, but never of my invincible greatness of mind." In short, Sancho gave the wagoner and the keeper the two pieces. The first harnessed his mules, and the last thanked Don Quixote for his noble bounty, and promised to acquaint the king himself with his heroic action when he came to court. "Well," said Don Quixote, "if his majesty should chance to inquire who the person was that did this thing, tell him it was the Knight of the Lions; a name I intend henceforth to take up, in lieu of that which I hitherto assumed, of the Knight of the Woeful Figure; in which proceeding I do but conform to the ancient custom of knights-errant, who changed their names as often as they pleased, or as it suited with their advantage."

After this, the wagon made the best of its way, as Don Quixote, Sancho, and the gentleman in green did of theirs. The latter for a great while was so taken up with making his observations on Don Quixote, that he had not time to speak a syllable; not knowing what opinion to have of a person, in whom he discovered such a mixture of good sense and extravagance. He was a stranger to the first part of his history; for had he read it, he could not have wondered either at his words or actions: but not knowing the nature of his madness, he took him to be wise and distracted by fits, since in his discourse he still expressed himself justly and handsomely enough; but in his actions all was wild, extravagant and unaccountable. "For," said the gentleman to himself, "can there be anything more foolish, than for this man to put on his helmet full of curds, and then believe them conveyed there by enchanters; or anything more extravagant than forcibly to endeavour to fight with lions?" In the midst of this soliloquy, Don Quixote interrupted him. "Without doubt, sir," said he, "you take me for a downright madman, and indeed my actions seem to speak me no less. But for all that, give me leave to tell you, I am not so mad, nor is my understanding so defective, as I suppose you may fancy. What a noble figure does the gallant knight make, who in the midst of some spacious place transfixes a furious bull with his lance in the view of his prince! What a noble figure makes the knight, who before the ladies, at a harmless tournament, comes prancing through the lists enclosed in shining steel; or those court champions, who in exercises of martial kind, or that at least are such in appearance, show their activity: and though all they do is nothing but for recreation, are thought the ornament of a prince's court! But a much nobler figure is the knight-errant, who, fired with the thirst of glorious fame, wanders through deserts, through solitary wildernesses, through woods, through crossways, over mountains and valleys, in quest of perilous adventures, resolved to bring them to a happy conclusion. Yes, I say, a nobler figure is a knight-errant, succouring a widow in some depopulate place, than the court knight making his addresses to the city dames. Every knight has his particular employment. Let the courtier wait on the ladies; let him with splendid equipage adorn his prince's court, and with a magnificent table support poor gentlemen. Let him give birth to feasts and tournaments, and show his grandeur, liberality, and munificence, and especially his piety; in all these things he fulfils the duties of his station.

"But as for the knight-errant, let him search into all the corners of the world, enter into the most intricate labyrinths, and every hour be ready to attempt impossibility itself. Let him in desolate wilds baffle the rigour of the weather, the scorching heat of the sun's fiercest beams, and the inclemency of winds and snow: let lions never fright him, dragons daunt him, nor evil spirits deter him. To go in quest of these, to meet, to dare, to conflict, and to overcome them all, is his principal and proper office. Since then my stars have decreed me to be one of these adventurous knights, I think myself obliged to attempt everything that seems to come within the

verge of my profession. This, sir, engaged me to encounter those lions just now, judging it to be my
immediate business, though I was sensible of the extreme rashness of the undertaking. For well I know,
that valour is a virtue situated between the two
vicious extremes of cowardice and temerity. But
certainly it is not so ill for a valiant man to rise to a
degree of rashness, as it is to fall short and border
upon cowardice. For as it is easier for a prodigal to
become liberal, than a miser; so it is easier for the
hardy and rash person to be reduced to true bravery,
than for the coward ever to rise to that virtue: and
therefore in thus attempting adventures, believe me,
it is better to exceed the bounds a little, and overdo,
rather than underdo the thing; because it sounds
better in people's ears to hear it said, how that
such a knight is rash and hardy, than such a knight
is dastardly and timorous." "For my part, sir," answered the gentleman in green, "I think all you have
said and done is agreeable to the exactest rules of
reason; and I believe, if the laws and ordinances of
knight-errantry were lost, they might be all recovered from you, your breast seeming to be the
safe repository and archive where they are lodged.
But it grows late, let us make a little more haste to
get to our village." . . .

Where you find the grounds of the braying adven-
tures, that of the puppet-player, and the memorable
divining of the fortune-telling ape.

By this time, it began to grow dark, and they
arrived at the inn. Sancho was very well pleased to
be at his journey's end, and the more, that his master
took the house for a real inn, and not for a castle, as
he used to do. . . .

Presently enters a fellow dressed in trowsers and
doublet, all of chamois leather, and calling out as
if he were somebody, "Landlord," cried he, "have
you any lodgings? For here comes the fortune-telling
ape, and the puppet-show of 'Melisandra's deliverance.'" "Body of me," cried the innkeeper, "who is
here, Master Peter? We shall have a merry night,
faith! Honest Master Peter, you are welcome with
all my heart. But where is the ape, and the show,
that I cannot see them?" "They will be here presently," said Peter. "I only came before to see if you
had any lodgings." "Lodging, man," said the innkeeper, "zookers! I would turn out the Duke of Alva
himself, rather than Mr. Peter should want room.
Come, come, bring in your things, for here are guests
in the house to-night that will be good customers to
you, I warrant you." "That is a good hearing," said
Peter, "and to encourage them I will lower my
prices; and if I can but get my charges to-night, I
will look for no more; so I will hasten forward the
cart." This said, he ran out of the door again. . . .

Master Peter came back with his puppet-show
and his ape, in a cart. The ape was pretty lusty,
without any tail, and his buttocks bare as a felt. Yet
he was not very ugly neither. Don Quixote no sooner
saw him, but coming up to him, "Mr. Fortune-teller,"
said he, "will you be pleased to tell us what fish we
shall catch, and what will become of us? and here
is your fee." Saying this, he ordered Sancho to
deliver Mr. Peter two reals. "Sir," answered Peter,
"this animal gives no account of things to come, he
knows something indeed of matters past, and a little
of the present." "Odds bobs!" quoth Sancho, "I
would not give a brass jack to know what is past;
for who knows that better than myself; I am not so
foolish as to pay for what I know already: but since
you say he has such a knack at guessing the present,
let goodman ape tell me what my wife Teresa is
doing, and what she is about, and here is my two
reals." "I will have nothing of you beforehand," said
Master Peter; so clapping himself on his left shoulder, up skipped the ape thither, at one frisk, and
laying his mouth to his ear grated his teeth; and
having made apish grimaces and a chattering noise
for a minute or two, with another skip down he
leaped upon the ground. Immediately upon this,
Master Peter ran to Don Quixote, and fell on his
knees, and embracing his legs, "Oh glorious restorer
of knight-errantry," cried he, "I embrace these legs,
as I would the pillars of Hercules. Who can sufficiently extol the great Don Quixote de la Mancha,
the reviver of drooping hearts, the prop and stay of
the falling, the raiser of the fallen, and the staff of
comfort to the weak and afflicted!"

At these words Don Quixote stood amazed,
Sancho quaked, the page wondered, the innkeeper
stared, all astonished at Master Peter's speech; who
then turning to Sancho, "And thou honest Sancho
Pança," said he, "the best squire to the best knight
in the world, bless thy kind stars, for thy good spouse
Teresa is a good housewife, and is at this instant
dressing a pound of flax, by the same token, she has
standing by her, on her left hand, a large broken-
mouth jug, which holds a pretty scantling of wine,
to cheer up her spirits." "By yea and nay," quoth
Sancho, "that is likely enough, for she is a true soul,
and a jolly soul; were it not for a spice of jealousy
that she has now and then, I would not change her
for the giantess Andondona herself, who, as my
master says, was as clever a piece of woman's flesh
as ever went upon two legs. Well, much good may
it do thee, honest Teresa; thou art resolved to provide for one, I find, though thy heirs starve for it."
"Well," said Don Quixote, "great is the knowledge
procured by reading, travel, and experience; what
on earth but the testimony of my own eyes could
have persuaded me that apes had the gift of divina-

tion! I am indeed the same Don Quixote de la Mancha, mentioned by this ingenious animal, though I must confess somewhat undeserving of so great a character as it has pleased him to bestow on me: but nevertheless I am not sorry to have charity and compassion bear so great a part in my commendation, since my nature has always disposed me to do good to all men, and hurt to none. . . . No more of this at present, let us now see the puppet-show: I fancy we shall find something in it worth seeing."

"Something!" said Master Peter, "sir, you shall see a thousand things worth seeing. I tell you, sir, I defy the world to show such another. I say no more, *Operibus credite, et non verbis.* But now let us begin, for it grows late, and we have much to do, say, and show." Don Quixote and Sancho complied, and went into the room where the show stood, with a good number of small wax-lights glimmering round about, that made it shine gloriously. Master Peter got to his station within, being the man that was to move the puppets; and his boy stood before to tell what the puppets said, and, with a white wand in his hand, to point at the several figures as they came in and out, and explain the mystery of the show. Then all the audience having taken their places, the boy, who was the mouth of the motion, began a story, that shall be heard or seen by those who will take the pains to read or hear the next chapter.

A pleasant account of the puppet-play, with other very good things truly.

The Tyrians and the Trojans were all silent; that is, the ears of all the spectators hung on the mouth of the interpreter of the show, when in the first place they had a loud flourish of kettle-drums and trumpets within the machine, and then several discharges of artillery; which prelude being soon over, "Gentlemen," cried the boy, raising his voice, "we present you here with a true history taken out of the chronicles of France, and the Spanish ballads, sung even by the boys about the streets, and in everybody's mouth; it tells you how Don Gayferos delivered his wife Melisandra, that was a prisoner among the Moors in Spain, in the city of Sansuena, now called Saragossa. Now, gallants, the first figure we present you with is Don Gayferos playing at Tables.

"Gentlemen, in the next place, mark that personage that peeps out there with a crown on his head and a sceptre in his hand. It is the Emperor Charlemagne, fair Melisandra's reputed father, who, vexed at the idleness and negligence of his son-in-law, comes to chide him; and pray observe with what passion and earnestness he rates him, as if he had a mind to lend him half-a-dozen sound raps over the pate with his sceptre. Nay, some authors do not stick to tell ye, he gave him as many, and well laid on too; and after he had told him how his honour lay a-bleeding, till he had delivered his wife out of durance, among many other pithy sayings, 'Look to it,' quoth he to him as he went, 'I will say no more.' Mind how the emperor turns his back upon him, and how he leaves Don Gayferos nettled and in the dumps. Now see how he starts up, and in a rage throws the tables one way, and whirls the men another; and calling for his arms with all haste, borrows his cousin-german Orlando's sword, Durindana, who withal offers to go along with him in this difficult adventure, but the valorous enraged knight will not let him, and says, he is able to deliver his wife himself, without his help, though they kept her down in the very centre of the earth. And now he is going to put on his armour in order to begin his journey.

"Now, gentlemen, cast your eyes upon yon tower; you are to suppose it one of the towers of the castle of Saragossa, now called the Aljaferia. That lady, whom you see in the balcony there, in a Moorish habit, is the peerless Melisandra, that casts many a heavy look towards France, thinking of Paris and her husband, the only comfort in her imprisonment. But now, silence, gentlemen, pray silence; here is an accident wholly new, the like perhaps never heard of before: do not you see that Moor who comes a-tiptoe creeping and stealing along with his finger in his mouth behind Melisandra? Hear what a smack he gives on her sweet lips, and see how she spits and wipes her mouth with her white smock sleeve: see how she takes on and tears her lovely hair for very madness, as if it were to blame for this affront. Next pray observe that grave Moor that stands in the open gallery: that is Marsilius, the king of Sansuena, who having been an eye-witness of the sauciness of the Moor, ordered him immediately to be apprehended, though his kinsman and great favourite, to have two hundred lashes given him, then to be carried through the city, with criers before to proclaim his crime, the rods of justice behind. And look how all this is put in execution sooner almost than the fact is committed: for your Moors, you must know, do not use any form of indictment as we do, neither have they any legal trials." "Child, child," said Don Quixote, "go on directly with your story, and do not keep us here with your excursions and ramblings out of the road: I tell you there must be a formal process and legal trial to prove matters of fact." "Boy," said the master from behind the show, "do as the gentleman bids you. Do not run so much upon flourishes, but follow your plain song, without venturing on counter-points, for fear of spoiling all." "I will, sir," quoth the boy, and so proceeding:

"Now, sirs, he that you see there a-horseback, wrapt up in the Gascoigne cloak, is Don Gayferos himself, whom his wife, now revenged on the Moor for his impudence, seeing him from the battlements of the tower, takes him for a stranger, and talks with him as such.

"I omit the rest, not to tire you with a long story. It is sufficient, that he makes himself known to her, as you may guess by the joy she shows; and accord-
10 ingly now see how she lets herself down from the balcony, to come at her loving husband, and get behind him; but unhappily, alas, one of the skirts of her gown is caught upon one of the spikes of the balcony, and there she hangs and hovers in the air miserably, without being able to get down. But see how Heaven is merciful, and sends relief in the greatest distress! Now Don Gayferos rides up to her, and not fearing to tear her rich gown, lays hold of it, and at one pull brings her down; and then at one
20 lift sets her astride upon his horse's crupper, bidding her to sit fast, and clasp her arms about him, that she might not fall, for the lady Melisandra was not used to that kind of riding.

"Observe now, gallants, how the horse neighs, and shows how proud he is of the burden of his brave master and fair mistress. Look now how they turn their backs, and leave the city, and gallop it merrily away towards Paris. Peace be with you, for a peer-less couple of true lovers! may ye get safe and sound
30 into your own country, without any let or ill chance in your journey, and live as long as Nestor in peace and quietness among your friends and relations." "Plainness, boy," cried Mr. Peter, "none of your flights, I beseech you, for affectation is the Devil." The boy answered nothing, but going on: "Now, sirs," quoth he, "some of those idle people, that love to pry into everything, happened to spy Melisandra as she was making her escape, and ran presently and gave Marsilius notice of it: whereupon he straight
40 commanded to sound an alarm; and now mind what a din and hurly-burly there is, and how the city shakes with the ring of the bells backwards in all the mosques!" "There you are out, boy," said Don Quixote: "the Moors have no bells, they only use kettle-drums, and a kind of shawms like our waits or hautboys; so that your ringing of bells in San-suena is a mere absurdity, good Mr. Peter." "Nay, sir," said Mr. Peter, "giving over ringing; if you stand upon trifles with us, we shall never please you.
50 Do not be so severe a critic: are there not a thousand plays that pass with great success and applause, though they have many greater absurdities, and nonsense in abundance? On, boy, on, let there be as many impertinences as moats in the sun; no matter, so I get the money." "Well said," answered Don Quixote. "And now, sirs," quoth the boy, "observe what a vast company of glittering horse comes pour-

ing out of the city, in pursuit of the Christian lovers; what a dreadful sound of trumpets, and clarions, and drums, and kettle-drums there is in the air. I fear 60 they will overtake them, and then will the poor wretches be dragged along most barbarously at the tails of their horses, which would be sad indeed."

Don Quixote, seeing such a number of Moors, and hearing such an alarm, thought it high time to assist the flying lovers; and starting up, "It shall never be said while I live," cried he aloud, "that I suffered such a wrong to be done to so famous a knight and so daring a lover as Don Gayferos. For-bear then your unjust pursuit, ye base rascals: stop, 70 or prepare to meet my furious resentment." Then drawing out his sword, to make good his threats, at one spring he gets to the show, and with a violent fury lays at the Moorish puppets, cutting and slash-ing in a most terrible manner; some he overthrows, and beheads others; maims this, and cleaves that in pieces. Among the rest of his merciless strokes, he thundered one down with a mighty force, that had not Mr. Peter luckily ducked and squatted down, it had certainly chopped off his head as easily as one 80 might cut an apple. "Hold, hold, sir," cried the puppet-player, after the narrow escape, "hold for pity's sake. What do you mean, sir? These are no real Moors that you cut and hack so, but poor harm-less puppets made of pasteboard. Think of what you do, you ruin me for ever. Oh that ever I was born! you have broke me quite." But Don Quixote, without minding his words, doubled and redoubled his blows so thick, and laid about him so outrageously, that in less than two credos he had cut all the strings and 90 wires, mangled the puppets, and spoiled and de-molished the whole motion. King Marsilius was in a grievous condition. The Emperor Charlemagne's head and crown were cleft in two. The whole audi-ence was in a sad consternation. The ape scampered off to the top of the house. Sancho was in a terrible fright, for, as he swore after the hurricane was over, he had never seen his master in such a rage be-fore. . . .

What happened to Don Quixote with the fair huntress.

It happened that the next day about sunset, as 100 they were coming out of a wood, Don Quixote cast his eyes around a verdant meadow, and at the further end of it descried a company, whom upon nearer view he judged to be persons of quality, that were taking the diversion of hawking; approaching nearer yet, he observed among them a very fine lady upon a white pacing mare, in green trappings, and a saddle-cloth of silver. The lady herself was dressed in green, so rich and so gay, that nothing could be finer. She rode with a goss-hawk on her left fist, by 110 which Don Quixote judged her to be of quality, and mistress of the train that attended; as indeed she was. Thereupon calling to his squire, "Son Sancho," cried he, "run and tell that lady on the palfrey with the goss-hawk on her fist, that I the 'Knight of the Lions' humbly salute her highness; and that if she pleases to give me leave, I should be proud to receive her commands, and have the honour of waiting on her, and kissing her fair hands. But take special care, Sancho, how thou deliverest thy message, and be sure do not lard my compliments with any of thy proverbs." "Why this to me?" quoth Sancho. "Marry, you need not talk of larding, as if I had never went ambassador before to a high and mighty dame." "I do not know that ever thou didst," replied Don Quixote, "at least on my account, unless it were when I sent thee to Dulcinea." "It may be so," quoth Sancho; "but a good paymaster needs no surety; and where there is plenty the guests cannot be empty: that is to say, I need none of your telling, nor tutoring about that matter: for, as silly as I look, I know something of everything." "Well, well, I believe it," said Don Quixote; "go then in a good hour, and Heaven inspire and guide thee."

Sancho put on, forcing Dapple from his old pace to a gallop; and approaching the fair huntress, he alighted, and falling on his knees, "Fair lady," quoth he, "that knight yonder, called 'the Knight of the Lions,' is my master: I am his squire, Sancho Pança by name. This same 'Knight of the Lions,' who but the other day was called 'the Knight of the Woeful Figure,' has sent me to tell you, that, so please your Worship's Grace to give him leave, with your good liking, to do as he has a mind; which, as he says, and as I believe, is only to serve your high-flown beauty, and be your 'ternal' vassal; you may chance to do a thing that would be for your own good, and he would take it for a hugeous kindness at your hands." "Indeed, honest squire," said the lady, "you have acquitted yourself of your charge with all the graceful circumstances which such an embassy requires: rise, pray rise; for it is by no means fit the squire to so great a knight as 'the Knight of the Woeful Figure,' to whose name and merit we are no strangers, should remain on his knees. Rise then, and desire your master, by all means to honour us with his company, that my Lord Duke and I may pay him our respects at a house we have hard by." . . . Sancho was overjoyed to find himself so much in the Duchess's favour, for he was ever a cordial friend to a plentiful way of living, and therefore never failed to take such opportunities by the foretop, wherever he met them.

Now the history tells us, that before they got to the castle, the Duke rode away from them, to instruct his servants how to behave themselves towards Don Quixote; so that no sooner did the Knight come near the gates, but he was met by two of the Duke's lacqueys or grooms in long vests, like nightgowns, of fine crimson satin. These suddenly took him in their arms, and lifting him from his horse without any further ceremony, "Go, great and mighty sir," said they, "and help my Lady Duchess down." Thereupon Don Quixote went and offered to do it; and many compliments and much ceremony passed on both sides: but in conclusion the Duchess's earnestness prevailed; for she would not alight from her palfrey but in the arms of her husband, excusing herself from incommoding so great a knight with so insignificant a burden. With that the Duke took her down. And now, being entered into a large courtyard, there came two beautiful damsels, who threw a long mantle of fine scarlet over Don Quixote's shoulders. In an instant, all the galleries about the courtyard were crowded with men and women, the domestics of the Duke, who cried, "Welcome, welcome, the flower and cream of knight-errantry!" Then most, if not all of them, sprinkled bottles of sweet water upon Don Quixote, the Duke, and Duchess: all which agreeably surprised the Don, and this was indeed the first day he knew and firmly believed himself to be a real knight-errant, and that his knighthood was more than fancy; finding himself treated just as he had read the brothers of the order were entertained in former ages.

Sancho was so transported, that he even forsook his beloved Dapple, to keep close to the Duchess, and entered the castle with the company: but his conscience flying in his face for leaving that dear companion of his alone, he went to a reverend old waiting-woman, who was one of the Duchess's retinue, and whispering her in the ear, "Mrs. Gonzales, or Mrs.—pray forsooth may I crave your name?" "Donna Rodriguez de Grijalva is my name," said the old duenna; "what is your business with me, friend?" "Pray now, mistress," quoth Sancho, "do so much as go out at the castle-gate, where you will find a dapple ass of mine; see him into the stable, or else put him in yourself; for, poor thing, it is main fearful and timersome, and cannot abide to be alone in a strange place." . . .

Don Quixote was led up a stately staircase, and then into a noble hall sumptuously hung with rich gold brocade. There his armour was taken off by six young damsels, that served him instead of pages, all of them fully instructed by the Duke and Duchess how to behave themselves so towards Don Quixote, that he might look on his entertainment as conformable to those which the famous knights-errant received of old. . . . They desired he would give them leave to take off his clothes, and put on him a clean shirt. But he would by no means permit it, giving them to understand, that modesty was as commendable a virtue in a knight as valour; and therefore he desired them to leave the shirt. . . .

Don Quixote then dressed himself, put on his belt and sword, threw his scarlet cloak over his shoulders, and clapped on a monteer cap of green velvet, which had been left him by the damsels. Thus accoutred, he entered the stateroom, where he found the damsels ranged in two rows, attending with water, and all necessaries to wash him in state; and having done him that office, with many humble courtesies and solemn ceremonies, immediately twelve pages with the gentleman-sewer at the head of them, came to conduct him to supper, letting him know that the Duke and Duchess expected him. Accordingly, they led him in great pomp, some walking before and some behind, into another room, where a table was magnificently set out.

As soon as he approached, the Duke and the Duchess came as far as the door to receive him, and with them a grave clergyman, one of those that assume to govern great men's houses, and who, not being nobly born themselves, do not know how to instruct those that are, but would have the liberality of the great measured by the narrowness of their own souls, making those whom they govern stingy, when they pretend to teach them frugality. One of these in all likelihood was this grave ecclesiastic, who came with the Duke to receive Don Quixote.

After a thousand courtly compliments on all sides, Don Quixote at last approached the table, between the Duke and the Duchess, and here arose a fresh contest; for the Knight, being offered the upper end of the table, thought himself obliged to decline it. However he could not withstand the Duke's pressing importunities, but was forced at last to comply. The parson sat right against him, and the Duke and the Duchess on each side. . . .

The Duchess asked Don Quixote, what news he had of the Lady Dulcinea, and how long it was since he had sent her any giants or robbers for a present, not doubting but that he had lately subdued many such? "Alas! madam," answered he, "my misfortunes have had a beginning, but, I fear, will never have an end. I have vanquished giants, elves, and cut-throats, and sent them to the mistress of my soul, but where shall they find her? She is enchanted, madam, and transformed to the ugliest piece of rusticity that can be imagined." "I do not know, sir," quoth Sancho; "when I saw her last she seemed to be the finest creature in the 'versal' world; thus far, at least, I can safely vouch for her upon my own knowledge, that for activity of body, and leaping, the best tumbler of them all does not go beyond her. Upon my honest word, madam Duchess, she will vault from the ground upon her ass like a cat." "Have you seen her enchanted?" said the Duke. "Seen her!" quoth Sancho; "and who the devil was the first that hit upon this trick of her enchantment,

think you, but I? She is as much enchanted as my father."

The churchman hearing them talk of giants, elves, and enchantments, began to suspect this was Don Quixote de la Mancha, whose history the Duke so often used to read, though he had several times reprehended him for it; telling him, it was a folly to read such follies. Being confirmed in his suspicion, he addressed himself very angrily to the Duke. "My Lord," said he, "your Grace will have a large account to give one day, for soothing this poor man's follies. I suppose this same Don Quixote, or Don Quite Sot, or whatever you are pleased to call him, cannot be quite so besotted as you endeavour to make him, by giving him such opportunities to run on in his fantastical humours." Then, directing his discourse to Don Quixote, "Hark ye," said he; "goodman Addlepate, who has put it into your crown that you are a knight-errant, that you vanquish giants and robbers? Go, go, get you home again, look after your children, if you have any, and what honest business you have to do, and leave wandering about the world, building castles in the air, and making yourself a laughing-stock to all that know you, or know you not. Where have you found, in the name of mischief, that there ever has been, or are now, any such thing as knights-errant? Where will you meet with giants in Spain, or monsters in La Mancha? Where shall one find your enchanted Dulcineas, and all those legions of whimsies and chimeras that are talked of on your account, but in your own empty skull?"

Don Quixote gave this reverend person the hearing with great patience. But at last, seeing him silent, without minding his respect to the Duke and Duchess, up he started with indignation and fury in his looks, and said—but his answer deserves a chapter by itself.

Don Quixote's answer to his reprover, with other grave and merry accidents.

Don Quixote being thus suddenly got up, shaking from head to foot for madness, as if he had quicksilver in his bones, cast an angry look on his indiscreet censor, and with an eager delivery, sputtering and stammering with choler, "This place," cried he, "the presence of these noble persons, and the respect I have always had for your function, check my just resentment, and tie up my hands from taking the satisfaction of a gentleman. For these reasons, and since every one knows that you gownmen, as well as women, use no other weapon but your tongues, I will fairly engage you upon equal terms, and combat you at your own weapon. I should rather have expected sober admonitions from a man of your cloth, than infamous reproaches. Charitable and wholesome correction ought to be managed at another rate, and with more moderation. The least that can be said of this reproof which you have given me here so bitterly, and in public, is, that it has exceeded the bounds of Christian correction, and a gentle one had been much more becoming. Is it fit, that without any insight into the offence which you reprove, you should, without any more ado, call the offender fool, sot, and addlepate? Pray, sir, what foolish action have you seen me do, that should provoke you to give me such ill language, and bid me so magisterially go home to look after my wife and children, before you know whether I have any? Do not you think those deserve as severe a censure, who screw themselves into other men's houses, and pretend to rule the master? A fine world it is truly, when a poor pedant, who has seen no more of it than lies within twenty or thirty leagues about him, shall take upon him to prescribe laws to knight-errantry, and judge of those who profess it! You, forsooth, esteem it an idle undertaking, and time lost, to wander through the world, though scorning its pleasures, and sharing the hardships and toils of it, by which the virtuous aspire to the high seat of immortality. If persons of honour, knights, lords, gentlemen, or men of any birth, should take me for a fool or a coxcomb, I should think it an irreparable affront. But for mere scholars, that never trod the paths of chivalry, to think me mad, I despise and laugh at it. I am a knight, and a knight will I die, if so it please Omnipotence. Some choose the high road of haughty ambition; others the low ways of base servile flattery; a third sort take the crooked path of deceitful hypocrisy; and a few, very few, that of true religion. I, for my own part, guided by my stars, follow the narrow track of knight-errantry; and, for the exercise of it, I despise riches, but not honour. I have redressed grievances, and righted the injured, chastised the insolent, vanquished giants, and trod elves and hobgoblins under my feet! I am in love, but no more than the profession of knight-errantry obliges me to be; yet I am none of this age's vicious lovers, but a chaste Platonic. My intentions are all directed to virtuous ends, and to do no man wrong, but good to all the world. And now let your Graces judge, most excellent Duke and Duchess, whether a person who makes it his only study to practise all this, deserves to be upbraided for a fool."

"Well said, i'faith!" quoth Sancho, "say no more for yourself, my good lord and master, stop when you are well, for there is not the least matter to be added more on your side, either in word, thought, or deed. Besides, since Mr. Parson has had the face to say point-blank as one may say, that there neither are, nor ever were, any knights-errant in the world,

no marvel he does not know what he says." "What," said the clergyman, "I warrant you are that Sancho Pança, to whom they say your master has promised an island?" "Ay, marry am I," answered Sancho, "and I am he that deserves it as well as another body; and I am one of those of whom they say, Keep with good men, and thou shalt be one of them; and of those of whom it is said again, Not with whom thou wert bred, but with whom thou hast fed; as also, Lean against a good tree, and it will shelter thee. I have leaned and stuck close to my good master, and kept him company this many a month; and now he and I are all one; and I must be as he is, if it be Heaven's blessed will; and so he lives and I live, he will not want kingdoms to rule, nor shall I want islands to govern."

"That thou shalt not, honest Sancho," said the Duke; "for I, on the great Don Quixote's account, will now give thee the government of an odd one of my own of no small consequence." "Down, down on thy knees, Sancho," cried Don Quixote, "and kiss his Grace's feet for this favour." Sancho did accordingly: but when the clergyman saw it, he got up in a great heat. . . . The Duchess was ready to die with laughing at Sancho, whom she thought a more pleasant fool, and a greater madman than his master; and she was not the only person at that time of this opinion. In short, Don Quixote being pacified, they made an end of dinner. . . .

The relishing conference which the Duchess and her women held with Sancho Pança, worth your reading and observation.

The story afterwards informs us, that Sancho slept not a wink all that afternoon, but waited on the Duchess as he had promised. Being mightily taken with his comical discourse, she ordered him to take a low chair and sit by her; but Sancho, who knew better things, absolutely declined it, till she pressed him again to sit as he was a governor, and speak as he was a squire; in both which capacities he deserved the very seat of Cid Ruy Dias, the famous champion. Sancho shrugged up his shoulders and obeyed, and all the Duchess's women standing round about her to give her silent attention, she began the conference.

"Now that we are private," said she, "and nobody to overhear us, I would desire you, my Lord Governor, to resolve me of some doubts. . . . I think I hear something whisper me in the ear, and say, if Don Quixote de la Mancha be such a shallow-brain, why does Sancho Pança, who knows him to be so, wait upon this madman, and rely thus upon his vain extravagant promises? I can only infer from this, that the man is more a fool than the master; and if so will not Madam Duchess be thought as mad as

either of them, to bestow the government of an island, or the command of others, on one who cannot govern himself?" "By our Lady," quoth Sancho, "your scruple comes in pudding-time. But it need not whisper in your ear, it may even speak plain, and as loud as it will. I am a fool, that is certain, for, if I had been wise, I had left my master many a fair day since; but it was my luck and my vile errantry, and that is all that can be said of it. I
10 must follow him through thick and thin. We are both town-born children; I have eaten his bread, I love him well, and there is no love lost between us. He pays me very well, he has given me three colts, and I am so very true and trusty to him, that nothing but death can part us. And if your High and Mightiness does not think fit to let me have this same government, why, so be it; with less was I born, and with less shall I die; it may be for the good of my conscience to go without it. I am a fool,
20 it is true, but yet I understand the meaning of the saying, The pismire had wings to do her hurt; and Sancho the squire may sooner get to heaven than Sancho the governor. There is as good bread baked here as in France, and Joan is as good as my lady in the dark. In the night all cats are grey. Unhappy is he that wants his breakfast at two in the afternoon. It is always good fasting after a good breakfast. There is no man has a stomach a yard bigger than another, but let it be never so big, there will
30 be hay and straw enough to fill it. A bellyful is a bellyful. The sparrow speeds as well as the sparrow-hawk. Good serge is fine, but coarse cloth is warm; and four yards of the one are as long as four yards of the other. When the hour is come we must all be packed off; the prince and the prick-louse go the same way at last: the road is no fairer for the one than the other. The Pope's body takes up no more room than the sexton's, though one be taller; for when they come to the pit, all are alike, and so
40 good-night or good-morrow, which you please. And let me tell you again, if you do not think fit to give me an island, because I am a fool, I will be so wise not to care whether you do or no."

Sancho's proverbial aphorisms were no small diversion to the Duchess. "You know," said she, "honest Sancho, that the promise of a gentleman or knight must be as precious and sacred to him as his life; I make no question, then, but that my Lord Duke, who is also a knight, though not of your
50 master's order, will infallibly keep his word with you in respect of your government. Take courage, then, Sancho, for when you least dream of it, in spite of all the envy and malice of the world, you will suddenly see yourself in full possession of your government, and seated in your chair of state in your rich robes, with all your marks and ornaments

of power about you. But be sure to administer true justice to your vassals, who by their loyalty and discretion will merit no less at your hands."

"As for the governing part," quoth Sancho, "let me 60 alone, I was ever charitable and good to the poor, and scorn to take the bread out of another man's mouth. On the other side, by our Lady, they shall play me no foul play. I am an old cur at a crust, and can sleep dog-sleep when I list. I can look sharp as well as another, and let me alone to keep the cob-webs out of my eyes. I know where the shoe wrings me. I will know who and who is together. Honesty is the best policy. I will stick to that. The good shall have my hand and heart, but the bad 70 neither foot nor fellowship. And in my mind, the main point in this post of governing, is to make a good beginning. I will lay my life, that as simple as Sancho sits here, in a fortnight's time he will manage ye this same island as rightly as a sheaf of barley." "You say well, Sancho," said the Duchess, "for time ripens all things. No man is born wise; bishops are made of men, and not of stones." . . .

Sancho kissed the Duchess's hand once more, and begged her Worship's Grace that special care might 80 be taken of his Dapple, for that he was the light of his eyes. "What is that Dapple?" asked the Duchess. "My beast, if it like your honour," answered Sancho; "my ass I would say, saving your presence; but because I will not call him ass, which is so common a name among men, I call him Dapple." . . . "Well," said the Duchess, "your ass may go with you to the government, and there you may feed, and pamper him, and make as much of him as you please." "Adad! my lady," quoth Sancho, "do not let your 90 worship think this will be a strange matter neither. I have seen more asses than one go to a government before now: and if mine goes too, it will be no new thing I trow." . . .

The instructions which Don Quixote gave Sancho Pança, before he went to the government of his island, with other matters of moment.

The day after, the Duke bid Sancho prepare, and be in a readiness to take possession of his government; for now his islanders wished as heartily for him, as they did for rain in a dry summer. . . . "Well then," quoth Sancho, "let me have this island, and I will do my best to be such a governor, that, 100 in spite of rogues, I shall not want a small nook in heaven one day or other. It is not out of covetousness neither, that I would leave my little cot, and set up for somebody, but merely to know what kind of thing it is to be a governor." "Oh! Sancho," said the Duke, "when once you have had a taste of it, you will never leave licking your fingers, it is so sweet and bewitching a thing to command and be obeyed. I am confident, when your master comes to be an Emperor (as he cannot fail to be, according to the course of his affairs) he will never by any consideration be persuaded to abdicate; his only grief will be, that he was one no sooner."

"Troth, sir," replied Sancho, "I am of your mind; it is a dainty thing to command, though it were but a flock of sheep." "Oh! Sancho," cried the Duke, "let me live and die with thee: for thou hast an insight into everything. I hope thou wilt prove as good a governor as thy wisdom bespeaks thee. But no more at this time,—to-morrow, without further delay, you may set forward to your island, and shall be furnished this afternoon with equipage and dress answerable to your post, and all other necessaries for your journey." . . .

By this time Don Quixote arrived, and hearing how suddenly Sancho was to go to his government, with the Duke's permission, he took him aside to give him some good instructions for his conduct in the discharge of his office.

Being entered Don Quixote's chamber, and the door shut, he almost forcibly obliged Sancho to sit by him; and then, with a grave deliberate voice, he thus began.

"First of all, O my son, fear God; for the fear of God is the beginning of wisdom, and wisdom will never let thee go astray.

"Secondly, consider what thou wert, and make it thy business to know thyself, which is the most difficult lesson in the world. Yet from this lesson thou wilt learn to avoid the frog's foolish ambition of swelling to rival the bigness of the ox; else the consideration of your having been a hog-driver, will be, to the wheel of your fortune, like the peacock's ugly feet."

"True," quoth Sancho, "but I was then but a little boy; for when I grew up to be somewhat bigger, I drove geese, and not hogs, but methinks that is nothing to the purpose; for all governors cannot come from kings and princes." . . .

"Be well-pleased with the meanness of thy family, Sancho, nor think it a disgrace to own thyself derived from labouring men; for, if thou art not ashamed of it thyself, nobody else will strive to make thee so. Endeavour rather to be esteemed humble and virtuous, rather than proud and vicious. The number is almost infinite of those who, from low and vulgar births, have been raised to the highest dignities, to the papal chair, and the imperial throne; and this I could prove by examples enough to tire thy patience. . . .

"If thou sendest for thy wife, as it is not fit a man in thy station should be long without his wife, and she ought to partake of her husband's good fortune, teach her, instruct her, polish her the best thou canst, till her native rusticity is refined to a handsomer behaviour; for often an ill-bred wife throws down all that a good and discreet husband can build up. . . .

"Let the tears of the poor find more compassion, though not more justice, than the informations of the rich.

"When the severity of the law is to be softened, let pity, not bribes, be the motive.

"Revile not with words those whom their crimes oblige thee to punish in deed; for the punishment is enough to the wretches, without the addition of ill language.

"If thou observest these rules, Sancho, thy days shall be long, thy fame eternal, thy recompense full, and thy felicity unspeakable. Thou shalt marry thy children and thy grandchildren to thy heart's desire; they shall want no titles: beloved of all men, thy life shall be peaceable, thy death in a good and venerable old age, and the offspring of thy grandchildren, with their soft youthful hands shall close thy eyes." . . .

After dinner Don Quixote gave Sancho, in writing, the copy of his verbal instructions, ordering him to get somebody to read them to him. But the squire had no sooner got them, but he dropped the paper, which fell into the Duke's hands; who, communicating the same to the Duchess, they found a fresh occasion of admiring the mixture of Don Quixote's good sense and extravagance: and so carrying on the humour, they sent Sancho that afternoon, with a suitable equipage, to the place he was to govern, which, wherever it lay, was to be an island to him. . . .

How the great Sancho Pança took possession of his island, and in what manner he began to govern.

Sancho, with all his attendants, came to a town that had about a thousand inhabitants, and was one of the best where the Duke had any power: they gave him to understand, that the name of the place was the island of Barataria, either because the town was called Barataria, or because the government cost him so cheap. As soon as he came to the gates (for it was walled) the chief officers and inhabitants, in their formalities, came out to receive him, the bells rung, and all the people gave general demonstrations of their joy. The new governor was then carried in mighty pomp to the great church, to give Heaven thanks; and after some ridiculous ceremonies, they delivered him the keys of the gates, and received him as a perpetual governor of the island of Barataria. In the meantime, the garb, the port, the huge beard, and the short and thick

96–97. **or because . . . so cheap.** Spanish *borato* means cheap.

shape of the new Governor, made every one who knew nothing of the jest wonder, and even those who were privy to the plot, who were many, were not a little surprised.

In short, from the church they carried him to the court of justice; where, when they had placed him in his seat, "My Lord Governor," said the Duke's steward to him, "it is an ancient custom here, that he who takes possession of this famous island, must
10 answer to some difficult and intricate question that is propounded to him; and by the return he makes, the people feel the pulse of his understanding, and by an estimate of his abilities, judge whether they ought to rejoice, or to be sorry for his coming."

All the while the steward was speaking, Sancho was staring on an inscription in large characters on the wall over against his seat, and as he could not read, he asked, what was the meaning of that which he saw painted there upon the wall. "Sir," said
20 they, "it is an account of the day when your Lordship took possession of this island, and the inscription runs thus: 'This day, being such a day of this month, in such a year, the Lord Don Sancho Pança took possession of this island, which may he long enjoy.'" "And who is he," asked Sancho, "whom they call Don Sancho Pança?" "Your Lordship," answered the steward; "for we know of no other Pança in this island but yourself, who now sits in this chair." "Well, friend," said Sancho, "pray take
30 notice, that Don does not belong to me, nor was it borne by any of my family before me. Plain Sancho Pança is my name; my father was called Sancho, my grandfather Sancho; and all of us have been Panças, without any Don or Donna added to our name. Now do I already guess your Dons are as thick as stones in this island. But it is enough that Heaven knows my meaning; if my government happens but to last four days to an end, it shall go hard but I will clear the island of those swarms of Dons
40 that must needs be as troublesome as so many flesh-flies." . . .

Sancho was conducted from the court of justice to a sumptuous palace; where, in a spacious room, he found the cloth laid, and a most neat and magnificent entertainment prepared. As soon as he entered, the wind music played, and four pages waited on him, in order to the washing his hands; which he did with a great deal of gravity. And now the instruments ceasing, Sancho sat down at the upper
50 end of the table; for there was no seat but there, and the cloth was only laid for one. A certain personage, who afterwards appeared to be a physician, came and stood at his elbow, with a whalebone wand in his hand. Then they took off a curious white cloth that lay over the dishes on the table, and discovered great variety of fruit, and other eatables. One that looked like a student, said grace; a page put a laced

bib under Sancho's chin; and another, who did the office of sewer, set a dish of fruit before him. But
69 he had hardly put one bit into his mouth, before the physician touched the dish with his wand, and then it was taken away by a page in an instant. Immediately another with meat was clapped in the place; but Sancho no sooner offered to taste it, but the doctor with the wand conjured it away as fast as the fruit. Sancho was amazed at this sudden removal, and looking about him on the company, asked them whether they used to tantalize people at that rate, feeding their eyes, and starving their bellies.

70 "My Lord Governor," answered the physician, "you are to eat here no otherwise than according to the use and custom of other islands where there are governors. I am a doctor of physic, my Lord, and have a salary allowed me in this island, for taking charge of the Governor's health, and I am more careful of it than of my own; studying night and day his constitution, that I may the better know what to prescribe when he falls sick. Now the chief thing I do, is to attend him always at his meals, to
80 let him eat what I think convenient for him, and to prevent his eating what I imagine to be prejudicial to his health, and offensive to his stomach. Therefore I now ordered the fruit to be taken away, because it is too cold and moist; and the other dish, because it is as much too hot, and overseasoned with spices, which are apt to increase thirst; and he that drinks much, destroys and consumes the radical moisture, which is the fuel of life." "So then," quoth Sancho, "this dish of roasted partridges here can do me no
90 manner of harm." "Hold," said the physician, "the Lord Governor shall not eat of them, while I live to prevent it." "Why so?" cried Sancho. "Because," answered the doctor, "our great master, Hippocrates, the north star and luminary of physic, says in one of his aphorisms, *Omnis saturatio mala, perdicis autem pessima*: that is, all repletion is bad, but that of partridges is worst of all." "If it be so," said Sancho, "let Mr. Doctor see which of all these dishes on the table will do me most good and least harm,
100 and let me eat my belly full of that, without having it whisked away with his wand. For, by my hopes, and the pleasures of government, as I live, I am ready to die with hunger; and not to allow me to eat any victuals (let Mr. Doctor say what he will) is the way to shorten my life, and not to lengthen it." "Very true, my Lord," replied the physician. . . . "Therefore what I would advise at present, as a fit diet for the Governor, for the preservation and support of his health, is a hundred of small wafers, and
110 a few thin slices of marmalade, to strengthen his stomach, and help digestion."

Sancho hearing this, leaned back upon his chair, and looking earnestly in the doctor's face, very seriously asked him, what his name was, and where he

had studied? "My Lord," answered he, "I am called Doctor Pedro Rezio de Aguero. The name of the place where I was born is Tirteafuera, and lies between Caraquel and Almodabar del Campo, on the right hand; and I took my degree of doctor in the university of Osuna." "Hark you," said Sancho, in a mighty chafe, "Mr. Dr. Pedro Rezio de Aguero, born at Tirteafuera, that lies between Caraquel and Almodabar del Campo, on the right hand, and who took your degree of doctor at the university of Osuna, and so forth, take yourself away! Avoid the room this moment, or by the sun's light, I'll get me a good cudgel, and beginning with your carcase, will so belabour and rib-roast all the physic-mongers in the island, that I will not leave therein one of the tribe of those, I mean that are ignorant quacks; for, as for learned and wise physicians, I will make much of them, and honour them like so many angels.". . .
The physician was terrified, seeing the Governor in such a heat, and would that moment have slunk out of the room, had not the sound of a post-horn in the street been heard that moment; whereupon the steward immediately looking out of the window, turned back, and said, there was an express come from the Duke, doubtless with some dispatch of importance.

Presently the messenger entered sweating, with haste and concern in his looks, and pulling a packet out of his bosom, delivered it to the Governor. Sancho gave it to the steward, and ordered him to read the direction, which was this: "To Don Sancho Pança, Governor of the island of Barataria, to be delivered into his own hands, or those of his secretary." "Who is my secretary?" cried Sancho. "It is I, my Lord," answered one that was by, "for I can write and read, and am a Biscainer." "That last qualification is enough to make thee set up for secretary to the emperor himself," said Sancho. "Open the letter then, and see what it says." The new secretary did so, and having perused the dispatch by himself, told the Governor, that it was a business that was to be told only in private: Sancho ordered every one to leave the room except the steward and the carver, and then the secretary read what follows:

"I have received information, my Lord Don Sancho Pança, that some of our enemies intend to attack your island with great fury, one of these nights: You ought therefore to be watchful, and stand upon your guard, that you may not be found unprovided. I have also had intelligence from faithful spies, that there are four men got into the town in disguise, to murder you; your abilities being regarded as a great obstacle to the enemies' designs. Look about you, take heed how you admit strangers to speak with you, and eat nothing that is laid before you. I will take care to send you assistance, if you stand in need of it: And in everything I rely on your prudence. From our castle, the 16th of August, at four in the morning.

"Your friend,
"THE DUKE."

Sancho was astonished at the news, and those that were with him seemed no less concerned. But at last, turning to the steward, "I will tell you," said he, "what is first to be done in this case, and that with all speed; clap me that same Doctor Rezio in a dungeon; for if anybody has a mind to kill me, it must be he, and that with a lingering death, the worst of deaths, hunger-starving. . . . Secretary, do you send my Lord Duke an answer, and tell him, his order shall be fulfilled in every part without fail. Remember me kindly to my Lady Duchess, . . . and I will be mindful to serve her to the best of my power: and when your hand is in, you may crowd in my service to my Master Don Quixote de la Mancha, that he may see I am neither forgetful nor ungrateful; the rest I leave to you; put in what you will, and do your part like a good secretary, and a staunch Biscainer. Now take away here, and bring me something to eat; and then you shall see I am able to deal with all the spies, wizards, and cut-throat dogs that dare to meddle with me and my island. . . .

"I intend to clear this island of all filth and rubbish, of all rogues and vagrants, idle knaves and sturdy beggars. For I would like you to know, my good friends, that your slothful, lazy, lewd people in a commonwealth, are like drones in a bee-hive, that waste and devour the honey which the labouring bees gather. I design to encourage husbandmen, preserve the privileges of the gentry, reward virtuous persons, and, above all things, reverence religion, and have regard to the honour of religious men. What think you of this, my good friends? Do I talk to the purpose, or do I talk idly?" "You speak so well, my Lord Governor," answered the steward, "that I stand in admiration to hear a man so unlettered as you are (for I believe your Lordship cannot read at all) utter so many notable things, and in every word a sentence; far from what they who sent you hither, and they who are here present, ever expected from your understanding. But every day produces some new wonder, jests are turned into earnest, and those who designed to laugh at others, happened to be laughed at themselves.". . .

A continuation of Sancho Pança's government, with other passages, such as they are.

At last the Lord Governor was pleased to rise; and, by Dr. Pedro Rezio's order, they brought him for his breakfast a little conserve, and a draught of fair water, which he would have exchanged with all his heart for a good luncheon of bread, and a bunch of grapes; but seeing he could not help himself, he was forced to make the best of a bad market, and seem to be content, though full sore against his will and appetite; for the doctor made him believe, that to eat but little, and that which was dainty, enlivened the spirits, and sharpened the wit, and consequently such a sort of diet was most proper for persons in authority and weighty employments, wherein there is less need of the strength of the body than of that of the mind. This sophistry served to famish Sancho, who, half-dead with hunger, cursed in his heart both the government and him that had given it him. However, hungry as he was, by the strength of his slender breakfast, he failed not to give audience that day; and the first that came before him was a stranger, who put the following case to him, the steward and the rest of the attendants being present.

"My Lord," said he, "a large river divides in two parts one and the same lordship. I beg your honour to lend me your attention, for it is a case of great importance, and some difficulty. Upon this river there is a bridge; at one end of which there stands a gallows, and a kind of court of justice, where four judges used to sit, for the execution of a certain law made by the lord of the land and river, which runs thus:

" 'Whoever intends to pass from one end of this bridge to the other, must first upon his oath declare whither he goes, and what his business is. If he swear truth, he may go on; but if he swear false, he shall be hanged, and die without remission upon the gibbet at the end of the bridge.'

"After due promulgation of this law, many people, notwithstanding its severity, adventured to go over this bridge, and as it appeared they swore true, the judges permitted them to pass unmolested. It happened one day that a certain passenger being sworn, declared, that by the oath he had taken, he was come to die upon that gallows, and that was all his business.

"This put the judges to a nonplus; 'for,' said they, 'if we let this man pass freely, he is forsworn, and according to the letter of the law he ought to die; if we hang him, he has sworn truth, seeing he swore he was to die on that gibbet; and then by the same law we should let him pass.'

"Now your Lordship's judgment is desired what the judges ought to do with this man. For they are still at a standing, not knowing what to determine in this case; and having been informed of your sharp wit, and great capacity in resolving difficult questions, they sent me to beseech your Lordship, in their names, to give your opinion in so intricate and knotty a case."

"To deal plainly with you," answered Sancho;

"those worshipful judges that sent you hither might as well have spared themselves the labour; for I am more inclined to dulness I assure you than sharpness: however, let me hear your question once more, that I may thoroughly understand it, and perhaps I may at last hit the nail on the head." The man repeated the question again and again; and when he had done, "To my thinking," said Sancho, "this question may be presently answered, as thus: the man swore he came to die on the gibbet, and if he dies there, he swore true, and according to the law he ought to be free, and go over the bridge. On the other side, if you do not hang him, he swore false, and by the same law he ought to be hanged." "It is as your Lordship says," replied the stranger, "you have stated the case right." "Why then," said Sancho, "even let that part of the man that swore true freely pass; and hang the other part of the man that swore false, and so the law will be fulfilled." "But then, my Lord," replied the stranger, "the man must be divided into two parts, which if we do, he certainly dies, and the law, which must every tittle of it be observed, is not put in execution."

"Well, hark you me, honest man," said Sancho, "either I am a very dunce, or there is as much reason to put this same person you talk of to death as to let him live and pass the bridge; for if the truth saves him, the lie condemns him. Now the case stands thus, I would have you tell those gentlemen that sent you to me, since there is as much reason to bring him off, as to condemn him, that they even let him go free; for it is always more commendable to do good than hurt. And this I would give you under my own hand, if I could write. Nor do I speak this of my own head; but I remember one precept, among many others, that my master Don Quixote gave me the night before I went to govern this island, which was, that when the scale of justice is even, or a case is doubtful, we should prefer mercy before rigour; and it has pleased God I should call it to mind so luckily at this juncture." "For my part," said the steward, "this judgment seems to me so equitable, that I do not believe Lycurgus himself, who gave laws to the Lacedæmonians, could ever have decided the matter better than the great Sancho has done.". . .

The toilsome end and conclusion of Sancho Pança's government.

It was now but the seventh night, after so many days of his government, when the careful Governor had betaken himself to his repose, sated not with bread and wine, but cloyed with hearing causes, pronouncing sentences, making statutes, and putting out orders and proclamations: scarce was sleep, in spite of wakeful hunger, beginning to close his eyes, when, of a sudden, he heard a great noise of bells, and most dreadful out-cries, as if the whole island had been sinking. Presently he started, and sat up in his bed, and listened with great attention, to try if he could learn how far this uproar might concern him. But while he was thus hearkening in the dark, a great number of drums and trumpets were heard, and that sound being added to the noise of the bells and the cries, gave so dreadful an alarm, that his fear and terror increased, and he was in a sad consternation. Up he leaped out of his bed, and put on his slippers, the ground being damp, and without anything else in the world on but his shirt, ran and opened his chamber-door, and saw about twenty men come running along the galleries with lighted links in one hand, and drawn swords in the other, all crying out, "Arm! my Lord Governor, arm! a world of enemies are got into the island, and we are undone, unless your valour and conduct relieve us." Thus bawling and running with great fury and disorder, they got to the door where Sancho stood quite scared out of his senses. "Arm, arm, this moment, my Lord!" cried one of them, "if you have not a mind to be lost with the whole island."

"What would you have me arm for?" quoth Sancho. "Do I know anything of arms or fighting, think ye? why do not ye rather send for Don Quixote, my Master, he will dispatch your enemies in a trice? Alas! as I am a sinner to Heaven, I understand nothing of this hasty service." "For shame, my Lord Governor," said another, "what a faint-heartedness is this! See, we bring you here arms offensive and defensive; arm yourself, and march to the market-place. Be our leader and captain as you ought, and show yourself a Governor." "Why then, arm me, and good luck attend me," quoth Sancho; with that they brought him two large shields, which they had provided, and without letting him put on his other clothes, clapped them over his shirt, and tied the one behind upon his back, and the other before upon his breast, having got his arms through some holes made on purpose. Now the shields being fastened to his body, as hard as cords could bind them, the poor Governor was cased up and immured as straight as an arrow, without being able so much as to bend his knees, or stir a step. Then, having put a lance into his hand for him to lean upon, and keep himself up, they desired him to march, and lead them on, and put life into them all, telling him that they did not doubt of victory, since they had him for their commander. "March!" quoth Sancho, "how do you think I am able to do it, squeezed as I am? These boards stick so plaguy close to me, I cannot so much as bend the joints of my knees; you must even carry me in your arms, and lay me across or set me upright, before some passage, and I will make good that spot of ground, either with this lance or my body." "Fie, my Lord Governor," said another, "it is

more your fear than your armour that stiffens your legs, and hinders you from moving. Move, move, march on, it is high time, the enemy grows stronger, and the danger presses."

The poor Governor, thus urged and upbraided, endeavoured to go forwards; but the first motion he made, threw him to the ground at his full length, so heavily, that he gave over all his bones for broken; and there he lay like a huge tortoise in his shell, or a flitch of bacon clapped between two boards, or like a boat overturned upon a flat, with the keel upwards. Nor had those drolling companions the least compassion upon him as he lay; quite contrary, having put out their lights, they made a terrible noise, and clattered with their swords, and trampled to and again upon the poor Governor's body, and laid on furiously with their swords upon his shields, insomuch, that if he had not shrunk his head into them for shelter, he had been in a woeful condition. Squeezed up in his narrow shell, he was in a grievous fright, and a terrible sweat, praying from the bottom of his heart, for deliverance from the cursed trade of governing islands. Some kicked him, some stumbled and fell upon him, and one among the rest jumped full upon him, and there stood for some time, as on a watch-tower, like a general encouraging his soldiers, and giving orders, crying out, "There boys, there! the enemies charge most on that side, make good that breach, secure that gate, down with those scaling ladders, fetch fire-balls, more granadoes, burning pitch, rosin, and kettles of scalding oil. Intrench yourselves, get beds, quilts, cushions, and barricade the streets;" in short, he called for all the instruments of death, and all the engines used for the defence of a city that is besieged and stormed

Sancho lay snug, though sadly bruised, and while he endured all quietly, "Oh that it would please the Lord," quoth he to himself, "that this island were but taken, or that I were fairly dead, or out of this peck of troubles." At last Heaven heard his prayers; and, when he least expected it, he heard them cry, "Victory! victory! the enemy is routed. Now, my Lord Governor, rise, come and enjoy the fruits of conquest, and divide the spoils taken from the enemy, by the valour of your invincible arms." "Help me up," cried poor Sancho in a doleful tone; and when they had set him on his legs, "Let all the enemy I have routed," quoth he, "be nailed to my forehead: I will divide no spoils of enemies: but if I have one friend here, I only beg he would give me a draught of wine to comfort me, and help me to dry up the sweat that I am in; for I am all over water." Thereupon they wiped him, gave him wine and took off his shields: after that, as he sat upon his bed, what with his fright, and what with the toil he had endured, he fell into a swoon, insomuch that those who acted this scene, began to repent they had carried it so far. But Sancho recovering from his fit in a little time, they also recovered from their uneasiness. Being come to himself, he asked what it was o'clock? They answered, it was now break of day. He said nothing; but, without any words, began to put on his clothes. While this was doing, and he continued seriously silent, all the eyes of the company were fixed upon him, wondering what could be the meaning of his being in such haste to put on his clothes.

At last, he made an end of dressing himself, and creeping along softly (for he was too much bruised to go along very fast), he got to the stable, followed by all the company; and coming to Dapple, he embraced the quiet animal, gave him a loving kiss on the forehead, and, with tears in his eyes, "Come hither," said he, "my friend, thou faithful companion, and fellow-sharer in my travels and miseries; when thee and I consorted together, and all my cares were but to mend thy furniture, and feed thy little carcase, then happy were my days, my months, and years. But since I forsook thee, and clambered up the towers of ambition and pride, a thousand woes, a thousand torments, and four thousand tribulations have haunted and worried my soul." While he was talking thus, he fitted on his pack-saddle, nobody offering to say anything to him. This done, with a great deal of difficulty he mounted his ass, and then addressing himself to the steward, the secretary, the gentleman-waiter, and Dr. Pedro Rezio, and many others that stood by, "Make way, gentlemen," said he, "and let me return to my former liberty. Let me go that I may seek my old course of life, and rise again from that death that buries me here alive. I was not born to be a Governor, nor to defend islands nor cities from enemies that break in upon them. I know better what belongs to ploughing, delving, pruning, and planting of vineyards, than how to make laws, and defend countries and kingdoms. St. Peter is very well at Rome; which is as much as to say, let every one stick to the calling he was born to. A spade does better in my hand than a Governor's truncheon; and I had rather fill my belly with a mess of plain porridge, than lie at the mercy of a coxcombly physic-monger that starves me to death. I had rather solace myself under the shade of an oak in summer, and wrap up my corpse in a double sheep-skin in the winter at my liberty, than lay me down with the slavery of a government in fine holland-sheets, and case my hide in furs and richest sables. Heaven be with you, gentle-folks, and pray tell my Lord Duke from me, that naked I was born, and naked I am at present. I have neither won nor lost, which is as much as to say, without a penny I came to this government, and without a penny I leave it, quite contrary to what governors of islands use to do, when they leave them. Clear the way,

then, I beseech you, and let me pass; I must get myself wrapped up all over in cerecloth; for I do not think I have a sound rib left, thanks to the enemies that have walked over me all night long."

"This must not be, my Lord Governor," said Dr. Rezio, "for I will give your Honour a balsamic drink, that is a specific against falls, dislocations, contusions, and all manner of bruises, and that will presently restore you to your former health and strength. And then for your diet, I promise to take a new course with you, and to let you eat abundantly of whatsoever you please." "It is too late, Mr. Doctor," answered Sancho; "you should as soon make me turn Turk, as hinder me from going. No, no, these tricks shall not pass upon me again, you shall as soon make me fly to heaven without wings, as get me to stay here, or ever catch me nibbling at a government again, though it were served up to me in a covered dish. I am of the blood of the Panças, and we are all wilful and positive. If once we cry Odd, it shall be odd in spite of all mankind, though it be even. Go to, then: let the pismire leave behind him in this stable, those wings that lifted him up in the air to be a prey to martlets and sparrows. Fair and softly. Let me now tread again on plain ground; though I may not wear pinked Cordovan leather-pumps, I shall not want a pair of sandals to my feet. Every sheep to her mate. Let not the cobbler go beyond his last; and so let me go, for it is late." "My Lord Governor," said the steward, "though it grieves us to part with your Honour, your sense and Christian behaviour engaging us to covet your company, yet we would not presume to stop you against your inclination: but you know that every Governor, before he leaves the place he has governed, is bound to give an account of his administration. Be pleased therefore to do so for the ten days you have been among us, and then peace be with you." "No man has power to call me to an account," replied Sancho, "unless it be by my Lord Duke's appointment. Now to him it is that I am going, and to him I will give a fair and square account. And indeed, going away so bare as I do, there needs no greater signs that I have governed like an angel." "In truth," said Dr. Rezio, "the great Sancho is in the right; and I am of opinion, we ought to let him go; for certainly the Duke will be very glad to see him." Thereupon they all agreed to let him pass, offering first to attend him, and supply him with whatever he might want in his journey, either for entertainment or conveniency. Sancho told them, that all he desired was a little corn for his ass, and half a cheese, and half a loaf for himself; having occasion for no other provisions in so short a journey. With that they all embraced him, and he embraced them all, not without tears in

94. **the ten days**; but Sancho governed only seven days.

his eyes, leaving them in admiration of the good sense which he discovered both in his discourse and unalterable resolution. . . .

How Don Quixote took his leave of the Duke.

Don Quixote thought it now time to leave the idle life he led in the castle, believing it a mighty fault, thus to shut himself up, and indulge his sensual appetite among the tempting varieties of dainties and delights, which the Lord and Lady of the place provided for his entertainment, as a knight-errant; and he thought he was to give a strict account to Heaven for a course of life so opposite to his active profession. Accordingly, one day he acquainted the Duke and Duchess with his sentiments, and begged their leave to depart. They both seemed very unwilling to part with him, but yet at last yielded to his entreaties. . . .

Don Quixote, having taken his solemn leave of the Duke and Duchess over-night, left his apartment the next morning, and appeared in his armour in the courtyard, the galleries all round about being filled at the same time with the people of the house; the Duke and Duchess being also got thither to see him: Sancho was upon his Dapple, with his cloak-bag, his wallet, and his provision, very brisk and cheerful. . . . Then Don Quixote bowed his head, and after he had made a low obeisance to the Duke, the Duchess, and all the company, he turned about with Rozinante; and Sancho following him on Dapple, they left the castle, and took the road for Saragossa. . . .

Of an unlucky adventure, which Don Quixote laid most to heart of any that had yet befallen him.

Now it happened one morning that Don Quixote going abroad to take the air upon the seashore, armed at all points, according to his custom (his arms, as he said, being his best attire, as combat was his refreshment), he spied a knight riding towards him, armed like himself from head to foot, with a bright moon blazoned on his shield, who coming within hearing, called out to him, "Illustrious, and never-sufficiently extolled Don Quixote de la Mancha, I am the Knight of the White Moon, whose incredible achievements, perhaps, have reached thy ears. Lo, I am come to enter into combat with thee, and to compel thee by dint of sword, to own and acknowledge my mistress, by whatever name and dignity she be distinguished, to be without any degree of comparison, more beautiful than thy Dulcinea del Toboso. Now if thou wilt fairly confess this truth, thou freest thyself from certain death, and me from the trouble of taking or giving thee thy life. If not, the conditions of our combat are these: if victory be on my side, thou shalt be obliged immediately to forsake thy arms, and the quest of adventures, and to return to thy own home, where thou shalt engage to live quietly and peaceably for the space of one whole year, without laying hand on thy sword, to the improvement of thy estate, and the salvation of thy soul. But if thou comest off conqueror, my life is at thy mercy, my horse and arms shall be thy trophy, and the fame of all my former exploits, by the lineal descent of conquest, be vested in thee as victor. Consider what thou hast to do, and let thy answer be quick, for my dispatch is limited to this very day."

Don Quixote was amazed and surprised as much at the arrogance of the Knight of the White Moon's challenge, as at the subject of it; so with a solemn and austere address, "Knight of the White Moon," said he, "whose achievements have as yet been kept from my knowledge, it is more than probable, that you have never seen the illustrious Dulcinea; for had you ever viewed her perfections, you had there found arguments enough to convince you, that no beauty past, present, or to come, can parallel hers; and therefore, without giving you directly the lie, I only tell thee, knight, thou art mistaken, and this position I will maintain by accepting your challenge on your conditions, except that article of your exploits descending to me; for, not knowing what character your actions bear, I shall rest satisfied with the fame of my own, by which, such as they are, I am willing to abide. And since your time is so limited, choose your ground, and begin your career as soon as you will, and expect to be met with a fair field and no favour: to whom God shall give her, St. Peter give his blessing."

Don Quixote making some short ejaculations to Heaven and his mistress, as he always used upon these occasions, began his career, without either sound of trumpet or any other signal. His adversary was no less forward; for setting spurs to his horse, which was much the swifter, he met Don Quixote before he had run half his career, so forcibly, that without making use of his lance, which it is thought he lifted up on purpose, he overthrew the Knight of la Mancha and Rozinante, both coming to the ground with a terrible fall.

The Knight of the White Moon got immediately upon him, and clapping the point of his lance to his face, "Knight," cried he, "you are vanquished, and a dead man, unless you immediately fulfil the conditions of your combat." Don Quixote, bruised and stunned with his fall, without lifting up his beaver, answered in a faint hollow voice, as if he had spoken out of a tomb, "Dulcinea del Toboso is the most beautiful woman in the world, and I the most unfortunate knight upon the earth. It were unjust that such perfection should suffer through my weakness. No, pierce my body with thy lance, Knight, and let my life expire with my honour." "Not so rigorous neither," replied the conqueror, "let the fame of the Lady Dulcinea del Toboso remain entire and unblemished; provided the great Don Quixote return home for a year, as we agreed before the combat, I am satisfied.". . . To which Don Quixote answered, that upon condition he should be enjoined nothing to the prejudice of Dulcinea, he would, upon the faith of a true knight, be punctual in the performance of everything else. This acknowledgment being made, the Knight of the White Moon turned about his horse, and . . . rode at a hand-gallop into the city. . . .

Don Quixote was lifted up, and upon taking off his helmet, they found him pale, and in a cold sweat. As for Rozinante, he was in so bad a plight, that he could not stir for the present. Then, as for Sancho, he was in so heavy a taking, that he knew not what to do, nor what to say; he was sometimes persuaded he was in a dream, sometimes he fancied this rueful adventure was all witchcraft and enchantment. In short, he found his master discomfited in the face of the world, and bound to good behaviour, and to lay aside his arms for a whole year. Now he thought his glory eclipsed, his hopes of greatness vanished into smoke, and his master's promises like his bones, put out of joint by that cursed fall, which he was afraid had at once crippled Rozinante and his master. At last, the vanquished knight was put into a chair, and they carried him into town. . . .

An account of the Knight of the White Moon and other passages.

Don Antonio Moreno followed the Knight of the White Moon to his inn, whither he was attended by a troublesome rabble of boys. The knight being got to his chamber, where his squire waited to take off his armour, Don Antonio came in, declaring he would not be shook off, till he had discovered who he was. The knight finding that the gentleman would not leave him: "Sir," said he, "since I lie under no obligation of concealing myself, if you please, while my man disarms me, you shall hear the whole truth of the story.

"You must know, sir, I am called the Bachelor Carrasco: I live in the same town with this Don Quixote, whose unaccountable frenzy has moved all his neighbours, and me among the rest, to endeavour by some means to cure his madness; in order to which, believing that rest and ease would prove the surest remedy, I bethought myself of this present stratagem. . . . For I know him to be so nicely punctual in whatever his word and honour is engaged for, that he will undoubtedly perform his promise. This, sir, is the sum of the whole story, and I beg the favour of you to conceal me from Don Quixote, that my project may not be ruined, . . .

30. **Don Antonio Moreno;** who had seen the combat.

and that the honest gentleman, who is naturally a man of good parts, may recover his understanding.". . .

Six days did Don Quixote keep his bed, very dejected, sullen, and out of humour, and full of severe and black reflections on his fatal overthrow. Sancho was his comforter, and among other his crumbs of comfort, "My dear master," quoth he, "cheer up, come pluck up a good heart, and be thankful for coming off no worse. Why, a man has broke his neck with a less fall, and you have not so much as a broken rib. Consider, sir, that they that game, sometimes must lose; we must not always look for bacon where we see the hooks. Come, sir, cry a fig for the doctor, since you will not need him this bout; let us jog home fair and softly, without thinking any more of sauntering up and down, nobody knows whither, in quest of adventures and bloody noses. Why, sir, I am the greatest loser, if you go to that, though it is you that are in the worst pickle. It is true, I was weary of being a governor, and gave over all thoughts that way; but yet I never parted with my inclination of being an earl; and now, if you miss being a king, by casting off your knight-errantry, poor I may go whistle for my earldom." "No more of that, Sancho," cried Don Quixote; "I shall only retire for a year, and then reassume my honourable profession, which will undoubtedly secure me a kingdom, and thee an earldom." "Heaven grant it may," quoth Sancho, "and no mischief betide us: Hope well, and have well, says the proverb.". . .

Two days after, Don Quixote, being somewhat recovered . . . and having caused his armour to be laid on Dapple, set forwards on his journey home: Sancho thus being forced to trudge after him on foot. . . .

How Don Quixote fell sick, made his last will, and died.

As all human things, especially the lives of men, are transitory, their very beginnings being but steps to their dissolution; so Don Quixote, who was no way exempted from the common fate, was snatched away by death, when he least expected it. Whether his sickness was the effect of his melancholy reflections, or whether it was so pre-ordained by Heaven, most certain it is, he was seized with a violent fever, that confined him to his bed six days.

All that time his good friends, the curate, bachelor, and barber, came often to see him, and his trusty squire Sancho Pança never stirred from his bedside.

They conjectured that his sickness proceeded from the regret of his defeat, and his being disappointed of Dulcinea's disenchantment; and accordingly they left nothing unessayed to divert him. The bachelor begged him to pluck up a good heart, and rise, that they might begin their pastoral life . . . but this had no effect on Don Quixote, for he still continued dejected. A physician was sent for, who, upon feeling his pulse, did not very well like it; and therefore desired him of all things to provide for his soul's health, for that of his body was in a dangerous condition. Don Quixote heard this with much more temper than those about him; for his niece, his housekeeper, and his squire fell a-weeping as bitterly as if he had been laid out already. The physician was of opinion, that mere melancholy and vexation had brought him to his approaching end. Don Quixote desired them to leave him a little, because he found himself inclinable to rest; they retired, and he had a hearty sleep of about six hours which the maid and niece were afraid had been his last.

At length he waked, and with a loud voice, "Blessed be the Almighty," cried he, "for this great benefit He has vouchsafed to do me! Infinite are His mercies; they are greater, and more in number than the sins of men." The niece hearkening very attentively to these words of her uncle, and finding more sense in them than there was in his usual talk, at least since he had fallen ill: "What do you say, Sir," said she, "has any thing extraordinary happened? What mercies are these you mention?"

"Mercies," answered he, "that Heaven has this moment vouchsafed to show me, in spite of all my iniquities. My judgment is returned clear and undisturbed and that cloud of ignorance is now removed, which the continual reading of those damnable books of knight-errantry had cast over my understanding. Now, I perceive their nonsense and impertinence, and am only sorry the discovery happens so late, when I want time to make amends by those studies that should enlighten my soul, and prepare me for futurity. I find, niece, my end approaches; but I would have it such, that though my life has got me the character of a madman I may deserve a better at my death. Dear child," continued he, "send for my honest friend the curate, the bachelor Carrasco, and Mr. Nicholas the barber, for I intend to make my confession and my will." His niece was saved the trouble of sending, for presently they all three came in; which Don Quixote perceiving, "My good friends," said he, "I have happy news to tell you; I am no longer Don Quixote de la Mancha, but Alonso Quixano, the same whom the world for his fair behaviour has been formerly pleased to call the Good. I now declare myself an enemy to Amadis de Gaul, and his whole generation; all profane stories of knight-errantry, all romances I detest. I have a true sense of the danger of reading them, and of all my past follies, and through Heaven's mercy, and my own experience, I abhor them." His three friends were not a little surprised to hear him talk at this rate, and concluded some new frenzy had possessed

him. "What now?" said Samson to him. "What is all this to the purpose, Signor Don Quixote? We have just had the news that the Lady Dulcinea is disenchanted; and now we are upon the point of turning shepherds, to sing, and live like princes, you are dwindled down to a hermit."

"No more of that, I beseech you," replied Don Quixote; "all the use I shall make of these follies at present, is to heighten my repentance; and though they have hitherto proved prejudicial, yet, by the assistance of Heaven, they may turn to my advantage at my death: I find it comes fast upon me; therefore, pray, gentlemen, let us be serious. I want a priest to receive my confession, and a scrivener to draw up my will. There is no trifling at a time like this; I must take care of my soul; and therefore pray let the scrivener be sent for, while Mr. Curate prepares me by confession."

Don Quixote's words put them all into such admiration, that they stood gazing upon one another; they thought they had reason to doubt of the return of his understanding, and yet they could not help believing him. They were also apprehensive he was near the point of death, considering the sudden recovery of his intellects; and he delivered himself after that with so much sense, discretion, and piety, and showed himself so resigned to the will of Heaven, that they made no scruple to believe him restored to his perfect judgment at last. The curate thereupon cleared the room of all the company but himself and Don Quixote, and then confessed him. In the meantime the bachelor ran for the scrivener, and presently brought him with him; and Sancho Pança being informed by the bachelor how ill his master was, and finding his niece and housekeeper all in tears, began to make wry faces, and fall a-crying. The curate having heard the sick person's confession, came out and told them, that the good Alonso Quixano was very near his end, and certainly in his senses; and therefore, they had best go in, that he might make his will. These dismal tidings opened the sluices of the housekeeper's, the niece's, and the good squire's swollen eyes, so that a whole inundation of tears burst out of those flood-gates, and a thousand sighs from their hearts; for indeed, either as Alonso Quixano, or as Don Quixote de la Mancha, as it has been observed, the sick gentleman had always showed himself such a good-natured man, and of so agreeable a behaviour, that he was not only beloved by his family, but by every one that knew him.

The scrivener, with the rest of the company, then went into the chamber, and the preamble and former part of the will being drawn, and the testator having recommended his soul to Heaven, and bequeathed his body to the earth, according to custom, he came to the legacies, as follows:

"Item, I give and bequeath to Sancho Pança,

whom in my madness I made my squire, whatever money he has, or may have of mine in his hands; and whereas there are reckonings and accounts to be adjusted between us, for what he has received and disbursed; my will and pleasure is, that whatever may remain due to me, which can be but small, be enjoyed by him as my free gift, without any let or molestation, and much good may it do him. And as, when I was mad, he was through my means made governor of an island, I would now, in my right senses, give him the government of a kingdom, were it in my power, in consideration of his integrity and faithfulness. And now, my friend," said he, turning to Sancho, "pardon me that I have brought upon thee, as well as myself, the scandal of madness, by drawing thee into my own errors, and persuading thee that there have been and still are knights-errant in the world." "Woe's me, my dear master's worship!" cried Sancho, all in tears, "do not die this bout, but even take my counsel, and live on many years; it is the maddest trick a man can ever play in his whole life, to let his breath sneak out of his body without any more ado, and without so much as a rap over the pate, or a kick on the guts; to go out like the snuff of a farthing candle, and die merely of the mulligrubs, or the sullens. For shame, sir, do not give way to sluggishness, but get out of your doleful dumps, and rise. Is this a time to lie honing and groaning a-bed, when we should be in the fields in our shepherd's clothing, as we had resolved? Ten to one but behind some bush, or under some hedge, we may find the Lady Madam Dulcinea, stripped of her enchanted rags, and as fine as a queen. Mayhaps you take it to heart, that you were unhorsed, and a little crupper-scratched the other day; but if that be all, lay the blame upon me, and say it was my fault, in not girting Rozinante tight enough. You know too, there is nothing more common in your errantry-books, than for the knights to be every foot jostled out of the saddle. There is nothing but ups and downs in this world, and he that is cast down to-day, may be a cock-a-hoop to-morrow." "Even so," said Samson, "honest Sancho has a right notion of the matter." "Soft and fair, gentleman," replied Don Quixote, "never look for birds of this year in the nests of the last: I was mad, but I am now in my senses; I was once Don Quixote de la Mancha but am now, as I said before, the plain Alonso Quixano, and I hope the sincerity of my words, and my repentance, may restore me to the same esteem you have had for me before; and so, Mr. Scrivener, pray go on."

"Item, I constitute and appoint Antonia Quixano, my niece here present, sole heiress of all my estate both real and personal after all my just debts and legacies, bequeathed by these presents, shall have been payed, satisfied, and deducted, out of the best of my goods and chattels; and the first of that kind to be discharged shall be the salary due to my house-keeper, together with twenty ducats over and above her wages; which said sum I leave and bequeath her to buy her mourning.

"Item, I appoint Mr. Curate, and Mr. Samson Carrasco the bachelor, here present, to be the executors of this my last will and testament.

"Item, it is my will, that if my niece Antonia Quixano be inclinable to marry, it be with none but a person, who, upon strict inquiry, shall be found never to have read a book of knight-errantry in his life; and in case it appears, that he has been conversant in such books, and that she persists in her resolution to marry him, she is then to forfeit all right and title to my bequest, which in such case, my executors are hereby empowered to dispose of to pious uses, as they shall think most proper.

"Item, I entreat the said executors, that if at any time they happen to meet with the author of a book now extant, entitled, 'The Second Part of the Achievements of Don Quixote de la Mancha,' they would from me most heartily beg his pardon for my being undesignedly the occasion of his writing such a parcel of impertinences as is contained in that book; for it is the greatest burthen to my departing soul, that ever I was the cause of his making such a thing public."

Having finished the will he fell into a swooning fit, and extended his body to the full length in the bed. All the company were troubled and alarmed, and ran to his assistance: however, he came to himself at last; but relapsed into the like fits almost every hour, for the space of three days that he lived after he had made his will. . . .

Thus died that ingenious gentleman Don Quixote de la Mancha, whose native place Cid Hamet has not thought fit directly to mention, with design that all the towns and villages in La Mancha should contend for the honour of giving him birth, as the seven cities of Greece did for Homer.

Baldassare Castiglione

1478–1529

Cervantes' satire of the medieval knight and his chivalric code was in part the attack of Renaissance reason on the naïve idealism of the Middle Ages, and in part a sign that knighthood had lost its authority in a world where national monarchies had displaced feudalism. As strong kings destroyed the power of the barons, the nobles flocked to the kings' courts, where they exchanged armor and lance for ruffles and rapier, if not also for the poet's pen. The dashing knight, proud of his independence, became a graceful courtier most valuable as a decoration for his monarch's retinue.

The ideal of the Renaissance gentleman is summarized in *The Courtier* (1514) by the Italian Castiglione. The author was himself a graceful fixture at the elegant court of Guidobaldo, Duke of Urbino. He had enjoyed a classical education at Milan and served as soldier to the Duke of that city, but the Dukes of Urbino employed him as suave ambassador to Henry VII of England and Charles V of Spain. His death in 1529 was said to have been hastened by his shame at being falsely accused of treachery.

Castiglione made himself the arbiter of social elegance for all of Europe through his charming Platonic dialogue, *The Courtier,* in which a group of distinguished ladies and gentlemen of his day supposedly debate the qualities of the perfect courtier in the drawing room of the gracious Duchess of Urbino. The characters, especially the ladies, emerge as witty artistic creations in the lively give-and-take, designed as a model of polite conversation. No phase of aristocratic life from boudoir to throne room is overlooked in their discussions. Born to nobility for noble instincts and to wealth for freedom from toil, Castiglione's gentleman is to realize Cicero's ideal of *humanitas* through a classical education and through service to the state as chivalrous soldier and wise political adviser. Culture of body and mind is to produce the well-rounded aristocrat, whose instincts are further refined by the influence of a good and beautiful woman. Attempting to realize an ideal of beauty in his whole behavior, the courtier is to be the embodiment of grace and virtue, the accomplished swordsman, the exquisite poet or musician, the Platonic lover, the loyal friend. And beside him stands his noble consort, the bright but prudent lady who inspires and complements his stately character. The code of Castiglione was soon accepted as law by the ruder courts to the north, and the Seigneur de Bayard in France and Sir Philip Sidney in England gave Europe living models of the new ideal.*

The Book of the Courtier

BOOK ONE

14.

T HIS Courtier of ours should be nobly born and of gentle race; because it is far less unseemly for one of ignoble birth to fail in worthy deeds, than for one of noble birth, who, if he strays from the path of his predecessors, stains his family name, and not only fails to achieve but loses what has been achieved already; for noble birth is like a bright lamp that manifests and makes visible good and evil deeds, and kindles and stimulates to virtue both 10 by fear of shame and by hope of praise. And since

* To emphasize the qualities of the courtier and the concept of Platonic love, the dialogue background is omitted from these excerpts. *The Book of the Courtier.* Translated by Leonard Opdycke, copyright 1929 by Horace Liveright, New York.

this splendor of nobility does not illumine the deeds of the humbly born, they lack that stimulus and fear of shame, nor do they feel any obligation to advance beyond what their predecessors have done; while to the nobly born it seems a reproach not to reach at least the goal set them by their ancestors. And thus it nearly always happens that both in the profession of arms and in other worthy pursuits the most famous men have been of noble birth, because nature has implanted in everything that hidden seed 20 which gives a certain force and quality of its own essence to all things that are derived from it, and makes them like itself: as we see not only in the breeds of horses and of other animals, but also in trees, the shoots of which nearly always resemble the trunk; and if they sometimes degenerate, it arises from poor cultivation. And so it is with men, who if rightly trained are nearly always like those from whom they spring, and often better; but if there be no one to give them proper care, they 30 become like savages and never reach perfection.

It is true that, by favor of the stars or of nature, some men are endowed at birth with such graces that they seem not to have been born, but rather as if some god had formed them with his very hands and adorned them with every excellence of mind and body. So too there are many men so foolish and rude that one cannot but think that nature brought them into the world out of contempt or mockery. . . . There is a middle state between perfect grace 40 on the one hand and senseless folly on the other; and those who are not thus perfectly endowed by nature, with study and toil can in great part polish and amend their natural defects. Besides his noble birth, then, I would have the Courtier favored in this regard also, and endowed by nature not only with talent and beauty of person and feature, but with a certain grace and (as we say) air that shall make him at first sight pleasing and agreeable to all who see him; and I would have this an ornament 50 that should dispose and unite all his actions, and in his outward aspect give promise of whatever is worthy the society and favor of every great lord.

17. But to come to some details, I am of opinion that the principal and true profession of the Courtier ought to be that of arms; which I would have him follow actively above all else, and be known among others as bold and strong, and loyal to whomsoever he serves. And he will win a reputation for these good qualities by exercising them at all times and in 60 all places, since one may never fail in this without severest censure. And just as among women, their fair fame once sullied never recovers its first lustre, so the reputation of a gentleman who bears arms, if once it be in the least tarnished with cowardice or other disgrace, remains forever infamous before the world and full of ignominy. Therefore the more

our Courtier excels in this art, the more he will be worthy of praise; and yet I do not deem essential in him that perfect knowledge of things and those other qualities that befit a commander; since this would be too wide a sea, let us be content, as we have said, with perfect loyalty and unconquered courage, and that he be always seen to possess them. For the courageous are often recognized even more in small things than in great; and frequently in perils of importance and where there are many spectators, some men are to be found, who, although their hearts be dead within them, yet, moved by shame or by the presence of others, press forward almost with their eyes shut, and do their duty God knows how. While on occasions of little moment, when they think they can avoid putting themselves in danger without being detected, they are glad to keep safe. But those who, even when they do not expect to be observed or seen or recognized by anyone, show their ardor and neglect nothing, however paltry, that may be laid to their charge,—they have that strength of mind which we seek in our Courtier. . . .

Therefore let the man we are seeking, be very bold, stern, and always among the first, where the enemy are to be seen; and in every other place, gentle, modest, reserved, above all things avoiding ostentation and that impudent self-praise by which men ever excite hatred and disgust in all who hear them.

20. Coming to the bodily frame, I say it is enough if this be neither extremely short nor tall, for both of these conditions excite a certain contemptuous surprise, and men of either sort are gazed upon in much the same way that we gaze on monsters. Yet if we must offend in one of the two extremes, it is preferable to fall a little short of the just measure of height than to exceed it, for besides often being dull of intellect, men thus huge of body are also unfit for every exercise of agility, which thing I should much wish in the Courtier. And so I would have him well built and shapely of limb, and would have him show strength and lightness and suppleness, and know all bodily exercises that befit a man of war; whereof I think the first should be to handle every sort of weapon well on foot and on horse, to understand the advantages of each, and especially to be familiar with those weapons that are ordinarily used among gentlemen; for besides the use of them in war, where such sublety in contrivance is perhaps not needful, there frequently arise differences between one gentleman and another, which perhaps result in duels often fought with such weapons as happen at the moment to be within reach: thus knowledge of this kind is a very safe thing. Nor am I one of those who say that skill is forgotten in the hour of need; for he whose skill forsakes him at such

a time, indeed gives token that he has already lost heart and head through fear.

22. There are also many other exercises, which although not immediately dependent upon arms, yet are closely connected therewith, and greatly foster manly sturdiness; and one of the chief among these seems to me to be the chase, because it bears a certain likeness to war: and truly it is an amusement for great lords and befitting a man at court, and furthermore it is seen to have been much cultivated among the ancients. It is fitting also to know how to swim, to leap, to run, to throw stones, for besides the use that may be made of this in war, a man often has occasion to show what he can do in such matters; whence good esteem is to be won, especially with the multitude, who must be taken into account withal. Another admirable exercise, and one very befitting a man at court, is the game of tennis, in which are well shown the disposition of the body, the quickness and suppleness of every member, and all those qualities that are seen in nearly every other exercise. Nor less highly do I esteem vaulting on horse, which although it be fatiguing and difficult, makes a man very light and dexterous more than any other thing; and besides its utility, if this lightness is accompanied by grace, it is to my thinking a finer show than any of the others.

Our Courtier having once become more than fairly expert in these exercises, I think he should leave the others on one side: such as turning summersaults, rope-walking, and the like, which savor of the mountebank and little befit a gentleman.

But since one cannot devote himself to such fatiguing exercises continually, and since repetition becomes very tiresome and abates the admiration felt for what is rare, we must always diversify our life with various occupations. For this reason I would have our Courtier sometimes descend to quieter and more tranquil exercises, and in order to escape envy and to entertain himself agreeably with everyone, let him do whatever others do, yet never departing from praiseworthy deeds, and governing himself with that good judgment which will keep him from all folly; but let him laugh, jest, banter, frolic, and dance, yet in such fashion that he shall always appear genial and discreet, and that everything he may do or say shall be stamped with grace.

26. . . . Having often considered whence this grace springs, laying aside those men who have it by nature, I find one universal rule concerning it, which seems to me worth more in this matter than any other in all things human that are done or said: and that is to avoid affectation to the uttermost and as it were a very sharp and dangerous rock; and, to use possibly a new word, to practice in everything a certain nonchalance that shall conceal design and show that what is done and said is done without

effort and almost without thought. From this I believe grace is in large measure derived, because everyone knows the difficulty of those things that are rare and well done, and therefore facility in them excites the highest admiration; while on the other hand, to strive and as the saying is to drag by the hair, is extremely disgraceful, and makes us esteem everything slightly, however great it be. . . .

27. . . . In nonchalance (which is praiseworthy in itself), I do not think that it is less a vice of affectation to let the clothes fall from one's back, than in care of dress (which also is praiseworthy in itself), to hold the head stiff for fear of disarranging one's locks, or to carry a mirror in the peak of one's cap and a comb in one's sleeve, and to have a valet follow one about the streets with sponge and brush: for such care in dress and such nonchalance both touch upon excess, which is always offensive and contrary to that pure and charming simplicity which is pleasing to the human mind. . . .

33. . . . What is chiefly important for the Courtier, in order to speak and write well, is knowledge; for he who is ignorant and has nothing in his mind that merits being heard, can neither say it nor write it.

Next he must arrange in good order what he has to say or write; then express it well in words, which (if I do not err) ought to be precise, choice, rich, and rightly formed, but above all, in use even among the masses; because such words as these make the grandeur and pomp of speech, if the speaker has good sense and carefulness, and knows how to choose the words most expressive of his meaning, and to exalt them, to mould them like wax to his will, and to arrange them in such position and order that they shall at a glance show and make known their dignity and splendor, like pictures placed in good and proper light.

And this I say as well of writing as of speaking: in which however some things are required that are not needful in writing,—such as a good voice, not too thin and soft like a woman's, nor yet so stern and rough as to smack of the rustic's,—but sonorous, clear, sweet, and well sounding, with distinct enunciation, and with proper bearing and gestures; which I think consist in certain movements of the whole body, not affected or violent, but tempered by a calm face and with a play of the eyes that shall give an effect of grace, accord with the words, and as far as possible express also, together with the gestures, the speaker's intent and feeling.

But all these things would be vain and of small moment, if the thoughts expressed by the words were not beautiful, ingenious, acute, elegant, and grave,—according to the need.

34. . . . Nor would I have him speak always of grave matters, but of amusing things, of games, jests, and waggery, according to the occasion; and in no place let him show vanity or childish folly. And again when he is speaking on an obscure or difficult subject, I would have him carefully explain his meaning with precision of both word and thought, and make every ambiguity clear and plain with a certain touch of unpedantic care. Likewise, where there is occasion, let him know how to speak with dignity and force, to arouse those emotions that are part of our nature, and to kindle them or to move them according to the need. Sometimes, with that simple candor that makes it seem as if nature herself were speaking, let him know how to soften them, and as it were to intoxicate them with sweetness, and so easily withal that the listener shall think that with very little effort he too could reach that excellence, and when he tries, shall find himself very far behind. . . .

41. In this way we avoid and hide affectation, and you can now see how opposed and destructive it is to grace in every office as well of the body as the mind: whereof we have thus far spoken little, and yet we must not omit it, for since the mind is of far more worth than the body, it deserves to be more cultivated and adorned. And as to what ought to be done in the case of our Courtier, we will lay aside the precepts of the many sage philosophers who write of this matter and define the properties of the mind and discuss so subtly about their rank,—and keeping to our subject, we will in a few words declare it to be enough that he be (as we say) an honest and upright man; for in this are included prudence, goodness, strength and temperance of mind, and all the other qualities that are proper to a name so honored. And I esteem him alone to be a true moral philosopher, who wishes to be good; and in this regard he needs few other precepts than that wish. And therefore Socrates was right in saying that he thought his teachings bore good fruit indeed whenever they incited anyone to understand and teach virtue: for they who have reached the goal of desiring nothing more ardently than to be good, easily acquire knowledge of everything needful therefor; so we will discuss this no further.

44. I would have him more than passably accomplished in letters, at least in those studies that are called the humanities, and conversant not only with the Latin language but with the Greek, for the sake of the many different things that have been admirably written therein. Let him be well versed in the poets, and not less in the orators and historians, and also proficient in writing verse and prose, especially in this vulgar tongue of ours; for besides the enjoyment he will find in it, he will by this means never lack agreeable entertainment with ladies, who are usually fond of such things. And if other occupations or want of study prevent his reaching such

perfection as to render his writings worthy of great praise, let him be careful to suppress them so that others may not laugh at him, and let him show them only to a friend whom he can trust: because they will at least be of this service to him, that the exercise will enable him to judge the work of others. For it very rarely happens that a man who is not accustomed to write, however learned he may be, can ever quite appreciate the toil and industry of writers, or taste the sweetness and excellence of style, and those latent niceties that are often found in the ancients. . . .

47. You must know that I am not content with the Courtier unless he be also a musician and unless, besides understanding and being able to read notes, he can play upon divers instruments. For if we consider rightly, there is to be found no rest from toil or medicine for the troubled spirit more becoming and praiseworthy in time of leisure, than this; and especially in courts, where besides the relief from tedium that music affords us all, many things are done to please the ladies, whose tender and gentle spirit is easily penetrated by harmony and filled with sweetness. Thus it is no marvel that in both ancient and modern times they have always been inclined to favor musicians, and have found refreshing spiritual food in music. . . .

52. . . . It is fitting for our Courtier to have knowledge of painting also, as being honorable and useful and highly prized in those times when men were of far greater worth than now they are. And if he should never derive from it other use or pleasure than the help it affords in judging the merit of statues ancient and modern, of vases, buildings, medals, cameos, intaglios, and the like,—it also enables him to appreciate the beauty of living bodies, not only as to delicacy of face but as to symmetry of all the other parts, both in men and in every other creature. Thus you see how a knowledge of painting is a source of very great pleasure. And let those think of this, who so delight in contemplating a woman's beauty that they seem to be in paradise, and yet cannot paint; which if they could do, they would have much greater pleasure, because they would more perfectly appreciate that beauty which engenders such satisfaction in their hearts.

BOOK TWO

17. But not even all these qualities in our Courtier will suffice to win universal favor of lords, cavaliers, and ladies, unless he has also a gentle and amiable manner in daily talk. And I verily believe it to be difficult to give any rule for this, because of the infinite variety of things that arise in conversation, and because among all the men on earth no two are found who have minds quite alike. So whoever has to prepare himself for conversation with many, must needs be guided by his own judgment, and distinguishing the differences between one man and another, must daily change his style and method according to the character of the person with whom he has to converse. . . .

18. I think that the conversation which the Courtier ought most to try in every way to make acceptable, is that which he holds with his prince; and although this word "conversation" implies a certain equality that seems impossible between a lord and his inferior, yet we will call it so for the present. Therefore, besides daily showing everyone that he possesses the worth we have already described, I would have the Courtier strive, with all the thoughts and forces of his mind, to love and almost to adore the prince whom he serves, above every other thing, and mould his wishes, habits, and all his ways to his prince's liking. . . .

Moreover it is possible without flattery to obey and further the wishes of him we serve, for I am speaking of those wishes that are reasonable and right, or of those that in themselves are neither good nor evil, such as would be a liking for play or a devotion to one kind of exercise above another. And I would have the Courtier bend himself to this even if he be by nature alien to it, so that on seeing him his lord shall always feel that he will have something agreeable to say; which will come about if he has the good judgment to perceive what his prince likes, and the wit and prudence to bend himself thereto, and a deliberate purpose to like that which perhaps he by nature dislikes. And adopting these precautions he will never be out of humor or melancholy before his prince, nor so taciturn as many are who seem to bear a grudge against their patrons, which is a truly odious thing. He will not be given to evil speaking, especially against his own lords; which often happens, for in courts there seems to rage a fury of such sort that those who have been most favored by their lord and have been raised to eminence from the lowest estate, are always complaining and speaking ill of him; which is unseemly not only in such as these, but even in those who chance to have been ill used. . . .

20. . . . To have the favor of princes, there is no better way than to deserve it. And when we see another man who is pleasing to a prince for any reason, we must not think to reach the same height ourselves by imitating him, for all things are not proper to all men. Thus there will sometimes be found a man who by nature is so ready at jesting that whatever he may say carries laughter with it, and he seems to have been born solely for that; and if another man, who has a sober habit of mind (however excellently endowed) tries to do the like, it will fall so cold and flat as to disgust those who

hear him, and he will prove exactly like that ass who tried to copy the dogs by frolicking with their master. Hence every man must understand himself and his own powers, and govern himself accordingly, and consider what things he ought to imitate, and what things he ought not.

38. I do not care at present to go more into detail in speaking of things that are too well known, such as that our Courtier ought not avow himself a great eater or drinker, or given to excess in any evil habit, or vile and ungoverned in his life, with certain peasant ways that recall the hoe and plough a thousand miles away; because a man of this kind may not hope to become a good Courtier, but can be set to no more fitting business than feeding sheep. . . . Wherefore the Courtier ought to shun these odious ways, and to praise the fine achievements of other men with kindness and good will; and although he may feel that he is admirable and far superior to all, yet he ought to appear not to think so.

But since such complete perfection as this is very rarely and perhaps never found in human nature, a man who is conscious of being lacking in some particular, ought not to despond thereat or lose hope of reaching a high standard, even though he cannot attain that perfect and supreme excellence to which he aspires. For in every art there are many grades that are honorable besides the highest, and whoever aims at the highest will seldom fail to rise more than half-way.

BOOK FOUR

5. I think that the aim of the perfect Courtier, which has not been spoken of till now, is to win for himself, by means of the accomplishments ascribed to him, the favor and mind of the prince whom he serves, that he may be able to say, and always shall say, the truth about everything which is fitting for the prince to know, without fear or risk of giving offence thereby; and that when he sees his prince's mind inclined to do something wrong, he may be quick to oppose, and gently to make use of the favor acquired by his good accomplishments, so as to banish every bad intent and lead his prince into the path of virtue. . . .

49. . . . By reviewing what has thus far been said, we might conclude that a Courtier who has to allure his prince to virtue by his worth and authority, must almost of necessity be old (because knowledge very rarely comes before years, and especially in those things that are learned by experience),— I do not know how becoming it is for him (being advanced in age) to be in love. For love does not sit well upon old men, and those things which in young men are delights, courtesies, and elegances very pleasing to women, in old men are extrava-

gances and ridiculous incongruities, and for him who practices them win hatred from women and derision from others. . . .

51. . . . I say, then, that according to the definition of the ancient sages love is naught but a certain desire to enjoy beauty; and as desire longs only for things that are perceived, perception must needs always precede desire, which by its nature wishes good things, but in itself is blind and does not perceive them. Therefore nature has so ordained that to every faculty of perception there is joined a certain faculty of appetite; and since in our soul there are three modes of perceiving, that is, by sense, by reason, and by intellect: from sense springs appetite, which we have in common with the brutes; from reason springs choice, which is peculiar to man; from the intellect, by which man is able to commune with the angels, springs will. Thus, just as sense perceives only things that are perceptible by the senses, appetite desires the same only; and just as intellect is directed solely to the contemplation of things intellectual, the will feeds only upon spiritual benefits. Being by nature rational and placed as a mean between these two extremes, man can at pleasure (by descending to sense or mounting to intellect) turn his desires now in the one direction and now in the other. In these two ways, therefore, it is possible to desire beauty, which universal name applies to all things (whether natural or artificial) that are framed in good proportion and due measure according to their nature.

52. But speaking of the beauty we have in mind, which is only that which is seen in the bodies and especially in the faces of men, and which excites this ardent desire that we call love,—we will say that it is an effluence of divine goodness, and that although it is diffused like the sun's light upon all created things, yet when it finds a face well proportioned and framed with a certain pleasant harmony of various colors embellished by lights and shadows and by an orderly distance and limit of outlines, it infuses itself therein and appears most beautiful, and adorns and illumines that object whereon it shines with grace and wonderful splendor, like a sunbeam falling on a beautiful vase of polished gold set with precious gems. Thus it agreeably attracts the eyes of men, and entering thereby, it impresses itself upon the soul, and stirs and delights her with a new sweetness throughout, and by kindling her it excites in her a desire for its own self.

Then, being seized with desire to enjoy this beauty as something good, if the soul allows herself to be guided by the judgment of sense, she runs into very grievous errors, and judges that the body wherein the beauty is seen is the chief cause thereof; and hence, in order to enjoy that beauty, she deems it necessary to join herself as closely to that body as she can; which is false: and accordingly, whoever thinks to enjoy the beauty by possessing the body deceives himself, and is moved, not by true perception through reasonable choice, but by false opinion through sensual appetite: wherefore the pleasure also that results therefrom is necessarily false and vicious. . . .

53. The cause, then, of this havoc in the minds of men is chiefly sense, which is very potent in youth, because the vigor of flesh and blood at that period gives to it as much strength as it takes away from reason, and hence easily leads the soul to follow appetite. For, finding herself plunged into an earthly prison and deprived of spiritual contemplation by being set the task of governing the body, the soul cannot of herself clearly comprehend the truth; wherefore, in order to have perception of things, she must needs go begging first notions from the senses, and so she believes them and bows before them and allows herself to be guided by them, especially when they have so much vigor that they almost force her; and as they are fallacious, they fill her with errors and false opinions.

Hence it nearly always happens that young men are wrapped in this love which is sensual and wholly rebellious to reason, and thus they become unworthy to enjoy the graces and benefits which love bestows upon its true subjects; nor do they feel any pleasures in love beyond those which the unreasoning animals feel, but anguish far more grievous.

This premise being admitted then,—and it is most true,—I say that the contrary happens to those who are of maturer age. For if such as these (when the soul is already less weighed down by bodily heaviness and when the natural heat begins to become tepid) are inflamed by beauty and turn thereto a desire guided by rational choice,—they are not deceived, and possess beauty perfectly. Therefore their possession of it always brings them good; because beauty is good, and hence true love of beauty is most good and holy, and always works for good in the mind of those who restrain the perversity of sense with the bridle of reason; which the old can do much more easily than the young.

57. . . . Beauty springs from God, and is like a circle of which goodness is the center. And hence, as there can be no circle without a center, there can be no beauty without goodness. Thus a wicked soul rarely inhabits a beautiful body, and for that reason outward beauty is a true sign of inward goodness. And this grace is impressed upon bodies, more or less, as an index of the soul, whereby she is known outwardly, as in the case of trees, in which the beauty of the blossom gives token of the excellence of the fruit. . . .

58. . . . The ugly are therefore for the most part wicked too, and the beautiful are good: and we may say that beauty is the pleasant, gay, acceptable, and desirable face of good, and that ugliness is the dark, disagreeable, unpleasant, and sad face of evil. And if you will consider all things, you will find that those which are good and useful always have a charm of beauty also. . . .

62. Therefore, when the gracious aspect of some fair woman meets his view, accompanied with such sweet behavior and gentle manners that he, as an adept in love, feels that his spirit accords with hers: as soon as he finds that his eyes lay hold upon her image and carry it to his heart; and that his soul begins to contemplate her with pleasure and to feel that influence within which stirs and warms it little by little; and that those quick spirits which shine out through the eyes continually add fresh tinder to the fire;—he ought at this first stage to provide a speedy cure, and arouse his reason, and therewith arm the fortress of his heart, and so shut the way to sense and appetite that they cannot enter there by force or trickery. Thus, if the flame is extinguished, the danger is extinguished also; but if it survives or grows, then the Courtier, feeling himself caught, must resolve on shunning wholly every stain of vulgar love, and thus enter on the path of divine love, with reason for guide. And first he must consider that the body wherein this beauty shines is not the fountain whence it springs, but rather that beauty (being an incorporeal thing and, as we have said, a heavenly beam) loses much of its dignity when it finds itself joined to vile and corruptible matter; for the more perfect it is the less it partakes thereof, and is most perfect when wholly separate therefrom. And he must consider that just as one cannot hear with the palate or smell with the ears, so too can beauty in no wise be enjoyed, nor can the desire which it excites in our minds be satisfied, by means of touch, but by that sense of which this beauty is the very object, namely, the power of vision.

Therefore let him shun the blind judgment of sense, and with his eyes enjoy the splendor of his lady, her grace, her amorous sparkle, the laughs, the ways, and all the other pleasant ornaments of her beauty. Likewise with his hearing let him enjoy the sweetness of her voice, the concord of her words, the harmony of her music (if this beloved be a musician). Thus will he feed his soul on sweetest food by means of these two senses—which have little of the corporeal and are ministers of reason—without passing in his desire for the body to any appetite less than seemly.

Next let him obey, please, and honor his lady with all reverence, and hold her dearer than himself, and prefer her conveniences and pleasures to his own, and love in her not less the beauty of mind than that of body. Therefore let him take care not to leave her to fall into any kind of error, but by admonition and good advice let him always seek to lead her on to modesty, to temperance, to true chastity, and see to it that no thoughts find place in her except those that are pure and free from every stain of vice; and by thus sowing virtue in the garden of her fair mind, he will gather fruits of fairest behavior too, and will taste them with wonderful delight. And this will be the true engendering and manifesting of beauty in beauty, which by some is said to be the end of love.

In such fashion will our Courtier be most acceptable to his lady, and she will always show herself obedient, sweet, and affable to him, and as desirous of pleasing him as of being loved by him; and the wishes of both will be most virtuous and harmonious, and they themselves will thus be very happy.

67. But besides these blessings the lover will find another much greater still, if he will employ this love as a step to mount to one much higher; which he will succeed in doing if he continually considers within himself how narrow a restraint it is to be always occupied in contemplating the beauty of one body only; and therefore, in order to escape such close bonds as these, in his thought he will little by little add so many ornaments, that by heaping all beauties together he will form a universal concept, and will reduce the multitude of these beauties to the unity of that single beauty which is spread over human nature at large. In this way he will no longer contemplate the particular beauty of one woman, but that universal beauty which adorns all bodies; and thus, bewildered by this greater light, he will not heed the lesser, and glowing with a purer flame, he will esteem lightly that which at first he so greatly prized. . . .

68. Therefore when our Courtier shall have reached this goal, although he may be called a very happy lover by comparison with those who are plunged in the misery of sensual love, still I would have him not rest content, but press boldly on following along the lofty path after the guide who leads him to the goal of true felicity. And thus, instead of going outside himself in thought (as all must needs do who choose to contemplate bodily beauty only), let him have recourse to himself, in order to contemplate that beauty which is seen by the eyes of the mind, which begin to be sharp and clear when those of the body lose the flower of their loveliness. Then the soul,—freed from vice, purged by studies of true philosophy, versed in spiritual life, and practiced in matters of the intellect, devoted to the contemplation of her own substance,—as if awakened from deepest sleep, opens those eyes which all possess but few use, and sees in herself a ray of that light which is the true image of the angelic beauty communicated to her, and of which she then communicates a faint shadow to the body. Grown blind to things earthly, the soul thus becomes very keen-sighted to things heavenly; and sometimes, when the motive forces of the body are absorbed by earnest contemplation or fettered by sleep, being unhampered by them, she is conscious of a certain far-off perfume of true angelic beauty, and ravished by the splendor of that light, she begins to kindle and pursues it so eagerly that she almost becomes phrensied with desire to unite herself to that beauty, thinking that she has found God's footstep, in the contemplation of which she seeks to rest as in her beatific end. And thus, glowing in this most happy flame, she rises to her noblest part, which is the intellect; and here, no longer darkened by the gloomy night of things earthly, she sees the divine beauty; but still she does not yet quite enjoy it perfectly, because she contemplates it in her own particular intellect only, which cannot be capable of the vast universal beauty.

Wherefore, not well content with this boon, love gives the soul a greater felicity; for just as from that particular beauty of one body it guides her to the universal beauty of all bodies, so in the highest stage of perfection it guides her from the particular to the universal intellect. Hence the soul, kindled by the most sacred fire of true divine love, flies to unite herself with the angelic nature, and not only quite forsaken sense, but has no longer need of reason's discourse; for, changed into an angel, she understands all things intelligible, and without veil or cloud views the wide sea of pure divine beauty, and receives it into herself, and enjoys that supreme felicity of which the senses are incapable.

Edmund Spenser

c. 1552–1599

It was the English essayist Charles Lamb (1775–1834) who first referred to Spenser as "the poet's poet," and the phrase has come to be the most celebrated cliché ever applied to this fine Renaissance figure. But cliché or not, Lamb's words possess an almost fatal accuracy in determining the limits of Spenser's achievement. There is now no question about Spenser's greatness; he ranks among the first dozen English poets. But his qualities have never made him popular save among the experts, however valiantly his supporters have striven to make him current gold among the people. He is far too complex, too academic, too involved and wordy, too remote, too unemotional, too courtly. Chaucer was even more of a courtier, with a courtier's basic point of view, but he had the common touch that raises him above Spenser as a human artist as well as endearing him to all who can read him. Yet it is difficult to name any other poet in English literature who so happily blended into a finished product of art most of the requirements of poetry: a prodigal poetic imagination; a most sensitively attuned musical perception; a sense of the vivid, the pictorial, the colorful; and an enormous capacity for sheer technical virtuosity. Therefore even if a casual reader of poetry may not essay *The Faerie Queene* or the *Amoretti*, or the *Epithalamion*, any true student of poetry assuredly will.

Beside such positive virtues and sterling achievements the facts of his life seem unimportant, and yet they must be considered as contributing much to his work. He was born about 1552, the son of a clothier in London; he attended the Merchant Taylors' School and then Pembroke Hall in Cambridge University, where he received the master's degree in 1576. At the university his college was very much under Calvinistic influence, an influence which is at once apparent to a reader of *The Faerie Queene*. After his graduation, Spenser retired for a few years to Lancashire, where he lived with relatives. From this period we hear about his love for and possible marriage with a Lancashire girl, known ever since merely as Rosalind, who appears in his first long poem, the collection of ingenious, thoughtful, and often profound pastoral eclogues entitled *The Shepheardes Calender* (1579). To her Spenser addressed his four Platonic *Hymns in Honor of Love and Beautie*, written early though not published until 1596.

He returned to London in the late 1570's and entered the service of the powerful Earl of Leicester, whose nephew, Sir Philip Sidney—the traditional epitome of the Elizabethan gentleman—was not only a talented poet and critic of the time but also an old university friend of Spenser's. Through Sidney and another friend, the scholar and critic Gabriel Harvey (another college mate), Spenser came into contact with the literary group known as the Areopagus. While it is not clear that Spenser was ever an official member of this group, it is evident that he sympathized with many of the views of these men, who were essentially classicists in poetry, deprecating the crudeness of English prosody. Yet Spenser, for all his classicism, never turned against his native English tongue, whose ancient forms particularly attracted him. Wisely or not, he adopted a pseudo-archaic vocabulary and spelling and grammar, particularly evident in *The Shepheardes Calender* and *The Faerie Queene*. Such a style may have contributed antique charm but assuredly militated against his popularity and readability in quarters which might otherwise have supported him better.

Spenser's association with Leicester brought him into opposition to the faction of Lord Burleigh, the great power behind the throne in Queen Elizabeth's reign; and when Leicester went into political eclipse, Spenser's opportunities for the political preferment he craved were very much lessened, although he continued to seek them through flattery of the Queen in his works. In 1580 he went to Ireland as secretary to Lord Grey de Wilton,

Lord Deputy of Ireland, a Puritan administrator of considerable severity whom Spenser immortalized as Artegal (or Justice) in the fifth book of *The Faerie Queene*. Indeed, Spenser seems to have sympathized with his superior to the extent that he profited by the prevailing English tendency to exploit Ireland in feudal manner, for he became the owner of an estate at Kilcolman in Munster and lived the life of an English landholder in constant conflict with his Irish neighbors. He returned to England in 1589–1590 to gain what advantages he might achieve from the publication of the first three books of *The Faerie Queene*, which, whatever their true poetic excellence, were nevertheless intended to assist Spenser in a political way. They brought fame and a pension but no preferment at court; and so, after writing a lament on the poetry of the times, *The Tears of the Muses*, and a satire on the court, *Prosopopoia*, or *Mother Hubbard's Tale*, he returned to Ireland and celebrated his return in another court satire, *Colin Clout's Come Home Again*. All three of the works just named belong to the years between 1590 and 1593.

After his marriage to Elizabeth Boyle (1594) he published two of his finest works, the sonnet-sequence *Amoretti* and the noble marriage-ode, *Epithalamion*, and went back to London once more to present the second three books of *The Faerie Queene* (1596). But again no preferment was forthcoming, and so in the following year Spenser and his family returned to Ireland. Here in 1598–1599 came a serious rebellion of the Irish, and although Spenser and his family were able to flee, their home was attacked and burned. Spenser himself sickened shortly thereafter and died on January 16, 1599. He was buried in Westminster Abbey not far from the tomb of Geoffrey Chaucer, his most illustrious immediate predecessor in English literature and the English poet who had exerted the greatest influence upon him.

It was Spenser's keenest disappointment that he never had the recognition at court that was bestowed on others much less worthy than he. As we look back at him in the rich setting of the Renaissance, this disappointment is perhaps comprehensible, but it is difficult for us to sympathize with it. Spenser's true calling was, after all, that of poet; and, however incomplete his achievement in terms of the grand plans he had in mind, none today can deny his solid worth and his absolute sincerity as poet supreme. Courtiers come and go, "packs and sects of great ones, that ebb and flow by the moon," but *The Faerie Queene*, the *Amoretti*, and the *Epithalamion* are still fixed in the firmament.

The Faerie Queene

Spenser published the first three books of *The Faerie Queene* in 1590; the second three appeared in 1596. We know, however, that he was working on his poem in the late 1570's. Under the date of January 23, 1589, he wrote an epistle to Sir Walter Raleigh, the famous Elizabethan courtier and man of letters, setting forth in it the plan

and purpose of *The Faerie Queene*. The text of this letter is subjoined:

"Sir, knowing how doubtfully all allegories may be construed, and this booke of mine which I have entituled the *Faery Queene*, being a continued allegory, or darke conceit, I have thought good, as well for avoyding of gealous opinions and misconstructions, as also for your better light in reading thereof (being so by you commanded) to discover unto you the general intention and meaning, which in the whole course thereof I have fashioned, without expressing of any particular purposes, or by accidents therein occasioned. The generall end therefore of all the booke is to fashion a gentleman or noble person in vertuous and gentle discipline: which for that I conceived shoulde be most plausible and pleasing, being coloured with an historicall fiction, the which the most part of men delight to read, rather for variety of manner than for profite of the ensample, I chose the historye of King Arthure, as most fitte for the excellency of his person, being made famous by many men's former workes, and also furthest from the daunger of envy, and suspition of present time. In which I have followed all the antique Poets historicall: first Homere, who in the Persons of Agamemnon and Ulysses hath ensampled a good governour and a vertuous man, the one in his Ilias, the other in his Odysseis; then Virgil, whose like intention was to doe in the person of Aeneas; after him Ariosto comprised them both in his Orlando: and lately Tasso dissevered them againe, and formed both parts in two persons, namely that part which they in Philosophy call Ethice, or vertues of a private man, coloured in his Rinaldo; the other named Politice in his Godfredo. By ensample of which excellente poets, I labour to pourtraict in Arthure, before he was king, the image of a brave knight, perfected in the twelve private morall vertues, as Aristotle hath devised; the which is the purpose of these first twelve bookes: which if I finde to be well accepted, I may be perhaps encoraged to frame the other part of pollicticke vertues in his person, after that hee came to be king.

"To some, I know, this methode will seeme displesaunt, which had rather have good discipline delivered plainly in way of precepts, or sermoned at large, as they use, then thus clowdily enwrapped in Allegoricall devises. But such, me seeme, should be satisfide with the use of these dayes, seeing all things accounted by their showes, and nothing esteemed of, that is not delightfull and pleasing to commune sence. For this cause is Xenophon preferred before Plato, for that the one, in the exquisite depth of his judgement, formed a commune welth, such as it should be; but the other in the person of Cyrus, and the Persians, fashioned a governement, such as might best be: so much more profitable and gratious is doctrine by ensample, then by rule. So haue I laboured to doe in the person of Arthure: whome I conceive, after his long education by Timon, to whom he was by Merlin delivered to be brought up, so soone as he was borne of the Lady Igrayne, to have seene in a dream or vision the Faery Queene, with whose excellent beauty ravished, he awaking resolved to seeke her out;

and so being by Merlin armed, and by Timon thoroughly instructed, he went to seeke her forth in Faerye land. In that Faery Queene I meane glory in my generall intention, but in my particular I conceive the most excellent and glorious person of our soveraine the Queene, and her kingdome in Faery land. And yet, in some places els, I doe otherwise shadow her. For considering she beareth two persons, the one of a most royall Queene or Empresse, the other of a most vertuous and beautifull Lady, this latter part in some places I doe expresse in Belphoebe, fashioning her name according to your owne excellent conceipt of Cynthia (Phoebe and Cynthia being both names of Diana). So in the person of Prince Arthure I sette forth magnificence in particular, which vertue for that (according to Aristotle and the rest) it is the perfection of all the rest, and conteineth in it them all, therefore in the whole course I mention the deedes of Arthure applyable to that vertue, which I write of in that booke. But of the xii. other vertues, I make xii. other knights the patrones, for the more variety of the history: of which these three bookes contayn three. The first of the knight of the Redcrosse, in whome I expresse holynes: The seconde of Sir Guyon, in whome I sette forth temperaunce: The third of Britomartis, a lady knight, in whom I picture chastity. But, because the beginning of the whole worke seemeth abrupte, and as depending upon other antecedents, it needs that ye know the occasion of these three knights' severall adventures. For the methode of a poet historical is not such, as of an historiographer. For an historiographer discourseth of affayres orderly as they were donne, accounting as well the times as the actions; but a poet thrusteth into the middest, even where it most concerneth him, and there recoursing to the thinges forepaste, and divining of thinges to come, maketh a pleasing analysis of all.

"The beginning therefore of my history, if it were to be told by an historiographer, should be the twelfth booke, which is the last; where I devise that the Faery Queene kept her annuall feaste xii. dayes; uppon which xii. severall dayes, the occasions of the xii. several adventures hapned, which, being undertaken by xii. severall knights, are in these xii. books severally handled and discoursed. The first was this. In the beginning of the feast, there presented himselfe a tall clownishe younge man, who, falling before the Queene of Faeries, desired a boone (as the manner then was) which during that feast she might not refuse: which was that hee might have the atchievement of any adventure, which during that feaste should happen: that being graunted, he rested him on the floore, unfitte through his rusticity for a better place. Soone after entred a faire ladye in mourning weedes, riding on a white asse, with a dwarfe behind her leading a warlike steed, that bore the armes of a knight, and his spear in the dwarfes hand. Shee, falling before the Queene of Faeries, complayned that her father and mother, an ancient king and queene, had bene by an huge dragon many years shut up in a brasen castle, who thence suffred them not to yssew; and therefore besought the Faery Queene to assygne her some one of her knights to take on him that exployt. Presently that clownish person, upstarting, desired that adventure: whereat the Queene much wondering, and the lady much gainesaying, yet he earnestly importuned his desire. In the end the lady told him, that unlesse that armour which she brought, would serve him (that is, the armour of a Christian man specified by Saint Paul, vi. Ephes.) that he could not succeed in that enterprise: which being forthwith put upon him, with dewe furnitures thereunto, he seemed the goodliest man in al that company, and was well liked of the lady. And eftesoones taking on him knighthood, and mounting on that straunge courser, he went forth with her on that adventure: where beginneth the first booke, viz.

A gentle knight was pricking on the playne, etc.

"The second day there came in a palmer, bearing an infant with bloody hands, whose parents he complained to have bene slayn by an enchaunteresse called Acrasia; and therefore craved of the Faery Queene, to appoint him some knight to performe that adventure; which being assigned to Sir Guyon, he presently went forth with that same palmer: which is the beginning of the second booke, and the whole subject thereof. The third day there came in a groome, who complained before the Faery Queene, that a vile enchaunter, called Busirane, had in hand a most faire lady, called Amoretta, whom he kept in most grievous torment, because she would not yield him the pleasure of her body. Whereupon Sir Scudamour, the lover of that lady, presently tooke on him that adventure. But being unable to performe it by reason of the hard enchauntments, after long sorrow, in the end met with Britomartis, who succoured him, and reskewed his love.

"But by occasion hereof many other adventures are intermedled; but rather as accidents then intendments: as the love of Britomart, the overthrow of Marinell, the misery of Florimell, the vertuousnes of Belphoebe, the lasciviousnes of Hellenora, and many the like.

"Thus much, Sir, I have briefly overronne, to direct your understanding to the welhead of the history, that from thence gathering the whole intention of the conceit ye may, as in a handfull, gripe al the discourse, which otherwise may happily seeme tedious and confused. So, humbly craving the continuance of your honorable favour towards me, and th' eternall establishment of your happines, I humbly take leave."

So much for the plans. Of the twelve projected books of *The Faerie Queene*, Spenser completed only six. Parts of a seventh survive. Book One, of the Red Cross Knight, treats of Holiness; Book Two, of Guyon, represents Temperance; Book Three, of Britomart, Chastity; Book Four, of Cambel and Telamond, Friendship; Book Five, of Artegal, Justice; and Book Six, of Calidore, Courtesy. In all these books, a threefold allegory is discernible, on moral, religious, and political levels; as Spenser is writing in the Elizabethan age, the religious and political implications coincide. But the general reader is probably wise if he adheres to the moral allegory and accepts the other allegories as incidental interpretations only. He will then catch sight of the forest in spite of the trees and will be in a position to admire the warm, colorful nar-

rative, the remarkable ability of the lines to evoke sensuous appeal, and the rich *décor* with which the whole epic is furnished lavishly. Here the Renaissance love of adornment is given its best expression.

BOOK I

CANTO ONE

The patron of true Holinesse
Foule Errour doth defeate:
Hypocrisie, him to entrappe,
Doth to his home entreate.

1

A GENTLE knight was pricking on the plaine,
   Ycladd in mightie armes and silver shielde,
Wherein old dints of deepe woundes did remaine,
The cruell markes of many 'a bloudy fielde;
Yet armes till that time did he never wield: 5
His angry steede did chide his foming bitt,
As much disdayning to the curbe to yield:
Full jolly knight he seemd, and faire did sitt,
As one for knightly giusts and fierce encounters fitt.

2

But on his brest a bloodie crosse he bore,   10
The deare remembrance of his dying Lord,
For whose sweete sake that glorious badge he wore,
And dead as living ever him ador'd:
Upon his shield the like was also scor'd,
For soveraine hope, which in his helpe he had: 15
Right faithfull true he was in deede and word,
But of his cheere did seeme too solemne sad;
Yet nothing did he dread, but ever was ydrad.

3

Upon a great adventure he was bond,
That greatest Gloriana to him gave,   20
That greatest glorious queene of Faery Lond,
To winne him worshippe, and her grace to have,
Which of all earthly thinges he most did crave;
And ever as he rode his hart did earne
To prove his puissance in battell brave   25
Upon his foe, and his new force to learne;
Upon his foe, a dragon horrible and stearne.

4

A lovely ladie rode him faire beside,
Upon a lowly asse more white than snow,
Yet she much whiter, but the same did hide   30

8. **jolly,** fair and bold; cf. the French *joli.* 17. **cheere,** countenance, expression. 18. **ydrad,** feared, dreaded. "He feared nothing but was always himself feared." 20–21. **Gloriana . . . Faery Lond;** see Spenser's epistle to Sir Walter Raleigh, p. 11:397. 27. **dragon,** here the personification of Sin, mentioned in the Apocalypse. 28. **lovely ladie,** Una, the personification of Truth. 29. **asse,** symbolic of humility and, like the "bloodie crosse" (l. 10) belonging to the Red Cross Knight, of Christ's atonement.

Under a vele, that wimpled was full low,
And over all a blacke stole shee did throw:
As one that inly mourned, so was she sad,
And heavie sate upon her palfrey slow:
Seemed in heart some hidden care she had;   35
And by her in a line a milkewhite lambe she lad.

5

So pure and innocent, as that same lambe,
She was in life and every vertuous lore,
And by descent from royall lynage came
Of ancient kinges and queenes, that had of yore   40
Their scepters stretcht from east to westerne shore,
And all the world in their subjection held,
Till that infernall feend with foule uprore
Forwasted all their land, and them expeld:
Whom to avenge, she had this knight from far compeld.   45

6

Behind her farre away a dwarfe did lag,
That lasie seemd, in being ever last,
Or wearied with bearing of her bag
Of needments at his backe. Thus as they past,
The day with cloudes was suddeine overcast,   50
And angry Jove an hideous storme of raine
Did poure into his lemans lap so fast,
That everie wight to shrowd it did constrain,
And this faire couple eke to shroud themselves were fain.

7

Enforst to seeke some covert nigh at hand,   55
A shadie grove not farr away they spide,
That promist ayde the tempest to withstand:
Whose loftie trees, yclad with sommers pride,
Did spred so broad, that heavens light did hide,
Not perceable with power of any starr: 60
And all within were pathes and alleies wide,
With footing worne, and leading inward farr:
Faire harbour that them seemes, so in they entred ar.

8

And foorth they passe, with pleasure forward led,
Joying to heare the birdes sweete harmony,   65
Which, therein shrouded from the tempest dred,
Seemd in their song to scorne the cruell sky.
Much can they praise the trees so straight and hy,
The sayling pine, the cedar proud and tall,

The vine-propp elme, the poplar never dry,   70
The builder oake, sole king of forrests all,
The aspine good for staves, the cypress funerall,

9

The laurell, meed of mightie conquerours
And poets sage, the firre that weepeth still,
The willow worne of forlorne paramours,   75
The eugh obedient to the benders will,
The birch for shaftes, the sallow for the mill,
The mirrhe sweete bleeding in the bitter wound,
The warlike beech, the ash for nothing ill,
The fruitfull olive, and the platane round,   80
The carver holme, the maple seeldom inward sound.

10

Led with delight, they thus beguile the way,
Untill the blustring storme is overblowne;
When, weening to returne whence they did stray,
They cannot finde that path, which first was showne,
But wander too and fro in waies unknowne,   86
Furthest from end then, when they neerest weene,
That makes them doubt, their wits be not their owne:
So many pathes, so many turnings seene,
That which of them to take, in diverse doubt they been.   90

11

At last resolving forward still to fare,
Till that some end they finde, or in or out,
That path they take, that beaten seemd most bare,
And like to lead the labyrinth about;
Which when by tract they hunted had throughout,
At length it brought them to a hollowe cave,   96
Amid the thickest woods. The champion stout
Eftsoones dismounted from his courser brave,
And to the dwarfe a while his needlesse spere he gave.

12

'Be well aware,' quoth then that ladie milde,   100
'Least suddaine mischiefe ye too rash provoke:
The danger hid, the place unknowne and wilde,
Breeds dreadfull doubts: oft fire is without smoke,
And perill without show: therefore your stroke,
Sir knight, with-hold, till further tryall made.'   105
'Ah, ladie,' sayd he, 'shame were to revoke
The forward footing for an hidden shade:
Vertue gives her selfe light, through darknesse for to wade.'

13

'Yea, but,' quoth she, 'the perill of this place
I better wot then you; though nowe too late   110

---

36. **in a line,** by a cord.   46. **dwarfe,** personifying Prudence.   52. **lemans lap,** lover's lap; that is, the Earth. Jove (l. 51) personifies the heavens in general.   68–81. **praise the trees.** The following catalogue of trees is something of a convention among medieval and classical authors; probably the most famous such passage preceding Spenser is that in Chaucer's *Parliament of Fowls*, ll. 171–182.   69. **sayling;** that is, used in sailing.

76. **eugh,** yew tree.   81. **holme,** a kind of oak, the wood of which was used for knife handles.

To wish you backe returne with foule disgrace,
Yet wisedome warnes, whilest foot is in the gate,
To stay the steppe, ere forced to retrate.
This is the wandring wood, this Errours den,
A monster vile, whom God and man does hate: 115
Therefore I read beware.' 'Fly, fly!' quoth then
The fearefull dwarfe: 'this is no place for living
    men.'

14

But full of fire and greedy hardiment,
The youthfull knight could not for ought be staide,
But forth unto the darksom hole he went,   120
And looked in: his glistring armor made
A little glooming light, much like a shade,
By which he saw the ugly monster plaine,
Halfe like a serpent horribly displaide,
But th' other halfe did womans shape retaine,   125
Most lothsom, filthie, foule, and full of vile disdaine.

15

And as she lay upon the durtie ground,
Her huge long taile her den all overspred,
Yet was in knots and many boughtes upwound,
Pointed with mortall sting. Of her there bred   130
A thousand yong ones, which she dayly fed,
Sucking upon her poisnous dugs, eachone
Of sundrie shapes, yet all ill favored:
Soone as that uncouth light upon them shone,
Into her mouth they crept, and suddain all were
    · gone.   135

16

Their dam upstart, out of her den effraide,
And rushed forth, hurling her hideous taile
About her cursed head, whose folds displaid
Were stretcht now forth at length without entraile.
She lookt about, and seeing one in mayle,   140
Armed to point, sought backe to turne againe;
For light she hated as the deadly bale,
Ay wont in desert darknes to remaine,
Where plain none might her see, nor she see any
    plaine.

17

Which when the valiant Elfe perceived, he lept   145
As lion fierce upon the flying pray,
And with his trenchand blade her boldly kept
From turning backe, and forced her to stay:
Therewith enrag'd she loudly gan to bray,
And turning fierce, her speckled taile advaunst,   150
Threatning her angrie sting, him to dismay:

Who, nought aghast, his mightie hand enhaunst:
The stroke down from her head unto her shoulder
    glaunst.

18

Much daunted with that dint, her sence was dazd,
Yet kindling rage her selfe she gathered round,   155
And all attonce her beastly bodie raizd
With doubled forces high above the ground:
Tho, wrapping up her wrethed sterne arownd,
Lept fierce upon his shield, and her huge traine
All suddenly about his body wound,   160
That hand or foot to stirr he strove in vaine:
God helpe the man so wrapt in Errours endless
    traine.

19

His lady, sad to see his sore constraint,
Cride out, 'Now, now, sir knight, shew what ye bee:
Add faith unto your force, and be not faint: 165
Strangle her, els she sure will strangle thee.'
That when he heard, in great perplexitie,
His gall did grate for griefe and high disdaine;
And knitting all his force, got one hand free,
Wherewith he grypt her gorge with so great paine,
That soone to loose her wicked bands did her con-
    straine.   171

20

Therewith she spewd out of her filthie maw
A floud of poyson horrible and blacke,
Full of great lumps of flesh and gobbets raw,
Which stunck so vildly, that it forst him slacke   175
His grasping hold, and from her turne him backe:
Her vomit full of books and papers was,
With loathly frogs and toades, which eyed did lacke,
And creeping sought way in the weedy gras:
Her filthie parbreake all the place defiled has.   180

21

As when old father Nilus gins to swell
With timely pride above the Aegyptian vale,
His fattie waves doe fertile slime outwell,
And overflow each plaine and lowly dale:
But when his later spring gins to avale,   185
Huge heapes of mudd he leaves, wherin there breed
Ten thousand kindes of creatures, partly male
And partly femall, of his fruitful seed;
Such ugly monstrous shapes elswher may no man
    reed.

---

116. **read**, counsel, advise. 129. **boughtes**, coils. 136. **upstart**, started up. 139. **entraile**, coiling. 141. **to point**, correctly and completely. 145. **Elfe**. The Red Cross Knight was of elfin birth.

158. **Tho**, then. 177. **books and papers**, the various pamphlets of the time attacking the Church of England, as well as the administration of Elizabeth herself. 180. **parbreake**, vomit. 185. **spring . . . avale**, flood begins to subside. The River Nile is here portrayed as a river-god. 189. **reed**, know about, perceive.

22

The same so sore annoyed has the knight,   190
That, welnigh choked with the deadly stinke,
His forces faile, ne can no lenger fight.
Whose corage when the feend perceivd to shrinke,
She poured forth out of her hellish sinke
Her fruitfull cursed spawne of serpents small,   195
Deformed monsters, fowle, and blacke as inke,
Which swarming all about his legs did crall,
And him encombred sore, but could not hurt at all.

23

As gentle shepheard in sweete eventide,
When ruddy Phebus gins to welke in west,   200
High on an hill, his flocke to vewen wide,
Markes which doe byte their hasty supper best;
A cloud of cumbrous gnattes doe him molest,
All striving to infixe their feeble stinges,
That from their noyance he no where can rest,   205
But with his clownish hands their tender wings
He brusheth oft, and oft doth mar their murmurings.

24

Thus ill bestedd, and fearefull more of shame
Then of the certeine perill he stood in,
Halfe furious unto his foe he came,   210
Resolvd in minde all suddenly to win,
Or soone to lose, before he once would lin;
And stroke at her with more than manly force,
That from her body, full of filthie sin,
He raft her hatefull heade without remorse: 215
A streame of cole black blood forth gushed from her corse.

25

Her scattred brood, soone as their parent deare
They saw so rudely falling to the ground,
Groning full deadly, all with troublous feare,
Gathred themselves about her body round,   220
Weening their wonted entrance to have found
At her wide mouth: but being there withstood,
They flocked all about her bleeding wound,
And sucked up their dying mothers bloud,
Making her death their life, and eke her hurt their good.   225

26

That detestable sight him much amazde,
To see th'unkindly impes, of heaven accurst,
Devoure their dam; on whom while so he gazd,
Having all satisfide their bloudy thurst,
Their bellies swolne he saw with fulnesse burst,   230

And bowels gushing forth: well worthy end
Of such as drunke her life, the which them nurst!
Now needeth him no lenger labour spend;
His foes have slaine themselves, with whom he should contend.

27

His ladie, seeing all that chaunst, from farre,   235
Approcht in hast to greet his victorie,
And saide, 'Faire knight, borne under happie starre,
Who see your vanquisht foes before you lye,
Well worthie be you of that armory,
Wherein ye have great glory wonne this day,   240
And proov'd your strength on a strong enimie,
Your first adventure: many such I pray,
And henceforth ever wish that like succeed it may.'

28

Then mounted he upon his steede againe,
And with the lady backward sought to wend;   245
That path he kept which beaten was most plaine,
Ne ever would to any by way bend,
But still did follow one unto the end,
The which at last out of the wood them brought.
So forward on his way (with God to frend)   250
He passed forth, and new adventure sought:
Long way he traveiled, before he heard of ought.

29

At length they chaunst to meet upon the way
An aged sire, in long blacke weedes yclad,
His feete all bare, his beard all hoarie gray,   255
And by his belt his booke he hanging had;
Sober he seemde, and very sagely sad,
And to the ground his eyes were lowly bent,
Simple in shew, and voide of malice bad,
And all the way he prayed as he went,   260
And often knockt his brest, as one that did repent.

30

He faire the knight saluted, louting low,
Who faire him quited, as that courteous was;
And after asked him, if he did know
Of straunge adventures, which abroad did pas.   265
'Ah! my dear sonne,' quoth he, 'how should, alas!
Silly old man, that lives in hidden cell,
Bidding his beades all day for his trespas,
Tydings of warre and worldly trouble tell?   269
With holy father sits not with such thinges to mell.

31

'But if of daunger, which hereby doth dwell,
And homebredd evil ye desire to heare,

199 ff. **As gentle shepheard**, etc. Note the classical, or Homeric, simile in this stanza. The same thing was observable in Stanza 21 (ll. 181–189). 200. **welke**, fade, decline. 212. **lin**, stop, desist. 227. **th'unkindly impes**, the unnatural young.

239. **armory**, armor bearing the Christian symbol. 256. **his booke**, his prayer-book or Bible. 263. **quited**, returned; that is, the greeting. 270. **With holy . . . mell**, "It is not fitting for a holy father to concern himself with such things."

Of a straunge man I can you tidings tell,
That wasteth all this countrie farre and neare.'
'Of such,' saide he, 'I chiefly doe inquere,   275
And shall you well rewarde to shew the place,
In which that wicked wight his dayes doth weare:
For to all knighthood it is foule disgrace,
That such a cursed creature lives so long a space.'

32

'Far hence,' quoth he, 'in wastfull wildernesse,   280
His dwelling is, by which no living wight
May ever passe, but through great distresse.'
'Now,' saide the ladie, 'draweth toward night,
And well I wote, that of your later fight
Ye all forwearied be: for what so strong,   285
But, wanting rest, will also want of might?
The Sunne, that measures heaven all day long,
At night doth baite his steedes the ocean waves
    emong.

33

'Then with the Sunne take, sir, your timely rest,
And with new day new worke at once begin: 290
Untroubled night, they say, gives counsell best.'
'Right well, sir knight, ye have advised bin,'
Quoth then that aged man; 'the way to win
Is wisely to advise: now day is spent;
Therefore with me ye may take up your in   295
For this same night.' The knight was well content:
So with that godly father to his home they went.

34

A little lowly hermitage it was,
Downe in a dale, hard by a forests side,
Far from resort of people, that did pas   300
In traveill to and froe: a litle wyde
There was an holy chappell edifyde,
Wherein the hermite dewly wont to say
His holy thinges each morne and even-tyde:
Thereby a christall streame did gently play,   305
Which from a sacred fountaine welled forth alway.

35

Arrived there, the little house they fill,
Ne looke for entertainment, where none was:
Rest is their feast, and all thinges at their will;
The noblest mind the best contentment has.   310
With faire discourse the evening so they pas:
For that olde man of plesing wordes had store,
And well could file his tongue as smooth as glas:
He told of saintes and popes, and evermore
He strowd an Ave-Mary after and before.   315

295. **in,** lodging; cf. the modern *inn.* 314-315. **saintes . . . Ave-Mary.** Inasmuch as this "holy man" proves to be Archimago, the symbol of hypocrisy, we may interpret these lines as attacks on the Catholic Church.

36

The drouping night thus creepeth on them fast,
And the sad humor loading their eye liddes,
As messenger of Morpheus, on them cast
Sweet slombring deaw, the which to sleep them
    biddes:
Unto their lodgings then his guestes he riddes: 320
Where when all drownd in deadly sleepe he findes,
He to his studie goes, and there amiddes
His magick bookes and artes of sundrie kindes,
He seekes out mighty charmes, to trouble sleepy
    mindes.

37

Then choosing out few words most horrible,   325
(Let none them read) thereof did verses frame;
With which and other spelles like terrible,
He bad awake blacke Plutoes griesly dame,
And cursed heven, and spake reprochful shame
Of highest God, the Lord of life and light: 330
A bold bad man, that dar'd to call by name
Great Gorgon, prince of darknes and dead night,
At which Cocytus quakes, and Styx is put to flight.

38

And forth he cald out of deepe darknes dredd
Legions of sprights, the which, like litle flyes   335
Fluttring about his ever damned hedd,
Awaite whereto their service he applyes,
To aide his friendes, or fray his enimies:
Of those he chose out two, the falsest twoo,
And fittest for to forge true-seeming lyes;   340
The one of them he gave a message too,
The other by him selfe staide, other worke to doo.

39

He, making speedy way through spersed ayre,
And through the world of waters wide and deepe,
To Morpheus house doth hastily repaire.   345
Amid the bowels of the earth full steepe,
And low, where dawning day doth never peepe,
His dwelling is; there Tethys his wet bed
Doth ever wash, and Cynthia still doth steepe
In silver deaw his ever-drouping hed,   350
Whiles sad Night over him her mantle black doth
    spred.

40

Whose double gates he findeth locked fast,
The one fair fram'd of burnisht yvory,

317. **sad humor,** heavy moisture. A "dry" brain was not supposed to sleep well; note l. 376. 328. **Plutoes griesly dame,** Proserpine, goddess of Death and the Underworld. 332. **Gorgon,** Demogorgon, a demon of great supernatural powers. 343. **He,** the messenger of Archimago. **spersed,** scattered, rarefied. 348. **Tethys.** In classical mythology Tethys was actually the wife of Oceanus, but here she represents the god himself, and is spoken of as male.

The other all with silver overcast;
And wakeful dogges before them farre doe lye,   355
Watching to banish Care their enimy,
Who oft is wont to trouble gentle Sleepe.
By them the sprite doth passe in quietly,
And unto Morpheus comes, whom drowned deepe
In drowsie fit he findes: of nothing he takes keepe.

41

And more, to lulle him in his slumber soft,   361
A trickling streame from high rock tumbling downe,
And ever drizling raine upon the loft,
Mixt with a murmuring winde, much like the sowne
Of swarming bees, did cast him in a swowne: 365
No other noyse, nor peoples troublous cryes,
As still are wont t'annoy the walled towne,
Might there be heard: but careless Quiet lyes,
Wrapt in eternall silence farre from enimyes.

42

The messenger approaching to him spake,   370
But his waste wordes retourned to him in vaine:
So sound he slept, that nought mought him awake.
Then rudely he him thrust, and pusht with paine,
Whereat he gan to stretch: but he againe
Shooke him so hard, that forced him to speake.   375
As one then in a dreame, whose dryer braine
Is tost with troubled sights and fancies weake,
He mumbled soft, but would not all his silence
    breake.

43

The sprite then gan more boldly him to wake,
And threatned unto him the dreaded name
Of Hecate: whereat he gan to quake,   380
And, lifting up his lompish head, with blame
Halfe angrie asked him, for what he came.
'Hether,' quoth he, 'me Archimago sent,
He that the stubborne sprites can wisely tame;   385
He bids thee to him send for his intent
A fit false dreame, that can delude the sleepers sent.'

44

The god obayde, and calling forth straight way
A diverse dreame out of his prison darke,
Delivered it to him, and downe did lay   390
His heavie head, devoide of carefull carke;
Whose sences all were straight benumbd and starke.
He, backe returning by the yvorie dore,
Remounted up as light as chearefull larke,
And on his little winges the dreame he bore   395
In hast unto his lord, where he him left afore.

45

Who all this while, with charmes and hidden artes,
Had made a lady of that other spright,
And fram'd of liquid ayre her tender partes,
So lively and so like in all mens sight,   400
That weaker sence it could have ravisht quight:
The maker selfe, for all his wondrous witt,
Was nigh beguiled with so goodly sight:
Her all in white he clad, and over it
Cast a black stole, most like to seem for Una fit.   405

46

Now when that ydle dreame was to him brought,
Unto that Elfin knight he bad him fly,
Where he slept soundly, void of evil thought,
And with false shewes abuse his fantasy,
In sort as he him schooled privily: 410
And that new creature, borne without her dew,
Full of the makers guyle, with usage sly
He taught to imitate that lady trew,
Whose semblance she did carrie under feigned hew.

47

Thus well instructed, to their worke they haste,   415
And comming where the knight in slumber lay,
The one upon his hardie head him plaste,
And made him dreame of loves and lustfull play,
That nigh his manly hart did melt away,
Bathed in wanton blis and wicked joy.   420
Then seemed him his lady by him lay,
And to him playnd, how that false winged boy
Her chaste hart had subdewd to learne Dame Pleas-
    ures toy.

48

And she her selfe, of beautie soveraigne queene,
Fayre Venus, seemde unto his bed to bring   425
Her, whom he, waking, evermore did weene
To bee the chastest flowre that aye did spring
On earthly braunch, the daughter of a king,
Now a loose leman to vile service bound:
And eke the Graces seemed all to sing   430
Hymen iö Hymen, dauncing all around,
Whylst freshest Flora her with yvie girlond crownd.

49

In this great passion of unwonted lust,
Or wonted feare of doing ought amis,
He started up, as seeming to mistrust   435
Some secret ill, or hidden foe of his:
Lo! there before his face his ladie is,
Under black stole hyding her bayted hooke,

---

376. See note to l. 317.   393. **yvorie dore.** False dreams passed out through the ivory door; true ones came out through the door of horn overlaid with silver (l. 354).

410. **In sort as,** according to the method.   411. **without her dew,** not befitting her due, unnaturally.   422. **playnd,** complained. **false winged boy,** Cupid, the god of love.   431. *Hymen iö Hymen,* the Greek wedding chant addressed to Hymen, god of marriage.

St. George and the dragon, by the German artist Albrecht Dürer. This is one of a series of woodcuts by Dürer on the same theme.

And as halfe blushing offred him to kis,
With gentle blandishment and lovely looke,   440
Most like that virgin true, which for her knight him
 took.

50

All cleane dismayd to see so uncouth sight,
And halfe enraged at her shameless guise,
He thought have slaine her in his fierce despight;
But hastie heat tempring with sufferance wise,   445
He stayde his hand, and gan himselfe advise
To prove his sense, and tempt her faigned truth.
Wringing her hands in wemens pitteous wise,
Tho can she weepe, to stirre up gentle ruth,   449
Both for her noble blood, and for her tender youth.

51

And sayd, 'Ah sir, my liege lord and my love,
Shall I accuse the hidden cruell fate,
And mightie causes wrought in heaven above,

449. **Tho . . . weepe,** then did she weep. 454. **blind god,** Cupid;
see note to l. 422.

Or the blind god, that doth me thus amate,
For hoped love to winne me certaine hate?   455
Yet thus perforce he bids me do, or die.
Die is my dew: yet rew my wretched state
You, whom my hard avenging destinie
Hath made judge of my life or death indifferently.

52

'Your owne deare sake forst me at first to leave   460
My fathers kingdom'—There she stopt with teares;
Her swollen hart her speech seemd to bereave;
And then againe begonne: 'My weaker yeares,
Captiv'd to fortune and frayle worldly feares,
Fly to your fayth for succour and sure ayde: 465
Let me not die in languor and long teares.'
'Why, dame,' quoth he, 'what hath ye thus dismayd?
What frayes ye, that were wont to comfort me af-
 frayd?'

53

'Love of your selfe,' she saide, 'and deare constraint,
Lets me not sleepe, but waste the wearie night   470
In secret anguish and unpittied plaint,
Whiles you in carelesse sleepe are drowned quight.'
Her doubtfull words made that redoubted knight
Suspect her truth: yet since no untruth he knew,
Her fawning love with foule disdainefull spight   475
He would not shend, but said, 'Deare dame, I rew,
That for my sake unknowne such griefe unto you
 grew.

54

'Assure your selfe, it fell not all to ground;
For all so deare as life is to my hart,
I deeme your love, and hold me to you bound;   480
Ne let vaine feares procure your needlesse smart,
Where cause is none, but to your rest depart.'
Not all content, yet seemd she to appease
Her mournefull plaintes, beguiled of her art,
And fed with words, that could not chose but please;
So slyding softly forth, she turnd as to her ease.   486

55

Long after lay he musing at her mood,
Much griev'd to thinke that gentle dame so light,
For whose defence he was to shed his blood.
At last dull warines of former fight   490
Having yrockt a sleepe his irkesome spright,
That troublous dreame gan freshly tosse his braine
With bowres, and beds, and ladies deare delight:
But when he saw his labour all was vaine,
With that misformed spright he backe returnd
 againe.   495

494. **he,** the dream spirit, who returned to Archimago with the spirit
impersonating Una.

CANTO TWO

The guilefull great enchaunter parts
The Redcrosse Knight from Truth:
Into whose stead faire Falsehood steps,
And werkes him woeful ruth.

1

By this the northerne wagoner had set
His sevenfold teme behind the stedfast starre,
That was in ocean waves yet never wet,
But firme is fixt, and sendeth light from farre
To al that in the wide deepe wandring arre: 5
And chearefull Chaunticlere with his note shrill
Had warned once, that Phoebus fiery carre
In hast was climbing up the easterne hill,
Full envious that night so long his roome did fill:

2

When those accursed messengers of hell,   10
That feigning dreame, and that faire-forged spright,
Came to their wicked maister, and gan tel
Their bootelesse paines, and ill succeeding night:
Who, all in rage to see his skilfull might
Deluded so, gan threaten hellish paine   15
And sad Proserpines wrath, them to affright.
But when he saw his threatning was but vaine,
He cast about, and searcht his baleful bokes againe.

3

Eftsoones he tooke that miscreated faire,
And that false other spright, on whom he spred   20
A seeming body of the subtile aire,
Like a young squire, in loves and lustyhed
His wanton daies that ever loosely led,
Without regard of armes and dreaded fight:
Those twoo he tooke, and in a secrete bed,   25
Covered with darkenes and misdeeming night,
Them both together laid, to joy in vaine delight.

4

Forthwith he runnes with feigned faithfull hast
Unto his guest, who, after troublous sights
And dreames, gan now to take more sound repast;   30
Whom suddenly he wakes with fearful frights,
As one aghast with feends or damned sprights,
And to him cals: 'Rise, rise, unhappy swaine,

5

That here wex old in sleepe, whiles wicked wights
Have knit themselves in Venus shameful chaine;   35
Come, see, where your false lady doth her honor
     staine.'

All in amaze he suddenly up start
With sword in hand, and with the old man went;
Who soone him brought into a secret part,
Where that false couple were full closely ment   40
In wanton lust and leud embracement:
Which when he saw, he burnt with gealous fire,
The eie of reason was with rage yblent,
And would have slaine them in his furious ire,
But hardly was restreined of that aged sire.   45

6

Retourning to his bed in torment great,
And bitter anguish of his guilty sight,
He could not rest, but did his stout heart eat,
And wast his inward gall with deepe despight,
Yrkesome of life, and too long lingring night.   50
At last faire Hesperus in highest skie
Had spent his lampe, and brought forth dawning
     light;
Then up he rose, and clad him hastily;
The dwarfe him brought his steed: so both away do
     fly.

7

Now when the rosy fingred Morning faire,   55
Weary of aged Tithones saffron bed,
Had spred her purple robe through deawy aire,
And the high hils Titan discovered,
The royall virgin shooke of drousyhed,
And rising forth out of her baser bowre,   60
Lookt for her knight, who far away was fled,
And for her dwarfe, that wont to wait each howre:
Then gan she wail and weepe, to see that woeful
     stowre.

8

And after him she rode with so much speede,
As her slowe beast could make; but all in vaine: 65
For him so far had borne his light-foot steede,
Pricked with wrath and fiery fierce disdaine,
That him to follow was but fruitlesse paine;
Yet she her weary limbes would never rest,
But every hil and dale, each wood and plaine,   70
Did search, sore grieved in her gentle brest,
He so ungently left her, whome she loved best.

Head-verse. **ruth,** ruefulness, wretchedness.   **1. northerne wagoner,**
the constellation of Boötes, the Charioteer, who drives Ursa Major,
the Great Bear—a constellation known in Middle English and
Elizabethan times as Charles' (or Arthur's) wain or wagon. The
great star in Boötes is Arcturus.   **2. sevenfold teme.** The constellation of Ursa Major (Charles' wain or the modern Big Dipper) has
seven major stars. **stedfast starre,** Polaris, the Pole Star, the brightest
star in the adjacent constellation of Ursa Minor, which is so close to
the northern celestial pole that its motion is extremely slow—to the
ancients it never moved.   **3. in ocean waves . . . wet.** In temperate
northern latitudes Ursa Major never sets.   **26. misdeeming night,**
night which causes misunderstanding or error.

40. **ment,** mingled, blended.   43. **yblent,** blinded.   50. **Yrkesome,**
wearied.   55. **rosy fingred,** the fixed Homeric epithet for the dawn
or morning.   56. **Tithones,** the lover of Aurora, goddess of the Dawn.
Aurora was able to obtain for Tithonus the gift of immortality from
Jove, but she forgot to ask for eternal youth.   63. **stowre,** misfortune,
hardship.

9

But subtill Archimago, when his guests
He saw divided into double parts,
And Una wandring in woods and forrests,　75
Th' end of his drift, he praisd his divelish arts,
That had such might over true meaning harts:
Yet rests not so, but other meanes doth make,
How he may worke unto her further smarte:
For her he hated as the hissing snake,　80
And in her many troubles did most pleasure take.

10

He then devisde himselfe how to disguise;
For by his mighty science he could take
As many formes and shapes in seeming wise,
As ever Proteus to himselfe could make:　85
Sometime a fowle, sometime a fish in lake,
Now like a foxe, now like a dragon fell,
That of himselfe he ofte for feare would quake,
And oft would flie away. O who can tell
The hidden powre of herbes, and might of magick spel?　90

11

But now seemde best, the person to put on
Of that good knight, his late beguiled guest:
In mighty armes he was yclad anon,
And silver shield; upon his coward brest
A bloody crosse, and on his craven crest　95
A bounch of heares discoloured diversly:
Full jolly knight he seemde, and wel addrest,
And when he sate uppon his courser free,
Saint George himselfe ye would have deemed him to be.

12

But he, the knight whose semblaunt he did beare,
The true Saint George, was wandred far away,　101
Still flying from his thoughts and gealous feare;
Will was his guide, and griefe led him astray.
At last him chaunst to meete upon the way
A faithlesse Sarrazin, all armde to point,　105
In whose great shield was writ with letters gay
Sans foy; full large of limbe and every joint
He was, and cared not for God or man a point.

13

Hee had a faire companion of his way,
A goodly lady clad in scarlot red,　110

99. Saint George, the patron saint of England, with whom the Red Cross Knight is later to be identified. 100. semblaunt, semblance or resemblance. 105. Sarrazin. The Saracen was originally a follower of Islam, but in the later romances the term is generalized to apply to any heathen warrior. 107. Sans foy, without faith. The three brothers Sansfoy, Sansjoy, and Sansloy together typify heathen vices—they are faithless, joyless, and lawless. 110. goodly lady, Duessa (Falsehood), who hypocritically assumes the name Fidessa (Faith).

Purfled with gold and pearle of rich assay;
And like a Persian mitre on her hed
Shee wore, with crowns and owches garnished,
The which her lavish lovers to her gave:
Her wanton palfrey all was overspred　115
With tinsell trappings, woven like a wave,
Whose bridle rung with golden bels and bosses brave.

14

With faire disport and courting dalliaunce
She intertainde her lover all the way:
But when she saw the knight his speare advaunce,
Shee soone left of her mirth and wanton play,　121
And bad her knight addresse him to the fray:
His foe was nigh at hand. He prickte with pride
And hope to winne his ladies hearte that day,
Forth spurred fast: adowne his coursers side　125
The red blood trickling staind the way, as he did ride.

15

The Knight of the Redcrosse, when he him spide
Spurring so hote with rage dispiteous,
Gan fairely couch his speare, and towards ride:
Soone meete they both, both fell and furious,　130
That, daunted with theyr forces hideous,
Their steeds doe stagger, and amazed stand,
And eke themselves, too rudely rigorous,
Astonied with the stroke of their owne hand,
Doe backe rebutte, and ech to other yealdeth land.

16

As when two rams, stird with ambitious pride,　136
Fight for the rule of the rich fleeced flocke,
Their horned fronts so fierce on either side
Doe meete, that, with the terror of the shocke
Astonied, both stand sencelesse as a blocke,　140
Forgetfull of the hanging victory:
So stood these twaine, unmoved as a rocke,
Both staring fierce, and holding idely
The broken reliques of their former cruelty.

17

The Sarrazin, sore daunted with the buffe,　145
Snatcheth his sword, and fiercely to him flies;
Who well it wards, and quyteth cuff with cuff:
Each others equall puissaunce envies,
And through their iron sides with cruell spies
Does seeke to perce: repining courage yields　150

112. mitre, used here in the general sense of a conical-shaped headdress. The epithet Persian has reference to its richness of material and brilliance of color. 113. owches, jewels, gems. 118. dalliaunce. This word is almost never used in the medieval romances without the suggestion of love-play. 123. prickte, spurred on, excited. 135. rebutte, recoil. 147. quyteth, returns. 148. envies, imparts hate. 149. spies, metaphorically used for "eyes" or perhaps "fingers."

No foote to foe. The flashing fier flies,
As from a forge, out of their burning shields,
And streams of purple bloud new dies the verdant
    fields.

18

'Curse on that Crosse,' quoth then the Sarrazin,
'That keepes thy body from the bitter fitt!   155
Dead long ygoe, I wote, thou haddest bin,
Had not that charme from thee forwarned itt:
But yet I warne thee now assured sitt,
And hide thy head.' Therewith upon his crest
With rigor so outrageous he smitt,   160
That a large share it hewd out of the rest,
And glauncing downe his shield, from blame him
    fairely blest.

19

Who thereat wondrous wroth, the sleeping spark
Of native vertue gan eftsoones revive,
And at his haughty helmet making mark,   165
So hugely stroke, that it the steele did rive,
And cleft his head. He, tumbling downe alive,
With bloudy mouth his mother earth did kis,
Greeting his grave: his grudging ghost did strive
With the fraile flesh; at last it flitted is,   170
Whether the soules doe fly of men that live amis.

20

The lady, when she saw her champion fall,
Like the old ruines of a broken towre,
Staid not to waile his woefull funerall,
But from him fled away with all her powre;   175
Who after her as hastily gan scowre,
Bidding the dwarfe with him to bring away
The Sarrazins shield, signe of the conqueroure.
Her soone he overtooke, and bad to stay,
For present cause was none of dread her to dis-
    may.   180

21

Shee, turning backe with ruefull countenaunce,
Cride, 'Mercy, mercy, sir, vouchsafe to showe
On silly dame, subject to hard mischaunce,
And to your mighty will!' Her humblesse low,
In so ritch weedes and seeming glorious show,   185
Did much enmove his stout heroicke heart,
And said, 'Deare dame, your suddein overthrow
Much rueth me; but now put feare apart,
And tel, both who ye be, and who that tooke your
    part.'

22

Melting in teares, then gan shee thus lament: 190
'The wreched woman, whom unhappy howre

Hath now made thrall to your commandement,
Before that angry heavens list to lowre,
And Fortune false betraide me to your powre,
Was, (O what now availeth that I was?)   195
Borne the sole daughter of an emperour,
He that the wide west under his rule has,
And high hath set his throne where Tiberis doth pas.

23

'He, in the first flowre of my freshest age,
Betrothed me unto the onely haire   200
Of a most mighty king, most rich and sage;
Was never prince so faithfull and so faire,
Was never prince so meek and debonaire;
But ere my hoped day of spousall shone,
My dearest lord fell from high honors staire,   205
Into the hands of hys accursed fone,
And cruelly was slaine, that shall I ever mone.

24

'His blessed body, spoild of lively breath,
Was afterward, I know not how, convaid
And fro me hid: of whose most innocent death   210
When tidings came to mee, unhappy maid,
O how great sorrow my sad soule assaid!
Then forth I went his woefull corse to find,
And many yeares throughout the world I straid,
A virgin widow, whose deepe wounded mind   215
With love, long time did languish as the striken hind.

25

'At last it chauncéd this proud Sarazin
To meete me wandring; who perforce me led
With him away, but yet could never win
The fort, that ladies hold in soveraigne dread.   220
There lies he now with foule dishonor dead,
Who, whiles he liv'de, was called proud Sansfoy;
The eldest of three brethren, all three bred
Of one bad sire, whose youngest is Sansjoy,
And twixt them both was born the bloudy bold
    Sansloy.   225

26

'In this sad plight, friendlesse, unfortunate,
Now miserable I Fidessa dwell,
Craving of you, in pitty of my state,
To doe none ill, if please ye not doe well.'
He in great passion al this while did dwell,   230
More busying his quicke eies, her face to view,
Then his dull cares, to heare what shee did tell;
And said, 'Faire lady, hart of flint would rew
The undeserved woes and sorrowes which ye shew.

155. **bitter fitt,** death-blow. 159. **hide,** shield. 162. **blame . . . blest,** kept him well from harm.

198. **Tiberis,** the River Tiber in Rome; the reference, however, is to the papal dominions or Catholicism. 200. **haire,** heir. 206. **fone,** foes, enemies. 212. **assaid,** assailed, attacked.

27

'Henceforth in safe assuraunce may ye rest,   235
Having both found a new friend you to aid,
And lost an old foe, that did you molest:
Better new friend than an old foe is said.'
With chaunge of chear the seeming simple maid
Let fal her eien, as shamefast, to the earth,   240
And yeelding soft, in that she nought gainsaid,
So forth they rode, he feining seemely merth,
And shee coy lookes: so dainty, they say, maketh
    derth.

28

Long time they thus together traveiled,
Til, weary of their way, they came at last   245
Where grew two goodly trees, that faire did spred
Their armes abroad, with gray mosse overcast,
And their greene leaves, trembling with every blast,
Made a calme shadowe far in compasse round:
The fearfull shepheard, often there aghast,   250
Under them never sat, ne wont there sound
His mery oaten pipe, but shund th'unlucky ground.

29

But this good knight, soone as he them can spie,
For the coole shade him thither hastly got:
For golden Phoebus, now ymounted hie,   255
From fiery wheeles of his faire chariot
Hurled his beame so scorching cruell hot,
That living creature mote it not abide;
And his new lady it endured not.
There they alight, in hope themselves to hide   260
From the fierce heat, and rest their weary limbs a
    tide.

30

Faire seemely plesaunce each other makes,
With goodly purposes, there as they sit:
And in his falsed fancy he her takes
To be the fairest wight that lived yit;   265
Which to expresse, he bends his gentle wit,
And thinking of those braunches greene to frame
A girlond for her dainty forehead fit,
He pluckt a bough; out of whose rifte there came
Smal drops of gory bloud, that trickled down the
    same.   270

31

Therewith a piteous yelling voice was heard,
Crying, 'O spare with guilty hands to teare
My tender sides in this rough rynd embard;
But fly, ah! fly far hence away, for feare

239. **chear**, expression, countenance. 243. **dainty . . . derth**, apparently a proverb meaning "Coyness or delicacy brings poverty (unsatisfied desire)." 270. **gory**, in this instance probably "clotted." 273. **embard**, confined, enclosed.

Least to you hap that happened to me heare,   275
And to this wretched lady, my deare love;
O too deare love, love bought with death too deare!'
Astond he stood, and up his heare did hove,
And with that suddein horror could no member
    move.

32

At last, whenas the dreadfull passion   280
Was overpast, and manhood well awake,
Yet musing at the straunge occasion,
And doubting much his sence, he thus bespake:
'What voice of damned ghost from Limbo lake,
Or guilefull spright wandring in empty aire,   285
Both which fraile men doe oftentimes mistake,
Sends to my doubtfull eares these speaches rare,
And ruefull plaints, me bidding guiltlesse blood to
    spare?'

33

Then groning deep: 'Nor damned ghost,' quoth he,
'Nor guileful sprite to thee these words doth speake,
But once a man, Fradubio, now a tree;   291
Wretched man, wretched tree! whose nature weake
A cruell witch, her cursed wil to wreake,
Hath thus transformd, and plast in open plaines,
Where Boreas doth blow full bitter bleake,   295
And scorching sunne does dry my secret vaines:
For though a tree I seme, yet cold and heat me
    paines.'

34

'Say on, Fradubio, then, or man or tree,'
Quoth then the knight; 'by whose mischievous arts
Art thou misshapen thus, as now I see?   300
He oft finds med'cine who his griefe imparts;
But double griefs afflict concealing harts,
As raging flames who striveth to suppresse.'
'The author then,' said he, 'of all my smarts,
Is one Duessa, a false sorceresse,   305
That many errant knights hath broght to wretched-
    nesse.

35

'In prime of youthly yeares, when corage hott
The fire of love and joy of chevalree
First kindled in my brest, it was my lott
To love this gentle lady, whome ye see   310
Now not a lady, but a seeming tree;
With whome as once I rode accompanyde,
Me chaunced of a knight encountred bee,
That had a like faire lady by his syde;
Lyke a faire lady, but did fowle Duessa hyde.   315

291. **Fradubio**, "Brother Doubt," the symbolizing of uncertainty and skepticism.

36

'Whose forged beauty he did take in hand
All other dames to have exceded farre;
I in defence of mine did likewise stand,
Mine, that did then shine as the morning starre:
So both to batteil fierce arraunged arre;   320
In which his harder fortune was to fall
Under my speare: such is the dye of warre:
His lady, left as a prise martiall,
Did yield her comely person, to be at my call.

37

'So doubly lov'd of ladies unlike faire,   325
Th'one seeming such, the other such indeede,
One day in doubt I cast for to compare,
Whether in beauties glorie did exceede;
A rosy girlond was the victors meede.
Both seemde to win, and both seemde won to bee,
So hard the discord was to be agreede: 331
Fraelissa was as faire as faire mote bee,
And ever false Duessa seemde as faire as shee.

38

'The wicked witch, now seeing all this while
The doubtfull ballaunce equally to sway,   335
What not by right, she cast to win by guile;
And by her hellish science raisd streight way
A foggy mist, that overcast the day,
And a dull blast, that, breathing on her face,
Dimmed her former beauties shining ray,   340
And with foule ugly forme did her disgrace:
Then was she fayre alone, when none was faire in
place.

39

'Then cride she out, "Fye, fye! deformed wight,
Whose borrowed beautie now appeareth plaine
To have before bewitched all mens sight;   345
O leave her soone, or let her soone be slaine."
Her loathly visage viewing with disdaine,
Eftsoones I thought her such as she me told,
And would have kild her; but with faigned paine
The false witch did my wrathfull hand with-hold:
So left her, where she now is turnd to mould.   351

40

'Thensforth I tooke Duessa for my dame,
And in the witch unweeting joyd long time,
Ne ever wist but that she was the same:
Till on a day (that day is everie prime,   355
When witches wont do penance for their crime)

316. **take in hand**, maintain, insist. 328. **Whether**, which one (of two)? 332. **Fraelissa**. The name is probably suggested by the adjective *frail*. 339. **her**, Fraelissa's. 355. **everie prime**, always springtime. 356. **witches . . . crime**. It was an old belief that spring enforced penance on all witches for crimes committed during the preceding autumn and winter seasons.

I chaunst to see her in her proper hew,
Bathing her selfe in origane and thyme:
A filthy foule old woman I did vew,
That ever to have toucht her I did deadly rew.   360

41

'Her neather partes misshapen, monstruous,
Were hidd in water, that I could not see,
But they did seeme more foule and hideous,
Then womans shape man would beleeve to bee.
Thensforth from her most beastly companie   365
I gan refraine, in minde to slipp away,
Soone as appeard safe opportunitie:
For danger great, if not assurd decay,
I saw before mine eyes, if I were knowne to stray.

42

'The divelish hag, by chaunges of my cheare,   370
Perceiv'd my thought; and drownd in sleepie night,
With wicked herbes and oyntments did besmeare
My body all, through charmes and magicke might,
That all my senses were bereaved quight:
Then brought she me into this desert waste,   375
And by my wretched lovers side me pight,
Where now enclosd in wooden wals full faste,
Banisht from living wights, our wearie daies we
waste.'

43

'But how long time,' said then the Elfin knight,
'Are you in this misformed hous to dwell?'   380
'We may not chaunge,' quoth he, 'this evill plight
Till we be bathed in a living well;
That is the terme prescribed by the spell.'
'O how,' sayd he, 'mote I that well out find,
That may restore you to your wonted well?'   385
'Time and suffised fates to former kynd
Shall us restore; none else from hence may us un-
bynd.'

44

The false Duessa, now Fidessa hight,
Heard how in vaine Fradubio did lament,
And knew well all was true. But the good knight   390
Full of sad feare and ghastly dreriment,
When all this speech the living tree had spent,
The bleeding bough did thrust into the ground,
That from the blood he might be innocent.   394
And with fresh clay did close the wooden wound:
Then turning to his lady, dead with feare her fownd.

45

Her seeming dead he fownd with feigned feare,
As all unweeting of that well she knew,
And paynd himselfe with busie care to reare
Her out of careless swowne. Her eylids blew,   400
And dimmed sight, with pale and deadly hew,

At last she up gan lift: with trembling cheare
Her up he tooke, too simple and too trew,
And oft her kist. At length, all passed feare,
He set her on her steede, and forward forth did
    beare.   405

[The action in Cantos III–VI is concerned with the
separate adventures of Una and the Red Cross Knight,
who meet again, however, in Canto VII. And in Canto
XI Una comes to her native land, in the company of the
Red Cross Knight; but they find their way barred by a
monstrous dragon, which the Red Cross Knight kills after
a terrific two-day struggle in which the Red Cross Knight
is refreshed by fruit from the Tree of Life. We come then
to Canto XII.]

CANTO TWELVE

Fayre Una to the Redcrosse Knight
   Betrouthed is with joy:
Though false Duessa, it to barre,
   Her false sleightes doe imploy.

1

Behold! I see the haven nigh at hand,
To which I meane my wearie course to bend;
Vere the maine shete, and beare up with the land,
The which afore is fayrly to be kend,
And seemeth safe from storms that may offend: 5
There this fayre virgin, wearie of her way,
Must landed bee, now at her journeyes end;
There eke my feeble barke a while may stay,
Till mery wynd and weather call her thence away.

2

Scarsely had Phoebus in the glooming east   10
Yett harnessed his fyrie-footed teeme,
Ne reard above the earth his flaming creast,
When the last deadly smoke aloft did steeme,
That signe of last outbreathed life did seeme
Unto the watchman on the castle wall;   15
Who thereby dead that balefull beast did deeme,
And to his lord and lady lowd gan call,
To tell, how he had seene the dragons fatall fall.

3

Uprose with hasty joy, and feeble speed,
That aged syre, the lord of all that land,   20
And looked forth, to weet if trew indeed
Those tydinges were, as he did understand:
Which whenas trew by tryall he out fond,
He badd to open wyde his brasen gate,
Which long time had beene shut, and out of hond 25
Proclaymed joy and peace through all his state;
For dead now was their foe, which them forrayed
    late.

4

Then gan triumphant trompets sownd on hye,
That sent to heven the ecchoed report
Of their new joy, and happie victory   30
Gainst him, that had them long opprest with tort,
And fast imprisoned in sieged fort.
Then all the people, as in solemne feast,
To him assembled with one full consort,
Rejoycing at the fall of that great beast,   35
From whose eternall bondage now they were re-
    least.

5

Forth came the auncient lord and aged queene,
Arayd in antique robes downe to the grownd,
And sad habiliments right well beseene:
A noble crew about them waited rownd   40
Of sage and sober peres, all gravely gownd;
Whom far before did march a goodly band
Of tall young men, all hable armes to sownd;
But now they laurell braunches bore in hand,
Glad signe of victory and peace in all their land. 45

6

Unto that doughtie conquerour they came,
And him before themselves prostrating low,
Their lord and patrone loud did him proclame,
And at his feet their lawrell boughes did throw.
Soone after them, all dauncing on a row,   50
The comely virgins came, with girlands dight,
As fresh as flowres in medow greene doe grow,
When morning deaw upon their leaves doth light:
And in their handes sweet timbrels all upheld on
    hight.

7

And them before, the fry of children yong   55
Their wanton sportes and childish mirth did play,
And to the maydens sownding tymbrels song,
In well attuned notes, a joyous lay,
And made delightfull musick all the way,
Untill they came where that faire virgin stood. 60
As fayre Diana, in fresh sommers day,
Beholdes her nymphs enraung'd in shady wood,
Some wrestle, some do run, some bathe in christall
    flood;

8

So she beheld those maydens meriment   64
With chearefull vew; who, when to her they came,
Themselves to ground with gracious humblesse bent,
And her ador'd by honorable name,
Lifting to heven her everlasting fame:
Then on her head they sett a girlond greene,

---

43. **hable,** able, enabled. **sownd,** make trial of.

And crowned her twixt earnest and twixt game; 70
Who, in her self-resemblance well beseene,
Did seeme, such as she was, a goodly maiden
    queene.

9

And after all the raskall many ran,
Heaped together in rude rablement,
To see the face of that victorious man; 75
Whom all admired, as from heaven sent,
And gazd upon with gaping wonderment.
But when they came where that dead dragon lay,
Stretcht on the ground in monstrous large extent,
The sight with ydle feare did them dismay, 80
Ne durst approach him nigh, to touch, or once assay.

10

Some feard and fledd; some feard, and well it faynd;
One, that would wiser seeme then all the rest,
Warnd him not touch, for yet perhaps remaynd
Some lingering life within his hollow brest, 85
Or in his wombe might lurke some hidden nest
Of many dragonettes, his fruitfull seede;
Another saide, that in his eyes did rest
Yet sparckling fyre, and badd thereof take heed;
Another said, he saw him move his eyes indeed. 90

11

One mother, whenas her foolehardy chyld
Did come to neare, and with his talants play,
Halfe dead through feare, her litle babe revyld,
And to her gossibs gan in counsell say:
'How can I tell, but that his talants may 95
Yet scratch my sonne, or rend his tender hand?'
So diversly them selves in vaine they fray;
Whiles some more bold, to measure him nigh stand,
To prove how many acres he did spred of land.

12

Thus flocked all the folke him rownd about, 100
The whiles that hoarie king, with all his traine,
Being arrived where that champion stout
After his foes defeasaunce did remaine,
Him goodly greetes, and fayre does entertayne
With princely gifts of yvory and gold, 105
And thousand thankes him yeeldes for all his paine:
Then when his daughter deare he does behold,
Her dearely doth imbrace, and kisseth manifold.

13

And after to his pallace he them bringes,
With shaumes, and trompets, and with clarions
    sweet; 110

And all the way the joyous people singes,
And with their garments strowes the paved street;
Whence mounting up, they fynd purveyaunce meet
Of all that royall princes court became,
And all the floore was underneath their feet 115
Bespredd with costly scarlott of great name,
On which they lowly sitt, and fitting purpose frame.

14

What needes me tell their feast and goodly guize,
In which was nothing riotous nor vaine?
What needes of dainty dishes to devize, 120
Of comely services, or courtly trayne?
My narrow leaves cannot in them contayne
The large discourse of roiall princes state.
Yet was their manner then but bare and playne:
For th'antique world excesse and pryde did hate;
Such proud luxurious pompe is swollen up but
    late. 126

15

Then, when with meates and drinkes of every kinde
Their fervent appetites they quenched had,
That auncient lord gan fit occasion finde,
Of straunge adventures, and of perils sad, 130
Which in his travell him befallen had,
For to demaund of his renowned guest:
Who then with utt'rance grave, and count'nance
    sad,
From poynt to poynt, as is before exprest,
Discourst his voyage long, according his request. 135

16

Great pleasure, mixt with pittifull regard,
That godly king and queene did passionate,
Whyles they his pitifull adventures heard,
That oft they did lament his lucklesse state,
And often blame the too importune fate, 140
That heapd on him so many wrathfull wreakes;
For never gentle knight, as he of late,
So tossed was in Fortunes cruell freakes;
And all the while salt teares bedeawed the hearers
    cheaks.

17

Then sayd the royall pere in sober wise: 145
'Dear sonne, great beene the evils which ye bore
From first to last in your late enterprise,
That I note whether praise or pitty more:
For never living man, I weene, so sore
In sea of deadly daungers was distrest; 150
But since now safe ye seised have the shore,
And well arrived are, (High God be blest!)
Let us devize of ease and everlasting rest.'

73. raskall, rude populace. 86. wombe, belly. 92. talants, talons, claws. 94. gossibs, close friends or acquaintances. 110. shaumes, shawms, an ancient reed instrument resembling the modern oboe.

120. devize, describe. 137. passionate, experience with intense feeling. 141. wreakes, adventures leading to expeditions in foreign lands. 148. note, do not know. 153. devize of, make plans for.

18

'Ah! dearest lord,' said then that doughty knight,
'Of ease or rest I may not yet devize;   155
For by the faith which I to armes have plight,
I bownden am streight after this emprize,
As that your daughter can ye well advize,
Backe to retourne to that great Faery Queene,
And her to serve six yeares in warlike wize,   160
Gainst that proud Paynim King that works her
        teene:
Therefore I ought crave pardon, till I there have
        beene.'

19

'Unhappy falls that hard necessity,'
Quoth he, 'the troubler of my happy peace,
And vowed foe of my felicity;   165
Ne I against the same can justly preace:
But since that band ye cannot now release,
Nor doen undoe, (for vowes may not be vayne)
Soone as the terme of those six yeares shall cease,
Ye then shall hether backe retourne agayne,   170
The marriage to accomplish vowd betwixt you
        twayn.

20

'Which, for my part, I covet to performe,
In sort as through the world I did proclame,
That who so kild that monster most deforme,
And him in hardy battayle overcame,   175
Should have mine onely daughter to his dame,
And of my kingdome heyre apparaunt bee:
Therefore since now to thee perteynes the same,
By dew desert of noble chevalree,
Both daughter and eke kingdome, lo! I yield to
        thee.'   180

21

Then forth he called that his daughter fayre,
The fairest Un', his onely daughter deare,
His onely daughter and his only hayre;
Who forth proceeding with sad sober cheare,
As bright as doth the morning starre appeare   185
Out of the east, with flaming lockes bedight,
To tell that dawning day is drawing neare,
And to the world does bring long wished light:
So faire and fresh that lady shewd her selfe in sight:

22

So faire and fresh, as freshest flowre in May;   190
For she had layd her mournfull stole aside,
And widow-like sad wimple throwne away,
Wherewith her heavenly beautie she did hide,
Whiles on her wearie journey she did ride;
And on her now a garment she did weare   195
All lilie white, withoutten spot or pride,

That seemd like silke and silver woven neare,
But neither silke nor silver therein did appeare.

23

The blazing brightnesse of her beauties beame,
And glorious light of her sunshyny face,   200
To tell, were as to strive against the streame:
My ragged rimes are all too rude and bace,
Her heavenly lineaments for to enchace.
Ne wonder; for her own deare loved knight,
All were she daily with himselfe in place,   205
Did wonder much at her celestiall sight:
Oft had he seene her faire, but never so faire dight.

24

So fairely dight, when she in presence came,
She to her syre made humble reverence,
And bowed low, that he right well became,   210
And added grace unto her excellence:
Who with great wisedome and grave eloquence
Thus gan to say—But eare he thus had sayd,
With flying speede, and seeming great pretence,
Came running in, much like a man dismayd,   215
A messenger with letters, which his message sayd.

25

All in the open hall amazed stood
At suddeinnesse of that unwary sight,
And wondred at his breathlesse hasty mood.
But he for nought would stay his passage right,   220
Till fast before the king he did alight;
Where falling flat, great humblesse he did make,
And kist the ground whereon his foot was pight;
Then he to his handes that writt he did betake,
Which he disclosing, read thus, as the paper spake:

26

'To thee, most mighty king of Eden fayre,   226
Her greeting sends in these sad lines addrest
The wofull daughter and forsaken heyre
Of that great Emperour of all the West;
And bids thee be advized for the best,   230
Ere thou thy daughter linck in holy band
Of wedlocke to that new unknowen guest:
For he already plighted his right hand
Unto another love, and to another land.

27

'To me, sad mayd, or rather widow sad,   235
He was affyaunced long time before,
And sacred pledges he both gave, and had,
False erraunt knight, infamous, and forswore!
Witnesse the burning altars, which he swore,
And guilty heavens of his bold perjury,   240
Which though he hath polluted oft of yore,

218. **unwary,** unexpected and uncomprehended.

Yet I to them for judgement just doe fly,
And them conjure t'avenge this shamefull inhury.

28

'Therefore since mine he is, or free or bond,
Or false or trew, or living or else dead,   245
Withhold, O soverayne prince, your hasty hond
From knitting league with him, I you aread;
Ne weene my right with strength adowne to tread,
Through weakenesse of my widowhed or woe:
For Truth is strong, her rightfull cause to plead, 250
And shall finde friends, if need requireth soe.
So bids thee well to fare, thy neither friend nor foe,
                                        FIDESSA.'

29

When he these bitter byting wordes had red,
The tydings straunge did him abashed make,
That still he sate long time astonished,   255
As in great muse, ne word to creature spake.
At last his solemne silence thus he brake,
With doubtfull eyes fast fixed on his guest:
'Redoubted knight, that for myne only sake
Thy life and honor late adventurest,   260
Let nought be hid from me, that ought to be ex-
          prest.

30

'What meane these bloody vowes and idle threats,
Throwne out from womanish impatient mynd?
What hevens? what altars? what enraged heates,
Here heaped up with termes of love unkynd,   265
My conscience cleare with guilty bands would bynd?
High God be witnesse, that I guiltlesse ame!
But if your selfe, sir knight, ye faulty fynd,
Or wrapped be in loves of former dame,
With cryme doe not it cover, but disclose the
          same.'   270

31

To whom the Redcrosse Knight this answere sent:
'My lord, my king, be nought hereat dismayed,
Till well ye wote by grave intendiment,
What woman, and wherefore, doth me upbrayd
With breach of love and loialty betrayd.   275
It was in my mishaps, as hitherward
I lately traveild, that unwares I strayd
Out of my way, through perils straunge and hard;
That day should faile me ere I had them all declard.

32

'There did I find, or rather I was fownd   280
Of this false woman, that Fidessa hight;
Fidessa hight the falsest dame on grownd,
Most false Duessa, royall richly dight.

That easy was t'inveigle weaker sight:
Who by her wicked arts and wiely skill,   285
Too false and strong for earthly skill or might,
Unwares me wrought unto her wicked will,
And to my foe betrayd, when least I feared ill.'

33

Then stepped forth the goodly royall mayd,
And on the ground her selfe prostrating low,   290
With sober countenaunce thus to him sayd:
'O pardon me, my soveraine lord, to sheow
The secret treasons, which of late I know
To have been wrought by that false sorceresse.
Shee, onely she, it is, that earst did throw   295
This gentle knight into so great distresse,
That death him did awaite in daily wretchednesse.

34

'And now it seemes, that she suborned hath
This crafty messenger with letters vaine,
To worke new woe and improvided scath,   300
By breaking of the band betwixt us twaine;
Wherein she used hath the practicke paine
Of this false footman, clokt with simplenesse,
Whome if ye please for to discover plaine,
Ye shall him Archimago find, I ghesse,   305
The falsest man alive; who tries, shall find no lesse.'

35

The king was greatly moved at her speach,
And, all with sudden indignation fraight,
Bad on that messenger rude hands to reach.
Eftsoons the gard, which on his state did wait,   310
Attacht that faytor false, and bound him strait:
Who, seeming sorely chauffed at his band,
As chained beare, whom cruell dogs doe bait,
With ydle force did faine them to withstande,
And often semblaunce made to scape out of their
          hand.   315

36

But they him layd full low in dungeon deepe,
And bound him hand and foote with yron chains,
And with continual watch did warely keepe:
Who then would thinke, that by his subtile trains
He could escape fowle death or deadly pains?   320
Thus when that princes wrath was pacifide,
He gan renew the late forbidden bains,
And to the knight his daughter deare he tyde,
With sacred rites and vowes for ever to abyde.

37

His owne two hands the holy knotts did knitt,   325
That none but death for ever can divide;

---

247. **aread,** counsel you, charge you.

302. **practicke,** actual. 308. **fraight,** fraught, loaded down with
311. **faytor,** agent, doer. 322. **bains,** banns (of marriage).

His owne two hands, for such a turne most fitt,
The housling fire did kindle and provide,
And holy water thereon sprinckled wide;
At which the bushy teade a groome did light,   330
And sacred lamp in secret chamber hide,
Where it should not be quenched day nor night,
For feare of evill fates, but burnen ever bright.

38

Then gan they sprinckle all the posts with wine,
And made great feast to solemnize that day: 335
They all perfumde with frankincense divine,
And precious odours fetcht from far away,
That all the house did sweat with great aray:
And all the while sweete musicke did apply
Her curious skill, the warbling notes to play,   340
To drive away the dull melancholy;
The whiles one sung a song of love and jollity.

39

During the which there was an heavenly noise
Heard sownd through all the pallace pleasantly,
Like as it had bene many an angels voice   345
Singing before th' Eternall Majesty,
In their trinall triplicities on hye;
Yett wist no creature, whence that hevenly sweet
Proceeded, yet each one felt secretly,
Himselfe thereby refte of his sences meet,   350
And ravishd with rare impression in his sprite.

40

Great joy was made that day of young and old,
And solemne feast proclayme throughout the land,
That their exceeding merth may not be told:
Suffice it heare by signes to understand   355
The usuall joyes at knitting of loves band.
Thrise happy man the knight himselfe did hold,
Possessed of his ladies hart and hand,
And ever, when his eie did her behold,
His heart did seeme to melt in pleasures manifold.

41

Her joyous presence and sweet company   361
In full content he there did long enjoy,
Ne wicked envy, ne vile gealosy,
His deare delights were hable to annoy:
Yet, swimming in that sea of blisfull joy,   365
He nought forgott, how he whilome had sworne,
In case he could that monstrous beast destroy,
Unto his Faery Queene backe to retourne:
The whice he shortly did, and Una left to mourne.

328. **housling,** sacramental.   330. **teade,** torch.   334. **posts;** that is, the posts of the bed.   347. **trinall triplicities,** threefold trinities, a reference to the ninefold arrangement of the angels in Heaven.

42

Now strike your sailes, yee jolly mariners,   370
For we be come unto a quiet rode,
Where we must sand some of our passengers,
And light this weary vessell of her lode.
Here she a while may make her safe abode,
Till she repaired have her tackles spent,   375
And wants supplide; and then againe abroad
On the long voiage whereto she is bent:
Well may she speede, and fairely finish her intent.

Niccolò Machiavelli

1469–1527

The political revolution of the Renaissance brought powerful national monarchies to Western Europe out of the decay of medieval feudalism. In Italy, however, the commercial rivalry of the major cities hindered nationalism and produced instead autocratic princes ruling powerful independent city-states, and it was an Italian, Niccolò Machiavelli, who codified the new philosophy of ruthless power politics in his frankly pragmatic treatise, *The Prince* (1513).

Since the term "machiavellian" in English has become synonymous with unscrupulous cunning, it is important to observe that Machiavelli was no more than a product of his time and that his amoral justification of political expediency sprang from his training and experience. The son of a prominent jurist, he emerged from obscurity at thirty to play an active role in Florentine politics in the era of the Medici. Well schooled in the Latin and Italian classics, he was always more interested in the historians, especially Livy, than in the poets and playwrights. Although he wrote verse and produced in *La Mandragola* (1524) one of the wittiest and most cynical comedies of modern times, the majority of his writings are historical and political. But in them the new, free spirit of Humanism expresses itself through his independent criticism of the feudal nobility, the temporal power of the Church, and the philosophy of scholasticism. His plea for a strong central government reflected his contempt for the political anarchy of the Middle Ages.

Machiavelli entered public life with the expulsion of the Medici from Florence in 1494. Between 1498 and 1512 he was secretary to the Ten of War and Peace, who controlled the military affairs of the city. He worked diligently at diplomatic missions, which took him beyond Italy to the French courts of Louis XII and Louis XIII as well as to Switzerland and Germany. But the embassy most influential in shaping his political views was one to Cesare Borgia, the unscrupulous military dictator who built a brief empire in central Italy by conscienceless murder of his enemies and dubious allies. As the prag-

372. **sand,** discharge.

matic philosophy of Machiavelli matured, he came to see Cesare Borgia as the model prince who would allow no moral considerations to impede the growth of his power. Following the example of Borgia, he organized a national militia for Florence and chose a murderous aide of Borgia's to be its leader. But this army was unable to withstand the Medici when they marched on Florence in 1512, and with the fall of the Ten Machiavelli lost his political influence and was even imprisoned for a time. Although he performed minor political duties thereafter, his later years were spent largely in retirement with his wife and children at his villa near San Casciano.

Machiavelli's political philosophy is contained in his monumental *Discourses on the First Ten Books of Livy* and his famous short treatise, *The Prince*. The first builds from an analysis of political elements in the ancient Roman historian a theory of the evolution of a republic, and the second implements autocratic government with a science of statecraft. *The Prince* is the great document of the centralization of government in Renaissance Europe and reveals Machiavelli's longing for a strong leader to unify Italy as England, France, and Spain had been unified. For a time Cesare Borgia seemed about to do this, and even after his fall he seemed to Machiavelli to have pointed the way.

The ideal prince should have the Roman virtue of *virtus,** and the shifts of fortune require that he should be ready to adjust his principles to any necessity. Hence, he should keep his word only if it is expedient and resort to cruelty and even murder if his objective requires it. Being skeptical of the intelligence and worth of common men, Machiavelli places faith in a strong ruler more clever but no more virtuous than his subjects, who justifies his ruthless rise to power by his success in maintaining order. Although the practical truth of *The Prince* has been amply supported by political dictators in our own century, and although its theory may harmonize with a biological explanation of man's social and political behavior, this cold-blooded treatise must shock readers who believe in a moral order in the universe and the rights and integrity of the common man.

The Prince

XIV. Of the Duties of a Prince Relative to His Military Force.

PRINCES ought to make the art of war their sole study and occupation, for it is peculiarly the science of those who govern. War, and the several sorts of discipline and institutions relative to it, should be his only study, the only profession he should follow, and the object he ought always to have in view. By this means princes can maintain possession of their dominions; and private individuals

* This means literally "manliness"; hence the characteristics of a man, such as strength, alertness, courage, and resourcefulness.
*The Prince.*³ Translator anonymous.

are sometimes raised thereby to supreme authority; whilst, on the other hand, we frequently see princes shamefully reduced to nothing by suffering themselves to be enfeebled by slothful inactivity. I repeat, therefore, that by a neglect of this art it is that states are lost, and by cultivating it they are acquired. . . .

We cannot establish a comparison between men who are armed and those who are not so; and it would be equally absurd to suppose that the disarmed should command and the others obey. A prince who is ignorant of the art of war can never enjoy repose or safety amongst armed subjects; he will always be to them an object of contempt, as they to him will justly be subjects of suspicion; how is it possible then that they should act in concert? In short, a prince who does not understand the art of war can never be esteemed by his troops, nor can he ever confide in them.

It is necessary therefore that princes should pay their whole attention to the art of war, which includes mental labour and study as well as the military exercise. To begin with the latter, the prince should take the utmost care that his troops be well disciplined and regularly exercised. The chase is well adapted to inure the body of fatigue and to all the intemperances of weather. This exercise will also teach him to observe the sources and situations, as well as the nature of rivers and marshes; to measure the extent of plains and the declivity of mountains. By these means he will acquire a knowledge of the topography of a country which he has to defend, and will easily habituate himself to select the places where war may be best carried on. . . .

As to that part of military science which is learned in the closet, a prince ought to read history and to pay particular attention to the achievements of great generals and the cause of their victories and defeats; but above all he should follow the example of those great men who, when they select a model, resolve to follow in his steps. It was thus that Alexander the Great immortalized himself by following the example of Achilles, Caesar by imitating Alexander, and Scipio by copying Cyrus. . . .

XV. *What Deserves Praise or Blame in Men, and Above All in Princes.* It now remains to show in what manner a prince should behave to his subjects and friends. This matter having been already discussed by others, it may seem arrogant in me to pursue it farther, especially if I should differ in opinion from them; but as I write only for those who possess sound judgment, I thought it better to treat this subject as it really is, in fact, than to amuse the imagination with visionary models of republics and governments which have never existed. For the manner in which men now live is so different from the manner in which they ought to live that he who deviates from the common course of practice and endeavours to act as duty dictates necessarily ensures his own destruction. Thus, a good man, and one who wishes to prove himself so in all respects, must be undone in a contest with so many who are evilly disposed. A prince who wishes to maintain his power ought therefore to learn that he should not be always good and must use that knowledge as circumstances and the exigencies of his own affairs may seem to require.

Laying aside, then, the false ideas which have been formed as to princes, and adhering only to those which are true, I say, that all men, and especially princes, are marked and distinguished by some quality or other which entails either reputation or dishonour. For instance, men are liberal or parsimonious, honourable or dishonourable, effeminate or pusillanimous, courageous or enterprising, humane or cruel, affable or haughty, wise or debauched, honest or dishonest, good tempered or surly, sedate or inconsiderate, religious or impious, and so forth.

It would, doubtless, be happy for a prince to unite in himself every species of good quality; but as our nature does not allow so great a perfection, a prince should have prudence enough to avoid those defects and vices which may occasion his ruin; and as to those who can only compromise his safety and the possession of his dominions, he ought, if possible, to guard against them; but if he cannot succeed in this, he need not embarrass himself in escaping the scandal of those vices, but should devote his whole energies to avoid those which may cause his ruin. He should not shrink from encountering some blame on account of vices which are important to the support of his states; for everything well considered, there are some things having the appearance of virtues, which would prove the ruin of a prince, should he put them into practice, and others upon which, though seemingly bad and vicious, his actual welfare and security entirely depend.

xvi. *Of Liberality and Economy.* To begin with the first qualities of the above-mentioned, I must observe that it is for the interest of a prince to be accounted liberal, but dangerous so to exercise his liberality that he is thereby neither feared nor respected. I will explain myself. If a prince be only liberal as far as it suits his purposes, that is to say, within certain bounds, he will please but few and will be called selfish. A prince who wishes to gain the reputation of being liberal should be regardless of expense; but then to support this reputation, he will often be reduced to the necessity of levying taxes on his subjects and adopting every species of fiscal resource which cannot fail to make him odious. Besides exhausting the public treasury by his prodigality, his credit will be destroyed, and he will run the risk of losing his dominions on the first reverse

of fortune, his liberality, as it always happens, having ensured him more enemies than friends. And which is worse, he cannot retrace his steps and replenish his finances without being charged with avarice.

A prince, therefore, who cannot be liberal without prejudicing his state should not trouble himself much about the imputation of being covetous; for he will be esteemed liberal in time, when people see that by parsimony he has improved his revenue, become able to defend his dominions, and even to undertake useful enterprises without the aid of new taxes. Then the many from whom he takes nothing will deem him sufficiently liberal, and the few only whose expectations he has failed to realize will accuse him of avarice. In our times we have seen no great exploits performed except by those who have been accounted avaricious; all the others have failed. Julius II attained the pontifical chair by means of his bounty; but he judged rightly in supposing that in order to enable him to prosecute the war against France, it would do him injury to preserve his reputation for liberality. By his parsimony he was able to support the expense of all his wars without the imposition of new taxes. The present king of Spain could never have accomplished all his great enterprises if he had any ambition to be thought liberal.

A prince, then, who would avoid poverty and always be in a condition to defend his dominions without imposing new taxes on his subjects should care little for being charged with avarice, since the imputed vice may be the very means of securing the prosperity and stability of his government.

It may however be alleged that Caesar would never have attained the empire but by his liberality, and that many others have arrived at the highest honours by the same means. I answer, you are either in possession of dominion already, or you are not. In the first place, liberality would be prejudicial; in the second, the reputation of it is serviceable and necessary. Caesar endeavored to appear liberal whilst he aspired to the empire of Rome. But if he had lived longer, he would have lost that reputation for liberality which had paved him the way to empire, or he would have lost himself in the attempt to preserve it.

There have been, however, some princes who have performed splendid actions and who have distinguished themselves by their liberality; but then their prodigality did not come from the public purse. Such were Cyrus, Alexander, and Caesar. A prince

76. **Julius II.** The great beautifier of Rome was also an able statesman, who really founded the Papal States and sought to drive the French from Italy. 82. **The present king of Spain,** Ferdinand of Aragon (reigned 1479–1516), who unified Spain by his marriage to Isabella of Castile and drove the Moors from Spain (1492).

ought to be very sparing of his own and his subjects' property; but he should be equally lavish of that which he takes from the enemy if he desires to be popular with his troops; for that will not diminish his reputation, but rather add to it. He who is too liberal cannot long continue so; he will become poor and contemptible unless he grinds his subjects with new taxes— which cannot fail to render him odious to them. Now there is nothing a prince ought to dread so much as his subjects' hatred; unless, indeed, it be their contempt. And both these evils may be occasioned by over liberality. If he must choose between extremes, it is better to submit to the imputation of parsimony than to make a show of liberality; since the first, though it may not be productive of honour, never gives birth to hatred and contempt.

XVII. *Of Cruelty and Clemency, and Whether it is Better to be Loved Than Feared.* To proceed to other qualities which are requisite in those who govern. A prince ought unquestionably to be merciful, but should take care how he executes his clemency. Caesar Borgia was accounted cruel; but it was to that cruelty that he was indebted for the advantage of uniting Romagna to his other dominions and of establishing in that province peace and tranquillity, of which it had been so long deprived. And, everything well considered, it must be allowed that this prince showed greater clemency than the people of Florence, who, to avoid the reproach of cruelty, suffered Pistoia to be destroyed. When it is necessary for a prince to restrain his subjects within the bounds of duty, he should not regard the imputation of cruelty, because by making a few examples he will find that he really showed more humanity in the end than he who by too great indulgence suffers disorders to arise, which commonly terminate in rapine and murder. For such disorders disturb a whole community, whilst punishments inflicted by the prince affect only a few individuals.

This is particularly true with respect to a new prince, who can scarcely avoid the reproach of cruelty, every new government being replete with dangers. . . .

A prince, however, should not be afraid of phantoms of his own raising; neither should he lend too ready an ear to terrifying tales which may be told him, but should temper his mercy with prudence, in such a manner that too much confidence may not put him off his guard, nor causeless jealousies make him insupportable. There is a medium between a foolish security and an unreasonable distrust.

It has been sometimes asked whether it is better to be loved than feared; to which I answer that one should wish to be both. But as that is a hard matter to accomplish, I think that, if it is necessary to make a selection, it is safer to be feared than be loved. For

it may be truly affirmed of mankind in general that they are ungrateful, fickle, timid, dissembling, and self-interested; so long as you can serve them, they are entirely devoted to you; their wealth, their blood, their lives, and even their offspring are at your disposal when you have no occasion for them; but in the day of need they turn their back upon you. The prince who relies on professions courts his own destruction, because the friends whom he acquires by means of money alone, and whose attachment does not spring from a regard for personal merit, are seldom proof against reverse of fortune, but abandon their benefactor when he most requires their services. Men are generally more inclined to submit to him who makes himself dreaded than to one who merely strives to be beloved; and the reason is obvious, for friendship of this kind, being a mere moral tie, a species of duty resulting from a benefit, cannot endure against the calculations of interest: whereas fear carries with it the dread of punishment, which never loses its influence. A prince, however, ought to make himself feared in such a manner that, if he cannot gain the love, he may at least avoid the hatred, of his subjects; and he may attain this object by respecting his subjects' property and the honour of their wives. If he finds it absolutely necessary to inflict the punishment of death, he should avow the reason for it, and, above all things, he should abstain from touching the property of the condemned party. For certain it is that men sooner forget the death of their relations than the loss of their patrimony. Besides, when he once begins to live by means of rapine, many occasions offer for seizing the wealth of his subjects; but there will be little or no necessity for shedding blood.

But when a prince is at the head of his army and has under his command a multitude of soldiers, he should make little account of being esteemed cruel; such a character will be useful to him, by keeping his troops in obedience and preventing every species of faction.

Hannibal, among many other admirable talents, possessed in a high degree that of making himself feared by his troops; insomuch that, having led a very large army composed of all kinds of people into a foreign country, he never had occasion, either in prosperity or adversity, to punish the least disorder or the slightest want of discipline: and this can only be attributed to his extreme severity, and such other qualities as caused him to be feared and respected by his soldiers, and without which his extraordinary talents and courage would have been unavailing. . . .

I conclude, then, with regard to the question whether it is better to be loved than feared,—that it depends on the inclinations of the subjects themselves, whether they will love their prince or not;

but the prince has it in his own power to make them fear him, and if he is wise, he will rather rely on his own resources than on the caprice of others, remembering that he should at the same time so conduct himself as to avoid being hated.

XVIII. *Whether a Prince is Obliged by His Promise.* It is unquestionably very praiseworthy in princes to be faithful to their engagements; but among those of the present day, who have been distinguished for great exploits, few indeed have been remarkable for this virtue or have scrupled to deceive others who may have relied on their good faith.

It should, therefore, be known that there are two ways of deciding any contest: the one by laws, the other by force. The first is peculiar to men, the second to beasts; but when laws are not sufficiently powerful, it is necessary to recur to force: a prince ought therefore to understand how to use both these descriptions of arms. This doctrine is admirably illustrated to us by the ancient poets in the allegorical history of the education of Achilles, and many other princes of antiquity, by the centaur Chiron, who, under the double form of man and beast, taught those who were destined to govern that it was their duty to use by turns the arms adapted to both these natures, seeing that one without the other cannot be of any durable advantage. Now, as a prince must learn how to act the part of a beast sometimes, he should make the fox and the lion his patterns. The first can but feebly defend himself against the wolf, and the latter readily falls into such snares as are laid for him. From the fox, therefore, a prince will learn dexterity in avoiding snares; and from the lion, how to employ his strength to keep the wolves in awe. But they who entirely rely upon the lion's strength will not always meet with success: in other words, a prudent prince cannot and ought not to keep his word, except when he can do it without injury to himself, or when the circumstances under which he contracted the engagement still exist.

I should be cautious in inculcating such a precept if all men were good; but as the generality of mankind are wicked and ever ready to break their words, a prince should not pique himself in keeping his more scrupulously, especially as it is always easy to justify a breach of faith on his part. I could give numerous proofs of this and show numberless engagements and treaties which have been violated by the treachery of princes, and that those who enacted the part of the fox have always succeeded best in their affairs. It is necessary, however, to disguise the appearance of craft, and thoroughly to understand the art of feigning and dissembling; for men are generally so simple and so weak that he who wishes to deceive easily finds dupes.

One example, taken from the history of our own times, will be sufficient. Pope Alexander VI played during his whole life a game of deception; and notwithstanding his faithless conduct was extremely well known, his artifices always proved successful. Oaths and protestations cost him nothing; never did a prince so often break his word or pay less regard to his engagements. This was because he so well understood this chapter in the art of government.

It is not necessary, however, for a prince to possess all the good qualities I have enumerated, but it is indispensable that he should appear to have them. I will even venture to affirm that it is sometimes dangerous to use, though it is always useful to seem to possess them. A prince should earnestly endeavour to gain the reputation of kindness, clemency, piety, justice, and fidelity to his engagements. He ought to possess all these good qualities, but still retain such power over himself as to display their opposites whenever it may be expedient. I maintain that a prince, and especially a new prince, cannot with impunity exercise all the virtues, because his own self-preservation will often compel him to violate the laws of charity, religion, and humanity. He should habituate himself to bend easily to the various circumstances which may from time to time surround him. In a word, it will be as useful to him to persevere in the path of rectitude, while he feels no inconvenience in doing so, as to know how to deviate from it when circumstances dictate such a course. He should make it a rule, above all things, never to utter anything which does not breathe of kindness, justice, good faith, and piety. This last quality it is most important for him to appear to possess, as men in general judge more from appearances than from reality. All men have eyes, but few have the gift of penetration. Every one sees your exterior, but few can discern what you have in your heart; and those few dare not oppose the voice of the multitude, who have the majesty of their prince on their side. Now, in forming a judgment of the minds of men, and more especially of princes, as we cannot recur to any tribunal, we must attend only to results. Let it then be the prince's chief care to maintain his authority; the means he employs, be what they may, will for this purpose always appear honourable and meet applause; for the vulgar are ever caught by appearances and judge only by the event. And as the world is chiefly composed of such as are called the vulgar, the voice of the few is seldom or never heard or regarded.

There is a prince now alive (whose name it may

57. **Pope Alexander VI,** a scandalous pope (1492–1503), ruthless and immoral, the father of Cesare Borgia, whose attempted conquest of the Romagna inspired *The Prince.* 107. **a prince now alive,** Ferdinand of Aragon and Castile, who had conquered the kingdoms of Naples and Navarre.

not be proper to mention) who ever preaches the doctrines of peace and good faith; but if he had observed either the one or the other, he would long ago have lost both his reputation and dominions.

XIX. *That it is Necessary to Avoid Being Hated and Despised.* Having distinctly considered the principal qualities with which a prince should be endowed, I shall briefly discuss the rest in a general discourse under the following heads, viz., that a prince ought sedulously to avoid everything which may make him odious or despicable. If he succeed in this, he may fill his part with reasonable success and need not fear danger from the infamy of other vices.

Nothing, in my opinion, renders a prince so odious as the violation of the right of property and a disregard to the honour of married women. Subjects will live contentedly enough under a prince who invades neither their property nor their honour; and then he will only have to contend against the pretensions of a few ambitious persons, whom he can easily find means to restrain.

A prince whose conduct is light, inconstant, pusillanimous, irresolute, and effeminate is sure to be despised. These defects he ought to shun as he would so many rocks, and endeavour to display a character for courage, gravity, energy, and magnificence in all his actions. His decisions in matters between individuals should be irrevocable, so that none may dare to think of abusing or deceiving him. By these means he will conciliate the esteem of his subjects and prevent any attempts to subvert his authority. He will then have less to apprehend from external enemies, who will be cautious in their attacks upon a prince who has secured the affection of his subjects. A prince has two things to guard against, the machinations of his own subjects and the attempts of powerful foreigners. The latter he will be able to repel by means of good friends and good troops; and these he will be sure to have as long as his arms are respectable. Besides, internal peace can only be interrupted by conspiracies, which are only dangerous when they are encouraged and supported by foreign powers. The latter, however, dare not stir if the prince but conform to the rules I have laid down. . . .

With regard to his subjects, if all be at peace without his dominions, a prince has nothing to dread but secret conspiracies, from which he may always secure himself by avoiding whatever can render him odious or contemptible. Conspiracies are seldom formed except against princes whose ruin and death would be acceptable to the people; otherwise men would not expose themselves to the dangers inseparable from such machinations.

History is filled with conspiracies; but how few have been crowned with success? No one can carry on such a design alone, nor trust any accomplices but malcontents. These frequently denounce their confederates and frustrate their designs in the hope of obtaining a large remuneration from him against whom they are leagued; so that those with whom you are necessarily associated in a conspiracy are placed between the temptation of a considerable reward and the dread of a great danger; so that to keep the secret it must either be entrusted to a very extraordinary friend or an irreconcilable enemy of the prince.

In short, conspirators live in continual fear, jealousy, and suspicion, whilst the prince is supported by all the splendour and majesty of the government, the laws, the customs, and the assistance of his friends, not to mention the affection which subjects naturally entertain towards those who govern them. So that conspirators have reason to fear both before and after the execution of their designs, for when the people have been once exasperated, there is no resource left to which they may fly. Of this I might give many examples, but I shall content myself with one only which occurred in the last century.

Hannibal Bentivoglio, the grandfather of the reigning prince of Bologna, had been murdered by the Canneschi, and the only member of the family who survived was John Bentivoglio, then an infant in the cradle. The people rose against the conspirators and massacred the whole family of the murderers; and in order still more strongly to show their attachment to the house of Bentivoglio, as there was none of the family left who was capable of governing the state, the Bolognese, having received information that a natural son of that prince then lived at Florence, sent deputies thither to demand him, though he lived in that city under the name of an artisan who passed for his father, and to him they confided the direction of the state till John Bentivoglio should be of age to govern.

A prince has therefore little to fear from conspiracies when he possesses the affections of the people; but he has no resource left if this support should fail him. Content the people and manage the nobles, and you have the maxim of wise governors.

France holds the first rank amongst well-governed states. One of the wisest institutions they possess is unquestionably that of the parliaments, whose object is to watch over the security of the government and the liberties of the people. The founders of this institution were aware, on the one hand, of the insolence and ambition of the nobles and, on the other, of the excess to which the people are liable to be transported against them, and they endeavoured to restrain both without the intervention of the king, who never could have taken part with the people, as he must thereby render the nobles discontented; nor could he favour the latter, without exciting the hatred of the people. Upon this account they have instituted an authority which, without the interference of the king, may favour the people and repress the insolence of the nobles. It must be confessed that nothing is more likely to give consistency to the government and ensure the tranquillity of the people. And we may learn from hence that princes should reserve to themselves distribution of favours and employments, and leave to the magistrates the care of pronouncing punishments, and, indeed, the general disposal of all things likely to excite discontent. . . .

XXI. *By What Means a Prince May Become Esteemed.* Nothing is more likely to make a prince esteemed than great enterprises and extraordinary actions. Ferdinand, the present king of Spain, may be considered as a new prince, because he has advanced himself from a petty state to be the most renowned monarch in Christendom. Now, if we examine his actions, they all deserve to be accounted great, and some of them indeed are splendid.

Scarcely was this prince seated on the throne when he turned his arms against the kingdom of Granada; and this war laid the foundation of his greatness, in which he met with no impediment, for the nobles of Castile were so intent on the invasion that they wholly disregarded his political innovations. In the meantime he insensibly established a dominion over them by maintaining armies at the expense of the church and people and by disciplining them in such a manner as afterwards made his power irresistible. Afterwards, in order that he might undertake enterprises still more brilliant, he dexterously assumed the mask of religion, and, by a cruel piety, drove the Moors out of his dominions. The means he took for this enterprise were, without doubt, barbarous; yet the exploit was extraordinary and almost unexampled.

Ferdinand, under the same cloak of religion, afterwards attacked Africa, Italy, and France, always having some great design in agitation, the event of which kept his subjects in continual suspense and admiration. And those enterprises succeeded each other so speedily that his subjects had no leisure to think of other matters, much less to engage in conspiracies against him.

It is also of great service to a prince to afford rare examples of civil administration, especially when it is necessary to reward or punish in an exemplary manner, for the extraordinary good or evil his subjects may have done . . . A prince should also invest his actions with a character of greatness, and above all things, avoid weakness and indecision. He must be a firm friend or an open foe; otherwise he will with difficulty conciliate his subjects. Should two powerful neighbours go to war, he must declare

for one of them or he will inevitably become the prey of the conqueror; and the vanquished party will be gratified at his ruin, and thus he will lose all protection; for the conqueror will despise a doubtful friend, who may abandon him on the first reverse of fortune, and the vanquished will never pardon him for remaining a tranquil spectator of his defeat.

When Antiochus marched into Greece on the invitation of the Etolians to drive out the Romans, he sent ambassadors to the Achaians, friends of the latter, to secure their neutrality. The Romans, on the other hand, demanded their assistance. The affair being taken into deliberation in the council of the Achaians, the Roman envoy spoke after the ambassador of Antiochus, and said, "You are advised to remain neutral, as the safest mode of conduct; and I assure you there can be none so bad; for you will inevitably remain at the mercy of the conqueror, whoever he may be, and will thus have two chances to one against you."

They can be no real friends who ask you to stand neuter. This consideration alone ought to open the eyes of a prince to the consequences of such conduct. Irresolute princes frequently embrace a neutrality to avoid some present inconvenience; but they meet their ruin by such a course. A bold adhesion to one party secures friendship by the tie of gratitude and leaves but little to fear from the mercy of the conqueror; first, because men are seldom so wholly destitute of honour as to repay benefits by so revolting ingratitude: secondly, because victory is rarely so very complete as to place the conqueror in a state to violate all the laws of propriety. If, on the other hand, he whose fortune the prince espouses should be vanquished, he may in time retrieve his losses and acknowledge this mark of preference and esteem.

A prince ought never, as I have already observed, unless under the pressure of circumstances, to espouse the part of a neighbouring state more powerful than himself, because he lies at the mercy of his neighbour should he be the conqueror. Thus the Venetians were ruined by unnecessarily allying themselves with France against the duke of Milan. The Florentines, on the other hand, could not be blamed for embracing the cause of the pope and the king of Spain, when they marched their forces against Lombardy; because by adopting this step, they yielded to the dictates of necessity. After all, no party can be absolutely sure of success, and sometimes one danger is avoided only to encounter a greater; the utmost human prudence can do in such extremities is to choose the lesser evil.

Princes ought to honour talents and protect the

65. Antiochus. Antiochus III, the ancient Seleucid emperor (reigned 223–187 B.C.), was driven from Greece by the Romans in 191 B.C.

arts, particularly commerce and agriculture. It is peculiarly important that those who follow such pursuits should be secure from all dread of being overcharged with taxes and despoiled of their lands after they have improved them by superior cultivation. Finally, they should not neglect to entertain the people at certain periods of the year with festivals and shows, and they should honour with their presence the different trading companies and corporations, and display on such occasions the greatest affability and facility of access, always remembering to support their station with becoming dignity, which should never be lost sight of, under any circumstances.

Hugo Grotius

1583–1645

If nationalistic monarchy found a cynical textbook in Machiavelli, the Renaissance also laid the foundation of international law in the *Rights of War and Peace* (1625) of Hugo Grotius. Grotius (or Huig van Groot, as he was known in his native Holland) is thought of today as a jurist alone, but his life reveals the diversity of interests and abilities characteristic of the titans of the Renaissance. Though his father had served four times as burgomaster of Leyden, the brilliant youth entered the university there at the age of twelve with a thirst for the classics rather than the law and with a talent for writing Latin verses. Later in life he was to vary his legal and diplomatic duties with learned commentaries on classical authors, translations of Greek tragedians, and essays on Christian faith. His achievements as poet and historian were as much admired by his contemporaries as were his legal dissertations.

But he was trained as a lawyer and pleaded his first case at seventeen. On a visit to France the youthful prodigy was dubbed "The Miracle of Holland" by King Henry IV for his theses in jurisprudence. At thirty he was made pensionary (chief magistrate) of Rotterdam, but, becoming involved in the religious controversy of the Remonstrants and Anti-remonstrants that wracked Holland at this time, he was sentenced to life imprisonment by the Anti-remonstrants. Through the ingenuity of his faithful wife he escaped from prison in a chest of linen and thereafter lived abroad in France and Sweden. He served as Swedish ambassador to France between 1635 and the year of his death.

Although Grotius had an active career as advocate and diplomat, he was at heart a theorist about law. Living in an age when the Christian code of medieval warfare and statecraft had given way to the unscrupulous "natural" code of the jungle among the new nations, he had seen the shocking application of Machiavelli's philosophy in the Thirty Years' War in Germany. Convinced that a new code must come to regulate the ambitions and conflicts of nations, he sought his authority in the concept of a rational human nature common to all men which predicates a moral order in the universe older than man himself. Like the Rationalists of the eighteenth century, he appealed to reason rather than religious faith to justify his argument for a universal code and held up the example of ancient lawgivers to prove its permanent truth.

Every man must live in society with other men and hence must observe moral laws that make that society possible. These higher laws demand that men and the groupings of men called nations deny their predatory urges for the good of the whole. The higher law founded upon reason is simply the ethical reflection of the rational principle upon which the whole universe operates. This law of nature is imperfectly embodied in the law of nations (*ius gentium*) because of the variations of custom, but it must lie behind the law of nations and in general motivate their behavior if civilization is to survive. Grotius, then, was no mere idealist, insisting that men and nations should be better than they are. He knew that even the most reckless rulers of his day realized the need to modify Machiavelli in practice and stopped short of the utterly lawless behavior that he condoned, even as they might violate the codes that they could not entirely deny. Upon this sensible basis Grotius set forth his *Rights of War and Peace*.

Rights of War and Peace

I. THE RATIONAL BASIS OF INTERNATIONAL LAW

1.

THE Civil Law, both that of Rome, and that of each nation in particular, has been treated of, with a view either to illustrate it or to present it in a compendious form, by many. But International Law, that which regards the mutual relations of several Peoples, or Rulers of Peoples, whether it proceed from nature, or be instituted by divine command, or introduced by custom and tacit compact, has been touched on by few, and has been by no one treated as a whole in an orderly manner. And yet that this be done concerns the human race.

3. And such a work is the more necessary on this account; that there are not wanting persons in our own time, and there have been also in former times persons, who have despised what has been done in this province of jurisprudence, so far as to hold that no such thing existed, except as a mere name. Every

*Rights of War and Peace.*⁸ Translated by William Whewell.

one can quote the saying of Euphemius in Thucydides;—that for a king or a city which has an empire to maintain, nothing is unjust which is useful: and to the same effect is the saying that, for those who have supreme power, the equity is where the strength is: and that other, that state affairs cannot be carried on without doing some wrong. To this we must add that the controversies which arise between peoples and kings have commonly war for their arbiter. And that war is far from having anything to do with rights is not only the opinion of the vulgar, but even learned and prudent men often let fall expressions which favour such an opinion. It is very usual to put rights and arms in opposition to each other.

5. But since our discussion of Rights is worthless if there are no Rights, it will serve both to recommend our work and to protect it from objections, if we refute briefly this very grave error. And that we may not have to deal with a mob of opponents, let us appoint them an advocate to speak for them. And whom can we select for this office fitter than Carneades, who had made such wonderful progress in his suspension of opinion, the supreme aim of his Academical Philosophy, that he could work the machinery of his eloquence for falsehood as easily as for truth. He, then, undertook to argue against justice; and especially the kind of justice of which we here treat; and in doing so, he found no argument stronger than this:—that men had, as utility prompted, established Rights, different as their manners differed; and even in the same society often changed with the change of times: but Natural Law there is none: for all creatures, men and animals alike, are impelled by nature to seek their own gratification: and thus, either there is no such thing as justice, or if it exist, it is the height of folly, since it does harm to itself in aiming at the good of others.

6. But what the philosopher here says, and what the poet follows:—"By naked nature ne'er was understood what's just and right"—must by no means be admitted. For man is an animal indeed, but an animal of an excellent kind, differing much more from all other tribes of animals than they differ from one another; which appears by the evidence of many actions peculiar to the human species. And among these properties which are peculiar to man is a desire for society; that is, a desire for a life spent in common with fellowmen; and not merely spent somehow, but spent tranquilly and in a manner corresponding to the character of his intellect. This desire the Stoics called οἰκείωσις, the domestic instinct, or feeling of kindred. And therefore the as-

sertion that by nature every animal is impelled only to seek its own advantage or good, if stated so generally as to include man, cannot be conceded.

7. And indeed even in other animals, as well as in man, their desire of their own individual good is tempered by a regard, partly for their offspring, partly for others of their own species; which in them, indeed, we perceive to proceed from some intelligence outside themselves; because with regard to other acts not at all more difficult than those an equal degree of intelligence does not appear. The same is to be said of infants, in which, previous to all teaching, we see a certain disposition to do good to others, as is sagaciously remarked by Plutarch: as for example, compassion breaks out spontaneously at that age. But inasmuch as a man of full age has the knowledge which enables him to act similarly in similar cases, and along with that, a peculiar and admirable appetite for society, and has also language, an instrument of this desire, given to him alone of all animals, it is reasonable to assume that he has a faculty of knowing and acting according to general principles; and such tendencies as agree with this faculty do not belong to all animals, but are peculiar attributes of human nature.

8. And this tendency to the conservation of society, which we have now expressed in a rude manner, and which tendency is in agreement with the nature of the human intellect, is the source of *Jus*, or Natural Law, properly so called. To this *Jus* belong the rule of abstaining from that which belongs to other persons, and, if we have in our possession anything of another's, the restitution of it, or of any gain which we have made from it, the fulfilling of promises, and the reparation of damage done by fault, and the recognition of certain things as meriting punishment among men.

9. From this signification has flowed another larger sense of *Jus*: for, inasmuch as man is superior to other animals, not only in the social impulse of which we have spoken, but in his judgment and power of estimating advantages and disadvantages; and in these, not only present good and ill, but also future good and ill, and what may lead to each; we may understand that it is congruous to human nature to follow, in such matters also, a judgment rightly framed; not to be misled by fear or by the temptation of present pleasure, nor to be carried away by blind and thoughtless impulse; and that what is plainly repugnant to such judgment, is also contrary to *Jus*, that is, to Natural Human Law.

10. And to this exercise of judgment pertains a reasonable and thoughtful assignment to each individual and each body of men of the things which peculiarly belong to them; by which exercise of judgment in some cases, the wiser man is preferred to the less wise; in others, our neighbour to a

1–2. the saying . . . in Thucydides; in Book VI, 85. 22–23. Carneades, the Skeptic (c. 213–129 B.C.), founder of the Third Academy in Athens. 40–41. "By naked . . . and right." Horace, I *Satires*, iii, 113.

II : 422

stranger; in others, a poor man to a rich man; according as the nature of each act and each thing requires. And this some persons have treated as a part of *Jus* properly and strictly so called; although *Jus* properly so called is really very different in its nature, and has this for its special office; to leave to another what is his, to give to him what we owe.

11. And what we have said would still have great weight, even if we were to grant what we cannot grant without wickedness, that there is no God, or that He bestows no regard on human affairs. But inasmuch as we are assured of the contrary of this, partly by reason, partly by constant tradition, confirmed by many arguments and by miracles attested by all ages, it follows that God, as the author of our being, to Whom we owe ourselves and all that we have, is to be obeyed by us without exception, especially since He has, in many ways, shown Himself both supremely good and supremely powerful: wherefore He is able to bestow upon those who obey Him the highest rewards, even eternal ones, as being Himself eternal; and He must be supposed to be willing as well as able to do this; and the more so, if He have promised such rewards in plain language; which we Christians believe, resting our belief on the indubitable faith of testimonies.

12. And here we are brought to another origin of *Jus*, besides that natural source; namely, the free will of God, to which, as our reason irresistibly tells us, we are bound to submit ourselves. But even that Natural Law of which we have spoken, whether it be that which binds together communities or that looser kind (which enjoins duties), although it do proceed from the internal principles of man, may yet be rightly ascribed to God; because it was by His will that such principles came to exist in us. And in this sense, Chrysippus and the Stoics said that the origin of *Jus*, or Natural Law, was not to be sought in any other quarter than in Jove himself; and it may be probably conjectured that the Latins took the word *Jus* from the name *Jove*.

15. In the next place, since it is comfortable to Natural Law to observe compacts (for some mode of obliging themselves was necessary among men, and no other natural mode could be imagined), Civil Rights were derived from this source, mutual compact. For those who had joined any community or put themselves in subjection to any man or men, either expressly promised or from the nature of the case must have been understood to promise tacitly that they would conform to that which either the majority of the community or those to whom the power was assigned should determine.

16. And therefore what Carneades said (as above), and what others also have said, as Horace, that utility is the mother of justice and right, if we are to speak accurately, is not true. For the Mother of Right, that is, of Natural Law, is Human Nature; for this would lead us to desire mutual society, even if it were not required for the supply of other wants; and the Mother of Civil Laws is Obligation by mutual compact; and since mutual compact derives its force from Natural Law, Nature may be said to be the Grandmother of Civil Laws. But Natural Law (which impels us to society) is reinforced by Utility. For the Author of Nature ordained that we should, as individuals, be weak and in need of many things to make life comfortable, in order that we might be the more impelled to cling to society. But Utility is the occasion of Civil Laws; for the association or subjection by mutual compact, of which we have just spoken, was at the first instituted for the sake of some utility. And accordingly, they who prescribe laws for others, in doing this, aim, or ought to aim at some Utility, to be produced to them for whom they legislate.

17. Further: as the Laws of each Community regard the Utility of that Community, so also between different Communities, Laws might be established, and it appears that Laws have been established, which enjoined the Utility, not of special communities, but of that great aggregate System of Communities. And this is what is called the Law of Nations, or International Law; when we distinguish it from Natural Law. And this part of Law is omitted by Carneades, who divides all Law into Natural Law and the Civil Laws of special peoples; while yet, inasmuch as he was about to treat of that Law which obtains between one people and another (for then follows an oration concerning war and acquisitions by war), he was especially called upon to make mention of Law of this kind.

18. And it is without any good reason that Carneades maintains, as we have said (5), that justice is folly. For since, by his own confession, that Citizen is not foolish who in a Civil Community obeys the Civil Law, although in consequence of such respect for the Law he may lose something which is useful to himself: so too that People is not foolish which does not so estimate its own utility as, on account of that, to neglect the common Laws between People and People. The reason of the thing is the same in both cases. For as a citizen who violates the Civil Law for the sake of present utility destroys that institution in which the perpetual utility of himself and his posterity is bound up; so too a people which violates the Laws of Nature and Nations beats down the bulwark of its own tranquillity for future time. And even if no utility were to arise from the observation of Law, it would be a point, not of folly, but of wisdom, to which we feel ourselves drawn by nature.

19. And therefore neither is that other saying of Horace universally true: "'Twas fear of wrong that

made us make our laws;" an opinion which one of the interlocutors in Plato's *Republic* explains in this way: that Laws were introduced from the fear of receiving wrong, and that men are driven to practise justice by a certain compulsion. For that applies to those institutions and laws only which were devised for the more easy maintenance of rights: as when many, individually feeble, fearing to be oppressed by those who were stronger, combined to establish judicial authorities, and to uphold them by their common strength; that those whom they could not resist singly, they might, united, control. And we may accept in this sense, and in no other, what is also said in Plato, that Right is that which the stronger party likes: namely, that we are to understand that Rights do not attain their external end, except they have force to back them. Thus Solon did great things, as he himself boasted, "by linking Force in the same yoke with Law."

20. But still Rights, even unsupported by force, are not destitute of all effect: for Justice, the observance of Rights, brings security to the conscience; while injustice inflicts on it tortures and wounds, such as Plato describes as assaulting the bosoms of tyrants. The conscience of honest men approves justice, condemns injustice. And what is the greatest point, injustice has for its enemy, justice, for its friend, God, who reserves His judgments for another life, yet in such a manner that He often exhibits their power in this life; of which we have many examples in history.

21. The reason why many persons, while they require justice as necessary in private citizens, commit the error of thinking it superfluous in a People or the Ruler of a People is this: in the first place, that in their regard to rights they look at nothing but the utility which arises from rights, which in the case of private citizens is evident, since they are separately too weak to protect themselves: while great States, which seem to embrace within them all that is requisite to support life in comfort, do not appear to have need of that virtue which regards extraneous parties, and is called justice.

22. But, not to repeat what I have already said, that Rights are not established for the sake of utility alone, there is no State so strong that it may not at some time need the aid of others external to itself, either in the way of commerce or in order to repel the force of many foreign nations combined against it. And hence we see that Leagues of alliance are sought even by the most powerful Peoples and Kings; which can have no force according to the principles of those who confine rights within the boundary of the State alone. It is most true (as Cicero says)

that everything loses its certainty at once if we give up the belief in rights.

28. I, for the reasons which I have stated, holding it to be most certain that there is among nations a common law of Rights which is of force with regard to war and in war, saw many and grave causes why I should write a work on that subject. For I saw prevailing throughout the Christian world a license in making war of which even barbarous nations would have been ashamed; recourse being had to arms for slight reasons or no reason; and when arms were once taken up, all reverence for divine and human law was thrown away, just as if men were thenceforth authorized to commit all crimes without restraint.

46. Passages of history are of twofold use to us; they supply both examples of our arguments, and judgment upon them with regard to examples; in proportion as they belong to better times and better nations, they have the more authority; and therefore we have preferred those taken from the Greeks and the Romans. Nor are the judgments delivered in such histories to be despised, especially when many of them agree; for Natural Law, as we have said, is in a certain measure, to be proved by such consent; and as to the Law of Nations, there is no other way of proving it.

II. NATURAL LAW AND WAR

1. Natural Law is the Dictate of Right Reason, indicating that any act, from its agreement or disagreement with the rational nature (of man) has in it a moral turpitude or a moral necessity; and consequently that such act is forbidden or commanded by God, the Author of nature.

Acts concerning which there is such a Dictate are obligatory (morally necessary) or are unlawful in themselves, and are therefore understood as necessarily commanded or forbidden by God; and in this character, Natural Law differs, not only from Human Law, but from Positive Divine Law, which does not forbid or command acts which, in themselves and by their own nature, are either obligatory or unlawful; but by forbidding them makes them unlawful, by commanding them makes them obligatory.

In order to understand Natural Law, we must remark that some things are said to be according to Natural Law which are not so properly, but, as the schools love to speak, reductively, Natural Law not opposing them; as we have said that some things are called just which are not unjust. And again, by an abuse of expression, some things are said to be according to Natural Law which reason shows to be decent, or better than their opposites, though not obligatory.

It is to be remarked also that Natural Law deals not only with things made by nature herself, but

---

2. in Plato's *Republic*; II, 359 B. 18–19. "by linking . . . with Law. " Quoted by Plutarch, *Life of Solon*, 86 c.

with things produced by the act of man. Thus property, as it now exists, is the result of human will: but being once introduced, Natural Law itself shows that it is unlawful for me to take what is yours against your will.

Natural Law is so immutable that it cannot be changed by God himself. For though the power of God be immense, there are some things to which it does not extend: because if we speak of those things being done, the words are mere words and have no meaning, being self-contradictory. Thus God Himself cannot make twice two not be four; and, in like manner, He cannot make that which is intrinsically bad, not be bad. For as the essence of things, when they exist and by which they exist, does not depend on anything else, so is it with the properties which follow that essence: and such a property is the baseness of certain actions when compared with the nature of rational beings. And God Himself allows Himself to be judged of by this rule.

Yet sometimes, in acts directed by Natural Law, there is an appearance of change which may mislead the unwary, when in fact it is not Natural Law which is changed, but the thing about which that Law is concerned. Thus, if a creditor gives me a receipt for my debt, I am no longer bound to pay him; not that Natural Law has ceased to command me to pay what I owe, but because I have ceased to owe it. So if God command any one to be slain or his goods to be taken, this does not make lawful homicide or theft, which words involve crime: but the act will no longer be homicide or theft, being authorized by the supreme Lord of life and of goods. . . .

2. In the first principle of nature (Self-preservation) there is nothing which is repugnant to war. Indeed, all things rather favour it: for the end of war, the preservation of life and limb and the retention or acquisition of things useful to life agree entirely with that of principle. And if force be requisite for this purpose, still there is in this nothing at variance with nature; for all animals are provided by nature with means for the very purpose of self-defense. . . .

Again, Right Reason and the nature of Society, which are next to be considered, do not prohibit all force, but that only which is repugnant to Society; that is, that which is used to attack the rights of others. For Society has for its object, that every one may have what is his own in safety, by the common help and agreement. Which consideration would still have place, even if property were not introduced; for even then, each one would have a property in his life, limbs, liberty; and these could not be attacked without wrong done to him. And also to use things which lay in common, and to take as much of them as nature should require, would be the right

of the person who first took occupation of them; and he who should prevent the exercise of this right, would do the occupier wrong. And this is much more easily understood now, when property has taken a shape by law or usage: as Cicero says.

Therefore it is not contrary to the nature of Society to take care of the future for one's self, so that the rights of others be not infringed: and thus, even force which does not violate the right of another is not unjust.

Lope de Vega

1562–1635

The romantic temperament of Spain finds its best expression in the ebullient plays of Lope de Vega. Behind him lay a century of dramatic evolution, but in Lope the Spanish theater reached maturity. His extravagant genius contributed brilliantly to most literary forms of his day, but his best and most voluminous output was reserved for drama, whether the religious *autos sacramentales,* or "cloak-and-sword *comedias*" of manners and intrigue, or the historical plays that revealed his patriotic fervor. His long, teeming life is more romantic and amazing than any single thing he wrote, and through all its inconsistencies shines his passionate faith in the Catholic religion and the high destiny of his beloved Spain.

Lope Felix de Vega Carpio is an almost exact contemporary of Shakespeare, but two more different playwrights in temperament, career, and artistic objectives could hardly be imagined. Beside the modest, thoughtful Englishman with his thirty-odd plays that carefully study human character, set the dashing Spaniard of a thousand plays turned out at breathless speed in oft-repeated molds. Even as a peasant boy, Lope dictated verses before he could write and at twelve completed his first play, which was acted by a prominent company. The youthful prodigy was sent to the University of Alcalá de Henares by a bishop whom he served as page, but it is probable that he left before obtaining his degree to take part in a naval expedition. By 1585 he had established himself as poet and playwright in Madrid, but a disappointment in love and his vengeful libel of the girl's family led to his exile from the city for eight years. He broke this exile only to elope with the daughter of Philip ii's King-at-Arms, but cut short his honeymoon to enlist with the Spanish Armada. He dispelled his grief at the defeat of the Armada and at the death of his brother by writing a narrative poem in eleven cantos on the return voyage.

Upon his arrival in Spain, Lope plunged into writing for the stage. The death of his wife in 1595 removed the last barrier to the dissipation to which his passionate nature had long been predisposed. A series of scandalous intrigues was not interrupted by a second marriage for money, and his new wife denounced in vain his liaisons with several mistresses. His illegitimate children were the gossip of his enemies, but no amount of attack could threaten his commanding eminence in literature. In the midst of this wanton life Lope suddenly turned devout and took holy orders in 1614. But this whim did not last long, and a rash of religious writing was followed by more of the libertine. Only in his seventies did a series of misfortunes—the death of his brilliant son, the elopement of a daughter with an older man—lead him to a pious end. Characteristically, he went to extremes in his repentance, beating himself until the walls of his room were spotted with blood. His death soon after was followed by a magnificent funeral.

Lope's total production is almost beyond belief; during nearly seventy years he never stopped writing. His miscellaneous works alone—epics, odes, sonnets, elegies, eclogues, romances, burlesques—fill twenty-one huge volumes. One scholar has estimated that he wrote over twenty-one million lines of verse. Since the majority of his plays have been lost, the exact number of them can never be known. At the age of seventy he claimed to have written fifteen hundred, and a disciple set the figure at eighteen hundred, plus four hundred *autos sacramentales*. Later scholars have reduced this number considerably, but the extant, genuine plays of Lope number 475 —in itself the most amazing dramatic output of all time. No wonder Cervantes, who was not always his friend, called Lope the 'Monster of Nature.'

Obviously Lope could not have thought through these plays individually: many are variations on each other, rushed through to appease an insatiable public. His themes are the standard Spanish loyalties—passionate romantic love for a fair lady, unquestioning Catholic faith, undying devotion to king and country. The intensity of these sentiments is revealed in set speeches, often rhetorical to the point of bombast. His characters too are conventionalized—the wise and beneficent king, the haughty and sometimes villainous nobleman whose defeat represents the death of feudalism, the proud peasant, the dashing young hero, his chaste and high-spirited lady, and above all the clever *gracioso*, or clown, whose buffoonery and realistic comments on the romantic characters bring the plays down to earth and comedy. In some respects Lope's plays are surprisingly modern: they are shorter than Shakespeare's, running to three acts rather than five; they are seldom either tragedies or comedies, but tragicomedies essentially serious in tone while relieved by humor and a happy ending; and their respectful treatment of commoners is much more appealing than Shakespeare's aristocratic contempt for the rabble. On the other hand, the high-flown speeches irritate our common sense, and the stock characters and sentiments are poor substitutes for the subtle psychology of Shakespeare and the broad philosophy of Molière. The prodigal Lope appeals through his sheer high spirits and flashes of poetry, not through the force of his ideas.

Of the many classes of his *comedias*, The Sheep Well (*Fuente Ovejuna*) excellently represents his chronicle plays. It has been chosen because of its strikingly modern subject—the uprising of a community against injustice and the common loyalty of its members to each other. It has no hero or heroine in the conventional sense; the hero is the town, *Fuente Ovejuna*, victorious over a hateful villain. This grand theme takes on an epic character in the communal solidarity of the last scene. The work was first published in 1619 and was probably written in that decade. Its revival in modern times was due to Russian critics who saw in its theme a parallel with the Soviet Revolution.

The Sheep Well

PERSONS

THE KING, FERDINAND OF ARAGON
QUEEN ISABELLA OF CASTILE
DON MANRIQUE, MASTER OF SANTIAGO
RODRIGO TÉLLEZ GIRÓN, GRAND MASTER OF CALATRAVA
THE COMMANDER FERNÁN GÓMEZ DE GUZMÁN
FLORES } *his retainers*
ORTUÑO }
CIMBRANOS, *a soldier*
A Judge
Two Regidors of Ciudad Real
ESTEBAN } *Alcaldes of Fuente Ovejuna*
ALONSO }
JUAN ROJO } *Regidors*
CUADRADO }
Another Regidor of Fuente Ovejuna
FRONDOSO }
MENGO } *peasants*
BARRILDO }
LEONELO, *a student*
A Farmer
A Soldier
LAURENCIA }
PASCUALA } *peasants girls*
JACINTA }
A Boy
Musicians, Soldiers, Farmers, Villagers and Attendants

The scene is laid in Almagro, the village of Fuente Ovejuna (meaning "Sheep Well"), the country round about Ciudad Real, and at the itinerant Royal Court in Castile. Time: 1476.

ACT FIRST

SCENE ONE. *A street in Almagro*

(*The* COMMANDER *enters with* FLORES *and* OR-
TUÑO, *servants.*)

COMMANDER.

Does the Master know I have come to town?
FLORES. He does, sir.
ORTUÑO. The years will bring discretion.
COMMANDER. I am Fernán Gómez de Guzmán.
FLORES. To-day youth may serve as his excuse.
COMMANDER. If he is ignorant of my name, let him
respect the dignity of the High Commander.
ORTUÑO. He were ill advised to fail in courtesy.
COMMANDER. Or he will gain little love. Courtesy
10 is the key to favor while discourtesy is stupidity that
breeds enmity.
ORTUÑO. Should a rude oaf hear how roundly he
was hated, with the whole world at his heels not to
bark but to bite, he would die sooner than convict
himself a boor.
FLORES. Slight no man. Among equals pride is
folly but toward inferiors it becomes oppression.
Here neglect is want of care. The boy has not yet
learned the price of favor.
20 COMMANDER. The obligation which he assumed
with the sword the day that the cross of Calatrava
was fixed upon his breast, bound him to humility
and love.
FLORES. He can intend no despite that his quick
spirit shall not presently make appear.
ORTUÑO. Return, sir, nor stay upon his pleasure.
COMMANDER. I have come to know this boy.
(*Enter the* MASTER OF CALATRAVA *and* Attendants.)
MASTER. A thousand pardons, Fernán Gómez de
Guzmán! I am advised of your arrival in the city.
30 COMMANDER. I had just complaint of you, for my
affection and our birth are holy ties, being as we
are the one Master of Calatrava, and the other Commander, who subscribes himself yours wholly.
MASTER. I had no thought of this purposed honor,
Fernando, hence a tardy welcome. Let me embrace
you once again.
COMMANDER. Vying in honor. I have staked my
own on your behalf in countless causes, even answering during your minority before the Pope at Rome.
40 MASTER. You have indeed. By the holy token that
we bear above our hearts, I repay your love, and
honor you as I should my father.
COMMANDER. I am well content.
MASTER. What news of the war at the front?
COMMANDER. Attend and learn your obligation.
MASTER. Say I am already in the field.
COMMANDER. Noble Master
Don Rodrigo Téllez Girón,

To power and rule exalted
Through bravery of a mighty sire   50
Who eight years since
Renounced the Mastership,
Devising it to you,
As was confirmed by oaths and surety
Of Kings and High Commanders,
Even the Sovereign Pontiff,
Pius the Second,
Concurring by his bull,
And later Paul, succeeding him,
Decreeing holily   60
That Don Juan Pacheco,
Noble Master of Santiago,
Should co-adjutor be
With you to serve,
Till now, his death recorded,
All government and rule
Descend upon your head,
Sole and supreme
Despite your untried years.
Wherefore take counsel,   70
Harkening to the voice of honor,
And follow the commitment
Of kin and allies, wisely led.
Henry the Fourth is dead.
Let all his lieges
Bend the knee forthwith
To Alonso, King of Portugal,
Heir by right in Castile
Through his wife
In tie of marriage,   80
Though Ferdinand,
Lord of Aragon,
Like right maintains
By title of his wife,
Isabella.
Yet to our eyes
The line of her succession is not clear,
Nor can we credit
Shadow of deception
In the right descent   90
Of Juana, now secure
Under the protection of your cousin,
Who loves you as a brother.
Therefore summon all the Knights
Of Calatrava to Almagro,
Thence to reduce
Ciudad Real,
Which guards the pass
Dividing Andalusia from Castile,
On both   100
Frowning impartially.
Few men will gain the day.
For want of soldiers
The people mount the walls,
Aided by errant knights

Faithful to Isabella,
And so pledged to Ferdinand
As King.
Strike terror, Rodrigo,
To the hearts of those who say
That this great cross
Rests heavily
Upon the sagging bosom of a child.
Consider the Counts of Ureña,
10 From whom you spring,
Flaunting the laurels of their might
Upon the heights of fame,
Nor neglect to emulate
The Marquises of Villena,
With other gallant captains
Whose names in manifold
Brighten the outstretched wings
Of reputation.
Unsheathe your virgin sword
20 Till in battle, like the cross,
It drip with blood.
Of this red cross,
Blasoned on the breast,
Breathes there no votary
Whose drawn sword flashes white.
At the breast the one,
At the side the other
Must glow and flame with red!
So crown, valiant Girón,
30 With deeds
The immortal temple
Reared stone by stone
By your great ancestors.
   MASTER. Fernán Gómez,
I shall march with you
Because our cause is just,
And with my kin bear arms.
If I must pass,
Then shall I pass at Ciudad Real
40 As a lightning stroke,
Cleaving as I pass,
While my scant years proclaim
To friend and foe alike
That when my uncle died
Was no mortality of valor.
I draw my sword
That men may see it shine,
Livid with the passion of the cross,
Maculately red.
50 Where hold you residence?
Send on your vassals
To combat in my train.
   COMMANDER. Few but faithful serve,
Who will contend like lions
In battle.
Fuente Ovejuna is a town
Of simple folk,

Unskilled in warfare,
Rather with plough and spade
Tilling the fields. 60
   COMMANDER. Favored possession
In these troubled times,
Pastoral, serene!
Gather your men;
Let none remain unarmed.
   MASTER. Today I spur my horse
And level my eager lance.

SCENE TWO. *The Square of Fuente Ovejuna.*

(PASCUALA *and* LAURENCIA *enter.*)

LAURENCIA. I prayed he would never come back.
PASCUALA. When I brought the word I knew it
would grieve you. 70
LAURENCIA. Would to God he had never seen
Fuente Ovejuna!
PASCUALA. Laurencia, many a girl has made a pre-
tense of saying no, yet all the while her heart has
been as soft as butter in her.
LAURENCIA. I am a live-oak, gnarled and twisted.
PASCUALA. Yes, but why refuse a drink of water?
LAURENCIA. I do, be the sun never so hot, though
you may not believe it. Why love Fernando? He's no
husband. 80
PASCUALA. No, woman.
LAURENCIA. And amen! Plenty of girls in the vil-
lage have trusted the Commander to their harm.
PASCUALA. It will be a miracle if you escape.
LAURENCIA. You are blind, because I have avoided
him a full month now, Pascuala, and no quarter.
Flores, who lays his snares, and that villain Ortuño,
offered me a waist, a necklace and a head-dress.
They praised Fernando, their master, and pictured
him so great that I blushed at his very glory, but for 90
all that they could not move me.
PASCUALA. But where was this?
LAURENCIA. Down by the brook there, a week
gone yesterday.
PASCUALA. You're already lost, Laurencia.
LAURENCIA. No, no, no!
PASCUALA. Maybe the priest might believe your
story.
LAURENCIA. I am too innocent for the priest. In
His Name, Pascuala, but of a morning rising early 100
I had rather set me a slice of ham on the fire to
munch with a crust of bread of my own kneading,
filching a glass meanwhile out of the old stopped
butt, once mother's back is turned, to wet my thirst,
and then climb to watch the cow thrash through the
cabbages, all foaming at the mouth come noonday,
while I hearten myself with a bit of eggplant and
a strip of bacon after hard walking, and return
weary toward supper-time to nibble the raisins,

home-grown in our own vineyard, which God fend the hail from, sitting me down with a dish of salad and pepper and olive oil, and so to bed tired at nightfall, in contentment and peace, with a prayer on my lips to be preserved from the men, devils, God knows, every one, than I would deliver myself up to their wiles for all their love and fury. What they want is to undo us, joy in the night and at dawning a maid's mourning.

10   PASCUALA. You are right, Laurencia, for a sated lover flies faster than a farm sparrow. In the winter when the fields are bare they sing 'tweet' under the eaves till they come by the crumbs from the farmer's board, but when the fields are green and frost has been forgotten, instead of fluttering down to sing 'tweet' they hop up to the roof-tree and cry 'twit,' and 'twit' it is at you standing down below, make the most that you can of their twitting. Men are the same. When they need us we are their very lives,
20 their heart, their soul, their entire being, but their hunger satisfied off they fly and leave us, too, with the echo of their twitting. So I say no man can be trusted.

   (MENGO, BARRILDO *and* FRONDOSO *enter.*)

   FRONDOSO. You defeat yourself, Barrildo.

   BARRILDO. Two judges are here who can decide between us.

   MENGO. Agree upon the forfeit and then we'll call in the girls. If they favor me, you hand me both your shirts, with whatever else you have on your
30 backs, in need of victory.

   BARRILDO. Agreed. But what will you give if you lose?

   MENGO. My rebeck of old box, which is worth more than a granary, for Gods knows its like cannot be bought in the village.

   BARRILDO. Fairly said and offered.

   FRONDOSO. Done!—God save you, ladies.

   LAURENCIA. Frondoso calls us ladies.

   FRONDOSO. The flattery of the age.
40 The blind we say are one-eyed,
The cross-eyed merely squint,
Pupils equal masters
While cripples barely limp;
The spendthrift fools call "open,"
The dumb now hold their tongues,
Bullies out-vie brave men,
Shouters shame the grave men,
And as for saving
Praise the miser—
50 None so active as the meddler
To promote the common good.
Gossips will "talk freely,"
While concede we must
The quarrelsome are just.

33. old box; that is, boxwood.

Boasters display their courage,
The shrinking coward "retires,"
The impudent grow witty,
The taciturn sit pretty,
All hail the idiot.
Gamblers, pray, "look forward,"   60
The bald deserve respect,
Admit the ass is graceful,
That large feet proclaim the faithful,
While a blotched and pimpled face-full
Is a scientific indication
Of a sluggish circulation.
The lie to-day a truth is,
Rudeness clever youth is,
And if you have a hump,
Why follow your bent   70
All the way over,
Without stooping
Moreover,
And so to conclude
I call you ladies,
For otherwise there is no telling what names I might
    call you.

   LAURENCIA. In the city praise may be the fashion, Frondoso, but by my faith we have a contrary custom in the country, where words are sharp and 80 barbed, upon tongues that are calloused to use them.

   FRONDOSO. Who speaks knows.

   LAURENCIA. Turn all in reverse.
Know and be a bore,
Work and you have luck,
The prudent are faint-hearted,
The upright reek with muck.
Advice to-day spells insult,
Charity rank waste,
Be fair and painted ugly,   90
Be good, what wretched taste!
Truth is made for boobies,
No purity wins rubies,
While as for giving,
'Tis a veil for sinful living,
Fie, fie the hypocrite!
Disparage true worth always.
Dub simple faith imbecility,
Flat cowardice amiability,
Nor ever be fearful   100
Against the innocent
To speak an ear-full.
No woman is honest,
No beauty is chaste,
And as for virtue
There is not enough to hurt you,
For in the country
A curse
Turns merit to reverse.

   MENGO. Devil of a girl!   110

   BARRILDO. On my soul, she is too quick for us!

MENGO. A pinch of spice plashed into the holy water the day of her christening.

LAURENCIA. Well, well, since you question us, let us have it without delay and judge truly.

FRONDOSO. I'll set out the argument.

LAURENCIA. Plant in season, then, and begin.

FRONDOSO. Attend, Laurencia.

LAURENCIA. Oh, I'll have an answer for you some day.

10 FRONDOSO. Be fair, be just.

LAURENCIA. What is this wager?

FRONDOSO. Barrildo and I oppose Mengo.

LAURENCIA. Mengo is right. So, there!

BARRILDO. A fact is certain and plain which he denies.

MENGO. I deny it because it's a lie and they wander from the mark.

LAURENCIA. Explain.

BARRILDO. He maintains there is no such thing as 20 love.

LAURENCIA. Then it takes hold of one mightily.

BARRILDO. Yes, though it be blind, for without love the world would never go on.

MENGO. I say little, not being able to read, though I could learn, but if the elements make the world and our bodies are made of the elements which war against each other unceasingly, causing anger and discord, then where is love?

BARRILDO. Mengo, the world is love, here and here-30 after, not discord. Harmony is love. Love is a reaching out.

MENGO. A pulling in, according to nature, which governs all things through the resemblances that are. Love is a looking to its own, it's preservation. I raise my hand to my face to prevent the blow, I move my feet to remove me from danger to my body, my eye-lids close to shield my sight through the attraction of a mutual love.

PASCUALA. He admits it's love, so what then? 40 There's an end.

MENGO. We love ourselves, no one else, that's flat.

PASCUALA. Mengo, what a lie! And God forgive me. The love a man bears for a woman, or a beast for its mate, is a fierce, consuming passion.

MENGO. Self-love, interest, not pure love. What is love?

LAURENCIA. A running after beauty.

MENGO. But why run after beauty?

LAURENCIA. For the thrill and the pleasure, boy.

50 MENGO. True. And the pleasure a man seeks for himself.

LAURENCIA. True again.

MENGO. So that self-love seeks its own delight?

LAURENCIA. Granted.

MENGO. Therefore there is no love, only we like what we like, and we intend in all things to get it, to seek delight, our delight.

BARRILDO. One day the priest preached in the village about a man named Plato who had taught men how to love, but what Plato loved, he said, was the 60 soul and the virtue that was hidden in it.

PASCUALA. So the fathers teach the children in 'cademies and schools.

LAURENCIA. Yes, and don't you listen to any nonsense, either. Mengo, thank God you never knew the curse of love.

MENGO. Were you ever in love?

LAURENCIA. In love with my honor, always.

FRONDOSO. Come, come, ladies! Decide, decide.

BARRILDO. Who wins? 70

PASCUALA. Let the priest or the sacristan cook up a reply, for Laurencia loves too much and I not a little, so how can we, siding both ways, decide?

FRONDOSO. They laugh at us.

(*Enter* FLORES.)

FLORES. God guard the fair!

PASCUALA. This man is from the Commander.

LAURENCIA. Why so brash, old goshawk, in the village?

FLORES. You meet me as a soldier.

LAURENCIA. From Don Fernando? 80

FLORES. The war is done, though it has cost us blood, and armies of our friends.

FRONDOSO. Say what of note our band achieved.

FLORES. I will, and that better than another, having seen it with my own eyes.
Beleaguering the city
Of Ciudad Real,
By charter royal,
The valiant Master mustered in
Two thousand foot, 90
Bravest among his vassals,
Beside three hundred horse,
Churchmen and laymen,
For the crimson cross
Summons to its aid
Those who profess it on their breasts
Though robed and habited for prayer,
Crusading oft in holy cause,
Ruthless to slay the Moor.
Boldly the lad rode forth, 100
His tunic green
Embroidered with golden scrolls,
While silken cords
Caught up his sleeves,
Stayed sixfold
Above his iron gauntlets.
His steed was sturdy stout,
A dappled roan
Bred beside the Betis,
Drinking of the willing stream 110
And pasturing on lush meadows,
But now in panoply of white
Bedecked, patterns of net

Flecking the snowy pools
That gemmed his mottled hide
From plumed crest
Down to the buckskin tail-piece.
At equal pace
The Commander Fernán Gómez
Bestrid a piebald charger,
Black of mane, the tail coal black,
White foaming at the nostril.
10 A Turkish coat of mail he wore,
Breastplate and corselet
Glowing bright orange,
Relieved with pearls and gold.
White plumes
Topped off his helmet,
Pallid plumes wind-blown,
Striking dismay,
The while his puissant arm
Banded now red, now white,
20 Brandished an ash-tree,
Famous as his lance
Even to Granada.
The city flew to arms,
Vain boasts of loyalty
With greed contending,
Some fearful for their homes,
Some of their treasure.
The Master breached those walls,
Flung back those surly churls,
30 And the heads
Of the rebel leaders,
As of those conspiring there
Against his dignity,
With a blow
Severed from the body.
We gagged the common folk,
Then beat them openly,
So in that town
The Master is feared and praised
40 Conjointly.
Though few in years,
By deeds, by valor and by victory
Nature in him has forged
A bolt from heaven
To rive Africa,
Her blue moon senescent
To the red cross bowed,
Obeisant.
Rich the promise
50 Of the rape of this fair city,
With apportionment
Of present gain
To him and the Commander.
Now hear the music sound, for zest in victory adds
    sweetest savor.

45. **Africa;** that is, Moslem Morocco.

(*The* COMMANDER *enters with* ORTUÑO *and* Musicians, *accompanied by* JUAN ROJO, *Regidor*, ESTEBAN *and* ALONSO, *Alcaldes.*)

Song

Welcome, great Commander,
Many times a victor,
Guzmáns, arm, to battle!
Girónes, strike, to battle!
Doves in peace,   60
Mighty in repose.
Forward to the conflict,
Strong of limb as oak-trees,
Drive the Moors before you
From Ciudad Real.
Flaunt your pennons proudly
In Fuente Ovejuna,
Valiant Fernán Gómez,
Glorious Conqueror!

COMMANDER. Acknowledgment and thanks in this 70
    our town
Receive in token of the love you show.
    ALONSO. Accept this rustic tribute to renown,
Proffered how simply. These poor meadows grow
Scant sustenance of woe.
    ESTEBAN.   Welcome accept
To Fuente Ovejuna, whose elders glow
    With pride, offering homely gifts, yet ept
To please, as pod or sprout or root, in carts
Heaped high with ruddy fruits, the produce rept 80
    From field and orchard, ripening in our hearts,
Mellowed in crib and barnyard. First, car one
Twin hampers bears of jars, baked for these marts,
    Whereto are added geese that sleekly run
Long necks from tangling nets, and shrilly shriek
Cackles of praise, paeans of booty won.
    Ten salted hogs bid the next wagon creak,
Bulging with fatty trimmings and dried meat;
The skins like amber shine, side, haunch and breek.
    A hundred pair of capon follow, treat 90
For the belly, plump hens torn from the cock
Through all the eager farms, tender and meet
    For axing. Arms we lack, nor bring we stock
Of blooded steeds, nor harness for the bold,
For such in rustic hands were cheat and mock
    Of love's pure gold which in our hearts is told.
Twelve wine-skins next appear, with beady wine
Filled full, in winter enemy of cold
    And friendly to the soldier, ally in line
Of battle, or on defense trusty like steel, 100
Tempering courage, for temper springs of wine.
    Unnumbered cheeses, last, jounce past awheel,
With products of the churn and dairy days,
True tokens of the love the people feel
Toward you and yours, harvests of heart-felt praise.
    COMMANDER. Thanks and be gone, Alcaldes of
this town. Be gone assured of favor.

ALONSO. Rest, Master, in enjoyment of our love. These cat-tails before the door and this coarse sedge grass should bear pearls to match your deserving, as indeed we pray, and yet fall short of the devotion of the village.

COMMANDER. I accept the gifts right gladly. So get you gone.

ESTEBAN. The singers will repeat the refrain.

Song
Welcome, great Commander,
10 *Many times a victor,*
Men and fields mowed down!   (*Exeunt.*)

COMMANDER. The girls stay behind.

LAURENCIA. No, Your Excellency.

COMMANDER. By the Lord you do! No airs nor graces! These are soldiers here.

LAURENCIA. Pascuala, he looks your way.

PASCUALA. Do you teach me to be modest?

COMMANDER. I look your way, little chuck with the crook, and tend to this burr of the pasture, till 20 she open to me.

PASCUALA. We grew here, Master.

COMMANDER. Pass into the house where my men will keep you safe.

LAURENCIA. If the Alcaldes go in so will we, because one is my father, but a girl by herself is just a girl and must be careful.

COMMANDER. A word, Flores.

FLORES. Master?

COMMANDER. How? What mean these green-30 briers?

FLORES. Walk straight in, girls. Come!

LAURENCIA. You let go!

FLORES. Any fool can walk.

PASCUALA. You'll lock the door if we do go in.

FLORES. Pass and taste the spoils of war. Come!

COMMANDER (*aside to* ORTUÑO). Throw the bolt, Ortuño, once they're inside.   (*Exit.*)

LAURENCIA. You hurt us, Flores.

ORTUÑO. These cheeses came in no cart.

40 PASCUALA. No, and we are not for you, either, so get out!

FLORES. What can you do with a girl?

LAURENCIA. Your master has his fill to-day for one stomach.

ORTUÑO. He's a judge of meat and prefers you, though the carts pass.

LAURENCIA. Then let him burst! (*The girls go out.*)

FLORES. What will the Master say with never a sight of a woman for good cheer? They laugh at us.

SCENE THREE. *A tent prepared for audience.*

(*Enter the* KING DON FERDINAND OF ARAGON *and* QUEEN ISABELLA, *accompanied by* DON MANRIQUE *and* Attendants.)

ISABELLA. To prepare is wise. Sire, harry Alonso 50 of Portugal where he has pitched his tents, for a ready offense averts the threatened injury.

THE KING. Navarre and Aragon despatch swift aid and succor. Under my command the Castilian bands shall be reformed. Success lies in prevention.

ISABELLA. Majesty, prevail by strategy.

DON MANRIQUE. Two Regidors of Ciudad Real crave audience.

THE KING. Admit them to our presence.
    (*Enter* Two Regidors *of Ciudad Real.*)

FIRST REGIDOR. Great Ferdinand the Catholic our 60
    King,
Posting from Aragon to high Castile
On warlike service and the common weal,
Humble petition to thy sword we bring
For vengeance, urging here the patent royal
Bestowed on Ciudad Real, thy city,
Foully wronged. To be thy city was our joy,
Thy will our law, proclaimed in kingly charter;
But blows of fate laid low our fealty.
A froward youth, Rodrigo Téllez Girón,   70
Master of Calatrava, with naked sword
Carves out addition to his wide domain,
Wasting our homes, our lands and revenues.
We met his treacherous assault, and force
Opposed to force, by threat and fear undaunted,
Till blood in rivers ran adown our streets,
Alas but vainly! The day we lost, and he,
Pricked on by the Commander Fernán Gómez,
Cunning in council, governs the city,
While we, enslaved, lament our injuries.   80

THE KING. Where dwells this Fernán Gómez?

FIRST REGIDOR. Sire, Fuente Ovejuna is his seat,
Wherein he rules amid his seignories.
He governs there, there does he his will,
Raining down blows upon his abject thralls
Beyond endurance.

THE KING. Name your captain.

SECOND REGIDOR.   Sire,
None lives. Not one, alas, of noble blood
Survives unwounded, untaken or unslain.   90

ISABELLA. This cause demands an instant remedy.
The walls may be surrendered to the foe,
Who thus will boldly dominate the pass,
Entering Extremadura from the side
Of Portugal.

THE KING. Set forth at once, Manrique,
And with two chosen companies chastise
This arrogance, denying let or stay.
The Count of Cabra shall by our command
As swiftly follow, bravest of the house   100
Of Córdoba.
The front of tyranny must bow
And pride lie low
In the presence of our majesty.

ISABELLA. Depart ambassador of victory. (*Exeunt.*)

SCENE FOUR. *A river bank near Fuente Ovejuna. Trees and bushes.*

(LAURENCIA *and* FRONDOSO *enter.*)

LAURENCIA. I had not wrung the sheets, you saucy Frondoso, when you drove me from the river bank with spying. While we gaze the country-side talks and waits on tip-toe. The sturdiest of our lads, your jacket is the gayest and the costliest, so others note what you do, and not a girl in the village nor herdsman on the hills nor down in the river bottoms but swears we are one and of right ought to be joined, while Juan Chamorro, the sacristan, leaves his piping to publish the banns, for love, they say, goes first to church. Ah, wine burst the vaults in August, and burst every pot with must but I heed them not nor attend to their chatter, though it be time, methinks, and time soon for our own good to put an end to all this idle talk and pother.

FRONDOSO. Laughing Laurencia, I die while you smile. Though I say nothing you will not hear me, till at last I have scarcely strength even to mutter. I would be your husband but you repay with taunts my faith and loyalty.

LAURENCIA. I encourage you all I can.

FRONDOSO. It's not enough. When I think of you I cannot eat, drink, or sleep. I starve yet love an angel. God knows I die.

LAURENCIA. Cross yourself, Frondoso, or else bethink you of some charm.

FRONDOSO. There's a charm for two doves at the church, love, that makes them one. God set us beak to beak!

LAURENCIA. Speak to your master, Juan Rojo, if you will, and can summon the courage, else I must, since he is my uncle. Pray for the day, and hope.

FRONDOSO. Look! The Commander!

LAURENCIA. Stalking deer. Hide in the bushes.

FRONDOSO. Big bucks are hard to hide.

(*The* COMMANDER *enters.*)

COMMANDER. Aha! Following the fawn, I hit upon the doe.

LAURENCIA. I was resting from washing and return to the brookside now, Commander.

COMMANDER. Sweet Laurencia, stay, nor obscure the beauty heaven has granted to my sight. If you have escaped my hand till now, the woods and the fields will befriend us, for they are accomplices of love. Bend your pride and let your cheek flush as it has never done yet in the village. Sebastiana, who was Pedro Redondo's wife, has been mine, and so has the chit who wedded Martín del Pozo. I came upon her two nights a bride, and she opened to me fondly.

LAURENCIA. My lord, they had opened to so many that their fondness was no longer in question. Ask the village. God grant you luck with the deer. The cross on your breast proclaims you are no tempter of women.

COMMANDER. You protest too much, lass. I put down my cross-bow. With my hands I will subdue these pretty wiles.

LAURENCIA. No, no! What would you? Let go!

(FRONDOSO *re-enters and seizes the cross-bow.*)

COMMANDER. Struggle is useless.

FRONDOSO. (Aside) I take the bow. Heaven grant I do not shoot.

COMMANDER. Yield! Have done!

LAURENCIA. Heaven help me now!

COMMANDER. We are alone, no one will hear—

FRONDOSO. Noble Commander, loose that girl, or your breast shall be my mark, though the cross shine clear upon it.

COMMANDER. The dog insults me!

FRONDOSO. Here is no dog. Laurencia, flee!

LAURENCIA. Frondoso, you take care.

FRONDOSO. Go! (LAURENCIA *goes.*)

COMMANDER. Only a fool deprives himself of his sword, which I, god or devil, put by, fearing to fright the chase!

FRONDOSO. By God above, Commander, if I loose this string I'll gyve you like a hawk!

COMMANDER. Betrayed! Traitorous hind, deliver up that cross-bow. Dog, set down!

FRONDOSO. To be shot through? Hardly. Love is a warrior that yields his throne to none.

COMMANDER. Shall a knight valiant in battle be foiled by a dumb peasant? Stay, wretch! On guard! —for I forget my rank and station.

FRONDOSO. I do not. I am a swain, but since I will to live, I take the cross-bow with me.

COMMANDER. Ignominy, shame! I will have vengeance to the hilt. Quickly I vanish.

ACT SECOND

SCENE ONE. *Square in Fuente Ovejuna.*

(ESTEBAN *enters with a* Regidor.)

ESTEBAN. Better touch the reserve no further. The year bodes ill with threat of foul weather, so let the grain be impounded though there be mutiny among the people.

REGIDOR. I am of your mind if the village may be governed in peace.

ESTEBAN. Then speak to Fernán Gómez. These astrologers with their harangues pretend they know secrets God only knows. Not a scrap can they read of the future, unholy fabricators of what was and what shall be, when to their eyes even the present is blank,

For their ignorance is rank.

Can they bring the clouds indoors and lay the stars upon the table? How do they peer into heaven and yet come down with such dire disasters? These fellows tell us how and when to sow, here with the grain, there with the barley and the vegetables, the squash, mustard, and cucumber—

As squashes add them to the number.
Next they predict a man will die and one does in Transylvania, or the vineyards shall suffer drought, or people take to beer in far-off Germany; also cherries will freeze and impoverish the neighbors in Gascony, while there will be a plague of tigers in Hyrcania. So or not so, pray remember—

The year ends with December.

(LEONELO, *a student, enters with* BARRILDO.)

LEONELO. I grant this town nothing, upon a review, but as the plain seat of stupidity.

BARRILDO. How did you fare in Salamanca?

LEONELO. That is no simple story.

BARRILDO. By this you must be a complete Bártulo.

LEONELO. Not even a barber by this. In our faculty few trim knowledge from the course.

BARRILDO. You return to us a scholar.

LEONELO. No, but I have learned what it is wise to know.

BARRILDO. With all the printing of books nowadays a man might pick up a few and be wise.

LEONELO. We know less than we did when there was less knowledge, for the bulk of learning is so great no man can compass it. Confusion results from excess, all the stir goes to froth, while those who read befuddle their heads with endless pages and become literal slaves. The art of printing has raised up a thousand geniuses over night. To be sure it spreads and conserves the Holy Scriptures, that they may be known of all and endure, but this invention of Guttenberg, that famous German of Mayence, has in fact devitalized glory. Many a man of repute has proved a very fool when his books have been printed, or else suffered the mortification of having simpletons issue theirs in his name. Others have set down arrant nonsense and credited it to their enemies out of spite, to whose undoing it circulates and appals the world.

BARRILDO. I can find no words to argue with you.

LEONELO. The ignorant have the learned at their mercy.

BARRILDO. Leonelo, on every account printing is a mighty invention.

LEONELO. For centuries the world did very well without it, and to this hour it has not produced one Jerome nor a second Augustine. The men were saints.

BARRILDO. Sit down and rest, for my head is dizzy opposing you.

(JUAN ROJO *and* A Farmer *enter.*)

JUAN ROJO: There is not a dower on four of these farms if the fields continue as they are, and this may be seen on all sides, far and near, for all is one.

FARMER. What word of the Commander?

JUAN ROJO. Would Laurencia had never set foot by the river!

FARMER. I could dangle him gladly from that olive-tree, savage, unbridled and lewd!

(*The* COMMANDER *enters with* ORTUÑO *and* FLORES.)

COMMANDER. Heaven for the just!

REGIDOR. Commander!

COMMANDER. God's body, why do you stand?

ESTEBAN. Señor, where the custom is to sit, we stand.

COMMANDER. I tell you to sit down.

ESTEBAN. As honorable men we cannot do you honor, having none.

COMMANDER. Sit down while I talk with you!

ESTEBAN. Shall we discuss my hound, sir?

COMMANDER. Alcalde, these true men of mine praise the rare virtue of the animal.

ESTEBAN. The beast is swift. In God's name but he can overtake a thief or harry a coward right cruelly.

COMMANDER. I would set him on a graceful hare that these days lopes before me.

ESTEBAN. Done, if you will lead us to the hare.

COMMANDER. Oh, speaking of your daughter—

ESTEBAN. My daughter?

COMMANDER. Yes, why not? The hare.

ESTEBAN. My daughter is not your quarry.

COMMANDER. Alcalde, pray you prevail upon her.

ESTEBAN. How?

COMMANDER. She plumes herself before me. A wife, and a proud one, of a councillor who attends before me now, and listens, at my every look darts kindling glances.

ESTEBAN. She does ill. You, Señor, do ill also, speaking thus freely.

COMMANDER. Oh, what rustic virtue! Here, Flores, get him the book of *Politics*, and let him perfect himself in Aristotle.

ESTEBAN. Señor, the town would live in the reflection of your honor. There be men in Fuente Ovejuna.

LEONELO. I never read of such a tyrant.

COMMANDER. What have I said, in faith, to which you take exception, Regidor?

JUAN ROJO. You have spoken ill. Speak well, for it is not meet you level at our honor.

COMMANDER. Your honor? Good! Are we importing friars to Calatrava?

REGIDOR. There be those that be content to wear the cross, though the heart be not too pure.

COMMANDER. I do not injure you, mingling my blood with yours.

JUAN ROJO. A smirch is no hidden stain.

COMMANDER. In doing my will I accord your wives honor.

ESTEBAN. The very words spell dishonor, while your deeds pass all remedy.

COMMANDER. Obstinate dolt! Ah, better the cities where men of parts and renown wreak their will and their pleasure! There husbands give thanks when their wives sacrifice upon the altar.

ESTEBAN. They do no such service, if with this you would move us. God rules, too, in the cities, and justice is swift.

COMMANDER. Get up and get out.

ESTEBAN. We have said what you have heard.

COMMANDER. Out of the square straight! Let not one remain behind!

ESTEBAN. We firmly take our leave.

COMMANDER. What? In company?

FLORES. By the rood, hold your hand!

COMMANDER. These hinds would slander me, defiling the square with lies, departing together.

ORTUÑO. Pray be patient.

COMMANDER. I marvel that I am so calm! Walk each one by himself, apart. Let no man speak till his door has shut behind him!

LEONELO. Great God, can they stomach this?

ESTEBAN. My path lies this way.

(ESTEBAN, JUAN ROJO, Regidor, LEONELO *and the* Peasants *go out, leaving the* COMMANDER, FLORES *and* ORTUÑO.)

COMMANDER. What shall we do with these knaves?

ORTUÑO. Their speech offends you and you by no means hide your unwillingness to hear it.

COMMANDER. Do they compare themselves with me?

FLORES. Perversity of man.

COMMANDER. Shall that peasant retain my crossbow and not be punished while I live?

FLORES. Last night we took him, as we thought, at Laurencia's door, and I gave an oaf who was his double a slash that married his two ears.

COMMANDER. Can you find no trace of that Frondoso?

FLORES. They say he remains in these parts still.

COMMANDER. And dares remain, who has attempted my life?

FLORES. Like a silly bird or a fish, a decoy will tempt him and he will fall into the lure.

COMMANDER. That a laborer, a stripling of the soil should aim a cross-bow at a captain before whose sword Córdoba and Granada tremble! Flores, the end of the world has come!

FLORES. Blame love, for it knows no monopoly of daring.

ORTUÑO. Seeing he lived, I took it as a token of your kindly disposition.

COMMANDER. Ortuño, the smile is false. Dirk in hand, within these two hours would I ransack the place, but vengeance yields the rein to reason until the hour shall come. Which of you had a smile of Pascuala?

FLORES. She says she intends to marry.

COMMANDER. How far is she prepared to go?

FLORES. She will advise you anon when she can accept a favor.

COMMANDER. How of Olalla?

ORTUÑO. Fair words.

COMMANDER. Buxom and spirited! How far?

ORTUÑO. She says her husband has been uneasy these past days, suspicious of my messages, and of your hovering about, attended. As soon as his fears are allayed, you shall have a sign.

COMMANDER. On the honor of a knight 'tis well! These rustics have sharp eyes and commonly are evil-minded.

ORTUÑO. Evil-minded, ill-spoken and ill-favored.

COMMANDER. Say not so of Inés.

FLORES. Which one?

COMMANDER. Antón's wife. Aha!

FLORES. Yes, she will oblige any day. I saw her in the corral, which you can enter secretly.

COMMANDER. These easy girls we requite but poorly. Flores, may women never learn the worth of the wares they sell!

FLORES. No pain wipes out the sweetness wholly. To prevail quickly, cheats the expectation, but, as philosophers agree, women desire the men as they are desired, nor can form be without substance, at which we should not complain, nor wonder.

COMMANDER. A man who is fiercely swept by love finds solace in a speedy yielding to desire, but afterward despises the object, for the road to forgetfulness even under the star of honor, is to hold oneself cheap before love's importuning.

(CIMBRANOS, *a soldier, enters, armed.*)

CIMBRANOS. Where is the Commander?

ORTUÑO. Behold him, if you have the faculty of sight.

CIMBRANOS. Oh, gallant Fernán Gómez,
Put off the rustic cap
For the morion of steel
And change the cloak
For armor!
The Master of Santiago
And the Count of Cabra,
By the title of the Castilian Queen,
Lay siege to Don Rodrigo Girón
In Ciudad Real,
And short his shrift unaided
Before their approaching powers,
Forfeiting the spoils so dearly won
At cost of blood of Calatrava.
Already from the battlements
Our sentinels descry
Pennons and banners,
The castles and the lions,
Quartered with the bars of Aragon.
What though the King of Portugal

Heap on Girón vain honors?
Vanquished, the Master must creep home
To Almagro, wounded,
Abandoning the city.
To horse, to horse, Señor!
At sight of you
The enemy will fly
Headlong into Castile,
Nor pause this side surrender.

10   COMMANDER. Hold and speak no more!
Stay for me.
Ortuño, sound the trumpet
Here in the square.
What soldiers
Are billeted with me?
   ORTUÑO. A troop of fifty men.
   COMMANDER. To horse every one!
   CIMBRANOS. Spur apace or Ciudad Real
Falls to the King

20   COMMANDER. That shall never be.   (*Exeunt.*)

SCENE TWO. *Open country, fields or meadow.*

(MENGO *enters with* LAURENCIA *and* PASCUALA,
running.)

PASCUALA. Don't leave us.
MENGO. What's the matter?
LAURENCIA. Mengo, we seek the village in groups, when there's no man to go with us, for fear of the Commander.
MENGO. How can the ugly devil torment so many?
LAURENCIA. He is upon us night and day.
MENGO. Oh, would heaven send a bolt to strike him where he stands!

30   LAURENCIA. He's an unchained beast, poison, arsenic and pestilence throughout the land.
MENGO. Laurencia, they say Frondoso pointed an arrow at his breast for your sake, here in this very meadow.
LAURENCIA. Mengo, I hated all men till then, but since that day I relent. Frondoso had courage; it will cost him his life.
MENGO. He must fly these fields, that's sure.
LAURENCIA. I love him enough to advise it, but
40 he'll have no counsel of me, storming and raging and turning away. The Commander swears he will hang him feet upward.
PASCUALA. I say hang the Commander.
MENGO. Stone him I say. God knows but I will up and at him with a rock I saved at the sheep-fold that will land him a crack that will crush his skull in! He's wickeder than Gabalus that old Roman.
LAURENCIA. The one that was so wicked was Heliogabalus. He was a man.
50   MENGO. Whoever he was, call him Gab or Gal,

49. **Heliogabalus,** a Roman emperor (218–222 A.D.), distinguished for his debauchery, extravagance, and cruelty.

his scurvy memory yields to this. You know history. Was there ever a man like Fernán Gómez?
PASCUALA. No, he's no man. There must be tigers in him.

(JACINTA *enters.*)

JACINTA. Help in God's name, if you are women!
LAURENCIA. Why, what's this, Jacinta?
PASCUALA. We are all your friends.
JACINTA. The Commander's men, on their way to Ciudad Real, armed with villainy when it should be steel, would seize me and take me to him.   60
LAURENCIA. God help you, Jacinta! With you, pray he be merciful, but I choose rather to die than be taken!   (*Exit.*)
PASCUALA. Jacinta, being no man I cannot save you.   (*Exit.*)
MENGO. I can because I am a man in strength and in name. Jacinta, stand beside me.
JACINTA. Are you armed?
MENGO. Twice. I have two arms.
JACINTA. You will need more.   70
MENGO. Jacinta, the ground bears stones.

(FLORES *and* ORTUÑO *enter.*)

FLORES. Did you think you could run away from us?
JACINTA. Mengo, I am dead with fear!
MENGO. Friends, these are poor peasant girls.
ORTUÑO. Do you assume to defend her?
MENGO. I do, so please you, since I am her relative and must protect her, if that may be.
FLORES. Kill him straightway!
MENGO. Strike me heaven, but I am in a rage! You   80
can put a cord around my neck but, by God, I'll sell my life dear!

(*The* COMMANDER *and* CIMBRANOS *enter.*)

COMMANDER. Who calls? What says this turd?
FLORES. The people of this town, which we should raze for there is no health in it, insult our arms.
MENGO. Señor, if pity can prevail in the face of injustice, reprove these soldiers who would force this peasant girl in your name, though spouse and parents be bred to honor, and grant me license straight   90
to lead her home unharmed.
COMMANDER. I will grant them license straight to harm you for your impudence. Let go that sling.
MENGO. Señor—
COMMANDER. Flores, Ortuño and Cimbranos, it will serve to tie his hands.
MENGO. Is this the voice of honor?
COMMANDER. What do these sheep of Fuente Ovejuna think of me?
MENGO. Señor, have I offended you, or mayhap   100
the village, in anything?
FLORES. Shall we kill him?
COMMANDER. It would soil your arms which we shall stain with redder blood.

ORTUÑO. We wait your orders, sir.

COMMANDER. Flog him without mercy. Tie him to that oak-tree, baring his back, and with the reins—

MENGO. No, no, for you are noble!

COMMANDER. Flog him till the rivets start from the straps!

MENGO. My God, can such things be?

(*They lead him off.*)

COMMANDER. Pretty peasant, draw near daintily. 10 Who would prefer a farmer to a valiant nobleman?

JACINTA. But will you heal my honor, taking me for yourself?

COMMANDER. Truly I do take you.

JACINTA. No, I have an honorable father, sir, who may not equal you in birth, but in virtue he is the first.

COMMANDER. These are troubled days nor will this rude peasantry salve my outraged spirit. Pass with me under the trees.

20 JACINTA. I?

COMMANDER. This way.

JACINTA. Look what you do!

COMMANDER. Refuse and I spurn you. You shall be the slut of the army.

JACINTA. No power of lust can overcome me.

COMMANDER. Silence and go before.

JACINTA. Pity, Señor!

COMMANDER. Pity have I none.

JACINTA. I appeal from your wickedness to God!

(*Exit the* COMMANDER, *haling her out.*)

SCENE THREE. *Room in Juan Rojo's house.*

(LAURENCIA *and* FRONDOSO *enter.*)

30 LAURENCIA. Through fields of danger
My love comes to me.

FRONDOSO. The hazard bear witness
To the love that I bear.
The Commander has vanished
O'er the brow of the hill
And I, the slave of beauty,
Lose all sense of fear,
Seeing him disappear.

LAURENCIA. Speak ill of no man.
40 To pray for his end
Postpones it, my friend.

FRONDOSO. Eternally.
And may he live a thousand years,
And every one bear joy!
I'll pray for his soul also
And may the pious litany
Bite, sear and destroy!
Laurencia, if my love
Live in your heart,
50 Let me enter there, love,

To dwell loyally.
The town counts us one,
Yet by the book we are twain.
Will you, I wonder,
Say yes,
Compulsion under?

LAURENCIA. Say for me to the town
Oh yes, yes and yes
Again and again!

FRONDOSO. I kiss your feet   60
For this new miracle of mercy.
Beauty grants me joy
In words grace conjures.

LAURENCIA. Flatter me no more,
But speak to my father
And win my uncle's praise.
Oh, speak,
Frondoso,
Oh may we marry, oh Frondoso,
It will be heaven   70
To be your wife!

FRONDOSO. In God we trust.   (*Hides himself.*)

(*Enter* ESTEBAN *and* JUAN ROJO, *Regidor.*)

ESTEBAN. His departure outraged the square, and indeed it was most unseemly behavior. Such tyranny stuns as a blow; even poor Jacinta must pay the price of his madness.

JUAN ROJO. Spain turns already to the Catholic Kings, a name by which our rulers have come to be known, and the nation renders obedience to their laws. They have appointed the Master of Santiago   80 Captain General of Ciudad Real, despatching him forthwith against Girón's oppression of the town. But my heart aches for Jacinta, being as she is an honest girl.

ESTEBAN. They beat Mengo soundly.

JUAN ROJO. I never saw dye, black or red, to rival his flesh.

ESTEBAN. Peace and no more, for my blood boils, or else congeals at his name. Have I authority or a staff of office?   90

JUAN ROJO. The man cannot control his servants.

ESTEBAN. On top of all this they chanced on Pedro Redondo's wife one day in the very bottom of the valley, and after he insulted her she was turned over to the men.

JUAN ROJO. Who is listening concealed?

FRONDOSO. I, a petitioner.

JUAN ROJO. Granted, Frondoso. Your father brought you to be, but I have brought you to be what you are, a prop and support, who is my very   100 son in the house.

FRONDOSO. Assured, Alcalde, of permission, I speak as one by birth honorable, and not obscure.

ESTEBAN. You have suffered wrong at the hand of Fernán Gómez?

FRONDOSO. More than a little.

ESTEBAN. My heart records it. The man is surely mad.

FRONDOSO. Señor, appealing to a father,
Serving a daughter,
I beg her hand
Not all a stranger.
Pardon presumption though it be extreme;
Boldly I speak for men shall count me bold.

ESTEBAN. By that word, Frondoso,
10 You renew my life,
Brushing aside
The apprehension of the years.
Now heaven be praised, my son,
For your proposal seals our honor,
Which may love guard jealously.
Apprise your father straight
Of this new promised joy,
For my consent stays
But his approbation,
20 In whose fair prospect
Beams my happiness.

JUAN ROJO. The maid must consent also.

ESTEBAN. Her consent should precede
And has preceded indeed,
Because a faithful lover
Is prophet and recorder.
I have taken an oath to bestow some right good maravedis upon a good young man.

FRONDOSO. I seek no dower. Gold, they say, makes
30 the day dull.

JUAN ROJO. So long as he does not court the wine-skins, you may dower him without stint or mercy.

ESTEBAN. I will speak to my daughter that assurance may be doubly sure.

FRONDOSO. Do, pray, for violence has no part in love.

ESTEBAN. Dearest daughter Laurencia!

LAURENCIA. Oh, father?

ESTEBAN. She approves for she answers before I
40 speak!—Dearest daughter Laurencia, step apart a moment. Frondoso, who is an honest lad, if one there be in Fuente Ovejuna, inquires of me as to your friend Gila, whom he would honor as a wife.

LAURENCIA. Gila a wife?

ESTEBAN. Is she a fitting mate, a proper wife?

LAURENCIA. Yes, father, oh she is! Of course!

ESTEBAN. Of course she is ugly, as ugly as they come, which led me to suggest, Laurencia, that Frondoso look at you.

50 LAURENCIA. Father, be serious as becomes your office.

ESTEBAN. Do you love him?

LAURENCIA. I have favored him and am myself favored. But you knew!

ESTEBAN. Shall I say yes?

LAURENCIA. Yes, father, for me.

28. maravedis, Spanish coins.

ESTEBAN. The yes will do for us both. Come, we will seek his father.

JUAN ROJO. Instantly.

ESTEBAN. My boy, to return to the dower. I can af- 60 ford, yes, and I pledge, four thousand maravedis.

FRONDOSO. Señor, I am your son now and you offend me.

ESTEBAN. A day and pride abates, lad, but if you marry without a dower, by my faith, many a day will succeed and the abatement not be mended.
      (*Exeunt* ESTEBAN *and* JUAN ROJO.)

LAURENCIA. Frondoso, bliss!

FRONDOSO. Yes, triply.
In a single moment
I feel so happy 70
I could die with pleasure!
Bliss it must be
Shared among three.
I look at you and laugh,
Laugh my heart out.
Oh, what treasure
I drink in at a glance
Now love comes to me,
Laurencia!   (*Exeunt.*)

SCENE FOUR. *Ciudad Real. The walls.*

(*The* MASTER, *the* COMMANDER, FLORES *and*
ORTUÑO *enter.*)

COMMANDER. Fly, sir! There is no remedy. 80

MASTER. The wall giving way, the weight of the enemy undoes us.

COMMANDER. We have bled them and cost them many lives.

MASTER. The banner of Calatrava shall not trail among their spoils, though it were recompense turning all to glory.

COMMANDER. Our league, Girón, crumbles and lies lifeless.

MASTER. Can we outstrip fortune, though she be 90 blind, favoring us to-day, to-day to leave us?

VOICES (*within*). Hail, Victory! Hail, the Crown of Castile!

MASTER. The pennons show upon the battlements while all the windows of the towers thrust banners forth, proclaiming the victory.

COMMANDER. Much joy may they have of the day! By my soul, a day of slaughter!

MASTER. Fernán Gómez, I'll to Calatrava.

COMMANDER. And I to Fuente Ovejuna. Stay upon 100 your cousin of Portugal, or, weighing adversity, yield allegiance to the Catholic King.

MASTER. I shall apprise you with despatch.

COMMANDER. Time is a hard general.

MASTER. God grant me few years like this, fertile in undeception.   (*Exeunt.*)

SCENE FIVE. *Esteban's house in Fuente Ovejuna.*

(*Enter the wedding-train,* Musicians, MENGO, FRONDOSO, LAURENCIA, PASCUALA, BARRILDO, ESTEBAN *and* JUAN ROJO.)

MUSICIANS. Joy to the bride
And long life beside!
Long life!

MENGO. A clever boy thought that up! Oh, that boy is clever!

BARRILDO. He could troll it out at any wedding.

FRONDOSO. Mengo sings only to the lash because he says it has more tang to it.

MENGO. Yes, and I know a young chap in the val-
10 ley, not meaning you of course, who would make a nice dish for the Commander.

BARRILDO. Enough of gloom and amen, seeing that a ferocious barbarian offers at our honor.

MENGO. I believe a hundred soldiers whipped me that day, and all I had was a sling that I gave up to protect me. However, I know a man, not mentioning names, who was full of honor and pursued with a syringe loaded with dye and some herbs that caused him great pain, and oh my, the pain that they caused
20 him! How that man did suffer!

BARRILDO. By way of jest. It was done as a laughing matter.

MENGO. As it came out afterwards. At the time he never laughed nor even suspected, but felt much better without the dye, though while it was in, death was preferable.

FRONDOSO. A song would be preferable, or anything. Come, let it be a good one, Mengo.

MENGO. Good! Do you invite me?
30 *Bride and groom*
Must dwell together.
Pray God neither one of them
Dare fight or row it.
Let both die
Just too tired out to live,
A long time after
They have forgotten all about it—
I mean the wedding.

FRONDOSO. God help the poet who made that up!
40 BARRILDO. He needs more help.

MENGO. Oh, that reminds me! Did you ever see a baker baking buns? He dips the dough into the oil until the pot is full, and then some swell up, some come out askew and twisted, leaning to the right, tumbling to the left, some scorched, some burned, some uneatable. Well, a poet's subject is his dough, he plops a verse onto the paper hoping it will turn out sweet, and his friends all tell him so, but when he tries to sell it he has to eat it himself, for the
50 world is too wise to buy or else hasn't the money.

BARRILDO. You came to the wedding so as not to give the bride and groom a chance to talk.

LAURENCIA. Uncle, you must be kissed. And you, too, Father—

JUAN ROJO. Not on the hand. May your father's hand be your protection, and Frondoso's also, in the hour of need.

ESTEBAN. Rojo, heaven protect her and her husband on whom I invoke an everlasting benison.

FRONDOSO. Ever to share with you. 60

JUAN ROJO. Come all now, play and sing, for they are as good as one.

MUSICIANS. *O maiden fair*
With the flowing hair,
Shun Fuente Ovejuna!
A warrior knight
Awaits thee there,
Waits the maid with the flowing hair
With the Cross of Calatrava.
Oh, hide in the shade 70
By the branches made!
Why, lovely maiden,
Why afraid?
Against desire
No wall may aid
'Gainst the Knight of Calatrava.
Thou grim knight spare
Frail beauty there
By Fuente Ovejuna!
No screen can hide, 80
No mountain bare,
No ocean bar love anywhere
'Gainst the Knight of Calatrava.
Here in the shade,
Shall love's debt be paid,
O peerless maiden,
Why afraid?
Against desire
No wall may aid
'Gainst the Knight of Calatrava. 90

(*The* COMMANDER, FLORES, ORTUÑO *and* CIMBRANOS *enter.*)

COMMANDER. Let all in the house stand still on pain of death.

JUAN ROJO. Señor, though this be no play, your command shall be obeyed. Will you sit down? Why all these arms and weapons? We question not, for you bring home victory.

FRONDOSO. I am dead unless heaven helps me.

LAURENCIA. Stand behind me, Frondoso.

COMMANDER. No, seize and bind him.

JUAN ROJO. Surrender, boy, 'tis best. 100

FRONDOSO. Do you want them to kill me?

JUAN ROJO. Why, pray?

COMMANDER. I am no man to take life unjustly, for, if I were, my soldiers would have run him through ere this, forwards or rearwards. Throw him into prison where his own father shall pronounce sentence upon him, chained in his dank cell.

PASCUALA. This is a wedding, Señor.

COMMANDER. What care I for weddings? Is this your occupation in the village?

PASCUALA. Pardon him, Señor, if he has done wrong, being who you are.

COMMANDER. Pascuala, he has done no wrong to me, but offense to the Master, Téllez Girón, whom God preserve. He has mocked his law, scoffed at his rule, and punishment must be imposed as a most dire example, or there will be those to rise against the Master, seeing that one afternoon, but shortly gone, flower of these loyal and faithful vassals, he dared take aim, pointing the cross-bow at the bosom of the High Commander.

ESTEBAN. If a father-in-law may offer a word of excuse, his dudgeon was not strange but manly, taking umbrage as a lover. You would deprive him of his wife. Small wonder the man should defend her!

COMMANDER. Alcalde, the truth is not in you.

ESTEBAN. Be just, Señor.

COMMANDER. I had no thought to deprive him of his wife, nor could so have done, he having none.

ESTEBAN. But you had the thought, which shall suffice. Henceforth enough! A King and Queen rule now in Castile whose firm decrees shall bring this rioting to cease, nor will they stay their hands, these wars once ended, nor suffer arrogance to overpower their towns and villages, crucifying the people cruelly. Upon his breast the King will place a cross, and on that royal breast it shall be the symbol, too, of honor!

COMMANDER. Death to presumption! Wrest the staff from him.

ESTEBAN. Señor, I yield it up, commanded.

COMMANDER. Beat him with it while he capers about this stable. Have at him smartly!

ESTEBAN. Still we suffer your authority. I am ready. Begin!

PASCUALA. They beat an old man?

LAURENCIA. Yes, because he is my father. Beat him, avenging yourself on me!

COMMANDER. Arrest her, and let ten soldiers guard this sinful maid! (*Exeunt* COMMANDER *and Train.*)

ESTEBAN. Justice, descend this day from heaven! (*Exit.*)

PASCUALA. No wedding but a shambles. (*Exit.*)

BARRILDO. And not a man of us said a word!

MENGO. I have had my beating already and you can still see purple enough on me to outfit a Cardinal, without the trouble of sending to Rome. Try, if you don't believe it, what a thorough job they can do.

JUAN ROJO. We must all take counsel.

MENGO. My counsel, friends, is to take nothing but forget it. I know which side I am on, though I don't say, for it's scaled like a salmon. Never again will any man get me to take it! Nor woman either.

ACT THIRD

SCENE ONE. *A room in the Town Hall at Fuente Ovejuna.*

(ESTEBAN, ALONSO *and* BARRILDO *enter.*)

ESTEBAN. Is the Town Board assembled?

BARRILDO. Not a person can be seen.

ESTEBAN. Bravely we face danger!

BARRILDO. All the farms had warning.

ESTEBAN. Frondoso is a prisoner in the tower and my daughter Laurencia in such plight that she is lost save for the direct interposition of heaven.

(JUAN ROJO *enters with the* Second Regidor.)

JUAN ROJO. Who complains aloud when silence is salvation? Peace, in God's name, peace!

ESTEBAN. I will shout to the clouds till they re-echo my complaints while men marvel at my silence.

(*Enter* MENGO *and Peasants.*)

MENGO. We came to attend the meeting.

ESTEBAN. Farmers of this village, an old man whose grey beard is bathed in tears, inquires what rites, what obsequies we poor peasants, assembled here, shall prepare for our ravished homes, bereft of honor? And if life be honor, how shall we fare since there breathes not one among us whom this savage has not offended? Speak! Who but has been wounded deeply, poisoned in respect? Lament now, yes, cry out! Well? If all be ill, how then say well? Well, there is work for men to do.

JUAN ROJO. The direst that can be. Since by report it is published that Castile is subject now to a King, who shall presently make his entrance into Córdoba, let us despatch two Regidors to that city to cast themselves at his feet and demand remedy.

BARRILDO. King Ferdinand is occupied with the overthrow of his enemies, who are not few, so that his commitments are warlike entirely. It were best to seek other succor.

REGIDOR. If my voice have any weight, I declare the independence of the village.

JUAN ROJO. How can that be?

MENGO. On my soul, my back tells me the Town Board will be informed as to that directly.

REGIDOR. The tree of our patience has been cut down, the ship of our joy rides storm-tossed, emptied of its treasure. They have rept the daughter from one who is Alcalde of this town in which we dwell, breaking his staff over his aged head. Could a slave be scorned more basely?

JUAN ROJO. What would you have the people do?

REGIDOR. Die or rain death on tyrants! We are many while they are few.

BARRILDO. Lift our hands against our Lord and Master?

ESTEBAN. Only the King is our master, save for

God, never these devouring beasts. If God be with us, what have we to fear?

MENGO. Gentlemen, I advise caution in the beginning and ever after. Although I represent only the very simplest laborers, who bear the most, believe me we find the bearing most unpleasant.

JUAN ROJO. If our wrongs are so great, we lose nothing with our lives. An end, then! Our homes and vineyards burn. Vengeance on the tyrants!

(*Enter* LAURENCIA, *her hair disheveled.*)

10 LAURENCIA. Open, for I have need of the support of men! Deeds, or I cry out to heaven! Do you know me?

ESTEBAN. Martyr of God, my daughter?

JUAN ROJO. This is Laurencia.

LAURENCIA. Yes, and so changed that, gazing, you doubt still!

ESTEBAN. My daughter!

LAURENCIA. No, no more! Not yours.

ESTEBAN. Why, light of my eyes, why, pride of
20 the valley?

LAURENCIA. Ask not, reckon not,
Here be it known
Tyrants reign o'er us,
We are ruled by traitors,
Justice is there none.
I was not Frondoso's,
Yours to avenge me,
Father, till the night
I was yours
30 Though he was my husband,
You the defender
Guarding the bride.
As well might the noble pay for the jewel lost in the
    merchant's hand!
I was lost to Fernán Gómez,
Haled to his keep,
Abandoned to wolves.
A dagger at my breast
Pointed his threats,
40 His flatteries, insults, lies,
To overcome my chastity
Before his fierce desires.

My face is bruised and bloody in this court of honest men. Some of you are fathers, some have daughters. Do your hearts sink within you, supine and cowardly crew? You are sheep, sheep! Oh, well-named, Village of Fuente Ovejuna, the Sheep Well! Sheep, sheep, sheep! Give me iron, for senseless stones can wield none, nor images, nor pillars—
50 jasper though they be—nor dumb living things that lack the tiger's heart that follows him who steals its young, rending the hunter limb from limb upon the very margin of the raging sea, seeking the pity of the angry waves.
But you are rabbits, farmers,
Infidels in Spain,

Your wives strut before you
With the cock upon their train!
Tuck your knitting in your belts,
Strip off your manly swords,
60 For, God living, I swear
That your women dare
Pluck these fearsome despots,
Beard the traitors there!
No spinning for our girls;
Heave stones and do not blench.
Can you smile, men?
Will you fight?
Caps we'll set upon you,
The shelter of a skirt,
70 Be heirs, boys, to our ribbons,
The gift of the maidenry,

For now the Commander will hang Frondoso from a merlon of the tower, without let or trial, as presently he will string you all, you race of half-men, for the women will leave this village, nor one remain behind! To-day the age of amazons returns, we lift our arms and strike against this villainy, and the crash of our blows shall amaze the world!

ESTEBAN. Daughter, I am no man to bear names
80 calmly, opprobrious and vile. I will go and beard this despot, though the united spheres revolve against me.

JUAN ROJO. So will I, for all his pride and knavery.

REGIDOR. Let him be surrounded and cut off.

BARRILDO. Hang a cloth from a pike as our banner and cry "Death to Monsters!"

JUAN ROJO. What course shall we choose?

MENGO. To be at them, of course. Raise an uproar
90 and with it the village, for every man will take an oath and be with you that to the last traitor the oppressors shall die.

ESTEBAN. Seize swords and spears, cross-bows, pikes and clubs.

MENGO. Long live the King and Queen!

ALL. Live our lords and masters!

MENGO. Death to cruel tyrants!

ALL. To cruel tyrants, death!

(*Exeunt all but* LAURENCIA.)

LAURENCIA. March on, and heaven march before 100
you! (*At the door.*) Hello! Ho, women of this town! Draw near! Draw near for the salvation of your honor!

(PASCUALA, JACINTA *and various* Women *enter.*)

PASCUALA. Who calls us? Where are the men to-day?

LAURENCIA. Behold them down that street, marching to murder Fernán Gómez. Yes, old men, young men, and troops of eager boys, like furies run to meet him! Shall they share all the glory of this mighty day, when we women can boast wrongs that 110 match and outstrip theirs?

JACINTA. What can we do?

LAURENCIA. Fall in behind me and we will do a deed that shall re-echo round the sphere! Jacinta, you have been most deeply wronged; lead forth a squadron of our girls.

JACINTA. You have borne no less.

LAURENCIA. Oh, Pascuala, for a flag!

PASCUALA. Tie a cloth upon this lance to flourish. We shall have our banner.

10 LAURENCIA. Stay not even for that, for now it comes to me:—Every woman her headdress! Wave, banners, wave!

PASCUALA. Name a captain and march!

LAURENCIA. We need no captain.

PASCUALA. No? Wave, banners!

LAURENCIA. When my courage is up I laugh at the Cid and pale Rodomonte!   (*Exeunt.*)

SCENE TWO. *Hall in the Castle of the* COMMANDER. (FLORES. ORTUÑO, CIMBRANOS *and the* COMMANDER *enter. Also* FRONDOSO, *his hands bound.*)

COMMANDER. And by the cord that dangles from his hands

20 Let him be hung until cut down by death.

FRONDOSO. My Lord, you shame your worth.

COMMANDER. String him up on the battlements without further word.

FRONDOSO. I had no thought, my Lord, against your life.

FLORES. What is this noise outside?
                    (*Noise and uproar.*)

COMMANDER. I hear voices.

FLORES. Do they threaten your justice, sire?

ORTUÑO. They are breaking down the gates.
                    (*Knocking and blows.*)

30 COMMANDER. The gate of my castle, the seat of the Commandery?

FLORES. The people fill the court.

JUAN ROJO (*within*). Push, smash, pull down, burn, destroy!

ORTUÑO. I like not their numbers.

COMMANDER. Shall these hinds come against me?

FLORES. Such passing fury sweeps them that all the outer doors are already beaten in!

COMMANDER. Undo this bumpkin. Frondoso, speak

40 to this Alcalde. Warn him of his peril.

FRONDOSO. Sire, what they do, remember is done in love.   (*Exit.*)

MENGO (*within*). Hail, Ferdinand and Isabella, and let the last traitor die!

FLORES. Señor, in God's name you had best conceal your person.

COMMANDER. If they persevere we can hold this room, for the doors are strong. They will turn back as quickly as they came.

FLORES. When the people rise and screw their 50 courage to the point, they never stop short of rapine and blood.

COMMANDER. Behind this grating as a barricade we can defend ourselves right stoutly.

FRONDOSO (*within*). Free Fuente Ovejuna!

COMMANDER. What a leader for these swine! I will out and fall upon them.

FLORES. I marvel at your courage.

ESTEBAN. (*Entering.*) Now we meet the tyrant and his minions face to face! Death to the traitor! 60 All for Fuente Ovejuna!
                    (*Enter the* Peasants.)

COMMANDER. Hold, my people! Stay!

ALL. Wrongs hold not. Vengeance knows no stay!

COMMANDER. Tell your wrongs, and on the honor of a knight I'll requite them, every one.

ALL. Fuente Ovejuna! Long live Ferdinand, our King!

Death to traitors and unbelievers!

COMMANDER. Will you not hear me? I lift my voice. I am your lord and master.   70

ALL. No, our lords and masters are the Catholic Kings!

COMMANDER. Stay a little.

ALL. All for Fuente Ovejuna! Die, Fernán Gómez!
                    (*Exeunt after breaking through the bars.*)
                    (*The* Women *enter, armed.*)

LAURENCIA. Stop here and challenge fortune, no women but an army.

PASCUALA. Any that shows herself a woman by mercy, shall swallow the enemy's blood!

JACINTA. We shall spit his body on our pikes.

PASCUALA. As one we stand behind you.   80

ESTEBAN (*within*). Die, traitor though Commander!

COMMANDER. I die! O God, have pity in Thy clemency!

BARRILDO (*within*). Flores next!

MENGO. Have at him, for he landed on me with a thousand whacks.

FRONDOSO. I'll draw his soul out like a tooth!

LAURENCIA. They need us there!

PASCUALA. Let them go on! We guard the door.   90

BARRILDO (*within*). No prayers, no mercy, vermin!

LAURENCIA. Pascuala, I go with my sword drawn, not sheathed!   (*Exit.*)

BARRILDO (*within*). Down with Ortuño!

FRONDOSO. Slash him across the cheek.
                    (FLORES *enters, fleeing, pursued by* MENGO.)

FLORES. Pity, Mengo! I was not to blame.

MENGO. To be a pimp was bad enough, but why the devil lay on me?

16–17. **the Cid and pale Rodomonte,** the bold hero of the Spanish epic and the boastful villain of Ariosto's *Orlando Furioso.*

79. **spit;** that is, thrust the pikes through his body like a spit through a roast.

PASCUALA. Mengo, give this man to the women.
Stay, Stay!

MENGO. 'Fore God I will! And no punishment
could be worse.

PASCUALA. Be well avenged!

MENGO. Believe me!

JACINTA. Run him through!

FLORES. What? Pity, women!

JACINTA. His courage well becomes him.

10 PASCUALA. So he has tears?

JACINTA. Kill him, viper of the vile!

PASCUALA. Down, wretch, and die!

FLORES. Pity, women, pity!

(ORTUÑO *enters, pursued by* LAURENCIA.)

ORTUÑO. I am not the man, I was not guilty!

LAURENCIA. In, women, and dye your conquering
swords in traitor's blood. Prove all your courage!

PASCUALA. Die dealing death!

ALL. All for Fuente Ovejuna! Hail, King Ferdinand! (*Exeunt.*)

SCENE THREE. *Near Ciudad Real.*

(*Enter the* KING DON FERDINAND OF ARAGON *and*
QUEEN ISABELLA OF CASTILE, *accompanied by* DON
MANRIQUE, MASTER OF SANTIAGO.)

20 MANRIQUE. Convenient haste hard following on
command,
The victory was gained at little cost,
With show of slight resistance. Eagerly
We crave a fresh assault to try our prowess.
The Count of Cabra consolidates the front
And fends a counter-stroke, keeping the field.

KING. The troops are well disposed. By our decree
He shall continue in his tents, the line
Reforming, holding the pass. An evil wind
30 Sweeps up from Portugal, where armed Alfonso
Levies further powers. Cabra shall remain
The head and forefront of our valor here,
Watchful as diligent, that men may see
The danger fly before the sentinel
And peace return with plenty to the land.

(*Enter* FLORES, *wounded.*)

FLORES. King Ferdinand the Catholic,
By right acclaim in Castile crowned,
In token of thy majesty
Oh hear the foulest treachery
40 Done yet by man from where the sun
Springs in the wakening east
To the lands of westering night!

KING. If there be warrant, speak.

FLORES. O thou great King, my wounds speak,
Admitting no delay
To close my story
With my life.
I come from Fuente Ovejuna,

Where the wretched hinds of the village
Have basely murdered their liege lord 50
In one general mutiny.
Perfidious folk,
They slew Fernán Gómez
As vassals moving upon slight cause,
Fixing upon him
The name of Tyrant,
Thenceforward their excuse.
They broke down his doors,
Closing their ears
To his free knightly pledge 60
To do each and all
Full justice,
Steeling their hearts against him,
And with unseemly rage
Tearing the cross from his breast,
Inflicting cruel wounds.
After which they cast him from a high window to
the ground where he was caught on pikes and
swordpoints by the women. They bore him in dead
and the most revengeful pulled at his beard and 70
hair, defacing every feature, for their fury waxed to
such extremity that they sliced off his ears neatly.
They beat down his scutcheon with staves and boast
outright that they will set the royal arms above the
portal where their lord's should be, full in the square
of the village. They sacked the keep as a fallen foe's,
and, exulting, raped his goods and properties. These
things I saw, hidden—unhappy was my lot!—and
so remained till nightfall, escaping to lay my prayer
before you. Justice, Sire, that swift penalty may fall 80
upon these offending churls! Bloodshed this day
cries out to God and challenges your rigor!

KING. No violence, no cruelty so dire
Escapes the inquest of our royal eye.
I marvel greatly at this villainy,
Wherefore to-day a judge shall be despatched
To verify the tale, and punishment
Mete out unto the guilty as example.
A captain, too, shall march in his escort
Securing the sentence, for mutiny 90
The bolder grown, bolder the chastisement.
Look to his wounds. (*Exeunt.*)

SCENE FOUR. *The Square in Fuente Ovejuna.*

(*The* Peasants *enter, men and women, bearing
the head of* FERNÁN GÓMEZ *on a pike.*)

MUSICIANS. *Hail, Ferdinand!*
Isabella, hail!
Death, tyrant band!

BARRILDO. Let's hear from Frondoso.

FRONDOSO. I've made a song and, if it's wrong,
You correct it as it goes along.
Hail, Isabella!
'Tis plain to be seen

Two can make one,
A King and a Queen.
When they die—
This to you, Saint Michael—
Just lift them both up to the sky.
Sweep the land clean,
O King and Queen!

LAURENCIA. See what you can do, Barrildo.

BARRILDO. Silence, then, while I get a rhyme in
my head.

PASCUALA. If you keep your head it will be twice
as good.

BARRILDO. *Hail to the King and Queen,*
For they are very famous!
They have won
And so they will not blame us.
May they always win,
Conquer giants
And a dwarf or two.
Down with tyrants!
And now I'm through.

MUSICIANS. *Hail, Ferdinand!*
Isabella, hail!
Death, tyrant band!

LAURENCIA. Mengo next!

FRONDOSO. Now Mengo!

MENGO. I'm a poet that is one.

PASCUALA. You're the back of the belly.

MENGO. *Oh, one Sunday morning*
The rascal beat me
From behind!
'Twas no way to treat me,
Most unkind.
How it hurt to seat me!
Glory to the Christian Kings!—
The wife must mind.

MUSICIAN. *Hail, Ferdinand!*
Isabella, hail!
Death, tyrant band!

ESTEBAN. You can take the head off the spear now.

MENGO. He might have been hung for his looks.
Phew!

(JUAN ROJO *enters with a shield bearing the royal*
arms.)

REGIDOR. Here come the arms!

ESTEBAN. Let all the people see.

JUAN ROJO. Where shall the arms be set?

REGIDOR. Before the town-hall, here, above the
door.

ESTEBAN. Noble escutcheon, hail!

BARRILDO. That is a coat of arms!

FRONDOSO. I see the light to-day, for the sun begins to shine.

ESTEBAN. Hail Castile and hail León!
Hail the bars of Aragon!
May tyrants die!
Hear, Fuente Ovejuna,

Follow counsel of the wise,
Nor hurt shall lie;
King and Queen must needs inquire
Right and wrong as they transpire,
Passing near-by.
Loyalty our hearts inspire.

FRONDOSO. That's a problem too. What shall our
story be?

ESTEBAN. Let us all agree to die, if it must be,
crying Fuente Ovejuna, and may no word of this
affair pass beyond that ever.

FRONDOSO. Besides it is the truth, for what was
done, Fuente Ovejuna did it, every man and woman.

ESTEBAN. Then that shall be our answer?

ALL. Yes!

ESTEBAN. Now I shall be the Judge and rehearse us
all in what we best had do. Mengo, put you to the
torture first.

MENGO. Am I the only candidate?

ESTEBAN. This is but talk, lad.

MENGO. All the same let's get through with it, and
quickly.

ESTEBAN. Who killed the Commander?

MENGO. Fuente Ovejuna killed him.

ESTEBAN. I'll put you to the torture.

MENGO. You will on your life, sir.

ESTEBAN. Confess, conscienceless hind!

MENGO. I do. What of it?

ESTEBAN. Who killed the Commander?

MENGO. Fuente Ovejuna.

ESTEBAN. Rack him again! Turn the wheel once
more.

MENGO. You oblige me.

ESTEBAN. Reduce him to carrion and let him go.

(*Enter* CUADRADO, REGIDOR.)

CUADRADO. What is this meeting?

FRONDOSO. Why so grave, Cuadrado?

CUADRADO. The King's Judge is here.

ESTEBAN. All to your homes, and quickly!

CUADRADO. A Captain comes with him also.

ESTEBAN. Let the devil appear! You know what
you are to say?

CUADRADO. They are going through the village prepared to take a deposition of every soul.

ESTEBAN. Have no fear.—Mengo, who killed the
Commander?

MENGO. Fuente Ovejuna. Ask me who!

(*Exeunt.*)

SCENE FIVE. *Almagro. A room in the Castle.*

(*The* MASTER *enters with a* Soldier.)

MASTER. Such news cannot be! To end like this?
I have a mind to run you through for your insolence.

SOLDIER. I was sent, Master, without malice.

MASTER. Can a mad handful of louts be moved to
such fury? I will take five hundred men forthwith

and burn the village, leaving no memory of those paths that were so basely trod.

SOLDIER. Master, be not so moved, for they have committed themselves to the King, whose power is not to be gainsaid lightly.

MASTER. How can they commit themselves to the King when they are vassals of Calatrava?

SOLDIER. That, Master, you will discuss with the King.

MASTER. No, for the land is his and all that it contains. I do obeisance to the Crown, and if they have submitted to the King I will subdue my rage and betake me to his presence as to a father's. My fault is grievous, in whose palliation I plead my untried years. I hang my head at this mischance of honor, but again to stumble were clear dishonor, yes, and certain death. (*Exeunt.*)

SCENE SIX. *The Square of Fuente Ovejuna. Before the Town Hall.*

(*Enter* LAURENCIA.)

LAURENCIA. Loving, that the beloved should suffer pain
A grinding sorrow fastens on the heart,
Fearing the loved must bear alone the smart
Care weighs the spirit down and hope lies slain.
The firm assurance, watchful to attain,
Doubting falters, and hastens to depart,
Nor is it folly in the brave to start
And tremble, promised boon transformed to bane.
I love my husband dearly. Now I see
Harpies of Vengeance rise before my sight
Unshapely, and my hope breathes a faint breath.
Only his good I seek. Oh, set him free
Ever with me to tremble in the night,
Or take him from me, so you take me, death!

(*Enter* FRONDOSO.)

FRONDOSO. Linger not, Laurencia.

LAURENCIA. My dear husband, fly danger, for I am its very heart.

FRONDOSO. Are you one to reject the homage of a lover?

LAURENCIA. My love, I fear for you, and you are my constant care.

FRONDOSO. Laurencia, I am so happy that surely this moment heaven smiles upon us both.

LAURENCIA. You see what has happened to the others, and how this judge proceeds firmly, with all severity? Save yourself before it is too late. Fly and avoid the danger!

FRONDOSO. What do you expect in such an hour? Shall I disappear and leave the peril to others, besides absenting myself from your sight? No, counsel me courage, for in danger a man betrays his blood, which is as it should be, come what may. (*Cries within.*)

I hear cries. They have put a man to the torture unless my ears deceive me. Listen and be still!

(*The* Judge *speaks within and Voices are heard in response.*)

JUDGE. Old man, I seek only the truth. Speak!

FRONDOSO. An old man tortured?

LAURENCIA. What barbarity!

ESTEBAN. Ease me a little.

JUDGE. Ease him. Who killed Fernando?

ESTEBAN. Fuente Ovejuna.

LAURENCIA. Good, father! Glory and praise!

FRONDOSO. Praise God he had the strength!

JUDGE. Take that boy there. Speak, you pup, for you know! Who was it? He says nothing. Put on the pressure there.

BOY. Judge, Fuente Ovejuna.

JUDGE. Now by the King, carls, I'll hang you to the last man! Who killed the Commander?

FRONDOSO. They torture the child and he replies like this?

LAURENCIA. There is courage in the village.

FRONDOSO. Courage and heart.

JUDGE. Peasants, be obstinate and this instrument brings death. So prepare! Who killed the Commander?

PASCUALA. Judge, Fuente Ovejuna.

JUDGE. Have no mercy.

FRONDOSO. I cannot think, my mind is blank!

LAURENCIA. Frondoso, Pascuala will not tell them.

FRONDOSO. The very children hold their peace!

JUDGE. They thrive upon it. —More! More!

PASCUALA. Oh, God in heaven!

JUDGE. Again, and answer me! Is she deaf?

PASCUALA. I say Fuente Ovejuna.

JUDGE. Seize that plump lad, half undressed already.

LAURENCIA. It must be Mengo! Poor Mengo!

FRONDOSO. He can never hold out.

MENGO. Oh, oh, oh!

JUDGE. Let him have it.

MENGO. Oh!

JUDGE. Prod his memory.

MENGO. Oh, oh!

JUDGE. Who slew the Commander, slave?

MENGO. Oh, oh! I can't get it out! I'll tell you—

JUDGE. Loosen that hand.

FRONDOSO. We are lost!

JUDGE. Let him have it on the back!

MENGO. No, for I'll give up everything!

JUDGE. Who killed him?

MENGO. Judge, Fuente Ovejuna.

JUDGE. Have these rogues no nerves that they can laugh at pain? The most likely, too, lie by instinct. I will no more to-day. To the street!

FRONDOSO. Now God bless Mengo! I was afraid, transfixed, but that lad is a cure for fear.

(BARRILDO *and the* Regidor *enter with* MENGO.)

BARRILDO. Good, Mengo, good!

REGIDOR. You have delivered us.

BARRILDO. Mengo, bravo!

FRONDOSO. We cheer you.

MENGO. Oh, oh! Not much.

BARRILDO. Drink, my friend, and eat. Come, come!

MENGO. Oh, oh! What have you got?

BARRILDO. Sweet lemon peel.

MENGO. Oh, oh!

10 FRONDOSA. Drink, drink. Take this.

BARRILDO. He does, too.

FRONDOSO. He takes it well. Down it goes.

LAURENCIA. Give him another bite.

MENGO. Oh, oh!

BARRILDO. Drink this for me.

LAURENCIA. Swallowed without a smile.

FRONDOSO. A sound answer deserves a round drink.

REGIDOR. Another, son?

MENGO. Oh, oh! Yes, yes!

20 FRONDOSO. Drink, for you deserve it.

LAURENCIA. He collects for every pang.

FRONDOSO. Throw a coat around him or he will freeze.

BARRILDO. Have you had enough?

MENGO. No, three more. Oh, oh!

FRONDOSO. He is asking for the wine.

BARRILDO. Yes, let him drink as much as he likes for one good turn begets another. What's the matter now?

30 MENGO. It leaves a taste in my mouth. Oh, I'm catching cold!

FRONDOSO. Another drink will help. Who killed the Commander?

MENGO. Fuente Ovejuna.

(*Exeunt the* Regidor, MENGO *and* BARRILDO.)

FRONDOSO. He has earned more than they give him. Ah, love, as you are mine confess to me. Who killed the Commander?

LAURENCIA. Love, Fuente Ovejuna.

FRONDOSO. Who?

40 LAURENCIA. Don't you think you can torture me. Fuente Ovejuna.

FRONDOSO. It did? How did I get you, then?

LAURENCIA. Love, I got you.   (*Exeunt.*)

SCENE SEVEN. *The open country.*

(*Enter the* KING *and* QUEEN, *meeting.*)

ISABELLA. Meeting, Sire, we crown our fortunes gladly.

KING. In union lies a more enduring glory.
Passing to Portugal the direct path
Leads me to you.

ISABELLA. To my heart, Majesty,

50 Turning away from conquest gratefully.

KING. What news of the war in Castile?

ISABELLA. Peace succeeds and the land lies ready, expecting the plough.

KING. Now my eyes light upon a living miracle, the consummation of a queenly peace.

(*Enter* DON MANRIQUE.)

MANRIQUE. The Master of Calatrava begs audience, having journeyed to your presence from his seat.

ISABELLA. I have a mind to greet this gentleman.

MANRIQUE. Majesty, his years are few, yet they 60 have proved his valor great.   (*Exit.*)

(*Enter the* MASTER.)

MASTER. Rodrigo Téllez Girón,
Master of Calatrava,
Humbly kneels repentant
And pardon begs, foredone.
False counsels proffered one
By one seduced my heart
To deeds disloyal and rash;
Now end all as begun
When a too ready ear   70
In Fernando placed its trust,
That false and unjust knight.
Pardon, Sire, past fear!
In mercy hold me dear,
Oh grant me royal favor,
To pay in loyalty
Forever rendered here!
Upon Granada's plain
When sounds the wild alarm
My valor shall wreak harm,   80
My sword-strokes fall amain
And through that fell champaign
Dart wounds to the enemy
Till the cross of victory
Red o'er the merlons reign.
Five hundred men in steel
I shall lead to smite your foes
Upon my life and oath, or close
My eyes in death! Here I kneel,
Never to displease you more.   90

KING. Rise, Master. Having tendered your allegiance you shall be received royally.

MASTER. Every word is balm.

ISABELLA. Few speak as bravely as they fight.

MASTER. Esther has returned to earth to wed a Christian Xerxes.

(DON MANRIQUE *enters.*)

MANRIQUE. Sire, the Judge that was despatched to Fuente Ovejuna has arrived with the process to report to Your Majesty.

KING (*to the* MASTER). These aggressors, being 100 of the Commandery, fall within your province.

95–96. **Esther has returned . . . Xerxes.** The Jewish maiden became the wife of the Persian king, according to the Biblical account.

MASTER. Sire, I yield to you, else were bloody vengeance taken for the death of the Commander.

KING (*to the* QUEEN). Then the decision rests with me?

ISABELLA. I grant it willingly though the right were mine of God.

(*Enter* Judge.)

JUDGE. I journeyed to Fuente Ovejuna in prosecution of your command probing all with due diligence and care. Having verified the crime, no writ or indictment has issued, inasmuch as with one accord and most singular fortitude, to all my questions as to the murderer the answer was always Fuente Ovejuna. Three hundred were put to torture, to the degree that forced them each to speak, without profit, Sire, of one word other than I have told you. Boys of ten were delivered to the rack, without yielding so much as a whisper, nor could they be moved by flattery or gold. Wherefore, this is my report, the evidence having failed; either you must pardon the village or wipe it out to the last man. They have followed me to your feet that in your own person you may pronounce judgment.

KING. If they seek our presence, let them appear before us, every one.

(*Enter* ESTEBAN *and* ALONSO, *Alcaldes,* JUAN ROJO *and* CUADRADO, *Regidors,* LAURENCIA, FRONDOSO, MENGO *and* Peasants, *both men and women.*)

LAURENCIA. Are those the King and Queen?

FRONDOSO. The power and majesty of Castile!

LAURENCIA. How beautiful, how wonderful! Saint Antonio, bless them both!

ISABELLA. Are these the people of the village?

ESTEBAN. Majesty, Fuente Ovejuna humbly kneels at your feet in allegiance. The mad tyranny and fierce cruelty of the dead Commander, raining insults through the farms, themselves provoked his death. He ravished our homes, forced our daughters, and knew no heart nor mercy.

FRONDOSO. This simple girl, O Queen, who is mine by rite of heaven, and has brought me all happiness, which surely must be matchless, on my wedding-night, as if it had been his very own, he bore off to his keep, and but that she is secure in honor, basely that night he had deflowered her.

MENGO. I know something as to that, with your permission, Queen, because you must be anxious to hear from me, seeing the bloody tanning that I got. I stood up for a girl in the village when the Commander went along the way to her undoing, the scurvy Nero, and then he took it out on me, and there never was a more thorough job at bottom. Three men paid it their attention, good pay at all three, since when, if you ask the explanation, I paid more for balm and ointment, with the powder and the myrtle I applied, than I could sell my sheep-cot for.

ESTEBAN. Sire, we yield ourselves to you. You are our King, and in witness of submission we have placed your arms above our doors. Have mercy, Sire, for our excuse is our extremity, which deserves your clemency.

KING. As no indictment is set down, although the fault be grave, it shall be pardoned. Since you yield yourselves to me, I further take the town under my protection, for in the Crown henceforth its charter shall abide, under such time as God in His mercy shall vouchsafe you a new Commander.

FRONDOSO. When his Majesty speaks
His voice we obey.
"Fuente Ovejuna" ends.
Friends, approve the play.

William Shakespeare

1564–1616

For an English-speaking person it is virtually impossible to say anything about Shakespeare now that has not already been said, even to excess. About a century after his death he was exalted into the first rank of English writers; and today only a habitual dissident would challenge his right to first place, for Shakespeare's catalog of created men and women is amazing in its scope, his knowledge of human beings uncanny, and his powers of expression, particularly in the dramatic field, unmatched for consistent effectiveness. In the long and distinguished course of English literature, one poet may surpass Shakespeare as a narrative writer, another as a lyric singer, another as a philosopher, another as a symbolist; yet none combines so powerfully a greater number of literary gifts in such an unforgettable medium.

Viewed against the background of world literature, Shakespeare's position is scarcely less high, for, although his range and power may sometimes remain uncomprehended by minds which are controlled by rules and objective standards, his sheer dynamic qualities are enough to inspire awe. It was not always thus, to be sure. Shakespeare was a professional man of the theater at a time when the theater depended upon royal or noble patronage, and he was willing to serve unashamedly the ends of patriotism and nationalism; he was not a man of academic learning and he was not an aristocrat. During the seventeenth century, therefore, even his English fellow countrymen considered him far too irregular and crude in style to bear the stamp of greatness. And even today one finds occasionally a disbeliever who is convinced that the great plays bearing the name of Shakespeare could never have been written by a commoner from a small provincial town, who never saw learning in one of the universities. Such narrow objections we can ignore, for it is an old rule that genius can break out anywhere, and that any man, if he be wise enough, can learn all about the world without benefit of books.

Besides, we know that there was such an individual as William Shakespeare, even if we know very little about the man's true personality. His biography must rest upon a minimum of facts and a maximum of inference and speculation. His parents in Stratford-on-Avon were solid enough citizens, but Shakespeare early contracted what we must regard as an unhappy and unfortunate marriage and may have fallen into difficulties with the local law. At any rate, he came up to London before he was thirty and in one way or another found himself a member of the theatrical profession, where he won the patronage of certain influential people at the court of Queen Elizabeth, served his apprenticeship as playwright, did some acting when the occasion arose, and finally emerged as a master playwright on his own during the early 1590's. His career as playwright and sometimes as actor continued for some twenty years and was clearly a successful one. Near the age of fifty he retired to Stratford, where he died on his fifty-second birthday, the day of St. George, the patron saint of England.

The First Folio edition of Shakespeare's plays, published in 1623, contains thirty-six dramas. Some of these he doubtless wrote in collaboration with other writers, particularly at the beginning and the end of his career. It was thus that he served his apprenticeship and learned his business. In his later years, we think, he sometimes allowed a younger playwright to work with him; it was the approved practice. It is not necessary, however, to consider such details here; it is quite sufficient to observe that the name of Shakespeare, applied to these thirty-six plays, indicates that he had a major interest in all of them, actually composing alone the great majority of them. In all the famous ones, the impress of the master is not to be mistaken. His great period, from *Romeo and Juliet* through *The Tempest*, runs from about 1596 to about 1612. During these years he also wrote a sequence of over one hundred and fifty sonnets of remarkable poetic achievement; and in the early 1590's he was responsible for two long narrative poems, *The Rape of Lucrece* and *Venus and Adonis;* but these lie outside the field of our immediate preoccupation. Taken alone, however, they would in themselves have established their author as one of the great poets of his age.

It is on his dramas, of course, that Shakespeare's position in world literature must rest. As exemplars of one of the greatest ages of dramatic writing anywhere, they brook no rivals. In substance they embrace, as Polonius in *Hamlet* puts it, "tragedy, comedy, history, pastoral, pastoral-comical, historical-pastoral, tragical-historical, tragical-comical-historical-pastoral, scene individable, or poem unlimited: Seneca cannot be too heavy, nor Plautus too light." Their multitudinous characters comprise the greatest single gallery of humanity in the annals of dramatic literature. Their thoughts and passions include all human experience; they pass from the trivial to the earthy, from the earthy to the ideal, from the pathetic

to the sublime and back again. Their humor—and Shakespeare was potentially one of the world's great humorists —covers everything from low comedy or farce to the most brittle of courtly witticisms. In portraying these characteristics, Shakespeare is ever ready to exhibit his most priceless gift—the expression of this universality of life in a magnificent language which, whether ugly or beautiful, whether base or noble, is so completely inevitable as to defy either imitation or improvement.

Printed quarto editions of *Hamlet,* the most famous play in the civilized world, appeared in 1602, 1603, 1605, and 1611; and the play of course appeared in the great First Folio edition of 1623, but its composition and production probably took place sometime in 1601 or 1602. The work was based in part on an English revenge-tragedy of some dozen years earlier, most likely by Thomas Kyd; and the ultimate source of the story is the Scandinavian tale of Amlethus or Hamlet told in the chronicle of Saxo Grammaticus, a Danish cleric and scholar of about 1200. The Danish saga was known to Renaissance Europe through a French translation by Belleforest (1570).

An enormous amount of research and scholarship has been expended on the problem of the genesis of *Hamlet,* as well as on the thorny matter of the interpretation of the character of the title role. No single generally satisfactory answer is forthcoming to either of these questions. We cannot tell how much or how little Shakespeare depended upon the earlier English play (the *Ur-Hamlet*); nor, indeed, is it known precisely what was in this play beyond the theme of Hamlet's revenge upon the murderer of his father. A later German dramatic representation of the story, *Der bestrafte Brudermord* (1710), which is supposed to have been based upon an English play (probably, though only probably, the *Ur-Hamlet*), has fratricide instead as the chief motif. Since some doubt has been thrown upon Shakespeare's knowledge of French, it is uncertain to what extent he drew upon Belleforest's version. As to the interpretation of Hamlet's character, it remains to this day an intensely subjective matter; it has been now romantic, now melodramatic, now allegorical, now realistic. The problems of the genesis of the play are, after all, academic problems. But the fascination exerted upon audiences, readers, and players by the role of Hamlet, easily the most celebrated of all modern dramatic roles, has been almost from the beginning a universal matter. Of the tribe of actors it can truly be said, "they all want to play Hamlet." For, whatever else his qualities, Hamlet has always typified the man who would and who would not, the man who tries to sidestep the unpleasant aspects of life and yet knows that he cannot, who hesitates to act but who, despite "the slings and arrows of outrageous fortune," is able to act sufficiently so that the objective of his life is achieved even though he himself is lost. All this even the casual reader of Shakespeare will discern—this, and the magnificent driving dramatic poetry, which has made *Hamlet* for all English-speaking people one of the greatest source-books of quotation.

Hamlet, Prince of Denmark

DRAMATIS PERSONAE

CLAUDIUS, *king of Denmark*
HAMLET, *son to the late, and nephew to the present king*
POLONIUS, *lord chamberlain*
HORATIO, *friend to Hamlet*
LAERTES, *son to Polonius*
VOLTIMAND,
CORNELIUS,
ROSENCRANTZ,
GUILDEN-
STERN,
OSRIC,
A Gentleman
} *courtiers*
A Priest
MARCELLUS } *officers*
BERNARDO
FRANCISCO, *a soldier*

REYNALDO, *servant to Polonius*
Players
Two Clowns, *grave-diggers*
FORTINBRAS, *prince of Norway*
A Captain
English Ambassadors

GERTRUDE, *queen of Denmark, and mother to Hamlet*
OPHELIA, *daughter to Polonius*

Lords, Ladies, Officers, Soldiers, Sailors, Messengers, and other Attendants
Ghost of Hamlet's Father

SCENE: *Denmark*

ACT I

SCENE 1. *Elsinore. A platform before the castle.*

(FRANCISCO *at his post. Enter to him* BERNARDO.)

BERNARDO.

WHO'S there?
FRANCISCO. Nay, answer me; stand, and unfold yourself.
BERNARDO. Long live the king!
FRANCISCO. Bernardo?
BERNARDO. He.
FRANCISCO. You come most carefully upon your hour.
BERNARDO. 'Tis now struck twelve; get thee to bed, Francisco.

FRANCISCO. For this relief much thanks: 'tis bitter cold,
And I am sick at heart.
BERNARDO. Have you had quiet guard?
FRANCISCO. Not a mouse stirring.
BERNARDO. Well, good night. 11
If you do meet Horatio and Marcellus,
The rivals of my watch, bid them make haste.
FRANCISCO. I think I hear them. Stand, ho! 14
Who's there?
(*Enter* HORATIO *and* MARCELLUS.)
HORATIO. Friends to this ground.
MARCELLUS. And liegemen to the Dane.
FRANCISCO. Give you good night.
MARCELLUS. O, farewell, honest soldier:
Who hath relieved you?
FRANCISCO. Bernardo has my place.
Give you good night. (*Exit.*)
MARCELLUS. Holla! Bernardo!
BERNARDO. Say,
What, is Horatio there?
HORATIO. A piece of him.
BERNARDO. Welcome, Horatio: welcome, good Marcellus. 20
MARCELLUS. What, has this thing appeared again tonight?
BERNARDO. I have seen nothing.
MARCELLUS. Horatio says 'tis but our fantasy,
And will not let belief take hold of him
Touching this dreadful sight, twice seen of us:
Therefore I have entreated him along
With us to watch the minutes of this night;
That if again this apparition come,
He may approve our eyes and speak to it.
HORATIO. Tush, tush, 'twill not appear.
BERNARDO. Sit down awhile;
And let us once again assail your ears, 31
That are so fortified against our story,
What we have two nights seen.
HORATIO. Well, sit we down,
And let us hear Bernardo speak of this.
BERNARDO. Last night of all, 35
When yond same star that's westward from the pole
Had made his course to illume that part of heaven
Where now it burns, Marcellus and myself,
The bell then beating one,—
(*Enter* Ghost.)
MARCELLUS. Peace, break thee off; look, where it comes again! 40
BERNARDO. In the same figure, like the king that's dead.

Hamlet, Prince of Denmark. The text used here is that of the Globe edition of Shakespeare, with certain emendations by Hardin Craig. Note, too, that the line numbering follows that of the Globe edition. *Act I, Scene 1. Stage directions: Elsinore . . . platform.* The platform is a level spot on the battlements of the castle. Elsinore, now Helsingör, was in the Middle Ages a rather important seaport of Denmark, controlling the approaches from the North Sea to the western Baltic. **2. me,** emphatic. Evidently Francisco is on guard-duty. **3. Long . . . king.** This seems to be the pass-word.

16. **Give you;** that is, God give you. 19. **A piece of him,** a casual answer. Horatio, like Hamlet, has his moments of flippancy. 29. **approve,** justify, corroborate. 36. **yond same star.** It was customary in the Middle Ages to use the constellation of Ursa Major, the "Big Dipper," to calculate time, inasmuch as it was a prominent constellation always to be seen above the horizon in the northern hemisphere.

MARCELLUS. Thou art a scholar; speak to it, Horatio.   42

BERNARDO. Looks it not like the king? mark it, Horatio.

HORATIO. Most like; it harrows me with fear and wonder.

BERNARDO. It would be spoke to.

MARCELLUS.   Question it, Horatio. 45

HORATIO. What art thou that usurp'st this time of night,
Together with that fair and warlike form
In which the majesty of buried Denmark
Did sometimes march? by Heaven, I charge thee, speak!

MARCELLUS. It is offended.

BERNARDO.   See, it stalks away! 50

HORATIO. Stay! speak, speak! I charge thee, speak!
                    (*Exit* Ghost.)

MARCELLUS. 'Tis gone, and will not answer.

BERNARDO. How now, Horatio! you tremble and look pale:
Is not this something more than fantasy?
What think you on 't?

HORATIO. Before my God, I might not this believe
Without the sensible and true avouch
Of mine own eyes.

MARCELLUS.   Is it not like the king?

HORATIO. As thou art to thyself;
Such was the very armour he had on,   60
When he the ambitious Norway combated;
So frowned he once, when, in an angry parle,
He smote the sledded Polacks on the ice.
'Tis strange.

MARCELLUS. Thus twice before, and just at this dead hour,
With martial stalk hath he gone by our watch.

HORATIO. In what particular thought to work I know not;
But in the gross and scope of my opinion,
This bodes some strange eruption to our state.

MARCELLUS. Good now, sit down, and tell me, he that knows,   70
Why this same strict and most observant watch
So nightly toils the subject of the land,
And why such daily cast of brazen cannon,
And foreign mart for implements of war;
Why such impress of shipwrights, whose sore task
Does not divide the Sunday from the week;
What might be toward, that this sweaty haste 77

Doth make the night joint-laborer with the day:
Who is't that can inform me?

HORATIO.   That can I;
At least, the whisper goes so. Our last king,   80
Whose image even but now appeared to us,
Was, as you know, by Fortinbras of Norway,
Thereto pricked on by a most emulate pride,
Dared to the combat; in which our valiant Hamlet—
For so this side of our known world esteemed him—
Did slay this Fortinbras; who, by a sealed compact,
Well ratified by law and heraldry,
Did forfeit, with his life, all those his lands
Which he stood seized of, to the conqueror:
Against the which, a moiety competent   90
Was gaged by our king; which had returned
To the inheritance of Fortinbras,
Had he been vanquisher; as, by the same covenant,
And carriage of the article designed,
His fell to Hamlet. Now, sir, young Fortinbras,
Of unimproved mettle hot and full,
Hath in the skirts of Norway here and there
Sharked up a list of lawless resolutes,
For food and diet, to some enterprise
That hath a stomach in 't; which is no other— 100
As it doth well appear unto our state—
But to recover of us, by strong hand
And terms compulsatory, those foresaid lands
So by his father lost: and this, I take it,
Is the main motive of our preparations,
The source of this our watch and the chief head
Of this post-haste and romage in the land.

BERNARDO. I think it be no other but e'en so:
Well may it sort that this portentous figure
Comes armed through our watch; so like the king 110
That was and is the question of these wars.

HORATIO. A mote it is to trouble the mind's eye.
In the most high and palmy state of Rome,
A little ere the mightiest Julius fell,
The graves stood tenantless and the sheeted dead
Did squeak and gibber in the Roman streets:
As stars with trains of fire and dews of blood,
Disasters in the sun; and the moist star
Upon whose influence Neptune's empire stands
Was sick almost to doomsday with eclipse: 120
And even the like precurse of fierce events,

42. **scholar.** In the Middle Ages, only clerics or scholars knew Latin, a language which was necessary to exorcise any spirit of the dead. 45. **It . . . spoke to.** It was the general belief that no ghost would address a living person unless spoken to first. 49. **sometimes,** now "sometime," meaning "formerly." 57. **sensible,** perceived by the senses. 62. **angry parle,** a parley or conference which breaks up in a fight. 63. **sledded Polacks,** men from Poland on sledges. 68. **gross and scope,** general range or drift. 70. **Good now,** a phrase expressing entreaty or argument. 72. **toils,** causes labor, makes work for. 75. **impress,** impressment, kidnaping. 77. **toward,** about to happen.

83. **emulate,** ambitious. 87. **law and heraldry,** civil as well as feudal law. 89. **seized,** possessed, endowed. 90. **moiety competent,** an adequate or sufficient amount. 91. **gaged,** pledged. 93. **covenant,** joint bargain. 94. **carriage,** substance, import. 96. **unimproved,** not turned to account or use. **hot and full,** full of fight. 98. **sharked up,** collected in hit-or-miss fashion. **resolutes,** adventurers, desperate men. 99. **food and diet,** hired only by giving them sustenance, not money. 100. **stomach,** opportunity for courage, but with a punning reference to "food and diet" in the preceding line. 107. **romage,** hustle and bustle. 113. **palmy state,** triumphant sovereignty. 114. **Julius,** Julius Caesar. 117. **As . . . blood.** There is probably a loss of some lines between this clause and the preceding. **stars . . . fire,** comets. 118. **Disasters,** unfavorable aspects—an astrological term. **moist star,** the moon, governing tides—hence the reference to Neptune's empire (the sea), in l. 119.

As harbingers preceding still the fates
And prologue to the omen coming on,
Have heaven and earth together demonstrated
Unto our climatures and countrymen.—
But soft, behold! lo, where it comes again!
      (*Re-enter* Ghost.)
I'll cross it, though it blast me. Stay, illusion!
If thou hast any sound, or use of voice,
Speak to me:
If there be any good thing to be done,   130
That may to thee do ease and grace to me,
Speak to me: (*Cock crows.*)
If thou art privy to thy country's fate,
Which, happily, foreknowing may avoid,
O, speak!
Or if thou hast uphoarded in thy life
Extorted treasure in the womb of earth,
For which, they say, you spirits oft walk in death,
Speak of it: stay, and speak! Stop it, Marcellus.   139
    MARCELLUS. Shall I strike at it with my partisan?
    HORATIO. Do, if it will not stand.
    BERNARDO.   'Tis here!
    HORATIO.   'Tis here!
                (*Exit* Ghost.)
    MARCELLUS. 'Tis gone!
We do it wrong, being so majestical,
To offer it the show of violence;
For it is, as the air, invulnerable,
And our vain blows malicious mockery.
    BERNARDO. It was about to speak, when the cock
      crew.
    HORATIO. And then it started like a guilty thing
Upon a fearful summons. I have heard,
The cock, that is the trumpet to the morn,   150
Doth with his lofty and shrill-sounding throat
Awake the god of day; and, at his warning,
Whether in sea or fire, in earth or air,
The extravagant and erring spirit hies
To his confine; and of the truth herein
This present object made probation.
    MARCELLUS. It faded on the crowing of the cock.
Some say that ever 'gainst that season comes
Wherein our Saviour's birth is celebrated,
The bird of dawning singeth all night long: 160
And then, they say, no spirit dare stir abroad;
The nights are wholesome; then no planets strike,

128–129. **If thou . . . speak.** In this passage Horatio mentions the
causes for a ghost's walking, as the Elizabethan age believed them
to be. Note that the manner of his address is that of an ancient charm.
134. **happily,** by chance, haply. 140. **partisan,** a long-handled spear
with a blade projecting laterally. 143. **majestical,** domineering,
importunate. 147. **cock crew.** It was the belief that walking ghosts
always returned to their graves after the first cock-crow (about one
o'clock in the morning). 154. **extravagant,** wandering abroad—the
same as erring. 156. **probation,** proof, corroboration. 162. **planets
strike.** Planets, particularly certain ones such as Mars, Mercury, and
Saturn, were considered malignant to individuals born in an inauspi-
cious hour, and so could bring down pestilence or mortal accidents
upon those people, especially at night.

No fairy takes, nor witch hath power to charm,
So hallowed and so gracious is the time.
    HORATIO. So I have heard and do in part believe it.
But, look, the morn, in russet mantle clad,
Walks o'er the dew of yon high eastward hill:
Break we our watch up; and by my advice,
Let us impart what we have seen tonight
Unto young Hamlet; for, upon my life,   170
This spirit, dumb to us, will speak to him.
Do you consent we shall acquaint him with it,
As needful in our loves, fitting our duty?
    MARCELLUS. Let's do 't, I pray; and I this morning
      know
Where we shall find him most conveniently.
                (*Exeunt.*)

SCENE 2. *A room of state in the castle.*

(*Enter the* KING, QUEEN, HAMLET, POLONIUS, LA-
ERTES, VOLTIMAND, CORNELIUS, *Lords, and Attend-
ants.*)
    KING. Though yet of Hamlet our dear brother's
      death
The memory be green, and that it us befitted
To bear our hearts in grief and our whole kingdom
To be contracted in one brow of woe,
Yet so far hath discretion fought with nature
That we with wisest sorrow think on him,
Together with remembrance of ourselves.
Therefore our sometime sister, now our queen,
The imperial jointress to this warlike state,
Have we, as 'twere with a defeated joy,—   10
With an auspicious and a dropping eye,
With mirth in funeral and with dirge in marriage,
In equal scale weighing delight and dole,—
Taken to wife: nor have we herein barred
Your better wisdoms, which have freely gone
With this affair along. For all, our thanks.
Now follows, that you know, young Fortinbras,
Holding a weak supposal of our worth,
Or thinking by our late dear brother's death
Our state to be disjoint and out of frame,   20
Colleagued with the dream of his advantage,
He hath not failed to pester us with message,
Importing the surrender of those lands
Lost by his father, with all bonds of law,
To our most valiant brother. So much for him.
Now for ourself and for this time of meeting:
Thus much the business is: we have here writ
To Norway, uncle of young Fortinbras,—
Who, impotent and bed-rid, scarcely hears
Of this his nephew's purpose,—to suppress   30

163. **takes,** charms, bewitches. 164. **gracious,** full of grace.
Act I, Scene 2. 9. **jointress,** dowager, literally a female joiner—
a legal term designating a widow who enjoys an estate settled upon
her by her husband's death. 17. **that;** as often in Shakespeare, "that
which." 18. **weak supposal,** low estimate. 21. **Colleagued,** added
to. **dream . . . advantage,** vision of success. 23. **Importing,** referring to.

His further gait herein; in that the levies,
The lists and full proportions, are all made
Out of his subject: and we here dispatch
You, good Cornelius, and you, Voltimand,
For bearers of this greeting to old Norway;
Giving to you no further personal power
To business with the king, more than the scope
Of these delated articles allow.
Farewell, and let your haste commend your duty.

CORNELIUS AND VOLTIMAND. In that and all things
    will we show our duty.   40

KING. We doubt it nothing; heartily farewell.
        (*Exeunt* VOLTIMAND *and* CORNELIUS.)
And now, Laertes, what's the news with you?
You told us of some suit; what is 't, Laertes?
You cannot speak of reason to the Dane,
And lose your voice: what wouldst thou beg, Laertes,
That shall not be my offer, not thy asking?
The head is not more native to the heart,
The hand more instrumental to the mouth,
Than is the throne of Denmark to thy father.
What wouldst thou have, Laertes?

LAERTES.   My dread lord, 50
Your leave and favor to return to France,
From whence though willingly I came to Denmark,
To show my duty in your coronation,
Yet now, I must confess, that duty done,
My thoughts and wishes bend again toward France
And bow them to your gracious leave and pardon.

KING. Have you your father's leave? What says
    Polonius?

POLONIUS. He hath, my lord, wrung from me my
    slow leave
By laborsome petition, and at last
Upon his will I sealed my hard consent: 60
I do beseech you, give him leave to go.

KING. Take thy fair hour, Laertes; time be thine,
And thy best graces spend it at thy will!
But now, my cousin Hamlet, and my son,—

HAMLET (*aside*). A little more than kin, and less
    than kind.

KING. How is it that the clouds still hang on you?

HAMLET. Not so, my lord; I am too much i' the
    sun.

---

31. **gait,** proceeding. 32. **proportions,** estimate and allocation of forces or supplies for carrying on war, logistics. 38. **delated,** expressly stated. 44. **Dane,** the Danish king. 45. **lose your voice,** speak in vain. 56. **leave and pardon,** permission to leave the country. 62. **Take . . . hour,** enjoy the opportunities and privileges of youth. 65. **A little . . . kind.** There is a play of words in this famous opening line in Hamlet's role. The general sense is, "my relation to you (kith) has become more than a normal kinship; it has become more than natural (kind)." The pun comes largely on the word "kind," which still kept some vestiges of its older meaning of "natural" but which tended to have the meaning of the word at the present time. 67. **too much i' the sun,** another equivocal phrase: "I am too much out of doors"; that is, "I am at sea"; "I am too much in the sun of your grace," definitely ironical; and "I am too much of a son to you." Obviously Hamlet is implying that he is bewildered, discontented at the turn of events, dispossessed of his heritage, and entrapped in an unnatural double relationship of stepson and nephew.

QUEEN. Good Hamlet, cast thy nighted color off,
And let thine eye look like a friend on Denmark.
Do not for ever with thy vailed lids   70
Seek for thy noble father in the dust:
Thou know'st 'tis common: all that lives must die,
Passing through nature to eternity.

HAMLET. Ay, madam, it is common.

QUEEN.   If it be,
Why seems it so particular with thee?

HAMLET. Seems, madam! nay, it is; I know not
    'seems.'
'Tis not alone my inky cloak, good mother,
Nor customary suits of solemn black,
Nor windy suspiration of forced breath,
No, nor the fruitful river in the eye,   80
Nor the dejected 'havior of the visage,
Together with all forms, moods, shapes of grief,
That can denote me truly: these indeed seem,
For they are actions that a man might play:
But I have that within which passeth show;
These but the trappings and the suits of woe.

KING. 'Tis sweet and commendable in your nature,
    Hamlet,
To give these mourning duties to your father:
But, you must know, your father lost a father;
That father lost, lost his, and the survivor bound   90
In filial obligation for some term
To do obsequious sorrow: but to persevere
In obstinate condolement is a course
Of impious stubbornness; 'tis unmanly grief:
It shows a will most incorrect to Heaven,
A heart unfortified, a mind impatient,
An understanding simple and unschooled:
For what we know must be and is as common
As any the most vulgar thing to sense,
Why should we in our peevish opposition   100
Take it to heart? Fie! 'tis a fault to Heaven,
A fault against the dead, a fault to nature,
To reason most absurd; whose common theme
Is death of fathers, and who still hath cried,
From the first corse till he that died today,
'This must be so.' We pray you, throw to earth
This unprevailing woe, and think of us
As of a father; for let the world take note,
You are the most immediate to our throne;
And with no less nobility of love   110
Than that which dearest father bears his son,
Do I impart toward you. For your intent

---

68. **nighted color,** Hamlet is traditionally dressed in black, as befits a mourning son; Queen Gertrude is not. 70. **vailed,** downcast. 74. **common,** a commonplace remark; a frequent situation, and, possibly, a vulgar action on the part of the Queen, though the last meaning is probably a modern interpretation only. 79. **windy suspiration,** loud sighs. **forced breath,** produced by distress of the heart. 92. **obsequious,** dutiful, ceremonially appropriate. 93. **condolement,** sorrowing. 95. **incorrect,** untrained, uncorrected, undisciplined. 99. **vulgar thing,** common experience. 107. **unprevailing,** unavailing. 110. **nobility,** high degree. 112. **impart.** Supply "love" between "impart" and "toward."

In going back to school in Wittenberg,
It is most retrograde to our desire:
And we beseech you, bend you to remain
Here, in the cheer and comfort of our eye,
Our chiefest courtier, cousin, and our son.

QUEEN. Let not thy mother lose her prayers, Hamlet:
I pray thee, stay with us; go not to Wittenberg.

HAMLET. I shall in all my best obey you, madam.

KING. Why, 'tis a loving and a fair reply: 121
Be as ourself in Denmark. Madam, come;
This gentle and unforced accord of Hamlet
Sits smiling to my heart: in grace whereof,
No jocund health that Denmark drinks today,
But the great cannon to the clouds shall tell,
And the king's rouse the heavens shall bruit again,
Re-speaking earthly thunder. Come away.

(*Exeunt all but* HAMLET.)

HAMLET. O, that this too too solid flesh would melt,
Thaw and resolve itself into a dew! 130
Or that the Everlasting had not fixed
His canon 'gainst self-slaughter! O God! God!
How weary, stale, flat, and unprofitable,
Seem to me all the uses of this world!
Fie on 't! ah fie! 'tis an unweeded garden,
That grows to seed; things rank and gross in nature
Possess it merely. That it should come to this!
But two months dead; nay, not so much, not two:
So excellent a king; that was, to this,
Hyperion to a satyr; so loving to my mother 140
That he might not beteem the winds of Heaven
Visit her face too roughly. Heaven and earth!
Must I remember? why, she would hang on him,
As if increase of appetite had grown
By what it fed on: and yet, within a month—
Let me not think on 't—Frailty, thy name is woman!—
A little month, or ere those shoes were old
With which she followed my poor father's body,
Like Niobe, all tears:—why she, even she—
O God! a beast, that wants discourse of reason, 150
Would have mourned longer—married with my uncle,
My father's brother, but no more like my father
Than I to Hercules: within a month:

---

113. **Wittenberg,** the famous university of northern Germany, founded in 1502 and later the center of German Reformation Protestantism. 115. **bend you,** incline yourself. 117. **cousin,** the usual term of courteous address by a king to the nobility of his kingdom. 127. **rouse,** draft of liquor, toast. **bruit again,** echo. 137. **merely,** completely, entirely. 140. **Hyperion,** the god of the sun in the ancient pantheon of Greek mythology (i.e., before the advent of Zeus as king of the gods). In later myth his functions were taken over by Apollo, god of the sun, divine inspiration, and beauty. 141. **beteem,** allow, permit. 149. **Niobe,** daughter of Tantalus, who boasted that she had more sons and daughters than Leto; for this Apollo and Artemis (Diana) slew all her children. Zeus later turned her into a stone. She became in classical myth a symbol of the bereaved mother much as Rachel in Matthew 2:18 is a symbol. 150. **discourse of reason,** process or faculty of reason.

Ere yet the salt of most unrighteous tears
Had left the flushing in her galled eyes,
She married. O, most wicked speed, to post
With such dexterity to incestuous sheets!
It is not nor it cannot come to good:
But break, my heart; for I must hold my tongue.

(*Enter* HORATIO, MARCELLUS, *and* BERNARDO.)

HORATIO. Hail to your lordship!

HAMLET. I am glad to see you well:
Horatio,—or I do forget myself. 161

HORATIO. The same, my lord, and your poor servant ever.

HAMLET. Sir, my good friend; I'll change that name with you:
And what make you from Wittenberg, Horatio?
Marcellus?

MARCELLUS. My good lord—

HAMLET. I am very glad to see you. Good even, sir.
But what, in faith, make you from Wittenberg?

HORATIO. A truant disposition, good my lord.

HAMLET. I would not hear your enemy say so, 170
Nor shall you do mine ear that violence,
To make it truster of your own report
Against yourself: I know you are no truant.
But what is your affair in Elsinore?
We'll teach you to drink deep ere you depart.

HORATIO. My lord, I came to see your father's funeral.

HAMLET. I pray thee, do not mock me, fellow-student;
I think it was to see my mother's wedding.

HORATIO. Indeed, my lord, it followed hard upon.

HAMLET. Thrift, thrift, Horatio! the funeral baked meats 180
Did coldly furnish forth the marriage tables.
Would I had met my dearest foe in Heaven
Or ever I had seen that day, Horatio!
My father!—methinks I see my father.

HORATIO. Where, my lord?

HAMLET. In my mind's eye, Horatio.

HORATIO. I saw him once; he was a goodly king.

HAMLET. He was a man, take him for all in all,
I shall not look upon his like again.

HORATIO. My lord, I think I saw him yesternight.

HAMLET. Saw? who? 190

HORATIO. My lord, the king your father.

HAMLET. The king my father!

HORATIO. Season your admiration for a while
With an attent ear, till I may deliver,
Upon the witness of these gentlemen,
This marvel to you.

---

156. **post,** hasten. 163. **I'll . . . you,** "I will be your servant; you will be my friend." 164. **make you,** are you doing? 180. **baked meats,** meat pies; in Shakespeare's time, as always, a favorite English dish. 182. **dearest,** most respected and most cordially hated; according to some, "direst." 192. **Season your admiration,** moderate your wonder and astonishment. 193. **deliver,** reveal.

HAMLET.   For God's love, let me hear.

HORATIO. Two nights together had these gentle-
men,
Marcellus and Bernardo, on their watch,
In the dead vast and middle of the night,
Been thus encountered. A figure like your father,
Armed at point exactly, cap-a-pe,   200
Appears before them, and with solemn march
Goes slow and stately by them: thrice he walked
By their oppressed and fear-surprised eyes,
Within his truncheon's length; whilst they, distilled
Almost to jelly with the act of fear,
Stand dumb and speak not to him. This to me
In dreadful secrecy impart they did;
And I with them the third night kept the watch:
Where, as they had delivered, both in time,   209
Form of the thing, each word made true and good,
The apparition comes: I knew your father;   211
These hands are not more like.

HAMLET.   But where was this?

MARCELLUS. My lord, upon the platform where we
watched.

HAMLET. Did you not speak to it?

HORATIO.   My lord, I did;
But answer made it none: yet once methought
It lifted up it head and did address
Itself to motion, like as it would speak;
But even then the morning cock crew loud,
And at the sound it shrunk in haste away,
And vanished from our sight.

HAMLET.   'Tis very strange.   220

HORATIO. As I do live, my honored lord, 'tis true;
And we did think it writ down in our duty
To let you know of it.

HAMLET. Indeed, indeed, sirs, but this troubles me.
Hold you the watch tonight?

MARCELLUS AND BERNARDO. We do, my lord.

HAMLET. Armed, say you?

MARCELLUS AND BERNARDO. Armed, my lord.

HAMLET. From top to toe?

MARCELLUS AND BERNARDO. My lord, from head to
foot.

HAMLET. Then saw you not his face?   229

HORATIO. O, yes, my lord; he wore his beaver up.

HAMLET. What, looked he frowningly?

HORATIO. A countenance more in sorrow than
anger.   232

HAMLET. Pale or red?

HORATIO.   Nay, very pale.

HAMLET.   And fixed his eyes upon you?

HORATIO. Most constantly.

HAMLET.   I would I had been there.

HORATIO. It would have much amazed you.

HAMLET. Very like, very like. Stayed it long?

HORATIO. While one with moderate haste might tell
a hundred.

MARCELLUS AND BERNARDO. Longer, longer.

HORATIO. Not when I saw it.

HAMLET.   His beard was grizzled,—no?

HORATIO. It was, as I have seen it in his life,   241
A sable silvered.

HAMLET.   I will watch tonight;
Perchance 'twill walk again.

HORATIO.   I warrant it will.

HAMLET. If it assume my noble father's person,
I'll speak to it, though Hell itself should gape
And bid me hold my peace. I pray you all,
If you have hitherto concealed this sight,
Let it be tenable in your silence still;
And whatsoever else shall hap tonight,
Give it an understanding, but no tongue: 250
I will requite your loves. So, fare you well:
Upon the platform, 'twixt eleven and twelve,
I'll visit you.

ALL.   Our duty to your honor.

HAMLET. Your loves, as mine to you; farewell.

(*Exeunt all but* HAMLET.)

My father's spirit in arms! all is not well;
I doubt some foul play: would the night were come!
Till then sit still, my soul: foul deeds will rise,
Though all the earth o'erwhelm them, to men's eyes.

(*Exit.*)

SCENE 3. *A room in Polonius's house.*

(*Enter* LAERTES *and* OPHELIA.)

LAERTES. My necessaries are embarked: farewell;
And sister, as the winds give benefit
And convoy is assistant, do not sleep,
But let me hear from you.

OPHELIA.   Do you doubt that?

LAERTES. For Hamlet and the trifling of his favor,
Hold it a fashion and a toy in blood,
A violet in the youth of primy nature,
Forward, not permanent, sweet, not lasting,
The perfume and suppliance of a minute;
No more.

OPHELIA. No more but so?

LAERTES.   Think it no more: 10
For nature, crescent, does not grow alone
In thews and bulk, but, as this temple waxes,
The inward service of the mind and soul
Grows wide withal. Perhaps he loves you now,
And now no soil nor cautel doth besmirch

242. **sable**, in heraldry, the color black.
Act I, Scene 3.   3. **convoy is assistant**, means of transportation are
ready.   6. **fashion**, custom, prevailing usage. **toy in blood**, a passing
amorous fancy.   7. **primy nature**, nature in the prime.   8. **Forward**,
precocious.   9. **suppliance of a minute**, diversion to while away a
minute.   11. **crescent**, growing, waxing.   12. **thews**, sinews, muscles.
temple, the body; cf. I Corinthians, 6:19: "know you not that your
body is the temple of the Holy Ghost?"   15. **soil**, blemish, defile-
ment. **cautel**, trick, deceitful manner.

200. **at point exactly**, precisely according to etiquette. **cap-a-pe**, from
head to foot.   203. **oppressed**, distressed.   204. **truncheon**, officer's
staff. **distilled**, softened, weakened.   205. **act**, action, effects.   216.
It, its.   230. **beaver**, visor of the helmet.

The virtue of his will: but you must fear,
His greatness weighed, his will is not his own;
For he himself is subject to his birth:
He may not, as unvalued persons do,
Carve for himself; for on his choice depends   20
The safety and health of this whole state;
And therefore must his choice be circumscribed
Unto the voice and yielding of that body
Whereof he is the head. Then if he says he loves you,
It fits your wisdom so far to believe it
As he in his particular act and place
May give his saying deed; which is no further
Than the main voice of Denmark goes withal.
Then weigh what loss your honor may sustain,
If with too credent ear you list his songs,   30
Or lose your heart, or your chaste treasure open
To his unmastered importunity.
Fear it, Ophelia, fear it, my dear sister,
And keep you in the rear of your affection,
Out of the shot and danger of desire.
The chariest maid is prodigal enough,
If she unmask her beauty to the moon:
Virtue itself 'scapes not calumnious strokes:
The canker galls the infants of the spring,
Too oft before their buttons be disclosed,   40
And in the morn and liquid dew of youth
Contagious blastments are most imminent.
Be wary then; best safety lies in fear:
Youth to itself rebels, though none else near.

    OPHELIA. I shall the effect of this good lesson keep,
As watchman to my heart. But, good my brother,
Do not, as some ungracious pastors do,
Show me the steep and thorny way to Heaven;
Whiles, like a puffed and reckless libertine,
Himself the primrose path of dalliance treads,   50
And recks not his own rede.

    LAERTES.   O, fear me not.
I stay too long: but here my father comes.
               (*Enter* POLONIUS.)
A double blessing is a double grace;
Occasion smiles upon a second leave.

    POLONIUS. Yet here, Laertes! aboard, aboard, for
      shame!
The wind sits in the shoulder of your sail,
And you are stayed for. There; my blessing with thee!
And these few precepts in thy memory
See thou character. Give thy thoughts no tongue,

Nor any unproportioned thought his act.   60
Be thou familiar, but by no means vulgar.
Those friends thou hast, and their adoption tried,
Grapple them to thy soul with hoops of steel;
But do not dull thy palm with entertainment
Of each new-hatched, unfledged comrade. Beware
Of entrance to a quarrel, but being in,
Bear 't that the opposed may beware of thee.
Give every man thy ear, but few thy voice;
Take each man's censure, but reserve thy judgment.
Costly thy habit as thy purse can buy,   70
But not expressed in fancy; rich, not gaudy;
For the apparel oft proclaims the man,
And they in France of the best rank and station
Are of a most select and generous chief in that.
Neither a borrower nor a lender be;
For loan oft loses both itself and friend,
And borrowing dulls the edge of husbandry.
This above all: to thine own self be true,
And it must follow, as the night the day,
Thou canst not then be false to any man.   80
Farewell: my blessing season this in thee!

    LAERTES. Most humbly do I take my leave, my
      lord.

    POLONIUS. The time invites you; go; your servants
      tend.

    LAERTES. Farewell, Ophelia; and remember well
What I have said to you.

    OPHELIA.   'Tis in my memory locked,
And you yourself shall keep the key of it.

    LAERTES. Farewell.   (*Exit.*)

    POLONIUS. What is 't, Ophelia, he hath said to you?

    OPHELIA. So please you, something touching the
      Lord Hamlet.

    POLONIUS. Marry, well bethought: 90
'Tis told me, he hath very oft of late
Given private time to you; and you yourself
Have of your audience been most free and bounte
    ous:
If it be so, as so 'tis put on me,
And that in way of caution, I must tell you,
You do not understand yourself so clearly
As it behoves my daughter and your honor.
What is between you? Give me up the truth.

    OPHELIA. He hath, my lord, of late made many
      tenders
Of his affection to me.   100

    POLONIUS. Affection! Pooh! You speak like a green
      girl,
Unsifted in such perilous circumstance.
Do you believe his tenders, as you call them?

---

16. **virtue . . . will,** good intentions. 19. **unvalued persons,** persons of no social rank. 23. **voice and yielding,** support, approval. 27. **deed,** effect. 32. **unmastered,** unrestrained. 36. **chariest,** most scrupuously or painfully modest. 39. **canker . . . spring,** the canker-worm injures the young plants of spring. 40. **buttons,** buds. 41. **liquid dew,** dew that is fresh. 42. **blastments,** blights. 47. **ungracious,** graceless. 51. **recks . . . rede,** heeds not his own advice. 53. **double,** etc. Laertes has evidently already said good-by to his father. 54. **Occasion,** opportunity. 58. **precepts,** etc. It is in keeping with Polonius' penchant for platitudes that the maxims he gives here are age-old. Still, the expression of them is memorable. 59. **character,** inscribe (v.). The accent of this word came on the second syllable.

60. **unproportioned,** immoderate, vulgar. 61. **familiar,** friendly. **vulgar,** common, cheap. 64. **dull thy palm,** make thyself less sensitive. 65. **unfledged,** immature, untried. 69. **censure,** opinion, criticism. 71. **expressed in fancy,** fantastic in design. 74. **chief,** mainly, principally (adv.). 77. **husbandry,** thrift, economy. 81. **season,** mature (v.), develop. 94. **put on me,** impressed on me. 99. **tenders,** offers. 102. **unsifted,** untried, untested.

OPHELIA. I do not know, my lord, what I should
  think.

POLONIUS. Marry, I'll teach you: think yourself a
  baby;
That you have taken these tenders for true pay,
Which are not sterling. Tender yourself more dearly;
Or—not to crack the wind of the poor phrase,
Running it thus—you'll tender me a fool.

OPHELIA. My lord, he hath importuned me with
  love   110
In honorable fashion.

POLONIUS. Ay, fashion you may call it; go to, go to.

OPHELIA. And hath given countenance to his
  speech, my lord,
With almost all the holy vows of Heaven.

POLONIUS. Ay, springes to catch woodcocks. I do
  know,
When the blood burns, how prodigal the soul
Lends the tongue vows: these blazes, daughter,
Giving more light than heat, extinct in both,
Even in their promise, as it is a-making,
You must not take for fire. From this time,   120
Be somewhat scanter of your maiden presence;
Set your entreatments at a higher rate
Than a command to parley. For Lord Hamlet,
Believe so much in him, that he is young,
And with a larger tether may he walk
Than may be given you: in few, Ophelia,
Do not believe his vows; for they are brokers,
Not of that dye which their investments show,
But mere implorators of unholy suits,
Breathing like sanctified and pious bawds,   130
The better to beguile. This is for all:
I would not, in plain terms, from this time forth,
Have you so slander any moment leisure,
As to give words or talk with the Lord Hamlet.
Look to 't, I charge you; come your ways.

OPHELIA. I shall obey, my lord.   (*Exeunt.*)

SCENE 4. *The platform.*

(*Enter* HAMLET, HORATIO, *and* MARCELLUS.)

HAMLET. The air bites shrewdly; it is very cold.

HORATIO. It is a nipping and an eager air.

HAMLET. What hour now?

HORATIO.   I think it lacks of twelve.

MARCELLUS.   No, it is struck.

HORATIO. Indeed? I heard it not; then it draws near
  the season
Wherein the spirit held his wont to walk.

(*A flourish of trumpets, and ordnance shot off,
within.*)
What does this mean, my lord?

HAMLET. The king doth wake tonight and takes his
  rouse,
Keeps wassail, and the swaggering up-spring reels;
And, as he drains his draughts of Rhenish down,   10
The kettle-drum and trumpet thus bray out
The triumph of his pledge.

HORATIO.   Is it a custom?

HAMLET. Ay, marry, is 't:
But to my mind, though I am native here
And to the manner born, it is a custom
More honored in the breach than the observance.
This heavy-headed revel east and west
Makes us traduced and taxed of other nations:
They clepe us drunkards, and with swinish phrase
Soil our addition; and indeed it takes   20
From our achievements, though performed at height,
The pith and marrow of our attribute.
So, oft it chances in particular men,
That for some vicious mole of nature in them,
As, in their birth—wherein they are not guilty,
Since nature cannot choose his origin—
By the o'ergrowth of some complexion,
Oft breaking down the pales and forts of reason,
Or by some habit that too much o'erleavens
The form of plausive manners, that these men,   30
Carrying, I say, the stamp of one defect,
Being nature's livery, or fortune's star,—
Their virtues else—be they as pure as grace,
As infinite as man may undergo—
Shall in the general censure take corruption
From that particular fault: the dram of eale
Doth all the noble substance of a doubt
To his own scandal.

HORATIO.   Look, my lord, it comes!

Act I, Scene 4. 8. **wake,** stay awake, hold revel. **rouse,** drinking-bout, carouse. 9. **wassail,** carousal. **up-spring,** a wild German folk-dance which generally concluded festivities. **reels, reels** through. 12. **triumph . . . pledge,** the glory of his promised achievement. 15. **to the manner born,** destined by birth to be subject to the custom (manner). 18. **taxed** of, censured by. 19. **clepe,** call. **with swinish phrase,** by calling us swine. 20. **addition,** title. 22. **attribute,** reputation. 24. **mole of nature,** natural blemish. 27. **complexion,** the particular combination and balance of the four physical humors of medieval physiology which went to constitute a person's temperament and character. 28. **pales,** palings, fences, stockades of a fortification. 29. **o'erleavens,** makes too light. 30. **plausive,** pleasing. 32. **nature's livery,** endowment from nature. 34. **undergo,** bear the weight of. 36–38. **dram . . . scandal.** This difficult passage has had a variety of interpretations, largely because of the obscurity of "eale"; that which makes the best sense is "a dram of evil can by a (mere) doubt put to scandal all noble qualities." It is noteworthy that the entire preceding passage from ll. 17–38 inclusive was omitted from the First Folio of 1623, probably because the then Queen of England was Danish.

105. **Marry,** a mild oath by the Virgin Mary. 106. **tenders,** promises to pay, promissory notes; a pun on *tenders* in l. 99. 107. **sterling,** legal currency, legal tender. **Tender,** hold, consider. 108. **crack the wind,** to run until it is broken-winded. 109. **tender . . . fool,** show me a fool for a daughter, or possibly, deliver me an illegitimate child. The various uses of the word *tender* (ll. 99, 103, 106, 107, and 109) afford an excellent example of the Elizabethan conceit based upon the pun. 112. **fashion,** mere form and pretense. **go to,** a mild term of reproach or teasing. 115. **springes,** snares. **woodcocks,** a game-bird noted for the ease with which it can be caught, hence a symbol of stupidity and gullibility. 122. **entreatments,** conversations, interviews. 123. **command to parley,** a mere invitation to talk. 124. **so much in him,** this much concerning him. 126. **in few,** in a few words, briefly. 127. **brokers,** go-betweens, bawds. 128. **dye,** color, hue, kind. **investments,** clothing. 129. **implorators,** solicitors of. 130. **Breathing,** speaking low. 133. **slander,** debase, bring disgrace upon. Insert "of" between "moment" and "leisure."

HAMLET. Angels and ministers of grace defend us!
Be thou a spirit of health or goblin damned,   40
Bring with thee airs from Heaven or blasts from Hell,
Be thy intents wicked or charitable,
Thou comest in such a questionable shape
That I will speak to thee: I'll call thee Hamlet,
King, father, royal Dane: O, answer me!
Let me not burst in ignorance; but tell
Why thy canonized bones, hearsed in death,
Have burst their cerements; why the sepulchre,
Wherein we saw thee quietly inurned,
Hath oped his ponderous and marble jaws,   50
To cast thee up again. What may this mean,
That thou, dead corse, again in complete steel
Revisitest thus the glimpses of the moon,
Making night hideous; and we fools of nature
So horridly to shake our disposition
With thoughts beyond the reaches of our souls?
Say, why is this? Wherefore? What should we do?
(Ghost *beckons* HAMLET.)
  HORATIO. It beckons you to go away with it,
As if some impartment did desire
To you alone.
  MARCELLUS. Look, with what courteous action   60
It waves you to a more removed ground:
But do not go with it.
  HORATIO.   No, by no means.
  HAMLET. It will not speak; then I will follow it.
  HORATIO. Do not, my lord.
  HAMLET.   Why, what should be the fear?
I do not set my life at a pin's fee;
And for my soul, what can it do to that,
Being a thing immortal as itself?
It waves me forth again; I'll follow it.
  HORATIO. What if it tempt you toward the flood,
my lord,
Or to the dreadful summit of the cliff   70
That beetles o'er his base into the sea,
And there assume some other horrible form,
Which might deprive your sovereignty of reason
And draw you into madness? think of it:
The very place puts toys of desperation,
Without more motive, into every brain
That looks so many fathoms to the sea
And hears it roar beneath.
  HAMLET.   It waves me still.
Go on; I'll follow thee.   79
  MARCELLUS. You shall not go, my lord.

  HAMLET.   Hold off your hands.
  HORATIO. Be ruled; you shall not go.
  HAMLET.   My fate cries out,
And makes each petty artery in this body
As hardy as the Nemean lion's nerve.
Still am I called. Unhand me, gentlemen.
By Heaven, I'll make a ghost of him that lets me!
I say, away! Go on; I'll follow thee.
(*Exeunt* Ghost *and* HAMLET.)
  HORATIO. He waxes desperate with imagination.
  MARCELLUS. Let's follow; 'tis not fit thus to obey
him.
  HORATIO. Have after. To what issue will this come?
  MARCELLUS. Something is rotten in the state of
Denmark.   90
  HORATIO. Heaven will direct it.
  MARCELLUS.   Nay, let's follow him.
(*Exeunt.*)

SCENE 5. *Another part of the platform.*

(*Enter* Ghost *and* HAMLET.)
  HAMLET. Where wilt thou lead me? Speak; I'll go
no further.
  GHOST. Mark me.
  HAMLET.   I will.
  GHOST.   My hour is almost come,
When I to sulphurous and tormenting flames
Must render up myself.
  HAMLET.   Alas, poor ghost!
  GHOST. Pity me not, but lend thy serious hearing
To what I shall unfold.
  HAMLET.   Speak; I am bound to hear.
  GHOST. So art thou to revenge, when thou shalt
hear.
  HAMLET. What?
  GHOST.   I am thy father's spirit,
Doomed for a certain term to walk the night,   10
And for the day confined to fast in fires,
Till the foul crimes done in my days of nature
Are burnt and purged away. But that I am forbid
To tell the secrets of my prison-house,
I could a tale unfold whose lightest word
Would harrow up thy soul, freeze thy young blood,
Make thy two eyes, like stars, start from their
spheres,
Thy knotted and combined locks to part
And each particular hair to stand on end,

---

39. **ministers of grace,** messengers bearing the grace (of God). 43. **questionable,** calling for questions and conversation. 47. **canonized,** buried according to the canons and sacraments of the Church. 48. **cerements,** grave-clothes. 53. **glimpses of the moon,** that which the moon sees by night—the earth. 54. **fools of nature,** persons limited in intelligence or perception by nature. 59. **impartment,** communication. 61. **removed,** remote. 65. **fee,** value. 73. **deprive . . . reason.** It was believed that evil spirits, masquerading as the ghost of a loved one, could often produce madness in a human being by luring him to some kind of physical or mental destruction. 75. **toys of desperation,** freakish notions of madness and suicide.

83. **Nemean lion,** one of the monsters slain by the Greek hero Hercules as one of his famous Twelve Labors. **nerve,** sinew, tendon. Arteries, in medieval physiology, were supposed to carry the spirits (animal, vital, and natural) to the appropriate parts of the body. Hamlet is saying that his arteries are tensed as powerfully as the sinews of the fabulous lion. 85. **lets,** hinders. 89. **issue,** outcome. 91. **it,** the outcome.
Act I, Scene 5. 11. **fast,** to do without food, of course; but it is likely that the word was used in Shakespeare's time to denote any kind of penance. 17. **spheres,** orbits, orbs. 18. **knotted,** intricately arranged, a reference to the Elizabethan lord's elaborate coiffure.

Like quills upon the fretful porpentine: 20
But this eternal blazon must not be
To ears of flesh and blood. List, list, O, list!
If thou didst ever thy dear father love—
    HAMLET. O God!
    GHOST. Revenge his foul and most unnatural murder.
    HAMLET. Murder!
    GHOST. Murder most foul, as in the best it is;
But this most foul, strange and unnatural.
    HAMLET. Haste me to know 't, that I, with wings as swift
As meditation or the thoughts of love,   30
May sweep to my revenge.
    GHOST.   I find thee apt;
And duller shouldst thou be than the fat weed
That roots itself with ease on Lethe wharf,
Wouldst thou not stir in this. Now, Hamlet, hear:
'Tis given out that, sleeping in my orchard,
A serpent stung me; so the whole ear of Denmark
Is by a forged process of my death
Rankly abused: but know, thou noble youth,
The serpent that did sting thy father's life
Now wears his crown.
    HAMLET.   O my prophetic soul!   40
My uncle!
    GHOST. Ay, that incestuous, that adulterate beast,
With witchcraft of his wit, with traitorous gifts,—
O wicked wit and gifts, that have the power
So to seduce! won to his shameful lust
The will of my most seeming-virtuous queen:
O Hamlet, what a falling-off was there!
From me, whose love was of that dignity
That it went hand in hand even with the vow
I made to her in marriage, and to decline   50
Upon a wretch whose natural gifts were poor
To those of mine!
But virtue, as it never will be moved,
Though lewdness court it in a shape of Heaven,
So lust, though to a radiant angel linked,
Will sate itself in a celestial bed,
And prey on garbage.
But, soft! methinks I scent the morning air;
Brief let me be. Sleeping within my orchard,
My custom always of the afternoon,   60
Upon my secure hour thy uncle stole,
With juice of cursed hebenon in a vial,
And in the porches of my ears did pour
The leperous distilment; whose effect

Holds such an enmity with blood of man
That swift as quicksilver it courses through
The natural gates and alleys of the body,
And with a sudden vigor it doth posset
And curd, like eager droppings into milk,
The thin and wholesome blood: so did it mine: 70
And a most instant tetter barked about,
Most lazar-like, with vile and loathsome crust,
All my smooth body.
Thus was I, sleeping, by a brother's hand
Of life, of crown, of queen, at once dispatched:
Cut off even in the blossoms of my sin,
Unhouseled, disappointed, unaneled,
No reckoning made, but sent to my account
With all my imperfections on my head:
O, horrible! O, horrible! most horrible!   80
If thou hast nature in thee, bear it not;
Let not the royal bed of Denmark be
A couch for luxury and damned incest.
But, howsoever thou pursuest this act,
Taint not thy mind, nor let thy soul contrive
Against thy mother aught: leave her to Heaven
And to those thorns that in her bosom lodge,
To prick and sting her. Fare thee well at once!
The glow-worm shows the matin to be near,
And 'gins to pale his uneffectual fire: 90
Adieu, adieu! Hamlet, remember me.   (_Exit._)
    HAMLET. O all you host of Heaven! O earth! what else?
And shall I couple Hell? O, fie! Hold, hold, my heart;
And you, my sinews, grow not instant old,
But bear me stiffly up. Remember thee!
Ay, thou poor ghost, while memory holds a seat
In this distracted globe. Remember thee!
Yea, from the table of my memory
I'll wipe away all trivial fond records,
All saws of books, all forms, all pressures past,   100
That youth and observation copied there;
And thy commandment all alone shall live
Within the book and volume of my brain,
Unmixed with baser matter: yes, by Heaven!
O most pernicious woman!
O villain, villain, smiling, damned villain!
My tables,—meet it is I set it down,
That one may smile, and smile, and be a villain;
At least I'm sure it may be so in Denmark:
                        (_Writing._)
So, uncle, there you are. Now to my word;   110

20. **porpentine,** porcupine. 21. **eternal blazon,** revelation of the hereafter, proclamation of eternity. 25. **unnatural murder,** referring to fratricide. 32. **fat weed,** probably foul weeds that grow along rotting wharves or piles of wood, possibly the asphodel plant. 33. **Lethe wharf,** the bank of the River Lethe, which, in classical mythology, was the river of forgetfulness in the realms of Hades, abode of the dead. 37. **process,** official report. 38. **abused,** deceived. 42. **adulterate,** adulterous. 61. **secure,** unsuspecting, confident. 62. **hebenon,** probably henbane, possibly hemlock or yew-sap. 64. **leperous,** producing leprosy.

68. **posset,** curdle, coagulate. 69. **eager,** sour, acid, bitter; compare the French _aigre_. 71. **tetter barked about,** a weeping eruption encased. _Bark_ is a transitive verb. 72. **lazar-like,** leper-like. 77. **Unhouseled . . . unaneled,** without having received the Eucharist, without equipment for my last journey (disappointed), and without having received extreme unction. 83. **luxury,** lechery, lust. 85. **Taint . . . mind,** do not degrade thy character, do nothing unnatural in pursuit of your revenge. 89. **matin,** daybreak. 90. **uneffectual fire,** the cold light of morning. 93. **couple,** add. 97. **distracted globe,** confused head, bewildered brain. 98. **table,** writing-tablet. 100. **saws,** sayings. **pressures,** impressions stamped. 110. **word,** watchword.

It is 'Adieu, adieu! remember me.'
I have sworn 't.

MARCELLUS AND HORATIO (*within*). My Lord, my
    lord,—

MARCELLUS (*within*). Lord Hamlet,—

HORATIO (*within*).   Heaven secure him!

HAMLET. So be it!

HORATIO (*within*). Hillo, ho, ho, my lord!

HAMLET. Hillo, ho, ho, boy! come, bird, come.
    (*Enter* HORATIO *and* MARCELLUS.)

MARCELLUS. How is 't, my noble lord?

HORATIO.   What news,
    my lord?

HAMLET. O, wonderful!

HORATIO.   Good my lord, tell it.

HAMLET. No; you'll reveal it.

HORATIO. Not I, my lord, by Heaven.

MARCELLUS.   Nor I, my lord. 120

HAMLET. How say you, then; would heart of man
    once think it?
But you'll be secret?

HORATIO AND MARCELLUS. Ay, by Heaven, my lord.

HAMLET. There's never a villain dwelling in all
    Denmark
But he's an arrant knave.

HORATIO. There needs no ghost, my lord, come
    from the grave   125
To tell us this.

HAMLET.   Why, right; you are i' the right;
And so, without more circumstance at all,
I hold it fit that we shake hands and part:
You, as your business and desire shall point you;
For every man has business and desire,   130
Such as it is; and for mine own poor part,
Look you, I'll go pray.

HORATIO. These are but wild and whirling words,
    my lord.

HAMLET. I'm sorry they offend you, heartily;
Yes, 'faith, heartily.

HORATIO.   There's no offence, my lord.

HAMLET. Yes, by Saint Patrick, but there is, Hora-
    tio,
And much offence, too. Touching this vision here,
It is an honest ghost, that let me tell you:
For your desire to know what is between us,
O'ermaster 't as you may. And now, good friends, 140
As you are friends, scholars and soldiers,
Give me one poor request.

HORATIO. What is 't, my lord? we will.

HAMLET. Never make known what you have seen
    tonight.

MARCELLUS AND HORATIO. My lord, we will not.

HAMLET.   Nay,
    but swear 't.

HORATIO.   In faith,
My lord, not I.

MARCELLUS. Nor I, my lord, in faith.

HAMLET. Upon my sword.

MARCELLUS.   We have sworn, my
    lord, already.

HAMLET. Indeed, upon my sword, indeed.

GHOST (*beneath*).   Swear.

HAMLET. Ah, ha, boy! say'st thou so? art thou
    there, truepenny?   150
Come on—you hear this fellow in the cellarage—
Consent to swear.

HORATIO.   Propose the oath, my lord.

HAMLET. Never to speak of this that you have seen,
Swear by my sword.

GHOST (*beneath*). Swear.

HAMLET. Hic et ubique? then we'll shift our
    ground.
Come hither, gentlemen,
And lay your hands again upon my sword:
Never to speak of this that you have heard,
Swear by my sword.   160

GHOST (*beneath*). Swear.

HAMLET. Well said, old mole! canst work i' the
    earth so fast?
A worthy pioner! Once more remove, good friends.

HORATIO. O day and night, but this is wondrous
    strange!

HAMLET. And therefore as a stranger give it wel-
    come.
There are more things in heaven and earth, Horatio,
Than are dreamt of in your philosophy.
But come;
Here, as before, never, so help you mercy,
How strange or odd soe'er I bear myself,   170
As I perchance hereafter shall think meet
To put an antic disposition on,
That you, at such times seeing me, never shall
With arms encumbered thus, or this headshake,
Or by pronouncing of some doubtful phrase,
As 'Well, well, we know,' or 'We could, an if we
    would,'
Or 'If we list to speak,' or 'There be, an if they
    might,'
Or such ambiguous giving out, to note

---

114. **Hillo, ho, ho!** The falconer's call to his falcon, to bring it back to his wrist. 124. **arrant,** thoroughgoing. 127. **more circumstance,** more beating about the bush. 136. **Saint Patrick.** In early Christian tradition, St. Patrick of Ireland was keeper of Purgatory and patron saint of all errors and confusion. 138. **honest,** real, true.

147. **sword.** In making such an oath, the swearer was to hold the sword upright (point down), so that the blade and the hilt would form an image of the Cross. 150. **truepenny,** a colloquial word meaning "good fellow," "good old man," or something of the sort. 156. **Hic et ubique,** here, there, and everywhere. 163. **pioner,** a military digger, miner, or sapper. 172. **put . . . disposition,** assume a fantastic manner. This passage indicates clearly that Hamlet's madness is feigned. 174. **encumbered,** folded, intertwined. 176. **an if,** if. 178. **giving out,** utterance, expression of information. **note,** indicate, show.

That you know aught of me: this not to do,
So grace and mercy at your most need help you,   180
Swear.
   GHOST (*beneath*). Swear.
   HAMLET. Rest, rest, perturbed spirit! (*They swear*). So, gentlemen,
With all my love I do commend me to you:
And what so poor a man as Hamlet is
May do, to express his love and friending to you,
God willing, shall not lack. Let us go in together;
And still your fingers on your lips, I pray.
The time is out of joint: O cursed spite,
That ever I was born to set it right!   190
Nay, come, let's go together.   (*Exeunt.*)

ACT II

SCENE 1. *A room in Polonius's house.*

(*Enter* POLONIUS *and* REYNALDO.)

   POLONIUS. Give him this money and these notes, Reynaldo.
   REYNALDO. I will, my lord.
   POLONIUS. You shall do marvellous wisely, good Reynaldo,
Before you visit him, to make inquire
Of his behavior.
   REYNALDO.   My lord, I did intend it.
   POLONIUS. Marry, well said; very well said. Look you, sir,
Inquire me first what Danskers are in Paris;
And how, and who, what means, and where they keep,
What company, at what expense; and finding
By this encompassment and drift of question   10
That they do know my son, come you more nearer
Than your particular demands will touch it:
Take you, as 'twere, some distant knowledge of him;
As thus, 'I know his father and his friends,
And in part him;' do you mark this, Reynaldo?
   REYNALDO. Ay, very well, my lord.
   POLONIUS. 'And in part him; but', you may say, 'not well:
But, if 't be he I mean, he's very wild;
Addicted so and so:' and there put on him
What forgeries you please; marry, none so rank   20
As may dishonor him; take heed of that;
But, sir, such wanton, wild and usual slips

As are companions noted and most known
To youth and liberty.
   REYNALDO.   As gaming, my lord.
   POLONIUS. Ay, or drinking, fencing, swearing, quarrelling,
Drabbing; you may go so far.
   REYNALDO. My lord, that would dishonor him.
   POLONIUS. 'Faith, no; as you may season it in the charge.
You must not put another scandal on him,
That he is open to incontinency;   30
That's not my meaning; but breathe his faults so quaintly
That they may seem the taints of liberty,
The flash and outbreak of a fiery mind,
A savageness in unreclaimed blood,
Of general assault.
   REYNALDO.   But, my good lord,—
   POLONIUS. Wherefore should you do this?
   REYNALDO.   Ay, my lord.
I would know that.
   POLONIUS.   Marry, sir, here's my drift;
And, I believe, it is a fetch of wit:
You laying these slight sullies on my son,
As 'twere a thing a little soiled i' the working,   40
Mark you,
Your party in converse, him you would sound,
Having ever seen in the prenominate crimes
The youth you breathe of guilty, be assured
He closes with you in this consequence;
'Good sir,' or so, or 'friend,' or 'gentleman,'
According to the phrase or the addition
Of man and country.
   REYNALDO.   Very good, my lord.
   POLONIUS. And then, sir, does he this—he does—
what was I about to say? By the mass, I was
about to say something; where did I leave?   51
   REYNALDO. At 'closes in the consequence,' at 'friend or so,' and 'gentleman.'
   POLONIUS. At 'closes in the consequence,' ay, marry;
He closes thus: 'I know the gentleman;
I saw him yesterday, or t'other day,
Or then, or then; with such, or such; and, as you say,
There was a' gaming; there o'ertook in 's rouse;
There falling out at tennis:' or perchance,
'I saw him enter such a house of sale,'   60

---

186. **friending**, friendliness.
Act II, Scene 1. 7. **me**, this so-called "ethical dative," common in Elizabethan English, is to be disregarded in reading. **Danskers**, Danes; but the true meaning is "inhabitants of Dantzig." 8. **keep**, dwell, live. 10. **encompassment**, round-about talking, circumlocution. **drift**, direction, course, trend. 11–12. **come . . . it**, cease direct questioning and come nearer to the facts by assuming an imperfect knowledge of Laertes. 13. **Take**, assume, pretend. 19. **put on**, impute to, ascribe to. 20. **forgeries**, fictions, invented tales. **rank**, excessive. 22. **wanton**, unrestrained, unlicensed.

25. **fencing**, an allusion to the bad reputation of professional fencers and schools of fencing in Elizabethan times. 26. **Drabbing**, whoring, frequenting brothels. 30. **incontinency**, unchastity, sexual unrestraint. 31. **quaintly**, delicately, subtly. 32. **taints of liberty**, defects arising from freedom. 34. **unreclaimed**, tamed. 35. **general assault**, a tendency that attacks all untrained youth. 38. **fetch of wit**, clever trick. 43. **ever**, at any time. **prenominate**, afore-mentioned. 45. **closes . . . consequence**, agrees with you in this conclusion. 47. **addition**, title. 49–51. **And then, sir . . . leave.** Polonius' mind begins to wander at this point, and so Shakespeare reverts to prose. 58. **o'ertook in 's rouse**, overcome by his drinking.

Videlicet, a brothel, or so forth.
See you now;
Your bait of falsehood takes this carp of truth:
And thus do we of wisdom and of reach,
With windlasses and with assays of bias,
By indirections find directions out:
So by my former lecture and advice,
Shall you my son. You have me, have you not?
    REYNALDO. My lord, I have.
    POLONIUS.   God be wi' you; fare
you well.
    REYNALDO. Good my lord!   70
    POLONIUS. Observe his inclination in yourself.
    REYNALDO. I shall, my lord.
    POLONIUS. And let him ply his music.
    REYNALDO.   Well, my lord.
    POLONIUS. Farewell!   (*Exit* REYNALDO.)
    (*Enter* OPHELIA.)
                How now, Ophelia! What's
the matter?
    OPHELIA. O, my lord, my lord, I have been so af-
frighted!
    POLONIUS. With what, i' the name of God?
    OPHELIA. My lord, as I was sewing in my closet,
Lord Hamlet, with his doublet all unbraced,
No hat upon his head; his stockings fouled,
Ungartered, and down-gyved to his ancle;   80
Pale as his shirt; his knees knocking each other;
And with a look so piteous in purport
As if he had been loosed out of Hell
To speak of horrors,—he comes before me.
    POLONIUS. Mad for thy love?
    OPHELIA.   My lord, I do not know;
But truly I do fear it.
    POLONIUS.   What said he?
    OPHELIA. He took me by the wrist and held me
hard;
Then goes he to the length of all his arm;
And, with his other hand thus o'er his brow,
He falls to such perusal of my face   90
As he would draw it. Long stayed he so;
At last, a little shaking of mine arm
And thrice his head thus waving up and down,
He raised a sigh so piteous and profound
As it did seem to shatter all his bulk
And end his being: that done, he lets me go;
And, with his head over his shoulder turned,
He seemed to find his way without his eyes;

For out of doors he went without their helps,
And, to the last, bended their light on me.   100
    POLONIUS. Come, go with me: I will go seek the
        king.
This is the very ecstasy of love,
Whose violent property fordoes itself
And leads the will to desperate undertakings
As oft as any passion under Heaven
That does afflict our natures. I am sorry.
What, have you given him any hard words of late?
    OPHELIA. No, my good lord, but, as you did com-
mand,
I did repel his letters and denied
His access to me.
    POLONIUS.   That hath made him mad.   110
I am sorry that with better heed and judgment
I had not quoted him: I feared he did but trifle,
And meant to wreck thee; but, beshrew my jealousy!
By Heaven, it is as proper to our age
To cast beyond ourselves in our opinions
As it is common for the younger sort
To lack discretion. Come, go we to the king;
This must be known; which, being kept close, might
    move
More grief to hide than hate to utter love. (*Exeunt.*)

SCENE 2. *A room in the castle.*

    (*Enter* KING, QUEEN, ROSENCRANTZ, GUILDENSTERN,
and Attendants.)
    KING. Welcome, dear Rosencrantz and Guilden-
stern!
Moreover that we much did long to see you,
The need we have to use you did provoke
Our hasty sendir.g. Something have you heard
Of Hamlet's transformation; so call it,
Sith nor the exterior nor the inward man
Resembles that it was. What it should be,
More than his father's death, that thus hath put him
So much from the understanding of himself,
I cannot dream of: I entreat you both,   10
That, being of so young days brought up with him,
And sith so neighbored to his youth and havior,
That you vouchsafe your rest here in our court
Some little time: so by your companies
To draw him on to pleasures, and to gather,
So much as from occasion you may glean,
Whether aught, to us unknown, afflicts him thus,
That, opened, lies within our remedy.

---

61. **Videlicet,** namely. 64. **reach,** capacity, range, ability. 65.
windlasses, round-about paths. **assays of bias,** attempts resembling
the course of a ball in the old game of bowls. These balls were
weighted on one side and therefore did not travel in a straight line,
but rather on the bias. 66. **indirections,** devious courses. **directions,**
straight courses, therefore the truth. 67. **lecture,** warning, instruction. 68. **have me,** understand me. 71. **Observe . . . yourself,** test
his conduct by studying your own. 77. **closet,** private room or
apartment. 78. **doublet,** close-fitting coat. **unbraced,** unfastened.
80. **down-gyved,** fallen to the ankles, where they seem like gyves or
fetters. 95. **bulk,** body.

102. **ecstasy,** the kind of madness arising from a domination by love,
amounting to one's being beside oneself. 103. **property,** nature,
quality. **fordoes,** destroys, ruins. 113. **beshrew my jealousy,** curse
my officious suspicions! 115. **cast beyond,** overshoot, miscalculate.
118–119. **might . . . love,** this might cause more grief to others by
hiding the knowledge of Hamlet's love for Ophelia than hatred to
Polonius and his family by revealing it.
Act II, Scene 2. 6. **Sith,** since. 11. **of so young . . . him,** from
such early youth. 13. **vouchsafe your rest,** please to remain.

QUEEN. Good gentlemen, he hath much talked of
you;
And sure I am two men there are not living   20
To whom he more adheres. If it will please you
To show us so much gentry and good will
As to expend your time with us awhile,
For the supply and profit of our hope,
Your visitation shall receive such thanks
As fits a king's remembrance.
ROSENCRANTZ.   Both your majesties
Might, by the sovereign power you have of us,
Put your dread pleasures more into command
Than to entreaty.
GUILDENSTERN. But we both obey,
And here give up ourselves, in the full bent   30
To lay our service freely at your feet,
To be commanded.
KING. Thanks, Rosencrantz and gentle Guilden-
stern.
QUEEN. Thanks, Guildenstern and gentle Rosen-
crantz:
And I beseech you instantly to visit
My too much changed son. Go, some of you,
And bring these gentlemen where Hamlet is.
GUILDENSTERN. Heavens make our presence and
our practices
Pleasant and helpful to him!
QUEEN.   Ay, amen!
(*Exeunt* ROSENCRANTZ, GUILDENSTERN, *and*
some Attendants.)
(*Enter* POLONIUS)
POLONIUS. The ambassadors from Norway, my
good lord,   40
Are joyfully returned.
KING. Thou still hast been the father of good news.
POLONIUS. Have I, my lord? I assure my good liege,
I hold my duty, as I hold my soul,
Both to my God and to my gracious king:
And I do think, or else this brain of mine
Hunts not the trail of policy so sure
As it hath used to do, that I have found
The very cause of Hamlet's lunacy.
KING. O speak of that; that do I long to hear.   50
POLONIUS. Give first admittance to the ambassa-
dors;
My news shall be the fruit of that great feast.
KING. Thyself do grace to them, and bring them in.
(*Exit* POLONIUS.)
He tells me, my dear Gertrude, he hath found
The head and source of all your son's distemper.
QUEEN. I doubt it is no other but the main;
His father's death, and our o'erhasty marriage.
KING. Well, we shall sift him.

(*Re-enter* POLONIUS, *with* VOLTIMAND
and CORNELIUS.)
Welcome, my good friends!
Say, Voltimand, what from our brother Norway?
VOLTIMAND. Most fair return of greetings and de-
sires.   60
Upon our first, he sent out to suppress
His nephew's levies; which to him appeared
To be a preparation 'gainst the Polack;
But, better looked into, he truly found
It was against your highness: whereat grieved,
That so his sickness, age, and impotence
Was falsely borne in hand, sends out arrests
On Fortinbras; which he, in brief, obeys;
Receives rebuke from Norway, and in fine
Makes vow before his uncle never more   70
To give the assay of arms against your majesty.
Whereon old Norway, overcome with joy,
Gives him three thousand crowns in annual fee,
And his commission to employ those soldiers,
So levied as before, against the Polack:
With an entreaty, herein further shown,
(*Giving a paper,*)
That it might please you to give quiet pass
Through your dominions for this enterprise,
On such regards of safety and allowance
As therein are set down.
KING.   It likes us well;   80
And at our more considered time we'll read,
Answer, and think upon this business.
Meantime we thank you for your well-took labor;
Go to your rest; at night we'll feast together:
Most welcome home!
(*Exeunt* VOLTIMAND *and* CORNELIUS.)
POLONIUS.   This business is well ended.
My liege, and madam, to expostulate
What majesty should be, what duty is,
Why day is day, night night, and time is time,
Were nothing but to waste night, day, and time.
Therefore, since brevity is the soul of wit,   90
And tediousness the limbs and outward flourishes,
I will be brief; your noble son is mad:
Mad call I it; for, to define true madness,
What is 't but to be nothing else but mad?
But let that go.
QUEEN.   More matter, with less art.
POLONIUS. Madam, I swear I use no art at all.
That he is mad, 'tis true: 'tis true 'tis pity;
And pity 'tis 'tis true: a foolish figure;
But farewell it, for I will use no art.
Mad let us grant him, then: and now remains   100
That we find out the cause of this effect,

---

67. **borne in hand,** led on, deluded.   69. **in fine,** finally.   71. **assay,**
trial.   79. **safety and allowance,** pledges of safety to the country and
terms of permission for the troops to pass through.   81. **considered,**
suitable.   90. **wit,** good sense and judgment.   91. **flourishes,** showy
ornament.   98. **figure,** figure of speech.

---

22. **gentry,** courtesy.   24. **supply and profit,** aid and successful outcome.   30. **in the full bent,** to the utmost of our abilities.   47.
policy, conduct of public affairs.   56. **main,** chief point, chief concern.

Or rather say, the cause of this defect,
For this effect defective comes by cause:
Thus it remains, and the remainder thus.
Perpend.
I have a daughter—have while she is mine—
Who, in her duty and obedience, mark,
Hath given me this: now gather, and surmise.   109
                    (*Reads.*)
'To the celestial and my soul's idol, the most beauti-
fied Ophelia,'—That's an ill phrase, a vile phrase;
'beautified' is a vile phrase: but you shall hear. Thus:
                    (*Reads.*)
'In her excellent white bosom, these, etc.'
    QUEEN. Came this from Hamlet to her?
    POLONIUS. Good madam, stay awhile; I will be
        faithful.   (*Reads.*)
            'Doubt that the stars are fire;
                Doubt that the sun doth move;
                Doubt truth to be a liar;
                But never doubt I love.   119
'O dear Ophelia, I am ill at these numbers; I have
not art to reckon my groans; but that I love thee best,
O most best, believe it. Adieu.
            'Thine evermore, most dear lady, whilst
                this machine is to him,
                            HAMLET.'
This, in obedience, hath my daughter shown me,
And more above, hath his solicitings,
As they fell out by time, by means and place,
All given to mine ear.
    KING.   But how hath she
Received his love?
    POLONIUS.   What do you think of me?
    KING. As of a man faithful and honorable.   130
    POLONIUS. I would fain prove so. But what might
        you think,
When I had seen this hot love on the wing—
As I perceived it, I must tell you that,
Before my daughter told me—what might you,
Or my dear majesty your queen here, think,
If I had played the desk or table-book,
Or given my heart a winking, mute and dumb,
Or looked upon this love with idle sight;
What might you think? No, I went round to work,
And my young mistress thus I did bespeak: 140
'Lord Hamlet is a prince, out of thy star;
This must not be:' and then I prescripts gave her,
That she should lock herself from his resort,
Admit no messengers, receive no tokens.

Which done, she took the fruits of my advice;
And he, repulsed—a short tale to make—
Fell into a sadness, then into a fast,
Thence to a watch, thence into a weakness,
Thence to a lightness, and, by this declension,
Into the madness wherein now he raves,   150
And all we mourn for.
    KING.   Do you think 'tis this?
    QUEEN. It may be, very likely.
    POLONIUS. Hath there been such a time—I'd fain
        know that—
That I have positively said 'Tis so,'
When it proved otherwise?
    KING.   Not that I know.
    POLONIUS (*pointing to his head and shoulder*).
        Take this from this, if this be otherwise:
If circumstances lead me, I will find
Where truth is hid, though it were hid indeed
Within the centre.
    KING.   How may we try it further?
    POLONIUS. You know, sometimes he walks four
        hours together   160
Here in the lobby.
    QUEEN.   So he does indeed.
    POLONIUS. At such a time I'll loose my daughter
        to him:
Be you and I behind an arras then;
Mark the encounter: if he love her not
And be not from his reason fallen thereon,
Let me be no assistant for a state,
But keep a farm and carters.
    KING.   We will try it.
    QUEEN. But, look, where sadly the poor wretch
        comes reading.
    POLONIUS. Away, I do beseech you, both away:
I'll board him presently.
            (*Exeunt* KING, QUEEN, *and* Attendants.)
            (*Enter* HAMLET, *reading.*)
                        O, give me leave: 170
How does my good Lord Hamlet?
    HAMLET. Well, God-a-mercy.
    POLONIUS. Do you know me, my lord?
    HAMLET. Excellent well; you are a fishmonger.
    POLONIUS. Not I, my lord.
    HAMLET. Then I would you were so honest a man.
    POLONIUS. Honest, my lord!
    HAMLET. Ay, sir; to be honest, as this world goes,
is to be one man picked out of ten thousand.
    POLONIUS. That's very true, my lord.   180
    HAMLET. For if the sun breed maggots in a dead

---

105. **Perpend**, consider, attend. 120. **ill . . . numbers**, unskilled
in making these verses. 121. **reckon**, number metrically, that is, scan.
124. **machine**, bodily frame. 126. **more above**, moreover. 127.
fell out, happened, occurred. **means**, opportunity of access. 136.
played . . . table-book, kept things shut up in my desk or notebook.
137. **given . . . winking**, given my heart a signal to remain silent.
139. **round**, straight, directly. 140. **bespeak**, address. 141. **out of
thy star**, above thee in position; thy fortune is not to compete with
such a high destiny.

148. **watch**, wakefulness, sleeplessness. 149. **lightness**, light-headed-
ness, giddiness. **declension**, decline, deterioration. 159. **centre**,
middle point of the earth. 163. **arras**, tapestry; Arras, in northern
France, was famous for its tapestries. 164. **encounter**, style and
manner of conversation at the meeting. 170. **board**, accost, address.
174. **fishmonger**, in Elizabethan slang, a bawd, a pimp.

dog, being a god kissing carrion,—Have you a daughter?

POLONIUS. I have, my lord.

HAMLET. Let her not walk i' the sun: conception is a blessing: but not as your daughter may conceive. Friend, look to 't.

POLONIUS (aside). How say you by that? Still harping on my daughter; yet he knew me not at first; he said I was a fishmonger: he is far gone, far gone: and truly in my youth I suffered much extremity for love; very near this. I'll speak to him again. What do you read, my lord?

HAMLET. Words, words, words.

POLONIUS. What is the matter, my lord? 195

HAMLET. Between who?

POLONIUS. I mean, the matter that you read, my lord.

HAMLET. Slanders, sir: for the satirical rogue says here that old men have grey beards, that their faces are wrinkled, their eyes purging thick amber and plum-tree gum and that they have a plentiful lack of wit, together with most weak hams: all which, sir, though I most powerfully and potently believe, yet I hold it not honesty to have it thus set down, for yourself, sir, should be old as I am, if like a crab you could go backward.

POLONIUS (aside). Though this be madness, yet there is method in 't. Will you walk out of the air, my lord?

HAMLET. Into my grave. 210

POLONIUS. Indeed, that is out o' the air. (Aside.) How pregnant sometimes his replies are! a happiness that often madness hits on, which reason and sanity could not so prosperously be delivered of. I will leave him, and suddenly contrive the means of meeting between him and my daughter.—My honorable lord, I will most humbly take my leave of you.

HAMLET. You cannot, sir, take from me any thing that I will more willingly part withal: except my life, except my life, except my life. 220

POLONIUS. Fare you well, my lord.

HAMLET. These tedious old fools!

(Enter ROSENCRANTZ and GUILDENSTERN.)

POLONIUS. You go to seek the Lord Hamlet; there he is.

ROSENCRANTZ (to POLONIUS). God save you, sir!

(Exit POLONIUS.)

GUILDENSTERN. My honored lord!

ROSENCRANTZ. My most dear lord!

HAMLET. My excellent good friends! How dost thou, Guildenstern? Ah, Rosencrantz! Good lads, how do ye both? 230

ROSENCRANTZ. As the indifferent children of the earth.

GUILDENSTERN. Happy, in that we are not over-happy;
On fortune's cap we are not the very button.

HAMLET. Nor the soles of her shoe?

ROSENCRANTZ. Neither, my lord.

HAMLET. Then you live about her waist, or in the middle of her favors?

GUILDENSTERN. 'Faith, her privates we.

HAMLET. In the secret parts of fortune? O, most true; she is a strumpet.
What's the news? 240

ROSENCRANTZ. None, my lord, but that the world's grown honest.

HAMLET. Then is Doomsday near: but your news is not true. Let me question more in particular: what have you, my good friends, deserved at the hands of fortune, that she sends you to prison hither?

GUILDENSTERN. Prison, my lord!

HAMLET. Denmark's a prison.

ROSENCRANTZ. Then is the world one. 250

HAMLET. A goodly one, in which there are many confines, wards, and dungeons, Denmark being one o' the worst.

ROSENCRANTZ. We think not so, my lord.

HAMLET. Why, then, 'tis none to you; for there is nothing either good or bad, but thinking makes it so: to me it is a prison.

ROSENCRANTZ. Why then, your ambition makes it one; 'tis too narrow for your mind. 259

HAMLET. O God, I could be bounded in a nut-shell and count myself a king of infinite space, were it not that I have bad dreams.

GUILDENSTERN. Which dreams indeed are ambition, for the very substance of the ambitious is merely the shadow of a dream.

HAMLET. A dream itself is but a shadow.

ROSENCRANTZ. Truly, and I hold ambition of so airy and light a quality that it is but a shadow's shadow. 268

182. **god kissing carrion,** the sun-god shining on a dead body; the phrase, however, has had several readings, emendations, and interpretations and is one of the most difficult cruxes in the text of *Hamlet*. 185. **i' the sun,** suggesting "in the sunshine of princely favors." But the sun was long regarded as a powerful agent in the stimulation of conception. Possibly, too, there is a pun here on the word *sun* to suggest the eventuality of Hamlet, the son, as the impregnator of Ophelia. There is in all likelihood, moreover, a clear play on the two common meanings of *conception*. Hamlet, in his "mad speech," is given to all kinds of double-talk. 188. **by,** concerning, in reference to. 195. **matter,** substance (of what you are reading). 196. **Between who?** Hamlet is deliberately choosing another meaning of *matter*, denoting an issue or dispute. 198 ff. **the satirical rogue,** etc. Resemblance has been pointed out between these lines and the tenth satire of the Roman poet Juvenal, but there were any number of similar descriptions of old age from the Middle Ages to Shakespeare's time, and it is certainly impossible to deduce from these lines what particular book Hamlet was reading. 200. **purging,** discharging, excreting. 204. **honesty,** decency. 213. **happiness,** felicity of expression. 214. **prosperously,** successfully. 220. **withal,** with.

231. **indifferent,** ordinary, average. 264. **very . . . ambitious,** the elusive and hypothetically substantial thing which the ambitious pursue, like "the bubble reputation" in *As You Like It*, Act II, Scene 7, l. 152.

II : 464

HAMLET. Then are our beggars bodies, and our monarchs and outstretched heroes the beggars' shadows. Shall we to the court? for, by my fay, I cannot reason.

ROSENCRANTZ AND GUILDENSTERN. We'll wait upon you.

HAMLET. No such matter: I will not sort you with the rest of my servants, for, to speak to you like an honest man, I am most dreadfully attended. But, in the beaten way of friendship, what make you at Elsinore?

ROSENCRANTZ. To visit you, my lord; no other occasion. 279

HAMLET. Beggar that I am, I am even poor in thanks; but I thank you: and sure, dear friends, my thanks are too dear a halfpenny. Were you not sent for? Is it your own inclining? Is it a free visitation? Come, deal justly with me: come, come; nay, speak.

GUILDENSTERN. What should we say, my lord?

HAMLET. Why, any thing, but to the purpose. You were sent for; and there is a kind of confession in your looks which your modesties have not craft enough to color: I know the good king and queen have sent for you. 291

ROSENCRANTZ. To what end, my lord?

HAMLET. That you must teach me. But let me conjure you, by the rights of our fellowship, by the consonancy of our youth, by the obligation of our ever-preserved love, and by what more dear a better proposer could charge you withal, be even and direct with me, whether you were sent for, or no?

ROSENCRANTZ (aside to GUILDENSTERN). What say you? 300

HAMLET (aside). Nay, then, I have an eye of you.—If you love me, hold not off.

GUILDENSTERN. My lord, we were sent for.

HAMLET. I will tell you why; so shall my anticipation prevent your discovery, and your secrecy to the king and queen moult no feather. I have of late—but wherefore I know not—lost all my mirth, forgone all custom of exercises; and indeed it goes so heavily with my disposition that this goodly frame, the earth, seems to me a sterile promontory, this most excellent canopy, the air, look you, this brave o'erhanging firmament, this majestical roof fretted with golden fire, why, it appears no other thing to me than a foul and pestilent congregation of vapors. What a piece of work is a man! how noble in reason! how infinite in faculty! in form and moving how express and ad-

mirable! in action how like an angel! in apprehension how like a god! the beauty of the world! the paragon of animals! And yet, to me, what is this quintessence of dust? Man delights not me; no, nor woman neither, though by your smiling you seem to say so. 323

ROSENCRANTZ. My lord, there was no such stuff in my thoughts.

HAMLET. Why did you laugh then, when I said, 'man delights not me'? 327

ROSENCRANTZ. To think, my lord, if you delight not in man, what lenten entertainment the players shall receive from you: we coted them on the way; and hither are they coming, to offer you service. 331

HAMLET. He that plays the king shall be welcome; his majesty shall have tribute of me; the adventurous knight shall use his foil and target; the lover shall not sigh gratis; the humorous man shall end his part in peace; the clown shall make those laugh whose lungs are tickle o' the sere; and the lady shall say her mind freely, or the blank verse shall halt for 't. What players are they? 340

ROSENCRANTZ. Even those you were wont to take delight in, the tragedians of the city.

HAMLET. How chances it they travel? their residence, both in reputation and profit, was better both ways. 345

ROSENCRANTZ. I think their inhibition comes by the means of the late innovation.

HAMLET. Do they hold the same estimation they did when I was in the city? are they so followed? 350

ROSENCRANTZ. No, indeed, are they not.

HAMLET. How comes it? do they grow rusty?

ROSENCRANTZ. Nay, their endeavor keeps in the wonted pace: but there is, sir, an aery of children, little eyases, that cry out on the top of the question, and are most tyranically clapped for 't: these are now the fashion, and so berattle the common stages—so

319. apprehension, understanding, comprehension. 321. quintessence, in ancient philosophy this was the fifth essence which transcended the four elements of earth, air, fire, and water, and yet was supposed to be latent in all existing things. 329. lenten, meager, sparse, barren. 330. coted, overtook and passed beyond. 334. foil and target, sword and shield. 338. tickle o' the sere, easy on the trigger. 338–340. lady . . . for 't, the lady (fond of talking) will have the opportunity to talk, blank verse or no blank verse. 344. residence, remaining in one place. 346. inhibition, formal prohibition from acting plays either in the city or at court. 347. innovation. This is probably an allusion to the introduction into Elizabethan plays of satire on persons still living or to the establishing of the Children of the Revels in Blackfriars' Theatre, which took place in January 1603; if the latter, it is a valuable clue to the dating of Hamlet. The children's troupe was so successful that it drove the professional adult actors to the "roads" and provinces for a time. This is, in other words, a direct reference to the so-called "War of the Theatres." 352–379. How comes . . . load too. This is probably the most famous passage in Elizabethan literature dealing with the War of the Theatres, which lasted through the first three or four years of the sixteenth century. 354. aery, nest. 355. eyases, young hawks. 355–356. cry . . . question. This difficult passage has been variously interpreted: "to speak in a high key dominating conversation" and "to shout loudly in controversy." 356. tyranically, outrageously. 358. berattle, fill with noise. common stages, public theaters.

272. fay, faith. reason, argue. 273. wait upon you, accompany you. 274. sort, class, group (v.). 276. dreadfully attended, poorly or meanly attended (with servants). 277. in the beaten . . . friendship, as a matter of general course among friends. what make you, what are you doing? 282. dear a halfpenny, dear at the cost of a halfpenny. 284. free, voluntary. 294. conjure, adjure, implore. 295. consonancy . . . youth, the fact that our ages are the same. 297. better proposer, one more skillful in finding suggestions. 305. prevent your discovery, forestall your disclosure. 313. fretted, adorned. 318. express, exact, accurate; but the meaning is obscure.

they call them—that many wearing rapiers are afraid of goose-quills and dare scarce come thither. 360

HAMLET. What, are they children? who maintains 'em? how are they escoted? Will they pursue the quality no longer than they can sing? will they not say afterwards, if they should grow themselves to common players—as it is most like, if their means are no better—their writers do them wrong, to make them exclaim against their own succession? 368

ROSENCRANTZ. 'Faith, there has been much to do on both sides; and the nation holds it no sin to tarre them to controversy: there was, for a while, no money bid for argument, unless the poet and the player went to cuffs in the question.

HAMLET. Is 't possible? 374

GUILDENSTERN. O, there has been much throwing about of brains.

HAMLET. Do the boys carry it away?

ROSENCRANTZ. Ay, that they do, my lord; Hercules and his load too. 379

HAMLET. It is not very strange; for mine uncle is king of Denmark, and those that would make mows at him while my father lived, give twenty, forty, fifty, an hundred ducats a-piece for his picture in little. 'Sblood, there is something in this more than natural, if philosophy could find it out. 385

(*Flourish of trumpets within.*)

GUILDENSTERN. There are the players.

HAMLET. Gentlemen, you are welcome to Elsinore. Your hands, come then: the appurtenance of welcome is fashion and ceremony: let me comply with you in this garb, lest my extent to the players, which, I tell you, must show fairly outward, should more appear like entertainment than yours. You are welcome: but my uncle-father and aunt-mother are deceived. 394

GUILDENSTERN. In what, my dear lord?

HAMLET. I am but mad north-north-west: when the wind is southerly I know a hawk from a handsaw.

(*Re-enter* POLONIUS.)

POLONIUS. Well be with you, gentlemen!

HAMLET. Hark you, Guildenstern; and you too: at each ear a hearer: that great baby you see there is not yet out of his swaddling-clouts. 401

ROSENCRANTZ. Happily he's the second time come to them; for they say an old man is twice a child.

HAMLET. I will prophesy he comes to tell me of the players; mark it. You say right, sir: o' Monday morning; 'twas so indeed.

POLONIUS. My lord, I have news to tell you.

HAMLET. My lord, I have news to tell you. When Roscius was an actor in Rome,— 410

POLONIUS. The actors are come hither, my lord.

HAMLET. Buz, buz!

POLONIUS. Upon mine honor,—

HAMLET. Then came each actor on his ass,—

POLONIUS. The best actors in the world, either for tragedy, comedy, history, pastoral, pastoral-comical, historical-pastoral, tragical-historical, tragical-comical-historical-pastoral, scene individable, or poem unlimited: Seneca cannot be too heavy, nor Plautus too light. For the law of writ and the liberty, these are the only men. 421

HAMLET. O Jephthah, judge of Israel, what a treasure hast thou!

POLONIUS. What a treasure had he, my lord?

HAMLET. Why,

'One fair daughter, and no more,
The which he loved passing well.'

POLONIUS (*aside*). Still on my daughter.

HAMLET. Am I not i' the right, old Jephthah?

POLONIUS. If you call me Jephthah, my lord, I have a daughter that I love passing well. 431

HAMLET. Nay, that follows not.

POLONIUS. What follows, then, my lord?

HAMLET. Why,

'As by lot, God wot,'

and then, you know,

359–360. **many . . . goose-quills,** many men of fashion (wearing rapiers) are afraid to patronize the theater lest they be satirized by the playwrights who write for the children's companies. The goose-quill implies satire. 362. **escoted,** maintained, kept. 363–364. **no longer . . . sing,** until their voices change. 365. **common,** regular. 368. **exclaim against,** run down, detract. **succession,** future careers. 371. **tarre,** set on, as dogs are set on a victim. 372. **argument,** the plot of a play. 373. **question,** dispute, controversy. 377. **carry it away,** win the day, succeed in their plan. 378–379. **Hercules . . . load.** The Globe Theater in Elizabethan London had for its sign Hercules bearing the world on his shoulder. 382. **ducats,** coins worth 9 s., 4d. apiece. 383. **in little,** in miniature. 390. **comply,** etc. A good example of the elaborate formality of court manners. **garb,** manner. **extent,** showing of kindness. 396. **I . . . north-north-west,** "I am mad in only one point of the compass," that is, in only one direction. 397. **hawk from a handsaw.** Critics have emended *handsaw,* to *hernshaw,* "young heron," or *hawk* to *hack* ("pickaxe") to bring conformity to the two elements in this statement; but in view of Hamlet's assumed eccentricity of speech, neither emendation seems necessary.

401. **swaddling-clouts,** diapers. 402. **Happily,** fortunately, by chance. 407. **o' Monday morning,** an inconsequential phrase to mislead the officiously listening Polonius. 410. **Roscius,** the most famous Roman actor known to us. 412. **Buz, buz.** This is considered a piece of Oxford slang common in the Elizabethan age to denote stale news. 414. **came . . . ass.** This, as well as several other phrases in Hamlet's speeches in this scene, is probably a quotation from an old play now unidentified. 418. **scene individable,** a play observing the so-called unity of place, with no change of scene permitted. **poem unlimited,** a play disregarding the unities of both time and place. **Seneca,** the famous Roman playwright of the first century after Christ, noted for his tragedies of terror. **Plautus,** a Roman writer of high comedy, who flourished about 200 B.C. Both Seneca and Plautus served as models to the Elizabethan writers of tragedy and comedy, respectively. 420. **law . . . liberty,** generally taken to mean the obligation to be faithful to the text of written plays while at the same time reserving the right to improvise; or it may refer to the distinction between plays written according to rules and those free from such regulation (the classical vs. the romantic manner). 422. **Jephthah,** judge of Israel. There was a popular Elizabethan ballad, *Jephthah's Daughter,* which recounted the affecting story of Jephthah's sacrifice of his daughter to fulfill his vow to God, as told in the Biblical book of Judges. Hamlet quotes from the ballad.

'It came to pass, as most like it was,'—
the first row of the pious chanson will show you
more; for look, where my abridgement comes.   439

(*Enter four or five* Players.)

You are welcome, masters; welcome, all. I am glad
to see thee well. Welcome, good friends. O, my old
friend! thy face is valanced since I saw thee last:
comest thou to beard me in Denmark? What, my
young lady and mistress! By 'r lady, your ladyship is
nearer to Heaven than when I saw you last, but the
altitude of a chopine. Pray God, your voice, like a
piece of uncurrent gold, be not cracked within the
ring. Masters, you are all welcome. We'll e'en to 't
like French falconers, fly at anything we see: we'll
have a speech straight: come, give us a taste of your
quality; come, a passionate speech.   452

FIRST PLAYER. What speech, my lord?

HAMLET. I heard thee speak me a speech once, but
it was never acted; or, if it was, not above once; for
the play, I remember, pleased not the million; 'twas
caviare to the general: but it was—as I received it,
and others, whose judgments in such matters cried in
the top of mine—an excellent play, well digested in
the scenes, set down with as much modesty as   461
cunning. I remember, one said there were no sallets
in the lines to make the matter savory, nor no matter
in the phrase that might indict the author of affectation; but called it an honest method, as wholesome as
sweet, and by very much more handsome than fine.
One speech in it I chiefly loved: 'twas Aeneas's tale
to Dido; and thereabout of it especially, where he
speaks of Priam's slaughter: if it live in your memory,
begin at this line: let me see, let me see—   471

'The rugged Pyrrhus, like the Hyrcanian beast,'—
it is not so:—it begins with Pyrrhus:—
'The rugged Pyrrhus, he whose sable arms,
Black as his purpose, did the night resemble
When he lay couched in the ominous horse,
Hath now this dread and black complexion smeared
With heraldry more dismal; head to foot

Now is he total gules; horridly tricked
With blood of fathers, mothers, daughters, sons,   480
Baked and impasted with the parching streets,
That lend a tyrranous and damned light
To their lord's murder: roasted in wrath and fire,
And thus o'er-sized with coagulate gore,
With eyes like carbuncles, the hellish Pyrrhus
Old grandsire Priam seeks.'
So, proceed you.

POLONIUS. 'Fore God, my lord, well spoken, with
good accent and good discretion.

FIRST PLAYER.   'Anon he finds him   490
Striking too short at Greeks; his antique sword,
Rebellious to his arm, lies where it falls,
Repugnant to command: unequal matched,
Pyrrhus at Priam drives; in rage strikes wide;
But with the whiff and wind of his fell sword
The unnerved father falls. Then senseless Ilium,
Seeming to feel this blow, with flaming top
Stoops to his base, and with a hideous crash
Takes prisoner Pyrrhus' ear: for, lo! his sword,
Which was declining on the milky head   500
Of reverend Priam, seemed i' the air to stick:
So, as a painted tyrant, Pyrrhus stood,
And like a neutral to his will and matter,
Did nothing.
But, as we often see, against some storm,
A silence in the heavens, the rack stand still,
The bold winds speechless and the orb below
As hush as death, anon the dreadful thunder
Doth rend the region, so, after Pyrrhus' pause,   509
Aroused vengeance sets him new a-work;
And never did the Cyclops' hammers fall
On Mars's armour forged for proof eterne
With less remorse than Pyrrhus' bleeding sword
Now falls on Priam.
Out, out, thou strumpet, Fortune! All you gods,
In general synod, take away her power;
Break all the spokes and fellies from her wheel,
And bowl the round nave down the hill of Heaven,
As low as to the fiends!'

POLONIUS. This is too long.   520

HAMLET. It shall be to the barber's, with your
beard. Prithee, say on: he's for a jig or a tale of
bawdry, or he sleeps: say on: come to Hecuba.

FIRST PLAYER. 'But who, O, who had seen the
mobled queen—'

---

438. **row,** stanza.   439. **abridgement comes,** the opportunity comes to
cut short this conversation.   442. **valanced,** fringed with a beard.
447. **chopine,** a shoe raised by great thickness of the heel, much the
fashion in Renaissance Italy, particularly in Venice.   448. **uncurrent,**
not passing currency, not valid. **cracked . . . ring.** In the center of a
Renaissance coin were rings enclosing the head of the sovereign
reigning; if the coin was cracked within these rings, it was unfit for
currency.   451. **straight,** immediately, at once.   457. **caviare . . .
general,** not relished by the common people, like caviar.   459. **cried
. . . mine,** spoke with greater authority than mine.   460. **digested,**
arranged.   461. **modesty,** moderation. **cunning,** skill.   462. **sallets,**
salads; here for spicy improprieties.   464. **indict,** convict.   466–467.
as wholesome . . . fine. Its virtue lay not in its elaborate ornament
or decoration but in its simplicity and order.   468. **Aeneas's tale,**
etc. The lines recited below by Hamlet are an imitation of an older
play by Marlowe and Nashe called *Dido, Queen of Carthage.* The introduction of a play within a play by Shakespeare is most skillfully
handled.   472. **Pyrrhus,** a Greek hero of the Trojan War, the slayer
of King Priam of Troy (l. 469). **Hyrcanian beast,** tiger.   476. **ominous horse,** Trojan horse.

479. **total gules,** entirely red; gules is the term in heraldry for the
color red. **tricked,** spotted, smeared, decorated.   481. **impasted,**
made into a paste.   484. **o'er-sized,** covered over with a size or glue.
493. **Repugnant,** resisting by fighting.   496. **senseless Ilium,** insensible Troy.   502. **painted tyrant,** tyrant in a picture.   503. **matter,** task, business.   505. **against,** before.   506. **rack,** mass of clouds.
509. **region,** the sky.   512. **proof eterne,** eternal resistance to attack.
516. **synod,** assembly.   517. **fellies,** pieces of wood joined together
to make the rim of a wheel.   518. **nave,** hub of a wheel.   522. **jig,**
comic performance given at the end or between the acts of a play,
usually featured by a lively dance—later, the dance itself.   523.
Hecuba, the wife of Priam and Queen of Troy.   525. **mobled,** muf-
fled.

HAMLET. 'The mobled queen?'

POLONIUS. That's good; 'mobled queen' is good.

FIRST PLAYER. 'Run barefoot up and down, threatening the flames

With bisson rheum; a clout upon that head

Where late the diadem stood, and for a robe,   530

About her lank and all o'er-teemed loins,

A blanket, in the alarm of fear caught up;

Who this had seen, with tongue in venom steeped,

'Gainst Fortune's state would treason have pronounced:

But if the gods themselves did see her then

When she saw Pyrrhus make malicious sport

In mincing with his sword her husband's limbs,

The instant burst of clamor that she made,

Unless things mortal move them not at all,

Would have made milch the burning eyes of Heaven,

And passion in the gods.'   541

POLONIUS. Look, whether he has not turned his color and has tears in 's eyes. Pray you, no more.

HAMLET. 'Tis well; I'll have thee speak out the rest soon. Good my lord, will you see the players well bestowed? Do you hear, let them be well used; for they are the abstract and brief chronicles of the time: after your death you were better have a bad epitaph than their ill report while you live.   551

POLONIUS. My lord, I will use them according to their desert.

HAMLET. God's bodykins, man, much better: use every man after his desert, and who should 'scape whipping? Use them after your own honor and dignity: the less they deserve, the more merit is in your bounty. Take them in.

POLONIUS. Come, sirs.   559

HAMLET. Follow him, friends: we'll hear a play tomorrow.

(*Exit* POLONIUS *with all the* Players *but the first.*)

Dost thou hear me, old friend; can you play the Murder of Gonzago?

FIRST PLAYER. Ay, my lord.

HAMLET. We'll ha't tomorrow night. You could, for a need, study a speech of some dozen or sixteen lines, which I would set down and insert in 't, could you not?

FIRST PLAYER. Ay, my lord.   569

HAMLET. Very well. Follow that lord; and look you mock him not.   (*Exit first* Player.)

My good friends, I'll leave you till night: you are welcome to Elsinore.

ROSENCRANTZ. Good my lord!

HAMLET. Ay, so, God be wi' ye.

(*Exeunt* ROSENCRANTZ *and* GUILDENSTERN.)

Now I am alone.

O, what a rogue and peasant slave am I!   576

Is it not monstrous that this player here,

But in a fiction, in a dream of passion,

Could force his soul so to his own conceit

That from her working all his visage wanned,

Tears in his eyes, distraction in 's aspect,

A broken voice, and his whole function suiting   582

With forms to his conceit? and all for nothing!

For Hecuba!

What's Hecuba to him, or he to Hecuba,

That he should weep for her? What would he do,

Had he the motive and the cue for passion

That I have? He would drown the stage with tears

And cleave the general ear with horrid speech,   589

Make mad the guilty and appal the free,

Confound the ignorant, and amaze indeed

The very faculties of eyes and ears.

Yet I,

A dull and muddy-mettled rascal, peak,

Like John-a-dreams, unpregnant of my cause,

And can say nothing: no, not for a king,

Upon whose property and most dear life

A damned defeat was made. Am I a coward?

Who calls me villain? breaks my pate across?

Plucks off my beard, and blows it in my face?   600

Tweaks me by the nose? gives me the lie i' the throat,

As deep as to the lungs? who does me this?

Ha!

'Swounds, I should take it: for it cannot be

But I am pigeon-livered and lack gall

To make oppression bitter, or ere this

I should have fatted all the region kites

With this slave's offal: bloody, bawdy villain!

Remorseless, treacherous, lecherous, kindless villain!

O, vengeance!   610

Why, what an ass am I! This is most brave,

That I, the son of a dear father murdered,

Prompted to my revenge by Heaven and Hell,

Must, like a whore, unpack my heart with words,

And fall a-cursing, like a very drab,

A scullion!

529. **bisson rheum,** blinding tears. **clout,** rag. 531. **o'er-teemed,** worn out by child-bearing. 534. **state,** power, majesty. 540. **milch,** moist with tears. 542. **turned,** changed. 548. **abstract,** summarizing account, epitome. 554. **God's bodykins,** by God's little body; the diminutive merely weakens the severity of the oath. 567. **dozen . . . lines.** There have been many guesses as to which were the "dozen or sixteen" lines inserted by Hamlet; the general opinion is that they come in the speech of Lucianus; Act III, Scene 2, ll. 266 ff.

576. **peasant,** base (used here as an adjective). 579. **conceit,** imagination. 580. **wanned,** grew pale and wan. 582–583. **his whole function . . . conceit,** his whole being responding with forms appropriate to his thoughts. 590. **free,** free from guilt, innocent. 594. **muddy-mettled,** dull-spirited, ineffectual. **peak,** mope, pine. 595. **John-a-dreams,** a generic name in Elizabethan English for the visionary and the dreamer. **unpregnant of,** not quickened or made alive by. 597. **property,** proprietorship (of kingship as well as life). 598. **defeat,** destruction. 605. **pigeon-livered.** It was the belief in Elizabethan England that the pigeon had no gall-bladder, and therefore could secrete no gall. Gall in the human system produces bitterness, according to further belief. 607. **region kites,** the predatory birds of the sky. 609. **kindless,** unnatural. 616. **scullion,** kitchen-servant.

Fie upon 't! foh! About, my brain! I have heard
That guilty creatures sitting at a play
Have by the very cunning of the scene
Been struck so to the soul that presently   620
They have proclaimed their malefactions;
For murder, though it have no tongue, will speak
With most miraculous organ. I'll have these players
Play something like the murder of my father
Before mine uncle: I'll observe his looks;
I'll tent him to the quick; if he but blench,
I know my course. The spirit that I have seen
May be the devil: and the devil hath power
To assume a pleasing shape; yea, and perhaps,
Out of my weakness and my melancholy,   630
As he is very potent with such spirits,
Abuses me to damn me: I'll have grounds
More relative than this: the play's the thing
Wherein I'll catch the conscience of the king. (*Exit.*)

ACT III

Scene 1. *A room in the castle*

(*Enter* KING, QUEEN, POLONIUS, OPHELIA, ROSEN-
CRANTZ, *and* GUILDENSTERN.)
KING. And can you, by no drift of circumstance,
Get from him why he puts on this confusion,
Grating so harshly all his days of quiet
With turbulent and dangerous lunacy?
    ROSENCRANTZ. He does confess he feels himself
        distracted;
But from what cause he will by no means speak.
    GUILDENSTERN. Nor do we find him forward to be
        sounded,
But, with a crafty madness, keeps aloof,
When we would bring him on to some confession
Of his true state.
    QUEEN.   Did he receive you well?   10
    ROSENCRANTZ. Most like a gentleman.
    GUILDENSTERN. But with much forcing of his dis-
        position.
    ROSENCRANTZ. Niggard of question; but, of our
        demands,
Most free in his reply.
    QUEEN.   Did you assay him
To any pastime?
    ROSENCRANTZ. Madam, it so fell out, that certain
        players
We o'er-raught on the way: of these we told him;

And there did seem in him a kind of joy
To hear of it: they are about the court.
And, as I think, they have already order   20
This night to play before him.
    POLONIUS.   'Tis most true:
And he beseeched me to entreat your majesties
To hear and see the matter.
    KING. With all my heart; and it doth much content
        me
To hear him so inclined.
Good gentlemen, give him a further edge,
And drive his purpose on to these delights.
    ROSENCRANTZ. We shall, my lord.
        (*Exeunt* ROSENCRANTZ *and* GUILDENSTERN.)
    KING.   Sweet Gertrude, leave us too;
For we have closely sent for Hamlet hither,
That he, as 'twere by accident, may here   30
Affront Ophelia:
Her father and myself, lawful espials,
Will so bestow ourselves that, seeing, unseen,
We may of their encounter frankly judge,
And gather by him, as he is behaved,
If 't be the affliction of his love or no
That thus he suffers for.
    QUEEN.   I shall obey you.
And for your part, Ophelia, I do wish
That your good beauties be the happy cause
Of Hamlet's wildness: so shall I hope your virtues   40
Will bring him to his wonted way again,
To both your honors.
    OPHELIA.   Madam, I wish it may.
                    (*Exit* QUEEN.)
    POLONIUS. Ophelia, walk you here. Gracious, so
        please you,
We will bestow ourselves. (*To* OPHELIA.) Read on
        this book;
That show of such an exercise may color
Your loneliness. We are oft to blame in this,—
'Tis too much proved—that with devotion's visage
And pious action we do sugar o'er
The devil himself.
    KING (*aside*). O, 'tis too true!
How smart a lash that speech doth give my con-
        science!   50
The harlot's cheek, beautied with plastering art,
Is not more ugly to the thing that helps it
Than is my deed to my most painted word:
O heavy burthen!—

617. **About,** get about your business! 626. **tent,** probe (v.). 628. **May be the devil.** As pointed out in the notes to Act I, Scene 4, l. 71, the habit of the devil of going about as a ghost of some loved one was firmly fixed in the Elizabethan mind. 631. **spirits,** the afore-mentioned humors (l. 630). 632. **Abuses,** deceives. 633. **relative,** closely related, germane.
Act III, Scene 1. 1. **drift of circumstance,** roundabout or devious method. 7. **forward,** willing. 12. **forcing of his disposition,** effort of temper and will. 13. **Niggard of question,** not inclined to conversation. 14. **assay,** challenge, tempt. 17. **o'er-raught,** overtook.

26. **edge,** incitement. 29. **closely,** secretly. 31. **Affront,** confront. 32. **lawful espials,** legitimate spies. 40. **wildness,** madness. 43. **Gracious,** your Grace, gracious one. Polonius is addressing the king. 45. **exercise,** act of devotion. 52. **ugly to,** ugly in comparison to. **thing,** the cosmetic. 54. **O heavy burthen!** This sudden expression of repentance by the king has the practical dramatic purpose of satisfying the audience of King Claudius' guilt. Moreover, the suddenness would not disturb an Elizabethan audience, because it was a current psychological belief that a sudden shift of spirits in the human body could bring about sudden conflicting moods.

POLONIUS. I hear him coming: let's withdraw, my
   lord.   (*Exeunt* KING *and* POLONIUS.)
             (*Enter* HAMLET.)

HAMLET. To be, or not to be: that is the question,
Whether 'tis nobler in the mind to suffer
The slings and arrows of outrageous fortune,
Or to take arms against a sea of troubles,
And by opposing end them? To die; to sleep;   60
No more; and by a sleep to say we end
The heart-ache and the thousand natural shocks
That flesh is heir to, 'tis a consummation
Devoutly to be wished. To die, to sleep;
To sleep: perchance to dream; ay, there's the rub;
For in that sleep of death what dreams may come
When we have shuffled off this mortal coil,
Must give us pause: there's the respect
That makes calamity of so long life;
For who would bear the whips and scorns of time, 70
The oppressor's wrong, the proud man's contumely,
The pangs of despised love, the law's delay,
The insolence of office and the spurns
That patient merit of the unworthy takes,
When he himself might his quietus make
With a bare bodkin? who would fardels bear,
To grunt and sweat under a weary life,
But that the dread of something after death,
The undiscovered country from whose bourn
No traveller returns, puzzles the will   80
And makes us rather bear those ills we have
Than fly to others that we know not of?
Thus conscience does make cowards of us all;
And thus the native hue of resolution
Is sicklied o'er with the pale cast of thought,
And enterprises of great pitch and moment
With this regard their currents turn awry,
And lose the name of action.—Soft you now!
The fair Ophelia! Nymph, in thy orisons
Be all my sins remembered.

OPHELIA.   Good my lord,   90
How does your honor for this many a day?

HAMLET. I humbly thank you; well, well, well.

59. **sea**, etc. The curious mixed metaphor in this line has suggested
the possibility that "sea" should be emended to "siege."   65. **rub**, in
the game of bowls, an obstacle or hazard.   67. **shuffled off,** sloughed
off or cast off. **coil**, turmoil; or the figure here may be that of the body
wrapped around the soul like a coil of rope. Numerous emendations
have been suggested, but the entire line has become so familiar as it
stands that tampering with it would be mere pedantry.   68. **respect,**
consideration.   69. Insert "a" between "long" and "life."   73.
office, either office or office-holders; probably both meanings are
appropriate.   74. **takes**, takes from; the "from" is expressed as "of"
in this same line.   75. **quietus**, a legal term signifying acquittance;
here used metaphorically for death.   76. **fardels**, burdens.   79.
bourn, boundary.   83. **conscience**, both in our modern sense of our
"psychological monitor" against wrongdoing and in the old (medieval) sense of tender feelings, which makes us timid about any kind
of radical action.   85. **sicklied o'er**, given a sickly tinge. **cast**, shade
of color.   86. **pitch**, height; the metaphor is from falconry. **moment**,
importance.   87. **regard**, consideration, respect. **currents**, courses.
89. **orisons**, prayers.

OPHELIA. My lord, I have remembrances of yours,
That I have longed long to re-deliver;
I pray you, now receive them.

HAMLET.   No, not I;
I never gave you aught.

OPHELIA. My honored lord, you know right well
   you did;
And, with them, words of so sweet breath composed
As made the things more rich: their perfume lost,
Take these again; for to the noble mind   100
Rich gifts wax poor when givers prove unkind.
There, my lord.

HAMLET. Ha, ha! are you honest?

OPHELIA. My lord!

HAMLET. Are you fair?

OPHELIA. What means your lordship?

HAMLET. That if you be honest and fair, your honesty should admit no discourse to your beauty.

OPHELIA. Could beauty, my lord, have better commerce than with honesty?   110

HAMLET. Ay, truly; for the power of beauty will
sooner transform honesty from what it is to a bawd
than the force of honesty can translate beauty into
his likeness: this was sometime a paradox, but now
the time gives it proof. I did love you once.

OPHELIA. Indeed, my lord, you made me believe so.

HAMLET. You should not have believed me; for
virtue cannot so inoculate our old stock but we shall
relish of it: I loved you not.   120

OPHELIA. I was the more deceived.

HAMLET. Get thee to a nunnery; why wouldst thou
be a breeder of sinners? I am myself indifferent honest; but yet I could accuse me of such things that it
were better my mother had not borne me: I am very
proud, revengeful, ambitious, with more offences at
my beck than I have thoughts to put them in, imagination to give them shape, or time to act them in.
What should such fellows as I do crawling between
earth and Heaven? We are arrant knaves, all; believe
none of us. Go thy ways to a nunnery. Where's your
father?   133

OPHELIA. At home, my lord.

HAMLET. Let the doors be shut upon him, that he
may play the fool no where but in 's own house. Farewell.

OPHELIA. O, help him, you sweet heavens!

103. **honest**, sincere, truthful; but also with the idea of chastity in a
woman.   105. **fair**, just, honorable.   107. **honest and fair,** chaste and
beautiful; note the play on words in reference to ll. 103 and 105
above.   108. **honesty**, chastity. **discourse to**, familiar intercourse
with.   110. **commerce**, intercourse.   115. **time**, the (present) time.
119. **inoculate**, graft; the metaphor is from horticulture.   120. **but
we . . . it,** but we still have a taste of the old stock.   128. **beck**,
command.   133. **Where's your father?** At this point it has been a
tradition for Polonius to stick his head out from behind the tapestry
so that Hamlet catches sight of him. Ophelia's lie ("At home, my
lord") therefore convinces Hamlet of her unreliability. It is to be
noticed that from this point in the play Hamlet's feigned madness
assumes a more violent form.

HAMLET. If thou dost marry, I'll give thee this plague for thy dowry: be thou as chaste as ice, as pure as snow, thou shalt not escape calumny. Get thee to a nunnery, go; farewell. Or, if thou wilt needs marry, marry a fool; for wise men know well enough what monsters you make of them. To a nunnery, go, and quickly too. Farewell. 146

OPHELIA. O heavenly powers, restore him!

HAMLET. I have heard of your paintings too, well enough; God has given you one face, and you make yourselves another; you jig, you amble, and you lisp, and nick-name God's creatures, and make your wantonness your ignorance. Go to, I'll no more on 't; it hath made me mad. I say, we will have no more marriages; those that are married already, all but one, shall live; the rest shall keep as they are. To a nunnery, go. (Exit.)

OPHELIA. O, what a noble mind is here o'erthrown! 158
The courtier's, soldier's, scholar's, eye, tongue, sword;
The expectancy and rose of the fair state, 160
The glass of fashion and the mould of form,
The observed of all observers, quite, quite down!
And I, of ladies most deject and wretched,
That sucked the honey of his music vows,
Now see that noble and most sovereign reason,
Like sweet bells jangled, out of tune and harsh;
That unmatched form and feature of blown youth
Blasted with ecstasy: O, woe is me,
To have seen what I have seen, see what I see!

(Re-enter KING and POLONIUS.)

KING. Love! his affections do not that way tend; 170
Nor what he spake, though it lacked form a little,
Was not like madness. There's something in his soul,
O'er which his melancholy sits on brood;
And I do doubt the hatch and the disclose
Will be some danger: which for to prevent,
I have in quick determination
Thus set it down: he shall with speed to England,
For the demand of our neglected tribute:
Haply the seas and countries different
With variable objects shall expel 180
This something-settled matter in his heart,
Whereon his brains still beating puts him thus
From fashion of himself. What think you on't?

POLONIUS. It shall do well: but yet I do believe
The origin and commencement of his grief

Sprung from neglected love. How now, Ophelia!
You need not tell us what Lord Hamlet said;
We heard it all. My lord, do as you please;
But, if you hold it fit, after the play
Let his queen mother all alone entreat him 190
To show his grief: let her be round with him;
And I'll be placed, so please you, in the ear
Of all their conference. If she find him not,
To England send him, or confine him where
Your wisdom best shall think.

KING. It shall be so:
Madness in great ones must not unwatched go.
(Exeunt.)

SCENE 2. A hall in the castle.

(Enter HAMLET and Players.)

HAMLET. Speak the speech, I pray you, as I pronounced it to you, trippingly on the tongue: but if you mouth it, as many of your players do, I had as lief the town-crier spoke my lines. Nor do not saw the air too much with your hand, thus, but use all gently; for in the very torrent, tempest, and, as I may say, the whirlwind of passion, you must acquire and beget a temperance that may give it smoothness. O, it offends me to the soul to hear a robustious 10 periwig-pated fellow tear a passion to tatters, to very rags, to split the ears of the groundlings, who for the most part are capable of nothing but inexplicable dumb-shows and noise: I would have such a fellow whipped for o'erdoing Termagant; it out-Herods Herod: pray you, avoid it.

FIRST PLAYER. I warrant your honor. 17

HAMLET. Be not too tame neither, but let your own discretion be your tutor: suit the action to the word, the word to the action; with this special observance, that you o'erstep not the modesty of nature: for anything so overdone is from the purpose of playing, whose end, both at the first and now, was and is, to hold, as 't were, the mirror up to nature; to show virtue her own feature, scorn her own image, and the very age and body of the time his form and pressure. Now this overdone, or come tardy off, though it 28

145. monsters, referring to the horns which grow on the foreheads of all cuckolds. 150. jig, move with jerky motions, probably a reference to the dance which takes place in the dramatic trifle known as the jig (see note to Act II, Scene 2, l. 522). 152–153. make . . . ignorance, excuse your wantonness on the grounds of your ignorance. 156. one, King Claudius. 160. expectancy, source of hope for the future. 167. feature, whole shape of the body, figure and stature as well. 168. ecstasy, madness. 174. disclose, that which will be disclosed when the shell is broken; the image seems to be that of an egg. 180. variable, various. 183. puts . . . himself, keeps him out of his natural manner or condition.

193. find him, find him out, discover what is wrong with him. Act III, Scene 2. 10. robustious, violent, boisterous. 12. groundlings, members of the audience who stood in the "yard" (i.e., on the floor) of the theater; they constituted the less discriminating portion of the spectators. 13. capable of, susceptible to, comprehending. 16. Termagant, a god of the Saracens. He appears in the medieval St. Nicholas play; one of the characters in the play, leaving Termagant in charge of some goods, returns to find them stolen, whereupon he beats the pagan divinity most lustily, and the vociferous howling of the god is received by the audience with the greatest delight. Herod, the king of Judaea who played a part in the early years of the story of Jesus, also appeared in medieval plays, where his part was played with great sound and fury. 17. warrant, promise. 26. age and body, generation. 27. pressure, stamp, impressed character. 28. come tardy off, badly timed and inadequately done.

make the unskilful laugh, cannot but make the judicious grieve; the censure of the which one must in your allowance o'erweigh a whole theatre of others. O, there be players that I have seen play, and heard others praise, and that highly, not to speak it profanely, that, neither having the accent of Christians nor the gait of Christian, pagan, nor man, have so strutted and bellowed that I have thought some of nature's journeymen had made men and not made them well, they imitated humanity so abominably. 39

FIRST PLAYER. I hope we have reformed that indifferently with us, sir. 41

HAMLET. O, reform it altogether. And let those that play your clowns speak no more than is set down for them; for there be of them that will themselves laugh, to set on some quantity of barren spectators to laugh too; though, in the meantime, some necessary question of the play be then to be considered: that's villainous, and shows a most pitiful ambition in the fool that uses it. Go, make you ready. 50

(*Exeunt* Players.)

(*Enter* POLONIUS, ROSENCRANTZ, *and* GUILDENSTERN.)

How now, my lord! will the king hear this piece of work?

POLONIUS. And the queen too, and that presently.

HAMLET. Bid the players make haste.

(*Exit* POLONIUS.)

Will you two help to hasten them?

ROSENCRANTZ AND GUILDENSTERN. We will, my lord.

(*Exeunt* ROSENCRANTZ *and* GUILDENSTERN.)

HAMLET. What ho! Horatio!

(*Enter* HORATIO.)

HORATIO. Here, sweet lord, at your service.

HAMLET. Horatio, thou art e'en as just a man
As e'er my conversation coped withal. 60

HORATIO. O, my dear lord,—

HAMLET. Nay, do not think I flatter;
For what advancement may I hope from thee
That no revenue hast but thy good spirits,
To feed and clothe thee? Why should the poor be flattered?
No, let the candied tongue lick absurd pomp,

And crook the pregnant hinges of the knee
Where thrift may follow fawning. Dost thou hear?
Since my dear soul was mistress of her choice
And could of men distinguish, her election
Hath sealed thee for herself; for thou hast been 70
As one, in suffering all, that suffers nothing,
A man that fortune's buffets and rewards
Hast ta'en with equal thanks: and blest are those
Whose blood and judgment are so well commingled,
That they are not a pipe for fortune's finger
To sound what stop she please. Give me that man
That is not passion's slave, and I will wear him
In my heart's core, ay, in my heart of heart,
As I do thee.—Something too much of this.—
There is a play tonight before the king; 80
One scene of it comes near the circumstance
Which I have told thee of my father's death:
I prithee, when thou seest that act afoot,
Even with the very comment of thy soul
Observe mine uncle: if his occulted guilt
Do not itself unkennel in one speech,
It is a damned ghost that we have seen,
And my imaginings are as foul
As Vulcan's stithy. Give him heedful note;
For I mine eyes will rivet to his face, 90
And after we will both our judgments join
In censure of his seeming.

HORATIO. Well, my lord;
If he steal aught the whilst this play is playing,
And 'scape detecting, I will pay the theft.

HAMLET. They are coming to the play; I must be idle:
Get you a place.

(*Danish march. A flourish. Enter* KING, QUEEN, POLONIUS, OPHELIA, ROSENCRANTZ, GUILDENSTERN, *and others.*)

KING. How fare our cousin Hamlet?

HAMLET. Excellent, i' faith; of the chameleon's dish: I eat the air, promise-crammed; you cannot feed capons so. 100

KING. I have nothing with this answer, Hamlet; these words are not mine.

HAMLET. No, nor mine now. (*To* POLONIUS.) My lord, you played once i' the university, you say?

---

31. **the which one,** one of whom (the judicious). 38. **journeymen,** laborers hired by the day—not yet masters of their trade. 41. **indifferently,** fairly well, tolerably. 43. **clowns.** Evidently the parts played by the clowns in the Elizabethan theater were often not written down at all—they were allowed the broadest latitude in ad-libbing —and their jests were often unpremeditated interruptions to serious actions. But during the time of Shakespeare there was more and more of a tendency to fix the parts by writing them down, so as to inhibit the often unlicensed range of the star comedian. 44. **of.** Insert "some" before "of." 46. **barren,** devoid of wit or intelligence or taste. 59. **just,** honest, reliable. 60. **conversation,** intercourse, experience. **coped,** met, encountered. 63. **revenue.** Note that this word is accented on the second syllable.

66. **pregnant,** receptive, inclined to fawn. 67. **thrift,** profit, success. 76. **stop,** the hole in a wind instrument for controlling the sound. 77. **passion's slave,** etc. The whole passage, from lines 59 to 79, has been considered as evidence for Shakespeare's conception of Hamlet as a man in whom reason and emotions were not kept in even balance and who for this reason came to grief in the pinch. Obviously he is far less even-tempered than Horatio; but then Horatio did not have the same provocations. 84. **very comment,** inward and wise criticism of the self. 85. **occulted,** hidden. 89. **stithy,** smithy; *stith* is the old word for *anvil.* 91–92. **judgments . . . seeming,** judgments and criticism of his behavior and appearance. 95. **idle,** crazy, unable to attend to anything serious. 98. **chameleon's dish.** Chameleons were popularly supposed to subsist on nothing but air. 101. **have nothing with,** make nothing of. 102. **are not mine,** are of no significance to me.

POLONIUS. That did I, my lord; and was accounted a good actor.

HAMLET. What did you enact?

POLONIUS. I did enact Julius Caesar: I was killed i' the Capitol; Brutus killed me.

HAMLET. It was a brute part of him to kill so capital a calf there. Be the players ready? 111

ROSENCRANTZ. Ay, my lord; they stay upon your patience.

QUEEN. Come hither, my dear Hamlet, sit by me.

HAMLET. No, good mother, here's metal more attractive.

POLONIUS (*to the* KING). O, ho! do you mark that?

HAMLET. Lady, shall I lie in your lap?

(*Lying down at* OPHELIA's *feet*.)

OPHELIA. No, my lord. 120

HAMLET. I mean, my head upon your lap?

OPHELIA. Ay, my lord.

HAMLET. Do you think I meant country matters?

OPHELIA. I think nothing, my lord.

HAMLET. That's a fair thought to lie between maids' legs.

OPHELIA. What is, my lord?

HAMLET. Nothing.

OPHELIA. You are merry, my lord.

HAMLET. Who, I? 130

OPHELIA. Ay, my lord.

HAMLET. O God, your only jig-maker. What should a man do but be merry? for, look you, how cheerfully my mother looks, and my father died within these two hours.

OPHELIA. Nay, 'tis twice two months, my lord. 136

HAMLET. So long? Nay then, let the devil wear black, for I'll have a suit of sables. O heavens! die two months ago, and not forgotten yet? Then there's hope a great man's memory may outlive his life half a year: but, by 'r lady, he must build churches, then; or else shall he suffer not thinking on, with the hobby-horse, whose epitaph is 'For, O, for, O, the hobby-horse is forgot.' 145

Hautboys play. The dumb-show enters.

Enter a King *and a* Queen *very lovingly; the* Queen *embracing him, and he her. She kneels, and makes show of protestation unto him. He takes her up, and declines his head upon her neck: lays him down upon a bank of flowers: she, seeing him asleep, leaves him. Anon comes in a fellow, takes off his crown, kisses it, and pours poison in the* King's *ears,*

and exit. The Queen *returns; finds the* King *dead, and makes passionate action. The* Poisoner, *with some two or three* Mutes, *comes in again, seeming to lament with her. The dead body is carried away. The* Poisoner *woos the* Queen *with gifts: she seems loath and unwilling awhile, but in the end accepts his love.*

(*Exeunt.*)

OPHELIA. What means this, my lord?

HAMLET. Marry, this is miching mallecho; it means mischief.

OPHELIA. Belike this show imports the argument of the play. 150

(*Enter* Prologue.)

HAMLET. We shall know by this fellow: the players cannot keep counsel; they'll tell all.

OPHELIA. Will he tell us what this show meant?

HAMLET. Ay, or any show that you'll show him: be not you ashamed to show, he'll not shame to tell you what it means.

OPHELIA. You are naught, you are naught; I'll mark the play.

PROLOGUE. For us, and for our tragedy,
Here stooping to your clemency, 160
We beg your hearing patiently. (*Exit.*)

HAMLET. Is this a prologue, or the posy of a ring?

OPHELIA. 'Tis brief, my lord.

HAMLET. As woman's love.

(*Enter two* Players, King *and* Queen.)

PLAYER KING. Full thirty times hath Phoebus' cart gone round
Neptune's salt wash and Tellus' orbed ground,
And thirty dozen moons with borrowed sheen
About the world have times twelve thirties been,
Since love our hearts and Hymen did our hands
Unite commutual in most sacred bands. 170

PLAYER QUEEN. So many journeys may the sun and moon
Make us again count o'er ere love be done!
But, woe is me, you are so sick of late,
So far from cheer and from your former state,
That I distrust you. Yet, though I distrust,
Discomfort you, my lord, it nothing must;
For women's fear and love holds quantity;
In neither aught, or in extremity.
Now, what my love is, proof hath made you know;
And as my love is sized, my fear is so: 180
Where love is great, the littlest doubts are fear;
Where little fears grow great, great love grows there.

132. **your only,** only your. 138. **suit of sables,** garments trimmed with sable fur, but Hamlet is playing on the other meaning of sable, the heraldic term for black. 144. **hobby-horse . . . 'forgot.'** This is evidently an allusion to a popular song of the time (quoted partially in *Love's Labour's Lost*, Act III, Scene 1, l. 30). The hobby-horse was a character which appeared, in the English folk-plays, in the Morris Dance; it is believed to be a reincarnation of the eight-legged steed ridden by Woden, king of the ancient Germanic gods. 145. ff. *Stage Direction: Hautboys,* wooden double-reed wind-instruments of a high pitch, the ancestor of the modern oboe.

147. **miching mallecho,** sneaking (or mincing) mischief; the latter word is supposed to be derived from the Spanish *malhecho.* 157. **naught,** improper, bad. The entire dialogue between Ophelia and Hamlet in this scene is extremely broad and risqué. 160. **stooping,** bowing. 162. **posy,** motto. 166. **Tellus' orbed ground.** Tellus was in classical mythology an ancient goddess of the earth, which—since the earth had been demonstrated to be round—is referred to here as "orbed ground." 167. **borrowed,** reflected. 169. **Hymen,** god of marriage in classical mythology. 170. **commutual,** intensely mutual. 175. **distrust,** am anxious about, worry about. 177. **holds quantity,** keeps proportion between.

PLAYER KING. 'Faith, I must leave thee, love, and
    shortly too;
My operant powers their functions leave to do:
And thou shalt live in this fair world behind,
Honored, beloved; and haply one as kind
For husband shalt thou—
    PLAYER QUEEN.   O, confound the rest!
Such love must needs be treason in my breast:
In second husband let me be accursed!   189
None wed the second but who killed the first.
    HAMLET (*aside*). Wormwood, wormwood.
    PLAYER QUEEN. The instances that second marriage
      move
Are base respects of thrift, but none of love:
A second time I kill my husband dead,
When second husband kisses me in bed.
    PLAYER KING. I do believe you think what now you
      speak;
But what we do determine oft we break.
Purpose is but the slave to memory,
Of violent birth, but poor validity;
Which now, like fruit unripe, sticks on the tree;   200
But fall, unshaken, when they mellow be.
Most necessary 'tis that we forget
To pay ourselves what to ourselves is debt:
What to ourselves in passion we propose,
The passion ending, doth the purpose lose.
The violence of either grief or joy
Their own enactures with themselves destroy:
Where joy most revels, grief doth most lament;
Grief joys, joy grieves, on slender accident.
This world is not for aye, nor 'tis not strange   210
That even our loves should with our fortunes change;
For 'tis a question left us yet to prove,
Whether love lead fortune, or else fortune love.
The great man down, you mark his favorite flies;
The poor advanced makes friends of enemies.
And hitherto doth love on fortune tend;
For who not needs shall never lack a friend,
And who in want a hollow friend doth try,
Directly seasons him his enemy.
But, orderly to end where I begun,   220
Our wills and fates do so contrary run
That our devices still are overthrown;
Our thoughts are ours, their ends none of our own;
So think thou wilt no second husband wed;
But die thy thoughts when thy first lord is dead.

PLAYER QUEEN. Nor earth to me give food, nor
    Heaven light!
Sport and repose lock from me day and night!
To desperation turn my trust and hope!
An anchor's cheer in prison be my scope!
Each opposite that blanks the face of joy   230
Meet what I would have well and it destroy!
Both here and hence pursue me lasting strife,
If, once a widow, ever I be wife!
    HAMLET. If she should break it now!
    PLAYER KING. 'Tis deeply sworn. Sweet, leave me
      here awhile;
My spirits grow dull, and fain I would beguile
The tedious day with sleep.   (*Sleeps.*)
    PLAYER QUEEN.   Sleep rock thy brain;
And never come mischance between us twain!
                      (*Exit.*)
    HAMLET. Madam, how like you this play?   239
    QUEEN. The lady doth protest too much, methinks.
    HAMLET. O, but she'll keep her word.
    KING. Have you heard the argument? Is there no
offence in 't?
    HAMLET. No, no, they do but jest, poison in jest;
no offence i' the world.
    KING. What do you call the play?   246
    HAMLET. The Mouse-trap. Marry, how? Tropi-
cally. The play is the image of a murder done in
Vienna: Gonzago is the duke's name; his wife,
Baptista: you shall see anon; 'tis a knavish piece of
work: but what o' that? your majesty and we that
have free souls, it touches us not; let the galled jade
wince, our withers are unwrung.
               (*Enter* LUCIANUS.)
This is one Lucianus, nephew to the king.
    OPHELIA. You are as good as a chorus, my lord.   255
    HAMLET. I could interpret between you and your
love, if I could see the puppets dallying.
    OPHELIA. You are keen, my lord, you are keen.
    HAMLET. It would cost you a groaning to take off
my edge.   260
    OPHELIA. Still better, and worse.
    HAMLET. So you must take your husbands. Begin,
murderer; pox, leave thy damnable faces, and begin.

---

184. **operant,** active, operating. **leave,** cease.   187. **confound,** strike
dumb.   191. **Wormwood.** The Old English drink, *wermod*, was a
spirituous liquor closely related to absinthe, and noted for its bitter
taste. Hence, the relation of this word to bitterness, although it should
be remarked that it has no relation to worms—the form *wormwood*
is due to a process known as folk etymology. In actual fact, the immediate descendant of this drink is the wine known as vermouth.
192. **instances,** inducements, motives.   193. **respects of thrifts,** considerations of material interest.   207. **enactures,** fulfillments.   219.
seasons, matures. Insert "as" between "him" and "his."

229. **anchor's,** anchorite's. **cheer,** fare, subsistence.   230. **opposite,**
opponent, adversary. **blanks,** causes to grow pale.   248. **tropically,**
figuratively, metaphorically; a *trope* is a figure of speech. **image,**
dramatic representation.   249. **Gonzago.** There was an actual murder of a Duke Gonzago of Urbano, Italy, in 1538 accomplished by
pouring a lethal lotion in his ears. A tragedy was written on the incident some time later in the century.   253. **galled jade,** a broken-
down horse whose hide has been irritated to the point of inflammation
by saddle or harness (galled). **withers,** the area between a horse's
shoulder-blades. **unwrung,** not wrung or twisted or cramped.   255.
chorus. In many Elizabethan plays—for example, Shakespeare's
Henry V—the action was explained and commented upon by an
actor known as the Chorus. At a puppet-show, on the other hand, the
action was explained by a so-called "interpreter," which explains
the reference in l. 256.   261. **Still better, and worse,** more shrewd
but less proper.   263. **pox,** an imprecation, referring since early times
to either the Black Death (bubonic plague) or syphilis.

Come: 'the croaking raven doth bellow for revenge.'

LUCIANUS. Thoughts black, hands apt, drugs fit,
    and time agreeing;
Confederate season, else no creature seeing;
Thou mixture rank, of midnight weeds collected,
With Hecate's ban thrice blasted, thrice infected,
Thy natural magic and dire property,   270
On wholesome life usurp immediately.

                (*Pours the poison into the sleeper's ears.*)

HAMLET. He poisons him i' the garden for 's estate.
His name's Gonzago: the story is extant, and writ in
choice Italian: you shall see anon how the murderer
gets the love of Gonzago's wife.

OPHELIA. The king rises.

HAMLET. What, frighted with false fire?

QUEEN. How fares my lord?

POLONIUS. Give o'er the play.

KING. Give me some light: away!   280

ALL. Lights, lights, lights!

              (*Exeunt all but* HAMLET *and* HORATIO.)

HAMLET. Why, let the stricken deer go weep,
    The hart ungalled play;
    For some must watch, while some must
        sleep:
    So runs the world away.
Would not this, sir, and a forest of feathers—if the
rest of my fortunes turn Turk with me—with two
Provincial roses on my razed shoes, get me a fellowship in a cry of players, sir?

HORATIO. Half a share.   290

HAMLET. A whole one, I.
    For thou dost know, O Damon dear,
        This realm dismantled was
    Of Jove himself; and now reigns here
        A very, very—pajock.

HORATIO. You might have rhymed.

HAMLET. O good Horatio, I'll take the ghost's word
for a thousand pound. Didst perceive?

HORATIO. Very well, my lord.

264–265. **'the croaking . . . revenge,'** suggested by the lines of the
older anonymous play, the *True Tragedie of Richard the Third*: "The
screeking raven sits croaking for revenge. Whole herds of beasts come
bellowing for revenge." 267. **Confederate,** conspiring to assist the
murderer. 269. **Hecate,** in classical mythology the goddess of witchcraft and sorcery. **ban,** curse. 277. **false fire,** either "fireworks" or
"blank cartridges." 282–285. **Why, let . . . world away,** probably
a quotation from another popular song of the times, with reference to
the belief that a wounded deer always retires to the woods to die,
weeping before his death. 286. **this,** i.e., the play. **feathers,** referring
to the plumes worn by Elizabethan actors portraying men of distinction. 287. **Turn Turk with,** go back on; the Turk was to Elizabethan England a symbol of cruelty and treachery. 288. **Provincial
roses,** roses either from Provins or Provence in France. **razed,** cut or
slashed for purposes of ornament. 289. **fellowship . . . players,**
partnership in a theatrical company. **cry,** the baying of a pack of
hounds. 290. **Half a share,** a reference to the practice in dramatic
companies of the time of dividing the ownership into a number of
shares among the householders. 292–295. **For thou . . . pajock,**
evidently an excerpt from an old ballad about Damon and Pythias.
293. **dismantled,** stripped, divested. 295. **pajock,** probably a peacock, a bird with a bad reputation.

HAMLET. Upon the talk of the poisoning.

HORATIO. I did very well note him.   301

HAMLET. Ah, ha! Come, some music! come, the
recorders!
    For if the king like not the comedy,
        Why then, belike, he likes it not, perdy.
Come, some music!

      (*Re-enter* ROSENCRANTZ *and* GUILDENSTERN.)

GUILDENSTERN. Good my lord, vouchsafe me a
word with you.

HAMLET. Sir, a whole history.

GUILDENSTERN. The king, sir—   310

HAMLET. Ay, sir, what of him?

GUILDENSTERN. Is in his retirement marvellous distempered.

HAMLET. With drink, sir?

GUILDENSTERN. No, my lord, rather with choler.

HAMLET. Your wisdom should show itself more
richer to signify this to his doctor; for, for me to put
him to his purgation would perhaps plunge him into
far more choler.   319

GUILDENSTERN. Good my lord, put your discourse
into some frame and start not so wildly from my
affair.

HAMLET. I am tame, sir; pronounce.

GUILDENSTERN. The queen, your mother, in most
great affliction of spirit, hath sent me to you.

HAMLET. You are welcome.   325

GUILDENSTERN. Nay, good my lord, this courtesy is
not of the right breed. If it shall please you to make
me a wholesome answer, I will do your mother's
commandment; if not, your pardon and my return
shall be the end of the business.

HAMLET. Sir, I cannot.   331

GUILDENSTERN. What, my lord?

HAMLET. Make you a wholesome answer; my wit's
diseased; but, sir, such answer as I can make, you
shall command; or, rather, as you say, my mother:
therefore no more, but to the matter; my mother, you
say,—

ROSENCRANTZ. Then thus she says; your behavior
hath struck her into amazement and admiration. 339

HAMLET. O wonderful son, that can so astonish a
mother! But is there no sequel at the heels of this
mother's admiration? Impart.

ROSENCRANTZ. She desires to speak with you in her
closet, ere you go to bed.

HAMLET. We shall obey, were she ten times our
mother. Have you any further trade with us?

ROSENCRANTZ. My lord, you once did love me.

HAMLET. So I do still, by these pickers and stealers.

---

303. **recorders,** wind-instruments like the flute. 305. **perdy,** a corruption of the French oath, *par dieu!* 315. **choler,** strictly speaking,
a bilious disorder; but the later meaning of anger is also implicit.
321. **frame,** order, shape. 328. **wholesome,** sensible. 337. **matter,**
business in hand. 339. **admiration,** wonder, amazement. 348.
pickers and stealers, hands, from the catechism, "to keep my hands
from picking and stealing."

ROSENCRANTZ. Good my lord, what is your cause of distemper? you do, surely, bar the door upon your own liberty, if you deny your griefs to your friend.

HAMLET. Sir, I lack advancement.

ROSENCRANTZ. How can that be, when you have the voice of the king himself for your succession in Denmark?

HAMLET. Ay, sir, but 'While the grass grows,'—the proverb is something musty. 359

(*Re-enter* Players *with recorders.*)
O, the recorders! let me see one. To withdraw with you:—why do you go about to recover the wind of me, as if you would drive me into a toil?

GUILDENSTERN. O, my lord, if my duty be too bold, my love is too unmannerly. 364

HAMLET. I do not well understand that. Will you play upon this pipe?

GUILDENSTERN. My lord, I cannot.

HAMLET. I pray you.

GUILDENSTERN. Believe me, I cannot.

HAMLET. I do beseech you. 370

GUILDENSTERN. I know no touch of it, my lord.

HAMLET. 'Tis as easy as lying: govern these ventages with your fingers and thumb, give it breath with your mouth, and it will discourse most eloquent music. Look you, these are the stops.

GUILDENSTERN. But these cannot I command to any utterance of harmony; I have not the skill. 378

HAMLET. Why, look you now, how unworthy a thing you make of me! You would play upon me; you would seem to know my stops; you would pluck out the heart of my mystery; you would sound me from my lowest note to the top of my compass: and there is much music, excellent voice, in this little organ; yet cannot you make it speak. 'Sblood, do you think I am easier to be played on than a pipe? Call me what instrument you will, though you can fret me, yet you cannot play upon me.

(*Enter* POLONIUS.)
God bless you, sir! 390

POLONIUS. My lord, the queen would speak with you, and presently.

HAMLET. Do you see yonder cloud that's almost in the shape of a camel?

POLONIUS. By the mass, and 'tis like a camel, indeed.

HAMLET. Methinks it is like a weasel.

POLONIUS. It is backed like a weasel.

HAMLET. Or like a whale?

POLONIUS. Very like a whale. 399

HAMLET. Then I will come to my mother by and by. They fool me to the top of my bent. I will come by and by.

POLONIUS. I will say so.

HAMLET. By and by is easily said. (*Exit* POLONIUS.)
Leave me, friends.
(*Exeunt all but* HAMLET.)
'Tis now the very witching time of night,
When churchyards yawn and Hell itself breathes out
Contagion to this world: now could I drink hot blood,
And do such bitter business as the day
Would quake to look on. Soft! now to my mother.
O heart, lose not thy nature; let not ever 411
The soul of Nero enter this firm bosom:
Let me be cruel, not unnatural:
I will speak daggers to her, but use none;
My tongue and soul in this be hypocrites;
How in my words soever she be shent,
To give them seals never, my soul, consent! (*Exit.*)

SCENE. 3. *A room in the castle.*

(*Enter* KING, ROSENCRANTZ, *and* GUILDENSTERN.)
KING. I like him not, nor stands it safe with us
To let his madness range. Therefore prepare you;
I your commission will forthwith dispatch,
And he to England shall along with you:
The terms of our estate may not endure
Hazard so near us as doth hourly grow
Out of his lunacies.

GUILDENSTERN. We will ourselves provide:
Most holy and religious fear it is
To keep those many many bodies safe
That live and feed upon your majesty. 10

ROSENCRANTZ. The single and peculiar life is
bound,
With all the strength and armor of the mind,
To keep itself from noyance; but much more
That spirit upon whose weal depend and rest
The lives of many. The cease of majesty
Dies not alone; but, like a gulf, doth draw
What's near it with it: it is a massy wheel,
Fixed on the summit of the highest mount,
To whose huge spokes ten thousand lesser things
Are mortised and adjoined; which, when it falls, 20

356. **voice,** support. 358. **'While the grass grows—'** The rest of the proverb goes, 'the silly (empty) horse starves.' Hamlet may be destroyed while waiting to succeed to the throne. 360. **withdraw,** speak in private. 361. **recover the wind,** in nautical phraseology, to get back on the windward side. 362. **toil,** snare, trap. 363–364. **if my duty . . . unmannerly,** if I am being too bold in my duty, it is because of my love for you. 373. **ventages,** the stops or finger holes of the recorder. 384. **compass,** range of voice. 385. **organ,** any musical instrument; here, the recorder. 388. **fret.** There is here a play on the meaning of the word as "irritate" and the "piece of wood" which regulates the fingering.

401. **top . . . bent,** limit of endurance, the extent to which a bow can be bent. 402. **by and by,** immediately. 406. **witching time,** the time when spells are cast, from midnight until one o'clock in the morning. 412. **soul of Nero.** It should be recalled that the Roman emperor Nero had his mother, Agrippina, murdered. 416. **shent,** rebuked, insulted. 417. **give them seals,** confirm them by some irrevocable deed.
Act III, Scene 3. 5. **estate,** state. 8. **fear,** caution. 11. **single and peculiar,** individual and private. 13. **noyance,** harm. 16. **gulf,** whirlpool.

Each small annexment, petty consequence,
Attends the boisterous ruin. Never alone
Did the king sigh, but with a general groan.

KING. Arm you, I pray you, to this speedy voyage;
For we will fetters put upon this fear,
Which now goes too free-footed.

ROSENCRANTZ AND GUILDENSTERN. We will haste us.

(*Exeunt* ROSENCRANTZ *and* GUILDENSTERN.)

(*Enter* POLONIUS.)

POLONIUS. My lord, he's going to his mother's
closet:
Behind the arras I'll convey myself,
To hear the process; I'll warrant she'll tax him home:
And, as you said, and wisely was it said,   30
'Tis meet that some more audience than a mother,
Since nature makes them partial, should o'erhear
The speech of vantage. Fare you well, my liege:
I'll call upon you ere you go to bed,
And tell you what I know.

KING.   Thanks, dear my lord.

(*Exit* POLONIUS.)

O, my offence is rank, it smells to Heaven;
It hath the primal eldest curse upon 't,
A brother's murder. Pray can I not,
Though inclination be as sharp as will:
My stronger guilt defeats my strong intent;   40
And, like a man to double business bound,
I stand in pause where I shall first begin,
And both neglect. What if this cursed hand
Were thicker than itself with brother's blood,
Is there not rain enough in the sweet heavens
To wash it white as snow? Whereto serves mercy
But to confront the visage of offence?
And what's in prayer but this two-fold force,
To be forestalled ere we come to fall,   49
Or pardoned being down? Then I'll look up;
My fault is past. But, O, what form of prayer
Can serve my turn? 'Forgive me my foul murder'?
That cannot be; since I am still possessed
Of those effects for which I did the murder,
My crown, mine own ambition and my queen.
May one be pardoned and retain the offence?
In the corrupted currents of this world
Offence's gilded hand may shove by justice,
And oft 'tis seen the wicked prize itself
Buys out the law: but 'tis not so above;   60
There is no shuffling, there the action lies
In his true nature; and we ourselves compelled,
Even to the teeth and forehead of our faults,
To give in evidence. What then? what rests?

Try what repentance can: what can it not?
Yet what can it when one can not repent?
O wretched state! O bosom black as death!
O limed soul, that, struggling to be free,
Art more engaged! Help, angels! Make assay!
Bow, stubborn knees; and, heart with strings of
steel,   70
Be soft as sinews of the new-born babe!
All may be well.   (*Retires and kneels.*)

(*Enter* HAMLET.)

HAMLET. Now might I do it pat, now he is praying;
And now I'll do 't. And so he goes to Heaven;
And so am I revenged. That would be scanned:
A villain kills my father; and for that,
I, his sole son, do this same villain send
To Heaven.
O, this is hire and salary, not revenge.
He took my father grossly, full of bread;   80
With all his crimes broad blown, as flush as May;
And how his audit stands who knows save Heaven?
But in our circumstance and course of thought,
'Tis heavy with him: and am I then revenged,
To take him in the purging of his soul,
When he is fit and seasoned for his passage?
No!
Up, sword; and know thou a more horrid hent:
When he is drunk asleep, or in his rage,
Or in the incestuous pleasure of his bed;   90
At gaming, swearing, or about some act
That has no relish of salvation in 't;
Then trip him, that his heels may kick at Heaven,
And that his soul may be as damned and black
As Hell, whereto it goes. My mother stays:
This physic but prolongs thy sickly days.   (*Exit.*)

KING (*rising*). My words fly up, my thoughts remain below:
Words without thoughts never to Heaven go. (*Exit.*)

SCENE 4. *The Queen's closet.*

(*Enter* QUEEN *and* POLONIUS.)

POLONIUS. He will come straight. Look you lay
home to him:

---

24. **Arm,** prepare.   28. **convey,** betake, with the suggestion of secrecy or stealth.   29. **process,** interview, business. **tax him home,** reprove him up to the hilt.   33. **of vantage,** from a vantage point.   39. **sharp as will,** though his desire be as strong as his determination. 47. **confront,** oppose directly.   55. **ambition,** the realization of ambition.   56. **offence,** the benefits derived from the offence.   58. **gilded hand,** hand offering gold as a bribe.   61. **shuffling,** escaping by trickery. **lies,** is sustainable.

68. **limed,** caught as with the bird lime.   69. **assay,** trial.   73–95. **Now might I . . . days.** This is generally considered the critical point in the delineation of Hamlet's character. One group of students of the play believes that Hamlet refrains from killing the king through sheer weakness of will and is here merely rationalizing his conduct and finding excuses for not doing his duty. But a more recent group insists that Hamlet is delaying only to make his revenge more complete by not sending the King to Heaven, for it was believed that anyone dying while engaged in prayer—provided the prayer was sincere—would not die in sin and so would certainly be received in Heaven.   75. **would be scanned,** would need to be looked into. 80. **full of bread,** full of physical appetites and life.   81. **broad blown,** in full bloom. **flush,** lusty.   83. **in our circumstance . . . thought,** as we see it in our situation in life.   88. **hent,** seizing.   89. **drunk asleep,** in a drunken sleep. **rage,** sexual passion.   96. **physic,** purging by prayer.
Act III, Scene 4.   1. **lay home,** talk plainly.

Tell him his pranks have been too broad to bear with,
And that your grace hath screened and stood be-
     tween
Much heat and him. I'll sconce me even here.
Pray you, be round with him.
    HAMLET (*within*). Mother, mother, mother!
    QUEEN.   I'll warrant you,
Fear me not: withdraw, I hear him coming.
         (POLONIUS *hides behind the arras.*)
         (*Enter* HAMLET.)
    HAMLET. Now, mother, what's the matter?
    QUEEN. Hamlet, thou hast thy father much of-
     fended.
    HAMLET. Mother, you have my father much of-
     fended.   10
    QUEEN. Come, come, you answer with an idle
     tongue.
    HAMLET. Go, go, you question with a wicked
     tongue.
    QUEEN. Why, how now, Hamlet?
    HAMLET.   What's the matter now?
    QUEEN. Have you forgot me?
    HAMLET.   No, by the rood, not so:
You are the queen, your husband's brother's wife;
And—would it were not so!—you are my mother.
    QUEEN. Nay, then, I'll set those to you that can
     speak.
    HAMLET. Come, come, and sit you down; you shall
     not budge;
You go not till I set you up a glass
Where you may see the inmost part of you.   20
    QUEEN. What wilt thou do? thou wilt not murder
me? Help, help, ho!
    POLONIUS (*behind*). What, ho! help, help, help!
    HAMLET (*drawing*). How now! a rat? Dead, for a
     ducat, dead!
            (*Makes a pass through the arras.*)
    POLONIUS (*behind*). O, I am slain! (*Falls and dies.*)
    QUEEN. O me, what hast thou done?
    HAMLET.   Nay, I know not;
Is it the king?
    QUEEN. O, what a rash and bloody deed is this!
    HAMLET. A bloody deed! almost as bad, good
     mother,
As kill a king, and marry with his brother.
    QUEEN. As kill a king!
    HAMLET.   Ay, lady, 'twas my word.   30
    (*Lifts up the arras and discovers* POLONIUS.)
Thou wretched, rash, intruding fool, farewell!
I took thee for thy better: take thy fortune;
Thou find'st to be too busy is some danger.
Leave wringing of your hands: peace! sit you down,
And let me wring your heart; for so I shall,

If it be made of penetrable stuff,
If damned custom have not brassed it so
That it be proof and bulwark against sense.
    QUEEN. What have I done, that thou darest wag
     thy tongue
In noise so rude against me?
    HAMLET.   Such an act   40
That blurs the grace and blush of modesty,
Calls virtue hypocrite, takes off the rose
From the fair forehead of an innocent love
And sets a blister there, makes marriage-vows
As false as dicers' oaths: O, such a deed
As from the body of contraction plucks
The very soul, and sweet religion makes
A rhapsody of words: Heaven's face doth glow;
Yea, this solidity and compound mass,
With tristful visage, as against the doom,   50
Is thought-sick at the act.
    QUEEN.   Ay me, what act,
That roars so loud, and thunders in the index?
    HAMLET. Look here, upon this picture, and on this.
The counterfeit presentment of two brothers.
See, what a grace was seated on this brow:
Hyperion's curls; the front of Jove himself;
An eye like Mars, to threaten and command;
A station like the herald Mercury
New-lighted on a heaven-kissing hill;
A combination and a form indeed,   60
Where every god did seem to set his seal,
To give the world assurance of a man;
This was your husband. Look you now, what follows:
Here is your husband; like a mildewed ear,
Blasting his wholesome brother. Have you eyes?
Could you on this fair mountain leave to feed,
And batten on this moor? Ha! have you eyes?
You cannot call it love; for at your age
The hey-day in the blood is tame, it's humble,
And waits upon the judgment: and what judgment 70
Would step from this to this? Sense, sure, you have,
Else could you not have motion; but sure, that sense
Is apoplex'd; for madness would not err,
Nor sense to ecstasy was ne'er so thralled
But it reserved some quantity of choice,

---

37. **brassed,** brazoned, hardened. 38. **proof,** armor, protection. **sense,** feeling. 44. **sets a blister,** brands as a harlot. 46. **contraction,** pledge, betrothal. 48. **rhapsody,** fantastic expression. 49. **this solidity . . . mass,** the solid earth itself. 50. **tristful,** full of sadness. **the doom,** Judgment Day. 51. **thought-sick,** sick with worry and anxiety. 52. **index,** prelude or preface. 54. **counterfeit presentment,** pictorial representation—the two pictures are thought of by some as miniatures carried about by Hamlet and by others as portraits on the wall. 56. **Hyperion,** the sun god; see Act I, Scene 2, l. 140 and note. 58. **station,** manner of standing, stance. 64. **mildewed ear.** The figure is suggested by the story of Joseph as told in Genesis, 41:5–7, in which the diseased ears of grain spread their blight to the healthy ears. 67. **batten,** feed, pasture (v.). 71–72. **Sense . . . motion.** Sense and motion are functions of the "middle" or the sensible soul, since the possession of sense is a necessary basis for motion. 73. **apoplex'd,** paralyzed (as a result of apoplexy). Elizabethan medicine classified mental disease into three kinds: apoplexy, ecstasy, and possession by a devil.

---

2. **broad,** unrestrained. 4. **heat,** the King's anger. **sconce,** ensconce, place, hide. 26. **Is it the king?** Hamlet, thinking the man hiding to be the king, nevertheless does not hesitate to strike, which suggests that he is not the weakling often portrayed.

To serve in such a difference. What devil was 't
That thus hath cozened you at hoodman-blind?
Eyes without feeling, feeling without sight,
Ears without hands or eyes, smelling sans all,
Or but a sickly part of one true sense   80
Could not so mope.
O shame! where is thy blush? Rebellious Hell,
If thou canst mutine in a matron's bones,
To flaming youth let virtue be as wax,
And melt in her own fire; proclaim no shame
When the compulsive ardor gives the charge,
Since frost itself as actively doth burn
And reason pandars will.

    QUEEN.   O Hamlet, speak no more:
Thou turnest mine eyes into my very soul;
And there I see such black and grained spots
As will not leave their tinct.

    HAMLET.   Nay, but to live   91
In the rank sweat of an enseamed bed,
Stewed in corruption, honeying and making love
Over the nasty sty,—

    QUEEN.   O speak to me no more;
These words, like daggers, enter in mine ears;
No more, sweet Hamlet!

    HAMLET.   A murderer and a villain;
A slave that is not twentieth part the tithe
Of your precedent lord; a vice of kings;
A cutpurse of the empire and the rule,
That from a shelf the precious diadem stole,   100
And put it in his pocket!

    QUEEN.   No more!

    HAMLET. A king of shreds and patches,—
            (*Enter* Ghost.)
Save me, and hover o'er me with your wings,
You heavenly guards! What would your gracious
       figure?

    QUEEN. Alas, he's mad!

    HAMLET. Do you not come your tardy son to chide,
That, lapsed in time and passion, lets go by
The important acting of your dread command?
O, say!

    GHOST. Do not forget: this visitation   110
Is but to whet thy almost blunted purpose.
But, look, amazement on thy mother sits:

O, step between her and her fighting soul:
Conceit in weakest bodies strongest works:
Speak to her, Hamlet.

    HAMLET.   How is it with you, lady?

    QUEEN. Alas, how is 't with you,
That you do bend your eye on vacancy
And with the incorporal air do hold discourse?
Forth at your eyes your spirits wildly peep;
And, as the sleeping soldiers in the alarm,   120
Your bedded hair, like life in excrements,
Start up, and stand on end. O gentle son,
Upon the heat and flame of thy distemper
Sprinkle cool patience. Whereon do you look?

    HAMLET. On him, on him! Look you, how pale he
       glares!
His form and cause conjoined, preaching to stones,
Would make them capable. Do not look upon me;
Lest with this piteous action you convert
My stern effects: then what I have to do   129
Will want true color; tears perchance for blood.

    QUEEN. To whom do you speak this?

    HAMLET.   Do you see
       nothing there?

    QUEEN. Nothing at all; yet all that is I see.

    HAMLET. Nor did you nothing hear?

    QUEEN.   No, nothing but ourselves.

    HAMLET. Why, look you there! look, how it steals
       away!
My father, in his habit as he lived!
Look, where he goes, even now, out at the portal!
            (*Exit* Ghost.)

    QUEEN. This is the very coinage of your brain:
This bodiless creation ecstasy
Is very cunning in.

    HAMLET.   Ecstasy!
My pulse, as yours, doth temperately keep time,   140
And makes as healthful music: it is not madness
That I have uttered: bring me to the test,
And I the matter will re-word, which madness
Would gambol from. Mother, for love of grace,
Lay not that flattering unction to your soul,
That not your trespass, but my madness speaks:
It will but skin and film the ulcerous place,
Whiles rank corruption, mining all within,
Infects unseen. Confess yourself to Heaven;
Repent what's past; avoid what is to come;   150
And do not spread the compost on the weeds,

---

77. **cozened,** tricked, deceived. **hoodman-blind,** the old game of blind man's buff. 79. **sans,** without. 83. **mutine,** mutiny, rebellion against convention. 86. **charge,** command. 88. **reason pandars will.** Normally reason is supposed to guide the will in the direction of good; but here reason has been perverted and serves only to cater to the baser instincts and desires of the will. 90. **grained,** dyed in grain. 92. **enseamed,** spotted with grease and dirt. Hamlet's imagination in respect to his mother's marriage-bed is of a distinctly morbid nature. 98. **precedent lord,** Hamlet's father. **vice of kings,** buffoon or clown of kings; in the medieval morality plays a vice was often portrayed as a clown or jester. 102. **shreds and patches,** motley, the variegated costume of the medieval Vice in the morality plays—see note to l. 98. 107. **lapsed . . . passion,** having allowed time to pass and passion to cool. 108. **important,** urgent, demanding. 112. **amazement,** frenzy, distraction, hysteria.

114. **Conceit,** imagination. 118. **incorporal,** immaterial, unsubstantial. 121. **bedded,** laid down in smooth layers—an interesting reference to the kind of hairdress affected by the Elizabethan gentleman. **excrements.** The hair was believed to be an excrement, or voided part, of the human body. 126. **conjoined,** united. 127. **capable,** susceptible. 128–129. **convert . . . effects,** divert me from my serious duty. 130. **want true color,** lack good reason so that I shall shed tears instead of blood. 143. **re-word,** repeat. 145. **unction,** ointment used either medicinally or as a religious sacrament; the implication here is that forgiveness for sin is not so easy to achieve. 148. **mining,** undermining. 150. **what is to come,** the unseen future.

To make them ranker. Forgive me this my virtue;
For in the fatness of these pursy times
Virtue itself of vice most pardon beg,
Yea, curb and woo for leave to do him good.
    QUEEN. O Hamlet, thou hast cleft my heart in
        twain.
    HAMLET. O, throw away the worser part of it,
And live the purer with the other half.
Good night: but go not to mine uncle's bed;
Assume a virtue, if you have it not.   160
That monster, custom, who all sense doth eat,
Of habits devil, is angel yet in this,
That to the use of actions fair and good
He likewise gives a frock or livery,
That aptly is put on. Refrain tonight,
And that shall lend a kind of easiness
To the next abstinence: the next more easy;
For use almost can change the stamp of nature,
And either (master) the devil, or throw him out
With wondrous potency. Once more, good night: 170
And when you are desirous to be blessed,
I'll blessing beg of you. For this same lord,
                (*Pointing to* POLONIUS)
I do repent: but Heaven hath pleased it so,
To punish me with this and this with me,
That I must be their scourge and minister.
I will bestow him, and will answer well
The death I gave him. So, again, good night.
I must be cruel, only to be kind:
Thus bad begins and worse remains behind.
One word more, good lady.
    QUEEN.   What shall I do?   180
    HAMLET. Not this, by no means, that I bid you do:
Let the bloat king tempt you again to bed:
Pinch wanton on your cheek; call you his mouse;
And let him, for a pair of reechy kisses,
Or paddling in your neck with his damned fingers,
Make you to ravel all this matter out,
That I essentially am not in madness,
But mad in craft. 'Twere good you let him know;
For who, that's but a queen, fair, sober, wise,
Would from a paddock, from a bat, a gib,   190
Such dear concernings hide? who would do so?
No, in despite of sense and secrecy,
Unpeg the basket on the house's top,
Let the birds fly, and, like the famous ape,

To try conclusions, in the basket creep,
And break your own neck down.
    QUEEN. Be thou assured, if words be made of
        breath,
And breath of life, I have no life to breathe
What thou hast said to me.
    HAMLET. I must to England; you know that?
    QUEEN.   Alack, 200
I had forgot: 'tis so concluded on.
    HAMLET. There's letters sealed: and my two
        schoolfellows,
Whom I will trust as I will adders fanged,
They bear the mandate; they must sweep my way,
And marshal me to knavery. Let it work;
For 'tis the sport to have the enginer
Hoist with his own petar: and 't shall go hard
But I will delve one yard below their mines,
And blow them at the moon: O, 'tis most sweet,
When in one line two crafts directly meet.   210
This man shall set me packing:
I'll lug the guts into the neighbor room.
Mother, good night. Indeed this counsellor
Is now most still, most secret and most grave,
Who was in life a foolish prating knave.
Come, sir, to draw toward an end with you.
Good night, mother.
(*Exeunt severally;* HAMLET *dragging in* POLONIUS.)

ACT IV

SCENE 1. *A room in the castle.*

(*Enter* KING, QUEEN, ROSENCRANTZ, *and*
            GUILDENSTERN.)
    KING. There's matter in these sighs, these profound
        heaves:
You must translate; 'tis fit we understand them.
Where is your son?
    QUEEN. Bestow this place on us a little while.
        (*Exeunt* ROSENCRANTZ *and* GUILDENSTERN.)
Ah, mine own lord, what have I seen tonight!
    KING. What, Gertrude? How does Hamlet?
    QUEEN. Mad as the sea and wind, when both con-
        tend
Which is the mightier: in his lawless fit,
Behind the arras hearing something stir,
Whips out his rapier, cries, 'A rat, a rat!'   10
And, in this brainish apprehension, kills

---

153. **fatness,** grossness. **pursy,** short-winded, corpulent. 155. **curb,** bow. 163. **use,** custom. 169. (**master**). This word has been restored by virtually all editors. 176. **answer,** account for. 184. **reechy,** foul, stinking. 187. **essentially,** in my true nature. 190. **paddock,** toad. **gib.** A gib (short for Gilbert) is a tom (short for Thomas) cat. 191. **dear concernings,** important affairs. 194. **famous ape.** This seems to be an old folk tale, difficult to identify except through passing references. We are indebted to Sir John Suckling, the graceful and attractive Cavalier poet of the seventeenth century for the following details: "It is the story of the jackanapes and the partridges; thou starest after a beauty till it be lost to thee, then let'st out another, and starest after that till it be gone too."

195. **conclusions,** experiments. 204. **sweep my way,** clear my path. 206. **enginer,** the constructor of military works, or perhaps an artilleryman. 207. **Hoist,** lifted, blown up. **petar,** petard, a small engine of war used to blow in a door or gate or effect a breach in a fortified wall; perhaps it may mean a case full of explosive materials. At any rate, the expression has become proverbial for "the biter bit!" 210. **two crafts,** two acts of guile; also, in double meaning, "two ships." 211. **set me packing,** set me to making schemes. 216. **draw,** drag; but there is a quibble on the sense of "draw."
Act IV, Scene I. 11. **brainish apprehension,** headstrong, passionate, compulsion.

The unseen good old man.

    KING.   O heavy deed!
It had been so with us, had we been there:
His liberty is full of threats to all;
To you yourself, to us, to every one.
Alas, how shall this bloody deed be answered?
It will be laid to us, whose providence
Should have kept short, restrained and out of haunt,
This mad young man: but so much was our love,
We would not understand what was most fit;   20
But, like the owner of a foul disease,
To keep it from divulging, let it feed
Even on the pith of life. Where is he gone?

    QUEEN. To draw apart the body he hath killed:
O'er whom his very madness, like some ore
Among a mineral of metals base,
Shows itself pure; he weeps for what is done.

    KING. O Gertrude, come away!
The sun no sooner shall the mountains touch,
But we will ship him hence: and this vile deed   30
We must, with all our majesty and skill,
Both countenance and excuse. Ho, Guildenstern!

    (*Re-enter* ROSENCRANTZ *and* GUILDENSTERN.)
Friends both, go join you with some further aid:
Hamlet in madness hath Polonius slain,
And from his mother's closet hath he dragged him:
Go seek him out; speak fair, and bring the body
Into the chapel. I pray you, haste in this.

    (*Exeunt* ROSENCRANTZ *and* GUILDENSTERN.)
Come, Gertrude, we'll call up our wisest friends;
And let them know, both what we mean to do,   39
And what's untimely done, (so viperous slander),
Whose whisper o'er the world's diameter,
As level as the cannon to his blank,
Transports his poisoned shot, may miss our name,
And hit the woundless air. O, come away!
My soul is full of discord and dismay.   (*Exeunt.*)

SCENE 2. *Another room in the castle.*

(*Enter* HAMLET.)

    HAMLET. Safely stowed.

    ROSENCRANTZ AND GUILDENSTERN (*within*). Hamlet! Lord Hamlet!

    HAMLET. But soft, what noise? who calls on Hamlet? O, here they come.

    (*Enter* ROSENCRANTZ *and* GUILDENSTERN.)

    ROSENCRANTZ. What have you done, my lord, with the dead body?

    HAMLET. Compounded it with dust, whereto 'tis kin.

    ROSENCRANTZ. Tell us where 'tis, that we may take it thence
And bear it to the chapel.

17. providence, foresight, foreknowledge. 18. short; that is, on a short tether. 42. blank, a white spot in the center of a target, the bull's-eye. 44. woundless, invulnerable.

    HAMLET. Do not believe it.

    ROSENCRANTZ. Believe what?   10

    HAMLET. That I can keep your counsel and not mine own. Besides, to be demanded of a sponge! what replication should be made by the son of a king?

    ROSENCRANTZ. Take you me for a sponge, my lord?

    HAMLET. Ay, sir, that soaks up the king's countenance, his rewards, his authorities. But such officers do the king best service in the end: he keeps them, like an ape, in the corner of his jaw; first mouthed, to be last swallowed: when he needs what you have gleaned, it is but squeezing you, and, sponge, you shall be dry again.   23

    ROSENCRANTZ. I understand you not, my lord.

    HAMLET. I am glad of it: a knavish speech sleeps in a foolish ear.

    ROSENCRANTZ. My lord, you must tell us where the body is, and go with us to the king.

    HAMLET. The body is with the king, but the king is not with the body. The king is a thing—

    GUILDENSTERN. A thing, my lord!   31

    HAMLET. Of nothing: bring me to him. Hide fox, and all after.   (*Exeunt.*)

SCENE 3. *Another room in the castle.*

(*Enter* KING, *attended.*)

    KING. I have sent to seek him, and to find the body.
How dangerous is it that this man goes loose!
Yet must not we put the strong law on him:
He's loved of the distracted multitude,
Who like not in their judgment, but their eyes;
And where 'tis so, the offender's scourge is weighed,
But never the offence. To bear all smooth and even,
This sudden sending him away must seem
Deliberate pause: diseases desperate grown
By desperate appliance are relieved,   10
Or not at all.

    (*Enter* ROSENCRANTZ.)
          How now! what hath befallen?

    ROSENCRANTZ. Where the dead body is bestowed, my lord,
We cannot get from him.

Act IV, Scene 2. 11. keep your counsel. Hamlet is aware of the treachery of Rosencrantz and Guildenstern, but says nothing about it. 12. demanded of, questioned by. 13. replication, reply. 17. countenance, favor, patronage. authorities, backing, support. 29–30. body . . . body. This ambiguous line has received many interpretations: "The body lies in death with the king, my father; but my father walks disembodied"; "Claudius has the bodily possession of kingship, but kingliness, or justice of inheritance, is not with him"; "The King is still alive in his body, but he is not with the dead body of Polonius." 32–33. Hide . . . after, a signal cry in the old game of hide-and-seek.
Act IV, Scene 3. 4. distracted, without the ability to form correct or logical judgments—a characteristic attitude of both the Middle Ages and the Renaissance toward the democratic spirit. 6. scourge, punishment. 9. Deliberate pause, considered action.

KING. But where is he?

ROSENCRANTZ. Without, my lord; guarded, to know
your pleasure.

KING. Bring him before us.

ROSENCRANTZ. Ho, Guildenstern! bring in my lord.

(*Enter* HAMLET *and* GUILDENSTERN.)

KING. Now, Hamlet, where's Polonius?

HAMLET. At supper.

KING. At supper! where?   19

HAMLET. Not where he eats, but where he is eaten:
a certain convocation of politic worms are e'en at
him. Your worm is your only emperor for diet: we
fat all creatures else to fat us, and we fat ourselves
for maggots; your fat king and your lean beggar is
but variable service, two dishes, but to one table;
that's the end.   26

KING. Alas, alas!

HAMLET. A man may fish with the worm that hath
eat of a king, and eat of the fish that hath fed of
that worm.   30

KING. What dost thou mean by this?

HAMLET. Nothing but to show you how a king may
go a progress through the guts of a beggar.

KING. Where is Polonius?

HAMLET. In Heaven; send thither to see: if your
messenger find him not there, seek him i' the other
place yourself. But indeed, if you find him not within
this month, you shall nose him as you go up the
stairs into the lobby.

KING. Go seek him there.   40

(*To some* Attendants.)

HAMLET. He will stay till you come.

(*Exeunt* Attendants.)

KING. Hamlet, this deed, for thine especial
safety,—

Which we do tender, as we dearly grieve
For that which thou hast done,—must send thee
hence
With fiery quickness: therefore prepare thyself;
The bark is ready, and the wind at help,
The associates tend, and everything is bent
For England.

HAMLET.   For England!

KING.   Ay, Hamlet.

HAMLET.   Good.

KING. So is it, if thou knewest our purposes.

HAMLET. I see a cherub that sees them. But, come;
for England!

Farewell, dear mother.

KING. Thy loving father, Hamlet.   52

HAMLET. My mother: father and mother is man
and wife; man and wife is one flesh; and so, my
mother. Come, for England!   (*Exit.*)

21. convocation . . . worms, a jesting allusion to the Diet of Worms
(1521), from which Luther departed to continue the German Reformation. politic, crafty. 25. variable service, a variety of dishes, a
change of diet. 33. progress, a royal journey of state. 43. tender,
hold dear, value. 50. cherub, the angel of knowledge.

KING. Follow him at foot; tempt him with speed
aboard;

Delay it not; I'll have him hence tonight:
Away! for every thing is sealed and done
That else leans on the affair: pray you, make haste.

(*Exeunt* ROSENCRANTZ *and* GUILDENSTERN.)

And, England, if my love thou holdest at aught—   60
As my great power thereof may give thee sense,
Since yet thy cicatrice looks raw and red
After the Danish sword, and thy free awe
Pays homage to us—thou mayst not coldly set
Our sovereign process; which imports at full,
By letters congruing to that effect,
The present death of Hamlet. Do it, England:
For like the hectic in my blood he rages,
And thou must cure me: till I know 'tis done,   69
Howe'er my haps, my joys were ne'er begun. (*Exit.*)

SCENE 4. *A plain in Denmark.*

(*Enter* FORTINBRAS, *a Captain, and* Soldiers,
marching.)

FORTINBRAS. Go, captain, from me greet the Danish king;

Tell him that, by his license, Fortinbras
Craves the conveyance of a promised march
Over his kingdom. You know the rendezvous.
If that his majesty would aught with us,
We shall express our duty in his eye;
And let him know so.

CAPTAIN.   I will do 't, my lord.

FORTINBRAS. Go softly on.

(*Exeunt* FORTINBRAS *and* Soldiers.)

(*Enter* HAMLET, ROSENCRANTZ, GUILDENSTERN, *and*
Others.)

HAMLET. Good sir, whose powers are these?

CAPTAIN. They are of Norway, sir.   10

HAMLET. How purposed, sir, I pray you?

CAPTAIN. Against some part of Poland.

HAMLET. Who commands them, sir?

CAPTAIN. The nephew to old Norway, Fortinbras.

HAMLET. Goes it against the main of Poland, sir,
Or for some frontier?

CAPTAIN. Truly to speak, and with no addition,
We go to gain a little patch of ground
That hath in it no profit but the name.
To pay five ducats, five, I would not farm it;   20
Nor will it yield to Norway or the Pole
A ranker rate, should it be sold in fee.

56. at foot, close behind, on his heels. 63. free awe, awe not inspired
by threat of force. 65. process, formal command, mandate. 68.
hectic, fever. 70. haps, fortunes.
Act IV, Scene 4. 2. license, leave. 3. conveyance, convoy, escort.
6. in his eye, in his presence. 8. softly, slowly. 15. main, the chief
part of the country, the country itself. 17. addition, amplification,
elaboration. 20. farm it, take a lease of it. 22. ranker, higher,
better. in fee, in fee simple, outright.

HAMLET. Why, then the Polack never will defend it.

CAPTAIN. Yes, it is already garrisoned.

HAMLET. Two thousand souls and twenty thousand ducats
Will not debate the question of this straw:
This is the imposthume of much wealth and peace,
That inward breaks, and shows no cause without
Why the man dies. I humbly thank you, sir.

CAPTAIN. God be wi' you, sir.   (*Exit.*)

ROSENCRANTZ. Will 't please you go, my lord?   30

HAMLET. I'll be with you straight. Go a little be-
fore.   (*Exeunt all except* HAMLET.)
How all occasions do inform against me,
And spur my dull revenge! What is a man,
If his chief good and market of his time
Be but to sleep and feed? a beast, no more.
Sure, he that made us with such large discourse,
Looking before and after, gave us not
That capability and god-like reason
To fust in us unused. Now, whether it be
Bestial oblivion, or some craven scruple   40
Of thinking too precisely on the event,
A thought which, quartered, hath but one part wis-
dom
And ever three parts coward, I do not know
Why yet I live to say 'This thing's to do';
Sith I have cause and will and strength and means
To do 't. Examples gross as earth exhort me:
Witness this army of such mass and charge
Led by a delicate and tender prince,
Whose spirit with divine ambition puffed
Makes mouths at the invisible event,   50
Exposing what is mortal and unsure
To all that fortune, death and danger dare,
Even for an egg-shell. Rightly to be great
Is not to stir without great argument,
But greatly to find quarrel in a straw
When honor's at the stake. How stand I then,
That have a father killed, a mother stained,
Excitements of my reason and my blood,
And let all sleep? while, to my shame, I see
The imminent death of twenty thousand men,
That, for a fantasy and trick of fame,   61
Go to their graves like beds, fight for a plot
Whereon the numbers cannot try the cause,
Which is not tomb enough and continent
To hide the slain? O, from this time forth,
My thoughts be bloody, or be nothing worth! (*Exit.*)

SCENE 5. *Elsinore. A room in the castle.*

(*Enter* QUEEN, HORATIO, *and* a Gentleman.)

QUEEN. I will not speak with her.

GENTLEMAN. She is importunate, indeed distract:
Her mood will needs be pitied.

QUEEN.   What would she have?

GENTLEMAN. She speaks much of her father; says she hears
There's tricks i' the world; and hems, and beats her heart;
Spurns enviously at straws; speaks things in doubt,
That carry but half sense: her speech is nothing,
Yet the unshaped use of it doth move
The hearers to collection; they aim at it,   9
And botch the words up fit to their own thoughts;
Which, as her winks, and nods, and gestures yield them,
Indeed would make one think there might be thought,
Though nothing sure, yet much unhappily.

HORATIO. 'Twere good she were spoken with: for she may strew
Dangerous conjectures in ill-breeding minds.

QUEEN. Let her come in.

(*Exit* HORATIO.)
To my sick soul, as sin's true nature is,
Each toy seems prologue to some great amiss:
So full of artless jealousy is guilt,
It spills itself in fearing to be spilt.   20

(*Re-enter* HORATIO, *with* OPHELIA.)

OPHELIA. Where is the beauteous majesty of Denmark?

QUEEN. How now, Ophelia!

OPHELIA (*sings*). How should I your true love know
            From another one?
        By his cockle hat and staff,
            And his sandal shoon.

QUEEN. Alas, sweet lady, what imports this song?

OPHELIA. Say you? nay, pray you, mark.
        He is dead and gone, lady,
            He is dead and gone;   30
        At his head a grass-green turf,
            At his heels a stone.

QUEEN. Nay, but, Ophelia,—

26. debate . . . straw, settle this trivial matter. 27. imposthume, a purulent abscess or swelling. 32. occasions, happenings, events. inform against, show up, betray; Hamlet is becoming impatient at his own dilatory behavior. 34. chief good . . . time, profit derived from selling (making use) of his time. 36. discourse, power of reasoning. 39. fust, grow moldy, decay. 41. event, outcome. 45. Sith, since. 54. argument, cause, reason. 58. Excitements of, incentives, inspirations to. blood, passion. 61. trick, toy, trifle. 64. continent, containing, holding (adj.)

Act IV, Scene 5. 5. tricks, deceptions, deceits. 6. Spurns enviously, kicks spitefully. 8. unshaped, unformed, artless. 9. collection, inference. aim, guess. 10. botch, patch. 11. yield, bring them forth. 13. nothing, not at all. 18. toy, trifle. great amiss, great disaster, calamity. 19–20. So full . . . spilt. Guilt is so full of suspicion that it unskilfully betrays itself in fearing to be revealed. 25. cockle hat, a hat worn with a cockle-shell attached to it, as a sign that the wearer had been on a pilgrimage to the famous shrine of Saint James (Santiago) of Compostella. In medieval romances the dress of a pilgrim, or palmer, was a conventional disguise for a lover. 26. shoon, the old *n* plural of shoe.

OPHELIA. Pray you, mark
 (*Sings*). White his shroud as the mountain snow,—
 (*Enter* KING.)
QUEEN. Alas, look here, my lord.
OPHELIA (*sings*). Larded with sweet flowers;
 Which bewept to the grave did
 go
 With true-love showers.
KING. How do you, pretty lady? 40
OPHELIA. Well, God 'ild you! They say the owl was a baker's daughter. Lord, we know what we are, but know not what we may be. God be at your table!
KING. Conceit upon her father.
OPHELIA. Pray you, let's have no words of this; but when they ask you what it means, say you this:
 (*Sings*). Tomorrow is Saint Valentine's
 day,
 All in the morning betime,
 And I a maid at your window,
 To be your Valentine. 51
 Then up he rose, and donned
 his clothes,
 And dupped the chamber-
 door;
 Let in the maid, that out a maid
 Never departed more.
KING. Pretty Ophelia!
OPHELIA. Indeed, la, without an oath, I'll make an end on 't:
 (*Sings*). By Gis and by Saint Charity,
 Alack, and fie for shame! 60
 Young men will do 't, if they
 come to 't;
 By cock, they are to blame,
 Quoth she, 'Before you tumbled
 me,
 You promised me to wed.'
 'So would I ha' done, by yonder
 sun,
 An thou hadst not come to
 my bed.'
KING. How long hath she been thus?
OPHELIA. I hope all will be well. We must be patient; but I cannot choose but weep, to think they should lay him i' the cold ground. My brother shall know of it: and so I thank you for your good counsel.

Come, my coach! Good night, ladies; good night, sweet ladies; good night, good night. (*Exit.*) 74
KING. Follow her close; give her good watch, I pray you.
 (*Exit* HORATIO.)
O, this is the poison of deep grief; it springs
All from her father's death. O Gertrude, Gertrude,
When sorrows come, they come not single spies,
But in battalions. First, her father slain:
Next, your son gone; and he most violent author 80
Of his own just remove: the people muddied,
Thick and unwholesome in their thoughts and whispers,
For good Polonius' death; and we have done but greenly,
In hugger-mugger to inter him: poor Ophelia
Divided from herself and her fair judgment,
Without the which we are pictures, or mere beasts:
Last, and as much containing as all these,
Her brother is in secret come from France;
Feeds on his wonder, keeps himself in clouds,
And wants not buzzers to infect his ear 90
With pestilent speeches of his father's death;
Wherein necessity, of matter beggared,
Will nothing stick our person to arraign
In ear and ear. O my dear Gertrude, this,
Like to a murdering-piece, in many places
Gives me superfluous death.
 (*A noise within.*)
QUEEN. Alack, what noise is this?
KING. Where are my Switzers? Let them guard the door.
 (*Enter another* Gentleman.)
What is the matter?
GENTLEMAN. Save yourself, my lord:
The ocean, overpeering of his list,
Eats not the flats with more impetuous haste
Than young Laertes, in a riotous head, 101
O'erbears your officers. The rabble call him lord;
And, as the world were now but to begin,
Antiquity forgot, custom not known,
The ratifiers and props of every word,
They cry, 'Choose we: Laertes shall be king':
Caps, hands, and tongues, applaud it to the clouds:
'Laertes shall be king, Laertes king!' 108
QUEEN. How cheerfully on the false trail they cry!
O, this is counter, you false Danish dogs!

37. **Larded,** decorated, garnished. 41. **God 'ild,** God yield or reward. 42. **owl . . . daughter,** referring to an old medieval legend that a baker's daughter, refusing bread to Christ, was turned into an owl. 45. **Conceit . . . father,** her imagination is directed toward her dead father. 51. **Valentine,** according to the old tradition, the first girl seen by a man on the morning of St. Valentine's Day was his valentine or sweetheart. Ophelia makes the legend work in reverse. 53. **dupped,** opened. 59. **Gis,** a corruption of Jesus. 62. **cock,** a perversion of God used in oaths. 66. **An,** if.

83. **greenly,** foolishly, in immature fashion. 84. **hugger-mugger,** secret and confused haste. 89. **in clouds,** invisible. 90. **buzzers,** gossipers, tattletales. 93. **nothing stick,** not hesitate in any way. 94. **in ear and ear,** in everybody's ear. 95. **murdering-piece,** a small cannon loaded with many small missiles, a kind of cannonized shotgun. 97. **Switzers,** Swiss guards, mercenaries. 99. **overpeering of his list,** overflowing his boundaries. 101. **head,** armed force. 102. **O'erbears,** overcomes, seduces. 105. **word,** title, custom. 110. **counter,** an old hunting term indicating that the trail is being followed in a direction opposite to that taken by the game.

KING. The doors are broke.

(*Noise within.*)

(*Enter* LAERTES, *armed;* Danes *following.*)

LAERTES. Where is this king? Sirs, stand you all
    without.

DANES. No, let's come in.

LAERTES.   I pray you, give me leave.

DANES. We will, we will.

(*They retire without the door.*)

LAERTES. I thank you: keep the door. O thou vile
    king,
Give me my father!

KING.   Calmly, good Laertes.

LAERTES. That drop of blood that's calm proclaims
    me bastard,
Cries cuckold to my father, brands the harlot
Even here, between the chaste unsmirched brow
Of my true mother.

KING.   What is the cause, Laertes,
That thy rebellion looks so giant-like?   121
Let him go, Gertrude; do not fear our person:
There's such divinity doth hedge a king,
That treason can but peep to what it would,
Acts little of his will. Tell me, Laertes,
Why thou art thus incensed. Let him go, Gertrude.
Speak, man.

LAERTES.   Where is my father?

KING.   Dead.

QUEEN.   But not by him.

KING. Let him demand his fill.

LAERTES. How came he dead? I'll not be juggled
    with: 130
To Hell, allegiance! vows, to the blackest devil!
Conscience and grace, to the profoundest pit!
I dare damnation. To this point I stand,
That both the worlds I give to negligence,
Let come what comes; only I'll be revenged
Most thoroughly for my father.

KING.   Who shall stay you?

LAERTES. My will, not all the world:
And for my means, I'll husband them so well,
They shall go far with little.

KING.   Good Laertes,
If you desire to know the certainty   140
Of your dear father's death, is 't writ in your revenge,
That, swoopstake, you will draw both friend and foe,
Winner and loser?

LAERTES.   None but his enemies.

KING.   Will you know them then?

LAERTES. To his good friends thus wide I'll ope
    my arms;
And like the kind life-rendering pelican,

Repast them with my blood.

KING.   Why, now you speak
Like a good child and a true gentleman.
That I am guiltless of your father's death,
And am most sensibly in grief for it,   150
It shall as level to your judgment pierce
As day does to your eye.

DANES (*within*).   Let her come in.

LAERTES. How now! what noise is that?

(*Re-enter* OPHELIA.)

O heat, dry up my brains! tears seven times salt,
Burn out the sense and virtue of mine eye!
By Heaven, thy madness shall be paid with weight,
Till our scale turn the beam. O rose of May!
Dear maid, kind sister, sweet Ophelia!
O heavens! is 't possible, a young maid's wits
Should be as mortal as an old man's life?   160
Nature is fine in love, and where 'tis fine,
It sends some precious instance of itself
After the thing it loves.

OPHELIA (*sings*). They bore him barefaced on the
            bier;
        Hey non nonny, nonny, hey
           nonny;
        And in his grave rained many
           a tear:——

Fare you well, my dove!

LAERTES. Hadst thou thy wits, and didst persuade
    revenge,
It could not move thus.

OPHELIA (*sings*). You must sing a-down a-down,
        An you call him a-down-a.   171
O how the wheel becomes it! It is the false steward,
that stole his master's daughter.

LAERTES. This nothing's more than matter.

OPHELIA. There's rosemary, that's for remembrance; pray, love, remember: and there is pansies,
that's for thoughts.

LAERTES. A document in madness, thoughts and
remembrance fitted.   179

OPHELIA. There's fennel for you, and columbines:
there's rue for you; and here's some for me: we may
call it herb-grace o' Sundays: O, you must wear your
rue with a difference. There's a daisy: I would give

146. **pelican,** an allusion to the old belief that a pelican fed its young with its own blood. 147. **repast,** feed. 150. **sensibly,** feelingly. 154. **heat,** emotion, passion—both of which were supposed to generate heat. 172. **wheel,** possibly a refrain; possibly referring to a spinning-wheel which accompanied the singing of the song. **false steward.** The exact story to which this is an allusion is not precisely known, but the false steward is a stock figure in medieval romances and ballads. 175. **rosemary,** used as a symbol of remembrance both at weddings and at funerals. 177. **pansies,** symbols of love and courtship. 178. **document,** a lesson or piece of instruction. 180. **fennel,** the symbol of flattery. **columbines,** symbols of unchastity and ingratitude. 181. **rue,** the symbol of repentance; when mingled with holy water it was called "herb of grace." But Ophelia is probably playing on the two meanings of the word: "repentant" and "having pity." 183. **difference,** in heraldry, a distinction in the coats of arms for different branches of the family.

122. **fear,** have fears for. 132. **grace,** God's favor. 134. **both the worlds . . . negligence,** I have contempt for both the present and the hereafter. 142. **swoopstake,** one who gathers all his winnings at dice in one swoop; hence, any indiscriminate action.

you some violets, but they withered all when my father died: they say he made a good end,—   186
(*Sings*): For bonny sweet Robin is all my joy.

LAERTES. Thought and affliction, passion, Hell itself,
She turns to favor and to prettiness.   189

OPHELIA (*sings*).   And will he not come again?
And will he not come again?
No, no, he is dead:
Go to thy death-bed:
He never will come again.

His beard was as white as snow,
All flaxen was his poll;
He is gone, he is gone,
And we cast away moan:
God ha' mercy on his soul!

And of all Christian souls, I pray God. God be wi' ye.
(*Exit.*)

LAERTES. Do you see this, O God?   201

KING. Laertes, I must commune with your grief,
Or you deny me right. Go but apart,
Make choice of whom your wisest friends you will,
And they shall hear and judge 'twixt you and me:
If by direct or by collateral hand
They find us touched, we will our kingdom give,
Our crown, our life, and all that we call ours,
To you in satisfaction; but if not,
Be you content to lend your patience to us,   210
And we shall jointly labor with your soul
To give it due content.

LAERTES.   Let this be so;
His means of death, his obscure funeral—
No trophy, sword, nor hatchment o'er his bones,
No noble rite nor formal ostentation—
Cry to be heard, as 'twere from heaven to earth,
That I must call 't in question.

KING.   So you shall;
And where the offence is let the great axe fall.
I pray you, go with me.   (*Exeunt.*)

SCENE 6. *Another room in the castle.*

(*Enter* HORATIO *and a* Servant.)

HORATIO. What are they that would speak
with me?

SERVANT. Sailors, sir: they say they have letters
for you.

HORATIO. Let them come in.   (*Exit* Servant.)
I do not know from what part of the world
I should be greeted, if not from lord Hamlet.

(*Enters* Sailors.)

FIRST SAILOR. God bless you, sir.

HORATIO. Let him bless thee too.

FIRST SAILOR. He shall, sir, an 't please him.
There's a letter for you, sir; it comes from the ambassador that was bound for England; if your name
be Horatio, as I am let to know it is.   11

HORATIO (*reads*). 'Horatio, when thou shalt have
overlooked this, give these fellows some means to
the king: they have letters for him. Ere we were two
days old at sea, a pirate of very warlike appointment
gave us chase. Finding ourselves too slow of sail, we
put on a compelled valor, and in the grapple I
boarded them: on the instant they got clear of our
ship; so I alone became their prisoner. They have
dealt with me like thieves of mercy: but they knew
what they did; I am to do a good turn for them. Let
the king have the letters I have sent; and repair thou
to me with as much speed as thou wouldst fly death.
I have words to speak in thine ear will make thee
dumb; yet are they much too light for the bore of
the matter. These good fellows will bring thee where
I am. Rosencrantz and Guildenstern hold their course
for England; of them I have much to tell thee. Farewell.   30
'He that thou knowest thine,
HAMLET.'
Come, I will make you way for these your letters;
And do 't the speedier, that you may direct me
To him from whom you brought them.   (*Exeunt.*)

SCENE 7. *Another room in the castle.*

(*Enter* KING *and* LAERTES.)

KING. Now must your conscience my acquittance
seal,
And you must put me in your heart for friend,
Sith you have heard, and with a knowing ear,
That he which hath your noble father slain
Pursued my life.

LAERTES.   It well appears: but tell me
Why you proceeded not against these feats,
So crimeful and so capital in nature,
As by your safety, wisdom, all things else,
You mainly were stirred up.

KING.   O, for two special reasons;
Which may to you, perhaps, seem much unsinewed,
But yet to me they are strong. The queen his mother
Lives almost by his looks; and for myself—   12

---

184. **daisy,** symbol of faithlessness and dissembling; **violets,** on the
other hand, symbolize constancy and sincerity. 187. **For bonny
. . . joy,** probably a line from a Robin Hood ballad.   188. **Thought,**
melancholy thoughts. 189. **favor,** attraction, charm. 190–199.
And will . . . soul, a popular song of the time entitled *The Merry
Milkmaids* or, somewhat confusingly, *The Milkmaids' Dumps.* 196.
poll, head. 203. **right,** my rights. 206. **collateral,** indirect. 207.
touched, implicated, involved. 214. **hatchment,** in heraldry, a
tablet displaying the armorial bearings of a deceased person.

Act IV, Scene 6. 14. **means,** access. 16. **appointment,** equipment
and manner. 21. **thieves of mercy.** This is an old rhetorical device,
thieves of mercy equals *merciful thieves.* 27. **bore,** caliber, scope.
Act IV, Scene 7. 1. **conscience,** knowledge that a thing is true.
9. **mainly,** greatly, mightily.

My virtue or my plague, be it either which—
She's so conjunctive to my life and soul,
That, as the star moves not but in his sphere,
I could not but by her. The other motive,
Why to a public count I might not go,
Is the great love the general gender bear him;
Who, dipping all his faults in their affection,
Would, like the spring that turneth wood to stone,
Convert his gyves to graces; so that my arrows,   21
Too slightly timbered for so loud a wind,
Would have reverted to my bow again,
And not where I had aimed them.

LAERTES. And so have I a noble father lost;
A sister driven into desperate terms,
Whose worth, if praises may go back again,
Stood challenger on mount of all the age
For her perfections: but my revenge will come.

KING. Break not your sleeps for that: you must not
          think   30
That we are made of stuff so flat and dull
That we can let our beard be shook with danger
And think it pastime. You shortly shall hear more:
I loved your father, and we love ourself;
And that, I hope, will teach you to imagine—
               (*Enter a* Messenger.)
How now! what news?

MESSENGER.   Letters, my lord, from Hamlet:
This to your majesty; this to the queen.

KING. From Hamlet! who brought them?

MESSENGER. Sailors, my lord, they say; I saw them
          not: 39
They were given me by Claudio; he received them
Of him that brought them.

KING.   Laertes, you shall hear them.
Leave us.   (*Exit* MESSENGER.)
(*Reads*). 'High and mighty, You shall know I am set
naked on your kingdom. Tomorrow shall I beg leave
to see your kingly eyes: when I shall, first asking your
pardon thereunto, recount the occasion of my sudden
and more strange return.

                              HAMLET.'
What should this mean? Are all the rest come back?
Or is it some abuse, and no such thing?   51

LAERTES. Know you the hand?

KING.   'Tis Hamlet's character. 'Naked!'
And in a postscript here, he says 'alone.'
Can you advise me?

LAERTES. I'm lost in it, my lord. But let him come;
It warms the very sickness in my heart,

That I shall live and tell him to his teeth,
'Thus didst thou.'

KING.   If it be so, Laertes—
As how should it be so? how otherwise?—
Will you be ruled by me?

LAERTES.   Ay, my lord;   60
So you will not o'errule me to a peace.

KING. To thine own peace. If he be now returned,
As checking at his voyage, and that he means
No more to undertake it, I will work him
To an exploit, now ripe in my device,
Under the which he shall not choose but fall:
And for his death no wind of blame shall breathe,
But even his mother shall uncharge the practice
And call it accident.

LAERTES.   My lord, I will be ruled;
The rather, if you could devise it so   70
That I might be the organ.

KING.   It falls right.
You have been talked of since your travel much,
And that in Hamlet's hearing, for a quality
Wherein, they say, you shine; your sum of parts
Did not together pluck such envy from him
As did that one, and that, in my regard,
Of the unworthiest siege.

LAERTES.   What part is that, my lord?

KING. A very riband in the cap of youth,
Yet needful too; for youth no less becomes
The light and careless livery that it wears   80
Than settled age his sables and his weeds,
Importing health and graveness. Two months since,
Here was a gentleman of Normandy:—
I've seen myself, and served against, the French,
And they can well on horseback: but this gallant
Had witchcraft in 't; he grew upon his seat;
And to such wondrous doing brought his horse,
As had he been incorpsed and demi-natured
With the brave beast: so far he topped my thought,
That I, in forgery of shapes and tricks,   90
Came short of what he did.

LAERTES.   A Norman was 't?

KING. A Norman.

LAERTES. Upon my life, Lamond.

KING.   The very same.

14. **conjunctive,** conformable, closely joined. 16. Insert "be" between "but" and "by." 17. **count,** account, reckoning. 18. **general gender,** the common people. 20. **spring,** snare so heavily limed as to cake wood. 26. **terms,** state, condition. 28. **on mount,** set up on high as a model. 37. **to the queen.** The content of Hamlet's letter to his mother is never told; in fact, the missive seems to have slipped completely from Shakespeare's mind. 40. **Claudio.** This character does not appear on the stage at any time in the play. 44. **naked,** without retinue or followers. 51. **abuse,** deception. 53. **character,** handwriting.

59. **how should . . . otherwise?** How can this be true? And yet, with this evidence of the letter, can Hamlet's return be anything but true? 63. **checking at,** in falconry, the term used to denote the action of a bird's leaving the pursuit of the quarry in order to attack a passing bird. 68. **uncharge the practice,** not object to the plan. 71. **organ,** instrument, means, agent. 77. **siege,** rank, seat. 81. **sables . . . weeds,** rich garments and clothing appropriate to old age. 82. **health,** wealth and prosperity, worldly success. 85. **can well,** know well how to perform, are skilled. 88. **incorpsed and demi-natured,** inclosed in one body and nearly of one nature, as a centaur contains the man and the horse in one body and is chiefly horselike. 90. **forgery,** invention. 93. **Lamond.** Pietro Monte, instructor to the Master of Horse at the court of Louis XII, King of France in Shakespeare's day, is very likely disguised here under the name of Lamond.

LAERTES. I know him well: he is the brooch indeed
And gem of all the nation.
KING. He made confession of you,
And gave you such a masterly report
For art and exercise in your defence
And for your rapier most especial.
That he cried out, 'twould be a sight indeed,   100
If one could match you: the scrimers of their nation,
He swore, had neither motion, guard, nor eye,
If you opposed them. Sir, this report of his
Did Hamlet so envenom with his envy
That he could nothing do but wish and beg
Your sudden coming o'er, to play with him.
Now, out of this,—
     LAERTES.   What out of this, my lord?
     KING. Laertes, was your father dear to you?
Or are you like the painting of a sorrow,
A face without a heart?
     LAERTES.   Why ask you this?   110
     KING. Not that I think you did not love your father;
But that I know love is begun by time;
And that I see, in passages of proof,
Time qualifies the spark and fire of it.
There lives within the very flame of love
A kind of wick or snuff that will abate it;
And nothing is at a like goodness still;
For goodness, growing to a plurisy,
Dies in his own too much: that we would do,
We should do when we would; for this 'would'
          changes   120
And hath abatements and delays as many
As there are tongues, are hands, are accidents;
And then this 'should' is like a spendthrift sigh,
That hurts by easing. But, to the quick o' the ulcer:—
Hamlet comes back; what would you undertake,
To show yourself your father's son in deed
More than in words?
     LAERTES.   To cut his throat i' the church.
     KING. No place, indeed, should murder sanctuarize;
Revenge should have no bounds. But, good Laertes,
Will you do this, keep close within your chamber.   130
Hamlet returned shall know you are come home:
We'll put on those shall praise your excellence
And set a double varnish on the fame
The Frenchman gave you, bring you in fine together
And wager on your heads: he, being remiss,

Most generous and free from all contriving,
Will not peruse the foils; so that, with ease,
Or with a little shuffling, you may choose
A sword unbated, and in a pass of practice
Requite him for your father.
     LAERTES.   I will do 't: 140
And, for that purpose, I'll anoint my sword.
I bought an unction of a mountebank,
So mortal that, but dip a knife in it,
Where it draws blood no cataplasm so rare,
Collected from all simples that have virtue
Under the moon, can save the thing from death
That is but scratched withal: I'll touch my point
With this contagion, that, if I gall him slightly
It may be death.
     KING.   Let's further think of this;
Weigh what convenience both of time and means   150
May fit us to our shape: if this should fail,
And that our drift look through our bad performance,
'Twere better not assayed: therefore this project
Should have a back or second, that might hold,
If this should blast in proof. Soft! let me see:
We'll make a solemn wager on your cunnings:
I ha 't:
When in your motion you are hot and dry—
As make your bouts more violent to that end—
And that he calls for drink, I'll have prepared him   160
A chalice for the nonce, whereon but sipping,
If he by chance escape your venomed stuck,
Our purpose may hold there.
          (Enter QUEEN.)
                    How now, sweet queen!
     QUEEN. One woe doth tread upon another's heel,
So fast they follow: your sister's drowned, Laertes.
     LAERTES. Drowned! O, where?
     QUEEN. There is a willow grows aslant a brook,
That shows his hoar leaves in the glassy stream;
There with fantastic garlands did she make
Of crow-flowers, nettles, daisies, and long purples   170
That liberal shepherds give a grosser name,
But our cold maids do dead men's fingers call them;
There, on the pendent boughs her coronet weeds
Clambering to hang, an envious sliver broke;
When down her weedy trophies and herself
Fell in the weeping brook. Her clothes spread wide;
And, mermaid-like, awhile they bore her up:

96. **confession of you,** a report of you. 98. **art and exercise,** skillful exercise. **defence,** self-defence with sword and rapier. 101. **scrimers,** fencers. 106. **play,** fence. 113. **passages of proof,** proved instances or occasions. 117. **still,** ever, always. 118. **plurisy,** excess, plethora. 119. **his own too much,** its own excess. 121. **abatements,** diminutions, losses. 122. **accidents,** events, happenings. 123. **spendthrift.** There was an old belief that each sigh cost the human heart a drop of blood. 124. **quick o' the ulcer,** the core of the abscess, the heart of the matter. 128. **sanctuarize,** protect from punishment. In medieval times, certain religious places were endowed with the privilege of sanctuary; all criminals taking refuge in those places were immune from arrest pending consideration of their cases by church authorities.

139. **unbated,** not blunted or dulled. **pass of practice,** an unexpected and treacherous thrust. 144. **cataplasm,** a plaster used as a poultice. 145. **simples,** herbs, recipes, prescriptions. 146. **Under the moon.** To pick an herb by moonlight was to enhance its medicinal effects. 148. **gall,** scratch, graze. 151. **shape,** planned action. 152. **drift . . . performance,** intention be revealed through our bungling. 155. **blast in proof,** burst or explode in testing, as a cannon. 156. **cunnings,** skills. 162. **stuck,** thrust; cf. Italian *stoccado*. 167. **willow,** dramatically appropriate, for this tree was a symbol of forsaken love 170. **crow-flowers,** buttercups. **long purples,** the early purple orchis. 171. **liberal,** free- or broad-spoken. 173. **coronet,** garlanded; an adjective here. 174. **sliver,** branch; **envious,** in the sense of evil, malicious.

Which time she chanted snatches of old tunes;
As one incapable of her own distress,
Or like a creature native and indued   180
Unto that element: but long it could not be
Till that her garments, heavy with their drink,
Pulled the poor wretch from her melodious lay
To muddy death.

LAERTES.   Alas, then, she is drowned?
QUEEN. Drowned, drowned.
LAERTES. Too much of water hast thou, poor
    Ophelia,
And therefore I forbid my tears: but yet
It is our trick; nature her custom holds,
Let shame say what it will: when these are gone,
The woman will be out. Adieu, my lord: 190
I have a speech of fire, that fain would blaze,
But that this folly douts it.   (*Exit.*)
KING.   Let's follow, Gertrude:
How much I had to do to calm his rage!
Now fear I this will give it start again;
Therefore let's follow.   (*Exeunt.*)

ACT V

SCENE 1. *A churchyard.*

(*Enter two* Clowns, *with spades, etc.*)

FIRST CLOWN. Is she to be buried in Christian burial that wilfully seeks her own salvation?

SECOND CLOWN. I tell thee she is; and therefore make her grave straight: the crowner hath sat on her, and finds it Christian burial.   5

FIRST CLOWN. How can that be, unless she drowned herself in her own defence?

SECOND CLOWN. Why, 'tis found so.

FIRST CLOWN. It must be 'se offendendo'; it cannot be else. For here lies the point: if I drown myself wittingly, it argues an act: and an act hath three branches: it is, to act, to do, and to perform: argal, she drowned herself wittingly.   14

SECOND CLOWN. Nay, but hear you, goodman delver,—

FIRST CLOWN. Give me leave. Here lies the water; good; here stands the man: good; if the man go to this water, and drown himself, it is, will he, nill he, he goes,—mark you that; but if the water come to him and drown him, he drowns not himself: argal, he that is not guilty of his own death shortens not his own life.

SECOND CLOWN. But is this law?   23

FIRST CLOWN. Ay, marry, is 't; crowner's quest law.

SECOND CLOWN. Will you ha' the truth on 't? If this had not been a gentlewoman, she should have been buried out o' Christian burial.   28

FIRST CLOWN. Why, there thou sayest: and the more pity that great folk should have countenance in this world to drown or hang themselves, more than their even Christian. Come, my spade. There is no ancient gentleman but gardeners, ditchers, and grave-makers: they hold up Adam's profession.

SECOND CLOWN. Was he a gentleman?

FIRST CLOWN. A' was the first that ever bore arms.

SECOND CLOWN. Why, he had none.   39

FIRST CLOWN. What, art a heathen? How dost thou understand the Scripture? The Scripture says 'Adam digged': could he dig without arms? I'll put another question to thee: if thou answerest me not to the purpose, confess thyself—   44

SECOND CLOWN. Go to.

FIRST CLOWN. What is he that builds stronger than either the mason, the shipwright, or the carpenter?

SECOND CLOWN. The gallows-maker, for that frame outlives a thousand tenants.   50

FIRST CLOWN. I like thy wit well, in good faith: the gallows does well: but how does it well? it does well to those who do ill: now thou dost ill to say the gallows is built stronger than the church: argal, the gallows may do well to thee. To 't again, come.

SECOND CLOWN. 'Who builds stronger than a mason, a shipwright, or a carpenter?'

FIRST CLOWN. Ay, tell me that, and unyoke.

SECOND CLOWN. Marry, now I can tell.   60

FIRST CLOWN. To 't.

SECOND CLOWN. Mass, I cannot tell.

(*Enter* HAMLET *and* HORATIO, *at a distance.*)

FIRST CLOWN. Cudgel thy brains no more about it, for your dull ass will not mend his pace with beating; and, when you are asked the question next, say 'a grave-maker': the houses that he makes last till doomsday. Go, get thee to Yaughan: fetch me a stoup of liquor.   (*Exit second* Clown.)
(*He digs and sings.*)

179. incapable, unable to comprehend. 180. indued, endowed with qualities enabling her to live in water. 186–187. Too much of water . . . tears. Evidently puns and conceits of this sort were not considered inappropriate for even the most solemn occasions in Elizabethan courtly fashion. 188. trick, way, the way of the world. 189–190. when these . . . will be out, when these tears have been shed, my womanlike feelings will be satisfied. 192. douts it, does it out, suppresses or extinguishes it.
Act V, Scene 1. Stage Direction: Clowns. The word *clown* was used to denote a peasant as well as a professional humorous character; the gravediggers here are of the rustic type of clown. 4. straight, straightway, immediately. crowner, coroner. 9. 'se offendendo.' The grave-digger means '*se defendendo*,' a term used in verdicts of justifiable homicides committed in self-defense. 12. three branches, a broad take-off on legal language. 13. argal, a corruption of the Latin *ergo*, "therefore." The clown may perhaps be unwittingly committing a pun on "argue."

24. quest, inquest. 29. there thou sayest, that's right, "you've got something there." 31. countenance, privilege, the "face" to do something. 32. even Christian, fellow Christian. 44. confess thyself. "And be hanged" completes the quotation. 59. unyoke, after your effort you may unharness your oxen. 62. Mass, by the Mass. 68. Yaughan, probably a London tavern-keeper of some sort of note, but the word has been subjected to much scrutiny. stoup, a two-quart measure.

In youth, when I did love, did love,
  Methought it was very sweet,   70
To contract, O, the time, for, ah, my behove,
  O, methought, there was nothing meet.

HAMLET. Has this fellow no feeling of his business, that he sings at grave-making?

HORATIO. Custom hath made it in him a property of easiness.

HAMLET. 'Tis e'en so: the hand of little employment hath the daintier sense.

FIRST CLOWN (*sings*).
  But age, with his stealing steps,
    Hath clawed me in his clutch,   80
  And hath shipped me intil the land,
    As if I had never been such.

           (*Throws up a skull.*)

HAMLET. That skull had a tongue in it, and could sing once; how the knave jowls it to the ground, as if it were Cain's jaw-bone, that did the first murder! It might be the pate of a politician, which this ass now o'erreaches; one that might circumvent God, might it not?

HORATIO. It might, my lord.   89

HAMLET. Or of a courtier; which could say 'Good morrow, sweet lord! How dost thou, good lord?' This might be my lord such-a-one, that praised my lord such-a-one's horse, when he meant to beg it; might it not?

HORATIO. Ay, my lord.   95

HAMLET. Why, e'en so: and now my Lady Worm's; chapless, and knocked about the mazzard with a sexton's spade: here's fine revolution, an we had the trick to see 't. Did these bones cost no more the breeding, but to play at loggats with 'em? mine ache to think on 't.   101

FIRST CLOWN (*sings*).
  A pick-axe, and a spade, a spade,
    For and a shrouding sheet:
  O, a pit of clay for to be made
    For such a guest is meet.

      (*Throws up another skull.*)

HAMLET. There's another: why may not that be the skull of a lawyer? Where be his quiddities now, his quillets, his cases, his tenures, and his tricks? why does he suffer this rude knave to knock him about the sconce with a dirty shovel, and will not tell him of his action of battery? Hum! This fellow might be in's time a great buyer of land, with his statutes, his recognizances, his fines, his double vouchers, his recoveries: is this the fine of his fines, and the recovery of his recoveries, to have his fine pate full of fine dirt? will his vouchers vouch him no more of his purchases, and double ones too, than the length and breadth of a pair of indentures? The very conveyances of his lands will hardly lie in this box; and must the 121 inheritor himself have no more, ha?

HORATIO. Not a jot more, my lord.

HAMLET. Is not parchment made of sheepskins? 123

HORATIO. Ay, my lord, and of calf-skins too.

HAMLET. They are sheep and calves which seek out assurance in that. I will speak to this fellow. Whose grave's this, sirrah?

FIRST CLOWN. Mine, sir.

  (*Sings*). O, a pit of clay for to be made
      For such a guest is meet.   130

HAMLET. I think it be thine, indeed, for thou liest in 't.

FIRST CLOWN. You lie out on 't, sir, and therefore it is not yours: for my part, I do not lie in 't, and yet it is mine.

HAMLET. Thou dost lie in 't, to be in 't and say it is thine; 'tis for the dead, not for the quick; therefore thou liest.

FIRST CLOWN. 'Tis a quick lie, sir; 'twill away again, from me to you.   140

HAMLET. What man dost thou dig it for?

FIRST CLOWN. For no man, sir.

HAMLET. What woman, then?

FIRST CLOWN. For none, neither.

HAMLET. Who is to be buried in 't?

FIRST CLOWN. One that was a woman, sir; but, rest her soul, she's dead.   147

HAMLET. How absolute the knave is! we must speak by the card, or equivocation will undo us. By

---

69 ff. **In youth . . . As if I had never been such.** These two stanzas, plus some nonsensical variations as sung by the clown, are from a popular song of the Tudor period attributed to Lord Vaux and printed in Tottel's famous *Miscellany* of English lyric poetry in 1557. The *O*'s and *ah*'s in ll. 71 and 72 are evidently grunts from the clown as he labors to dig the grave. 71. **behove**, benefit. 76. **property of easiness**, a habit to which he easily conforms. 84. **jowls**, dashes, hurls. 85. **Cain's jaw-bone.** It was a popular confusion that led to the belief that Cain slew his brother Abel (Genesis, 4:8) with the jaw-bone of an ass; actually, the legend is that it was Samson who slew a thousand Philistines with this surprising implement (see Judges, 15:15). 87. **politician**, a schemer or intriguer. **o'erreaches**, a play on the literal meaning of "reaching over" and "circumventing" or "defeating." 97. **chapless**, without a lower jaw. 98. **mazzard**, head. 100. **loggats**, an old English country game based on the principle of horseshoe pitching, in which six sticks are thrown as nearly as possible against a stake in the ground or a block of wood fixed to the floor. 103. **For and**, in addition to.

107. **quiddities**, subtleties, quibbles, quirks. 108. **quillets**, verbal niceties and hair splittings. **tenures**, either the actual holding of a piece of property or an office or else the conditions and terms governing such holding. 110. **sconce**, head. 114. **statutes, recognizances**, legal terms involved in the possession and transfer of land. 115. **fines**, ends, with ensuing obvious puns. 115. **vouchers**, persons called upon to guarantee the title to land. **recoveries**, the process for transfer of an entailed estate. 119. **indentures . . . conveyances**, contracts and deeds of transfer. 124. **calf-skins**, parchments. 132. **liest**, etc. There follows now a series of puns on *lie*. 139. **quick**, live; there is a pun in the next line. 148. **absolute**, literal, positive. 149. **by the card**, by the compass; that is, precisely, accurately. The mariner's card was marked with all the points of the compass. **equivocation**, ambiguity, double-talk.

the Lord, Horatio, these three years I have taken note of it: the age is grown so picked that the toe of the peasant comes so near the heel of the courtier, he galls his kibe. How long hast thou been a grave-maker?

FIRST CLOWN. Of all the days i' the year, I came to 't that day that our last king Hamlet overcame Fortinbras.   157

HAMLET. How long is that since?

FIRST CLOWN. Cannot you tell that? every fool can tell that: it was the very day that young Hamlet was born; he that is mad, and sent into England.

HAMLET. Ay, marry, why was he sent into England?

FIRST CLOWN. Why, because he was mad: he shall recover his wits there; or, if he do not, it's no great matter there.

HAMLET. Why?

FIRST CLOWN. 'Twill not be seen in him there; there the men are as mad as he.   170

HAMLET. How came he mad?

FIRST CLOWN. Very strangely, they say.

HAMLET. How strangely?

FIRST CLOWN. Faith, e'en with losing his wits.

HAMLET. Upon what ground?

FIRST CLOWN. Why, here in Denmark: I have been sexton here, man and boy, thirty years.

HAMLET. How long will a man lie i' the earth ere he rot?   179

FIRST CLOWN. I' faith, if he be not rotten before he die—as we have many pocky corses now-a-days, that will scarce hole the laying in—he will last you some eight year or nine year: a tanner will last you nine year.   184

HAMLET. Why he more than another?

FIRST CLOWN. Why, sir, his hide is so tanned with his trade, that he will keep out water a great while; and your water is a sore decayer of your whoreson dead body. Here's a skull now; this skull has lain in the earth three and twenty years.   191

HAMLET. Whose was it?

FIRST CLOWN. A whoreson mad fellow's it was: whose do you think it was?

HAMLET. Nay, I know not.

FIRST CLOWN. A pestilence on him for a mad rogue! a' poured a flagon of Rhenish on my head once. This same skull, sir, was Yorick's skull, the king's jester.

HAMLET. This?   200

FIRST CLOWN. E'en that.

HAMLET. Let me see. (*Takes the skull.*) Alas, poor Yorick! I knew him, Horatio: a fellow of infinite jest, of most excellent fancy: he hath borne me on his back a thousand times; and now, how abhorred in my imagination it is! my gorge rises at it. Here hung those lips that I have kissed I know not how oft. Where be your gibes now? your gambols? your songs? your flashes of merriment, that were wont to set the table on a roar? Not one now, to mock your own grinning? quite chap-fallen? Now get you to my lady's chamber, and tell her, let her paint an inch thick, to this favor she must come; make her laugh at that. Prithee, Horatio, tell me one thing.

HORATIO. What's that, my lord?

HAMLET. Dost thou think Alexander looked o' this fashion i' the earth?

HORATIO. E'en so.   220

HAMLET. And smelt so? pah!

(*Puts down the skull.*)

HORATIO. E'en so, my lord.

HAMLET. To what base uses we may return, Horatio! Why may not imagination trace the noble dust of Alexander, till he find it stopping a bung-hole? 226

HORATIO. 'Twere to consider too curiously, to consider so.

HAMLET. No, faith, not a jot; but to follow him thither with modesty enough, and likelihood to lead it: as thus: Alexander died, Alexander was buried, Alexander returneth into dust; the dust is earth; of earth we make loam; and why of that loam, whereto he was converted, might they not stop a beer-barrel?

Imperious Caesar, dead and turned to clay,
Might stop a hole to keep the wind away:
O, that that earth, which kept the world in awe,   238
Should patch a wall to expel the winter's flaw!
But soft! but soft! aside; here comes the king.

(*Enter Priests, etc., in procession; the corpse of Ophelia;* LAERTES *and* Mourners, *following:* KING, QUEEN; *their trains, etc.*)

The queen, the courtiers: who is this they follow? 241
And with such maimed rites? This doth betoken
The corse they follow did with desperate hand
Fordo it own life: 'twas of some estate.
Couch we awhile, and mark.

(*Retiring with* HORATIO.)

LAERTES. What ceremony else?

HAMLET.   That is Laertes,
A very noble youth: mark.

LAERTES.   What ceremony else?

150. three years. Some have seen in this an allusion to the poor laws of 1601 (which would date Hamlet as late as 1604). In any event, such laws were regarded by the nobility as dangerous concessions to the common herd; and it must be remembered that Hamlet, throughout the scene with the gravedigger, is the somewhat condescending young aristocrat. 152. picked, finicky, fastidious. 153. kibe, chilblain, sore heel. 177. thirty years. This is manifestly a confirmation of the fact that Hamlet is thirty years of age at the time of the action of the play. 181. pocky, rotten, diseased. 198. Yorick. Will Kemp was the great comedian of the Elizabethan stage; Yorick is supposed to be Will Tarleton, Kemp's celebrated predecessor.

215. favor, countenance, face, expression. 227. curiously, minutely, pedantically. 230. modesty, moderation, restraint. 236. Imperious, imperial. 239. flaw, a gust of wind. 244. Fordo, destroy. it, its. 245. Couch, lie low, hide.

FIRST PRIEST. Her obsequies have been as far en-
        larged
As we have warranty: her death was doubtful;
And, but that great command o'ersways the order, 251
She should in ground unsanctified have lodged
Till the last trumpet; for charitable prayers,
Shards, flints and pebbles should be thrown on her:
Yet here she is allowed her virgin crants,
Her maiden strewments and the bringing home
Of bell and burial.
    LAERTES. Must there no more be done?
    FIRST PRIEST.   No more be done:
We should profane the service of the dead
To sing a requiem and such rest to her   260
As to peace-parted souls.
    LAERTES.   Lay her in the earth:
And from her fair and unpolluted flesh
May violets spring! I tell thee, churlish priest,
A ministering angel shall my sister be,
When thou liest howling.
    HAMLET.   What, the fair Ophelia!
    QUEEN. Sweets to the sweet: farewell!
                (Scattering flowers.)
I hoped thou shouldst have been my Hamlet's wife;
I thought thy bride-bed to have decked, sweet maid,
And not have strewed thy grave.
    LAERTES.   O, treble woe
Fall ten times treble on that cursed head,   270
Whose wicked deed thy most ingenious sense
Deprived thee of! Hold off the earth awhile,
Till I have caught her once more in mine arms:
                (Leaps into the grave.)
Now pile your dust upon the quick and dead,
Till of this flat a mountain you have made,
To o'ertop old Pelion, or the skyish head
Of blue Olympus.
    HAMLET (advancing). What is he whose grief
Bears such an emphasis? whose phrase of sorrow
Conjures the wandering stars, and makes them stand
Like wonder-wounded hearers? This is I,   280
Hamlet the Dane.
                (Leaps into the grave.)
    LAERTES.   The devil take thy soul!
                (Grappling with him.)
    HAMLET. Thou pray'st not well.
I prithee, take thy fingers from my throat;
For, though I am not splenitive and rash,

Yet have I in me something dangerous,
Which let thy wiseness fear: hold off thy hand.
    KING. Pluck them asunder.
    QUEEN.   Hamlet, Hamlet!
    ALL. Gentlemen,—
    HORATIO.   Good my lord, be quiet.
    (The Attendants part them, and they come out of
the grave.)
    HAMLET. Why, I will fight with him upon this
        theme
Until my eyelids will no longer wag.   290
    QUEEN. O my son, what theme?
    HAMLET. I loved Ophelia: forty thousand brothers
Could not, with all their quantity of love,
Make up my sum. What wilt thou do for her?
    KING. O, he is mad, Laertes.
    QUEEN. For love of God, forbear him.
    HAMLET. 'Swounds, show me what thou 'lt do:
Woo 't weep? woo 't fight? woo 't fast? woo 't tear thy-
        self?
Woo 't drink up eisel? eat a crocodile?
I'll do 't. Dost thou come here to whine?   300
To outface me with leaping in her grave?
Be buried quick with her, and so will I:
And, if thou prate of mountains, let them throw
Millions of acres on us, till our ground,
Singeing his pate against the burning zone,
Make Ossa like a wart! Nay, an thou 'lt mouth,
I'll rant as well as thou.
    QUEEN.   This is mere madness:
And thus awhile the fit will work on him;
Anon, as patient as the female dove,
When that her golden couplets are disclosed,
His silence will sit drooping.
    HAMLET.   Hear you, sir;   311
What is the reason that you use me thus?
I loved you ever: but it is no matter;
Let Hercules himself do what he may,
The cat will mew and dog will have his day. (Exit.)
    KING. I pray you, good Horatio, wait upon him.
                (Exit HORATIO.)
    (To LAERTES.) Strengthen your patience in our last
        night's speech;
We'll put the matter to the present push.
Good Gertrude, set some watch over your son.
This grave shall have a living monument: 320
An hour of quiet shortly shall we see;
Till then, in patience our proceeding be. (Exeunt.)

---

249. **enlarged,** extended; a reference to the fact that suicides are not
given full burial rites, although it is not at all clear that Ophelia
committed suicide. 250. **doubtful,** suspicious. 254. **Shards,** broken
bits of pottery or stone. 255. **crants,** garlands hung upon the biers
of unmarried women. 256. **strewments,** strewing of flowers. 256–
257. **bringing home . . . burial,** the funeral procession to the church.
261. **peace-parted,** a reference to the *Nunc Dimittis;* see Luke 2:29:
"Lord, lettest now thy servant depart in peace." 271. **ingenious
sense,** reason. 276. **Pelion . . . Olympus,** two famous mountains
of northern Greece. 279. **wandering stars,** planets. 284. **splenitive,**
quick-tempered, irritable.

290. **wag,** move. The word did not have the somewhat ridiculous
sense it now has. 293. **quantity,** possibly used in an ironical sense,
implying that a brother's love is, beside a lover's, comparatively
small. 296. **forbear,** leave alone. 298. **Woo't,** wilt thou, dost thou
wish. 299. **eisel,** vinegar. 310. **golden couplets.** The female pigeon
is popularly supposed to lay two eggs, and her young, when newly
hatched, are covered with a fine golden-colored down. 317. **in,** by
referring to or remembering. 318. **present push,** immediate test.
320. **living,** lasting.

SCENE 2. *A hall in the castle.*

(*Enter* HAMLET *and* HORATIO.)

HAMLET. So much for this, sir: now shall you see the other;
You do remember all the circumstance?

HORATIO. Remember it, my lord!

HAMLET. Sir, in my heart there was a kind of fighting,
That would not let me sleep: methought I lay
Worse than the mutines in the bilboes. Rashly,
And praised be rashness for it, let us know,
Our indiscretion sometimes serves us well,
When our deep plots do pall: and that should teach us
There's a divinity that shapes our ends,   10
Rough-hew them how we will,—

HORATIO.   That is most certain.

HAMLET. Up from my cabin,
My sea-gown scarfed about me, in the dark
Groped I to find out them; had my desire,
Fingered their packet, and in fine withdrew
To mine own room again; making so bold,
My fears forgetting manners, to unseal
Their grand commission; where I found, Horatio,—
O royal knavery!—an exact command,
Larded with many several sorts of reasons   20
Importing Denmark's health and England's too,
With, ho! such bugs and goblins in my life,
That, on the supervise, no leisure bated,
No, not to stay the grinding of the axe,
My head should be struck off.

HORATIO.   Is 't possible?

HAMLET. Here's the commission: read it at more leisure.
But wilt thou hear me how I did proceed?

HORATIO. I beseech you.

HAMLET. Being thus be-netted round with villanies,—
Ere I could make a prologue to my brains,   30
They had begun the play—I sat me down,
Devised a new commission, wrote it fair:
I once did hold it, as our statists do,
A baseness to write fair and labored much
How to forget that learning, but, sir, now
It did me yeoman's service: wilt thou know
The effect of what I wrote?

HORATIO.   Ay, good my lord.

HAMLET. An earnest conjuration from the king,
As England was his faithful tributary,
As love between them like the palm might flourish,   40
As peace should still her wheaten garland wear
And stand a comma 'tween their amities,
And many such-like 'As'es of great charge,
That, on the view and knowing of these contents,
Without debatement further, more or less,
He should the bearers put to sudden death,
Not shriving-time allowed.

HORATIO.   How was this sealed?

HAMLET. Why, even in that was Heaven ordinant.
I had my father's signet in my purse,
Which was the model of that Danish seal;   50
Folded the writ up in form of the other,
Subscribed it, gave 't the impression, placed it safely,
The changeling never known. Now, the next day,
Was our sea-fight; and what to this was sequent
Thou know'st already.

HORATIO. So Guildenstern and Rosencrantz go to 't.

HAMLET. Why, man, they did make love to this employment;
They are not near my conscience; their defeat
Does by their own insinuation grow:
'Tis dangerous when the baser nature comes   60
Between the pass and fell incensed points
Of mighty opposites.

HORATIO.   Why, what a king is this!

HAMLET. Does it not, thinkest thee, stand me now upon—
He that hath killed my king and whored my mother,
Popped in between the election and my hopes,
Thrown out his angle for my proper life,
And with such cozenage—is 't not perfect conscience,
To quit him with this arm? and is 't not to be damned,
To let this canker of our nature come
In further evil?   70

HORATIO. It must be shortly known to him from England
What is the issue of the business there.

HAMLET. It will be short: the interim is mine;
And a man's life's no more than to say 'One.'
But I am very sorry, good Horatio,
That to Laertes I forgot myself;

Act V, Scene 2. 6. **mutines,** mutineers, rebels. **bilboes,** shackles. 9. **pall,** fail. 11. **Rough-hew,** to shape roughly, perhaps to bungle or botch. 13. **sea-gown,** a coarse, high-collared, short-sleeved overgarment, reaching below the knees, much used by Elizabethan seamen. 15. **Fingered,** pilfered, stole. 20. **Larded,** interspersed. 22. **such bugs . . . my life,** such imaginary dangerous qualities in my way of living. 23. **supervise,** perusal. **leisure bated,** delay allowed. 30–31. **prologue . . . play;** that is, before I could begin to think I had already reached a decision. 33. **statists,** statesmen. 34. **fair,** clearly, legibly. 36. **yeoman's service,** loyal, faithful, and energetic service.

41. **wheaten garland,** a symbol of peace. 42. **comma,** the slightest possible break. 43. **'As'es,'** no doubt the "whereases" of a legal document. 48. **ordinant,** directing, guiding. 54. **sequent,** subsequent, following. 58. **defeat,** destruction and death. 59. **insinuation,** interference, meddling. 61. **pass,** thrust; a term of fencing. **fell incensed,** fiercely angered. 63. **stand me . . . upon,** incumbent upon me, my duty. 65. **election.** The Danish throne in early medieval times, like that of the Anglo-Saxons, was hereditary on approval of the earls and nobles—in this sense, there was an election of the king. 66. **angle,** fish-hook. **proper,** own. 67. **cozenage,** trickery. 68. **quit,** pay off, requite. 69. **canker,** a worm which eats buds and leaves; possibly used here in the secondary sense of "ulcer."

For, by the image of my cause, I see
The portraiture of his: I'll court his favors:
But, sure, the bravery of his grief did put me
Into a towering passion.

HORATIO.   Peace! who comes here?   80
                    (*Enter* OSRIC.)

OSRIC. Your lordship is right welcome back to Denmark.

HAMLET. I humbly thank you, sir. Dost know this water-fly?

HORATIO. No, my good lord.

HAMLET. Thy state is the more gracious; for 'tis a vice to know him. He hath much land, and fertile: let a beast be lord of beasts, and his crib shall stand at the king's mess: 'tis a chough; but, as I say, spacious in the possession of dirt.   90

OSRIC. Sweet lord, if your lordship were at leisure, I should impart a thing to you from his majesty.

HAMLET. I will receive it, sir, with all diligence of spirit. Put your bonnet to his right use; 'tis for the head.

OSRIC. I thank your lordship, it is very hot.

HAMLET. No, believe me, 'tis very cold; the wind is northerly.

OSRIC. It is indifferent cold, my lord, indeed.   100

HAMLET. But yet methinks it is very sultry and hot for my complexion.

OSRIC. Exceedingly, my lord; it is very sultry,—as 'twere,—I cannot tell how. But, my lord, his majesty bade me signify to you that he has laid a great wager on your head: sir, this is the matter,—

HAMLET. I beseech you, remember—   108
          (HAMLET *moves him to put on his hat.*)

OSRIC. Nay, good my lord; for mine ease, in good faith. Sir, here is newly come to court Laertes; believe me, an absolute gentleman, full of most excellent differences, of very soft society and great showing: indeed, to speak feelingly of him, he is the card or calendar of gentry, for you shall find in him the continent of what part a gentleman would see.   116

HAMLET. Sir, his definement suffers no perdition

in you; though, I know, to divide him inventorially would dizzy the arithmetic of memory, and yet but yaw neither, in respect of his quick sail. But, in the verity of extolment, I take him to be a soul of great article; and his infusion of such dearth and rareness, as, to make true diction of him, his semblable in his mirror; and who else would trace him, his umbrage, nothing more.   126

OSRIC. Your lordship speaks most infallibly of him.

HAMLET. The concernancy, sir? why do we wrap the gentleman in our more rawer breath?

OSRIC. Sir?   130

HORATIO. Is 't not possible to understand in another tongue? You will do 't, sir, really.

HAMLET. What imports the nomination of this gentleman?

OSRIC. Of Laertes?

HORATIO. His purse is empty already; all's golden words are spent.

HAMLET. Of him, sir.

OSRIC. I know you are not ignorant—   139

HAMLET. I would you did, sir; yet, in faith, if you did, it would not much approve me. Well, sir?

OSRIC. You are not ignorant of what excellence Laertes is—

HAMLET. I dare not confess that, lest I should compare with him in excellence; but, to know a man well, were to know himself.

OSRIC. I mean, sir, for his weapon; but in the imputation laid on him by them, in his meed he's unfellowed.   150

HAMLET. What's his weapon?

OSRIC. Rapier and dagger.

HAMLET. That's two of his weapons: but, well.

OSRIC. The king, sir, hath wagered with him six Barbary horses; against the which he has imponed, as I take it, six French rapiers and poniards, with their assigns, as girdle, hangers, and so: three of the carriages, in faith, are very dear to fancy, very responsive to the hilts, most delicate carriages, and of very liberal conceit.   160

HAMLET. What call you the carriages?

---

79. **bravery,** bravado, showy swaggering. 84. **water-fly,** idle, vain, buzzing, or chattering person. Osric is a beautiful example of the social climber among courtiers. 89. **crib . . . mess,** his eating-place will be at the king's table. He would be one of a group of persons, usually four in number, assigned to a table at a royal banquet. Hamlet implies that Osric's social climbing will undoubtedly bring him material success. **chough,** jackdaw, a chattering, noisy bird; possibly also a pun on "chuff," a boor or churl. 90. **spacious . . . possession,** amply possessed. 100. **indifferent,** moderately, somewhat. 108. **remember,** remember thy courtesy; a conventional invitation for a subordinate to keep his hat on. 109. **for mine ease,** a conventional reply to the conventional invitation just mentioned. Osric knows all the answers expected of polite society. 112. **differences,** peculiarities. **soft,** gentle, refined. 113. **showing,** distinguished appearance. 114. **feelingly,** with just appreciation of his refinement. **card,** map, model. 115. **continent,** that which contains fully, the sum and substance. 117. **definement,** definition, description. **perdition,** loss, diminution. Hamlet is deliberately talking in extremely artificial language to show his ironic contempt of Osric's character.

118. **divide him inventorially,** to itemize all his good points. 120. **yaw,** in nautical terms, an unsteady movement of a ship. Dowden's note on this difficult metaphor is worth quoting: "To enumerate in detail the perfections of Laertes would bewilder the computations of memory, yet for all that—in spite of their calculations—the enumeration would stagger to and fro (yaw), and so fall behind, in comparison with Laertes's quick sailing." 122. **article,** importance. 123. **infusion,** infused temperament, or character imparted by nature. **dearth,** scarcity, rareness. 126. **umbrage,** shadow. 128. **concernancy,** import. 129. **breath,** speech. 131–132. **Is 't . . . tongue,** "Is it not possible for you to understand your jargon when someone else uses it?" 133. **What imports . . . gentleman?** What is this gentleman's name? 141. **approve,** commend. 146–147. **but, to know . . . himself,** to know a man as excellent would be to know Laertes. 149. **imputation,** reputation. 150. **meed,** merit. 156. **imponed,** wagered, bet. 158. **hangers,** straps on the sword-belt from which the sword hung. 159. **dear to fancy,** expensively fashioned. **responsive,** suited to, corresponding well to. 160. **delicate;** that is, in workmanship.

HORATIO. I knew you must be edified by the margent ere you had done.

OSRIC. The carriages, sir, are the hangers.

HAMLET. The phrase would be more german to the matter, if we could carry cannon by our sides: I would it might be hangers till then. But, on: six Barbary horses against six French swords, their assigns, and three liberal-conceited carriages; that's the French bet against the Danish. Why is this 'imponed', as you call it? 171

OSRIC. The king, sir, hath laid, that in a dozen passes between yourself and him, he shall not exceed you three hits: he hath laid on twelve for nine; and it would come to immediate trial, if your lordship would vouchsafe the answer.

HAMLET. How if I answer 'no'?

OSRIC. I mean, my lord, the opposition of your person in trial. 179

HAMLET. Sir, I will walk here in the hall: if it please his majesty, 'tis the breathing-time of day for me; let the foils be brought, the gentleman willing, and the king hold his purpose, I will win for him an I can; if not, I will gain nothing but my shame and the odd hits. 185

OSRIC. Shall I re-deliver you e'en so?

HAMLET. To this effect, sir; after what flourish your nature will.

OSRIC. I commend my duty to your lordship.

HAMLET. Yours, yours. (*Exit* OSRIC.) He does well to commend it himself; there are no tongues else for 's turn.

HORATIO. This lapwing runs away with the shell on his head. 194

HAMLET. He did comply with his dug, before he sucked it. Thus has he—and many more of the same breed that I know the drossy age dotes on—only got the tune of the time and outward habit of encounter; a kind of yesty collection, which carries them through and through the most fond and winnowed opinions; and do but blow them to their trial, the bubbles are out. 202

(*Enter a* Lord.)

LORD. My lord, his majesty commended him to you by young Osric, who brings back to him, that you attend him in the hall: he sends to know if your pleasure hold to play with Laertes, or that you will take longer time.

HAMLET. I am constant to my purposes; they fol-

---

163. **margent**, margin, marginal notes. 165. **german**, germane, related to, appropriate to. 176. **answer**, encounter. 181. **breathing-time**, exercise-period. 193. **lapwing**, or peewit; this bird has the habit of drawing a visitor away from its nest, and, when newly hatched, of running about with some of its shell still on its head. 195. **comply . . . dug**, he (Osric) no doubt paid compliments to his mother's breast. 197. **drossy**, cheap, frivolous. 199. **yesty**, frothy, yeasty. 201. **fond and winnowed**, both foolish and sensible; they are capable of saying both wise and foolish things. 202. **blow them . . . bubbles are out**, put them to the test and their ignorance is exposed.

---

low the king's pleasure: if his fitness speaks, mine is ready; now or whensoever, provided I be so able as now. 211

LORD. The king and queen and all are coming down.

HAMLET. In happy time.

LORD. The queen desires you to use some gentle entertainment to Laertes before you fall to play

HAMLET. She well instructs me. (*Exit* Lord.)

HORATIO. You will lose this wager, my lord.

HAMLET. I do not think so; since he went into France, I have been in continual practice; I shall win at the odds. But thou wouldst not think how ill all's here about my heart: but it is no matter.

HORATIO. Nay, good my lord,— 224

HAMLET. It is but foolery; but it is such a kind of gain-giving, as would perhaps trouble a woman.

HORATIO. If your mind dislike any thing, obey it: I will forestall their repair hither, and say you are not fit. 229

HAMLET. Not a whit, we defy augury: there's a special providence in the fall of a sparrow. If it be now, 'tis not to come; if it be not to come, it will be now; if it be not now, yet it will come: the readiness is all: since no man has aught of what he leaves, what is 't to leave betimes? Let be. 235

(*Enter* KING, QUEEN, LAERTES, Lords, OSRIC, *and* Attendants *with foils, etc.*)

KING. Come, Hamlet, come, and take this hand from me.

(*The* KING *puts* LAERTES's *hand into* HAMLET's.)

HAMLET. Give me your pardon, sir: I've done you wrong;
But pardon 't, as you are a gentleman.
This presence knows,
And you must needs have heard, how I am punished 240
With sore distraction. What I have done,
That might your nature, honor and exception
Roughly awake, I here proclaim was madness.
Was 't Hamlet wronged Laertes? Never Hamlet;
If Hamlet from himself be ta'en away,
And when he's not himself does wrong Laertes,
Then Hamlet does it not, Hamlet denies it.
Who does it, then? His madness: if it be so,
Hamlet is of the faction that is wronged;
His madness is poor Hamlet's enemy. 250
Sir, in this audience,
Let my disclaiming from a purposed evil
Free me so far in your most generous thoughts,
That I have shot mine arrow o'er the house,
And hurt my brother.

---

214. **In happy time**, a conventional courtesy phrase. 226. **gain-giving**, misgiving. 239. **presence**, not only the royal presence itself but also the assembling of the entire court. 242. **exception**, disapproval.

LAERTES.   I am satisfied in nature,
Whose motive, in this case, should stir me most
To my revenge: but in my terms of honor
I stand aloof; and will no reconcilement,
Till by some elder masters, of known honor,
I have a voice and precedent of peace,   260
To keep my name ungored. But till that time,
I do receive your offered love like love,
And will not wrong it.
    HAMLET.   I embrace it freely;
And will this brother's wager frankly play.
Give us the foils. Come on.
    LAERTES.   Come, one for me.
    HAMLET. I'll be your foil, Laertes: in mine igno-
        rance
Your skill shall, like a star i' the darkest night,
Stick fiery off indeed.
    LAERTES.   You mock me, sir.
    HAMLET. No, by this hand.
    KING. Give them the foils, young Osric. Cousin
        Hamlet,   270
You know the wager?
    HAMLET.   Very well, my lord;
Your grace hath laid the odds o' the weaker side.
    KING. I do not fear it; I have seen you both:
But since he is bettered, we have therefore odds.
    LAERTES. This is too heavy, let me see another.
    HAMLET. This likes me well. These foils have all
        a length?   (They prepare to play.)
    OSRIC. Ay, my good lord.
    KING. Set me the stoups of wine upon that table.
If Hamlet give the first or second hit,
Or quit in answer of the third exchange,   280
Let all the battlements their ordnance fire;
The king shall drink to Hamlet's better breath;
And in the cup an union shall he throw,
Richer than that which four successive kings
In Denmark's crown have worn. Give me the cups;
And let the kettle to the trumpet speak,
The trumpet to the cannoneer without,
The cannons to the heavens, the heavens to the earth,
'Now the king drinks to Hamlet.' Come, begin:
And you, the judges, bear a wary eye.   290
    HAMLET. Come on, sir.
    LAERTES.   Come, my lord.
                            (They play.)
    HAMLET.   One.
    LAERTES.   No.
    HAMLET.   Judgment.
    OSRIC. A hit, a very palpable hit.
    LAERTES.   Well; again.

    KING. Stay; give me drink. Hamlet, this pearl is
        thine;
Here's to thy health.
    (Trumpets sound, and cannon shot off within.)
                    Give him the cup.
    HAMLET. I'll play this bout first; set it by awhile.
Come. (They play.) Another hit; what say you?
    LAERTES. A touch, a touch, I do confess.
    KING. Our son shall win.
    QUEEN.   He's fat, and scant of breath.
Here, Hamlet, take my napkin, rub thy brows: 299
The queen carouses to thy fortune, Hamlet.
    HAMLET. Good madam!
    KING.   Gertrude, do not drink.
    QUEEN. I will, my lord; I pray you, pardon me.
    KING (aside). It is the poisoned cup; it is too late.
    HAMLET. I dare not drink yet, madam; by and by.
    QUEEN. Come, let me wipe thy face.
    LAERTES. My lord, I'll hit him now.
    KING.   I do not think 't.
    LAERTES (aside). And yet 'tis almost 'gainst my
        conscience.
    HAMLET. Come, for the third, Laertes: you do but
        dally;
I pray you, pass with your best violence;
I am afeard you make a wanton of me.   310
    LAERTES. Say you so? come on.
                            (They play.)
    OSRIC. Nothing, neither way.
    LAERTES. Have at you now!
    (LAERTES wounds HAMLET; then, in scuffling,
they change rapiers, and HAMLET wounds LAERTES.)
    KING.   Part them; they are incensed.
    HAMLET. Nay, come, again.
                            (The QUEEN falls.)
    OSRIC.   Look to the queen there, ho!
    HORATIO. They bleed on both sides. How is it, my
        lord?
    OSRIC. How is 't, Laertes?
    LAERTES. Why, as a woodcock to mine own
        springe, Osric;
I am justly killed with mine own treachery.
    HAMLET. How does the queen?
    KING.   She swounds to see them bleed.
    QUEEN. No, no, the drink, the drink,—O my dear
        Hamlet,—   320
The drink, the drink! I am poisoned!   (Dies.)
    HAMLET. O villany! Ho! let the door be locked:
Treachery! Seek it out.

255. nature. Laertes replies that he is personally satisfied, but he
feels nevertheless that his honor must be satisfied by the rules of
the "code of honor." 260. voice, authority, authoritative statement.
266. foil. There is here a quibble on foil in the sense of "contrast"
and of "blunted rapier." 268. Stick fiery off, shine forth brilliantly.
283. union, pearl. 286. kettle, kettle-drum.

293. pearl is thine. At this point the King puts the poison in Hamlet's
cup. 298. fat. Richard Burbage, the original Hamlet, was a corpulent man; some editors, however, prefer to think of fat merely as
"soft, out of condition," or perhaps "sweating." Some would emend
the word to "faint." 300. carouses, drinks a toast. 310. wanton,
spoiled child, sissy. 314. ho! probably "stop!" in the sense of "stop
the contest!" 317. woodcock, a slang expression for a blockhead;
the woodcock was considered a particularly stupid, gullible bird.
springe, snare, trap. 319. swounds, swoons, faints.

LAERTES. It is here, Hamlet: Hamlet, thou art
    slain;
No medicine in the world can do thee good;
In thee there is not half an hour of life;
The treacherous instrument is in thy hand,
Unbated and envenomed: the foul practice
Hath turned itself on me; lo, here I lie,   329
Never to rise again: thy mother's poisoned:
I can no more: the king, the king's to blame.
    HAMLET. The point envenomed too! . . .
Then, venom, to thy work!
                    (*Stabs the* KING.)
    ALL. Treason! Treason!
    KING. O, yet defend me, friends; I am but hurt.
    HAMLET. Here, thou incestuous, murderous,
    damned Dane,
Drink off this potion. Is thy union here?
Follow my mother.   (KING *dies.*)
    LAERTES.   He is justly served;
It is a poison tempered by himself.
Exchange forgiveness with me, noble Hamlet:
Mine and my father's death come not upon thee, 341
Nor thine on me!   (*Dies.*)
    HAMLET. Heaven make thee free of it! I follow
    thee.
I am dead, Horatio. Wretched queen, adieu!
You that look pale and tremble at this chance,
That are but mutes or audience to this act,
Had I but time—as this fell sergeant, death,
Is strict in his arrest—O, I could tell you—
But let it be. Horatio, I am dead;
Thou livest; report me and my cause aright
To the unsatisfied.
    HORATIO.   Never believe it: 351
I am more an antique Roman than a Dane:
Here's yet some liquor left.
    HAMLET.   As thou 'rt a man,
Give me the cup; let go; by Heaven, I'll have 't.
O good Horatio, what a wounded name,
Things standing thus unknown, shall live behind me!
If thou didst ever hold me in thy heart,
Absent thee from felicity awhile,
And in this harsh world draw thy breath in pain,
To tell my story.
            (*March afar off, and shot within.*)
            What warlike noise is this?
    OSRIC. Young Fortinbras, with conquest come from
    Poland,   361
To the ambassadors of England gives
This warlike volley.
    HAMLET.   O, I die, Horatio;
The potent poison quite o'ercrows my spirit;

I cannot live to hear the news from England;
But I do prophesy the election lights
On Fortinbras: he has my dying voice;
So tell him, with the occurrents, more and less,
Which have solicited. The rest is silence.   (*Dies.*)
    HORATIO. Now cracks a noble heart. Good night,
    sweet prince;   370
And flights of angels sing thee to thy rest!
Why does the drum come hither?   (*March within.*)
    (*Enter* FORTINBRAS, *the* English Ambassadors, *and
others.*)
    FORTINBRAS. Where is this sight?
    HORATIO.   What is it ye would see?
If aught of woe or wonder, cease your search.
    FORTINBRAS. This quarry cries on havoc. O proud
    death,
What feast is toward in thine eternal cell,
That thou so many princes at a shot
So bloodily hast struck?
    FIRST AMBASSADOR.   The sight is dismal;
And our affairs from England come too late:
The ears are senseless that should give us hearing,
To tell him his commandment is fulfilled,   381
That Rosencrantz and Guildenstern are dead:
Where should we have our thanks?
    HORATIO.   Not from his mouth,
Had it the ability of life to thank you:
He never gave commandment for their death.
But since, so jump upon this bloody question,
You from the Polack wars, and you from England,
Are here arrived, give order that these bodies
High on a stage be placed to the view;   389
And let me speak to the yet unknowing world
How these things came about: so shall you hear
Of carnal, bloody, and unnatural acts,
Of accidental judgments, casual slaughters,
Of deaths put on by cunning and forced cause,
And, in this upshot, purposes mistook
Fallen on the inventors' heads: all this can I
Truly deliver.
    FORTINBRAS.   Let us haste to hear it,
And call the noblest to the audience.
For me, with sorrow I embrace my fortune:
I have some rights of memory in this kingdom,   400
Which now to claim my vantage doth invite me.
    HORATIO. Of that I shall have also cause to speak,
And from his mouth whose voice will draw on more:
But let this same be presently performed,
Even while men's minds are wild; lest more mis-
    chance,
On plots and errors, happen.

---

328. **Unbated**, with the foil removed. **practice**, plot, stratagem, sharp or treacherous doings. 339. **tempered**, mixed, prepared. 346. **mutes**, actors or players to whom no lines are assigned. 347. **sergeant**, sheriff's officer, officer of the law. 352. **Roman**. It was the Roman custom for a subordinate to follow his master in death. 364. **o'ercrows**, crows over, gloats over, triumphs over.

368. **occurrents**, events, incidents, happenings. 369. **solicited**, moved, caused. 375. **quarry**, heap of dead. **cries on havoc**, calls for slaughter. 376. **toward**, to come. 383. **his mouth**; that is, the King's. 386. **jump**, immediately following. **question**, dispute. 393. **casual**, accidental, chance. 400. **of memory**, traditional. 403. **draw on more**, lead more to speak. 406. **On**, in addition to, on top of; possibly, on account of.

FORTINBRAS.   Let four captains
Bear Hamlet, like a soldier, to the stage;
For he was likely, had he been put on,
To have proved most royally: and, for his passage,
The soldiers' music and the rites of war   410
Speak loudly for him.

409. **passage**, passing, death.

Take up the bodies: such a sight as this
Becomes the field, but here shows much amiss.
Go, bid the soldiers shoot.

(*A* dead march. Exeunt, bearing off the dead
bodies; after which a peal of ordnance is shot off.*)*

413. **field**, battlefield.

"Four Soldiers," engraving by the German Master M Z, who was active about 1500. From the Art Institute of Chicago.

Nicolaus Copernicus

1473–1543

The greatest of the Humanists, inspired by the literary achievements and ethical teachings of the ancients, had no interest in natural science, which seemed irrelevant to their exploration of human nature. Through the influence of Petrarch and Erasmus, who dismissed it with contempt, science was neglected for generations. But the new intellectual freedom eventually led to a renewal of scientific speculation in the sixteenth century and the discoveries upon which modern science is founded.

Copernicus, the Polish astronomer, was not a scientist in the modern sense but half churchman and half Humanist, who was led to revolutionize our view of the heavens not by a telescope but by developing the suggestion of an ancient philosopher. At Cracow and later Bologna he studied Ptolemaic astronomy along with canon law and medicine and pursued his interest in the stars through a life crowded with administrative duties. Early in his studies he became skeptical of the geocentric astronomy of the Middle Ages because of its complexity and was aroused by finding that some ancient followers of Pythagoras believed the sun to be the center of our universe. With meager instruments he began to observe the heavens and eventually verified this heliocentric view to his own satisfaction. He cautiously announced his refutation of the orthodox theory in a manuscript first circulated in 1530, but not until 1543, the year of his death, did a disciple venture to publish his treatise, *De Revolutionibus Orbium Celestium.*

Although some churchmen were shocked by this reversal of traditional authority, Copernicus protected himself from persecution by announcing his theory as a hypothesis based on mathematical calculation rather than the result of scientific observation. It sprang from his search for a simpler explanation of the motions of the planets than the complicated Ptolemaic system provided. Such reasoning reminds one of Dante, who also demanded that a Christian universe should be neat and simple. The quest of Copernicus for simplicity actually led him into error, for he insisted, like Dante, upon circular orbits for his planets, because God would necessarily give a perfect order to his creation. It remained for Johannes Kepler, his successor, to substitute direct observation for reasoning and to prove that the orbits of the planets are elliptical. Scientific method lagged behind scientific findings, which in the sixteenth century had still the quality of magnificent accidents. But the great discovery of Copernicus was a major step in the long development of modern science.

The Revolutions of the Heavenly Bodies

I CAN well believe, most holy father, that certain people, when they hear of my attributing motion to the earth in these books of mine, will at once declare that such an opinion ought to be rejected. Now, my own theories do not please me so much as not to consider what others may judge of them. Accordingly, when I began to reflect upon what those persons who accept the stability of the earth, as confirmed by the opinion of many centuries, would say when I claimed that the earth moved, I hesitated for a long time as to whether I should publish that which I have written to demonstrate its motion, or whether it would not be better to follow the example of the Pythagoreans, who used to hand down the secrets of philosophy to their relatives and friends only in oral form. As I well considered all this, I was almost impelled to put the finished work wholly aside, through the scorn I had reason to anticipate on account of the newness and apparent contrariness of my theory to reason.

My friends, however, dissuaded me from such a course and admonished me that I ought to publish my book, which had lain concealed in my possession not only nine years, but already into four times the ninth year. Not a few other distinguished and very learned men asked me to do the same thing, and told me that I ought not, on account of my anxiety, to delay any longer in consecrating my work to the general service of mathematicians.

But your holiness will perhaps not so much wonder that I have dared to bring the results of my night labors to the light of day, after having taken so much care in elaborating them, but is waiting instead to hear how it entered my mind to imagine that the earth moved, contrary to the accepted opinion of mathematicians—nay, almost contrary to ordinary human understanding. Therefore I will not conceal from your holiness that what moved me to consider another way of reckoning the motions of the heavenly bodies was nothing else than the fact that the mathematicians do not agree with one another in their investigations. In the first place, they are so uncertain about the motions of the sun and moon that they cannot find out the length of a full year. In the second place, they apply neither the same laws of cause and effect in determining the

The Revolutions of the Heavenly Bodies. 8 Translated by William S. Knickerbocker. Reprinted by permission of Appleton-Century-Crofts, Inc.
14. **Pythagoreans,** followers of the Greek philosopher, **Pythagoras** (sixth century B.C.).

motions of the sun and moon and of the five planets, nor the same proofs. Some employ only concentric circles, others use eccentric and epicyclic ones, with which, however, they do not fully attain the desired end. They could not even discover nor compute the main thing—namely, the form of the universe and the symmetry of its parts. It was with them as if some should, from different places, take hands, feet, head, and other parts of the body, which although very beautiful, were not drawn in their proper relations, and, without making them in any way correspond, should construct a monster instead of a human being.

Accordingly, when I had long reflected on this uncertainty of mathematical tradition, I took the trouble to read again the books of all the philosophers I could get hold of, to see if some one of them had not once believed that there were other motions of the heavenly bodies. First I found in Cicero that Hicetas had believed in the motion of the earth. Afterwards I found in Plutarch, likewise, that some others had held the same opinion. This induced me also to begin to consider the movability of the earth, and, although the theory appeared contrary to reason, I did so because I knew that others before me had been allowed to assume rotary movements at will, in order to explain the phenomena of these celestial bodies. I was of the opinion that I, too, might be permitted to see whether, by presupposing motion in the earth, more reliable conclusions than hitherto reached could not be discovered for the rotary motions of the spheres. And thus, acting on the hypothesis of the motion which, in the following book, I ascribe to the earth, and by long and continued observations, I have finally discovered that if the motion of the other planets be carried over to the relation of the earth and this is made the basis for the rotation of every star, not only will the phenomena of the planets be explained thereby, but also the laws and the size of the stars; all their spheres and the heavens themselves will appear so harmoniously connected that nothing could be changed in any part of them without confusion in the remaining parts and in the whole universe.

That the universe is spherical

First we must remark that the universe is spherical in form, partly because this form being a perfect whole requiring no joints, is the most complete of all, partly because it makes the most capacious form, which is best suited to contain and preserve everything; or again because all the constituent parts of the universe, that is the sun, moon, and the planets appear in this form; or because everything strives to

20. **Hicetas**, a Pythagorean philosopher of Syracuse, probably antedating Aristotle, who is mentioned in Cicero's *Academica*, ii, 39.

attain this form, as appears in the case of drops of water and other fluid bodies if they attempt to define themselves. So no one will doubt that this form belongs to the heavenly bodies.

That the earth is also spherical

That the earth is also spherical is therefore beyond question, because it presses from all sides upon its center. Although by reason of the elevations of the mountains and the depressions of the valleys a perfect circle cannot be understood, yet this does not affect the general spherical nature of the earth. This appears in the following manner. To those who journey towards the North the north pole of the daily revolution of the heavenly sphere seems gradually to rise, while the opposite seems to sink. Most of the stars in the region of the Bear seem not to set, while some of the southern stars seem not to rise at all. So Italy does not see Canopes, which is visible to the Egyptians. And Italy sees the outermost star of the Stream, which our region of a colder zone does not know. On the other hand, to those who go towards the South the others seem to rise and those to sink which are high in our region. Moreover, the inclination of the Poles to the diameter of the earth bears always the same relation, which could happen only in the case of a sphere. So it is evident that the earth is included between the two poles, and is therefore spherical in form. Let us add that the inhabitants of the East do not observe the eclipse of the sun or of the moon which occurs in the evening, and the inhabitants of the West those which occur in the morning, while those who dwell between see those later and these earlier. That the water also has the same form can be observed from ships, in that the land which cannot be seen from the deck is visible from the mast-tree. And conversely, if a light be placed at the mast-head it seems to those who remain on the shores gradually to sink and at last still sinking to disappear. It is clear that the water also, according to its nature, continually presses like the earth downward and does not rise above its banks higher than its convexity permits. So the land extends above the ocean as much as the land happens to be higher.

Whether the earth has a circular motion, and concerning the location of the earth

As it has been already shown that the earth has the form of a sphere, we must consider whether a movement also coincides with this form, and what place the earth holds in the universe. Without this there will be no secure results to be obtained in regard to the heavenly phenomena. The great majority of authors, of course, agree that the earth stands still in the center of the universe, and consider it inconceivable and ridiculous to suppose the opposite.

But if the matter is carefully weighed it will be seen that the question is not yet settled and therefore by no means to be regarded lightly. Every change of place which is observed is due to a movement of the observed object or of the observer, or to movements of both, naturally in different directions, for if the observed object and the observer move in the same manner and in the same direction, no movement will be seen. Now it is from the earth that the revolution of the heavens is observed, and it is produced for our eyes. Therefore, if the earth undergoes no movement this movement must take place in everything outside of the earth, but in the opposite direction than if everything on the earth moved, and of this kind is the daily revolution. So this appears to affect the whole universe, that is, everything outside the earth with the single exception of the earth itself. If, however, one should admit that this movement was not peculiar to the heavens, but that the earth revolved from west to east, and if this was carefully considered in regard to the apparent rising and setting of the sun, the moon, and the stars, it would be discovered that this was the real situation. Since the sky, which contains and shelters all things, is the common seat of all things, it is not easy to understand why motion should not be ascribed rather to the thing contained than to the containing, to the located rather than to the location. From this supposition follows another question of no less importance, concerning the place of the earth, although it has been accepted and believed by almost all that the earth occupies the middle of the universe. But if one should suppose that the earth is not at the center of the universe, that, however, the distance between the two is not great enough to be measured on the orbits of the fixed stars, but would be noticeable and perceptible on the orbit of the sun or of the planets: and if one was further of the opinion that the movements of the planets appeared to be irregular, as if they were governed by a center other than the earth, then such a one could perhaps have given the true reasons for the apparently irregular movement. For since the planets appear now nearer and now farther from the earth, this shows necessarily that the center of their revolutions is not the center of the earth: although it does not settle whether the earth increases and decreases the distance from them or they their distance from the earth.

Refutation of the argument of the ancients that the earth remains still in the middle of the universe, as if it were its center

From this and similar reasons it is supposed that the earth rests at the center of the universe and that there is no doubt of the fact. But if one believed that the earth revolved, he would certainly be of the opinion that this movement was natural and not arbitrary. For whatever is in accord with nature produces results which are the opposite of those produced by force. Things upon which force or an outside power has acted must be injured and cannot long endure: what happens by nature, however, preserves itself well and exists in the best condition. So Ptolemy feared without good reason that the earth and all earthly objects subject to the revolution would be destroyed by the act of nature, since this latter is opposed to artificial acts, or to what is produced by the human spirit. But why did not he fear the same, and in a much higher degree, of the universe, whose motion must be as much more rapid as the heavens are greater than the earth? Or has the heaven become so immense because it has been driven outward from the center by the inconceivable power of the revolution; while if it stood still, on the contrary, it would collapse and fall together? But surely if this is the case the extent of the heavens would increase infinitely. For the more it is driven higher by the outward force of the movement, so much the more rapid will the movement become, because of the ever-increasing circle which must be traversed in 24 hours; and, conversely, if the movement grows, the immensity of the heavens grows. So the velocity would increase the size and the size would increase the velocity unendingly. According to the physical law that the endless cannot wear away nor in any way move, the heavens must necessarily stand still.

But it is said that beyond the sky no body, no place, no vacant space, in fact nothing at all exists; then it is strange that something should be enclosed by nothing. But if the heaven is endless and is bounded only by the inner hollow, perhaps this establishes all the more clearly the fact that there is nothing outside the heavens, because everything is within it, but the heaven must then remain unmoved. The highest proof on which one supports the finite character of the universe is its movement. But whether the universe is endless or limited we will leave to the physiologues; this remains sure for us that the earth enclosed between the poles is bounded by a spherical surface. Why therefore should we not take the position of ascribing to a movement conformable to its nature and corresponding to its form, rather than suppose that the whole universe whose limits are not and cannot be known moves? And why will we not recognize that the appearance of a daily revolution belongs to the heavens, but the actuality to the earth; and that the relation is similar to that of which one says: "We run out of the harbor, the lands and cities retreat from us." Because if a ship sails along quietly, everything outside of it appears to those on board as if it moved with the motion of the boat, and the boatman thinks that the boat with all on board is standing still, this

Copernicus, from a biography of the astronomer by Pierre Gassendi published in 1655.

same thing may hold without doubt of the motion of the earth, and it may seem as if the whole universe revolved. What shall we say, however, of the clouds and other things floating, falling or raising in the air—except that not only does the earth move with the watery elements belonging with it, but also a large part of the atmosphere, and whatever else is in any way connected with the earth; whether it is because the air immediately touching the earth
10 has the same nature as the earth, or that the motion has become imparted to the atmosphere. A like astonishment must be felt if that highest region of the air be supposed to follow the heavenly motion, as shown by those suddenly appearing stars which the Greeks call comets or bearded stars, which belong to that region and which rise and set like other stars. We may suppose that part of the atmosphere, because of its great distance from the earth, has become free from the earthly motion. So the atmos-
20 phere which lies close to the earth and all things floating in it would appear to remain still, unless driven here and there by the wind or some other outside force, which chance may bring into play; for how is the wind in the air different from the current in the sea? We must admit that the motion of things

rising and falling in the air is in relation to the universe a double one, being always made up of a rectilinear and a circular movement. Since that which seeks of its own weight to fall is essentially earthy, so there is no doubt that these follow the
30 same natural law as their whole; and it results from the same principle that those things which pertain to fire are forcibly driven on high. Earthly fire is nourished with earthly stuff, and it is said that the flame is only burning smoke. But the peculiarity of the fire consists in this that it expands whatever it seizes upon, and it carries this out so consistently that it can in no way and by no machinery be prevented from breaking its bonds and completing its work. The expanding motion, however, is directed
40 from the center outward; therefore, if any earthly material is ignited it moves upward. So to each single body belongs a single motion, and this is evinced preferably in a circular direction as long as the single body remains in its natural place and its entirety. In this position the movement is the circular movement, which, as far as the body itself is concerned, is as if it did not occur. The rectilinear motion, however, seizes upon those bodies which have wandered or have been driven from their
50 natural position or have been in any way disturbed. Nothing is so much opposed to the order and form of the world as the displacement of one of its parts. Rectilinear motion takes place only when objects are not properly related, and are not complete according to their nature because they have separated from their whole and have lost their unity. Moreover, objects which have been driven outward or away, leaving out of consideration the circular motion, do not obey a single, simple, and regular motion, since they
60 cannot be controlled simply by their lightness or by the force of their weight, and if in falling they have at first a slow movement the rapidity of the motion increases as they fall, while in the case of earthly fire, which is forced upwards—and we have no means of knowing any other kind of fire—we will see that its motion is slow as if its earthly origin thereby showed itself. The circular motion, on the other hand, is always regular, because it is not subject to an intermittent cause. Those other objects,
70 however, would cease to be either light or heavy in respect to their natural movement if they reached their own place, and thus they would fit into that movement. Therefore, if the circular movement is to be ascribed to the universe as a whole and the rectilinear to the parts, we might say that the revolution is to the straight line as the natural state is to sickness. That Aristotle divided motion into three sorts, that from the center out, that inward toward the center, and that around about the center appears
80 to be merely a logical convenience, just as we distinguish point, line, and surface, although one can-

not exist without the others, and none of them are found apart from bodies. This fact is also to be considered, that the condition of immovability is held to be nobler and more divine than that of change and inconstancy, which latter therefore should be ascribed rather to the earth than to the universe, and I would add also that it seems inconsistent to attribute motion to the containing and locating element rather than to the contained and located object, which the earth is. Finally since the planets plainly are at one time nearer and at another time farther from the earth, it would follow, on the theory that the universe revolves, that the movement of the one and same body which is known to take place about a center, that is the center of the earth, must also be directed toward the center from without and from the center outward. The movement about the center must therefore be made more general, and it suffices if that single movement be about its own center. So it appears from all these considerations that the movement of the earth is more probable than its fixity, especially in regard to the daily revolution, which is most peculiar to the earth.

Giordano Bruno

c. 1548–1600

Among those who were inspired by Copernicus to further speculation about the universe was an earnest Dominican friar named Giordano Bruno, who produced an exposition of the Copernican theory in 1584. Educated as a churchman at Naples, he had been forced to flee from Italy and renounce his monastic order, because his reason led him to deny the doctrine of transubstantiation, the miracle of the eucharist by which the bread and wine are transformed into the body and blood of Jesus. But so strong was his love of Italy that he could find no spiritual peace in exile and lectured his way discontentedly through Calvinist Switzerland, Anglican England, and Lutheran Germany without sympathy for any of the Protestant sects. At last his homesickness and poverty made him return to Italy as tutor to a Venetian gentleman, who was soon so scandalized by his heresies that he turned him over to the Inquisition. Frightened, Bruno abjectly recanted his blasphemy against the Pope and orthodox dogma and for eight long years languished in prison, until at last he defiantly reaffirmed his faith in a new conception of the universe and was burned at the stake as an arrogant heretic on February 17, 1600.

This great martyr to the new science was not a scientist but a philosopher whose passionate imagination was led by Copernicus to a new idea of the universe that later science was laboriously to confirm. His metaphysical speculations are spread through many treatises, but his major hypothesis is contained in *On the Infinite*

(1584). Copernicus had destroyed the medieval notion that the earth must be the center of the universe because man, the lord of the earth, was the climax of God's creation. But in making the sun the center of things he had still assumed a finite universe operated by simple and rational laws not unlike those accepted by Dante. Bruno, with a sudden poetic vision, jumped from the idea of the earth as center to the idea of no center at all. Because the nearness of man to his own earth had made it seem larger than the sun, which seemed to revolve about it, might not the nearness of our sun to us have misled Copernicus to assume that the more distant stars revolved about our sun? As the imagination of Bruno freed itself from medieval dogma, he announced the heresy that the stars are suns like our sun, which seem smaller and much less bright only because they are farther away from us. Once released from the snug medieval conception of a finite universe, he began to see stars beyond stars and concluded that the universe is infinite and that the stars are all moving in space, fixed only in their relation to each other. Having destroyed the Christian distinction between Earth and Heaven and dotted the universe with an infinity of worlds, he was led to assume that these other worlds might be inhabited by living things as is our own. God is accordingly not the special father of his human creatures on this planet, but the single unifying soul of this infinite universe. "Nature is God in things!"

The poetic soul of Bruno, if it lost the mystical vision of Christianity, found a new excitement in the vision of a still greater God who appears everywhere in every natural force. So Bruno passed from the idea of an infinite universe and an infinite relativity among its parts to a triumphant pantheism. He was still a religious thinker at heart, though his imagination led him to two key principles of modern science.

Of the Infinite Universe and Innumerable Worlds

A PREFATORY DEDICATION

I KNOW myself to be for the most part accounted a sophist, more desirous to appear subtle than to be really solid; an ambitious fellow, that studies rather to set up a new and false sect than to confirm the ancient and true doctrine; a deceiver, that aims at purchasing brightness to his own fame by engaging others in the darkness of error; a restless spirit, that overturns the edifice of sound discipline and makes himself a founder to some hut of perversity. But so may all the holy Deities deliver me from those that unjustly hate me, so may my own God be ever propitious to me, so may the Governors of this our globe show me their favor, so may the stars furnish me with such a seed for the field and with

Of the Infinite Universe and Innumerable Worlds.[8] Translated by John Toland.

such a field for the seed, that the world may reap the useful and glorious fruit of my labor, by awakening the genius and opening the understanding of such as are deprived of light: so may all these things happen, I say, as it is most certain that I neither fain nor pretend. If I err, I am far from thinking that I do so; and whether I speak or write, I dispute not for the mere love of victory (for I look upon all reputation and conquest to be hateful to God, to be most vile and dishonorable, without Truth) but it is for the love of true WISDOM, and by the studious admiration of this mistress, that I fatigue, that I disquiet, that I torment myself.

This will be made evident by the demonstrative arguments I offer, drawn from lively reasons; as these are derived from regulated sense, which is informed by positive Ideas, that like so many ambassadresses are sent abroad from the subjects of nature: being obvious to those that seek for them, clear to those that conceive them, distinct to those that consider them, and certain to those that comprehend them. But it is time that I present you with my Contemplations about *the infinite Universe and innumerable Worlds.*

In this dialogue then you'll find, first, that the inconstancy of our senses shows they are not the principle of certitude, which is only acquired by a kind of comparison, or by conferring one sensible object, or one sense with another; and so it is concluded that the same truth may be in different subjects, as in the sensible object and in the understanding.

Secondly, you come to the beginning of the demonstration for the infinity of the universe, whereof the first argument alleged is, that those who by their imaginations would set walls or bounds to it are not able themselves to assign or fix the extremities of it. . . .

The topic of the sixth argument is that by making the world finite, a vacuum cannot be avoided, if that be void where there is nothing; though we shall evince this void to be impossible. . . .

The eighth argument is that none of the senses excludes infinity, since we cannot deny it, merely because not comprehended by any of our senses; but rather assert it, because by it the senses are comprehended, and reason comes to their help to confirm it: nay, if we further consider, our senses do ever suppose infinity, since we always see one thing terminated by another thing; and that we never perceived anything by internal or external sense that was not terminated by a thing like itself or by some other thing different from itself. . . . Even by what we see, then, we ought rather to infer infinity than otherwise, because nothing occurs in nature that is not terminated by another and no one thing whatsoever is terminated by itself. . . .

[Many other arguments follow.]

Here you'll meet with the reasons why we should not fear that any part of this Universe should fall or fly off, that the least particle should be lost in empty space or be truly annihilated. Here you'll perceive the reason of that vicissitude which may be observed in the constant change of all things, whereby it happens that there is nothing so ill but may befall us or be prevented, nor anything so good but may be lost or obtained by us; since in this infinite field the parts and modes do perpetually vary, though the substance and the whole do eternally persevere the same.

From this contemplation (if we do but rightly consider) it will follow that we ought never to be dispirited by any strange accidents through excess of fear or pain, nor ever be elated by any prosperous event through excess of hope or pleasure; whence we have the way to true Morality, and, by following it, we would become the magnanimous despisers of what men of childish thoughts do fondly esteem, and the wise judges of the history of nature which is written in our minds, and the strict executioners of those divine laws which are engraven in the center of our hearts. We would know that it is no harder thing to fly from hence up to Heaven than to fly from heaven back again to the Earth, that ascending thither and descending hither are all one; that we are no more circumferential to the other Globes than they are to us, nor they more central to us than we are to them, and that none of them is more above the stars than we, as they are no less than we covered over or comprehended by the sky. Behold us therefore free from envying them! behold us delivered from the vain anxiety and foolish care of desiring to enjoy that good afar off which in as great a degree we may possess so near at hand, and even at home! Behold us freed from the terror that they should fall upon us, anymore than we should hope that we might fall upon them; since every one as well as all of those globes are sustained by infinite Ether, in which this our animal freely runs, and keeps to his prescribed course, as the rest of the planets do to theirs.

Did we but consider and comprehend all this, oh! to what much further considerations and comprehensions should we be carried! as we might be sure to obtain that happiness by virtue of this science, which in other sciences is sought after in vain. This is that philosophy which opens the senses, which satisfies the mind, which enlarges the understanding, and which leads man to the only true beatitude whereof he's capable according to his natural state and constitution; for it frees him from the solicitous pursuit of pleasure and from the anxious apprehensions of pain, making him enjoy the good things of the present hour, and not to fear more than he hopes from the future; since that same providence, or fate, or fortune, which causes the vicissitudes of our particular being will not let us know more of the one than we are ignorant of the other. At first sight, indeed, we are apt to be dubious and perplexed: but when we more profoundly consider the essence and accidents of that matter into which we are mutable, we'll find that there is no death attending ours or the substance of any other thing; since nothing is substantially diminished, but only everything changing form by its perpetual motion in this infinite space. And seeing that everything is subject to a good and most perfect efficient cause, we ought neither to believe nor to hope otherwise than that as everything proceeds from what is good, so the whole must needs be good, in a good state, and to a good purpose: the contrary of which appears only to them who consider no more than is just before them, as the beauty of an edifice is not manifest to one that has seen only some small portion of the same, as a stone, the plastering, or part of a wall; but is most charming to him that saw the whole and had leisure to observe the symmetry of the parts.

We fear not therefore that what is accumulated in this world should by the malice of some wandering spirit or by the wrath of some evil genius be shaken and scattered, as it were into smoke or dust, out of this cupola of the sky, and beyond the starry mantle of the firmament; nor that the nature of things can otherwise come to be annihilated in substance, than as it seems to our eyes that the air contained in the concavity of a bubble is become nothing when that bubble is burst; because we know that in the world one thing ever succeeds another, there being no utmost bottom, whence, as by the hand of an artificer, things are irreparably struck into nothing. There are no ends, limits, margins, or walls that keep back or subtract any parcel of the infinite abundance of things. Thence it is that the earth and sea are ever equally fertile, and thence the perpetual brightness of the sun; eternal fuel circulating to those devouring fires, and a supply of waters being eternally furnished to the evaporated seas, from the infinite and ever-renewing magazine of matter. . . .

Look to it now, Gentlemen Astrologers, with your humble servants the Natural Philosophers, and see to what use you can put your Circles that are described by the imaginary nine moveable Spheres, in which you so imprison your brains that you seem to me like so many parrots in their cages, hopping and dancing from one perch to another, yet always turning and winding within the same wires. But be it known unto you that so great an Emperor has not so narrow a palace, so miserable a throne, so low a tribunal, so scanty a court, so little and weak a representative; as that a fancy can bring it forth, a dream overlay it, madness repair it, a chimera shatter it, a disaster lessen it, another accident increase

it, and a thought make it perfect again, being brought together by a blast and made solid by a shake. It is, on the contrary, an immense portraiture, an admirable image, an exalted figure, a most high vestige, an infinite representation of an infinite original, and a spectacle befitting the excellence and eminence of Him that can neither be imagined, nor conceived, nor comprehended.

Thus the excellence of God is magnified, and the grandeur of his Empire made manifest. He's not glorified in one but in numberless Suns, not in one Earth or in one World, but in ten hundred thousand, in infinite Globes: so that this faculty of the intellect is not vain or arbitrary, that ever will and can add space to space, quantity to quantity, unity to unity, number to number. By this science we are loosened from the chains of a most narrow dungeon and set at liberty to rove in a most august empire. We are removed from conceited boundaries and poverty to the innumerable riches of an infinite space, of so worthy a field, and of such beautiful worlds.

Sir Francis Bacon

1561–1626

Francis Bacon had the outstanding intellect of Elizabethan England, and his achievements in a wide variety of fields reflect the ideal versatility of the Renaissance man. His own age knew him as a statesman who rose to political heights as lord chancellor of James I. He is popularly remembered as the author of some pithy and worldly-wise essays on moral subjects. A few enthusiastic but misguided scholars have even credited him with writing the plays of Shakespeare. But he thought of himself as a philosopher and aspired to review and renew all the sciences in the manner of Aristotle. Perhaps his greatest service to Western culture lay in articulating a scientific method and bridging the gap between Renaissance scientists and modern science.

This ambitious thinker was ideally trained for his remarkable career. His distinguished father, Sir Nicholas Bacon, was Lord Keeper of the Seal under Elizabeth and educated his two promising sons, Anthony and Francis, at Cambridge. Anthony's later career in politics was only slightly less distinguished than his younger brother's. Francis left Cambridge at fourteen to study law and interrupted his law preparation a year later to join a diplomatic embassy to France. He was admitted to the bar in 1582 and soon entered Parliament. With the accession of James I in 1603 he rose rapidly to a commanding political position. He was knighted and eventually created Baron Verulam. Between 1607 and 1618 he rose from solicitor-general through the offices of attorney-general, privy councilor, and Lord Keeper of the Seal to be lord chancellor of England.

Three years later he fell suddenly from this eminence when he was accused of having taken bribes; he confessed to the charge and was deprived of all his offices and even barred from court and Parliament. Deeply impressed by the political philosophy of Machiavelli, he had long preached a pragmatic morality in his essays and had apparently applied it to his own political activities. It was regrettable that the great thinker of this age should have stooped to dishonesty in his public career but it is by no means inconsistent with his completely materialistic philosophy. In the five years remaining to him he pursued his legal and scientific studies and died of a chill contracted in experimenting with snow as a preservative of meat.

At no time in his life was Bacon too busy to study and write. The three editions of his *Essays* belong to the three periods of his career: his political apprenticeship (1597), his rise to power (1612), and his disgrace and retirement (1625). These little epigrammatic studies offer highly practical wisdom on many subjects: marriage and the single life, youth and age, love and friendship, health and riches, ambition, superstition, and the nature of man. Bacon's clear-cut, aphoristic style concentrates a world of common sense in a few memorable sentences.

But the *Essays* were merely relaxation for his energetic mind. His philosophy he committed to Latin in which language he projected a thorough review of existing sciences as well as the discovery of new knowledge by a new organon, or method of approaching the facts of nature. He planned his total scientific compendium as the *Great Instauration,* or renovation, of natural knowledge. The first part, *The Advancement of Learning* (1605), was first published in English and only later formed part of the larger scheme when elaborated as *De Augmentis Scientiarum.* It gave a review of the state of knowledge in Bacon's time and suggested a system of classifying the various branches of learning. The second part, the *Novum Organum* (1620), described the new method of true science in opposition to older methods beclouded by phantoms, or "idols," of the mind. This greatest of all Bacon's works divorced science from superstition, theology, and even philosophy as older ages had known it. Although Bacon was not himself free from a priori reasoning about science and understood the experimental method only imperfectly, he paved the way for the modern science of the seventeenth century. The later parts of his *Magna Instauratio* are only fragments of his projected study of nature by the new method. The most intriguing of all his works is the *New Atlantis* (1624), a utopian sketch that describes an ideal commonwealth of scholars pursuing a scientific analysis of nature for the profit of mankind. Bacon's vision bore fruit in 1662 with the establishment in London of the Royal Society for Improving Natural Knowledge.

As an enthusiastic pioneer, Bacon promised far more than he achieved. Misinterpreting nature as a simple phenomenon, he lived to see that no one man could explore it all. A more serious defect was his disregard of the hypothesis as the starting point of scientific method. He despised mere authority and syllogistic reasoning so

much that he placed too great trust in the mere observation of natural things. Demanding certainty rather than probability, he failed to see that the scientist must begin with a probable assumption, or hypothesis, to guide his experiment. He was right in affirming that science reaches its conclusions by induction, finding general truths in particular instances. He was right in condemning the reverse reasoning from generals to particulars, but he slighted the role of scientific imagination in initiating the observation of particulars. Still he cleared the ground of older prejudices, and his magnificent plea for observing facts without preconceptions makes him the most revered spokesman for science in the Renaissance.

Novum Organum

1.

MAN, being the servant and interpreter of Nature, can do and understand so much and so much only as he has observed in fact or in thought of the course of nature: beyond this he neither knows anything nor can do anything.

2. Neither the naked hand nor the understanding left to itself can effect much. It is by instruments and helps that the work is done, which are as much wanted for the understanding as for the hand. And as the instruments of the hand either give motion or guide it, so the instruments of the mind supply either suggestions for the understanding or cautions.

3. Human knowledge and human power meet in one; for where the cause is not known the effect cannot be produced. Nature to be commanded must be obeyed; and that which in contemplation is as the cause is in operation as the rule.

4. Towards the effecting of works, all that man can do is to put together or put asunder natural bodies. The rest is done by nature working within. . . .

26. The conclusions of human reason as ordinarily applied in matter of nature, I call for the sake of distinction *Anticipations of Nature* (as a thing rash or premature). That reason which is elicited from facts by a just and methodical process, I call *Interpretation of Nature.*

27. Anticipations are a ground sufficiently firm for consent; for even if men went mad all after the same fashion, they might agree one with another well enough.

28. For the winning of assent, indeed, anticipations are far more powerful than interpretations; because being collected from a few instances, and those for the most part of familiar occurrence, they straightway touch the understanding and fill the

Novum Organum.[3] Translated by James Spedding.

imagination; whereas interpretations on the other hand, being gathered here and there from very various and widely dispersed facts, cannot suddenly strike the understanding; and therefore they must needs, in respect of the opinions of the time, seem harsh and out of tune; much as the mysteries of faith do.

29. In sciences founded on opinions and dogmas, the use of anticipations and logic is good; for in them the object is to command assent to the proposition, not to master the thing.

30. Though all the wits of all the ages should meet together and combine and transmit their labours, yet will no great progress ever be made in science by means of anticipations; because radical errors in the first concoction of the mind are not to be cured by the excellence of functions and remedies subsequent.

31. It is idle to expect any great advancement in science from the superinducing and engrafting of new things upon old. We must begin anew from the very foundations, unless we would revolve for ever in a circle with mean and contemptible progress.

32. The honour of the ancient authors, and indeed of all, remains untouched; since the comparison I challenge is not of wits or faculties, but of ways and methods, and the part I take upon myself is not that of a judge, but of a guide.

33. This must be plainly avowed: no judgment can be rightly formed either of my method or of the discoveries to which it leads, by means of anticipations (that is to say, of the reasoning which is now in use); since I cannot be called on to abide by the sentence of a tribunal which is itself on its trial. . . .

36. One method of delivery alone remains to us; which is simply this: we must lead men to the particulars themselves, and their series and order; while men on their side must force themselves for awhile to lay their notions by and begin to familiarize themselves with facts.

37. The doctrine of those who have denied that certainty could be attained at all, has some agreement with my way of proceeding at the first setting out; but they end in being infinitely separated and opposed. For the holders of that doctrine assert simply that nothing can be known; I also assert that not much can be known in nature by the way which ɪs now in use. But then they go on to destroy the authority of the senses and understanding; whereas I proceed to devise and supply helps for the same.

38. The idols and false notions which are now in possession of the human understanding, and have taken deep root therein, not only so beset men's minds that truth can hardly find entrance, but even after entrance obtained, they will again in the very instauration of the sciences meet and trouble us, unless men being forewarned of the danger fortify themselves as far as may be against their assaults.

39. There are four classes of Idols which beset men's minds. To these for distinction's sake I have assigned names,—calling the first class *Idols of the Tribe;* the second, *Idols of the Cave;* the third, *Idols of the Market-place;* the fourth, *Idols of the Theatre.* . . .

41. The Idols of the Tribe have their foundation in human nature itself, and in the tribe or race of men. For it is a false assertion that the sense of man is the measure of things. On the contrary, all perceptions as well of the sense as of the mind are according to the measure of the universe. And the human understanding is like a false mirror, which, receiving rays irregularly, distorts and discolours the nature of things by mingling its own nature with it.

42. The Idols of the Cave are the idols of the individual man. For every one (besides the errors common to human nature in general) has a cave or den of his own, which refracts and discolours the light of nature; owing either to his own proper and peculiar nature; or to his education and conversation with others; or to the reading of books, and the authority of those whom he esteems and admires; or to the differences of impressions, accordingly as they take place in a mind preoccupied and predisposed or in a mind indifferent and settled; or the like. So that the spirit of man (according as it is meted out to different individuals) is in fact a thing variable and full of perturbation, and governed as it were by chance. Whence it was well observed by Heraclitus that men look for sciences in their own lesser worlds, and not in the greater or common world.

43. There are also Idols formed by the intercourse and association of men with each other, which I call Idols of the Market-place, on account of the commerce and consort of men there. For it is by discourse that men associate; and words are imposed according to the apprehension of the vulgar. And therefore the ill and unfit choice of words wonderfully obstructs the understanding. Nor do the definitions or explanations wherewith in some things learned men are wont to guard and defend themselves, by any means set the matter right. But words plainly force and overrule the understanding, and throw all into confusion, and lead men away into numberless empty controversies and idle fancies.

44. Lastly, there are Idols which have immigrated into men's minds from the various dogmas of philosophies, and also from wrong laws of demonstration. These I call Idols of the Theatre; because in my judgment all the received systems are but so many stage-plays, representing worlds of their own creation after an unreal and scenic fashion. Nor is it

88. **Heraclitus,** the Greek philosopher of Ephesus (fl. 515 B.C.), who taught that man's narrow experience gives him a false belief in the permanence of external things.

only of the systems now in vogue, or only of the ancient sects and philosophies, that I speak; for many more plays of the same kind may yet be composed and in like artificial manner set forth; seeing that errors the most widely different have nevertheless causes for the most part alike. Neither again do I mean this only of entire systems, but also of many principles and axioms in science, which by tradition, credulity, and negligence have come to be received. But of these several kinds of Idols I must speak more largely and exactly, that the understanding may be duly cautioned.

45. The human understanding is of its own nature prone to suppose the existence of more order and regularity in the world than it finds. And though there be many things in nature which are singular and unmatched, yet it devises for them parallels and conjugates and relatives which do not exist. Hence the fiction that all celestial bodies move in perfect circles; spirals and dragons being (except in name) utterly rejected. Hence too the element of Fire with its orb is brought in, to make up the square with the other three which the sense perceives. Hence also the ratio of density of the so-called elements is arbitrarily fixed at ten to one. And so on of other dreams. And these fancies affect not dogmas only, but simple notions also.

46. The human understanding when it has once adopted an opinion (either as being the received opinion or as being agreeable to itself) draws all things else to support and agree with it. And though there be a greater number and weight of instances to be found on the other side, yet these it either neglects and despises, or else by some distinction sets aside and rejects; in order that by this great and pernicious predetermination the authority of its former conclusions may remain inviolate. And therefore it was a good answer that was made by one who when they showed him hanging in a temple a picture of those who had paid their vows as having escaped shipwreck, and would have him say whether he did not now acknowledge the power of the gods,— "Aye," asked he again, "but where are they painted that were drowned after their vows?" And such is the way of all superstition, whether in astrology, dreams, omens, divine judgments, or the like; wherein men, having a delight in such vanities, mark the events where they are fulfilled, but where they fail, though this happen much oftener, neglect and pass them by. But with far more subtlety does this mischief insinuate itself into philosophy and the sciences; in which the first conclusion colours and brings into conformity with itself all that come after, though far sounder and better. Besides, independently of that delight and vanity which I have described, it is the peculiar and perpetual error of the human intellect to be more moved and excited by affirmatives than by negatives; whereas it ought properly to hold itself indifferently disposed towards both alike. Indeed in the establishment of any true axiom, the negative instance is the more forcible of the two.

47. The human understanding is moved by those things most which strike and enter the mind simultaneously and suddenly, and so fill the imagination; and then it feigns and supposes all other things to be somehow, though it cannot see how, similar to those few things by which it is surrounded. But for that going to and fro to remote and heterogeneous instances, by which axioms are tried as in the fire, the intellect is altogether slow and unfit, unless it be forced thereto by severe laws and overruling authority.

48. The human understanding is unquiet; it cannot stop or rest, and still presses onward, but in vain. Therefore it is that we cannot conceive of any end or limit to the world; but always as of necessity it occurs to us that there is something beyond. Neither again can it be conceived how eternity has flowed down to the present day; for that distinction which is commonly received of infinity in time past and in time to come can by no means hold; for it would thence follow that one infinity is greater than another, and that infinity is wasting away and tending to become finite. The like subtlety arises touching the infinite divisibility of lines, from the same inability of thought to stop. But this inability interferes more mischievously in the discovery of causes: for although the most general principles in nature ought to be held merely positive, as they are discovered, and cannot with truth be referred to a cause; nevertheless the human understanding being unable to rest still seeks something prior in the order of nature. And then it is that in struggling towards that which is further off it falls back upon that which is more nigh at hand; namely, on final causes: which have relation clearly to the nature of man rather than to the nature of the universe; and from this source have strangely defiled philosophy. But he is no less an unskilled and shallow philosopher who seeks causes of that which is most general, than he who in things subordinate and subaltern omits to do so.

49. The human understanding is no dry light, but receives an infusion from the will and affections; whence proceed sciences which may be called "sciences as one would." For what a man had rather were true he more readily believes. Therefore he rejects difficult things from impatience of research; sober things, because they narrow hope; the deeper things of nature, from superstition; the light of experience, from arrogance and pride, lest his mind should seem to be occupied with things mean and transitory; things not commonly believed, out of deference to the opinion of the vulgar. Numberless in

short are the ways, and sometimes imperceptible, in which the affections colour and infect the understanding. . . .

96. We have as yet no natural philosophy that is pure; all is tainted and corrupted; in Aristotle's school by logic; in Plato's by natural theology; in the second school of Platonists, such as Proclus and others, by mathematics, which ought only to give definiteness to natural philosophy, not to generate or give it birth. From a natural philosophy pure and unmixed, better things are to be expected.

97. No one has yet been found so firm of mind and purpose as resolutely to compel himself to sweep away all theories and common notions, and to apply the understanding, thus made fair and even, to a fresh examination of particulars. Thus it happens that human knowledge, as we have it, is a mere medley and ill-digested mass, made up of much credulity and much accident, and also of the childish notions which we at first imbibed. . . .

99. Again, even in the great plenty of mechanical experiments, there is yet a great scarcity of those which are of most use for the information of the understanding. For the mechanic, not troubling himself with the investigation of truth, confines his attention to those things which bear upon his particular work, and will not either raise his mind or stretch out his hand for anything else. But then only will there be good ground of hope for the further advance of knowledge, when there shall be received and gathered together into natural history a variety of experiments, which are of no use in themselves, but simply serve to discover causes and axioms; which I call *Experimenta lucifera,*" experiments of *light,* to distinguish them from those which I call *fructifera,*" experiments of *fruit.*

Now experiments of this kind have one admirable property and condition; they never miss or fail. For since they are applied, not for the purpose of producing any particular effect, but only of discovering the natural cause of some effect, they answer the end equally well whichever way they turn out; for they settle the question. . . .

104. The understanding must not however be allowed to jump and fly from particulars to remote axioms and of almost the highest generality (such as the first principles, as they are called, of arts and things), and taking stand upon them as truths that cannot be shaken, proceed to prove and frame the middle axioms by reference to them; which has been the practice hitherto; the understanding being not only carried that way by a natural impulse, but also by the use of syllogistic demonstration trained and inured to it. But then, and then only, may we hope well of the sciences, when in a just scale of ascent, and by successive steps not interrupted or broken, we rise from particulars to lesser axioms; and then

to middle axioms, one above the other; and last of all to the most general. For the lowest axioms differ but slightly from bare experience, while the highest and most general (which we now have) are notional and abstract and without solidity. But the middle are the true and solid and living axioms, on which depend the affairs and fortunes of men; and above them again, last of all, those which are indeed the most general; such I mean as are not abstract, but of which those intermediate axioms are really limitations.

The understanding must not therefore be supplied with wings, but rather hung with weights, to keep it from leaping and flying. Now this has never yet been done; when it is done, we may entertain better hopes of the sciences.

Martin Luther

1483–1546

Although preceded by various heretical movements within the Roman Church, the Protestant Reformation is officially dated from the posting of Luther's Ninety-five Theses at the German town of Wittenberg in 1517. Luther's attack on papal indulgences led to the suppressive Diet of Worms, and this in turn led to the protest of nineteen German states against obstructions to the Lutheran movement, which gave rise to the term "protestant." Luther was originally innocent of any intent to secede from the Church, and only a chain of circumstances pushed him to the crucial step of an open break.

The son of pious but humble parents, he had secured a schooling at Magdeburg and Eisenach only with the aid of a benevolent patron, but at the University of Erfurt he distinguished himself as a brilliant Latin scholar. Intended for the law, he turned to divinity and eventually entered the Augustine monastery at Erfurt in 1505 because of a long trial of conscience. Having overcome his fears for his soul through deep repentance of his sins, he was ordained priest and became professor of philosophy at Wittenberg.

A trip to Rome on church business in 1510 aroused the ire of the austere preacher against the worldliness and luxury of church leaders. When in 1514 the Humanistic Pope Leo x, a son of Lorenzo de' Medici, resolved to complete the building of Saint Peter's at Rome, he issued a bull granting papal indulgence to all contributors to the building fund. A Dominican friar, John Tetzel, was authorized to preach the indulgence in northern Germany. His appearance near Wittenberg in October 1517 stirred Luther to a furious attack on the sale of papal indulgences, stated in the Ninety-five Theses that he posted on the door of the castle church. With guarded words he argued that salvation comes through inner repentance rather than from an external act of penance. This distinction assumed a personal and direct relationship between the Christian and his God and led eventually to Luther's denying the need of the Church as intermediary.

Although his propositions were denounced as heretical, Luther refused to recant and ignored a summons to Rome and two papal bulls issued against him, since he was protected by German princes who resented the political and taxational power of Rome in their states. As the controversy spread, he grew bolder and more radical in his attack on the authority of the Pope. His defiant appearance before the Diet of Worms was followed by his establishment of an independent German church with a new service that he completed in 1529. The Lutheran Church assumed its official status in 1530 through the publication of the Augsburg Confession, composed by his friend and great disciple, Philip Melanchthon. Yet for all his insistence on freedom of conscience, Luther refused to unite his movement with the Swiss Protestantism of Ulrich Zwingli because of differences over points of doctrine. Although he denounced the intolerance of Rome, he has been criticized for being no more tolerant of those who disagreed with him.

By 1525, Luther's break with Rome was largely completed, and his remaining years were devoted to shaping his church and to writing. In 1534 he completed his translation of the Bible, which remains the standard Protestant version in German. From time to time he composed hymns for a Protestant hymnal (*Eine feste Burg, Aus tiefer Not*), which reveal his deep love of music. But the most attractive product of his last twenty years was his *Table Talk*, actually his casual conversation as it was taken down by twelve devoted disciples. Married in 1525 to a former nun, he made their home an open house for his followers, who have left a charming impression of the domestic quiet and scholarly ease of Luther's later years. In the varied *Table Talk* we see the humanity of the man, his mellow delight in living, his robust piety, and even his occasional coarseness. Only Boswell's *Johnson* equals the frankness of this personal reporting.

Table Talk

11.

I HAVE grounded my preaching upon the literal word; he that pleases may follow me; he that will not may stay. I call upon St. Peter, St. Paul, Moses, and all the Saints to say whether they ever fundamentally comprehended one single word of God without studying it over and over and over again. The Psalm says: *His understanding is infinite.* The saints, indeed, know God's word, and can discourse of it, but the practice is another matter; therein we shall ever remain scholars.

*Table Talk.*³ Translated by William Hazlitt.

The school theologians have a fine similitude hereupon, that it is as with a sphere or globe, which, lying on a table, touches it only with one point, yet it is the whole table which supports the globe. Though I am an old doctor of divinity, to this day I have not got beyond the children's learning—the Ten Commandments, the Belief, and the Lord's Prayer; and these I understand not so well as I should, though I study them daily, praying, with my son John and my daughter Magdalen. If I thoroughly appreciated these first words of the Lord's Prayer, *Our Father, which art in Heaven,* and really believed that God, who made heaven and earth and all creatures, and has all things in his hand, was my Father, then should I certainly conclude with myself that I also am a lord of heaven and earth, that Christ is my brother, Gabriel my servant, Raphael my coachman, and all the angels my attendants at need, given unto me by my heavenly Father to keep me in the path, that unawares I knock not my foot against a stone. But that our faith may be exercised and confirmed, our heavenly Father suffers us to be cast into dungeons or plunged in water. So we may see how finely we understand these words, and how belief shakes, and how great our weakness is, so that we begin to think—Ah, who knows how far that is true which is set forth in the Scriptures?

12. No greater mischief can happen to a Christian people than to have God's word taken from them, or falsified, so that they no longer have it pure and clear. God grant we and our descendants be not witnesses of such a calamity.

20. Oh! how great and glorious a thing it is to have before one the Word of God! With that we may at all times feel joyous and secure; we need never be in want of consolation, for we see before us, in all its brightness, the pure and right way. He who loses sight of the word of God falls into despair; the voice of heaven no longer sustains him; he follows only the disorderly tendency of his heart, and of world vanity, which lead him on to his destruction.

33. In all sciences, the ablest professors are they who have thoroughly mastered the texts. A man, to be a good jurisconsult, should have every text of the law at his fingers' ends; but in our time, the attention is applied rather to glosses and commentaries. When I was young, I read the Bible over and over and over again, and was so perfectly acquainted with it that I could, in an instant, have pointed to any verse that might have been mentioned. I then read the commentators, but I soon threw them aside, for I found therein many things my conscience could not approve, as being contrary to the sacred text. 'Tis always better to see with one's own eyes than with those of other people.

39. I never thought the world had been so

wicked, when the Gospel began, as now I see it is; I rather hoped that every one would have leaped for joy to have found himself freed from the filth of the pope, from his lamentable molestations of poor troubled consciences, and that through Christ they would by faith obtain the celestial treasure they sought after before with such vast cost and labour, though in vain. And especially I thought the bishops and universities would with joy of heart have received the true doctrines, but I have been lamentably deceived. Moses and Jeremiah, too, complained they had been deceived.

58. The ungodly papists prefer the authority of the church far above God's Word; a blasphemy abominable and not to be endured; wherewith, void of all shame and piety, they spit in God's face. Truly, God's patience is exceeding great, in that they be not destroyed; but so it always has been.

63. All the works of God are unsearchable and unspeakable, no human sense can find them out; faith only takes hold of them without human power or aid. No mortal creature can comprehend God in his majesty, and therefore did he come before us in the simplest manner, and was made man, ay, sin, death, and weakness.

In all things, in the least creatures and in their members, God's almighty power and wonderful works clearly shine. For what man, how powerful, wise, and holy soever, can make out of one fig a fig-tree, or another fig? or out of one cherry-stone a cherry or a cherry-tree? or what man can know how God creates and preserves all things and makes them grow?

Neither can we conceive how the eye sees or how intelligible words are spoken plainly when only the tongue moves and stirs in the mouth; all which are natural things, daily seen and acted. How then should we be able to comprehend or understand the secret counsels of God's majesty, or search them out with our human sense, reason, or understanding. Should we then admire our own wisdom? I, for my part, admit myself a fool, and yield myself captive.

67. When one asked where God was before heaven was created, St. Augustin answered: He was in himself. When another asked me the same question, I said: He was building Hell for such idle, presumptuous, fluttering, and inquisitive spirits as you. After he had created all things, he was everywhere, and yet he was nowhere, for I cannot take hold of him without the Word. But he will be found there where he has engaged to be. The Jews found him at Jerusalem by the throne of grace (Exod. xxv.) We find him in the Word and faith, in baptism and the sacraments; but in his majesty, he is nowhere to be found.

91. God, in this world, has scarce the tenth part of the people; the smallest number only will be saved. The world is exceeding ungodly and wicked; who would believe our people should be so unthankful towards the gospel?

100. Our loving Lord God wills that we eat, drink, and be merry, making use of his creatures, for therefore he created them. He will not that we complain, as if he had not given sufficient, or that he could not maintain our poor carcases; he asks only that we acknowledge him for our God, and thank him for his gifts.

123. Dr. Jonas, inviting Luther to dinner, caused a bunch of ripe cherries to be hung over the table where they dined, in remembrance of the creation, and as a suggestion to his guests to praise God for creating such fruits. But Luther said: Why not rather remember this in one's children, that are the fruit of one's body? For these are far more excelling creatures of God than all the fruits of trees. In them we see God's power, wisdom, and art, who made them all out of nothing, gave them life and limbs, exquisitely constructed, and will maintain and preserve them. Yet how little do we regard this. When people have children, all the effect is to make them grasping, raking together all they can to leave behind them. They do not know that before a child comes into the world, it has its lot assigned already, and that it is ordained and determined what and how much it shall have. In the married state we find that the conception of children depends not on our will and pleasure; we never know whether God will give us a son or a daughter. All this goes on without our counsel. My father and mother did not imagine they should have brought a spiritual overseer into the world. 'Tis God's work only, and this we cannot enter into. I believe that, in the life to come, we shall have nothing to do, but to meditate on and marvel at our Creator and his creatures.

171. Idolatry is all manner of seeming holiness and worshipping, let these counterfeit spiritualities shine outwardly as glorious and fair as they may; in a word, all manner of devotion in those that would serve God without Christ the Mediator, his Word and command. In Popedom it was held a work of the greatest sanctity for the monks to sit in their cells and meditate of God and of his wonderful works; to be kindled with zeal, kneeling on their knees, praying, and having their imaginary contemplations of celestial objects with such supposed devotion that they wept for joy. In these their conceits, they banished all desires and thoughts of women, and what else is temporal and evanescent. They seemed to meditate only of God and of his wonderful works. Yet all these seeming holy actions of devotion, which the wit and wisdom of man holds to be angelical sanctity, are nothing else but works of the flesh. All manner of religion, where people serve God without his Word and command, is simply

idolatry, and the more holy and spiritual such a religion seems, the more hurtful and venomous it is; for it leads people away from the faith of Christ, and makes them rely and depend upon their own strength, works, and righteousness.

In like manner, all kinds of orders of monks, fasts, prayers, hairy shirts, the austerities of the Capuchins, who in Popedom are held to be the most holy of all, are mere works of the flesh; for the monks hold they are holy, and shall be saved, not through Christ, whom they view as a severe and angry judge, but through the rules of their order.

No man can make the papists believe that the private mass is the greatest blaspheming of God, and the highest idolatry upon earth, an abomination the like to which has never been in Christendom since the time of the apostles; for they are blinded and hardened therein, so that their understanding and knowledge of God and of all divine matters is perverted and erroneous. They hold that to be the most upright and greatest service of God which, in truth, is the greatest and most abominable idolatry. And again, they hold that for idolatry which, in truth, is the upright and most acceptable service of God, the acknowledging Christ and believing in him. But we that truly believe in Christ and are of his mind, we, God be praised, know and judge all things, but are judged of no human creature.

178. The papists took the invocation of saints from the heathen, who divided God into numberless images and idols, and ordained to each its particular office and work.

These the papists, void of all shame and Christianity, imitated, thereby denying God's almighty power; every man, out of God's Word, spinning to himself a particular opinion, according to his own fancy; as one of their priests, celebrating mass, when about to consecrate many oblations at the altar at once, thought it would not be congruously spoken, or according to grammar rules, to say, "This is my body," so said, "These are my bodies;" and afterwards highly extolled his device, saying: "If I had not been so good a grammarian, I had brought in a heresy and consecrated but one oblation."

Such like fellows does the world produce; grammarians, logicians, rhetoricians, and philosophers, all falsifying the Holy Writ and sophisticating it with their arts, whereas it ought to remain every point in its own place whereto God ordered and appointed it. Divinity should be empress, and philosophy and other arts merely servants, not to govern and master her, as Servetus, Campanus, and other seducers would do. God preserve his church, which by him is carried as a child in the mother's womb, and defend her from such philosophical divinity.

The invocation of saints is a most abominable blindness and heresy; yet the papists will not give up. The Pope's greatest profit arises from the dead; for the calling on dead saints brings him infinite sums of money and riches, far more than he gets from the living. But thus goes the world; superstition, unbelief, false doctrine, idolatry obtain more credit and profit than the upright, true, and pure religion.

250. No sinner can escape his punishment, unless he be sorry for his sins. For though one go scot-free for awhile, yet at last he will be snapped, as the Psalm says: "God indeed is still judge on earth."

Our Lord God suffers the ungodly to be surprised and taken captive in very slight and small things, when they think not of it, when they are most secure and live in delight and pleasure, leaping for joy. In such manner was the Pope surprised by me, about his indulgences and pardons, comparatively a slight matter.

574. The greatest punishment God can inflict on the wicked is when the church, to chastise them, delivers them over to Satan, who, with God's permission, kills them or makes them undergo great calamities. Many devils are in woods, in waters, in wildernesses, and in dark pooly places, ready to hunt and prejudice people; some are also in the thick black clouds which cause hail, lightnings, and thunderings and poison the air, the pastures, and grounds. When these things happen, then the philosophers and physicians say it is natural, ascribing it to the planets and showing I know not what reasons for such misfortunes and plagues as ensue.

581. August 25, 1538, the conversation fell upon witches who spoil milk, eggs, and butter in farmyards. Dr. Luther said: "I should have no compassion on these witches; I would burn all of them. We read in the old law that the priests threw the first stone at such malefactors. 'Tis said this stolen butter turns rancid and falls to the ground when any one goes to eat it. He who attempts to counteract and chastise these witches is himself corporeally plagued and tormented by their master, the devil. Sundry schoolmasters and ministers have often experienced this. Our ordinary sins offend and anger God. What, then, must be his wrath against witchcraft, which we may justly designate high treason against divine majesty, a revolt against the infinite power of God. The jurisconsults who have so learnedly and pertinently treated of rebellion, affirm that the subject who rebels against his sovereign, is worthy of death. Does not witchcraft, then, merit death, which is a revolt of the creature against the Creator, a denial to God of the authority it accords to the demon?"

591. A pastor, near Torgau, came to Luther and complained that the devil tormented him without intermission. The Doctor replied: He plagues and harasses me too, but I resist him with the arms of

faith. I know of one person at Magdeburg who put Satan to the rout by spitting at him; but this example is not to be lightly followed; for the devil is a presumptuous spirit, and not disposed to yield. We run great risk when, with him, we attempt more than we can do. One man, who relied implicitly on his baptism, when the devil presented himself to him, his head furnished with horns, tore off one of the horns; but another man, of less faith, who attempted the same thing, was killed by the devil.

605. I would rather die through the devil than through the Emperor or Pope; for then I should die through a great and mighty prince of the world. But if he eat a bit of me, 'twill be his bane; he shall spew me out again; and, at the day of judgment, I in requital will devour him.

672. Erasmus is very pitiful with his prefaces, though he tries to smooth them over; he appears to see no difference between Jesus Christ our Saviour and the wise pagan legislator Solon. He sneers at St. Paul and St. John; and ventures to say that the Epistle to the Romans, whatever it might have been at a former period, is not applicable to the present state of things. Shame upon thee, accursed wretch! 'Tis a mere Momus, making his mows and mocks at everything and everybody, at God and man, at papist and protestant, but all the while using such shuffling and double-meaning terms, that no one can lay hold of him to any effectual purpose. Whenever I pray, I pray for a curse upon Erasmus.

721. The state of matrimony is the chief in the world after religion; but people shun it because of its inconveniences, like one who, running out of the rain, falls into the river. We ought herein to have more regard to God's command and ordinance, for the sake of the generation and the bringing up of children, than to our untoward humours and cogitations; and further, we should consider that it is a physic against sin and unchastity. None, indeed, should be compelled to marry; the matter should be left to each man's conscience, for bride-love may not be forced. God has said: "It is not good that the man should be alone;" and St. Paul compares the church to a spouse, or bride and a bridegroom. But let us ever take heed that, in marrying, we esteem neither money nor wealth, great descent, nobility, nor lasciviousness.

726. Marrying cannot be without women, nor can the world subsist without them. To marry is physic against incontinence. A woman is, or at least should be, a friendly, courteous, and merry companion in life, whence they are named by the Holy Ghost house-honours, the honour and ornament of the house, and inclined to tenderness, for there-unto are they chiefly created, to bear children and be the pleasure, joy, and solace of their husbands.

25. **Momus,** the Greek god of mockery and censure.

728. On what pretence can man have interdicted marriage, which is a law of nature? 'Tis as though we were forbidden to eat, to drink, to sleep. That which God has ordained and regulated is no longer a matter of the human will, which we may adopt or reject with impunity. 'Tis the most certain sign of God's enmity to Popedom that he has allowed it to assail the conjugal union of the sexes.

732. 'Tis a grand thing for a married pair to live in perfect union, but the devil rarely permits this. When they are apart, they cannot endure the separation, and when they are together, they cannot endure the always seeing one another. 'Tis as the poet says: *Nec tecum vivere possum, nec sine te.* Married people must assiduously pray against these assaults of the devil. I have seen marriages where, at first, husband and wife seemed as though they would eat one another up: in six months they have separated in mutual disgust. 'Tis the devil inspires this evanescent ardour in order to divert the parties from prayer.

739. There was at Frankfort-on-the-Oder, a schoolmaster, a pious and learned man, whose heart was fervently inclined to theology, and who had preached several times with great applause. He was called to the dignity of deacon, but his wife, a violent, fierce woman, would not consent to his accepting the charge, saying she would not be the wife of a minister.

It became a question what was the poor man to do? Which was he to renounce, his preachership or his wife? Luther at first said jocosely: "Oh, if he has married, as you tell me, a widow, he must needs obey her." But, after awhile, he resumed severely: "The wife is bound to follow her husband, not the husband his wife. This must be an ill woman, nay, the devil incarnate, to be ashamed of a charge with which our Lord and his apostles were invested. If she were my wife, I should shortly say to her: 'Wilt thou follow me, aye or no? Reply forthwith,' and if she replied no, I would leave her and take another wife."

752. The reproduction of mankind is a great marvel and mystery. Had God consulted me in the matter, I should have advised him to continue the generation of the species by fashioning them of clay, in the way Adam was fashioned; as I should have conselled him also to let the sun remain always suspended over the earth, like a great lamp, maintaining perpetual light and heat.

840. Music is one of the best arts; the notes give life to the text; it expels melancholy, as we see in king Saul. Kings and princes ought to maintain music, for great potentates and rulers should protect good and liberal arts and laws; though private

70. *Nec tecum . . . sine te,* "I cannot live with you, nor without you." (See Martial, XII, 47.)

people have desire thereunto and love it, yet their ability is not adequate. We read in the Bible, that the good and godly kings maintained and paid singers. Music is the best solace for a sad and sorrowful mind; by it the heart is refreshed and settled again in peace.

John Milton

1608–1674

The separation of the English Church from Rome by Henry VIII was largely a political move; the true Protestant movement in England came with the radical nonconformists of the sixteenth century, who denounced the intermediation of any church, Catholic or Anglican, between man and his Maker. Inspired by Calvin, English Protestants placed a terrifying personal responsibility on man, weighed down with a depraved nature since Adam's original sin. Confronted with a powerful and even angry God, they sought to free themselves from the taint of worldliness and renounced the show of ecclesiastical vestments and fashionable dress alike to signalize the austerity of their reformed way of life. Since they wished to purify the English Church by replacing ritual with direct spiritual contact with God, they were called the Puritans. Aspiring to a theocratic state of their own and faced with persecution, they came to constitute a political party, which precipitated the Civil War of 1642–1649 in England and ruled under Cromwell for a decade (1649–1659).

Despite the sternness of their way of life, the Puritans were not without a feeling for art and beauty. Indeed, John Milton showed that a magnificent epic poem could be built upon the Calvinist doctrine of human depravity and original sin. This great Puritan poet was scarcely typical of his sect, and yet he was all his life a dissenter and nonconformist, who took an active part in the government of Cromwell. An earnest conscience had led him to renounce his Anglican background and embrace the principles of the Puritans. His father, a prosperous and cultured scrivener, educated the sensitive, artistic youth at St. Paul's School and Christ's College, Cambridge, where he considered for a time a career in the Anglican Church. But his disgust with the High Church tyranny at Cambridge led him to retire with an M.A. degree in 1632 to pursue study and writing on his father's estate at Horton, twenty miles from London. To his Horton period (1632–1637) belong the best of his minor poems: the companion pieces *L'Allegro* and *Il Penseroso* (1632), the masque *Comus* (1634), and the pastoral elegy *Lycidas* (1637) in memory of his college mate Edward King. His Latin poems, though now little read, are among the finest in the Latin revival. His interest in the culture of Renaissance Italy led him to take a leisurely tour through Paris, Genoa, Florence, and Venice, which he cut short in 1639 with the rumor of civil war at home.

The second period of his career (1639–1660) corresponds to the period of civil war and the Puritan Commonwealth in England, and it converted the accomplished young man, half Puritan in his abstemious living, half Cavalier in his elegant tastes, into the mature and ardent spokesman for Cromwell's Puritan theocracy. Serving first as private tutor in London and later as Latin Secretary to the Commission of Foreign Affairs, Milton supported the cause with a series of prose tracts that crowded poetry out of his life for twenty years. These tracts began in 1641 with *Of Reformation Touching Church Discipline in England,* which pleaded for the complete abolishment of Catholic ritual and the episcopal system from the Church. His unsuccessful marriage in 1643 to Mary Powell, a girl half his age, probably led to his tract, *The Doctrine and Discipline of Divorce Restored, to the Good of Both Sexes,* in which he argued that incompatibility of temperaments was as just ground for divorce as infidelity. When he was threatened with censorship for his advanced views, he replied with the best of his prose writings, *Areopagitica* (1644), a memorable plea for freedom of the press. The deep-seated independence of his spirit flared into a fiery radicalism in political and ecclesiastical matters, and he militantly supported the execution of Charles I in his *Tenure of Kings and Magistrates* (1649). But most of the prose writings of his second period lack general interest today. The death of his first wife in 1652 left him three small daughters to rear; and his second wife, whom he married in 1656, died in childbirth a year later. In addition to this, his eyesight had been failing throughout this period, so that by 1652 he was totally blind and had to perform his duties as Secretary through an assistant.

With restoration of the monarchy under Charles II, Milton lost his power and became for a time a fugitive from the vengeful Cavaliers. But this reversal of fortune returned his interests to poetry and led to his major poems of the last period (1660–1671). Dictating his verses to his three unappreciative daughters or his kindly third wife, he first delivered his masterpiece, *Paradise Lost* (1667). To this he added by 1671 a shorter epic of the triumph of Christ over Satan, *Paradise Regained,* and a Biblical tragedy in classical form, *Samson Agonistes,* in which the blind but still resisting Samson represents the blind Milton, unyielding to the end. Though he lived to see the Puritan cause in eclipse, his later years were sustained by his faith in himself and his poetry. Posterity has justified his faith.

Paradise Lost

Milton chose the most ambitious and forbidding of all literary forms, the epic, to give the Protestant world a noble counterpart of Dante's *Divine Comedy.* Beginning as a Calvinist, the English poet pushed his rebellion from Catholicism even further and ended as a member of no sect but rather a Protestant extremist of individual nature. *Paradise Lost* rings with the prophetic strain, as he musters his burning religious faith, his classical learning, and masterful poetic skill for an apocalyptic account of what he considered the greatest event in human history, the fall of Adam, which has encumbered man with the taint of sin from that day to this. Few poets have dared to undertake such a cosmic theme. In the vastness of his design and the sublime heights of his vision he makes demands on his reader that put him beyond popular appeal. In the words of Dr. Johnson, *"Paradise Lost* is one of the books which the reader admires and lays down, and forgets to take up again. None ever wished it longer than it is. We read Milton for instruction, retire harassed and overburdened, and look elsewhere for recreation; we desert our master, and seek for companions." The Olympian heights of Aeschylus are not easily scaled; the terrifying depths of Dante's Inferno demand hardy spirits. Milton brought the Olympian nobility of the ancients to the Christian tale of man's first fall. We must rise above everyday thought and feeling if we are to grasp his moral message and lofty poetic dream.

His purpose is simply stated: "to justify the ways of God to men," by proving that evil came not from God but from a counterspirit as evil as God is good and loving and merciful. His plot is the simple story of the tempting of Eve and Adam and of their expulsion from Eden, but he prefixes to this an account of how evil was born with the rebellion of Satan and his cohorts against the power of God in Heaven. Sworn to everlasting war with his Maker, Satan seduces the newly created man and woman in Paradise to sin, but for his arrogance is reduced to the mean estate of serpent. Man, on the other hand, is comforted with the promise of a Saviour in God's own Son.

Milton's first source was the Bible, and his poem is filled with allusions to both the Old and the New Testaments. There is much of Dante too in his description of Hell, and a strongly Calvinist interpretation of original sin and salvation by atonement. But Milton belonged also to the Renaissance and reveals on every page his classical learning and especially his indebtedness to Homer. The epic invocation; the beginning *in medias res* with the actual fall of Satan; the throwback narratives in the discussions of Adam, Eve, and the Angel; the roll call of the leaders; the epic commonplaces and elaborate similes, all remind us of the influence of Homer and Virgil in Renaissance epics. But the poem is a religious epic, not a national one, and is built around no one hero, as are the *Iliad* and the *Odyssey*. Indeed, the arch villain is the best-defined character in the poem, and the heroic treatment of Satan may suggest Milton's unconscious sympathy with a fellow rebel. *Paradise Lost* is a work of Milton's own conception, and he matched his grand intent with a noble style. His blank verse strides across older limitations to form actual paragraphs, by which larger units of narrative and thought can be developed in melodious language. The perfect harmony of thought and expression within this free framework has produced a lofty, if austere, poetic creation.

BOOK I

The Argument

This first Book proposes, first in brief, the whole subject, man's disobedience, and the loss thereupon of Paradise wherein he was placed: then touches the prime cause of his fall, the serpent, or rather Satan in the serpent; who revolting from God, and drawing to his side many legions of angels, was by the command of God driven out of Heaven with all his crew into the great deep. Which action past over, the poem hastes into the midst of things, presenting Satan with his angels now fallen into Hell, described here, not in the centre (for Heaven and Earth may be supposed as yet not made, certainly not yet accursed) but in a place of utter darkness, fitliest called Chaos: here Satan with his angels lying on the burning lake, thunder-struck and astonished, after a certain space recovers, as from confusion, calls up him who next in order and dignity lay by him; they confer of their miserable fall. Satan awakens all his legions, who lay till then in the same manner confounded; they rise, their numbers, array of battle, their chief leaders named, according to the idols known afterwards in Canaan and the countries adjoining. To these Satan directs his speech, comforts them with hope yet of regaining Heaven, but tells them lastly of a new world and new kind of creature to be created, according to an ancient prophecy or report in Heaven; for that angels were long before this visible creation, was the opinion of many ancient fathers. To find out the truth of this prophecy, and what to determine thereon he refers to a full council. What his associates thence attempt. Pandemonium, the palace of Satan, rises, suddenly built out of the deep: the infernal peers there sit in council.

O F man's first disobedience, and the fruit
Of that forbidden tree, whose mortal taste
Brought Death into the world, and all our woe,
With loss of Eden, till one greater Man
Restore us, and regain the blissful seat, 5
Sing, Heavenly Muse! that on the secret top

The Argument. **into the midst of things,** a translation of *in medias res* from Horace's *Ars Poetica,* the critical principle that an epic poem should begin in the midst of an action and later, by an "epic throwback," recount the antecedent action. This is the plan followed by Milton; Books v and vi, as in the *Odyssey,* the *Iliad,* and the *Aeneid,* put the earliest part of the story into the mouth of a narrator who took part in the antecedent action. **Pandemonium,** literally, (the place) of all demons. **1. man's . . . disobedience.** Milton conceived the fall of man as a nobler subject than the wrath of Achilles in the *Iliad,* and the greater man (l. 4)—that is, Christ—a greater figure than Odysseus or Ulysses. **6. Heavenly Muse,** not merely the classical Muse of Greek and Latin poetry, but rather the holy spirit that inspired Moses, David, and the prophets; in fact, Milton implicitly contrasts these with the pagan divinities. In Renaissance tradition, however, the ninth Muse, Urania, was the inspirer of all great men; it is therefore likely that Milton, with his Renaissance leanings, had Urania in mind at this point.

Of Oreb, or of Sinai, didst inspire
That shepherd, who first taught the chosen seed,
In the beginning how the Heavens and Earth
Rose out of Chaos: or if Sion Hill   10
Delight thee more, and Siloa's brook that flowed
Fast by the oracle of God; I thence
Invoke thy aid to my adventurous song,
That with no middle flight intends to soar
Above th' Aonian Mount, while it pursues   15
Things unattempted yet in prose or rhyme.
And chiefly Thou, O Spirit, that dost prefer
Before all temples th' upright heart and pure,
Instruct me, for Thou know'st; Thou from the first
Wast present, and with mighty wings outspread   20
Dove-like satst brooding on the vast abyss
And mad'st it pregnant: what in me is dark
Illumine, what is low raise and support,
That to the highth of this great argument
I may assert Eternal Providence,   25
And justify the ways of God to men.
    Say first, for Heaven hides nothing from thy view
Nor the deep tract of Hell, say first what cause
Moved our grand parents in that happy state,
Favoured of Heaven so highly, to fall off   30
From their Creator, and trangress His will
For one restraint, lords of the world besides?
Who first seduced them to that foul revolt?
The infernal serpent; he it was, whose guile,
Stirred up with envy and revenge, deceived   35
The mother of mankind, what time his pride
Had cast him out from Heaven, with all his host
Of rebel angels, by whose aid aspiring
To set himself in glory above his peers,
He trusted to have equalled the most High,   40
If He opposed; and with ambitious aim
Against the throne and monarchy of God
Raised impious war in Heaven and battle proud
With vain attempt. Him the Almighty Power

Hurled headlong flaming from the ethereal sky 45
With hideous ruin and combustion down
To bottomless perdition, there to dwell
In adamantine chains and penal fire,
Who durst defy the Omnipotent to arms.
Nine times the space that measures day and night 50
To mortal men, he with his horrid crew
Lay vanquished, rolling in the fiery gulf
Confounded though immortal; but his doom
Reserved him to more wrath; for now the thought
Both of lost happiness and lasting pain   55
Torments him; round he throws his baleful eyes
That witnessed huge affliction and dismay
Mixed with obdurate pride and steadfast hate:
At once as far as angel's ken he views
The dismal situation waste and wild,   60
A dungeon horrible, on all sides round,
As one great furnace flamed, yet from those flames
No light, but rather darkness visible
Served only to discover sights of woe,
Regions of sorrow, doleful shades, where peace   65
And rest can never dwell, hope never comes
That comes to all; but torture without end
Still urges, and a fiery deluge, fed
With ever-burning sulphur unconsumed:
Such place Eternal Justice had prepared   70
For those rebellious, here their prison ordained
In utter darkness, and their portion set
As far removed from God and light of Heaven
As from the centre thrice to th' utmost pole.
O how unlike the place from whence they fell!   75
There the companions of his fall, o'erwhelmed
With floods and whirlwinds of tempestuous fire,
He soon discerns, and weltering by his side
One next himself in power, and next in crime,
Long after known in Palestine, and named   80

---

7. **Oreb,** Horeb, the mountain near Mount Sinai on which God spoke to Moses from the burning bush, as told in Exodus, 3. It was atop Mount Sinai that Moses received from God the laws to govern the Hebrews, as told in Exodus, 19. 8. **That shepherd,** Moses, to whom was attributed the authorship of the Book of Genesis, which includes the story of the Creation. 10. **Sion Hill,** the hill on which Jerusalem was built. 11. **Siloa's brook,** a stream which flowed near the hill on which the Temple was built in Jerusalem. 15. **Aonian Mount,** Mount Helicon in Boeotia, Greece, which was sacred to the Muses; but Milton insists that his inspiration is higher than that of the classical poets, whence the preposition "Above." 17. **Spirit,** the Spirit of God which in the Creation moved upon the Face of the Waters (see Genesis, 1, 2); perhaps we may read it here as "The Holy Ghost." 21. **Dove-like;** cf. Luke, 3:22: "And the Holy Ghost descended in a bodily shape like a dove." 26. **justify . . . men.** The purpose of Milton in writing the epic. 32. **For one restraint,** because of one prohibition. 34. **infernal serpent.** It was a common belief in the Renaissance and later Middle Ages that devils became like serpents, dragons, worms, or creeping and crawling things. This reference of course anticipates the later event recounted in Book x, 509–540, when Satan and his entire concourse of devils are reduced to serpent-forms.

45. ff. **Hurled headlong,** etc. Cf. Isaiah, 14:12: "How art thou fallen from Heaven, O Lucifer, son of the morning!" and Jude, 1: 6: "angels which kept not their first estate . . . in everlasting chains, under darkness." 50. **Nine times,** etc. Milton is probably reminded here of the ancient Greek legend, as told by Hesiod, where Zeus, newly established King of the Gods, hurled the vanquished Titans into Tartarus; their fall took nine days and nights. There are many such classical "recalls" in Milton's epic poetry. 63. **darkness visible,** an ancient but always effective poetic paradox. 64. **discover,** reveal, disclose. 66–67. **hope . . . comes,** an obvious reminiscence of Dante's "All hope abandon, ye who enter here!" in the *Inferno*, III, 9. 68. **urges,** pushes, drives. 72. **utter,** outer, remote; not "absolute." 74. **centre . . . pole.** Although Milton knew well enough the new cosmogony based upon the Copernican system, in which the planets revolve about the sun as their center, he adopted for the purposes of his plot in *Paradise Lost* the old Ptolemaic system. In this system the center was the circle of the stellar universe, and at the center of this circle was the Earth; around it, each on its own orbit, revolved the planets, and there was a special sphere for the fixed stars. Above was Heaven; at the opposite extreme was Hell, formed out of Chaos. The radius of the stellar circle was one-third the distance from Heaven to Hell. Throughout *Paradise Lost*, therefore, Milton used the term *centre* to mean the Earth. The utmost pole is a part of Milton's special conception of the created, or stellar, universe as encased in a shell with a lower pole sunk in Chaos and an upper pole pointing toward, but not touching, Heaven.

Beëlzebub. To whom the Arch-Enemy,
And thence in Heaven called Satan, with bold words
Breaking the horrid silence thus began:
   'If thou beest he; but O, how fallen! how changed
From him, who in the happy realms of light   85
Clothed with transcendent brightness didst outshine
Myriads though bright: if he whom mutual league,
United thoughts and counsels, equal hope,
And hazard in the glorious enterprise,
Joined with me once, now misery hath joined   90
In equal ruin: into what pit thou seest
From what highth fallen, so much the stronger
        proved
He with His thunder: and till then who knew
The force of those dire arms? yet not for those,
Nor what the potent victor in his rage   95
Can else inflict, do I repent or change,
Though changed in outward lustre: that fixed mind
And high disdain, from sense of injured merit,
That with the mightiest raised me to contend,
And to the fierce contention brought along   100
Innumerable force of spirits armed
That durst dislike His reign, and me preferring,
His utmost power with adverse power opposed
In dubious battle on the plains of Heaven,
And shook His throne. What though the field be
        lost?   105
All is not lost; the unconquerable will,
And study of revenge, immortal hate,
And courage never to submit or yield:
And what is else not to be overcome.
That glory never shall His wrath or might   110
Extort from me. To bow and sue for grace
With suppliant knee, and deify His power
Who from the terror of this arm so late
Doubted His empire, that were low indeed,
That were an ignominy and shame beneath   115
This downfall; since by Fate the strength of gods
And this empyreal substance cannot fail,
Since through experience of this great event
In arms not worse, in foresight much advanced,
We may with more successful hope resolve   120
To wage by force or guile eternal war
Irreconcilable, to our grand Foe,
Who now triumphs, and in th' excess of joy
Sole reigning holds the tyranny of Heaven.'
   So spake th' apostate angel, though in pain,   125
Vaunting aloud, but racked with deep despair;
And him thus answered soon his bold compeer:

'O Prince, O Chief of many thronèd Powers,
That led th' embattled Seraphim to war
Under thy conduct, and in dreadful deeds   130
Fearless, endangered Heaven's perpetual King;
And put to proof His high supremacy,
Whether upheld by strength, or chance, or Fate,
Too well I see and rue the dire event,
That with sad overthrow and foul defeat   135
Hath lost us Heaven, and all this mighty host
In horrible destruction laid thus low,
As far as Gods and Heavenly Essences
Can perish: for the mind and spirit remains
Invincible, and vigor soon returns,   140
Though all our glory extinct, and happy state
Here swallowed up in endless misery.
But what if He our conqueror (whom I now
Of force believe almighty, since no less
Than such could have o'erpowered such force as
        ours),   145
Have left us this our spirit and strength entire
Strongly to suffer and support our pains,
That we may so suffice His vengeful ire,
Or do Him mightier service as His thralls
By right of war, whate'er His business be   150
Here in the heart of Hell to work in fire,
Or do His errands in the gloomy deep;
What can it then avail though yet we feel
Strength undiminished, or eternal being
To undergo eternal punishment?'   155
   Whereto with speedy words the arch-fiend replied:
'Fallen cherub, to be weak is miserable,
Doing or suffering; but of this be sure,
To do aught good never will be our task,
But ever to do ill our sole delight,   160
As being the contrary to His high will
Whom we resist. If then His Providence
Out of our evil seek to bring forth good,
Our labour must be to pervert that end,
And out of good still to find means of evil;   165
Which oft-times may succeed, so as perhaps
Shall grieve Him, if I fail not, and disturb
His inmost counsels from their destined aim.
But see, the angry victor hath recalled
His ministers of vengeance and pursuit   170
Back to the gates of Heaven; the sulphurous hail
Shot after us in storm, o'erblown hath laid
The fiery surge, that from the precipice
Of Heaven received us falling, and the thunder,

81. **Beelzebub,** considered the captain of the first of the nine orders of Devils, and generally placed second in rank to Satan himself. 92. **so much the stronger proved.** Observe the backward-pointing allusion to the Battle in Heaven, which is described later in the poem (Book VI). 98. **injured merit.** The emphasis in the poem on Satan's abilities and merit gives his character tragic implications. 107. **study,** pursuit of, zeal for. 114. **Doubted,** feared for. 115. **ignominy.** The third syllable of this word was frequently dropped in seventeenth-century English, with a resulting pronunciation of *ignomy*.

128–129. **Powers . . . Seraphim.** Milton follows the celestial hierarchy described by Dante in his *Paradiso*,XXVIII. The order presents (1) Seraphim; (2) Cherubim; (3) Thrones; (4) Dominions; (5) Virtues; (6) Powers; (7) Principalities; (8) Archangels; (9) Angels. 138. **Heavenly Essences,** the supernaturally material bodies of spirits. There is some doubt in the minds of the demons themselves whether or not their essences are perishable; note Book II, lines 99 and 145–154 below. 144. **Of force,** of necessity, necessarily. 148. **so suffice . . . ire.** Milton follows Dante in believing that evil spirits are sometimes permitted to wander and thereby carry out the judgments of God. 158. **Doing or suffering,** that is, whether active or passive.

Winged with red lightning and impetuous rage, 175
Perhaps hath spent his shafts, and ceases now
To bellow through the vast and boundless deep.
Let us not slip the occasion, whether scorn,
Or satiate fury yield it from our Foe.
Seest thou yon dreary plain, forlorn and wild, 180
The seat of desolation, void of light,
Save what the glimmering of these livid flames
Casts pale and dreadful? Thither let us tend
From off the tossing of these fiery waves,
There rest, if any rest can harbour there, 185
And reassembling our afflicted powers,
Consult how we may henceforth most offend
Our Enemy, our own loss how repair,
How overcome this dire calamity,
What reinforcement we may gain from hope, 190
If not what resolution from despair.'

　　Thus Satan talking to his nearest mate
With head up-lift above the wave, and eyes
That sparkling blazed, his other parts besides
Prone on the flood, extended long and large 195
Lay floating many a rood, in bulk as huge
As whom the fables name of monstrous size,
Titanian, or Earth-born, that warred on Jove,
Briareos or Typhon, whom the den
By ancient Tarsus held, or that sea-beast 200
Leviathan, which God of all His works
Created hugest that swim the ocean stream:
Him haply slumbering on the Norway foam
The pilot of some small night-foundered skiff,
Deeming some island, oft, as seamen tell, 205
With fixed anchor in his scaly rind
Moors by his side under the lee, while night
Invests the sea, and wishéd morn delays:
So stretched out huge in length the arch-fiend lay
Chained on the burning lake, nor ever thence 210
Had risen or heaved his head, but that the will
And high permission of all-ruling Heaven
Left him at large to his own dark designs,
That with reiterated crimes he might
Heap on himself damnation, while he sought 215
Evil to others, and enraged might see
How all his malice served but to bring forth
Infinite goodness, grace and mercy shown
On man by him seduced, but on himself
Treble confusion, wrath and vengeance poured. 220

Forthwith upright he rears from off the pool
His mighty stature; on each hand the flames
Driven backward slope their pointing spires, and
　　rolled
In billows, leave in the midst a horrid vale.
Then with expanded wings he steers his flight 225
Aloft, incumbent on the dusky air
That felt unusual weight, till on dry land
He lights, if it were land that ever burned
With solid, as the lake with liquid fire;
And such appeared in hue, as when the force 230
Of subterranean wind transports a hill
Torn from Pelorus, or the shattered side
Of thundering Aetna, whose combustible
And fuelled entrails thence conceiving fire,
Sublimed with mineral fury, aid the winds, 235
And leave a singéd bottom all involved
With stench and smoke; such resting found the sole
Of unblessed feet. Him followed his next mate,
Both glorying to have scaped the Stygian flood
As gods, and by their own recovered strength, 240
Not by the sufferance of supernal power.
　　'Is this the region, this the soil, the clime,'
Said then the lost archangel, 'this the seat
That we must change for Heaven, this mournful
　　gloom
For that celestial light? Be it so, since He 245
Who now is Sovereign can dispose and bid
What shall be right: farthest from Him is best;
Whom reason hath equalled, force hath made su-
　　preme
Above His equals. Farewell, happy fields!
Where Joy forever dwells. Hail, horrors! hail, 250
Infernal world! and thou profoundest Hell,
Receive thy new possessor: one who brings
A mind not to be changed by place or time.
The mind is its own place, and in itself
Can make a Heaven of Hell, a Hell of Heaven. 255
What matter where, if I be still the same,
And what I should be, all but less than He
Whom thunder hath made greater? Here at least
We shall be free; the Almighty hath not built
Here for His envy, will not drive us hence: 260
Here we may reign secure, and in my choice
To reign is worth ambition, though in Hell:
Better to reign in Hell than serve in Heaven.
But wherefore let we then our faithful friends,
The associates and copartners of our loss 265
Lie thus astonished on the oblivious pool,

186. **afflicted,** conquered, cast down. 199. **Briareos or Typhon,** in Greek myth, two monsters. Briareos had a hundred hands; Typhon a hundred fire-breathing heads. They attempted to overthrow the sovereignty of Zeus, king of the gods of Olympus. Typhon lived in Cilicia, of which the ancient city of Tarsus was capital; the locale is, of course, Asia Minor. 201. **Leviathan.** There is more than one Biblical allusion to the monster Leviathan; Milton seems here to be thinking of that in Isaiah, 27:1: ". . . the piercing serpent, even Leviathan, that crooked serpent; and he shall slay the dragon that is in the sea." There is a very ancient tradition of the sea-monster or sea-serpent so large that he is often mistaken for an island, to the disaster of mariners; the Middle Ages often used this monster as symbol of the Devil, as in the Medieval Bestiary. Note l. 204.

232. **Pelorus,** the northeastern cape on the island of Sicily, near the great volcano Aetna (l. 233). 235. **Sublimed,** purified by incandescence—an alchemical term. 239. **Stygian flood,** a lake derived from the river Styx of the classical Underworld. 242. **clime,** region. 254–255. **mind . . . Heaven,** a favorite idea of thinking men in the Renaissance, an idea antithetical to current beliefs in the Middle Ages—perhaps we can call it an unshakable trait in the modern mind, though analogies can be found in ancient literature. 266. **oblivious,** bestowing forgetfulness or oblivion.

And call them not to share with us their part
In this unhappy mansion, or once more
With rallied arms to try what may be yet
Regained in Heaven, or what more lost in Hell?' 270
So Satan spake, and him Beëlzebub
Thus answered: 'Leader of those armies bright,
Which but the Omnipotent none could have foiled,
If once they hear that voice, their liveliest pledge
Of hope in fears and dangers, heard so oft 275
In worst extremes, and on the perilous edge
Of battle when it raged, in all assaults
Their surest signal, they will soon resume
New courage and revive, though now they lie
Groveling and prostrate on yon lake of fire, 280
As we erewhile, astounded and amazed,
No wonder, fallen such a pernicious highth.'
He scarce had ceased when the superior fiend
Was moving toward the shore; his ponderous shield
Ethereal temper, massy, large and round, 285
Behind him cast; the broad circumference
Hung on his shoulders like the moon, whose orb
Through optic glass the Tuscan artist views
At evening from the top of Fesolè,
Or in Valdarno, to descry new lands, 290
Rivers or mountains in her spotty globe.
His spear, to equal which the tallest pine
Hewn on Norwegian hills, to be the mast
Of some dread Ammiral, were but a wand,
He walked with to support uneasy steps 295
Over the burning marl, not like those steps
On Heaven's azure, and the torrid clime
Smote on him sore besides, vaulted with fire;
Natheless he so endured, till on the beach
Of that inflamed sea, he stood and called 300
His legions, angel forms, who lay entranced
Thick as autumnal leaves that strow the brooks
In Vallombrosa, where the Etrurian shades
High overarched embower; or scattered sedge
Afloat, when with fierce winds Orion armed 305
Hath vexed the Red Sea coast, whose waves o'er-
threw
Busiris and his Memphian chivalry,
While with perfidious hatred they pursued

The sojourners of Goshen, who beheld
From the safe shore their floating carcasses 310
And broken chariot-wheels, so thick bestrown
Abject and lost lay these, covering the flood,
Under amazement at their hideous change.
He called so loud, that all the hollow deep
Of Hell resounded: 'Princes, Potentates, 315
Warriors, the flower of Heaven, once yours, now lost,
If such astonishment as this can seize
Eternal spirits; or have ye chosen this place
After the toil of battle to repose
Your wearied virtue, for the ease you find 320
To slumber here, as in the vales of Heaven?
Or in this abject posture have ye sworn
To adore the Conqueror? Who now beholds
Cherub and seraph rolling in the flood
With scattered arms and ensigns, till anon 325
His swift pursuers from Heaven's gates discern
Th' advantage, and descending tread us down
Thus drooping, or with linkéd thunderbolts
Transfix us to the bottom of this gulf.
Awake! arise! or be forever fallen!' 330
They heard, and were abashed, and up they
sprung
Upon the wing, as when men wont to watch
On duty, sleeping found by whom they dread,
Rouse and bestir themselves ere well awake.
Nor did they not perceive the evil plight 335
In which they were, or the fierce pains not feel;
Yet to their General's voice they soon obeyed
Innumerable. As when the potent rod
Of Amram's son in Egypt's evil day
Waved round the coast, up called a pitchy cloud 340
Of locusts, warping on the eastern wind,
That o'er the realm of impious Pharaoh hung
Like night, and darkened all the land of Nile:
So numberless were those bad angels seen
Hovering on wing under the cope of Hell 345
'Twixt upper, nether, and surrounding fires;
Till, as a signal given, th' uplifted spear
Of their great Sultan waving to direct
Their course, in even balance down they light
On the firm brimstone, and fill all the plain; 350
A multitude, like which the populous north
Poured never from her frozen loins, to pass
Rhene or the Danaw, when her barbarous sons
Came like a deluge on the south, and spread
Beneath Gibraltar to the Lybian sands. 355
Forthwith from every squadron and each band
The heads and leaders thither haste where stood
Their great commander; Godlike shapes and forms

276. edge, front-line in battle. 282. pernicious, death-dealing. 285. Ethereal temper, tempered into a subtle, superearthly texture. 288. optic glass, telescope. Tuscan artist, the Italian astronomer and physicist Galileo (1564–1642), whom Milton had met at Florence on his travels to Italy; he was an ardent defender of the Copernican theory of astronomy (see note to 74 above). 289. Fesolè, Fiesole, a hill near Florence. 290. Valdarno, the valley of the Arno River, which flows through Florence. 294. Ammiral, admiral, but here applied to the flag-ship rather than to the officer himself. 303. Vallombrosa, a valley twenty miles east of Florence. Etruria is an ancient section of Italy comprising present-day Tuscany and a portion of Umbria. 305. Orion, in Greek legend a hunter who was transformed into a constellation, one of the most striking and famous in the northern heavens. 307. Busiris, a legendary king of England, not, however the Pharaoh who pursued the people of Israel, as told in Exodus, 14.

309. sojourners of Goshen. Before the Exodus from Egypt, the Israelites had inhabited a district of northern Egypt called Goshen. 339. Amram's son, Moses. For the account of the plague of locusts (ll. 340–341), see Exodus, 10:12–19. 353. Rhene . . . Danaw, the Rhine and Danube; the reference here is, of course, to the migrations of the Germanic barbarians, which extended even into northern Africa.

Excelling human, princely dignities,
And powers that erst in Heaven sat on thrones; 360
Though of their names in heavenly records now
Be no memorial, blotted out and rased
By their rebellion, from the Books of Life.
Nor had they yet among the sons of Eve 364
Got them new names, till wandering o'er the earth,
Through God's high sufferance for the trial of man,
By falsities and lies the greatest part
Of mankind they corrupted to forsake
God their Creator, and the invisible
Glory of Him, that made them, to transform 370
Oft to the image of a brute, adorned
With gay religions, full of pomp and gold,
And devils to adore for deities:
Then were they known to men by various names,
And various idols through the heathen world. 375
Say, Muse, their names then known, who first, who last,
Roused from the slumber, on that fiery couch,
At their great Emperor's call, as next in worth
Came singly where he stood on the bare strand,
While the promiscuous crowd stood yet aloof? 380
The chief were those who from the pit of Hell
Roaming to seek their prey on earth, durst fix
Their seats long after next the Seat of God,
Their altars by His altar, Gods adored
Among the nations round, and durst abide 385
Jehovah thundering out of Sion, throned
Between the Cherubim; yea, often placed
Within His sanctuary itself their shrines,
Abominations; and with cursèd things
His holy rites, and solemn feasts profaned, 390
And with their darkness durst affront His light.
First *Moloch*, horrid king besmeared with blood
Of human sacrifice, and parents' tears,
Though for the noise of drums and timbrels loud
Their children's cries unheard, that passed through fire 395
To his grim idol. Him the Ammonite
Worshipped in Rabba and her watery plain,
In Argob and in Basan, to the stream
Of utmost Arnon. Nor content with such

Audacious neighbourhood, the wisest heart 400
Of Solomon he led by fraud to build
His Temple right against the Temple of God
On that opprobrious hill, and made his grove
The pleasant valley of Hinnom, Tophet thence
And black Gehenna called, the type of Hell. 405
Next *Chemos*, th' obscene dread of Moab's sons,
From Aroar to Nebo, and the wild
Of southmost Abarim, in Hesebon
And Hornoaim, Seon's realm, beyond
The flowery dale of Sibma clad with vines, 410
And Eleale to th' Asphaltic Pool.
Peor his other name, when he enticed
Israel in Sittim on their march from Nile
To do him wanton rites, which cost them woe.
Yet thence his lustful orgies he enlarged 415
Even to that hill of scandal, by the grove
Of Moloch homicide, lust hard by hate;
Till good Josiah drove them thence to Hell.
With these came they, who from the bordering flood
Of old Euphrates to the brook that parts 420
Egypt from Syrian ground, had general names
Of Baalim and Ashtaroth, those male,
These feminine. For spirits when they please
Can either sex assume, or both; so soft
And uncompounded is their essence pure, 425
Not tied or manacled with joint or limb,
Nor founded on the brittle strength of bones,
Like cumbrous flesh; but in what shape they choose
Dilated or condensed, bright or obscure,
Can execute their airy purposes, 430
And works of love or enmity fulfill.
For those the race of Israel oft forsook
Their living strength, and unfrequented left
His righteous altar, bowing lowly down
To bestial gods; for which their heads as low 435

401. **Solomon . . . fraud.** King Solomon was persuaded by some of his multitudinous wives to build a temple to Moloch. 403. **that opprobrious hill,** the Mount of Olives, so-called not from its association with the story of Christ but because it was the site of Solomon's temple to Moloch. 404. **valley . . . Tophet.** A place of sacrifice to Moloch was appointed in the valley of Hinnom (called in Greek Gehenna); this place was called Tophet, and it was later the place of incineration for all the city refuse of Jerusalem. 406. **Chemos,** a god of the Moabites, another ancient tribe living east of the River Jordan. 407–411. **Aroar . . . Asphaltic Pool,** the names of towns and mountains in the Jordan River district extending south to the Dead Sea, or Asphaltic Pool, so-called because of the large amount of bitumen found in it. 413–414. **Israel . . . woe.** At Shittim, during the wanderings of the Jewish people, thousands of them were executed for taking Moabitish wives and for worshiping Baal-peor (note l. 412), god of the Moabites; see Numbers, 25. It is clear that every one of the gods and peoples mentioned by Milton in this passage was defeated by the Hebrews' Jehovah. 416. **hill of scandal,** the Mount of Olives; see l. 403 above. 418. **Josiah,** King of Isreal, called "good" because he restored the worship of Jehovah. 420–421. **Euphrates . . . Syrian ground.** In King David's time the Euphrates River bounded Palestine to the east, and Besor Brook, named in I Samuel, 30:10, separated Palestine from Egypt to the south. 422. **Baalim and Ashtaroth,** collective names for manifestations of the sun-god and the moon-goddess. 423–424. **spirits . . . assume.** The power of demons to metamorphose themselves is traceable in both Greek and Hebrew legend from time immemorial.

376. **Say . . . names.** This roll-call of leaders was no doubt suggested to Milton by the naming and numbering of the Greek and Trojan warriors in the second book of the *Iliad*. It was the belief that the rebel Angels lost their original names at the time of the War in Heaven. Milton has named them after famous heathen gods. 383. **next the Seat.** Milton is referring to the numerous occasions in Hebrew history when, as in the reign of Solomon, shrines to foreign gods were erected in or near the Temple of Jehovah. His bitterness toward the desecration of the Temple is indicated by lines 387 ff. 392. **Moloch,** originally a fire-god worshiped by the sacrifice of infants incinerated in the heated arms of his statue. He was a god of the Ammonites, who occupied land to the south and east of Palestine; see I Kings, 11:7. 394–395. **noise . . . unheard.** When the children were sacrificed to Moloch, drums and cymbals were sounded to drown out the victims' cries. 397. **Rabba,** the ancient capital of the Ammonites; other Ammonite place-names are Argob (398), Basan (398), and Arnon (399), all situated east of the River Jordan.

Bowed down in battle, sunk before the spear
Of despicable foes. With these in troop
Came *Astoreth*, whom the Phoenicians called
Astarte, queen of Heaven, with crescent horns;
To whose bright image nightly by the moon   440
Sidonian virgins paid their vows and songs,
In Sion also not unsung, where stood
Her temple on the offensive mountain, built
By that uxorious king, whose heart though large,
Beguiled by fair idolatresses, fell   445
To idols foul. *Thammuz* came next behind,
Whose annual wound in Lebanon allured
The Syrian damsels to lament his fate
In amorous ditties all a summer's day,
While smooth *Adonis* from his native rock   450
Ran purple to the sea, supposed with blood
Of Thammuz yearly wounded: the love-tale
Infected Sion's daughters with like heat,
Whose wanton passions in the sacred porch
Ezekiel saw, when by the vision led   455
His eye surveyed the dark idolatries
Of alienated Judah. Next came one
Who mourned in earnest, when the captive Ark
Maimed his brute image, head and hands lopped off
In his own temple, on the grunsel edge,   460
Where he fell flat, and shamed his worshippers:
Dagon his name, sea monster, upward man
And downward fish: yet had his temple high
Reared in Azotus, dreaded through the coast
Of Palestine, in Gath and Ascalon,   465
And Accaron and Gaza's frontier bounds.
Him followed *Rimmon*, whose delightful seat
Was fair Damascus, on the fertile banks
Of Abbana and Pharphar, lucid streams.
He also against the house of God was bold: 470
A leper once he lost and gained a king,
Ahaz his sottish conqueror, whom he drew
God's altar to disparage and displace
For one of Syrian mode, whereon to burn
His odious offerings, and adore the gods   475

Whom he had vanquished. After these appeared
A crew who, under names of old renown,
Osiris, Isis, Orus and their train
With monstrous shapes and sorceries abused
Fanatic Egypt and her priests, to seek   480
Their wandering gods, disguised in brutish forms
Rather than human. Nor did Israel scape
The infection when their borrowed gold composed
The calf in Oreb: and the rebel king
Doubled that sin in Bethel and in Dan,   485
Likening his Maker to the grazed ox,
Jehovah, who in one night when he passed
From Egypt marching, equalled with one stroke
Both her first-born and all her bleating gods.
Belial came last, than whom a spirit more lewd 490
Fell not from Heaven, or more gross to love
Vice for itself: to him no temple stood
Or altar smoked; yet who more oft than he
In temples and at altars, when the priest
Turns atheist, as did Eli's sons, who filled   495
With lust and violence the house of God.
In courts and palaces he also reigns
And in luxurious cities, where the noise
Of riot ascends above their loftiest towers,
And injury and outrage: and when night   500
Darkens the streets, then wander forth the sons
Of Belial, flown with insolence and wine.
Witness the streets of Sodom, and that night
In Gibeah, when the hospitable door
Exposed a matron to avoid worse rape.   505
These were the prime in order and in might;
The rest were long to tell, though far renowned,
The Ionian gods, of *Javan's* issue held
Gods, yet confessed later than Heaven and earth
Their boasted parents; *Titan*, Heaven's first-born 510
With his enormous brood, and birthright seized

---

438. **Astarte,** the Phoenician goddess of beauty and love, comparable to the classical Venus or Aphrodite.   441. **Sidonian,** from the Phoenician city of Sidon.   444. **that uxorious king,** Solomon. In addition to the temple of Moloch already mentioned (l. 403 above and note), Solomon also erected a temple to Astarte.   446. **Thammuz,** the Phoenician equivalent of the Greek Adonis, whose death in classical legend symbolized the coming of Autumn. He was once a river-god whose name was given to a river in Lebanon; this river brings down a quantity of red mud in a freshet, whence the references to Adonis and the annual wound (ll. 447 and 450 ff.).   453. **Sion's daughters,** the women of Jerusalem. The passing of Adonis was celebrated by wholesale lamentation on the part of women, for Adonis (Thammuz) symbolized not only the regenerative powers of nature through love and beauty, but also the spring and summer seasons.   455. **Ezekiel saw,** see Ezekiel, 8:14.   460. **grunsel edge,** threshold; see I Samuel, 5:4. 462. **Dagon,** a sea-god of the Philistines, who occupied the coast of ancient Palestine.   464-466. **Azotus . . . Gaza,** the five chief cities of the Philistines.   467. **Rimmon,** a god of ancient Damascus.   471. **A leper,** the Syrian general Naaman, who was cured by bathing in the River Jordan; see II Kings, 16.   472. **Ahaz,** King of Judah (see II Kings, 16).

481. **brutish forms.** The famous Egyptian deities mentioned in l. 478 were in the following animal shapes: Osiris was a bull; Isis, a cow; and Orus, a solar animal.   484. **The calf in Oreb,** the heretical worship of this image by the Israelites, during the absence of Moses, is told in Exodus, 32. **the rebel king,** Jereboam, who rebelled with Ten Tribes of Israel against Rehoboam, son of Solomon, and established idolatry with two golden calves as the object of worship in Bethel and Dan, two northern cities. The story is told in I Kings, 12:28-33. 487-488. **Jehovah . . . equalled.** By slaying the first-born in the tenth plague (as told in Exodus, 12), Jehovah made equal in death the first-born and the false gods themselves.   490. **Belial,** the prince of the third order of demons.   495-496. **Eli's sons . . . God.** See I Samuel, ii, 12-17, where the sons of the High Priest Eli are likened to "the sons of Belial [i.e., worthlessness]; they knew not the Lord." 498. **luxurious,** lecherous, lustful.   501-502. **sons of Belial,** a common nickname among the Puritans for the courtiers and followers of King Charles I; these lines are then a slap at roistering Cavaliers. 502. **flown,** flushed.   503. **Sodom,** the "wicked city" of the plain, destroyed with its sister-city Gomorrah (see Genesis, 29:1-11).   504-505. **Gibeah . . . rape;** see Judges, 19.   508. **Ionian,** Greek. **Javan,** son of Japhet, and therefore grandson of Noah (Genesis, 10:2); he was considered in legend the founder of the Greeks.   509-510. **confessed . . . parents.** In Greek mythology, Heaven and Earth were the parents of the first gods, the Titans; but Milton shares the belief that all pagan divinities have been human beings deified by man.   510. **Titan,** the first son of Uranus (Heaven) and Ge (Earth).

By younger *Saturn,* he from mightier *Jove,*
His own and Rhea's son, like measure found;
So Jove usurping reigned: these first in Crete
And Ida known, thence on the snowy top   515
Of cold Olympus ruled the middle air,
Their highest Heaven; or on the Delphian cliff,
Or in Dodona, and through all the bounds
Of Doric land; or who with Saturn old
Fled over Adria to the Hesperian fields,   520
And o'er the Celtic roamed the utmost isles.
All these and more came flocking; but with looks
Downcast and damp, yet such wherein appeared
Obscure some glimpse of joy, to have found their
  chief
Not in despair, to have found themselves not lost 525
In loss itself; which on his countenance cast
Like doubtful hue: but he his wonted pride
Soon recollecting, with high words, that bore
Semblance of worth, not substance, gently raised
Their fainting courage, and dispelled their fears. 530
Then straight commands that at the warlike sound
Of trumpets loud and clarions be upreared
His mighty standard; that proud honour claimed
Azazel at his right, a Cherub tall:
Who forthwith from the glittering staff unfurled 535
The imperial ensign, which full high advanced
Shone like a meteor streaming to the wind
With gems and golden lustre rich imblazed,
Seraphic arms and trophies: all the while
Sonorous metal blowing martial sounds: 540
At which the universal host upsent
A shout that tore Hell's concave, and beyond
Frighted the reign of Chaos and old Night.
All in a moment through the gloom were seen
Ten thousand banners rise into the air   545
With orient colours waving: with them rose
A forest huge of spears; and thronging helms
Appeared, and serried shields in thick array
Of depth immeasurable: anon they move
In perfect phalanx to the Dorian mood   550
Of flutes and soft recorders; such as raised

To highth of noblest temper heroes old
Arming to battle, and instead of rage
Deliberate valour breathed, firm and unmoved
With dread of death to flight or foul retreat,   555
Nor wanting power to mitigate and 'suage
With solemn touches, troubled thoughts, and chase
Anguish and doubt and fear and sorrow and pain
From mortal or immortal minds. Thus they
Breathing united force with fixed thought   560
Moved on in silence to soft pipes that charmed
Their painful steps o'er the burnt soil; and now
Advanced in view they stand, a horrid front
Of dreadful length and dazzling arms, in guise
Of warriors old with ordered spear and shield,   565
Awaiting what command their mighty chief
Had to impose: he through the armed files
Darts his experienced eye, and soon traverse
The whole battalion views, their order due,
Their visages and stature as of Gods,   570
Their number last he sums. And now his heart
Distends with pride, and hardening in his strength
Glories: for never since created man,
Met such embodied force, as named with these
Could merit more than that small infantry   575
Warred on by cranes: tough all the giant brood
Of Phlegra with the heroic race were joined
That fought at Thebes and Ilium, on each side
Mixed with auxiliar gods; and what resounds
In fable or romance of Uther's son   580
Begirt with British and Armoric knights;
And all who since, baptized or infidel
Jousted in Aspramont or Montalban,
Damasco, or Marocco, or Trebisond,
Or whom Biserta sent from Afric shore   585
When Charlemain with all his peerage fell
By Fontarabbia. Thus far these beyond
Compare of mortal prowess, yet observed
Their dread commander; he above the rest
In shape and gesture proudly eminent   590
Stood like a tower; his form had yet not lost
All her original brightness, nor appeared
Less than archangel ruined, and th' excess

512. **Saturn,** a younger brother of Titan, who supplanted him and was in turn supplanted by his son Zeus (Jove or Jupiter). 514 ff. **these first,** etc. Milton is here surveying the range of the gods of Olympus throughout the Greek world from Crete to the north. 515. **Ida.** According to Greek legend, Zeus was born on Mount Ida and established his dwelling on Mount Olympus. 517. **Delphian cliff,** in northern Greece, famous as the site of the most celebrated oracle of Apollo. 518. **Dodona,** also in northern Greece, the site of an oracle of Zeus. 520. **Adria,** the Adriatic Sea. **Hesperian fields,** Italy, where the older Greek gods were worshiped by the Romans. 521. **Celtic . . . isles,** France and Spain, primarily, although Britain may be included. 534. **Azazel,** a name taken from Leviticus, 16:8; he is here the lord of demons on Earth, and one of the four standard-bearers of Satan. 536. **advanced,** raised. 543. **reign of Chaos.** Milton is here anticipating his account in Book II, lines 890–1009. 546. **orient,** bright, pertaining to the dawn. 550. **phalanx,** body of troops in close, serried lines. **Dorian mood,** that ancient scale of music considered appropriate for martial effects. 551. **recorders,** early wind instruments somewhat like the flute.

563. **horrid,** bristling with spears. 568. **traverse,** across. 573. **since created man,** since man was created. 575. **small infantry.** In classical legend the Pigmies of Ethiopia waged continual war with the cranes that attacked them. 576. **giant brood,** the Titans were defeated by the Olympian gods at Phlegra, a promontory in Macedonia. 578. **Thebes and Ilium,** in Greek heroic legend, the two cities about which were centered, respectively, the War of the Seven against Thebes and the Trojan War. 580. **Uther's son,** King Arthur of British legendry, at one time the hero of a projected epic poem by Milton. 581. **Armoric,** Breton, from Brittany. 583–584. **Aspramont . . . Trebisond.** Places associated with contests celebrated in the medieval romances and the chronicles of the Crusades. Aspramont was near Nice, France; Montalban, or Montauban, is in southern France not far from Toulouse; Trebisond, or Trebizond, is on the southern shores of the Black Sea. Morocco and Damascus need no comment. 585. **Biserta,** the modern Bizerte, in northern Africa; it was in the Middle Ages an important center of western Moslem civilization. 587. **Fontarabbia,** actually some forty miles from Roncevals, site of the famous battle on which is based the *Song of Roland.*

Of glory obscured: as when the sun new risen
Looks through the horizontal misty air   595
Shorn of his beams, or from behind the moon
In dim eclipse disastrous twilight sheds
On half the nations, and with fear of change
Perplexes monarchs. Darkened so, yet shone
Above them all the archangel: but his face   600
Deep scars of thunder had entrenched, and care
Sat on his faded cheek, but under brows
Of dauntless courage, and considerate pride
Waiting revenge: cruel his eye, but cast
Signs of remorse and passion to behold   605
The fellows of his crime, the followers rather
(Far other once beheld in bliss) condemned
Forever now to have their lot in pain,
Millions of spirits for his fault amerced
Of Heaven, and from eternal splendors flung   610
For his revolt, yet faithful how they stood,
Their glory withered. As when Heaven's fire
Hath scathed the forest oaks, or mountain pines
With singéd top their stately growth, though bare,
Stands on the blasted heath. He now prepared   615
To speak; whereat their doubled ranks they bend
From wing to wing, and half enclose him round
With all his peers: attention held them mute.
Thrice he essayed, and thrice in spite of scorn,
Tears such as angels weep, burst forth: at last   620
Words interwove with sighs found out their way:
  'O myriads of immortal spirits, O powers
Matchless, but with the Almighty, and that strife
Was not inglorious, though the event was dire,
As this place testifies, and this dire change   625
Hateful to utter: but what power of mind
Foreseeing or presaging, from the depth
Of knowledge past or present, could have feared,
How such united force of gods, how such
As stood like these, could ever know repulse?   630
For who can yet believe, though after loss,
That all these puissant legions, whose exile
Hath emptied Heaven, shall fail to re-ascend
Self-raised, and re-possess their native seat?
For me, be witness all the host of Heaven,   635
If counsels different, or danger shunned
By me, have lost our hopes. But he who reigns
Monarch in Heaven, till then as one secure
Sat on His throne, upheld by old repute,
Consent or custom, and his regal state   640
Put forth at full, but still His strength concealed,
Which tempted our attempt, and wrought our fall.
Henceforth His might we know, and know our own
So as not either to provoke, or dread
New war, provoked; our better part remains   645
To work in close design, by fraud or guile

What force effected not: that He no less
At length from us may find, who overcomes
By force, hath overcome but half his foe.
Space may produce new worlds; whereof so rife   650
There went a fame in Heaven that He ere long
Intended to create, and therein plant
A generation, whom His choice regard
Should favour equal to the sons of Heaven:
Thither, if but to pry, shall be perhaps   655
Our first eruption, thither or elsewhere:
For this infernal pit shall never hold
Celestial spirits in bondage, nor the abyss
Long under darkness cover. But these thoughts
Full counsel must mature: peace is despaired,   660
For who can think submission? War then, War
Open or understood, must be resolved.'
  He spake: and to confirm his words, out flew
Millions of flaming swords, drawn from the thighs
Of mighty Cherubim; the sudden blaze   665
Far round illumined Hell: highly they raged
Against the Highest, and fierce with grasped arms
Clashed on their sounding shields the din of war,
Hurling defiance toward the vault of Heaven.
  There stood a hill not far whose grisly top   670
Belched fire and rolling smoke; the rest entire
Shone with a glossy scurf, undoubted sign
That in his womb was hid metallic ore,
The work of sulphur. Thither winged with speed
A numerous brigad hastened. As when bands   675
Of pioners with spade and pickax armed
Forerun the royal camp, to trench a field,
Or cast a rampart. *Mammon* led them on,
Mammon, the least erected spirit that fell
From Heaven, for even in Heaven his looks and
        thoughts   680
Were always downward bent, admiring more
The riches of Heaven's pavement, trodden gold,
Than aught divine or holy else enjoyed
In vision beatific; by him first
Men also, and by his suggestion taught,   685
Ransacked the center, and with impious hands
Rifled the bowels of their mother Earth
For treasures better hid. Soon had his crew
Opened into the hill a spacious wound
And digged out ribs of gold. Let none admire   690
That riches grow in Hell; that soil may best
Deserve the precious bane. And here let those
Who boast in mortal things, and wondering tell

---

603. **considerate**, based on well-founded thought. 609. **amerced**, punished (a legal term). 642. **tempted our attempt**. Note the play on words. 646. **close**, secret.

651. **fame**, rumor, report. 674. **work of sulphur**. It was an old belief of alchemy that all minerals came from a combination of sulphur and mercury. 675. **brigad**, brigade; the accent is on the first syllable. 676. **pioners**, soldiers whose duty it was to dig trenches, lay roads and mines (sappers), or do anything else pertaining to military engineering labor battalions. 678. **Mammon**. The name is derived from an Aramaic word meaning wealth or riches, but was believed in the Middle Ages to be the name of a devil. 690. **admire**, wonder (v.). 692. **bane**, evil, curse; not the old meaning of 'slayer.'

Of Babel, and the works of Memphian kings,
Learn how their greatest monuments of fame, 695
And strength and art are easily outdone
By spirits reprobate, and in an hour
What in an age they with incessant toil
And hands innumerable scarce perform.
Nigh on the plain in many cells prepared, 700
That underneath had veins of liquid fire
Sluiced from the lake, a second multitude
With wondrous art founded the massy ore,
Severing each kind, and scummed the bullion dross:
A third as soon had formed within the ground 705
A various mould, and from the boiling cells
By strange conveyance filled each hollow nook,
As in an organ from one blast of wind
To many a row of pipes the sound-board breathes.
Anon out of the earth a fabric huge 710
Rose like an exhalation, with the sound
Of dulcet symphonies and voices sweet,
Built like a temple, where pilasters round
Were set, and Doric pillars overlaid
With golden architrave; nor did there want 715
Cornice or frieze, with bossy sculptures graven;
The roof was fretted gold. Not Babylon,
Nor great Alcairo such magnificence
Equalled in all their glories, to enshrine
Belus or Serapis their gods, or seat 720
Their kings, when Egypt with Assyria strove
In wealth and luxury. The ascending pile
Stood fixed her stately highth, and straight the doors
Opening their brazen folds discover, wide
Within, her ample spaces, o'er the smooth 725
And level pavement: from the arched roof
Pendant by subtle magic many a row
Of starry lamps and blazing cressets fed
With naphtha and asphaltus yielded light
As from a sky. The hasty multitude 730
Admiring entered, and the work some praise
And some the architect: his hand was known
In Heaven by many a towered structure high,
Where sceptered angels held their residence,
And sat as princes, whom the supreme King 735
Exalted to such power, and gave to rule,
Each in his hierarchy, the Orders bright.
Nor was his name unheard or unadored

In ancient Greece; and in Ausonian land
Men called him *Mulciber*; and how he fell 740
From Heaven, they fabled, thrown by angry Jove
Sheer o'er the crystal battlements: from morn
To noon he fell, from noon to dewy eve,
A summer's day; and with the setting sun
Dropped from the zenith like a falling star, 745
On Lemnos the Aegaean Isle: thus they relate,
Erring; for he with his rebellious rout
Fell long before; nor aught availed him now
To have built in Heaven high towers; nor did he scape
By all his engines, but was headlong sent 750
With his industrious crew to build in Hell.
Meanwhile the winged heralds by command
Of sovereign power, with awful ceremony
And trumpets' sound throughout the host proclaim
A solemn council forthwith to be held 755
At *Pandemonium*, the high capital
Of Satan and his peers: their summons called
From every band and squared regiment
By place or choice the worthiest; they anon
With hundreds and with thousands trooping came
Attended: all access was thronged, the gates 761
And porches wide, but chief the spacious hall
(Though like a covered field, where champions bold
Wont ride in armed, and at the Soldan's chair
Defied the best of Paynim chivalry 765
To mortal combat or career with lance)
Thick swarmed, both on the ground and in the air,
Brushed with the hiss of rustling wings. As bees
In spring time, when the sun with Taurus rides,
Pour forth their populous youth about the hive 770
In clusters; they among fresh dews and flowers
Fly to and fro, or on the smoothed plank,
The suburb of their straw-built citadel,
New rubbed with balm, expatiate and confer
Their state affairs. So thick the airy crowd 775
Swarmed and were straitened; till the signal given,
Behold a wonder! they but now who seemed
In bigness to surpass Earth's giant sons
Now less than smallest dwarfs, in narrow room
Throng numberless, like that pygmean race 780
Beyond the Indian mount, or Faery elves,
Whose midnight revels, by a forest-side
Or fountain some belated peasant sees,

694. **Babel,** the first city built in the kingdom of Nimrod, famous for the unfinished Tower which was to reach to Heaven. 709. **sound-board.** The word is used here with specific reference to the organ; in which the sound-board is the surface which transmits air from the bellows to the pipes of the instrument. 713–716. **pilasters . . . frieze.** The materials described are elements of particular significance to later Renaissance, or baroque, architecture. 718. **Alcairo,** Cairo, Egypt. 720. **Belus or Serapis,** the Assyrian god Bel and the Egyptian deity, respectively. 728. **cressets,** fire-baskets for illumination. 737. **Each . . . hierarchy.** See note to l. 128 above.

739. **Ausonian land,** an ancient name for what is now Italy. 740. **Mulciber,** Vulcan or the Greek Hephaestos. 756. **Pandemonium,** the place of all demons. 764. **wont,** was wont, was accustomed to. **Soldan,** sultan, Saracen potentate. 765. **Paynim chivalry,** etc., an allusion to tournaments or conflicts between Christian and pagan knights, as told in the medieval romances or in medieval chronicles about the Crusaders. 769. **Taurus,** the second constellation of the Zodiac. The sun is in this constellation from about April 20 to May 20; in other words, the constellation is a symbol of springtime. 774. **expatiate,** walk abroad. 780. **pygmean race,** etc. See note to l. 575 above.

Or dreams he sees, while overhead the moon
Sits arbitress, and nearer to the Earth   785
Wheels her pale course, they on their mirth and
    dance
Intent, with jocund music charm his ear;
At once with joy and fear his heart rebounds.
Thus incorporeal spirits to smallest forms
Reduced their shapes immense, and were at large,
Though without number still amidst the hall   791
Of that infernal court. But far within
And in their own dimensions like themselves
The great Seraphic Lords and Cherubim
In close recess and secret conclave sat   795
A thousand demi-gods on golden seats,
Frequent and full. After short silence then
And summons read, the great consult began.

BOOK II

The Argument

The consultation begun, Satan debates whether another battle is to be hazarded for the recovery of
Heaven: some advise it, others dissuade; a third proposal
is preferred, mentioned before by Satan, to search the
truth of that prophecy or tradition in Heaven concerning
another world, and another kind of creature equal or
not much inferior to themselves, about this time to be
created: their doubt who shall be sent on this difficult
search; Satan their chief undertakes alone the voyage,
is honoured and applauded. The council thus ended, the
rest betake them several ways and to several employments, as their inclinations lead them, to entertain the
time till Satan return. He passes on his journey to Hell
Gates, finds them shut, and who sat there to guard them,
by whom at length they are opened, and discover to him
the great gulf between Hell and Heaven; with what difficulty he passes through, directed by Chaos, the power
of that place, to the sight of this new world which he
sought.

High on a throne of royal state, which far
Outshone the wealth of Ormus and of Ind,
Or where the gorgeous East with richest hand
Showers on her kings barbaric pearl and gold,
Satan exalted sat, by merit raised   5
To that bad eminence; and from despair
Thus high uplifted beyond hope, aspires
Beyond thus high, insatiate to pursue
Vain war with Heaven, and by success untaught
His proud imaginations thus displayed: 10
    'Powers and Dominions, Deities of Heaven,
For since no deep within her gulf can hold

Immortal vigor, though oppressed and fallen,
I give not Heaven for lost. From this descent
Celestial virtues rising, will appear   15
More glorious and more dread than from no fall,
And trust themselves to fear no second fate:
Me though just right, and the fixed laws of Heaven
Did first create your leader, next, free choice,
With what besides, in counsel or in fight,   20
Hath been achieved of merit, yet this loss
Thus far at least recovered, hath much more
Established in a safe unenvied throne
Yielded with full consent. The happier state
In Heaven, which follows dignity, might draw   25
Envy from each inferior; but who here
Will envy whom the highest place exposes
Foremost to stand against the Thunderer's aim
Your bulwark, and condemns to greatest share
Of endless pain? where there is then no good   30
For which to strive, no strife can grow up there
From Faction; for none sure will claim in Hell
Precedence, none, whose portion is so small
Of present pain, that with ambitious mind
Will covet more. With this advantage then   35
To union, and firm faith, and firm accord,
More than can be in Heaven, we now return
To claim our just inheritance of old,
Surer to prosper than prosperity
Could have assured us; and by what best way,   40
Whether of open war or covert guile,
We now debate; who can advise, may speak.'
    He ceased, and next him Moloch, sceptered king,
Stood up, the strongest and the fiercest spirit
That fought in Heaven; now fiercer by despair: 45
His trust was with th' Eternal to be deemed
Equal in strength, and rather than be less
Cared not to be at all; with that care lost
Went all his fear: of God, or Hell, or worse
He recked not, and these words thereafter spake:
    'My sentence is for open war. Of wiles,   51
More unexpert, I boast not: them let those
Contrive who need, or when they need, not now.
For while they sit contriving, shall the rest,
Millions that stand in arms, and longing wait   55
The signal to ascend, sit lingering here
Heaven's fugitives, and for their dwelling place
Accept this dark, opprobrious den of shame,
The prison of His tyranny who reigns
By our delay? no, let us rather choose   60
Armed with Hell-flames and fury all at once
O'er Heaven's high towers to force resistless way,
Turning our tortures into horrid arms

795. **close recess,** secret meeting-place. **conclave,** inner chamber.
797. **frequent,** crowded. 798. **consult,** consultation, meeting. 2.
Ormus, Ormuz, an ancient and very rich trading city on an island
in the Persian Gulf. **Ind,** India. 9. **success,** experience, consequence.

15. **virtues,** rank in the hierarchy of Hell. 25. **dignity,** worth, merit.
28. **Thunderer,** an epithet applied particularly to Jove (Jupiter or
Zeus), although Thor, in the Germanic Pantheon, was also associated with thunder. Satan is here clearly picturing God as a tyrant
like Zeus or Thor. 51. **sentence,** opinion, decision. 52. **unexpert,**
inexperienced.

Against the torturer; when to meet the noise
Of His almighty engine He shall hear   65
Infernal thunder, and for lightning see
Black fire and horror shot with equal rage
Among His angels; and His throne itself
Mixed with Tartarean sulphur, and strange fire,
His own invented torments. But perhaps   70
The way seems difficult and steep to scale
With upright wing against a higher foe.
Let such bethink them, if the sleepy drench
Of that forgetful lake benumb not still,
That in our proper motion we ascend   75
Up to our native seat: descent and fall
To us is adverse. Who but felt of late
When the fierce foe hung on our broken rear
Insulting, and pursued us through the deep,
With what compulsion and laborious flight   80
We sunk thus low? The ascent is easy, then;
The event is feared; should we again provoke
Our stronger, some worse way His wrath may find
To our destruction, if there be in Hell
Fear to be worse destroyed; what can be worse   85
Than to dwell here, driven out from bliss, con-
          demned
In this abhorred deep to utter woe,
Where pain of unextinguishable fire
Must exercise us without hope of end,
The vassals of His anger, when the scourge   90
Inexorably, and the torturing hour,
Calls us to penance? More destroyed than thus
We should be quite abolished and expire.
What fear we then? what doubt we to incense
His utmost ire? which to the highth enraged,   95
Will either quite consume us, and reduce
To nothing this essential, happier far
Than miserable to have eternal being:
Or if our substance be indeed divine,
And cannot cease to be, we are at worst   100
On this side nothing; and by proof we feel
Our power sufficient to disturb His Heaven,
And with perpetual inroads to alarm,
Though inaccessible, His fatal throne:
Which if not victory is yet revenge.'   105
          He ended frowning, and his look denounced
Desperate revenge, and battle dangerous
To less than gods. On the other side up rose
Belial, in act more graceful and humane;
A fairer person lost not Heaven; he seemed   110
For dignity composed and high exploit:
But all was false and hollow; though his tongue
Dropped manna, and could make the worse appear
The better reason, to perplex and dash

Maturest counsels: for his thoughts were low;   115
To vice industrious, but to nobler deeds
Timorous and slothful; yet he pleased the ear,
And with persuasive accent thus began:
          'I should be much for open war, O Peers,
As not behind in hate; if what was urged   120
Main reason to persuade immediate war,
Did not dissuade me most, and seem to cast
Ominous conjecture on the whole success:
When he who most excels in fact of arms,
In what he counsels and in what excels   125
Mistrustful, grounds his courage on despair
And utter dissolution, as the scope
Of all his aim, after some dire revenge.
First, what revenge? the towers of Heaven are filled
With armed watch, that render all access   130
Impregnable; oft on the bordering deep
Encamp their legions, or with obscure wing
Scout far and wide into the realm of night,
Scorning surprise. Or could we break our way
By force, and at our heels all Hell should rise   135
With blackest insurrection, to confound
Heaven's purest light, yet our great Enemy
All incorruptible would on His throne
Sit unpolluted, and the ethereal mould
Incapable of stain would soon expel   140
Her mischief, and purge off the baser fire
Victorious. Thus repulsed, our final hope
Is flat despair; we must exasperate
The Almighty Victor to spend all His rage,
And that must end us, that must be our cure,   145
To be no more; sad cure. For who would lose,
Though full of pain, this intellectual being,
Those thoughts that wander through Eternity,
To perish rather, swallowed up and lost
In the wide womb of uncreated night,   150
Devoid of sense and motion? and who knows,
Let this be good, whether our angry Foe
Can give it, or will ever? how He can
Is doubtful; that He never will is sure.
Will He, so wise, let loose at once His ire,   155
Belike through impotence, or unaware,
To give His enemies their wish, and end
Them in His anger, whom His anger saves
To punish endless? wherefore cease we then?
Say they who counsel war, we are decreed,   160
Reserved and destined to eternal woe;
Whatever doing, what can we suffer more,
What can we suffer worse? is this then worst,
Thus sitting, thus consulting, thus in arms?
What when we fled amain, pursued and struck   165
With Heaven's afflicting thunder, and besought
The deep to shelter us? this Hell then seemed
A refuge from those wounds; or when we lay
Chained on the burning lake? that sure was worse.

69. **Tartarean.** Milton in characteristic fashion conceives of Hell as
identical with the classical Tartarus. The forgetful lake (74) is another classical reminiscence or recall.   89. **exercise,** agitate, torment.
97. **essential,** being, substance (sb.).   104. **fatal,** established by fate.
106. **denounced,** threatened.

124. **fact,** deed.

What if the breath that kindled those grim fires 170
Awaked should blow them into sevenfold rage
And plunge us in the flames? or from above
Should intermitted vengeance arm again
His red right hand to plague us? what if all
Her stores were opened, and this firmament 175
Of Hell should spout her cataracts of fire,
Impendent horrors, threatening hideous fall
One day upon our heads; while we perhaps
Designing or exhorting glorious war,
Caught in a fiery tempest shall be hurled 180
Each on his rock transfixed, the sport and prey
Of racking whirlwinds, or forever sunk
Under yon boiling ocean, wrapped in chains;
There to converse with everlasting groans,
Unrespited, unpitied, unreprieved, 185
Ages of hopeless end; this would be worse.
War therefore, open or concealed, alike
My voice dissuades; for what can force or guile
With Him, or who deceive His mind, whose eye
Views all things at one view? He from Heaven's
    highth 190
All these our motions vain, sees and derides;
Not more almighty to resist our might
Than wise to frustrate all our plots and wiles.
Shall we then live thus vile, the race of Heaven
Thus trampled, thus expelled to suffer here 195
Chains and these torments? better these than worse,
By my advice; since Fate inevitable
Subdues us, and omnipotent decree,
The Victor's will. To suffer, as to do,
Our strength is equal, nor the law unjust 200
That so ordains: this was at first resolved,
If we were wise, against so great a foe
Contending, and so doubtful what might fall.
I laugh, when those who at the spear are bold
And venturous, if that fail them, shrink and fear 205
What yet they know must follow, to endure
Exile, or ignominy, or bonds, or pain,
The sentence of their Conqueror: this is now
Our doom, which if we can sustain and bear,
Our supreme Foe in time may much remit 210
His anger, and perhaps thus far removed
Not mind us not offending, satisfied
With what is punished; whence these raging fires
Will slacken, if His breath stir not their flames.
Our purer essence then will overcome 215
Their noxious vapour, or inured not feel,
Or changed at length, and to the place conformed
In temper and in nature, will receive
Familiar the fierce heat, and void of pain;
This horror will grow mild, this darkness light, 220
Besides what hope the never-ending flight

181. **Each . . . transfixed;** like Prometheus in Greek legend or Ajax
in the story of the Trojan War. 191. **All . . . derides.** Cf. Psalms,
2:4: "He that sitteth in the heavens shall laugh; the Lord shall have
them in derision." 216. **inured,** accustomed. 218. **temper,** temperament.

Of future days may bring, what chance, what
    change
Worth waiting, since our present lot appears
For happy though but ill, for ill not worst,
If we procure not to ourselves more woe.' 225
    Thus Belial with words clothed in reason's garb
Counselled ignoble ease, and peaceful sloth,
Not peace; and after him thus Mammon spake:
    'Either to disenthrone the king of Heaven
We war, if war be best, or to regain 230
Our own right lost: him to unthrone we then
May hope, when everlasting Fate shall yield
To fickle chance, and Chaos judge the strife:
The former vain to hope argues as vain
The latter; for what place can be for us 235
Within Heaven's bound, unless Heaven's Lord su-
    preme
We overpower? Suppose He should relent
And publish grace to all, on promise made
Of new subjection; with what eyes could we
Stand in His presence humble, and receive 240
Strict laws imposed, to celebrate His throne
With warbled hymns, and to His Godhead sing
Forced Hallelujahs; while He lordly sits
Our envied Sovereign, and His altar breathes
Ambrosial odours and ambrosial flowers, 245
Our servile offerings? This must be our task
In Heaven, this our delight; how wearisome
Eternity so spent in worship paid
To whom we hate. Let us not then pursue
By force impossible, by leave obtained 250
Unacceptable, though in Heaven, our state
Of splendid vassalage, but rather seek
Our own good from ourselves, and from our own
Live to ourselves, though in this vast recess,
Free, and to none accountable, preferring 255
Hard liberty before the easy yoke
Of servile pomp. Our greatness will appear
Then most conspicuous, when great things of small,
Useful of hurt, prosperous of adverse
We can create, and in what place soe'er 260
Thrive under evil, and work ease out of pain
Through labour and endurance. This deep world
Of darkness do we dread? How oft amidst
Thick clouds and dark doth Heaven's all-ruling Sire
Choose to reside, His glory unobscured, 265
And with the majesty of darkness round
Covers His throne; from whence deep thunders roar
Mustering their rage, and Heaven resembles Hell?
As He our darkness, cannot we His light
Imitate when we please? This desert soil 270
Wants not her hidden lustre, gems and gold;
Nor want we skill or art, from whence to raise
Magnificence; and what can Heaven show more?

245. **ambrosial,** yielding ambrosia, the food of the gods in Olympus
and the perfume of wine poured in libations to them. 249. **pursue,**
seek to obtain.

Our torments also may in length of time
Become our elements, these piercing fires 275
As soft as now severe, our temper changed
Into their temper; which must needs remove
The sensible of pain. All things invite
To peaceful counsels, and the settled state
Of order, how in safety best we may 280
Compose our present evils, with regard
Of what we are and where, dismissing quite
All thoughts of war; ye have what I advise.'
    He scarce had finished, when such murmur filled
The assembly, as when hollow rocks retain 285
The sound of blustering winds, which all night long
Had roused the sea, now with hoarse cadence lull
Seafaring men o'erwatched, whose bark by chance
Or pinnace anchors in a craggy bay
After the tempest: such applause was heard 290
As Mammon ended, and his sentence pleased,
Advising peace: for such another field
They dreaded worse than Hell: so much the fear
Of thunder and the sword of Michael
Wrought still within them; and no less desire 295
To found this nether empire, which might rise
By policy, and long process of time,
In emulation opposite to Heaven.
Which when Beëlzebub perceived, than whom,
Satan except, none higher sat, with grave 300
Aspect he rose, and in his rising seemed
A pillar of state; deep on his front engraven
Deliberation sat and public care;
And princely counsel in his face yet shone,
Majestic though in ruin: sage he stood 305
With Atlantean shoulders fit to bear
The weight of mightiest monarchies; his look
Drew audience and attention still as night
Or summer's noon-tide air, while thus he spake:
    'Thrones and Imperial Powers, off-spring of
       Heaven, 310
Ethereal Virtues; or these titles now
Must we renounce, and changing style be called
Princes of Hell? for so the popular vote
Inclines, here to continue, and build up here
A growing empire, doubtless, while we dream, 315
And know not that the King of Heaven hath doomed
This place our dungeon, not our safe retreat
Beyond His potent arm, to live exempt
From Heaven's high jurisdiction, in new league

Banded against His throne, but to remain 320
In strictest bondage, though thus far removed,
Under th' inevitable curb, reserved
His captive multitude; for He, be sure,
In highth or depth, still first and last will reign
Sole king, and of His kingdom lose no part 325
By our revolt, but over Hell extend
His empire, and with iron sceptre rule
Us here, as with his golden those in Heaven.
What sit we then projecting peace and war?
War hath determined us, and foiled with loss 330
Irreparable; terms of peace yet none
Vouchsafed or sought. For what peace will be given
To us enslaved, but custody severe,
And stripes, and arbitrary punishment
Inflicted? and what peace can we return, 335
But to our power hostility and hate,
Untamed reluctance, and revenge though slow,
Yet ever plotting how the Conqueror least
May reap His conquest, and may least rejoice
In doing what we most in suffering feel? 340
Nor will occasion want, nor shall we need
With dangerous expedition to invade
Heaven, whose high walls fear no assault or siege,
Or ambush from the deep. What if we find
Some easier enterprise? There is a place 345
(If ancient and prophetic fame in Heaven
Err not), another world, the happy seat
Of some new race called *Man*, about this time
To be created like to us, though less
In power and excellence, but favored more 350
Of Him who rules above; so was His will
Pronounced among the gods, and by an oath,
That shook Heaven's whole circumference, con-
    firmed.
Thither let us bend all our thoughts, to learn
What creatures there inhabit, of what mould, 355
Or substance, how endued, and what their power,
And where their weakness, how attempted best,
By force or subtlety: though Heaven be shut,
And Heaven's high Arbitrator sit secure
In His own strength, this place may lie exposed, 360
The utmost border of His Kingdom, left
To their defence who hold it; here perhaps
Some advantageous act may be achieved
By sudden onset, either with Hell fire
To waste His whole creation, or possess 365
All as our own, and drive as we were driven,
The puny habitants, or if not drive,
Seduce them to our party, that their God
May prove their foe, and with repenting hand
Abolish His own works. This would surpass 370

275. **Become our elements.** It was the tradition that devils had immediate power over the four terrestrial elements of earth, air, fire, and water—an explanation of the essential hostility of these elements, when unchecked, toward mankind. 288. **o'erwatched,** worn out from watching. 294. **Michael,** the chief warrior in the hosts of Heaven; this archangel's combat with Satan in that battle is described later in Book VI. 297. **policy,** statesmanship. 302. **front,** forehead, brow. 306. **Atlantean,** like Atlas, who in Greek mythology held up the sky on his shoulders. 311. **Virtues,** one of the orders on the celestial hierarchy; see note to Book I, l. 128 above. 312. **style,** the formal term of address to one of royal or noble birth 315. **doubtless.** Note the sarcasm.

324. **first and last.** See Revelation, 1:2, 21:6, and 22:13: "I am Alpha and Omega, the beginning and the end, the first and last." 327. **iron sceptre.** See Psalms, 2:9: "Thou shalt break them with a rod of iron." 336. **to our power,** to the limit of our power. 346. **fame,** report. 356. **endued,** invested or gifted with qualities of mind.

Common revenge, and interrupt His joy
In our confusion, and our joy upraise
In His disturbance; when His darling sons
Hurled headlong to partake with us, shall curse
Their frail original, and faded bliss,   375
Faded so soon. Advise if this be worth
Attempting, or to sit in darkness here
Hatching vain empires.' Thus Beëlzebub
Pleaded his devilish counsel, first devised
By Satan, and in part proposed: for whence   380
But from the author of all ill could spring
So deep a malice, to confound the race
Of mankind in one root, and Earth with Hell
To mingle and involve, done all to spite
The great Creator? But their spite still serves   385
His glory to augment. The bold design
Pleased highly those infernal states, and joy
Sparkled in all their eyes; with full assent
They vote; whereat his speech he thus renews:
  'Well have ye judged, well ended long debate,
Synod of Gods, and like to what ye are,   391
Great things resolved, which from the lowest deep
Will once more lift us up, in spite of Fate,
Nearer our ancient seat; perhaps in view
Of those bright confines, whence with neighboring
    arms   395
And opportune excursion we may chance
Re-enter Heaven; or else in some mild zone
Dwell not unvisited of Heaven's fair light
Secure, and at the brightening orient beam
Purge off this gloom; the soft delicious air,   400
To heal the scar of these corrosive fires
Shall breathe her balm. But first, whom shall we
    send
In search of this new world, whom shall we find
Sufficient? who shall tempt with wandering feet
The dark unbottomed infinite abyss   405
And through the palpable obscure find out
His uncouth way, or spread his airy flight
Upborne with indefatigable wings
Over the vast abrupt, ere he arrive
The happy isle; what strength, what art can then
Suffice, or what evasion bear him safe   411
Through the strict sentries and stations thick
Of angels watching round? Here he had need
All circumspection, and we now no less
Choice in our suffrage; for on whom we send,   415
The weight of all and our last hope relies.'

375. original, "original parent" rather than "original state"—in other
words, Adam. 379. first devised; see Book I, ll. 650–654 above.
387. states, estates, authorities, as in the modern "three estates."
391. Synod, any kind of assembly, as used here. 394. seat, established home. 405. abyss, the undefined portion of the cosmic space
between Heaven and Hell. 407. uncouth, unknown, uncertain. 409.
abrupt, here a noun meaning the space or gulf in Chaos between Hell
and Earth. arrive, reach. 410. isle. The Earth and its universe is
likened to an island in the great ocean of Chaos. 412. sentries. This
word should probably be read in the old form "senteries," inasmuch
as the three syllables are necessary for the meter.

  This said, he sat; and expectation held
His look suspense, awaiting who appeared
To second, or oppose, or undertake
The perilous attempt; but all sat mute,   420
Pondering the danger with deep thoughts; and each
In other's countenance read his own dismay
Astonished: none among the choice and prime
Of those Heaven-warring champions could be found
So hardy as to proffer or accept   425
Alone the dreadful voyage; till at last
Satan, whom now transcendent glory raised
Above his fellows, with monarchal pride
Conscious of highest worth, unmoved thus spake:
  'O Progeny of Heaven, empyreal Thrones,   430
With reason hath deep silence and demur
Seized us, though undismayed; long is the way
And hard, that out of Hell leads up to light;
Our prison strong, this huge convex of fire,
Outrageous to devour, immures us round   435
Ninefold, and gates of burning adamant
Barred over us prohibit all egress.
These passed, if any pass, the void profound
Of unessential Night receives him next
Wide gaping, and with utter loss of being   440
Threatens him, plunged in that abortive gulf.
If thence he scape into whatever world,
Or unknown region, what remains him less
Than unknown dangers and as hard escape.
But I should ill become this throne, O Peers,   445
And this imperial sovereignty, adorned
With splendor, armed with power, if aught pro-
    posed
And judged of public moment, in the shape
Of difficulty or danger could deter
Me from attempting. Wherefore do I assume   450
These royalties, and not refuse to reign,
Refusing to accept as great a share
Of hazard as of honour, due alike
To him who reigns, and so much to him due
Of hazard more, as he above the rest   455
High honoured sits? Go therefore, mighty Powers,
Terror of Heaven, though fallen; intend at home,
While here shall be our home, what best may ease
The present misery, and render Hell
More tolerable; if there be cure or charm   460
To respite or deceive, or slack the pain
Of this ill mansion: intermit no watch
Against a wakeful foe, while I abroad
Through all the coasts of dark destruction seek
Deliverance for us all: this enterprise   465
None shall partake with me.' Thus saying rose

432–433. long is the way, etc., an obvious reminiscence of the words
of the Cumaean Sibyl to Aeneas in Virgil's *Aeneid*, in which she warns
him that the descent to Hades is easy but the return long and difficult. 434. convex, used here for a sphere entire. 439. unessential,
lacking substance, material or essence; formless. 457. intend, consider, deliberate. 461. deceive, beguile. 462. mansion, seat; see
l. 394 above and note.

The monarch, and prevented all reply,
Prudent, lest from his resolution raised
Others among the chief might offer now
(Certain to be refused) what erst they feared; 470
And so refused might in opinion stand
His rivals, winning cheap the high repute
Which he through hazard huge must earn. But they
Dreaded not more the adventure than his voice
Forbidding; and at once with him they rose; 475
Their rising all at once was as the sound
Of thunder heard remote. Towards him they bend
With awful reverence prone; and as a god
Extol him equal to the Highest in Heaven:
Nor failed they to express how much they praised,
That for the general safety he despised 481
His own: for neither do the spirits damned
Lose all their virtue; lest bad men should boast
Their specious deeds on Earth, which glory excites,
Or close ambition varnished o'er with zeal. 485
Thus they their doubtful consultations dark
Ended, rejoicing in their matchless chief:
As when from mountain-tops the dusky clouds
Ascending, while the north wind sleeps, o'erspread
Heaven's cheerful face, the lowering element 490
Scowls o'er the darkened landscape snow, or shower;
If chance the radiant sun with farewell sweet
Extend his evening beam, the fields revive,
The birds their notes renew, and bleating herds
Attest their joy, that hill and valley rings. 495
O shame to men! Devil with devil damned
Firm concord holds, men only disagree
Of creatures rational, though under hope
Of Heavenly Grace; and, God proclaiming peace,
Yet live in hatred, enmity, and strife 500
Among themselves, and levy cruel wars,
Wasting the Earth, each other to destroy:
As if (which might induce us to accord)
Man had not hellish foes enow besides,
That day and night for his destruction wait. 505
    The Stygian council thus dissolved; and forth
In order came the grand Infernal Peers,
Midst came their mighty paramount, and seemed
Alone the antagonist of Heaven, nor less
Than Hell's dread emperor with pomp supreme, 510
And God-like imitated state; him round
A globe of fiery Seraphim enclosed
With bright emblazonry, and horrent arms.
Then of their session ended they bid cry
With trumpet's regal sound the great result: 515
Toward the four winds four speedy Cherubim
Put to their mouths the sounding alchemy
By herald's voice explained: the hollow abyss

468. **raised,** heightened, emboldened. 484. **specious,** showy, ostentatious. 507. **Peers.** No doubt Milton has in mind the English House of Peers or Lords in Parliament. 508. **Midst,** amidst, in the midst. **paramount,** chief, leader. 512. **globe,** a solid body of soldiers. 513. **horrent,** bristling. 517. **alchemy.** "Alchemy" gold, so-called, was an alloy much like brass used particularly in wind-instruments.

Heard far and wide, and all the host of Hell
With deafening shout, returned them loud acclaim.
Thence more at ease their minds and somewhat
    raised 521
By false presumptuous hope, the rangéd powers
Disband, and wandering each his several way
Pursues, as inclination or sad choice
Leads him perplexed, where he may likeliest find
Truce to his restless thoughts, and entertain 526
The irksome hours, till his great chief return.
Part on the plain, or in the air sublime
Upon the wing, or in swift race contend,
As at the Olympian games or Pythian fields; 530
Part curb their fiery steeds, or shun the goal
With rapid wheels, or fronted brigades form.
As when to warn proud cities war appears
Waged in the troubled sky, and armies rush
To battle in the clouds, before each van 535
Prick forth the airy knights, and couch their spears
Till thickest legions close; with feats of arms
From either end of Heaven the welkin burns.
Others with vast Typhaean rage more fell
Rend up both rocks and hills, and ride the air 540
In whirlwind; Hell scarce holds the wild uproar,—
As when Alcides from Oechalia crowned
With conquest, felt the envenomed robe, and tore
Through pain up by the roots Thessalian pines,
And Lichas from the top of Oeta threw 545
Into the Euboic Sea. Others more mild,
Retreated in a silent valley, sing
With notes angelical to many a harp
Their own heroic deeds and hapless fall
By doom of battle; and complain that Fate 550
Free Virtue should enthrall to Force or Chance.
Their song was partial, but the harmony
(What could it less when spirits immortal sing?)
Suspended Hell, and took with ravishment 554
The thronging audience. In discourse more sweet
(For eloquence the soul, song charms the sense),
Others apart sat on a hill retired,
In thoughts more elevate, and reasoned high
Of Providence, Foreknowledge, Will, and Fate,
Fixed Fate, freewill, foreknowledge absolute, 560
And found no end, in wandering mazes lost.
Of good and evil much they argued then,
Of happiness and final misery,

522. **powers,** armies. 530. **Olympian . . . Pythian,** the famous athletic meets of ancient Greece. 531. **shun the goal.** The reference here is to the chariot race, in which the driver wheeled as closely as possible to the turning-posts in the course without, of course, touching it. 539. **Typhaean;** see Book I, note to l. 199. 543. **Alcides,** etc. Hercules, son of Alcaeus (Alcides), returning with his bride Deianira from one of his successful exploits, slew with a poisoned arrow the centaur Nessus, who had attempted to abduct the bride. Dying, Nessus told Deianira to give her husband a robe anointed with his blood. The centaur's blood was itself fatally poisonous. The victim Hercules, maddened by the pain, threw his servant Lichas (545) into the sea. 560. **Fate, freewill, foreknowledge,** "predestination."

Passion and apathy, and glory and shame,
Vain wisdom all, and false philosophy: 565
Yet with a pleasing sorcery could charm
Pain for a while or anguish, and excite
Fallacious hope, or arm the obdured breast
With stubborn patience as with triple steel.
Another part in squadrons and gross bands,   570
On bold adventure to discover wide
That dismal world, if any clime perhaps
Might yield them easier habitation, bend
Four ways their flying march, along the banks
Of four infernal rivers that disgorge   575
Into the burning lake their baleful streams—
Abhorred *Styx*, the flood of deadly hate,
Sad *Acheron* of sorrow, black and deep;
Cocytus, named of lamentation loud
Heard on the rueful stream; fierce *Phlegeton*,   580
Whose waves of torrent fire inflame with rage.
Far off from these a slow and silent stream,
Lethe, the river of Oblivion, rolls
Her watery labyrinth, whereof who drinks,
Forthwith his former state and being forgets,   585
Forgets both joy and grief, pleasure and pain.
Beyond this flood a frozen Continent
Lies dark and wild, beat with perpetual storms
Of whirlwind and dire hail, which on firm land
Thaws not, but gathers heap, and ruin seems   590
Of ancient pile; all else deep snow and ice,
A gulf profound as that Serbonian bog
Betwixt Damiata and Mount Casius old,
Where armies whole have sunk: the parching air
Burns frore, and cold performs the effect of fire.   595
Thither by Harpy-footed Furies haled,
At certain revolutions all the damned
Are brought: and feel by turns the bitter change
Of fierce extremes, extremes by change more fierce,
From beds of raging fire to starve in ice   600
Their soft ethereal warmth, and there to pine
Immovable, infixed, and frozen round,
Periods of time, thence hurried back to fire.
They ferry over this Lethean sound
Both to and fro, their sorrow to augment,   605
And wish and struggle, as they pass, to reach
The tempting stream, with one small drop to lose
In sweet forgetfulness all pain and woe,
All in one moment, and so near the brink;
But Fate withstands, and to oppose th' attempt   610

Medusa with Gorgonian terror guards
The ford, and of itself the water flies
All taste of living wight, as once it fled
The lip of Tantalus. Thus roving on
In confused march forlorn, the adventurous bands
With shuddering horror pale and eyes aghast   616
Viewed first their lamentable lot, and found
No rest: through many a dark and dreary vale
They passed, and many a region dolorous,
O'er many a frozen, many a fiery Alp,   620
Rocks, caves, lakes, fens, bogs, dens, and shades of
    death,
A universe of death, which God by curse
Created evil, for evil only good,
Where all life dies, death lives, and Nature breeds,
Perverse, all monstrous, all prodigious things,   625
Abominable, unutterable, and worse
Than fables yet have feigned, or fear conceived,
Gorgons and Hydras, and Chimeras dire.
    Meanwhile the Adversary of God and Man,   629
Satan, with thoughts inflamed of highest design,
Puts on swift wings, and toward the Gates of Hell
Explores his solitary flight; sometimes
He scours the right hand coast, sometimes the left,
Now shaves with level wing the deep, then soars
Up to the fiery concave towering high.   635
As when far off at sea a fleet descried
Hangs in the clouds, by equinoctial winds
Close sailing from Bengala, or the Isles
Of Ternate and Tidore, whence merchants bring
Their spicy drugs: they on the trading flood   640
Through the wide Ethiopian to the Cape
Ply stemming nightly toward the Pole, so seemed
Far off the flying fiend: at last appear
Hell-bounds high reaching to the horrid roof,
And thrice three-fold the Gates; three folds were
    brass,   645
Three iron, three of adamantine rock,
Impenetrable, impaled with circling fire,
Yet unconsumed. Before the Gates there sat
On either side a formidable shape;
The one seemed woman to the waist, and fair,   650
But ended foul in many a scaly fold
Voluminous and vast, a serpent armed

564. **apathy,** here, the absence of passion, an ideal of ancient Stoic philosophy.   570. **gross,** large.   575. **four infernal rivers.** These are enumerated below as Styx (577); Acheron (578); Cocytus (579); and Phlegeton (580). These were all, of course, from classical mythology. 592. **Serbonian bog,** Serbonis Lake, which had the deceitful appearance of solid ground but was in reality a dangerous quagmire.   595. **frore,** frozen.   596. **Furies,** the Eumenides of Greek tradition, who avenged unnatural crimes. They are described as monstrous birds with the faces of women and huge claw-like feet, like the Harpies. 600. **starve,** die, kill (when used transitively, as here).

611. **Medusa with Gorgonian terror.** In Greek mythology, Medusa was the monstrous Gorgon, with snaky locks and aspect so terrifying that one glance at it was sufficient to turn the beholder to stone. She was slain by Perseus, who attacked her with the aid of a mirror. 614. **Tantalus.** For offending Hera, or Juno, queen of the gods of Olympus, this legendary king was punished in Hades by the torture of ever unsatisfied hunger and thirst; cf. our *tantalize.* 620. **Alp,** any high mountain.   628. **Gorgons . . . Hydras . . . Chimeras,** generalized names for various monsters of the classical Underworld. 632. **Explores,** pursues uncertainly.   638–639. **Bengala . . . Ternate . . . Tidore.** In order, these are the names of an arm of the Indian ocean (the Bay of Bengal) and two small islands in the Dutch East Indies (in the Molucca group).   641. **Ethiopian,** the Indian Ocean. The allusions in these lines are striking evidence of the newly-discovered trading centers in the Far East.

With mortal sting: about her middle round
A cry of Hell-hounds never ceasing barked   654
With wide Cerberean mouths full loud, and rung
A hideous peal: yet, when they list, would creep,
If aught disturbed their noise, into her womb,
And kennel there, yet there still barked and howled
Within unseen. Far less abhorred than these
Vexed Scylla bathing in the sea that parts   660
Calabria from the hoarse Trinacrian shore:
Nor uglier follow the night-hag, when called
In secret, riding through the air she comes
Lured with the smell of infant blood, to dance
With Lapland witches, while the labouring moon
Eclipses at their charms. The other shape,   666
If shape it might be called that shape had none
Distinguishable in member, joint, or limb,
Or substance might be called that shadow seemed,
For each seemed either: black it stood as night,   670
Fierce as ten Furies, terrible as Hell,
And shook a dreadful dart; what seemed his head
The likeness of a kingly crown had on.
Satan was now at hand, and from his seat
The monster moving onward came as fast,   675
With horrid strides, Hell trembled as he strode.
The undaunted fiend what this might be admired,
Admired, not feared; God and His Son except,
Created thing naught valued he nor shunned;
And with disdainful look thus first began: 680
'Whence and what art thou, execrable shape,
That darest, though grim and terrible, advance
Thy miscreated front athwart my way
To yonder Gates? through them I mean to pass,
That be assured! without leave asked of thee: 685
Retire, or taste thy folly, and learn by proof,
Hell-born, not to contend with spirits of Heaven!'
    To whom the goblin, full of wrath, replied:
'Art thou that traitor angel, art thou he,
Who first broke peace in Heaven and faith, till then
Unbroken, and in proud rebellious arms   691
Drew after him the third part of Heaven's sons
Conjured against the Highest, for which both thou
And they, outcast from God, are here condemned
To waste eternal days in woe and pain?   695
And reckonest thou thyself with spirits of Heaven,
Hell-doomed, and breathest defiance here and scorn,
Where I reign king, and to enrage thee more,
Thy king and lord? Back to thy punishment,

False fugitive, and to thy speed add wings,   700
Lest with a whip of scorpions I pursue
Thy lingering, or with one stroke of this dart
Strange horror seize thee, and pangs unfelt before!'
    So spake the grisly terror, and in shape,
So speaking and so threatening, grew tenfold   705
More dreadful and deform: on the other side
Incensed with indignation Satan stood
Unterrified, and like a comet burned,
That fires the length of Ophiuchus huge
In the Arctic sky, and from his horrid hair   710
Shakes pestilence and war. Each at the head
Levelled his deadly aim; their fatal hands
No second stroke intend, and such a frown
Each cast at th' other, as when two black clouds,
With Heaven's artillery fraught, come rattling on
Over the Caspian, then stand front to front   716
Hovering a space, till winds the signal blow
To join their dark encounter in mid-air:
So frowned the mighty combatants, that Hell
Grew darker at their frown, so matched they stood;
For never but once more was either like   721
To meet so great a foe: and now great deeds
Had been achieved, whereof all Hell had rung,
Had not the snaky sorceress that sat
Fast by Hell Gate, and kept the fatal key,   725
Risen, and with hideous outcry rushed between.
    'O Father, what intends thy hand,' she cried,
'Against thy only son? What fury, O son,
Possesses thee to bend that mortal dart
Against thy father's head? and knowest for whom?
For Him who sits above and laughs the while   731
At thee ordained His drudge, to execute
Whate'er His wrath, which He calls Justice, bids,
His wrath which one day will destroy ye both!'
    She spake, and at her words the hellish pest   735
Forbore, then these to her Satan returned:
    'So strange thy outcry, and thy words so strange
Thou interposest, that my sudden hand
Prevented spares to tell thee yet by deeds
What it intends; till first I know of thee,   740
What thing thou art, thus double-formed, and why
In this infernal vale first met thou callest
Me father, and that phantasm call'st my son?
I know thee not, nor ever saw till now
Sight more detestable than him and thee.'   745
    To whom thus the portress of Hell Gate replied:
'Hast thou forgot me, then, and do I seem
Now in thine eye so foul, once deemed so fair
In Heaven, when at the Assembly, and in sight
Of all the Seraphim with thee combined   750
In bold conspiracy against Heaven's king,

---

655. **Cerberean mouths**, maws like those of Cerberus, the famous three-headed monster and Hell-hound in classical mythology. 660. **Scylla**, a female sea-monster destructive to sea-faring men. 662. **night-hag**, Hecate, a goddess of the classical Underworld; in later European folklore she is queen of the witches, as in Shakespeare's *Macbeth*. 665. **Lapland**. In Milton's time this remote section of the northland was believed to be the abode of witches. 677. **admired**, wondered at. 688. **goblin**, fiend—much more awe-inspiring than the modern "goblin." 692. **third . . . sons**, referring doubtless to the dragon seen by Saint John in the Apocalypse, "whose tail drew the third part of the stars of Heaven, and did cast them to Earth." See Revelation, 12:3–4. 693. **Conjured**, drawn together by an oath.

709. **Ophiuchus**, the constellation of the Serpent in the northern hemisphere, a long and sprawling aggregation of undistinguished stars. 716. **Caspian**. This great inland sea of southeastern Russia has long had the reputation of being stormy. 722. **meet . . . foe.** Both Satan and Death were, of course, still to meet Christ.

All on a sudden miserable pain
Surprised thee, dim thine eyes, and dizzy swum
In darkness, while thy head flames thick and fast
Threw forth, till on the left side opening wide, 755
Likest to thee in shape and countenance bright,
Then shining heavenly fair, a goddess armed
Out of thy head I sprung; amazement seized
All the Host of Heaven; back they recoiled afraid
At first, and called me *Sin,* and for a sign 760
Portentous held me; but familiar grown,
I pleased, and with attractive graces won
The most averse, thee chiefly, who full oft
Thyself in me thy perfect image viewing
Becam'st enamoured, and such joy thou took'st 765
With me in secret, that my womb conceived
A growing burden. Meanwhile War arose,
And fields were fought in Heaven; wherein re-
      mained
(For what could else) to our Almighty Foe
Clear victory, to our part loss and rout 770
Through all th' Empyrean: down they fell,
Driven headlong from the pitch of Heaven, down
Into this deep, and in the general fall
I also; at which time this powerful key
Into my hand was given, with charge to keep 775
These Gates forever shut, which none can pass
Without my opening. Pensive here I sat
Alone, but long I sat not, till my womb
Pregnant by thee, and now excessive grown,
Prodigious motion felt and rueful throes. 780
At last this odious offspring whom thou seest,
Thine own begotten, breaking violent way,
Tore through my entrails, that with fear and pain
Distorted, all my nether shape thus grew
Transformed: but he, my inbred enemy, 785
Forth issued, brandishing his fatal dart
Made to destroy: I fled, and cried out *Death;*
Hell trembled at the hideous name, and sighed
From all her caves, and back resounded *Death.*
I fled, but he pursued (though more, it seems, 790
Inflamed with lust than rage) and swifter far,
Me overtook, his mother all dismayed,
And in embraces forcible and foul
Engendering with me, of that rape begot
These yelling monsters that with ceaseless cry 795
Surround me, as thou saw'st, hourly conceived
And hourly born, with sorrow infinite
To me, for when they list into the womb
That bred them they return, and howl and gnaw
My bowels, their repast; then bursting forth 800
Afresh with conscious terrors vex me round,
That rest or intermission find I none.

758. **Out of thy head,** etc. Milton has borrowed this idea from the
Greek legend according to which Pallas Athene (Minerva) sprang
full-fledged from the head of Zeus. 768. **fields,** battles. 781.
odious offspring, a personification of the old Biblical idea that "the
wages of Sin is Death."

"The Temptation of Adam and Eve," by Albrecht Dürer.
This engraving was made in 1504.

Before mine eyes in opposition sits
Grim *Death,* my son and foe, who sets them on,
And me his parent would full soon devour 805
For want of other prey, but that he knows
His end with mine involved; and knows that I
Should prove a bitter morsel, and his bane,
Whenever that shall be; so Fate pronounced.
But thou, O father, I forewarn thee, shun 810
His deadly arrow; neither vainly hope
To be invulnerable in those bright arms,
Though tempered heavenly, for that mortal dint,
Save He who reigns above, none can resist.'
    She finished, and the subtle fiend his lore 815
Soon learned, now milder, and thus answered
      smooth:
'Dear daughter, since thou claimest me for thy sire,
And my fair son here show'st me, the dear pledge
Of dalliance had with thee in Heaven, and joys
Then sweet, now sad to mention, through dire
      change 820
Befallen us unforeseen, unthought of, know
I come no enemy, but to set free
From out this dark and dismal house of pain,
Both him and thee, and all the heavenly host
Of spirits that in our just pretenses armed 825
Fell with us from on high: from them I go

825. **pretenses,** legal claims.

This uncouth errand sole, and one for all
Myself expose, with lonely steps to tread
The unfounded deep, and through the void immense
To search with wandering quest a place foretold
Should be, and, by concuring signs, ere now   831
Created vast and round, a place of bliss
In the purlieus of Heaven, and therein placed
A race of upstart creatures, to supply
Perhaps our vacant room, though more removed,
Lest Heaven surcharged with potent multitude   836
Might hap to move new broils: be this or aught
Than this more secret now designed, I haste
To know, and this once known, shall soon return,
And bring ye to the place where thou and Death
Shall dwell at ease, and up and down unseen   841
Wing silently the buxom air, embalmed
With odours; there ye shall be fed and filled
Immeasurably, all things shall be your prey.'
He ceased, for both seemed highly pleased, and
      Death   845
Grinned horrible a ghastly smile, to hear
His famine should be filled, and blessed his maw
Destined to that good hour; no less rejoiced
His mother bad, and thus bespake her sire:
'The key of this infernal pit by due,   850
And by command of Heaven's all-powerful king
I keep, by Him forbidden to unlock
These adamantine Gates; against all force
Death ready stands to interpose his dart,
Fearless to be o'ermatched by living might.   855
But what owe I to His commands above
Who hates me, and hath hither thrust me down
Into this gloom of Tartarus profound,
To sit in hateful office here confined,
Inhabitant of Heaven, and heavenly-born,   860
Here in perpetual agony and pain,
With terrors and with clamors compassed round
Of mine own brood, that on my bowels feed:
Thou art my father, thou my author, thou
My being gavest me; whom should I obey   865
But thee, whom follow? thou wilt bring me soon
To that new world of light and bliss, among
The gods who live at ease, where I shall reign
At thy right hand voluptuous, as beseems
Thy daughter and thy darling, without end.'   870
      Thus saying, from her side the fatal key,
Sad instrument of all our woe, she took;
And towards the Gate rolling her bestial train,
Forthwith the huge portcullis high up drew,
Which but herself not all the Stygian powers   875
Could once have moved; then in the key-hole turns
The intricate wards, and every bolt and bar

827. uncouth, unknown. 829. unfounded, without foundations or bottom. deep, Chaos. 842. buxom, yielding, unresisting. 869. right hand voluptuous. Sin is picturing herself as eventually sitting in her true nature at the right hand of Satan, just as Christ is described in the scriptures as sitting after the Day of Judgment at the right hand of God.

Of massy iron or solid rock with ease
Unfastens: on a sudden open fly
With impetuous recoil and jarring sound   880
The infernal doors, and on their hinges grate
Harsh thunder, that the lowest bottom shook
Of Erebus. She opened, but to shut
Excelled her power: the Gates wide open stood,
That with extended wings a bannered host   885
Under spread ensigns marching might pass through
With horse and chariots ranked in loose array;
So wide they stood, and like a furnace-mouth
Cast forth redounding smoke and ruddy flame.
Before their eyes in sudden view appear   890
The secrets of the hoary deep, a dark
Illimitable ocean without bound,
Without dimension, where length, breadth, and
      highth,
And time and place are lost; where eldest Night
And Chaos, ancestors of Nature, hold   895
Eternal anarchy, amidst the noise
Of endless wars, and by confusion stand.
For hot, cold, moist, and dry, four champions fierce
Strive here for mastery, and to battle bring
Their embryon atoms; they around the flag   900
Of each his faction, in their several clans,
Light-armed or heavy, sharp, smooth, swift or slow,
Swarm populous, unnumbered as the sands
Of Barca or Cyrene's torrid soil,
Levied to side with warring winds, and poise   905
Their lighter wings. To whom these most adhere,
He rules a moment; Chaos umpire sits,
And by decision more embroils the fray
By which he reigns: next him high arbiter
Chance governs all. Into this wide abyss,   910
The womb of Nature and perhaps her grave,
Of neither sea, nor shore, nor air, nor fire,
But all these in their pregnant causes mixed
Confusedly, and which thus must ever fight,
Unless the almighty Maker them ordain   915
His dark materials to create more worlds,
Into this wild abyss the wary fiend
Stood on the brink of Hell and looked a while,
Pondering his voyage: for no narrow frith
He had to cross. Nor was his ear less pealed   920
With noises loud and ruinous (to compare
Great things with small) than when Bellona storms,
With all her battering engines bent to raze
Some capital city, or less than if this frame
Of Heaven were falling, and these elements   925
In mutiny had from her axle torn
The steadfast Earth. At last his sail-broad vans
He spreads for flight, and in the surging smoke
Uplifted spurns the ground, thence many a league

883. Erebus, darkness. 889. redounding, billowing. 904. Barca, the Libyan desert between Egypt and Tunis. Cyrene, an ancient city near the site of the present Tripoli. 920. pealed, struck by noise. 922. Bellona, the Roman goddess of war, partner of Mars.

As in a cloudy chair ascending rides   930
Audacious, but that seat soon failing, meets
A vast vacuity; all unawares
Fluttering his pennons vain plumb down he drops
Ten thousand fathom deep, and to this hour
Down had been falling, had not by ill chance   935
The strong rebuff of some tumultuous cloud
Instinct with fire and nitre hurried him
As many miles aloft: that fury stayed,
Quenched in a boggy Syrtis, neither sea,
Nor good dry land: nigh foundered on he fares,   940
Treading the crude consistence, half on foot,
Half flying; behoves him now both oar and sail.
As when a gryphon through the wilderness
With winged course o'er hill or moory dale,
Pursues the Arimaspian, who by stealth   945
Had from his wakeful custody purloined
The guarded gold: so eagerly the fiend
O'er bog or steep, through strait, rough, dense, or
      rare,
With head, hands, wings, or feet pursues his way,
And swims or sinks, or wades, or creeps, or flies:
At length a universal hubbub wild   951
Of stunning sounds and voices all confused
Borne through the hollow dark assaults his ear
With loudest vehemence: thither he plies,
Undaunted to meet there whatever power   955
Or spirit of the nethermost abyss
Might in that noise reside, of whom to ask
Which way the nearest coast of darkness lies
Bordering on light; when straight behold the throne
Of Chaos, and his dark pavilion spread   960
Wide on the wasteful deep; with him enthroned
Sat sable-vested Night, eldest of things,
The consort of his reign; and by them stood
Orcus and *Ades*, and the dreaded name
Of *Demogorgon;* Rumor next and Chance,   965
And Tumult and Confusion all embroiled,
And Discord with a thousand various mouths.
   To whom Satan turning boldly, thus: 'Ye Powers
And Spirits of this nethermost abyss,
Chaos and ancient Night, I come no spy,   970
With purpose to explore or to disturb
The secrets of your realm, but by constraint
Wandering this darksome desert, as my way
Lies through your spacious empire up to light,
Alone, and without guide, half lost, I seek   975
What readiest path leads where your gloomy bounds

Confine with Heaven; or if some other place
From your dominion won, the ethereal King
Possesses lately, thither to arrive
I travel this profound, direct my course;   980
Directed, no mean recompense it brings
To your behoof, if I that region lost,
All usurpation thence expelled, reduce
To her original darkness and your sway
(Which is my present journey) and once more   985
Erect the standard there of ancient Night;
Yours be the advantage all, mine the revenge.'
   Thus Satan; and him thus the anarch old
With faltering speech and visage incomposed
Answered: 'I know thee, stranger, who thou art,
That mighty leading Angel, who of late   991
Made head against Heaven's King, though over-
      thrown.
I saw and heard, for such a numerous host
Fled not in silence through the frighted deep
With ruin upon ruin, rout on rout,   995
Confusion worse confounded; and Heaven's Gates
Poured out by millions her victorious bands
Pursuing. I upon my frontiers here
Keep residence; if all I can will serve,
That little which is left so to defend   1000
Encroached on still through our intestine broils
Weakening the sceptre of old Night: first Hell
Your dungeon stretching far and wide beneath;
Now lately Heaven and Earth, another world
Hung o'er my realm, linked in a golden chain   1005
To that side Heaven from whence your legions fell:
If that way be your walk, you have not far;
So much the nearer danger; go and speed;
Havoc and spoil and ruin are my gain.'
   He ceased; and Satan stayed not to reply,   1010
But glad that now his sea should find a shore,
With fresh alacrity and force renewed
Springs upward like a pyramid of fire
Into the wild expanse, and through the shock
Of fighting elements, on all sides round   1015
Environed wins his way; harder beset
And more endangered, than when Argo passed
Through Bosphorus betwixt the jostling rocks:
Or when Ulysses on the larboard shunned
Charybdis, and by the other whirlpool steered.   1020
So he with difficulty and labour hard
Moved on, with difficulty and labour he;
But he once past, soon after when Man fell,
Strange alteration! Sin and Death amain
Following his track, such was the will of Heaven,
Paved after him a broad and beaten way   1026

939. **Syrtis**, quicksands off the coast of northern Africa near Tripoli.
943. **gryphon**, or griffin, a fabulous monster with a lion's body and an
eagle's head and wings. 945. **Arimaspian**, one-eyed people of
Scythia who, according to tradition, fought against the gryphons to
obtain the gold treasure which the monsters guarded—another of a
long line of tales about unusual creatures keeping watch over hoards
of treasure. 964. **Orcus**, a personification in Roman myth of the
Underworld. **Ades**, a similar personification of Death. 965. **Demogorgon**, a mysterious infernal deity originating in the early days of
the Roman empire who was so powerful as to control the destinies of
both gods and men.

977. **Confine**, have borders with. 988. **anarch.** Chaos is the king of
misrule. 989. **incomposed**, not "discomposed" but rather "not composed at all." 1005. **golden chain.** According to classical legend,
Zeus drew the gods, the Earth, the sea, and the whole universe upon
a single golden chain, which integrated all existence. 1017. **Argo,**
the ship which the Greek hero Jason used to sail to his adventure of
the Golden Fleece. 1020. **Charybdis,** see note to 660 above.

Over the dark abyss, whose boiling gulf
Tamely endured a bridge of wondrous length
From Hell continued reaching the utmost orb
Of this frail world; by which the spirits perverse
With easy intercourse pass to and fro   1031
To tempt or punish mortals, except whom
God and good angels guard by special grace.
But now at last the sacred influence
Of light appears, and from the walls of Heaven
Shoots far into the bosom of dim Night   1036
A glimmering dawn; here Nature first begins
Her farthest verge, and Chaos to retire,
As from her outmost works, a broken foe,
With tumult less and with less hostile din,   1040
That Satan with less toil, and now with ease
Wafts on the calmer wave by dubious light
And like a weather-beaten vessel holds
Gladly the port, though shrouds and tackle torn;
Or in the emptier waste, resembling air,   1045
Weighs his spread wings, at leisure to behold
Far off the empyreal Heaven, extended wide
In circuit, undetermined square or round,
With opal towers and battlements adorned
Of living sapphire, once his native seat;   1050
And fast by hanging in a golden chain
This pendant world, in bigness as a star
Of smallest magnitude close by the moon.
Thither, full fraught with mischievous revenge,
Accursed, and in a cursèd hour he hies.   1055

[Since Milton chose to plunge at once into the middle
of the action of his epic, the narrative substance of a part
of the Books following is necessarily concerned with sum-
ming up the earlier stages of the story. These also tell of
the temptation of Adam and Eve by Satan and of their
repentance for their sin. In the eleventh book God accepts
their prayers, "but declares that they must no longer
abide in Paradise; sends Michael with a band of Cherubim to dispossess them . . ." Michael descends to Eden,
breaks to Adam and Eve the news of their banishment,
yet of their ultimate redemption, then, taking Adam upon
a high hill, unfolds to him in a vision all that shall happen
on earth down to the time of the Flood.]

BOOK XII

The Argument

The Angel Michael continues from the Flood to relate
what shall succeed; then, in the mention of *Abraham,*
comes by degrees to explain, who that Seed of the
woman shall be, which was promised Adam and Eve in
the Fall; His Incarnation, Death, Resurrection, and Ascension; the state of the Church till His Second Coming.
Adam, greatly satisfied and re-comforted by these relations and promises, descends the hill with Michael;
wakens Eve, who all this while had slept, but with gentle

1029. **orb,** the outermost sphere of those which surround the earth,
according to the old cosmogony.   1039. **her,** Nature's.

dreams composed to quietness of mind and submission.
Michael in either hand leads them out of Paradise, the
fiery sword waving behind them, and the Cherubim taking their stations to guard the place.

As one who in his journey bates at noon,
Though bent on speed, so here the Archangel
           paused
Betwixt the world destroyed and world restored,
If Adam aught perhaps might interpose;
Then with transition sweet new speech resumes: 5
   'Thus thou hast seen one world begin and end;
And Man as from a second stock proceed.
Much thou hast yet to see, but I perceive
Thy mortal sight to fail; objects divine
Must needs impair and weary human sense: 10
Henceforth what is to come I will relate,
Thou therefore give due audience, and attend.
This second source of men, while yet but few,
And while the dread of Judgment past remains
Fresh in their minds, fearing the Deity,   15
With some regard to what is just and right
Shall lead their lives, and multiply apace,
Labouring the soil, and reaping plenteous crop,
Corn, wine and oil; and from the herd or flock,
Oft sacrificing bullock, lamb, or kid,   20
With large wine-offerings poured, and sacred feast,
Shall spend their days in joy unblamed, and dwell
Long time in peace by families and tribes
Under paternal rule; till one shall rise
Of proud ambitious heart, who not content   25
With fair equality, fraternal state,
Will arrogate Dominion undeserved
Over his brethren, and quite dispossess
Concord and Law of Nature from the Earth;
Hunting (and men, not beasts, shall be his game)
With war and hostile snare such as refuse   31
Subjection to his empire tyrannous:
A mighty hunter thence he shall be styled
Before the Lord, as in despite of Heaven,
Or from Heaven claiming second sovereignty;   35
And from rebellion shall derive his name,
Though of rebellion others he accuse.
He with a crew, whom like ambition joins
With him or under him to tyrannize,
Marching from Eden towards the West, shall find
The plain, wherein a black bituminous gürge   41
Boils out from under ground, the mouth of Hell;
Of brick, and of that stuff they cast to build
A city and tower, whose top may reach to Heaven;
And get themselves a name, lest far dispersed   45
In foreign lands their memory be lost,
Regardless whether good or evil fame.
But God, who oft descends to visit men

1. **bates,** abates speed, pauses.   5. **transition,** summary, epitome.
18. **Labouring,** working, used here transitively.   24. **one,** Nimrod.
The story is told in Genesis, 10:9 ff.

Unseen, and through their habitations walks
To mark their doings, them beholding soon,   50
Comes down to see their city, ere the tower
Obstruct Heaven Towers, and in derision sets
Upon their tongues a various spirit to rase
Quite out their native language, and instead
To sow a jangling noise of words unknown: 55
Forthwith a hideous gabble rises loud
Among the builders; each to other calls
Not understood, till hoarse, and all in rage,
As mocked they storm; great laughter was in
    Heaven,
And looking down, to see the hubbub strange   60
And hear the din; thus was the building left
Ridiculous, and the work Confusion named.'
    Whereto thus Adam fatherly displeased:
'O execrable son, so to aspire
Above his brethren, to himself assuming   65
Authority usurped, from God not given:
He gave us only over beast, fish, fowl
Dominion absolute; that right we hold
By His donation; but Man over men
He made not Lord; such title to Himself   70
Reserving, human left from human free.
But this usurper his encroachment proud
Stays not on Man; to God his tower intends
Siege and defiance: wretched man! what food
Will he convey up thither to sustain   75
Himself and his rash army, where thin air
Above the clouds will pine his entrails gross,
And famish him of breath, if not of bread?'
    To whom thus Michael: 'Justly thou abhorrest
That son, who on the quiet state of men   80
Such trouble brought, affecting to subdue
Rational Liberty; yet know withal,
Since thy original lapse, true Liberty
Is lost, which always with right Reason dwells
Twinned, and from her hath no dividual being: 85
Reason in Man obscured, or not obeyed,
Immediately inordinate desires
And upstart passions catch the government
From Reason, and to servitude reduce
Man till then free. Therefore since he permits   90
Within himself unworthy powers to reign
Over free Reason, God in judgment just
Subjects him from without to violent lords;
Who oft as undeservedly enthrall
His outward freedom: tyranny must be,   95
Though to the tyrant thereby no excuse.
Yet sometimes nations will decline so low
From virtue, which is reason, that no wrong,
But Justice, and some fatal curse annexed,

Deprives them of their outward liberty,   100
Their inward lost: witness the irreverent son
Of him who built the Ark, who for the shame
Done to his father, heard this heavy curse,
Servant of Servants, on his vicious race.
Thus will this latter, as the former world,   105
Still tend from bad to worse, till God at last,
Wearied with their iniquities, withdraw
His presence from among them, and avert
His holy eyes; resolving from thenceforth
To leave them to their own polluted ways;   110
And one peculiar nation to select
From all the rest, of whom to be invoked,
A nation from one faithful man to spring:
Him on this side Euphrates yet residing,
Bred up in idol-worship; O that men   115
(Canst thou believe?) should be so stupid grown,
While yet the Patriarch lived, who scaped the Flood,
As to forsake the living God, and fall
To worship their own work in wood and stone
For gods! yet him God the most High vouchsafes
To call by vision from his Father's house,   121
His kindred and false gods, into a land
Which He will show him, and from him will raise
A mighty nation, and upon him shower
His benediction so, that in his seed   125
All nations shall be blessed; he straight obeys,
Not knowing to what land, yet firm believes:
I see him, but thou canst not, with what faith
He leaves his gods, his friends, and native soil,
Ur of Chaldaea, passing now the ford   130
To Haran, after him a cumbrous train
Of herds and flocks, and numerous servitude;
Not wandering poor, but trusting all his wealth
With God, who called him, in a land unknown.
Canaan he now attains; I see his tents   135
Pitched about Sechem, and the neighbouring plain
Of Moreh; there by promise he receives
Gift to his progeny of all that land;
From Hamath northward to the desert south
(Things by their name I call, though yet unnamed),
From Hermon east to the great Western Sea,   141
Mount Hermon, yonder Sea, each place behold
In prospect, as I point them; on the shore

---

53. **various spirit,** a spirit of contention, at variance with order and conformity. 61–62. **building . . . Confusion,** the Tower of Babel, the "confusion of tongues"; see Genesis, 11:2–9. 83–85. **Liberty . . . twinned.** The coupling of Liberty and Reason is virtually a commonplace in Milton's political and social views.

101. **irreverent son,** Ham, son of Noah, and father of Canaan. Note Genesis, 9:25: "And Noah said, 'Cursed be Canaan; a servant of servants shall he be unto his brethren.' " Ham became the ancestral progenitor of all the colored peoples of the world. 111. **one peculiar nation,** Israel. 113. **one faithful man,** Abraham. 130–131. **Ur . . . Haran.** The ancient city of Ur has been tentatively located on the western shore of the River Euphrates not far down the river from Babylon. **Haran** was across the river. 132. **servitude,** a collective noun for servants. 136. **Sechem,** or Shechem, the site of Abraham's first encampment in the land of Canaan; it is the present town of Nablus, between Mounts Ebal and Gerizim. 139. **Hamath,** on the River Orontes in eastern Syria; it is named in Numbers, 34:8 as the northern boundary-mark of the ancient land of Canaan. 141. **Hermon,** the highest mountain in Palestine, northeast of the Sea of Galilee. **Western Sea,** the Mediterranean.

Mount Carmel; here the double-founted stream
Jordan, true limit eastward; but his sons   145
Shall dwell to Senir, that long ridge of hills.
This ponder, that all nations of the Earth
Shall in his seed be blessed; by that seed
Is meant thy great Deliverer, who shall bruise
The Serpent's head; whereof to thee anon   150
Plainlier shall be revealed. This Patriarch blest,
Whom faithful *Abraham* due time shall call,
A son, and of his son a grandchild leaves,
Like him in faith, in wisdom, and renown;
The grandchild with twelve sons increased, departs
From Canaan, to a land hereafter called   156
Egypt, divided by the River Nile;
See where it flows, disgorging at seven mouths
Into the Sea; to sojourn in that land
He comes, invited by a younger son   160
In time of dearth, a son whose worthy deeds
Raise him to be the second in that realm
Of Pharaoh; there he dies, and leaves his race
Growing into a nation, and now grown
Suspected to a sequent king, who seeks   165
To stop their overgrowth, as inmate guests
Too numerous; whence of guests he makes them
      slaves
Inhospitably, and kills their infant males;
Till by two brethren (those two brethren call
Moses and *Aaron*) sent from God to claim   170
His people from enthrallment, they return
With glory and spoil back to their Promised Land.
But first the lawless tyrant, who denies
To know their God, or message to regard,
Must be compelled by signs and judgments dire;
To blood unshed the rivers must be turned,   176
Frogs, lice, and flies must all his palace fill
With loathed intrusion, and fill all the land;
His cattle must of rot and murrain die,
Botches and blains must all his flesh emboss,   180
And all his people; thunder mixed with hail,
Hail mixed with fire must rend the Egyptian sky
And wheel on the Earth, devouring where it rolls;
What it devours not, herb, or fruit, or grain,
A darksome cloud of locusts swarming down   185
Must eat, and on the ground leave nothing green:
Darkness must overshadow all his bounds,
Palpable darkness, and blot out three days;
Last with one midnight stroke all the first-born
Of Egypt must lie dead. Thus with ten wounds   190
The river-dragon, tamed at length, submits
To let his sojourners depart, and oft
Humbles his stubborn heart, but still as ice

144. **Mount Carmel,** a high cape projecting from the shore of Palestine into the Mediterranean.   146. **Senir,** a peak in the Mount Hermon range.   153. **A son,** Isaac.   175 ff. **signs and judgments,** the Ten Plagues; see Exodus, 7:19 ff.   180. **emboss,** cover with swellings and abscesses.   190-191. **Thus . . . the river-dragon;** see Ezekiel, 29:3: "Behold, I am against thee, Pharaoh King of Egypt, the great dragon that lieth in the midst of his rivers."

More hardened after thaw, till in his rage,
Pursuing whom he late dismissed, the Sea   195
Swallows him with his host, but them lets pass
As on dry land between two crystal walls,
Awed by the rod of Moses so to stand
Divided, till his rescued gain their shore:
Such wondrous power God to His saint will lend,
Though present in His Angel, who shall go   201
Before them in a cloud, and pillar of fire,
By day a cloud, by night a pillar of fire,
To guide them in their journey, and remove
Behind them, while the obdurate king pursues: 205
All night he will pursue, but his approach
Darkness defends between till morning-watch;
Then through the fiery pillar and the cloud,
God looking forth will trouble all his host
And craze their chariot-wheels; when by command
Moses once more his potent rod extends   211
Over the Sea; the Sea his rod obeys;
On their embattled ranks the waves return,
And overwhelm their war: the race elect
Safe towards Canaan from the shore advance   215
Through the wild desert, not the readiest way,
Lest entering on the Canaanite alarmed
War terrify them inexpert, and fear
Return them back to Egypt, choosing rather
Inglorious life with servitude; for life   220
To noble and ignoble is more sweet
Untrained in arms, where rashness leads not on.
This also shall they gain by their delay
In the wide wilderness; there they shall found
Their government, and their great senate choose
Through the Twelve Tribes, to rule by laws or-
      dained: 226
God from the Mount of Sinai, whose gray top
Shall tremble, He descending, will Himself
In thunder, lightning, and loud trumpet's sound
Ordain them Laws; part such as appertain   230
To civil justice, part religious rites
Of sacrifice, informing them, by types
And shadows, of that destined seed to bruise
The Serpent, by what means He shall achieve
Mankind's deliverance. But the voice of God   235
To mortal ear is dreadful; they beseech

202-203. **cloud . . . fire.** When the Israelites were on their way out of Egypt to the Promised Land, as told in Exodus, 13:21 ff., God showed them the way by leading them in the form of a cloud by day and a pillar of fire by night.   207. **defends,** prevents, forbids—by interposing Himself between the Israelites and the pursuing Egyptians.   210. **craze,** shatter, destroy.   213-214. **embattled . . . war.** The destruction of the hosts of Pharoah in the Red Sea is told in Exodus, 14.   218. **War,** armies, military forces.   225. **senate.** According to Exodus, 24:1-9 and Numbers, 11:16-30, there were seventy elders who witnessed some of the more important acts of Moses. No doubt it was from the nature of this group that Milton used the word *senate.*   236. **mortal . . . dreadful.** The beliefs that the voice of God is too mighty for mortal hearing and the sight of God too dazzling for mortal eyes are both too ancient for mere tracing; no doubt Milton is remembering the passage from Exodus, 20:19: "Speak thou with us, and we will hear; but let not God speak with us, lest we die."

That Moses might report to them His will,
And terror cease; He grants what they besought,
Instructed that to God is no access
Without mediator, whose high office now   240
Moses in figure bears, to introduce
One greater, of whose day he shall foretell,
And all the prophets in their age the times
Of great *Messiah* shall sing. Thus laws and rites
Established, such delight hath God in men   245
Obedient to His will, that He vouchsafes
Among them to set up His tabernacle,
The holy One with mortal men to dwell:
By his prescript a sanctuary is framed
Of cedar, overlaid with gold, therein   250
An Ark, and in the Ark His testimony,
The records of His covenant, over these
A mercy-seat of gold between the wings
Of two bright Cherubim, before him burn
Seven lamps, as in a zodiac representing   255
The heavenly fires; over the tent a cloud
Shall rest by day, a fiery gleam by night,
Save when they journey, and at length they come,
Conducted by His Angel to the land
Promised to Abraham and his seed: the rest   260
Were long to tell, how many battles fought,
How many kings destroyed, and kingdoms won,
Or how the Sun shall in mid-Heaven stand still
A day entire, and night's due course adjourn,
Man's voice commanding, Sun in Gibeon stand,   265
And thou, Moon, in the vale of Ajalon,
Till Israel overcome; so call the third
From Abraham, son of Isaac, and from him
His whole descent, who thus shall Canaan win.'
    Here Adam interposed. 'O sent from Heaven,   270
Enlightener of my darkness, gracious things
Thou hast revealed, those chiefly which concern
Just Abraham and his seed: now first I find
Mine eyes true opening, and my heart much eased,
Erewhile perplexed with thoughts what would be-
    come   275
Of me and all Mankind; but now I see
His day, in whom all nations shall be blessed,
Favour unmerited by me, who sought
Forbidden knowledge by forbidden means.
This yet I apprehend not, why to those   280
Among whom God will deign to dwell on Earth
So many and so various laws are given;
So many laws argue so many sins
Among them; how can God with such reside?'
    To whom thus Michael: 'Doubt not but that sin
Will reign among them, as of thee begot,   286
And therefore was Law given them to evince

Their natural pravity, by stirring up
Sin against Law to fight; that when they see
Law can discover Sin, but not remove,   290
Save by those shadowy expiations weak,
The blood of bulls and goats, they may conclude
Some blood more precious must be paid for Man,
Just for unjust, that in such righteousness
To them by Faith imputed, they may find   295
Justification toward God, and peace
Of Conscience, which the law by ceremonies
Cannot appease, nor Man the moral part
Perform, and not performing cannot live.
So Law appears imperfect, and but given   300
With purpose to resign them in full time
Up to a better covenant, disciplined
From shadowy types to Truth, from flesh to spirit,
From imposition of strict laws, to free
Acceptance of large Grace, from servile Fear   305
To filial, works of law to works of faith.
And therefore shall not Moses, though of God
Highly beloved, being but the minister
Of Law, his people into Canaan lead;
But *Joshua*, whom the Gentiles Jesus call,   310
His name and office bearing, who shall quell
The adversary Serpent, and bring back
Through the world's wilderness long wandered Man
Safe to eternal Paradise of rest.
Meanwhile they in their earthly Canaan placed   315
Long time shall dwell and prosper, but when sins
National interrupt their public peace,
Provoking God to raise them enemies:
From whom as oft he saves them penitent
By judges first, then under kings; of whom   320
The second, both for piety renowned
And puissant deeds, a promise shall receive
Irrevocable, that his regal throne
Forever shall endure; the like shall sing
All prophecy, that of the royal stock   325
Of David (so I name this king) shall rise
A Son, the Woman's seed to thee foretold,
Foretold to Abraham, as in whom shall trust
All nations, and to kings foretold, of kings
The last, for of his reign shall be no end.   330
But first a long succession must ensue,
And his next son, for wealth and wisdom famed,
The clouded Ark of God till then in tents
Wandering shall in a glorious temple enshrine.
Such follow him, as shall be registered   335
Part good, part bad, of bad the longer scroll,
Whose foul idolatries, and other faults
Heaped to the popular sum, will so incense
God, as to leave them, and expose their land,

240. mediator. Moses is regarded as the first mediator between God
and Man. 249–256. sanctuary . . . fires. The description of God's
Tabernacle given in this passage is based on Exodus, 25. 263.
Sun . . . stand still. When Joshua was fighting the armies of the
Five Kings in Gibeah, the Sun, by God's intervention, stood still
until the Israelites had defeated their enemies. See Joshua, 10:12–13.

291. shadowy, symbolic. 298. nor Man the moral part, etc. The
meaning is that no mere man can perform all the moral obligations
of Moses' law. 321. second, King David. 332. next son, King
Solomon. 337. foul idolatries. The defections of Solomon are explained in Book I, ll. 399–403 and notes.

Their city, His temple, and His holy Ark,   340
With all His sacred things, a scorn and prey
To that proud city, whose high walls thou saw'st
Left in confusion, Babylon thence called.
There in captivity He lets them dwell
The space of seventy years, then brings them back,
Remembering mercy, and His covenant sworn 346
To David, established as the days of Heaven.
Returned from Babylon by leave of kings
Their lords, whom God disposed, the house of God
They first re-edify, and for a while   350
In mean estate live moderate, till grown
In wealth and multitude, factious they grow;
But first among the priests dissension springs,
Men who attend the Altar, and should most
Endeavour Peace; their strife pollution brings 355
Upon the Temple itself: at last they seize
The sceptre, and regard not David's sons,
Then lose it to a stranger, that the true
Anointed King *Messiah* might be born
Barred of His right; yet at His birth a star 360
Unseen before in Heaven proclaims Him come,
And guides the eastern sages, who inquire
His place, to offer incense, myrrh, and gold;
His place of birth a solemn angel tells
To simple shepherds, keeping watch by night; 365
They gladly thither haste, and by a choir
Of squadroned angels hear His carol sung.
A virgin is His mother, but His sire
The power of the Most High; He shall ascend
The throne hereditary, and bound His reign 370
With Earth's wide bounds, His glory with the
     Heavens.'
He ceased, discerning Adam with such joy
Surcharged, as had like grief been dewed in tears,
Without the vent of words, which these he breathed:
  'O Prophet of glad tidings, finisher 375
Of utmost hope! now clear I understand
What oft my steadiest thoughts have searched in
     vain,
Why our great expectation should be called
The seed of woman: Virgin Mother, hail!
High in the love of Heaven, yet from my loins 380
Thou shalt proceed, and from thy womb the Son

347. **days of Heaven.** The Captivity of the Jews in Babylon (from 606 to 536 B.C.) is construed as fulfilling God's covenant with David to make "his throne as the days of Heaven." See Psalms, 89:29. 348. **kings,** Cyrus the Great, Darius, and Artaxerxes. 353. **dissension springs.** The serious factional disputes between rival claimants for the High Priesthood of Israel are recounted in the apocryphal Book of II Maccabees, 3 and 4. 356. **they,** the Asmonean family, who held control of the High Priesthood from 153 to 35 B.C. 357. **David's sons,** represented by Zerubbabel, who brought back the returning Hebrews to Jerusalem; he was a direct descendant of David. 358. **a stranger,** probably King Antiochus the Great, who held Palestine against Judas Maccabeus and his successors until the time of Christ. 360. **Barred . . . right.** Christ, as the descendant of David, was born King of the Jews, although he was barred from his occupancy of the throne. 364. **solemn,** appropriate to a religious rite or ceremony. 366. **thither,** to the place of the nativity. 374. **which,** of which.

Of God Most High; so God with Man unites.
Needs must the Serpent now his capital bruise
Expect with mortal pain: say where and when
Their fight, what stroke shall bruise the Victor's
     heel.' 385
  To whom thus Michael: 'Dream not of their fight,
As of a duel, or the local wounds
Of head or heel: not therefore joins the Son
Manhood to Godhead, with more strength to foil
Thy enemy; nor so is overcome 390
Satan, whose fall from Heaven, a deadlier bruise,
Disabled not to give thee thy death's wound:
Which He, who comes thy Saviour, shall recure,
Not by destroying Satan, but his works
In thee and in thy seed; nor can this be, 395
But by fulfilling that which thou didst want,
Obedience to the Law of God, imposed
On penalty of death, and suffering death,
The penalty to thy transgression due,
And due to theirs which out of thine will grow: 400
So only can high Justice rest appaid.
The Law of God exact He shall fulfill
Both by obedience and by love, though love
Alone fulfill the Law; thy punishment
He shall endure by coming in the flesh 405
To a reproachful life and cursed death,
Proclaiming life to all who shall believe
In His redemption, and that His obedience
Imputed becomes theirs by faith, His merits
To save them, not their own, through legal works.
For this He shall live hated, be blasphemed, 411
Seized on by force, judged, and to death condemned
A shameful and accursed, nailed to the Cross
By His own nation, slain for bringing life;
But to the Cross He nails thy Enemies, 415
The Law that is against thee, and the sins
Of all Mankind, with Him there crucified,
Never to hurt them more who rightly trust
In this His satisfaction; so He dies,
But soon revives, Death over Him no power 420
Shall long usurp; ere the third dawning light
Return, the stars of morn shall see Him rise
Out of His grave, fresh as the dawning light,
Thy ransom paid, which Man from death redeems,
His death for Man, as many as offered life 425
Neglect not, and the benefit embrace
By faith not void of works: this God-like act
Annuls thy doom, the death thou shouldst have died,
In sin forever lost from life; this act
Shall bruise the head of Satan, crush his strength
Defeating Sin and Death, his two main arms, 431
And fix far deeper in his head their stings

383. **capital,** a play on words, referring to the fact that the injury to Satan was not only a chief injury but was sustained in the head (Lat. *caput*). 393. **recure,** heal. 401. **appaid,** satisfied, requited. 409. **His merits.** This should be construed as a direct object of *believes* in line 407. 424. **Thy,** referring not only to Adam but to all Mankind.

Than temporal death shall bruise the Victor's heel,
Or theirs' whom He redeems, a death like sleep,
A gentle wafting to immortal life.   435
Nor after resurrection shall He stay
Longer on Earth than certain times to appear
To His disciples, men who in His life
Still followed Him; to them shall leave in charge
To teach all nations what of Him they learned   440
And His salvation, them who shall believe
Baptizing in the profluent stream, the sign
Of washing them from guilt of sin to life
Pure, and in mind prepared, if so befall,
For death, like that which the Redeemer died.   445
All nations they shall teach; for from that day
Not only to the sons of Abraham's loins
Salvation shall be preached, but to the sons
Of Abraham's faith wherever through the world;
So in His seed all nations shall be blest.   450
Then to the Heaven of Heavens He shall ascend
With victory, triumphing through the air
Over His foes and thine; there shall surprise
The Serpent, prince of air, and drag in chains
Through all His realm, and there confounded leave;
Then enter into glory, and resume   456
His seat at God's right hand, exalted high
Above all names in Heaven; and thence shall come,
When this world's dissolution shall be ripe,
With glory and power to judge both quick and dead,
To judge the unfaithful dead, but to reward   461
His faithful, and receive them into bliss,
Whether in Heaven or Earth, for then the Earth
Shall all be Paradise, far happier place
Than this of Eden, and far happier days.'   465
   So spake the Archangel Michael, then paused,
As at the world's great period; and our sire,
Replete with joy and wonder thus replied:
'O goodness infinite, goodness immense!
That all this good of evil shall produce,   470
And evil turn to good; more wonderful
Than that which by Creation first brought forth
Light out of darkness! full of doubt I stand,
Whether I should repent me now of sin
By me done and occasioned, or rejoice   475
Much more, that much more good thereof shall
      spring,
To God more glory, more goodwill to men
From God, and over wrath grace shall abound.
But say, if our Deliverer up to Heaven
Must re-ascend, what will betide the few   480
His faithful, left among the unfaithful herd,
The enemies of truth; who then shall guide
His people, who defend? Will they not deal

Worse with His followers than with Him they dealt?'
   'Be sure they will,' said the Angel; 'but from
      Heaven   485
He to His own a Comforter will send,
The promise of the Father, who shall dwell
His Spirit within them, and the law of faith
Working through love, upon their hearts shall write,
To guide them in all truth, and also arm   490
With spiritual armor, able to resist
Satan's assaults, and quench his fiery darts,
What Man can do against them, not afraid,
Though to the death, against such cruelties
With inward consolations recompensed,   495
And oft supported so as shall amaze
Their proudest persecutors: for the Spirit
Poured first on His apostles, whom He sends
To evangelize the nations, then on all
Baptized, shall them with wondrous gifts endue   500
To speak all tongues, and do all miracles,
As did their Lord before them. Thus they win
Great numbers of each nation to receive
With joy the tidings brought from Heaven: at length
Their ministry performed, and race well run,   505
Their doctrine and their story written left,
They die; but in their room, as they forewarn,
Wolves shall succeed for teachers, grievous wolves,
Who all the sacred mysteries of Heaven
To their own vile advantages shall turn   510
Of lucre and ambition, and the truth
With superstitions and traditions taint,
Left only in those written records pure,
Though not but by the Spirit understood.
Then shall they seek to avail themselves of names,
Places and titles, and with these to join   516
Secular power, though feigning still to act
By spiritual, to themselves appropriating
The Spirit of God, promised alike and given
To all believers; and from that pretense,   520
Spiritual laws by carnal power shall force
Out every conscience; laws which none shall find
Left them enrolled, or what the Spirit within
Shall on the heart engrave. What will they then
But force the spirit of Grace itself, and bind   525
His consort Liberty; what, but unbuild
His living temples, built by Faith to stand,
Their own faith, not another's: for on Earth
Who against faith and conscience can be heard
Infallible? yet many will presume: 530
Whence heavy persecution shall arise
On all who in the worship persevere
Of Spirit and Truth; the rest, far greater part,
Will deem in outward rites and specious forms
Religion satisfied; Truth shall retire   535

442. **profluent,** running; according to Milton the ideal baptism could be performed only in running water. 446 ff. **All nations,** etc. See Galatians, 3:8: "And the scripture, foreseeing that God would justify the heathen through faith, preached before the gospel unto Abraham, saying, 'In thee shall all nations be blessed.'"

525. **force . . . Grace.** Cf. II Corinthians, 3:17: "Now the Lord is that Spirit; and where the Spirit of the Lord is, there is Liberty." 527. **living temples.** According to St. Paul (I Corinthians, 6:19), the human body is a "temple of the Holy Ghost."

Bestuck with slanderous darts, and works of Faith
Rarely be found: so shall the world go on,
To good malignant, to bad men benign,
Under her own weight groaning, till the day
Appear of respiration to the just,   540
And vengeance to the wicked, at return
Of Him so lately promised to thy aid,
The Woman's seed, obscurely then foretold,
Now amplier known thy Saviour and thy Lord,
Last in the clouds from Heaven to be revealed   545
In glory of the Father, to dissolve
Satan with his perverted world, then raise
From the conflagrant mass, purged and refined,
New Heavens, new Earth, ages of endless date
Founded in righteousness and peace and love,   550
To bring forth fruits, joy and eternal bliss.'
   He ended; and thus Adam last replied:
'How soon hath thy prediction, Seer blest,
Measured this transient world, the race of Time,
Till Time stand fixed; beyond is all abyss,   555
Eternity, whose end no eye can reach.
Greatly instructed I shall hence depart,
Greatly in peace of thought, and have my fill
Of knowledge, what this vessel can contain;
Beyond which was my folly to aspire.   560
Henceforth I learn, that to obey is best,
And love with fear the only God, to walk
As in His presence, ever to observe
His Providence, and on Him sole depend,
Merciful over all His works, with good   565
Still overcoming evil, and by small
Accomplishing great things, by things deemed weak
Subverting worldly strong, and worldly wise
By simple meek; that suffering for Truth's sake
Is fortitude to highest victory,   570
And to the faithful, Death the Gate of Life;
Taught this by His example whom I now
Acknowledge my Redeemer ever blest.'
   To whom thus also the Angel last replied:
'This having learned, thou hast attained the sum
Of wisdom; hope no higher, though all the stars   576
Thou knew'st by name, and all the ethereal Powers,
All secrets of the deep, all Nature's works,
Or works of God in Heaven, air, Earth, or sea,
And all the riches of this world enjoy'dst,   580
And all the rule, one empire; only add
Deeds to thy knowledge answerable, add Faith,
Add Virtue, Patience, Temperance; add Love,
By name to come called Charity, the soul
Of all the rest: then wilt thou not be loath   585
To leave this Paradise, but shalt possess
A Paradise within thee, happier far.
Let us descend now therefore from this top
Of speculation; for the hour precise
Exacts our parting hence; and see the guards,   590

By me encamped on yonder hill, expect
Their motion, at whose front a flaming sword,
In signal of remove, waves fiercely round;
We may no longer stay: go, waken Eve;
Her also I with gentle dreams have calmed,   595
Portending good, and all her spirits composed
To meek submission: thou at season fit
Let her with thee partake what thou hast heard,
Chiefly what may concern her faith to know,
The great deliverance by her Seed to come   600
(For by the Woman's Seed) on all Mankind.
That ye may live, which will be many days,
Both in one Faith unanimous though sad,
With cause for evils past, yet much more cheered
With meditation on the happy end.'   605
   He ended, and they both descend the hill;
Descended, Adam to the bower where Eve
Lay sleeping ran before, but found her waked;
And thus with words not sad she him received:
   'Whence thou return'st, and whither went'st, I
        know;   610
For God is also in sleep, and dreams advise,
Which he hath sent propitious, some great good
Presaging, since with sorrow and heart's distress
Wearied I fell asleep: but now lead on;
In me is no delay; with thee to go,   615
Is to stay here; without thee here to stay
Is to go hence unwilling; thou to me
Art all things under Heaven, all places thou,
Who for my wilful crime art banished hence.
This further consolation yet secure   620
I carry hence; though all by me is lost,
Such favor I unworthy am vouchsafed,
By me the promised Seed shall all restore.'
   So spake our mother Eve, and Adam heard
Well pleased, but answered not; for now too nigh
The Archangel stood, and from the other hill   626
To their fixed station, all in bright array
The Cherubim descended; on the ground
Gliding meteorous, as evening mist
Risen from a river o'er the marish glides,   630
And gathers ground fast at the laborer's heel
Homeward returning. High in front advanced,
The brandished sword of God before them blazed
Fierce as a comet; which with torrid heat,
And vapor as the Libyan air adust,   635
Began to parch that temperate clime; whereat
In either hand the hastening Angel caught
Our lingering parents, and to the Eastern Gate
Led them direct, and down the cliff as fast
To the subjected plain; then disappeared.   640

611. **God . . . advise.** There is a trace of classical paganism in this
statement, although it is a belief often found in rabbinical lore. 630.
marish, marsh, swampland. 632. **advanced,** held aloft. 635.
adust, burned, scorched. Milton conceives of the sword of God as
burning Paradise as a blast from the Libyan desert can scorch the
land. Note the choice of brand for sword in l. 643, which conforms
etymologically to the idea. 640. **subjected,** lying below.

540. **respiration,** refreshment, encouragement. 559. **this vessel,**
Adam's body. 589. **speculation,** looking out.

They looking back, all the eastern side beheld
Of Paradise, so late their happy seat,
Waved over by that flaming brand, the Gate
With dreadful faces thronged and fiery arms;
Some natural tears they dropped, but wiped them
    soon;   645
The world was all before them, where to choose
Their place of rest, and Providence their guide;
They, hand in hand, with wandering steps and slow,
Through Eden took their solitary way.

Jonathan Edwards

1703–1758

The dominance of the national Anglican Church in English religious and political life from the time of Queen Elizabeth brought restriction and even persecution to other Christian sects, both Catholic and Protestant. As English explorers opened up the New World to colonization, the religious minorities came to seek havens along the stern Atlantic coast of North America, which the national government encouraged with grants of land. Catholics settled Maryland, but the religious migration was essentially Protestant, as Puritans founded Massachusetts and Quakers the friendly colony of Pennsylvania. Since the Puritans still held the conservative view that the civil government could control the consciences of men and punish violations of religious decrees, Massachusetts became a theocratic state which the Quakers and Roger Williams found as intolerant and oppressive as the Anglican government in England.

Many fire-breathing divines arose in Puritan New England to preach the austere Calvinist doctrine which was embodied in the civil legislation of the colonies. John Cotton, Thomas Hooker, Richard Mather, and Increase Mather were seventeenth-century predecessors of Jonathan Edwards, in whom the Puritan tradition found its greatest American spokesman. The son of a distinguished minister of Windsor, Connecticut, he was educated at Yale and prepared himself for the ministry there. Taking over the pastorate of his maternal grandfather at Northampton, Massachusetts, in 1726, Edwards was roused by the moral lethargy of the community to preach a series of terrifying sermons on the damnation awaiting sinners who did not follow stern Puritan rules of conduct. For twenty years he electrified not only his own community but all of New England with his discourses on "the Great Awakening" necessary in the souls of his contemporaries to the evils in man's nature and the hellfire that lay beyond the grave.

The best known of these grim warnings is *Sinners in the Hands of an Angry God*, preached at Enfield, Connecticut, on July 8, 1741. Taking his text from Deuteronomy ("Their foot shall slide in due time"), he develops the idea that "there is nothing that keeps wicked men at any moment out of hell, but the mere pleasure of God." Moreover, "the God that holds you over the pit of hell, much as one holds a spider, or some loathsome insect over the fire, abhors you, and is dreadfully provoked." This shocking message sent the Enfield congregation into hysteria as the austere minister read it calmly without gesture or modulation of voice. "There was such a breathing of distress, and weeping, that the preacher was obliged to speak to the people and desire silence that he might be heard."

The "Great Awakening" took the form of an avalanche of conversions to the pious life. Northampton was only one community whipped into a fervor of conscience by the Calvinist Savonarola. This emotional approach to salvation was justified by Edwards in his *Treatise concerning Religious Affections* (1746), which argued that knowledge of the gospel was not enough, but that a spiritual awakening to divine love shown in a radical change in living was essential to church membership. When he demanded that sinners, regardless of social position, should be disciplined by the community, his Northampton flock grew wary and awakened from their nightmare of holiness to dismiss Edwards from his pastorate (1750). His *Farewell Sermon* appealed to a Higher Judge above the congregation that had condemned him. Thereafter he served for six years as missionary to the Indians in the frontier town of Stockbridge and was called to the presidency of Princeton only two months before his death in March 1758.

Although Edwards is popularly remembered for his brimstone sermons, he was also a great theologian and Christian philosopher. His treatise on *Freedom of Will* (1754) argued for predestination along orthodox Calvinist lines against the views of the Dutch theologian, Arminius, who favored the free will of man to choose good or evil. Despite his sternness, Edwards was a humanitarian in his approach to his fellow men and was known as a staunch friend as well as an affectionate husband and father. Though he may have smugly lectured his contemporaries on Puritan principles, his own life was a model one.

Sinners in the Hands of an Angry God

DEUT. XXXII. 35

—Their foot shall slide in due time.—

In this verse is threatened the vengeance of God on the wicked unbelieving Israelites, who were God's visible people, and who lived under the means of grace; but who, notwithstanding all God's wonderful works towards them, remained (as ver. 28.) void of counsel, having no understanding in them. Under all the cultivations of heaven, they brought forth bitter and poisonous fruit; as in the two verses

Sinners in the Hands of an Angry God.[A] Preached at Enfield, Connecticut, July 8, 1741.

next preceding the text.—The expression I have chosen for my text, *Their foot shall slide in due time,* seems to imply the following things, relating to the punishment and destruction to which these wicked Israelites were exposed.

1. That they were always exposed to *destruction;* as one that stands or walks in slippery places is always exposed to fall. This is implied in the manner of their destruction coming upon them, being represented by their foot sliding. The same is expressed, Psalm lxxiii. 18. "Surely thou didst set them in slippery places; thou castedst them down into destruction."

2. It implies, that they were always exposed to sudden unexpected destruction. As he that walks in slippery places is every moment liable to fall, he cannot foresee one moment whether he shall stand or fall the next; and when he does fall, he falls at once without warning: Which is also expressed in Psalm lxxiii. 18, 19. "Surely thou didst set them in slippery places; thou castedst them down into destruction: How are they brought into desolation as in a moment!"

3. Another thing implied is, that they are liable to fall *of themselves,* without being thrown down by the hand of another; as he that stands or walks on slippery ground needs nothing but his own weight to throw him down.

4. That the reason why they are not fallen already, and do not fall now, is only that God's appointed time is not come. For it is said, that when that due time, or appointed time comes, *their foot shall slide.* Then they shall be left to fall, as they are inclined by their own weight. God will not hold them up in these slippery places any longer, but will let them go; and then, at that very instant, they shall fall into destruction; as he that stands on such slippery declining ground, on the edge of a pit, he cannot stand alone, when he is let go he immediately falls and is lost.

The observation from the words that I would now insist upon is this.—"There is nothing that keeps wicked men at any one moment out of hell, but the mere pleasure of God"—By the *mere* pleasure of God, I mean his *sovereign* pleasure, his arbitrary will, restrained by no obligation, hindered by no manner of difficulty, any more than if nothing else but God's mere will had in the least degree, or in any respect whatsoever, any hand in the preservation of wicked men one moment.—The truth of this observation may appear by the following considerations.

1. There is no want of *power* in God to cast wicked men into hell at any moment. Men's hands cannot be strong when God rises up. The strongest have no power to resist him, nor can any deliver out of his hands.—He is not only able to cast wicked men into hell, but he can most easily do it. Sometimes an earthly prince meets with a great deal of difficulty to subdue a rebel, who has found means to fortify himself, and has made himself strong by the number of his followers. But it is not so with God. There is no fortress that is any defence from the power of God. Though hand join in hand, and vast multitudes of God's enemies combine and associate themselves, they are easily broken in pieces. They are as great heaps of light chaff before the whirlwind; or large quantities of dry stubble before devouring flames. We find it easy to tread on and crush a worm that we see crawling on the earth; so it is easy for us to cut or singe a slender thread that any thing hangs by: thus easy is it for God, when he pleases, to cast his enemies down to hell. What are we, that we should think to stand before him, at whose rebuke the earth trembles, and before whom the rocks are thrown down?

2. They *deserve* to be cast into hell; so that divine justice never stands in the way, it makes no objection against God's using his power at any moment to destroy them. Yea, on the contrary, justice calls aloud for an infinite punishment of their sins. Divine justice says of the tree that brings forth such grapes of Sodom, "Cut it down, why cumbereth it the ground?" Luke xiii. 7. The sword of divine justice is every moment brandished over their heads, and it is nothing but the hand of arbitrary mercy, and God's mere will, that holds it back.

3. They are already under a sentence of *condemnation* to hell. They do not only justly deserve to be cast down thither, but the sentence of the law of God, that eternal and immutable rule of righteousness that God has fixed between him and mankind, is gone out against them, and stands against them; so that they are bound over already to hell. John iii. 18. "He that believeth not is condemned already." So that every unconverted man properly belongs to hell; that is his place; from thence he is, John viii. 23. "Ye are from beneath:" And thither he is bound; it is the place that justice, and God's word, and the sentence of his unchangeable law assign to him.

4. They are now the objects of that very same *anger* and wrath of God, that is expressed in the torments of hell. And the reason why they do not go down to hell at each moment, is not because God, in whose power they are, is not then very angry with them; as he is with many miserable creatures now tormented in hell, who there feel and bear the fierceness of his wrath. Yea, God is a great deal more angry with great numbers that are now on earth: yea, doubtless, with many that are now in this congregation, who it may be are at ease, than he is with many of those who are now in the flames of hell.

So that it is not because God is unmindful of their wickedness, and does not resent it, that he does not let loose his hand and cut them off. God is not altogether such an one as themselves, though they may imagine him to be so. The wrath of God burns against them, their damnation does not slumber; the pit is prepared, the fire is made ready, the furnace is now hot, ready to receive them; the flames do now rage and glow. The glittering sword is whet, and held over them, and the pit hath opened its mouth under them.

5. The *devil* stands ready to fall upon them, and seize them as his own, at what moment God shall permit him. They belong to him; he has their souls in his possession, and under his dominion. The scripture represents them as his goods, Luke xi. 12. The devils watch them; they are ever by them at their right hand; they stand waiting for them, like greedy hungry lions that see their prey, and expect to have it, but are for the present kept back. If God should withdraw his hand, by which they are restrained, they would in one moment fly upon their poor souls. The old serpent is gaping for them; hell opens its mouth wide to receive them; and if God should permit it, they would be hastily swallowed up and lost.

6. There are in the souls of wicked men those hellish *principles* reigning, that would presently kindle and flame out into hell fire, if it were not for God's restraints. There is laid in the very nature of carnal men, a foundation for the torments of hell. There are those corrupt principles, in reigning power in them, and in full possession of them, that are seeds of hell fire. These principles are active and powerful, exceeding violent in their nature, and if it were not for the restraining hand of God upon them, they would soon break out, they would flame out after the same manner as the same corruptions, the same enmity does in the hearts of damned souls, and would beget the same torments as they do in them. The souls of the wicked are in scripture compared to the troubled sea, Isa. lvii. 20. For the present, God restrains their wickedness by his mighty power, as he does the raging waves of the troubled sea, saying, "Hitherto shalt thou come, but no further;" but if God should withdraw that restraining power, it would soon carry all before it. Sin is the ruin and misery of the soul; it is destructive in its nature; and if God should leave it without restraint, there would need nothing else to make the soul perfectly miserable. The corruption of the heart of man is immoderate and boundless in its fury; and while wicked men live here, it is like fire pent up by God's restraints, whereas if it were let loose, it would set on fire the course of nature; and as the heart is now a sink of sin, so if sin was not restrained, it would

immediately turn the soul into a fiery oven, or a furnace of fire and brimstone.

7. It is no security to wicked men for one moment, that there are no visible means of death at hand. It is no security to a natural man, that he is now in health, and that he does not see which way he should now immediately go out of the world by any accident, and that there is no visible danger in any respect in his circumstances. The manifold and continual experience of the world in all ages, shows this is no evidence, that a man is not on the very brink of eternity, and that the next step will not be into another world. The unseen, unthought-of ways and means of persons going suddenly out of the world are innumerable and inconceivable. Unconverted men walk over the pit of hell on a rotten covering, and there are innumerable places in this covering so weak that they will not bear their weight, and these places are not seen. The arrows of death fly unseen at noon-day; the sharpest sight cannot discern them. God has so many different unsearchable ways of taking wicked men out of the world and sending them to hell, that there is nothing to make it appear, that God had need to be at the expence of a miracle, or go out of the ordinary course of his providence, to destroy any wicked man, at any moment. All the means that there are of sinners going out of the world, are so in God's hands, and so universally and absolutely subject to his power and determination, that it does not depend at all the less on the mere will of God, whether sinners shall at any moment go to hell, than if means were never made use of, or at all concerned in the case.

8. Natural men's prudence and care to preserve their own lives, or the care of others to preserve them, do not secure them a moment. To this, divine providence and universal experience do also bear testimony. There is this clear evidence that men's own wisdom is no security to them from death; that if it were otherwise we should see some difference between the wise and politic men of the world, and others, with regard to their liableness to early and unexpected death: but how is it in fact? Eccles. ii. 16. "How dieth the wise man? even as the fool."

9. All wicked men's pains and *contrivance* which they use to escape hell, while they continue to reject Christ, and so remain wicked men, do not secure them from hell one moment. Almost every natural man that hears of hell, flatters himself that he shall escape it; he depends upon himself for his own security; he flatters himself in what he has done, in what he is now doing, or what he intends to do. Every one lays out matters in his own mind how he shall avoid damnation, and flatters himself that he contrives well for himself, and that his schemes will not fail. They hear indeed that there are but few

saved, and that the greater part of men that have died heretofore are gone to hell; but each one imagines that he lays out matters better for his own escape than others have done. He does not intend to come to that place of torment; he says within himself, that he intends to take effectual care, and to order matters so for himself as not to fail.

But the foolish children of men miserably delude themselves in their own schemes, and in confidence in their own strength and wisdom; they trust to nothing but a shadow. The greater part of those who heretofore have lived under the same means of grace, and are now dead, are undoubtedly gone to hell; and it was not because they were not as wise as those who are now alive: it was not because they did not lay out matters as well for themselves to secure their own escape. If we could speak with them, and inquire of them, one by one, whether they expected, when alive, and when they used to hear about hell, ever to be the subjects of that misery: we doubtless, should hear one and another reply, "No, I never intended to come here: I had laid out matters otherwise in my mind; I thought I should contrive well for myself: I thought my scheme good. I intended to take effectual care; but it came upon me unexpected; I did not look for it at that time, and in that manner; it came as a thief: Death outwitted me: God's wrath was too quick for me. Oh, my cursed foolishness! I was flattering myself, and pleasing myself with vain dreams of what I would do hereafter; and when I was saying, Peace and safety, then suddenly destruction came upon me."

10. God has laid himself under *no obligation*, by any promise to keep any natural man out of hell one moment. God certainly has made no promises either of eternal life, or of any deliverance or preservation from eternal death, but what are contained in the covenant of grace, the promises that are given in Christ, in whom all the promises are yea and amen. But surely they have no interest in the promises of the covenant of grace who are not the children of the covenant, who do not believe in any of the promises, and have no interest in the Mediator of the covenant.

So that, whatever some have imagined and pretended about promises made to natural men's earnest seeking and knocking, it is plain and manifest, that whatever pains a natural man takes in religion, whatever prayers he makes, till he believes in Christ, God is under no manner of obligation to keep him a moment from eternal destruction.

So that, thus it is that natural men are held in the hand of God, over the pit of hell; they have deserved the fiery pit, and are already sentenced to it; and God is dreadfully provoked, his anger is as great towards them as to those that are actually suffering the executions of the fierceness of his wrath in hell, and they have done nothing in the least to appease or abate that anger, neither is God in the least bound by any promise to hold them up one moment; the devil is waiting for them, hell is gaping for them, the flames gather and flash about them, and would fain lay hold on them, and swallow them up; the fire pent up in their own hearts is struggling to break out: and they have no interest in any Mediator, there are no means within reach that can be any security to them. In short, they have no refuge, nothing to take hold of; all that preserves them every moment is the mere arbitrary will, and uncovenanted, unobliged forbearance of an incensed God.

APPLICATION

The use of this awful subject may be for awakening unconverted persons in this congregation. This that you have heard is the case of every one of you that are out of Christ.—That world of misery, that lake of burning brimstone, is extended abroad under you. There is the dreadful pit of the glowing flames of the wrath of God; there is hell's wide gaping mouth open; and you have nothing to stand upon, nor any thing to take hold of; there is nothing between you and hell but the air; it is only the power and mere pleasure of God that holds you up.

You probably are not sensible of this; you find you are kept out of hell, but do not see the hand of God in it; but look at other things, as the good state of your bodily constitution, your care of your own life, and the means you use for your own preservation. But indeed these things are nothing; if God should withdraw his hand, they would avail no more to keep you from falling, than the thin air to hold up a person that is suspended in it.

Your wickedness makes you as it were heavy as lead, and to tend downwards with great weight and pressure towards hell; and if God should let you go, you would immediately sink and swiftly descend and plunge into the bottomless gulf, and your healthy constitution, and your own care and prudence, and best contrivance, and all your righteousness, would have no more influence to uphold you and keep you out of hell, than a spider's web would have to stop a fallen rock. Were it not for the sovereign pleasure of God, the earth would not bear you one moment; for you are a burden to it; the creation groans with you; the creature is made subject to the bondage of your corruption, not willingly; the sun does not willingly shine upon you to give you light to serve sin and Satan; the earth does not willingly yield her increase to satisfy your lusts; nor is it willingly a stage for your wickedness to be acted upon; the air does not willingly serve you for breath to maintain the flame of life in your vitals, while you spend your life in the service of God's enemies. God's creatures are good, and were made for men to serve God with, and do not willingly subserve to any other purpose, and groan when they are abused to purposes so directly contrary to their nature and end. And the world would spew you out, were it not for the sovereign hand of him who hath subjected it in hope. There are black clouds of God's wrath now hanging directly over your heads, full of the dreadful storm, and big with thunder; and were it not for the restraining hand of God, it would immediately burst forth upon you. The sovereign pleasure of God, for the present, stays his rough wind; otherwise it would come with fury, and your destruction would come like a whirlwind, and you would be like the chaff of the summer threshing floor.

The wrath of God is like great waters that are dammed for the present; they increase more and more, and rise higher and higher, till an outlet is given; and the longer the stream is stopped, the more rapid and mighty is its course, when once it is let loose. It is true, that judgment against your evil works has not been executed hitherto; the floods of God's vengeance have been withheld; but your guilt in the mean time is constantly increasing, and you are every day treasuring up more wrath; the waters are constantly rising, and waxing more and more mighty; and there is nothing but the mere pleasure of God, that holds the waters back, that are unwilling to be stopped, and press hard to go forward. If God should only withdraw his hand from the floodgate, it would immediately fly open, and the fiery floods of the fierceness and wrath of God, would rush forth with inconceivable fury, and would come upon you with omnipotent power; and if your strength were ten thousand times greater than it is, yea, ten thousand times greater than the strength of the stoutest, sturdiest devil in hell, it would be nothing to withstand or endure it.

The bow of God's wrath is bent, and the arrow made ready on the string, and justice bends the arrow at your heart, and strains the bow, and it is nothing but the mere pleasure of God, and that of any angry God, without any promise or obligation at all, that keeps the arrow one moment from being made drunk with your blood. Thus all you that never passed under a great change of heart, by the mighty power of the Spirit of God upon your souls; all you that were never born again, and made new creatures, and raised from being dead in sin, to a state of new, and before altogether unexperienced light and life, are in the hands of an angry God. However you may have reformed your life in many things, and may have had religious affections, and may keep up a form of religion in your families and closets, and in the house of God, it is nothing but his mere pleasure that keeps you from being this moment swallowed up in everlasting destruction. However unconvinced you may now be of the truth of what you hear, by and by you will be fully convinced of it. Those that are gone from being in the like circumstances with you, see that it was so with them; for destruction came suddenly upon most of them; when they expected nothing of it, and while they were saying, Peace and safety: now they see, that those things on which they depended for peace and safety, were nothing but thin air and empty shadows.

The God that holds you over the pit of hell, much as one holds a spider, or some loathsome insect over the fire, abhors you, and is dreadfully provoked: his wrath towards you burns like fire; he looks upon you as worthy of nothing else, but to be cast into the fire; he is of purer eyes than to bear to have you in his sight; you are ten thousand times more abominable in his eyes, than the most hateful venomous serpent is in ours. You have offended him infinitely more than ever a stubborn rebel did his prince; and yet it is nothing but his hand that holds you from falling into the fire every moment. It is to be ascribed to nothing else, that you did not go to hell the last night; that you was suffered to awake again in this world, after you closed your eyes to sleep. And there is no other reason to be given, why you have not dropped into hell since you arose in the morning, but that God's hand has held you up. There is no other reason to be given why you have not gone to hell, since you have sat here in the house of God, provoking his pure eyes by your sinful wicked manner of attending his solemn worship. Yea, there is nothing else that is to be given as a reason why you do not this very moment drop down into hell.

O sinner! Consider the fearful danger you are in: it is a great furnace of wrath, a wide and bottomless pit, full of the fire of wrath, that you are held over in the hand of that God, whose wrath is provoked and incensed as much against you, as against many of the damned in hell. You hang by a slender thread, with the flames of divine wrath flashing about it, and ready every moment to singe it, and burn it asunder; and you have no interest in any Mediator, and nothing to lay hold of to save yourself, nothing to keep off the flames of wrath, nothing of your own, nothing that you ever have done, nothing that you can do, to induce God to spare you one moment. . . .

Therefore, let every one that is out of Christ, now awake and fly from the wrath to come. The wrath of Almighty God is now undoubtedly hanging over a great part of this congregation: Let every one fly out of Sodom: "Haste and escape for your lives, look not behind you, escape to the mountain, lest you be consumed."

Francesco Petrarca

1304–1374

The father of the Renaissance, as Petrarch is often called, is best remembered today, not as the enthusiastic popularizer of the ancient classics, but as the exquisite poet of the sonnets to Laura. This irony reflects the continuous conflict in his own nature between the scholarly recluse and the graceful poet and man of the world. Petrarch's father, a political exile from Florence who settled at Avignon, intended his son for the law and was so angry to find him neglecting his legal studies at Bologna in order to read Roman literature that he summarily burned his precious books, except for a Virgil and a Cicero that Francesco begged him to spare. But he eventually abandoned the youth to his own interests, and Francesco took minor orders in the Church to gain leisure for study and literature. Yet Petrarch lived as well the fashionable life of a dandy at Avignon, which had taken on great luster as the seat of the papacy during the "Babylonian Captivity."

To this aspect of his career belongs his love for Laura, whom he first saw at the Church of St. Clara in Avignon on Good Friday, April 6, 1327. Whether or not she was that Laura de Sade, wife of a gentleman of the city, as later scholars supposed her to be, she soon became the shining center of Petrarch's love life, so that she remained the ideal source of his poetic inspiration long after her death in the plague of 1348. To her he directed the 331 poems of his *Canzoniere* in Italian, 287 of them in the sonnet form that he popularized for later poets of the Renaissance in Italy, France, England, and Spain. Rearranged in the order of their likely composition, these exquisite lyrics trace the whole progress of his passion, from his first sight of Laura to his lingering grief at her death. The various moods of the distracted lover, here frustrated by his beloved's marriage to another, are revealed through a subtle analysis of mental states. The reality and intensity of the poet's emotions are not injured by his care to preserve Laura's anonymity or by her apparent indifference to his earnest attentions.

To his worldly self belongs also his ambition for fame as an epic poet. Infatuated with the stately refinement of Cicero and Virgil, Petrarch turned from Italian to a stiff sort of Latin in his epistles to friends of his own day and Horace's and in his dull Latin epic on Scipio Africanus, entitled *Africa* (1339). In an age newly aware of the treasures of antiquity, this polished imitation of Virgil gained great fame and led to the crowning of Petrarch as supreme poet of the Christian world by the University of Paris and the Roman Senate on the Capitoline Hill on April 8, 1341. This great triumph, which appealed to his abundant vanity, marked the climax of his worldly life. Princes vied with popes for the honor of knowing him and for the favor of his Latin pen.

But even as he was winning his fame, he frequently fled from society to his secluded farm in the valley of Vaucluse, where his best works were written. The death of Laura and many of his closest friends in 1348 brought a real turning point in his career. The characteristics of the retiring scholar which his father had found in the teen-age youth led him to forsake the social and political world for study and meditation in his library. Although he performed minor diplomatic missions for the city of Milan in his later years, we think of the older Petrarch at work in his Venetian palace or on the little farm in the Euganean hills where he died. Appropriately, he was found in his library with his head at rest on an open book. Unlike some Humanists who followed him, Petrarch was not a deep thinker and made little use of the knowledge he absorbed from the ancients. But his romantic enthusiasm for their literary form and pagan ideas made him the first spokesman of their message to modern times.

Vision

WHEN I behold this fickle trustles state
  Of vaine worlds glorie, flitting too and fro,
And mortall men tossed by troublous fate
  In restles seas of wretchedness and woe;
I wish I might this wearie life forgoe,   5
  And shortly turne unto my happie rest,
Where my free spirite might not anie moe
  Be vext with sights, that doe her peace molest,
And ye, faire ladie, in whose bounteous brest
  All heavenly grace and vertue shrinèd is,   10
When ye these rythmes doo read, and vew the rest,
  Loath this base world, and thinke of heavens blis:
And though ye be the fairest of God's creatures,
Yet thinke, that Death shall spoyle your goodly
    features.

Love's Inconsistency

I FIND no peace, and all my war is done;
  I fear and hope, I burn, and freeze like ice;
  I fly aloft, yet can I not arise;
And nought I have, and all the world I seize on,
That locks nor loseth, holdeth me in prison,   5
  And holds me not, yet can I scape no wise:
Nor letteth me live, nor die, at my devise,
And yet of death it giveth me occasion.
Without eye I see; without tongue I plain:
  I wish to perish, yet I ask for health;   10
  I love another, and I hate myself;
I feed me in sorrow, and laugh in all my pain.
  Lo, thus displeaseth me both death and life,
  And my delight is causer of this strife.

Vision. Translated by Edmund Spenser.
1. **fickle,** uncertain.
Love's Inconsistency. Translated by Sir Thomas Wyatt.

Signs of Love

IF amorous faith, a heart of guileless ways,
　　Soft langours, courteously controlled desire,
　And virtuous will, kindled with noble fire,
And lengthened wanderings in a lightless maze;
If thoughts, which evermore the brow displays,　　5
　Or words that faint and brokenly suspire,
　Still checked with fear and shame; if hues no
　　　higher
Than the pale violet hath, or love displays;
If holding some one than one's self more dear,
　If sorrowing and sighing evermore,　　　　　10
　If chewing grief, and rage, and many a cross,
If burning far away, and freezing near,
　Are signs that Love consumes me to the core,
　Yours, lady, is the fault and mine the loss.

The Beauty
and Virtue of Laura

SAY from what part of heaven 'twas Nature drew,
　　From what idea, that so perfect mold
　　To form such features, bidding us behold,
In charms below, what she above could do?
What fountain nymph, what dryad maid e'er threw
　Upon the wind such tresses of pure gold?　　6
　What heart such numerous virtues can unfold?
Although the chiefest all my fond hopes slew.
He for celestial charms may look in vain
　Who has not seen my fair one's radiant eyes,　10
　And felt their glances pleasingly beguile.
How Love can heal his wounds, then wound again,
　He only knows who knows how sweet her sighs,
　　How sweet her converse, and how sweet her
　　　smile.

Wherein His Heart,
by Laura Rejected,

MUST OF A CERTAINTY
PERISH UNLESS SHE RELENT

A THOUSAND times, O my sweet warrior,
　　Burning to purchase peace of those proud
　　　eyes,
Have I held forth the heart your heart denies,
Which your nobility will not bend for.
And if some other lady love it more,　　　　5
Vain is her hope and false: what you despise

Signs of Love. Translated by C. B. Cayley.
The Beauty and Virtue of Laura. Translated by John Nott.
Wherein His Heart, By Laura Rejected. . . . Translated by Joseph
Auslander. Reprinted from *The Sonnets of Petrarch,* published by
Longmans, Green and Company, Ltd., copyright 1931.

I must disdain, since what you do not prize
I spurn, and what you hate cannot adore.
Exiled by me, what then if it shall find
With you no word of mercy now or later,　　　10
And so, when others call it, stay behind,
Afraid to go, afraid of its dear hater?
Though guilt to both of us must be assigned,
It loves you more, and thus your guilt is greater.

Wherein
He Pursues Solitude,

BUT LOVE SHADOWS
HIM EVERYWHITHER

A LONE, thought-sick, I pace where none has been
　　Roaming the desert with dull steps and slow,
And still glance warily about to know
If the herd follows, if the world has seen:
How else the hoofprint of the Philistine　　　5
Escape, but in some cave with grief to go!
I look distraught and haggard: I must show
No one how keen Love's tooth is, O how keen!
Meseems the very mountains and the shores,
Rivers and woods must guess the secret I　　　10
So seek to hide from men by desert doors—
O tell me where beneath a savage sky
Is any space the foot of Love ignores,
But with Love's whisper and my soul's rings high!

Wherein
He Tells the Course

OF TRUE LOVE

IF this should not be Love, O God, what shakes
　　me?
If Love it is, what strange, what rich delight!
If Love be kind, why has it fangs to bite?
If cruel, why so sweet the barb that rakes me?　　4
If Love I crave, why this lament that breaks me?
If not, what tears or sighs can mend my plight?
O Death in Life, dear pain, where lies thy might
If I refuse the doom that overtakes me?
If I consent, without a cause I grieve:
So in a tempest do my fortunes heave,　　　　10
By winds contrary and by waters tost;
So, in a stupor, like a blind man lost
In mischievous error, lured from doubt to doubt,
June freezes, January thaws me out.

Wherein He Pursues Solitude . . . ; *Wherein He Tells the Course
of True Love.* Translated by Joseph Auslander. Reprinted from *The
Sonnets of Petrarch,* published by Longmans, Green and Company,
Ltd., copyright 1931.

Wherein
He Envies

WHATSOEVER OF LOVELY
IN NATURE
HER PRESENCE MAKES LOVELIER

O RICH and happy flowers forever apart
    On which my pensive Lady puts her heel!
O golden acres privileged to feel
Her phrase, her footprint pressed upon your heart!
Trees silver green with April's earliest art;   5
Pale passionate violets; dark grove that can steal
Only so much of sun as may reveal
Your swarthy steeples in a radiant dart!
O comely landscape! O translucent stream
Mirroring her pure face, her intense eyes   10
And seizing all alive their bluest beam!
I envy you your crystal burglaries!
No rock, however cold, but with my theme
Shall henceforth kindle and consume in sighs!

If It Be Destined

I F it be destined that my Life, from thine
    Divided, yet with thine shall linger on
Till, in the later twilight of Decline,
    I may behold those Eyes, their luster gone;
When the gold tresses that enrich thy brow   5
    Shall all be faded into silver-gray,
From which the wreaths that well bedeck them now
    For many a Summer shall have fallen away;
Then should I dare to whisper in your ears
    The pent-up Passion of so long ago,   10
That Love which hath survived the wreck of years
    Hath little else to pray for, or bestow,
Thou wilt not to the broken heart deny
The boon of one too-late relenting Sigh.

The Death-Bed
of Laura

N o power of darkness, with ill influence, dared
    Within a space so holy to intrude,
Till Death his terrible triumph had declared.
    Then hushed was all lament, all fear subdued;
Each on those beauteous features gazed intent,   5
    And from despair was armed with fortitude.

Wherein He Envies. . . . Translated by Joseph Auslander. Reprinted from *The Sonnets of Petrarch*, published by Longmans, Green and Company, Ltd., copyright 1931.
If It Be Destined. Translated by Edward Fitzgerald.
The Death-Bed of Laura. Translated by Lady Dacre.

As a pure flame that not by force is spent,
    But faint and fainter softly dies away
Passed gently forth in peace the soul, content;
    And as a light of clear and steady ray.   10
When fails the source from which its brightness flows,
    She to the last held on her wonted way.
Pale was she? no; but white as shrouding snows,
    That, when the winds are lulled, fall silently,
She seemed as one o'erwearied to repose.   15
E'en as in balmy slumbers lapt to lie
(The spirit parted from the form below),
    In her appeared what th'unwise term to die;
And Death sate beauteous on her beauteous brow.

On the Announcement
of the Death of Laura

A LAS! that touching glance, that beauteous face!
    Alas! that dignity with sweetness fraught!
    Alas! that speech which tamed the wildest thought!
That roused the coward, glory to embrace;
Alas! that smile which in me did encase   5
    The fatal dart, whence here I hope for naught.
Oh! hadst thou earlier our regions sought,
The world had then confessed thy sovereign grace!
In thee I breathed; life's flame was nursed by thee,
    For I was thine; and since of thee bereaved,   10
    Each other woe hath lost its venomed sting:
My soul's blest joy! when last thy voice on me
    In music fell, my heart sweet hope conceived;
    Alas! thy words have sped on zephyrs' wing!

He Thanks Her
that from Time to Time

SHE RETURNS TO CONSOLE HIM
WITH HER PRESENCE

W HEN welcome slumber locks my torpid frame,
    I see thy spirit in the midnight dream;
    Thine eyes that still in living lustre beam:
In all but frail mortality the same.
Ah! then, from earth and all its sorrows free,   5
    Methinks I meet thee in each former scene,
    Once the sweet shelter of a heart serene;
Now vocal only while I weep for thee.
For thee!—ah, no! From human ills secure,

On the Announcement of the Death of Laura. Translated by Susan Wollaston.
He Thanks Her that from Time to Time. . . . Translated by Anne Bannerman.

Thy hallowed soul exults in endless day;   10
'Tis I who linger on the toilsome way.
No balm relieves the anguish I endure,
Save the fond feeble hope that thou art near
To soothe my sufferings with an angel's tear.

Wherein
Laura Is Forever

A PRESENT APPARITION

IF the lone bird lament or the green leaves
   Shiver beneath the summer's soft caresses,
Or rapid streams flash from dark wildernesses
Churning the rock that with my sorrow grieves,
While Love his slow eternal elegy weaves,   5
Then, then I see her whom this blind earth presses!
Those eyes like wells of stars, those golden tresses,
That voice like tears, that silver breast which heaves:
"Unhappy soul, why weep? Ah why, sad lover,
Thus, thus with anguish and remorse devour   10
Your splendid manhood in its perfect flower?
Yet light and warmth its radiance recover:
Bewail me not: the brightness that seemed over
Has burst into one white perpetual hour!"

Wherein Soaring
in an Ecstasy

OF THOUGHT TO HEAVEN
HE ENCOUNTERS LAURA

AN ecstasy of thought praised me where
   She wanders, that shall no more walk with
     me:
There!—lovelier, humbler—there, ah there I see—
I see her in the third celestial sphere!
She takes my hand and whispers, "With me here   5
Thou shalt again taste pure felicity:
For I am she that pained thee, even she
That perished in the blossom of her year.
My bliss no mortal hope has ever spanned;
Thee only I await, and that sweet veil   10
Thou didst so love, my body's golden shell."—
Why did she stop? Ah why release my hand?
Alas! Her tones, her touch beyond control
Had swept me heavenward, snatched my ravished
     soul!

Wherein Laura Is Forever a Present Apparition; Wherein Soaring in an Ecstasy. . . . Translated by Joseph Auslander. From *The Sonnets of Petrarch,* published by Longmans, Green and Company, Ltd., copyright 1931.

The Spring Returns,

BUT NOT TO HIM RETURNS

THE spring returns, the spring wind softly blow-
   ing
Sprinkles the grass with gleam and glitter of showers,
Powdering pearl and diamond, dripping with
   flowers,
Dropping wet flowers, dancing the winter's going;
The swallow twitters, the groves of midnight are
   glowing   5
With nightingale music and madness; the sweet fierce
   powers
Of Love flame up through the earth; the seed-soul
   towers
And trembles; Nature is filled to overflowing . . .
The spring returns, but there is no returning
Of spring for me. O heart with anguish burning!   10
She that unlocked all April in a breath
Returns not . . . And these meadows, blossoms,
   birds,
These lovely gentle girls—words, empty words,
As bitter as the black estates of death!

Wherein
He Makes Confession

AND INTREATS
THE LORD'S GRACE

WEEPING, I still regret the years that went
   In empty sacrifice to mortal things;
No swooping starward, though my soul had wings
Which might have brushed Thy burning element.
O Thou, that know'st so well how I repent,   5
Sovereign of space, immortal King of Kings,
Succour the soul torn with self-torturings—
To Thee it turns: O prove Thou provident!
To my war-shattered life appoint Thou still
Death as the port of peace; and if my course   10
Was idle, let it find a quiet hill!
O for the brief remainder, let remorse
Not darken, let Thy hand the end fulfill!
Thou know'st in Thee alone rests my resource!

The Spring Returns . . . ; Wherein He Makes Confession. . . . Translated by Joseph Auslander. Reprinted from *The Sonnets of Petrarch,* published by Longmans, Green and Company, Ltd., copyright 1931.

François Villon

1431–c.1461

Although he lived out his brief and disreputable life a full century after Petrarch and Boccaccio, Villon is as much the last voice of the French Middle Ages as he is the harbinger of the Renaissance. He was well educated but in the ecclesiastical curriculum of the conservative University of Paris, whose solemn pedantry Rabelais was to satirize a century later. Born François de Montcorbier, the future poet apparently lost his father early in life and owed his education to a kindly priest, Guillaume de Villon, whose name he took in gratitude. His mother, to whom he refers affectionately in a famous poem, was an unlettered woman who contributed nothing to his intellectual development.

François was a brilliant but reckless student, who took his bachelor's degree at eighteen and his master of arts three years later. But he always preferred the company of rogues and sharpers in the streets and taverns of Paris to the dull scholars of the university. Several of these low characters had fancy criminal records ending with the gibbet, and Villon himself narrowly escaped hanging more than once. Others were simply rollicking students who excelled in drinking, gluttony, and debauchery. Villon tells us of many mistresses of his own who must have inspired his lusty poems in praise of women. Of all these, only one, Catherine de Vaucelles, aroused anything like real love. But her mercenary nature made her indifferent to the indigent poet of the city streets, and she was apparently the cause of his downfall. A brawl with a rival for her affections ended in the death of a priest and the banishment of Villon for six months. When powerful patrons persuaded the French king to relax the sentence, Villon returned to Paris and a life of crime as one leader of a notorious gang. Burglaries committed against churches and even the university treasury led to his arrest and two sentences to death. But he avoided them both with the assistance of the new king, Louis XI, and apparently died of tuberculosis and a general physical collapse brought on by years of dissipation and eventual starvation.

Despite his short and turbulent life, Villon found time to become an exquisite poet, the supreme master of that delicate and complex French form, the ballade. The slender volume of his verses is addressed to the people of Paris in the form of two fanciful wills or *Testaments*, the *Greater* and the *Lesser*. As he makes his imaginary bequests in rhyme, he runs through all classes of the medieval city but shows more love for shifty-eyed criminals and humble chimney sweeps than for scholars and elegant nobles. Villon, the best of the vagabond poets, brings a teeming medieval metropolis to life in his graceful, melodious stanzas.

No, I Am Not As Others Are

No, I am not, as others are,
　Child of the angels, with a wreath
Of planets or of any star.
My father's dead, and lies beneath
The churchyard stone: God rest his breath!　5
I know that my poor old mother
(And she too knows) must come to death,
And that her son must follow her.

I know that rich and poor and all,
Foolish and wise, and priest and lay,　10
Mean folk and noble, great and small,
High and low, fair and foul, and they
That wore rich clothing on the way,
Being of whatever stock or stem,
And are coiffed newly every day,　15
Death shall take every one of them.

Paris and Helen are both dead.
Whoever dies, dies with much pain;
For when his wind and breath are sped
His gall breaks on his heart, and then　20
He sweats, God knows that sweat of men!
Then shall he pray against his doom
Child, brother, sister, all in vain:
None will be surety in his room.

Death makes him tremble and turn pale,　25
His veins stretch and his nose fall in,
His flesh grow moist and his neck swell,
Joints and nerves lengthen and wax thin;
Body of woman, that hath been
Soft, tender, precious, smooth and even,　30
Must thou be spoiled in bone and skin?
Yes, or else go alive to heaven.

His Mother's Service to Our Lady

LADY of Heaven and earth, and therewithal
　Crowned Empress of the nether clefts of
　　Hell,—
I, thy poor Christian, on thy name do call,
　Commending me to thee, with thee to dwell,
　Albeit in nought I be commendable.　5
But all mine undeserving may not mar
Such mercies as thy sovereign mercies are;

No, I Am Not As Others Are. Translated by Arthur Symons.
His Mother's Service To Our Lady. Translated by D. G. Rossetti.

Without the which (as true words testify)
No soul can reach thy Heaven so fair and far.
   Even in this faith I choose to live and die. 10

Unto thy Son say thou that I am His,
   And to me graceless make Him gracious.
Sad Mary of Egypt lacked not of that bliss,
   Nor yet the sorrowful clerk Theophilus,
Whose bitter sins were set aside even thus 15
Though to the Fiend his bounden service was.
Oh help me, lest in vain for me should pass
   (Sweet Virgin that shalt have no loss thereby!)
The blessed Host and sacring of the Mass.
   Even in this faith I choose to live and die. 20

A pitiful poor woman, shrunk and old,
   I am, and nothing learn'd in letter-lore.
Within my parish-cloister I behold
   A painted Heaven where harps and lutes adore,
And eke an Hell whose damned folk seethe full
      sore: 25
One bringeth fear, the other joy to me.
That joy, great Goddess, make thou mine to be,—
   Thou of whom all must ask it even as I;
And that which faith desires, that let it see.
   For in this faith I choose to live and die. 30

O excellent Virgin Princess! thou didst bear
King Jesus, the most excellent comforter,
Who even of this our weakness craved a share
   And for our sake stooped to us from on high,
Offering to death His young life sweet and fair. 35
Such as He is, Our Lord, I Him declare,
   And in this faith I choose to live and die.

The Ballad
of Dead Ladies

TELL me now in what hidden way is
   Lady Flora the lovely Roman?
Where's Hipparchia, and where is Thais,
   Neither of them the fairer woman?
   Where is Echo, beheld of no man, 5
Only heard on river and mere,—
   She whose beauty was more than human? . . .
But where are the snows of yester-year?

Where's Heloïse, the learned nun,
   For whose sake Abeillard, I ween, 10

14. **Theophilus,** a legendary churchman who, like Faust, sold his soul to the devil, but later did penance for thirty days and was redeemed upon the intercession of the Virgin. 19. **sacring,** the consecrated elements of the mass.
The Ballad of Dead Ladies. Translated by D. G. Rossetti.

Lost manhood and put priesthood on?
   (From Love he won such dule and teen!)
   And where, I pray you, is the Queen
Who willed that Buridan should steer
   Sewed in a sack's mouth down the Seine? . . .
But where are the snows of yester-year? 16

White Queen Blanche, like a queen of lilies,
   With a voice like any mermaidèn,—
Bertha Broadfoot, Beatrice, Alice,
   And Ermengarde the lady of Maine,— 20
   And that good Joan whom Englishmen
At Rouen doomed and burned her there,—
   Mother of God, where are they then? . . .
But where are the snows of yester-year?

Nay, never ask this week, fair lord, 25
   Where they are gone, nor yet this year,
Save with this much for an overword,—
   But where are the snows of yester-year?

Ballad
of the Women
of Paris

ALBEIT the Venice girls get praise
   For their sweet speech and tender air,
And though the old women have wise ways
   Of chaffering for amorous ware,
   Yet at my peril dare I swear, 5
Search Rome, where God's grace mainly tarries,
   Florence and Savoy, everywhere,
There's no good girl's lip out of Paris.

The Naples women, as folk prattle,
   Are sweetly spoken and subtle enough; 10
German girls are good at tattle,

28. It is enough to know of these ladies that they were all beautiful or otherwise wonderful, and all dead. But for the curious the following may be added (on the authority of J. U. Nicholson in his *Complete Works of François Villon*): **Flora** was the name of many Roman courtesans, here especially the first of them for whom an annual festival was established. **Hipparchia** may be the mistress of the Greek philosopher Crates. **Thais** was a mistress of Alexander the Great. **Echo** was the Greek nymph changed into an echo. **Heloïse,** daughter of Canon Fulbert, was the beloved of the medieval churchman Abelard. **Queen Marguerite** of Navarre, notorious as an adulteress, was popularly thought to have commanded the death of Jehan Buridan, a rector of the University of Paris and learned doctor. **Queen Blanche** of Castile was supposed to have enjoyed singing the songs that her lover, King Tibalt of Navarre, composed for her. **Bertha Broadfoot** was the mother of Charlemagne. **Beatrice** may be the wife of Charles de France, son of Louis VIII. **Alice** may be Alix de Champagne, wife of Louis VII. **Ermengarde** is probably the daughter of Hélie de la Flèche, Count of Maine. **Joan** is of course Joan of Arc. *Ballad of the Women of Paris.* Translated by Algernon Charles Swinburne.

And Prussians make their boast thereof;
 Take Egypt for the next remove,
Or that waste land the Tartar harries,
 Spain or Greece, for the matter of love,   15
There's no good girl's lip out of Paris.

Breton and Swiss know nought of the matter,
 Gascony girls or girls of Toulouse;
Two fisherwomen with a half-hour's chatter
 Would shut them up by threes and twos;   20
 Calais, Lorraine, and all their crews,
(Names enow the mad song marries.)
 England and Picardy, search them and choose,
There's no good girl's lip out of Paris.

Prince, give praise to our French ladies   25
 For the sweet sound their speaking carries;
'Twixt Rome and Cadiz many a maid is,
 But no good girl's lip out of Paris.

The Tree of Love

I HAVE a tree, a graft of Love,
 That in my heart has taken root;
Sad are the buds and blooms thereof,
 And bitter sorrow is its fruit;
 Yet, since it was a tender shoot,   5
So greatly hath its shadow spread,
That underneath all joy is dead,
 And all my pleasant days are flown,
Nor can I slay it, nor instead
 Plant any tree, save this alone.   10

Ah, yet, for long and long enough
 My tears were rain about its root,
And though the fruit be harsh thereof,
 I scarcely looked for better fruit
 Than this, that carefully I put   15
In garner, for the bitter bread
Whereon my weary life is fed:
 Ah, better were the soil unsown
That bears such growths; but Love instead
 Will plant no tree, but this alone.   20

Ah, would that this new spring, whereof
 The leaves and flowers flush into shoot,
I might have succor and aid of Love,
 To prune these branches at the root,
 That long have borne such bitter fruit,   25
And graft a new bough, comfortèd
With happy blossoms white and red;
 So pleasure should for pain atone,

The Tree of Love. Translated by Andrew Lang. From *The Poetical Works of Andrew Lang.* Reprinted by permission of Longmans, Green and Company, Ltd., and the representatives of the late Andrew Lang.

Nor Love slay this tree, nor instead
 Plant any tree, but this alone.   30

L'envoy

Princes, by whom my hope is fed,
My heart thee prays in lowlihead
 To prune the ill boughs overgrown,
Nor slay Love's tree, nor plant instead
 Another tree, save this alone.

Ballad Written for a Bridegroom

Which Villon gave to a gentleman newly married to send to his wife whom he had won with the sword.

AT daybreak, when the falcon claps his wings,
 No whit for grief, but noble heart and
 high,
With loud glad noise he stirs himself and springs,
 And takes his meat and toward his lure draws
 nigh;
 Such good I wish you! Yea, and heartily   5
I am fired with hope of true love's meed to get;
 Know that Love writes it in his book; for why,
This is the end for which we twain are met.

Mine own heart's lady with no gainsayings
 You shall be always wholly till I die;   10
And in my right against all bitter things
 Sweet laurel with fresh rose its force shall try;
 Seeing reason wills not that I cast love by
(Nor here with reason shall I chide or fret)
 Nor cease to serve, but serve more constantly;   15
This is the end for which we twain are met.

And, which is more, when grief about me clings
 Through Fortune's fit or fume of jealousy,
Your sweet kind eye beats down her threatenings
 As wind doth smoke; such power sits in your eye.
 Thus in your field my seed of harvestry   21
Thrives, for the fruit is like me that I set;
 God bids me tend it with good husbandry;
This is the end for which we twain are met.

Princess, give ear to this my summary;   25
 That heart of mine your heart's love should forget,
Shall never be: like trust in you put I:
 This is the end for which we twain are met.

Ballad Written for a Bridegroom. Translated by Algernon Charles Swinburne. Addressed to Robert d'Estouteville, who won the hand of Ambroise de Lore at a great tournament in 1446. The French original of this poem includes the bride's name as an acrostic in the first two stanzas.

Rondel

GOOD-BY, the tears are in my eyes;
    Farewell, farewell, my prettiest;
Farewell, of women born the best;
Good-bye! the saddest of good-byes.
Farewell! with many vows and sighs   5
    My sad heart leaves you to your rest;
Farewell! the tears are in my eyes;
Farewell! from you my miseries
    Are more than now may be confessed,
    And most by thee have I been blessed,   10
Yea, and for thee have wasted sighs;
Good-bye! the last of my good-byes.

To Death,
of His Lady

DEATH, of thee do I make my moan,
    Who hadst my lady away from me,
Nor wilt assuage thine enmity
Till with her life thou hast mine own;
For since that hour my strength has flown.   5
    Lo! what wrong was her life to thee,
                                Death?

Two we were, and the heart was one;
    Which now being dead, dead I must be,
    Or seem alive as lifelessly   10
As in the choir the painted stone,
                                Death!

Villon's Straight Tip
to All Cross Coves

SUPPOSE you screeve? or go cheap-jack?
    Or fake the broads? or fig a nag?
Or thimble-rig? or knap a yack?
    Or pitch a snide? or smash a rag?
    Suppose you duff? or nose and lag?   5
Or get the straight, and land your pot?

Rondel. Translated by Andrew Lang. From *The Poetical Works of Andrew Lang.* Reprinted by permission of Longmans, Green and Company, Ltd., and the representatives of the late Andrew Lang. *To Death, of His Lady.* Translated by D. G. Rossetti. *Villon's Straight Tip to All Cross Coves.* Translated by W. E. Henley. Reprinted by permission of Charles Scribner's Sons. Villon's cynical advice to his underworld friends has been amusingly translated by Henley into English thieves' slang of an older day. Some of the expressions—land your pot, melt the swag, booze cops the lot—are still intelligible enough. With the others the *Oxford English Dictionary* will help those who want to know just which skin-games and crimes Villon is reviewing. But regardless of how much "dough" they may bring in, "booze and the blowens cop the lot."

How do you melt the multy swag?
Booze and the blowens cop the lot.

Fiddle, or fence, or mace, or mack;
    Or moskeneer, or flash the drag;   10
Dead-lurk a crib, or do a crack;
    Pad with a slang, or chuck a fag;
    Bonnet, or tout, or mump and gag;
Rattle the tats, or mark the spot;
    You can not bank a single stag;   15
Booze and the blowens cop the lot.

Suppose you try a different tack,
    And on the square you flash your flag?
At penny-a-lining make your whack,
    Or with the mummers mug and gag?   20
    For nix, for nix the dibbs you bag!
At any graft, no matter what,
    Your merry goblins soon stravag:
Booze and the blowens cop the lot.

The Moral

It's up the spout and Charley Wag   25
With wipes and tickers and what not.
    Until the squeezer nips your scrag,
Booze and the blowens cop the lot.

The Dispute
of the Heart and Body
of François Villon

WHO is this I hear?—Lo, this is I, thine
                                heart,
    That holds on merely now by a slender string.
Strength fails me, shape and sense are rent apart,
    The blood in me is turned to a bitter thing,
    Seeing thee skulk here like a dog shivering.—
Yea, and for what?—For that thy sense found
                                sweet.—   6
What irks it thee?—I feel the sting of it.—
    Leave me at peace.—Why?—Nay now, leave me
    at peace;
I will repent when I grow ripe in wit.—
    I say no more.—I care not though thou cease.—

What are thou, trow?—A man worth praise, per-
                                fay.—   11
    This is thy thirtieth year of wayfaring.—
'Tis a mule's age.—Art thou a boy still?—Nay.—
    Is it hot lust that spurs thee with its sting,

The Dispute of the Heart and Body of François Villon. Translated by Algernon Charles Swinburne. Debate poems of this kind were common in medieval literature and, in the case of such works as the Middle English *Debate of the Body and Soul,* were used as vehicles for sermons on hell and damnation.

Grasping thy throat? Know'st thou not any-
        thing?—   15
Yea, black and white, when milk is specked with
        flies,
I can make out.—No more?—Nay, in no wise.
    Shall I begin again the count of these?—
Thou art undone.—I will make shift to rise.—
    I say no more.—I care not though thou cease.—

I have the sorrow of it, and thou the smart.   21
    Wert thou a poor mad fool or weak of wit,
Then might'st thou plead this pretext with thine
        heart;
    But if thou know not good from evil a whit,
    Either thy head is hard as stone to hit,   25
Or shame, not honor, gives thee most content.
What canst thou answer to this argument?—
    When I am dead I shall be well at ease.—
God! What good hope!—Thou art over eloquent.—
    I say no more.—I care not though thou cease.—

Whence is this ill?—From sorrow and not from sin.
    When Saturn packed my wallet up for me   32
I well believe he put these ills therein.—
    Fool, wilt thou make thy servant lord of thee?
    Hear now the wise king's counsel; thus saith he;
All power upon the stars a wise man hath;   36
There is no planet that shall do him scathe.—
    Nay, as they made me I grow and I decrease.—
What say'st thou?—Truly this is all my faith.—   39
    I say no more.—I care not though thou cease.—

Wouldst thou live still?—God help me that I may!—
Then thou must—What? turn penitent and gray?—
Read always—What?—Grave words and good to say;
    Leave off the ways of fools, lest they displease.—
Good; I will do it.—Wilt thou remember?—Yea.—
Abide not till there come an evil day.   46
    I say no more.—I care not though thou cease.

Epistle
in Form of a Ballad
to His Friends

Have pity, pity, friends, have pity on me,
        Thus much at least, may it please you,
        of your grace!
I lie not under hazel or hawthorn-tree
    Down in this dungeon ditch, mine exile's place
    By leave of God and fortune's foul disgrace.   5

32. **Saturn,** the Roman god honored in the Saturnalia with feasting, drinking, and general carousal. 35. **wise king's counsel;** a reference to Solomon.
Epistle in the Form of a Ballad to His Friends. Translated by Algernon Swinburne.

Girls, lovers, glad young folk and newly wed,
Jumpers and jugglers, tumbling heel o'er head,
    Swift as a dart, and sharp as needle-ware,
Throats clear as bells that ring the kine to shed,
    Your poor old friend, what, will you leave him
        there?   10

Singers that sing at pleasure, lawlessly,
    Light, laughing, gay of word and deed, that race
And run like folk light-witted as ye be
    And have in hand nor current coin nor base,
    Ye wait too long, for now he's dying apace.   15
Rhymers of lays and roundels sung and read,
Ye'll brew him broth too late when he lies dead.
    Nor wind nor lightning, sunbeam nor fresh air,
May pierce the thick wall's bound where lies his
        bed;
    Your poor old friend, what, will you leave him
        there?   20

O noble folk, from tithes and taxes free,
    Come and behold him in this piteous case,
Ye that nor king nor emperor holds in fee,
    But only God in heaven; behold his face
    Who needs must fast, Sundays and holidays,   25
Which makes his teeth like rakes; and when he hath
        fed
With never a cake for banquet but dry bread,
    Must drench his bowels with much cold watery
        fare,
With board nor stool, but low on earth instead;
    Your poor old friend, what, will you leave him
        there?   30

Princes afore-named, old and young foresaid,
Get me the king's seal and my pardon sped,
    And hoist me in some basket up with care:
So swine will help each other ill bested,
For where one squeaks they run in heaps ahead,   35
    Your poor old friend, what, will you leave him
        there?

Ballad
of the Gibbet

An epitaph in the form of a ballad that François Villon wrote of himself and his company, they expecting shortly to be hanged.

Brothers and men that shall after us be,
        Let not your hearts be hard to us:
For pitying this our misery
    Ye shall find God the more piteous.

Ballad of the Gibbet. Translated by Andrew Lang. From *The Poetical Works of Andrew Lang.* Reprinted by permission of Longmans, Green and Company, Ltd., and the representatives of the late Andrew Lang.

Look on us six that are hanging thus,   5
And for the flesh that so much we cherished
How it is eaten of birds and perished,
    And ashes and dust fill our bones' place,
Mock not at us that so feeble be,
    But pray God pardon us out of His grace.   10

Listen, we pray you, and look not in scorn,
    Though justly, in sooth, we are cast to die;
Ye wot no man so wise is born
    That keeps his wisdom constantly.
    Be ye then merciful, and cry   15
To Mary's Son that is piteous,
That His mercy take no stain from us,
    Saving us out of the fiery place.
We are but dead, let no soul deny
    To pray God succor us out of His grace.   20

The rain out of heaven has washed us clean,
    The sun has scorched us black and bare,
Ravens and rooks have pecked at our eyne,
    And feathered their nests with our beards and
        hair.
    Round are we tossed, and here and there,   25
This way and that, at the wild wind's will,
Never a moment my body is still;
    Birds they are busy about my face.
Live not as we, not fare as we fare;
    Pray God pardon us out of His grace.   30

L'envoy

Prince Jesus, Master of all, to thee
We pray Hell gain no mastery,
    That we come never anear that place;
And ye men, make no mockery,
    Pray God pardon us out of His grace.

Pierre de Ronsard

1524–1585

From Villon to Ronsard is a long step out of the uncouth Middle Ages of France into the elegant Renaissance. In contrast to the underworld that Villon knew, Ronsard grew up at the court of Francis I, where he served as page boy to the Dauphin. In later life he was the favorite of six French kings and numbered both Elizabeth of England and Mary of Scotland among his patrons. But deafness cut short his hope for a diplomatic career, and he turned to scholarship and poetry. Schooled in Greek as well as in Latin, he turned against the medieval poetic tradition and was fired by the urge to establish in modern France a school of poetry equal to the ancients in genius and refinement. With other enthusiasts among his friends he formed the circle of seven scholar-poets called the Pleiades. These earnest

young men developed a common doctrine of art based on imitation of the classics and slaved at writing correct verses with almost religious zeal.

Of this group, only Ronsard revealed the genius of a first-rate poet, and even he was hampered at first by his subjection to ancient models. Indeed he shows the best and worst features of the typical Renaissance poet, who was both inspired and restrained by a worship of antiquity. His careful but affected copies of Pindar, Anacreon, and Horace lack personal conviction, and his attempt in the *Franciade* (1572) to produce a classical epic on royal demand ended in embarrassing failure. But during the last ten years of his life Ronsard relaxed his rigid compliance with the forms of ancients and, enkindled by his late love for Hélène de Surgères, wrote a series of exquisite sonnets to her, illuminated by personal feeling and a sure command of poetic language. Although Petrarch inspired them, these melodious lyrics express the delicate sentiments of a court poet who has at last dared to speak for himself. His classical imitations had a revolutionary effect on the course of French poetry, but his reputation today rests on a few lyrics in which he told his own love story. Reworked beyond recognition in the next generation by the ponderous classicist Malherbe, they were rediscovered in their original form as recently as 1827 by the great critic Sainte-Beuve.

Summer's Revel

Oh! but my mind is weary!
    Long I have conned the dreary
      Tomes of Aratus.
Surely 'tis time to play now!
Ho! to the fields away now!   5
Shall we not live to-day now?
    What though dull fools berate us!

What is the use of learning,
When it but brings new yearning
    Problems to tease us?   10
When, or at eve or morning,
Soon, but without a warning,
Pleadings and pity scorning,
    Orcus the dark shall seize us.

Corydon, lead the way, and   15
Find where good wine's to pay, and
    Cool me a flagon!
Then in vine-trellised bowers,
Bedded on thick-strewn flowers,
Hours upon idle hours   20
    Sweetly shall haste or lag on.

Summer's Revel. Translated by Curtis Hidden Page. From *Songs and Sonnets of Pierre de Ronsard*, by Curtis Hidden Page. Reprinted by permission of Mrs. Alice T. Loomis.
3. **Aratus** (c. 315–245 B.C.), a minor Greek poet. 14. **Orcus,** the land of the dead.

Artichokes bring me, mellow
Apricots, melons yellow,
   Creams, and strawberries.
These have the sweetest savor   25
Eaten in forest cave, or
Lying by brooks that rave or
   Streamlet that singing tarries.

Now in my youth's fresh buoyance
Laughter shall wait on joyance,   30
   Wine shall flow fast now;
Lest, when my life grows colder,
Sickness, by age made bolder,
Say, as he taps my shoulder:
   "Come, friend—you've drunk your last now."

Fragment of a Sonnet

NATURE withheld Cassandra in the skies,
   For more adornment, a full thousand years;
She took their cream of Beauty's fairest dyes,
And shaped and tinted her above all Peers:
Meanwhile Love kept her dearly with his wings,   5
And underneath their shadow filled her eyes
With such a richness that the cloudy Kings
Of high Olympus uttered slavish sighs.
When from the Heavens I saw her first descend,
My heart took fire, and only burning pains,   10
They were my pleasures—they my Life's sad end;
Love poured her beauty into my warm veins.

Love's Charming

MAID of fifteen, in childlike beauty dight,
   Fair head with crinkled ringlets golden-
     tressed,
   Rose-petalled forehead, cheeks like amethyst,
Laughter that lifts the soul to Heaven's delight;
And neck like snow, and throat than milk more
     white,   5
   And heart full-blossomed neath a budding breast—
   Beauty divine in human form expressed,
And virtue worthy of that beauty bright—
An eye whose light can change the night to day,
   A gentle hand that smooths away my care,   10
   Yet holds my life caught in its fingers' snare;
Withal a voice that's ever fain to sing,
   Still stopped by smiles, or sweet sighs languish-
     ing—
   These are the spells that charmed my wits away.

Fragment of a Sonnet. Translated by John Keats.
Love's Charming. Translated by Curtis Hidden Page. From *Songs and Sonnets of Pierre de Ronsard*, by Curtis Hidden Page. Reprinted by permission of Mrs. Alice T. Loomis.

To His Young Mistress

FAIR flower of fifteen springs, that still
   Art scarcely blossomed from the bud,
Yet hast such store of evil will,
   A heart so full of hardihood,
     Seeking to hide in friendly wise   5
     The mischief of your mocking eyes.

If you have pity, child, give o'er,
   Give back the heart you stole from me,
Pirate, setting so little store
   On this your captive from Love's sea,   10
     Holding his misery for gain,
     And making pleasure of his pain.

Another, not so fair of face,
   But far more pitiful than you,
Would take my heart, if of his grace,   15
   My heart would give her of Love's due;
     And she shall have it, since I find
     That you are cruel and unkind.

Nay, I would rather that I died,
   Within your white hands prisoning,   20
Would rather that it still abide
   In your ungentle comforting,
     Than change its faith, and seek to her
     That is more kind, but not so fair.

Even unto Death

To think one thought a hundred hundred ways,
   'Neath two loved eyes to lay your heart quite
     bare,
   To drink the bitter liquor of despair
And eat forever ashes of lost days—
In spirit and flesh to know youth's bloom decays,   5
   To die of pain, yet swear no pain is there,
   The more you sue, to move the less your fair,
Yet make her wish, the law your life obeys—
Anger that passes, faith that cannot move;
   Far dearer than yourself your foe to love;   10
   To build a thousand vain imaginings,
To long to plead, yet fear to voice a breath,
   In ruin of all hope to hope all things—
These are the signs of love—love even to death.

To His Young Mistress. Translated by Andrew Lang. From *The Poetical Works of Andrew Lang*. Reprinted by permission of Longmans, Green and Company, Ltd., and the representatives of the late Andrew Lang.
Even unto Death. Translated by Curtis Hidden Page. From *Songs and Sonnets of Pierre de Ronsard*, by Curtis Hidden Page. Reprinted by permission of Mrs. Alice T. Loomis.

Love's Flower

TAKE thou this rose, sweet even as thou art,
 Thou rose of roses rarest, loveliest,
 Thou flower of freshest flowers, whose fragrance
  blest
Enwraps me, ravished from myself apart.
Take thou this rose, and with it take my heart,   5
 My heart that hath no wings, unto thy breast,
 So constant that its faith stands manifest,
Though wounded sore with many a cruel dart.
The rose and I are diverse in one thing:
 Each morning's rose at eve lies perishing,   10
 While countless mornings see my love new-born
But never night shall see its life decay. . . .
 Ah! would that love, new-blossomed in the morn,
 Even as a flower had lasted but a day.

Roses

I SEND you here a wreath of blossoms blown,
 And woven flowers at sunset gathered,
 Another dawn had seen them ruined, and shed
Loose leaves upon the grass at random strown.
By this, their sure example, be it known,   5
 That all your beauties, now in perfect flower,
 Shall fade as these, and wither in an hour.
Flower-like, and brief of days, as the flower sown.
Ah, time is flying, lady—time is flying;
 Nay, 'tis not time that flies but we that go,   10
Who in short space shall be in churchyard lying,
 And of our loving parley none shall know,
Nor any man consider what we were;
Be therefore kind, my love, whilst thou art fair.

The Rose

SEE, Mignonne, hath not the Rose,
 That this morning did unclose
 Her purple mantle to the light,
Lost before the day be dead,
The glory of her raiment red,   5
 Her color, bright as yours is bright?

Ah, Mignonne, in how few hours
The petals of her purple flowers
 All have faded, fallen, died;

Love's Flower. Translated by Curtis Hidden Page. From *Songs and Sonnets of Pierre de Ronsard*, by Curtis Hidden Page. Reprinted by permission of Mrs. Alice T. Loomis.
Roses; The Rose. Translated by Andrew Lang. From *The Poetical Works of Andrew Lang*. Reprinted by permission of Longmans, Green and Co., Ltd., and the representatives of the late Andrew Lang.

Sad Nature, mother ruinous,   10
That seest thy fair child perish thus
 'Twixt matin song and even-tide.

Hear me, my darling, speaking sooth,
Gather the fleet flower of your youth,
 Take ye your pleasure at the best;   15
Be merry ere your beauty flit,
For length of days will tarnish it
 Like roses that were loveliest.

The Poet's Gift

THAT century to century may tell
 The perfect love Ronsard once bore to you,
 How he was reason-reft for love of you
And thought it freedom in your chains to dwell;
That age on age posterity full well   5
 May know my veins were filled with beauty of
  you
 And that my heart's one wish was only you,
I bring for gift to you this immortelle.
Long will it live in freshness of its prime.
 And you shall live, through me, long after death—
 So can the well-skilled lover conquer Time,   11
Who loving you all virtue followeth.
 Like Laura, you shall live the cynosure
 Of earth, so long as pens and books endure.

Of His Lady's Old Age

WHEN you are very old, at evening
 You'll sit and spin beside the fire, and
  say,
Humming my songs, "Ah well, ah well-a-day!
When I was young, of me did Ronsard sing."
None of your maidens that doth hear the thing,   5
 Albeit with her weary task foredone,
 But wakens at my name, and calls you one
Blest, to be held in long remembering.

I shall be low beneath the earth, and laid
On sleep, a phantom in the myrtle shade,   10
 While you beside the fire, a grandame gray;
My love, your pride, remember and regret;
Ah, love me, love! we may be happy yet,
 And gather roses, while 'tis called to-day.

The Poet's Gift. Translated by Curtis Hidden Page. From *Songs and Sonnets of Pierre de Ronsard*, by Curtis Hidden Page. Reprinted by permission of Mrs. Alice T. Loomis.
Of His Lady's Old Age. Translated by Andrew Lang. From *The Poetical Works of Andrew Lang*. Reprinted by permission of Longmans, Green and Company, Ltd., and the representatives of the late Andrew Lang.

To His Valet

I WANT three days to read the Iliad through!
  So, Corydon, close fast my chamber door.
If anything should bother me before
I've done, I swear you'll have somewhat to rue!
No! not the servant, nor your mate, nor you   5
  Shall come to make the bed or clean the floor.
  I must have three good quiet days—or four.
Then I'll make merry for a week or two.
Ah! but—if any one should come from HER,
  Admit him quickly! Be no loiterer,   10
  But come and make me brave for his receiving.
But no one else!—not friends or nearest kin!
  Though an Olympian God should seek me, leaving
  His Heaven, shut fast the door! Don't let him in!

The Revenge

FAIR rebel to thyself and Time,
  Who laugh'st at all my tears,
When thou has lost thy youthful prime,
  And age his trophy rears,

Weighing thy inconsiderate pride,   5
  Thou shalt in vain accuse it:
"Why beauty am I now denied,
  Or knew not then to use it?"

Then shall I wish, ungentle Fair,
  Thou in like flames may'st burn!   10
Venus, if just, will hear my prayer,
  And I shall laugh my turn.

Deadly Kisses

AH, take these lips away; no more,
  No more such kisses give to me.
My spirit faints for joy; I see
Through mists of death the dreamy shore,
And meadows by the water-side,   5
  Where all about the Hollow Land
Fare the sweet singers that have died,
  With their lost ladies, hand in hand;
Ah, Love, how fireless are their eyes,
  How pale their lips that kiss and smile.   10
  So mine must be in little while
If thou wilt kiss me in such wise.

To His Valet. Translated by Curtis Hidden Page. From *Songs and Sonnets of Pierre de Ronsard*, by Curtis Hidden Page. Reprinted by permission of Mrs. Alice T. Loomis.
The Revenge. Translated by Thomas Stanley.
Deadly Kisses. Translated by Andrew Lang. From *The Poetical Works of Andrew Lang.* Reprinted by permission of Longmans, Green and Company, Ltd., and the representatives of the late Andrew Lang.

His Lady's Death

TWAIN that were foes, while Mary lived, are fled;
  One laurel-crowned abides in heaven, and one
  Beneath the earth has fared, a fallen sun,
A light of love among the loveless dead.
The first is Chastity, that vanquished   5
  The archer Love, that held joint empery
  With the sweet beauty that made war on me,
When laughter of lips with laughing eyes was wed.

Their strife the Fates have closed, with stern control,
The earth holds her fair body, and her soul   10
  An angel with glad angels triumpheth;
Love has no more than he can do; desire
Is buried, and my heart a faded fire,
  And for Death's sake, I am in love with Death

His Lady's Tomb

As in the gardens, all through May, the rose,
  Lovely, and young, and fair apparelled,
  Makes sunrise jealous of her rosy red,
When dawn upon the dew of dawning glows;
Graces and Loves within her breast repose,   5
  The woods are faint with the sweet odor shed,
  Till rains and heavy suns have smitten dead
The languid flower, and the loose leaves unclose,—

So this, the perfect beauty of our days,
When earth and heaven were vocal of her praise,   10
  The fates have slain, and her sweet soul reposes;
And tears I bring, and sighs, and on her tomb
Pour milk, and scatter buds of many a bloom,
  That dead, as living, she may be with roses.

Transit Mundus

ANOTHER Winter comes. The last comes soon, I
  know.
For six and fifty years have blanched my head with
  snow.
The time is here to say, Farewell, to love and song,
And take my leave of life's best days, for oh! how
  long! . . .   4

His Lady's Death; His Lady's Tomb. Translated by Andrew Lang. From *The Poetical Works of Andrew Lang.* Reprinted by permission of Longmans, Green and Company, Ltd., and the representatives of the late Andrew Lang.
Transit Mundus. Translated by Curtis Hidden Page. From *Songs and Sonnets of Pierre de Ronsard*, by Curtis Hidden Page. Reprinted by permission of Mrs. Alice T. Loomis. *Transit mundus* means the world passes by.

Yet I have lived. So much stands safe beyond recall.
I grudge not life its joys. I have tasted one and all,
Nor e'er refrained my hand from pleasures within
    reach,
Save but as Reason set due measure unto each.
The part assigned me I have played on this life's
    stage
In costume fitted to the times and to my age.   10

I've seen the morning dawn, and evening come
    again.
I've seen the storm, the lightning-flash, the hail, the
    rain.
Peoples I've seen, and kings!—For twenty years now
    past
I've seen each day rise upon France as though her
    last.
Wars I have seen, and strife of words, and terms of
    truce   15
First made and then unmade again, then made by
    ruse
To break and make again! . . . I've seen that neath
    the moon
All was but change and chance, and danced to
    Fortune's tune.
Though man seek Prudence out for guide, it boots
    him naught;
Fate ineluctable doth hold him chained and caught,
Bound hand and foot, in prison; and all he may pro-
    pose   21
Fortune and Fate, wisely mayhap, themselves dis-
    pose.

Full-feasted of the world, even as a wedding-guest
Goes from the banquet-hall, I go to my long rest;
As from a king's great feast, I go not with ill grace
Though after me one come, and take the abandoned
    place.

English Lyricists

The English Renaissance produced a great chorus of lyric voices extending from Wyatt and Surrey at the court of Henry VIII to Herrick and Waller well over a century later. A flood of spontaneous song characterized the writing of this long period, its plays and romances as well as its exquisite sonnet sequences. It overflows into the prose, whether in the ornate diction of Sidney's *Arcadia*, overladen with dainty figures of speech, or the simple music of the King James version of the Bible. At their best, Renaissance lyrics were written to be sung, and the lovely songs in Shakespeare's plays have inspired composers from his day to ours.

The favorite lyric form was the sonnet, introduced from Italy by Sir Thomas Wyatt around 1535; and many a poet's love affair, real or imagined, was embodied in a sonnet cycle after the manner of Petrarch, Boccaccio, and Ronsard. Sidney wrote his to Stella, Spenser to Elizabeth, Samuel Daniel to Delia, Thomas Lodge to Phyllis, Shakespeare to a mysterious youth and an equally mysterious "dark lady." Wyatt had adhered to the Italian sonnet form of Petrarch, with its sharp division between the octave (rhymed *abbaabba*) and the sestet (*cdecde,* or some variation thereof), which came to be called the Italian sonnet in English. Surrey experimented with variations of the fourteen-line stanza closer to the simplicity of English verse and developed a so-called English form (*ababcdcdefefgg*), which was later popularized by Shakespeare.

The early lyrics of the Renaissance were the work of gentleman-amateurs and circulated in manuscript among their friends, often until after the poets' deaths. Many were lost because they eluded publication, while others found their way into later anthologies, such as *Tottel's Miscellany* (1557), *The Paradise of Dainty Devices* (1576), and *England's Helicon* (1600). Even the sonnets of Shakespeare, although they were published as a separate volume in 1609, were written at least ten years before.

These Shakespearean sonnets offer a perennial enigma to literary scholars. Of the 154 in the collection, the first 126 are addressed to a young man of noble birth and great beauty in terms of idealistic affection, while the last twenty-eight are in praise of a dark-haired lady, who apparently scorned the poet's devotion. The nature of Shakespeare's attachment to the well-endowed youth has occasioned as much scholarly argument as has his identity. A cryptic dedication of the poems by the publisher to "Mr. W. H., the onlie begetter of these ensuing sonnets," has inspired attempts to identify the young man with various patrons of the poet—Henry Wriothesley, Earl of Southampton, and William, Lord Herbert, among others—but none of these theories has been generally accepted. The ordinary reader can brush aside such speculations and be happy to find in this uneven cycle some of the noblest and most musical sonnets in the language.

The graceful lyrics of Ben Jonson (1573–1637) were the least characteristic of all his many writings. This blunt, pugnacious commoner began his career as a bricklayer and common soldier in English wars on the Continent, but he improved his early schooling at Westminster by private study, until he became the most scholarly of all Elizabethan playwrights. His natural talent for the stage was obstructed by his classical theories in the heavy, stilted tragedies, *Sejanus* and *Cataline;* but in his classical comedies, such as *Volpone* and *The Alchemist,* it united with his skill in social satire to produce a brilliant and biting comedy of humors. Though the pedantic Jonson admired Shakespeare, he could never quite forgive the lack of ancient learning in his great contemporary.

Jonson outlived Shakespeare by twenty years, and during that period presided over a circle of devoted friends and disciples, who were proud to call themselves "the tribe of Ben." Their favorite haunt was the Devil Tavern, where the flow of wine and wit betrayed their devotion to the Greek Anacreon and Roman Horace. It was a Royalist stronghold on the eve of Puritan revolution, the resort of brilliant young cynics bred on the pagan philosophies of antiquity.

The finest artist in this remarkable tribe was Robert Herrick (1591–1674), the exquisite poet who carries the pagan spirit of Jonson through the seventeenth century. Yet his carefree delight in the physical world was complicated in later life by a career in the church, which actually rounded out his varied experience. Reared in the rustic setting of a charming village near London, which he often remembered in his verses, Herrick was educated at St. John's College, Cambridge, and became attached to Jonson and his classical circle in London. Failure at court led him to take orders in the Anglican Church and accept exile from city society in the provincial parish of Dean Prior. During the Puritan regime his Royalist sympathies lost him his church position, but he returned to it after the Restoration in 1662.

Herrick published only one volume of verses, the *Hesperides* (1648), which immediately followed his ejection from his church post, but contributions to other collections brought his total to about 1300 poems. Of these some are the "noble numbers" inspired by his serious life as a clergyman, but the best loved are the melodious little pastoral lyrics which praise natural, happy living in the sophisticated accents of a rollicking cavalier. Herrick is the poet of spring sunshine and May wine, of youthful love and laughter. He bids us live for today, free from care for the future, which may bring sadness and decay but is sure to bring a heaven above as rich and happy as our heaven on earth. His pagan love songs, brimful of color and spontaneous life, have the perennial charm of youth in their graceful meters.

John Donne (1573–1631) was also a preacher and poet, but his serious side won out, even in the most mundane of his love lyrics. Educated at both Oxford and Cambridge, he at first studied law and served as secretary to the Lord Keeper of the Great Seal. But dismissal from this post for an indiscretion led him to seek security in a church career. Ordained an Anglican priest in 1615, he served as dean of St. Paul's from 1621 until his death and became renowned for the most brilliant sermons of his generation.

Donne's poems belong to his youth, though they were not published until after his death. Written in a time when Petrarchian sonnets and convivial Anacreontics were all the rage, they break sharply with the graceful court fashion in their subtle, cynical reasoning and crabbed, whimsical style. Intellect in Donne has by no means submerged emotion, but it cramps and confines it and sometimes warps it into bizarre or perverse forms. His love poems are full of cutting irony; his satires are sometimes pointed and direct, sometimes complicated by odd bits of learning and excessive intellectual refinement. He deliberately tangles his ideas in obscurities and refuses to give us the melody of which he was abundantly capable. In this fondness for the unusual he predicts the so-called metaphysical poets of the seventeenth century, Herbert, Crashaw, and Vaughan, whose serious and difficult verses match subtle introspection with a taut and crotchety style. Yet Donne's intellect and individual manner have inspired a large school of poets in the twentieth century, and it is now the fashion to praise him.

WILLIAM SHAKESPEARE

from *Love's Labor's Lost*

WHEN icicles hang by the wall,
  And Dick the shepherd blows his nail,
And Tom bears logs into the hall,
  And milk comes frozen home in pail,
When blood is nipped and ways be foul,   5
Then nightly sings the staring owl,
"Tu-whit, tu-who!" A merry note,
While greasy Joan doth keel the pot.

When all aloud the wind doth blow,
  And coughing drowns the parson's saw,   10
And birds sit brooding in the snow,
  And Marian's nose looks red and raw,
When roasted crabs hiss in the bowl,
Then nightly sings the staring owl,
"Tu-whit, tu-who!" A merry note,   15
While greasy Joan doth keel the pot.

from *The Two Gentlemen of Verona*

WHO is Silvia? What is she,
  That all our swains commend her?
Holy, fair, and wise is she;
  The heaven such grace did lend her,
That she might admiréd be.   5

Is she kind as she is fair?
  For beauty lives with kindness.
Love doth to her eyes repair,
  To help him of his blindness;
And, being helped, inhabits there.   10

Then to Silvia let us sing,
  That Silvia is excelling;
She excels each mortal thing
  Upon the dull earth dwelling.
To her let us garlands bring.

Love's Labor's Lost. **2. blows his nail**, blows on his fingers to warm them. **8. keel**, cool by stirring to prevent its boiling over. **13. crabs**, hot crabapples to flavor the ale.

from *The Merchant of Venice*

TELL me where is fancy bred,
    Or in the heart, or in the head?
How begot, how nourishèd?
        Reply, reply.
It is engend'red in the eyes,   5
With gazing fed; and fancy dies
In the cradle where it lies.
Let us all ring fancy's knell;
I'll begin it—Ding, dong, bell.
        Ding, dong, bell.

from *Much Ado about Nothing*

SIGH no more, ladies, sigh no more;
    Men were deceivers ever;
One foot in sea, and one on shore,
    To one thing constant never.
Then sigh not so, but let them go,   5
    And be you blithe and bonny,
Converting all your sounds of woe
    Into "Hey nonny, nonny!"

Sing no more ditties, sing no moe
    Of dumps so dull and heavy;   10
The fraud of men was ever so,
    Since summer first was leavy.
Then sigh not so, but let them go,
    And be you blithe and bonny,
Converting all your sounds of woe   15
    Into "Hey nonny, nonny!"

from *As You Like It*

UNDER the greenwood tree
    Who loves to lie with me,
And turn his merry note
    Unto the sweet bird's throat,
Come hither, come hither, come hither!   5
    Here shall he see
        No enemy
But winter and rough weather.

Who doth ambition shun,
    And loves to live i' the sun,   10
Seeking the food he eats,
    And pleased with what he gets,
Come hither, come hither, come hither!
    Here shall he see
        No enemy   15
But winter and rough weather.

It was a lover and his lass,
    With a hey, and a ho, and a hey nonino,
That o'er the green corn-field did pass
    In the spring time, the only pretty ring time,
    When birds do sing, hey ding a ding, ding!   5
Sweet lovers love the spring.

Between the acres of the rye,
    With a hey, and a ho, and a hey nonino,
These pretty country folks would lie,
    In spring time, the only pretty ring time,   10
    When birds do sing, hey ding a ding, ding!
Sweet lovers love the spring.

This carol they began that hour,
    With a hey, and a ho, and a hey nonino,
How that a life was but a flower   15
    In spring time, the only pretty ring time,
    When birds do sing, hey ding a ding, ding!
Sweet lovers love the spring.

And therefore take the present time,
    With a hey, and a ho, and a hey nonino,   20
For love is crownéd with the prime
    In spring time, the only pretty ring time,
    When birds do sing, hey ding, a ding, ding!
Sweet lovers love the spring.

    Blow, blow, thou winter wind,
    Thou art not so unkind
        As man's ingratitude;
    Thy tooth is not so keen,
    Because thou art not seen,   5
        Although thy breath be rude.
Heigh-ho! sing, heigh-ho! unto the green holly:
Most friendship is feigning, most loving mere folly:
    Then, heigh-ho, the holly!
        This life is most jolly.   10

    Freeze, freeze, thou bitter sky,
    That dost not bite so nigh
        As benefits forgot:
    Though thou the waters warp,
    Thy sting is not so sharp   15
        As friend remember'd not.
Heigh-ho! sing, &c.

from *Twelfth Night*

O MISTRESS mine, where are you roaming?
    O, stay and hear; your true love's coming,
    That can sing both high and low.
Trip no further, pretty sweeting,

Journey's end in lovers meeting,　　　　5
　　Every wise man's son doth know.

What is love? 'Tis not hereafter;
Present mirth hath present laughter;
　　What's to come is still unsure.
In delay there lies no plenty;　　　　10
Then come kiss me, sweet-and-twenty,
　　Youth's a stuff will not endure.

from *Measure for Measure*

TAKE, oh, take those lips away,
　　That so sweetly were forsworn;
And those eyes, the break of day,
　　Lights that do mislead the morn.
But my kisses bring again,　　　　5
　　Bring again;
Seals of love, but sealed in vain,
　　Sealed in vain.

from *Cymbeline*

HARK, hark! The lark at heaven's gate sings,
　　And Phoebus 'gins arise,
His steeds to water at those springs
　　On chaliced flowers that lies;
And winking Mary-buds begin　　　　5
　　To ope their golden eyes.
With every thing that pretty is,
　　My lady sweet, arise!
　　　　Arise, arise!

Fear no more the heat o' the sun,
　　Nor the furious winter's rages;
Thou thy worldly task hast done,
　　Home art gone, and ta'en thy wages.
Golden lads and girls all must,　　　　5
As chimney-sweepers, come to dust.

Fear no more the frown o' the great;
　　Thou art past the tyrant's stroke;
Care no more to clothe and eat;
　　To thee the reed is as the oak.　　　　10
The scepter, learning, physic, must
All follow this, and come to dust.

Fear no more the lightning-flash,
　　Nor the all-dreaded thunder-stone;
Fear not slander, censure rash;　　　　15

Cymbeline. 4. chaliced flowers; like cups full of dew being dried by the sun.

Thou hast finished joy and moan.
All lovers young, all lovers must
Consign to thee, and come to dust.

No exorciser harm thee!
　　Nor no witchcraft charm thee!　　　　20
Ghost unlaid forbear thee!
　　Nothing ill come near thee!
Quiet consummation have;
　　And renownéd be thy grave!

from *The Winter's Tale*

WHEN daffodils begin to peer,
　　With hey! the doxy over the dale,
Why, then comes in the sweet o' the year;
　　For the red blood reigns in the winter's pale.

The white sheet bleaching on the hedge,　　　　5
　　With hey! the sweet birds, oh, how they sing!
Doth set my pugging tooth on edge;
　　For a quart of ale is a dish for a king.

The lark, that tirra-lirra chants,
　　With hey! with hey! the thrush and the jay,　　　　10
Are summer songs for me and my aunts,
　　While we lie tumbling in the hay.

from *The Tempest*

FULL fathom five thy father lies:
　　Of his bones are coral made;
Those are pearls that were his eyes;
　　Nothing of him that doth fade,
But doth suffer a sea-change　　　　5
Into something rich and strange.
Sea-nymphs hourly ring his knell:
Hark! now I hear them—Ding, dong, bell!

Sonnets

18

SHALL I compare thee to a summer's day?
　　Thou art more lovely and more temperate:
Rough winds do shake the darling buds of May,
And summer's lease hath all too short a date:
Sometime too hot the eye of heaven shines,　　　　5
And often is his gold complexion dimm'd;
And every fair from fair sometime declines,
By chance or nature's changing course untrimm'd;

The Winter's Tale. 2. doxy, prostitute. 7. **pugging tooth,** urge to thieving. 11. **aunts,** thieves' slang for prostitutes.
Sonnet 18. 7. fair, beautiful person. 8. **untrimm'd,** deprived of beauty.

But thy eternal summer shall not fade
Nor lose possession of that fair thou owest; 10
Nor shall Death brag thou wander'st in his shade,
When in eternal lines to time thou growest:
　So long as men can breathe or eyes can see,
　So long lives this, and this gives life to thee.

29

When, in disgrace with fortune and men's eyes,
I all alone beweep my outcast state
And trouble deaf heaven with my bootless cries
And look upon myself and curse my fate,
Wishing me like to one more rich in hope, 5
Featured like him, like him with friends possess'd,
Desiring this man's art and that man's scope,
With what I most enjoy contented least;
Yet in these thoughts myself almost despising,
Haply I think on thee, and then my state, 10
Like to the lark at break of day arising
From sullen earth, sings hymns at heaven's gate;
　For thy sweet love remember'd such wealth brings
　That then I scorn to change my state with kings.

30

When to the sessions of sweet silent thought
I summon up remembrance of things past,
I sigh the lack of many a thing I sought,
And with old woes new wail my dear time's waste:
Then can I drown an eye, unused to flow, 5
For precious friends hid in death's dateless night,
And weep afresh love's long since cancell'd woe,
And moan the expense of many a vanish'd sight:
Then can I grieve at grievances foregone,
And heavily from woe to woe tell o'er 10
The sad account of fore-bemoanèd moan,
Which I new pay as if not paid before.
　But if the while I think on thee, dear friend,
　All losses are restored and sorrows end.

33

Full many a glorious morning have I seen
Flatter the mountain-tops with sovereign eye,
Kissing with golden face the meadows green,
Gilding pale streams with heavenly alchemy;
Anon permit the basest clouds to ride 5
With ugly rack on his celestial face,
And from the forlorn world his visage hide,
Stealing unseen to west with this disgrace:
Even so my sun one early morn did shine
With all-triumphant splendor on my brow; 10
But out, alack! he was but one hour mine;
The region cloud hath mask'd him from me now.
　Yet him for this my love no whit disdaineth;
　Suns of the world may stain when heaven's sun
　　staineth.

Sonnet 18.　14. this, poem.
Sonnet 33.　6. rack, high, broken clouds.

54

O, how much more doth beauty beauteous seem
By that sweet ornament which truth doth give!
The rose looks fair, but fairer we it deem
For that sweet odour which doth in it live.
The canker-blooms have full as deep a dye 5
As the perfumed tincture of the roses,
Hang on such thorns and play as wantonly
When summer's breath their masked buds discloses:
But, for their virtue only is their show,
They live unwoo'd and unrespected fade, 10
Die to themselves. Sweet roses do not so;
Of their sweet deaths are sweetest odours made:
　And so of you, beauteous and lovely youth,
　When that shall fade, my verse distills your truth.

55

Not marble, nor the gilded monuments
Of princes, shall outlive this powerful rhyme;
But you shall shine more bright in these contents
Than unswept stone besmear'd with sluttish time.
When wasteful war shall statues overturn, 5
And broils root out the work of masonry,
Nor Mars his sword nor war's quick fire shall burn
The living record of your memory.
'Gainst death and all-oblivious enmity
Shall you pace forth; your praise shall still find room
Even in the eyes of all posterity 11
That wear this world out to the ending doom.
　So, till the judgement that yourself arise,
　You live in this, and dwell in lovers' eyes.

60

Like as the waves make towards the pebbled shore,
So do our minutes hasten to their end;
Each changing place with that which goes before,
In sequent toil all forwards do contend.
Nativity, once in the main of light, 5
Crawls to maturity, wherewith being crown'd,
Crooked eclipses 'gainst his glory fight,
And Time that gave doth now his gift confound.
Time doth transfix the flourish set on youth
And delves the parallels in beauty's brow, 10
Feeds on the rarities of nature's truth,
And nothing stands but for his scythe to mow:
　And yet to times in hope my verse shall stand,
　Praising thy worth, despite his cruel hand.

64

When I have seen by Time's fell hand defaced
The rich proud cost of outworn buried age;
When sometime lofty towers I see down-razed

Sonnet 54.　5. canker-blooms, the dog rose, with color but no scent.
Sonnet 60.　5. the main of light, the sun.　10. delves the parallels,
digs the furrows.

And brass eternal slave to mortal rage;
When I have seen the hungry ocean gain   5
Advantage on the kingdom of the shore,
And the firm soil win of the watery main,
Increasing store with loss and loss with store;
When I have seen such interchange of state,
Or state itself confounded to decay;   10
Ruin hath taught me thus to ruminate,
That Time will come and take my love away.
    This thought is as a death, which cannot choose
    But weep to have that which it fears to lose.

66

Tired with all these, for restful death I cry,
As, to behold desert a beggar born,
And needy nothing trimm'd in jollity,
And purest faith unhappily forsworn,
And gilded honour shamefully misplaced,   5
And maiden virtue rudely strumpeted,
And right perfection wrongfully disgraced,
And strength by limping sway disabled,
And art made tongue-tied by authority,
And folly, doctor-like, controlling skill,   10
And simple truth miscall'd simplicity,
And captive good attending captain ill:
    Tired with all these, from these would I be gone,
    Save that, to die, I leave my love alone

73

That time of year thou mayst in me behold
When yellow leaves, or none, or few, do hang
Upon those boughs which shake against the cold,
Bare ruin'd choirs, where late the sweet birds sang.
In me thou see'st the twilight of such day   5
As after sunset fadeth in the west,
Which by and by black night doth take away,
Death's second self, that seals up all in rest.
In me thou see'st the glowing of such fire
That on the ashes of his youth doth lie,   10
As the death-bed whereon it must expire,
Consumed with that which it was nourish'd by.
    This thou perceivest, which makes thy love more
        strong
    To love that well which thou must leave ere long.

95

How sweet and lovely dost thou make the shame
Which, like a canker in the fragrant rose,
Doth spot the beauty of thy budding name!
O, in what sweets doth thou thy sins enclose!
That tongue that tells the story of thy days,   5
Making lascivious comments on thy sport,
Cannot dispraise but in a kind of praise;
Naming thy name blesses an ill report.
O, what a mansion have those vices got
Which for their habitation chose out thee,   10

Sonnet 66. **1. these,** injustices that follow.

Where beauty's veil doth cover every blot,
And all things turn to fair that eyes can see!
    Take heed, dear heart, of this large privilege;
    The hardest knife ill-used doth lose his edge.

102

My love is strengthen'd, though more weak in seem-
        ing;
I love not less, though less the show appear:
That love is merchandized whose rich esteeming
The owner's tongue doth publish everywhere.
Our love was new and then but in the spring   5
When I was wont to greet it with my lays,
As Philomel in summer's front doth sing
And stops her pipe in growth of riper days:
Not that the summer is less pleasant now
Than when her mournful hymns did hush the night,
But that wild music burthens every bough   11
And sweets grown common lose their dear delight.
    Therefore like her I sometime hold my tongue,
    Because I would not dull you with my song.

104

To me, fair friend, you never can be old,
For as you were when first your eye I eyed,
Such seems your beauty still. Three winters cold
Have from the forests shook three summers' pride,
Three beauteous springs to yellow autumn turn'd   5
In process of the seasons have I seen.
Three April perfumes in three hot Junes burn'd,
Since first I saw you fresh, which yet are green.
Ah! yet doth beauty, like a dial-hand,
Steal from his figure, and no pace perceived;   10
So your sweet hue, which methinks still doth stand,
Hath motion, and mine eye may be deceived:
    For fear of which, hear this, thou age unbred;
    Ere you were born was beauty's summer dead.

106

When in the chronicle of wasted time
I see descriptions of the fairest wights,
And beauty making beautiful old rhyme
In praise of ladies dead and lovely knights,
Then, in the blazon of sweet beauty's best,   5
Of hand, of foot, of lip, of eye, of brow,
I see their antique pen would have express'd
Even such a beauty as you master now.
So all their praises are but prophecies
Of this our time, all you prefiguring;   10
And, for they look'd but with divining eyes,
They had not skill enough your worth to sing:
    For we, which now behold these present days,
    Have eyes to wonder, but lack tongues to praise.

109

O, never say that I was false of heart,
Though absence seem'd my flame to qualify.

A French fifteenth-century drawing of three ladies.

As easy might I from myself depart
As from my soul, which in thy breast doth lie:
That is my home of love: if I have ranged,   5
Like him that travels, I return again,
Just to the time, not with the time exchanged,
So that myself bring water for my stain.
Never believe, though in my nature reign'd
All frailties that besiege all kinds of blood,   10
That it could so preposterously be stain'd,
To leave for nothing all thy sum of good!
    For nothing this wide universe I call,
    Save thou, my rose; in it thou art my all.

116

Let me not to the marriage of true minds
Admit impediments. Love is not love
Which alters when it alteration finds,
Or bends with the remover to remove:
O, no! it is an ever-fixéd mark   5
That looks on tempests and is never shaken;
It is the star to every wandering bark,
Whose worth's unknown, although his height be
    taken.
Love's not Time's fool, though rosy lips and cheeks
Within his bending sickle's compass come;   10
Love alters not with his brief hours and weeks,
But bears it out even to the edge of doom.
    If this be error and upon me proved,
    I never writ, nor no man ever loved.

121

'Tis better to be vile than vile esteem'd,
When not to be receives reproach of being,
And the just pleasure lost which is so deem'd
Not by our feeling but by others' seeing:
For why should others' false adulterate eyes   5
Give salutation to my sportive blood?
Or on my frailties why are frailer spies,
Which in their wills count bad what I think good?
No, I am that I am, and they that level
At my abuses reckon up their own: 10
I may be straight, though they themselves be bevel;
By their rank thoughts my deeds must not be shown;

Unless this general evil they maintain,
All men are bad, and in their badness reign.

BEN JONSON

To the Memory of My Beloved, Master William Shakespeare

To draw no envy, Shakespeare, on thy name,
    Am I thus ample to thy book and fame;
While I confess thy writings to be such
As neither man, nor muse, can praise too much.
'Tis true, and all men's suffrage. But these ways   5
Were not the paths I meant unto thy praise;
For silliest ignorance on these may light,
Which, when it sounds at best, but echoes right;
Or blind affection, which doth ne'er advance
The truth, but gropes, and urgeth all by chance;   10
Or crafty malice might pretend this praise,
And think to ruin, where it seemed to raise.
These are, as some infamous bawd or whore
Should praise a matron. What could hurt her more?
But thou art proof against them, and, indeed,   15
Above the ill fortune of them, or the need.
I therefore will begin. Soul of the age!
The applause, delight, the wonder of our stage!
My Shakespeare, rise! I will not lodge thee by
Chaucer, or Spenser, or bid Beaumont lie   20
A little further, to make thee a room;
Thou art a monument without a tomb,
And art alive still while thy book doth live
And we have wits to read and praise to give.
That I not mix thee so, my brain excuses,   25
I mean with great, but disproportioned Muses;
For if I thought my judgment were of years,
I should commit thee surely with thy peers,
And tell how far thou didst our Lyly outshine,
Or sporting Kyd, or Marlowe's mighty line.   30
And though thou hadst small Latin and less Greek,
From thence to honor thee, I would not seek
For names; but call forth thundering Aeschylus,
Euripides, and Sophocles to us;
Pacuvius, Accius, him of Cordova dead,   35
To life again, to hear thy buskin tread,
And shake a stage; or, when thy socks were on,

To the Memory of My Beloved, Master William Shakespeare. Prefixed to the first complete edition of Shakespeare's plays, 1623. 2. **ample,** contributing something additional to. 20. **Chaucer, Spenser, Beaumont,** all of whom were buried in Westminster Abbey. 30. **Kyd,** Thomas Kyd (1557?–1595?), an early English playwright. 35. **Pacuvius, Accius,** Roman tragedians of the second century B.C. **him of Cordova dead.** Seneca, born in Córdoba, Spain, was the classical inspiration of Elizabethan tragedy. 36. **buskin.** Buskin and sock were ancient symbols of tragedy and comedy, after the footgear worn by Greek actors.

Leave thee alone for the comparison
Of all that insolent Greece or haughty Rome
Sent forth, or since did from their ashes come.   40
Triumph, my Britain, thou hast one to show
To whom all scenes of Europe homage owe.
He was not of an age, but for all time!
And all the Muses still were in their prime,
When, like Apollo, he came forth to warm   45
Our ears, or like a Mercury to charm!
Nature herself was proud of his designs
And joyed to wear the dressing of his lines!
Which were so richly spun, and woven so fit,
As, since, she will vouchsafe no other wit.   50
The merry Greek, tart Aristophanes,
Neat Terence, witty Plautus, now not please,
But antiquated and deserted lie,
As they were not of Nature's family.
Yet must I not give Nature all; thy art,   55
My gentle Shakespeare, must enjoy a part.
For though the poet's matter nature be,
His art doth give the fashion; and, that he
Who casts to write a living line, must sweat
(Such as thine are) and strike the second heat   60
Upon the Muses' anvil; turn the same
(And himself with it) that he thinks to frame,
Or, for the laurel, he may gain a scorn;
For a good poet's made, as well as born.
And such wert thou! Look how the father's face   65
Lives in his issue; even so the race
Of Shakespeare's mind and manners brightly shines
In his well turnèd, and true filèd lines;
In each of which he seems to shake a lance,
As brandished at the eyes of ignorance.   70
Sweet Swan of Avon! what a sight it were
To see thee in our waters yet appear,
And make those flights upon the banks of Thames,
That so did take Eliza, and our James!
But stay, I see thee in the hemisphere   75
Advanced, and made a constellation there!
Shine forth, thou Star of poets, and with rage
Or influence, chide or cheer the drooping stage,
Which, since thy flight from hence, hath mourned
    like night,
And despairs day, but for thy volume's light.

Song: to Celia

COME, my Celia, let us prove,
   While we may, the sports of love.
Time will not be ours forever;
He, at length, our good will sever;

Spend not then his gifts in vain.   5
Suns that set may rise again;
But if once we lose this light,
'Tis with us perpetual night.
Why should we defer our joys?
Fame and rumor are but toys.   10
Cannot we delude the eyes
Of a few poor household spies?
Or his easier ears beguile,
Thus removèd by our wile?
'Tis no sin love's fruit to steal;   15
But the sweet theft to reveal,
To be taken, to be seen,
These have crimes accounted been.

Song to Celia

DRINK to me only with thine eyes,
   And I will pledge with mine;
Or leave a kiss but in the cup,
   And I'll not look for wine.
The thirst that from the soul doth rise   5
   Doth ask a drink divine;
But might I of Jove's nectar sup,
   I would not change for thine.
I sent thee late a rosy wreath,
   Not so much honoring thee   10
As giving it a hope, that there
   It could not withered be.
But thou thereon didst only breathe,
   And sent'st it back to me;
Since when it grows, and smells, I swear,   15
   Not of itself, but thee.

Simplex Munditiis

STILL to be neat, still to be drest,
   As you were going to a feast;
Still to be powdered, still perfumed;
Lady, it is to be presumed,
Though art's hid causes are not found,   5
All is not sweet, all is not sound.

Give me a look, give me a face
That makes simplicity a grace;
Robes loosely flowing, hair as free.
Such sweet neglect more taketh me   10
Than all the adulteries of art;
They strike mine eyes, but not my heart.

69. **shake a lance**; pun on "shake spear."   71. **Sweet Swan of Avon.**
The river Avon flows through Stratford, Shakespeare's birthplace.
74. **Eliza, James,** Queen Elizabeth and King James I.

Song to Celia. 13. his; a reference to her husband.
Simplex Munditiis. Inspired by Horace's Ode 1, 5.

Epitaph
on Elizabeth L. H.

WOULD'ST thou hear what man can say
  In a little? Reader, stay.
Underneath this stone doth lie
As much beauty as could die,
Which in life did harbor give   5
To more virtue than doth live.

If at all she had a fault,
Leave it buried in this vault.
One name was Elizabeth,
The other, let it sleep with death!   10
Fitter, where it died, to tell,
Than that it lived at all. Farewell!

It Is Not Growing
Like a Tree

IT is not growing like a tree
  In bulk, doth make men better be;
Or standing long an oak, three hundred year,
To fall a log at last, dry, bald, and sear:
    A lily of a day   5
    Is fairer far in May;
  Although it fall and die that night,
  It was the plant and flower of light.
In small proportions we just beauties see,
And in short measures life may perfect be.

A Song

OH, do not wanton with those eyes,
  Lest I be sick with seeing,
Nor cast them down, but let them rise,
  Lest shame destroy their being.
O, be not angry with those fires,   5
  For then their threats will kill me;
Nor look too kind on my desires,
  For then my hopes will spill me.
O, do not steep them in my tears,
  For so will sorrow stay me;   10
Nor spread them as distract with fears—
  Mine own enough betray me.

It Is Not Growing Like a Tree. From *A Pindaric Ode on the Death of H. Morison.*

JOHN DONNE

Song

GO and catch a falling star,
    Get with child a mandrake root,
Tell me where all past years are,
  Or who cleft the devil's foot;
Teach me to hear mermaids singing.   5
Or to keep off envy's stinging,
        And find
        What wind
Serves to advance an honest mind.

If thou be'st born to strange sights, 10
  Things invisible go see,
Ride ten thousand days and nights
  Till Age snow white hairs on thee;
Thou, when thou return'st, wilt tell me
All strange wonders that befell thee, 15
        And swear
        No where
Lives a woman true and fair.

If thou find'st one, let me know;
  Such a pilgrimage were sweet.   20
Yet do not; I would not go,
  Though at next door we might meet.
Though she were true when you met her,
And last till you write your letter,
        Yet she   25
        Will be
False, ere I come, to two or three.

The Ecstasy

WHERE, like a pillow on a bed,
    A pregnant bank swelled up, to rest
The violet's reclining head,
  Sat we two, one another's best.
Our hands were firmly cemented   5
  With a fast balm, which thence did spring,
Our eye-beams twisted, and did thread
  Our eyes, upon one double string;
So t' intergraft our hands, as yet
  Was all the means to make us one,   10
And pictures in our eyes to get
  Was all our propagation.

Song. 2. mandrake, an herb of southern Europe with a forked root resembling a human figure, the object of many superstitions.

As 'twixt two equal armies, fate
  Suspends uncertain victory,
Our souls (which to advance their state, 15
  Were gone out) hung 'twixt her, and me.
And whil'st our souls negotiate there,
  We like sepulchral statues lay;
All day, the same our postures were,
  And we said nothing, all the day. 20
If any, so by love refined
  That he soul's language understood,
And by good love were grown all mind,
  Within convenient distance stood,
He (though he knew not which soul spake, 25
  Because both meant, both spake the same)
Might thence a new concoction take,
  And part far purer than he came.
This Ecstasy doth unperplex
  (We said) and tell us what we love; 30
We see by this, it was not sex,
  We see, we saw not what did move:
But as all several souls contain
  Mixtures of things, they know not what,
Love, these mixed souls, doth mix again, 35
  And makes both one, each this and that.
A single violet transplant,
  The strength, the color, and the size,
(All which before was poor, and scant)
  Redoubles still, and multiplies. 40
When love, with one another so
  Interinanimates two souls,
That abler soul, which thence doth flow,
  Defects of loneliness controls.
We then, who are this new soul, know 45
  Of what we are composed, and made,
For, th' atomies of which we grow,
  Are souls, whom no change can invade.
But O alas, so long, so far
  Our bodies why do we forbear? 50
They are ours, though they are not we; we are
  The intelligences, they the sphere.
We owe them thanks, because they thus,
  Did us, to us, at first convey,
Yielded their forces, sense, to us, 55
  Nor are dross to us, but allay.
On man heaven's influence works not so,
  But that it first imprints the air,
So soul into the soul may flow,
  Though it to body first repair. 60
As our blood labors to beget
  Spirits, as like souls as it can,
Because such fingers need to knit
  That subtle knot, which makes us man:

---

32. **We see . . . did move.** We see now that we did not see then
what moved us to love.   33. **several,** separate.   56. **allay,** alloy.

So must pure lovers' souls descend 65
  T' affections, and to faculties,
Which sense may reach and apprehend,
  Else a great prince in prison lies.
T' our bodies turn we then, that so
  Weak men on love revealed may look; 70
Love's mysteries in souls do grow,
  But yet the body is his book.
And if some lover, such as we,
  Have heard this dialogue of one,
Let him still mark us, he shall see 75
  Small change, when we're to bodies gone.

Love's Infiniteness

IF yet I have not all thy love,
  Dear, I shall never have it all,
I cannot breathe one other sigh, to move,
Nor can intreat one other tear to fall,
And all my treasure, which should purchase thee, 5
Sighs, tears, and oaths, and letters, I have spent.
Yet no more can be due to me,
Than at the bargain made was meant;
If then thy gift of love were partial,
That some to me, some should to others fall, 10
  Dear, I shall never have thee all.

Or if then thou gavest me all,
All was but all, which thou hadst then;
But if in thy heart, since, there be or shall,
New love created be, by other men, 15
Which have their stocks entire, and can in tears,
In sighs, in oaths, and letters outbid me,
This new love may beget new fears,
For, this love was not vowed by thee;
And yet it was, thy gift being general, 20
The ground, thy heart is mine, what ever shall
  Grow there, dear; I should have it all.

Yet I would not have all yet;
He that hath all can have no more,
And since my love doth every day admit 25
New growth, thou shouldst have new rewards in
    store;
Thou canst not every day give me thy heart,
If thou canst give it, then thou never gavest it;
Love's riddles are, that though thy heart depart,
It stays at home, and thou with losing savest it; 30
But we will have a way more liberal,
Then changing hearts, to join them, so we shall
  Be one, and one another's all.

The Funeral

WHOEVER comes to shroud me, do not harm
　　Nor question much
That subtle wreath of hair about mine arm;
The mystery, the sign you must not touch,
　　For 'tis my outward soul, 5
Viceroy to that which, unto heav'n being gone,
　　Will leave this to control
And keep these limbs, her provinces, from dissolu-
　　tion.

For if the sinewy thread my brain lets fall
　　Through every part 10
Can tie those parts, and make me one of all;
Those hairs, which upward grew, and strength and
　　art
　　Have from a better brain,
Can better do 't: except she meant that I
　　By this should know my pain, 15
As prisoners then are manacled, when they're
　　condemned to die.

Whate'er she meant by 't, bury it with me,
　　For since I am
Love's martyr, it might breed idolatry
If into other hands these reliques came 20
　　As 't was humility
To afford to it all that a soul can do,
　　So 't is some bravery
That, since you would have none of me, I bury
　　some of you.

Death

DEATH, be not proud, though some have called
　　thee
Mighty and dreadful, for thou art not so;
For those whom thou think'st thou dost overthrow
Die not, poor Death; nor yet canst thou kill me.
From rest and sleep, which but thy picture be, 5
Much pleasure; then from thee much more must
　　flow;
And soonest our best men with thee do go—
Rest of their bones and souls' delivery!
Thou'rt slave to fate, chance, kings, and desperate
　　men,
And dost with poison, war, and sickness dwell; 10
And poppy or charms can make us sleep as well
And better than thy stroke. Why swell'st thou then?
One short sleep past, we wake eternally,
And Death shall be no more: Death, thou shalt die!

The Argument
of His Book

I SING of brooks, of blossoms, birds, and bowers,
　Of April, May, of June and July flowers;
I sing of May-poles, hock-carts, wassails, wakes,
Of bridegrooms, brides, and of their bridal cakes;
I write of youth, of love, and have access 5
By these to sing of cleanly wantonness;
I sing of dews, of rains, and, piece by piece,
Of balm, of oil, of spice and ambergris;
I sing of times trans-shifting, and I write
How roses first came red and lilies white; 10
I write of groves, of twilight, and I sing
The Court of Mab, and of the Fairy King.
I write of hell; I sing (and ever shall)
Of heaven, and hope to have it after all.

An Ode
for Ben Jonson

AH, Ben!
　　Say how or when
Shall we, thy guests,
Meet at those lyric feasts,
Made at the Sun, 5
The Dog, the Triple Tun;
Where we such clusters had,
As made us nobly wild, not mad?
And yet each verse of thine
Out-did the meat, out-did the frolic wine. 10

My Ben!
Or come again,
Or send to us
Thy wit's great overplus;
But teach us yet 15
Wisely to husband it,
Lest we that talent spend;
And having once brought to an end
That precious stock, the store
Of such a wit the world should have no more.

The Argument of His Book. 3. hock-carts, the last carts loaded at
the harvest home festival. wakes, parish festivals.
An Ode for Ben Jonson. 5–6. the Sun, the Dog, the Triple Tun,
three London taverns. 7. clusters; of grapes; hence, wine.

The Night Piece,
to Julia

Her eyes the glow-worm lend thee;
    The shooting stars attend thee;
  And the elves also,
  Whose little eyes glow
Like the sparks of fire, befriend thee.   5

No will-o'-the-wisp mislight thee,
Nor snake or slow-worm bite thee;
  But on, on thy way
  Not making a stay,
Since ghosts there's none to affright thee.   10

Let not the dark thee cumber;
What though the moon does slumber?
  The stars of the night
Will lend thee their light,
Like tapers clear without number.   15

Then, Julia, let me woo thee,
Thus, thus to come unto me;
  And when I shall meet
  Thy silv'ry feet,
My soul I'll pour into thee.

Delight in Disorder

A sweet disorder in the dress
  Kindles in clothes a wantonness.
A lawn about the shoulders thrown
Into a fine distraction;
An erring lace, which here and there   5
Enthrals the crimson stomacher;
A cuff neglectful, and thereby
Ribbands to flow confusedly;
A winning wave, deserving note,
In the tempestuous petticoat;   10
A careless shoestring, in whose tie
I see a wild civility;—
Do more bewitch me, than when art
Is too precise in every part.

Upon Julia's Clothes

When as in silks my Julia goes,
    Then, then, methinks, how sweetly flows
The liquefaction of her clothes.

Next, when I cast mine eyes, and see
That brave vibration, each way free,   5
Oh, how that glittering taketh me!

Cherry-Ripe

Cherry-ripe, ripe, ripe, I cry,
  Full and fair ones; come and buy!
If so be you ask me where
They do grow, I answer, there,
Where my Julia's lips do smile;   5
There's the land, or cherry-isle,
Whose plantations fully show
All the year where cherries grow.

Upon Mistress
Susanna Southwell
Her Feet

Her pretty feet
    Like snails did creep
A little out, and then,
As if they playéd at bo-peep,
Did soon draw in again.   5

To Daffodils

Fair daffodils, we weep to see
    You haste away so soon;
As yet the early-rising sun
Has not attained his noon.
      Stay, stay   5
    Until the hasting day
      Has run
    But to the evensong;
And, having prayed together, we
    Will go with you along.   10
We have short time to stay, as you,
    We have as short a spring;
As quick a growth to meet decay,
    As you, or anything.
      We die   15
    As your hours do, and dry
      Away
    Like to the summer's rain;
Or as the pearls of morning's dew,
    Ne'er to be found again.

To the Virgins
to Make Much of Time

Gather ye rosebuds while ye may,
    Old Time is still a-flying;
And this same flower that smiles today,
    Tomorrow will be dying.

Cherry Ripe. 1. Cherry-ripe . . . ; like the cherry-seller in the London streets.

The glorious lamp of heaven, the sun,   5
  The higher he's a-getting,
The sooner will his race be run,
  And nearer he's to setting.

That age is best which is the first,
  When youth and blood are warmer;   10
But being spent, the worse and worst
  Times still succeed the former.

Then be not coy, but use your time,
  And while ye may, go marry;
For, having lost but once your prime,   15
  You may forever tarry.

To Dianeme

SWEET, be not proud of those two eyes,
  Which star-like sparkle in their skies:
Nor be you proud that you can see
All hearts your captives; yours, yet free.
Be you not proud of that rich hair,   5
Which wantons with the Love-sick air:
When as that Ruby, which you wear,
Sunk from the tip of your soft ear,
Will last to be a precious stone,
When all your world of beauty's gone.   10

To Anthea, Who May Command Him Anything

BID me to live, and I will live
  Thy protestant to be:
Or bid me love, and I will give
  A loving heart to thee.

A heart as soft, a heart as kind,   5
  A heart as sound and free,
As in the whole world thou canst find,
  That heart I'll give to thee.

Bid that heart stay, and it will stay,
  To honor thy decree: 10
Or bid it languish quite away,
  And 't shall do so for thee.

Bid me to weep, and I will weep,
  While I have eyes to see:
And having none, yet I will keep   15
  A heart to weep for thee.

Bid me despair, and I'll despair,
  Under that cypress tree:

Or bid me die, and I will dare
  E'en Death, to die for thee.   20

Thou art my life, my love, my heart,
  The very eyes of me:
And hast command of every part,
  To live and die for thee.

To Electra

I DARE not ask a kiss;
  I dare not beg a smile;
Lest having that, or this,
  I might grow proud the while.

No, no, the utmost share   5
  Of my desire shall be
Only to kiss that Air
  That lately kissèd thee.

To Primroses
Filled with Morning-dew

WHY do ye weep, sweet babes? can tears
      Speake grief in you,
    Who were but born
  Just as the modest morn
  Teemed her refreshing dew?   5
Alas, you have not known that shower
    That mars a flower;
    Nor felt the unkind
  Breath of a blasting wind;
  Nor are ye worn with years;   10
    Or warped, as we,
  Who think it strange to see,
Such pretty flowers, like to orphans young,
To speak by tears, before ye have a tongue.

Speak, whimpering younglings, and make known
    The reason why   16
    Ye droop and weep;
  Is it for want of sleep?
  Or childish lullaby?
Or that ye have not seen as yet   20
    The violet?
  Or brought a kiss
From that sweetheart to this?
No, no, this sorrow shown
    By your tears shed,   25
  Would have this lecture read,
That things of greatest, so of meanest worth,
Conceived with grief are, and with tears brought
    forth.

To Daisies,
Not to Shut So Soon

SHUT not so soon; the dull-eyed night
  Has not as yet begun
To make a seizure on the light,
  Or to seal up the sun.

No marigolds yet closéd are;   5
  No shadows great appear;
Nor doth the early shepherds' star
  Shine like a spangle here.

Stay but till my Julia close
  Her life-begetting eye;   10
And let the whole world then dispose
  Itself to live or die.

The Fairies

IF ye will with Mab find grace,
  Set each platter in his place:
Rake the fire up, and get
Water in, ere sun be set.
Wash your pails, and cleanse your dairies;   5
Sluts are loathsome to the fairies:
Sweep your house: Who doth not so,
Mab will pinch her by the toe.

The Hag

THE hag is astride
  This night for to ride,
The devil and she together;
  Through thick and through thin,
  Now out, and then in,   5
Though ne'er so foul be the weather.

  A thorn or a burr
  She takes for a spur,
With a lash of a bramble she rides now;
  Through brakes and through briars,   10
  O'er ditches and mires,
She follows the spirit that guides now.

  No beast for his food
  Dares now range the wood,
But hushed in his lair he lies lurking: 15
  While mischiefs by these,
  On land and on seas,
At noon of night are a-working.

The Hag. 18. noon of night, midnight.

The storm will arise
And trouble the skies   20
This night; and, more for the wonder,
  The ghost from the tomb
  Affrighted shall come,
Called out by the clap of the thunder.

His Prayer
for Absolution

FOR those my unbaptizéd rimes,
  Writ in my wild, unhallowed times,
For every sentence, clause, and word
That's not inlaid with thee, my Lord,
Forgive me, God, and blot each line   5
Out of my book that is not thine.
But if, 'mongst all, thou find'st here one
Worthy thy benediction,
That one of all the rest shall be
The glory of my work and me.

Litany
to the Holy Spirit

IN the hour of my distress,
  When temptations me oppress,
And when I my sins confess,
    Sweet Spirit, comfort me!

When I lie within my bed,   5
Sick in heart and sick in head,
And with doubts discomfortéd,
    Sweet Spirit, comfort me!

When the house doth sigh and weep,
And the world is drowned in sleep,   10
Yet mine eyes the watch do keep,
    Sweet Spirit, comfort me!

When the artless doctor sees
No one hope, but of his fees,
And his skill runs on the lees,   15
    Sweet Spirit, comfort me!

When his potion and his pill,
His, or none, or little skill,
Meet for nothing but to kill,
    Sweet Spirit, comfort me!   20

When the passing bell doth toll,
And the furies in a shoal
Come to fright a parting soul,
    Sweet Spirit, comfort me!

When the tapers now burn blue,
And the comforters are few,
And that number more than true,
    Sweet Spirit, comfort me!

When the priest his last hath prayed,   30
And I nod to what is said,
'Cause my speech is now decayed,
    Sweet Spirit, comfort me!

When, God knows, I'm tossed about
Either with despair or doubt;
Yet before the glass be out,   35
    Sweet Spirit, comfort me!

35. **the glass,** the hour-glass.

When the tempter me pursu'th   25
With the sins of all my youth,
And half damns me with untruth,
    Sweet Spirit, comfort me!   40

When the flames and hellish cries
Fright mine ears and fright mine eyes,
And all terrors me surprise,
    Sweet Spirit, comfort me!

When the Judgment is revealed,   45
And that opened which was sealed,
When to Thee I have appealed,
    Sweet Spirit, comfort me!

GENERAL INDEX

The name of an author represented by selections appears in capitals and small capitals (SHAKESPEARE, WILLIAM): the number in boldface after the name is the page on which his biographical sketch begins.

Selections that are reprinted in this book are listed in boldface italic; the number in boldface after the title is the page on which the selection begins; the other numbers are pages on which it is mentioned. A few selections without titles are listed according to first lines.

Aage and Else, **249**
Abgesang, 151
Abu Bekr, 25
Actors, of Renaissance, 279, 280
Advancement of Learning, The, 506
Africa, 548
Agincourt, battle of, 269
Agricola, Georg, 277
Aladdin and His Lamp, 28
Albertus Magnus, 8, 15, 265, 277
ALBRECHT VON JOHANNSDORF, 152
Alcuin, 8
Alexander VI, Pope, 275
Ali Baba and the Forty Thieves, 28
Allah, in *Koran,* 25
Allegory, Puritan, 286
Amadis of Gaul, 286, 347
Amoretti, 396
Anglican Church, origin of, 276
Anglo-Saxon, epic poetry, 6–8
Anti-remonstrants, 421
Antwerp, as commercial center, 266
Apocalyptic Utterances, The, 48
Aquinas, Thomas, 8, 15, 265
Aquino, Maria d', 301
Arabian Nights, The, 20, 28, 29
Arabian Nights Entertainment, The, 20
Arabic, use of in *Koran,* 25
Arabs, scientific knowledge of, 19, 277; in Spain, 269
Aragon, 269
Areopagitica, 514
Argument of His Book, The, 571
Arianism, 65
Ariosto, Ludovico, 278, 281
Aristotle, criticism of in Renaissance, 277
Arius, 65
Armada, Spanish, 425
As You Like It, songs from, **563**
Athanasius, 65
Attila, in *The Nibelungenlied,* 125
Aubade, 151
Aucassin and Nicolete, **137,** 138
Augsburg, as commercial center, 266

Augsburg Confession, 276, 510
Author to the Reader, The, **325**
Autobiography, revival of in Renaissance, 278
Autobiography, of Cellini, 282
Autos sacramentales, 425, 426
Averroës, 19, 277
Avicenna, 19, 277
Avignon, papacy of, 9, 275, 548

Babylonian Captivity, 9, 275, 548
BACON, FRANCIS, 285, **505;** and scientific method, 278
Bacon, Roger, 8, 265; and experimental method, 277
Bagdad, 19
Ballad, folk type, 247; minstrel type, 247
Ballad of Dead Ladies, The, **553**
Ballad of Sir Tannhäuser, The, **153**
Ballad of the Gibbet, **556**
Ballad of the Women of Paris, The, **553**
Ballad Written for a Bridegroom, **554**
Ballade, used by Villon, 282, 552
Ballads, popular, discussed, 246–248; origin of, 12–13; publication of, 248
Bardi, 266
Beauty and Virtue of Laura, The, **549**
Bede, 8
Beowulf, 8, 10, **125**
Beowulf, as epic hero, 126
Bible, 47, 63; influence of on Milton, 515; influence of on Saint Francis, 74; lay interpretation of, 275; relation to *Koran,* 25; translated by Luther, 510
Biography, 278
Bishop Golias. *See* Golias.
Blacks, in Florentine politics, 158
Blow, blow, thou winter wind, 563
BOCCACCIO, GIOVANNI, 280, **300;** and Greek Renaissance, 273
Boethius, 8; influence of on Chaucer, 202
Boniface VIII, Pope, 275
Bonnie George Campbell, **258**
Bonny Barbara Allan, **256**
Book of the Courtier, The, 272, 282, **389**
Book of the Duchess, The, 202

Borgia, Cesare, 414–415
Bourgeoisie, 9, 272
Brant, Sebastian, 294
Bride of Ribe, The, **256**
Bruni, Leonardo, 273
BRUNO, GIORDANO, 277, **503**
Budé, Guillaume, 282
Bunyan, John, 286
Burbage, James, 279
BURGRAVE OF LÜENZ, THE, 153
Burgundy, Dukes of, 269
Byzantine Empire, arts of, 19; fall of, 21, 267

Caedmon, 8
Caedmonian cycle, 10
Calderón de la Barca, Pedro, 288
Calvin, John, 276
Calvinism, in England, 514; influence on Spenser, 396; origin and spread of, 276
Camoëns, Luis de, 269
Campaldino, battle of, 158
Canossa, 4
Canterbury Tales, The, **203**; composition of, 202–203
Capitalism, and development of monarchy, 267; rise of in Renaissance, 266–267
Carmina Burana, 289
CASTIGLIONE, BALDASSARE, 272, 282, **388**
Castile, 269
Catholic Church, and Arian heresy, 65; attitude of Erasmus toward, 293; and Avignonese papacy, 275; and Ghibellines, 158; and Great Schism, 275; and Guelphs, 158; and Nicaean Creed, 65; organization of, 2–3; and origin of drama, 13; and Reformation, 275–276; significance of in Middle Ages, 2; temporal power of in Middle Ages, 4. *See* also Christian Church, Papacy, Pope.
Cellini, Benvenuto, 273, 278, 282
CERVANTES, MIGUEL DE, 286–288, **346**, **388**
Chansons de geste, 10; described, 111
Chante-fable form, 137
Charlemagne, campaign of in Spain (778), 110; government of, 6, 8; in *The Song of Roland,* 111
Charles I, king of Spain, 269
Charles V, Holy Roman Emperor, 269
Charles VIII, king of France, 282
CHAUCER, GEOFFREY, **201**; compared to Dante, 23; compared to Spenser, 395–396
Cherry-Ripe, **572**
Child, Francis J., and collection of ballads, 246
Children's Crusade, 21
Chivalry, decline of, 271; effect of on literature, 9; in medieval romance, 10–11; of Minnesingers, 151; satirized by Cervantes, 346–347; satirized in *Aucassin and Nicolete,* 137; in *Sir Gawain and the Green Knight,* 88; in Spain, 286
Chrestien de Troyes, 11

Christian Church, and *Divine Comedy,* 159; Eastern, 19; establishment of, 48
Christianity, ideals of in Matthew, 48; recognized by Constantine, 65; in *The Song of Roland,* 111
Chrysoloras, Emanuel, 273
City-states, Italian, 268
Clergy, Catholic, decline of temporal power, 271; influence on medieval literature, 14–15; and writing of romances, 12
Colet, John, 283; and Erasmus, 293
Colin Clout's Come Home Again, 396
Columbus, Christopher, 267
Comedias. See Comedy, Spanish.
Comedy, of Ben Jonson, 285; Spanish, 288
Commedia. See Divine Comedy, The.
Commerce, of Renaissance Europe, 266–267
Comus, 286, **514**
Confessions of Golias, The, **289**
Consolation of Philosophy, The. See De Philosophiae Consolatione.
Constantine, Emperor, 65
Constantinople, capture of by Turks, 21
Conte del Graal, 15
Copernican theory, expounded by Bruno, 503
COPERNICUS, NICOLAUS, 277, **499**
Corinthians, Paul's Epistles to, 48. *See* **First Epistle of Paul to the Corinthians.**
Counter-Reformation, history of, 276; in Spain, 269
Courtiers, and English literature, 283; Italian, 282; position of in Renaissance, 271; and Renaissance monarchs, 272; as seen by Castiglione, 388–389
Cradle, The, **308**
Crécy, battle of, 269
Cromwell, Oliver, 514
Crusader Hymns, 151
Crusades, 21
Cymbeline, songs from, **564**
Cynewulf, 8
Cynewulfian cycle, 10

DANTE ALIGHIERI, **157**, 265; compared to Chaucer, 23; influence of on Boccaccio, 301; influence of on Milton, 515; love for Beatrice, 158; medievalism of, 10; and writing of *Divine Comedy,* 158–159
De Contemptu Mundi, 9
De Monarchia, 158
De Philosophiae Consolatione, 8, 202
De Revolutionibus Orbium Celestium. See Revolution of the Heavenly Bodies, The.
Deadly Kisses, **560**
Death, **571**
Death-Bed of Laura, The, **550**
Decameron, 280, 301
Delight in Disorder, **572**
DELLA MIRANDOLA, PICO, 273, **291**
Denmark, ballads of, 246–247
Devotion to the Cross, The, 288

Dialogue, use of in medieval teaching, 18–19
DIETMAR VON AIST, 151
Dietrich Saga, 125
Discourses on the First Ten Books of Livy, 415
Dispute of the Heart and the Body of François Villon, The, 555
Divan, The, 44
Divine Comedy, The, 160; interpretation of, 158–159; numerical symbols in, 159
Don Federigo's Falcon, 303
Don Quixote de la Mancha, 286–288, **347**
DONNE, JOHN, 283, **562**
Drama, development of in Middle Ages, 13; Elizabethan, 285; French, 279; of Lope de Vega, 426; and Puritan opposition, 286; Renaissance, 279–280; of Shakespeare, 285, 447–448; Spanish, 279–280, 288, 425–426
Du Bellay, Jean, 309
Duns Scotus, 8, 15, 265

Eastern Orthodox Church, 19
Ecclesiastical History of the English People, 8
Ecstasy, The, 569
Eddic Poems. *See Edda.*
Education, effect of Renaissance on, 275
Edward, 249
Edward III, king of England, 88; and Chaucer, 201
EDWARDS, JONATHAN, 276, **543**
Einhard, 110
Elckerlijk. See Everyman.
Elder Edda, 125
Elizabeth, queen of England, 269, 283; and drama, 279; and English Reformation, 276
Emperor of the Romans. *See Charlemagne.*
England, ballads of, 246–248; colonization by, 267; history of during Renaissance, 268–269; and Hundred Years' War, 267; Reformation in, 276; Renaissance drama of, 279; Renaissance literature of, 283–286
Epic, early medieval, 6–8, 10; Germanic, 125; *Song of Roland* as, 111; *The Nibelungenlied* as, 125
Epic form, as *chanson de geste,* 111
Epic lays, French, 110
Epics, of Ariosto and Tasso, 281
Epistle in the Form of a Ballad to His Friends, 556
Epistle to the Corinthians, I, 48
Epitaph on Elizabeth L. H., 569
Epithalamion, 396
ERASMUS, DESIDERIUS, 275, **293**; as northern Humanist, 273–274
Essay, use by Montaigne, 278
Essays (of Francis Bacon), 506
Essays (of Michel de Montaigne), 325
Euphues, or the Anatomy of Wit, 285
Euphuism, 285
Eusebius, 65
Even unto Death, 558

Everyman, 13
Exempla, 12

Fabliau, 12
Faerie Queene, The, 272, 285, **396**
Fairies, The, 574
Fear no more the heat o' the sun, **564**
Feast of Bricriu, The, 88
Ferdinand, king of Spain, 269
Feudal nobility, decline of, 271
Feudal system. *See Feudalism.*
Feudalism, decline of, 266–267; organization of, 3–4; significance of in Middle Ages, 2; struggle of with Church, 4
Fiammetta. *See Aquino, Maria d'.*
Fiammetta, La, 301
Ficino, Marsilio, 273
Filocolo, Il, 301
Filostrato, Il, 301
Fioretti di San Francesco. *See Little Flowers, The.*
Firdousi, 19, 20
First Epistle of Paul to the Corinthians, 63
Fitzgerald, Edward, 37, 38
Florence, 10; commerce of with east, 266; Medici rule of, 268; plague of, 301; politics of, 414–415; and start of Renaissance, 265
Fragment of a Sonnet, 558
Framework device, use of in *The Arabian Nights,* 29; used by Boccaccio, 301; used by Chaucer, 203
France, Golden Age of, 269; history of during Renaissance, 269; and Hundred Years' War, 267; Renaissance drama of, 279; Renaissance literature of, 282–283
Franciade, 557
Franciscan Friars, founding of, 74; and Rabelais, 309
Franks, under Charlemagne, 8
Freedom of Will, 543
Freemen, in medieval society, 4
Friar Onion and the Relics of the Angel Gabriel, 305
Friendship, 325
Fuente Ovejuna. *See Sheep Well, The.*
Fuggers, 266
Full many a glorious morning have I seen, **565**
Funeral, The, 571

Galatea, 347
Galen, translated by Rabelais, 309
Galilei, Galileo, 277
Galland, Antoine, 28
Gama, Vasco da, 267, 269
Garden of Eden, as visualized by Dante, 159
Gargantua and Pantagruel, 274, 283, **310**; analyzed, 309–310
Gascons, attack on Charlemagne, 110
Genoa, 10; commerce of with East, 266

Germanic epic, 125

Germany, history of during Renaissance, 268. *See* Holy Roman Empire.

Ghibellines, 9, 158

Golden Age, of English literature, 269; of French art, 269; of Spanish art, 271

Goliardic verse, 289

Goliards. *See* WANDERING SCHOLARS.

Golias, Bishop, 289

Gospel According to Saint Matthew, The, 47, 48

GOTTFRIED VON STRASBURG, 11, 151

Granada, 269

Gray Friars. *See* Franciscan Friars.

Great Schism, 275

Greek literature, in Middle Ages, 272; rediscovery of, 273–274

Green Knight, The, 88

Gregory VII, Pope, 4

Grocyn, William, 283

GROOT, HUIG VAN. *See* GROTIUS, HUGO.

GROTIUS, HUGO, 271, **421**

Grundtvig, Svend, 246

Guelphs, 9; and Dante, 158

Guilds, 9; and production of plays, 13

Guillaume de Lorris, 15–18

Guinevere, 11, 12

Gulistan, 20

HAFIZ, 19, 20, **44**

Hag, The, **574**

Hamlet, 285, **449**; analyzed, 448

HAMMERKEN, THOMAS. *See* THOMAS À KEMPIS

Hark, hark! The lark at heaven's gate sings, **564**

Haroun al-Raschid, 19, 20

He Thanks Her That from Time to Time . . . , **550**

Heaven, in Medieval teaching, 5–6; as visualized by Dante, 159

Heliand, 10

Heliocentric theory, 277

Hell, in medieval teaching, 5; as visualized by Dante, 159; *diagram of,* 175

Henry II, king of England, 4

Henry IV, Holy Roman Emperor, 4

Henry IV, king of France, 269; and Grotius, 421

Henry VII, king of England, 269

Henry VIII, king of England, 276, 283, 293

HERRICK, ROBERT, 283, **562**

Hidden lovers' woes, **157**

Hildebrandslied, 10

Hippocrates, translated by Rabelais, 309

His Lady's Death, **560**

His Lady's Tomb, **560**

His Mother's Service to Our Lady, **552**

His Prayer for Absolution, **574**

Historiography, contribution of Bede to, 8

Holy Grail, 12

Holy Roman Emperor, struggle with Pope, 158

Holy Roman Empire, and German weakness, 268; and Italy, 268

Homer, translated by Boccaccio, 301

Hora Novissima, 14

How sweet and lovely dost thou make the shame, **566**

Hrostvitha, 13

Huguenots, 269; and Massacre of St. Bartholomew's Day, 325; origin of, 276

Humanism, of Boccaccio, 300–301; development of, 272–274; of Erasmus, 293–294; French, 282–283; Italian, 280–281; origin of term, 273; of Pico della Mirandola, 291; of Rabelais, 309; of Wandering Scholars, 289

Humanists, Italian, 272–273; northern, 273–274; use of Latin by, 278; versatility of, 273

Hundred Years' War, 267, 269; and French Renaissance, 282

Huss, John, 10, 275

Hymns in Honor of Love and Beautie, 396

Idyll. *See* Pastoral.

If It Be Destined, **550**

Il Penseroso, 514

Imitatio Christi. See Imitation of Christ, The.

Imitation of Christ, The, **66**

Individualism, in Italian city-state, 10; in Renaissance literature, 278; of Renaissance man, 265–266

Induction, use of by Francis Bacon, 278, 506

Innocent III, Pope, 9; and Franciscan Order, 74

Inquisition, 503

Internationalism, of Grotius, 271

Invitation to Youth, The, **290**

Isabella, queen of Spain, 269

Islam, compared with Christianity, 20; compared with Medieval Europe, 19–20; penetration of into Europe, 21

It Is Not Growing Like a Tree, **569**

It was a lover and his lass, **563**

Italy, commerce of with East, 266; history of during Renaissance, 268; literature of, 280–281

James I, king of England, and Francis Bacon, 505

James II, king of England, 276

Jerusalem, destruction of in Matthew, 47

Jerusalem Delivered, 281

Jesuits, founding of, 276

Jesus, life of in Matthew, 48

Joan of Arc, 269

John, king of England, 4, 8–9

John of Salisbury, 15

Johnie Armstrong, **263**

JONSON, BEN, 285, **561**

Justinian, 19

Kemp Owyne, **262**

King, emergence of in England, 268–269; emergence of in France, 269; position of in medieval state, 3; position in Renaissance, 267ff.
Kingdom of God, 2, 4–5
Kingdom of Heaven Parables, The, 48
Kingdom of the Devil, 2, 4–5
Kings, and Reformation, 274–275
Kittredge, George L., 247
Knight's Tale, The, 202
Koran, The, 19, **25;** compared to New Testament, 20

La Boetie, Étienne de, 325
Labors of Persiles and Sigismunda, 347
L'Allegro, 514
Lancelot, 11, 12; as French chivalric hero, 89
Langton, Stephen, 4
Latin, use of by Humanists, 278
Laura, 548; death of in Florence, 301
Leiche, 151
Leicester, Earl of, 396
Leo x, Pope, 275, 509
Leonardo da Vinci, 273; scientific studies of, 277
Lepanto, battle of, 347
Let me not to the marriage of true minds, **567**
Life and Death of the Noble Brennenberger, **155**
Life Is a Dream, 288
Like as the waves make towards the pebbled shore, **565**
Litany to the Holy Spirit, **574**
Little Flowers of Saint Francis, The, **75**
Lorenzo the Magnificent. *See* Medici, Lorenzo de'.
Louis xi, king of France, 269; and Villon, 552
Louis xiv, king of France, 269
Love's Charming, **558**
Love's Flower, **559**
Love's Inconsistency, **548**
Love's Infiniteness, **570**
Love's Labour's Lost, song from, **562**
Loyola, Ignatius, 276
Lusiads, The, 269
Luther, Martin, 509; and start of Reformation, 275–276
Lutheran Church, establishment of, 276, 510
Lycidas, 286, 514
Lyly, John, 285
Lyric poetry, of Minnesingers, 151
Lyricists, English, 561–562

Machiavelli, Niccolò, 268, 282, **414;** influence on Bacon, 505
Magellan, Ferdinand, 267
Magna Charta, 8–9
Mandeville, Sir John, 18
Mandragola, 282
Map, Walter, 18
Marlowe, Christopher, 285

Martel, Charles, 21
Massacre of St. Bartholomew's Day, 325
Matthew. *See* **Gospel According to Saint Matthew, The.**
Measure for Measure, song from, **564**
Mecca, and writing of *Koran,* 25
Medici, banking house of, 266; in Florentine politics, 414–415
Medici, Cosimo de', 268, 273, 280
Medici, Lorenzo de', 268, 280–281, 291; *pictured,* 265
Medina, and writing of *Koran,* 25
Melanchthon, Philipp, 510
Merchant of Venice, The, song from, **563**
Meun, Jean de, 15–18
Michelangelo Buonarroti, 273
Middle Ages, daily life of, 6; defined, 2; essay on, 2–23; literature of, 6–19; meaning of, 21–23
Middle English, in *Sir Gawain and the Green Knight,* 88
Milton, John, 286, **514**
Minnelieder, 151
Minnesingers, The, 151, 265
Minstrel, as ballad maker, 247
Miracle plays, 13
Mohammed, and composition of *Koran,* 25; life and teachings of, 19
Mohammedanism. *See* Islam.
Mohammedans, and *The Arabian Nights,* 28; in Spain, 269
Monarchy. *See* King.
Monasticism, evolution of, 8–9
Montaigne, Michel de, 283, 324; on Humanism, 274
Montcorbier, François de. *See* **Villon, François.**
Moors, 21
Morality plays, 13
More, Sir Thomas, 283, 293, 294
Mountjoy, Lord, and Erasmus, 293
Much Ado about Nothing, song from, **563**
My love is strengthen'd though more weak in seeming, **566**

Nationalism, development of in Europe, 267–271; of the German Reformation, 268; and the Reformation, 274–275; and warfare, 271
Netherlands, in colonial race, 267
New Atlantis, 283, 506
New Testament, The, **47**
Nibelungenlied, The, 11, **125,** 126
Nicaea, Council of, 65
Nicaean Creed, The, 65, 66
Night Piece, to Julia, The, **572**
Nishapur, 37
No, I Am Not as Others Are, **552**
Norman Conquest, 111
Not marble, nor the gilded monuments, **565**

Novel, *Troilus and Criseyde* as, 19
Novum Organum, 278, 285, **506**

O, how much more doth beauty beauteous seem, **565**
O lady, long have I been fain, **151**
O mistress mine, where are you roaming? **563**
O, never say that I was false of heart, **566**
Ode for Ben Jonson, An, 571
Odes, of Hafiz. *See Divan, The.*
Of Age, 340
Of Democritus and Heraclitus, 326
Of His Lady's Old Age, 559
Of the Education of Children, 327
Of the Infinite Universe and Innumerable Worlds, 503
Of Three Commerces, 342
Old Testament, influence of on Matthew, 47
OMAR KHAYYAM, 19, 20, **37;** compared to Hafiz, 44
On Humility and Forgiveness, 48
On the Announcement of the Death of Laura, 550
Oration on the Dignity of Man, 273, 291, 292
Order of the Garter, 88
Order of Tertiaries, 74
Orlando Furioso, 281
Orleans, siege of, 269
Othman, Caliph, 25
Ottoman Turks, 21, 267
Ovid, influence of on medieval literature, 272
Oxford, 293

Palace School, 8
Papacy, condition of in Renaissance, 275–276; and Reformation, 274–275
Paradise, as visualized by Dante, 159; *diagram of,* 195
Paradise Lost, 286, **514;** analyzed, 514–515
Paradise Regained, 514
Pardoner's Tale, The, 202
Parliament of Fowls, The, 202
Parzifal, 151
Pastoral, use of by Spenser, 396
Patience, 88
Paul, life of, 48
Pauline Epistles, 48. *See **First Epistle of Paul to the Corinthians.***
Pearl, The, 88
PEARL POET, THE, 23, 88
Percy Manuscript, 246
Persia, medieval renaissance of, 19; Shirazists of, 20
Peruzzi, 266
PETRACCO, FRANCESCO. *See* PETRARCA, FRANCESCO.
PETRARCA, FRANCESCO, 280, **548;** as first Humanist, 273; friendship of with Boccaccio, 300–301
PETRARCH. *See* PETRARCA, FRANCESCO.
Philip II, king of Spain, 269
Philip III, king of Spain, 347

Philip IV, king of France, 275
Piers Plowman, 247
Piers Plowman Poet, 23
Pilatus, Leontius, 301
Pilgrim's Progress, The, 286
Pinzón, Martin, 267
Plantagenet, Richard, 202
Platonic Academy, 280, 286, 291; founding of, 273
Pleiades, 282, 557
Poetic Edda. See Elder Edda.
Poetry, of French Renaissance, 282–283; of Hafiz, 44; of Minnesingers, 151; of Omar Khayyam, 37–38; of Shakespeare, 448, 561; of Wandering Scholars, 289
Poet's Gift, The, **559**
Poitiers, battle of, 269
Poor Claras, 74
Pope, position of in medieval Church, 2–3; struggle of with Holy Roman Emperor, 4, 9, 158
Popes, of Renaissance, 275–276
Popular Ballads, British and Danish, 246
Portugal, 269
Portuguese, explorations of, 267
Porziuncula, 74
Praise of Folly, The, 274, 275, **294**
Predestination, defended by Edwards, 543
Prince, The, 268, 282, **415**
Prioress's Tale, The, 202
Prose, of Renaissance Italy, 282
Prose Edda. See Younger Edda.
Prosopopoia, 396
Protestantism, English, 514; and Erasmus, 293; Lutheran, 276. *See also* Reformation, Lutheranism, Calvinism, Puritanism.
Ptolemaic theory, 499; challenged by Copernicus, 277; and medieval Church, 158
Purgatory, in medieval teaching, 5; as visualized by Dante, 159; *diagram of,* 175
Puritanism, in England, 276, 514; literature of, 286; in North America, 276, 543
Purity, 88

Quixote, Don. See Don Quixote.

RABELAIS, FRANÇOIS, 283, **309;** as Humanist thinker, 274
Rationalism, of Erasmus, 293; of Montaigne, 324–325
Rebirth of learning. *See* Renaissance.
Reformation, Catholic. *See* Counter-Reformation.
Reformation, connection of with Renaissance, 275; English, 276; forerunners of, 275; French, 325; German, 276; history of, 274–276; influence on English literature, 286; and Martin Luther, 509–510
REINMAR VON HAGENAU, 152
Reliques of Ancient English Poetry, 247

Remonstrants, 421
Renaissance, commercial life of, 266–267; effect of on Reformation, 274; English, 269; English literature of, 283–286; essay on, 265–288; general features of, 265–266; Humanism of, 272–274; literature of, 278ff.; Spanish literature of, 286
Revenge, The, 560
Revolutions of the Heavenly Bodies, The, 277, 499
Richard II, 202
Riddles Wisely Expounded, 248
Rights of War and Peace, 271, 421
Robin Hood ballads, 247
Robin Hood's Death and Burial, 257
Roland, as epic hero, 111; described by Einhard, 110
Roman de la Rose, 12, 15–18, 265; influence of on Chaucer, 202
Romance, Celtic, 88; chivalric, 21; German, 151; medieval, emergence of, 10–12; Middle English, 88; moral, 12, 21, 88
Rondel, 555
RONSARD, PIERRE DE, 557
Rose, The, 559
Roses, 559
Rubaiyat, The, 37, 38
Rustum, 20

Sacraments, 2
Sadi, 19, 20
Saint Bartholomew's Day, Massacre of, 325
Saint Clara, 74
SAINT FRANCIS OF ASSISI, 74, 265; stigmata of, 75
Saint George, and English chivalry, 88
Samson Agonistes, 286, 514
Saracens, 21; in Spain, 110
Satan, fall of according to Dante, 159
Saul of Tarsus. See Paul.
Savonarola, Girolamo, 275
Scholasticism, in thirteenth century, 8–9
Scholastics, 21; attacked by Roger Bacon, 277; writings of, 8–9
Science, Arabic, 19; and medieval mind, 5; of Renaissance era, 276–278
Scientific method, formulated by Bacon, 278
Scop, 8
Scotland, ballads of, 246–247
Second Nun's Tale, The, 202
Sejanus, 285
Serfdom, 3–4
Shah Nameh, 20
Shahriar, Sultan, 29
SHAKESPEARE, WILLIAM, 279, 285, 447; compared to Lope de Vega, 425, 426; as lyric poet, 561
Shall I compare thee to a summer's day? 564
Sheep Well, The, 288, 426; proletariat in, 272
Sheherazade, 29
SHEMSUDDIN MOHAMMED. See HAFIZ.
Shepheardes Calender, 285, 396

Ship of Fools, 294
Shiraz, 44; and Persian literature, 20
Sidney, Sir Philip, 389, 396
Siegfried, as epic hero, 125
Sigh no more, ladies, sigh no more, 563
Signs of Love, 549
Simplex Munditiis, 568
Sinners in the Hands of an Angry God, 276, 543
Sir Gawain and the Green Knight, 88, 89; as moral romance, 12
Sir Luno and the Mermaid, 261
Sir Patrick Spens, 252
Skepticism, of Montaigne, 324–325
Song, 569
Song, A, 569
Song of Roland, The, 10, 110, 111
Song of the Open Road, A, 289
Song: To Celia, 568
Song to Celia, 568
Sonnet, use of by English lyricists, 561; use of by Petrarch, 19
Sonnets, of Petrarch, 548; of Petrarch and Boccaccio, 280; of Shakespeare, 564; of Spenser, 396
Spain, and Columbus, 267; history of during Renaissance, 269–271; Renaissance drama of, 279–280; Renaissance literature of, 286–288
SPENSER, EDMUND, 285, 395; and courtly ideals, 272
Spring Returns, but Not to Him Returns, 551
Spruch, 151
Stratford-on-Avon, 285, 448
Sufism, and Hafiz, 44; of Persian writers, 20
Summer's Revel, 557
Suras, 25
Surrey, Earl of, 283
Switzerland, and Calvinist reforms, 276
Symphonia Platonis et Aristotelis, 291

Table Talk, 510
Tagelied, 151
Take, oh, take those lips away, 564
Tamerlane. See Timur.
Tannhäuser. See *Ballad of Sir Tannhäuser, The.*
Tasso, Torquato, 278, 281
Te Deum, 14
Tears of the Muses, The, 396
Teatro Olimpico, 279
Tell me where is fancy bred, 563
Tempest, The, song from, 564
Ten of War and Peace, 414–415
Tenure of Kings and Magistrates, 514
Terza rima, developed by Dante, 159
Teseide, 301
Testaments, 552
Tetzel, John, 509
That time of year thou mayest in me behold, 566
That We Taste Nothing Pure, 341
Theaters, in Renaissance Italy, 279

Theodoric the Great, 125
Theodosius, Emperor, 2
There's No Lust Like to Poetry, 291
Thomas à Becket, Archbishop, 4
THOMAS À KEMPIS, 15, 66
Thomas Rymer, 251
Thousand and One Nights, The. See Arabian Nights, The.
Three Rings, The, 301
Timur, 44
Tired with all these, for restful death I cry, **566**
'Tis better to be vile than vile esteem'd, **567**
To Anthea, Who May Command Him Anything, 573
To Daffodils, 572
To Daisies, Not to Shut So Soon, 574
To Death, of His Lady, 555
To Dianeme, 573
To Electra, 573
To His Valet, 560
To His Young Mistress, 558
To me, fair friend, you never can be old, **566**
To my lady's bower I crept, **151**
To Primroses Filled with Morning-dew, 573
To the Memory of My Beloved, Master William Shakespeare, 567
To the Virgins to Make Much of Time, 572
Tours, battle of, 21
Tragedy, of Marlowe, 285; of Shakespeare, 447
Transit Mundus, 560
Treatise Concerning Religious Affections, 543
Tree of Love, The, 554
Trent, Council of, 276
Tristan, 11, 12, 151
Tristram Shandy, 310
Troilus and Criseyde, 202; as modern novel, 19
Tudors, 269
Turk and Gawain, The, 88
Turks, Ottoman. *See Ottoman Turks.*
Turpin of Rheims, Archbishop, 111
Twelfth Night, song from, **563**
Two Gentlemen of Verona, The, song from, **562**

Under the greenwood tree, **563**
University Wits, 285
Universities, and Humanism, 273–274
Upon Julia's Clothes, 572
Upon Mistress Susanna Southwell Her Feet, 572
Urbino, Guidobaldo, Duke of, 389
Utopia, 283

Vagantes. See WANDERING SCHOLARS, THE.
Valla, Lorenzo, 273
Vassals, 3
VEGA, LOPE DE, 272, 279, 288, **425**

Venice, 10; commerce of with East, 266
Vernacular, use of in Renaissance, 279
Vesalius, Andreas, 277
Villein. *See Serfdom.*
VILLON, FRANÇOIS, 282, 552
Villon's Straight Tip to All Cross Coves, **555**
Vincent of Beauvais, 8, 15
Virgil, 272; in *Divine Comedy,* 159
Vision, 548
Vita Nuova, 158
Volpone, 285
Volsungasaga, 11, 125

Waldensians, 275
Waldo, Peter, 275
WALTHER VON DER VOGELWEIDE, 11, 151, 152, 153
WANDERING SCHOLARS, THE, **289**
War of the Roses, 267, 268
Went a maid fair to behold, **153**
What sweetness into that old word *woman* grew, 152
Whatever be my faults, one quality, 152
When daffodils begin to peer, **564**
When I have seen by Time's fell hand defaced, **565**
When icicles hang by the wall, **562**
When, in disgrace with fortune and men's eyes, **565**
When in the chronicle of wasted time, **566**
When to the sessions of sweet silent thought, **565**
Wherein He Envies Whatsoever of Lovely . . . , 550
Wherein He Makes Confession . . . , 551
Wherein He Pursues Solitude . . . , 549
Wherein He Tells the Course of True Love, 549
Wherein His Heart, by Laura Rejected . . . , 549
Wherein Laura Is Forever a Present Apparition, 551
Wherein Soaring in an Ecstasy . . . , 551
Whites, in Florentine politics, 158
Who is Sylvia? **562**
Who slays the lion, who slays the dragon? **153**
Wife of Usher's Well, The, **255**
"Will you take this wilding wreath?" **152**
William the Conqueror, 111, 268
Winter's Tale, The, song from, **564**
Wittenberg Church, and start of Reformation, 275, 509
WOLFRAM VON ESCHENBACH, 151, 157
Worms, Diet of, 510
Wyatt, Sir Thomas, 283
Wycliffe, John, 10, 275

Young Engel, 258
Younger Edda, 125

Zaid ibn Tabit, 25
Zwingli, Ulrich, 510

11 12 13 14 15 16 17 18 19 20 21 22 23 24 25   65 64 63